Collins

Collins
Italian
Dictionary

HarperCollins Publishers
Westerhill Road
Bishopbriggs
Glasgow
G64 2QT
Great Britain

First Edition 2006

© HarperCollins Publishers 2006

ISBN-13 978-0-00-723144-7
ISBN-10 0-00-723144-x

Collins® is a registered trademark of
HarperCollins Publishers Limited

www.collins.co.uk

A catalogue record for this book is
available from the British Library

Typeset by Thomas Callan

Printed and bound in Italy by
Legoprint S.P.A.

Acknowledgements
We would like to thank those
authors and publishers who kindly
gave permission for copyright
material to be used in the Collins
Word Web. We would also like to
thank Times Newspapers Ltd for
providing valuable data.

EDITORIAL DIRECTOR
Michela Clari

CONTRIBUTORS
G Bacchelli

EDITORIAL COORDINATION
Joyce Littlejohn

SERIES EDITOR
Lorna Knight

BASED ON THE COLLINS ITALIAN GEM
Catherine E Love
P L Rossi
D M Chaplin
F Villa
E Bilucaglia

INDICE

CONTENTS

I marchi registrati
I termini che a nostro parere costituiscono un marchio registrato sono stati designati come tali. In ogni caso, né la presenza né l'assenza di tale designazione implicano alcuna valutazione del loro reale stato giuridico.

Note on trademarks
Entered words that we have reason to believe constitute trademarks have been designated as such. However, neither the presence nor the absence of such designation should be regarded as affecting the legal status of any trademark.

CONTENTS

INTRODUZIONE

Vi ringraziamo di aver scelto il Dizionario inglese Collins e ci auguriamo che esso si riveli uno strumento utile e piacevole da usare nello studio, in vacanza e sul lavoro.

INTRODUCTION

We are delighted that you have decided to buy the Collins Italian Dictionary and hope you will enjoy and benefit from using it at school, at home, on holiday or at work.

William Collins' dream of knowledge for all began with the publication of his first book in 1819. A self-educated mill worker, he not only enriched millions of lives, but also founded a flourishing publishing house. Today, staying true to this spirit, Collins books are packed with inspiration, innovation, and practical expertise. They place you at the centre of a world of possibility and give you exactly what you need to explore it.

Language is the key to this exploration, and at the heart of Collins Dictionaries is language as it is really used. New words, phrases, and meanings spring up every day, and all of them are captured and analysed by the Collins Word Web. Constantly updated, and with over 2.5 billion entries, this living language resource is unique to our dictionaries.

Words are tools for life. And a Collins Dictionary makes them work for you.

Collins. Do more.

ABBREVIAZIONI

		ABBREVIATIONS
abbreviazione	*abbr*	abbreviation
aggettivo	*adj*	adjective
amministrazione	*Admin*	administration
avverbio	*adv*	adverb
aeronautica, viaggi aerei	*Aer*	flying, air travel
aggettivo	*ag*	adjective
agricoltura	*Agr*	agriculture
amministrazione	*Amm*	administration
anatomia	*Anat*	anatomy
architettura	*Archit*	architecture
articolo determinativo	*art def*	definite article
articolo indeterminativo	*art indef*	indefinite article
attributivo	*attrib*	attributive
ausiliare	*aus, aux*	auxiliary
automobile	*Aut*	motor car and motoring
avverbio	*av*	adverb
aeronautica, viaggi aerei	*Aviat*	flying, air travel
biologia	*Biol*	biology
botanica	*Bot*	botany
inglese britannico	*BRIT*	British English
consonante	*C*	consonant
chimica	*Chim, Chem*	chemistry
commercio, finanza	*Comm*	commerce, finance
comparativo	*compar*	comparative
informatica	*Comput*	computing
congiunzione	*cong, conj*	conjunction
edilizia	*Constr*	building
sostantivo usato come aggettivo, ma mai con funzione predicativa	*cpd*	compound element: noun used as adjective and which cannot follow the noun it qualifies
cucina	*Cuc, Culin*	cookery
davanti a	*dav*	before

ABBREVIAZIONI		ABBREVIATIONS
articolo determinativo	*def art*	definite article
determinativo; articolo, aggettivo dimostrativo o indefinito ecc	*det*	determiner: article, demonstrative etc
diminutivo	*dimin*	diminutive
diritto	*Dir*	law
economia	*Econ*	economics
edilizia	*Edil*	building
elettricità, elettronica	*Elettr, Elec*	electricity, electronics
esclamazione	*escl, excl*	exclamation
femminile	*f*	feminine
familiare (! da evitare)	*fam(!)*	colloquial usage (! particularly offensive)
ferrovia	*Ferr*	railways
senso figurato	*fig*	figurative use
fisiologia	*Fisiol*	physiology
fotografia	*Fot*	photography
verbo inglese la cui particella è inseparabile dal verbo	*fus*	(phrasal verb) where the particle cannot be separated from the main verb
nella maggior parte dei sensi; generalmente	*gen*	in most or all senses; generally
geografia, geologia	*Geo*	geography, geology
geometria	*Geom*	geometry
storia, storico	*Hist*	history, historical
impersonale	*impers*	impersonal
articolo indeterminativo	*indef art*	indefinite article
familiare (! da evitare)	*inf(!)*	colloquial usage (! particularly offensive)
infinito	*infin*	infinitive
informatica	*Inform*	computing

ABBREVIAZIONI

insegnamento, sistema scolastico e universitario	*Ins*	schooling, schools and universities
invariabile	*inv*	invariable
irregolare	*irreg*	irregular
grammatica, linguistica	*Ling*	grammar, linguistics
maschile	*m*	masculine
matematica	*Mat(h)*	mathematics
termine medico, medicina	*Med*	medical term, medicine
il tempo, meteorologia	*Meteor*	the weather, meteorology
maschile o femminile	*m/f*	masculine or feminine
esercito, linguaggio militare	*Mil*	military matters
musica	*Mus*	music
sostantivo	*n*	noun
nautica	*Naut*	sailing, navigation
numerale (aggettivo, sostantivo)	*num*	numeral adjective or noun
	o.s.	oneself
peggiorativo	*peg, pej*	derogatory, pejorative
fotografia	*Phot*	photography
fisiologia	*Physiol*	physiology
plurale	*pl*	plural
politica	*Pol*	politics
participio passato	*pp*	past participle
preposizione	*prep*	preposition
pronome	*pron*	pronoun
psicologia, psichiatria	*Psic, Psych*	psychology, psychiatry
tempo passato	*pt*	past tense
qualcosa	*qc*	
qualcuno	*qn*	
religione, liturgia	*Rel*	religions, church service
sostantivo	*s*	noun
	sb	somebody

ABBREVIATIONS

ABBREVIAZIONI		ABBREVIATIONS
insegnamento, sistema scolastico e universitario	*Scol*	schooling, schools and universities
singolare	*sg*	singular
soggetto (grammaticale)	*sog*	(grammatical) subject
	sth	something
congiuntivo	*sub*	subjunctive
soggetto (grammaticale)	*subj*	(grammatical) subject
superlativo	*superl*	superlative
termine tecnico, tecnologia	*Tecn, Tech*	technical term, technology
telecomunicazioni	*Tel*	telecommunications
tipografia	*Tip*	typography, printing
televisione	*TV*	television
tipografia	*Typ*	typography, printing
università	*Univ*	university
inglese americano	*US*	American English
vocale	*V*	vowel
verbo	*vb*	verb
verbo o gruppo verbale con funzione intransitiva	*vi*	verb or phrasal verb used intransitively
verbo pronominale o riflessivo	*vpr*	pronominal or reflexive verb
verbo o gruppo verbale con funzione transitiva	*vt*	verb or phrasal verb used transitively
zoologia	*Zool*	zoology
marchio registrato	®	registered trademark
introduce un'equivalenza culturale	≈	introduces a cultural equivalent

TRASCRIZIONE FONETICA

Consonanti		Consonants
Consonanti		**Consonants**

NB **p, b, t, d, k, g** sono seguite da un'aspirazione in inglese.

NB **p, b, t, d, k, g** are not aspirated in Italian.

padre	p	**pupp**y
bambino	b	**b**a**b**y
tu**tt**o	t	**t**en**t**
da**d**o	d	**d**a**dd**y
cane **ch**e	k	**c**ork **k**iss **ch**ord
gola **gh**iro	g	**g**a**g** **gu**ess
sano	s	**s**o ri**c**e ki**ss**
svago e**s**ame	z	cou**s**in bu**zz**
scena	ʃ	**sh**eep **s**ugar
	ʒ	plea**s**ure bei**ge**
pe**c**e lan**ci**are	tʃ	**ch**ur**ch**
giro **gi**oco	dʒ	**j**ud**ge** **g**eneral
a**f**a **f**aro	f	**f**arm ra**ff**le
vero bra**v**o	v	**v**ery re**v**
	θ	**th**in ma**th**s
	ð	**th**at o**th**er
le**tt**o a**l**a	l	**l**itt**l**e ba**ll**
gli	ʎ	mi**lli**on
rete a**r**co	r	**r**at **r**a**r**e
ramo mad**r**e	m	**m**u**mm**y co**mb**
no fuma**n**te	n	**n**o ra**n**
gnomo	ɲ	ca**ny**on
	ŋ	si**ng**i**ng** ba**n**k
	h	**h**at re**h**eat
bu**i**o p**i**acere	j	**y**et
u**o**mo g**u**aio	w	**w**all be**w**ail
	x	lo**ch**

Varie		**Miscellaneous**

per l'inglese: la "r" finale viene pronunciata se seguita da una vocale	r	
precede la sillaba accentata	'	precedes the stressed syllable

PHONETIC TRANSCRIPTION

Vocali		Vowels
NB La messa in equivalenza di certi suoni indica solo una rassomiglianza approssimativa.		NB The pairing of some vowel sounds only indicates approximate equivalence.
vino idea	i iː	heel bead
	ɪ	hit pity
stella edera	e	
epoca eccetto	ɛ	set tent
mamma amore	a æ	bat apple
	ɑː	after car calm
	ã	fiancé
	ʌ	fun cousin
müsli	y	
	ə	over above
	əː	urn fern work
rosa occhio	ɔ	wash pot
	ɔː	born cork
ponte ognuno	o	
föhn	ø	
utile zucca	u	full soot
	uː	boon lewd

Dittonghi		Diphthongs
	ɪə	beer tier
	ɛə	tear fair there
	eɪ	date plaice day
	aɪ	life buy cry
	au	owl foul now
	əu	low no
	ɔɪ	boil boy oily
	uə	poor tour

ITALIAN PRONUNCIATION

Vowels

Where the vowel **e** or the vowel **o** appears in a stressed syllable it can be either open [ε], [ɔ] or closed [e], [o]. As the open or closed pronunciation of these vowels is subject to regional variation, the distinction is of little importance to the user of this dictionary. Phonetic transcription for headwords containing these vowels will therefore only appear where other pronunciation difficulties are present.

Consonants

c before "e" or "i" is pronounced like the *"tch"* in match.
ch is pronounced like the *"k"* in "kit".
g before "e" or "i" is pronounced like the *"j"* in "jet".
gh is pronounced like the *"g"* in "get".
gl before "e" or "i" is normally pronounced like the *"lli"* in "million", and in a few cases only like the *"gl"* in "glove".
gn is pronounced like the *"ny"* in "canyon"
sc before "e" or "i" is pronounced *"sh"*.
z is pronounced like the *"ts"* in "stetson", or like the *"d's"* in "bird's-eye".

Headwords containing the above consonants and consonantal groups have been given full phonetic transcription in this dictionary.

NB All double written consonants in Italian are fully sounded: e.g. the **tt** in "tutto" is pronounced as in "hat trick".

ITALIAN VERB FORMS

1 Gerundio **2** Participio passato **3** Presente **4** Imperfetto **5** Passato remoto **6** Futuro **7** Condizionale **8** Congiuntivo presente **9** Congiuntivo passato **10** Imperativo

andare **3** vado, vai, va, andiamo, andate, vanno **6** andrò *ecc.* **8** vada **10** va'!, vada!, andate!, vadano!

apparire **2** apparso **3** appaio, appari *o* apparisci, appare *o* apparisce, appaiono *o* appariscono **5** apparvi *o* apparsi, apparisti, apparve *o* apparì *o* apparse, apparvero *o* apparirono *o* apparsero **8** appaia *o* apparisca

aprire **2** aperto **3** apro **5** aprii, apristi **8** apra

AVERE **3** ho, hai, ha, abbiamo, avete, hanno **5** ebbi, avesti, ebbe, avemmo, aveste, ebbero **6** avrò *ecc.* **8** abbia *ecc.* **10** abbi!, abbia!, abbiate!, abbiano!

bere **1** bevendo **2** bevuto **3** bevo *ecc.* **4** bevevo *ecc.* **5** bevvi *o* bevetti, bevesti **6** berrò *ecc.* **8** beva *ecc.* **9** bevessi *ecc.*

cadere **5** caddi, cadesti **6** cadrò *ecc.*

cogliere **2** colto **3** colgo, colgono **5** colsi, cogliesti **8** colga

correre **2** corso **5** corsi, corresti

cuocere **2** cotto **3** cuocio, cociamo, cuociono **5** cossi, cocesti

dare **3** do, dai, dà, diamo, date, danno **5** diedi *o* detti, desti **6** darò *ecc.* **8** dia *ecc.* **9** dessi *ecc.* **10** da'!, dai!, date!, diano!

dire **1** dicendo **2** detto **3** dico, dici, dice, diciamo, dite, dicono **4** dicevo *ecc.* **5** dissi, dicesti **6** dirò *ecc.* **8** dica, diciamo, diciate, dicano **9** dicessi *ecc.* **10** di'!, dica!, dite!, dicano!

dolere **3** dolgo, duoli, duole, dolgono **5** dolsi, dolesti **6** dorrò *ecc.* **8** dolga

dovere **3** devo *o* debbo, devi, deve, dobbiamo, dovete, devono *o* debbono **6** dovrò *ecc.* **8** debba, dobbiamo, dobbiate, devano *o* debbano

ESSERE **2** stato **3** sono, sei, è, siamo, siete, sono **4** ero, eri, era, eravamo, eravate, erano **5** fui, fosti, fu, fummo, foste, furono **6** sarò *ecc.* **8** sia *ecc.* **9** fossi, fossi, fosse, fossimo, foste, fossero **10** sii!, sia!, siate!, siano!

fare **1** facendo **2** fatto **3** faccio, fai, fa, facciamo, fate, fanno **4** facevo *ecc.* **5** feci, facesti **6** farò *ecc.* **8** faccia *ecc.* **9** facessi *ecc.* **10** fa'!, faccia!, fate!, facciano!

FINIRE **1** finendo **2** finito **3** finisco, finisci, finisce, finiamo, finite, finiscono **4** finivo, finivi, finiva, finivamo, finivate, finivano **5** finii, finisti, finì, finimmo, finiste, finirono **6** finirò, finirai, finirà, finiremo, finirete, finiranno **7** finirei, finiresti, finirebbe, finiremmo, finireste, finirebbero **8** finisca, finisca, finisca, finiamo, finiate, finiscano **9** finissi, finissi, finisse, finissimo, finiste, finissero **10** finisci!, finisca!, finite!, finiscano!

giungere **2** giunto **5** giunsi, giungesti

leggere **2** letto **5** lessi, leggesti

mettere **2** messo **5** misi, mettesti

morire **2** morto **3** muoio, muori, muore, moriamo, morite, muoiono **6** morirò *o* morrò *ecc.* **8** muoia

muovere **2** mosso **5** mossi, movesti

nascere **2** nato **5** nacqui, nascesti

nuocere **2** nuociuto **3** nuoccio, nuoci, nuoce, nociamo *o* nuociamo, nuocete, nuocciono **4** nuocevo *ecc.* **5** nocqui, nuocesti **6** nuocerò *ecc.* **7** nuoccia

offrire **2** offerto **3** offro **5** offersi *o* offrii, offristi **8** offra

parere **2** parso **3** paio, paiamo, paiono **5** parvi *o* parsi, paresti **6** parrò *ecc.* **8** paia, paiamo, paiate, paiano

PARLARE 1 parlando 2 parlato 3 parlo, parli, parla, parliamo, parlate, parlano 4 parlavo, parlavi, parlava, parlavamo, parlavate, parlavano 5 parlai, parlasti, parlò, parlammo, parlaste, parlarono 6 parlerò, parlerai, parlerà, parleremo, parlerete, parleranno 7 parlerei, parleresti, parlerebbe, parleremmo, parlereste, parlerebbero 8 parli, parli, parli, parliamo, parliate, parlino 9 parlassi, parlassi, parlasse, parlassimo, parlaste, parlassero 10 parla!, parli!, parlate!, parlino!

piacere 2 piaciuto 3 piaccio, piacciamo, piacciono 5 piacqui, piacesti 8 piacci *ecc.*

porre 1 ponendo 2 posto 3 pongo, poni, pone, poniamo, ponete, pongono 4 ponevo *ecc.* 5 posi, ponesti 6 porrò *ecc.* 8 ponga, poniamo, poniate, pongano 9 ponessi *ecc.*

potere 3 posso, puoi, può, possiamo, potete, possono 6 potrò *ecc.* 8 possa, possiamo, possiate, possano

prendere 2 preso 5 presi, prendesti

ridurre 1 riducendo 2 ridotto 3 riduco *ecc.* 4 riducevo *ecc.* 5 ridussi, riducesti 6 ridurrò *ecc.* 8 riduca *ecc.* 9 riducessi *ecc.*

riempire 1 riempiendo 3 riempio, riempi, riempie, riempiono

rimanere 2 rimasto 3 rimango, rimangono 5 rimasi, rimanesti 6 rimarrò *ecc.* 8 rimanga

rispondere 2 risposto 5 risposi, rispondesti

salire 3 salgo, sali, salgono 8 salga

sapere 3 so, sai, sa, sappiamo, sapete, sanno 5 seppi, sapesti 6 saprò *ecc.* 8 sappia *ecc.* 10 sappi!, sappia!, sappiate!, sappiano!

scrivere 2 scritto 5 scrissi, scrivesti

sedere 3 siedo, siedi, siede, siedono 8 sieda

spegnere 2 spento 3 spengo, spengono 5 spensi, spegnesti 8 spenga

stare 2 stato 3 sto, stai, sta, stiamo, state, stanno 5 stetti, stesti 6 starò *ecc.* 8 stia *ecc.* 9 stessi *ecc.* 10 sta'!, stia!, state!, stiano!

tacere 2 taciuto 3 taccio, tacciono 5 tacqui, tacesti 8 taccia

tenere 3 tengo, tieni, tiene, tengono 5 tenni, tenesti 6 terrò *ecc.* 8 tenga

trarre 1 traendo 2 tratto 3 traggo, trai, trae, traiamo, traete, traggono 4 traevo *ecc.* 5 trassi, traesti 6 trarrò *ecc.* 8 tragga 9 traessi *ecc.*

udire 3 odo, odi, ode, odono 8 oda

uscire 3 esco, esci, esce, escono 8 esca

valere 2 valso 3 valgo, valgono 5 valsi, valesti 6 varrò *ecc.* 8 valga

vedere 2 visto *o* veduto 5 vidi, vedesti 6 vedrò *ecc.*

VENDERE 1 vendendo 2 venduto 3 vendo, vendi, vende, vendiamo, vendete, vendono 4 vendevo, vendevi, vendeva, vendevamo, vendevate, vendevano 5 vendei *o* vendetti, vendesti, vendé *o* vendette, vendemmo, vendeste, venderono *o* vendettero 6 venderò, venderai, venderà, venderemo, venderete, venderanno 7 venderei, venderesti, venderebbe, venderemmo, vendereste, venderebbero 8 venda, venda, venda, vendiamo, vendiate, vendano 9 vendessi, vendessi, vendesse, vendessimo, vendeste, vendessero 10 vendi!, venda!, vendete!, vendano!

venire 2 venuto 3 vengo, vieni, viene, vengono 5 venni, venisti 6 verrò *ecc.* 8 venga

vivere 2 vissuto 5 vissi, vivesti

volere 3 voglio, vuoi, vuole, vogliamo, volete, vogliono 5 volli, volesti 6 vorrò *ecc.* 8 voglia *ecc.* 10 vogli!, voglia!, vogliate!, vogliano!

ENGLISH VERB FORMS

present	pt	pp	present	pt	pp
arise	arose	arisen	feed	fed	fed
awake	awoke	awoken	feel	felt	felt
be (am, is, are; being)	was, were	been	fight	fought	fought
			find	found	found
bear	bore	born(e)	flee	fled	fled
beat	beat	beaten	fling	flung	flung
become	became	become	fly	flew	flown
begin	began	begun	forbid	forbade	forbidden
bend	bent	bent	forecast	forecast	forecast
bet	bet, betted	bet, betted	forget	forgot	forgotten
			forgive	forgave	forgiven
bid (at auction, cards)	bid	bid	forsake	forsook	forsaken
			freeze	froze	frozen
bid (say)	bade	bidden	get	got	got, (US) gotten
bind	bound	bound			
bite	bit	bitten	give	gave	given
bleed	bled	bled	go (goes)	went	gone
blow	blew	blown	grind	ground	ground
break	broke	broken	grow	grew	grown
breed	bred	bred	hang	hung	hung
bring	brought	brought	hang (execute)	hanged	hanged
build	built	built	have (has; having)	had	had
burn	burnt, burned	burnt, burned			
			hear	heard	heard
burst	burst	burst	hide	hid	hidden
buy	bought	bought	hit	hit	hit
can	could	(been able)	hold	held	held
cast	cast	cast	hurt	hurt	hurt
catch	caught	caught	keep	kept	kept
choose	chose	chosen	kneel	knelt, kneeled	knelt, kneeled
cling	clung	clung			
come	came	come	know	knew	known
cost	cost	cost	lay	laid	laid
cost (work out price of)	costed	costed	lead	led	led
			lean	leant, leaned	leant, leaned
creep	crept	crept			
cut	cut	cut	leap	leapt, leaped	leapt, leaped
deal	dealt	dealt			
dig	dug	dug	learn	learnt, learned	learnt, learned
do (does)	did	done			
draw	drew	drawn	leave	left	left
dream	dreamed, dreamt	dreamed, dreamt	lend	lent	lent
			let	let	let
drink	drank	drunk	lie (lying)	lay	lain
drive	drove	driven	light	lit, lighted	lit, lighted
dwell	dwelt	dwelt			
eat	ate	eaten	lose	lost	lost
fall	fell	fallen	make	made	made

xvi

present	pt	pp	present	pt	pp
may	might	—	spell	spelt, spelled	spelt, spelled
mean	meant	meant	spend	spent	spent
meet	met	met	spill	spilt, spilled	spilt, spilled
mistake	mistook	mistaken			
mow	mowed	mown, mowed	spin	spun	spun
			spit	spat	spat
must	(had to)	(had to)	split	split	split
pay	paid	paid	spoil	spoiled, spoilt	spoiled, spoilt
put	put	put			
quit	quit, quitted	quit, quitted	spread	spread	spread
			spring	sprang	sprung
read	read	read	stand	stood	stood
rid	rid	rid	steal	stole	stolen
ride	rode	ridden	stick	stuck	stuck
ring	rang	rung	sting	stung	stung
rise	rose	risen	stink	stank	stunk
run	ran	run	stride	strode	stridden
saw	sawed	sawed, sawn	strike	struck	struck, stricken
say	said	said			
see	saw	seen	strive	strove	striven
seek	sought	sought	swear	swore	sworn
sell	sold	sold	sweep	swept	swept
send	sent	sent	swell	swelled	swollen, swelled
set	set	set			
sew	sewed	sewn	swim	swam	swum
shake	shook	shaken	swing	swung	swung
shear	sheared	shorn, sheared	take	took	taken
			teach	taught	taught
shed	shed	shed	tear	tore	torn
shine	shone	shone	tell	told	told
shoot	shot	shot	think	thought	thought
show	showed	shown	throw	threw	thrown
shrink	shrank	shrunk	thrust	thrust	thrust
shut	shut	shut	tread	trod	trodden
sing	sang	sung	wake	woke, waked	woken, waked
sink	sank	sunk			
sit	sat	sat	wear	wore	worn
slay	slew	slain	weave	wove, weaved	woven, weaved
sleep	slept	slept			
slide	slid	slid	wed	wedded, wed	wedded, wed
sling	slung	slung			
slit	slit	slit	weep	wept	wept
smell	smelt, smelled	smelt, smelled	win	won	won
			wind	wound	wound
sow	sowed	sown, sowed	wring	wrung	wrung
speak	spoke	spoken	write	wrote	written
speed	sped, speeded	sped, speeded			

A *abbr* (= *autostrada*) ≈ M (*motorway*)

○ **PAROLA CHIAVE**

a (*a + il* = **al**, *a + lo* = **allo**, *a + l'* = **all'**, *a + la* = **alla**, *a + i* = **ai**, *a + gli* = **agli**, *a + le* = **alle**) *prep*
1 (*stato in luogo*) at; (: *in*) in; **essere alla stazione** to be at the station; **essere a casa/a scuola/a Roma** to be at home/at school/in Rome; **è a 10 km da qui** it's 10 km from here, it's 10 km away
2 (*moto a luogo*) to; **andare a casa/a scuola** to go home/to school
3 (*tempo*) at; (*epoca, stagione*) in; **alle cinque** at five (o'clock); **a mezzanotte/Natale** at midnight/Christmas; **al mattino** in the morning; **a maggio/primavera** in May/spring; **a cinquant'anni** at fifty (years of age); **a domani!** see you tomorrow!
4 (*complemento di termine*) to; **dare qc a qn** to give sth to sb
5 (*mezzo, modo*) with, by; **a piedi/cavallo** on foot/horseback; **fatto a mano** made by hand, handmade; **una barca a motore** a motorboat; **a uno a uno** one by one; **all'italiana** the Italian way, in the Italian fashion
6 (*rapporto*) a, per; (: *con prezzi*) at; **prendo 850 euro al mese** I get 850 euros a o per month; **pagato a ore** paid by the hour; **vendere qc a 2 euro il chilo** to sell sth at 2 euros a o per kilo

abbagli'ante [abbaʎˈʎante] *ag* dazzling; **abbaglianti** *smpl* (*Aut*): **accendere gli abbaglianti** to put one's headlights on full (*BRIT*) o high (*US*) beam
abbagli'are [abbaʎˈʎare] *vt* to dazzle; (*illudere*) to delude
abbai'are *vi* to bark
abbando'nare *vt* to leave, abandon, desert; (*trascurare*) to neglect; (*rinunciare a*) to abandon, give up; **abbandonarsi** *vpr* to let o.s. go; **abbandonarsi a** (*ricordi, vizio*) to give o.s. up to
abbas'sare *vt* to lower; (*radio*) to turn down; **abbassarsi** *vpr* (*chinarsi*) to stoop; (*livello, sole*) to go down; (*fig: umiliarsi*) to demean o.s.; **~ i fari** (*Aut*) to dip o dim (*US*) one's lights
ab'basso *escl* **~ il re!** down with the king!
abbas'tanza [abbasˈtantsa] *av* (*a sufficienza*) enough; (*alquanto*) quite, rather, fairly; **non è ~ furbo** he's not shrewd enough; **un vino ~ dolce** quite a sweet wine; **averne ~ di qn/qc** to have had enough of sb/sth
ab'battere *vt* (*muro, casa*) to pull down; (*ostacolo*) to knock down; (*albero*) to fell; (: *vento*) to bring down; (*bestie da macello*) to slaughter; (*cane, cavallo*) to destroy, put down; (*selvaggina, aereo*) to shoot down; (*fig: malattia, disgrazia*) to lay low; **abbattersi** *vpr* (*avvilirsi*) to lose heart; **abbat'tuto, -a** *ag* (*fig*) depressed
abba'zia [abbatˈtsia] *sf* abbey
'abbia *vb vedi* **avere**
abbi'ente *ag* well-to-do, well-off; **abbienti** *smpl* **gli abbienti** the well-to-do
abbiglia'mento [abbiʎʎaˈmento] *sm* dress *no pl*; (*indumenti*) clothes *pl*; (*industria*) clothing industry
abbi'nare *vt* **~ (a)** to combine (with)
abboc'care *vi* (*pesce*) to bite; (*tubi*) to join; **~ (all'amo)** (*fig*) to swallow the bait
abbona'mento *sm* subscription; (*alle ferrovie ecc*) season ticket; **fare l'~** to take out a subscription (o season ticket)
abbo'narsi *vpr* **~ a un giornale** to take out a subscription to a newspaper; **~ al teatro/alle ferrovie** to take out a season ticket for the theatre/the train
abbon'dante *ag* abundant, plentiful; (*giacca*) roomy
abbon'danza [abbonˈdantsa] *sf* abundance; plenty
abbor'dabile *ag* (*persona*) approachable; (*prezzo*) reasonable

abbotto'nare vt to button up, do up

abbracci'are [abbrat't∫are] vt to embrace; (*persona*) to hug, embrace; (*professione*) to take up; (*contenere*) to include;
abbracciarsi vpr to hug o embrace (one another); **ab'braccio** sm hug, embrace

abbrevi'are vt to shorten; (*parola*) to abbreviate

abbreviazi'one [abbrevjat'tsjone] sf abbreviation

abbron'zante [abbron'dzante] ag tanning, sun cpd

abbronzarsi vpr to tan, get a tan

abbron'zato, -a [abbron'dzato] ag (sun)tanned

abbrusto'lire vt (*pane*) to toast; (*caffè*) to roast; **abbrustolirsi** vpr to toast; (*fig: al sole*) to soak up the sun

abbuf'farsi vpr (*fam*): **~ (di qc)** to stuff o.s. (with sth)

abdi'care vi to abdicate; **~ a** to give up, renounce

a'bete sm fir (tree); **abete rosso** spruce

'abile ag (*idoneo*): **~ (a qc/a fare qc)** fit (for sth/to do sth); (*capace*) able; (*astuto*) clever; (*accorto*) skilful; **~ al servizio militare** fit for military service; **abilità** sf inv ability; cleverness; skill

a'bisso sm abyss, gulf

abi'tante sm/f inhabitant

abi'tare vt to live in, dwell in ▷ vi **~ in campagna/a Roma** to live in the country/in Rome; **dove abita?** where do you live?; **abitazi'one** sf residence; house

'abito sm dress no pl; (*da uomo*) suit; (*da donna*) dress; (*abitudine, disposizione, Rel*) habit; **abiti** smpl (*vestiti*) clothes; **in ~ da sera** in evening dress

abitu'ale ag usual, habitual; (*cliente*) regular

abitual'mente av usually, normally

abitu'are vt: **~ qn a** to get sb used o accustomed to; **abituarsi a** to get used to, accustom o.s. to

abitudi'nario, -a ag of fixed habits ▷ sm/f regular customer

abi'tudine sf habit; **aver l'~ di fare qc** to be in the habit of doing sth; **d'~** usually; **per ~** from o out of habit

abo'lire vt to abolish; (*Dir*) to repeal

abor'tire vi (*Med*) to miscarry, have a miscarriage; (: *deliberatamente*) to have an abortion; (*fig*) to miscarry, fail; **a'borto** sm miscarriage; abortion

ABS [abiɛse] sigla m (= *Anti-Blockier System*) ABS

'abside sf apse

abu'sare vi **~ di** to abuse, misuse; (*alcool*) to take to excess; (*approfittare, violare*) to take advantage of

abu'sivo, -a ag unauthorized, unlawful; (**occupante**) **~ (di una casa)** squatter
    Attenzione! In inglese esiste la parola *abusive* che però vuol dire *ingiurioso*.

a.C. av abbr (= *avanti Cristo*) B.C.

a'cacia, -cie [a'kat∫a] sf (*Bot*) acacia

ac'cadde vb vedi **accadere**

acca'demia sf (*società*) learned society; (*scuola: d'arte, militare*) academy

acca'dere vb impers to happen, occur

accal'dato ag hot

accalo'rarsi vpr (*fig*) to get excited

accampa'mento sm camp

accamparsi vpr to camp

acca'nirsi vpr (*infierire*) to rage; (*ostinarsi*) to persist; **acca'nito, -a** ag (*odio, gelosia*) fierce, bitter; (*lavoratore*) assiduous, dogged; (*fumatore*) inveterate

ac'canto av near, nearby; **~ a** prep near, beside, close to

accanto'nare vt (*problema*) to shelve; (*somma*) to set aside

accappa'toio sm bathrobe

accarez'zare [akkaret'tsare] vt to caress, stroke, fondle; (*fig*) to toy with

acca'sarsi vpr to set up house; to get married

accasci'arsi [akka∫'∫arsi] vpr to collapse; (*fig*) to lose heart

accat'tone, -a sm/f beggar

accaval'lare vt (*gambe*) to cross

acce'care [att∫e'kare] vt to blind ▷ vi to go blind

ac'cedere [at't∫edere] vi **~ a** to enter; (*richiesta*) to grant, accede to

accele'rare [att∫ele'rare] vt to speed up ▷ vi (*Aut*) to accelerate; **~ il passo** to quicken one's pace; **accelera'tore** sm (*Aut*) accelerator

ac'cendere [at't∫endere] vt (*fuoco, sigaretta*) to light; (*luce, televisione*) to put on, switch on, turn on; (*Aut: motore*) to switch on; (*Comm: conto*) to open; (*fig: suscitare*) to inflame, stir up; **ha da ~?** have you got a light?; **non riesco ad ~ il riscaldamento** I can't turn the heating on; **accen'dino, accendi'sigaro** sm (cigarette) lighter

accen'nare [att∫en'nare] vt (*Mus*) to pick out the notes of; to hum ▷ vi **~ a** (*fig: alludere a*) to hint at; (: *far atto di*) to make as if; **~ un saluto** (*con la mano*) to make as if to wave; (*col capo*) to half nod; **accenna a piovere** it looks as if it's going to rain

ac'cenno [at't∫enno] sm (*cenno*) sign; nod; (*allusione*) hint

accensi'one [att∫en'sjone] sf (*vedi verbo*) lighting; switching on; opening; (*Aut*) ignition

ac'cento [at'tʃɛnto] sm accent; (Fonetica, fig) stress; (inflessione) tone (of voice)

accentu'are [attʃentu'are] vt to stress, emphasize; **accentuarsi** vpr to become more noticeable

accerchi'are [attʃer'kjare] vt to surround, encircle

accerta'mento [attʃerta'mento] sm check; assessment

accer'tare [attʃer'tare] vt to ascertain; (verificare) to check; (reddito) to assess; **accertarsi** vpr **accertarsi (di)** to make sure (of)

ac'ceso, -a [at'tʃeso] pp di **accendere** ▷ ag lit; on; open; (colore) bright

acces'sibile [attʃes'sibile] ag (luogo) accessible; (persona) approachable; (prezzo) reasonable

ac'cesso [at'tʃesso] sm (anche Inform) access; (Med) attack, fit; (impulso violento) fit, outburst

accessori smpl accessories

ac'cetta [at'tʃetta] sf hatchet

accet'tabile [attʃet'tabile] ag acceptable

accet'tare [attʃet'tare] vt to accept; **accettate carte di credito?** do you accept credit cards?; **~ di fare qc** to agree to do sth; **accettazi'one** sf acceptance; (locale di servizio pubblico) reception; **accettazione bagagli** (Aer) check-in (desk)

acchiap'pare [akkjap'pare] vt to catch

acciaie'ria [attʃaje'ria] sf steelworks sg

acci'aio [at'tʃajo] sm steel

acciden'tato, -a [attʃiden'tato] ag (terreno ecc) uneven

accigli'ato, -a [attʃiʎ'ʎato] ag frowning

ac'cingersi [at'tʃindʒersi] vpr **~ a fare qc** to be about to do sth

acciuf'fare [attʃuf'fare] vt to seize, catch

acci'uga, -ghe [at'tʃuga] sf anchovy

ac'cludere vt to enclose

accocco'larsi vpr to crouch

accogli'ente [akkoʎ'ʎɛnte] ag welcoming, friendly

ac'cogliere [ak'kɔʎʎere] vt (ricevere) to receive; (dare il benvenuto) to welcome; (approvare) to agree to, accept; (contenere) to hold, accommodate

ac'colgo ecc vb vedi **accogliere**

ac'colsi ecc vb vedi **accogliere**

accoltel'lare vt to knife, stab

accomoda'mento sm agreement, settlement

accomo'dante ag accommodating

accomo'darsi vpr (sedersi) to sit down; (entrare) to come in; **s'accomodi!** (venga avanti) come in!; (si sieda) take a seat!

accompagna'mento [akkompaɲɲa'mento] sm (Mus) accompaniment

accompa'gnare [akkompaɲ'ɲare] vt to accompany, come o go with; (Mus) to accompany; (unire) to couple; **~ la porta** to close the door gently

accompagna'tore, -trice sm/f companion; **~ turistico** courier

acconcia'tura [akkontʃa'tura] sf hairstyle

accondiscen'dente [akkondiʃʃen'dɛnte] ag affable

acconsen'tire vi **~ (a)** to agree o consent (to)

acconten'tare vt to satisfy; **accontentarsi** vpr **accontentarsi di** to be satisfied with, content o.s. with

ac'conto sm part payment; **pagare una somma in ~** to pay a sum of money as a deposit

acco'rato, -a ag heartfelt

accorci'are [akkor'tʃare] vt to shorten; **accorciarsi** vpr to become shorter

accor'dare vt to reconcile; (colori) to match; (Mus) to tune; (Ling) **~ qc con qc** to make sth agree with sth; (Dir) to grant; **accordarsi** vpr to agree, come to an agreement; (colori) to match

ac'cordo sm agreement; (armonia) harmony; (Mus) chord; **essere d'~** to agree; **andare d'~** to get on well together; **d'~!** all right!, agreed!; **accordo commerciale** trade agreement

ac'corgersi [ak'kɔrdʒersi] vpr **~ di** to notice; (fig) to realize

ac'correre vi to run up

ac'corto, -a pp di **accorgersi** ▷ ag shrewd; **stare ~** to be on one's guard

accos'tare vt (avvicinare) **~ qc a** to bring sth near to, put sth near to; (avvicinarsi a) to approach; (socchiudere: imposte) to half-close; (: porta) to leave ajar ▷ vi (Naut) to come alongside; **accostarsi** vpr **accostarsi a** to draw near, approach; (fig) to support

accredi'tare vt (notizia) to confirm the truth of; (Comm) to credit; (diplomatico) to accredit

ac'credito sm (Comm: atto) crediting; (: effetto) credit

accucci'arsi [akkut'tʃarsi] vpr (cane) to lie down

accu'dire vt (anche: vi **~ a**) to attend to

accumu'lare vt to accumulate; **accumularsi** vpr to accumulate; (Finanza) to accrue

accu'rato, -a ag (diligente) careful; (preciso) accurate

ac'cusa *sf* accusation; (*Dir*) charge; **la pubblica ~** the prosecution

accu'sare *vt* **~ qn di qc** to accuse sb of sth; (*Dir*) to charge sb with sth; **~ ricevuta di** (*Comm*) to acknowledge receipt of

accusa'tore, -'trice *sm/f* accuser ▷ *sm* (*Dir*) prosecutor

a'cerbo, -a [a'tʃɛrbo] *ag* bitter; (*frutta*) sour, unripe; (*persona*) immature

'acero ['atʃero] *sm* maple

a'cerrimo, -a [a'tʃɛrrimo] *ag* very fierce

a'ceto [a'tʃeto] *sm* vinegar

ace'tone [atʃe'tone] *sm* nail varnish remover

A.C.I. ['atʃi] *sigla m* = **Automobile Club d'Italia**

'acido, -a ['atʃido] *ag* (*sapore*) acid, sour; (*Chim*) acid ▷ *sm* (*Chim*) acid

'acino ['atʃino] *sm* berry; **acino d'uva** grape

'acne *sf* acne

'acqua *sf* water; (*pioggia*) rain; **acque** *sfpl* (*di mare, fiume ecc*) waters; **fare ~** (*Naut*) to leak, take in water; **~ in bocca!** mum's the word!; **acqua corrente** running water; **acqua dolce/salata** fresh/salt water; **acqua minerale/potabile/tonica** mineral/drinking/tonic water; **acque termali** thermal waters

a'cquaio *sm* sink

acqua'ragia [akkwa'radʒa] *sf* turpentine

a'cquario *sm* aquarium; (*dello zodiaco*): **A~** Aquarius

acquascooter [akkwas'kuter] *sm inv* Jet Ski®

ac'quatico, -a, -ci, -che *ag* aquatic; (*Sport, Scienza*) water *cpd*

acqua'vite *sf* brandy

acquaz'zone [akkwat'tsone] *sm* cloudburst, heavy shower

acque'dotto *sm* aqueduct; waterworks *pl*, water system

acque'rello *sm* watercolour

acqui'rente *sm/f* purchaser, buyer

acquis'tare *vt* to purchase, buy; (*fig*) to gain; **a'cquisto** *sm* purchase; **fare acquisti** to go shopping

acquo'lina *sf* **far venire l'~ in bocca a qn** to make sb's mouth water

a'crobata, -i, -e *sm/f* acrobat

a'culeo *sm* (*Zool*) sting; (*Bot*) prickle

a'cume *sm* acumen, perspicacity

a'custico, -a, ci, che *ag* acoustic ▷ *sf* (*scienza*) acoustics *sg*; (*di una sala*) acoustics *pl*; **cornetto ~** ear trumpet; **apparecchio ~** hearing aid

a'cuto, -a *ag* (*appuntito*) sharp, pointed; (*suono, voce*) shrill, piercing; (*Mat, Ling, Med*) acute; (*Mus*) high-pitched; (*fig: dolore, desiderio*) intense; (: *perspicace*) acute, keen

a'dagio [a'dadʒo] *av* slowly ▷ *sm* (*Mus*) adagio; (*proverbio*) adage, saying

adatta'mento *sm* adaptation

adat'tare *vt* to adapt; (*sistemare*) to fit; **adattarsi** *vpr* **adattarsi (a)** (*ambiente, tempi*) to adapt (to); (*essere adatto*) to be suitable (for)

a'datto, -a *ag* **~ (a)** suitable (for), right (for)

addebi'tare *vt* **~ qc a qn** to debit sb with sth

ad'debito *sm* (*Comm*) debit

adden'tare *vt* to bite into

adden'trarsi *vpr* **~ in** to penetrate, go into

addestra'mento *sm* training

addes'trare *vt* to train

ad'detto, -a *ag* **~ a** (*persona*) assigned to; (*oggetto*) intended for ▷ *sm* employee; (*funzionario*) attaché; **gli addetti ai lavori** authorized personnel; (*fig*) those in the know; **addetto commerciale** commercial attaché; **addetto stampa** press attaché

ad'dio *sm, escl* goodbye, farewell

addirit'tura *av* (*veramente*) really, absolutely; (*perfino*) even; (*direttamente*) directly, right away

addi'tare *vt* to point out; (*fig*) to expose

addi'tivo *sm* additive

addizi'one *sf* addition

addob'bare *vt* to decorate; **ad'dobbo** *sm* decoration

addolo'rare *vt* to pain, grieve; **addolorarsi (per)** to be distressed (by)

addolo'rato, -a *ag* distressed, upset; **l'Addolorata** (*Rel*) Our Lady of Sorrows

ad'dome *sm* abdomen

addomesti'care *vt* to tame

addomi'nale *ag* abdominal; **(muscoli mpl) addominali** stomach muscles

addormen'tare *vt* to put to sleep; **addormentarsi** *vpr* to fall asleep, go to sleep

ad'dosso *av* on; **mettersi ~ il cappotto** to put one's coat on; **~ a** (*sopra*) on; (*molto vicino*) right next to; **stare ~ a qn** (*fig*) to breathe down sb's neck; **dare ~ a qn** (*fig*) to attack sb

adeguarsi *vpr* to adapt

adegu'ato, -a *ag* adequate; (*conveniente*) suitable; (*equo*) fair

a'dempiere *vt* to fulfil, carry out

ade'rente *ag* adhesive; (*vestito*) close-fitting ▷ *sm/f* follower

ade'rire *vi* (*stare attaccato*) to adhere, stick; **~ a** to adhere to, stick to; (*fig: società, partito*) to join; (: *opinione*) to support; (*richiesta*) to agree to

adesi'one *sf* adhesion; (*fig*) agreement,

acceptance; **ade'sivo, -a** ag, sm adhesive

a'desso av (ora) now; (or ora, poco fa) just now; (tra poco) any moment now

adia'cente [adja'tʃɛnte] ag adjacent

adi'bire vt (usare): **~ qc a** to turn sth into

adole'scente [adoleʃˈʃɛnte] ag, sm/f adolescent

adope'rare vt to use

ado'rare vt to adore; (Rel) to adore, worship

adot'tare vt to adopt; (decisione, provvedimenti) to pass; **adot'tivo, -a** ag (genitori) adoptive; (figlio, patria) adopted; **adozi'one** sf adoption; **adozione a distanza** child sponsorship

adri'atico, -a, -ci, -che ag Adriatic ▷ sm **l'A~, il mare A~** the Adriatic, the Adriatic Sea

adu'lare vt to adulate, flatter

a'dultero, -a ag adulterous ▷ sm/f adulterer (adulteress)

a'dulto, -a ag adult; (fig) mature ▷ sm adult, grown-up

a'ereo, -a ag air cpd; (radice) aerial ▷ sm aerial; (aeroplano) plane; **aereo da caccia** fighter (plane); **aereo di linea** airliner; **aereo a reazione** jet (plane); **ae'robica** sf aerobics sg; **aero'nautica** sf (scienza) aeronautics sg; **aeronautica militare** air force

aero'porto sm airport; **all'~ per favore** to the airport, please

aero'sol sm inv aerosol

'afa sf sultriness

af'fabile ag affable

affaccen'dato, -a [affattʃen'dato] ag (persona) busy

affacci'arsi [affat'tʃarsi] vpr **~ (a)** to appear (at)

affa'mato, -a ag starving; (fig): **~ (di)** eager (for)

affan'noso, -a ag (respiro) difficult; (fig) troubled, anxious

af'fare sm (faccenda) matter, affair; (Comm) piece of business, (business) deal; (occasione) bargain; (Dir) case; (fam: cosa) thing; **affari** smpl (Comm) business sg; **Ministro degli Affari esteri** Foreign Secretary (BRIT), Secretary of State (US)

affasci'nante [affaʃʃi'nante] ag fascinating

affasci'nare [affaʃʃi'nare] vt to bewitch; (fig) to charm, fascinate

affati'care vt to tire; **affaticarsi** vpr (durar fatica) to tire o.s. out; **affati'cato, -a** ag tired

af'fatto av completely; **non ... ~** not ... at all; **niente ~** not at all

affer'mare vt (dichiarare) to maintain,

affirm; **affermarsi** vpr to assert o.s., make one's name known; **affer'mato, -a** ag established, well-known; **affermazi'one** sf affirmation, assertion; (successo) achievement

affer'rare vt to seize, grasp; (fig: idea) to grasp; **afferrarsi** vpr **afferrarsi a** to cling to

affet'tare vt (tagliare a fette) to slice; (ostentare) to affect

affetta'trice [affetta'tritʃe] sf meat slicer

affet'tivo, -a ag emotional, affective

af'fetto sm affection; **affettu'oso, -a** ag affectionate

affezio'narsi [affettsjo'narsi] vpr **~ a** to grow fond of

affezio'nato, -a [affettsjo'nato] ag **~ a qn/qc** fond of sb/sth; (attaccato) attached to sb/sth

affia'tato, -a ag **essere molto affiatati** to get on very well

affibbi'are vt (fig: dare) to give

affi'dabile ag reliable

affida'mento sm (Dir: di bambino) custody; (fiducia): **fare ~ su qn** to rely on sb; **non dà nessun ~** he's not to be trusted

affi'dare vt **~ qc o qn a qn** to entrust sth o sb to sb; **affidarsi** vpr **affidarsi a** to place one's trust in

affi'lare vt to sharpen

affi'lato, -a ag (gen) sharp; (volto, naso) thin

affinché [affin'ke] cong in order that, so that

affit'tare vt (dare in affitto) to let, rent (out); (prendere in affitto) to rent; **af'fitto** sm rent; (contratto) lease

af'fliggere [af'fliddʒere] vt to torment; **affliggersi** vpr to grieve

af'flissi ecc vb vedi **affliggere**

afflosci'arsi [affloʃˈʃarsi] vpr to go limp

afflu'ente sm tributary

affo'gare vt, vi to drown

affol'lare vt to crowd; **affollarsi** vpr to crowd; **affol'lato, -a** ag crowded

affon'dare vt to sink

affran'care vt to free, liberate; (Amm) to redeem; (lettera) to stamp; (: meccanicamente) to frank (BRIT), meter (US)

af'fresco, -schi sm fresco

affret'tarsi vpr to hurry; **~ a fare qc** to hurry o hasten to do sth

affret'tato, -a ag (veloce: passo, ritmo) quick, fast; (frettoloso: decisione) hurried, hasty; (: lavoro) rushed

affron'tare vt (pericolo ecc) to face; (nemico) to confront; **affrontarsi** vpr (reciproco) to come to blows

affumi'cato, -a ag (prosciutto, aringa ecc) smoked

affuso'lato, -a ag tapering

Af'ganistan sm l'~ Afghanistan

a'foso, -a ag sultry, close

'Africa sf l'~ Africa; **afri'cano, -a** ag, sm/f African

a'genda [a'dʒɛnda] sf diary

Attenzione! In inglese esiste la parola agenda che però vuol dire ordine del giorno.

a'gente [a'dʒɛnte] sm agent; **agente di cambio** stockbroker; **agente di polizia** police officer; **agente segreto** secret agent; **agen'zia** sf agency; (succursale) branch; **agenzia immobiliare** estate agent's (office) (BRIT), real estate office (US); **agenzia di collocamento/stampa** employment/press agency; **agenzia viaggi** travel agency

agevo'lare [adʒevo'lare] vt to facilitate, make easy

agevolazi'one [adʒevolat'tsjone] sf (facilitazione economica) facility; **agevolazione di pagamento** payment on easy terms; **agevolazioni creditizie** credit facilities; **agevolazioni fiscali** tax concessions

a'gevole [a'dʒevole] ag easy; (strada) smooth

agganci'are [aggan'tʃare] vt to hook up; (Ferr) to couple

ag'geggio [ad'dʒeddʒo] sm gadget, contraption

agget'tivo [addʒet'tivo] sm adjective

agghiacci'ante [aggjat'tʃante] ag chilling

aggior'nare [addʒor'nare] vt (opera, manuale) to bring up-to-date; (seduta ecc) to postpone; **aggiornarsi** vpr to bring (o keep) o.s. up-to-date; **aggior'nato, -a** ag up-to-date

aggi'rare [addʒi'rare] vt to go round; (fig: ingannare) to trick; **aggirarsi** vpr to wander about; **il prezzo s'aggira sul milione** the price is around the million mark

aggi'ungere [ad'dʒundʒere] vt to add

aggi'unsi ecc [ad'dʒunsi] vb vedi **aggiungere**

aggius'tare [addʒus'tare] vt (accomodare) to mend, repair; (riassettare) to adjust; (fig: lite) to settle

aggrap'parsi vpr ~ **a** to cling to

aggra'vare vt (aumentare) to increase; (appesantire: anche fig) to weigh down, make heavy; (pena) to make worse; **aggravarsi** vpr to worsen, become worse

aggre'dire vt to attack, assault

aggressi'one sf aggression; (atto) attack, assault

aggres'sivo, -a ag aggressive

aggres'sore sm aggressor, attacker

aggrot'tare vt ~ **le sopracciglia** to frown

aggrovigliarsi vpr (fig) to become complicated

aggu'ato sm trap; (imboscata) ambush; **tendere un ~ a qn** to set a trap for sb

agguer'rito, -a ag fierce

agi'ato, -a [a'dʒato] ag (vita) easy; (persona) well-off, well-to-do

'agile ['adʒile] ag agile, nimble

'agio ['adʒo] sm ease, comfort; **mettersi a proprio ~** to make o.s. at home o comfortable; **agi** smpl comforts; **mettersi a proprio ~** to make o.s. at home o comfortable; **dare ~ a qn di fare qc** to give sb the chance of doing sth

a'gire [a'dʒire] vi to act; (esercitare un'azione) to take effect; (Tecn) to work, function; ~ **contro qn** (Dir) to take action against sb

agi'tare [adʒi'tare] vt (bottiglia) to shake; (mano, fazzoletto) to wave; (fig: turbare) to disturb; (: incitare) to stir (up); (: dibattere) to discuss; **agitarsi** vpr (mare) to be rough; (malato, dormitore) to toss and turn; (bambino) to fidget; (emozionarsi) to get upset; (Pol) to agitate; **agi'tato, -a** ag rough; restless; fidgety; upset, perturbed

'aglio ['aʎʎo] sm garlic

a'gnello [an'ɲɛllo] sm lamb

'ago (pl **'aghi**) sm needle

ago'nistico, -a, -ci, -che ag athletic; (fig) competitive

agopun'tura sf acupuncture

a'gosto sm August

a'grario, -a ag agrarian, agricultural; (riforma) land cpd

a'gricolo, -a ag agricultural, farm cpd; **agricol'tore** sm farmer; **agricol'tura** sf agriculture, farming

agri'foglio [agri'fɔʎʎo] sm holly

agritu'rismo sm farm holidays pl

agrodolce ag bittersweet; (salsa) sweet and sour

a'grume sm (spesso al pl: pianta) citrus; (: frutto) citrus fruit

a'guzzo, -a [a'guttso] ag sharp

'ahi escl (dolore) ouch!

'Aia sf l'~ the Hague

'aids abbr m o f Aids

airbag sm inv air bag

ai'rone sm heron

aiu'ola sf flower bed

aiu'tante sm/f assistant ▷ sm (Mil) adjutant; (Naut) master-at-arms; **aiutante di campo** aide-de-camp

aiu'tare vt to help; ~ **qn (a fare)** to help sb

(to do); **aiutarsi** *vpr* to help each other; **~ qn in qc/a fare qc** to help sb with sth/to do sth; **può aiutarmi?** can you help me?

ai'uto *sm* help, assistance, aid; *(aiutante)* assistant; **venire in ~ di qn** to come to sb's aid; **aiuto chirurgo** assistant surgeon

'ala *(pl* **'ali)** *sf* wing; **fare ~** to fall back, make way; **ala destra/sinistra** *(Sport)* right/left wing

ala'bastro *sm* alabaster

a'lano *sm* Great Dane

'alba *sf* dawn

alba'nese *ag, sm/f, sm* Albanian

Alba'nia *sf* **l'~** Albania

albe'rato, -a *ag (viale, piazza)* lined with trees, tree-lined

al'bergo, -ghi *sm* hotel; **albergo della gioventù** youth hostel

'albero *sm* tree; *(Naut)* mast; *(Tecn)* shaft; **albero genealogico** family tree; **albero a gomiti** crankshaft; **albero maestro** mainmast; **albero di Natale** Christmas tree; **albero di trasmissione** transmission shaft

albi'cocca, -che *sf* apricot

'album *sm* album; **album da disegno** sketch book

al'bume *sm* albumen

'alce ['altʃe] *sm* elk

'alcol *sm inv* = **alcool**

al'colico, -a, -ci, -che *ag* alcoholic ▷ *sm* alcoholic drink

alcoliz'zato, -a [alkolid'dzato] *sm/f* alcoholic

'alcool *sm inv* alcohol

al'cuno, -a *(det: dav sm:* **alcun** + *C, V,* **alcuno** + *s impura, gn, pn, ps, x, z; dav sf:* **alcuna** + *C,* **alcun'** + *V)* det *(nessuno):* **non ... ~** no, not any; **alcuni, e** *det pl* some, a few; **non c'è alcuna fretta** there's no hurry, there isn't any hurry; **senza alcun riguardo** without any consideration ▷ *pron pl* **alcuni, e** some, a few

alfa'betico, -a, ci, che *ag* alphabetical

alfa'beto *sm* alphabet

'alga, -ghe *sf* seaweed *no pl*, alga

'algebra ['aldʒebra] *sf* algebra

Alge'ria [aldʒe'ria] *sf* **l'~** Algeria

alge'rino, -a [aldʒe'rino] *ag, sm/f* Algerian

ali'ante *sm (Aer)* glider

'alibi *sm inv* alibi

a'lice [a'litʃe] *sf* anchovy

ali'eno, -a *ag (avverso):* **~ (da)** opposed (to), averse (to) ▷ *sm/f* alien

alimen'tare *vt* to feed; *(Tecn)* to feed; to supply; *(fig)* to sustain ▷ *ag* food *cpd*; **alimentari** *smpl* foodstuffs; *(anche:*

negozio di alimentari) grocer's shop;
alimentazi'one *sf* feeding; supplying; sustaining; *(gli alimenti)* diet

a'liquota *sf* share; *(d'imposta)* rate; **aliquota d'imposta** tax rate

alis'cafo *sm* hydrofoil

'alito *sm* breath

all. *abbr (= allegato)* encl.

allaccia'mento [allattʃa'mento] *sm* *(Tecn)* connection

allacci'are [allat'tʃare] *vt (scarpe)* to tie, lace (up); *(cintura)* to do up, fasten; *(luce, gas)* to connect; *(amicizia)* to form

allaccia'tura [allattʃa'tura] *sf* fastening

alla'gare *vt* to flood; **allagarsi** *vpr* to flood

allar'gare *vt* to widen; *(vestito)* to let out; *(aprire)* to open; *(fig: dilatare)* to extend; **allargarsi** *vpr (gen)* to widen; *(scarpe, pantaloni)* to stretch; *(fig: problema, fenomeno)* to spread

allar'mare *vt* to alarm

al'larme *sm* alarm; **allarme aereo** air-raid warning

allat'tare *vt* to breed

alle'anza [alle'antsa] *sf* alliance

alle'arsi *vpr* to form an alliance; **alle'ato, -a** *ag* allied ▷ *sm/f* ally

alle'gare *vt (accludere)* to enclose; *(Dir: citare)* to cite, adduce; *(denti)* to set on edge; **alle'gato, -a** *ag* enclosed ▷ *sm* enclosure; *(di e-mail)* attachment; **in allegato** enclosed

allege'rire [alleddʒe'rire] *vt* to lighten, make lighter; *(fig: lavoro, tasse)* to reduce

alle'gria *sf* gaiety, cheerfulness

al'legro, -a *ag* cheerful, merry; *(un po' brillo)* merry, tipsy; *(vivace: colore)* bright ▷ *sm (Mus)* allegro

allena'mento *sm* training

alle'nare *vt* to train; **allenarsi** *vpr* to train; **allena'tore** *sm (Sport)* trainer, coach

allen'tare *vt* to slacken; *(disciplina)* to relax; **allentarsi** *vpr* to become slack; *(ingranaggio)* to work loose

aller'gia, -'gie [aller'dʒia] *sf* allergy; **al'lergico, -a, -ci, -che** *ag* allergic; **sono allergico alla penicillina** I'm allergic to penicillin

alles'tire *vt (cena)* to prepare; *(esercito, nave)* to equip, fit out; *(spettacolo)* to stage

allet'tante *ag* attractive, alluring

alle'vare *vt (animale)* to breed, rear; *(bambino)* to bring up

allevi'are *vt* to alleviate

alli'bito, -a *ag* astounded

alli'evo *sm* pupil; *(apprendista)* apprentice; *(Mil)* cadet

alliga'tore *sm* alligator

alline'are vt (persone, cose) to line up; (Tip) to align; (fig: economia, salari) to adjust, align; **allinearsi** vpr to line up; (fig: a idee): **allinearsi a** to come into line with

al'lodola sf (sky)lark

alloggi'are [allod'dʒare] vt to accommodate ▷ vi to live; **al'loggio** sm lodging, accommodation (BRIT), accommodations (US)

allonta'nare vt to send away, send off; (impiegato) to dismiss; (pericolo) to avert, remove; (estraniare) to alienate; **allontanarsi** vpr **allontanarsi (da)** to go away (from); (estraniarsi) to become estranged (from)

al'lora av (in quel momento) then ▷ cong (in questo caso) well then; (dunque) well then, so; **la gente d'~** people then o in those days; **da ~ in poi** from then on

al'loro sm laurel

'alluce ['allutʃe] sm big toe

alluci'nante [allutʃi'nante] ag awful; (fam) amazing

allucinazi'one [allutʃinat'tsjone] sf hallucination

al'ludere vi ~ **a** to allude to, hint at

allu'minio sm aluminium (BRIT), aluminum (US)

allun'gare vt to lengthen; (distendere) to prolong, extend; (diluire) to water down; **allungarsi** vpr to lengthen; (ragazzo) to stretch, grow taller; (sdraiarsi) to lie down, stretch out

al'lusi ecc vb vedi **alludere**

allusi'one sf hint, allusion

alluvi'one sf flood

al'meno av at least ▷ cong **(se)** ~ if only; **(se) ~ piovesse!** if only it would rain!

a'logeno, -a [a'lɔdʒeno] ag **lampada alogena** halogen lamp

a'lone sm halo

'Alpi sfpl **le ~** the Alps

alpi'nismo sm mountaineering, climbing; **alpi'nista, -i, -e** sm/f mountaineer, climber

al'pino, -a ag Alpine; mountain cpd; **alpini** smpl (Mil) Italian Alpine troops

alt escl halt!, stop!

alta'lena sf (a funi) swing; (in bilico) seesaw

al'tare sm altar

alter'nare vt to alternate; **alternarsi** vpr to alternate; **alterna'tiva** sf alternative; **alterna'tivo, -a** ag alternative

al'terno, -a ag alternate; **a giorni alterni** on alternate days, every other day

al'tero, -a ag proud

al'tezza [al'tettsa] sf height; width, breadth; depth; pitch; (Geo) latitude;

(titolo) highness; (fig: nobiltà) greatness; **essere all'~ di** to be on a level with; (fig) to be up to o equal to

al'ticcio, -a, -ci, -ce [al'tittʃo] ag tipsy

alti'tudine sf altitude

'**alto, -a** ag high; (persona) tall; (tessuto) wide, broad; (sonno, acque) deep; (suono) high(-pitched); (Geo) upper; (settentrionale) northern ▷ sm top (part) ▷ av high; (parlare) aloud, loudly; **il palazzo è ~ 20 metri** the building is 20 metres high; **ad alta voce** aloud; **a notte alta** in the dead of night; **in ~** up, upwards; at the top; **dall'~ in o al basso** up and down; **degli alti e bassi** (fig) ups and downs; **alta fedeltà** high fidelity, hi-fi; **alta finanza/società** high finance/society; **alta moda** haute couture

altopar'lante sm loudspeaker

altopi'ano (pl **altipi'ani**) sm plateau, upland plain

altret'tanto, -a ag, pron as much; (pl) as many ▷ av equally; **tanti auguri! — grazie, ~** all the best! — thank you, the same to you

altri'menti av otherwise

○ PAROLA CHIAVE

'**altro, -a** det **1** (diverso) other, different; **questa è un'altra cosa** that's another o a different thing

2 (supplementare) other; **prendi un altro cioccolatino** have another chocolate; **hai avuto altre notizie?** have you had any more o any other news?

3 (nel tempo): **l'altro giorno** the other day; **l'altr'anno** last year; **l'altro ieri** the day before yesterday; **domani l'altro** the day after tomorrow; **quest'altro mese** next month

4: **d'altra parte** on the other hand ▷ pron **1** (persona, cosa diversa o supplementare): **un altro, un'altra** another (one); **lo farà un altro** someone else will do it; **altri, e** others; **gli altri** (la gente) others, other people; **l'uno e l'altro** both (of them); **aiutarsi l'un l'altro** to help one another; **da un giorno all'altro** from day to day; (nel giro di 24 ore) from one day to the next; (da un momento all'altro) any day now

2 (sostantivato: solo maschile) something else; (: in espressioni interrogative) anything else; **non ho altro da dire** I have nothing else o I don't have anything else to say; **più che altro** above all; **se non altro** at least; **tra l'altro** among other things; **ci mancherebbe altro!** that's all we need!; **non faccio altro che lavorare** I do nothing but work; **contento? — altro che!** are you pleased? — and how!; vedi **senza**; **noialtri**; **voialtri**; **tutto**

al'trove av elsewhere, somewhere else
altru'ista, -i, -e ag altruistic
a'lunno, -a sm/f pupil
alve'are sm hive
al'zare [al'tsare] vt to raise, lift; (issare) to hoist; (costruire) to build, erect; **alzarsi** vpr to rise; (dal letto) to get up; (crescere) to grow tall (o taller); **~ le spalle** to shrug one's shoulders; **alzarsi in piedi** to stand up, get to one's feet
a'maca, -che sf hammock
amalga'mare vt to amalgamate; **amalgamarsi** vpr to amalgamate
a'mante ag **~ di** (musica ecc) fond of ▷ sm/f lover/mistress
a'mare vt to love; (amico, musica, sport) to like; **amarsi** vpr to love each other
amareggi'ato, -a [amared'dʒato] ag upset, saddened
ama'rena sf sour black cherry
ama'rezza [ama'rettsa] sf bitterness
a'maro, -a ag bitter ▷ sm bitterness; (liquore) bitters pl
amaz'zonico, -a, -ci, che [amad'dzɔniko] ag Amazonian; Amazon cpd
ambasci'ata [ambaʃʃata] sf embassy; (messaggio) message; **ambascia'tore, -'trice** sm/f ambassador/ambassadress
ambe'due ag inv **~ i ragazzi** both boys ▷ pron inv both
ambienta'lista, -i, e ag environmental ▷ sm/f environmentalist
ambien'tare vt to acclimatize; (romanzo, film) to set; **ambientarsi** vpr to get used to one's surroundings
ambi'ente sm environment; (fig: insieme di persone) milieu; (stanza) room
am'biguo, -a ag ambiguous
ambizi'one [ambit'tsjone] sf ambition; **ambizi'oso, -a** ag ambitious
'ambo ag inv both ▷ sm (al gioco) double
'ambra sf amber; **ambra grigia** ambergris
ambu'lante ag itinerant ▷ sm peddler
ambu'lanza [ambu'lantsa] sf ambulance; **chiamate un ~** call an ambulance
ambula'torio sm (studio medico) surgery
A'merica sf l'**~** America; l'**~ latina** Latin America; **ameri'cano, -a** ag, sm/f American
ami'anto sm asbestos
ami'chevole [ami'kevole] ag friendly
ami'cizia [ami'tʃittsja] sf friendship; **amicizie** sfpl (amici) friends
a'mico, -a, -ci, -che sm/f friend;

(fidanzato) boyfriend/girlfriend; **amico del cuore** bosom friend
'amido sm starch
ammac'care vt (pentola) to dent; (persona) to bruise
ammacca'tura sf dent; bruise
ammaes'trare vt (animale) to train
ammai'nare vt to lower, haul down
amma'larsi vpr to fall ill; **amma'lato, -a** ag ill, sick ▷ sm/f sick person; (paziente) patient
ammanet'tare vt to handcuff
ammas'sare vt (ammucchiare) to amass; (raccogliere) to gather together; **ammassarsi** vpr to pile up; to gather
ammat'tire vi to go mad
ammaz'zare [ammat'tsare] vt to kill; **ammazzarsi** vpr (uccidersi) to kill o.s.; (rimanere ucciso) to be killed; **ammazzarsi di lavoro** to work o.s. to death
am'mettere vt to admit; (riconoscere: fatto) to acknowledge, admit; (permettere) to allow, accept; (supporre) to suppose
amminis'trare vt to run, manage; (Rel, Dir) to administer; **amministra'tore** sm administrator; (di condominio) flats manager; **amministratore delegato** managing director; **amministrazi'one** sf management; administration
ammi'raglio [ammi'raʎʎo] sm admiral
ammi'rare vt to admire; **ammirazi'one** sf admiration
am'misi ecc vb vedi **ammettere**
ammobili'ato, -a ag furnished
am'mollo sm **lasciare in ~** to leave to soak
ammo'niaca sf ammonia
ammo'nire vt (avvertire) to warn; (rimproverare) to admonish; (Dir) to caution
ammonizi'one [ammonit'tsjone] sf (monito: anche Sport) warning; (rimprovero) reprimand; (Dir) caution
ammon'tare vi **~ a** to amount to ▷ sm (total) amount
ammorbi'dente sm fabric conditioner
ammorbi'dire vt to soften
ammortizza'tore sm (Aut, Tecn) shock-absorber
ammucchi'are [ammuk'kjare] vt to pile up, accumulate
ammuf'fire vi to go mouldy (BRIT) o moldy (US)
ammuto'lire vi to be struck dumb
amne'sia sf amnesia
amnis'tia sf amnesty
'amo sm (Pesca) hook; (fig) bait
a'more sm love; **amori** smpl love affairs; **il tuo bambino è un ~** your baby's a darling; **fare l'~ o all'~** to make love; **per ~ o per forza** by hook or by crook; **amor proprio**

self-esteem, pride

amo'roso, -a ag (affettuoso) loving, affectionate; (d'amore: sguardo) amorous; (: poesia, relazione) love cpd

'ampio, -a ag wide, broad; (spazioso) spacious; (abbondante: vestito) loose; (: gonna) full; (: spiegazione) ample, full

am'plesso sm intercourse

ampli'are vt (ingrandire) to enlarge; (allargare) to widen; **ampliarsi** vpr to grow, increase

amplifica'tore sm (Tecn, Mus) amplifier

ampu'tare vt (Med) to amputate

A.N. sigla f (= Alleanza Nazionale) Italian right-wing party

anabbaglianti smpl dipped (BRIT) o dimmed (US) headlights

anaboliz'zante ag anabolic ▷ sm anabolic steroid

anal'colico, -a, -ci, -che ag non-alcoholic ▷ sm soft drink

analfa'beta, -i, -e ag, sm/f illiterate

anal'gesico, -a, -ci, -che [anal'dʒɛziko] ag, sm analgesic

a'nalisi sf inv analysis; (Med: esame) test; **analisi del sangue** blood test sg

analiz'zare [analid'dzare] vt to analyse; (Med) to test

a'nalogo, -a, -ghi, -ghe ag analogous

'ananas sm inv pineapple

anar'chia [anar'kia] sf anarchy; **a'narchico, -a, -ci, -che** ag anarchic(al) ▷ sm/f anarchist

anarco-insurreziona'lista ag anarcho-revolutionary

'A.N.A.S. sigla f (= Azienda Nazionale Autonoma delle Strade) national roads department

anato'mia sf anatomy

'anatra sf duck

'anca, -che sf (Anat) hip

'anche ['anke] cong (inoltre, pure) also, too; (perfino) even; **vengo anch'io** I'm coming too; **~ se** even if

an'cora av still; (di nuovo) again; (di più) some more; (persino): **~ più forte** even stronger; **non ~** not yet; **~ una volta** once more, once again; **~ un po'** a little more; (di tempo) a little longer

an'dare sm **a lungo ~** in the long run ▷ vi to go; (essere adatto): **~ a** to suit; (piacere): **il suo comportamento non mi va** I don't like the way he behaves; **ti va di ~ al cinema?** do you feel like going to the cinema?; **andarsene** to go away; **questa camicia va lavata** this shirt needs a wash o should be washed; **~ a cavallo** to ride; **~ in macchina/aereo** to go by car/plane; **~ a fare qc** to go and do sth; **~ a pescare/sciare** to go fishing/skiing; **~ a male** to go bad; **come va?** (lavoro, progetto) how are things?; **come va? — bene, grazie!** how are you? — fine, thanks!; **va fatto entro oggi** it's got to be done today; **ne va della nostra vita** our lives are at stake; **an'data** sf going; (viaggio) outward journey; **biglietto di sola andata** single (BRIT) o one-way ticket; **biglietto di andata e ritorno** return (BRIT) o round-trip (US) ticket

andrò ecc vb vedi andare

a'neddoto sm anecdote

a'nello sm ring; (di catena) link; **anelli** smpl (Ginnastica) rings

a'nemico, -a, -ci, -che ag anaemic

aneste'sia sf anaesthesia

'angelo ['andʒelo] sm angel; **angelo custode** guardian angel

anghe'ria [ange'ria] sf vexation

angli'cano, -a ag Anglican

anglo'sassone ag Anglo-Saxon

'angolo sm corner; (Mat) angle; **angolo cottura** (di appartamento ecc) cooking area

an'goscia, -sce [an'gɔʃʃa] sf deep anxiety, anguish no pl

angu'illa sf eel

an'guria sf watermelon

'anice ['anitʃe] sm (Cuc) aniseed; (Bot) anise

'anima sf soul; (abitante) inhabitant; **non c'era ~ viva** there wasn't a living soul; **anima gemella** soul mate

ani'male sm, ag animal; **animale domestico** pet

anna'cquare vt to water down, dilute

annaffi'are vt to water; **annaffia'toio** sm watering can

an'nata sf year; (importo annuo) annual amount; **vino d'~** vintage wine

anne'gare vt, vi to drown

anne'rire vt to blacken ▷ vi to become black

annien'tare vt to annihilate, destroy

anniver'sario sm anniversary; **anniversario di matrimonio** wedding anniversary

'anno sm year; **ha 8 anni** he's 8 (years old)

anno'dare vt to knot, tie; (fig: rapporto) to form

annoi'are vt to bore; **annoiarsi** vpr to be bored

> Attenzione! In inglese esiste il verbo to annoy che però vuol dire dare fastidio a.

anno'tare vt (registrare) to note, note down; (commentare) to annotate

annu'ale ag annual

annu'ire vi to nod; (acconsentire) to agree

annul'lare vt to annihilate, destroy;

(contratto, francobollo) to cancel; (matrimonio) to annul; (sentenza) to quash; (risultati) to declare void

annunci'are [annun'tʃare] vt to announce; (dar segni rivelatori) to herald

an'nuncio [an'nuntʃo] sm announcement; (fig) sign; **annunci economici** classified advertisements, small ads; **annunci mortuari** (colonna) obituary column; **annuncio pubblicitario** advertisement

'annuo, -a ag annual, yearly

annu'sare vt to sniff, smell; **~ tabacco** to take snuff

a'nomalo, -a ag anomalous

a'nonimo, -a ag anonymous ▷ sm (autore) anonymous writer (o painter ecc); **società anonima** (Comm) joint stock company

anores'sia sf anorexia

ano'ressico, -a, ci, che ag anorexic

anor'male ag abnormal ▷ sm/f subnormal person

ANSA sigla f (= Agenzia Nazionale Stampa Associata) press agency

'ansia sf anxiety

ansi'mare vi to pant

ansi'oso, -a ag anxious

'anta sf (di finestra) shutter; (di armadio) door

An'tartide sf l'~ Antarctica

an'tenna sf (Radio, TV) aerial; (Zool) antenna, feeler; (Naut) yard; **antenna parabolica** satellite dish

ante'prima sf preview; **anteprima di stampa** (Inform) print preview

anteri'ore ag (ruota, zampa) front; (fatti) previous, preceding

antiade'rente ag non-stick

antibi'otico, -a, -ci, -che ag, sm antibiotic

anti'camera sf anteroom; **fare ~** to wait (for an audience)

antici'pare [antitʃi'pare] vt (consegna, visita) to bring forward, anticipate; (somma di denaro) to pay in advance; (notizia) to disclose ▷ vi to be ahead of time; **an'ticipo** sm anticipation; (di denaro) advance; **in anticipo** early, in advance; **occorre che prenoti in anticipo?** do I need to book in advance?

an'tico, -a, -chi, -che ag (quadro, mobili) antique; (dell'antichità) ancient; **all'antica** old-fashioned

anticoncezio'nale [antikontʃettsjo'nale] sm contraceptive

anticonfor'mista, -i, -e ag, sm/f nonconformist

anti'corpo sm antibody

antidolo'rifico, -ci sm painkiller

anti'doping sm drug testing ▷ ag inv **test ~ drugs** (BRIT) o drug (US) test

an'tifona sf (Mus, Rel) antiphon; **capire l'~** (fig) to take the hint

anti'forfora ag inv anti-dandruff

anti'furto sm anti-theft device

anti'gelo [anti'dʒelo] ag inv **(liquido) ~** (per motore) antifreeze; (per cristalli) de-icer

antiglobalizzazione [antiglobaliddzat'tsjone] ag inv **movimento ~** anti-globalization movement

An'tille sfpl **le ~** the West Indies

antin'cendio [antin'tʃendjo] ag inv fire cpd

anti'nebbia sm inv (anche: **faro ~**: Aut) fog lamp

antinfiamma'torio, -a ag, sm anti-inflammatory

antio'rario [antio'rarjo] ag **in senso ~** anticlockwise

anti'pasto sm hors d'œuvre

antipa'tia sf antipathy, dislike; **anti'patico, -a, -ci, -che** ag unpleasant, disagreeable

antiproi'ettile ag inv bulletproof

antiquari'ato sm antique trade; **un oggetto d'~** an antique

anti'quario sm antique dealer

anti'quato, -a ag antiquated, old-fashioned

anti'rughe ag inv (crema, prodotto) anti-wrinkle

antitraspi'rante ag antiperspirant

anti'vipera ag inv **siero ~** remedy for snake bites

antivirus [anti'virus] sm inv antivirus software no pl ▷ ag inv antivirus

antolo'gia, -'gie [antolo'dʒia] sf anthology

anu'lare ag ring cpd ▷ sm third finger

'anzi ['antsi] av (invece) on the contrary; (o meglio) or rather, or better still

anzi'ano, -a [an'tsjano] ag old; (Amm) senior ▷ sm/f old person; senior member

anziché [antsi'ke] cong rather than

a'patico, -a, -ci, -che ag apathetic

'ape sf bee

aperi'tivo sm apéritif

aperta'mente av openly

a'perto, -a pp di **aprire** ▷ ag open; **all'~** in the open (air); **è ~ al pubblico?** is it open to the public?; **quando è ~ il museo?** when is the museum open?

aper'tura sf opening; (ampiezza) width; (Fot) aperture; **apertura alare** wing span; **apertura mentale** open-mindedness

ap'nea sf **immergersi in ~** to dive without breathing apparatus

a'postrofo sm apostrophe

ap'paio *ecc vb vedi* **apparire**

ap'palto *sm* (*Comm*) contract; **dare/prendere in ~ un lavoro** to let out/undertake a job on contract

appannarsi *vpr* to mist over; to grow dim

apparecchi'are [apparek'kjare] *vt* to prepare; (*tavola*) to set ▷ *vi* to set the table

appa'recchio [appa'rekkjo] *sm* piece of apparatus, device; (*aeroplano*) aircraft *inv*; **apparecchio acustico** hearing aid; **apparecchio telefonico** telephone; **apparecchio televisivo** television set

appa'rente *ag* apparent

appa'rire *vi* to appear; (*sembrare*) to seem, appear

apparta'mento *sm* flat (*BRIT*), apartment (*US*)

appar'tarsi *vpr* to withdraw

apparte'nere *vi* **~ a** to belong to

ap'parvi *ecc vb vedi* **apparire**

appassio'nare *vt* to thrill; (*commuovere*) to move; **appassionarsi** *vpr* **appassionarsi a qc** to take a great interest in sth; **appassio'nato, -a** *ag* passionate; (*entusiasta*): **appassionato (di)** keen (on)

appas'sire *vi* to wither

appas'sito, -a *ag* dead

ap'pello *sm* roll-call; (*implorazione, Dir*) appeal; **fare ~ a** to appeal to

ap'pena *av* (*a stento*) hardly, scarcely; (*solamente, da poco*) just ▷ *cong* as soon as; **(non) ~ furono arrivati ...** as soon as they had arrived ...; **~ ... che** *o* **quando** no sooner ... than

ap'pendere *vt* to hang (up)

appen'dice [appen'ditʃe] *sf* appendix; **romanzo d'~** popular serial

appendi'cite [appendi'tʃite] *sf* appendicitis

Appen'nini *smpl* **gli ~** the Apennines

appesan'tire *vt* to make heavy; **appesantirsi** *vpr* to grow stout

appe'tito *sm* appetite

appic'care *vt* **~ il fuoco a** to set fire to, set on fire

appicci'care [appittʃi'kare] *vt* to stick; **appiccicarsi** *vpr* to stick; (*fig: persona*) to cling

appiso'larsi *vpr* to doze off

applau'dire *vt, vi* to applaud; **ap'plauso** *sm* applause

appli'care *vt* to apply; (*regolamento*) to enforce; **applicarsi** *vpr* to apply o.s.

appoggi'are [appod'dʒare] *vt* (*mettere contro*): **~ qc a qc** to lean *o* rest sth against sth; (*fig: sostenere*) to support; **appoggiarsi** *vpr* **appoggiarsi a** to lean against; (*fig*) to rely upon; **ap'poggio** *sm* support

apposita'mente *av* specially; (*apposta*) on purpose

ap'posito, -a *ag* appropriate

ap'posta *av* on purpose, deliberately

appos'tarsi *vpr* to lie in wait

ap'prendere *vt* (*imparare*) to learn

appren'dista, -i, -e *sm/f* apprentice

apprensi'one *sf* apprehension

apprez'zare [appret'tsare] *vt* to appreciate

appro'dare *vi* (*Naut*) to land; (*fig*): **non ~ a nulla** to come to nothing

approfit'tare *vi* **~ di** to make the most of; (*peg*) to take advantage of

approfon'dire *vt* to deepen; (*fig*) to study in depth

appropri'ato, -a *ag* appropriate

approssima'tivo, -a *ag* approximate, rough; (*impreciso*) inexact, imprecise

appro'vare *vt* (*condotta, azione*) to approve of; (*candidato*) to pass; (*progetto di legge*) to approve

appunta'mento *sm* appointment; (*amoroso*) date; **darsi ~** to arrange to meet (one another); **ho un ~ con...** I have an appointment with ...; **vorrei prendere un ~** I'd like to make an appointment

ap'punto *sm* note; (*rimprovero*) reproach ▷ *av* (*proprio*) exactly, just; **per l'~!, ~!** exactly!

apribot'tiglie [apribot'tiʎʎe] *sm inv* bottle opener

a'prile *sm* April

a'prire *vt* to open; (*via, cadavere*) to open up; (*gas, luce, acqua*) to turn on ▷ *vi* to open; **aprirsi** *vpr* to open; **aprirsi a qn** to confide in sb, open one's heart to sb; **a che ora aprite?** what time do you open?

apris'catole *sm inv* tin (*BRIT*) *o* can opener

APT *sigla f* (= *Azienda di Promozione Turistica*) ≈ tourist board

aquagym [akkwa'dʒim] *sf* aquaerobics

'aquila *sf* (*Zool*) eagle; (*fig*) genius

aqui'lone *sm* (*giocattolo*) kite; (*vento*) North wind

A/R *abbr* = **andata e ritorno** (*biglietto*) return ticket (*BRIT*), round-trip ticket (*US*)

A'rabia Sau'dita *sf* **l'~** Saudi Arabia

'arabo, -a *ag, sm/f* Arab ▷ *sm* (*Ling*) Arabic

a'rachide [a'rakide] *sf* peanut

ara'gosta *sf* crayfish; lobster

a'rancia, -ce [a'rantʃa] *sf* orange; **aranci'ata** *sf* orangeade; **aranci'one** *ag inv* (*color*) **arancione** bright orange

a'rare *vt* to plough (*BRIT*), plow (*US*)

a'ratro *sm* plough (*BRIT*), plow (*US*)

a'razzo [a'rattso] *sm* tapestry

arbi'trare *vt* (*Sport*) to referee; to umpire; (*Dir*) to arbitrate

arbi'trario, -a ag arbitrary

'arbitro sm arbiter, judge; (Dir) arbitrator; (Sport) referee; (: Tennis, Cricket) umpire

ar'busto sm shrub

archeolo'gia [arkeolo'dʒia] sf arch(a)eology; **arche'ologo, -a, -gi, -ghe** sm/f arch(a)eologist

architet'tare [arkitet'tare] vt (fig: ideare) to devise; (: macchinare) to plan, concoct

archi'tetto [arki'tetto] sm architect; **architet'tura** sf architecture

ar'chivio [ar'kivjo] sm archives pl; (Inform) file

'arco sm (arma, Mus) bow; (Archit) arch; (Mat) arc

arcoba'leno sm rainbow

arcu'ato, -a ag curved, bent

'ardere vt, vi to burn

ar'desia sf slate

'area sf area; (Edil) land, ground; **area di rigore** (Sport) penalty area; **area di servizio** (Aut) service area

a'rena sf arena; (per corride) bullring; (sabbia) sand

are'narsi vpr to run aground

argente'ria [ardʒente'ria] sf silverware, silver

Argen'tina [ardʒen'tina] sf **l'~** Argentina; **argen'tino, -a** ag, sm/f Argentinian

ar'gento [ar'dʒento] sm silver; **argento vivo** quicksilver

ar'gilla [ar'dʒilla] sf clay

'argine ['ardʒine] sm embankment, bank; (diga) dyke, dike

argo'mento sm argument; (motivo) motive; (materia, tema) subject

'aria sf air; (espressione, aspetto) air, look; (Mus: melodia) tune; (di opera) aria; **mandare all'~ qc** to ruin o upset sth; **all'~ aperta** in the open (air)

'arido, -a ag arid

arieggi'are [arjed'dʒare] vt (cambiare aria) to air; (imitare) to imitate

ari'ete sm ram; (Mil) battering ram; (dello zodiaco): **A~** Aries

a'ringa, -ghe sf herring inv

arit'metica sf arithmetic

'arma, -i sf weapon, arm; (parte dell'esercito) arm; **chiamare alle armi** to call up (BRIT), draft (US); **sotto le armi** in the army (o forces); **alle armi!** to arms!; **arma atomica/nucleare** atomic/nuclear weapon; **arma da fuoco** firearm; **armi di distruzione di massa** weapons of mass destruction

arma'dietto sm (di medicinali) medicine cabinet; (in palestra ecc) locker; (in cucina) (kitchen) cupboard

ar'madio sm cupboard; (per abiti) wardrobe; **armadio a muro** built-in cupboard

ar'mato, -a ag **~ (di)** (anche fig) armed (with); ▷ sf (Mil) army; (Naut) fleet; **rapina a mano armata** armed robbery

arma'tura sf (struttura di sostegno) framework; (impalcatura) scaffolding; (Storia) armour no pl, suit of armour

armis'tizio [armis'tittsjo] sm armistice

armo'nia sf harmony

ar'nese sm tool, implement; (oggetto indeterminato) thing, contraption; **male in ~** (malvestito) badly dressed; (di salute malferma) in poor health; (povero) down-at-heel

'arnia sf hive

a'roma, -i sm aroma; fragrance; **aromi** smpl (Cuc) herbs and spices; **aromatera'pia** sf aromatherapy

'arpa sf (Mus) harp

arrabbi'are vi (cane) to be affected with rabies; **arrabbiarsi** vpr (essere preso dall'ira) to get angry, fly into a rage; **arrabbi'ato, -a** ag rabid, with rabies; furious, angry

arrampi'carsi vpr to climb (up)

arrangiarsi vpr to manage, do the best one can

arreda'mento sm (studio) interior design; (mobili ecc) furnishings pl

arre'dare vt to furnish

ar'rendersi vpr to surrender

arres'tare vt (fermare) to stop, halt; (catturare) to arrest; **arrestarsi** vpr (fermarsi) to stop; **ar'resto** sm (cessazione) stopping; (fermata) stop; (cattura, Med) arrest; **subire un arresto** to come to a stop o standstill; **mettere agli arresti** to place under arrest; **arresti domiciliari** house arrest sg

arre'trare vt, vi to withdraw; **arre'trato, -a** ag (lavoro) behind schedule; (paese, bambino) backward; (numero di giornale) back cpd; **arretrati** smpl arrears

arric'chire [arrik'kire] vt to enrich; **arricchirsi** vpr to become rich

arri'vare vi to arrive; (accadere) to happen, occur; **~ a** (livello, grado ecc) to reach; **a che ora arriva il treno da Londra?** what time does the train from London arrive?; **non ci arrivo** I can't reach it; (fig: non capisco) I can't understand it

arrive'derci [arrive'dertʃi] escl goodbye!

arri'vista, -i, -e sm/f go-getter

ar'rivo sm arrival; (Sport) finish, finishing line

arro'gante ag arrogant

arros'sire vi (per vergogna, timidezza) to blush, flush; (per gioia, rabbia) to flush

arros'tire vt to roast; (pane) to toast; (ai

ferri) to grill
ar'rosto sm, ag inv roast
arroto'lare vt to roll up
arroton'dare vt (forma, oggetto) to round; (stipendio) to add to; (somma) to round off
arruggi'nito, -a [arrudd'ʒin'nito] ag rusty
'arsi vb vedi **ardere**
'arte sf art; (abilità) skill
ar'teria sf artery; **arteria stradale** main road
'artico, -a, -ci, -che ag Arctic
articolazi'one sf articulation; (Anat, Tecn) joint
ar'ticolo sm article; **articolo di fondo** (Stampa) leader, leading article
artifici'ale [artifi'tʃale] ag artificial
artigia'nato [artidʒa'nato] sm craftsmanship; craftsmen pl
artigi'ano, -a [arti'dʒano] sm/f craftsman/woman
ar'tista, -i, -e sm/f artist; **ar'tistico, -a, -ci, -che** ag artistic
ar'trite sf (Med) arthritis
a'scella [aʃ'ʃella] sf (Anat) armpit
ascen'dente [aʃʃen'dɛnte] sm ancestor; (fig) ascendancy; (Astr) ascendant
ascen'sore [aʃʃen'sore] sm lift
a'scesso [aʃ'ʃɛsso] sm (Med) abscess
asciugaca'pelli [aʃʃugaka'pelli] sm hair-drier
asciuga'mano [aʃʃuga'mano] sm towel
asciu'gare [aʃʃu'gare] vt to dry; **asciugarsi** vpr to dry o.s.; (diventare asciutto) to dry
asci'utto, -a [aʃ'ʃutto] ag dry; (fig: magro) lean; (: burbero) curt; **restare a bocca asciutta** (fig) to be disappointed
ascol'tare vt to listen to
as'falto sm asphalt
'Asia sf l'~ Asia; **asi'atico, -a, -ci, -che** ag, sm/f Asiatic, Asian
a'silo sm refuge, sanctuary; **~ (d'infanzia)** nursery(-school); **asilo nido** crèche; **asilo politico** political asylum
'asino sm donkey, ass
ASL sigla f (= Azienda Sanitaria Locale) local health centre
'asma sf asthma
as'parago, -gi sm asparagus no pl
aspet'tare vt to wait for; (anche Comm) to await; (aspettarsi) to expect ▷ vi to wait; **aspettami, per favore** wait for me, please
as'petto sm (apparenza) aspect, appearance, look; (punto di vista) point of view; **di bell'~** good-looking
aspira'polvere sm inv vacuum cleaner
aspi'rare vt (respirare) to breathe in, inhale; (apparecchi) to suck (up) ▷ vi **~ a** to

aspire to
aspi'rina sf aspirin
'aspro, -a ag (sapore) sour, tart; (odore) acrid, pungent; (voce, clima, fig) harsh; (superficie) rough; (paesaggio) rugged
assaggi'are [assad'dʒare] vt to taste; **posso assaggiarlo?** can I have a taste?; **assaggino** [assad'dʒino] sm **assaggini** (Cuc) selection of first courses; **solo un assaggino** just a little
as'sai av (molto) a lot, much; (: con ag) very; (a sufficienza) enough ▷ ag inv (quantità) a lot of, much; (numero) a lot of, many; **~ contento** very pleased
as'salgo ecc vb vedi **assalire**
assa'lire vt to attack, assail
assal'tare vt (Mil) to storm; (banca) to raid; (treno, diligenza) to hold up
as'salto sm attack, assault
assassi'nare vt to murder; to assassinate; (fig) to ruin; **assas'sino, -a** ag murderous ▷ sm/f murderer; assassin
'asse sm (Tecn) axle; (Mat) axis ▷ sf board; **asse** sf **da stiro** ironing board
assedi'are vt to besiege
asse'gnare [assen'nare] vt to assign, allot; (premio) to award
as'segno [as'senno] sm allowance; (anche: **~ bancario**) cheque (BRIT), check (US); **contro ~** cash on delivery; **posso pagare con un ~?** can I pay by cheque?; **assegno circolare** bank draft; **assegni familiari** ≈ child benefit no pl; **assegno sbarrato** crossed cheque; **assegno di viaggio** traveller's cheque; **assegno a vuoto** dud cheque; **assegno di malattia/di invalidità** sick pay/disability benefit
assem'blea sf assembly
assen'tarsi vpr to go out
as'sente ag absent; (fig) faraway, vacant; **as'senza** sf absence
asse'tato, -a ag thirsty, parched
assicu'rare vt (accertare) to ensure; (infondere certezza) to assure; (fermare, legare) to make fast, secure; (fare un contratto di assicurazione) to insure; **assicurarsi** vpr (accertarsi): **assicurarsi (di)** to make sure (of); (contro il furto ecc): **assicurarsi (contro)** to insure o.s. (against); **assicurazi'one** sf assurance; insurance
assi'eme av (insieme) together; **~ a** (together) with
assil'lare vt to pester, torment
assis'tente sm/f assistant; **assistente sociale** social worker; **assistente di volo** (Aer) steward/stewardess
assis'tenza [assis'tɛntsa] sf assistance; **~ ospedaliera** free hospital treatment;

~ sociale welfare services *pl*; **assistenza sanitaria** health service

as'sistere *vt* (*aiutare*) to assist, help; (*curare*) to treat ▷ *vi* **~ (a qc)** (*essere presente*) to be present (at sth), to attend (sth)

'**asso** *sm* ace; **piantare qn in ~** to leave sb in the lurch

associ'are [asso't∫are] *vt* to associate; **associarsi** *vpr* to enter into partnership; **associarsi a** to become a member of, join; (*dolori, gioie*) to share in; **~ qn alle carceri** to take sb to prison

associazi'one [assot∫at'tsjone] *sf* association; (*Comm*) association, society; **~ a delinquere** (*Dir*) criminal association

as'solsi *ecc vb vedi* **assolvere**

assoluta'mente *av* absolutely

asso'luto, -a *ag* absolute

assoluzi'one [assolut'tsjone] *sf* (*Dir*) acquittal; (*Rel*) absolution

as'solvere *vt* (*Dir*) to acquit; (*Rel*) to absolve; (*adempiere*) to carry out, perform

assomigli'are [assomiλ'λare] *vi* **~ a** to resemble, look like; **assomigliarsi** *vpr* to look alike; (*nel carattere*) to be alike

asson'nato, -a *ag* sleepy

asso'pirsi *vpr* to doze off

assor'bente *ag* absorbent ▷ *sm*: **assorbente interno** tampon; **assorbente esterno/igienico** sanitary towel

assor'bire *vt* to absorb

assor'dare *vt* to deafen

assorti'mento *sm* assortment

assor'tito, -a *ag* assorted; matched, matching

assuefazi'one [assuefat'tsjone] *sf* (*Med*) addiction

as'sumere *vt* (*impiegato*) to take on, engage; (*responsabilità*) to assume, take upon o.s.; (*contegno, espressione*) to assume, put on; (*droga*) to consume

as'sunsi *ecc vb vedi* **assumere**

assurdità *sf inv* absurdity; **dire delle ~** to talk nonsense

as'surdo, -a *ag* absurd

'**asta** *sf* pole; (*vendita*) auction

as'temio, -a *ag* teetotal ▷ *sm/f* teetotaller
> Attenzione! In inglese esiste la parola *abstemious* che però vuol dire *moderato*.

aste'nersi *vpr* **~ (da)** to abstain (from), refrain (from); (*Pol*) to abstain (from)

aste'risco, -schi *sm* asterisk

'**astice** ['astit∫e] *sm* lobster

astig'matico, -a, ci, che *ag* astigmatic

asti'nenza [asti'nɛntsa] *sf* abstinence; **essere in crisi di ~** to suffer from withdrawal symptoms

as'tratto, -a *ag* abstract

'**astro...** *prefisso*: **astrolo'gia** [astrolo'dʒia] *sf* astrology; **astro'nauta, -i, -e** *sm/f* astronaut; **astro'nave** *sf* space ship; **astrono'mia** *sf* astronomy; **astro'nomico, -a, -ci, -che** *ag* astronomic(al)

as'tuccio [as'tutt∫o] *sm* case, box, holder

as'tuto, -a *ag* astute, cunning, shrewd

A'tene *sf* Athens

'**ateo, -a** *ag, sm/f* atheist

at'lante *sm* atlas

at'lantico, -a, -ci, -che *ag* Atlantic ▷ *sm* **l'A~, l'Oceano A~** the Atlantic, the Atlantic Ocean

at'leta, -i, -e *sm/f* athlete; **at'letica** *sf* athletics *sg*; **atletica leggera** track and field events *pl*; **atletica pesante** weightlifting and wrestling

atmos'fera *sf* atmosphere

a'tomico, -a, -ci, -che *ag* atomic; (*nucleare*) atomic, atom *cpd*, nuclear

'**atomo** *sm* atom

'**atrio** *sm* entrance hall, lobby

a'troce [a'trot∫e] *ag* (*che provoca orrore*) dreadful; (*terribile*) atrocious

attac'cante *sm/f* (*Sport*) forward

attacca'panni *sm* hook, peg; (*mobile*) hall stand

attac'care *vt* (*unire*) to attach; (*cucendo*) to sew on; (*far aderire*) to stick (on); (*appendere*) to hang (up); (*assalire: anche fig*) to attack; (*iniziare*) to begin, start; (*fig: contagiare*) to pass on ▷ *vi* to stick, adhere; **attaccarsi** *vpr* to stick, adhere; (*trasmettersi per contagio*) to be contagious; (*afferrarsi*): **attaccarsi (a)** to cling (to); (*fig: affezionarsi*): **attaccarsi (a)** to become attached (to); **~ discorso** to start a conversation; **at'tacco, -chi** *sm* (*azione offensiva: anche fig*) attack; (*Med*) attack, fit; (*Sci*) binding; (*Elettr*) socket

atteggia'mento [attedd ʒa'mento] *sm* attitude

at'tendere *vt* to wait for, await ▷ *vi* **~ a** to attend to

atten'dibile *ag* (*storia*) credible; (*testimone*) reliable

atten'tato *sm* attack; **~ alla vita di qn** attempt on sb's life

at'tento, -a *ag* attentive; (*accurato*) careful, thorough; **stare ~ a qc** to pay attention to sth; **~!** be careful!

attenzi'one [atten'tsjone] *sf* attention; **~!** watch out!, be careful!; **attenzioni** *sfpl* (*premure*) attentions; **fare ~ a** to look out for; **coprire qn di attenzioni** to lavish attentions on sb

atter'raggio [atter'radd ʒo] *sm* landing

atter'rare vt to bring down ▷ vi to land

at'tesa sf waiting; (tempo trascorso aspettando) wait; **essere in ~ di qc** to be waiting for sth

at'tesi ecc vb vedi **attendere**

at'teso, -a pp di **attendere**

'attico, -ci sm attic

attil'lato, -a ag (vestito) close-fitting

'attimo sm moment; **in un ~** in a moment

atti'rare vt to attract

atti'tudine sf (disposizione) aptitude; (atteggiamento) attitude

attività sf inv activity; (Comm) assets pl

at'tivo, -a ag active; (Comm) profit-making, credit cpd ▷ sm (Comm) assets pl; **in ~** in credit

'atto sm act; (azione, gesto) action, act, deed; (Dir: documento) deed, document; **atti** smpl (di congressi ecc) proceedings; **mettere in ~** to put into action; **fare ~ di fare qc** to make as if to do sth; **atto di morte/di nascita** death/birth certificate

at'tore, -'trice sm/f actor/actress

at'torno av round, around, about; **~ a** round, around, about

attrac'care vt, vi (Naut) to dock, berth

at'tracco, -chi sm (Naut) docking no pl; berth

at'trae ecc vb vedi **attrarre**

attra'ente ag attractive

at'traggo ecc vb vedi **attrarre**

at'trarre vt to attract

at'trassi ecc vb vedi **attrarre**

attraver'sare vt to cross; (città, bosco, fig: periodo) to go through; (fiume) to run through

attra'verso prep through; (da una parte all'altra) across

attrazi'one [attrat'tsjone] sf attraction

at'trezzo sm tool, instrument; (Sport) piece of equipment

at'trice [at'tritʃe] sf vedi **attore**

attu'ale ag (presente) present; (di attualità) topical

> Attenzione! In inglese esiste la parola actual che però vuol dire effettivo.

attualità sf inv topicality; (avvenimento) current event

attual'mente av at the moment, at present

> Attenzione! In inglese esiste la parola actually che però vuol dire effettivamente oppure veramente.

attu'are vt to carry out

attu'tire vt to deaden, reduce

'audio sm (TV, Radio, Cine) sound

audiovi'sivo, -a ag audiovisual

audizi'one [audit'tsjone] sf hearing; (Mus) audition

augu'rare vt to wish; **augurarsi qc** to hope for sth

au'guri smpl best wishes; **fare gli ~ a qn** to give sb one's best wishes; **tanti ~!** best wishes!; (per compleanno) happy birthday!

'aula sf (scolastica) classroom; (universitaria) lecture theatre; (di edificio pubblico) hall

aumen'tare vt, vi to increase; **au'mento** sm increase

au'rora sf dawn

ausili'are ag, sm, sm/f auxiliary

Aus'tralia sf **l'~** Australia; **australi'ano, -a** ag, sm/f Australian

'Austria sf **l'~** Austria; **aus'triaco, -a, -ci, -che** ag, sm/f Austrian

au'tentico, -a, -ci, -che ag authentic, genuine

au'tista, -i sm driver

'auto sf inv car

autoabbron'zante sm, ag self-tan

autoade'sivo, -a ag self-adhesive ▷ sm sticker

autobio'grafico, -a, ci, che ag autobiographic(al)

'autobus sm inv bus

auto'carro sm lorry (BRIT), truck

autocertificazi'one [autotʃertifikat'tsjone] sf self-declaration

autodistrut'tivo, -a ag self-destructive

auto'gol sm inv own goal

au'tografo, -a ag, sm autograph

auto'grill® sm inv motorway restaurant

auto'matico, -a, -ci, -che ag automatic ▷ sm (bottone) snap fastener; (fucile) automatic

auto'mobile sf (motor) car

automobi'lista, -i, -e sm/f motorist

auto'leggio sm car hire

autono'mia sf autonomy; (di volo) range

au'tonomo, -a ag autonomous, independent

autop'sia sf post-mortem, autopsy

auto'radio sf inv (apparecchio) car radio; (autoveicolo) radio car

au'tore, -'trice sm/f author

autoreggente [autored'dʒente] ag **calze autoreggenti** hold ups

auto'revole ag authoritative; (persona) influential

autoricari'cabile ag **scheda ~** top-up card

autori'messa sf garage

autorità sf inv authority

autoriz'zare [autorid'dzare] vt (permettere) to authorize; (giustificare) to allow, sanction

autos'contro sm dodgem car (BRIT), bumper car (US)

autoscu'ola sf driving school
autos'tima sf self-esteem
autos'top sm hitchhiking;
autostop'pista, -i, -e sm/f hitchhiker
autos'trada sf motorway (BRIT),
highway (US); **autostrada informatica**
information superhighway

● **AUTOSTRADE**
●
● You have to pay to use Italian
● motorways. They are indicated by an "A"
● followed by a number on a green sign.
● The speed limit on Italian motorways
● is 130 kph.

auto'velox® sm inv (police) speed camera
autovet'tura sf (motor) car
au'tunno sm autumn
avam'braccio [avam'brattʃo] (pl (f) **-cia**)
sm forearm
avangu'ardia sf vanguard
a'vanti av (stato in luogo) in front; (moto:
andare, venire) forward; (tempo: prima)
before ▷ prep (luogo): **~ a** before, in front
of; (tempo): **~ Cristo** before Christ ▷ escl
(entrate) come (o go) in!; (Mil) forward!;
(coraggio) come on! ▷ sm inv (Sport)
forward; **~ e indietro** backwards and
forwards; **andare ~** to go forward;
(continuare) to go on; (precedere) to go
(on) ahead; (orologio) to be fast; **essere ~
negli studi** to be well advanced with one's
studies
avan'zare [avan'tsare] vt (spostare
in avanti) to move forward, advance;
(domanda) to put forward; (promuovere) to
promote; (essere creditore): **~ qc da qn** to be
owed sth by sb ▷ vi (andare avanti) to move
forward, advance; (progredire) to make
progress; (essere d'avanzo) to be left, remain
ava'ria sf (guasto) damage; (: meccanico)
breakdown
a'varo, -a ag avaricious, miserly ▷ sm
miser

PAROLA CHIAVE

a'vere sm (Comm) credit; **gli averi** (ricchezze)
wealth sg
▷ vt 1 (possedere) to have; **ha due
bambini/una bella casa** she has (got)
two children/a lovely house; **ha i capelli
lunghi** he has (got) long hair; **non ho da
mangiare/bere** I've (got) nothing to eat/
drink, I don't have anything to eat/drink
2 (indossare) to wear, have on; **aveva una
maglietta rossa** he was wearing o he had
on a red tee-shirt; **ha gli occhiali** he wears

o has glasses
3 (ricevere) to get; **hai avuto l'assegno?**
did you get o have you had the cheque?
4 (età, dimensione) to be; **ha 9 anni** he
is 9 (years old); **la stanza ha 3 metri di
lunghezza** the room is 3 metres in length;
vedi **fame; paura** ecc
5 (tempo): **quanti ne abbiamo oggi?**
what's the date today?; **ne hai per molto?**
will you be long?
6 (fraseologia): **avercela con qn** to be
angry with sb; **cos'hai?** what's wrong o
what's the matter (with you)?; **non ha
niente a che vedere o fare con me** it's
got nothing to do with me
▷ vb aus 1 to have; **aver bevuto/
mangiato** to have drunk/eaten
2 (+ da + infinito): **avere da fare qc** to have
to do sth; **non hai che da chiederlo** you
only have to ask him

aviazi'one [avjat'tsjone] sf aviation; (Mil)
air force
'avido, -a ag eager; (peg) greedy
avo'cado sm avocado
a'vorio sm ivory
Avv. abbr = **avvocato**
avvantaggi'are [avvantad'dʒare]
vt to favour; **avvantaggiarsi** vpr
**avvantaggiarsi negli affari/sui
concorrenti** to get ahead in business/of
one's competitors
avvele'nare vt to poison
av'vengo ecc vb vedi **avvenire**
avveni'mento sm event
avve'nire vi, vb impers to happen, occur
▷ sm future
av'venni ecc vb vedi **avvenire**
avven'tato, -a ag rash, reckless
avven'tura sf adventure; (amorosa) affair
avventu'rarsi vpr to venture
avventu'roso, -a ag adventurous
avve'rarsi vpr to come true
av'verbio sm adverb
avverrò ecc vb vedi **avvenire**
avver'sario, -a ag opposing ▷ sm
opponent, adversary
avver'tenza [avver'tentsa] sf
(ammonimento) warning; (cautela) care;
(premessa) foreword; **avvertenze** sfpl
(istruzioni per l'uso) instructions
avverti'mento sm warning
avver'tire vt (avvisare) to warn; (rendere
consapevole) to inform, notify; (percepire)
to feel
avvi'are vt (mettere sul cammino) to direct;
(impresa, trattative) to begin, start; (motore)
to start; **avviarsi** vpr to set off, set out
avvici'nare [avvitʃi'nare] vt to bring

near; (trattare con: persona) to approach;
avvicinarsi vpr **avvicinarsi (a qn/qc)** to
approach (sb/sth), draw near (to sb/sth)
avvi'lito, -a ag discouraged
avvin'cente ag captivating
avvi'sare vt (far sapere) to inform;
(mettere in guardia) to warn; **av'viso** sm
warning; (annuncio) announcement;
(: affisso) notice; (inserzione pubblicitaria)
advertisement; **a mio avviso** in my
opinion; **avviso di chiamata** (servizio)
call waiting; (segnale) call waiting signal;
avviso di garanzia (Dir) notification (of
impending investigation and of the right to
name a defence lawyer)

Attenzione! In inglese esiste la parola
advice che però vuol dire *consiglio*.

avvis'tare vt to sight
avvi'tare vt to screw down (o in)
avvo'cato, -'essa sm/f (Dir) barrister
(BRIT), lawyer; (fig) defender, advocate
av'volgere [av'vɔldʒere] vt to roll up;
(avviluppare) to wrap up; **avvolgersi** vpr
(avvilupparsi) to wrap o.s. up; **avvol'gibile**
sm roller blind (BRIT), blind
av'volsi ecc vb vedi **avvolgere**
avvol'toio sm vulture
aza'lea [addza'lea] sf azalea
azi'enda [ad'dzjɛnda] sf business, firm,
concern; **azienda agricola** farm
azi'one [at'tsjone] sf action; (Comm) share
a'zoto [ad'dzɔto] sm nitrogen
azzar'dare [addzar'dare] vt (soldi, vita) to
risk, hazard; (domanda, ipotesi) to hazard,
venture; **azzardarsi** vpr **azzardarsi a fare**
to dare (to) do
az'zardo [ad'dzardo] sm risk
azzec'care [attsek'kare] vt (risposta ecc)
to get right
azzuf'farsi [attsuf'farsi] vpr to come to
blows
az'zurro, -a [ad'dzurro] ag blue ▷ sm
(colore) blue; **gli azzurri** (Sport) the Italian
national team

b

'babbo sm (fam) dad, daddy; **Babbo
Natale** Father Christmas
baby'sitter ['beɪbɪsɪtəʳ] sm/f inv baby-
sitter
'bacca, -che sf berry
baccà' sm dried salted cod; (fig: peg)
dummy
bac'chetta [bak'ketta] sf (verga) stick, rod;
(di direttore d'orchestra) baton; (di tamburo)
drumstick; **~ magica** magic wand
ba'checa, -che [ba'kɛka] sf (mobile)
showcase, display case; (Univ, in ufficio)
notice board (BRIT), bulletin board (US)
baci'are [ba'tʃare] vt to kiss; **baciarsi** vpr
to kiss (one another)
baci'nella [batʃi'nɛlla] sf basin
ba'cino [ba'tʃino] sm basin; (Mineralogia)
field, bed; (Anat) pelvis; (Naut) dock
'bacio ['batʃo] sm kiss
'baco, -chi sm worm; **baco da seta**
silkworm
ba'dare vi (fare attenzione) to take care, be
careful; (occuparsi di): **~ a** to look after, take
care of; (dare ascolto): **~ a** to pay attention
to; **bada ai fatti tuoi!** mind your own
business!
'baffi smpl moustache sg; (di animale)
whiskers; **ridere sotto i ~** to laugh up
one's sleeve; **leccarsi i ~** to lick one's lips
bagagli'aio [bagaʎ'ʎajo] sm luggage van

(BRIT) o car (US); (Aut) boot (BRIT), trunk (US)

ba'gaglio [ba'ɡaʎʎo] sm luggage no pl, baggage no pl; **fare/disfare i bagagli** to pack/unpack; **i nostri bagagli non sono arrivati** our luggage has not arrived; **può mandare qualcuno a prendere i nostri bagagli?** could you send someone to collect our luggage?; **bagaglio a mano** hand luggage

bagli'ore [baʎ'ʎore] sm flash, dazzling light; **un ~ di speranza** a ray of hope

ba'gnante [baɲ'ɲante] sm/f bather

ba'gnare [baɲ'ɲare] vt to wet; (inzuppare) to soak; (innaffiare) to water; (fiume) to flow through; (: mare) to wash, bathe; **bagnarsi** vpr to get wet; (al mare) to go swimming o bathing; (in vasca) to have a bath

ba'gnato, -a [baɲ'ɲato] ag wet

ba'gnino [baɲ'ɲino] sm lifeguard

'bagno ['baɲɲo] sm bath; (stanza) bathroom; (toilette) toilet; **bagni** smpl (stabilimento) baths; **fare il ~** to have a bath; (nel mare) to go swimming o bathing; **dov'è il ~?** where's the toilet?; **fare il ~ a qn** to give sb a bath; **mettere a ~** to soak; **~ schiuma** bubble bath

bagnoma'ria [baɲɲoma'ria] sm **cuocere a ~** to cook in a double saucepan

bagnoschi'uma [baɲɲoskj'uma] sm inv bubble bath

'baia sf bay

balbet'tare vi to stutter, stammer; (bimbo) to babble ▷ vt to stammer out

bal'canico, -a, ci, che ag Balkan

bal'cone sm balcony; **avete una camera con ~?** do you have a room with a balcony?

bal'doria sf **fare ~** to have a riotous time

ba'lena sf whale

ba'leno sm flash of lightning; **in un ~** in a flash

bal'lare vt, vi to dance

balle'rina sf dancer; ballet dancer; (scarpa) ballet shoe

balle'rino sm dancer; ballet dancer

bal'letto sm ballet

'ballo sm dance; (azione) dancing no pl; **essere in ~** (fig: persona) to be involved; (: cosa) to be at stake

balne'are ag seaside cpd; (stagione) bathing

'balsamo sm (aroma) balsam; (lenimento, fig) balm

bal'zare [bal'tsare] vi to bounce; (lanciarsi) to jump, leap; **'balzo** sm bounce; jump, leap; (del terreno) crag

bam'bina ag, sf vedi **bambino**

bam'bino, -a sm/f child

'bambola sf doll

bambù sm bamboo

ba'nale ag banal, commonplace

ba'nana sf banana

'banca, -che sf bank; **banca dati** data bank

banca'rella sf stall

banca'rotta sf bankruptcy; **fare ~** to go bankrupt

ban'chetto [ban'ketto] sm banquet

banchi'ere [ban'kjɛre] sm banker

ban'china [ban'kina] sf (di porto) quay; (per pedoni, ciclisti) path; (di stazione) platform; **~ cedevole** (Aut) soft verge (BRIT) o shoulder (US)

'banco, -chi sm bench; (di negozio) counter; (di mercato) stall; (di officina) (work-)bench; (Geo, banca) bank; **banco di corallo** coral reef; **banco degli imputati** dock; **banco di prova** (fig) testing ground; **banco dei testimoni** witness box; **banco dei pegni** pawnshop; **banco di nebbia** bank of fog

'Bancomat® sm inv automated banking; (tessera) cash card

banco'nota sf banknote

'banda sf band; (di stoffa) band, stripe; (lato, parte) side; **~ perforata** punch tape

bandi'era sf flag, banner

ban'dito sm outlaw, bandit

'bando sm proclamation; (esilio) exile, banishment; **~ alle chiacchiere!** that's enough talk!; **bando di concorso** announcement of a competition

bar sm inv bar

'bara sf coffin

ba'racca, -che sf shed, hut; (peg) hovel; **mandare avanti la ~** to keep things going

ba'rare vi to cheat

'baratro sm abyss

ba'ratto sm barter

ba'rattolo sm (di latta) tin; (di vetro) jar; (di coccio) pot

'barba sf beard; **farsi la ~** to shave; **farla in ~ a qn** (fig) to do sth to sb's face; **che ~!** what a bore!

barbabi'etola sf beetroot (BRIT), beet (US); **barbabietola da zucchero** sugar beet

barbi'ere sm barber

bar'bone sm (cane) poodle; (vagabondo) tramp

'barca, -che sf boat; **barca a motore** motorboat; **barca a remi** rowing boat; **barca a vela** sail(ing) boat

barcol'lare vi to stagger

ba'rella sf (lettiga) stretcher

ba'rile sm barrel, cask

ba'rista, -i, -e sm/f barman/maid; (proprietario) bar owner

ba'rocco, -a, -chi, -che *ag, sm* baroque
ba'rometro *sm* barometer
ba'rone *sm* baron; **baro'nessa** *sf* baroness
'barra *sf* bar; (*Naut*) helm; (*linea grafica*) line, stroke
bar'rare *vt* to bar
barri'carsi *vpr* to barricade o.s.
barri'era *sf* barrier; (*Geo*) reef
ba'ruffa *sf* scuffle
barzel'letta [bardzel'letta] *sf* joke, funny story
ba'sare *vt* to base, found; **basarsi** *vpr* **basarsi su** (*fatti, prove*) to be based o founded on; (: *persona*) to base one's arguments on
'basco, -a, -schi, -sche *ag* Basque ▷ *sm* (*copricapo*) beret
'base *sf* base; (*fig: fondamento*) basis; (*Pol*) rank and file; **di ~** basic; **in ~ a** on the basis of, according to; **a ~ di caffè** coffee-based
'baseball ['beisbɔːl] *sm* baseball
ba'sette *sfpl* sideburns
ba'silica, -che *sf* basilica
ba'silico *sm* basil
basket ['basket] *sm* basketball
bas'sista, -i, -e *sm/f* bass player
'basso, -a *ag* low; (*di statura*) short; (*meridionale*) ▷ *sm* bottom, lower part; (*Mus*) bass; **la bassa Italia** southern Italy
bassorili'evo *sm* bas-relief
bas'sotto, -a *ag* squat ▷ *sm* (*cane*) dachshund
'basta *escl* (that's) enough!, that will do!
bas'tardo, -a *ag* (*animale, pianta*) hybrid, crossbreed; (*persona*) illegitimate, bastard; (*peg*) ▷ *sm/f* illegitimate child, bastard (*peg*)
bas'tare *vi, vb impers* to be enough, be sufficient; **~ a qn** to be enough for sb; **basta chiedere** o **che chieda a un vigile** you have only to o need only ask a policeman; **basta così, grazie** that's enough, thanks
basto'nare *vt* to beat, thrash
baston'cino [baston'tʃino] *sm* (*Sci*) ski pole; **bastoncini di pesce** fish fingers
bas'tone *sm* stick; **~ da passeggio** walking stick
bat'taglia [bat'taʎʎa] *sf* battle; fight
bat'tello *sm* boat
bat'tente *sm* (*imposta: di porta*) wing, flap; (: *di finestra*) shutter; (*batacchio: di porta*) knocker; (: *di orologio*) hammer; **chiudere i battenti** (*fig*) to shut up shop
'battere *vt* to beat; (*grano*) to thresh; (*percorrere*) to scour ▷ *vi* (*bussare*) to knock; (*urtare*): **~ contro** to hit o strike against;

(*pioggia, sole*) to beat down; (*cuore*) to beat; (*Tennis*) to serve; **battersi** *vpr* to fight; **~ le mani** to clap; **~ i piedi** to stamp one's feet; **~ a macchina** to type; **~ bandiera italiana** to fly the Italian flag; **~ in testa** (*Aut*) to knock; **in un batter d'occhio** in the twinkling of an eye
batte'ria *sf* battery; (*Mus*) drums *pl*
bat'terio *sm* bacterium
batte'rista, -i, -e *sm/f* drummer
bat'tesimo *sm* (*rito*) baptism; christening
battez'zare [batted'dzare] *vt* to baptize; to christen
batti'panni *sm inv* carpet-beater
battis'trada *sm inv* (*di pneumatico*) tread; (*di gara*) pacemaker
'battito *sm* beat, throb; **battito cardiaco** heartbeat
bat'tuta *sf* blow; (*di macchina da scrivere*) stroke; (*Mus*) bar; beat; (*Teatro*) cue; (*frase spiritosa*) witty remark; (*di caccia*) beating; (*Polizia*) combing, scouring; (*Tennis*) service
ba'tuffolo *sm* wad
ba'ule *sm* trunk; (*Aut*) boot (*BRIT*), trunk (*US*)
'bava *sf* (*di animale*) slaver, slobber; (*di lumaca*) slime; (*di vento*) breath
bava'glino [bavaʎ'ʎino] *sm* bib
ba'vaglio [ba'vaʎʎo] *sm* gag
'bavero *sm* collar
ba'zar [bad'dzar] *sm inv* bazaar
BCE *sigla f* (= *Banca centrale europea*) ECB
be'ato, -a *ag* blessed; (*fig*) happy; **~ te!** lucky you!
bec'care *vt* to peck; (*fig: raffreddore*) to catch; **beccarsi** *vpr* (*fig*) to squabble; **beccarsi qc** to catch sth
beccherò *ecc* [bekke'rɔ] *vb vedi* **beccare**
'becco, -chi *sm* beak, bill; (*di caffettiera ecc*) spout; lip
be'fana *sf* hag, witch; **la B~** old woman who, according to legend, brings children their presents at the Epiphany; (*Epifania*) Epiphany

● **BEFANA**
●
● The **Befana** is a national holiday on the
● feast of the Epiphany. It takes its name
● from **la Befana**, the old woman who,
● according to Italian legend comes down
● the chimney during the night leaving
● gifts for children who have been good,
● and coal for those who have not.

bef'fardo, -a *ag* scornful, mocking
'begli ['beʎʎi] *ag vedi* **bello**
'bei *ag vedi* **bello**

beige [bɛʒ] *ag inv* beige
bel *ag vedi* **bello**
be'lare *vi* to bleat
'belga, -gi, -ghe *ag, sm/f* Belgian
'Belgio ['bɛldʒo] *sm* **il ~** Belgium
'bella *sf* (*Sport*) decider; *vedi anche* **bello**
bel'lezza [bel'lettsa] *sf* beauty

  PAROLA CHIAVE

'bello, -a (*ag: dav sm* **bel** + C, **bell'** + V,
bello + *s impura, gn, pn, ps, x, z, pl* **bei** +
C, **begli** + *s impura ecc o* V) *ag* 1 (*oggetto,
donna, paesaggio*) beautiful, lovely; (*uomo*)
handsome; (*tempo*) beautiful, fine, lovely;
le belle arti fine arts
2 (*quantità*): **una bella cifra** a considerable
sum of money; **un bel niente** absolutely
nothing
3 (*rafforzativo*): **è una truffa bella e
buona!** it's a real fraud!; **è bell'e finito** it's
already finished
▷ *sm* 1 (*bellezza*) beauty; (*tempo*) fine
weather
2: **adesso viene il bello** now comes the
best bit; **sul più bello** at the crucial point;
cosa fai di bello? are you doing anything
interesting?
▷ *av* **fa bello** the weather is fine, it's fine

'belva *sf* wild animal
belve'dere *sm inv* panoramic viewpoint
benché [ben'ke] *cong* although
'benda *sf* bandage; (*per gli occhi*) blindfold;
ben'dare *vt* to bandage; to blindfold
'bene *av* well; (*completamente, affatto*):
è ben difficile it's very difficult ▷ *ag inv*
gente ~ well-to-do people ▷ *sm* good;
beni *smpl* (*averi*) property *sg*, estate *sg*;
io sto ~/poco ~ I'm well/not very well;
va ~ all right; **volere un ~ dell'anima a
qn** to love sb very much; **un uomo per ~**
a respectable man; **fare ~** to do the right
thing; **fare ~ a** (*salute*) to be good for; **fare
del ~ a qn** to do sb a good turn; **beni di
consumo** consumer goods
bene'detto, -a *pp di* **benedire** ▷ *ag*
blessed, holy
bene'dire *vt* to bless; to consecrate
benedu'cato, -a *ag* well-mannered
benefi'cenza [benefi'tʃentsa] *sf* charity
bene'ficio [bene'fitʃo] *sm* benefit; **con ~
d'inventario** (*fig*) with reservations
be'nessere *sm* well-being
benes'tante *ag* well-to-do
be'nigno, -a [be'niɲɲo] *ag* kind, kindly;
(*critica ecc*) favourable; (*Med*) benign
benve'nuto, -a *ag, sm* welcome; **dare il ~
a qn** to welcome sb

ben'zina [ben'dzina] *sf* petrol (*BRIT*), gas
(*US*); **fare ~** to get petrol (*BRIT*) o gas (*US*);
sono rimasto senza ~ I have run out of
petrol (*BRIT*) o gas (*US*); **benzina verde**
unleaded (petrol); **benzi'naio** *sm* petrol
(*BRIT*) o gas (*US*) pump attendant
'bere *vt* to drink; **darla a ~ a qn** (*fig*) to fool
sb; **vuoi qualcosa da ~?** would you like
a drink?
ber'lina *sf* (*Aut*) saloon (car) (*BRIT*), sedan
(*US*)
Ber'lino *sf* Berlin
ber'muda *smpl* (*calzoncini*) Bermuda
shorts
ber'noccolo *sm* bump; (*inclinazione*) flair
ber'retto *sm* cap
berrò *ecc vb vedi* **bere**
ber'saglio [ber'saʎʎo] *sm* target
besciamella [beʃʃa'mɛlla] *sf* béchamel
sauce
bes'temmia *sf* curse; (*Rel*) blasphemy
bestemmi'are *vi* to curse, swear; to
blaspheme ▷ *vt* to curse, swear at; to
blaspheme
'bestia *sf* animal; **andare in ~** (*fig*) to fly
into a rage; **besti'ale** *ag* beastly; animal
cpd; (*fam*): **fa un freddo bestiale** it's
bitterly cold; **besti'ame** *sm* livestock;
(*bovino*) cattle *pl*
be'tulla *sf* birch
be'vanda *sf* drink, beverage
'bevo *ecc vb vedi* **bere**
be'vuto, -a *pp di* **bere**
'bevvi *ecc vb vedi* **bere**
bianche'ria [bjanke'ria] *sf* linen; **~
da donna** ladies' underwear, lingerie;
biancheria femminile lingerie;
biancheria intima underwear
bi'anco, -a, -chi, -che *ag* white; (*non
scritto*) blank ▷ *sm* white; (*intonaco*)
whitewash ▷ *sm/f* white, white man/
woman; **in ~** (*foglio, assegno*) blank; (*notte*)
sleepless; **in ~ e nero** (*TV, Fot*) black and
white; **mangiare in ~** to follow a bland
diet; **pesce in ~** boiled fish; **andare in
~** (*non riuscire*) to fail; **bianco dell'uovo**
egg-white
biasi'mare *vt* to disapprove of, censure
'Bibbia *sf* (*anche fig*) bible
bibe'ron *sm inv* feeding bottle
'bibita *sf* (soft) drink
biblio'teca, -che *sf* library; (*mobile*)
bookcase
bicarbo'nato *sm* **~ (di sodio)** bicarbonate
(of soda)
bicchi'ere [bik'kjɛre] *sm* glass
bici'cletta [bitʃi'kletta] *sf* bicycle; **andare
in ~** to cycle
bidè *sm inv* bidet

bi'dello, -a *sm/f* (*Ins*) janitor

bi'done *sm* drum, can; (*anche*: ~ dell'immondizia) (dust)bin; (*fam*: truffa) swindle; fare un ~ a qn (*fam*) to let sb down; to cheat sb

bien'nale *ag* biennial

● BIENNALE DI VENEZIA

The Biennale di Venezia is an international contemporary art festival, which takes place every two years at Giardini in Venice. In its current form, it includes exhibits by artists from the many countries taking part, a thematic exhibition and a section for young artists.

bifamili'are *ag* ≈ semi-detached house

bifor'carsi *vpr* to fork

bigiotte'ria [bidʒotte'ria] *sf* costume jewellery; (*negozio*) jeweller's (*selling only costume jewellery*)

bigliet'taio, -a *sm/f* (*in treno*) ticket inspector; (*in autobus*) conductor

bigliette'ria [biʎʎette'ria] *sf* (*di stazione*) ticket office; booking office; (*di teatro*) box office

bigli'etto [biʎ'ʎetto] *sm* (*per viaggi, spettacoli ecc*) ticket; (*cartoncino*) card; (*anche*: ~ di banca) (bank)note; biglietto d'auguri greetings card; biglietto di visita visiting card; biglietto d'andata e ritorno return (ticket), round-trip ticket (*us*); biglietto di sola andata single (ticket)

bignè [bin'ɲe] *sm inv* cream puff

bigo'dino *sm* roller, curler

bi'gotto, -a *ag* over-pious ▷ *sm/f* church fiend

bi'kini *sm inv* bikini

bi'lancia, -ce [bi'lantʃa] *sf* (*pesa*) scales *pl*; (: *di precisione*) balance; (*dello zodiaco*): B~ Libra; bilancia commerciale balance of trade; bilancia dei pagamenti balance of payments

bi'lancio [bi'lantʃo] *sm* (*Comm*) balance(-sheet); (*statale*) budget; fare il ~ di (*fig*) to assess; bilancio consuntivo (*final*) balance; bilancio preventivo budget

bili'ardo *sm* billiards *sg*; billiard table

bi'lingue *ag* bilingual

bilo'cale *sm* two-room flat (*Brit*) o apartment (*us*)

bi'nario, -a *ag* (*sistema*) binary ▷ *sm* (*railway*) track o line; (*piattaforma*) platform; da che ~ parte il treno per Londra? which platform does the train for London go from?; binario morto dead-end track

bi'nocolo *sm* binoculars *pl*

bio... *prefisso*; biodegra'dabile *ag* biodegradable; biodi'namico, -a, -ci, -che *ag* biodynamic; biogra'fia *sf* biography; biolo'gia *sf* biology

bio'logico, -a, -ci, -che *ag* (*scienze, fenomeni ecc*) biological; (*agricoltura, prodotti*) organic; guerra biologica biological warfare

bi'ondo, -a *ag* blond, fair

biotecnologia [bioteknolo'dʒia] *sf* biotechnology

biri'chino, -a [biri'kino] *ag* mischievous ▷ *sm/f* scamp, little rascal

bi'rillo *sm* skittle (*BRIT*), pin (*US*)

'biro® *sf inv* biro®

'birra *sf* beer; a tutta ~ (*fig*) at top speed; birra chiara/scura ≈ lager/stout; birre'ria *sf* ≈ bierkeller

bis *escl*, *sm inv* encore

bis'betico, -a, -ci, -che *ag* ill-tempered, crabby

bisbigli'are [bisbiʎ'ʎare] *vt*, *vi* to whisper

'bisca, -sche *sf* gambling-house

'biscia, -sce ['biʃʃa] *sf* snake; biscia d'acqua grass snake

biscot'tato, -a *ag* crisp; fette biscottate rusks

bis'cotto *sm* biscuit

bisessu'ale *ag*, *sm/f* bisexual

bises'tile *ag* anno ~ leap year

bis'nonno, -a *sm/f* great grandfather/grandmother

biso'gnare [bizoɲ'ɲare] *vb impers* bisogna che tu parta/lo faccia you'll have to go/do it; bisogna parlargli we'll (o I'll) have to talk to him

bi'sogno [bi'zoɲɲo] *sm* need; ha ~ di qualcosa? do you need anything?

bis'tecca, -che *sf* steak, beefsteak

bisticci'are [bistit'tʃare] *vi* to quarrel, bicker; bisticciarsi *vpr* to quarrel, bicker

'bisturi *sm* scalpel

'bivio *sm* fork; (*fig*) dilemma

biz'zarro, -a [bid'dzarro] *ag* bizarre, strange

blate'rare *vi* to chatter

blin'dato, -a *ag* armoured

bloc'care *vt* to block; (*isolare*) to isolate, cut off; (*porto*) to blockade; (*prezzi, beni*) to freeze; (*meccanismo*) to jam; bloccarsi *vpr* (*motore*) to stall; (*freni, porta*) to jam, stick; (*ascensore*) to stop, get stuck

blocche'rò *ecc* [blokke'rɔ] *vb vedi* bloccare

bloc'chetto [blok'ketto] *sm* notebook; (*di biglietti*) book

'blocco, -chi sm block; (Mil) blockade; (dei fitti) restriction; (quadernetto) pad; (fig: unione) coalition; (il bloccare) blocking; isolating, cutting-off; blockading; freezing; jamming; **in ~** (nell'insieme) as a whole; (Comm) in bulk; **blocco cardiaco** cardiac arrest; **blocco stradale** road block

blu ag inv, sm dark blue

'blusa sf (camiciotto) smock; (camicetta) blouse

'boa sm inv (Zool) boa constrictor; (sciarpa) feather boa ▷ sf buoy

bo'ato sm rumble, roar

bob [bɔb] sm inv bobsleigh

'bocca, -che sf mouth; **in ~ al lupo!** good luck!

boc'caccia, -ce [bok'kattʃa] sf (malalingua) gossip; **fare le boccacce** to pull faces

boc'cale sm jug; **boccale da birra** tankard

boc'cetta [bot'tʃetta] sf small bottle

'boccia, -ce ['bɔttʃa] sf bottle; (da vino) decanter, carafe; (palla) bowl; **gioco delle bocce** bowls sg

bocci'are [bot'tʃare] vt (proposta, progetto) to reject; (Ins) to fail; (Bocce) to hit

bocci'olo [bot'tʃɔlo] sm bud

boc'cone sm mouthful, morsel

boicot'tare vt to boycott

'bolla sf bubble; (Med) blister; **bolla di consegna** (Comm) delivery note; **bolla papale** papal bull

bol'lente ag boiling; boiling hot

bol'letta sf bill; (ricevuta) receipt; **essere in ~** to be hard up

bollet'tino sm bulletin; (Comm) note; **bollettino meteorologico** weather report; **bollettino di spedizione** consignment note

bollicina [bolli'tʃina] sf bubble

bol'lire vt, vi to boil

bolli'tore sm (Cuc) kettle; (per riscaldamento) boiler

'bollo sm stamp; **bollo per patente** driving licence tax; **bollo postale** postmark

'bomba sf bomb; **bomba atomica** atom bomb; **bomba a mano** hand grenade; **bomba ad orologeria** time bomb

bombarda'mento sm bombardment; bombing

bombar'dare vt to bombard; (da aereo) to bomb

'bombola sf cylinder

bombo'letta sf aerosol

bomboni'era sf box of sweets (as souvenir at weddings, first communions etc)

bo'nifico, -ci sm (riduzione, abbuono)

discount; (versamento a terzi) credit transfer

bontà sf goodness; (cortesia) kindness; **aver la ~ di fare qc** to be good o kind enough to do sth

borbot'tare vi to mumble

'borchia ['bɔrkja] sf stud

bor'deaux [bor'dɔ] ag inv, sm inv maroon

'bordo sm (Naut) ship's side; (orlo) edge; (striscia di guarnizione) border, trim; **a ~ di** (nave, aereo) aboard, on board; (macchina) in

bor'ghese [bor'geze] ag (spesso peg) middle-class; bourgeois; **abito ~** civilian dress

'borgo, -ghi sm (paesino) village; (quartiere) district; (sobborgo) suburb

boro'talco sm talcum powder

bor'raccia, -ce [bor'rattʃa] sf canteen, water-bottle

'borsa sf bag; (anche: **~ da signora**) handbag; (Econ): **la B~ (valori)** the Stock Exchange; **borsa dell'acqua calda** hot-water bottle; **borsa nera** black market; **borsa della spesa** shopping bag; **borsa di studio** grant; **borsel'lino** sm purse; **bor'setta** sf handbag

'bosco, -schi sm wood

bos'niaco, -a, ci, che ag, sm/f Bosnian

'Bosnia Erze'govina ['bɔsnja erdze'govina] sf **la ~** Bosnia Herzegovina

Bot, bot sigla m inv (= buono ordinario del Tesoro) short-term Treasury bond

bo'tanica sf botany

bo'tanico, -a, -ci, -che ag botanical ▷ sm botanist

'botola sf trap door

'botta sf blow; (rumore) bang

'botte sf barrel, cask

bot'tega, -ghe sf shop; (officina) workshop

bot'tiglia [bot'tiʎʎa] sf bottle; **bottiglie'ria** sf wine shop

bot'tino sm (di guerra) booty; (di rapina, furto) loot

'botto sm bang; crash; **di ~** suddenly

bot'tone sm button; **attaccare ~ a qn** (fig) to buttonhole sb

bo'vino, -a ag bovine; **bovini** smpl cattle

box [bɔks] sm inv (per cavalli) horsebox; (per macchina) lock-up; (per macchina da corsa) pit; (per bambini) playpen

boxe [bɔks] sf boxing

'boxer ['bɔkser] sm inv (cane) boxer ▷ smpl (mutande): **un paio di ~** a pair of boxer shorts

BR sigla fpl = **Brigate Rosse**

brac'cetto [brat'tʃetto] sm **a ~** arm in arm

braccia'letto sm bracelet, bangle

bracci'ata [brat'tʃata] *sf* (*nel nuoto*) stroke

'**braccio** ['brattʃo] (*pl(f)* **braccia**) *sm* (*Anat*) arm; (*pl(m)* bracci: *di gru, fiume*) arm; (: *di edificio*) wing; **braccio di mare** sound; **bracci'olo** *sm* (*appoggio*) arm

'**bracco, -chi** *sm* hound

'**brace** ['bratʃe] *sf* embers *pl*

braci'ola [bra'tʃɔla] *sf* (*Cuc*) chop

'**branca, -che** *sf* branch

'**branchia** ['brankja] *sf* (*Zool*) gill

'**branco, -chi** *sm* (*di cani, lupi*) pack; (*di pecore*) flock; (*peg: di persone*) gang, pack

bran'dina *sf* camp bed (BRIT), cot (US)

'**brano** *sm* piece; (*di libro*) passage

Bra'sile *sm* **il ~** Brazil; **brasili'ano, -a** *ag, sm/f* Brazilian

'**bravo, -a** *ag* (*abile*) clever, capable, skilful; (*buono*) good, honest; (: *bambino*) good; (*coraggioso*) brave; **~!** well done!; (*a teatro*) bravo!

bra'vura *sf* cleverness, skill

Bre'tagna [bre'taɲɲa] *sf* **la ~** Brittany

bre'tella *sf* (*Aut*) link; **bretelle** *sfpl* (*di calzoni*) braces

'**bretone** *ag, sm/f* Breton

'**breve** *ag, sm/f* brief, short; **in ~** in short

brevet'tare *vt* to patent

bre'vetto *sm* patent; **brevetto di pilotaggio** pilot's licence (BRIT) o license (US)

'**bricco, -chi** *sm* jug; **bricco del caffè** coffeepot

'**briciola** ['britʃola] *sf* crumb

'**briciolo** ['britʃolo] *sm* (*specie fig*) bit

'**briga, -ghe** *sf* (*fastidio*) trouble, bother; **pigliarsi la ~ di fare qc** to take the trouble to do sth

bri'gata *sf* (*Mil*) brigade; (*gruppo*) group, party; **Brigate Rosse** (*Pol*) Red Brigades

'**briglia** ['briʎʎa] *sf* rein; **a ~ sciolta** at full gallop; (*fig*) at full speed

bril'lante *ag* bright; (*anche fig*) brilliant; (*che luccica*) shining ▷ *sm* diamond

bril'lare *vi* to shine; (*mina*) to blow up ▷ *vt* (*mina*) to set off

'**brillo, -a** *ag* merry, tipsy

'**brina** *sf* hoarfrost

brin'dare *vi* **a qn/qc** to drink to o toast sb/sth

'**brindisi** *sm inv* toast

bri'oche [bri'ɔʃ] *sf inv* brioche

bri'tannico, -a, -ci, -che *ag* British

'**brivido** *sm* shiver; (*di ribrezzo*) shudder; (*fig*) thrill

brizzo'lato, -a [brittso'lato] *ag* (*persona*) going grey; (*barba, capelli*) greying

'**brocca, -che** *sf* jug

'**broccoli** *smpl* broccoli *sg*

'**brodo** *sm* broth; (*per cucinare*) stock; **brodo ristretto** consommé

bron'chite [bron'kite] *sf* (*Med*) bronchitis

bronto'lare *vi* to grumble; (*tuono, stomaco*) to rumble

'**bronzo** ['brondzo] *sm* bronze

'**browser** ['brauzer] *sm inv* (*Inform*) browser

brucia'pelo [brutʃa'pelo]: **a ~** *av* point-blank

bruci'are [bru'tʃare] *vt* to burn; (*scottare*) to scald ▷ *vi* to burn; **bruciarsi** *vpr* to burn o.s.; (*fallire*) to ruin one's chances; **~ le tappe** (*fig*) to shoot ahead; **bruciarsi la carriera** to ruin one's career

'**bruco, -chi** *sm* caterpillar; grub

'**brufolo** *sm* pimple, spot

'**brullo, -a** *ag* bare, bleak

'**bruno, -a** *ag* brown, dark; (*persona*) dark(-haired)

'**brusco, -a, -schi, -sche** *ag* (*sapore*) sharp; (*modi, persona*) brusque, abrupt; (*movimento*) abrupt, sudden

bru'sio *sm* buzz, buzzing

bru'tale *ag* brutal

'**brutto, -a** *ag* ugly; (*cattivo*) bad; (*malattia, strada, affare*) nasty, bad; **~ tempo** bad weather

Bru'xelles [bry'sɛl] *sf* Brussels

BSE [biɛsse'e] *sigla f* (= *encefalopatia spongiforme bovina*) BSE

'**buca, -che** *sf* hole; (*avvallamento*) hollow; **buca delle lettere** letterbox

buca'neve *sm inv* snowdrop

bu'care *vt* (*forare*) to make a hole (*o holes*) in; (*pungere*) to pierce; (*biglietto*) to punch; **bucarsi** *vpr* (*di eroina*) to mainline; **~ una gomma** to have a puncture

bu'cato *sm* (*operazione*) washing; (*panni*) wash, washing

'**buccia, -ce** ['buttʃa] *sf* skin, peel

bucherò *ecc* [buke'rɔ] *vb vedi* **bucare**

'**buco, -chi** *sm* hole

bud'dismo *sm* Buddhism

bu'dino *sm* pudding

'**bue** *sm* ox; **carne di ~** beef

bu'fera *sf* storm

'**buffo, -a** *ag* funny; (*Teatro*) comic

bu'gia, -'gie [bu'dʒia] *sf* lie; **dire una ~** to tell a lie; **bugi'ardo, -a** *ag* lying, deceitful ▷ *sm/f* liar

'**buio, -a** *ag* dark ▷ *sm* dark, darkness

'**bulbo** *sm* (*Bot*) bulb; **bulbo oculare** eyeball

Bulga'ria *sf* **la ~** Bulgaria

'**bulgaro, -a** *ag, sm/f, sm* Bulgarian

buli'mia *sf* bulimia; **bu'limico, -a, -ci, -che** *ag* bulimic

bul'lone *sm* bolt

buona'notte *escl* good night! ▷ *sf* **dare la**

~ a to say good night to
buona'sera *escl* good evening!
buongi'orno [bwon'dʒorno] *escl* good
morning (*o* afternoon)!
buongus'taio, -a *sm/f* gourmet

 PAROLA CHIAVE

bu'ono, -a (*ag: dav sm* **buon** + C *o* V, **buono**
+ *s impura, gn, pn, ps, x, z; dav sf* **buon'** +V) *ag*
1 (*gen*) good; **un buon pranzo/ristorante**
a good lunch/restaurant; **(stai) buono!**
behave!
2 (*benevolo*): **buono (con)** good (to), kind
(to)
3 (*giusto, valido*) right; **al momento buono**
at the right moment
4 (*adatto*): **buono a/da** fit for/to; **essere
buono a nulla** to be no good *o* use at
anything
5 (*auguri*): **buon anno!** happy New Year!;
buon appetito! enjoy your meal!; **buon
compleanno!** happy birthday!; **buon
divertimento!** have a nice time!; **buona
fortuna!** good luck!; **buon riposo!** sleep
well!; **buon viaggio!** bon voyage!, have a
good trip!
6: **a buon mercato** cheap; **di buon'ora**
early; **buon senso** common sense; **alla
buona** *ag* simple
▷ *av* in a simple way, without any fuss ▷ *sm*
1 (*bontà*) goodness, good
2 (*Comm*) voucher, coupon; **buono di
cassa** cash voucher; **buono di consegna**
delivery note; **buono del Tesoro** Treasury
bill

buon'senso *sm* = **buon senso**
burat'tino *sm* puppet
'burbero, -a *ag* surly, gruff
buro'cratico, -a, ci, che *ag* bureaucratic
burocra'zia [burokrat'tsia] *sf*
bureaucracy
bur'rasca, -sche *sf* storm
'burro *sm* butter
bur'rone *sm* ravine
bus'sare *vi* to knock
'bussola *sf* compass
'busta *sf* (*da lettera*) envelope; (*astuccio*)
case; **in ~ aperta/chiusa** in an unsealed/
sealed envelope; **busta paga** pay packet
busta'rella *sf* bribe, backhander
bus'tina *sf* (*piccola busta*) envelope; (*di cibi,
farmaci*) sachet; (*Mil*) forage cap; **bustina
di tè** tea bag
'busto *sm* bust; (*indumento*) corset, girdle;
a mezzo ~ (*foto*) half-length
but'tare *vt* to throw; (*anche: ~ via*) to
throw away; **~ giù** (*scritto*) to scribble
down; (*cibo*) to gulp down; (*edificio*) to pull
down, demolish; (*pasta, verdura*) to put
into boiling water; **buttarsi** *vpr* (*saltare*) to
jump; **buttarsi dalla finestra** to jump out
of the window
byte ['bait] *sm inv* byte

C

to drop; (*anche*: **~ dal sonno**) to be falling asleep on one's feet; **~ dalle nuvole** (*fig*) to be taken aback

cadrò *ecc vb vedi* **cadere**

ca'duta *sf* fall; **la ~ dei capelli** hair loss

caffè *sm inv* coffee; (*locale*) café; **caffè corretto** espresso coffee with a shot of spirits; **caffè macchiato** coffee with a dash of milk; **caffè macinato** ground coffee

caffel'latte *sm inv* white coffee

caffetti'era *sf* coffeepot

'cagna ['kaɲɲa] *sf* (*Zool*, *peg*) bitch

CAI *sigla m* = **Club Alpino Italiano**

cala'brone *sm* hornet

cala'maro *sm* squid

cala'mita *sf* magnet

calamità *sf inv* calamity, disaster

ca'lare *vt* (*far discendere*) to lower; (*Maglia*) to decrease ▷ *vi* (*discendere*) to go (*o* come) down; (*tramontare*) to set, go down; **~ di peso** to lose weight

cal'cagno [kal'kaɲɲo] *sm* heel

cal'care *sm* (*incrostazione*) (lime)scale

'calce ['kaltʃe] *sm* **in ~** at the foot of the page ▷ *sf* lime; **calce viva** quicklime

calci'are [kal'tʃare] *vt*, *vi* to kick; **calcia'tore** *sm* footballer

'calcio ['kaltʃo] *sm* (*pedata*) kick; (*sport*) football, soccer; (*di pistola*, *fucile*) butt; (*Chim*) calcium; **calcio d'angolo** (*Sport*) corner (kick); **calcio di punizione** (*Sport*) free kick; **calcio di rigore** penalty

calco'lare *vt* to calculate, work out, reckon; (*ponderare*) to weigh (up); **calcola'tore, -'trice** *ag* calculating ▷ *sm* calculator; (*fig*) calculating person; **calcolatore elettronico** computer; **calcola'trice** *sf* calculator

'calcolo *sm* (*anche Mat*) calculation; (*infinitesimale ecc*) calculus; (*Med*) stone; **fare i propri calcoli** (*fig*) to weigh the pros and cons; **per ~** out of self-interest

cal'daia *sf* boiler

'caldo, -a *ag* warm; (*molto caldo*) hot; (*fig*: *appassionato*) keen; hearty ▷ *sm* heat; **ho ~** I'm warm; I'm hot; **fa ~** it's warm; it's hot

caleidos'copio *sm* kaleidoscope

calen'dario *sm* calendar

'calibro *sm* (*di arma*) calibre, bore; (*Tecn*) callipers *pl*; (*fig*) calibre; **di grosso ~** (*fig*) prominent

'calice ['kalitʃe] *sm* goblet; (*Rel*) chalice

Cali'fornia *sf* California

californi'ano, -a *ag* Californian

calligra'fia *sf* (*scrittura*) handwriting; (*arte*) calligraphy

'callo *sm* callus; (*ai piedi*) corn

'calma *sf* calm

ca'bina *sf* (*di nave*) cabin; (*da spiaggia*) beach hut; (*di autocarro*, *treno*) cab; (*di aereo*) cockpit; (*di ascensore*) cage; **cabi'nato** *sm* cabin cruiser; **cabina di pilotaggio** cockpit; **cabina telefonica** call *o* (tele)phone box

ca'cao *sm* cocoa

'caccia ['kattʃa] *sf* hunting; (*con fucile*) shooting; (*inseguimento*) chase; (*cacciagione*) game ▷ *sm inv* (*aereo*) fighter; (*nave*) destroyer; **caccia grossa** big-game hunting; **caccia all'uomo** manhunt

cacci'are [kat'tʃare] *vt* to hunt; (*mandar via*) to chase away; (*ficcare*) to shove, stick ▷ *vi* to hunt; **cacciarsi** *vpr* **dove s'è cacciata la mia borsa?** where has my bag got to?; **cacciarsi nei guai** to get into trouble; **~ fuori qc** to whip *o* pull sth out; **~ un urlo** to let out a yell; **caccia'tore** *sm* hunter; **cacciatore di frodo** poacher

caccia'vite [kattʃa'vite] *sm inv* screwdriver

'cactus *sm inv* cactus

ca'davere *sm* (dead) body, corpse

'caddi *ecc vb vedi* **cadere**

ca'denza [ka'dɛntsa] *sf* cadence; (*ritmo*) rhythm; (*Mus*) cadenza

ca'dere *vi* to fall; (*denti*, *capelli*) to fall out; (*tetto*) to fall in; **questa gonna cade bene** this skirt hangs well; **lasciar ~** (*anche fig*)

cal'mante *sm* tranquillizer

cal'mare *vt* to calm; (*lenire*) to soothe; **calmarsi** *vpr* to grow calm, calm down; (*vento*) to abate; (*dolori*) to ease

'calmo, -a *ag* calm, quiet

'calo *sm* (*Comm: di prezzi*) fall; (*: di volume*) shrinkage; (*: di peso*) loss

ca'lore *sm* warmth; heat; **in ~** (*Zool*) on heat

calo'ria *sf* calorie

calo'rifero *sm* radiator

calo'roso, -a *ag* warm

calpes'tare *vt* to tread on, trample on; **"è vietato ~ l'erba"** "keep off the grass"

ca'lunnia *sf* slander; (*scritta*) libel

cal'vizie [kal'vittsje] *sf* baldness

'calvo, -a *ag* bald

'calza ['kaltsa] *sf* (*da donna*) stocking; (*da uomo*) sock; **fare la ~** to knit; **calze di nailon** nylons, (nylon) stockings

calza'maglia [kaltsa'maʎʎa] *sf* tights *pl*; (*per danza, ginnastica*) leotard

calzet'tone [kaltset'tone] *sm* heavy knee-length sock

cal'zino [kal'tsino] *sm* sock

calzo'laio [kaltso'lajo] *sm* shoemaker; (*che ripara scarpe*) cobbler

calzon'cini [kaltson'tʃini] *smpl* shorts; **calzoncini da bagno** (swimming) trunks

cal'zone [kal'tsone] *sm* trouser leg; (*Cuc*) savoury turnover made with pizza dough; **calzoni** *smpl* (*pantaloni*) trousers (BRIT), pants (US)

camale'onte *sm* chameleon

cambia'mento *sm* change

cambi'are *vt* to change; (*modificare*) to alter, change; (*barattare*): **~ (qc con qn/qc)** to exchange (sth with sb/for sth) ▷ *vi* to change, alter; **cambiarsi** *vpr* (*d'abito*) to change; **~ casa** to move (house); **~ idea** to change one's mind; **~ treno** to change trains; **dove posso ~ dei soldi?** where can I change some money?; **ha da ~?** have you got any change?; **posso cambiarlo, per favore?** could I exchange this, please?

cambiava'lute *sm inv* exchange office

'cambio *sm* change; (*modifica*) alteration, change; (*scambio, Comm*) exchange; (*corso dei cambi*) rate (of exchange); (*Tecn, Aut*) gears *pl*; **in ~ di** in exchange for; **dare il ~ a qn** to take over from sb

'camera *sf* room; (*anche*: **~ da letto**) bedroom; (*Pol*) chamber, house; **camera ardente** mortuary chapel; **camera d'aria** inner tube; (*di pallone*) bladder; **camera di commercio** Chamber of Commerce; **Camera dei Deputati** Chamber of Deputies, ≈ House of Commons (BRIT),

≈ House of Representatives (US); **camera a gas** gas chamber; **camera a un letto/due letti** single/twin-bedded room; **camera matrimoniale** double room; **camera oscura** (*Fot*) dark room

> Attenzione! In inglese esiste la parola *camera*, che però significa *macchina fotografica*.

came'rata, -i, -e *sm/f* companion, mate ▷ *sf* dormitory

cameri'era *sf* (*domestica*) maid; (*che serve a tavola*) waitress; (*che fa le camere*) chambermaid

cameri'ere *sm* (man)servant; (*di ristorante*) waiter

came'rino *sm* (*Teatro*) dressing room

'camice ['kamitʃe] *sm* (*Rel*) alb; (*per medici ecc*) white coat

cami'cetta [kami'tʃetta] *sf* blouse

ca'micia, -cie [ka'mitʃa] *sf* (*da uomo*) shirt; (*da donna*) blouse; **camicia di forza** straitjacket; **camicia da notte** (*da donna*) nightdress; (*da uomo*) nightshirt

cami'netto *sm* hearth, fireplace

ca'mino *sm* chimney; (*focolare*) fireplace, hearth

'camion *sm inv* lorry (BRIT), truck (US)

camio'nista, -i *sm* lorry driver (BRIT), truck driver (US)

cam'mello *sm* (*Zool*) camel; (*tessuto*) camel hair

cammi'nare *vi* to walk; (*funzionare*) to work, go

cam'mino *sm* walk; (*sentiero*) path; (*itinerario, direzione, tragitto*) way; **mettersi in ~** to set o start off

camo'milla *sf* camomile; (*infuso*) camomile tea

ca'moscio [ka'moʃʃo] *sm* chamois; **di ~** (*scarpe, borsa*) suede *cpd*

cam'pagna [kam'paɲɲa] *sf* country, countryside; (*Pol, Comm, Mil*) campaign; **in ~** in the country; **andare in ~** to go to the country; **fare una ~** to campaign; **campagna pubblicitaria** advertising campaign

cam'pana *sf* bell; (*anche*: **~ di vetro**) bell jar; **campa'nello** *sm* (*all'uscio, da tavola*) bell

campa'nile *sm* bell tower, belfry

cam'peggio *sm* camping; (*terreno*) camp site; **fare (del) ~** to go camping

camper ['kamper] *sm inv* motor caravan (BRIT), motor home (US)

campio'nario, -a *ag* **fiera campionaria** trade fair ▷ *sm* collection of samples

campio'nato *sm* championship

campi'one, -'essa *sm/f* (*Sport*) champion ▷ *sm* (*Comm*) sample '**campo** sm field; (Mil) field; (accampamento) camp; (spazio delimitato: sportivo ecc) ground; field; (di quadro) background; **i campi** (campagna) the countryside; **campo da aviazione** airfield; **campo di battaglia** (Mil, fig) battlefield; **campo di concentramento** concentration camp; **campo da golf** golf course; **campo profughi** refugee camp; **campo sportivo** sports ground; **campo da tennis** tennis court; **campo visivo** field of vision

'**Canada** sm **il ~** Canada; **cana'dese** ag, sm/f Canadian ▷ sf (anche: **tenda canadese**) ridge tent

ca'**naglia** [ka'naʎʎa] sf rabble, mob; (persona) scoundrel, rogue

ca'**nale** sm (anche fig) channel; (artificiale) canal

'**canapa** sf hemp; **canapa indiana** (droga) cannabis

cana'**rino** sm canary

cancel'**lare** [kantʃel'lare] vt (con la gomma) to rub out, erase; (con la penna) to strike out; (annullare) to annul, cancel; (disdire) to cancel

cancelle'**ria** [kantʃelle'ria] sf chancery; (materiale per scrivere) stationery

can'**cello** [kan'tʃello] sm gate

'**cancro** sm (Med) cancer; (dello zodiaco): **C~** Cancer

candeg'**gina** [kanded'dʒina] sf bleach

can'**dela** sf candle; **candela (di accensione)** (Aut) spark(ing) plug

cande'**labro** sm candelabra

candeli'**ere** sm candlestick

candi'**dare** vt to present as candidate; **candidarsi** vpr to present o.s. as candidate

candi'**dato, -a** sm/f candidate; (aspirante a una carica) applicant

'**candido, -a** ag white as snow; (puro) pure; (sincero) sincere, candid

can'**dito, -a** ag candied

'**cane** sm dog; (di pistola, fucile) cock; **fa un freddo ~** it's bitterly cold; **non c'era un ~** there wasn't a soul; **cane da caccia/da guardia** hunting/guard dog; **cane lupo** Alsatian; **cane pastore** sheepdog

ca'**nestro** sm basket

can'**guro** sm kangaroo

ca'**nile** sm kennel; (di allevamento) kennels pl; **canile municipale** dog pound

'**canna** sf (pianta) reed; (: indica, da zucchero) cane; (bastone) stick, cane; (di fucile) barrel; (di organo) pipe; (fam: droga) joint; **canna fumaria** chimney flue; **canna da pesca** (fishing) rod; **canna da zucchero** sugar cane

cannel'**loni** smpl pasta tubes stuffed with sauce and baked

cannocchi'**ale** [kannok'kjale] sm telescope

can'**none** sm (Mil) gun; (Storia) cannon; (tubo) pipe, tube; (piega) box pleat; (fig) ace

can'**nuccia, -ce** [kan'nuttʃa] sf (drinking) straw

ca'**noa** sf canoe

'**canone** sm canon, criterion; (mensile, annuo) rent; fee

canot'**taggio** [kanot'taddʒo] sm rowing

canotti'**era** sf vest

ca'**notto** sm small boat, dinghy; canoe

can'**tante** sm/f singer

can'**tare** vt, vi to sing; **cantau'tore, -'trice** sm/f singer-composer

canti'**ere** sm (Edil) (building) site; (cantiere navale) shipyard

can'**tina** sf cellar; (bottega) wine shop; **cantina sociale** cooperative winegrowers' association

> ▐ Attenzione! In inglese esiste la parola canteen, che però significa mensa.

'**canto** sm song; (arte) singing; (Rel) chant; chanting; (poesia) poem, lyric; (parte di una poesia) canto; (parte, lato): **da un ~** on the one hand; **d'altro ~** on the other hand

canzo'**nare** [kantso'nare] vt to tease

can'**zone** [kan'tsone] sf song; (Poesia) canzone

'**caos** sm inv chaos; **ca'otico, -a, -ci, -che** ag chaotic

CAP sigla m = **codice di avviamento postale**

ca'**pace** [ka'patʃe] ag able, capable; (ampio, vasto) large, capacious; **sei ~ di farlo?** can you o are you able to do it?; **capacità** sf inv ability; (Dir, di recipiente) capacity

ca'**panna** sf hut

capan'**none** sm (Agr) barn; (fabbricato industriale) (factory) shed

ca'**parbio, -a** ag stubborn

ca'**parra** sf deposit, down payment

ca'**pello** sm hair; **capelli** smpl (capigliatura) hair sg

ca'**pezzolo** [ka'pettsolo] sm nipple

ca'**pire** vt to understand; **non capisco** I don't understand

capi'**tale** ag (mortale) capital; (fondamentale) main, chief ▷ sf (città) capital ▷ sm (Econ) capital

capi'**tano** sm captain

capi'**tare** vi (giungere casualmente) to happen to go, find o.s.; (accadere) to happen; (presentarsi: cosa) to turn up, present itself ▷ vb impers to happen; **mi è capitato un guaio** I've had a spot of trouble capi'tello sm (Archit) capital

ca'pitolo sm chapter

capi'tombolo sm headlong fall, tumble

'capo sm head; (persona) head, leader; (: in ufficio) head, boss; (: in tribù) chief; (di oggetti) head; top; end; (Geo) cape; **andare a ~** to start a new paragraph; **da ~** over again; **capo di bestiame** head inv of cattle; **capo di vestiario** item of clothing; **Capo'danno** sm New Year; **capo'giro** sm dizziness no pl; **capola'voro, -i** sm masterpiece; **capo'linea** (pl **capi'linea**) sm terminus; **capostazi'one** (pl **capistazi'one**) sm station master

capo'tavola (pl(m) capi'tavola) pl(f) inv sm/f (persona) head of the table; **sedere a ~** to sit at the head of the table

capo'volgere [kapo'voldʒere] vt to overturn; (fig) to reverse; **capovolgersi** vpr to overturn; (barca) to capsize; (fig) to be reversed

'cappa sf (mantello) cape, cloak; (del camino) hood

cap'pella sf (Rel) chapel

cap'pello sm hat

'cappero sm caper

cap'pone sm capon

cap'potto sm (over)coat

cappuc'cino [kapput'tʃino] sm (frate) Capuchin monk; (bevanda) cappuccino, frothy white coffee

cap'puccio [kap'puttʃo] sm (copricapo) hood; (della biro) cap

'capra sf (she-)goat

ca'priccio [ka'prittʃo] sm caprice, whim; (bizza) tantrum; **fare i capricci** to be very naughty; **capricci'oso, -a** ag capricious, whimsical; naughty

Capri'corno sm Capricorn

capri'ola sf somersault

capri'olo sm roe deer

'capro sm ~ **espiatorio** scapegoat

ca'prone sm billy-goat

'capsula sf capsule; (di arma, per bottiglie) cap

cap'tare vt (Radio, TV) to pick up; (cattivarsi) to gain, win

carabini'ere sm member of Italian military police force

● CARABINIERI
●
● Originally part of the armed forces, the
● **carabinieri** are police who perform
● both military and civil duties. They
● include paratroopers and mounted
● divisions.

ca'raffa sf carafe

Ca'raibi smpl **il mar dei ~** the Caribbean (Sea)

cara'mella sf sweet

ca'rattere sm character; (caratteristica) characteristic, trait; **avere un buon ~** to be good-natured; **carattere jolly** wild card; **caratte'ristica, -che** sf characteristic, trait, peculiarity; **caratte'ristico, -a, -ci, -che** ag characteristic

car'bone sm coal

carbu'rante sm (motor) fuel

carbura'tore sm carburettor

carce'rato, -a [kartʃe'rato] sm/f prisoner

'carcere ['kartʃere] sm prison; (pena) imprisonment

carci'ofo [kar'tʃofo] sm artichoke

cardel'lino sm goldfinch

car'diaco, -a, -ci, -che ag cardiac, heart cpd

cardi'nale ag, sm cardinal

'cardine sm hinge

'cardo sm thistle

ca'rente ag ~ **di** lacking in

cares'tia sf famine; (penuria) scarcity, dearth

ca'rezza [ka'rettsa] sf caress

'carica, -che sf (mansione ufficiale) office, position; (Mil, Tecn, Elettr) charge; **ha una forte ~ di simpatia** he's very likeable; vedi anche **carico**

caricabatte'ria sm inv battery charger

cari'care vt (merce, Inform) to load; (orologio) to wind up; (batteria, Mil) to charge

'carico, -a, -chi, -che ag (che porta un peso): ~ **di** loaded o laden with; (fucile) loaded; (orologio) wound up; (batteria) charged; (colore) deep; (caffè, tè) strong ▷ sm (il caricare) loading; (ciò che si carica) load; (fig: peso) burden, weight; **persona a ~** dependent; **essere a ~ di qn** (spese ecc) to be charged to sb

'carie sf (dentaria) decay

ca'rino, -a ag (grazioso) lovely, pretty, nice; (riferito a uomo, anche simpatico) nice

carità sf charity; **per ~!** (escl di rifiuto) good heavens, no!

carnagi'one [karna'dʒone] sf complexion

'carne sf flesh; (bovina, ovina ecc) meat; **non mangio ~** I don't eat meat; **carne di maiale/manzo/pecora** pork/beef/ mutton; **carne in scatola** tinned o canned meat; **carne tritata** o **macinata** mince (BRIT), hamburger meat (US), minced (BRIT) o ground (US) meat

carne'vale *sm* carnival

'**caro, -a** *ag* (amato) dear; (costoso) dear,
expensive; **è troppo ~** it's too expensive

ca'rogna [ka'roɲɲa] *sf* carrion; (anche: **fig**:
fam) swine

ca'rota *sf* carrot

caro'vana *sf* caravan

car'poni *av* on all fours

car'rabile *ag* suitable for vehicles; **"passo
~"** "keep clear"

carreggi'ata [karred'dʒata] *sf*
carriageway (BRIT), (road)way

car'rello *sm* trolley; (Aer) undercarriage;
(Cinema) dolly; (di macchina da scrivere)
carriage

carri'era *sf* career; **fare ~** to get on; **a gran
~** at full speed

carri'ola *sf* wheelbarrow

'**carro** *sm* cart, wagon; **carro armato**
tank; **carro attrezzi** breakdown van

car'rozza [kar'rottsa] *sf* carriage, coach

carrozze'ria [karrottse'ria] *sf* body,
coachwork (BRIT); (officina) coachbuilder's
workshop (BRIT), body shop

carroz'zina [karrot'tsina] *sf* pram (BRIT),
baby carriage (US)

'**carta** *sf* paper; (al ristorante) menu; (Geo)
map; plan; (documento) card; (costituzione)
charter; **carte** *sfpl* (documenti) papers,
documents; **alla ~** (al ristorante) à la
carte; **carta assegni** bank card; **carta
assorbente** blotting paper; **carta bollata**
o **da bollo** official stamped paper; **carta
(da gioco)** playing card; **carta di credito**
credit card; **carta (geografica)** map;
carta d'identità identity card; **carta
igienica** toilet paper; **carta d'imbarco**
(Aer, Naut) boarding card; **carta da lettere**
writing paper; **carta da pacchi** wrapping
paper; **carta da parati** wallpaper; **carta
libera** (Amm) unstamped paper; **carta
stradale** road map; **carta verde** (Aut)
green card; **carta vetrata** sandpaper;
carta da visita visiting card

car'taccia, -ce [kar'tattʃa] *sf* waste paper

carta'pesta *sf* papier-mâché

car'tella *sf* (scheda) card; (Inform, custodia:
di cartone) folder; (: di uomo d'affari ecc)
briefcase; (: di scolaro) schoolbag, satchel;
cartella clinica (Med) case sheet

cartel'lino *sm* (etichetta) label; (su porta)
notice; (scheda) card; **timbrare il ~**
(all'entrata) to clock in; (all'uscita) to clock
out; **cartellino di presenza** clock card,
timecard

car'tello *sm* sign; (pubblicitario) poster;
(stradale) sign, signpost; (Econ) cartel; (in
dimostrazioni) placard; **cartello stradale**
sign; **cartel'lone** *sm* (della tombola)
scoring frame; (Teatro) playbill; **tenere il
cartellone** (spettacolo) to have a long run;
cartellone pubblicitario advertising
poster

car'tina *sf* (Aut, Geo) map; **può
indicarmelo sulla ~?** can you show it to
me on the map?

car'toccio [kar'tottʃo] *sm* paper bag

cartole'ria *sf* stationer's (shop)

carto'lina *sf* postcard; **cartolina postale**
ready-stamped postcard

car'tone *sm* cardboard; (Arte) cartoon;
cartoni animati (Cinema) cartoons

car'tuccia, -ce [kar'tuttʃa] *sf* cartridge

'**casa** *sf* house; (in senso astratto) home;
(Comm) firm, house; **essere a ~** to be at
home; **vado a ~ mia/tua** I'm going home/
to your house; **vino della ~** house wine;
casa di cura nursing home; **casa editrice**
publishing house; **Casa delle Libertà**
centre-right coalition; **casa di riposo** (old
people's) home, care home; **case popolari**
≈ council houses (o flats) (BRIT), ≈ public
housing units (US); **casa dello studente**
student hostel

ca'sacca, -che *sf* military coat; (di fantino)
blouse

casa'linga, -ghe *sf* housewife

casa'lingo, -a, -ghi, -ghe *ag* household,
domestic; (fatto a casa) home-made;
(semplice) homely; (amante della casa)
home-loving

cas'care *vi* to fall; **cas'cata** *sf* fall;
(d'acqua) cascade, waterfall

cascherò *ecc* [kaske'rɔ] *vb vedi* **cascare**

'**casco, -schi** *sm* helmet; (del parrucchiere)
hair-drier; (di banane) bunch; **casco blu**
(Mil) blue helmet (UN soldier)

casei'ficio [kazei'fitʃo] *sm* creamery

ca'sella *sf* pigeon-hole; **casella postale**
post office box

ca'sello *sm* (di autostrada) toll-house

ca'serma *sf* barracks pl

ca'sino (fam) *sm* brothel; (confusione) row,
racket

casinò *sm inv* casino

'**caso** *sm* chance; (fatto, vicenda) event,
incident; (possibilità) possibility; (Med,

Ling) case; **a ~** at random; **per ~** by chance, by accident; **in ogni ~, in tutti i casi** in any case, at any rate; **al ~** should the opportunity arise; **nel ~ che** in case; **~ mai** if by chance; **caso limite** borderline case

caso'lare *sm* cottage

'**caspita** *escl (di sorpresa)* good heavens!; *(di impazienza)* for goodness' sake!

'**cassa** *sf* case, crate, box; *(bara)* coffin; *(mobile)* chest; *(involucro: di orologio ecc)* case; *(macchina)* cash register, till; *(luogo di pagamento)* checkout (counter); *(fondo)* fund; *(istituto bancario)* bank; **cassa automatica prelievi** cash dispenser; **cassa continua** night safe; **cassa mutua** *o* **malattia** health insurance scheme; **cassa integrazione: mettere in cassa integrazione** ≈ to lay off; **cassa di risparmio** savings bank; **cassa toracica** *(Anat)* chest

cassa'forte *(pl* **casse'forti)** *sf* safe; **lo potrebbe mettere nella ~?** could you put this in the safe, please?

cassa'panca *(pl* **cassa'panche** *o* **casse'panche)** *sf* settle

casseru'ola *sf* saucepan

cas'setta *sf* box; *(per registratore)* cassette; *(Cinema, Teatro)* box-office takings *pl*; **film di ~** box-office draw; **cassetta di sicurezza** strongbox; **cassetta delle lettere** letterbox

cas'setto *sm* drawer

cassi'ere, -a *sm/f* cashier; *(di banca)* teller

casso'netto *sm* wheelie-bin

cas'tagna [kas'taɲɲa] *sf* chestnut

cas'tagno [kas'taɲɲo] *sm* chestnut (tree)

cas'tano, -a *ag* chestnut (brown)

cas'tello *sm* castle; *(Tecn)* scaffolding

casti'gare *vt* to punish; **cas'tigo, -ghi** *sm* punishment

cas'toro *sm* beaver

casu'ale *ag* chance *cpd*; *(Inform)* random *cpd*

cataliza'tore [kataliddza'tore] *sm* *(anche fig)* catalyst; *(Aut)* catalytic converter

ca'talogo, -ghi *sm* catalogue

catarifran'gente [katarifran'dʒɛnte] *sm* *(Aut)* reflector

ca'tarro *sm* catarrh

ca'tastrofe *sf* catastrophe, disaster

catego'ria *sf* category

ca'tena *sf* chain; **catena di montaggio** assembly line; **catene da neve** *(Aut)* snow chains; **cate'nina** *sf (gioiello)* (thin) chain

cate'ratta *sf* cataract; *(chiusa)* sluice-gate

ca'tino *sm* basin

ca'trame *sm* tar

'**cattedra** *sf* teacher's desk; *(di docente)*

chair

catte'drale *sf* cathedral

catti'veria *sf* malice, spite; naughtiness; *(atto)* spiteful act; *(parole)* malicious *o* spiteful remark

cat'tivo, -a *ag* bad; *(malvagio)* bad, wicked; *(turbolento: bambino)* bad, naughty; *(: mare)* rough; *(odore, sapore)* nasty, bad

cat'tolico, -a, -ci, -che *ag, sm/f* (Roman) Catholic

cattu'rare *vt* to capture

'**causa** *sf* cause; *(Dir)* lawsuit, case, action; **a ~ di, per ~ di** because of; **fare** *o* **muovere ~ a qn** to take legal action against sb

cau'sare *vt* to cause

cau'tela *sf* caution, prudence

'**cauto, -a** *ag* cautious, prudent

cauzi'one [kaut'tsjone] *sf* security; *(Dir)* bail

'**cava** *sf* quarry

caval'care *vt (cavallo)* to ride; *(muro)* to sit astride; *(ponte)* to span; **caval'cata** *sf* ride; *(gruppo di persone)* riding party

cavalca'via *sm inv* flyover

cavalci'oni [kaval'tʃoni]: **a ~ di** *prep* astride

cavali'ere *sm* rider; *(feudale, titolo)* knight; *(soldato)* cavalryman; *(al ballo)* partner

caval'letta *sf* grasshopper

caval'letto *sm (Fot)* tripod; *(da pittore)* easel

ca'vallo *sm* horse; *(Scacchi)* knight; *(Aut: anche: ~ **vapore**)* horsepower; *(dei pantaloni)* crotch; **a ~** on horseback; **a ~ di** astride, straddling; **cavallo di battaglia** *(fig)* hobby-horse; **cavallo da corsa** racehorse; **cavallo a dondolo** rocking horse

ca'vare *vt (togliere)* to draw out, extract, take out; *(: giacca, scarpe)* to take off; *(: fame, sete, voglia)* to satisfy; **cavarsela** to manage, get on all right; *(scamparla)* to get away with it

cava'tappi *sm inv* corkscrew

ca'verna *sf* cave

'**cavia** *sf* guinea pig

cavi'ale *sm* caviar

ca'viglia [ka'viʎʎa] *sf* ankle

'**cavo, -a** *ag* hollow ▸ *sm (Anat)* cavity; *(corda, Elettr, Tel)* cable

cavo'letto *sm* **~ di Bruxelles** Brussels sprout

cavolfi'ore *sm* cauliflower

'**cavolo** *sm* cabbage; *(fam)*: **non m'importa un ~** I don't give a damn

'**cazzo** ['kattso] *sm (fam!: pene)* prick (!); **non gliene importa un ~** *(fig fam!)* he doesn't give a damn about it; **fatti i**

cazzi tuoi (fig fam!) mind your own damn business

C.C.D. sigla m (= Centro Cristiano Democratico) Italian political party of the centre

CD sm inv CD; (lettore) CD player

CD-Rom [tʃidi'rɔm] sm inv CD-ROM

C.D.U. sigla m (= Cristiano Democratici Uniti) Italian centre-right political party

ce [tʃe] pron, av vedi **ci**

Ce'cenia [tʃe'tʃɛnja] sf **la ~** Chechnya

ce'ceno, -a [tʃe'tʃɛno] sm/f, ag Chechen

'ceco, -a, -chi, -che ['tʃɛko] ag, sm/f Czech; **la Repubblica Ceca** the Czech Republic

'cedere ['tʃɛdere] vt (concedere posto) to give up; (Dir) to transfer, make over ▷ vi (cadere) to give way, subside; **~ (a)** to surrender (to), yield (to), give in (to)

'cedola ['tʃɛdola] sf (Comm) coupon; voucher

'ceffo ['tʃɛffo] (peg) sm ugly mug

cef'fone [tʃef'fone] sm slap, smack

cele'brare [tʃele'brare] vt to celebrate

'celebre ['tʃɛlebre] ag famous, celebrated

ce'leste [tʃe'lɛste] ag celestial; heavenly; (colore) sky-blue

'celibe ['tʃɛlibe] ag single, unmarried

'cella ['tʃɛlla] sf cell; **cella frigorifera** cold store

'cellula ['tʃɛllula] sf (Biol, Elettr, Pol) cell; **cellu'lare** sm cellphone

cellu'lite [tʃellu'lite] sf cellulite

cemen'tare [tʃemen'tare] vt (anche fig) to cement

ce'mento [tʃe'mento] sm cement; **cemento armato** reinforced concrete

'cena ['tʃena] sf dinner; (leggera) supper

ce'nare [tʃe'nare] vi to dine, have dinner

'cenere ['tʃenere] sf ash

'cenno ['tʃenno] sm (segno) sign, signal; (gesto) gesture; (col capo) nod; (con la mano) wave; (allusione) hint, mention; (breve esposizione) short account; **far ~ di sì/no** to nod (one's head)/shake one's head

censi'mento [tʃensi'mento] sm census

cen'sura [tʃen'sura] sf censorship; censor's office; (fig) censure

cente'nario, -a [tʃente'narjo] ag (che ha cento anni) hundred-year-old; (che ricorre ogni cento anni) centennial, centenary cpd ▷ sm/f centenarian ▷ sm centenary

cen'tesimo, -a [tʃen'tezimo] ag, sm hundredth; (di euro, dollaro) cent

cen'tigrado, -a [tʃen'tigrado] ag centigrade; **20 gradi centigradi** 20 degrees centigrade

cen'timetro [tʃen'timetro] sm centimetre

centi'naio [tʃenti'najo] sm (pl(f) **-aia**) sm **un ~ (di)** a hundred; about a hundred

'cento ['tʃɛnto] num a hundred, one hundred

cento'mila [tʃento'mila] num a o one hundred thousand; **te l'ho detto ~ volte** (fig) I've told you a thousand times

cen'trale [tʃen'trale] ag central ▷ sf: **centrale telefonica** (telephone) exchange; **centrale elettrica** electric power station; **centra'lino** sm (telephone) operator; **centra'lino** sm (telephone) exchange; (di albergo ecc) switchboard; **centralizzato, -a** [tʃentralid'dzato] ag central

cen'trare [tʃen'trare] vt to hit the centre of; (Tecn) to centre

cen'trifuga [tʃen'trifuga] sf spin-drier

'centro ['tʃɛntro] sm centre; **centro civico** civic centre; **centro commerciale** shopping centre; (città) commercial centre

'ceppo ['tʃeppo] sm (di albero) stump; (pezzo di legno) log

'cera ['tʃera] sf wax; (aspetto) appearance

ce'ramica, -che [tʃe'ramika] sf ceramic; (Arte) ceramics sg

cerbi'atto [tʃer'bjatto] sm (Zool) fawn

cer'care [tʃer'kare] vt to look for, search for ▷ vi **~ di fare qc** to try to do sth; **stiamo cercando un albergo/ristorante** we're looking for a hotel/restaurant

cercherò ecc [tʃerke'rɔ] vb vedi **cercare**

cerchia ['tʃerkja] sf circle

cerchietto [tʃer'kjetto] sm (per capelli) hairband

'cerchio ['tʃerkjo] sm circle; (giocattolo, di botte) hoop

cereali [tʃere'ali] smpl cereal sg

ceri'monia [tʃeri'mɔnja] sf ceremony

ce'rino [tʃe'rino] sm wax match

'cernia ['tʃɛrnja] sf (Zool) stone bass

cerni'era [tʃer'njera] sf hinge; **cerniera lampo** zip (fastener) (BRIT), zipper (US)

'cero ['tʃero] sm (church) candle

ce'rotto [tʃe'rɔtto] sm sticking plaster

certa'mente [tʃerta'mente] av certainly

certifi'cato sm certificate; **certificato medico** medical certificate; **certificato di nascita/di morte** birth/death certificate

◯ **PAROLA CHIAVE**

'certo, -a ['tʃɛrto] ag (sicuro): **certo (di/ che)** certain o sure (of/that)
▷ det 1 (tale) certain; **un certo signor Smith** a (certain) Mr Smith
2 (qualche: con valore intensivo) some; **dopo un certo tempo** after some time; **un fatto di una certa importanza** a matter of some importance; **di una certa età**

past one's prime, not so young
▷ *pron* **certi, e** *pl* some ▷ *av* (*certamente*) certainly; (*senz'altro*) of course; **di certo** certainly; **no (di) certo!, certo che no!** certainly not!; **sì certo** yes indeed, certainly

cer'vello, -i [tʃer'vɛllo] (*Anat*) (*pl(f)* **-a**) *sm* brain; **cervello elettronico** computer
'cervo, -a ['tʃɛrvo] *sm/f* stag/doe ▷ *sm* deer; **cervo volante** stag beetle
ces'puglio [tʃes'puʎʎo] *sm* bush
ces'sare [tʃes'sare] *vi, vt* to stop, cease; **~ di fare qc** to stop doing sth
ces'tino [tʃes'tino] *sm* basket; (*per la carta straccia*) wastepaper basket; **cestino da viaggio** (*Ferr*) packed lunch (*o* dinner)
'cesto ['tʃesto] *sm* basket
'ceto ['tʃɛto] *sm* (*social*) class
cetrio'lino [tʃetrio'lino] *sm* gherkin
cetri'olo [tʃetri'ɔlo] *sm* cucumber
Cfr. *abbr* (= *confronta*) cf.
CGIL *sigla f* (= *Confederazione Generale Italiana del Lavoro*) trades union organization
chat line [tʃæt'laen] *sf inv* chat room
chattare [tʃat'tare] *vi* (*Inform*) to chat online

Ⓞ **PAROLA CHIAVE**

che [ke] *pron* **1** (*relativo: persona: soggetto*) who; (: *oggetto*) whom, that; (: *cosa, animale*) which, that; **il ragazzo che è venuto** the boy who came; **l'uomo che io vedo** the man (whom) I see; **il libro che è sul tavolo** the book which *o* that is on the table; **il libro che vedi** the book (which *o* that) you see; **la sera che ti ho visto** the evening I saw you
2 (*interrogativo, esclamativo*) what; **che (cosa) fai?** what are you doing?; **a che (cosa) pensi?** what are you thinking about?; **non sa che (cosa) fare** he doesn't know what to do; **ma che dici!** what are you saying!
3 (*indefinito*): **quell'uomo ha un che di losco** there's something suspicious about that man; **un certo non so che** an indefinable something
▷ *det* **1** (*interrogativo: tra tanti*) what; (: *tra pochi*) which; **che tipo di film preferisci?** what sort of film do you prefer?; **che vestito ti vuoi mettere?** what (*o* which) dress do you want to put on?
2 (*esclamativo: seguito da aggettivo*) how; (: *seguito da sostantivo*) what; **che buono!** how delicious!; **che bel vestito!** what a lovely dress!
▷ *cong* **1** (*con proposizioni subordinate*) that;

credo che verrà I think he'll come; **voglio che tu studi** I want you to study; **so che tu c'eri** I know (that) you were there; **non che, non che sia sbagliato, ma ...** not that it's wrong, but ...
2 (*finale*) so that; **vieni qua, che ti veda** come here, so (that) I can see you
3 (*temporale*): **arrivai che eri già partito** you had already left when I arrived; **sono anni che non lo vedo** I haven't seen him for years
4 (*in frasi imperative, concessive*): **che venga pure!** let him come by all means!; **che tu sia benedetto!** may God bless you!
5 (*comparativo: con più, meno*) than; *vedi anche* **più**; **meno**; **così** *ecc*

chemiotera'pia [kemjotera'pia] *sf* chemotherapy
chero'sene [kero'zene] *sm* kerosene

Ⓞ **PAROLA CHIAVE**

chi [ki] *pron* **1** (*interrogativo: soggetto*) who; (: *oggetto*) who, whom; **chi è?** who is it?; **di chi è questo libro?** whose book is this?, whose is this book?; **con chi parli?** who are you talking to?; **a chi pensi?** who are you thinking about?; **chi di voi?** which of you?; **non so a chi rivolgermi** I don't know who to ask
2 (*relativo*) whoever, anyone who; **dillo a chi vuoi** tell whoever you like
3 (*indefinito*): **chi ... chi ...** some ... others ...; **chi dice una cosa, chi dice un'altra** some say one thing, others say another

chiacchie'rare [kjakkje'rare] *vi* to chat; (*discorrere futilmente*) to chatter; (*far pettegolezzi*) to gossip; **chi'acchiere** *sfpl* **fare due** *o* **quattro chiacchiere** to have a chat
chia'mare [kja'mare] *vt* to call; (*rivolgersi a qn*) to call (in), send for; **chiamarsi** *vpr* (*aver nome*) to be called; **come ti chiami?** what's your name?; **mi chiamo Paolo** my name is Paolo, I'm called Paolo; **~ alle armi** to call up; **~ in giudizio** to summon; **chia'mata** *sf* (*Tel*) call; (*Mil*) call-up
chia'rezza [kja'rettsa] *sf* clearness; clarity
chia'rire [kja'rire] *vt* to make clear; (*fig: spiegare*) to clear up, explain
chi'aro, -a ['kjaro] *ag* clear; (*luminoso*) clear, bright; (*colore*) pale, light
chi'asso ['kjasso] *sm* uproar, row
chi'ave ['kjave] *sf* key ▷ *ag inv* key *cpd*; **posso avere la mia ~?** can I have my key?; **chiave d'accensione** (*Aut*) ignition key;

chiave di volta keystone; **chiave inglese** monkey wrench

chi'azza ['kjattsa] *sf* stain; splash

'**chicco, -chi** ['kikko] *sm* grain; (*di caffè*) bean; **chicco d'uva** grape

chi'edere ['kjɛdere] *vt* (*per sapere*) to ask; (*per avere*) to ask for ▷ *vi* ~ **di qn** to ask after sb; (*al telefono*) to ask for *o* want sb; ~ **qc a qn** to ask sb sth; to ask sb for sth; **chiedersi** *vpr* **chiedersi (se)** to wonder (whether)

chi'esa ['kjɛza] *sf* church

chi'esi *ecc* ['kjɛzi] *vb vedi* **chiedere**

'**chiglia** ['kiʎʎa] *sf* keel

'**chilo** ['kilo] *sm* kilo; **chi'lometro** *sm* kilometre

'**chimica** ['kimika] *sf* chemistry

'**chimico, -a, -ci, -che** ['kimiko] *ag* chemical ▷ *sm/f* chemist

chi'nare [ki'nare] *vt* to lower, bend; **chinarsi** *vpr* to stoop, bend

chi'occiola ['kjɔttʃola] *sf* snail; (*di indirizzo e-mail*) at sign, @; **scala a ~** spiral staircase

chi'odo ['kjɔdo] *sm* nail; (*fig*) obsession; **chiodo di garofano** (*Cuc*) clove

chi'osco, -schi ['kjɔsko] *sm* kiosk, stall

chi'ostro ['kjɔstro] *sm* cloister

chiro'mante [kiro'mante] *sm/f* palmist

chirur'gia [kirur'dʒia] *sf* surgery; **chirurgia estetica** cosmetic surgery; **chi'rurgo, -ghi** *o* **gi** *sm* surgeon

chissà [kis'sa] *av* who knows, I wonder

chi'tarra [ki'tarra] *sf* guitar

chitar'rista, -i, e [kitar'rista] *sm/f* guitarist, guitar player

chi'udere ['kjudere] *vt* to close, shut; (*luce, acqua*) to put off, turn off; (*definitivamente: fabbrica*) to close down, shut down; (*strada*) to close; (*recingere*) to enclose; (*porre termine a*) to end ▷ *vi* to close, shut; to close down, shut down; to end; **chiudersi** *vpr* to shut, close; (*ritirarsi: anche fig*) to shut o.s. away; (*ferita*) to close up; **a che ora chiudete?** what time do you close?

chi'unque [ki'unkwe] *pron* (*relativo*) whoever; (*indefinito*) anyone, anybody; ~ **sia** whoever it is

'**chiusi** *ecc* ['kjusi] *vb vedi* **chiudere**

chi'uso, -a ['kjuso] *pp di* **chiudere** ▷ *sf* (*di corso d'acqua*) sluice, lock; (*recinto*) enclosure; (*di discorso ecc*) conclusion, ending; **chiu'sura** *sf* (*vedi* **chiudere**) closing; shutting; closing *o* shutting down; enclosing; putting *o* turning off; ending; (*dispositivo*) catch; fastening; fastener; **chiusura lampo®** zip (fastener) (BRIT), zipper (US)

C.I. *abbr* = **carta d'identità**

PAROLA CHIAVE

ci [tʃi] (*dav* lo, la, li, le, ne *diventa* **ce**) *pron* **1** (*personale: complemento oggetto*) us; (: *a noi: complemento di termine*) (to) us; (: *riflessivo*) ourselves; (: *reciproco*) each other, one another; (*impersonale*): **ci si veste** we get dressed; **ci ha visti** he's seen us; **non ci ha dato niente** he gave us nothing; **ci vestiamo** we get dressed; **ci amiamo** we love one another *o* each other

2 (*dimostrativo: di ciò, su ciò, in ciò ecc*) about (*o* on *o* of) it; **non so cosa farci** I don't know what to do about it; **che c'entro io?** what have I got to do with it?

▷ *av* (*qui*) here; (*lì*) there; (*moto attraverso luogo*): **ci passa sopra un ponte** a bridge passes over it; **non ci passa più nessuno** nobody comes this way any more; **esserci** *vedi* **essere**

cia'batta [tʃa'batta] *sf* slipper; (*pane*) ciabatta

ciam'bella [tʃam'bɛlla] *sf* (*Cuc*) ring-shaped cake; (*salvagente*) rubber ring

ci'ao ['tʃao] *escl* (*all'arrivo*) hello!; (*alla partenza*) cheerio! (BRIT), bye!

cias'cuno, -a [tʃas'kuno] (*det: dav sm:* **ciascun** +C, V, **ciascuno** +*s impura, gn, pn, ps, x, z; dav sf:* **ciascuna** +C, **ciascun'** +V) *det* every, each; (*ogni*) every ▷ *pron* each (one); (*tutti*) everyone, everybody

ci'barie [tʃi'barje] *sfpl* foodstuffs

ciber'nauta, -i, -e [tʃiber'nauta] *sm/f* Internet surfer

ciber'spazio [tʃiber'spattsjo] *sm* cyberspace

'**cibo** ['tʃibo] *sm* food

ci'cala [tʃi'kala] *sf* cicada

cica'trice [tʃika'tritʃe] *sf* scar

'**cicca** ['tʃikka] *sf* cigarette end

'**ciccia** ['tʃittʃa] (*fam*) *sf* fat

cicci'one, -a [tʃit'tʃone] *sm/f* (*fam*) fatty

cicla'mino [tʃikla'mino] *sm* cyclamen

ci'clismo [tʃi'klizmo] *sm* cycling; **ci'clista, -i, -e** *sm/f* cyclist

'**ciclo** ['tʃiklo] *sm* cycle; (*di malattia*) course

ciclomo'tore [tʃiklomo'tore] *sm* moped

ci'clone [tʃi'klone] *sm* cyclone

ci'cogna [tʃi'koɲɲa] *sf* stork

ci'eco, -a, -chi, -che ['tʃɛko] *ag* blind ▷ *sm/f* blind man/woman

ci'elo ['tʃɛlo] *sm* sky; (*Rel*) heaven

'**cifra** ['tʃifra] *sf* (*numero*) figure; numeral; (*somma di denaro*) sum, figure; (*monogramma*) monogram, initials *pl*; (*codice*) code, cipher

'ciglio, -i ['tʃiλλo] (*delle palpebre*) (*pl(f)* **ciglia**) *sm* (*margine*) edge, verge; (eye)lash; (eye)lid; (*sopracciglio*) eyebrow

'cigno ['tʃiɲɲo] *sm* swan

cigo'lare [tʃigo'lare] *vi* to squeak, creak

'Cile ['tʃile] *sm* **il ~** Chile

ci'leno, -a [tʃi'lɛno] *ag, sm/f* Chilean

cili'egia, -gie o **ge** [tʃi'ljɛdʒa] *sf* cherry

ciliegina [tʃilje'dʒina] *sf* glacé cherry

cilin'drata [tʃilin'drata] *sf* (*Aut*) (*cubic*) capacity; **una macchina di grossa ~ a** big-engined car

ci'lindro [tʃi'lindro] *sm* cylinder; (*cappello*) top hat

'cima ['tʃima] *sf* (*sommità*) top; (*di monte*) top, summit; (*estremità*) end; **in ~ a** at the top of; **da ~ a fondo** from top to bottom; (*fig*) from beginning to end

'cimice ['tʃimitʃe] *sf* (*Zool*) bug; (*puntina*) drawing pin (*BRIT*), thumbtack (*US*)

cimini'era [tʃimi'njɛra] *sf* chimney; (*di nave*) funnel

cimi'tero [tʃimi'tɛro] *sm* cemetery

'Cina ['tʃina] *sf* **la ~** China

cin'cin [tʃin'tʃin] *escl* cheers!

'cinema ['tʃinema] *sm inv* cinema

ci'nese [tʃi'nese] *ag, sm/f, sm* Chinese *inv*

'cinghia ['tʃiŋgja] *sf* strap; (*cintura, Tecn*) belt

cinghi'ale [tʃin'gjale] *sm* wild boar

cinguet'tare [tʃingwet'tare] *vi* to twitter

'cinico, -a, -ci, -che ['tʃiniko] *ag* cynical ▷ *sm/f* cynic

cin'quanta [tʃin'kwanta] *num* fifty; **cinquan'tesimo, -a** *num* fiftieth

cinquan'tina [tʃinkwan'tina] *sf* (*serie*): **una ~ (di)** about fifty; (*età*): **essere sulla ~** to be about fifty

'cinque ['tʃinkwe] *num* five; **avere ~ anni** to be five (years old); **il ~ dicembre 1998** the fifth of December 1998; **alle ~ (ora)** at five (o'clock)

cinque'cento [tʃinkwe'tʃɛnto] *num* five hundred ▷ *sm* **il C~** the sixteenth century

cin'tura [tʃin'tura] *sf* belt; **cintura di salvataggio** lifebelt (*BRIT*), life preserver (*US*); **cintura di sicurezza** (*Aut, Aer*) safety o seat belt

cintu'rino [tʃintu'rino] *sm* strap; **~ dell'orologio** watch strap

ciò [tʃɔ] *pron* this; that; **~ che** what; **~ nonostante** o **nondimeno** nevertheless, in spite of that

ci'occa, -che ['tʃɔkka] *sf* (*di capelli*) lock

ciocco'lata [tʃokko'lata] *sf* chocolate; (*bevanda*) (hot) chocolate; **cioccola'tino** *sm* chocolate

cioè [tʃo'ɛ] *av* that is (to say)

ci'otola ['tʃɔtola] *sf* bowl

ci'ottolo ['tʃɔttolo] *sm* pebble; (*di strada*) cobble(stone)

ci'polla [tʃi'polla] *sf* onion; (*di tulipano ecc*) bulb

cipol'lina [tʃipol'lina] *sf* **cipolline sottaceto** pickled onions

ci'presso [tʃi'prɛsso] *sm* cypress (tree)

'cipria ['tʃiprja] *sf* (*face*) powder

'Cipro ['tʃipro] *sm* Cyprus

'circa ['tʃirka] *av* about, roughly ▷ *prep* about, concerning; **a mezzogiorno ~** about midday

'circo, -chi ['tʃirko] *sm* circus

circo'lare [tʃirko'lare] *vi* to circulate; (*Aut*) to drive (along), move (along) ▷ *ag* circular ▷ *sf* (*Amm*) circular; (*di autobus*) circle (line)

'circolo ['tʃirkolo] *sm* circle

circon'dare [tʃirkon'dare] *vt* to surround; **circondarsi** *vpr* **circondarsi di** to surround o.s. with

circonvallazi'one [tʃirkonvallat'tsjone] *sf* ring road (*BRIT*), beltway (*US*); (*per evitare una città*) by-pass

circos'petto, -a [tʃirkos'petto] *ag* circumspect, cautious

circos'tante [tʃirkos'tante] *ag* surrounding, neighbouring

circos'tanza [tʃirkos'tantsa] *sf* circumstance; (*occasione*) occasion

cir'cuito [tʃir'kuito] *sm* circuit

CISL *sigla f* (= *Confederazione Italiana Sindacati Lavoratori*) trades union organization

cis'terna [tʃis'tɛrna] *sf* tank, cistern

'cisti ['tʃisti] *sf* cyst

cis'tite [tʃis'tite] *sf* cystitis

ci'tare [tʃi'tare] *vt* (*Dir*) to summon; (*autore*) to quote; (*a esempio, modello*) to cite

ci'tofono [tʃi'tɔfono] *sm* entry phone; (*in uffici*) intercom

città [tʃit'ta] *sf inv* town; (*importante*) city; **città universitaria** university campus

cittadi'nanza [tʃittadi'nantsa] *sf* citizens *pl*; (*Dir*) citizenship

citta'dino, -a [tʃitta'dino] *ag* town *cpd*; city *cpd* ▷ *sm/f* (*di uno Stato*) citizen; (*abitante di città*) townsman, city dweller

ci'uccio ['tʃuttʃo] *sm* (*fam*) comforter, dummy (*BRIT*), pacifier (*US*)

ci'uffo ['tʃuffo] *sm* tuft

ci'vetta [tʃi'vetta] *sf* (*Zool*) owl; (*fig: donna*) coquette, flirt ▷ *ag inv* **auto/nave ~** decoy car/ship

'civico, -a, -ci, -che ['tʃiviko] *ag* civic; (*museo*) municipal, town *cpd*

ci'vile [tʃi'vile] *ag* civil; (*non militare*) civilian; (*nazione*) civilized ▷ *sm* civilian

civiltà [tʃivil'ta] *sf* civilization; (*cortesia*) civility

'clacson *sm inv* (*Aut*) horn

clandes'tino, -a *ag* clandestine; (*Pol*) underground, clandestine; (*immigrato*) illegal ▷ *sm/f* stowaway; (*anche:* **immigrato ~**) illegal immigrant

'classe *sf* class; **di ~** (*fig*) with class; of excellent quality; **classe operaia** working class; **classe turistica** (*Aer*) economy class

'classico, -a, -ci, -che *ag* classical; (*tradizionale: moda*) classic(al) ▷ *sm* classic; classical author

clas'sifica *sf* classification; (*Sport*) placings *pl*

classifi'care *vt* to classify; (*candidato, compito*) to grade; **classificarsi** *vpr* to be placed

'clausola *sf* (*Dir*) clause

clavi'cembalo [klavi'tʃembalo] *sm* harpsichord

cla'vicola *sf* (*Anat*) collar bone

clic'care *vi* (*Inform*): **~ su** to click on

cli'ente *sm/f* customer, client

'clima, -i *sm* climate; **climatizzatore** *sm* air conditioning system

'clinica, -che *sf* (*scienza*) clinical medicine; (*casa di cura*) clinic, nursing home; (*settore d'ospedale*) clinic

clo'nare *vt* to clone; **clonazione** [klona'tsjone] *sf* cloning

'cloro *sm* chlorine

club *sm inv* club

c.m. *abbr* = **corrente mese**

cm *abbr* (= *centimetro*) cm

coalizi'one [koalit'tsjone] *sf* coalition

'COBAS *sigla mpl* (= *Comitati di base*) independent trades unions

'coca *sf* (*bibita*) Coke®; (*droga*) cocaine

coca'ina *sf* cocaine

cocci'nella [kottʃi'nɛlla] *sf* ladybird (*BRIT*), ladybug (*US*)

cocci'uto, -a [kot'tʃuto] *ag* stubborn, pigheaded

'cocco, -chi *sm* (*pianta*) coconut palm; (*frutto*): **noce di ~** coconut ▷ *sm/f* (*fam*) darling

cocco'drillo *sm* crocodile

cocco'lare *vt* to cuddle, fondle

cocerò *ecc* [kotʃe'rɔ] *vb vedi* **cuocere**

co'comero *sm* watermelon

'coda *sf* tail; (*fila di persone, auto*) queue (*BRIT*), line (*US*); (*di abiti*) train; **con la ~ dell'occhio** out of the corner of one's eye; **mettersi in ~** to queue up (*BRIT*), line up (*US*); to join the queue (*BRIT*) *o* line (*US*); **coda di cavallo** (*acconciatura*) ponytail

co'dardo, -a *ag* cowardly ▷ *sm/f* coward

'codice ['kɔditʃe] *sm* code; **codice di avviamento postale** postcode (*BRIT*), zip code (*US*); **codice a barre** bar code; **codice civile** civil code; **codice fiscale** tax code; **codice penale** penal code; **codice segreto** (*di tessera magnetica*) PIN (number); **codice della strada** highway code

coe'rente *ag* coherent

coe'taneo, -a *ag, sm/f* contemporary

'cofano *sm* (*Aut*) bonnet (*BRIT*), hood (*US*); (*forziere*) chest

'cogliere ['kɔʎʎere] *vt* (*fiore: frutto*) to pick, gather; (*sorprendere*) to catch, surprise; (*bersaglio*) to hit; (*fig: momento opportuno ecc*) to grasp, seize, take; (*: capire*) to grasp; **~ qn in flagrante** *o* **in fallo** to catch sb red-handed

co'gnato, -a [koɲ'ɲato] *sm/f* brother-/sister-in-law

co'gnome [koɲ'ɲome] *sm* surname

coinci'denza [kointʃi'dɛntsa] *sf* coincidence; (*Ferr, Aer, di autobus*) connection

coin'cidere [koin'tʃidere] *vi* to coincide

coin'volgere [koin'vɔldʒere] *vt* **~ in** to involve in

cola'pasta *sm inv* colander

co'lare *vt* (*liquido*) to strain; (*pasta*) to drain; (*oro fuso*) to pour ▷ *vi* (*sudore*) to drip; (*botte*) to leak; (*cera*) to melt; **~ a picco** *vt, vi* (*nave*) to sink

colazi'one [kolat'tsjone] *sf* breakfast; **fare ~** to have breakfast; **a che ora è servita la ~?** what time is breakfast?

co'lera *sm* (*Med*) cholera

'colgo *ecc vb vedi* **cogliere**

'colica *sf* (*Med*) colic

co'lino *sm* strainer

'colla *sf* glue; (*di farina*) paste

collabo'rare *vi* to collaborate; **~ a** to collaborate on; (*giornale*) to contribute to; **collabora'tore, -'trice** *sm/f* collaborator; contributor; **collaboratore esterno** freelance; **collaboratrice familiare** home help

col'lana *sf* necklace; (*collezione*) collection, series

col'lant [kɔ'lã] *sm inv* tights *pl*

col'lare *sm* collar

col'lasso *sm* (*Med*) collapse

collau'dare *vt* to test, try out

col'lega, -ghi, -ghe *sm/f* colleague

collega'mento *sm* connection; (*Mil*) liaison

colle'gare *vt* to connect, join, link; **collegarsi** *vpr* (*Radio, TV*) to link up; **collegarsi con** (*Tel*) to get through to

col'legio [kol'lɛdʒo] *sm* college; (*convitto*)

boarding school; **collegio elettorale** (*Pol*) constituency

'**collera** *sf* anger

col'**lerico, -a, -ci, -che** *ag* quick-tempered, irascible

col'**letta** *sf* collection

col'**letto** *sm* collar

collezio'**nare** [kollettsjo'nare] *vt* to collect

collezi'**one** [kollet'tsjone] *sf* collection

col'**lina** *sf* hill

col'**lirio** *sm* eyewash

'**collo** *sm* neck; (*di abito*) neck, collar; (*pacco*) parcel; **collo del piede** instep

colloca'**mento** *sm* (*impiego*) employment; (*disposizione*) placing, arrangement

collo'**care** *vt* (*libri, mobili*) to place; (*Comm: merce*) to find a market for

collocazi'**one** [kollokat'tsjone] *sf* placing; (*di libro*) classification

col'**loquio** *sm* conversation, talk; (*ufficiale, per un lavoro*) interview; (*Ins*) preliminary oral exam

col'**mare** *vt* ~ **di** (*anche fig*) to fill with; (*dare in abbondanza*) to load o overwhelm with

co'**lombo, -a** *sm/f* dove; pigeon

co'**lonia** *sf* colony; (*per bambini*) holiday camp; **(acqua di) ~** (eau de) cologne

co'**lonna** *sf* column; **colonna sonora** (*Cinema*) sound track; **colonna vertebrale** spine, spinal column

colon'**nello** *sm* colonel

colo'**rante** *sm* colouring

colo'**rare** *vt* to colour; (*disegno*) to colour in

co'**lore** *sm* colour; **a colori** in colour, colour *cpd*; **farne di tutti i colori** to get up to all sorts of mischief; **vorrei un ~ diverso** I'd like a different colour

colo'**rito, -a** *ag* coloured; (*viso*) rosy, pink; (*linguaggio*) colourful ▷ *sm* (*tinta*) colour; (*carnagione*) complexion

'**colpa** *sf* fault; (*biasimo*) blame; (*colpevolezza*) guilt; (*azione colpevole*) offence; (*peccato*) sin; **di chi è la ~?** whose fault is it?; **è ~ sua** it's his fault; **per ~ di** through, owing to; **col'pevole** *ag* guilty

col'**pire** *vt* to hit, strike; (*fig*) to strike; **rimanere colpito da qc** to be amazed o struck by sth

'**colpo** *sm* (*urto*) knock; (: *affettivo*) blow, shock; (: *aggressivo*) blow; (*di pistola*) shot; (*Med*) stroke; (*rapina*) raid; **di ~** suddenly; **fare ~** to make a strong impression; **colpo d'aria** chill; **colpo in banca** bank job o raid; **colpo basso** (*Pugilato, fig*) punch below the belt; **colpo di fulmine** love at

first sight; **colpo di grazia** coup de grâce; **colpo di scena** (*Teatro*) coup de théâtre; (*fig*) dramatic turn of events; **colpo di sole** sunstroke; **colpo di Stato** coup d'état; **colpo di telefono** phone call; **colpo di testa** (sudden) impulse o whim; **colpi di sole** (*nei capelli*) highlights

'**colsi** *ecc vb vedi* **cogliere**

coltel'**lata** *sf* stab

col'**tello** *sm* knife; **coltello a serramanico** clasp knife

colti'**vare** *vt* to cultivate; (*verdura*) to grow, cultivate

'**colto, -a** *pp di* **cogliere** ▷ *ag* (*istruito*) cultured, educated

'**coma** *sm inv* coma

comanda'**mento** *sm* (*Rel*) commandment

coman'**dante** *sm* (*Mil*) commander, commandant; (*di reggimento*) commanding officer; (*Naut, Aer*) captain

coman'**dare** *vi* to be in command ▷ *vt* to command; (*imporre*) to order, command; **~ a qn di fare** to order sb to do

combaci'**are** [komba'tʃare] *vi* to meet; (*fig: coincidere*) to coincide

com'**battere** *vt, vi* to fight

combi'**nare** *vt* to combine; (*organizzare*) to arrange; (*fam: fare*) to make, cause; **combinazi'one** *sf* combination; (*caso fortuito*) coincidence; **per combinazione** by chance

combus'**tibile** *ag* combustible ▷ *sm* fuel

 PAROLA CHIAVE

'**come** *av* **1** (*alla maniera di*) like; **ti comporti come lui** you behave like him o like he does; **bianco come la neve** (as) white as snow; **come se** as if, as though

2 (*in qualità di*) as a; **lavora come autista** he works as a driver

3 (*interrogativo*) how; **come ti chiami?** what's your name?; **come sta?** how are you?; **com'è il tuo amico?** what is your friend like?; **come?** (*prego?*) pardon?, sorry?; **come mai?** how come?; **come mai non ci hai avvertiti?** why on earth didn't you warn us?

4 (*esclamativo*): **come sei bravo!** how clever you are!; **come mi dispiace!** I'm terribly sorry!

▷ *cong* **1** (*in che modo*) how; **mi ha spiegato come l'ha conosciuto** he told me how he met him

2 (*correlativo*) as; (*con comparativi di maggioranza*) than; **non è bravo come pensavo** he isn't as clever as I thought; **è**

meglio di come pensassi it's better than I thought

3 (*appena che, quando*) as soon as; **come arrivò, iniziò a lavorare** as soon as he arrived, he set to work; *vedi* **così**; **tanto**

'comico, -a, -ci, -che *ag* (*Teatro*) comic; (*buffo*) comical ▷ *sm* (*attore*) comedian, comic actor

cominci'are [komin'tʃare] *vt, vi* to begin, start; **~ a fare/col fare** to begin to do/by doing; **a che ora comincia il film?** when does the film start?

comi'tato *sm* committee

comi'tiva *sf* party, group

co'mizio [ko'mittsjo] *sm* (*Pol*) meeting, assembly

com'media *sf* comedy; (*opera teatrale*) play; (: *che fa ridere*) comedy; (*fig*) playacting *no pl*

commemo'rare *vt* to commemorate

commen'tare *vt* to comment on; (*testo*) to annotate; (*Radio, TV*) to give a commentary on

commerci'ale [kommer'tʃale] *ag* commercial, trading; (*peg*) commercial

commercia'lista, -i, e [kommertʃa'lista] *sm/f* (*laureato*) graduate in economics and commerce; (*consulente*) business consultant

commerci'ante [kommer'tʃante] *sm/f* trader, dealer; (*negoziante*) shopkeeper

commerci'are [kommer'tʃare] *vt, vi* **~ in** to deal *o* trade in

com'mercio [kom'mertʃo] *sm* trade, commerce; **essere in ~** (*prodotto*) to be on the market *o* on sale; **essere nel ~** (*persona*) to be in business; **commercio al dettaglio/all'ingrosso** retail/wholesale trade; **commercio elettronico** e-commerce

com'messo, -a *pp di* **commettere** ▷ *sm/f* shop assistant (*BRIT*), sales clerk (*US*) ▷ *sm* (*impiegato*) clerk; **commesso viaggiatore** commercial traveller

commes'tibile *ag* edible

com'mettere *vt* to commit

com'misi *ecc vb vedi* **commettere**

commissari'ato *sm* (*Amm*) commissionership; (: *sede*) commissioner's office; **commissariato di polizia** police station

commis'sario *sm* commissioner; (*di pubblica sicurezza*) ≈ (police) superintendent (*BRIT*), ≈ (police) captain (*US*); (*Sport*) steward; (*membro di commissione*) member of a committee *o* board

commissi'one *sf* (*incarico*) errand; (*comitato, percentuale*) commission; (*Comm: ordinazione*) order; **commissioni** *sfpl* (*acquisti*) shopping *sg*; **commissioni bancarie** bank charges; **commissione d'esame** examining board

com'mosso, -a *pp di* **commuovere**

commo'vente *ag* moving

commozi'one [kommot'tsjone] *sf* emotion, deep feeling; **commozione cerebrale** (*Med*) concussion

commu'overe *vt* to move, affect; **commuoversi** *vpr* to be moved

como'dino *sm* bedside table

comodità *sf inv* comfort; convenience

'comodo, -a *ag* comfortable; (*facile*) easy; (*conveniente*) convenient; (*utile*) useful, handy ▷ *sm* comfort; convenience; **con ~** at one's convenience *o* leisure; **fare il proprio ~** to do as one pleases; **far ~** to be useful *o* handy

compa'gnia [kompaɲ'ɲia] *sf* company; (*gruppo*) gathering

com'pagno, -a [kom'paɲɲo] *sm/f* (*di classe, gioco*) companion; (*Pol*) comrade

com'paio *ecc vb vedi* **comparire**

compa'rare *vt* to compare

compara'tivo, -a *ag, sm* comparative

compa'rire *vi* to appear

com'parvi *ecc vb vedi* **comparire**

compassi'one *sf* compassion, pity; **avere ~ di qn** to feel sorry for sb, to pity sb

com'passo *sm* (pair of) compasses *pl*; callipers *pl*

compa'tibile *ag* (*scusabile*) excusable; (*conciliabile, Inform*) compatible

compa'tire *vt* (*aver compassione di*) to sympathize with, feel sorry for; (*scusare*) to make allowances for

com'patto, -a *ag* compact; (*roccia*) solid; (*folla*) dense; (*fig: gruppo, partito*) united

compen'sare *vt* (*equilibrare*) to compensate for, make up for; **~ qn di** (*rimunerare*) to pay *o* remunerate sb for; (*risarcire*) to pay compensation to sb for; (*fig: fatiche, dolori*) to reward sb for; **com'penso** *sm* compensation payment, remuneration; reward; **in compenso** (*d'altra parte*) on the other hand

compe'rare *vt* = **comprare**

'compere *sfpl* **fare ~** to do the shopping

compe'tente *ag* competent; (*mancia*) apt, suitable

com'petere *vi* to compete, vie; (*Dir: spettare*): **~ a** to lie within the competence of; **competizi'one** *sf* competition

compi'angere [kom'pjandʒere] *vt* to sympathize with, feel sorry for

'compiere *vt* (*concludere*) to finish, complete; (*adempiere*) to carry out, fulfil;

compiersi *vpr (avverarsi)* to be fulfilled, come true; **~ gli anni** to have one's birthday

compi'lare *vt (modulo)* to fill in; *(dizionario, elenco)* to compile

'compito *sm (incarico)* task, duty; *(dovere)* duty; *(Ins)* exercise; *(: a casa)* piece of homework; **fare i compiti** to do one's homework

comple'anno *sm* birthday

complessità *sf* complexity

comples'sivo, -a *ag (globale)* comprehensive, overall; *(totale: cifra)* total

com'plesso, -a *ag* complex ▷ *sm (Psic, Edil)* complex; *(Mus)* complex; *(: orchestrina)* band; *(: di musica pop)* group; **in** *o* **nel ~** on the whole; **complesso alberghiero** hotel complex; **complesso edilizio** building complex; **complesso vitaminico** vitamin complex

completa'mente *av* completely

comple'tare *vt* to complete

com'pleto, -a *ag* complete; *(teatro, autobus)* full ▷ *sm* suit; **al ~** full; *(tutti presenti)* all present; **completo da sci** ski suit

compli'care *vt* to complicate; **complicarsi** *vpr* to become complicated

'complice ['kɔmplitʃe] *sm/f* accomplice

complicità [komplitʃi'ta] *sf inv* complicity; **un sorriso/uno sguardo di ~** a knowing smile/look

complimen'tarsi *vpr* **~ con** to congratulate

compli'mento *sm* compliment; **complimenti** *smpl (cortesia eccessiva)* ceremony *sg*; *(ossequi)* regards, compliments; **complimenti!** congratulations!; **senza complimenti!** don't stand on ceremony!; make yourself at home!; help yourself!

complot'tare *vi* to plot, conspire

com'plotto *sm* plot, conspiracy

com'pone *ecc vb vedi* **comporre**

compo'nente *sm/f* member ▷ *sm* component

com'pongo *ecc vb vedi* **comporre**

componi'mento *sm (Dir)* settlement; *(Ins)* composition; *(poetico, teatrale)* work

com'porre *vt (musica, testo)* to compose; *(mettere in ordine)* to arrange; *(Dir: lite)* to settle; *(Tip)* to set; *(Tel)* to dial; **comporsi** *vpr* **comporsi di** to consist of, be composed of

comporta'mento *sm* behaviour

compor'tare *vt (implicare)* to involve; **comportarsi** *vpr* to behave

com'posi *ecc vb vedi* **comporre**

composi'tore, -'trice *sm/f* composer;

(Tip) compositor, typesetter

com'posto, -a *pp di* **comporre** ▷ *ag (persona)* composed, self-possessed; *(: decoroso)* dignified; *(formato da più elementi)* compound *cpd* ▷ *sm* compound

com'prare *vt* to buy; **dove posso ~ delle cartoline?** where can I buy some postcards?

com'prendere *vt (contenere)* to comprise, consist of; *(capire)* to understand

compren'sibile *ag* understandable

comprensi'one *sf* understanding

compren'sivo, -a *ag (prezzo):* **~ di** inclusive of; *(indulgente)* understanding

> Attenzione! In inglese esiste la parola *comprehensive*, che però in genere significa *completo*.

com'preso, -a *pp di* **comprendere** ▷ *ag (incluso)* included; **il servizio è ~?** is service included?

com'pressa *sf (Med: garza)* compress; *(: pastiglia)* tablet; *vedi anche* **compresso**

com'primere *vt (premere)* to press; *(Fisica)* to compress; *(fig)* to repress

compro'messo, -a *pp di* **compromettere** ▷ *sm* compromise

compro'mettere *vt* to compromise; **compromettersi** *vpr* to compromise o.s.

com'puter *sm inv* computer

comu'nale *ag* municipal, town *cpd,* ≈ borough *cpd*

co'mune *ag* common; *(consueto)* common, everyday; *(di livello medio)* average; *(ordinario)* ordinary ▷ *sm (Amm)* town council; *(: sede)* town hall ▷ *sf (di persone)* commune; **fuori del ~** out of the ordinary; **avere in ~** to have in common, share; **mettere in ~** to share

comuni'care *vt (notizia)* to pass on, convey; *(malattia)* to pass on; *(ansia ecc)* to communicate; *(trasmettere: calore ecc)* to transmit, communicate; *(Rel)* to administer communion to ▷ *vi* to communicate

comuni'cato *sm* communiqué; **comunicato stampa** press release

comunicazi'one [komunikat'tsjone] *sf* communication; *(annuncio)* announcement; *(Tel):* **dare la ~ a qn** to put sb through; **ottenere la ~** to get through; **comunicazione (telefonica)** (telephone) call

comuni'one *sf* communion; **comunione di beni** *(Dir)* joint ownership of property

comu'nismo *sm* communism

comunità *sf inv* community; **Comunità Europea** European Community

co'munque *cong* however, no matter how ▷ *av (in ogni modo)* in any case; *(tuttavia)* however, nevertheless

con prep with; **partire col treno** to leave by train; **~ mio grande stupore** to my great astonishment; **~ tutto ciò** for all that

con'cedere [kon't∫edere] vt (accordare) to grant; (ammettere) to admit, concede; **concedersi qc** to treat o.s. to sth, to allow o.s. sth

concentrarsi vpr to concentrate

concentrazi'one sf concentration

conce'pire [kont∫e'pire] vt (bambino) to conceive; (progetto, idea) to conceive (of); (metodo, piano) to devise

con'certo [kon't∫ɛrto] sm (Mus) concert; (: componimento) concerto

con'cessi ecc [kon't∫ɛssi] vb vedi **concedere**

con'cetto [kon't∫etto] sm (pensiero, idea) concept; (opinione) opinion

concezi'one [kont∫et'tsjone] sf conception

con'chiglia [kon'ki∆∆a] sf shell

conci'are [kon't∫are] vt (pelli) to tan; (tabacco) to cure; (fig: ridurre in cattivo stato) to beat up; **conciarsi** vpr (sporcarsi) to get in a mess; (vestirsi male) to dress badly

concili'are [kont∫i'ljare] vt to reconcile; (contravvenzione) to pay on the spot; (sonno) to be conducive to, induce; **conciliarsi qc** to gain o win sth (for o.s.); **conciliarsi qn** to win sb over; **conciliarsi con** to be reconciled with

con'cime [kon't∫ime] sm manure; (chimico) fertilizer

con'ciso, -a [kon't∫izo] ag concise, succinct

concitta'dino, -a [kont∫itta'dino] sm/f fellow citizen

con'cludere vt to conclude; (portare a compimento) to conclude, finish, bring to an end; (operare positivamente) to achieve ▷ vi (essere convincente) to be conclusive; **concludersi** vpr to come to an end, close

concor'dare vt (tregua, prezzo) to agree on; (Ling) to make agree ▷ vi to agree

con'corde ag (d'accordo) in agreement; (simultaneo) simultaneous

concor'rente sm/f competitor; (Ins) candidate; **concor'renza** sf competition

concorrenzi'ale [konkorren'tsjale] ag competitive

con'correre vi **~ (in)** (Mat) to converge o meet (in); **~ (a)** (competere) to compete (for); (: Ins: a una cattedra) to apply (for); (partecipare: a un'impresa) to take part (in), contribute (to); **con'corso, -a** pp di **concorrere** ▷ sm competition; (Ins) competitive examination; **concorso di colpa** (Dir) contributory negligence

con'creto, -a ag concrete

con'danna sf sentence; conviction; condemnation

condan'nare vt (Dir): **~ a** to sentence to; **~ per** to convict of; (disapprovare) to condemn

conden'sare vt to condense

condi'mento sm seasoning; dressing

con'dire vt to season; (insalata) to dress

condi'videre vt to share

condizio'nale [kondittsjo'nale] ag conditional ▷ sm (Ling) conditional ▷ sf (Dir) suspended sentence

condizio'nare [kondittsjo'nare] vt to condition; **ad aria condizionata** air-conditioned; **condiziona'tore** sm air conditioner

condizi'one [kondit'tsjone] sf condition

condogli'anze [kondo∆'∆antse] sfpl condolences

condo'minio sm joint ownership; (edificio) jointly-owned building

con'dotta sf (modo di comportarsi) conduct, behaviour; (di un affare ecc) handling; (di acqua) pipe; (incarico sanitario) country medical practice controlled by a local authority

condu'cente [kondu't∫ente] sm driver

con'duco ecc vb vedi **condurre**

con'durre vt to conduct; (azienda) to manage; (accompagnare: bambino) to take; (automobile) to drive; (trasportare: acqua, gas) to convey, conduct; (fig) to lead ▷ vi to lead

con'dussi ecc vb vedi **condurre**

confe'renza [konfe'rentsa] sf (discorso) lecture; (riunione) conference; **conferenza stampa** press conference

con'ferma sf confirmation

confer'mare vt to confirm

confes'sare vt to confess; **confessarsi** vpr to confess; **andare a confessarsi** (Rel) to go to confession

con'fetto sm sugared almond; (Med) pill

Attenzione! In inglese esiste la parola confetti, che però significa coriandoli.

confet'tura sf (gen) jam; (di arance) marmalade

confezio'nare [konfettsjo'nare] vt (vestito) to make (up); (merci, pacchi) to package

confezi'one [konfet'tsjone] sf (di abiti: da uomo) tailoring; (: da donna) dressmaking; (imballaggio) packaging; **confezioni per signora** ladies' wear; **confezioni da uomo** menswear; **confezione regalo** gift pack

confic'care vt **~ qc in** to hammer o drive sth into; **conficcarsi** vpr to stick

confi'dare vi **~ in** to confide in, rely on ▷ vt to confide; **confidarsi con qn** to confide

configu'rare vt (Inform) to set

configurazi'one [konfigurat'tsjone] sf configuration; (Inform) setting

confi'nare vi ~ **con** to border on ▷ vt (Pol) to intern; (fig) to confine

Confin'dustria sigla f (= Confederazione Generale dell'Industria Italiana) employers' association, ≈ CBI (BRIT)

con'fine sm boundary; (di paese) border, frontier

confis'care vt to confiscate

con'flitto sm conflict

conflu'enza [konflu'entsa] sf (di fiumi) confluence; (di strade) junction

con'fondere vt to mix up, confuse; (imbarazzare) to embarrass; **confondersi** vpr (mescolarsi) to mingle; (turbarsi) to be confused; (sbagliare) to get mixed up

confor'tare vt to comfort, console

confron'tare vt to compare

con'fronto sm comparison; **in** o **a ~ di** in comparison with, compared to; **nei miei** (o **tuoi** ecc) **confronti** towards me (o you ecc)

con'fusi ecc vb vedi **confondere**

confusi'one sf confusion; (chiasso) racket, noise; (imbarazzo) embarrassment

con'fuso, -a pp di **confondere** ▷ ag (vedi confondere) confused; embarrassed

conge'dare [kondʒe'dare] vt to dismiss; (Mil) to demobilize; **congedarsi** vpr to take one's leave

con'gegno [kon'dʒeɲɲo] sm device, mechanism

conge'lare [kondʒe'lare] vt to freeze; **congelarsi** vpr to freeze; **congela'tore** sm freezer

congesti'one [kondʒes'tjone] sf congestion

conget'tura [kondʒet'tura] sf conjecture

con'giungere [kon'dʒundʒere] vt to join (together); **congiungersi** vpr to join (together)

congiunti'vite [kondʒunti'vite] sf conjunctivitis

congiun'tivo [kondʒun'tivo] sm (Ling) subjunctive

congi'unto, -a [kon'dʒunto] pp di **congiungere** ▷ ag (unito) joined ▷ sm/f relative

congiunzi'one [kondʒun'tsjone] sf (Ling) conjunction

congi'ura [kon'dʒura] sf conspiracy

congratu'larsi vpr ~ **con qn per qc** to congratulate sb on sth

congratulazi'oni [kongratulat'tsjoni] sfpl congratulations

con'gresso sm congress

C.O.N.I. sigla m (= Comitato Olimpico Nazionale Italiano) Italian Olympic Games Committee

coni'are vt to mint, coin; (fig) to coin

co'niglio [ko'niʎʎo] sm rabbit

coniu'gare vt (Ling) to conjugate; **coniugarsi** vpr to get married

'coniuge ['kɔnjudʒe] sm/f spouse

connazio'nale [konnattsjo'nale] sm/f fellow-countryman/woman

connessi'one sf connection

con'nettere vt to connect, join ▷ vi (fig) to think straight

'cono sm cone; **cono gelato** ice-cream cone

co'nobbi ecc vb vedi **conoscere**

cono'scente [konoʃ'ʃente] sm/f acquaintance

cono'scenza [konoʃ'ʃentsa] sf (il sapere) knowledge no pl; (persona) acquaintance; (facoltà sensoriale) consciousness no pl; **perdere ~** to lose consciousness

co'noscere [ko'noʃʃere] vt to know; **ci siamo conosciuti a Firenze** we (first) met in Florence; **conoscersi** vpr to know o.s.; (reciproco) to know each other; (incontrarsi) to meet; **~ qn di vista** to know sb by sight; **farsi ~** (fig) to make a name for o.s.; **conosci'uto, -a** pp di **conoscere** ▷ ag well-known

con'quista sf conquest

conquis'tare vt to conquer; (fig) to gain, win

consa'pevole ag ~ **di** aware o conscious of

'conscio, -a, -sci, -sce ['kɔnʃo] ag ~ **di** aware o conscious of

consecu'tivo, -a ag consecutive; (successivo: giorno) following, next

con'segna [kon'seɲɲa] sf delivery; (merce consegnata) consignment; (custodia) care, custody; (Mil: ordine) orders pl; (: punizione) confinement to barracks; **pagamento alla ~** cash on delivery; **dare qc in ~ a qn** to entrust sth to sb

conse'gnare [konseɲ'ɲare] vt to deliver; (affidare) to entrust, hand over; (Mil) to confine to barracks

consegu'enza [konse'gwentsa] sf consequence; **per** o **di ~** consequently

con'senso sm approval, consent; **consenso informato** informed consent

consen'tire vi ~ **a** to consent o agree to ▷ vt to allow, permit

con'serva sf (Cuc) preserve; **conserva di frutta** jam; **conserva di pomodoro** tomato purée

conser'vante sm (per alimenti) preservative

conser'vare vt (Cuc) to preserve; (custodire) to keep; (: dalla distruzione ecc) to preserve, conserve

conserva'tore, -'trice sm/f (Pol) conservative

conserva'torio sm (di musica) conservatory

conservazi'one [konservat'tsjone] sf preservation; conservation

conside'rare vt to consider; (reputare) to consider, regard; **considerarsi** vpr to consider o.s.

consigli'are [konsiʎ'ʎare] vt (persona) to advise; (metodo, azione) to recommend, advise, suggest; **mi può ~ un buon ristorante?** can you recommend a good restaurant?; **con'siglio** sm (suggerimento) advice no pl, piece of advice; (assemblea) council; **consiglio d'amministrazione** board; **Consiglio d'Europa** Council of Europe; **Consiglio dei Ministri** (Pol): **il Consiglio dei Ministri** ≈ the Cabinet

consis'tente ag thick; solid; (fig) sound, valid

con'sistere vi ~ **in** to consist of

conso'lare ag consular ▷ vt (confortare) to console, comfort; (rallegrare) to cheer up; **consolarsi** vpr to be comforted; to cheer up

conso'lato sm consulate

consolazi'one [konsolat'tsjone] sf consolation, comfort

'console sm consul

conso'nante sf consonant

'consono, -a ag ~ **a** consistent with, consonant with

con'sorte sm/f consort

consta'tare vt to establish, verify

consu'eto, -a ag habitual, usual

consu'lente sm/f consultant

consul'tare vt to consult; **consultarsi** vpr **consultarsi con qn** to seek the advice of sb

consul'torio sm ~ **familiare** family planning clinic

consu'mare vt (logorare: abiti, scarpe) to wear out; (usare) to consume, use up; (mangiare, bere) to consume; (Dir) to consummate; **consumarsi** vpr to wear out; to be used up; (anche fig) to be consumed; (combustibile) to burn out

con'tabile ag accounts cpd, accounting ▷ sm/f accountant

contachi'lometri [kontaki'lɔmetri] sm inv ≈ mileometer

conta'dino, -a sm/f countryman/ woman, farm worker; (peg) peasant

contagi'are [konta'dʒare] vt to infect

contagi'oso, -a ag infectious; contagious

conta'gocce [konta'gottʃe] sm inv (Med) dropper

contami'nare vt to contaminate

con'tante sm cash; **pagare in contanti** to pay cash; **non ho contanti** I haven't got any cash

con'tare vt to count; (considerare) to consider ▷ vi to count, be of importance; ~ **su qn** to count o rely on sb; ~ **di fare qc** to intend to do sth; **conta'tore** sm meter

contat'tare vt to contact

con'tatto sm contact

'conte sm count

conteggi'are [konted'dʒare] vt to charge, put on the bill

con'tegno [kon'teɲɲo] sm (comportamento) behaviour; (atteggiamento) attitude; **darsi un ~** to act nonchalant; to pull o.s. together

contemporanea'mente av simultaneously; at the same time

contempo'raneo, -a ag, sm/f contemporary

conten'dente sm/f opponent, adversary

conte'nere vt to contain; **conteni'tore** sm container

conten'tezza [konten'tettsa] sf contentment

con'tento, -a ag pleased, glad; ~ **di** pleased with

conte'nuto sm contents pl; (argomento) content

con'tessa sf countess

contes'tare vt (Dir) to notify; (fig) to dispute

con'testo sm context

continen'tale ag, sm/f continental

conti'nente ag continent ▷ sm (Geo) continent; (: terra ferma) mainland

contin'gente [kontin'dʒente] ag contingent ▷ sm (Comm) quota; (Mil) contingent

continua'mente av (senza interruzione) continuously, nonstop; (ripetutamente) continually

continu'are vt to continue (with), go on with ▷ vi to continue, go on; ~ **a fare qc** to go on o continue doing sth

continuità sf continuity

con'tinuo, -a ag (numerazione) continuous; (pioggia) continual, constant; (Elettr): **corrente continua** direct current; **di ~** continually

'conto sm (calcolo) calculation; (Comm, Econ) account; (di ristorante, albergo) bill; (fig: stima) consideration, esteem; **il ~, per favore** can I have the bill, please?; **lo metta sul mio ~** put it on my bill; **fare i conti con qn** to settle one's account with sb; **fare ~ su qn/qc** to count o rely on sb; **rendere ~ a qn di qc** to be accountable to sb for sth; **tener ~ di qn/qc** to take sb/sth into account; **per ~ di** on behalf of; **per ~ mio** as far as I'm concerned; **a conti fatti, in fin dei conti** all things considered; **conto corrente** current account; **conto alla rovescia** countdown

con'torno sm (linea) outline, contour; (ornamento) border; (Cuc) vegetables pl

con'torto, -a pp di **contorcere**

contrabbandi'ere, -a sm/f smuggler

contrab'bando sm smuggling, contraband; **merce di ~** contraband, smuggled goods pl

contrab'basso sm (Mus) (double) bass

contraccambi'are vt (favore ecc) to return

contraccet'tivo, -a [kontrattʃet'tivo] ag, sm contraceptive

contrac'colpo sm rebound; (di arma da fuoco) recoil; (fig) repercussion

contrad'dire vt to contradict; **contraddirsi** vpr to contradict o.s.; (uso reciproco: persone) to contradict each other o one another; (: testimonianze ecc) to be contradictory

contraf'fare vt (persona) to mimic; (alterare: voce) to disguise; (firma) to forge, counterfeit

contraria'mente av **~ a** contrary to

contrari'are vt (contrastare) to thwart, oppose; (irritare) to annoy, bother

con'trario, -a ag opposite; (sfavorevole) unfavourable ▷ sm opposite; **essere ~ a qc** (persona) to be against sth; **in caso ~** otherwise; **avere qc in ~** to have some objection; **al ~** on the contrary

contrasse'gnare [kontrasseɲ'ɲare] vt to mark

contras'tare vt (avversare) to oppose; (impedire) to bar; (negare: diritto) to contest, dispute ▷ vi **~ (con)** (essere in disaccordo) to contrast (with); (lottare) to struggle (with)

contrat'tacco sm counterattack

contrat'tare vt, vi to negotiate

contrat'tempo sm hitch

con'tratto, -a pp di **contrarre** ▷ sm contract

contravvenzi'one [kontravven'tsjone] sf contravention; (ammenda) fine

contrazi'one [kontrat'tsjone] sf contraction; (di prezzi ecc) reduction

contribu'ente sm/f taxpayer; ratepayer (BRIT), property tax payer (US)

contribu'ire vi to contribute

'contro prep against; **~ di me/lui** against me/him; **pastiglie ~ la tosse** throat lozenges; **~ pagamento** (Comm) on payment ▷ prefisso: **controfi'gura** sf (Cinema) double

control'lare vt (accertare) to check; (sorvegliare) to watch, control; (tenere nel proprio potere, fig: dominare) to control; **controllarsi** vpr to control o.s.; **con'trollo** sm check; watch; control; **controllo delle nascite** birth control; **control'lore** sm (Ferr, Autobus) (ticket) inspector

contro'luce [kontro'lutʃe] sf inv (Fot) backlit shot ▷ av **(in) ~** against the light; (fotografare) into the light

contro'mano av **guidare ~** to drive on the wrong side of the road; (in un senso unico) to drive the wrong way up a one-way street

controprodu'cente [kontroprodu'tʃɛnte] ag counterproductive

contro'senso sm (contraddizione) contradiction in terms; (assurdità) nonsense

controspio'naggio [kontrospio'naddʒo] sm counterespionage

contro'versia sf controversy; (Dir) dispute

contro'verso, -a ag controversial

contro'voglia [kontro'voʎʎa] av unwillingly

contusi'one sf (Med) bruise

convale'scente [konvaleʃ'ʃɛnte] ag, sm/f convalescent

convali'dare vt (Amm) to validate; (fig: sospetto, dubbio) to confirm

con'vegno [kon'veɲɲo] sm (incontro) meeting; (congresso) convention, congress; (luogo) meeting place

conve'nevoli smpl civilities

conveni'ente ag suitable; (vantaggioso) profitable; (: prezzo) cheap

> Attenzione! In inglese esiste la parola convenient, che però significa comodo.

conve'nire vi (riunirsi) to gather, assemble; (concordare) to agree; (tornare utile) to be worthwhile ▷ vb impers **conviene fare questo** it is advisable to do this; **conviene andarsene** we should go; **ne convengo** I agree

con'vento sm (di frati) monastery; (di suore) convent

convenzio'nale [konventsjo'nale] ag conventional

convenzi'one [konven'tsjone] sf (Dir) agreement; (nella società) convention

conver'sare vi to have a conversation, converse

conversazi'one [konversat'tsjone] sf conversation; **fare ~** to chat, have a chat

conversi'one sf conversion; **conversione ad U** (Aut) U-turn

conver'tire vt (trasformare) to change; (Pol, Rel) to convert; **convertirsi** vpr **convertirsi (a)** to be converted (to)

con'vesso, -a ag convex

convin'cente [konvin'tʃɛnte] *ag* convincing

con'vincere [kon'vintʃere] *vt* to convince; **~ qn di qc** to convince sb of sth; **~ qn a fare qc** to persuade sb to do sth; **convincersi** *vpr* **convincersi (di qc)** to convince o.s. (of sth); **~ qn di qc** to convince sb of sth; **~ qn a fare qc** to convince sb to do sth

convi'vente *sm/f* common-law husband/wife

con'vivere *vi* to live together

convo'care *vt* to call, convene; (*Dir*) to summon

convulsi'one *sf* convulsion

coope'rare *vi* **~ (a)** to cooperate (in); **coopera'tiva** *sf* cooperative

coordi'nare *vt* to coordinate

co'perchio [ko'pɛrkjo] *sm* cover; (*di pentola*) lid

co'perta *sf* cover; (*di lana*) blanket; (*da viaggio*) rug; (*Naut*) deck

coper'tina *sf* (*Stampa*) cover, jacket

co'perto, -a *pp di* **coprire** ▷ *ag* covered; (*cielo*) overcast ▷ *sm* place setting; (*posto a tavola*) place; (*al ristorante*) cover charge; **~ di** covered in *o* with

coper'tone *sm* (*Aut*) rubber tyre

coper'tura *sf* (*anche Econ, Mil*) cover; (*di edificio*) roofing

'copia *sf* copy; **brutta/bella ~** rough/final copy

copi'are *vt* to copy

copi'one *sm* (*Cinema, Teatro*) script

'coppa *sf* (*bicchiere*) goblet; (*per frutta, gelato*) dish; (*trofeo*) cup, trophy; **coppa dell'olio** oil sump (*BRIT*) *o* pan (*US*)

'coppia *sf* (*di persone*) couple; (*di animali, Sport*) pair

coprifu'oco, -chi *sm* curfew

copri'letto *sm* bedspread

copripiu'mino *sm* duvet cover

co'prire *vt* to cover; (*occupare: carica, posto*) to hold; **coprirsi** *vpr* (*cielo*) to cloud over; (*vestirsi*) to wrap up, cover up; (*Econ*) to cover o.s.; **coprirsi di** (*macchie, muffa*) to become covered in

coque [kɔk] *sf* **uovo alla ~** boiled egg

co'raggio [ko'raddʒo] *sm* courage, bravery; **~!** (*forza!*) come on!; (*animo!*) cheer up!

co'rallo *sm* coral

Co'rano *sm* (*Rel*) Koran

co'razza [ko'rattsa] *sf* armour; (*di animali*) carapace, shell; (*Mil*) armour(-plating)

'corda *sf* cord; (*fune*) rope; (*spago, Mus*) string; **dare ~ a qn** to let sb have his (*o* her) way; **tenere sulla ~ a qn** to keep sb on tenterhooks; **tagliare la ~** to slip away, sneak off; **corda vocale** vocal cords

cordi'ale *ag* cordial, warm ▷ *sm* (*bevanda*) cordial

'cordless ['kɔːdlɪs] *sm inv* cordless phone

cor'done *sm* cord, string; (*linea: di polizia*) cordon; **cordone ombelicale** umbilical cord

Co'rea *sf* **la ~** Korea

coreogra'fia *sf* choreography

cori'andolo *sm* (*Bot*) coriander; **coriandoli** *smpl* confetti *sg*

cor'nacchia [kor'nakkja] *sf* crow

corna'musa *sf* bagpipes *pl*

cor'netta *sf* (*Mus*) cornet; (*Tel*) receiver

cor'netto *sm* (*Cuc*) croissant; (*gelato*) cone

cor'nice [kor'nitʃe] *sf* frame; (*fig*) setting, background

cornici'one [korni'tʃone] *sm* (*di edificio*) ledge; (*Archit*) cornice

'corno (*pl(f)* **-a**) *sm* (*Zool*) horn; (*pl(m)* **-i**: *Mus*) horn; **fare le corna a qn** to be unfaithful to sb

Corno'vaglia [korno'vaʎʎa] *sf* **la ~** Cornwall

cor'nuto, -a *ag* (*con corna*) horned; (*fam!: marito*) cuckolded ▷ *sm* (*fam!*) cuckold; (*: insulto*) bastard (!)

'coro *sm* chorus; (*Rel*) choir

co'rona *sf* crown; (*di fiori*) wreath

'corpo *sm* body; (*militare, diplomatico*) corps *inv*; **prendere ~** to take shape; **a ~ a ~** hand-to-hand; **corpo di ballo** corps de ballet; **corpo insegnante** teaching staff

corpora'tura *sf* build, physique

cor'reggere [kor'reddʒere] *vt* to correct; (*compiti*) to correct, mark

cor'rente *ag* (*acqua: di fiume*) flowing; (*: di rubinetto*) running; (*moneta, prezzo*) current; (*comune*) everyday ▷ *sm* **essere al ~ (di)** to be well-informed (about); **mettere al ~ (di)** to inform (of) ▷ *sf* (*d'acqua*) current, stream; (*spiffero*) draught; (*Elettr, Meteor*) current; (*fig*) trend, tendency; **la vostra lettera del 5 ~ mese** (*Comm*) your letter of the 5th of this month; **corrente alternata/continua** alternate/direct current; **corrente'mente** *av* commonly; **parlare una lingua correntemente** to speak a language fluently

'correre *vi* to run; (*precipitarsi*) to rush; (*partecipare a una gara*) to race, run; (*fig: diffondersi*) to go round ▷ *vt* (*Sport: gara*) to compete in; (*rischio*) to run; (*pericolo*) to face; **~ dietro a qn** to run after sb; **corre voce che ...** it is rumoured that ...

cor'ressi *ecc vb vedi* **correggere**

correzi'one [korret'tsjone] *sf* correction; marking; **correzione di bozze** proofreading

corri'doio *sm* corridor; (*in aereo, al cinema*)

aisle; **vorrei un posto sul ~** I'd like an aisle seat

corri'dore sm (Sport) runner; (: su veicolo) racer

corri'era sf coach (BRIT), bus

corri'ere sm (diplomatico, di guerra, postale) courier; (Comm) carrier

corri'mano sm handrail

corrispon'dente ag corresponding ▷ sm/f correspondent

corrispon'denza [korrispon'dɛntsa] sf correspondence

corris'pondere vi (equivalere): **~ (a)** to correspond (to) ▷ vt (stipendio) to pay; (fig: amore) to return

cor'rodere vt to corrode

cor'rompere vt to corrupt; (comprare) to bribe

cor'roso, -a pp di **corrodere**

cor'rotto, -a pp di **corrompere** ▷ ag corrupt

corru'gare vt to wrinkle; **~ la fronte** to knit one's brows

cor'ruppi ecc vb vedi **corrompere**

corruzi'one [korrut'tsjone] sf corruption; bribery

'corsa sf running no pl; (gara) race; (di autobus, taxi) journey, trip; **fare una ~** to run, dash; (Sport) to run a race; **corsa campestre** cross-country race

'corsi ecc vb vedi **correre**

cor'sia sf (Aut, Sport) lane; (di ospedale) ward

'Corsica sf **la ~** Corsica

cor'sivo sm cursive (writing); (Tip) italics pl

'corso, -a pp di **correre** ▷ sm course; (strada cittadina) main street; (di unità monetaria) circulation; (di titoli, valori) rate, price; **in ~** in progress, under way; (annata) current; **corso d'acqua** river, stream; (artificiale) waterway; **corso d'aggiornamento** refresher course; **corso serale** evening class

'corte sf (court)yard; (Dir, regale) court; **fare la ~ a qn** to court sb; **corte marziale** court-martial

cor'teccia, -ce [kor'tettʃa] sf bark

corteggi'are [korted'dʒare] vt to court

cor'teo sm procession

cor'tese ag courteous; **corte'sia** sf courtesy; **per cortesia ...** excuse me, please ...

cor'tile sm (court)yard

cor'tina sf curtain; (anche fig) screen

'corto, -a ag short; **essere a ~ di qc** to be short of sth; **corto circuito** short-circuit

'corvo sm raven

'cosa sf thing; (faccenda) affair, matter, business no pl; **(che) ~?** what?; **(che)**

cos'è? what is it?; **a ~ pensi?** what are you thinking about?

'coscia, -sce ['kɔʃʃa] sf thigh; **coscia di pollo** (Cuc) chicken leg

cosci'ente [koʃʃɛnte] ag conscious; **~ di** conscious o aware of

◯ **PAROLA CHIAVE**

così av 1 (in questo modo) like this, (in) this way; (in tal modo) so; **le cose stanno così** this is the way things stand; **non ho detto così!** I didn't say that!; **come stai? — (e) così** how are you? — so-so; **e così via** and so on; **per così dire** so to speak
2 (tanto) so; **così lontano** so far away; **un ragazzo così intelligente** such an intelligent boy
▷ ag inv (tale): **non ho mai visto un film così** I've never seen such a film ▷ cong 1 (perciò) so, therefore
2: **così ... come** as ... as; **non è così bravo come te** he's not as good as you; **così ... che** so ... that

cosid'detto, -a ag so-called

cos'metico, -a, -ci, -che ag, sm cosmetic

cos'pargere [kos'pardʒere] vt **~ di** to sprinkle with

cos'picuo, -a ag considerable, large

cospi'rare vi to conspire

'cossi ecc vb vedi **cuocere**

'costa sf (tra terra e mare) coast(line); (litorale) shore; (Anat) rib; **la C~ Azzurra** the French Riviera

cos'tante ag constant; (persona) steadfast ▷ sf constant

cos'tare vi, vt to cost; **quanto costa?** how much does it cost?; **~ caro** to be expensive, cost a lot

cos'tata sf (Cuc) large chop

costeggi'are [kosted'dʒare] vt to be close to; to run alongside

costi'ero, -a ag coastal, coast cpd

costitu'ire vt (comitato, gruppo) to set up, form; (elementi, parti: comporre) to make up, constitute; (rappresentare) to constitute; (Dir) to appoint; **costituirsi** vpr **costituirsi alla polizia** to give o.s. up to the police

costituzi'one [kostitut'tsjone] sf setting up; building up; constitution

'costo sm cost; **a ogni o qualunque ~, a tutti i costi** at all costs

'costola sf (Anat) rib

cos'toso, -a ag expensive, costly

cos'tringere [kos'trindʒere] vt **~ qn a fare qc** to force sb to do sth

costru'ire vt to construct, build;

costruzi'one sf construction, building
cos'tume sm (uso) custom; (foggia di vestire, indumento) costume; **costume da bagno** bathing o swimming costume (BRIT), swimsuit; (da uomo) bathing o swimming trunks pl
co'tenna sf bacon rind
coto'letta sf (di maiale, montone) chop; (di vitello, agnello) cutlet
co'tone sm cotton; **cotone idrofilo** cotton wool (BRIT), absorbent cotton (US)
'cotta sf (fam: innamoramento) crush
'cottimo sm **lavorare a ~** to do piecework
'cotto, -a pp di **cuocere** ▷ ag cooked; (fam: innamorato) head-over-heels in love; **ben ~** (carne) well done
cot'tura sf cooking; (in forno) baking; (in umido) stewing
co'vare vt to hatch; (fig: malattia) to be sickening for; (: odio, rancore) to nurse ▷ vi (fuoco, fig) to smoulder
'covo sm den
co'vone sm sheaf
'cozza ['kɔttsa] sf mussel
coz'zare [kot'tsare] vi **~ contro** to bang into, collide with
'crampo sm cramp; **ho un ~ alla gamba** I've got cramp in my leg
'cranio sm skull
cra'tere sm crater
cra'vatta sf tie
cre'are vt to create
'crebbi ecc vb vedi **crescere**
cre'dente sm/f (Rel) believer
cre'denza [kre'dɛntsa] sf belief; (armadio) sideboard
'credere vt to believe ▷ vi **~ in, ~ a** to believe in; **~ qn onesto** to believe sb (to be) honest; **~ che** to believe o think that; **credersi furbo** to think one is clever
'credito sm (anche Comm) credit; (reputazione) esteem, repute; **comprare a ~** to buy on credit
'crema sf cream; (con uova, zucchero ecc) custard; **crema pasticciera** confectioner's custard; **crema solare** sun cream
cre'mare vt to cremate
'crepa sf crack
cre'paccio [kre'pattʃo] sm large crack, fissure; (di ghiacciaio) crevasse
crepacu'ore sm broken heart
cre'pare vi (fam: morire) to snuff it, kick the bucket; **~ dalle risa** to split one's sides laughing
crêpe [krɛp] sf inv pancake
cre'puscolo sm twilight, dusk
'crescere ['kreʃʃere] vi to grow ▷ vt (figli) to raise
'cresima sf (Rel) confirmation

'crespo, -a ag (capelli) frizzy; (tessuto) puckered ▷ sm crêpe
'cresta sf crest; (di polli, uccelli) crest, comb
'creta sf chalk; clay
creti'nata sf (fam): **dire/fare una ~** to say/do a stupid thing
cre'tino, -a ag stupid ▷ sm/f idiot, fool
CRI sigla f = **Croce Rossa Italiana**
cric sm inv (Tecn) jack
cri'ceto [kri'tʃeto] sm hamster
crimi'nale ag, sm/f criminal
criminalità sf crime; **criminalità organizzata** organized crime
'crimine sm (Dir) crime
crip'tare vt (TV: programma) to encrypt
crisan'temo sm chrysanthemum
'crisi sf inv crisis; (Med) attack, fit; **crisi di nervi** attack o fit of nerves
cris'tallo sm crystal; **cristalli liquidi** liquid crystals
cristia'nesimo sm Christianity
cristi'ano, -a ag, sm/f Christian
'Cristo sm Christ
cri'terio sm criterion; (buon senso) (common) sense
'critica, -che sf criticism; **la ~** (attività) criticism; (persone) the critics pl; vedi anche **critico**
criti'care vt to criticize
'critico, -a, -ci, -che ag critical ▷ sm critic
cro'ato, -a ag, sm/f Croatian, Croat
Croa'zia [kroa'ttsja] sf Croatia
croc'cante ag crisp, crunchy
'croce ['krotʃe] sf cross; **in ~** (di traverso) crosswise; (fig) on tenterhooks; **Croce Rossa** Red Cross
croci'ata [kro'tʃata] sf crusade
croci'era [kro'tʃera] sf (viaggio) cruise; (Archit) transept
croci'fisso, -a pp di **crocifiggere**
crol'lare vi to collapse; **'crollo** sm collapse; (di prezzi) slump, sudden fall; **crollo in Borsa** slump in prices on the Stock Exchange
cro'mato, -a ag chromium-plated
'cromo sm chrome, chromium
'cronaca, -che sf (Stampa) news sg; (: rubrica) column; (TV, Radio) commentary; **fatto o episodio di ~** news item; **cronaca nera** crime news sg; crime column
'cronico, -a, -ci, -che ag chronic
cro'nista, -i sm (Stampa) reporter
cro'nometro sm chronometer; (a scatto) stopwatch
'crosta sf crust
cros'tacei [kros'tatʃei] smpl shellfish
cros'tata sf (Cuc) tart
cros'tino sm (Cuc) crouton; (: da antipasto) canapé

cruci'ale [kru'tʃale] *ag* crucial

cruci'verba *sm inv* crossword (puzzle)

cru'dele *ag* cruel

'crudo, -a *ag* (*non cotto*) raw; (*aspro*) harsh, severe

cru'miro (*peg*) *sm* blackleg (BRIT); scab

'crusca *sf* bran

crus'cotto *sm* (*Aut*) dashboard

CSI *sigla f inv* (= *Comunità Stati Indipendenti*) CIS

CSM [tʃiesse'emme] *sigla m* (= *consiglio superiore della magistratura*) Magistrates' Board of Supervisors

'Cuba *sf* Cuba

cu'bano, -a *ag, sm/f* Cuban

cu'betto *sm*; **cubetto di ghiaccio** ice cube

'cubico, -a, -ci, -che *ag* cubic

cu'bista, -i, -e *ag* (*Arte*) Cubist ▷ *sf* (*in discoteca*) podium dancer

'cubo, -a *ag* cubic ▷ *sm* cube; **elevare al ~** (*Mat*) to cube

cuc'cagna [kuk'kaɲɲa] *sf* **paese della ~** land of plenty; **albero della ~** greasy pole (*fig*)

cuc'cetta [kut'tʃetta] *sf* (*Ferr*) couchette; (*Naut*) berth

cucchiai'ata [kukja'jata] *sf* spoonful

cucchia'ino [kukkja'ino] *sm* teaspoon; coffee spoon

cucchi'aio [kuk'kjajo] *sm* spoon

'cuccia, -ce ['kuttʃa] *sf* dog's bed; **a ~!** down!

'cucciolo ['kuttʃolo] *sm* cub; (*di cane*) puppy

cu'cina [ku'tʃina] *sf* (*locale*) kitchen; (*arte culinaria*) cooking, cookery; (*le vivande*) food, cooking; (*apparecchio*) cooker; **cucina componibile** fitted kitchen; **cuci'nare** *vt* to cook

cu'cire [ku'tʃire] *vt* to sew, stitch; **cuci'trice** *sf* stapler

cucù *sm inv* cuckoo

'cuffia *sf* bonnet, cap; (*da infermiera*) cap; (*da bagno*) (bathing) cap; (*per ascoltare*) headphones *pl*, headset

cu'gino, -a [ku'dʒino] *sm/f* cousin

PAROLA CHIAVE

'cui *pron* 1 (*nei complementi indiretti: persona*) whom; (: *oggetto, animale*) which; **la persona/le persone a cui accennavi** the person/people you were referring to *o* to whom you were referring; **i libri di cui parlavo** the books I was talking about *o* about which I was talking; **il quartiere in cui abito** the district where I live; **la ragione per cui** the reason why

2 (*inserito tra articolo e sostantivo*) whose;

la donna i cui figli sono scomparsi the woman whose children have disappeared; **il signore, dal cui figlio ho avuto il libro** the man from whose son I got the book

culi'naria *sf* cookery

'culla *sf* cradle

cul'lare *vt* to rock

'culmine *sm* top, summit

'culo (*fam!*) *sm* arse (BRIT!), ass (US!); (*fig: fortuna*): **aver ~** to have the luck of the devil

'culto *sm* (*religione*) religion; (*adorazione*) worship, adoration; (*venerazione: anche fig*) cult

cul'tura *sf* culture; education, learning; **cultu'rale** *ag* cultural

cultu'rismo *sm* body-building

cumula'tivo, -a *ag* cumulative; (*prezzo*) inclusive; (*biglietto*) group *cpd*

'cumulo *sm* (*mucchio*) pile, heap; (*Meteor*) cumulus

cu'netta *sf* (*avvallamento*) dip; (*di scolo*) gutter

cu'ocere ['kwɔtʃere] *vt* (*alimenti*) to cook; (*mattoni ecc*) to fire ▷ *vi* to cook; **~ al forno** (*pane*) to bake; (*arrosto*) to roast; **cu'oco, -a, -chi, -che** *sm/f* cook; (*di ristorante*) chef

cu'oio *sm* leather; **cuoio capelluto** scalp

cu'ore *sm* heart; **cuori** *smpl* (*Carte*) hearts; **avere buon ~** to be kind-hearted; **stare a ~ a qn** to be important to sb

'cupo, -a *ag* dark; (*suono*) dull; (*fig*) gloomy, dismal

'cupola *sf* dome; cupola

'cura *sf* care; (*Med: trattamento*) (course of) treatment; **aver ~ di** (*occuparsi di*) to look after; **a ~ di** (*libro*) edited by; **cura dimagrante** diet

cu'rare *vt* (*malato, malattia*) to treat; (: *guarire*) to cure; (*aver cura di*) to take care of; (*testo*) to edit; **curarsi** *vpr* to take care of o.s.; (*Med*) to follow a course of treatment; **curarsi di** to pay attention to

curio'sare *vi* to look round, wander round; (*tra libri*) to browse; **~ nei negozi** to look *o* wander round the shops

curiosità *sf inv* curiosity; (*cosa rara*) curio, curiosity

curi'oso, -a *ag* curious; **essere ~ di** to be curious about

cur'sore *sm* (*Inform*) cursor

'curva *sf* curve; (*stradale*) bend, curve

cur'vare *vt* to bend ▷ *vi* (*veicolo*) to take a bend; (*strada*) to bend, curve; **curvarsi** *vpr* to bend; (*legno*) to warp

'curvo, -a *ag* curved; (*piegato*) bent

cusci'netto [kuʃʃi'netto] *sm* pad; (*Tecn*) bearing ▷ *ag inv* **stato ~** buffer state; **cuscinetto a sfere** ball bearing

cu'scino [kuʃʃino] *sm* cushion; (*guanciale*) pillow

cus'tode *sm/f* keeper, custodian

cus'todia *sf* care; (*Dir*) custody; (*astuccio*) case, holder

custo'dire *vt* (*conservare*) to keep; (*assistere*) to look after, take care of; (*fare la guardia*) to guard

CV *abbr* (= *cavallo vapore*) h.p.

cybercaffè [tʃiberkaˈfe] *sm inv* cybercafé

cybernauta, -i, -e *sm/f* Internet surfer

cyberspazio *sm* cyberspace

d

PAROLA CHIAVE

da (*da+il* = **dal**, *da+lo* = **dallo**, *da+l'* = **dall'**, *da+la* = **dalla**, *da+i* = **dai**, *da+gli* = **dagli**, *da+le* = **dalle**) *prep* 1 (*agente*) by; **dipinto da un grande artista** painted by a great artist

2 (*causa*) with; **tremare dalla paura** to tremble with fear

3 (*stato in luogo*) at; **abito da lui** I'm living at his house *o* with him; **sono dal giornalaio/da Francesco** I'm at the newsagent's/Francesco's (house)

4 (*moto a luogo*) to; (*moto per luogo*) through; **vado da Pietro/dal giornalaio** I'm going to Pietro's (house)/to the newsagent's; **sono passati dalla finestra** they came in through the window

5 (*provenienza, allontanamento*) from; **arrivare/partire da Milano** to arrive/depart from Milan; **scendere dal treno/dalla macchina** to get off the train/out of the car; **si trova a 5 km da qui** it's 5 km from here

6 (*tempo: durata*) for; (: *a partire da*: *nel passato*) since; (: *nel futuro*) from; **vivo qui da un anno** I've been living here for a year; **è dalle 3 che ti aspetto** I've been waiting for you since 3 (o'clock); **da oggi in poi** from today onwards; **da bambino** as a

child, when I (*o he ecc*) was a child
7 (*modo, maniera*) like; **comportarsi da uomo** to behave like a man; **l'ho fatto da me** I did it (by) myself
8 (*descrittivo*): **una macchina da corsa** a racing car; **una ragazza dai capelli biondi** a girl with blonde hair; **un vestito da 60 euro** a 60 euros dress

dà *vb vedi* **dare**

dac'capo *av* (*di nuovo*) (once) again; (*dal principio*) all over again, from the beginning

'dado *sm* (*da gioco*) dice *o* die; (*Cuc*) stock (BRIT) *o* bouillon (US) cube; (*Tecn*) (screw)nut; **dadi** *smpl* (game of) dice; **giocare a dadi** to play dice

'daino *sm* (fallow) deer *inv*; (*pelle*) buckskin

dal'tonico, -a, -ci, -che *ag* colour-blind

'dama *sf* lady; (*nei balli*) partner; (*gioco*) draughts *sg* (BRIT), checkers *sg* (US)

damigi'ana [dami'dʒana] *sf* demijohn

da'nese *ag* Danish ▷ *sm/f* Dane ▷ *sm* (*Ling*) Danish

Dani'marca *sf* **la ~** Denmark

dannazi'one *sf* damnation

danneggi'are [danned'dʒare] *vt* to damage; (*rovinare*) to spoil; (*nuocere*) to harm

'danno *sm* damage; (*a persona*) harm, injury; **danni** *smpl* (*Dir*) damages; **dan'noso, -a** *ag* **dannoso (a, per)** harmful (to), bad (for)

Da'nubio *sm* **il ~** the Danube

'danza ['dantsa] *sf* **la ~** dancing; **una ~** a dance

dan'zare [dan'tsare] *vt, vi* to dance

dapper'tutto *av* everywhere

dap'prima *av* at first

'dare *sm* (*Comm*) debit ▷ *vt* to give; (*produrre: frutti, suono*) to produce ▷ *vi* (*guardare*): **~ su** to look (out) onto; **darsi** *vpr* **darsi a** to dedicate o.s. to; **darsi al commercio** to go into business; **darsi al bere** to take to drink; **~ da mangiare a qn** to give sb sth to eat; **~ per certo qc** to consider sth certain; **~ per morto qn** to give sb up for dead; **darsi per vinto** to give in

'data *sf* date; **~ limite d'utilizzo** *or* **di consumo** best-before date; **data di nascita** date of birth; **data di scadenza** expiry date

'dato, -a *ag* (*stabilito*) given ▷ *sm* datum; **dati** *smpl* data *pl*; **~ che** given that; **un ~ di fatto** a fact; **dati sensibili** personal information

da'tore, -'trice *sm/f*; **datore di lavoro** employer

'dattero *sm* date

dattilogra'fia *sf* typing

datti'lografo, -a *sm/f* typist

da'vanti *av* in front; (*dirimpetto*) opposite ▷ *ag inv* front ▷ *sm* front; **~ a** in front of; facing, opposite; (*in presenza di*) before, in front of

davan'zale [davan'tsale] *sm* windowsill

dav'vero *av* really, indeed

d.C. *adv abbr* (= *dopo Cristo*) A.D.

'dea *sf* goddess

'debbo *ecc vb vedi* **dovere**

'debito, -a *ag* due, proper ▷ *sm* debt; (*Comm: dare*) debit; **a tempo ~** at the right time

'debole *ag* weak, feeble; (*suono*) faint; (*luce*) dim ▷ *sm* weakness; **debo'lezza** *sf* weakness

debut'tare *vi* to make one's debut

deca'denza [deka'dɛntsa] *sf* decline; (*Dir*) loss, forfeiture

decaffei'nato, -a *ag* decaffeinated

decapi'tare *vt* to decapitate, behead

decappot'tabile *ag, sf* convertible

de'cennio [de'tʃɛnnjo] *sm* decade

de'cente [de'tʃɛnte] *ag* decent, respectable, proper; (*accettabile*) satisfactory, decent

de'cesso [de'tʃɛsso] *sm* death

de'cidere [de'tʃidere] *vt* **~ qc** to decide on sth; (*questione, lite*) to settle sth; **~ di fare/ che** to decide to do/that; **~ di qc** (*cosa*) to determine sth; **decidersi (a fare)** to decide (to do), make up one's mind (to do)

deci'frare [detʃi'frare] *vt* to decode; (*fig*) to decipher, make out

deci'male [detʃi'male] *ag* decimal

'decimo, -a ['dɛtʃimo] *num* tenth

de'cina [de'tʃina] *sf* ten; (*circa dieci*): **una ~ (di)** about ten

de'cisi *ecc* [de'tʃizi] *vb vedi* **decidere**

decisi'one [detʃi'zjone] *sf* decision; **prendere una ~** to make a decision

deci'sivo, -a [detʃi'zivo] *ag* (*gen*) decisive; (*fattore*) deciding

de'ciso, -a [de'tʃizo] *pp di* **decidere**

decli'nare *vi* (*pendio*) to slope down; (*fig: diminuire*) to decline ▷ *vt* to decline

declinazi'one *sf* (*Ling*) declension

de'clino *sm* decline

decodifica'tore *sm* (*Tel*) decoder

decol'lare *vi* (*Aer*) to take off; **de'collo** *sm* take-off

deco'rare *vt* to decorate; **decorazi'one** *sf* decoration

de'creto *sm* decree; **decreto legge** *decree with the force of law*

'dedica, -che *sf* dedication

dedi'care *vt* to dedicate; **dedicarsi** *vpr* **dedicarsi a** to devote o.s. to

dedicherò ecc [dedike'rɔ] vb vedi **dedicare**

'**dedito, -a** ag ~ **a** (studio ecc) dedicated o devoted to; (vizio) addicted to

de'**duco** ecc vb vedi **dedurre**

de'**durre** vt (concludere) to deduce; (defalcare) to deduct

de'**dussi** ecc vb vedi **dedurre**

defici'**ente** [defi'tʃɛnte] ag (mancante): ~ **di** deficient in; (insufficiente) insufficient ▷ sm/f mental defective; (peg: cretino) idiot

'**deficit** ['dɛfitʃit] sm inv (Econ) deficit

defi'**nire** vt to define; (risolvere) to settle; **defini'tiva** sf **in** ~ (dopotutto) in the end; (dunque) hence; **defini'tivo, -a** ag definitive, final; **definizi'one** sf definition; settlement

defor'**mare** vt (alterare) to put out of shape; (corpo) to deform; (pensiero, fatto) to distort; **deformarsi** vpr to lose its shape

de'**forme** ag deformed; disfigured

de'**funto, -a** ag late cpd ▷ sm/f deceased

degene'**rare** [dedʒene'rare] vi to degenerate

de'**gente** [de'dʒɛnte] sm/f (in ospedale) in-patient

deglu'**tire** vt to swallow

de'**gnare** [deɲ'ɲare] vt ~ **qn della propria presenza** to honour sb with one's presence; **degnarsi** vpr **degnarsi di fare qc** to deign o condescend to do sth

'**degno, -a** ag dignified; ~ **di** worthy of; ~ **di lode** praiseworthy

de'**grado** sm; **degrado urbano** urban decline

'**delega, -ghe** sf (procura) proxy

dele'**terio, -a** ag damaging; (per salute ecc) harmful

del'**fino** sm (Zool) dolphin; (Storia) dauphin; (fig) probable successor

deli'**cato, -a** ag delicate; (salute) delicate, frail; (fig: gentile) thoughtful, considerate; (: che dimostra tatto) tactful

delin'**quente** sm/f criminal, delinquent; **delinquente abituale** regular offender, habitual offender; **delin'quenza** sf criminality, delinquency; **delinquenza minorile** juvenile delinquency

deli'**rare** vi to be delirious, rave; (fig) to rave

de'**lirio** sm delirium; (ragionamento insensato) raving; (fig): **andare/mandare in** ~ to go/send into a frenzy

de'**litto** sm crime

delizi'**oso, -a** ag delightful; (cibi) delicious

delta'**plano** sm hang-glider; **volo col** ~ hang-gliding

delu'**dente** ag disappointing

de'**ludere** vt to disappoint; **delusi'one** sf disappointment; **de'luso, -a** pp di **deludere**

'**demmo** vb vedi **dare**

demo'**cratico, -a, -ci, -che** ag democratic

democra'**zia** [demokrat'tsia] sf democracy

demo'**lire** vt to demolish

de'**monio** sm demon, devil; **il D~** the Devil

de'**naro** sm money

densi**tà** sf inv density

'**denso, -a** ag thick, dense

den'**tale** ag dental

'**dente** sm tooth; (di forchetta) prong; **al** ~ (Cuc: pasta) al dente; **denti del giudizio** wisdom teeth; **denti da latte** milk teeth; **denti'era** sf (set of) false teeth pl

denti'**fricio** [denti'fritʃo] sm toothpaste

den'**tista, -i, -e** sm/f dentist

'**dentro** av inside; (in casa) indoors; (fig: nell'intimo) inwardly ▷ prep ~ **(a)** in; **piegato in** ~ folded over; **qui/là** ~ in here/there; ~ **di sé** (pensare, brontolare) to oneself

de'**nuncia, -ce** o **cie** [de'nuntʃa] sf denunciation; declaration; **denuncia dei redditi** (income) tax return

denunci'**are** [denun'tʃare] vt to denounce; (dichiarare) to declare; (persona, smarrimento ecc) report; **vorrei** ~ **un furto** I'd like to report a theft

denu'**trito, -a** ag undernourished

denutrizi'**one** [denutrit'tsjone] sf malnutrition

deodo'**rante** sm deodorant

depe'**rire** vi to waste away

depi'**larsi** vpr ~ **(le gambe)** (con rasoio) to shave (one's legs); (con ceretta) to wax (one's legs)

depila'**torio, -a** ag hair-removing cpd, depilatory

dépli'**ant** [depli'ã] sm inv leaflet; (opuscolo) brochure

deplo'**revole** ag deplorable

de'**pone, de'pongo** ecc vb vedi **deporre**

de'**porre** vt (depositare) to put down; (rimuovere: da una carica) to remove; (: re) to depose; (Dir) to testify

depor'**tare** vt to deport

de'**posi** ecc vb vedi **deporre**

deposi'**tare** vt (gen, Geo, Econ) to deposit; (lasciare) to leave; (merci) to store; **depositarsi** vpr (sabbia, polvere) to settle

de'**posito** sm deposit; (luogo) warehouse; depot; (: Mil) depot; **deposito bagagli** left-luggage office

deposizi'**one** [depozit'tsjone] sf deposition; (da una carica) removal

depra'**vato, -a** ag depraved ▷ sm/f degenerate

depre'**dare** vt to rob, plunder

depressi'one *sf* depression

de'presso, -a *pp di* **deprimere** ▷ *ag* depressed

deprez'zare [depret'tsare] *vt* (*Econ*) to depreciate

depri'mente *ag* depressing

de'primere *vt* to depress

depu'rare *vt* to purify

depu'tato *sm* (*Pol*) deputy, ≈ Member of Parliament (*BRIT*), ≈ Member of Congress (*US*)

deragli'are [deraʎ'ʎare] *vi* to be derailed; **far ~** to derail

de'ridere *vt* to mock, deride

de'risi *ecc vb vedi* **deridere**

de'riva *sf* (*Naut, Aer*) drift; **andare alla ~** (*anche fig*) to drift

deri'vare *vi* **~ da** to derive from ▷ *vt* to derive; (*corso d'acqua*) to divert

derma'tologo, -a, -gi, -ghe *sm/f* dermatologist

deru'bare *vt* to rob

des'crivere *vt* to describe; **descrizi'one** *sf* description

de'serto, -a *ag* deserted ▷ *sm* (*Geo*) desert; **isola deserta** desert island

deside'rare *vt* to want, wish for; (*sessualmente*) to desire; **~ fare/che qn faccia** to want *o* wish to do/sb to do; **desidera fare una passeggiata?** would you like to go for a walk?

desi'derio *sm* wish; (*più intenso, carnale*) desire

deside'roso, -a *ag* **~ di** longing *o* eager for

desi'nenza [dezi'nɛntsa] *sf* (*Ling*) ending, inflexion

de'sistere *vi* **~ da** to give up, desist from

deso'lato, -a *ag* (*paesaggio*) desolate; (*persona: spiacente*) sorry

'dessi *ecc vb vedi* **dare**

'deste *ecc vb vedi* **dare**

desti'nare *vt* to destine; (*assegnare*) to appoint, assign; (*indirizzare*) to address; **~ qc a qn** to intend to give sth to sb, intend sb to have sth; **destina'tario, -a** *sm/f* (*di lettera*) addressee

destinazi'one [destinat'tsjone] *sf* destination; (*uso*) purpose

des'tino *sm* destiny, fate

destitu'ire *vt* to dismiss, remove

'destra *sf* (*mano*) right hand; (*parte*) right (side); (*Pol*): **la ~** the Right; **a ~** (*essere*) on the right; (*andare*) to the right

destreggi'arsi [destred'dʒarsi] *vpr* to manoeuvre (*BRIT*), maneuver (*US*)

des'trezza [des'trettsa] *sf* skill, dexterity

'destro, -a *ag* right, right-hand

dete'nuto, -a *sm/f* prisoner

deter'gente [deter'dʒɛnte] *ag* (*crema,*

latte) cleansing ▷ *sm* cleanser

> Attenzione! In inglese esiste la parola *detergent* che però significa *detersivo*.

determi'nare *vt* to determine

determina'tivo, -a *ag* determining; **articolo ~** (*Ling*) definite article

determi'nato, -a *ag* (*gen*) certain; (*particolare*) specific; (*risoluto*) determined, resolute

deter'sivo *sm* detergent

detes'tare *vt* to detest, hate

de'trae, de'traggo *ecc vb vedi* **detrarre**

de'trarre *vt* **~ (da)** to deduct (from), take away (from)

de'trassi *ecc vb vedi* **detrarre**

'detta *sf* **a ~ di** according to

det'taglio [det'taʎʎo] *sm* detail; (*Comm*): **il ~** retail; **al ~** (*Comm*) retail; separately

det'tare *vt* to dictate; **~ legge** (*fig*) to lay down the law; **det'tato** *sm* dictation

'detto, -a *pp di* **dire** ▷ *ag* (*soprannominato*) called, known as; (*già nominato*) above-mentioned ▷ *sm* saying; **~ fatto** no sooner said than done

devas'tare *vt* to devastate; (*fig*) to ravage

devi'are *vi* **~ (da)** to turn off (from) ▷ *vt* to divert; **deviazi'one** *sf* (*anche Aut*) diversion

'devo *ecc vb vedi* **dovere**

de'volvere *vt* (*Dir*) to transfer, devolve

de'voto, -a *ag* (*Rel*) devout, pious; (*affezionato*) devoted

devozi'one [devot'tsjone] *sf* devoutness; (*anche Rel*) devotion

PAROLA CHIAVE

di (*di+il* = **del**, *di+lo* = **dello**, *di+l'* = **dell'**, *di+la* = **della**, *di+i* = **dei**, *di+gli* = **degli**, *di+le* = **delle**) *prep* **1** (*possesso, specificazione*) of; (*composto da, scritto da*) by; **la macchina di Paolo/mio fratello** Paolo's/my brother's car; **un amico di mio fratello** a friend of my brother's, one of my brother's friends; **un quadro di Botticelli** a painting by Botticelli

2 (*caratterizzazione, misura*) of; **una casa di mattoni** a brick house, a house made of bricks; **un orologio d'oro** a gold watch; **un bimbo di 3 anni** a child of 3, a 3-year-old child

3 (*causa, mezzo, modo*) with; **tremare di paura** to tremble with fear; **morire di cancro** to die of cancer; **spalmare di burro** to spread with butter

4 (*argomento*) about, of; **discutere di sport** to talk about sport

5 (*luogo: provenienza*) from; out of; **essere**

di Roma to be from Rome; **uscire di casa** to come out of o leave the house **6** (*tempo*) in; **d'estate/d'inverno** in (the) summer/winter; **di notte** by night, at night; **di mattina/sera** in the morning/ evening; **di lunedì** on Mondays ▷ *det* (*una certa quantità di*) some; (: *negativo*) any; (*interrogativo*) any; some; **del pane** (some) bread; **delle caramelle** (some) sweets; **degli amici miei** some friends of mine; **vuoi del vino?** do you want some o any wine?

dia'bete *sm* diabetes *sg*
dia'betico, -a, ci, che *ag, sm/f* diabetic
dia'framma, -i *sm* (*divisione*) screen; (*Anat, Fot, contraccettivo*) diaphragm
di'agnosi [di'aɲɲozi] *sf* diagnosis *sg*
diago'nale *ag, sf* diagonal
dia'gramma, -i *sm* diagram
dia'letto *sm* dialect
di'alisi *sf* dialysis *sg*
di'alogo, -ghi *sm* dialogue
dia'mante *sm* diamond
di'ametro *sm* diameter
diaposi'tiva *sf* transparency, slide
di'ario *sm* diary
diar'rea *sf* diarrhoea
di'avolo *sm* devil
di'battito *sm* debate, discussion
'dice ['ditʃe] *vb vedi* **dire**
di'cembre [di'tʃɛmbre] *sm* December
dice'ria [ditʃe'ria] *sf* rumour, piece of gossip
dichia'rare [dikja'rare] *vt* to declare; **dichiararsi** *vpr* to declare o.s.; (*innamorato*) to declare one's love; **dichiararsi vinto** to acknowledge defeat; **dichiarazi'one** *sf* declaration; **dichiarazione dei redditi** statement of income; (*modulo*) tax return
dician'nove [ditʃan'nɔve] *num* nineteen
dicias'sette [ditʃas'sɛtte] *num* seventeen
dici'otto [di'tʃɔtto] *num* eighteen
dici'tura [ditʃi'tura] *sf* words *pl*, wording
'dico *ecc vb vedi* **dire**
didasca'lia *sf* (*di illustrazione*) caption; (*Cine*) subtitle; (*Teatro*) stage directions *pl*
di'eci ['djetʃi] *num* ten
di'edi *ecc vb vedi* **dare**
'diesel ['dizəl] *sm inv* diesel engine
dies'sino, -a *sm/f* member of the DS political party
di'eta *sf* diet; **essere a ~** to be on a diet
di'etro *av* behind; (*in fondo*) at the back ▷ *prep* behind; (*tempo: dopo*) after ▷ *sm* back, rear ▷ *ag inv* back *cpd*; **le zampe di ~** the hind legs; **~ richiesta** on demand; (*scritta*) on application

di'fendere *vt* to defend; **difendersi** *vpr* (*cavarsela*) to get by; **difendersi da/contro** to defend o.s. from/against; **difendersi dal freddo** to protect o.s. from the cold; **difen'sore, -a** *sm/f* defender; **avvocato difensore** counsel for the defence; **di'fesa** *sf* defence
di'fesi *ecc vb vedi* **difendere**
di'fetto *sm* (*mancanza*): **~ di** lack of; shortage of; (*di fabbricazione*) fault, flaw, defect; (*morale*) fault, failing, defect; (*fisico*) defect; **far ~** to be lacking; **in ~** at fault; in the wrong; **difet'toso, -a** *ag* defective, faulty
diffe'rente *ag* different
diffe'renza [diffe'rɛntsa] *sf* difference; **a ~ di** unlike
diffe'rire *vt* to postpone, defer ▷ *vi* to be different
diffe'rita *sf* **in ~** (*trasmettere*) prerecorded
dif'ficile [dif'fitʃile] *ag* difficult; (*persona*) hard to please, difficult (to please); (*poco probabile*): **è ~ che sia libero** it is unlikely that he'll be free ▷ *sm* difficult part; difficulty; **difficoltà** *sf inv* difficulty
diffi'dente *ag* suspicious, distrustful
diffi'denza *sf* suspicion, distrust
dif'fondere *vt* (*luce, calore*) to diffuse; (*notizie*) to spread, circulate; **diffondersi** *vpr* to spread
dif'fusi *ecc vb vedi* **diffondere**
dif'fuso, -a *pp di* **diffondere** ▷ *ag* (*malattia, fenomeno*) widespread
'diga, -ghe *sf* dam; (*portuale*) breakwater
dige'rente [didʒe'rɛnte] *ag* (*apparato*) digestive
dige'rire [didʒe'rire] *vt* to digest; **digesti'one** *sf* digestion; **diges'tivo, -a** *ag* digestive ▷ *sm* (after-dinner) liqueur
digi'tale [didʒi'tale] *ag* digital; (*delle dita*) finger *cpd*, digital ▷ *sf* (*Bot*) foxglove
digi'tare [didʒi'tare] *vt, vi* (*Inform*) to key (in)
digiu'nare [didʒu'nare] *vi* to starve o.s.; (*Rel*) to fast; **digi'uno, -a** *ag* **essere digiuno** not to have eaten ▷ *sm* fast; **a digiuno** on an empty stomach
dignità [diɲɲi'ta] *sf inv* dignity
'DIGOS ['digɔs] *sigla f* (= *Divisione Investigazioni Generali e Operazioni Speciali*) *police department dealing with political security*
digri'gnare [digriɲ'ɲare] *vt* **~ i denti** to grind one's teeth
dilapi'dare *vt* to squander, waste
dila'tare *vt* to dilate; (*gas*) to cause to expand; (*passaggio, cavità*) to open (up); **dilatarsi** *vpr* to dilate; (*Fisica*) to expand
dilazio'nare [dilattsjo'nare] *vt* to delay,

defer

di'lemma, -i sm dilemma

dilet'tante sm/f dilettante; (anche Sport) amateur

dili'gente [dili'dʒente] ag (scrupoloso) diligent; (accurato) careful, accurate

dilu'ire vt to dilute

dilun'garsi vpr (fig): ~ **su** to talk at length on o about

diluvi'are vb impers to pour (down)

di'luvio sm downpour; (inondazione, fig) flood

dima'grante ag slimming cpd

dima'grire vi to get thinner, lose weight

dime'nare vt to wave, shake; **dimenarsi** vpr to toss and turn; (fig) to struggle; ~ **la coda** (cane) to wag its tail

dimensi'one sf dimension; (grandezza) size

dimenti'canza [dimenti'kantsa] sf forgetfulness; (errore) oversight, slip; **per ~** inadvertently

dimenti'care vt to forget; **ho dimenticato la chiave/il passaporto** I forgot the key/my passport; **dimenticarsi** vpr **dimenticarsi di qc** to forget sth

dimesti'chezza [dimesti'kettsa] sf familiarity

di'mettere vt ~ **qn da** to dismiss sb from; (dall'ospedale) to discharge sb from; **dimettersi** vpr **dimettersi (da)** to resign (from)

dimez'zare [dimed'dzare] vt to halve

diminu'ire vt to reduce, diminish; (prezzi) to bring down, reduce ▷ vi to decrease, diminish; (rumore) to die down, die away; (prezzi) to fall, go down

diminu'tivo, -a ag, sm diminutive

diminuzi'one sf decreasing, diminishing

di'misi ecc vb vedi **dimettere**

dimissi'oni sfpl resignation sg; **dare** o **presentare le ~** to resign, hand in one's resignation

dimos'trare vt to demonstrate, show; (provare) to prove, demonstrate; **dimostrarsi** vpr **dimostrarsi molto abile** to show o.s. o prove to be very clever; **dimostra 30 anni** he looks about 30 (years old); **dimostrazi'one** sf demonstration; proof

di'namica sf dynamics sg

di'namico, -a, -ci, -che ag dynamic

dina'mite sf dynamite

'dinamo sf inv dynamo

dino'sauro sm dinosaur

din'torni smpl outskirts; **nei ~ di** in the vicinity o neighbourhood of

'dio (pl **'dei**) sm god; **D~** God; **gli dei** the gods; **D~ mio!** my goodness!, my God!

diparti'mento sm department

dipen'dente ag dependent ▷ sm/f employee; **dipendente statale** state employee

di'pendere vi ~ **da** to depend on; (finanziariamente) to be dependent on; (derivare) to come from, be due to

di'pesi ecc vb vedi **dipendere**

di'pingere [di'pindʒere] vt to paint

di'pinsi ecc vb vedi **dipingere**

di'pinto, -a pp di **dipingere** ▷ sm painting

di'ploma, -i sm diploma

diplo'matico, -a, -ci, -che ag diplomatic ▷ sm diplomat

diploma'zia [diplomat'tsia] sf diplomacy

di'porto: **imbarcazione da ~** sf pleasure craft

dira'dare vt to thin (out); (visite) to reduce, make less frequent; **diradarsi** vpr to disperse; (nebbia) to clear (up)

'dire vt to say; (segreto, fatto) to tell; ~ **qc a qn** to tell sb sth; ~ **a qn di fare qc** to tell sb to do sth; ~ **di sì/no** to say yes/no; **si dice che ...** they say that ...; **si ~bbe che ...** it looks (o sounds) as though ...; **dica, signora?** (in un negozio) yes, Madam, can I help you?; **come si dice in inglese...?** what's the English (word) for ...?

di'ressi ecc vb vedi **dirigere**

di'retta sf vedi **diretto**

di'retto, -a pp di **dirigere** ▷ ag direct ▷ sm (Ferr) through train

diret'tore, -'trice sm/f (di azienda) director; manager/ess; (di scuola elementare) head (teacher) (BRIT), principal (US); **direttore d'orchestra** conductor; **direttore vendite** sales director o manager

direzi'one [diret'tsjone] sf board of directors; management; (senso di movimento) direction; **in ~ di** in the direction of, towards

diri'gente [diri'dʒente] sm/f executive; (Pol) leader ▷ ag **classe ~** ruling class

di'rigere [di'ridʒere] vt to direct; (impresa) to run, manage; (Mus) to conduct; **dirigersi** vpr **dirigersi verso** o **a** to make o head for

dirim'petto av opposite; ~ **a** opposite, facing

di'ritto, -a ag straight; (onesto) straight, upright ▷ av straight, directly; **andare ~** to go straight on ▷ sm right side; (Tennis) forehand; (Maglia) plain stitch; (prerogativa) right; (leggi, scienza) law; **diritti** smpl (tasse) duty sg; **stare ~** to stand up straight; **aver ~ a qc** to be entitled to sth; **diritti d'autore** royalties

dirotta'mento sm; **dirottamento**

(aereo) hijack

dirot'tare vt (nave, aereo) to change the course of; (aereo sotto minaccia) to hijack; (traffico) to divert ▷ vi (nave, aereo) to change course; **dirotta'tore, -'trice** sm/f hijacker

di'rotto, -a ag (pioggia) torrential; (pianto) unrestrained; **piovere a ~** to pour; **piangere a ~** to cry one's heart out

di'rupo sm crag, precipice

di'sabile sm/f disabled person ▷ ag disabled; **i disabili** the disabled

disabi'tato, -a ag uninhabited

disabitu'arsi vpr **~ a** to get out of the habit of

disac'cordo sm disagreement

disadat'tato, -a ag (Psic) maladjusted

disa'dorno, -a ag plain, unadorned

disagi'ato, -a [diza'dʒato] ag poor, needy; (vita) hard

di'sagio [di'zadʒo] sm discomfort; (disturbo) inconvenience; (fig: imbarazzo) embarrassment; **essere a ~** to be ill at ease

disappro'vare vt to disapprove of; **disapprovazi'one** sf disapproval

disap'punto sm disappointment

disar'mare vt, vi to disarm; **di'sarmo** sm (Mil) disarmament

di'sastro sm disaster

disas'troso, -a ag disastrous

disat'tento, -a ag inattentive; **disattenzi'one** sf carelessness, lack of attention

disavven'tura sf misadventure, mishap

dis'capito sm **a ~ di** to the detriment of

dis'carica, -che sf (di rifiuti) rubbish tip o dump

di'scendere [diʃʃendere] vt to go (o come) down ▷ vi to go (o come) down; (strada) to go down; (smontare) to get off; **~ da** (famiglia) to be descended from; **~ dalla macchina/dal treno** to get out of the car/out of o off the train; **~ da cavallo** to dismount, get off one's horse

di'scesa [diʃʃesa] sf descent; (pendio) slope; **in ~** (strada) downhill cpd, sloping; **discesa libera** (Sci) downhill (race)

disci'plina [diʃʃi'plina] sf discipline

'disco, -schi sm disc; (Sport) discus; (fonografico) record; (Inform) disk; **disco orario** (Aut) parking disc; **disco rigido** (Inform) hard disk; **disco volante** flying saucer

disco'grafico, -a, ci, che ag record cpd, recording cpd ▷ sm record producer; **casa discografica** record(ing) company

dis'correre vi **~ (di)** to talk (about)

dis'corso, -a pp di **discorrere** ▷ sm speech; (conversazione) conversation, talk

disco'teca, -che sf (raccolta) record library; (locale) disco

discre'panza [diskre'pantsa] sf disagreement

dis'creto, -a ag discreet; (abbastanza buono) reasonable, fair

discriminazi'one [diskriminat'tsjone] sf discrimination

dis'cussi ecc vb vedi **discutere**

discussi'one sf discussion; (litigio) argument; **fuori ~** out of the question

dis'cutere vt to discuss, debate; (contestare) to question ▷ vi (conversare): **~ (di)** to discuss; (litigare) to argue

dis'detta sf (di prenotazione ecc) cancellation; (sfortuna) bad luck

dis'dire vt (prenotazione) to cancel; (Dir): **~ un contratto d'affitto** to give notice (to quit); **vorrei ~ la mia prenotazione** I want to cancel my booking

dise'gnare [dise̞ɲ'ɲare] vt to draw; (progettare) to design; (fig) to outline

disegna'tore, -'trice sm/f designer

di'segno [di'seɲɲo] sm drawing; design; outline; **disegno di legge** (Dir) bill

diser'bante sm weed-killer

diser'tare vt, vi to desert

dis'fare vt to undo; (valigie) to unpack; (meccanismo) to take to pieces; (neve) to melt; **disfarsi** vpr to come undone; (neve) to melt; **~ il letto** to strip the bed; **disfarsi di qn** (liberarsi) to get rid of sb; **dis'fatto, -a** pp di **disfare**

dis'gelo [diz'dʒelo] sm thaw

dis'grazia [diz'grattsja] sf (sventura) misfortune; (incidente) accident, mishap

disgu'ido sm hitch; **disguido postale** error in postal delivery

disgus'tare vt to disgust

dis'gusto sm disgust; **disgus'toso, -a** ag disgusting

disidra'tare vt to dehydrate

disimpa'rare vt to forget

disinfet'tante ag, sm disinfectant

disinfet'tare vt to disinfect

disini'bito, -a ag uninhibited

disinstal'lare vt (software) to uninstall

disinte'grare vt, vi to disintegrate; **disintegrarsi** vpr to disintegrate

disinteres'sarsi vpr **~ di** to take no interest in

disinte'resse sm indifference; (generosità) unselfishness

disintossicarsi vpr to clear out one's system; (alcolizzato, drogato) to be treated for alcoholism o drug addiction)

disin'volto, -a ag casual, free and easy

dismi'sura sf excess; **a ~** to excess, excessively

disoccu'pato, -a ag unemployed ▷ sm/f unemployed person; **disoccupazi'one** sf unemployment

diso'nesto, -a ag dishonest

disordi'nato, -a ag untidy; (privo di misura) irregular, wild

di'sordine sm (confusione) disorder, confusion; (sregolatezza) debauchery; **disordini** smpl (Pol ecc) disorder sg; (tumulti) riots

disorien'tare vt to disorientate

disorien'tato, -a ag disorientated

'dispari ag inv odd, uneven

dis'parte: in ~ av (da lato) aside, apart; **tenersi o starsene in ~** to keep to o.s., hold o.s. aloof

dispendi'oso, -a ag expensive

dis'pensa sf pantry, larder; (mobile) sideboard; (Dir) exemption; (Rel) dispensation; (fascicolo) number, issue

dispe'rato, -a ag (persona) in despair; (caso, tentativo) desperate

disperazi'one sf despair

dis'perdere vt (disseminare) to disperse; (Mil) to scatter, rout; (fig: consumare) to waste, squander; **disperdersi** vpr to disperse; to scatter; **dis'perso, -a** pp di **disperdere** ▷ sm/f missing person

dis'petto sm spite no pl, spitefulness no pl; **fare un ~ a qn** to play a (nasty) trick on sb; **a ~ di** in spite of; **dispet'toso, -a** ag spiteful

dispia'cere [dispjaˈtʃere] sm (rammarico) regret, sorrow; (dolore) grief; **dispiaceri** smpl (preoccupazioni) troubles, worries vi ~ **a** to displease vb impers **mi dispiace (che)** I am sorry (that); **le dispiace se...?** do you mind if...?

dis'pone, dis'pongo ecc vb vedi **disporre**

dispo'nibile ag available

dis'porre vt (sistemare) to arrange; (preparare) to prepare; (Dir) to order; (persuadere): ~ **qn a** to incline o dispose sb towards ▷ vi (decidere) to decide; (usufruire): ~ **di** to use, have at one's disposal; (essere dotato): ~ **di** to have

dis'posi ecc vb vedi **disporre**

disposi'tivo sm (meccanismo) device

disposizi'one [dispoziˈtsjone] sf arrangement, layout; (stato d'animo) mood; (tendenza) bent, inclination; (comando) order; (Dir) provision, regulation; **a ~ di qn** at sb's disposal

dis'posto, -a pp di **disporre**

disprez'zare [dispretˈtsare] vt to despise

dis'prezzo [dis'prettso] sm contempt

'disputa sf dispute, quarrel

dispu'tare vt (contendere) to dispute, contest; (gara) to take part in ▷ vi to

quarrel; ~ **di** to discuss; **disputarsi qc** to fight for sth

'disse vb vedi **dire**

dissente'ria sf dysentery

dissen'tire vi ~ **(da)** to disagree (with)

disse'tante ag refreshing

'dissi vb vedi **dire**

dissimu'lare vt (fingere) to dissemble; (nascondere) to conceal

dissi'pare vt to dissipate; (scialacquare) to squander, waste

dissu'adere vt ~ **qn da** to dissuade sb from

distac'care vt to detach, separate; (Sport) to leave behind; **distaccarsi** vpr to be detached; (fig) to stand out; **distaccarsi da** (fig: allontanarsi) to grow away from

dis'tacco, -chi sm (separazione) separation; (fig: indifferenza) detachment; (Sport): **vincere con un ~ di ...** to win by a distance of ...

dis'tante av far away ▷ ag ~ **(da)** distant (from), far away (from)

dis'tanza [disˈtantsa] sf distance

distanzi'are [distanˈtsjare] vt to space out, place at intervals; (Sport) to outdistance; (fig: superare) to outstrip, surpass

dis'tare vi **distiamo pochi chilometri da Roma** we are only a few kilometres (away) from Rome; **quanto dista il centro da qui?** how far is the town centre?

dis'tendere vt (coperta) to spread out; (gambe) to stretch (out); (mettere a giacere) to lay; (rilassare: muscoli, nervi) to relax; **distendersi** vpr (rilassarsi) to relax; (sdraiarsi) to lie down

dis'tesa sf expanse, stretch

dis'teso, -a pp di **distendere**

distil'lare vt to distil

distille'ria sf distillery

dis'tinguere vt to distinguish; **distinguersi** vpr (essere riconoscibile) to be distinguished; (emergere) to stand out, be conspicuous, distinguish o.s.

dis'tinta sf (nota) note; (elenco) list; **distinta di versamento** pay-in slip

distin'tivo, -a ag distinctive; distinguishing ▷ sm badge

dis'tinto, -a pp di **distinguere** ▷ ag (dignitoso ed elegante) distinguished; **"distinti saluti"** (in lettera) yours faithfully

distinzi'one [distinˈtsjone] sf distinction

dis'togliere [disˈtɔʎʎere] vt ~ **da** to take away from; (fig) to dissuade from

distorsi'one sf (Med) sprain; (Fisica, Ottica) distortion

dis'trarre vt to distract; (divertire) to entertain, amuse; **distrarsi** vpr (non *fare attenzione*) to be distracted, let one's mind wander; (*svagarsi*) to amuse o enjoy o.s.; **dis'tratto, -a** *pp di* **distrarre** ▷ *ag* absent-minded; (*disattento*) inattentive; **distrazi'one** *sf* absent-mindedness; inattention; (*svago*) distraction, entertainment

dis'tretto *sm* district

distribu'ire *vt* to distribute; (*Carte*) to deal (out); (*posta*) to deliver; (*lavoro*) to allocate, assign; (*ripartire*) to share out; **distribu'tore** *sm* (*di benzina*) petrol (BRIT) o gas (US) pump; (*Aut, Elettr*) distributor; **distributore automatico** vending machine

distri'care *vt* to disentangle, unravel; **districarsi** *vpr* (*tirarsi fuori*): **districarsi da** to get out of, disentangle o.s. from

dis'truggere [dis'truddʒere] *vt* to destroy; **distruzi'one** *sf* destruction

distur'bare *vt* to disturb, trouble; (*sonno, lezioni*) to disturb, interrupt; **disturbarsi** *vpr* to put o.s. out

dis'turbo *sm* trouble, bother, inconvenience; (*indisposizione*) (slight) disorder, ailment; **scusi il ~** I'm sorry to trouble you

disubbidi'ente *ag* disobedient

disubbi'dire *vi* **~ (a qn)** to disobey (sb)

disu'mano, -a *ag* inhuman

di'tale *sm* thimble

'dito (*pl(f)* **'dita**) *sm* finger; (*misura*) finger, finger's breadth; **dito (del piede)** toe

'ditta *sf* firm, business

ditta'tore *sm* dictator

ditta'tura *sf* dictatorship

dit'tongo, -ghi *sm* diphthong

di'urno, -a *ag* day *cpd*, daytime *cpd*

'diva *sf vedi* **divo**

di'vano *sm* sofa; divan; **divano letto** bed settee, sofa bed

divari'care *vt* to open wide

di'vario *sm* difference

diven'tare *vi* to become; **~ famoso/ professore** to become famous/a teacher

diversifi'care *vt* to diversify, vary; to differentiate; **diversificarsi** *vpr* **diversificarsi (per)** to differ (in)

diversità *sf inv* difference, diversity; (*varietà*) variety

di'versivo *sm* diversion, distraction

di'verso, -a *ag* (*differente*): **~ (da)** different (from); **diversi, -e** *det pl* several, various; (*Comm*) sundry *pron pl* several (people), many (people)

diver'tente *ag* amusing

diverti'mento *sm* amusement, pleasure; (*passatempo*) pastime, recreation

diver'tire *vt* to amuse, entertain;

divertirsi *vpr* to amuse o enjoy o.s.

di'videre *vt* (*anche Mat*) to divide; (*distribuire, ripartire*) to divide (up), split (up); **dividersi** *vpr* (*separarsi*) to separate; (*strade*) to fork

divi'eto *sm* prohibition; **"~ di sosta"** (*Aut*) "no parking"

divinco'larsi *vpr* to wriggle, writhe

di'vino, -a *ag* divine

di'visa *sf* (*Mil ecc*) uniform; (*Comm*) foreign currency

di'visi *ecc vb vedi* **dividere**

divisi'one *sf* division

'divo, -a *sm/f* star

divo'rare *vt* to devour

divorzi'are [divor'tsjare] *vi* **~ (da qn)** to divorce (sb)

di'vorzio [di'vɔrtsjo] *sm* divorce

divul'gare *vt* to divulge, disclose; (*rendere comprensibile*) to popularize

dizio'nario [ditsjo'narjo] *sm* dictionary

DJ [di'dʒei] *sigla m/f* (= *Disk Jockey*) DJ

do *sm* (*Mus*) C; (: *solfeggiando*) do(h)

dobbi'amo *vb vedi* **dovere**

D.O.C. [dɔk] *abbr* (= *denominazione di origine controllata*) label guaranteeing the quality of wine

'doccia, -ce ['dottʃa] *sf* (*bagno*) shower; **fare la ~** to have a shower

do'cente [do'tʃente] *ag* teaching ▷ *sm/f* teacher; (*di università*) lecturer

'docile ['dɔtʃile] *ag* docile

documen'tario *sm* documentary

documen'tarsi *vpr* **~ (su)** to gather information o material (about)

docu'mento *sm* document; **documenti** *smpl* (*d'identità ecc*) papers

dodi'cesimo, -a [dodi'tʃezimo] *num* twelfth

'dodici ['doditʃi] *num* twelve

do'gana *sf* (*ufficio*) customs *pl*; (*tassa*) (customs) duty; **passare la ~** to go through customs; **dogani'ere** *sm* customs officer

'doglie ['dɔʎʎe] *sfpl* (*Med*) labour *sg*, labour pains

'dolce ['doltʃe] *ag* sweet; (*carattere, persona*) gentle, mild; (*fig: mite: clima*) mild; (*non ripido: pendio*) gentle ▷ *sm* (*sapore dolce*) sweetness, sweet taste; (*Cuc: portata*) sweet, dessert; (: *torta*) cake; **dolcifi'cante** *sm* sweetener

'dollaro *sm* dollar

Dolo'miti *sfpl* **le ~** the Dolomites

do'lore *sm* (*fisico*) pain; (*morale*) sorrow, grief; **dolo'roso, -a** *ag* painful; sorrowful, sad

do'manda *sf* (*interrogazione*) question; (*richiesta*) demand; (: *cortese*) request;

(*Dir: richiesta scritta*) application; (*Econ*): **la ~** demand; **fare una ~ a qn** to ask sb a question; **fare ~ (per un lavoro)** to apply (for a job)

doman'dare *vt* (*per avere*) to ask for; (*per sapere*) to ask; (*esigere*) to demand; **domandarsi** *vpr* to wonder; to ask o.s.; **~ qc a qn** to ask sb for sth; to ask sb sth

do'mani *av* tomorrow ▷ *sm* **il ~** (*il futuro*) the future; (*il giorno successivo*) the next day; **~ l'altro** the day after tomorrow

do'mare *vt* to tame

doma'tore, -'trice *sm/f* (*gen*) tamer; **domatore di cavalli** horsebreaker; **domatore di leoni** lion tamer

domat'tina *av* tomorrow morning

do'menica, -che *sf* Sunday; **di o la ~** on Sundays

do'mestico, -a, -ci, -che *ag* domestic ▷ *sm/f* servant, domestic

domi'cilio [domi'tʃiljo] *sm* (*Dir*) domicile, place of residence

domi'nare *vt* to dominate; (*fig: sentimenti*) to control, master ▷ *vi* to be in the dominant position

do'nare *vt* to give, present; (*per beneficenza ecc*) to donate ▷ *vi* (*fig*): **~ a** to suit, become; **~ sangue** to give blood; **dona'tore, -'trice** *sm/f* donor; **donatore di sangue/di organi** blood/organ donor

dondo'lare *vt* (*cullare*) to rock; **dondolarsi** *vpr* to swing, sway; **'dondolo** *sm* **sedia/cavallo a dondolo** rocking chair/horse

'donna *sf* woman; **donna di casa** housewife; home-loving woman; **donna di servizio** maid

donnai'olo *sm* ladykiller

'donnola *sf* weasel

'dono *sm* gift

doping ['dɔpiŋ] *sm* doping

'dopo *av* (*tempo*) afterwards; (*più tardi*) later; (*luogo*) after, next ▷ *prep* after ▷ *cong* (*temporale*): **~ aver studiato** after having studied; **~ mangiato va a dormire** after having eaten *o* after a meal he goes for a sleep ▷ *ag inv* **il giorno ~** the following day; **un anno ~** a year later; **~ di me/lui** after me/him; **~, a ~!** see you later!

dopo'barba *sm inv* after-shave

dopodo'mani *av* the day after tomorrow

doposcì [dopoʃʃi] *sm inv* après-ski outfit

dopo'sole *sm inv* aftersun (lotion)

dopo'tutto *av* (*tutto considerato*) after all

doppi'aggio [dop'pjaddʒo] *sm* (*Cinema*) dubbing

doppi'are *vt* (*Naut*) to round; (*Sport*) to lap; (*Cinema*) to dub

'doppio, -a *ag* double; (*fig: falso*) double-dealing, deceitful ▷ *sm* (*quantità*): **il ~**

(**di**) twice as much (*o* many), double the amount (*o* number) of; (*Sport*) doubles *pl* ▷ *av* double

doppi'one *sm* duplicate (copy)

doppio'petto *sm* double-breasted jacket

dormicchi'are [dormik'kjare] *vi* to doze

dormigli'one, -a [dormiʎ'ʎone] *sm/f* sleepyhead

dor'mire *vt, vi* to sleep; **andare a ~** to go to bed; **dor'mita** *sf* **farsi una dormita** to have a good sleep

dormi'torio *sm* dormitory

dormi'veglia [dormi'veʎʎa] *sm* drowsiness

'dorso *sm* back; (*di montagna*) ridge, crest; (*di libro*) spine; **a ~ di cavallo** on horseback

do'sare *vt* to measure out; (*Med*) to dose

'dose *sf* quantity, amount; (*Med*) dose

do'tato, -a *ag* **~ di** (*attrezzature*) equipped with; (*bellezza, intelligenza*) endowed with; **un uomo ~** a gifted man

'dote *sf* (*di sposa*) dowry; (*assegnata a un ente*) endowment; (*fig*) gift, talent

Dott. *abbr* (= *dottore*) Dr.

dotto'rato *sm* degree; **dottorato di ricerca** doctorate, doctor's degree

dot'tore, -essa *sm/f* doctor; **chiamate un ~** call a doctor

○ **DOTTORE**

○ In Italy, anyone who has a degree in any
○ subject can use the title **dottore**. Thus
○ a person who is addressed as **dottore** is
○ not necessarily a doctor of medicine.

dot'trina *sf* doctrine

Dott.ssa *abbr* (= *dottoressa*) Dr.

'dove *av* (*gen*) where; (*in cui*) where, in which; (*dovunque*) wherever ▷ *cong* (*mentre, laddove*) whereas; **~ sei?/vai?** where are you?/are you going?; **dimmi dov'è** tell me where it is; **di ~ sei?** where are you from?; **per ~ si passa?** which way should we go?; **la città ~ abito** the town where *o* in which I live; **siediti ~ vuoi** sit wherever you like

do'vere *sm* (*obbligo*) duty ▷ *vt* (*essere debitore*): **~ qc (a qn)** to owe (sb) sth ▷ *vi* (*seguito dall'infinito: obbligo*) to have to; **rivolgersi a chi di ~** to apply to the appropriate authority *o* person; **lui deve farlo** he has to do it, he must do it; **quanto le devo?** how much do I owe you?; **è dovuto partire** he had to leave; **ha dovuto pagare** he had to pay; (*: intenzione*): **devo partire domani** I'm (due) to leave tomorrow; (*: probabilità*): **dev'essere tardi** it must be late; **come**

si deve (*lavorare, comportarsi*) properly; **una persona come si deve** a respectable person

dove'roso, -a *ag* (right and) proper

dovrò *ecc vb vedi* **dovere**

do'vunque *av* (*in qualunque luogo*) wherever; (*dappertutto*) everywhere; **~ io vada** wherever I go

do'vuto, -a *ag* (*causato*): **~ a** due to

doz'zina [dod'dzina] *sf* dozen; **una ~ di uova** a dozen eggs

dozzi'nale [doddzi'nale] *ag* cheap, second-rate

'drago, -ghi *sm* dragon

'dramma, -i *sm* drama; **dram'matico, -a, -ci, -che** *ag* dramatic

'drastico, -a, -ci, -che *ag* drastic

'dritto, -a *ag, av* = **diritto**

'droga, -ghe *sf* (*sostanza aromatica*) spice; (*stupefacente*) drug; **droghe leggere/ pesanti** soft/hard drugs

drogarsi *vpr* to take drugs

dro'gato, -a *sm/f* drug addict

droghe'ria [droge'ria] *sf* grocer's shop (*BRIT*), grocery (store) (*US*)

drome'dario *sm* dromedary

DS [di'ɛsse] *sigla mpl* (= *Democratici di Sinistra*) *Italian left-wing party*

'dubbio, -a *ag* (*incerto*) doubtful, dubious; (*ambiguo*) dubious ▷ *sm* (*incertezza*) doubt; **avere il ~ che** to be afraid that, suspect that; **mettere in ~ qc** to question sth

dubi'tare *vi* **~ di** to doubt; (*risultato*) to be doubtful of

Dub'lino *sf* Dublin

'duca, -chi *sm* duke

du'chessa [du'kessa] *sf* duchess

'due *num* two

due'cento [due'tʃɛnto] *num* two hundred ▷ *sm* **il D~** the thirteenth century

due'pezzi [due'pɛttsi] *sm* (*costume da bagno*) two-piece swimsuit; (*abito femminile*) two-piece suit

'dunque *cong* (*perciò*) so, therefore; (*riprendendo il discorso*) well (then) ▷ *sm inv* **venire al ~** to come to the point

du'omo *sm* cathedral

▎Attenzione! In inglese esiste la parola *dome*, che però significa *cupola*.

dupli'cato *sm* duplicate

'duplice ['duplitʃe] *ag* double, twofold; **in ~ copia** in duplicate

du'rante *prep* during

du'rare *vi* to last; **~ fatica a** to have difficulty in

du'rezza [du'rettsa] *sf* hardness; stubbornness; harshness; toughness

'duro, -a *ag* (*pietra, lavoro, materasso, problema*) hard; (*persona: ostinato*) stubborn, obstinate; (*severo*) harsh, hard; (*voce*) harsh; (*carne*) tough ▷ *sm* hardness; (*difficoltà*) hard part; (*persona*) tough guy; **tener ~** to stand firm, hold out; **~ d'orecchi** hard of hearing

DVD [divu'di] *sigla m* (= *digital versatile* (*or*) *video disc*) DVD; (*lettore*) DVD player

e (*dav V spesso* **ed**) *cong* and; **e lui?** what about him?; **e compralo!** well buy it then!

E *abbr* (= *est*) E

è *vb vedi* **essere**

eb'bene *cong* well (then)

'ebbi *ecc vb vedi* **avere**

e'braico, -a, -ci, -che *ag* Hebrew, Hebraic ▷ *sm* (*Ling*) Hebrew

e'breo, -a *ag* Jewish ▷ *sm/f* Jew/ess

EC *abbr* (= *Eurocity*) fast train connecting Western European cities

ecc. *av abbr* (= *eccetera*) etc

eccel'lente [ettʃel'lɛnte] *ag* excellent

ec'centrico, -a, -ci, -che [et'tʃɛntriko] *ag* eccentric

ecces'sivo, -a [ettʃes'sivo] *ag* excessive

ec'cesso [et'tʃɛsso] *sm* excess; **all'~** (*gentile, generoso*) to excess, excessively; **eccesso di velocità** (*Aut*) speeding

ec'cetera [et'tʃɛtera] *av* et cetera, and so on

ec'cetto [et'tʃɛtto] *prep* except, with the exception of; **~ che** except, other than; **~ che (non)** unless

eccezio'nale [ettʃettsjo'nale] *ag* exceptional

eccezi'one [ettʃet'tsjone] *sf* exception; (*Dir*) objection; **a ~ di** with the exception of, except for; **d'~** exceptional

ecci'tare [ettʃi'tare] *vt* (*curiosità, interesse*) to excite, arouse; (*folla*) to incite; **eccitarsi** *vpr* to get excited; (*sessualmente*) to become aroused

'ecco *av* (*per dimostrare*): **~ il treno!** here's o here comes the train!; (*dav pron*): **~mi!** here I am!; **~ne uno!** here's one (of them)!; (*dav pp*): **~ fatto!** there, that's it done!

ec'come *av* rather; **ti piace? — ~!** do you like it? — I'll say! o and how! o rather! (*BRIT*)

e'clisse *sf* eclipse

'eco (*pl(m)* **'echi**) *sm o f* echo

ecogra'fia *sf* (*Med*) scan

ecolo'gia [ekolo'dʒia] *sf* ecology

eco'logico, -a, ci, che [eko'lɔdʒiko] *ag* ecological

econo'mia *sf* economy; (*scienza*) economics *sg*; (*risparmio: azione*) saving; **fare ~** to economize, make economies; **eco'nomico, -a, -ci, -che** *ag* economic; (*poco costoso*) economical

ecstasy ['ekstazi] *sf* Ecstasy

'edera *sf* ivy

e'dicola *sf* newspaper kiosk o stand (*US*)

edi'ficio [edi'fitʃo] *sm* building

e'dile *ag* building *cpd*

Edim'burgo *sf* Edinburgh

edi'tore, -'trice *ag* publishing *cpd* ▷ *sm/f* publisher

> Attenzione! In inglese esiste la parola *editor*, che però significa *redattore*.

edizi'one [edit'tsjone] *sf* edition; (*tiratura*) printing; **edizione straordinaria** special edition

edu'care *vt* to educate; (*gusto, mente*) to train; **~ qn a fare** to train sb to do; **edu'cato, -a** *ag* polite, well-mannered; **educazi'one** *sf* education; (*familiare*) upbringing; (*comportamento*) (good) manners *pl*; **educazione fisica** (*Ins*) physical training o education

> Attenzione! In inglese esiste la parola *educated*, che però significa *istruito*.

educherò *ecc* [eduke'rɔ] *vb vedi* **educare**

effemi'nato, -a *ag* effeminate

efferve'scente [efferveʃ'ʃɛnte] *ag* effervescent

effet'tivo, -a *ag* (*reale*) real, actual; (*impiegato, professore*) permanent; (*Mil*) regular ▷ *sm* (*Mil*) strength; (*di patrimonio ecc*) sum total

ef'fetto *sm* effect; (*Comm: cambiale*) bill; (*fig: impressione*) impression; **in effetti** in fact, actually; **effetto serra** greenhouse effect; **effetti personali** personal effects, personal belongings

effi'cace [effi'katʃe] *ag* effective

effici'ente [effi'tʃɛnte] *ag* efficient

E'geo [e'dʒɛo] *sm* **l'~, il mare ~** the Aegean (Sea)

E'gitto [e'dʒitto] sm **l'~** Egypt

egizi'ano, -a [edʒit'tsjano] ag, sm/f Egyptian

'egli ['eʎʎi] pron he; **~ stesso** he himself

ego'ismo sm selfishness, egoism; **ego'ista, -i, -e** ag selfish, egoistic ▷ sm/f egoist

Egr. abbr = **egregio**

e'gregio, -a, -gi, -gie [e'grɛdʒo] ag (nelle lettere): **E~ Signore** Dear Sir

E.I. abbr = **Esercito Italiano**

elabo'rare vt (progetto) to work out, elaborate; (dati) to process

elasticiz'zato, -a [elastit'ʃid'dzato] ag stretch cpd

e'lastico, -a, -ci, -che ag elastic; (fig: andatura) springy; (: decisione, vedute) flexible ▷ sm (di gomma) rubber band; (per il cucito) elastic no pl

ele'fante sm elephant

ele'gante ag elegant

e'leggere [e'lɛddʒere] vt to elect

elemen'tare ag elementary; **le (scuole) elementari** sfpl primary (BRIT) o grade (US) school

ele'mento sm element; (parte componente) element, component, part; **elementi** smpl (della scienza ecc) elements, rudiments

ele'mosina sf charity, alms pl; **chiedere l'~** to beg

elen'care vt to list

elencherò ecc [elenke'rɔ] vb vedi **elencare**

e'lenco, -chi sm list; **elenco telefonico** telephone directory

e'lessi ecc vb vedi **eleggere**

eletto'rale ag electoral, election cpd

elet'tore, -'trice sm/f voter, elector

elet'trauto sm inv workshop for car electrical repairs; (tecnico) car electrician

elettri'cista, -i [elettri'tʃista] sm electrician

elettricità [elettritʃi'ta] sf electricity

e'lettrico, -a, -ci, -che ag electric(al)

elettriz'zante [elettrid'dzante] ag (fig) electrifying, thrilling

elettriz'zare [elettrid'dzare] vt to electrify; **elettrizzarsi** vpr to become charged with electricity

e'lettro... prefisso; **elettrodo'mestico, -a, -ci, -che** ag apparecchi **elettrodomestici** domestic (electrical) appliances; **elet'tronico, -a, -ci, -che** ag electronic

elezi'one [elet'tsjone] sf election; **elezioni** sfpl (Pol) election(s)

'elica, -che sf propeller

eli'cottero sm helicopter

elimi'nare vt to eliminate

elisoc'corso sm helicopter ambulance

el'metto sm helmet

elogi'are [elo'dʒare] vt to praise

elo'quente ag eloquent

e'ludere vt to evade

e'lusi ecc vb vedi **eludere**

e-mail [i'mɛil] sf inv (messaggio, sistema) e-mail ▷ ag inv (indirizzo) e-mail

emargi'nato, -a [emardʒi'nato] sm/f outcast; **emarginazione** [emardʒinat'tsjone] sf marginalization

embri'one sm embryo

emenda'mento sm amendment

emer'genza [emer'dʒɛntsa] sf emergency; **in caso di ~** in an emergency

e'mergere [e'mɛrdʒere] vi to emerge; (sommergibile) to surface; (fig: distinguersi) to stand out

e'mersi ecc vb vedi **emergere**

e'mettere vt (suono, luce) to give out, emit; (onde radio) to send out; (assegno, francobollo, ordine) to issue

emi'crania sf migraine

emi'grare vi to emigrate

emis'fero sm hemisphere; **emisfero australe** southern hemisphere; **emisfero boreale** northern hemisphere

e'misi ecc vb vedi **emettere**

emit'tente ag (banca) issuing; (Radio) broadcasting, transmitting ▷ sf (Radio) transmitter

emorra'gia, -'gie [emorra'dʒia] sf haemorrhage

emor'roidi sfpl haemorrhoids pl (BRIT), hemorrhoids pl (US)

emo'tivo, -a ag emotional

emozio'nante [emottsjo'nante] ag exciting, thrilling

emozionare [emottsjo'nare] vt (commuovere) to move; (agitare) to make nervous; (elettrizzare) to excite; **emozionarsi** vpr to be moved; to be nervous; to be excited; **emozionato, -a** [emottsjo'nato] ag (commosso) moved; (agitato) nervous; (elettrizzato) excited

emozi'one [emot'tsjone] sf emotion; (agitazione) excitement

enciclope'dia [entʃiklope'dia] sf encyclopaedia

endove'noso, -a ag (Med) intravenous

'E.N.E.L. ['enel] sigla m (= Ente Nazionale per l'Energia Elettrica) national electricity company

ener'getico, -a, ci, che [ener'dʒɛtiko] ag (risorse, crisi) energy cpd; (sostanza, alimento) energy-giving

ener'gia, -'gie [ener'dʒia] sf (Fisica) energy; (fig) energy, strength, vigour; **energia eolica** wind power; **energia solare** solar energy, solar power;

e'nergico, -a, -ci, -che *ag* energetic, vigorous

'enfasi *sf* emphasis; *(peg)* bombast, pomposity

en'nesimo, -a *ag (Mat, fig)* nth; **per l'ennesima volta** for the umpteenth time

e'norme *ag* enormous, huge

'ente *sm (istituzione)* body, board, corporation; *(Filosofia)* being; **enti pubblici** public bodies; **ente di ricerca** research organization

en'trambi, -e *pron pl* both (of them) ▷ *ag pl* ~ **i ragazzi** both boys, both of the boys

en'trare *vi* to go *(o come)* in; ~ **in** *(luogo)* to enter, go *(o come)* into; *(trovar posto, poter stare)* to fit into; *(essere ammesso a: club ecc)* to join, become a member of; ~ **in automobile** to get into the car; **far ~ qn** *(visitatore ecc)* to show sb in; **questo non c'entra** *(fig)* that's got nothing to do with it; **en'trata** *sf* entrance, entry; **dov'è l'entrata?** where's the entrance?; **entrate** *sfpl (Comm)* receipts, takings; *(Econ)* income *sg*

'entro *prep (temporale)* within

entusias'mare *vt* to excite, fill with enthusiasm; **entusiasmarsi** *vpr* **entusiasmarsi (per qc/qn)** to become enthusiastic (about sth/sb); **entusi'asmo** *sm* enthusiasm; **entusi'asta, -i, -e** *ag* enthusiastic ▷ *sm/f* enthusiast

epa'tite *sf* hepatitis

epide'mia *sf* epidemic

epiles'sia *sf* epilepsy

epi'lettico, -a, ci, che *ag, sm/f* epileptic

epi'sodio *sm* episode

'epoca, -che *sf (periodo storico)* age, era; *(tempo)* time; *(Geo)* age

ep'pure *cong* and yet, nevertheless

EPT *sigla m (= Ente Provinciale per il Turismo)* district tourist bureau

equa'tore *sm* equator

equazi'one [ekwat'tsjone] *sf (Mat)* equation

e'questre *ag* equestrian

equi'librio *sm* balance, equilibrium; **perdere l'equilibrare** to lose one's balance

e'quino, -a *ag* horse *cpd*, equine

equipaggia'mento [ekwipaddʒa'mento] *sm (operazione: di nave)* equipping, fitting out; (: *di spedizione, esercito)* equipping, kitting out; *(attrezzatura)* equipment

equipaggi'are [ekwipad'dʒare] *vt (di persone)* to man; *(di mezzi)* to equip; **equipaggiarsi** *vpr* to equip o.s.; **equi'paggio** *sm* crew

equitazi'one [ekwitat'tsjone] *sf* (horse-)riding

equiva'lente *ag, sm* equivalent

e'quivoco, -a, -ci, -che *ag* equivocal, ambiguous; *(sospetto)* dubious ▷ *sm* misunderstanding; **a scanso di equivoci** to avoid any misunderstanding; **giocare sull'**~ to equivocate

'equo, -a *ag* fair, just

'era *sf* era

'era *ecc vb vedi* **essere**

'erba *sf* grass; **in** ~ *(fig)* budding; **erbe aromatiche** herbs; **erba medica** lucerne; **er'baccia, -ce** *sf* weed

erboriste'ria *sf (scienza)* study of medicinal herbs; *(negozio)* herbalist's (shop)

e'rede *sm/f* heir; **eredità** *sf (Dir)* inheritance; *(Biol)* heredity; **lasciare qc in eredità a qn** to leave *o* bequeath sth to sb; **eredi'tare** *vt* to inherit; **eredi'tario, -a** *ag* hereditary

ere'mita, -i *sm* hermit

er'gastolo *sm (Dir: pena)* life imprisonment

'erica *sf* heather

er'metico, -a, -ci, -che *ag* hermetic

'ernia *sf (Med)* hernia

'ero *vb vedi* **essere**

e'roe *sm* hero

ero'gare *vt (somme)* to distribute; *(gas, servizi)* to supply

e'roico, -a, -ci, -che *ag* heroic

ero'ina *sf* heroine; *(droga)* heroin

erosi'one *sf* erosion

e'rotico, -a, -ci, -che *ag* erotic

er'rato, -a *ag* wrong

er'rore *sm* error, mistake; *(morale)* error; **per** ~ by mistake; **ci dev'essere un** ~ there must be some mistake; **errore giudiziario** miscarriage of justice

eruzi'one [erut'tsjone] *sf* eruption

esacer'bare [ezatʃer'bare] *vt* to exacerbate

esage'rare [ezadʒe'rare] *vt* to exaggerate ▷ *vi* to exaggerate; *(eccedere)* to go too far

esal'tare *vt* to exalt; *(entusiasmare)* to excite, stir

e'same *sm* examination; *(Ins)* exam, examination; **fare** *o* **dare un** ~ to sit *o* take an exam; **esame di guida** driving test; **esame del sangue** blood test

esami'nare *vt* to examine

esaspe'rare *vt* to exasperate; to exacerbate

esatta'mente *av* exactly; accurately, precisely

esat'tezza [ezat'tettsa] *sf* exactitude, accuracy, precision

e'satto, -a *pp di* **esigere** ▷ *ag (calcolo, ora)* correct, right, exact; *(preciso)* accurate,

precise; (*puntuale*) punctual
esau'dire *vt* to grant, fulfil
esauri'ente *ag* exhaustive
esauri'mento *sm* exhaustion;
esaurimento nervoso nervous
breakdown
esau'rire *vt* (*stancare*) to exhaust, wear
out; (*provviste, miniera*) to exhaust;
esaurirsi *vpr* to exhaust o.s., wear o.s.
out; (*provviste*) to run out; **esau'rito, -a**
ag exhausted; (*merci*) sold out; **registrare
il tutto esaurito** (*Teatro*) to have a full
house; **e'sausto, -a** *ag* exhausted
'esca (*pl* **'esche**) *sf* bait
'esce ['eʃʃe] *vb vedi* **uscire**
eschi'mese [eski'mese] *ag, sm/f* Eskimo
'esci ['eʃʃi] *vb vedi* **uscire**
escla'mare *vi* to exclaim, cry out
esclama'tivo, -a *ag* **punto ~** exclamation
mark
esclamazi'one *sf* exclamation
es'cludere *vt* to exclude
es'clusi *ecc vb vedi* **escludere**
esclusi'one *sf* exclusion; **a ~ di, fatta
~ per** except (for), apart from; **senza ~
(alcuna)** without exception; **procedere
per ~** to follow a process of elimination;
senza ~ di colpi (*fig*) with no holds barred;
esclusione sociale social exclusion
esclu'siva *sf* (*Dir, Comm*) exclusive o sole
rights *pl*
esclusiva'mente *av* exclusively, solely
esclu'sivo, -a *ag* exclusive
es'cluso, -a *pp di* **escludere**
'esco *vb vedi* **uscire**
escogi'tare [eskodʒi'tare] *vt* to devise,
think up
'escono *vb vedi* **uscire**
escursi'one *sf* (*gita*) excursion, trip;
(: *a piedi*) hike, walk; (*Meteor*) range;
escursione termica temperature range
esecuzi'one [ezekut'tsjone] *sf* execution,
carrying out; (*Mus*) performance;
esecuzione capitale execution
esegu'ire *vt* to carry out, execute; (*Mus*) to
perform, execute
e'sempio *sm* example; **per ~** for example,
for instance; **fare un ~** to give an example;
esem'plare *ag* exemplary ▷ *sm* example;
(*copia*) copy
eserci'tare [ezertʃi'tare] *vt* (*professione*)
to practise (BRIT), practice (US); (*allenare:
corpo, mente*) to exercise, train; (*diritto*)
to exercise; (*influenza, pressione*) to exert;
esercitarsi *vpr* to practise; **esercitarsi
alla lotta** to practise fighting
e'sercito [e'zɛrtʃito] *sm* army
eser'cizio [ezer'tʃittsjo] *sm* practice;
exercising; (*fisico: di matematica*) exercise;

(*Econ*) financial year; (*azienda*) business,
concern; **in ~** (*medico ecc*) practising;
esercizio pubblico (*Comm*) commercial
concern
esi'bire *vt* to exhibit, display; (*documenti*)
to produce, present; **esibirsi** *vpr* (*attore*)
to perform; (*fig*) to show off; **esibizi'one**
sf exhibition; (*di documento*) presentation;
(*spettacolo*) show, performance
esi'gente [ezi'dʒɛnte] *ag* demanding
e'sigere [e'zidʒere] *vt* (*pretendere*) to
demand; (*richiedere*) to demand, require;
(*imposte*) to collect
'esile *ag* (*persona*) slender, slim; (*stelo*) thin;
(*voce*) faint
esili'are *vt* to exile; **e'silio** *sm* exile
esis'tenza [ezis'tɛntsa] *sf* existence
e'sistere *vi* to exist
esi'tare *vi* to hesitate
'esito *sm* result, outcome
'esodo *sm* exodus
esone'rare *vt* to exempt
e'sordio *sm* debut
esor'tare *vt* **~ qn a fare** to urge sb to do
e'sotico, -a, -ci, -che *ag* exotic
es'pandere *vt* to expand; (*confini*) to
extend; (*influenza*) to extend, spread;
espandersi *vpr* to expand; **espansi'one**
sf expansion; **espansione di memoria**
(*Inform*) memory upgrade; **espan'sivo, -a**
ag expansive, communicative
espatri'are *vi* to leave one's country
espedi'ente *sm* expedient
es'pellere *vt* to expel
esperi'enza [espe'rjɛntsa] *sf* experience
esperi'mento *sm* experiment
es'perto, -a *ag, sm* expert
espi'rare *vt, vi* to breathe out
es'plicito, -a [es'plitʃito] *ag* explicit
es'plodere *vi* (*anche fig*) to explode ▷ *vt*
to fire
esplo'rare *vt* to explore
esplosi'one *sf* explosion
es'pone *ecc vb vedi* **esporre**
es'pongo, es'poni *ecc vb vedi* **esporre**
es'porre *vt* (*merci*) to display; (*quadro*)
to exhibit, show; (*fatti, idee*) to explain,
set out; (*porre in pericolo, Fot*) to expose:
esporsi *vpr* **esporsi a** (*sole, pericolo*) to
expose o.s. to; (*critiche*) to lay o.s. open to
espor'tare *vt* to export
es'pose *ecc vb vedi* **esporre**
esposizi'one [espozit'tsjone] *sf*
displaying; setting out; (*anche Fot*) exposure;
(*mostra*) exhibition; (*narrazione*) explanation, exposition
es'posto, -a *pp di* **esporre** ▷ *ag* **~ a nord**
facing north ▷ *sm* (*Amm*) statement,
account; (: *petizione*) petition

espressi'one sf expression

espres'sivo, -a ag expressive

es'presso, -a pp di **esprimere** ▷ ag express ▷ sm (lettera) express letter; (anche: **treno ~**) express train; (anche: **caffè ~**) espresso

es'primere vt to express; **esprimersi** vpr to express o.s.

es'pulsi ecc vb vedi **espellere**

espulsi'one sf expulsion

es'senza [es'sɛntsa] sf essence; **essenzi'ale** ag essential; **l'essenziale** the main o most important thing

○ **PAROLA CHIAVE**

'**essere** sm being; **essere umano** human being

▷ vb copulativo **1** (con attributo, sostantivo) to be; **sei giovane/simpatico** you are o you're young/nice; **è medico** he is o he's a doctor

2 (+ di: appartenere) to be; **di chi è la penna?** whose pen is it?; **è di Carla** it is o it's Carla's, it belongs to Carla

3 (+ di: provenire) to be; **è di Venezia** he is o he's from Venice

4 (data, ora): **è il 15 agosto/lunedì** it is o it's the 15th of August/Monday; **che ora è?, che ore sono?** what time is it?; **è l'una** it is o it's one o'clock; **sono le due** it is o it's two o'clock

5 (costare): **quant'è?** how much is it?; **sono 10 euro** it's 10 euros

▷ vb aus **1** (attivo): **essere arrivato/venuto** to have arrived/come; **è già partita** she has already left

2 (passivo) to be; **essere fatto da** to be made by; **è stata uccisa** she has been killed

3 (riflessivo): **si sono lavati** they washed, they got washed

4 (+ da + infinito): **è da farsi subito** it must be o is to be done immediately

▷ vi **1** (esistere, trovarsi) to be; **sono a casa** I'm at home; **essere in piedi/seduto** to be standing/sitting

2: **esserci**: **c'è** there is; **ci sono** there are; **che c'è?** what's the matter?, what is it?; **ci sono!** (fig: ho capito) I get it!; vedi anche **ci**

▷ vb impers **è tardi/Pasqua** it's late/Easter; **è possibile che venga** he may come; **è così** that's the way it is

'**essi** pron mpl vedi **esso**

'**esso, -a** pron it; (riferito a persona: soggetto) he/she; (: complemento) him/her

est sm east

es'tate sf summer

esteri'ore ag outward, external

es'terno, -a ag (porta, muro) outer, outside; (scala) outside; (alunno, impressione) external ▷ sm outside, exterior ▷ sm/f (allievo) day pupil; **all'~** outside; **per uso ~** for external use only; **esterni** smpl (Cinema) location shots

'**estero, -a** ag foreign ▷ sm **all'~** abroad

es'teso, -a pp di **estendere** ▷ ag extensive, large; **scrivere per ~** to write in full

es'tetico, -a, -ci, -che ag aesthetic ▷ sf (disciplina) aesthetics sg; (bellezza) attractiveness; **este'tista, -i, -e** sm/f beautician

es'tinguere vt to extinguish, put out; (debito) to pay off; **estinguersi** vpr to go out; (specie) to become extinct

es'tinsi ecc vb vedi **estinguere**

estin'tore sm (fire) extinguisher

estinzi'one sf putting out; (di specie) extinction

estir'pare vt (pianta) to uproot, pull up; (fig: vizio) to eradicate

es'tivo, -a ag summer cpd

es'torcere [es'tɔrtʃere] vt **~ qc (a qn)** to extort sth (from sb)

estradizi'one [estradit'tsjone] sf extradition

es'trae, es'traggo ecc vb vedi **estrarre**

es'traneo, -a ag foreign ▷ sm/f stranger; **rimanere ~ a qc** to take no part in sth

es'trarre vt to extract; (minerali) to mine; (sorteggiare) to draw

es'trassi ecc vb vedi **estrarre**

estrema'mente av extremely

estre'mista, -i, e sm/f extremist

estremità sf inv extremity, end ▷ sf pl (Anat) extremities

es'tremo, -a ag extreme; (ultimo: ora, tentativo) final, last ▷ sm extreme; (di pazienza, forze) limit, end; **estremi** smpl (Amm: dati essenziali) details, particulars; **l'~ Oriente** the Far East

estro'verso, -a ag, sm extrovert

età sf inv age; **all'~ di 8 anni** at the age of 8, at 8 years of age; **ha la mia ~** he (o she) is the same age as me o as I am; **raggiungere la maggiore ~** to come of age; **essere in ~ minore** to be under age

'**etere** sm ether

eternità sf eternity

e'terno, -a ag eternal

etero'geneo, -a [etero'dʒɛneo] ag heterogeneous

eterosessu'ale ag, sm/f heterosexual

'**etica** sf ethics sg; vedi anche **etico**

eti'chetta [eti'ketta] sf label; (cerimoniale): **l'~** etiquette

'etico, -a, -ci, -che *ag* ethical

eti'lometro *sm* Breathalyzer®

etimolo'gia, -'gie [etimolo'dʒia] *sf* etymology

Eti'opia *sf* l'~ Ethiopia

'etnico, -a, -ci, -che *ag* ethnic

e'trusco, -a, -schi, -sche *ag, sm/f* Etruscan

'ettaro *sm* hectare (= 10,000 m²)

'etto *sm abbr* (= *ettogrammo*) 100 grams

'euro *sm inv* (*divisa*) euro

Eu'ropa *sf* l'~ Europe

europarlamen'tare *sm/f* Member of the European Parliament, MEP

euro'peo, -a *ag, sm/f* European

eutana'sia *sf* euthanasia

evacu'are *vt* to evacuate

e'vadere *vi* (*fuggire*): ~ **da** to escape from ▷ *vt* (*sbrigare*) to deal with, dispatch; (*tasse*) to evade

evapo'rare *vi* to evaporate

e'vasi *ecc vb vedi* **evadere**

evasi'one *sf* (*vedi* evadere) escape; dispatch; **evasione fiscale** tax evasion

eva'sivo, -a *ag* evasive

e'vaso, -a *pp di* **evadere** ▷ *sm* escapee

e'vento *sm* event

eventu'ale *ag* possible

▎ Attenzione! In inglese esiste la parola *eventual*, che però significa *finale*.

eventual'mente *av* if necessary

▎ Attenzione! In inglese esiste la parola *eventually*, che però significa *alla fine*.

evi'dente *ag* evident, obvious

evidente'mente *av* evidently; (*palesemente*) obviously, evidently

evi'tare *vt* to avoid; ~ **di fare** to avoid doing; ~ **qc a qn** to spare sb sth

evoluzi'one [evolut'tsjone] *sf* evolution

e'volversi *vpr* to evolve

ev'viva *escl* hurrah!; ~ **il re!** long live the king!, hurrah for the king!

ex *prefisso* ex, former

'extra *ag inv* first-rate; top-quality ▷ *sm inv* extra; **extracomuni'tario, -a** *ag* from outside the EC ▷ *sm/f* non-EC citizen

extrater'restre *ag, sm/f* extraterrestrial

fa *vb vedi* **fare** ▷ *sm inv* (*Mus*) F; (: *solfeggiando la scala*) fa ▷ *av* **10 anni fa** 10 years ago

'fabbrica *sf* factory; **fabbri'care** *vt* to build; (*produrre*) to manufacture, make; (*fig*) to fabricate, invent

▎ Attenzione! In inglese esiste la parola *fabric*, che però significa *stoffa*.

fac'cenda [fat'tʃɛnda] *sf* matter, affair; (*cosa da fare*) task, chore

fac'chino [fak'kino] *sm* porter

'faccia, -ce [fat'tʃa] *sf* face; (*di moneta, medaglia*) side; **faccia a faccia** face to face

facci'ata [fat'tʃata] *sf* façade; (*di pagina*) side

'faccio [fat'tʃo] *vb vedi* **fare**

fa'cessi *ecc* [fa'tʃessi] *vb vedi* **fare**

fa'cevo *ecc* [fa'tʃevo] *vb vedi* **fare**

'facile [fat'tʃile] *ag* easy; (*disposto*): ~ **a** inclined to, prone to; (*probabile*): **è ~ che piova** it's likely to rain

facoltà *sf inv* faculty; (*autorità*) power

facolta'tivo, -a *ag* optional; (*fermata d'autobus*) request *cpd*

'faggio [fad'dʒo] *sm* beech

fagi'ano [fa'dʒano] *sm* pheasant

fagio'lino [fadʒo'lino] *sm* French (BRIT) o string bean

fagi'olo [fa'dʒolo] *sm* bean

'fai *vb vedi* **fare**

'fai-da-'te *sm inv* DIY, do-it-yourself

'falce [ˈfaltʃe] *sf* scythe; **falci'are** *vt* to cut; *(fig)* to mow down

falcia'trice [faltʃaˈtritʃe] *sf (per fieno)* reaping machine; *(per erba)* mowing machine

'falco, -chi *sm* hawk

'falda *sf* layer, stratum; *(di cappello)* brim; *(di cappotto)* tails *pl*; *(di monte)* lower slope; *(di tetto)* pitch

fale'gname [falenˈɲame] *sm* joiner

falli'mento *sm* failure; bankruptcy

fal'lire *vi (non riuscire)*: **~ (in)** to fail (in); *(Dir)* to go bankrupt ▷ *vt (colpo, bersaglio)* to miss

'fallo *sm* error, mistake; *(imperfezione)* defect, flaw; *(Sport)* foul; fault; **senza ~** without fail

falò *sm inv* bonfire

falsifi'care *vt* to forge; *(monete)* to forge, counterfeit

'falso, -a *ag* false; *(errato)* wrong; *(falsificato)* forged; fake; *(: oro, gioielli)* imitation *cpd* ▷ *sm* forgery; **giurare il ~** to commit perjury

'fama *sf* fame; *(reputazione)* reputation, name

'fame *sf* hunger; **aver ~** to be hungry

fa'miglia [faˈmiʎʎa] *sf* family

famili'are *ag (della famiglia)* family *cpd*; *(ben noto)* familiar; *(rapporti, atmosfera)* friendly; *(Ling)* informal, colloquial ▷ *sm/f* relative, relation

fa'moso, -a *ag* famous, well-known

fa'nale *sm (Aut)* light, lamp (BRIT); *(luce stradale, Naut)* light; *(di faro)* beacon

fa'natico, -a, -ci, -che *ag* fanatical; *(del teatro, calcio ecc)*: **~ di o per** mad o crazy about ▷ *sm/f* fanatic; *(tifoso)* fan

'fango, -ghi *sm* mud

'fanno *vb vedi* **fare**

fannul'lone, -a *sm/f* idler, loafer

fantasci'enza [fantaʃˈʃɛntsa] *sf* science fiction

fanta'sia *sf* fantasy, imagination; *(capriccio)* whim, caprice ▷ *ag inv* **vestito ~** patterned dress

fan'tasma, -i *sm* ghost, phantom

fan'tastico, -a, -ci, -che *ag* fantastic; *(potenza, ingegno)* imaginative

fan'tino *sm* jockey

fara'butto *sm* crook

fard *sm inv* blusher

 PAROLA CHIAVE

'fare *sm* 1 *(modo di fare)*: **con fare distratto** absent-mindedly; **ha un fare simpatico** he has a pleasant manner

2: **sul far del giorno/della notte** at daybreak/nightfall

▷ *vt* 1 *(fabbricare, creare)* to make; *(: casa)* to build; *(: assegno)* to make out; **fare un pasto/una promessa/un film** to make a meal/a promise/a film; **fare rumore** to make a noise

2 *(effettuare: lavoro, attività, studi)* to do; *(: sport)* to play; **cosa fa?** *(adesso)* what are you doing?; *(di professione)* what do you do?; **fare psicologia/italiano** *(Ins)* to do psychology/Italian; **fare un viaggio** to go on a trip o journey; **fare una passeggiata** to go for a walk; **fare la spesa** to do the shopping

3 *(funzione)* to be; *(Teatro)* to play, be; **fare il medico** to be a doctor; **fare il malato** *(fingere)* to act the invalid

4 *(suscitare: sentimenti)*: **fare paura a qn** to frighten sb; **(non) fa niente** *(non importa)* it doesn't matter

5 *(ammontare)*: **3 più 3 fa 6** 3 and 3 are o make 6; **fanno 3 euro** that's 3 euros; **Roma fa 2.000.000 di abitanti** Rome has 2,000,000 inhabitants; **che ora fai?** what time do you make it?

6 *(+ infinito)*: **far fare qc a qn** *(obbligare)* to make sb do sth; *(permettere)* to let sb do sth; **fammi vedere** let me see; **far partire il motore** to start (up) the engine; **far riparare la macchina/costruire una casa** to get o have the car repaired/a house built

7: **farsi: farsi una gonna** to make o.s. a skirt; **farsi un nome** to make a name for o.s.; **farsi la permanente** to get a perm; **farsi tagliare i capelli** to get one's hair cut; **farsi operare** to have an operation

8 *(fraseologia)*: **farcela** to succeed, manage; **non ce la faccio più** I can't go on; **ce la faremo** we'll make it; **me l'hanno fatta!** *(imbrogliare)* I've been done!; **lo facevo più giovane** I thought he was younger; **fare sì/no con la testa** to nod/shake one's head

▷ *vi* 1 *(agire)* to act, do; **fate come volete** do as you like; **fare presto** to be quick; **fare da** to act as; **non c'è niente da fare** it's no use; **saperci fare con qn/qc** to know how to deal with sb/sth; **faccia pure!** go ahead!

2 *(dire)* to say; **"davvero?" fece** "really?" he said

3: **fare per** *(essere adatto)* to be suitable for; **fare per fare qc** to be about to do sth; **fece per andarsene** he made as if to leave

4: **farsi: si fa così** you do it like this, this is the way it's done; **non si fa così!** *(rimprovero)* that's no way to behave!; **la festa non si fa** the party is off

5: fare a gara con qn to compete o vie with sb; **fare a pugni** to come to blows; **fare in tempo a fare** to be in time to do ▷ *vb impers* **fa bel tempo** the weather is fine; **fa caldo/freddo** it's hot/cold; **fa notte** it's getting dark ▷ *vpr* **farsi 1** (*diventare*) to become; **farsi prete** to become a priest; **farsi grande/vecchio** to grow tall/old

2 (*spostarsi*): **farsi avanti/indietro** to move forward/back

3 (*fam: drogarsi*) to be a junkie

far'falla *sf* butterfly

fa'rina *sf* flour

farma'cia, -'cie [farma'tʃia] *sf* pharmacy; (*negozio*) chemist's (shop) (BRIT); pharmacy; **farma'cista, -i, -e** *sm/f* chemist (BRIT), pharmacist

'farmaco, -ci o **chi** *sm* drug, medicine

'faro *sm* (*Naut*) lighthouse; (*Aer*) beacon; (*Aut*) headlight

'fascia, -sce ['faʃʃa] *sf* band, strip; (*Med*) bandage; (*di sindaco, ufficiale*) sash; (*parte di territorio*) strip, belt; (*di contribuenti ecc*) group, band; **essere in fasce** (*anche eec*) to be in one's infancy; **fascia oraria** time band

fasci'are [faʃʃare] *vt* to bind; (*Med*) to bandage

fa'scicolo [faʃʃikolo] *sm* (*di documenti*) file, dossier; (*di rivista*) issue, number; (*opuscolo*) booklet, pamphlet

'fascino ['faʃʃino] *sm* charm, fascination

fa'scismo [faʃʃizmo] *sm* fascism

'fase *sf* phase; (*Tecn*) stroke; **fuori ~** (*motore*) rough

fas'tidio *sm* bother, trouble; **dare ~ a qn** to bother o annoy sb; **sento ~ allo stomaco** my stomach's upset; **avere fastidi con la polizia** to have trouble o bother with the police; **fastidi'oso, -a** *ag* annoying, tiresome

> Attenzione! In inglese esiste la parola *fastidious*, che però significa *pignolo*.

'fata *sf* fairy

fa'tale *ag* fatal; (*inevitabile*) inevitable; (*fig*) irresistible

fa'tica, -che *sf* hard work, toil; (*sforzo*) effort; (*di metalli*) fatigue; **a ~** with difficulty; **fare ~ a fare qc** to have a job doing sth; **fati'coso, -a** *ag* tiring, exhausting; (*lavoro*) laborious

'fatto, -a *pp di* **fare** ▷ *ag* **un uomo ~** a grown man; **~ a mano/in casa** hand-/home-made ▷ *sm* fact; (*azione*) deed; (*avvenimento*) event, occurrence; (*di romanzo, film*) action, story; **cogliere qn sul ~** to catch sb red-handed; **il ~ sta** o **è**

che the fact remains o is that; **in ~ di** as for, as far as ... is concerned

fat'tore *sm* (*Agr*) farm manager; (*Mat, elemento costitutivo*) factor; **fattore di protezione** (*di lozione solare*) factor; **vorrei una crema solare con ~ di protezione 15** I'd like a factor 15 suntan cream

fatto'ria *sf* farm; farmhouse

> Attenzione! In inglese esiste la parola *factory*, che però significa *fabbrica*.

fatto'rino *sm* errand-boy; (*di ufficio*) office-boy; (*d'albergo*) porter

fat'tura *sf* (*Comm*) invoice; (*di abito*) tailoring; (*malia*) spell

fattu'rato *sm* (*Comm*) turnover

'fauna *sf* fauna

'fava *sf* broad bean

'favola *sf* (*fiaba*) fairy tale; (*d'intento morale*) fable; (*fandonia*) yarn; **favo'loso, -a** *ag* fabulous; (*incredibile*) incredible

fa'vore *sm* favour; **per ~** please; **fare un ~ a qn** to do sb a favour

favo'rire *vt* to favour; (*il commercio, l'industria, le arti*) to promote, encourage; **vuole ~?** won't you help yourself?; **favorisca in salotto** please come into the sitting room

fax *sm inv* fax; **mandare qc via ~** to fax sth

fazzo'letto [fattso'letto] *sm* handkerchief; (*per la testa*) (head)scarf; **fazzoletto di carta** tissue

feb'braio *sm* February

'febbre *sf* fever; **aver la ~** to have a high temperature; **febbre da fieno** hay fever

'feci *ecc* ['fɛtʃi] *vb vedi* **fare**

fecondazi'one [fekondat'tsjone] *sf* fertilization; **fecondazione artificiale** artificial insemination

fe'condo, -a *ag* fertile

'fede *sf* (*credenza*) belief, faith; (*Rel*) faith; (*fiducia*) faith, trust; (*fedeltà*) loyalty; (*anello*) wedding ring; (*attestato*) certificate; **aver ~ in qn** to have faith in sb; **in buona/cattiva ~** in good/bad faith; **"in ~"** (*Dir*) "in witness whereof"; **fe'dele** *ag* **fedele (a)** faithful (to) ▷ *sm/f* follower; **i fedeli** (*Rel*) the faithful

'federa *sf* pillowslip, pillowcase

fede'rale *ag* federal

'fegato *sm* liver; (*fig*) guts *pl*, nerve

'felce ['feltʃe] *sf* fern

fe'lice [fe'litʃe] *ag* happy; (*fortunato*) lucky; **felicità** *sf* happiness

felici'tarsi [felitʃi'tarsi] *vpr* (*congratularsi*): **~ con qn per qc** to congratulate sb on sth

fe'lino, -a *ag, sm* feline

'felpa *sf* sweatshirt

'femmina *sf* (*Zool, Tecn*) female; (*figlia*) girl, daughter; (*spesso peg*) woman;

femmi'nile *ag* feminine; (*sesso*) female; (*lavoro, giornale, moda*) woman's ▷ *sm* (*Ling*) feminine

'**femore** *sm* thighbone, femur

fe'nomeno *sm* phenomenon

feri'ale *ag* **giorno** ~ weekday

'**ferie** *sfpl* holidays (BRIT), vacation *sg* (US); **andare in** ~ to go on holiday o vacation

fe'rire *vt* to injure; (*deliberatamente*: Mil ecc) to wound; (*colpire*) to hurt; **ferirsi** *vpr* to hurt o.s., injure o.s; **fe'rita** *sf* injury, wound; **fe'rito, -a** *sm/f* wounded o injured man/woman

fer'maglio [fer'maʎʎo] *sm* clasp; (*per documenti*) clip

fer'mare *vt* to stop, halt; (*Polizia*) to detain, hold ▷ *vi* to stop; **fermarsi** *vpr* to stop, halt; **fermarsi a fare qc** to stop to do sth; **può fermarsi qui/all'angolo?** could you stop here/at the corner?

fer'mata *sf* stop; **fermata dell'autobus** bus stop

fer'menti *smpl* ~ **lattici** probiotic bacteria

fer'mezza [fer'mettsa] *sf* (*fig*) firmness, steadfastness

'**fermo, -a** *ag* still, motionless; (*veicolo*) stationary; (*orologio*) not working; (*saldo: anche fig*) firm; (*voce, mano*) steady ▷ *escl* stop!; keep still! ▷ *sm* (*chiusura*) catch, lock; (*Dir*): **fermo di polizia** police detention

fe'roce [fe'rɔtʃe] *ag* (*animale*) fierce, ferocious; (*persona*) cruel, fierce; (*fame, dolore*) raging; **le bestie feroci** wild animals

ferra'gosto *sm* (*festa*) feast of the Assumption; (*periodo*) August holidays *pl*

● FERRAGOSTO

● **Ferragosto**, August 15th, is a national
● holiday. Marking the Feast of the
● Assumption, its origins are religious
● but in recent years it has simply become
● the most important public holiday of
● the summer season. Most people take
● some extra time off work and head out
● of town to the holiday resorts.

ferra'menta *sfpl* **negozio di** ~ ironmonger's (BRIT), hardware shop o store (US)

'**ferro** *sm* iron; **una bistecca ai ferri** a grilled steak; **ferro battuto** wrought iron; **ferro da calza** knitting needle; **ferro di cavallo** horseshoe; **ferro da stiro** iron

ferro'via *sf* railway (BRIT), railroad (US); **ferrovi'ario, -a** *ag* railway *cpd* (BRIT), railroad *cpd* (US); **ferrovi'ere** *sm*

railwayman (BRIT), railroad man (US)

'**fertile** *ag* fertile

'**fesso, -a** *pp di* **fendere** ▷ *ag* (*fam: sciocco*) crazy, cracked

fes'sura *sf* crack, split; (*per gettone, moneta*) slot

'**festa** *sf* (*religiosa*) feast; (*pubblica*) holiday; (*compleanno*) birthday; (*onomastico*) name day; (*ricevimento*) celebration, party; **far** ~ to have a holiday; to live it up; **far** ~ **a qn** to give sb a warm welcome

festeggi'are [fested'dʒare] *vt* to celebrate; (*persona*) to have a celebration for

fes'tivo, -a *ag* (*atmosfera*) festive; **giorno** ~ holiday

'**feto** *sm* foetus (BRIT), fetus (US)

'**fetta** *sf* slice

fettuc'cine [fettut'tʃine] *sfpl* (*Cuc*) ribbon-shaped pasta

FF.SS. *abbr* = **Ferrovie dello Stato**

FI *sigla* = **Firenze** ▷ *abbr* (= Forza Italia) *Italian centre-right political party*

fi'aba *sf* fairy tale

fi'acca *sf* weariness; (*svogliatezza*) listlessness

fi'acco, -a, -chi, -che *ag* (*stanco*) tired, weary; (*svogliato*) listless; (*debole*) weak; (*mercato*) slack

fi'accola *sf* torch

fi'ala *sf* phial

fi'amma *sf* flame

fiam'mante *ag* (*colore*) flaming; **nuovo** ~ brand new

fiam'mifero *sm* match

fiam'mingo, -a, -ghi, -ghe *ag* Flemish ▷ *sm/f* Fleming ▷ *sm* (*Ling*) Flemish; **i Fiamminghi** the Flemish

fi'anco, -chi *sm* side; (*Mil*) flank; **di** ~ sideways, from the side; **a** ~ **a** ~ side by side

fi'asco, -schi *sm* flask; (*fig*) fiasco; **fare** ~ to fail

fia'tare *vi* (*fig: parlare*): **senza** ~ without saying a word

fi'ato *sm* breath; (*resistenza*) stamina; **avere il** ~ **grosso** to be out of breath; **prendere** ~ to catch one's breath

'**fibbia** *sf* buckle

'**fibra** *sf* fibre; (*fig*) constitution

fic'care *vt* to push, thrust, drive; **ficcarsi** *vpr* (*andare a finire*) to get to

ficcherò *ecc* [fikke'rɔ] *vb vedi* **ficcare**

'**fico, -chi** *sm* (*pianta*) fig tree; (*frutto*) fig; **fico d'India** prickly pear; **fico secco** dried fig

fidanza'mento [fidantsa'mento] *sm* engagement

fidan'zarsi [fidan'tsarsi] *vpr* to get engaged; **fidan'zato, -a** *sm/f* fiancé/

fiancée

fi'darsi vpr **~ di** to trust; **fi'dato, -a** ag reliable, trustworthy

fi'ducia [fi'dutʃa] sf confidence, trust; **incarico di ~** position of trust, responsible position; **persona di ~** reliable person

fie'nile sm barn; hayloft

fi'eno sm hay

fi'era sf fair

fi'ero, -a ag proud; (audace) bold

'fifa (fam) sf **aver ~** to have the jitters

fig. abbr (= figura) fig.

'figlia ['fiʎʎa] sf daughter

figli'astro, -a [fiʎ'ʎastro] sm/f stepson/daughter

'figlio ['fiʎʎo] sm son; (senza distinzione di sesso) child; **figlio di papà** spoilt, wealthy young man; **figlio unico** only child

fi'gura sf figure; (forma, aspetto esterno) form, shape; (illustrazione) picture, illustration; **far ~** to look smart; **fare una brutta ~** to make a bad impression

figu'rina sf figurine; (cartoncino) picture card

'fila sf row, line; (coda) queue; (serie) series, string; **di ~** in succession; **fare la ~** to queue; **in ~ indiana** in single file

fi'lare vt to spin ▷ vi (baco, ragno) to spin; (formaggio fuso) to go stringy; (discorso) to hang together; (fam: amoreggiare) to go steady; (muoversi a forte velocità) to go at full speed; **~ diritto** (fig) to toe the line; **~ via** to dash off

filas'trocca, -che sf nursery rhyme

filate'lia sf philately, stamp collecting

fi'letto sm (di vite) thread; (di carne) fillet

fili'ale ag filial ▷ sf (di impresa) branch

film sm inv film

'filo sm (anche fig) thread; (filato) yarn; (metallico) wire; (di lama, rasoio) edge; **per ~ e per segno** in detail; **con un ~ di voce** in a whisper; **filo d'erba** blade of grass; **filo interdentale** dental floss; **filo di perle** string of pearls; **filo spinato** barbed wire

fi'lone sm (di minerali) seam, vein; (pane) ≈ Vienna loaf; (fig) trend

filoso'fia sf philosophy; **fi'losofo, -a** sm/f philosopher

fil'trare vt, vi to filter

'filtro sm filter; **filtro dell'olio** (Aut) oil filter

fi'nale ag final ▷ sm (di opera) end, ending; (: Mus) finale ▷ sf (Sport) final; **final'mente** av finally, at last

fi'nanza [fi'nantsa] sf finance; **finanze** sfpl (di individuo, Stato) finances

finché [fin'ke] cong (per tutto il tempo che) as long as; (fino al momento in cui) until; **aspetta ~ io (non) sia ritornato** wait

until I get back

'fine ag (lamina, carta) thin; (capelli, polvere) fine; (vista, udito) keen, sharp; (persona: raffinata) refined, distinguished; (osservazione) subtle ▷ sf end ▷ sm aim, purpose; (esito) result, outcome; **secondo ~** ulterior motive; **in o alla ~** in the end, finally

fi'nestra sf window; **fines'trino** sm window; **vorrei un posto vicino al finestrino** I'd like a window seat

'fingere ['findʒere] vt to feign; (supporre) to imagine, suppose; **fingersi** vpr **fingersi ubriaco/pazzo** to pretend to be drunk/mad; **~ di fare** to pretend to do

fi'nire vt to finish ▷ vi to finish, end; **quando finisce lo spettacolo?** when does the show finish?; **~ di fare** (compiere) to finish doing; (smettere) to stop doing; **~ in galera** to end up o finish up in prison

finlan'dese ag, sm (Ling) Finnish ▷ sm/f Finn

Fin'landia sf **la ~** Finland

'fino, -a ag (capelli, seta) fine; (oro) pure; (fig: acuto) shrewd ▷ av (spesso troncato in **fin**: pure, anche) even ▷ prep (spesso troncato in **fin**: tempo): **fin quando?** till when?; (: luogo): **fin qui** as far as here; **~ a** (tempo) until, till; (luogo) as far as, (up) to; **fin da domani** from tomorrow onwards; **fin da ieri** since yesterday; **fin dalla nascita** from o since birth

fi'nocchio [fi'nɔkkjo] sm fennel; (fam: peg: omosessuale) queer

fi'nora av up till now

'finsi ecc vb vedi **fingere**

'finta sf pretence, sham; (Sport) feint; **far ~ (di fare)** to pretend (to do)

'finto, -a pp di **fingere** ▷ ag false; artificial

finzi'one [fin'tsjone] sf pretence, sham

fi'occo, -chi sm (di nastro) bow; (di stoffa, lana) flock; (di neve) flake; (Naut) jib; **coi fiocchi** (fig) first-rate; **fiocchi di avena** oatflakes; **fiocchi di granturco** cornflakes

fi'ocina ['fjɔtʃina] sf harpoon

fi'oco, -a, -chi, -che ag faint, dim

fi'onda sf catapult

fio'raio, -a sm/f florist

fi'ore sm flower; **fiori** smpl (Carte) clubs; **a fior d'acqua** on the surface of the water; **avere i nervi a fior di pelle** to be on edge; **fior di latte** cream; **fiori di campo** wild flowers

fioren'tino, -a ag Florentine

fio'retto sm (Scherma) foil

fio'rire vi (rosa) to flower; (albero) to blossom; (fig) to flourish

Fi'renze [fi'rɛntse] sf Florence

'firma sf signature

Attenzione! In inglese esiste la parola firm, che però significa ditta.

fir'mare vt to sign; **un abito firmato** a designer suit; **dove devo ~?** where do I sign?

fisar'monica, -che sf accordion

fis'cale ag fiscal, tax cpd; **medico ~** doctor employed by Social Security to verify cases of sick leave

fischi'are [fis'kjare] vi to whistle ▷ vt to whistle; (attore) to boo, hiss

fischi'etto [fis'kjetto] sm (strumento) whistle

'fischio ['fiskjo] sm whistle

'fisco sm tax authorities pl, ≈ Inland Revenue (BRIT), ≈ Internal Revenue Service (US)

'fisica sf physics sg

'fisico, -a, -ci, -che ag physical ▷ sm/f physicist ▷ sm physique

fisiotera'pia sf physiotherapy

fisiotera'pista sm/f physiotherapist

fis'sare vt to fix, fasten; (guardare intensamente) to stare at; (data, condizioni) to fix, establish, set; (prenotare) to book; **fissarsi** vpr **fissarsi su** (sguardo, attenzione) to focus on; (fig: idea) to become obsessed with

'fisso, -a ag fixed; (stipendio, impiego) regular ▷ av **guardare ~ qc/qn** to stare at sth/sb

'fitta sf sharp pain; vedi anche **fitto**

fit'tizio, -a ag fictitious, imaginary

'fitto, -a ag thick, dense; (pioggia) heavy ▷ sm depths pl, middle; (affitto, pigione) rent

fi'ume sm river

fiu'tare vt to smell, sniff; (animale) to scent; (fig: inganno) to get wind of, smell; **~ tabacco/cocaina** to take snuff/cocaine

fla'grante ag **cogliere qn in ~** to catch sb red-handed

fla'nella sf flannel

flash [flaʃ] sm inv (Fot) flash; (giornalistico) newsflash

'flauto sm flute

fles'sibile ag pliable; (fig: che si adatta) flexible

flessibili'tà sf (anche fig) flexibility

flessi'one sf (gen) bending; (Ginnastica: a terra) sit-up; (: in piedi) forward bend; (: sulle gambe) knee-bend; (diminuzione) slight drop, slight fall; (Ling) inflection; **fare una ~** to bend; **una ~ economica** a downward trend in the economy

'flettere vt to bend

'flipper sm inv pinball machine

F.lli abbr (= fratelli) Bros.

'flora sf flora

'florido, -a ag flourishing; (fig) glowing with health

'floscio, -a, -sci, -sce ['floʃʃo] ag (cappello) floppy, soft; (muscoli) flabby

'flotta sf fleet

'fluido, -a ag, sm fluid

flu'oro sm fluorine

'flusso sm flow; (Fisica, Med) flux; **~ e ri~** ebb and flow

fluvi'ale ag river cpd, fluvial

FMI sigla m (= Fondo Monetario Internazionale) IMF

'foca, -che sf (Zool) seal

fo'caccia, -ce [fo'kattʃa] sf kind of pizza; (dolce) bun

'foce ['fotʃe] sf (Geo) mouth

foco'laio sm (Med) centre of infection; (fig) hotbed

foco'lare sm hearth, fireside; (Tecn) furnace

'fodera sf (di vestito) lining; (di libro, poltrona) cover

fode'rare vt to line; to cover

'fodero sm (di spada) scabbard; (di pugnale) sheath; (di pistola) holster

'foga sf enthusiasm, ardour

'foglia ['fɔʎʎa] sf leaf; **foglia d'argento/ d'oro** silver/gold leaf

'foglio ['fɔʎʎo] sm (di carta) sheet (of paper); (di metallo) sheet; **foglio di calcolo** (Inform) spreadsheet; **foglio rosa** (Aut) provisional licence; **foglio di via** (Dir) expulsion order; **foglio volante** pamphlet

'fogna ['fɔɲɲa] sf drain, sewer

föhn [føːn] sm inv hair dryer

'folla sf crowd, throng

'folle ag mad, insane; (Tecn) idle; **in ~** (Aut) in neutral

fol'lia sf folly, foolishness; foolish act; (pazzia) madness, lunacy

'folto, -a ag thick

fon sm inv hair dryer

fondamen'tale ag fundamental, basic

fonda'mento sm foundation; **fondamenta** sfpl (Edil) foundations

fon'dare vt to found; (fig: dar base): **~ qc su** to base sth on

fon'dente ag **cioccolato ~** plain o dark chocolate

'fondere vt (neve) to melt; (metallo) to fuse, melt; (fig: colori) to merge, blend; (: imprese, gruppi) to merge ▷ vi to melt; **fondersi** vpr to melt; (fig: partiti, correnti) to unite, merge

'fondo, -a ag deep ▷ sm (di recipiente, pozzo) bottom; (di stanza) back; (quantità di liquido che resta, deposito) dregs pl; (sfondo) background; (unità immobiliare) property, estate; (somma di denaro) fund; (Sport)

long-distance race; **fondi** *smpl* (*denaro*)
funds; **a notte fonda** at dead of night; **in ~ a** at the bottom of; at the back of; (*strada*)
at the end of; **andare a ~** (*nave*) to sink;
conoscere a ~ to know inside out; **dar ~ a** (*fig: provviste, soldi*) to use up; **in ~** (*fig*)
after all, all things considered; **andare fino in ~ a** (*fig*) to examine thoroughly; **a ~ perduto** (*Comm*) without security; **fondi di magazzino** old o unsold stock *sg*; **fondi di caffè** coffee grounds; **fondo comune di investimento** investment trust

fondo'tinta *sm inv* (*cosmetico*) foundation

fo'netica *sf* phonetics *sg*

fon'tana *sf* fountain

'fonte *sf* spring, source; (*fig*) source ▷ *sm*:
fonte battesimale (*Rel*) font; **fonte energetica** source of energy

fo'raggio [fo'raddʒo] *sm* fodder, forage

fo'rare *vt* to pierce, make a hole in;
(*pallone*) to burst; (*biglietto*) to punch; **~ una gomma** to burst a tyre (*BRIT*) o tire
(*US*)

'forbici ['fɔrbitʃi] *sfpl* scissors

'forca, -che *sf* (*Agr*) fork, pitchfork;
(*patibolo*) gallows *sg*

for'chetta [for'ketta] *sf* fork

for'cina [for'tʃina] *sf* hairpin

fo'resta *sf* forest

foresti'ero, -a *ag* foreign ▷ *sm/f* foreigner

'forfora *sf* dandruff

'forma *sf* form; (*aspetto esteriore*) form,
shape; (*Dir: procedura*) procedure; (*per calzature*) last; (*stampo da cucina*) mould

formag'gino [formad'dʒino] *sm*
processed cheese

for'maggio [for'maddʒo] *sm* cheese

for'male *ag* formal

for'mare *vt* to form, shape, make; (*numero di telefono*) to dial; (*fig: carattere*) to form,
mould; **formarsi** *vpr* to form, take shape;
for'mato *sm* format, size; **formazi'one**
sf formation; (*fig: educazione*) training;
formazione professionale vocational
training

for'mica¹, -che *sf* ant

formica®² ['fɔrmika] *sf* (*materiale*)
Formica®

formi'dabile *ag* powerful, formidable;
(*straordinario*) remarkable

'formula *sf* formula; **formula di cortesia**
courtesy form

formu'lare *vt* to formulate; to express

for'naio *sm* baker

for'nello *sm* (*elettrico, a gas*) ring; (*di pipa*)
bowl

for'nire *vt* **~ qn di qc, ~ qc a qn** to provide
o supply sb with sth, supply sth to sb

'forno *sm* (*di cucina*) oven; (*panetteria*)
bakery; (*Tecn: per calce ecc*) kiln; (: *per metalli*) furnace; **forno a microonde**
microwave oven

'foro *sm* (*buco*) hole; (*Storia*) forum;
(*tribunale*) (law) court

'forse *av* perhaps, maybe; (*circa*) about;
essere in ~ to be in doubt

'forte *ag* strong; (*suono*) loud; (*spesa*)
considerable, great; (*passione, dolore*)
great, deep ▷ *av* strongly; (*velocemente*)
fast; (*a voce alta*) loud(ly); (*violentemente*)
hard ▷ *sm* (*edificio*) fort; (*specialità*) forte,
strong point; **essere ~ in qc** to be good
at sth

for'tezza [for'tettsa] *sf* (*morale*) strength;
(*luogo fortificato*) fortress

for'tuito, -a *ag* fortuitous, chance

for'tuna *sf* (*destino*) fortune, luck; (*buona sorte*) success, fortune; (*eredità, averi*)
fortune; **per ~** luckily, fortunately; **di ~**
makeshift, improvised; **atterraggio di ~** emergency landing; **fortu'nato, -a** *ag*
lucky, fortunate; (*coronato da successo*)
successful

'forza ['fɔrtsa] *sf* strength; (*potere*) power;
(*Fisica*) force; **forze** *sfpl* (*fisiche*) strength
sg; (*Mil*) forces *escl* come on!; **per ~** against
one's will; (*naturalmente*) of course; **a viva ~** by force; **a ~ di** by dint of; **~ maggiore**
circumstances beyond one's control; **la ~ pubblica** the police *pl*; **forze armate**
armed forces; **forze dell'ordine** the forces
of law and order; **Forza Italia** *Italian
centre-right political party*; **forza di pace**
peacekeeping force

for'zare [for'tsare] *vt* to force; **~ qn a fare**
to force sb to do

for'zista, -i, e [for'tsista] *ag* of Forza Italia
▷ *sm/f* member (o supporter) of Forza
Italia

fos'chia [fos'kia] *sf* mist, haze

'fosco, -a, -schi, -sche *ag* dark, gloomy

'fosforo *sm* phosphorous

'fossa *sf* pit; (*di cimitero*) grave; **fossa biologica** septic tank

fos'sato *sm* ditch; (*di fortezza*) moat

fos'setta *sf* dimple

'fossi *ecc vb vedi* **essere**

'fossile *ag, sm* fossil

'fosso *sm* ditch; (*Mil*) trench

'foste *ecc vb vedi* **essere**

'foto *sf* photo; **può farci una ~, per favore?** would you take a picture of us,
please? ▷ *prefisso*: **foto ricordo** souvenir
photo; **foto tessera** passport(-type)
photo; **foto'camera** *sf* **fotocamera digitale** digital camera; **foto'copia** *sf*
photocopy; **fotocopi'are** *vt* to photocopy;
fotocopia'trice [fotokopja'tritʃe]

sf photocopier; **fotogra'fare** *vt* to photograph; **fotogra'fia** *sf* (*procedimento*) photography; (*immagine*) photograph; **fare una fotografia** to take a photograph; **una fotografia a colori/in bianco e nero** a colour/black and white photograph; **foto'grafico, -a, ci, che** *ag* photographic; **macchina fotografica** camera; **fo'tografo, -a** *sm/f* photographer; **fotoro'manzo** *sm* romantic picture story

fou'lard [fu'lar] *sm inv* scarf

fra *prep* = **tra**

'fradicio, -a, -ci, -ce ['fraditʃo] *ag* (*molto bagnato*) soaking (wet); **ubriaco ~** blind drunk

'fragile ['fradʒile] *ag* fragile; (*fig: salute*) delicate

'fragola *sf* strawberry

fra'grante *ag* fragrant

frain'tendere *vt* to misunderstand

fram'mento *sm* fragment

'frana *sf* landslide; (*fig: persona*): **essere una ~** to be useless

fran'cese [fran'tʃeze] *ag* French ▷ *sm/f* Frenchman/woman ▷ *sm* (*Ling*) French; **i Francesi** the French

'Francia ['frantʃa] *sf* **la ~** France

'franco, -a, -chi, -che *ag* (*Comm*) free; (*sincero*) frank, open, sincere ▷ *sm* (*moneta*) franc; **farla franca** (*fig*) to get off scot-free; **prezzo ~ fabbrica** ex-works price; **franco di dogana** duty-free

franco'bollo *sm* (postage) stamp

'frangia, -ge ['frandʒa] *sf* fringe

frap'pé *sm* milk shake

'frase *sf* (*Ling*) sentence; (*locuzione, espressione, Mus*) phrase; **frase fatta** set phrase

'frassino *sm* ash (tree)

frastagli'ato, -a [frastaʎ'ʎato] *ag* (*costa*) indented, jagged

frastor'nare *vt* to daze; to befuddle

frastu'ono *sm* hubbub, din

'frate *sm* friar, monk

fratel'lastro *sm* stepbrother; (*con genitore in comune*) half-brother

fra'tello *sm* brother; **fratelli** *smpl* brothers; (*nel senso di fratelli e sorelle*) brothers and sisters

fra'terno, -a *ag* fraternal, brotherly

frat'tempo *sm* **nel ~** in the meantime, meanwhile

frat'tura *sf* fracture; (*fig*) split, break

frazi'one [frat'tsjone] *sf* fraction; (*di comune*) small town

'freccia, -ce ['frettʃa] *sf* arrow; **freccia di direzione** (*Aut*) indicator

fred'dezza [fred'dettsa] *sf* coldness

'freddo, -a *ag, sm* cold; **fa ~** it's cold; **aver ~** to be cold; **a ~** (*fig*) deliberately; **freddo'loso, -a** *ag* sensitive to the cold

fre'gare *vt* to rub; (*fam: truffare*) to take in, cheat; (: *rubare*) to swipe, pinch; **fregarsene** (*fam!*): **chi se ne frega?** who gives a damn (about it)?

fregherò *ecc* [frege'rɔ] *vb vedi* **fregare**

fre'nare *vt* (*veicolo*) to slow down; (*cavallo*) to rein in; (*lacrime*) to restrain, hold back ▷ *vi* to brake; **frenarsi** *vpr* (*fig*) to restrain o.s., control o.s.

'freno *sm* brake; (*morso*) bit; **tenere a ~** to restrain; **freno a disco** disc brake; **freno a mano** handbrake

frequen'tare *vt* (*scuola, corso*) to attend; (*locale, bar*) to go to, frequent; (*persone*) to see (often)

frequen'tato, -a *ag* (*locale*) busy

fre'quente *ag* frequent; **di ~** frequently

fres'chezza [fres'kettsa] *sf* freshness

'fresco, -a, -schi, -sche *ag* fresh; (*temperatura*) cool; (*notizia*) recent, fresh ▷ *sm* **godere il ~** to enjoy the cool air; **stare ~** (*fig*) to be in for it; **mettere al ~** to put in a cool place

'fretta *sf* hurry, haste; **in ~** in a hurry; **in ~ e furia** in a mad rush; **aver ~** to be in a hurry

'friggere ['friddʒere] *vt* to fry ▷ *vi* (*olio ecc*) to sizzle

'frigido, -a ['fridʒido] *ag* (*Med*) frigid

'frigo *sm* fridge

frigo'bar *sm inv* minibar

frigo'rifero, -a *ag* refrigerating ▷ *sm* refrigerator

fringu'ello *sm* chaffinch

'frissi *ecc vb vedi* **friggere**

frit'tata *sf* omelette; **fare una ~** (*fig*) to make a mess of things

frit'tella *sf* (*Cuc*) fritter

'fritto, -a *pp di* **friggere** ▷ *ag* fried ▷ *sm* fried food; **fritto misto** mixed fry

frit'tura *sf* (*Cuc*): **frittura di pesce** mixed fried fish

'frivolo, -a *ag* frivolous

frizi'one [frit'tsjone] *sf* friction; (*sulla pelle*) rub, rub-down; (*Aut*) clutch

friz'zante [frid'dzante] *ag* (*anche fig*) sparkling

fro'dare *vt* to defraud, cheat

'frode *sf* fraud; **frode fiscale** tax evasion

'fronda *sf* (leafy) branch; (*di partito politico*) internal opposition; **fronde** *sfpl* (*di albero*) foliage *sg*

fron'tale *ag* frontal; (*scontro*) head-on

'fronte *sf* (*Anat*) forehead; (*di edificio*) front, façade ▷ *sm* (*Mil, Pol, Meteor*) front; **a ~, di ~** facing, opposite; **di ~ a** (*posizione*) opposite, facing, in front of; (*a paragone di*) compared with

fronti'era sf border, frontier

'frottola sf fib

fru'gare vi to rummage ▷ vt to search

frugherò ecc [fruge'rɔ] vb vedi **frugare**

frul'lare vt (Cuc) to whisk ▷ vi (uccelli) to flutter; **frul'lato** sm milk shake; fruit drink; **frulla'tore** sm electric mixer

fru'mento sm wheat

fru'scio [fruʃʃio] sm rustle; rustling; (di acque) murmur

'frusta sf whip; (Cuc) whisk

frus'tare vt to whip

frus'trato, -a ag frustrated

'frutta sf fruit; (portata) dessert; **frutta candita** candied fruit; **frutta secca** dried fruit

frut'tare vi to bear dividends, give a return

frut'teto sm orchard

frutti'vendolo, -a sm/f greengrocer (BRIT), produce dealer (US)

'frutto sm fruit; (fig: risultato) result(s); (Econ: interesse) interest; (: reddito) income; **frutti di bosco** berries; **frutti di mare** seafood sg

FS abbr = **Ferrovie dello Stato**

fu vb vedi **essere** ▷ ag inv **il fu Paolo Bianchi** the late Paolo Bianchi

fuci'lare [futʃi'lare] vt to shoot

fu'cile [fu'tʃile] sm rifle, gun; (da caccia) shotgun, gun

'fucsia sf fuchsia

'fuga sf escape, flight; (di gas, liquidi) leak; (Mus) fugue; **fuga di cervelli** brain drain

fug'gire [fud'dʒire] vi to flee, run away; (fig: passar veloce) to fly ▷ vt to avoid

'fui vb vedi **essere**

fu'liggine [fu'liddʒine] sf soot

'fulmine sm thunderbolt; lightning no pl

fu'mare vi to smoke; (emettere vapore) to steam ▷ vt to smoke; **le dà fastidio se fumo?** do you mind if I smoke?; **fuma'tore, -'trice** sm/f smoker

fu'metto sm comic strip; **giornale** sm, **a fumetti** comic

'fummo vb vedi **essere**

'fumo sm smoke; (vapore) steam; (il fumare tabacco) smoking; **fumi** smpl (industriali ecc) fumes; **i fumi dell'alcool** the after-effects of drink; **vendere ~** to deceive, cheat; **fumo passivo** passive smoking

'fune sf rope, cord; (più grossa) cable

'funebre ag (rito) funeral; (aspetto) gloomy, funereal

fune'rale sm funeral

'fungere ['fundʒere] vi **~ da** to act as

'fungo, -ghi sm fungus; (commestibile) mushroom; **fungo velenoso** toadstool

funico'lare sf funicular railway

funi'via sf cable railway

'funsi ecc vb vedi **fungere**

funzio'nare [funtsjo'nare] vi to work, function; (fungere): **~ da** to act as; **come funziona?** how does this work?; **la TV non funziona** the TV isn't working

funzio'nario [funtsjo'narjo] sm official; **funzionario statale** civil servant

funzi'one [fun'tsjone] sf function; (carica) post, position; (Rel) service; **in ~ (meccanismo)** in operation; **in ~ di (come)** as; **fare la ~ di qn (farne le veci)** to take sb's place

fu'oco, -chi sm fire; (fornello) ring; (Fot, Fisica) focus; **dare ~ a qc** to set fire to sth; **far ~ (sparare)** to fire; **al ~!** fire!; **fuoco d'artificio** firework

fuorché [fwor'ke] cong, prep except

fu'ori av outside; (all'aperto) outdoors, outside; (fuori di casa, Sport) out; (esclamativo) get out! ▷ prep **~ (di)** out of, outside ▷ sm outside; **lasciar ~ qc/qn** to leave sth/sb out; **far ~ qn (fam)** to kill sb, do sb in; **essere ~ di sé** to be beside o.s.; **~ luogo (inopportuno)** out of place, uncalled for; **~ mano** out of the way, remote; **~ pericolo** out of danger; **~ uso** old-fashioned; obsolete; **fuorigi'oco** sm offside; **fuori'strada** sm (Aut) cross-country vehicle

'furbo, -a ag clever, smart; (peg) cunning

fu'rente ag **~ (contro)** furious (with)

fur'fante sm rascal, scoundrel

fur'gone sm van

'furia sf (ira) fury, rage; (fig: impeto) fury, violence; (fretta) rush; **a ~ di** by dint of; **andare su tutte le furie** to get into a towering rage; **furi'bondo, -a** ag furious

furi'oso, -a ag furious

'furono vb vedi **essere**

fur'tivo, -a ag furtive

'furto sm theft; **vorrei denunciare un ~** I'd like to report a theft; **furto con scasso** burglary

'fusa sfpl **fare le ~** to purr

fu'seaux smpl inv leggings

'fusi ecc vb vedi **fondere**

fu'sibile sm (Elettr) fuse

fusi'one sf (di metalli) fusion, melting; (colata) casting; (Comm) merger; (fig) merging

'fuso, -a pp di **fondere** ▷ sm (Filatura) spindle; **fuso orario** time zone

fus'tino sm (di detersivo) tub

'fusto sm stem; (Anat, di albero) trunk; (recipiente) drum, can

fu'turo, -a ag, sm future

'gabbia *sf* cage; (*da imballaggio*) crate; **gabbia dell'ascensore** lift (*BRIT*) o elevator (*US*) shaft; **gabbia toracica** (*Anat*) rib cage

gabbi'ano *sm* (sea)gull

gabi'netto *sm* (*Med ecc*) consulting room; (*Pol*) ministry; (*WC*) toilet, lavatory; (*Ins: di fisica ecc*) laboratory

'gaffe [gaf] *sf inv* blunder

ga'lante *ag* gallant, courteous; (*avventura*) amorous

ga'lassia *sf* galaxy

ga'lera *sf* (*Naut*) galley; (*prigione*) prison

'galla *sf* **a ~** afloat; **venire a ~** to surface, come to the surface; (*fig: verità*) to come out

galleggi'are [galled'dʒare] *vi* to float

galle'ria *sf* (*traforo*) tunnel; (*Archit, d'arte*) gallery; (*Teatro*) circle; (*strada coperta con negozi*) arcade

'Galles *sm* **il ~** Wales

gal'lina *sf* hen

'gallo *sm* cock

galop'pare *vi* to gallop

ga'loppo *sm* gallop; **al o di ~** at a gallop

'gamba *sf* leg; (*asta: di lettera*) stem; **in ~** (*in buona salute*) well; (*bravo, sveglio*) bright, smart; **prendere qc sotto ~** (*fig*) to treat sth too lightly

gambe'retto *sm* shrimp

'gambero *sm* (*di acqua dolce*) crayfish; (*di mare*) prawn

'gambo *sm* stem; (*di frutta*) stalk

'gamma *sf* (*Mus*) scale; (*di colori, fig*) range

'gancio ['gantʃo] *sm* hook

'gara *sf* competition; (*Sport*) competition; contest; match; (: *corsa*) race; **fare a ~** to compete, vie

ga'rage [ga'raʒ] *sm inv* garage

garan'tire *vt* to guarantee; (*debito*) to stand surety for; (*dare per certo*) to assure

garan'zia [garan'tsia] *sf* guarantee; (*pegno*) security

gar'bato, -a *ag* courteous, polite

gareggi'are [gared'dʒare] *vi* to compete

garga'rismo *sm* gargle; **fare i gargarismi** to gargle

ga'rofano *sm* carnation; **chiodo di ~** clove

'garza ['gardza] *sf* (*per bende*) gauze

gar'zone [gar'dzone] *sm* (*di negozio*) boy

gas *sm inv* gas; **sento odore di ~** I can smell gas; **a tutto ~** at full speed; **dare ~** (*Aut*) to accelerate

ga'solio *sm* diesel (oil)

gas'sato, -a *ag* fizzy

gas'trite *sf* gastritis

gastrono'mia *sf* gastronomy

gat'tino *sm* kitten

'gatto, -a *sm/f* cat, tomcat/she-cat; **gatto delle nevi** (*Aut, Sci*) snowcat; **gatto selvatico** wildcat

'gazza ['gaddza] *sf* magpie

gel [dʒɛl] *sm inv* gel

ge'lare [dʒe'lare] *vt, vi, vb impers* to freeze

gelate'ria [dʒelate'ria] *sf* ice-cream shop

gela'tina [dʒela'tina] *sf* gelatine; **gelatina esplosiva** dynamite; **gelatina di frutta** fruit jelly

ge'lato, -a [dʒe'lato] *ag* frozen ▷ *sm* ice cream

'gelido, -a ['dʒɛlido] *ag* icy, ice-cold

'gelo ['dʒɛlo] *sm* (*temperatura*) intense cold; (*brina*) frost; (*fig*) chill

gelo'sia [dʒelo'sia] *sf* jealousy

ge'loso, -a [dʒe'loso] *ag* jealous

'gelso ['dʒɛlso] *sm* mulberry (tree)

gelso'mino [dʒelso'mino] *sm* jasmine

ge'mello, -a [dʒe'mɛllo] *ag, sm/f* twin; **gemelli** *smpl* (*di camicia*) cufflinks; (*dello zodiaco*): **Gemelli** Gemini *sg*

'gemere ['dʒɛmere] *vi* to moan, groan; (*cigolare*) to creak

'gemma ['dʒɛmma] *sf* (*Bot*) bud; (*pietra preziosa*) gem

gene'rale [dʒene'rale] *ag, sm* general; **in ~** (*per sommi capi*) in general terms; (*di solito*) usually, in general

gene'rare [dʒene'rare] *vt* (*dar vita*) to give birth to; (*produrre*) to produce; (*causare*)

to arouse; (*Tecn*) to produce, generate;
generazi'one *sf* generation
'**genere** [ˈdʒɛnere] *sm* kind, type, sort;
(*Biol*) genus; (*merce*) article, product;
(*Ling*) gender; (*Arte, Letteratura*) genre;
in ~ generally, as a rule; **genere umano**
mankind; **generi alimentari** foodstuffs
ge'nerico, -a, -ci, -che [dʒeˈnɛriko] *ag*
generic; (*vago*) vague, imprecise
'**genero** [ˈdʒɛnero] *sm* son-in-law
gene'roso, -a [dʒeneˈroso] *ag* generous
ge'netica [dʒeˈnɛtika] *sf* genetics *sg*
ge'netico, -a, -ci, -che [dʒeˈnɛtiko] *ag*
genetic
gen'giva [dʒenˈdʒiva] *sf* (*Anat*) gum
geni'ale [dʒenˈjale] *ag* (*persona*) of genius;
(*idea*) ingenious, brilliant
'**genio** [ˈdʒɛnjo] *sm* genius; **andare a ~ a**
qn to be to sb's liking, appeal to sb
geni'tore [dʒeniˈtore] *sm* parent, father
o mother; **i miei genitori** my parents, my
father and mother
gen'naio [dʒenˈnajo] *sm* January
'**Genova** [ˈdʒɛnova] *sf* Genoa
'**gente** [ˈdʒɛnte] *sf* people *pl*
gen'tile [dʒenˈtile] *ag* (*persona, atto*) kind;
(: *garbato*) courteous, polite; (*nelle lettere*):
G~ Signore Dear Sir; (: *sulla busta*): **G~**
Signor Fernando Villa Mr Fernando Villa
genu'ino, -a [dʒenuˈino] *ag* (*prodotto*)
natural; (*persona, sentimento*) genuine,
sincere
geogra'fia [dʒeograˈfia] *sf* geography
geolo'gia [dʒeoloˈdʒia] *sf* geology
ge'ometra, -i, -e [dʒeˈɔmetra] *sm/f*
(*professionista*) surveyor
geome'tria [dʒeomeˈtria] *sf* geometry
ge'ranio [dʒeˈranjo] *sm* geranium
gerar'chia [dʒerarˈkia] *sf* hierarchy
'**gergo, -ghi** [ˈdʒɛrgo] *sm* jargon; slang
geria'tria [dʒerjaˈtria] *sf* geriatrics *sg*
Ger'mania [dʒerˈmanja] *sf* **la ~** Germany;
la ~ occidentale/orientale West/East
Germany
'**germe** [ˈdʒɛrme] *sm* germ; (*fig*) seed
germogli'are [dʒermoʎˈʎare] *vi* to sprout;
to germinate
gero'glifico, -ci [dʒeroˈglifiko] *sm*
hieroglyphic
ge'rundio [dʒeˈrundjo] *sm* gerund
'**gesso** [ˈdʒɛsso] *sm* chalk; (*Scultura, Med,*
Edil) plaster; (*statua*) plaster figure;
(*minerale*) gypsum
gesti'one [dʒesˈtjone] *sf* management
ges'tire [dʒesˈtire] *vt* to run, manage
'**gesto** [ˈdʒɛsto] *sm* gesture
Gesù [dʒeˈzu] *sm* Jesus
gesu'ita, -i [dʒezuˈita] *sm* Jesuit
get'tare [dʒetˈtare] *vt* to throw; (*anche:*

~ via) to throw away *o* out; (*Scultura*) to
cast; (*Edil*) to lay; (*acqua*) to spout; (*grido*)
to utter; **gettarsi** *vpr* **gettarsi in** (*fiume*)
to flow into; **~ uno sguardo su** to take a
quick look at
'**getto** [ˈdʒetto] *sm* (*di gas, liquido, Aer*) jet;
a ~ continuo uninterruptedly; **di ~** (*fig*)
straight off, in one go
get'tone [dʒetˈtone] *sm* token; (*per giochi*)
counter; (: *roulette ecc*) chip; **gettone**
telefonico telephone token
ghiacci'aio [gjatˈtʃajo] *sm* glacier
ghiacci'ato, -a *ag* frozen; (*bevanda*)
ice-cold
ghi'accio [ˈgjattʃo] *sm* ice
ghiacci'olo [gjatˈtʃolo] *sm* icicle; (*tipo di*
gelato) ice lolly (BRIT), Popsicle® (US)
ghi'aia [ˈgjaja] *sf* gravel
ghi'anda [ˈgjanda] *sf* (*Bot*) acorn
ghi'andola [ˈgjandola] *sf* gland
ghi'otto, -a [ˈgjotto] *ag* greedy; (*cibo*)
delicious, appetizing
ghir'landa [girˈlanda] *sf* garland, wreath
'**ghiro** [ˈgiro] *sm* dormouse
'**ghisa** [ˈgiza] *sf* cast iron
già [dʒa] *av* already; (*ex, in precedenza*)
formerly ▷ *escl* of course!, yes indeed!
gi'acca, -che [ˈdʒakka] *sf* jacket; **giacca**
a vento windcheater (BRIT), windbreaker
(US)
giacché [dʒakˈke] *cong* since, as
giac'cone [dʒakˈkone] *sm* heavy jacket
gi'ada [ˈdʒada] *sf* jade
giagu'aro [dʒaˈgwaro] *sm* jaguar
gi'allo [ˈdʒallo] *ag* yellow; (*carnagione*)
sallow ▷ *sm* yellow; (*anche:* **romanzo ~**)
detective novel; (*anche:* **film ~**) detective
film; **giallo dell'uovo** yolk
Giamaica [dʒaˈmaika] *sf* **la ~** Jamaica
Giap'pone [dʒapˈpone] *sm* Japan;
giappo'nese *ag, sm/f, sm* Japanese *inv*
giardi'naggio [dʒardiˈnaddʒo] *sm*
gardening
giardini'ere, -a [dʒardiˈnjɛre] *sm/f*
gardener
giar'dino [dʒarˈdino] *sm* garden; **giardino**
d'infanzia nursery school; **giardino**
pubblico public gardens *pl*, (public) park;
giardino zoologico zoo
giavel'lotto [dʒavelˈlotto] *sm* javelin
gigabyte [dʒigaˈbait] *sm inv* gigabyte
gi'gante, -'essa [dʒiˈgante] *sm/f* giant
▷ *ag* giant, gigantic; (*Comm*) giant-size
'**giglio** [ˈdʒiʎʎo] *sm* lily
gilè [dʒiˈle] *sm inv* waistcoat
gin [dʒin] *sm inv* gin
gine'cologo, -a, -gi, -ghe [dʒineˈkɔlogo]
sm/f gynaecologist
gi'nepro [dʒiˈnepro] *sm* juniper

gi'nestra [dʒi'nɛstra] sf (Bot) broom

Gi'nevra [dʒi'nevra] sf Geneva

gin'nastica sf gymnastics sg; (esercizio fisico) keep-fit exercises; (Ins) physical education

gi'nocchio [dʒi'nɔkkjo] (pl(m) **gi'nocchi**, o pl(f) **gi'nocchia**) sm knee; **stare in ~** to kneel, be on one's knees; **mettersi in ~** to kneel (down)

gio'care [dʒo'kare] vt to play; (scommettere) to stake, wager, bet; (ingannare) to take in ▷ vi to play; (a roulette ecc) to gamble; (fig) to play a part, be important; **~ a** (gioco, sport) to play; (cavalli) to bet on; **giocarsi la carriera** to put one's career at risk; **gioca'tore, -'trice** sm/f player; gambler

gio'cattolo [dʒo'kattolo] sm toy

giocherò ecc [dʒoke'rɔ] vb vedi **giocare**

gi'oco, -chi ['dʒɔko] sm game; (divertimento, Tecn) play; (al casinò) gambling; (Carte) hand; (insieme di pezzi ecc necessari per un gioco) set; **per ~** for fun; **fare il doppio ~ con qn** to double-cross sb; **i Giochi Olimpici** the Olympic Games; **gioco d'azzardo** game of chance; **gioco degli scacchi** chess set

giocoli'ere [dʒoko'ljɛre] sm juggler

gi'oia ['dʒɔja] sf joy, delight; (pietra preziosa) jewel, precious stone

gioielle'ria [dʒojelle'ria] sf jeweller's craft; jeweller's (shop)

gioielli'ere, -a [dʒojel'ljɛre] sm/f jeweller

gioi'ello [dʒo'jɛllo] sm jewel, piece of jewellery; **i miei gioielli** my jewels o jewellery; **gioielli** smpl (anelli, collane ecc) jewellery; **i gioielli della Corona** the crown jewels

Gior'dania [dʒor'danja] sf **la ~** Jordan

giorna'laio, -a [dʒorna'lajo] sm/f newsagent (BRIT), newsdealer (US)

gior'nale [dʒor'nale] sm (news) paper; (diario) journal, diary; (Comm) journal; **giornale di bordo** log; **giornale radio** radio news sg

giornali'ero, -a [dʒorna'ljɛro] ag daily; (che varia: umore) changeable ▷ sm day labourer

giorna'lismo [dʒorna'lizmo] sm journalism

giorna'lista, -i, -e [dʒorna'lista] sm/f journalist

gior'nata [dʒor'nata] sf day; **giornata lavorativa** working day

gi'orno ['dʒorno] sm day; (opposto alla notte) day, daytime; (anche: **luce del ~**) daylight; **al ~** per day; **di ~** by day; **al ~ d'oggi** nowadays

gi'ostra ['dʒɔstra] sf (per bimbi) merry-go-round; (torneo storico) joust

gi'ovane ['dʒovane] ag young; (aspetto) youthful ▷ sm/f youth/girl, young man/woman; **i giovani** young people

gio'vare [dʒo'vare] vi **~ a** (essere utile) to be useful to; (far bene) to be good for ▷ vb impers (essere bene, utile) to be useful; **giovarsi di qc** to make use of sth

giovedì [dʒove'di] sm inv Thursday; **di o il ~** on Thursdays

gioventù [dʒoven'tu] sf (periodo) youth; (i giovani) young people pl, youth

G.I.P. [dʒip] sigla m inv (= Giudice per le Indagini Preliminari) judge for preliminary enquiries

gira'dischi [dʒira'diski] sm inv record player

gi'raffa [dʒi'raffa] sf giraffe

gi'rare [dʒi'rare] vt (far ruotare) to turn; (percorrere, visitare) to go round; (Cinema) to shoot; to make; (Comm) to endorse ▷ vi to turn; (più veloce) to spin; (andare in giro) to wander, go around; **girarsi** vpr to turn; **~ attorno a** to go round; to revolve round; **al prossimo incrocio giri a destra/sinistra** turn right/left at the next junction; **far ~ la testa a qn** to make sb dizzy; (fig) to turn sb's head

girar'rosto [dʒirar'rɔsto] sm (Cuc) spit

gira'sole [dʒira'sole] sm sunflower

gi'revole [dʒi'revole] ag revolving, turning

gi'rino [dʒi'rino] sm tadpole

'giro ['dʒiro] sm (circuito, cerchio) circle; (di chiave, manovella) turn; (viaggio) tour, excursion; (passeggiata) stroll, walk; (in macchina) drive; (in bicicletta) ride; (Sport: della pista) lap; (di denaro) circulation; (Carte) hand; (Tecn) revolution; **prendere in ~ qn** (fig) to pull sb's leg; **fare un ~** to go for a walk (o a drive o a ride); **andare in ~** to go about, walk around; **a stretto ~ di posta** by return of post; **nel ~ di un mese** in a month's time; **essere nel ~** (fig) to belong to a circle (of friends); **giro d'affari** (Comm) turnover; **giro di parole** circumlocution; **giro di prova** (Aut) test drive; **giro turistico** sightseeing tour; **giro'collo** sm **a girocollo** crew-neck cpd

gironzo'lare [dʒirondzo'lare] vi to stroll about

'gita ['dʒita] sf excursion, trip; **fare una ~** to go for a trip, go on an outing

gi'tano, -a [dʒi'tano] sm/f gipsy

giù [dʒu] av down; (dabbasso) downstairs; **in ~** downwards, down; **~ di lì** (pressappoco) thereabouts; **~ per, cadere ~ per le scale** to fall down the stairs; **bambini dai 6 anni in ~** children aged 6 and under; **essere ~** (fig: di salute) to be run down; (: di spirito) to be depressed

giub'botto [dʒub'bɔtto] *sm* jerkin; **giubbotto antiproiettile** bulletproof vest; **giubbotto salvagente** life jacket

giudi'care [dʒudi'kare] *vt* to judge; *(accusato)* to try; *(lite)* to arbitrate in; **~ qn/qc bello** to consider sb/sth (to be) beautiful

gi'udice ['dʒuditʃe] *sm* judge; **giudice conciliatore** justice of the peace; **giudice istruttore** examining (BRIT) *o* committing (US) magistrate; **giudice popolare** member of a jury

giu'dizio [dʒu'dittsjo] *sm* judgment; *(opinione)* opinion; *(Dir)* judgment, sentence; (: *processo)* trial; (: *verdetto)* verdict; **aver ~** to be wise *o* prudent; **citare in ~** to summons

gi'ugno ['dʒuɲɲo] *sm* June

gi'ungere ['dʒundʒere] *vi* to arrive ▷ *vt* *(mani ecc)* to join; **~ a** to arrive at, reach

gi'ungla ['dʒungla] *sf* jungle

gi'unsi ecc ['dʒunsi] *vb vedi* **giungere**

giura'mento [dʒura'mento] *sm* oath; **giuramento falso** perjury

giu'rare [dʒu'rare] *vt* to swear ▷ *vi* to swear, take an oath

giu'ria [dʒu'ria] *sf* jury

giu'ridico, -a, -ci, -che [dʒu'ridiko] *ag* legal

giustifi'care [dʒustifi'kare] *vt* to justify; **giustificazi'one** *sf* justification; *(Ins)* (note of) excuse

gius'tizia [dʒus'tittsja] *sf* justice; **giustizi'are** *vt* to execute, put to death

gi'usto, -a ['dʒusto] *ag (equo)* fair, just; *(vero)* true, correct; *(adatto)* right, suitable; *(preciso)* exact, correct ▷ *av (esattamente)* exactly, precisely; *(per l'appunto, appena)* just; **arrivare ~** to arrive just in time; **ho ~ bisogno di te** you're just the person I need

glaci'ale [gla'tʃale] *ag* glacial

gli [ʎi] *(davV, gn s impura, gn, pn, ps, x, z) det mpl* the ▷ *pron (a lui)* to him; *(a esso)* to it; *(in coppia con lo, la, li, le, ne: a lui, a lei, a loro ecc)*: **~ele do** I'm giving them to him *(o* her *o* them); *vedi anche* **il**

glo'bale *ag* overall

'globo *sm* globe

'globulo *sm (Anat)*: **globulo rosso/bianco** red/white corpuscle

'gloria *sf* glory

'gnocchi ['ɲɔkki] *smpl (Cuc)* small dumplings made of semolina pasta or potato

'gobba *sf (Anat)* hump; *(protuberanza)* bump

'gobbo, -a *ag* hunchbacked; *(ricurvo)* round-shouldered ▷ *sm/f* hunchback

'goccia, -ce ['gottʃa] *sf* drop; **goccio'lare**

vi, vt to drip

go'dere *vi (compiacersi)*: **~ (di)** to be delighted (at), rejoice (at); *(trarre vantaggio)*: **~ di** to benefit from ▷ *vt* to enjoy; **godersi la vita** to enjoy life; **godersela** to have a good time, enjoy o.s.

godrò ecc *vb vedi* **godere**

'goffo, -a *ag* clumsy, awkward

'gola *sf (Anat)* throat; *(golosità)* gluttony, greed; *(di camino)* flue; *(di monte)* gorge; **fare ~** *(anche fig)* to tempt

golf *sm inv (Sport)* golf; *(maglia)* cardigan

'golfo *sm* gulf

go'loso, -a *ag* greedy

gomi'tata *sf* **dare una ~ a qn** to elbow sb; **farsi avanti a (forza o furia di) gomitate** to elbow one's way through; **fare a gomitate per qc** to fight to get sth

'gomito *sm* elbow; *(di strada ecc)* sharp bend

go'mitolo *sm* ball

'gomma *sf* rubber; *(per cancellare)* rubber, eraser; *(di veicolo)* tyre (BRIT), tire (US); **gomma americana** *o* **da masticare** chewing gum; **gomma a terra** flat tyre (BRIT) *o* tire (US); **ho una ~ a terra** I've got a flat tyre; **gom'mone** *sm* rubber dinghy

gonfi'are *vt (pallone)* to blow up, inflate; *(dilatare, ingrossare)* to swell; *(fig: notizia)* to exaggerate; **gonfiarsi** *vpr* to swell; *(fiume)* to rise; **'gonfio, -a** *ag* swollen; *(stomaco)* bloated; *(vela)* full; **gonfi'ore** *sm* swelling

'gonna *sf* skirt; **gonna pantalone** culottes *pl*

'gorgo, -ghi *sm* whirlpool

gorgogli'are [gorgoʎ'ʎare] *vi* to gurgle

go'rilla *sm inv* gorilla; *(guardia del corpo)* bodyguard

'gotico, -a, ci, che *ag, sm* Gothic

'gotta *sf* gout

gover'nare *vt (stato)* to govern, rule; *(pilotare, guidare)* to steer; *(bestiame)* to tend, look after

go'verno *sm* government

GPL *sigla m* (= *Gas di Petrolio Liquefatto)* LPG

GPS *sigla m* (= *Global Positioning System)* GPS

graci'dare [gratʃi'dare] *vi* to croak

'gracile ['gratʃile] *ag* frail, delicate

gradazi'one [gradat'tsjone] *sf (sfumatura)* gradation; **gradazione alcolica** alcoholic content, strength

gra'devole *ag* pleasant, agreeable

gradi'nata *sf* flight of steps; *(in teatro, stadio)* tiers *pl*

gra'dino *sm* step; *(Alpinismo)* foothold

gra'dire *vt (accettare con piacere)* to accept; *(desiderare)* to wish; **gradisce una tazza di tè?** would you like a cup of tea?

'grado *sm (Mat, Fisica ecc)* degree; *(stadio)*

degree, level; (*Mil*, *sociale*) rank; **essere in ~ di fare** to be in a position to do

gradu'ale *ag* gradual

graf'fetta *sf* paper clip

graffi'are *vt* to scratch; **graffiarsi** *vpr* to get scratched; (*con unghie*) to scratch o.s.

'graffio *sm* scratch

gra'fia *sf* spelling; (*scrittura*) handwriting

'grafico, -a, -ci, -che *ag* graphic ▷ *sm* graph; (*persona*) graphic designer

gram'matica, -che *sf* grammar

'grammo *sm* gram(me)

'grana *sf* (*granello, di minerali, corpi spezzati*) grain; (*fam: seccatura*) trouble; (: *soldi*) cash ▷ *sm inv* Parmesan (cheese)

gra'naio *sm* granary, barn

gra'nata *sf* (*proiettile*) grenade

Gran Bre'tagna [-bre'tanna] *sf* **la ~** Great Britain

'granchio ['grankjo] *sm* crab; (*fig*) blunder; **prendere un ~** (*fig*) to blunder

'grande (*qualche volta* **gran** + C, **grand'** + V) *ag* (*grosso, largo, vasto*) big, large; (*alto*) tall; (*lungo*) long; (*in sensi astratti*) great ▷ *sm/f* (*persona adulta*) adult, grown-up; (*chi ha ingegno e potenza*) great man/woman; **fare le cose in ~** to do things in style; **una gran bella donna** a very beautiful woman; **non è una gran cosa** *o* **un gran che** it's nothing special; **non ne so gran che** I don't know very much about it

gran'dezza [gran'dettsa] *sf* (*dimensione*) size; magnitude; (*fig*) greatness; **in ~ naturale** life-size(d)

grandi'nare *vb impers* to hail

'grandine *sf* hail

gra'nello *sm* (*di cereali, uva*) seed; (*di frutta*) pip; (*di sabbia, sale ecc*) grain

gra'nito *sm* granite

'grano *sm* (*in quasi tutti i sensi*) grain; (*frumento*) wheat; (*di rosario, collana*) bead; **grano di pepe** peppercorn

gran'turco *sm* maize

'grappa *sf* rough, strong brandy

'grappolo *sm* bunch, cluster

gras'setto *sm* (*Tip*) bold (type)

'grasso, -a *ag* fat; (*cibo*) fatty; (*pelle*) greasy; (*terreno*) rich; (*fig: guadagno, annata*) plentiful ▷ *sm* (*di persona, animale*) fat; (*sostanza che unge*) grease

'grata *sf* grating

gra'ticola *sf* grill

'gratis *av* free, for nothing

grati'tudine *sf* gratitude

'grato, -a *ag* grateful; (*gradito*) pleasant, agreeable

gratta'capo *sm* worry, headache

grattaci'elo [gratta'tʃɛlo] *sm* skyscraper

gratta e vinci ['gratta e 'vintʃi] *sm*

inv (*biglietto*) scratchcard; (*lotteria*) scratchcard lottery

grat'tare *vt* (*pelle*) to scratch; (*raschiare*) to scrape; (*pane, formaggio, carote*) to grate; (*fam: rubare*) to pinch ▷ *vi* (*stridere*) to grate; (*Aut*) to grind; **grattarsi** *vpr* to scratch o.s.; **grattarsi la pancia** (*fig*) to twiddle one's thumbs

grat'tugia, -gie [grat'tudʒa] *sf* grater; **grattugi'are** *vt* to grate; **pane grattugiato** breadcrumbs *pl*

gra'tuito, -a *ag* free; (*fig*) gratuitous

'grave *ag* (*danno, pericolo, peccato ecc*) grave, serious; (*responsabilità*) heavy, grave; (*contegno*) grave, solemn; (*voce, suono*) deep, low-pitched; (*Ling*): **accento ~** grave accent; **un malato ~** a person who is seriously ill

grave'mente *av* (*ammalato, ferito*) seriously

gravi'danza [gravi'dantsa] *sf* pregnancy

gravità *sf* seriousness; (*anche Fisica*) gravity

gra'voso, -a *ag* heavy, onerous

'grazia ['grattsja] *sf* grace; (*favore*) favour; (*Dir*) pardon

'grazie ['grattsje] *escl* thank you!; **~ mille!** *o* **tante!** *o* **infinite!** thank you very much!; **~ a** thanks to

grazi'oso, -a [grat'tsjoso] *ag* charming, delightful; (*gentile*) gracious

'Grecia ['grɛtʃa] *sf* **la ~** Greece; 'greco, -a, -ci, -che *ag*, *sm/f*, *sm* Greek

'gregge ['greddʒe] (*pl(f)* **-i**) *sm* flock

grembi'ule *sm* apron; (*sopravveste*) overall

'grembo *sm* lap; (*ventre della madre*) womb

'grezzo, -a ['greddzo] *ag* raw, unrefined; (*diamante*) rough, uncut; (*tessuto*) unbleached

gri'dare *vi* (*per chiamare*) to shout, cry (out); (*strillare*) to scream, yell ▷ *vt* to shout (out), yell (out); **~ aiuto** to cry *o* shout for help

'grido (*pl(m)* **-i**, *o pl(f)* **-a**) *sm* shout, cry; scream, yell; (*di animale*) cry; **di ~** famous

'grigio, -a, -gi, -gie ['gridʒo] *ag*, *sm* grey

'griglia ['griʎʎa] *sf* (*per arrostire*) grill; (*Elettr*) grid; (*inferriata*) grating; **alla ~** (*Cuc*) grilled

gril'letto *sm* trigger

'grillo *sm* (*Zool*) cricket; (*fig*) whim

'grinta *sf* grim expression; (*Sport*) fighting spirit

gris'sino *sm* bread-stick

Groen'landia *sf* **la ~** Greenland

gron'daia *sf* gutter

gron'dare *vi* to pour; (*essere bagnato*): **~ di** to be dripping with ▷ *vt* to drip with

'groppa *sf* (*di animale*) back, rump; (*fam*:

dell'uomo) back, shoulders pl

gros'sezza [gros'settsa] sf size; thickness

gros'sista, -i, -e sm/f (Comm) wholesaler

'grosso, -a ag big, large; (di spessore) thick; (grossolano: anche fig) coarse; (grave, insopportabile) serious, great; (tempo, mare) rough ▷ sm **il ~ di** the bulk of; **un pezzo ~** (fig) a VIP, a bigwig; **farla grossa** to do something very stupid; **dirle grosse** to tell tall stories; **sbagliarsi di ~** to be completely wrong

'grotta sf cave; grotto

grot'tesco, -a, -schi, -sche ag grotesque

gro'viglio [gro'viʎʎo] sm tangle; (fig) muddle

gru sf inv crane

'gruccia, -ce ['gruttʃa] sf (per camminare) crutch; (per abiti) coat-hanger

'grumo sm (di sangue) clot; (di farina ecc) lump

'gruppo sm group; **gruppo sanguigno** blood group

GSM sigla m (= Global System for Mobile Communication) GSM

guada'gnare [gwadaɲ'ɲare] vt (ottenere) to gain; (soldi, stipendio) to earn; (vincere) to win; (raggiungere) to reach

gua'dagno [gwa'daɲɲo] sm earnings pl; (Comm) profit; (vantaggio, utile) advantage, gain; **guadagno lordo/netto** gross/net earnings pl

gu'ado sm ford; **passare a ~** to ford

gu'ai escl **~ a te (o lui ecc)!** woe betide you (o him ecc)!

gu'aio sm trouble, mishap; (inconveniente) trouble, snag

gua'ire vi to whine, yelp

gu'ancia, -ce ['gwantʃa] sf cheek

guanci'ale [gwan'tʃale] sm pillow

gu'anto sm glove

guarda'linee sm inv (Sport) linesman

guar'dare vt (con lo sguardo: osservare) to look at; (film, televisione) to watch; (custodire) to look after, take care of ▷ vi to look; (badare): **~ a** to pay attention to; (luoghi: esser orientato): **~ a** to face; **guardarsi** vpr to look at o.s.; **guardarsi da** (astenersi) to refrain from; (stare in guardia) to beware of; **guardarsi dal fare** to take care not to do; **guarda di non sbagliare** try not to make a mistake; **~ a vista qn** to keep a close watch on sb

guarda'roba sm inv wardrobe; (locale) cloakroom

gu'ardia sf (individuo, corpo) guard; (sorveglianza) watch; **fare la ~ a qc/qn** to guard sth/sb; **stare in ~** (fig) to be on one's guard; **di ~** (medico) on call; **guardia carceraria** (prison) warder; **guardia del**

corpo bodyguard; **Guardia di finanza** (corpo) customs pl; (persona) customs officer; **guardia medica** emergency doctor service

guardi'ano, -a sm/f (di carcere) warder; (di villa ecc) caretaker; (di museo) custodian; (di zoo) keeper; **guardiano notturno** night watchman

guarigi'one [gwari'dʒone] sf recovery

gua'rire vt (persona, malattia) to cure; (ferita) to heal ▷ vi to recover, be cured; to heal (up)

guar'nire vt (ornare: abiti) to trim; (Cuc) to garnish

guasta'feste sm/f inv spoilsport

guastarsi vpr (cibo) to go bad; (meccanismo) to break down; (tempo) to change for the worse

gu'asto, -a ag (non funzionante) broken; (: telefono ecc) out of order; (andato a male) bad, rotten; (: dente) decayed, bad; (fig: corrotto) depraved ▷ sm breakdown; (avaria) failure; **guasto al motore** engine failure

gu'erra sf war; (tecnica: atomica, chimica ecc) warfare; **fare la ~ (a)** to wage war (against); **guerra mondiale** world war; **guerra preventiva** preventive war

'gufo sm owl

gu'ida sf (libro) guidebook; (persona) guide; (comando, direzione) guidance, direction; (Aut) driving; (tappeto: di tenda, cassetto) runner; **avete una ~ in italiano?** do you have a guidebook in Italian?; **c'è una ~ che parla italiano?** is there an Italian-speaking guide?; **guida a destra/a sinistra** (Aut) right-/left-hand drive; **guida telefonica** telephone directory; **guida turistica** tourist guide

gui'dare vt to guide; (squadra, rivolta) to lead; (auto) to drive; (aereo, nave) to pilot; **sai ~?** can you drive?; **guida'tore, -trice** sm/f (conducente) driver

guin'zaglio [gwin'tsaʎʎo] sm leash, lead

'guscio ['guʃʃo] sm shell

gus'tare vt (cibi) to taste; (: assaporare con piacere) to enjoy, savour; (fig) to enjoy, appreciate ▷ vi: **~ a** to please; **non mi**

gusta affatto I don't like it at all

'gusto sm taste; (sapore) flavour; (godimento) enjoyment; **che gusti avete?** which flavours do you have?; **al ~ di fragola** strawberry-flavoured; **mangiare di ~** to eat heartily; **prenderci ~: ci ha preso ~** he's acquired a taste for it, he's got to like it; **gus'toso, -a** ag tasty; (fig) agreeable

H, h ['akka] sf o m inv (lettera) H, h ▷ abbr (= ora) hr; (= etto, altezza) h; **H come hotel** ≈ H for Harry (BRIT), H for How (US)

ha, 'hai [a, ai] vb vedi **avere**

ha'cker [hæ'kəʳ] sm inv hacker

hall [hɔl] sf inv hall, foyer

hamburger [am'burger] sm inv (carne) hamburger; (panino) burger

'handicap ['handikap] sm inv handicap; **handicap'pato, -a** ag handicapped ▷ sm/f handicapped person, disabled person

'hanno ['anno] vb vedi **avere**

hard discount [ardi'kaunt] sm inv discount supermarket

hard disk [ar'disk] sm inv hard disk

hardware ['ardwer] sm inv hardware

hascisch [aʃ'ʃiʃ] sm hashish

Hawaii [a'vai] sfpl **le ~** Hawaii sg

help [ɛlp] sm inv (Inform) help

'herpes ['ɛrpes] sm (Med) herpes sg; **herpes zoster** shingles sg

'hi-fi ['haifai] sm inv, ag inv hi-fi

ho [ɔ] vb vedi **avere**

'hobby ['hɔbi] sm inv hobby

'hockey ['hɔki] sm hockey; **hockey su ghiaccio** ice hockey

home page ['houm'pɛidʒ] sf inv home page

Hong Kong ['ɔk̃ɔg] sf Hong Kong

'hostess ['houstis] sf inv air hostess (BRIT)

o stewardess
hot dog ['hɔtdɔg] *sm inv* hot dog
ho'tel *sm inv* hotel
humour ['hju:mǝ] *sm inv* (sense of)
humour
'humus *sm* humus
husky ['aski] *sm inv* (*cane*) husky *m inv*

i *det mpl* the
IC *abbr* (= *Intercity*) Intercity
ICI ['itʃi] *sigla f* (= *Imposta Comunale sugli Immobili*) ≈ Council Tax
i'cona *sf* (*Rel, Inform, fig*) icon
i'dea *sf* idea; (*opinione*) opinion, view; (*ideale*) ideal; **dare l'~ di** to seem, look like; **neanche** *o* **neppure per ~!** certainly not!; **idea fissa** obsession
ide'ale *ag, sm* ideal
ide'are *vt* (*immaginare*) to think up, conceive; (*progettare*) to plan
i'dentico, -a, -ci, -che *ag* identical
identifi'care *vt* to identify; **identificarsi** *vpr* **identificarsi (con)** to identify o.s. (with)
identità *sf inv* identity
ideolo'gia, -'gie [ideolo'dʒia] *sf* ideology
idio'matico, -a, -ci, -che *ag* idiomatic; **frase idiomatica** idiom
idi'ota, -i, -e *ag* idiotic ▷ *sm/f* idiot
'idolo *sm* idol
idoneità *sf* suitability
i'doneo, -a *ag* **~ a** suitable for, fit for; (*Mil*) fit for; (*qualificato*) qualified for
i'drante *sm* hydrant
idra'tante *ag* moisturizing ▷ *sm* moisturizer
i'draulico, -a, -ci, -che *ag* hydraulic ▷ *sm* plumber

idroe'lettrico, -a, -ci, -che *ag* hydroelectric

i'drofilo, -a *ag vedi* **cotone**

i'drogeno [i'drɔdʒeno] *sm* hydrogen

idrovo'lante *sm* seaplane

i'ena *sf* hyena

i'eri *av, sm* yesterday; **il giornale di ~** yesterday's paper; **~ l'altro** the day before yesterday; **~ sera** yesterday evening

igi'ene [i'dʒɛne] *sf* hygiene; **igiene pubblica** public health; **igi'enico, -a, -ci, -he** *ag* hygienic; (*salubre*) healthy

i'gnaro, -a [iɲ'ɲaro] *ag* **~ di** unaware of, ignorant of

i'gnobile [iɲ'ɲɔbile] *ag* despicable, vile

igno'rante [iɲɲo'rante] *ag* ignorant

igno'rare [iɲɲo'rare] *vt* (*non sapere, conoscere*) to be ignorant o unaware of, not to know; (*fingere di non vedere, sentire*) to ignore

i'gnoto, -a [iɲ'ɲɔto] *ag* unknown

PAROLA CHIAVE

il (*pl(m)* **i**; *diventa* **lo** (*pl* **gli**) *davanti a s impura, gn, pn, ps, x, z; f* **la** (*pl* **le**)) *det m* **1** the; **il libro/lo studente/l'acqua** the book/the student/the water; **gli scolari** the pupils

2 (*astrazione*): **il coraggio/l'amore/la giovinezza** courage/love/youth

3 (*tempo*): **il mattino/la sera** in the morning/evening; **il venerdì** *ecc* (*abitualmente*) on Fridays *ecc*; (*quel giorno*) on (the) Friday *ecc*; **la settimana prossima** next week

4 (*distributivo*) a, an; **2 euro il chilo/paio** 2 euros a o per kilo/pair

5 (*partitivo*) some, any; **hai messo lo zucchero?** have you added sugar?; **hai comprato il latte?** did you buy (some o any) milk?

6 (*possesso*): **aprire gli occhi** to open one's eyes; **rompersi la gamba** to break one's leg; **avere i capelli neri/il naso rosso** to have dark hair/a red nose

7 (*con nomi propri*): **il Petrarca** Petrarch; **il Presidente Bush** President Bush; **dov'è la Francesca?** where's Francesca?

8 (*con nomi geografici*): **il Tevere** the Tiber; **l'Italia** Italy; **il Regno Unito** the United Kingdom; **l'Everest** Everest

ille'gale *ag* illegal

illeg'gibile [illed'dʒibile] *ag* illegible

ille'gittimo, -a [ille'dʒittimo] *ag* illegitimate

il'leso, -a *ag* unhurt, unharmed

illimi'tato, -a *ag* boundless; unlimited

ill.mo *abbr* = **illustrissimo**

il'ludere *vt* to deceive, delude; **illudersi** *vpr* to deceive o.s., delude o.s.

illumi'nare *vt* to light up, illuminate; (*fig*) to enlighten; **illuminarsi** *vpr* to light up; **~ a giorno** to floodlight; **illuminazi'one** *sf* lighting; illumination; floodlighting; (*fig*) flash of inspiration

il'lusi *ecc vb vedi* **illudere**

illusi'one *sf* illusion; **farsi delle illusioni** to delude o.s.; **illusione ottica** optical illusion

il'luso, -a *pp di* **illudere**

illus'trare *vt* to illustrate; **illustrazi'one** *sf* illustration

il'lustre *ag* eminent, renowned; **illus'trissimo, -a** *ag* (*negli indirizzi*) very revered

imbal'laggio [imbal'laddʒo] *sm* packing *no pl*

imbal'lare *vt* to pack; (*Aut*) to race

imbalsa'mare *vt* to embalm

imbambo'lato, -a *ag* (*sguardo*) vacant, blank

imbaraz'zante [imbarat'tsante] *ag* embarrassing, awkward

imbaraz'zare [imbarat'tsare] *vt* (*mettere a disagio*) to embarrass; (*ostacolare movimenti*) to hamper

imbaraz'zato, -a [imbarat'tsato] *ag* embarrassed; **avere lo stomaco ~** to have an upset stomach

imba'razzo [imba'rattso] *sm* (*disagio*) embarrassment; (*perplessità*) puzzlement, bewilderment; **imbarazzo di stomaco** indigestion

imbar'care *vt* (*passeggeri*) to embark; (*merci*) to load; **imbarcarsi** *vpr* **imbarcarsi su** to board; **imbarcarsi per l'America** to sail for America; **imbarcarsi in** (*fig: affare ecc*) to embark on

imbarcazi'one [imbarkat'tsjone] *sf* (small) boat, (small) craft *inv*; **imbarcazione di salvataggio** lifeboat

im'barco, -chi *sm* embarkation; loading; boarding; (*banchina*) landing stage

imbas'tire *vt* (*cucire*) to tack; (*fig: abbozzare*) to sketch, outline

im'battersi *vpr* **~ in** (*incontrare*) to bump o run into

imbat'tibile *ag* unbeatable, invincible

imbavagli'are [imbavaʎ'ʎare] *vt* to gag

imbe'cille [imbe'tʃille] *ag* idiotic ▷ *sm/f* idiot; (*Med*) imbecile

imbian'care *vt* to whiten; (*muro*) to whitewash ▷ *vi* to become o turn white

imbian'chino [imbjan'kino] *sm* (house) painter, painter and decorator

imboc'care *vt* (*bambino*) to feed; (*entrare: strada*) to enter, turn into

imbocca'tura sf mouth; (di strada, porto) entrance; (Mus, del morso) mouthpiece

imbos'cata sf ambush

imbottigli'are [imbottiʎˈʎare] vt to bottle; (Naut) to blockade; (Mil) to hem in; **imbottigliarsi** vpr to be stuck in a traffic jam

imbot'tire vt to stuff; (giacca) to pad; **imbottirsi** vpr **imbottirsi di** (rimpinzarsi) to stuff o.s. with; **imbot'tito, -a** ag stuffed; (giacca) padded; **panino imbottito** filled roll

imbra'nato, -a ag clumsy, awkward ▷ sm/f clumsy person

imbrogli'are [imbroʎˈʎare] vt to mix up; (fig: raggirare) to deceive, cheat; (: confondere) to confuse, mix up; **imbrogli'one, -a** sm/f cheat, swindler

imbronci'ato, -a ag sulky

imbu'care vt to post; **dove posso ~ queste cartoline?** where can I post these cards?

imbur'rare vt to butter

im'buto sm funnel

imi'tare vt to imitate; (riprodurre) to copy; (assomigliare) to look like

immagazzi'nare [immagaddziˈnare] vt to store

immagi'nare [immadʒiˈnare] vt to imagine; (supporre) to suppose; (inventare) to invent; **s'immagini!** don't mention it!, not at all!; **immaginazi'one** sf imagination; (cosa immaginata) fancy

im'magine [imˈmadʒine] sf image; (rappresentazione grafica, mentale) picture

imman'cabile ag certain; unfailing

im'mane ag (smisurato) enormous; (spaventoso) terrible

immangi'abile [immanˈdʒabile] ag inedible

immatrico'lare vt to register; **immatricolarsi** vpr (Ins) to matriculate, enrol

imma'turo, -a ag (frutto) unripe; (persona) immature; (prematuro) premature

immedesi'marsi vpr ~ **in** to identify with

immediata'mente av immediately, at once

immedi'ato, -a ag immediate

im'menso, -a ag immense

im'mergere [imˈmɛrdʒere] vt to immerse, plunge; **immergersi** vpr to plunge; (sommergibile) to dive, submerge; (dedicarsi a): **immergersi in** to immerse o.s. in

immeri'tato, -a ag undeserved

immersi'one sf immersion; dive; (di sommergibile) submersion, dive; (di palombaro) dive

im'mettere vt ~ **(in)** to introduce (into); ~ **dati in un computer** to enter data on a computer

immi'grato, -a sm/f immigrant

immi'nente ag imminent

immischi'arsi vpr ~ **in** to interfere o meddle in

im'mobile ag motionless, still; **immobili'are** ag (Dir) property cpd

immon'dizia [immonˈdittsja] sf dirt, filth; (spesso al pl: spazzatura, rifiuti) rubbish no pl, refuse no pl

immo'rale ag immoral

immor'tale ag immortal

im'mune ag (esente) exempt; (Med, Dir) immune

immu'tabile ag immutable; unchanging

impacchet'tare [impakketˈtare] vt to pack up

impacci'ato, -a ag awkward, clumsy; (imbarazzato) embarrassed

im'pacco, -chi sm (Med) compress

impadro'nirsi vpr ~ **di** to seize, take possession of; (fig: apprendere a fondo) to master

impa'gabile ag priceless

impa'lato, -a ag (fig) stiff as a board

impalca'tura sf scaffolding

impalli'dire vi to turn pale; (fig) to fade

impa'nato, -a ag (Cuc) coated in breadcrumbs

impanta'narsi vpr to sink (in the mud); (fig) to get bogged down

impappi'narsi vpr to stammer, falter

impa'rare vt ~ to learn

impar'tire vt to bestow, give

imparzi'ale [imparˈtsjale] ag impartial, unbiased

impas'sibile ag impassive

impas'tare vt (pasta) to knead

impastic'carsi vpr to pop pills

im'pasto sm (l'impastare: di pane) kneading; (: di cemento) mixing; (pasta) dough; (anche fig) mixture

im'patto sm impact

impau'rire vt to scare, frighten ▷ vi (anche: **impaurirsi**) to become scared o frightened

impazi'ente [impaˈtsjente] ag impatient

impaz'zata [impatˈtsata] sf **all'~** (precipitosamente) at breakneck speed

impaz'zire [impatˈtsire] vi to go mad; ~ **per qn/qc** to be crazy about sb/sth

impec'cabile ag impeccable

impedi'mento sm obstacle, hindrance

impe'dire vt (vietare): ~ **a qn di fare** to prevent sb from doing; (ostruire) to obstruct; (*impacciare*) to hamper, hinder

impegnarsi *vpr* (*vincolarsi*): **~ a fare** to undertake to do; (*mettersi risolutamente*): **~ in qc** to devote o.s. to sth; **~ con qn** (*accordarsi*) to come to an agreement with sb

impegna'tivo, -a *ag* binding; (*lavoro*) demanding, exacting

impe'gnato, -a *ag* (*occupato*) busy; (*fig: romanzo, autore*) committed, engagé

im'pegno [im'peɲɲo] *sm* (*obbligo*) obligation; (*promessa*) promise, pledge; (*zelo*) diligence, zeal; (*compito, d'autore*) commitment

impel'lente *ag* pressing, urgent

impen'narsi *vpr* (*cavallo*) to rear up; (*Aer*) to nose up; (*fig*) to bridle

impensie'rire *vt* to worry; **impensierirsi** *vpr* to worry

impera'tivo, -a *ag, sm* imperative

impera'tore, -'trice *sm/f* emperor/ empress

imperdo'nabile *ag* unforgivable, unpardonable

imper'fetto, -a *ag* imperfect ▷ *sm* (*Ling*) imperfect (tense)

imperi'ale *ag* imperial

imperi'oso, -a *ag* (*persona*) imperious; (*motivo, esigenza*) urgent, pressing

imperme'abile *ag* waterproof ▷ *sm* raincoat

im'pero *sm* empire; (*forza, autorità*) rule, control

imperso'nale *ag* impersonal

imperso'nare *vt* to personify; (*Teatro*) to play, act (the part of)

imperter'rito, -a *ag* fearless, undaunted; impassive

imperti'nente *ag* impertinent

'impeto *sm* (*moto, forza*) force, impetus; (*assalto*) onslaught; (*fig: impulso*) impulse; (: *slancio*) transport; **con ~** energetically; vehemently

impet'tito, -a *ag* stiff, erect

impetu'oso, -a *ag* (*vento*) strong, raging; (*persona*) impetuous

impi'anto *sm* (*installazione*) installation; (*apparecchiature*) plant; (*sistema*) system; **impianto elettrico** wiring; **impianto di risalita** (*Sci*) ski lift; **impianto di riscaldamento** heating system; **impianto sportivo** sports complex

impic'care *vt* to hang; **impiccarsi** *vpr* to hang o.s.

impicci'arsi [impit'tʃarsi] *vpr* (*immischiarsi*): **~ (in)** to meddle (in); **impicciati degli affari tuoi!** mind your own business!

impicci'one, -a [impit'tʃone] *sm/f* busybody

impie'gare *vt* (*usare*) to use, employ; (*spendere: denaro, tempo*) to spend; (*investire*) to invest; **impie'gato, -a** *sm/f* employee

impi'ego, -ghi *sm* (*uso*) use; (*occupazione*) employment; (*posto di lavoro*) (regular) job, post; (*Econ*) investment

impieto'sire *vt* to move to pity; **impietosirsi** *vpr* to be moved to pity

impigli'arsi *vpr* to get caught up *o* entangled

impi'grirsi *vpr* to grow lazy

impli'care *vt* to imply; (*coinvolgere*) to involve

im'plicito, -a [im'plitʃito] *ag* implicit

implo'rare *vt* to implore; (*pietà ecc*) to beg for

impolve'rarsi *vpr* to get dusty

im'pone *ecc vb vedi* **imporre**

impo'nente *ag* imposing, impressive

im'pongo *ecc vb vedi* **imporre**

impo'nibile *ag* taxable ▷ *sm* taxable income

impopo'lare *ag* unpopular

im'porre *vt* to impose; (*costringere*) to force, make; (*far valere*) to impose, enforce; **imporsi** *vpr* (*persona*) to assert o.s.; (*cosa: rendersi necessario*) to become necessary; (*aver successo: moda, attore*) to become popular; **~ a qn di fare** to force sb to do, make sb do

impor'tante *ag* important; **impor'tanza** *sf* importance; **dare importanza a qc** to attach importance to sth; **darsi importanza** to give o.s. airs

impor'tare *vt* (*introdurre dall'estero*) to import ▷ *vi* to matter, be important ▷ *vb impers* (*essere necessario*) to be necessary; (*interessare*) to matter; **non importa!** it doesn't matter!; **non me ne importa!** I don't care!

im'porto *sm* (*total*) amount

importu'nare *vt* to bother

im'posi *ecc vb vedi* **imporre**

imposizi'one [impozit'tsjone] *sf* imposition; order, command; (*onere, imposta*) tax

imposses'sarsi *vpr* **~ di** to seize, take possession of

impos'sibile *ag* impossible; **fare l'~** to do one's utmost, do all one can

im'posta *sf* (*di finestra*) shutter; (*tassa*) tax; **imposta sul reddito** income tax; **imposta sul valore aggiunto** value added tax (*BRIT*), sales tax (*US*)

impos'tare *vt* (*imbucare*) to post; (*preparare*) to plan, set out; (*avviare*) to begin, start off; (*voce*) to pitch

impostazi'one [impostat'tsjone] *sf*
(*di lettera*) posting (BRIT), mailing (US);
(*di problema, questione*) formulation,
statement; (*di lavoro*) organization,
planning; (*di attività*) setting up; (*Mus:
di voce*) pitch; **impostazioni** *sfpl* (*di
computer*) settings

impo'tente *ag* weak, powerless; (*anche
Med*) impotent

imprati'cabile *ag* (*strada*) impassable;
(*campo da gioco*) unplayable

impre'care *vi* to curse, swear; **~ contro** to
hurl abuse at

imprecazi'one [imprekat'tsjone] *sf*
abuse, curse

impre'gnare [impreɲ'ɲare] *vt* **~ (di)**
(*imbevere*) to soak o impregnate (with);
(*riempire*) to fill (with)

imprendi'tore *sm* (*industriale*)
entrepreneur; (*appaltatore*) contractor;
piccolo ~ small businessman

im'presa *sf* (*iniziativa*) enterprise; (*azione*)
exploit; (*azienda*) firm, concern

impressio'nante *ag* impressive;
upsetting

impressio'nare *vt* to impress; (*turbare*)
to upset; (*Fot*) to expose; **impressionarsi** *vpr*
to be easily upset

impressi'one *sf* impression; (*fig:
sensazione*) sensation, feeling; (*stampa*)
printing; **fare ~** (*colpire*) to impress;
(*turbare*) to frighten, upset; **fare
buona/cattiva ~ a** to make a good/bad
impression on

impreve'dibile *ag* unforeseeable;
(*persona*) unpredictable

impre'visto, -a *ag* unexpected,
unforeseen ▷ *sm* unforeseen event; **salvo
imprevisti** unless anything unexpected
happens

imprigio'nare [impridʒo'nare] *vt* to
imprison

impro'babile *ag* improbable, unlikely

im'pronta *sf* imprint, impression, sign;
(*di piede, mano*) print; (*fig*) mark, stamp;
impronta digitale fingerprint

improvvisa'mente *av* suddenly;
unexpectedly

improvvi'sare *vt* to improvise

improv'viso, -a *ag* (*imprevisto*)
unexpected; (*subitaneo*) sudden; **all'~**
unexpectedly; suddenly

impru'dente *ag* unwise, rash

impu'gnare [impuɲ'ɲare] *vt* to grasp,
grip; (*Dir*) to contest

impul'sivo, -a *ag* impulsive

im'pulso *sm* impulse

impun'tarsi *vpr* to stop dead, refuse to
budge; (*fig*) to be obstinate

impu'tato, -a *sm/f* (*Dir*) accused,
defendant

 PAROLA CHIAVE

in (*in + il* = **nel**, *in + lo* = **nello**, *in + l'* = **nell'**, *in
+ la* = **nella**, *in + i* = **nei**, *in + gli* = **negli**, *in + le*
= **nelle**) *prep* **1** (*stato in luogo*) in; **vivere in
Italia/città** to live in Italy/town; **essere in
casa/ufficio** to be at home/the office; **se
fossi in te** if I were you

2 (*moto a luogo*) to; (: *dentro*) into; **andare
in Germania/città** to go to Germany/
town; **andare in ufficio** to go to the office;
entrare in macchina/casa to get into the
car/go into the house

3 (*tempo*) in; **nel 1989** in 1989; **in giugno/
estate** in June/summer

4 (*modo, maniera*) in; **in silenzio** in silence;
in abito da sera in evening dress; **in
guerra** at war; **in vacanza** on holiday;
Maria Bianchi in Rossi Maria Rossi née
Bianchi

5 (*mezzo*) by; **viaggiare in autobus/treno**
to travel by bus/train

6 (*materia*) made of; **in marmo** made of
marble, marble *cpd*; **una collana in oro** a
gold necklace

7 (*misura*) in; **siamo in quattro** there are
four of us; **in tutto** in all

8 (*fine*): **dare in dono** to give as a gift;
spende tutto in alcool he spends all his
money on drink; **in onore di** in honour of

inabi'tabile *ag* uninhabitable

inacces'sibile [inattʃes'sibile] *ag* (*luogo*)
inaccessible; (*persona*) unapproachable

inaccet'tabile [inattʃet'tabile] *ag*
unacceptable

ina'datto, -a *ag* **~ (a)** unsuitable o unfit
(for)

inadegu'ato, -a *ag* inadequate

inaffi'dabile *ag* unreliable

inami'dato, -a *ag* starched

inar'care *vt* (*schiena*) to arch; (*sopracciglia*)
to raise

inaspet'tato, -a *ag* unexpected

inas'prire *vt* (*disciplina*) to tighten up,
make harsher; (*carattere*) to embitter;
inasprirsi *vpr* to become harsher; to
become bitter; to become worse

inattac'cabile *ag* (*anche fig*) unassailable;
(*alibi*) cast-iron

inatten'dibile *ag* unreliable

inat'teso, -a *ag* unexpected

inattu'abile *ag* impracticable

inau'dito, -a *ag* unheard of

inaugu'rare *vt* to inaugurate, open;
(*monumento*) to unveil

inaugurazi'one [inaugurat'tsjone] *sf* inauguration; unveiling

incal'lito, -a *ag* calloused; *(fig)* hardened, inveterate; *(: insensibile)* hard

incande'scente [inkandeʃʃɛnte] *ag* incandescent, white-hot

incan'tare *vt* to enchant, bewitch; **incantarsi** *vpr (rimanere intontito)* to be spellbound; to be in a daze; *(meccanismo: bloccarsi)* to jam; **incan'tevole** *ag* charming, enchanting

in'canto *sm* spell, charm, enchantment; *(asta)* auction; **come per ~** as if by magic; **mettere all'~** to put up for auction

inca'pace [inka'patʃe] *ag* incapable

incarce'rare [inkartʃe'rare] *vt* to imprison

incari'care *vt* **~ qn di fare** to give sb the responsibility of doing; **incaricarsi di** to take care o charge of

in'carico, -chi *sm* task, job

incarta'mento *sm* dossier, file

incar'tare *vt* to wrap (in paper)

incas'sare *vt (merce)* to pack (in cases); *(gemma: incastonare)* to set; *(Econ: riscuotere)* to collect; *(Pugilato: colpi)* to take, stand up to; **in'casso** *sm* cashing, encashment; *(introito)* takings *pl*

incas'trare *vt* to fit in, insert; *(fig: intrappolare)* to catch; **incastrarsi** *vpr (combaciare)* to fit together; *(restare bloccato)* to become stuck

incate'nare *vt* to chain up

in'cauto, -a *ag* imprudent, rash

inca'vato, -a *ag* hollow; *(occhi)* sunken

incendi'are [intʃen'djare] *vt* to set fire to; **incendiarsi** *vpr* to catch fire, burst into flames

in'cendio [in'tʃendjo] *sm* fire

inceneri'tore [intʃeneri'tore] *sm* incinerator

in'censo [in'tʃenso] *sm* incense

incensu'rato, -a [intʃensu'rato] *ag (Dir)*: **essere ~** to have a clean record

incenti'vare [intʃenti'vare] *vt (produzione, vendite)* to boost; *(persona)* to motivate

incen'tivo [intʃen'tivo] *sm* incentive

incepparsi *vpr* to jam

incer'tezza [intʃer'tettsa] *sf* uncertainty

in'certo, -a [in'tʃerto] *ag* uncertain; *(irresoluto)* undecided, hesitating ▷ *sm* uncertainty

in'cetta [in'tʃetta] *sf* buying up; **fare ~ di qc** to buy up sth

inchi'esta [in'kjesta] *sf* investigation, inquiry

inchinarsi *vpr* to bend down; *(per riverenza)* to bow; *(: donna)* to curtsy

inchio'dare [inkjo'dare] *vt* to nail (down); **~ la macchina** *(Aut)* to jam on the brakes

inchi'ostro [in'kjɔstro] *sm* ink; **inchiostro simpatico** invisible ink

inciam'pare [intʃam'pare] *vi* to trip, stumble

inci'dente [intʃi'dɛnte] *sm* accident; **ho avuto un ~** I've had an accident; **incidente automobilistico** o **d'auto** car accident; **incidente diplomatico** diplomatic incident

in'cidere [in'tʃidere] *vi* **~ su** to bear upon, affect ▷ *vt (tagliare incavando)* to cut into; *(Arte)* to engrave; to etch; *(canzone)* to record

in'cinta [in'tʃinta] *ag f* pregnant

incipri'are [intʃi'prjare] *vt* to powder; **incipriarsi** ▷ *vpr* to powder one's face

in'circa [in'tʃirka] *av* **all'~** more or less, very nearly

in'cisi ecc [in'tʃizi] *vb vedi* **incidere**

incisi'one [intʃi'zjone] *sf* cut; *(disegno)* engraving; etching; *(registrazione)* recording; *(Med)* incision

in'ciso, -a [in'tʃizo] *pp di* **incidere** ▷ *sm* **per ~** incidentally, by the way

inci'tare [intʃi'tare] *vt* to incite

inci'vile [intʃi'vile] *ag* uncivilized; *(villano)* impolite

incl. *abbr* (= *incluso*) encl.

incli'nare *vt* to tilt; **inclinarsi** *vpr (barca)* to list; *(aereo)* to bank

in'cludere *vt* to include; *(accludere)* to enclose; **in'cluso, -a** *pp di* **includere** ▷ *ag* included; enclosed

incoe'rente *ag* incoherent; *(contraddittorio)* inconsistent

in'cognita [in'kɔɲɲita] *sf (Mat, fig)* unknown quantity

in'cognito, -a [in'kɔɲɲito] *ag* unknown ▷ *sm* **in ~** incognito

incol'lare *vt* to glue, gum; *(unire con colla)* to stick together

inco'lore *ag* colourless

incol'pare *vt* **~ qn di** to charge sb with

in'colto, -a *ag (terreno)* uncultivated; *(trascurato: capelli)* neglected; *(persona)* uneducated

in'colume *ag* safe and sound, unhurt

incom'benza [inkom'bɛntsa] *sf* duty, task

in'combere *vi (sovrastare minacciando)*: **~ su** to threaten, hang over

incominci'are [inkomin'tʃare] *vi, vt* to begin, start

incompe'tente *ag* incompetent

incompi'uto, -a *ag* unfinished, incomplete

incom'pleto, -a *ag* incomplete

incompren'sibile *ag* incomprehensible

inconce'pibile [inkontʃe'pibile] *ag*

inconceivable

inconcili'abile [inkontʃi'ljabile] *ag*
irreconcilable

inconclu'dente *ag* inconclusive; (*persona*)
ineffectual

incondizio'nato, -a [inkondittsjo'nato]
ag unconditional

inconfon'dibile *ag* unmistakable

inconsa'pevole *ag* **~ di** unaware of,
ignorant of

in'conscio, -a, -sci, -sce [in'kɔnʃo]
ag unconscious ▷ *sm* (*Psic*): **l'~** the
unconscious

inconsis'tente *ag* insubstantial;
unfounded

inconsu'eto, -a *ag* unusual

incon'trare *vt* to meet; (*difficoltà*) to meet
with; **incontrarsi** *vpr* to meet

in'contro *av* **~ a** (*verso*) towards ▷ *sm*
meeting; (*Sport*) match; meeting;
incontro di calcio football match

inconveni'ente *sm* drawback, snag

incoraggia'mento [inkoraddʒa'mento]
sm encouragement

incoraggi'are [inkorad'dʒare] *vt* to
encourage

incornici'are [inkorni'tʃare] *vt* to frame

incoro'nare *vt* to crown

in'correre *vi* **~ in** to meet with, run into

incosci'ente [inkoʃʃente] *ag* (*inconscio*)
unconscious; (*irresponsabile*) reckless,
thoughtless

incre'dibile *ag* incredible, unbelievable

in'credulo, -a *ag* incredulous, disbelieving

incremen'tare *vt* to increase; (*dar sviluppo
a*) to promote

incre'mento *sm* (*sviluppo*) development;
(*aumento numerico*) increase, growth

incresci'oso, -a [inkreʃʃoso] *ag* (*incidente
ecc*) regrettable

incrimi'nare *vt* (*Dir*) to charge

incri'nare *vt* to crack; (*fig: rapporti,
amicizia*) to cause to deteriorate;
incrinarsi *vpr* to crack; to deteriorate

incroci'are [inkro'tʃare] *vt* to cross;
(*incontrare*) to meet ▷ *vi* (*Naut, Aer*) to
cruise; **incrociarsi** *vpr* (*strade*) to cross,
intersect; (*persone, veicoli*) to pass each
other; **~ le braccia/le gambe** to fold one's
arms/cross one's legs

in'crocio [in'krotʃo] *sm* (*anche Ferr*)
crossing; (*di strade*) crossroads

incuba'trice [inkuba'tritʃe] *sf* incubator

'incubo *sm* nightmare

incu'rabile *ag* incurable

incu'rante *ag* **~ (di)** heedless (of), careless
(of)

incurio'sire *vt* to make curious;
incuriosirsi *vpr* to become curious

incursi'one *sf* raid

incur'vare *vt* to bend, curve; **incurvarsi**
vpr to bend, curve

incusto'dito, -a *ag* unguarded,
unattended

in'cutere *vt* **~ timore/rispetto a qn** to
strike fear into sb/command sb's respect

'indaco *sm* indigo

indaffa'rato, -a *ag* busy

inda'gare *vt* to investigate

in'dagine [in'dadʒine] *sf* investigation,
inquiry; (*ricerca*) research, study; **indagine
di mercato** market survey

indebi'tarsi *vpr* to run o get into debt

indebo'lire *vt, vi* (*anche*: **indebolirsi**) to
weaken

inde'cente [inde'tʃɛnte] *ag* indecent

inde'ciso, -a [inde'tʃizo] *ag* indecisive;
(*irresoluto*) undecided

indefi'nito, -a *ag* (*anche Ling*) indefinite;
(*impreciso, non determinato*) undefined

in'degno, -a [in'deɲɲo] *ag* (*atto*)
shameful; (*persona*) unworthy

indemoni'ato, -a *ag* possessed (by the
devil)

in'denne *ag* unhurt, uninjured

indenniz'zare [indennid'dzare] *vt* to
compensate

indetermina'tivo, -a *ag* (*Ling*) indefinite

'India *sf* **l'~** India; **indi'ano, -a** *ag* Indian
▷ *sm/f* (*d'India*) Indian; (*d'America*) Native
American, (American) Indian

indi'care *vt* (*mostrare*) to show, indicate;
(: *col dito*) to point to, point out;
(*consigliare*) to suggest, recommend;
indica'tivo, -a *ag* indicative ▷ *sm*
(*Ling*) indicative (mood); **indicazi'one**
sf indication; (*informazione*) piece of
information

'indice ['inditʃe] *sm* index; (*fig*) sign;
(*dito*) index finger, forefinger; **indice di
gradimento** (*Radio, TV*) popularity rating

indicherò *ecc* [indike'rɔ] *vb vedi* **indicare**

indi'cibile [indi'tʃibile] *ag* inexpressible

indietreggi'are [indietred'dʒare] *vi* to
draw back, retreat

indi'etro *av* back; (*guardare*) behind, back;
(*andare, cadere: anche:* **all'~**) backwards;
rimanere ~ to be left behind; **essere ~** (*col
lavoro*) to be behind; (*orologio*) to be slow;
rimandare qc ~ to send sth back

indi'feso, -a *ag* (*città ecc*) undefended;
(*persona*) defenceless

indiffe'rente *ag* indifferent

in'digeno, -a [in'didʒeno] *ag* indigenous,
native ▷ *sm/f* native

indigesti'one [indidʒes'tjone] *sf*
indigestion

indi'gesto, -a [indi'dʒɛsto] *ag* indigestible

indi'gnare [indiɲ'ɲare] vt to fill with indignation; **indignarsi** vpr to get indignant

indimenti'cabile ag unforgettable

indipen'dente ag independent

in'dire vt (concorso) to announce; (elezioni) to call

indi'retto, -a ag indirect

indiriz'zare [indirit'tsare] vt (dirigere) to direct; (mandare) to send; (lettera) to address

indi'rizzo [indi'rittso] sm address; (direzione) direction; (avvio) trend, course; **il mio ~ è...** my address is ...

indis'creto, -a ag indiscreet

indis'cusso, -a ag unquestioned

indispen'sabile ag indispensable, essential

indispet'tire vt to irritate, annoy ▷ vi (anche: **indispettirsi**) to get irritated o annoyed

individu'ale ag individual

individu'are vt (dar forma distinta a) to characterize; (determinare) to locate; (riconoscere) to single out

indi'viduo sm individual

indizi'ato, -a ag suspected ▷ sm/f suspect

in'dizio [in'dittsjo] sm (segno) sign, indication; (Polizia) clue; (Dir) piece of evidence

'indole sf nature, character

indolen'zito, -a [indolen'tsito] ag stiff, aching; (intorpidito) numb

indo'lore ag painless

indo'mani sm **l'~** the next day, the following day

Indo'nesia sf **l'~** Indonesia

indos'sare vt (mettere indosso) to put on; (avere indosso) to have on; **indossa'tore, -'trice** sm/f model

indottri'nare vt to indoctrinate

indovi'nare vt (scoprire) to guess; (immaginare) to imagine, guess; (il futuro) to foretell; **indovi'nello** sm riddle

indubbia'mente av undoubtedly

in'dubbio, -a ag certain, undoubted

in'duco ecc vb vedi **indurre**

indugi'are [indu'dʒare] vi to take one's time, delay

in'dugio [in'dudʒo] sm (ritardo) delay; **senza ~** without delay

indul'gente [indul'dʒɛnte] ag indulgent; (giudice) lenient

indu'mento sm article of clothing, garment

indu'rire vt to harden ▷ vi (anche: **indurirsi**) to harden, become hard

in'durre vt **~ qn a fare qc** to induce o persuade sb to do sth; **~ qn in errore** to mislead sb

in'dussi ecc vb vedi **indurre**

in'dustria sf industry; **industri'ale** ag industrial ▷ sm industrialist

inecce'pibile [inettʃe'pibile] ag unexceptionable

i'nedito, -a ag unpublished

ine'rente ag **~ a** concerning, regarding

i'nerme ag unarmed; defenceless

inerpi'carsi vpr **~ (su)** to clamber (up)

i'nerte ag inert; (inattivo) indolent, sluggish

ine'satto, -a ag (impreciso) inexact; (erroneo) incorrect; (Amm: non riscosso) uncollected

inesis'tente ag non-existent

inesperi'enza [inespe'rjɛntsa] sf inexperience

ines'perto, -a ag inexperienced

inevi'tabile ag inevitable

i'nezia [i'nɛttsja] sf trifle, thing of no importance

infagot'tare vt to bundle up, wrap up; **infagottarsi** vpr to wrap up

infal'libile ag infallible

infa'mante ag defamatory

in'fame ag infamous; (fig: cosa, compito) awful, dreadful

infan'gare vt to cover with mud; (fig: reputazione) to sully; **infangarsi** vpr to get covered in mud; to be sullied

infan'tile ag child cpd; childlike; (adulto, azione) childish; **letteratura ~** children's books pl

in'fanzia [in'fantsja] sf childhood; (bambini) children pl; **prima ~** babyhood, infancy

infari'nare vt to cover with (o sprinkle with o dip in) flour; **infarina'tura** sf (fig) smattering

in'farto sm (Med) heart attack

infasti'dire vt to annoy, irritate; **infastidirsi** vpr to get annoyed o irritated

infati'cabile ag tireless, untiring

in'fatti cong actually, as a matter of fact

> Attenzione! In inglese esiste l'espressione in fact che però vuol dire in effetti.

infatu'arsi vpr **~ di** to become infatuated with, fall for

infe'dele ag unfaithful

infe'lice [infe'litʃe] ag unhappy; (sfortunato) unlucky, unfortunate; (inopportuno) inopportune, ill-timed; (mal riuscito: lavoro) bad, poor

inferi'ore ag lower; (per intelligenza, qualità) inferior ▷ sm/f inferior; **~ a** (numero, quantità) less o smaller than;

(*meno buono*) inferior to; **~ alla media** below average; **inferiorità** *sf* inferiority

inferme'ria *sf* infirmary; (*di scuola, nave*) sick bay

infermi'ere, -a *sm/f* nurse

infermità *sf inv* illness; infirmity; **infermità mentale** mental illness; (*Dir*) insanity

in'fermo, -a *ag* (*ammalato*) ill; (*debole*) infirm

infer'nale *ag* infernal; (*proposito, complotto*) diabolical

in'ferno *sm* hell

inferri'ata *sf* grating

infes'tare *vt* to infest

infet'tare *vt* to infect; **infettarsi** *vpr* to become infected; **infezi'one** *sf* infection

infiam'mabile *ag* inflammable

infiam'mare *vt* to set alight; (*fig, Med*) to inflame; **infiammarsi** *vpr* to catch fire; (*Med*) to become inflamed; **infiammazi'one** *sf* (*Med*) inflammation

infie'rire *vi* **~ su** (*fisicamente*) to attack furiously; (*verbalmente*) to rage at

infi'lare *vt* (*ago*) to thread; (*mettere: chiave*) to insert; (*: anello, vestito*) to slip *o* put on; (*strada*) to turn into, take; **infilarsi** *vpr* **infilarsi in** to slip into; (*indossare*) to slip on; **~ l'uscio** to slip in; to slip out

infil'trarsi *vpr* to penetrate, seep through; (*Mil*) to infiltrate

infil'zare [infil'tsare] *vt* (*infilare*) to string together; (*trafiggere*) to pierce

'infimo, -a *ag* lowest

in'fine *av* finally; (*insomma*) in short

infinità *sf* infinity; (*in quantità*) **un'~ di** an infinite number of

infi'nito, -a *ag* infinite; (*Ling*) infinitive ▷ *sm* infinity; (*Ling*) infinitive; **all'~** (*senza fine*) endlessly

infinocchi'are [infinok'kjare] (*fam*) *vt* to hoodwink

infischi'arsi [infis'kjarsi] *vpr* **~ di** not to care about

in'fisso, -a (*pp*) *di* **infiggere** *sm* fixture; (*di porta, finestra*) frame

inflazi'one [inflat'tsjone] *sf* inflation

in'fliggere [in'fliddʒere] *vt* to inflict

in'flissi *ecc vb vedi* **infliggere**

influ'ente *ag* influential; **influ'enza** *sf* influence; (*Med*) influenza, flu

influen'zare [influen'tsare] *vt* to influence, have an influence on

influ'ire *vi* **~ su** to influence

in'flusso *sm* influence

infon'dato, -a *ag* unfounded, groundless

in'fondere *vt* **~ qc in qn** to instill sth in sb

infor'mare *vt* to inform, tell; **informarsi**

vpr **informarsi (di** *o* **su)** to inquire (about)

infor'matica *sf* computer science

informa'tivo, -a *ag* informative

infor'mato, -a *ag* informed; **tenersi ~** to keep o.s. (well-)informed

informa'tore *sm* informer

informazi'one [informat'tsjone] *sf* piece of information; **prendere informazioni sul conto di qn** to get information about sb; **chiedere un'~** to ask for (some) information

in'forme *ag* shapeless

informico'larsi *vpr* to have pins and needles

infortu'nato, -a *ag* injured, hurt ▷ *sm/f* injured person

infor'tunio *sm* accident; **infortunio sul lavoro** industrial accident, accident at work

infra'dito *sm inv* (*calzatura*) flip flop (BRIT), thong (US)

infrazi'one [infrat'tsjone] *sf* **~ a** breaking of, violation of

infredda'tura *sf* slight cold

infreddo'lito, -a *ag* cold, chilled

infu'ori *av* out; **all'~** outwards; **all'~ di** (*eccetto*) except, with the exception of

infuri'arsi *vpr* to fly into a rage

infusi'one *sf* infusion

in'fuso, -a *pp di* **infondere** ▷ *sm* infusion

Ing. *abbr* = **ingegnere**

ingaggi'are [ingad'dʒare] *vt* (*assumere con compenso*) to take on, hire; (*Sport*) to sign on; (*Mil*) to engage

ingan'nare *vt* to deceive; (*fisco*) to cheat; (*eludere*) to dodge, elude; (*fig: tempo*) to while away ▷ *vi* (*apparenza*) to be deceptive; **ingannarsi** *vpr* to be mistaken, be wrong

in'ganno *sm* deceit, deception; (*azione*) trick; (*menzogna, frode*) cheat, swindle; (*illusione*) illusion

inge'gnarsi [indʒeɲ'ɲarsi] *vpr* to do one's best, try hard; **~ per vivere** to live by one's wits

inge'gnere [indʒeɲ'ɲere] *sm* engineer; **~ civile/navale** civil/naval engineer; **ingegne'ria** *sf* engineering; **ingegnere genetica** genetic engineering

in'gegno [in'dʒeɲɲo] *sm* (*intelligenza*) intelligence, brains *pl*; (*capacità creativa*) ingenuity; (*disposizione*) talent; **inge'gnoso, -a** *ag* ingenious, clever

ingelo'sire [indʒelo'zire] *vt* to make jealous ▷ *vi* (*anche:* **ingelosirsi**) to become jealous

in'gente [in'dʒente] *ag* huge, enormous

ingenuità [indʒenui'ta] *sf* ingenuousness

in'genuo, -a [in'dʒɛnuo] *ag* naïve
▮ Attenzione! In inglese esiste la
parola *ingenious*, che però significa
ingegnoso.

inge'rire [indʒe'rire] *vt* to ingest

inges'sare [indʒes'sare] *vt* (*Med*) to put in plaster; **ingessa'tura** *sf* plaster

Inghil'terra [ingil'tɛrra] *sf* l'~ England

inghiot'tire [ingjot'tire] *vt* to swallow

ingial'lire [indʒal'lire] *vi* to go yellow

inginocchi'arsi [indʒinok'kjarsi] *vpr* to kneel (down)

ingiù [in'dʒu] *av* down, downwards

ingi'uria [in'dʒurja] *sf* insult; (*fig: danno*) damage

ingius'tizia [indʒus'tittsja] *sf* injustice

ingi'usto, -a [in'dʒusto] *ag* unjust, unfair

in'glese *ag* English ▷ *sm/f* Englishman/ woman ▷ *sm* (*Ling*) English; **gli Inglesi** the English; **andarsene** *o* **filare all'~** to take French leave

ingoi'are *vt* to gulp (down); (*fig*) to swallow (up)

ingol'farsi *vpr* to flood

ingom'brante *ag* cumbersome

ingom'brare *vt* (*strada*) to block; (*stanza*) to clutter up

in'gordo, -a *ag* ~ **di** greedy for; (*fig*) greedy *o* avid for

in'gorgo, -ghi *sm* blockage, obstruction; (*anche*: ~ **stradale**) traffic jam

ingoz'zarsi *vpr* ~ **(di)** to stuff o.s. (with)

ingra'naggio [ingra'naddʒo] *sm* (*Tecn*) gear; (*di orologio*) mechanism; **gli ingranaggi della burocrazia** the bureaucratic machinery

ingra'nare *vi* to mesh, engage ▷ *vt* to engage; ~ **la marcia** to get into gear

ingrandi'mento *sm* enlargement; extension

ingran'dire *vt* (*anche Fot*) to enlarge; (*estendere*) to extend; (*Ottica, fig*) to magnify ▷ *vi* (*anche*: **ingrandirsi**) to become larger *o* bigger; (*aumentare*) to grow, increase; (*espandersi*) to expand

ingras'sare *vt* to make fat; (*animali*) to fatten; (*lubrificare*) to oil, lubricate ▷ *vi* (*anche*: **ingrassarsi**) to get fat, put on weight

in'grato, -a *ag* ungrateful; (*lavoro*) thankless, unrewarding

ingredi'ente *sm* ingredient

in'gresso *sm* (*porta*) entrance; (*atrio*) hall; (*l'entrare*) entrance, entry; (*facoltà di entrare*) admission; **ingresso libero** admission free

ingros'sare *vt* to increase; (*folla, livello*) to swell ▷ *vi* (*anche*: **ingrossarsi**) to increase; to swell

in'grosso *av* **all'~** (*Comm*) wholesale;

(*all'incirca*) roughly, about

ingua'ribile *ag* incurable

'inguine *sm* (*Anat*) groin

ini'bire *vt* to forbid, prohibit; (*Psic*) to inhibit; **inibirsi** *vpr* to restrain o.s.

ini'bito, -a *ag* inhibited ▷ *sm/f* inhibited person

iniet'tare *vt* to inject; **iniezi'one** *sf* injection

ininterrotta'mente *av* non-stop, continuously

ininter'rotto, -a *ag* unbroken; uninterrupted

inizi'ale [init'tsjale] *ag, sf* initial

inizi'are [init'tsjare] *vi, vt* to begin, start; **a che ora inizia il film?** when does the film start?; ~ **qn a** to initiate sb into; (*pittura ecc*) to introduce sb to; ~ **a fare qc** to start doing sth

inizia'tiva [inittsja'tiva] *sf* initiative; **iniziativa privata** private enterprise

i'nizio [i'nittsjo] *sm* beginning; **all'~** at the beginning, at the start; **dare ~ a qc** to start sth, get sth going

innaffi'are *ecc* = **annaffiare** *ecc*

innamo'rarsi *vpr* ~ **(di qn)** to fall in love (with sb); **innamo'rato, -a** *ag* (*che nutre amore*): **innamorato (di)** in love (with); (*appassionato*): **innamorato di** very fond of ▷ *sm/f* lover; sweetheart

innanzi'tutto *av* first of all

in'nato, -a *ag* innate

innatu'rale *ag* unnatural

inne'gabile *ag* undeniable

innervo'sire *vt* ~ **qn** to get on sb's nerves; **innervosirsi** *vpr* to get irritated *o* upset

innes'care *vt* to prime

'inno *sm* hymn; **inno nazionale** national anthem

inno'cente [inno'tʃɛnte] *ag* innocent

in'nocuo, -a *ag* innocuous, harmless

innova'tivo, -a *ag* innovative

innume'revole *ag* innumerable

inol'trare *vt* (*Amm*) to pass on, forward

i'noltre *av* besides, moreover

inon'dare *vt* to flood

inoppor'tuno, -a *ag* untimely, ill-timed; inappropriate; (*momento*) inopportune

inorri'dire *vt* to horrify ▷ *vi* to be horrified

inosser'vato, -a *ag* (*non visto*) unobserved; (*non rispettato*) not observed, not kept

inossi'dabile *ag* stainless

INPS *sigla m* (= *Istituto Nazionale Previdenza Sociale*) social security service

inqua'drare *vt* (*foto, immagine*) to frame; (*fig*) to situate, set

inqui'eto, -a *ag* restless; (*preoccupato*) worried, anxious

inqui'lino, -a *sm/f* tenant
inquina'mento *sm* pollution
inqui'nare *vt* to pollute
insabbi'are *vt* (*fig: pratica*) to shelve; **insabbiarsi** *vpr* (*arenarsi: barca*) to run aground; (*fig: pratica*) to be shelved
insac'cati *smpl* (*Cuc*) sausages
insa'lata *sf* salad; **insalata mista** mixed salad; **insalata russa** (*Cuc*) Russian salad (*comprised of cold diced cooked vegetables in mayonnaise*); **insalati'era** *sf* salad bowl
insa'nabile *ag* (*piaga*) which cannot be healed; (*situazione*) irremediable; (*odio*) implacable
insa'puta *sf* **all'~ di qn** without sb knowing
inse'diarsi *vpr* to take up office; (*popolo, colonia*) to settle
in'segna [in'seɲɲa] *sf* sign; (*emblema*) sign, emblem; (*bandiera*) flag, banner
insegna'mento [inseɲɲa'mento] *sm* teaching
inse'gnante [inseɲ'ɲante] *ag* teaching ▷ *sm/f* teacher
inse'gnare [inseɲ'ɲare] *vt, vi* to teach; **~ a qn qc** to teach sb sth; **~ a qn a fare qc** to teach sb (how) to do sth
insegui'mento *sm* pursuit, chase
insegu'ire *vt* to pursue, chase
insena'tura *sf* inlet, creek
insen'sato, -a *ag* senseless, stupid
insen'sibile *ag* (*nervo*) insensible; (*persona*) indifferent
inse'rire *vt* to insert; (*Elettr*) to connect; (*allegare*) to enclose; (*annuncio*) to put in, place; **inserirsi** *vpr* (*fig*): **inserirsi in** to become part of
inservi'ente *sm/f* attendant
inserzi'one [inser'tsjone] *sf* insertion; (*avviso*) advertisement; **fare un'~ sul giornale** to put an advertisement in the paper
insetti'cida, -i [insetti'tʃida] *sm* insecticide
in'setto *sm* insect
insi'curo, -a *ag* insecure
insi'eme *av* together ▷ *prep* **~ a o con** together with ▷ *sm* whole; (*Mat, servizio, assortimento*) set; (*Moda*) ensemble, outfit; **tutti ~** all together; **tutto ~** all together; (*in una volta*) at one go; **nell'~** on the whole; **d'~** (*veduta ecc*) overall
in'signe [in'siɲɲe] *ag* (*persona*) famous, distinguished; (*città, monumento*) notable
insignifi'cante [insiɲɲifi'kante] *ag* insignificant
insinu'are *vt* (*introdurre*): **~ qc in** to slip o slide sth into; (*fig*) to insinuate, imply; **insinuarsi** *vpr* **insinuarsi in** to seep into;

(*fig*) to creep into; to worm one's way into
in'sipido, -a *ag* insipid
insis'tente *ag* insistent; persistent
in'sistere *vi* **~ su qc** to insist on sth; **~ in qc/a fare** (*perseverare*) to persist in sth/in doing
insoddis'fatto, -a *ag* dissatisfied
insoffe'rente *ag* intolerant
insolazi'one [insolat'tsjone] *sf* (*Med*) sunstroke
inso'lente *ag* insolent
in'solito, -a *ag* unusual, out of the ordinary
inso'luto, -a *ag* (*non risolto*) unsolved
in'somma *av* (*in conclusione*) in short; (*dunque*) well ▷ *escl* for heaven's sake!
in'sonne *ag* sleepless; **in'sonnia** *sf* insomnia, sleeplessness
insonno'lito, -a *ag* sleepy, drowsy
insoppor'tabile *ag* unbearable
in'sorgere [in'sordʒere] *vi* (*ribellarsi*) to rise up, rebel; (*apparire*) to come up, arise
in'sorsi *ecc vb vedi* **insorgere**
insospet'tire *vt* to make suspicious ▷ *vi* (*anche:* **insospettirsi**) to become suspicious
inspi'rare *vt* to breathe in, inhale
in'stabile *ag* (*carico, indole*) unstable; (*tempo*) unsettled; (*equilibrio*) unsteady
instal'lare *vt* to install
instan'cabile *ag* untiring, indefatigable
instau'rare *vt* to introduce, institute
insuc'cesso [insut'tʃesso] *sm* failure, flop
insuffici'ente [insuffi'tʃɛnte] *ag* insufficient; (*compito, allievo*) inadequate; **insuffici'enza** *sf* insufficiency; inadequacy; (*Ins*) fail; **insufficienza di prove** (*Dir*) lack of evidence; **insufficienza renale** renal insufficiency
insu'lina *sf* insulin
in'sulso, -a *ag* (*sciocco*) inane, silly; (*persona*) dull, insipid
insul'tare *vt* to insult, affront
in'sulto *sm* insult, affront
intac'care *vt* (*fare tacche*) to cut into; (*corrodere*) to corrode; (*fig: cominciare ad usare: risparmi*) to break into; (: *ledere*) to damage
intagli'are [intaʎ'ʎare] *vt* to carve
in'tanto *av* (*nel frattempo*) meanwhile, in the meantime; (*per cominciare*) just to begin with; **~ che** while
inta'sare *vt* to choke (up), block (up); (*Aut*) to obstruct, block; **intasarsi** *vpr* to become choked o blocked
intas'care *vt* to pocket
in'tatto, -a *ag* intact; (*puro*) unsullied
intavo'lare *vt* to start, enter into
inte'grale *ag* complete; (*pane, farina*)

wholemeal (BRIT), whole-wheat (US);
(Mat): **calcolo ~** integral calculus
inte'grante ag **parte ~** integral part
inte'grare vt to complete; (Mat) to
integrate; **integrarsi** vpr (persona) to
become integrated
integra'tore sm **integratori alimentari**
nutritional supplements
integrità sf integrity
'integro, -a ag (intatto, intero) complete,
whole; (retto) upright
intelaia'tura sf frame; (fig) structure,
framework
intel'letto sm intellect; **intellettu'ale** ag,
sm/f intellectual
intelli'gente [intelli'dʒɛnte] ag
intelligent
intem'perie sfpl bad weather sg
in'tendere vt (avere intenzione): **~ fare qc**
to intend o mean to do sth; (comprendere)
to understand; (udire) to hear; (significare)
to mean; **intendersi** vpr (conoscere):
intendersi di to know a lot about, be
a connoisseur of; (accordarsi) to get on
(well); **intendersela con qn** (avere una
relazione amorosa) to have an affair with sb;
intendi'tore, -'trice sm/f connoisseur,
expert
inten'sivo, -a ag intensive
in'tenso, -a ag intense
in'tento, -a ag (teso, assorto): **~ (a)** intent
(on), absorbed (in) ▷ sm aim, purpose
intenzio'nale [intentsjo'nale] ag
intentional
intenzi'one [inten'tsjone] sf intention;
(Dir) intent; **avere ~ di fare qc** to intend o
do sth, have the intention of doing sth
interat'tivo, -a ag interactive
intercet'tare [intertʃet'tare] vt to
intercept
intercity [ɪntəsɪ'tɪ] sm inv (Ferr) ≈ intercity
(train)
inter'detto, -a pp di **interdire** ▷ ag
forbidden, prohibited; (sconcertato)
dumbfounded ▷ sm (Rel) interdict
interes'sante ag interesting; **essere in
stato ~** to be expecting (a baby)
interes'sare vt to interest; (concernere) to
concern, be of interest to; (far intervenire):
~ qn a to draw sb's attention to ▷ vi **~ a**
to interest, matter to; **interessarsi** vpr
(mostrare interesse): **interessarsi a** to take
an interest in, be interested in; (occuparsi):
interessarsi di to take care of
inte'resse sm (anche Comm) interest
inter'faccia, -ce [inter'fattʃa] sf (Inform)
interface
interfe'renza [interfe'rɛntsa] sf
interference

interfe'rire vi to interfere
interiezi'one [interjet'tsjone] sf
exclamation, interjection
interi'ora sfpl entrails
interi'ore ag interior, inner, inside,
internal; (fig) inner
inter'medio, -a ag intermediate
inter'nare vt (arrestare) to intern; (Med) to
commit (to a mental institution)
inter'nauta sm/f Internet user
internazio'nale [internattsjo'nale] ag
international
'Internet ['internet] sf Internet; **in ~** on
the Internet
in'terno, -a ag (di dentro) internal,
interior, inner; (: mare) inland; (nazionale)
domestic; (allievo) boarding ▷ sm inside,
interior; (di paese) interior; (fodera) lining;
(di appartamento) flat (number); (Tel)
extension ▷ sm/f (Ins) boarder; **interni**
smpl (Cinema) interior shots; **all'~** inside;
Ministero degli Interni Ministry of the
Interior, ≈ Home Office (BRIT), Department
of the Interior (US)
in'tero, -a ag (integro, intatto) whole,
entire; (completo, totale) complete;
(numero) whole; (non ridotto: biglietto) full;
(latte) full-cream
interpel'lare vt to consult
interpre'tare vt to interpret; **in'terprete**
sm/f interpreter; (Teatro) actor/actress,
performer; (Mus) performer; **ci potrebbe
fare da interprete?** could you act as an
interpreter for us?
interregio'nale [interredʒo'nale] sm
train that travels between two or more regions
of Italy, stopping frequently
interro'gare vt to question; (Ins) to test;
interrogazi'one sf questioning no pl; (Ins)
oral test
inter'rompere vt to interrupt; (studi,
trattative) to break off, interrupt;
interrompersi vpr to break off, stop
interrut'tore sm switch
interruzi'one [interrut'tsjone] sf
interruption; break
interur'bana sf trunk o long-distance call
inter'vallo sm interval; (spazio) space, gap
interve'nire vi (partecipare): **~ a** to
take part in; (intromettersi: anche Pol)
to intervene; (Med: operare) to operate;
inter'vento sm participation;
(intromissione) intervention; (Med)
operation; **fare un intervento nel corso
di** (dibattito, programma) to take part in
inter'vista sf interview; **intervis'tare** vt
to interview
intes'tare vt (lettera) to address;
(proprietà): **~ a** to register in the name of;

~ **un assegno a qn** to make out a cheque to sb

intestato, -a *ag* (*proprietà, casa, conto*) in the name of; (*assegno*) made out to; **carta intestata** headed paper

intes'tino *sm* (*Anat*) intestine

intimidazi'one [intimidat'tsjone] *sf* intimidation

intimi'dire *vt* to intimidate ▷ *vi* (*intimidirsi*) to grow shy

intimità *sf* intimacy; privacy; (*familiarità*) familiarity

'intimo, -a *ag* intimate; (*affetti, vita*) private; (*fig: profondo*) inmost ▷ *sm* (*persona*) intimate *o* close friend; (*dell'animo*) bottom, depths *pl*; **parti intime** (*Anat*) private parts

in'tingolo *sm* sauce; (*pietanza*) stew

intito'lare *vt* to give a title to; (*dedicare*) to dedicate; **intitolarsi** *vpr* (*libro, film*) to be called

intolle'rabile *ag* intolerable

intolle'rante *ag* intolerant

in'tonaco, -ci *o* **chi** *sm* plaster

into'nare *vt* (*canto*) to start to sing; (*armonizzare*) to match; **intonarsi** *vpr* (*colori*) to go together; **intonarsi a** (*carnagione*) to suit; (*abito*) to go with, match

inton'tito, -a *ag* stunned, dazed; ~ **dal sonno** stupid with sleep

in'toppo *sm* stumbling block, obstacle

in'torno *av* around; ~ **a** (*attorno a*) around; (*riguardo, circa*) about

intossi'care *vt* to poison; **intossicazi'one** *sf* poisoning

intralci'are [intral'tʃare] *vt* to hamper, hold up

intransi'tivo, -a *ag, sm* intransitive

intrapren'dente *ag* enterprising, go-ahead

intra'prendere *vt* to undertake

intrat'tabile *ag* intractable

intratte'nere *vt* to entertain; to engage in conversation; **intrattenersi** *vpr* to linger; **intrattenersi su qc** to dwell on sth

intrave'dere *vt* to catch a glimpse of; (*fig*) to foresee

intrecci'are [intret'tʃare] *vt* (*capelli*) to plait, braid; (*intessere: anche fig*) to weave, interweave, intertwine

intri'gante *ag* scheming ▷ *sm/f* schemer, intriguer

in'trinseco, -a, -ci, -che *ag* intrinsic

in'triso, -a *ag* ~ (**di**) soaked (in)

intro'durre *vt* to introduce; (*chiave ecc*): ~ **qc in** to insert sth into; (*persone: far entrare*) to show in; **introdursi** *vpr* (*moda, tecniche*) to be introduced; **introdursi in** (*persona:*

penetrare) to enter; (: *entrare furtivamente*) to steal *o* slip into; **introduzi'one** *sf* introduction

in'troito *sm* income, revenue

intro'mettersi *vpr* to interfere, meddle; (*interporsi*) to intervene

in'truglio [in'truʎʎo] *sm* concoction

intrusi'one *sf* intrusion; interference

in'truso, -a *sm/f* intruder

intu'ire *vt* to perceive by intuition; (*rendersi conto*) to realize; **in'tuito** *sm* intuition; (*perspicacia*) perspicacity

inu'mano, -a *ag* inhuman

inumi'dire *vt* to dampen, moisten; **inumidirsi** *vpr* to become damp *o* wet

i'nutile *ag* useless; (*superfluo*) pointless, unnecessary

inutil'mente *av* unnecessarily; (*senza risultato*) in vain

inva'dente *ag* (*fig*) interfering, nosey

in'vadere *vt* to invade; (*affollare*) to swarm into, overrun; (*acque*) to flood

inva'ghirsi [inva'girsi] *vpr* ~ **di** to take a fancy to

invalidità *sf* infirmity; disability; (*Dir*) invalidity

in'valido, -a *ag* (*infermo*) infirm, invalid; (*al lavoro*) disabled; (*Dir: nullo*) invalid ▷ *sm/f* invalid; disabled person

in'vano *av* in vain

invasi'one *sf* invasion

inva'sore, invadi'trice [invadi'tritʃe] *ag* invading ▷ *sm* invader

invecchi'are [invek'kjare] *vi* (*persona*) to grow old; (*vino, popolazione*) to age; (*moda*) to become dated ▷ *vt* to age; (*far apparire più vecchio*) to make look older

in'vece [in'vetʃe] *av* instead; (*al contrario*) on the contrary; ~ **di** instead of

inve'ire *vi* ~ **contro** to rail against

inven'tare *vt* to invent; (*pericoli, pettegolezzi*) to make up, invent

inven'tario *sm* inventory; (*Comm*) stocktaking *no pl*

inven'tore *sm* inventor

invenzi'one [inven'tsjone] *sf* invention; (*bugia*) lie, story

inver'nale *ag* winter *cpd*; (*simile all'inverno*) wintry

in'verno *sm* winter

invero'simile *ag* unlikely

inversi'one *sf* inversion; reversal; **"divieto d'~"** (*Aut*) "no U-turns"

in'verso, -a *ag* opposite; (*Mat*) inverse ▷ *sm* contrary, opposite; **in senso ~** in the opposite direction; **in ordine ~** in reverse order

inver'tire *vt* to invert, reverse; ~ **la marcia** (*Aut*) to do a U-turn

investi'gare vt, vi to investigate;
investiga'tore, -'trice sm/f investigator,
detective; **investigatore privato** private
investigator

investi'mento sm (Econ) investment

inves'tire vt (denaro) to invest; (veicolo:
pedone) to knock down; (: altro veicolo)
to crash into; (apostrofare) to assail;
(incaricare): **~ qn di** to invest sb with

invi'are vt to send; **invi'ato, -a** sm/f
envoy; (Stampa) correspondent; **inviato
speciale** (Pol) special envoy; (di giornale)
special correspondent

in'vidia sf envy; **invidi'are** vt **invidiare
qn (per qc)** to envy sb for sth; **invidiare
qc a qn** to envy sb sth; **invidi'oso, -a** ag
envious

in'vio, -'vii sm sending; (insieme di merci)
consignment; (tasto) Return (key), Enter
(key)

invipe'rito, -a ag furious

invi'sibile ag invisible

invi'tare vt to invite; **~ qn a fare** to invite
sb to do; **invi'tato, -a** sm/f guest; **in'vito**
sm invitation

invo'care vt (chiedere: aiuto, pace) to cry
out for; (appellarsi: la legge, Dio) to appeal
to, invoke

invogli'are [invoʎ'ʎare] vt **~ qn a fare** to
tempt sb to do, induce sb to do

involon'tario, -a ag (errore)
unintentional; (gesto) involuntary

invol'tino sm (Cuc) roulade

in'volto sm (pacco) parcel; (fagotto) bundle

in'volucro sm cover, wrapping

inzup'pare [intsup'pare] vt to soak;
inzupparsi vpr to get soaked

'io pron I ▷ sm inv **l'~** the ego, the self; **~
stesso(a)** I myself

i'odio sm iodine

l'onio sm **lo ~, il mar ~** the Ionian (Sea)

ipermer'cato sm hypermarket

ipertensi'one sf high blood pressure,
hypertension

iper'testo sm hypertext

ip'nosi sf hypnosis; **ipnotiz'zare** vt to
hypnotize

ipocri'sia sf hypocrisy

i'pocrita, -i, -e ag hypocritical ▷ sm/f
hypocrite

ipo'teca, -che sf mortgage

i'potesi sf inv hypothesis

'ippica sf horseracing

'ippico, -a, -ci, -che ag horse cpd

ippocas'tano sm horse chestnut

ip'podromo sm racecourse

ippo'potamo sm hippopotamus

'ipsilon sm o m inv (lettera) Y, y; (: dell'alfabeto
greco) epsilon

IR abbr (= Interregionale) long distance train
which stops frequently

ira'cheno, -a [ira'kɛno] ag, sm/f Iraqi

l'ran sm **l'~** Iran

irani'ano, -a ag, sm/f Iranian

l'raq sm **l'~** Iraq

'iride sf (arcobaleno) rainbow; (Anat, Bot) iris

'iris sm inv iris

Ir'landa sf **l'~** Ireland; **l'~ del Nord**
Northern Ireland, Ulster; **la Repubblica
d'~** Eire, the Republic of Ireland; **irlan'dese**
ag Irish ▷ sm/f Irishman/woman; **gli
Irlandesi** the Irish

iro'nia sf irony; **i'ronico, -a, -ci, -che** ag
ironic(al)

irragio'nevole [irradʒo'nevole] ag
irrational; unreasonable

irrazio'nale [irrattsjo'nale] ag irrational

irre'ale ag unreal

irrego'lare ag irregular; (terreno) uneven

irremo'vibile ag (fig) unshakeable,
unyielding

irrequi'eto, -a ag restless

irresis'tibile ag irresistible

irrespon'sabile ag irresponsible

irri'gare vt (annaffiare) to irrigate; (fiume
ecc) to flow through

irrigi'dire [irridʒi'dire] vt to stiffen;
irrigidirsi vpr to stiffen

irri'sorio, -a ag derisory

irri'tare vt (mettere di malumore) to irritate,
annoy; (Med) to irritate; **irritarsi** vpr
(stizzirsi) to become irritated o annoyed;
(Med) to become irritated

ir'rompere vi **~ in** to burst into

irru'ente ag (fig) impetuous, violent

ir'ruppi ecc vb vedi **irrompere**

irruzi'one [irrut'tsjone] sf **fare ~ in** to
burst into; (polizia) to raid

is'crissi ecc vb vedi **iscrivere**

is'critto, -a pp di **iscrivere** ▷ sm/f
member; **per** o **in** writing

is'crivere vt to register, enter; (persona):
~ (a) to register (in), enrol (in); **iscriversi**
vpr **iscriversi (a)** (club, partito) to join;
(università) to register o enrol (at);
(esame, concorso) to register o enter (for);
iscrizi'one sf (epigrafe ecc) inscription; (a
scuola, società) enrolment, registration;
(registrazione) registration

Is'lam sm **l'~** Islam

Is'landa sf **l'~** Iceland

islan'dese ag Icelandic ▷ sm/f Icelander
▷ sm (Ling) Icelandic

'isola sf island; **isola pedonale** (Aut)
pedestrian precinct

isola'mento sm isolation; (Tecn)
insulation

iso'lante ag insulating ▷ sm insulator

iso'lare vt to isolate; (*Tecn*) to insulate; (: *acusticamente*) to soundproof; **isolarsi** vpr to isolate o.s.; **iso'lato, -a** ag isolated; insulated ▷ sm (*gruppo di edifici*) block

ispet'tore sm inspector

ispezio'nare [ispettsjo'nare] vt to inspect

'ispido, -a ag bristly, shaggy

ispi'rare vt to inspire

Isra'ele sm **l'~** Israel; **israeli'ano, -a** ag, sm/f Israeli

is'sare vt to hoist

istan'taneo, -a ag instantaneous ▷ sf (*Fot*) snapshot

is'tante sm instant, moment; **all'~, sull'~** instantly, immediately

is'terico, -a, -ci, -che ag hysterical

isti'gare vt to incite

is'tinto sm instinct

istitu'ire vt (*fondare*) to institute, found; (*porre: confronto*) to establish; (*intraprendere: inchiesta*) to set up

isti'tuto sm institute; (*di università*) department; (*ente, Dir*) institution; **istituto di bellezza** beauty salon; **istituto di credito** bank, banking institution; **istituto di ricerca** research institute

istituzi'one [istitut'tsjone] sf institution

'istmo sm (*Geo*) isthmus

'istrice ['istritʃe] sm porcupine

istru'ito, -a ag educated

istrut'tore, -'trice sm/f instructor ▷ ag **giudice ~** vedi **giudice**

istruzi'one sf education; training; (*direttiva*) instruction; **istruzioni** sfpl (*norme*) instructions; **istruzioni per l'uso** instructions for use; **~ obbligatoria** (*Scol*) compulsory education

I'talia sf **l'~** Italy

itali'ano, -a ag Italian ▷ sm/f Italian ▷ sm (*Ling*) Italian; **gli Italiani** the Italians

itine'rario sm itinerary

'ittico, -a, -ci, -che ag fish cpd; fishing cpd

lugos'lavia = **Jugoslavia**

IVA ['iva] sigla f (= *imposta sul valore aggiunto*) VAT

J

jazz [dʒaz] sm jazz

jeans [dʒinz] smpl jeans

jeep® [dʒip] sm inv jeep

'jogging ['dʒɔgin] sm jogging; **fare ~** to go jogging

'jolly ['dʒɔli] sm inv joker

joystick [dʒɔis'tik] sm inv joystick

ju'do [dʒu'dɔ] sm judo

Jugos'lavia [jugoz'lavja] sf (*Storia*): **la ~** Yugoslavia; **la ex-~** former Yugoslavia; **jugos'lavo, -a** ag, sm/f (*Storia*) Yugoslav(ian)

K   I

K, k ['kappa] *sf o m inv* (lettera) K, k ▷ *abbr*
(= *kilo-, chilo-*) k; (*Inform*) K; **K come**
Kursaal ≈ K for King
kamikaze [kami'kaddze] *sm inv* kamikaze
karaoke [ka'raoke] *sm inv* karaoke
karatè *sm* karate
ka'yak [ka'jak] *sm inv* kayak
Kenia ['kenja] *sm* **il ~** Kenya
kg *abbr* (= *chilogrammo*) kg
'killer *sm inv* gunman, hired gun
kitsch [kitʃ] *sm* kitsch
'kiwi ['kiwi] *sm inv* kiwi fruit
km *abbr* (= *chilometro*) km
K.O. [kappa'o] *sm inv* knockout
ko'ala [ko'ala] *sm inv* koala (bear)
koso'varo, -a [koso'varo] *ag, sm/f*
Kosovan
Ko'sovo *sm* Kosovo
'krapfen *sm inv* (*Cuc*) doughnut
Kuwait [ku'vait] *sm* **il ~** Kuwait

l' *det vedi* **la; lo; il**
la (*dav* **l'**) *det f* the ▷ *pron* (*oggetto: persona*)
her; (: *cosa*) it; (: *forma di cortesia*) you; *vedi*
anche **il**
là *av* there; **di là** (*da quel luogo*) from there;
(*in quel luogo*) in there; (*dall'altra parte*)
over there; **di là di** beyond; **per di là** that
way; **più in là** further on; (*tempo*) later
on; **fatti in là** move up; **là dentro/**
sopra/sotto in/up (*o* on)/under there;
vedi anche **quello**
'labbro (*pl*(*f*) **labbra**) (*solo nel senso Anat*)
sm lip
labi'rinto *sm* labyrinth, maze
labora'torio *sm* (*di ricerca*) laboratory;
(*di arti, mestieri*) workshop; **laboratorio**
linguistico language laboratory
labori'oso, -a *ag* (*faticoso*) laborious;
(*attivo*) hard-working
'lacca, -che *sf* lacquer
'laccio ['lattʃo] *sm* noose; (*legaccio, tirante*)
lasso; (*di scarpa*) lace; **laccio emostatico**
tourniquet
lace'rare [latʃe'rare] *vt* to tear to shreds,
lacerate; **lacerarsi** *vpr* to tear
'lacrima *sf* tear; **in lacrime** in tears;
lacri'mogeno, -a *ag* **gas lacrimogeno**
tear gas
la'cuna *sf* (*fig*) gap
'ladro *sm* thief

laggiù [lad'dʒu] *av* down there; (*di là*) over there

la'gnarsi [laɲ'ɲarsi] *vpr* ~ **(di)** to complain (about)

'lago, -ghi *sm* lake

la'guna *sf* lagoon

'laico, -a, -ci, -che *ag* (*apostolato*) lay; (*vita*) secular; (*scuola*) non-denominational ▷ *sm/f* layman/woman

'lama *sm inv* (*Zool*) llama; (*Rel*) lama ▷ *sf* blade

lamentarsi *vpr* (*emettere lamenti*) to moan, groan; (*rammaricarsi*): ~ **(di)** to complain (about)

lamen'tela *sf* complaining *no pl*

la'metta *sf* razor blade

'lamina *sf* (*lastra sottile*) thin sheet (*o* layer *o* plate); **lamina d'oro** gold leaf; gold foil

'lampada *sf* lamp; **lampada a gas** gas lamp; **lampada da tavolo** table lamp

lampa'dario *sm* chandelier

lampa'dina *sf* light bulb; **lampadina tascabile** pocket torch (BRIT) *o* flashlight (US)

lam'pante *ag* (*fig: evidente*) crystal clear, evident

lampeggi'are [lamped'dʒare] *vi* (*luce, fari*) to flash ▷ *vb impers* **lampeggia** there's lightning; **lampeggia'tore** *sm* (*Aut*) indicator

lampi'one *sm* street light *o* lamp (BRIT)

'lampo *sm* (*Meteor*) flash of lightning; (*di luce: fig*) flash

lam'pone *sm* raspberry

'lana *sf* wool; **pura ~ vergine** pure new wool; **lana d'acciaio** steel wool; **lana di vetro** glass wool

lan'cetta [lan'tʃetta] *sf* (*indice*) pointer, needle; (*di orologio*) hand

'lancia ['lantʃa] *sf* (*arma*) lance; (: *picca*) spear; (*di pompa antincendio*) nozzle; (*imbarcazione*) launch; **lancia di salvataggio** lifeboat

lanciafi'amme [lantʃa'fjamme] *sm inv* flamethrower

lanci'are [lan'tʃare] *vt* to throw, hurl, fling; (*Sport*) to throw; (*far partire: automobile*) to get up to full speed; (*bombe*) to drop; (*razzo, prodotto, moda*) to launch; **lanciarsi** *vpr* **lanciarsi contro/su** to throw *o* hurl *o* fling o.s. against/on; **lanciarsi in** (*fig*) to embark on

lanci'nante [lantʃi'nante] *ag* (*dolore*) shooting, throbbing; (*grido*) piercing

'lancio ['lantʃo] *sm* throwing *no pl*; throw; dropping *no pl*; drop; launching *no pl*; launch; **lancio del disco** (*Sport*) throwing the discus; **lancio del peso** putting the shot

'languido, -a *ag* (*fiacco*) languid, weak; (*tenero, malinconico*) languishing

lan'terna *sf* lantern; (*faro*) lighthouse

'lapide *sf* (*di sepolcro*) tombstone; (*commemorativa*) plaque

'lapsus *sm inv* slip

'lardo *sm* bacon fat, lard

lar'ghezza [lar'gettsa] *sf* width; breadth; looseness; generosity; **larghezza di vedute** broad-mindedness

'largo, -a, -ghi, -ghe *ag* wide; broad; (*maniche*) wide; (*abito: troppo ampio*) loose; (*fig*) generous ▷ *sm* width; breadth; (*mare aperto*): **il ~** the open sea ▷ *sf* **stare** *o* **tenersi alla larga (da qn/qc)** to keep one's distance (from sb/sth), keep away (from sb/sth); ~ **due metri** two metres wide; ~ **di spalle** broad-shouldered; **di larghe vedute** broad-minded; **su larga scala** on a large scale; **di manica larga** generous, open-handed; **al ~ di Genova** off (the coast of) Genoa; **farsi ~ tra la folla** to push one's way through the crowd

'larice ['laritʃe] *sm* (*Bot*) larch

larin'gite [larin'dʒite] *sf* laryngitis

'larva *sf* larva; (*fig*) shadow

la'sagne [la'zaɲɲe] *sfpl* lasagna *sg*

lasci'are [laʃʃare] *vt* to leave; (*abbandonare*) to leave, abandon, give up; (*cessare di tenere*) to let go of ▷ *vb aus* ~ **fare qn** to let sb do; ~ **andare** *o* **correre** *o* **perdere** to let things go their own way; ~ **stare qc/qn** to leave sth/sb alone; **lasciarsi** *vpr* (*persone*) to part; (*coppia*) to split up; **lasciarsi andare** to let o.s. go

'laser ['lazer] *ag, sm inv* **(raggio) ~** laser (beam)

lassa'tivo, -a *ag, sm* laxative

'lasso *sm*; **lasso di tempo** interval, lapse of time

lassù *av* up there

'lastra *sf* (*di pietra*) slab; (*di metallo, Fot*) plate; (*di ghiaccio, vetro*) sheet; (*radiografica*) X-ray (plate)

lastri'cato *sm* paving

late'rale *ag* lateral, side *cpd*; (*uscita, ingresso ecc*) side *cpd* ▷ *sm* (*Calcio*) half-back

la'tino, -a *ag, sm* Latin

lati'tante *sm/f* fugitive (from justice)

lati'tudine *sf* latitude

'lato, -a *ag* (*fig*) wide, broad ▷ *sm* side; (*fig*) aspect, point of view; **in senso ~** broadly speaking

'latta *sf* tin (plate); (*recipiente*) tin, can

lat'tante *ag* unweaned

'latte *sm* milk; **latte detergente** cleansing milk *o* lotion; **latte intero** full-cream milk;

latte a lunga conservazione UHT milk, long-life milk; **latte magro** o **scremato** skimmed milk; **latte in polvere** dried o powdered milk; **latte solare** suntan lotion; **latti'cini** smpl dairy products
lat'tina sf (di birra ecc) can
lat'tuga, -ghe sf lettuce
'laurea sf degree; **laurea in ingegneria** engineering degree; **laurea in lettere** ≈ arts degree

⊚ **LAUREA**

⊚
⊚ The **laurea** is awarded to students
⊚ who successfully complete their
⊚ degree courses. Traditionally,
⊚ this takes between four and six
⊚ years; a major element of the final
⊚ examinations is the presentation
⊚ and discussion of a dissertation. A
⊚ shorter, more vocational course of
⊚ study, taking from two to three years,
⊚ is also available; at the end of this time
⊚ students receive a diploma called the
⊚ **laurea breve**.

laure'arsi vpr to graduate
laure'ato, -a ag, sm/f graduate
'lauro sm laurel
'lauto, -a ag (pranzo, mancia) lavish
'lava sf lava
la'vabo sm washbasin
la'vaggio [la'vaddʒo] sm washing no pl; **lavaggio del cervello** brainwashing no pl; **lavaggio a secco** dry-cleaning
la'vagna [la'vaɲɲa] sf (Geo) slate; (di scuola) blackboard
la'vanda sf (anche Med) wash; (Bot) lavender; **lavande'ria** sf laundry; **lavanderia automatica** launderette; **lavanderia a secco** dry-cleaner's; **lavan'dino** sm sink
lavapi'atti sm/f dishwasher
la'vare vt to wash; **lavarsi** vpr to wash, have a wash; **~ a secco** to dry-clean; **lavarsi le mani/i denti** to wash one's hands/clean one's teeth
lava'secco sm o f inv dry cleaner's
lavasto'viglie [lavasto'viʎʎe] sm o f inv (macchina) dishwasher
lava'trice [lava'tritʃe] sf washing machine
lavo'rare vi to work; (fig: bar, studio ecc) to do good business ▷ vt to work; **lavorarsi qn** (persuaderlo) to work on sb; **~ a** to work on; **~ a maglia** to knit; **lavora'tivo, -a** ag working; **lavora'tore, -'trice** sm/f worker ▷ ag working

la'voro sm work; (occupazione) job, work no pl; (opera) piece of work, job; (Econ) labour; **che ~ fa?** what do you do?; **lavori forzati** hard labour sg; **lavoro interinale** o **in affitto** temporary work
le det fpl the ▷ pron (oggetto) them; (: a lei, a essa) (to) her; (: forma di cortesia) (to) you; vedi anche **il**
le'ale ag loyal; (sincero) sincere; (onesto) fair
lecca 'lecca sm inv lollipop
leccapi'edi (peg) sm/f inv toady, bootlicker
lec'care vt to lick; (gatto: latte ecc) to lick o lap up; (fig) to flatter; **leccarsi i baffi** to lick one's lips
leccherò ecc [lekke'rɔ] vb vedi **leccare**
'leccio ['lettʃo] sm holm oak, ilex
leccor'nia sf titbit, delicacy
'lecito, -a ['lɛtʃito] ag permitted, allowed
'lega, -ghe sf league; (di metalli) alloy
le'gaccio [le'gattʃo] sm string, lace
le'gale ag legal ▷ sm lawyer; **legaliz'zare** vt to authenticate; (regolarizzare) to legalize
le'game sm (corda, fig: affettivo) tie, bond; (nesso logico) link, connection
le'gare vt (prigioniero, capelli, cane) to tie (up); (libro) to bind; (Chim) to alloy; (fig: collegare) to bind, join ▷ vi (far lega) to unite; (fig) to get on well
le'genda [le'dʒenda] sf (di carta geografica ecc) = **leggenda**
'legge ['leddʒe] sf law
leg'genda [led'dʒenda] sf (narrazione) legend; (di carta geografica ecc) key, legend
'leggere ['leddʒere] vt, vi to read
legge'rezza [ledlʒe'rettsa] sf lightness; thoughtlessness; fickleness
leg'gero, -a [led'dʒero] ag light; (agile, snello) nimble, agile, light; (tè, caffè) weak; (fig: non grave, piccolo) slight; (: spensierato) thoughtless; (: incostante) fickle; free and easy; **alla leggera** thoughtlessly
leg'gio, -'gii [led'dʒio] sm lectern; (Mus) music stand
legherò ecc [lege'rɔ] vb vedi **legare**
legisla'tivo, -a [ledʒizla'tivo] ag legislative
legisla'tura [ledʒizla'tura] sf legislature
le'gittimo, -a [le'dʒittimo] ag legitimate; (fig: giustificato, lecito) justified, legitimate; **legittima difesa** (Dir) self-defence
'legna ['leɲɲa] sf firewood
'legno ['leɲɲo] sm wood; (pezzo di legno) piece of wood; **di ~** wooden; **legno compensato** plywood
'lei pron (soggetto) she; (oggetto: per dare rilievo, con preposizione) her; (forma di cortesia: anche: **L~**) you ▷ sm **dare del ~**

a qn to address sb as "lei"; **~ stessa** she herself; you yourself

---

● **LEI**
●
● **lei** is the third person singular pronoun.
● It is used in Italian to address an adult
● whom you do not know or with whom
● you are on formal terms.

---

lenta'mente av slowly
'lente sf (Ottica) lens sg; **lenti a contatto o corneali** contact lenses; **lenti (a contatto) morbide/rigide** soft/hard contact lenses; **lente d'ingrandimento** magnifying glass; **lenti** sfpl (occhiali) lenses
len'tezza [len'tettsa] sf slowness
len'ticchia [len'tikkja] sf (Bot) lentil
len'tiggine [len'tiddʒine] sf freckle
'lento, -a ag slow; (molle: fune) slack; (non stretto: vite, abito) loose ▷ sm (ballo) slow dance
'lenza ['lentsa] sf fishing-line
lenzu'olo [len'tswɔlo] sm sheet
le'one sm lion; (dello zodiaco): **L~** Leo
lepo'rino, -a ag **labbro ~** harelip
'lepre sf hare
'lercio, -a, -ci, -cie ['lɛrtʃo] ag filthy
lesi'one sf (Med) lesion; (Dir) injury, damage; (Edil) crack
les'sare vt (Cuc) to boil
'lessi ecc vb vedi **leggere**
'lessico, -ci sm vocabulary; lexicon
'lesso, -a ag boiled ▷ sm boiled meat
le'tale ag lethal; fatal
leta'maio sm dunghill
le'tame sm manure, dung
le'targo, -ghi sm lethargy; (Zool) hibernation
'lettera sf letter; **lettere** sfpl (letteratura) literature sg; (studi umanistici) arts (subjects); **alla ~** literally; **in lettere** in words, in full
letteral'mente av literally
lette'rario, -a ag literary
lette'rato, -a ag well-read, scholarly
lettera'tura sf literature
let'tiga, -ghe sf (barella) stretcher
let'tino sm cot (BRIT), crib (US); **lettino solare** sunbed
'letto, -a pp di **leggere** ▷ sm bed; **andare a ~** to go to bed; **letto a castello** bunk beds pl; **letto a una piazza** single; **letto a due piazze o matrimoniale** double bed
let'tore, -'trice sm/f reader; (Ins) (foreign language) assistant (BRIT), (foreign) teaching assistant (US) ▷ sm (Tecn): **~ ottico** optical character reader; **lettore CD** CD player; **lettore DVD** DVD player

let'tura sf reading

⚠ Attenzione! In inglese esiste la parola *lecture*, che però significa *lezione* oppure *conferenza*.

leuce'mia [leutʃe'mia] sf leukaemia
'leva sf lever; (Mil) conscription; **far ~ su qn** to work on sb; **leva del cambio** (Aut) gear lever
le'vante sm east; (vento) East wind; **il L~** the Levant
le'vare vt (occhi, braccio) to raise; (sollevare, togliere: tassa, divieto) to lift; (indumenti) to take off, remove; (rimuovere) to take away; (: dal di sopra) to take off; (: dal di dentro) to take out
leva'toio, -a ag **ponte ~** drawbridge
lezi'one [let'tsjone] sf lesson; (Univ) lecture; **fare ~** to teach; to lecture; **dare una ~ a qn** to teach sb a lesson; **lezioni private** private lessons
li pron pl (oggetto) them
lì av there; **di o da lì** from there; **per di lì** that way; **di lì a pochi giorni** a few days later; **lì per lì** there and then; at first; **essere lì (lì) per fare** to be on the point of doing, be about to do; **lì dentro** in there; **lì sotto** under there; **lì sopra** on there; up there; vedi anche **quello**
liba'nese ag, sm/f Lebanese inv
Li'bano sm **il ~** the Lebanon
'libbra sf (peso) pound
li'beccio [li'bettʃo] sm south-west wind
li'bellula sf dragonfly
libe'rale ag, sm/f liberal
liberaliz'zare [liberalid'dzare] vt to liberalize
libe'rare vt (rendere libero: prigioniero) to release; (: popolo) to free, liberate; (sgombrare: passaggio) to clear; (: stanza) to vacate; (produrre: energia) to release; **liberarsi** vpr **liberarsi di qc/qn** to get rid of sth/sb; **liberazi'one** sf liberation, freeing; release; rescuing

---

● **LIBERAZIONE**
●
● The **Liberazione** is a national
● holiday which falls on April 25th. It
● commemorates the liberation of Italy at
● the end of the Second World War.

'libero, -a ag free; (strada) clear; (non occupato: posto ecc) vacant; free; not taken; empty; not engaged; **~ di fare qc** free to do sth; **~ da** free from; **è ~ questo posto?** is this seat free?; **~ arbitrio** free will; **~ professionista** self-employed professional person; **~ scambio** free trade;

libertà sf inv freedom; (*tempo disponibile*) free time ▷ sfpl (*licenza*) liberties; **in libertà provvisoria/vigilata** released without bail/on probation

'Libia sf **la ~** Libya; **'libico, -a, -ci, -che** ag, sm/f Libyan

li'bidine sf lust

li'braio sm bookseller

li'brarsi vpr to hover

libre'ria sf (*bottega*) bookshop; (*mobile*) bookcase

▌ Attenzione! In inglese esiste la parola *library*, che però significa *biblioteca*.

li'bretto sm booklet; (*taccuino*) notebook; (*Mus*) libretto; **libretto degli assegni** cheque book; **libretto di circolazione** (*Aut*) logbook; **libretto di risparmio** (*savings*) bank-book, passbook; **libretto universitario** student's report book

'libro sm book; **libro di cassa** cash book; **libro mastro** ledger; **libro paga** payroll; **libro di testo** textbook

li'cenza [li'tʃɛntsa] sf (*permesso*) permission, leave; (*di pesca, caccia, circolazione*) permit, licence; (*Mil*) leave; (*Ins*) school leaving certificate; (*libertà*) liberty; licence; licentiousness; **andare in ~** (*Mil*) to go on leave

licenzia'mento [litʃentsja'mento] sm dismissal

licenzi'are [litʃen'tsjare] vt (*impiegato*) to dismiss; (*Comm: per eccesso di personale*) to make redundant; (*Ins*) to award a certificate to; **licenziarsi** vpr (*impiegato*) to resign, hand in one's notice; (*Ins*) to obtain one's school-leaving certificate

li'ceo [li'tʃɛo] sm (*Ins*) secondary (*BRIT*) o high (*US*) school (*for 14- to 19-year-olds*)

'lido sm beach, shore

Liechtenstein ['liktənstain] sm **il ~** Liechtenstein

li'eto, -a ag happy, glad; **"molto ~"** (*nelle presentazioni*) "pleased to meet you"

li'eve ag light; (*di poco conto*) slight; (*sommesso: voce*) faint, soft

lievi'tare vi (*anche fig*) to rise ▷ vt to leaven

li'evito sm yeast; **lievito di birra** brewer's yeast

'ligio, -a, -gi, -gie ['lidʒo] ag faithful, loyal

'lilla sm inv lilac

'lillà sm inv lilac

'lima sf file; **lima da unghie** nail file

limacci'oso, -a [limat'tʃoso] ag slimy; muddy

li'mare vt to file (down); (*fig*) to polish

limi'tare vt to limit, restrict; (*circoscrivere*) to bound, surround; **limitarsi** vpr **limitarsi nel mangiare** to limit one's

eating; **limitarsi a qc/a fare qc** to limit o.s. to sth/to doing sth

'limite sm limit; (*confine*) border, boundary; **limite di velocità** speed limit

limo'nata sf lemonade (*BRIT*), (lemon) soda (*US*); lemon squash (*BRIT*), lemonade (*US*)

li'mone sm (*pianta*) lemon tree; (*frutto*) lemon

'limpido, -a ag clear; (*acqua*) limpid, clear

'lince ['lintʃe] sf lynx

linci'are vt to lynch

'linea sf line; (*di mezzi pubblici di trasporto: itinerario*) route; (: *servizio*) service; **a grandi linee** in outline; **mantenere la ~** to look after one's figure; **aereo di ~** airliner; **nave di ~** liner; **volo di ~** scheduled flight; **linea aerea** airline; **linea di partenza/d'arrivo** (*Sport*) starting/finishing line; **linea di tiro** line of fire

linea'menti smpl features; (*fig*) outlines

line'are ag linear; (*fig*) coherent, logical

line'etta sf (*trattino*) dash; (*d'unione*) hyphen

lin'gotto sm ingot, bar

'lingua sf (*Anat, Cuc*) tongue; (*idioma*) language; **mostrare la ~** to stick out one's tongue; **di ~ italiana** Italian-speaking; **che lingue parla?** what languages do you speak?; **una ~ di terra** a spit of land; **lingua madre** mother tongue

lingu'aggio [lin'gwaddʒo] sm language

lingu'etta sf (*di strumento*) reed; (*di scarpa, Tecn*) tongue; (*di busta*) flap

'lino sm (*pianta*) flax; (*tessuto*) linen

li'noleum sm inv linoleum, lino

liposuzi'one [liposut'tsjone] sf liposuction

lique'fatto, -a pp di **liquefare**

liqui'dare vt (*società, beni: persona: uccidere*) to liquidate; (*persona: sbarazzarsene*) to get rid of; (*conto, problema*) to settle; (*Comm: merce*) to sell off, clear; **liquidazi'one** sf liquidation; settlement; clearance sale

liquidità sf liquidity

'liquido, -a ag, sm liquid; **liquido per freni** brake fluid

liqui'rizia [likwi'rittsja] sf liquorice

li'quore sm liqueur

'lira sf (*Storia: unità monetaria*) lira; (*Mus*) lyre; **lira sterlina** pound sterling

'lirico, -a, -ci, -che ag lyric(al); (*Mus*) lyric; **cantante/teatro ~** opera singer/house

Lis'bona sf Lisbon

'lisca, -sche sf (*di pesce*) fishbone

lisci'are [liʃ'ʃare] vt to smooth; (*fig*) to flatter

'liscio, -a, -sci, -sce ['liʃʃo] ag smooth;

(capelli) straight; (mobile) plain; (bevanda alcolica) neat; (fig) straightforward, simple ▷ av **andare ~** to go smoothly; **passarla liscia** to get away with it

'liso, -a ag worn out, threadbare

'lista sf (elenco) list; **lista elettorale** electoral roll; **lista delle spese** shopping list; **lista dei vini** wine list; **lista delle vivande** menu

lis'tino sm list; **listino dei cambi** (foreign) exchange rate; **listino dei prezzi** price list

'lite sf quarrel, argument; (Dir) lawsuit

liti'gare vi to quarrel; (Dir) to litigate

li'tigio [li'tidʒo] sm quarrel

lito'rale ag coastal, coast cpd ▷ sm coast

'litro sm litre

livel'lare vt to level, make level

li'vello sm level; (fig) level, standard; **ad alto ~** (fig) high-level; **livello del mare** sea level

'livido, -a ag livid; (per percosse) bruised, black and blue; (cielo) leaden ▷ sm bruise

Li'vorno sf Livorno, Leghorn

'lizza ['littsa] sf lists pl; **scendere in ~** to enter the lists

lo (dav s impura, gn, pn, ps, x, z; dav∨ **l'**) det m the ▷ pron (oggetto: persona) him; (: cosa) it; **lo sapevo** I knew it; **lo so** I know; **sii buono, anche se lui non lo è** be good, even if he isn't; vedi anche **il**

lo'cale ag local ▷ sm room; (luogo pubblico) premises pl; **locale notturno** nightclub; **località** sf inv locality

lo'canda sf inn

locomo'tiva sf locomotive

locuzi'one [lokut'tsjone] sf phrase, expression

lo'dare vt to praise

'lode sf praise; (Ins): **laurearsi con 110 e ~** ≈ to graduate with a first-class honours degree (BRIT), graduate summa cum laude (US)

'loden sm inv (stoffa) loden; (cappotto) loden overcoat

lo'devole ag praiseworthy

loga'ritmo sm logarithm

'loggia, -ge ['lɔddʒa] sf (Archit) loggia; (circolo massonico) lodge; **loggi'one** sm (di teatro): **il loggione** the Gods sg

'logico, -a, -ci, -che ['lɔdʒiko] ag logical

logo'rare vt to wear out; (sciupare) to waste; **logorarsi** vpr to wear out; (fig) to wear o.s. out

'logoro, -a ag (stoffa) worn out, threadbare; (persona) worn out

Lombar'dia sf **la ~** Lombardy

lom'bata sf (taglio di carne) loin

lom'brico, -chi sm earthworm

londi'nese ag London cpd ▷ sm/f Londoner

'Londra sf London

lon'gevo, -a [lon'dʒevo] ag long-lived

longi'tudine [londʒi'tudine] sf longitude

lonta'nanza [lonta'nantsa] sf distance; absence

lon'tano, -a ag (distante) distant, faraway; (assente) absent; (vago: sospetto) slight, remote; (tempo: remoto) far-off, distant; (parente) distant, remote ▷ av far; **è lontana la casa?** is it far to the house?, is the house far from here?; **è ~ un chilometro** it's a kilometre away o a kilometre from here; **più ~** farther; **da** o **di ~** from a distance; **~ da** a long way from; **è molto ~ da qui?** is it far from here?; **alla lontana** slightly, vaguely

lo'quace [lo'kwatʃe] ag talkative, loquacious; (fig: gesto ecc) eloquent

'lordo, -a ag dirty, filthy; (peso, stipendio) gross

'loro pron pl (oggetto, con preposizione) them; (complemento di termine) to them; (soggetto) they; (forma di cortesia: anche: **L~**) you; to you; **il(la) ~, i(le) ~** det their; (forma di cortesia: anche: **L~**) your ▷ pron theirs; (forma di cortesia: anche: **L~**) yours; **~ stessi(e)** they themselves; you yourselves

'losco, -a, -schi, -sche ag (fig) shady, suspicious

'lotta sf struggle, fight; (Sport) wrestling; **lotta libera** all-in wrestling; **lot'tare** vi to fight, struggle; to wrestle

lotte'ria sf lottery; (di gara ippica) sweepstake

'lotto sm (gioco) (state) lottery; (parte) lot; (Edil) site

● **LOTTO**

● The **Lotto** is an official lottery run by the
● Italian Finance Ministry. It consists of
● a weekly draw of numbers and is very
● popular.

lozi'one [lot'tsjone] sf lotion

lubrifi'cante sm lubricant

lubrifi'care vt to lubricate

luc'chetto [luk'ketto] sm padlock

lucci'care [luttʃi'kare] vi to sparkle, glitter, twinkle

'luccio ['luttʃo] sm (Zool) pike

'lucciola ['luttʃola] sf (Zool) firefly; glowworm

'luce ['lutʃe] sf light; (finestra) window; **alla ~ di** by the light of; **fare ~ su qc** (fig) to shed o throw light on sth; **~ del sole/della luna**

sun/moonlight

lucer'nario [lutʃer'narjo] *sm* skylight

lu'certola [lu'tʃertola] *sf* lizard

luci'dare [lutʃi'dare] *vt* to polish

lucida'trice [lutʃida'tritʃe] *sf* floor polisher

'lucido, -a ['lutʃido] *ag* shining, bright; (*lucidato*) polished; (*fig*) lucid ▷ *sm* shine, lustre; (*disegno*) tracing; **lucido per scarpe** shoe polish

'lucro *sm* profit, gain

'luglio ['luʎʎo] *sm* July

'lugubre *ag* gloomy

'lui *pron* (*soggetto*) he; (*oggetto: per dare rilievo, con preposizione*) him; **~ stesso** he himself

lu'maca, -che *sf* slug; (*chiocciola*) snail

lumi'noso, -a *ag* (*che emette luce*) luminous; (*cielo, colore, stanza*) bright; (*sorgente*) of light, light *cpd*; (*fig: sorriso*) bright, radiant

'luna *sf* moon; **luna nuova/piena** new/full moon; **luna di miele** honeymoon; **siamo in ~ di miele** we're on honeymoon

'luna park *sm inv* amusement park, funfair

lu'nare *ag* lunar, moon *cpd*

lu'nario *sm* almanac; **sbarcare il ~** to make ends meet

lu'natico, -a, -ci, -che *ag* whimsical, temperamental

lunedì *sm inv* Monday; **di** *o* **il ~** on Mondays

lun'ghezza [lun'gettsa] *sf* length; **lunghezza d'onda** (*Fisica*) wavelength

'lungo, -a, -ghi, -ghe *ag* long; (*lento: persona*) slow; (*diluito: caffè, brodo*) weak, watery, thin ▷ *sm* length ▷ *prep* along; **~ 3 metri** 3 metres long; **a ~** for a long time; **a ~ andare** in the long run; **di gran lunga** (*molto*) by far; **andare in ~** *o* **per le lunghe** to drag on; **saperla lunga** to know what's what; **in ~ e in largo** far and wide, all over; **~ il corso dei secoli** throughout the centuries

lungo'mare *sm* promenade

lu'notto *sm* (*Aut*) rear *o* back window; **lunotto termico** heated rear window

lu'ogo, -ghi *sm* place; (*posto: di incidente ecc*) scene, site; (*punto, passo di libro*) passage; **in ~ di** instead of; **in primo ~** in the first place; **aver ~** to take place; **dar ~ a** to give rise to; **luogo di nascita** birthplace; (*Amm*) place of birth; **luogo di provenienza** place of origin; **luogo comune** commonplace

'lupo, -a *sm/f* wolf

'luppolo *sm* (*Bot*) hop

'lurido, -a *ag* filthy

lusin'gare *vt* to flatter

Lussem'burgo *sm* (*stato*): **il ~** Luxembourg ▷ *sf* (*città*) Luxembourg

'lusso *sm* luxury; **di ~** luxury *cpd*; **lussu'oso, -a** *ag* luxurious

lus'suria *sf* lust

lus'trino *sm* sequin

'lutto *sm* mourning; **essere in/portare il ~** to be in/wear mourning

m. abbr = **mese**; **metro**; **miglia**; **monte**
ma cong but; **ma insomma!** for goodness
sake!; **ma no!** of course not!
'macabro, -a ag gruesome, macabre
macché [mak'ke] escl not at all!, certainly
not!
macche'roni [makke'roni] smpl macaroni
sg
'macchia ['makkja] sf stain, spot; (chiazza
di diverso colore) spot, splash, patch; (tipo
di boscaglia) scrub; **alla ~** (fig) in hiding;
macchi'are vt (sporcare) to stain, mark;
macchiarsi vpr (persona) to get o.s. dirty;
(stoffa) to stain; to get stained o marked
macchi'ato, -a [mak'kjato] ag (pelle, pelo)
spotted; **~ di** stained with; **caffè ~** coffee
with a dash of milk
'macchina ['makkina] sf machine;
(motore, locomotiva) engine; (automobile)
car; (fig: meccanismo) machinery; **andare
in ~** (Aut) to go by car; (Stampa) to go
to press; **macchina da cucire** sewing
machine; **macchina fotografica** camera;
macchina da presa cine o movie camera;
macchina da scrivere typewriter;
macchina a vapore steam engine
macchi'nario [makki'narjo] sm
machinery
macchi'nista, -i [makki'nista] sm (di
treno) engine-driver; (di nave) engineer

Macedonia [matʃe'dɔnja] sf **la ~**
Macedonia
mace'donia [matʃe'dɔnja] sf fruit salad
macel'laio [matʃel'lajo] sm butcher
macelle'ria sf butcher's (shop)
ma'cerie [ma'tʃerje] sfpl rubble sg, debris
sg
ma'cigno [ma'tʃiɲɲo] sm (masso) rock,
boulder
maci'nare [matʃi'nare] vt to grind; (carne)
to mince (BRIT), grind (US)
macrobi'otico, -a ag macrobiotic ⊳ sf
macrobiotics sg
Ma'donna sf (Rel) Our Lady
mador'nale ag enormous, huge
'madre sf mother; (matrice di bolletta)
counterfoil ⊳ ag inv mother cpd; **ragazza
~** unmarried mother; **scena ~** (Teatro)
principal scene; (fig) terrible scene
madre'lingua sf mother tongue, native
language
madre'perla sf mother-of-pearl
ma'drina sf godmother
maestà sf inv majesty
ma'estra sf vedi **maestro**
maes'trale sm north-west wind, mistral
ma'estro, -a sm/f (Ins: anche: **~ di scuola
o elementare**) primary (BRIT) o grade
school (US) teacher; (esperto) expert
⊳ sm (artigiano, fig: guida) master; (Mus)
maestro ⊳ ag (principale) main; (di grande
abilità) masterly, skilful; **maestra d'asilo**
nursery teacher; **~ di cerimonie** master of
ceremonies
'mafia sf Mafia
'maga sf sorceress
ma'gari escl (esprime desiderio): **~ fosse
vero!** if only it were true!; **ti piacerebbe
andare in Scozia? — ~!** would you like to
go to Scotland? — and how! ⊳ av (anche)
even; (forse) perhaps
magaz'zino [magad'dzino] sm
warehouse; **grande ~** department store
⚠ Attenzione! In inglese esiste la parola
magazine che però significa *rivista*.
'maggio ['maddʒo] sm May
maggio'rana [maddʒo'rana] sf (Bot)
(sweet) marjoram
maggio'ranza [maddʒo'rantsa] sf
majority
maggior'domo [maddʒor'dɔmo] sm
butler
maggi'ore [mad'dʒore] ag (comparativo:
più grande) bigger, larger; taller; greater;
(: più vecchio: sorella, fratello) older, elder;
(: di grado superiore) senior; (: più importante:
Mil, Mus) major; (superlativo) biggest,
largest; tallest; greatest; oldest, eldest
⊳ sm/f (di grado) superior; (di età) elder;

(*Mil*) major; (: *Aer*) squadron leader; **la maggior parte** the majority; **andare per la ~** (*cantante ecc*) to be very popular; **maggio'renne** *ag* of age ▷ *sm/f* person who has come of age

ma'gia [ma'dʒia] *sf* magic; **'magico, -a, -ci, -che** *ag* magic; (*fig*) fascinating, charming, magical

magis'trato [madʒis'trato] *sm* magistrate

'maglia ['maʎʎa] *sf* stitch; (*lavoro ai ferri*) knitting *no pl*; (*tessuto*) jersey; (*maglione*) jersey, sweater; (*di catena*) link; (*di rete*) mesh; **maglia diritta/rovescia** plain/purl; **magli'etta** *sf* (*canottiera*) vest; (*tipo camicia*) T-shirt

magli'one *sm* sweater, jumper

ma'gnetico, -a, -ci, -che *ag* magnetic

ma'gnifico, -a, -ci, -che [maɲ'ɲifiko] *ag* magnificent, splendid; (*ospite*) generous

ma'gnolia [maɲ'ɲɔlja] *sf* magnolia

'mago, -ghi *sm* (*stregone*) magician, wizard; (*illusionista*) magician

ma'grezza [ma'grettsa] *sf* thinness

'magro, -a *ag* (very) thin, skinny; (*carne*) lean; (*formaggio*) low-fat; (*fig: scarso, misero*) meagre, poor; (: *meschino: scusa*) poor, lame; **mangiare di ~** not to eat meat

'mai *av* (*nessuna volta*) never; (*talvolta*) ever; **non ... ~** never; **~ più** never again; **non sono ~ stato in Spagna** I've never been to Spain; **come ~?** why (*o* how) on earth?; **chi/dove/quando ~?** whoever/wherever/ whenever?

mai'ale *sm* (*Zool*) pig; (*carne*) pork

maio'nese *sf* mayonnaise

'mais *sm inv* maize

mai'uscolo, -a *ag* (*lettera*) capital; (*fig*) enormous, huge

mala'fede *sf* bad faith

malan'dato, -a *ag* (*persona: di salute*) in poor health; (: *di condizioni finanziarie*) badly off; (*trascurato*) shabby

ma'lanno *sm* (*disgrazia*) misfortune; (*malattia*) ailment

mala'pena *sf* **a ~** hardly, scarcely

ma'laria *sf* (*Med*) malaria

ma'lato, -a *ag* ill, sick; (*gamba*) bad; (*pianta*) diseased ▷ *sm/f* sick person; (*in ospedale*) patient; **malat'tia** *sf* (*infettiva ecc*) illness, disease; (*cattiva salute*) illness, sickness; (*di pianta*) disease

mala'vita *sf* underworld

mala'voglia [mala'vɔʎʎa] *sf* **di ~** unwillingly, reluctantly

Mala'ysia *sf* Malaysia

mal'concio, -a, -ci, -ce [mal'kontʃo] *ag* in a sorry state

malcon'tento *sm* discontent

malcos'tume *sm* immorality

mal'destro, -a *ag* (*inabile*) inexpert, inexperienced; (*goffo*) awkward

'male *av* badly ▷ *sm* (*ciò che è ingiusto, disonesto*) evil; (*danno, svantaggio*) harm; (*sventura*) misfortune; (*dolore fisico, morale*) pain, ache; **di ~ in peggio** from bad to worse; **sentirsi ~** to feel ill; **far ~** (*dolere*) to hurt; **far ~ alla salute** to be bad for one's health; **far del ~ a qn** to hurt *o* harm sb; **restare** *o* **rimanere ~** to be sorry; to be disappointed; to be hurt; **andare a ~** to go bad; **come va? — non c'è ~** how are you? — not bad; **avere mal di gola/testa** to have a sore throat/a headache; **aver ~ ai piedi** to have sore feet; **mal d'auto** carsickness; **mal di cuore** heart trouble; **male di dente** toothache; **mal di mare** seasickness

male'detto, -a *pp di* **maledire** ▷ *ag* cursed, damned; (*fig: fam*) damned, blasted

male'dire *vt* to curse; **maledizi'one** *sf* curse; **maledizione!** damn it!

maledu'cato, -a *ag* rude, ill-mannered

maleducazi'one [male,dukat'tsjone] *sf* rudeness

ma'lefico, -a, -ci, -che *ag* (*influsso, azione*) evil

ma'lessere *sm* indisposition, slight illness; (*fig*) uneasiness

malfa'mato, -a *ag* notorious

malfat'tore, -'trice *sm/f* wrongdoer

mal'fermo, -a *ag* unsteady, shaky; (*salute*) poor, delicate

mal'grado *prep* in spite of, despite ▷ *cong* although; **mio (*o* tuo *ecc*) ~** against my (*o* your *ecc*) will

ma'ligno, -a [ma'liɲɲo] *ag* (*malvagio*) malicious, malignant; (*Med*) malignant

malinco'nia *sf* melancholy, gloom; **malin'conico, -a, -ci, -che** *ag* melancholy

malincu'ore: **a ~** *av* reluctantly, unwillingly

malin'teso, -a *ag* misunderstood; (*riguardo, senso del dovere*) mistaken, wrong ▷ *sm* misunderstanding; **c'è stato un ~** there's been a misunderstanding

ma'lizia [ma'littsja] *sf* (*malignità*) malice; (*furbizia*) cunning; (*espediente*) trick; **malizi'oso, -a** *ag* malicious; cunning; (*vivace, birichino*) mischievous

malme'nare *vt* to beat up

ma'locchio [ma'lɔkkjo] *sm* evil eye

ma'lora *sf* **andare in ~** to go to the dogs

ma'lore *sm* (*sudden*) illness

mal'sano, -a *ag* unhealthy

'malta *sf* (*Edil*) mortar

mal'tempo *sm* bad weather

'malto sm malt

maltrat'tare vt to ill-treat

malu'more sm bad mood; (irritabilità) bad temper; (discordia) ill feeling; **di ~** in a bad mood

'malva sf (Bot) mallow ▷ ag, sm inv mauve

mal'vagio, -a, -gi, -gie [mal'vadʒo] ag wicked, evil

malvi'vente sm criminal

malvolenti'eri av unwillingly, reluctantly

'mamma sf mummy, mum; **~ mia!** my goodness!

mam'mella sf (Anat) breast; (di vacca, capra ecc) udder

mam'mifero sm mammal

ma'nata sf (colpo) slap; (quantità) handful

man'canza [man'kantsa] sf lack; (carenza) shortage, scarcity; (fallo) fault; (imperfezione) failing, shortcoming; **per ~ di tempo** through lack of time; **in ~ di meglio** for lack of anything better

man'care vi (essere insufficiente) to be lacking; (venir meno) to fail; (sbagliare) to be wrong, make a mistake; (non esserci) to be missing, not to be there; (essere lontano): **~ (da)** to be away (from) ▷ vt to miss; **~ di** to lack; **~ a** (promessa) to fail to keep; **tu mi manchi** I miss you; **mancò poco che morisse** he very nearly died; **mancano ancora 10 sterline** we're still £10 short; **manca un quarto alle 6** it's a quarter to 6

mancherò ecc [manke'rɔ] vb vedi **mancare**

'mancia, -ce ['mantʃa] sf tip; **quanto devo lasciare di ~?** how much should I tip?; **~ competente** reward

manci'ata [man'tʃata] sf handful

man'cino, -a [man'tʃino] ag (braccio) left; (persona) left-handed; (fig) underhand

manda'rancio [manda'rantʃo] sm clementine

man'dare vt to send; (far funzionare: macchina) to drive; (emettere) to send out; (: grido) to give, utter, let out; **~ a chiamare qn** to send for sb; **~ avanti** (fig: famiglia) to provide for; (: fabbrica) to run, look after; **~ giù** to send down; (anche fig) to swallow; **~ via** to send away; (licenziare) to fire

manda'rino sm mandarin (orange); (cinese) mandarin

man'data sf (quantità) lot, batch; (di chiave) turn; **chiudere a doppia ~** to double-lock

man'dato sm (incarico) commission; (Dir: provvedimento) warrant; (di deputato ecc) mandate; (ordine di pagamento) postal o money order; **mandato d'arresto** warrant for arrest

man'dibola sf mandible, jaw

'mandorla sf almond; **'mandorlo** sm almond tree

'mandria sf herd

maneggi'are [maned'dʒare] vt (creta, cera) to mould, work, fashion; (arnesi, utensili) to handle; (: adoperare) to use; (fig: persone, denaro) to handle, deal with; **ma'neggio** sm moulding; handling; use; (intrigo) plot, scheme; (per cavalli) riding school

ma'nesco, -a, -schi, -sche ag free with one's fists

ma'nette sfpl handcuffs

manga'nello sm club

mangi'are [man'dʒare] vt to eat; (intaccare) to eat into o away; (Carte, Scacchi ecc) to take ▷ vi to eat ▷ sm eating; (cibo) food; (cucina) cooking; **possiamo ~ qualcosa?** can we have something to eat?; **mangiarsi le parole** to mumble; **mangiarsi le unghie** to bite one's nails

man'gime [man'dʒime] sm fodder

'mango, -ghi sm mango

ma'nia sf (Psic) mania; (fig) obsession, craze; **ma'niaco, -a, -ci, -che** ag suffering from a mania; **maniaco (di)** obsessed (by), crazy (about)

'manica sf sleeve; (fig: gruppo) gang, bunch; (Geo): **la M~, il Canale della M~** the (English) Channel; **essere di ~ larga/ stretta** to be easy-going/strict; **manica a vento** (Aer) wind sock

mani'chino [mani'kino] sm (di sarto, vetrina) dummy

'manico, -ci sm handle; (Mus) neck

mani'comio sm mental hospital; (fig) madhouse

mani'cure sm o f inv manicure ▷ sf inv manicurist

mani'era sf way, manner; (stile) style, manner; **maniere** sfpl (comportamento) manners; **in ~ che** so that; **in ~ da** so as to; **in tutte le maniere** at all costs

manifes'tare vt to show, display; (esprimere) to express; (rivelare) to reveal, disclose ▷ vi to demonstrate; **manifestazi'one** sf show, display; expression; (sintomo) sign, symptom; (dimostrazione pubblica) demonstration; (cerimonia) event

mani'festo, -a ag obvious, evident ▷ sm poster, bill; (scritto ideologico) manifesto

ma'niglia [ma'niʎʎa] sf handle; (sostegno: negli autobus ecc) strap

manipo'lare vt to manipulate; (alterare: vino) to adulterate

man'naro: lupo ~ sm werewolf

'mano, -i sf hand; (strato: di vernice ecc) coat; **di prima ~** (notizia) first-hand; **di**

seconda ~ second-hand; **man ~** little by little, gradually; **man ~ che** as; **darsi** o **stringersi la ~** to shake hands; **mettere le mani avanti** (fig) to safeguard o.s.; **restare a mani vuote** to be left empty-handed; **venire alle mani** to come to blows; **a ~** by hand; **mani in alto!** hands up!

mano'dopera sf labour

ma'nometro sm gauge, manometer

mano'mettere vt (alterare) to tamper with; (aprire indebitamente) to break open illegally

ma'nopola sf (dell'armatura) gauntlet; (guanto) mitt; (di impugnatura) hand-grip; (pomello) knob

manos'critto, -a ag handwritten ▷ sm manuscript

mano'vale sm labourer

mano'vella sf handle; (Tecn) crank

ma'novra sf manoeuvre (BRIT), maneuver (US); (Ferr) shunting

man'sarda sf attic

mansi'one sf task, duty, job

mansu'eto, -a ag gentle, docile

man'tello sm cloak; (fig: di neve ecc) blanket, mantle; (Zool) coat

mante'nere vt to maintain; (adempiere: promesse) to keep, abide by; (provvedere a) to support, maintain; **mantenersi** vpr **mantenersi calmo/giovane** to stay calm/young

'Mantova sf Mantua

manu'ale ag manual ▷ sm (testo) manual, handbook

ma'nubrio sm handle; (di bicicletta ecc) handlebars pl; (Sport) dumbbell

manutenzi'one [manuten'tsjone] sf maintenance, upkeep; (d'impianti) maintenance, servicing

'manzo ['mandzo] sm (Zool) steer; (carne) beef

'mappa sf (Geo) map; **mappa'mondo** sm map of the world; (globo girevole) globe

mara'tona sf marathon

'marca, -che sf (Comm: di prodotti) brand; (contrassegno, scontrino) ticket, check; **prodotto di ~** (di buona qualità) high-class product; **marca da bollo** official stamp

mar'care vt (munire di contrassegno) to mark; (a fuoco) to brand; (Sport: gol) to score; (: avversario) to mark; (accentuare) to stress; **~ visita** (Mil) to report sick

marcherò ecc [marke'rɔ] vb vedi **marcare**

mar'chese, -a [mar'keze] sm/f marquis o marquess/marchioness

marchi'are [mar'kjare] vt to brand

'marcia, -ce ['martʃa] sf (anche Mus, Mil) march; (funzionamento) running; (il

camminare) walking; (Aut) gear; **mettere in ~** to start; **mettersi in ~** to get moving; **far ~ indietro** (Aut) to reverse; (fig) to back-pedal

marciapi'ede [martʃa'pjɛde] sm (di strada) pavement (BRIT), sidewalk (US); (Ferr) platform

marci'are [mar'tʃare] vi to march; (andare: treno, macchina) to go; (funzionare) to run, work

'marcio, -a, -ci, -ce ['martʃo] ag (frutta, legno) rotten, bad; (Med) festering; (fig) corrupt, rotten

mar'cire [mar'tʃire] vi (andare a male) to go bad, rot; (suppurare) to fester; (fig) to rot, waste away

'marco, -chi sm (unità monetaria) mark

'mare sm sea; **in ~** at sea; **andare al ~** (in vacanza ecc) to go to the seaside; **il M~ del Nord** the North Sea

ma'rea sf tide; **alta/bassa ~** high/low tide

mareggi'ata [mared'dʒata] sf heavy sea

mare'moto sm seaquake

maresci'allo [mareʃʃallo] sm (Mil) marshal; (: sottufficiale) warrant officer

marga'rina sf margarine

marghe'rita [marge'rita] sf (ox-eye) daisy, marguerite; (di stampante) daisy wheel

'margine ['mardʒine] sm margin; (di bosco, via) edge, border

mariju'ana [mæri'wa:nə] sf marijuana

ma'rina sf navy; (costa) coast; (quadro) seascape; **marina mercantile/militare** navy/merchant navy (BRIT) o marine (US)

mari'naio sm sailor

mari'nare vt (Cuc) to marinate; **~ la scuola** to play truant

ma'rino, -a ag sea cpd, marine

mario'netta sf puppet

ma'rito sm husband

ma'rittimo, -a ag maritime, sea cpd

marmel'lata sf jam; (di agrumi) marmalade

mar'mitta sf (recipiente) pot; (Aut) silencer; **marmitta catalitica** catalytic converter

'marmo sm marble

mar'motta sf (Zool) marmot

maroc'chino, -a [marok'kino] ag, sm/f Moroccan

Ma'rocco sm **il ~** Morocco

mar'rone ag inv brown ▷ sm (Bot) chestnut

> Attenzione! In inglese esiste la parola *maroon*, che però indica un altro colore, il rosso bordeaux.

mar'supio sm pouch; (per denaro) bum bag; (per neonato) sling

martedì sm inv Tuesday; **di** o **il ~** on

Tuesdays; **martedì grasso** Shrove Tuesday

martel'lare *vt* to hammer ▷ *vi* (*pulsare*) to throb; (: *cuore*) to thump

mar'tello *sm* hammer; (: *di uscio*) knocker; **martello pneumatico** pneumatic drill

'martire *sm/f* martyr

mar'xista, -i, -e *ag, sm/f* Marxist

marza'pane [martsa'pane] *sm* marzipan

'marzo ['martso] *sm* March

mascal'zone [maskal'tsone] *sm* rascal, scoundrel

mas'cara *sm inv* mascara

ma'scella [maʃʃella] *sf* (*Anat*) jaw

'maschera ['maskera] *sf* mask; (*travestimento*) disguise; (: *per un ballo ecc*) fancy dress; (*Teatro, Cinema*) usher/usherette; (*personaggio del teatro*) stock character; **masche'rare** *vt* to mask; (*travestire*) to disguise; to dress up; (*fig: celare*) to hide, conceal; (*Mil*) to camouflage; **mascherarsi da** to disguise o.s. as; to dress up as; (*fig*) to masquerade as

mas'chile [mas'kile] *ag* masculine; (*sesso, popolazione*) male; (*abiti*) men's; (*per ragazzi: scuola*) boys'

mas'chilista, -i, -e *ag, sm/f* (*uomo*) (male) chauvinist, sexist; (*donna*) sexist

'maschio, -a ['maskjo] *ag* (*Biol*) male; (*virile*) manly ▷ *sm* (*anche Zool, Tecn*) male; (*uomo*) man; (*ragazzo*) boy; (*figlio*) son

masco'lino, -a *ag* masculine

'massa *sf* mass; (*di errori ecc*) **una ~ di** heaps of, masses of; (*di gente*) mass, multitude; (*Elettr*) earth; **in ~** (*Comm*) in bulk; (*tutti insieme*) en masse; **adunata in ~** mass meeting; **di ~** (*cultura, manifestazione*) mass *cpd*

mas'sacro *sm* massacre, slaughter; (*fig*) mess, disaster

massaggi'are [massad'dʒare] *vt* to massage

mas'saggio [mas'saddʒo] *sm* massage; **massaggio cardiaco** cardiac massage

mas'saia *sf* housewife

masse'rizie [masse'rittsje] *sfpl* (household) furnishings

mas'siccio, -a, -ci, -ce [mas'sittʃo] *ag* (*oro, legno*) solid; (*palazzo*) massive; (*corporatura*) stout ▷ *sm* (*Geo*) massif

'massima *sf* (*sentenza, regola*) maxim; (*Meteor*) maximum temperature; **in linea di ~** generally speaking; *vedi* **massimo**

massi'male *sm* maximum

'massimo, -a *ag, sm* maximum; **al ~** at (the) most

'masso *sm* rock, boulder

masteriz'zare [masterid'dzare] *vt* (*CD, DVD*) to burn

masterizza'tore [masteriddza'tore] *sm* CD burner o writer

masti'care *vt* to chew

'mastice ['mastitʃe] *sm* mastic; (*per vetri*) putty

mas'tino *sm* mastiff

ma'tassa *sf* skein

mate'matica *sf* mathematics *sg*

mate'matico, -a, -ci, -che *ag* mathematical ▷ *sm/f* mathematician

materas'sino *sm* mat; **materasso gonfiabile** air bed

mate'rasso *sm* mattress; **materasso a molle** spring o interior-sprung mattress

ma'teria *sf* (*Fisica*) matter; (*Tecn, Comm*) material, matter *no pl*; (*disciplina*) subject; (*argomento*) subject matter, material; **in ~ di** (*per quanto concerne*) on the subject of; **materie prime** raw materials

materi'ale *ag* material; (*fig: grossolano*) rough, rude ▷ *sm* material; (*insieme di strumenti ecc*) equipment *no pl*, materials *pl*

maternità *sf* motherhood, maternity; (*reparto*) maternity ward

ma'terno, -a *ag* (*amore, cura ecc*) maternal, motherly; (*nonno*) maternal; (*lingua, terra*) mother *cpd*

ma'tita *sf* pencil; **matite colorate** coloured pencils; **matita per gli occhi** eyeliner (pencil)

ma'tricola *sf* (*registro*) register; (*numero*) registration number; (*nell'università*) freshman, fresher

ma'trigna [ma'trinna] *sf* stepmother

matrimoni'ale *ag* matrimonial, marriage *cpd*

matri'monio *sm* marriage, matrimony; (*durata*) marriage, married life; (*cerimonia*) wedding

mat'tina *sf* morning

'matto, -a *ag* mad, crazy; (*fig: falso*) false, imitation ▷ *sm/f* madman/woman; **avere una voglia matta di qc** to be dying for sth

mat'tone *sm* brick; (*fig*): **questo libro/ film è un ~** this book/film is heavy going

matto'nella *sf* tile

matu'rare *vi* (*anche*: **maturarsi**: *frutta, grano*) to ripen; (*ascesso*) to come to a head; (*fig: persona, idea, Econ*) to mature ▷ *vt* to ripen, to (make) mature

maturità *sf* maturity; (*di frutta*) ripeness, maturity; (*Ins*) school-leaving examination, ≈ GCE A-levels (*BRIT*)

ma'turo, -a *ag* mature; (*frutto*) ripe, mature

max. *abbr* (= *massimo*) max

maxischermo [maxis'kermo] *sm* giant screen

'mazza ['mattsa] *sf* (*bastone*) club;

(*martello*) sledge-hammer; (*Sport: da golf*) club; (: *da baseball, cricket*) bat

maz'zata [mat'tsata] *sf* (*anche fig*) heavy blow

'**mazzo** ['mattso] *sm* (*di fiori, chiavi ecc*) bunch; (*di carte da gioco*) pack

me *pron* me; **me stesso(a)** myself; **sei bravo quanto me** you are as clever as I (am) o as me

mec'canico, -a, -ci, -che *ag* mechanical ▷ *sm* mechanic; **può mandare un ~?** can you send a mechanic?

mecca'nismo *sm* mechanism

me'daglia [me'daʎʎa] *sf* medal

me'desimo, -a *ag* same; (*in persona*): **io ~ I** myself

'**media** *sf* average; (*Mat*) mean; (*Ins: voto*) end-of-term average; **le medie** *sfpl* = **scuola media**; **in ~** on average; *vedi anche* **medio**

medi'ante *prep* by means of

media'tore, -'trice *sm/f* mediator; (*Comm*) middle man, agent

medi'care *vt* to treat; (*ferita*) to dress

medi'cina [medi'tʃina] *sf* medicine; **medicina legale** forensic medicine

'**medico, -a, -ci, -che** *ag* medical ▷ *sm* doctor; **chiamate un ~** call a doctor; **medico generico** general practitioner, GP

medie'vale *ag* medieval

'**medio, -a** *ag* average; (*punto, ceto*) middle; (*altezza, statura*) medium ▷ *sm* (*dito*) middle finger; **licenza media** *leaving certificate awarded at the end of 3 years of secondary education*; **scuola media** *first 3 years of secondary school*

medi'ocre *ag* mediocre, poor

medi'tare *vt* to ponder over, meditate on; (*progettare*) to plan, think out ▷ *vi* to meditate

mediter'raneo, -a *ag* Mediterranean; **il (mare) M~** the Mediterranean (Sea)

me'dusa *sf* (*Zool*) jellyfish

mega'byte *sm inv* (*Comput*) megabyte

me'gafono *sm* megaphone

'**meglio** ['mɛʎʎo] *av, ag inv* better; (*con senso superlativo*) best ▷ *sm* (*la cosa migliore*): **il ~** the best (thing); **faresti ~ ad andartene** you had better leave; **alla ~** as best one can; **andar di bene in ~** to get better and better; **fare del proprio ~** to do one's best; **per il ~** for the best; **aver la ~ su qn** to get the better of sb

'**mela** *sf* apple; **mela cotogna** quince

mela'grana *sf* pomegranate

melan'zana [melan'dzana] *sf* aubergine (*BRIT*), eggplant (*US*)

melato'nina *sf* melatonin

'**melma** *sf* mud, mire

'**melo** *sm* apple tree

melo'dia *sf* melody

me'lone *sm* (musk)melon

'**membro** *sm* member (*pl(f)* **membra**) (*arto*) limb

memo'randum *sm inv* memorandum

me'moria *sf* memory; **memorie** *sfpl* (*opera autobiografica*) memoirs; **a ~** (*imparare, sapere*) by heart; **a ~ d'uomo** within living memory

mendi'cante *sm/f* beggar

 PAROLA CHIAVE

'**meno** *av* **1** (*in minore misura*) less; **dovresti mangiare meno** you should eat less, you shouldn't eat so much

2 (*comparativo*): **meno ... di** not as ... as, less ... than; **sono meno alto di te** I'm not as tall as you (are), I'm less tall than you (are); **meno ... che** not as ... as, less ... than; **meno che mai** less than ever; **è meno intelligente che ricco** he's more rich than intelligent; **meno fumo più mangio** the less I smoke the more I eat

3 (*superlativo*): **il meno dotato degli studenti** the least gifted of the students; **è quello che compro meno spesso** it's the one I buy least often

4 (*Mat*) minus; **8 meno 5** 8 minus 5, 8 take away 5; **sono le 8 meno un quarto** it's a quarter to 8; **meno 5 gradi** 5 degrees below zero, minus 5 degrees; **1 euro in meno** 1 euro less

5 (*fraseologia*): **quanto meno poteva telefonare** he could at least have phoned; **non so se accettare o meno** I don't know whether to accept or not; **fare a meno di qc/qn** to do without sth/sb; **non potevo fare a meno di ridere** I couldn't help laughing; **meno male!** thank goodness!; **meno male che sei arrivato** it's a good job that you've come

▷ *ag inv* (*tempo, denaro*) less; (*errori, persone*) fewer; **ha fatto meno errori di tutti** he made fewer mistakes than anyone, he made the fewest mistakes of all ▷ *sm inv* **1**: **il meno** (*il minimo*) the least; **parlare del più e del meno** to talk about this and that **2** (*Mat*) minus

▷ *prep* (*eccetto*) except (for), apart from; **a meno che, a meno di** unless; **a meno che non piova** unless it rains; **non posso, a meno di prendere ferie** I can't, unless I take some leave

meno'pausa *sf* menopause

'**mensa** *sf* (*locale*) canteen; (: *Mil*) mess; (: *nelle università*) refectory

men'sile *ag* monthly ▷ *sm* (*periodico*) monthly (magazine); (*stipendio*) monthly salary

'**mensola** *sf* bracket; (*ripiano*) shelf; (*Archit*) corbel

'**menta** *sf* mint; (*anche*: ~ **piperita**) peppermint; (*bibita*) peppermint cordial; (*caramella*) mint, peppermint

men'tale *ag* mental; **mentalità** *sf inv* mentality

'**mente** *sf* mind; **imparare/sapere qc a** ~ to learn/know sth by heart; **avere in** ~ **qc** to have sth in mind; **passare di** ~ **a qn** to slip sb's mind

men'tire *vi* to lie

'**mento** *sm* chin

'**mentre** *cong* (*temporale*) while; (*avversativo*) whereas

menù *sm inv* menu; **ci può portare il** ~? could we see the menu?; **menù turistico** set menu

menzio'nare [mentsjo'nare] *vt* to mention

men'zogna [men'tsoɲɲa] *sf* lie

mera'viglia [mera'viʎʎa] *sf* amazement, wonder; (*persona, cosa*) marvel, wonder; **a** ~ perfectly, wonderfully, wonder; **meravigli'are** *vt* to amaze, astonish; **meravigliarsi (di)** to marvel (at); (*stupirsi*) to be amazed (at), be astonished (at); **meravigli'oso, -a** *ag* wonderful, marvellous

mer'cante *sm* merchant; **mercante d'arte** art dealer

merca'tino *sm* (*rionale*) local street market; (*Econ*) unofficial stock market

mer'cato *sm* market; **mercato dei cambi** exchange market; **mercato nero** black market

'**merce** ['mɛrtʃe] *sf* goods *pl*, merchandise

mercé [mer'tʃe] *sf* mercy

merce'ria [mertʃe'ria] *sf* (*articoli*) haberdashery (BRIT), notions *pl* (US); (*bottega*) haberdasher's shop (BRIT), notions store (US)

mercoledì *sm inv* Wednesday; **di** o **il** ~ on Wednesdays; **mercoledì delle Ceneri** Ash Wednesday

mer'curio *sm* mercury

'**merda** (*fam!*) *sf* shit (!)

me'renda *sf* afternoon snack

meren'dina *sf* snack

meridi'ana *sf* (*orologio*) sundial

meridi'ano, -a *ag* meridian; midday *cpd*, noonday ▷ *sm* meridian

meridio'nale *ag* southern ▷ *sm/f* southerner

meridi'one *sm* south

me'ringa, -ghe *sf* (*Cuc*) meringue

meri'tare *vt* to deserve, merit ▷ *vb impers*

merita andare it's worth going

meri'tevole *ag* worthy

'**merito** *sm* merit; (*valore*) worth; **in** ~ **a** as regards, with regard to; **dare** ~ **a qn di** to give sb credit for; **finire a pari** ~ to finish joint first (*o* second *ecc*); to tie

mer'letto *sm* lace

'**merlo** *sm* (*Zool*) blackbird; (*Archit*) battlement

mer'luzzo [mer'luttso] *sm* (*Zool*) cod

mes'chino, -a [mes'kino] *ag* wretched; (*scarso*) scanty, poor; (*persona: gretta*) mean; (: *limitata*) narrow-minded, petty

mesco'lare *vt* to mix; (*vini, colori*) to blend; (*mettere in disordine*) to mix up, muddle up; (*carte*) to shuffle

'**mese** *sm* month

'**messa** *sf* (*Rel*) mass; (*il mettere*): **messa in moto** starting; **messa in piega** set; **messa a punto** (*Tecn*) adjustment; (*Aut*) tuning; (*fig*) clarification; **messa in scena** = **messinscena**

messag'gero [messad'dʒero] *sm* messenger

messaggino [messad'dʒino] *sm* (*di telefonino*) text (message)

mes'saggio [mes'saddʒo] *sm* message; **posso lasciare un** ~? can I leave a message?; **ci sono messaggi per me?** are there any messages for me?; **messaggio di posta elettronica** e-mail message

messag'gistica [messad'dʒistica] *sf* ~ **immediata** (*Inform*) instant messaging; **programma di** ~ **immediata** instant messenger

mes'sale *sm* (*Rel*) missal

messi'cano, -a *ag, sm/f* Mexican

'**Messico** *sm* **il** ~ Mexico

messin'scena [messin'ʃena] *sf* (*Teatro*) production

'**messo, -a** *pp di* **mettere** ▷ *sm* messenger

mesti'ere *sm* (*professione*) job; (: *manuale*) trade; (: *artigianale*) craft; (*fig: abilità nel lavoro*) skill, technique; **essere del** ~ to know the tricks of the trade

'**mestolo** *sm* (*Cuc*) ladle

mestruazi'one [mestruat'tsjone] *sf* menstruation

'**meta** *sf* destination; (*fig*) aim, goal

metà *sf inv* half; (*punto di mezzo*) middle; **dividere qc a** o **per** ~ to divide sth in half, halve sth; **fare a** ~ **(di qc con qn)** to go halves (with sb in sth); **a** ~ **prezzo** at half price; **a** ~ **strada** halfway

meta'done *sm* methadone

me'tafora *sf* metaphor

me'tallico, -a, -ci, -che *ag* (*di metallo*) metal *cpd*; (*splendore, rumore ecc*) metallic

me'tallo *sm* metal

metalmec'canico, -a, -ci, -che *ag* engineering *cpd* ▷ *sm* engineering worker

me'tano *sm* methane

me'ticcio, -a, -ci, -ce [me'tittʃo] *sm/f* half-caste, half-breed

me'todico, -a, -ci, -che *ag* methodical

'metodo *sm* method

'metro *sm* metre; (*nastro*) tape measure; (*asta*) (metre) rule

metropoli'tana *sf* underground, subway

'mettere *vt* to put; (*abito*) to put on; (: *portare*) to wear; (*installare: telefono*) to put in; (*fig: provocare*): **~ fame/allegria a qn** to make sb hungry/happy; (*supporre*): **mettiamo che ...** let's suppose *o* say that ...; **mettersi** *vpr* (*persona*) to put o.s.; (*oggetto*) to go; (*disporsi: faccenda*) to turn out; **mettersi a sedere** to sit down; **mettersi a letto** to get into bed; (*per malattia*) to take to one's bed; **mettersi il cappello** to put on one's hat; **mettersi a** (*cominciare*) to begin to, start to; **mettersi al lavoro** to set to work; **mettersi con qn** (*in società*) to team up with sb; (*in coppia*) to start going out with sb; **metterci: metterci molta cura/molto tempo** to take a lot of care/a lot of time; **ci ho messo 3 ore per venire** it's taken me 3 hours to get here; **mettercela tutta** to do one's best; **~ a tacere qn/qc** to keep sb/sth quiet; **~ su casa** to set up house; **~ su un negozio** to start a shop; **~ via** to put away

mezza'notte [meddza'nɔtte] *sf* midnight

'mezzo, -a ['mɛddzo] *ag* half; **un ~ litro/panino** half a litre/roll ▷ *av* half-; **~ morto** half-dead ▷ *sm* (*metà*) half; (*parte centrale: di strada ecc*) middle; (*per raggiungere un fine*) means *sg*; (*veicolo*) vehicle; (*nell'indicare l'ora*): **le nove e ~** half past nine; **~giorno e ~** half past twelve; **mezzi** *smpl* (*possibilità economiche*) means; **di mezza età** middle-aged; **un soprabito di mezza stagione** a spring (*o* autumn) coat; **di ~** middle, in the middle; **andarci di ~** (*patir danno*) to suffer; **levarsi** *o* **togliersi di ~** to get out of the way; **in ~ a** in the middle of; **per** *o* **a ~ di** by means of; **mezzi di comunicazione di massa** mass media *pl*; **mezzi pubblici** public transport *sg*; **mezzi di trasporto** means of transport

mezzogi'orno [meddzo'dʒorno] *sm* midday, noon; **a ~** at 12 (o'clock) *o* midday *o* noon; **il ~ d'Italia** southern Italy

mi (*dav lo, la, li, le, ne diventa* **me**) *pron* (*oggetto*) me; (*complemento di termine*) to me; (*riflessivo*) myself ▷ *sm* (*Mus*) E; (: *solfeggiando la scala*) mi

miago'lare *vi* to miaow, mew

'mica *av* (*fam*): **non ... ~** not ... at all; **non**

sono ~ stanco I'm not a bit tired; **non sarà ~ partito?** he wouldn't have left, would he?; **~ male** not bad

'miccia, -ce ['mittʃa] *sf* fuse

micidi'ale [mitʃi'djale] *ag* fatal; (*dannosissimo*) deadly

micro'fibra *sf* microfibre

mi'crofono *sm* microphone

micros'copio *sm* microscope

mi'dollo (*pl(f)* **midolla**) *sm* (*Anat*) marrow; **midollo osseo** bone marrow

mi'ele *sm* honey

'miglia ['miʎʎa] *sfpl di* **miglio**

migli'aio [miʎ'ʎajo] ((*pl*)*f* **migliaia**) *sm* thousand; **un ~ (di)** about a thousand; **a migliaia** by the thousand, in thousands

'miglio ['miʎʎo] *sm* (*Bot*) millet (*pl(f)* **miglia**) (*unità di misura*) mile; **~ marino** *o* **nautico** nautical mile

migliora'mento [miʎʎora'mento] *sm* improvement

miglio'rare [miʎʎo'rare] *vt, vi* to improve

migli'ore [miʎ'ʎore] *ag* (*comparativo*) better; (*superlativo*) best ▷ *sm* **il ~** the best (thing) ▷ *sm/f* **il(la) ~** the best (person); **il miglior vino di questa regione** the best wine in this area

'mignolo ['miɲɲolo] *sm* (*Anat*) little finger, pinkie; (: *dito del piede*) little toe

Mi'lano *sf* Milan

miliar'dario, -a *sm/f* millionaire

mili'ardo *sm* thousand million, billion (*us*)

mili'one *sm* million; **mille euro** one thousand euros

mili'tante *ag, sm/f* militant

mili'tare *vi* (*Mil*) to be a soldier, serve; (*fig: in un partito*) to be a militant ▷ *ag* military ▷ *sm* serviceman; **fare il ~** to do one's military service

'mille (*pl* **mila**) *num* a *o* one thousand; **dieci mila** ten thousand

mil'lennio *sm* millennium

millepi'edi *sm inv* centipede

mil'lesimo, -a *ag, sm* thousandth

milli'grammo *sm* milligram(me)

milli'metro *sm* millimetre

'milza ['miltsa] *sf* (*Anat*) spleen

mimetiz'zare [mimetid'dzare] *vt* to camouflage; **mimetizzarsi** *vpr* to camouflage o.s.

'mimo *sm* (*attore, componimento*) mime

mi'mosa *sf* mimosa

min. *abbr* (= *minuto, minimo*) min.

'mina *sf* (*esplosiva*) mine; (*di matita*) lead

mi'naccia, -ce [mi'nattʃa] *sf* threat; **minacci'are** *vt* to threaten; **minacciare qn di morte** to threaten to kill sb; **minacciare di fare qc** to threaten to do sth

mi'nare vt (Mil) to mine; (fig) to undermine

mina'tore sm miner

mine'rale ag, sm mineral

mine'rario, -a ag (delle miniere) mining; (dei minerali) ore cpd

mi'nestra sf soup; **minestra in brodo** noodle soup; **minestra di verdure** vegetable soup

minia'tura sf miniature

mini'bar sm inv minibar

mini'era sf mine

mini'gonna sf miniskirt

'minimo, -a ag minimum, least, slightest; (piccolissimo) very small, slight; (il più basso) lowest, minimum ▷ sm minimum; **al ~** at least; **girare al ~** (Aut) to idle

minis'tero sm (Pol, Rel) ministry; (governo) government; **M~ delle Finanze** Ministry of Finance, ≈ Treasury

mi'nistro sm (Pol, Rel) minister

mino'ranza [mino'rantsa] sf minority

mi'nore ag (comparativo) less; (più piccolo) smaller; (numero) lower; (inferiore) lower, inferior; (meno importante) minor; (più giovane) younger; (superlativo) least; smallest; lowest; youngest ▷ sm/f = **minorenne**

mino'renne ag under age ▷ sm/f minor, person under age

mi'nuscolo, -a ag (scrittura, carattere) small; (piccolissimo) tiny ▷ sf small letter

mi'nuto, -a ag tiny, minute; (pioggia) fine; (corporatura) delicate, fine ▷ sm (unità di misura) minute; **al ~** (Comm) retail

'mio (f **'mia**, pl **mi'ei** or **'mie**) det **il ~**, **la mia** ecc my ▷ pron **il ~**, **la mia** ecc mine; **i miei** my family; **un ~ amico** a friend of mine

'miope ag short-sighted

'mira sf (anche fig) aim; **prendere la ~** to take aim; **prendere di ~ qn** (fig) to pick on sb

mi'racolo sm miracle

mi'raggio [mi'raddʒo] sm mirage

mi'rare vi **~ a** to aim at

mi'rino sm (Tecn) sight; (Fot) viewer, viewfinder

mir'tillo sm bilberry (BRIT), blueberry (US), whortleberry

mi'scela [miʃʃela] sf mixture; (di caffè) blend

'mischia ['miskja] sf scuffle; (Rugby) scrum, scrummage

mis'cuglio [mis'kuʎʎo] sm mixture, hotchpotch, jumble

'mise vb vedi **mettere**

mise'rabile ag (infelice) miserable, wretched; (povero) poverty-stricken; (di scarso valore) miserable

mi'seria sf extreme poverty; (infelicità) misery

miseri'cordia sf mercy, pity

'misero, -a ag miserable, wretched; (povero) poverty-stricken; (insufficiente) miserable

'misi vb vedi **mettere**

mi'sogino [mi'zɔdʒino] sm misogynist

'missile sm missile

missio'nario, -a ag, sm/f missionary

missi'one sf mission

misteri'oso, -a ag mysterious

mis'tero sm mystery

'misto, -a ag mixed; (scuola) mixed, coeducational ▷ sm mixture

mis'tura sf mixture

mi'sura sf measure; (misurazione, dimensione) measurement; (taglia) size; (provvedimento) measure, step; (moderazione) moderation; (Mus) time; (: divisione) bar; (fig: limite) bounds pl, limit; **nella ~ in cui** inasmuch as, insofar as; **(fatto) su ~** made to measure

misu'rare vt (ambiente, stoffa) to measure; (terreno) to survey; (abito) to try on; (pesare) to weigh; (fig: parole ecc) to weigh up; (: spese, cibo) to limit ▷ vi to measure; **misurarsi** vpr **misurarsi con qn** to have a confrontation with sb; to compete with sb

'mite ag mild

'mitico, -a, -ci, -che ag mythical

'mito sm myth; **mitolo'gia, -'gie** sf mythology

'mitra sf (Rel) mitre ▷ sm inv (arma) sub-machine gun

mit'tente sm/f sender

mm abbr (= millimetro) mm

'mobile ag mobile; (parte di macchina) moving; (Dir: bene) movable, personal ▷ sm (arredamento) piece of furniture; **mobili** smpl (mobilia) furniture sg

mocas'sino sm moccasin

'moda sf fashion; **alla ~, di ~** fashionable, in fashion

modalità sf inv formality

mo'della sf model

mo'dello sm model; (stampo) mould ▷ ag inv model cpd

'modem sm inv modem

modera'tore, -'trice sm/f moderator

mo'derno, -a ag modern

mo'desto, -a ag modest

'modico, -a, -ci, -che ag reasonable, moderate

mo'difica, -che sf modification

modifi'care vt to modify, alter

'modo sm way, manner; (mezzo) means, way; (occasione) opportunity; (Ling) mood; (Mus) mode; **modi** smpl (comportamento) manners; **a suo ~, a ~ suo** in his own way;

ad o **in ogni ~** anyway; **di** o **in ~ che** so that; **in ~ da** so as to; **in tutti i modi** at all costs; (*comunque sia*) anyway; (*in ogni caso*) in any case; **in qualche ~** somehow or other; **per ~ di dire** so to speak; **modo di dire** turn of phrase

'**modulo** *sm* (*modello*) form; (*Archit, lunare, di comando*) module

'**mogano** *sm* mahogany

'**mogio, -a, -gi, -gie** ['mɔdʒo] *ag* down in the dumps, dejected

'**moglie** ['mɔʎʎe] *sf* wife

mo'ine *sfpl* cajolery *sg*; (*leziosità*) affectation *sg*

mo'lare *sm* (*dente*) molar

'**mole** *sf* mass; (*dimensioni*) size; (*edificio grandioso*) massive structure

moles'tare *vt* to bother, annoy; **mo'lestia** *sf* annoyance, bother; **recar molestia a qn** to bother sb; **molestie sessuali** sexual harassment *sg*

'**molla** *sf* spring; **molle** *sfpl* (*per camino*) tongs

mol'lare *vt* to release, let go; (*Naut*) to ease; (*fig: ceffone*) to give ▷ *vi* (*cedere*) to give in

'**molle** *ag* soft; (*muscoli*) flabby

mol'letta *sf* (*per capelli*) hairgrip; (*per panni stesi*) clothes peg

'**mollica, -che** *sf* crumb, soft part

mol'lusco, -schi *sm* mollusc

'**molo** *sm* mole, breakwater; jetty

moltipli'care *vt* to multiply; **moltiplicarsi** *vpr* to multiply; to increase in number; **moltiplicazi'one** *sf* multiplication

○ PAROLA CHIAVE

'**molto, -a** *det* (*quantità*) a lot of, much; (*numero*) a lot of, many; **molto pane/carbone** a lot of bread/coal; **molta gente** a lot of people, many people; **molti libri** a lot of books, many books; **non ho molto tempo** I haven't got much time; **per molto (tempo)** for a long time
▷ *av* **1** a lot, (very) much; **viaggia molto** he travels a lot; **non viaggia molto** he doesn't travel much o a lot
2 (*intensivo: con aggettivi, avverbi*) very; (: *con participio passato*) (very) much; **molto buono** very good; **molto migliore, molto meglio** much o a lot better
▷ *pron* much, a lot

momentanea'mente *av* at the moment, at present

momen'taneo, -a *ag* momentary, fleeting

mo'mento *sm* moment; **da un ~ all'altro**

at any moment; (*all'improvviso*) suddenly; **al ~ di fare** just as I was (o you were o he was *ecc*) doing; **per il ~** for the time being; **dal ~ che** ever since; (*dato che*) since; **a momenti** (*da un momento all'altro*) any time o moment now; (*quasi*) nearly

'**monaca, -che** *sf* nun

'**Monaco** *sf* Monaco; **Monaco (di Baviera)** Munich

'**monaco, -ci** *sm* monk

monar'chia *sf* monarchy

monas'tero *sm* (*di monaci*) monastery; (*di monache*) convent

mon'dano, -a *ag* (*anche fig*) worldly; (*anche:* **dell'alta società**) society *cpd*; fashionable

mondi'ale *ag* (*campionato, popolazione*) world *cpd*; (*influenza*) world-wide

'**mondo** *sm* world; (*grande quantità*): **un ~ di** lots of, a host of; **il bel ~** high society

mo'nello, -a *sm/f* street urchin; (*ragazzo vivace*) scamp, imp

mo'neta *sf* coin; (*Econ: valuta*) currency; (*denaro spicciolo*) (small) change; **moneta estera** foreign currency; **moneta legale** legal tender

mongol'fiera *sf* hot-air balloon

'**monitor** *sm inv* (*Tecn, TV*) monitor

monolo'cale *sm* studio flat

mono'polio *sm* monopoly

mo'notono, -a *ag* monotonous

monovo'lume *ag inv, sf inv* (**automobile**) **~** people carrier, MPV

mon'sone *sm* monsoon

monta'carichi [monta'kariki] *sm inv* hoist, goods lift

mon'taggio [mon'taddʒo] *sm* (*Tecn*) assembly; (*Cinema*) editing

mon'tagna [mon'taɲɲa] *sf* mountain; (*zona montuosa*): **la ~** the mountains *pl*; **andare in ~** to go to the mountains; **montagne russe** roller coaster *sg*, big dipper *sg* (*BRIT*)

monta'naro, -a *ag* mountain *cpd* ▷ *sm/f* mountain dweller

mon'tano, -a *ag* mountain *cpd*; alpine

mon'tare *vt* to go (o come) up; (*cavallo*) to ride; (*apparecchiatura*) to set up, assemble; (*Cuc*) to whip; (*Zool*) to cover; (*incastonare*) to mount, set; (*Cinema*) to edit; (*Fot*) to mount ▷ *vi* to go (o come) up; (*a cavallo*): **~ bene/male** to ride well/badly; (*aumentare di livello, volume*) to rise

monta'tura *sf* assembling *no pl*; (*di occhiali*) frames *pl*; (*di gioiello*) mounting, setting; (*fig*): **montatura pubblicitaria** publicity stunt

'**monte** *sm* mountain; **a ~** upstream; **mandare a ~ qc** to upset sth, cause sth to

fail; **il M~ Bianco** Mont Blanc; **monte di pietà** pawnshop; **monte premi** prize
mon'tone sm (Zool) ram; **carne di ~** mutton
montu'oso, -a ag mountainous
monu'mento sm monument
mo'quette [mɔ'ket] sf inv fitted carpet
'mora sf (del rovo) blackberry; (del gelso) mulberry; (Dir) delay; (: somma) arrears pl
mo'rale ag moral ▷ sf (scienza) ethics sg, moral philosophy; (complesso di norme) moral standards pl, morality; (condotta) morals pl; (insegnamento morale) moral ▷ sm morale; **essere giù di ~** to be feeling down
'morbido, -a ag soft; (pelle) soft, smooth

⬛ Attenzione! In inglese esiste la parola morbid, che però significa morboso.

mor'billo sm (Med) measles sg
'morbo sm disease
mor'boso, -a ag (fig) morbid
'mordere vt to bite; (addentare) to bite into
mori'bondo, -a ag dying, moribund
mo'rire vi to die; (abitudine, civiltà) to die out; **~ di fame** to die of hunger; (fig) to be starving; **~ di noia/paura** to be bored/scared to death; **fa un caldo da ~** it's terribly hot
mormo'rare vi to murmur; (brontolare) to grumble
'moro, -a ag dark(-haired), dark(-complexioned)
'morsa sf (Tecn) vice; (fig: stretta) grip
morsi'care vt to nibble (at), gnaw (at); (insetto) to sting
'morso, -a pp di **mordere** ▷ sm bite; (di insetto) sting; (parte della briglia) bit; **morsi della fame** pangs of hunger
morta'della sf (Cuc) mortadella (type of salted pork meat)
mor'taio sm mortar
mor'tale ag, sm mortal
'morte sf death
'morto, -a pp di **morire** ▷ ag dead ▷ sm/f dead man/woman; **i morti** the dead; **fare il ~** (nell'acqua) to float on one's back; **il Mar M~** the Dead Sea
mo'saico, -ci sm mosaic
'Mosca sf Moscow
'mosca, -sche sf fly; **mosca cieca** blind-man's-buff
mosce'rino [moʃʃe'rino] sm midge, gnat
mos'chea [mos'kɛa] sf mosque
'moscio, -a, -sci, -sce ['mɔʃʃo] ag (fig) lifeless
mos'cone sm (Zool) bluebottle; (barca) pedalo; (: a remi) kind of pedalo with oars
'mossa sf movement; (nel gioco) move
'mossi ecc vb vedi **muovere**

'mosso, -a pp di **muovere** ▷ ag (mare) rough; (capelli) wavy; (Fot) blurred
mos'tarda sf mustard; **mostarda di Cremona** pickled fruit with mustard
'mostra sf exhibition, show; (ostentazione) show; **in ~** on show; **far ~ di** (fingere) to pretend; **far ~ di sé** to show off
mos'trare vt to show; **può mostrarmi dov'è, per favore?** can you show me where it is, please?
'mostro sm monster; **mostru'oso, -a** ag monstrous
mo'tel sm inv motel
moti'vare vt (causare) to cause; (giustificare) to justify, account for
mo'tivo sm (causa) reason, cause; (movente) motive; (letterario) (central) theme; (disegno) motif, design, pattern; (Mus) motif; **per quale ~?** why?, for what reason?
'moto sm (anche Fisica) motion; (movimento, gesto) movement; (esercizio fisico) exercise; (sommossa) rising, revolt; (commozione) feeling, impulse ▷ sf inv (motocicletta) motorbike; **mettere in ~** to set in motion; (Aut) to start up
motoci'clista, -i, -e sm/f motorcyclist
mo'tore, -'trice ag motor; (Tecn) driving ▷ sm engine, motor; **a ~** motor cpd, power-driven; **~ a combustione interna/a reazione** internal combustion/jet engine; **motore di ricerca** (Inform) search engine; **moto'rino** sm moped; **motorino di avviamento** (Aut) starter
motos'cafo sm motorboat
'motto sm (battuta scherzosa) witty remark; (frase emblematica) motto, maxim
'mouse ['maus] sm inv (Inform) mouse
mo'vente sm motive
movi'mento sm movement; (fig) activity, hustle and bustle; (Mus) tempo, movement
mozi'one [mot'tsjone] sf (Pol) motion
mozza'rella [mottsa'rɛlla] sf mozzarella, a moist Neapolitan curd cheese
mozzi'cone [mottsi'kone] sm stub, butt, end; (anche: ~ **di sigaretta**) cigarette end
'mucca, -che sf cow; **mucca pazza** mad cow disease
'mucchio ['mukkjo] sm pile, heap; (fig): **un ~ di** lots of, heaps of
'muco, -chi sm mucus
'muffa sf mould, mildew
mug'gire [mud'dʒire] vi (vacca) to low, moo; (toro) to bellow; (fig) to roar
mu'ghetto [mu'getto] sm lily of the valley
mu'lino sm mill; **mulino a vento** windmill
'mulo sm mule
'multa sf fine

multi'etnico, -a, -ci, -che *ag* multiethnic

multirazziale [multirat'tsjale] *ag* multiracial

multi'sala *ag inv* multiscreen

multivitami'nico, -a, -ci, -che *ag* **complesso ~** multivitamin

'mummia *sf* mummy

'mungere ['mundʒere] *vt* (*anche fig*) to milk

munici'pale [munitʃi'pale] *ag* municipal; town *cpd*

muni'cipio [muni'tʃipjo] *sm* town council, corporation; (*edificio*) town hall

munizi'oni [munit'tsjoni] *sfpl* (*Mil*) ammunition *sg*

'munsi *ecc vb vedi* **mungere**

mu'oio *ecc vb vedi* **morire**

mu'overe *vt* to move; (*ruota, macchina*) to drive; (*sollevare: questione, obiezione*) to raise, bring up; (: *accusa*) to make, bring forward; **muoversi** *vpr* to move; **muoviti!** hurry up!, get a move on!

'mura *sfpl vedi* **muro**

mu'rale *ag* wall *cpd*; mural

mura'tore *sm* mason; bricklayer

'muro *sm* wall

'muschio ['muskjo] *sm* (*Zool*) musk; (*Bot*) moss

musco'lare *ag* muscular, muscle *cpd*

'muscolo *sm* (*Anat*) muscle

mu'seo *sm* museum

museru'ola *sf* muzzle

'musica *sf* music; **musica da ballo/ camera** dance/chamber music; **musi'cale** *ag* musical; **musi'cista, -i, -e** *sm/f* musician

'müsli ['mysli] *sm* muesli

'muso *sm* muzzle; (*di auto, aereo*) nose; **tenere il ~** to sulk

mussul'mano, -a *ag, sm/f* Muslim, Moslem

'muta *sf* (*di animali*) moulting; (*di serpenti*) sloughing; (*per immersioni subacquee*) diving suit; (*gruppo di cani*) pack

mu'tande *sfpl* (*da uomo*) (under)pants

'muto, -a *ag* (*Med*) dumb; (*emozione, dolore, Cinema*) silent; (*Ling*) silent, mute; (*carta geografica*) blank; **~ per lo stupore** *ecc* speechless with amazement *ecc*

'mutuo, -a *ag* (*reciproco*) mutual ▷ *sm* (*Econ*) (long-term) loan

N *abbr* (= *nord*) N

n. *abbr* (= *numero*) no.

'nafta *sf* naphtha; (*per motori diesel*) diesel oil

nafta'lina *sf* (*Chim*) naphthalene; (*tarmicida*) mothballs *pl*

'naia *sf* (*Mil*) slang term for national service

na'if [na'if] *ag inv* naïve

'nanna *sf* (*linguaggio infantile*): **andare a ~** to go to beddy-byes

'nano, -a *ag, sm/f* dwarf

napole'tano, -a *ag, sm/f* Neapolitan

'Napoli *sf* Naples

nar'ciso [nar'tʃizo] *sm* narcissus

nar'cotico, -ci *sm* narcotic

na'rice [na'ritʃe] *sf* nostril

nar'rare *vt* to tell the story of, recount; **narra'tiva** *sf* (*branca letteraria*) fiction

na'sale *ag* nasal

'nascere ['naʃʃere] *vi* (*bambino*) to be born; (*pianta*) to come o spring up; (*fiume*) to rise, have its source; (*sole*) to rise; (*dente*) to come through; (*fig: derivare, conseguire*): **~ da** to arise from, be born out of; **è nata nel 1952** she was born in 1952; **'nascita** *sf* birth

nas'condere *vt* to hide, conceal; **nascondersi** *vpr* to hide; **nascon'diglio** *sm* hiding place; **nascon'dino** *sm* (*gioco*) hide-and-seek; **nas'cosi** *ecc vb*

vedi **nascondere**; **nas'costo, -a** *pp di*
nascondere ▷ *ag* hidden; **di nascosto**
secretly

na'sello *sm* (*Zool*) hake

'naso *sm* nose

'nastro *sm* ribbon; (*magnetico, isolante,*
Sport) tape; **nastro adesivo** adhesive
tape; **nastro trasportatore** conveyor belt

nas'turzio [nas'turtsjo] *sm* nasturtium

na'tale *ag* of one's birth ▷ *sm* (*Rel*): **N~**
Christmas; (*giorno della nascita*) birthday;
nata'lizio, -a *ag* (*del Natale*) Christmas *cpd*

'natica, -che *sf* (*Anat*) buttock

'nato, -a *pp di* **nascere** ▷ *ag* **un attore ~ a**
born actor; **nata Pieri** née Pieri

na'tura *sf* nature; **pagare in ~** to pay in
kind; **natura morta** still life

natu'rale *ag* natural

natural'mente *av* naturally; (*certamente,*
sì) of course

natu'rista, -i, -e *ag, sm/f* naturist, nudist

naufra'gare *vi* (*nave*) to be wrecked;
(*persona*) to be shipwrecked; (*fig*) to fall
through; 'naufrago, -ghi *sm* castaway,
shipwreck victim

'nausea *sf* nausea; nause'ante *ag* (*odore*)
nauseating; (*sapore*) disgusting; (*fig*)
sickening

'nautico, -a, -ci, -che *ag* nautical

na'vale *ag* naval

na'vata *sf* (*anche:* **~ centrale**) nave; (*anche:*
~ laterale) aisle

'nave *sf* ship, vessel; **nave cisterna**
tanker; **nave da guerra** warship; **nave**
passeggeri passenger ship

na'vetta *sf* shuttle; (*servizio di*
collegamento) shuttle (service)

navi'cella [navi'tʃɛlla] *sf* (*di aerostato*)
gondola; **navicella spaziale** spaceship

navi'gare *vi* to sail; **~ in Internet** to surf
the Net; **navigazi'one** *sf* navigation

nazio'nale [nattsjo'nale] *ag* national ▷ *sf*
(*Sport*) national team; **nazionalità** *sf inv*
nationality

nazi'one [nat'tsjone] *sf* nation

naziskin ['nɑːtsiskin] *sm inv* Nazi
skinhead

NB *abbr* (= *nota bene*) NB

 PAROLA CHIAVE

ne *pron* **1** (*di lui, lei, loro*) of him/her/them;
about him/her/them; **ne riconosco la**
voce I recognize his (*o* her) voice
2 (*di questa, quella cosa*) of it; about it; **ne**
voglio ancora I want some more (of it *o*
them); **non parliamone più!** let's not talk
about it any more!
3 (*con valore partitivo*): **hai dei libri? — sì,**

ne ho have you any books? — yes, I have
(some); **hai del pane? — no, non ne ho**
have you any bread? — no, I haven't any;
quanti anni hai? — ne ho 17 how old are
you? — I'm 17
▷ *av* (*moto da luogo: da lì*) from there; **ne**
vengo ora I've just come from there

né *cong* **né ... né** neither ... nor; **né l'uno**
né l'altro lo vuole neither of them wants
it; **non parla né l'italiano né il tedesco**
he speaks neither Italian nor German, he
doesn't speak either Italian or German;
non piove né nevica it isn't raining or
snowing

ne'anche [ne'anke] *av, cong* not even;
non ... ~ not even; **~ se volesse**
potrebbe venire he couldn't come even
if he wanted to; **non l'ho visto — ~ io**
I didn't see him — neither did I *o* I didn't
either; **~ per idea** *o* **sogno!** not on your
life!

'nebbia *sf* fog; (*foschia*) mist

necessaria'mente [netʃessarjamente]
av necessarily

neces'sario, -a [netʃes'sarjo] *ag*
necessary

necessità [netʃessi'ta] *sf inv* necessity;
(*povertà*) need, poverty

necro'logio [nekro'lɔdʒo] *sm* obituary
notice

ne'gare *vt* to deny; (*rifiutare*) to deny,
refuse; **~ di aver fatto/che** to deny
having done/that; **nega'tivo, -a** *ag, sf, sm*
negative

negherò *ecc* [nege'rɔ] *vb vedi* **negare**

negli'gente [negli'dʒɛnte] *ag* negligent,
careless

negozi'ante [negot'tsjante] *sm/f* trader,
dealer; (*bottegaio*) shopkeeper (BRIT),
storekeeper (US)

negozi'are [negot'tsjare] *vt* to negotiate
▷ *vi* **~ in** to trade *o* deal in; **negozi'ato**
sm negotiation

ne'gozio [ne'gɔttsjo] *sm* (*locale*) shop
(BRIT), store (US)

'negro, -a *ag, sm/f* Negro

ne'mico, -a, -ci, -che *ag* hostile; (*Mil*)
enemy *cpd* ▷ *sm/f* enemy; **essere ~ di** to be
strongly averse *o* opposed to

nem'meno *av, cong* = **neanche**

'neo *sm* mole; (*fig*) (slight) flaw

'neon *sm* (*Chim*) neon

neo'nato, -a *ag* newborn ▷ *sm/f* newborn
baby

neozelan'dese [neoddzelan'dese] *ag*
New Zealand *cpd* ▷ *sm/f* New Zealander

'Nepal *sm* **il ~** Nepal

nep'pure *av, cong* = **neanche**

'nero, -a *ag* black; (*scuro*) dark ▷ *sm* black; **il Mar N~** the Black Sea

'nervo *sm* (*Anat*) nerve; (*Bot*) vein; **avere i nervi** to be on edge; **dare sui nervi a qn** to get on sb's nerves; **ner'voso, -a** *ag* nervous; (*irritabile*) irritable ▷ *sm* (*fam*): **far venire il nervoso a qn** to get on sb's nerves

'nespola *sf* (*Bot*) medlar; (*fig*) blow, punch

'nesso *sm* connection, link

 PAROLA CHIAVE

nes'suno, -a (*det: dav sm* **nessun** +C, V, **nessuno** +*s impura, gn, pn, ps, x, z; dav sf* **nessuna** +C, **nessun'** +V) *det* **1** (*non uno*) no; (, *espressione negativa* +) any; **non c'è nessun libro** there isn't any book, there is no book; **nessun altro** no one else, nobody else; **nessun'altra cosa** nothing else; **in nessun luogo** nowhere

2 (*qualche*) any; **hai nessuna obiezione?** do you have any objections?

▷ *pron* **1** (*non uno*) no one, nobody; (, *espressione negativa* +) any(one); (: *cosa*) none; (, *espressione negativa* +) any; **nessuno è venuto, non è venuto nessuno** nobody came

2 (*qualcuno*) anyone, anybody; **ha telefonato nessuno?** did anyone phone?

net'tare *vt* to clean

net'tezza [net'tettsa] *sf* cleanness, cleanliness; **nettezza urbana** cleansing department

'netto, -a *ag* (*pulito*) clean; (*chiaro*) clear, clear-cut; (*deciso*) definite; (*Econ*) net

nettur'bino *sm* dustman (*BRIT*), garbage collector (*US*)

neu'trale *ag* neutral

'neutro, -a *ag* neutral; (*Ling*) neuter ▷ *sm* (*Ling*) neuter

'neve *sf* snow; **nevi'care** *vb impers* to snow; **nevi'cata** *sf* snowfall

ne'vischio [ne'viskjo] *sm* sleet

ne'voso, -a *ag* snowy; snow-covered

nevral'gia [nevral'dʒia] *sf* neuralgia

nevras'tenico, -a, -ci, -che *ag* (*Med*) neurasthenic; (*fig*) hot-tempered

ne'vrosi *sf* neurosis

ne'vrotico, -a, ci, che *ag, sm/f* (*anche fig*) neurotic

'nicchia ['nikkja] *sf* niche; (*naturale*) cavity, hollow; **nicchia di mercato** (*Comm*) niche market

nicchi'are [nik'kjare] *vi* to shilly-shally, hesitate

'nichel ['nikel] *sm* nickel

nico'tina *sf* nicotine

'nido *sm* nest; **a ~ d'ape** (*tessuto ecc*) honeycomb *cpd*

 PAROLA CHIAVE

ni'ente *pron* **1** (*nessuna cosa*) nothing; **niente può fermarlo** nothing can stop him; **niente di niente** absolutely nothing; **nient'altro** nothing else; **nient'altro che** nothing but, just, only; **niente affatto** not at all, not in the least; **come se niente fosse** as if nothing had happened; **cose da niente** trivial matters; **per niente** (*gratis, invano*) for nothing

2 (*qualcosa*) **hai bisogno di niente?** do you need anything?

3: **non ... niente** nothing; (*espressione negativa* +) anything; **non ho visto niente** I saw nothing, I didn't see anything; **non ho niente da dire** I have nothing o haven't anything to say

▷ *sm* nothing; **un bel niente** absolutely nothing; **basta un niente per farla piangere** the slightest thing is enough to make her cry ▷ *av* (*in nessuna misura*): **non ... niente** not ... at all; **non è (per) niente buono** it isn't good at all

Ni'geria [ni'dʒɛrja] *sf* **la ~** Nigeria

'ninfa *sf* nymph

nin'fea *sf* water lily

ninna-'nanna *sf* lullaby

'ninnolo *sm* (*gingillo*) knick-knack

ni'pote *sm/f* (*di zii*) nephew/niece; (*di nonni*) grandson/daughter, grandchild

'nitido, -a *ag* clear; (*specchio*) bright

ni'trire *vi* to neigh

ni'trito *sm* (*di cavallo*) neighing *no pl*; neigh; (*Chim*) nitrite

nitroglice'rina [nitroglitʃe'rina] *sf* nitroglycerine

no *av* (*risposta*) no; **vieni o no?** are you coming or not?; **perché no?** why not?; **lo conosciamo? — tu no ma io sì** do we know him? — you don't but I do; **verrai, no?** you'll come, won't you?

'nobile *ag* noble ▷ *sm/f* noble, nobleman/woman

'nocca, -che *sf* (*Anat*) knuckle

'noccio *ecc* ['nɔttʃo] *vb vedi* **nuocere**

nocci'ola [not'tʃɔla] *ag inv* (*colore*) hazel, light brown ▷ *sf* hazelnut

noccio'lina [nottʃo'lina] *sf*; **nocciolina americana** peanut

'nocciolo ['nɔttʃolo] *sm* (*di frutto*) stone; (*fig*) heart, core

'noce ['notʃe] *sm* (*albero*) walnut tree ▷ *sf* (*frutto*) walnut; **noce di cocco** coconut; **noce moscata** nutmeg

no'cevo ecc [no't∫evo] vb vedi **nuocere**
no'civo, -a [no't∫ivo] ag harmful, noxious
'nocqui ecc vb vedi **nuocere**
'nodo sm (di cravatta, legname, Naut) knot; (Aut, Ferr) junction; (Med, Astr, Bot) node; (fig: legame) bond, tie; (: punto centrale) heart, crux; **avere un ~ alla gola** to have a lump in one's throat
no-'global sm/f anti-globalization protester ▷ ag (movimento, manifestante) anti-globalization
'noi pron (soggetto) we; (oggetto: per dare rilievo, con preposizione) us; **~ stessi(e)** we ourselves; (oggetto) ourselves
'noia sf (tedio) boredom; (disturbo, impaccio) bother no pl, trouble no pl; **avere qn/qc a ~** not to like sb/sth; **mi è venuto a ~** I'm tired of it; **dare ~ a** to annoy; **avere delle noie con qn** to have trouble with sb
noi'oso, -a ag boring; (fastidioso) annoying, troublesome

> Attenzione! In inglese esiste la parola noisy, che però significa rumoroso.

noleggi'are [noled'dʒare] vt (prendere a noleggio) to hire (BRIT), rent; (dare a noleggio) to hire out (BRIT), rent (out); (aereo, nave) to charter; **vorrei ~ una macchina** I'd like to hire a car; **no'leggio** sm hire (BRIT), rental; charter
'nomade ag nomadic ▷ sm/f nomad
'nome sm name; (Ling) noun; **in/a ~ di** in the name of; **di** o **per ~** (chiamato) called, named; **conoscere qn di ~** to know sb by name; **nome d'arte** stage name; **nome di battesimo** Christian name; **nome di famiglia** surname
no'mignolo [no'miɲɲolo] sm nickname
'nomina sf appointment
nomi'nale ag nominal; (Ling) noun cpd
nomi'nare vt to name; (eleggere) to appoint; (citare) to mention
nomina'tivo, -a ag (Ling) nominative; (Econ) registered ▷ sm (Ling: anche: **caso ~**) nominative (case); (Amm) name
non av not ▷ prefisso non-; vedi **affatto**; **appena** ecc
nonché [non'ke] cong (tanto più, tanto meno) let alone; (e inoltre) as well as
noncu'rante ag **~ (di)** careless (of), indifferent (to)
'nonno, -a sm/f grandfather/mother; (in senso più familiare) grandma/grandpa; **i nonni** smpl the grandparents
non'nulla sm inv **un ~** nothing, a trifle
'nono, -a ag, sm ninth
nonos'tante prep in spite of, notwithstanding ▷ cong although, even though
nontiscordardimé sm inv (Bot) forget-me-not

nord sm North ▷ ag inv north; northern; **il Mare del N~** the North Sea; **nor'dest** sm north-east; **nor'dovest** sm north-west
'norma sf (principio) norm; (regola) regulation, rule; (consuetudine) custom, rule; **a ~ di legge** according to law, as laid down by law; **norme per l'uso** instructions for use; **norme di sicurezza** safety regulations
nor'male ag normal; standard cpd
normal'mente av normally
norve'gese [norve'dʒese] ag, sm/f, sm Norwegian
Nor'vegia [nor'vedʒa] sf **la ~** Norway
nostal'gia [nostal'dʒia] sf (di casa, paese) homesickness; (del passato) nostalgia
nos'trano, -a ag local; national; home-produced
'nostro, -a det **il (la) ~(-a)** ecc our ▷ pron **il (la) ~(-a)** ecc ours ▷ sm **il ~** our money; our belongings; **i nostri** our family; our own people; **è dei nostri** he's one of us
'nota sf (segno) mark; (comunicazione scritta, Mus) note; (fattura) bill; (elenco) list; **degno di ~** noteworthy, worthy of note
no'taio sm notary
no'tare vt (segnare: errori) to mark; (registrare) to note (down), write down; (rilevare, osservare) to note, notice; **farsi ~** to get o.s. noticed
no'tevole ag (talento) notable, remarkable; (peso) considerable
no'tifica, -che sf notification
no'tizia [no'tittsja] sf (piece of) news sg; (informazione) piece of information; **notizi'ario** sm (Radio, TV, Stampa) news sg
'noto, -a ag (well-)known
notori'età sf fame; notoriety
no'torio, -a ag well-known; (peg) notorious
not'tambulo, -a sm/f night-bird; (fig)
not'tata sf night
'notte sf night; **di ~** at night; (durante la notte) in the night, during the night; **notte bianca** sleepless night
not'turno, -a ag nocturnal; (servizio, guardiano) night cpd
no'vanta num ninety; **novan'tesimo, -a** num ninetieth
'nove num nine
nove'cento [nove't∫ɛnto] num nine hundred ▷ sm **il N~** the twentieth century
no'vella sf (Letteratura) short story
no'vello, -a ag (piante, patate) new; (insalata, verdura) early; (sposo) newly-married
no'vembre sm November
novità sf inv novelty; (innovazione)

innovation; (*cosa originale, insolita*)
something new; (*notizia*) (piece of) news
sg; **le ~ della moda** the latest fashions

nozi'one [not'tsjone] *sf* notion, idea

'nozze ['nɔttse] *sfpl* wedding *sg*, marriage
sg; **nozze d'argento/d'oro** silver/golden
wedding *sg*

'nubile *ag* (*donna*) unmarried, single

'nuca *sf* nape of the neck

nucle'are *ag* nuclear

'nucleo *sm* nucleus; (*gruppo*) team,
unit, group; (*Mil, Polizia*) squad; **nucleo
familiare** family unit

nu'dista, -i, -e *sm/f* nudist

'nudo, -a *ag* (*persona*) bare, naked, nude;
(*membra*) bare, naked; (*montagna*) bare
▷ *sm* (*Arte*) nude

'nulla *pron, av* = **niente** ▷ *sm* = **il nulla**
nothing

nullità *sf inv* nullity; (*persona*) nonentity

'nullo, -a *ag* useless, worthless; (*Dir*) null
(and void); (*Sport*): **incontro ~** draw

nume'rale *ag, sm* numeral

nume'rare *vt* to number

nu'merico, -a, -ci, -che *ag* numerical

'numero *sm* number; (*romano, arabo*)
numeral; (*di spettacolo*) act, turn; **numero
civico** house number; **numero di scarpe**
shoe size; **numero di telefono** telephone
number; **nume'roso, -a** *ag* numerous,
many; (*con sostantivo sg*) large

nu'occio *ecc* ['nwɔttʃo] *vb vedi* **nuocere**

nu'ocere ['nwɔtʃere] *vi* **~ a** to harm,
damage

nu'ora *sf* daughter-in-law

nuo'tare *vi* to swim; (*galleggiare: oggetti*) to
float; **nuota'tore, -'trice** *sm/f* swimmer;
nu'oto *sm* swimming

nu'ova *sf* (*notizia*) (piece of) news *sg*; *vedi
anche* **nuovo**

nuova'mente *av* again

Nu'ova Ze'landa [-dze'landa] *sf* **la ~** New
Zealand

nu'ovo, -a *ag* new; **di ~** again; **~
fiammante** *o* **di zecca** brand-new

nutri'ente *ag* nutritious, nourishing

nutri'mento *sm* food, nourishment

nu'trire *vt* to feed; (*fig: sentimenti*) to
harbour, nurse; **nutrirsi** *vpr* **nutrirsi di** to
feed on, to eat

'nuvola *sf* cloud; **nuvo'loso, -a** *ag* cloudy

nuzi'ale [nut'tsjale] *ag* nuptial; wedding
cpd

'nylon ['nailən] *sm* nylon

O

o (*dav V spesso* **od**) *cong* or; **o ... o** either ...
or; **o l'uno o l'altro** either (of them)

O *abbr* (= *ovest*) W

'oasi *sf inv* oasis

obbedi'ente *ecc* = **ubbidiente** *ecc*

obbli'gare *vt* (*costringere*): **~ qn a fare**
to force *o* oblige sb to do; (*Dir*) to bind;
obbliga'torio, -a *ag* compulsory,
obligatory; **'obbligo, -ghi** *sm* obligation;
(*dovere*) duty; **avere l'obbligo di fare** to be
obliged to do; **essere d'obbligo** (*discorso,
applauso*) to be called for

o'beso, -a *ag* obese

obiet'tare *vt* **~ che** to object that; **~
su qc** to object to sth, raise objections
concerning sth

obiet'tivo, -a *ag* objective ▷ *sm* (*Ottica,
Fot*) lens *sg*, objective; (*Mil, fig*) objective

obiet'tore *sm* objector; **obiettore di
coscienza** conscientious objector

obiezi'one [objet'tsjone] *sf* objection

obi'torio *sm* morgue, mortuary

o'bliquo, -a *ag* oblique; (*inclinato*)
slanting; (*fig*) devious, underhand

oblite'rare *vt* (*biglietto*) to stamp;
(*francobollo*) to cancel

oblò *sm inv* porthole

'oboe *sm* (*Mus*) oboe

'oca (*pl* **'oche**) *sf* goose

occasi'one *sf* (*caso favorevole*) opportunity;

(*causa, motivo, circostanza*) occasion; (*Comm*) bargain; **d'~** (*a buon prezzo*) bargain *cpd*; (*usato*) secondhand

occhi'aia [okˈkjaja] *sf* **avere le occhiaie** to have shadows under one's eyes

occhi'ali [okˈkjali] *smpl* glasses, spectacles; **occhiali da sole/da vista** sunglasses/(prescription) glasses

occhi'ata [okˈkjata] *sf* look, glance; **dare un'~ a** to have a look at

occhi'ello [okˈkjɛllo] *sm* buttonhole; (*asola*) eyelet

'occhio [ˈɔkkjo] *sm* eye; **~!** careful!, watch out!; **a ~ nudo** with the naked eye; **a quattr'occhi** privately, tête-à-tête; **dare all'~ o nell'~ a qn** to catch sb's eye; **fare l'~ a qc** to get used to sth; **tenere d'~ qn** to keep an eye on sb; **vedere di buon/mal ~ qc** to look favourably/unfavourably on sth

occhio'lino [okkjoˈlino] *sm* **fare l'~ a qn** to wink at sb

occiden'tale [ottʃidenˈtale] *ag* western ▷ *sm/f* Westerner

occi'dente [ottʃiˈdɛnte] *sm* west; (*Pol*): **l'O~** the West; **a ~** in the west

occor'rente *ag* necessary ▷ *sm* all that is necessary

occor'renza [okkorˈrɛntsa] *sf* necessity, need; **all'~** in case of need

oc'correre *vi* to be needed, be required ▷ *vb impers* **occorre farlo** it must be done; **occorre che tu parta** you must leave, you'll have to leave; **mi occorrono i soldi** I need the money

▌ Attenzione! In inglese esiste il verbo *to occur*, che però significa *succedere*.

oc'culto, -a *ag* hidden, concealed; (*scienze, forze*) occult

occu'pare *vt* to occupy; (*manodopera*) to employ; (*ingombrare*) to occupy, take up; **occuparsi** *vpr* to occupy o.s., keep o.s. busy; (*impiegarsi*) to get a job; **occuparsi di** (*interessarsi*) to take an interest in; (*prendersi cura di*) to look after, take care of; **occu'pato, -a** *ag* (*Mil, Pol*) occupied; (*persona: affaccendato*) busy; (*posto, sedia*) taken; (*toilette, Tel*) engaged; **la linea è occupata** the line's engaged; **è occupato questo posto?** is this seat taken?; **occupazi'one** *sf* occupation; (*impiego, lavoro*) job; (*Econ*) employment

o'ceano [oˈtʃeano] *sm* ocean

'ocra *sf* ochre

'OCSE *sigla f* (= *Organizzazione per la Cooperazione e lo Sviluppo Economico*) OECD (*Organization for Economic Cooperation and Development*)

ocu'lare *ag* ocular, eye *cpd*; **testimone ~** eye witness

ocu'lato, -a *ag* (*attento*) cautious, prudent; (*accorto*) shrewd

ocu'lista, -i, -e *sm/f* eye specialist, oculist

odi'are *vt* to hate, detest

odi'erno, -a *ag* today's, of today; (*attuale*) present

'odio *sm* hatred; **avere in ~ qc/qn** to hate o detest sth/sb; **odi'oso, -a** *ag* hateful, odious

odo'rare *vt* (*annusare*) to smell; (*profumare*) to perfume, scent ▷ *vi* **~ (di)** to smell (of)

o'dore *sm* smell; **odori** *smpl* (*Cuc*) (aromatic) herbs

of'fendere *vt* to offend; (*violare*) to break, violate; (*insultare*) to insult; (*ferire*) to hurt; **offendersi** *vpr* (*con senso reciproco*) to insult one another; (*risentirsi*): **offendersi (di)** to take offence (at), be offended (by)

offe'rente *sm* (*in aste*): **al maggior ~** to the highest bidder

of'ferta *sf* offer; (*donazione, anche Rel*) offering; (*in gara d'appalto*) tender; (*in aste*) bid; (*Econ*) supply; **fare un'~** to make an offer; to tender; to bid; **"offerte d'impiego"** "situations vacant"; **offerta speciale** special offer

of'fesa *sf* insult, affront; (*Mil*) attack; (*Dir*) offence; *vedi anche* **offeso**

of'feso, -a *pp di* **offendere** ▷ *ag* offended; (*fisicamente*) hurt, injured ▷ *sm/f* offended party; **essere ~ con qn** to be annoyed with sb; **parte offesa** (*Dir*) plaintiff

offi'cina [offiˈtʃina] *sf* workshop

of'frire *vt* to offer; **offrirsi** *vpr* (*proporsi*) to offer (o.s.), volunteer; (*occasione*) to present itself; (*esporsi*): **offrirsi a** to expose o.s. to; **ti offro da bere** I'll buy you a drink

offus'care *vt* to obscure, darken; (*fig: intelletto*) to dim, cloud; (: *fama*) to obscure, overshadow; **offuscarsi** *vpr* to grow dark; to cloud, grow dim; to be obscured

ogget'tivo, -a [oddʒetˈtivo] *ag* objective

og'getto [odˈdʒɛtto] *sm* object; (*materia, argomento*) subject (matter); **oggetti smarriti** lost property *sg*

'oggi [ˈɔddʒi] *av, sm* today; **~ a otto** a week today; **oggigi'orno** *av* nowadays

OGM *sigla m* (= *organismo geneticamente modificato*) GMO

'ogni [ˈoɲɲi] *det* every, each; (*tutti*) all; (*con valore distributivo*) every; **~ uomo è mortale** all men are mortal; **viene ~ due giorni** he comes every two days; **~ cosa** everything; **ad ~ costo** at all costs, at any price; **in ~ luogo** everywhere; **~ tanto** every so often; **~ volta che** every time that

Ognis'santi [oɲɲisˈsanti] *sm* All Saints' Day

o'gnuno [oɲˈɲuno] *pron* everyone,

everybody

O'landa sf l'~ Holland; **olan'dese** ag Dutch ▷ sm (Ling) Dutch ▷ sm/f Dutchman/woman; **gli Olandesi** the Dutch

ole'andro sm oleander

oleo'dotto sm oil pipeline

ole'oso, -a ag oily; (che contiene olio) oil-yielding

ol'fatto sm sense of smell

oli'are vt to oil

oli'era sf oil cruet

Olim'piadi sfpl Olympic games; **o'limpico, -a, -ci, -che** ag Olympic

'olio sm oil; **sott'~** (Cuc) in oil; **~ di fegato di merluzzo** cod liver oil; **olio d'oliva** olive oil; **olio di semi** vegetable oil

o'liva sf olive; **o'livo** sm olive tree

'olmo sm elm

OLP sigla f (= Organizzazione per la Liberazione della Palestina) PLO

ol'traggio [ol'traddʒo] sm outrage; offence, insult; **~ a pubblico ufficiale** (Dir) insulting a public official; **oltraggio al pudore** (Dir) indecent behaviour

ol'tranza [ol'trantsa] sf **a ~** to the last, to the bitter end

'oltre av (più in là) further; (di più: aspettare) longer, more ▷ prep (di là da) beyond, over, on the other side of; (più di) more than, over; (in aggiunta a) besides; (eccetto): **~ a** except, apart from; **oltrepas'sare** vt to go beyond, exceed

o'maggio [o'maddʒo] sm (dono) gift; (segno di rispetto) homage, tribute; **omaggi** smpl (complimenti) respects; **rendere ~ a** to pay homage o tribute to; **in ~** (copia, biglietto) complimentary

ombe'lico, -chi sm navel

'ombra sf (zona non assolata, fantasma) shade; (sagoma scura) shadow; **sedere all'~** to sit in the shade; **restare nell'~** (fig) to remain in obscurity

om'brello sm umbrella; **ombrel'lone** sm beach umbrella

om'bretto sm eye shadow

O.M.C. sigla f (= Organizzazione Mondiale del Commercio) WTO

ome'lette [ɔmaˈlɛt] sf inv omelet(te)

ome'lia sf (Rel) homily, sermon

omeopa'tia sf homoeopathy

omertà sf conspiracy of silence

o'mettere vt to omit, leave out; **~ di fare** to omit o fail to do

omi'cida, -i, -e [omiˈtʃida] ag homicidal, murderous ▷ sm/f murderer/eress

omi'cidio [omiˈtʃidjo] sm murder; **omicidio colposo** culpable homicide

o'misi ecc vb vedi **omettere**

everybody

omissi'one sf omission; **omissione di soccorso** (Dir) failure to stop and give assistance

omogeneiz'zato [omodʒeneidˈdzato] sm baby food

omo'geneo, -a [omoˈdʒɛneo] ag homogeneous

o'monimo, -a sm/f namesake ▷ sm (Ling) homonym

omosessu'ale ag, sm/f homosexual

O.M.S. sigla f (= Organizzazione Mondiale della Sanità) WHO

On. abbr (Pol) = **onorevole**

'onda sf wave; **mettere** o **mandare in ~** (Radio, TV) to broadcast; **andare in ~** (Radio, TV) to go on the air; **onde corte/lunghe/medie** short/long/medium wave

'onere sm burden; **oneri fiscali** taxes

onestà sf honesty

o'nesto, -a ag (probo, retto) honest; (giusto) fair; (casto) chaste, virtuous

ONG sigla f inv **Organizzazione Non Governativa** NGO

onnipo'tente ag omnipotent

ono'mastico, -ci sm name-day

ono'rare vt to honour; (far onore a) to do credit to

ono'rario, -a ag honorary ▷ sm fee

o'nore sm honour; **in ~ di** in honour of; **fare gli onori di casa** to play host (o hostess); **fare ~ a** to honour; (pranzo) to do justice to; (famiglia) to be a credit to; **farsi ~** to distinguish o.s.; **ono'revole** ag honourable ▷ sm/f (Pol) ≈ Member of Parliament (BRIT), ≈ Congressman/woman (US)

on'tano sm (Bot) alder

'O.N.U. [ˈɔnu] sigla f (= Organizzazione delle Nazioni Unite) UN, UNO

o'paco, -a, -chi, -che ag (vetro) opaque; (metallo) dull, matt

o'pale sm o f opal

'opera sf work; (azione rilevante) action, deed, work; (Mus) work; opus; (: melodramma) opera; (: teatro) opera house; (ente) institution, organization; **opere pubbliche** public works; **opera d'arte** work of art; **opera lirica** (grand) opera

ope'raio, -a ag working-class; workers' ▷ sm/f worker; **classe operaia** working class

ope'rare vt to carry out, make; (Med) to operate on ▷ vi to operate, work; (rimedio) to act, work; (Med) to operate; **operarsi** vpr (Med) to have an operation; **operarsi d'appendicite** to have one's appendix out; **operazi'one** sf operation

ope'retta sf (Mus) operetta, light opera

opini'one *sf* opinion; **opinione pubblica** public opinion

'oppio *sm* opium

op'pongo *ecc vb vedi* **opporre**

op'porre *vt* to oppose; **opporsi** *vpr* **opporsi (a qc)** to oppose (sth); to object (to sth); **~ resistenza/un rifiuto** to offer resistance/refuse

opportu'nista, -i, -e *sm/f* opportunist

opportunità *sf inv* opportunity; (*convenienza*) opportuneness, timeliness

oppor'tuno, -a *ag* timely, opportune

op'posi *ecc vb vedi* **opporre**

opposizi'one [oppozit'tsjone] *sf* opposition; (*Dir*) objection

op'posto, -a *pp di* **opporre** ▷ *ag* opposite; (*opinioni*) conflicting ▷ *sm* opposite, contrary; **all'~** on the contrary

oppressi'one *sf* oppression

oppri'mente *ag* (*caldo, noia*) oppressive; (*persona*) tiresome; (*deprimente*) depressing

op'primere *vt* (*premere, gravare*) to weigh down; (*estenuare: caldo*) to suffocate, oppress; (*tiranneggiare: popolo*) to oppress

op'pure *cong* or (else)

op'tare *vi* **~ per** to opt for

o'puscolo *sm* booklet, pamphlet

opzi'one [op'tsjone] *sf* option

'ora *sf* (*60 minuti*) hour; (*momento*) time; **che ~ è?, che ore sono?** what time is it?; **a che ~ apre il museo/negozio?** what time does the museum/shop open?; **non veder l'~ di fare** to long to do, look forward to doing; **di buon'~** early; **alla buon'~!** at last!; **~ legale** *o* **estiva** summer time (BRIT), daylight saving time (US); **ora di cena** dinner time; **ora locale** local time; **ora di pranzo** lunchtime; **ora di punta** (*Aut*) rush hour

o'racolo *sm* oracle

o'rale *ag, sm* oral

o'rario, -a *ag* hourly; (*fuso, segnale*) time *cpd*; (*velocità*) per hour ▷ *sm* timetable, schedule; (*di ufficio, visite ecc*) hours *pl*, time(s *pl*); **in ~** on time

o'rata *sf* (*Zool*) sea bream

ora'tore, -'trice *sm/f* speaker; orator

'orbita *sf* (*Astr, Fisica*) orbit; (*Anat*) (eye-)socket

or'chestra [or'kɛstra] *sf* orchestra

orchi'dea [orki'dɛa] *sf* orchid

or'digno [or'diɲɲo] *sm* (*esplosivo*) explosive device

ordi'nale *ag, sm* ordinal

ordi'nare *vt* (*mettere in ordine*) to arrange, organize; (*Comm*) to order; (*prescrivere: medicina*) to prescribe; (*comandare*): **posso ~ per favore?** can I order now please?; **~ a qn di fare qc** to order *o* command sb to do sth; (*Rel*) to ordain

ordi'nario, -a *ag* (*comune*) ordinary; everyday; standard; (*grossolano*) coarse, common ▷ *sm* ordinary; (*Ins: di università*) full professor

ordi'nato, -a *ag* tidy, orderly

ordinazi'one [ordinat'tsjone] *sf* (*Comm*) order; (*Rel*) ordination; **eseguire qc su ~** to make sth to order

'ordine *sm* order; (*carattere*): **d'~ pratico** of a practical nature; **all'~** (*Comm: assegno*) to order; **di prim'~** first-class; **fino a nuovo ~** until further notice; **essere in ~** (*documenti*) to be in order; (*stanza, persona*) to be tidy; **mettere in ~** to put in order, tidy (up); **l'~ pubblico** law and order; **ordini (sacri)** (*Rel*) holy orders; **ordine del giorno** (*di seduta*) agenda; (*Mil*) order of the day; **ordine di pagamento** (*Comm*) order for payment

orec'chino [orek'kino] *sm* earring

o'recchio [o'rekkjo] (*pl(f)* **o'recchie**) *sm* (*Anat*) ear

orecchi'oni [orek'kjoni] *smpl* (*Med*) mumps *sg*

o'refice [o'refitʃe] *sm* goldsmith; jeweller; **orefice'ria** *sf* (*arte*) goldsmith's art; (*negozio*) jeweller's (shop)

'orfano, -a *ag* orphan(ed) ▷ *sm/f* orphan; **~ di padre/madre** fatherless/motherless

orga'netto *sm* barrel organ; (*fam: armonica a bocca*) mouth organ; (: *fisarmonica*) accordion

or'ganico, -a, -ci, -che *ag* organic ▷ *sm* personnel, staff

organi'gramma, -i *sm* organization chart

orga'nismo *sm* (*Biol*) organism; (*corpo umano*) body; (*Amm*) body, organism

organiz'zare [organid'dzare] *vt* to organize; **organizzarsi** *vpr* to get organized; **organizzazi'one** *sf* organization

'organo *sm* organ; (*di congegno*) part; (*portavoce*) spokesman, mouthpiece

'orgia, -ge [ˈɔrdʒa] *sf* orgy

or'goglio [or'ɡɔʎʎo] *sm* pride; **orgogli'oso, -a** *ag* proud

orien'tale *ag* oriental; eastern; east

orienta'mento *sm* positioning; orientation; direction; **senso di ~** sense of direction; **perdere l'~** to lose one's bearings; **orientamento professionale** careers guidance

orientarsi *vpr* to find one's bearings; (*fig: tendere*) to tend, lean; (: *indirizzarsi*): **~ verso** to take up, go in for

ori'ente *sm* east; **l'O~** the East, the Orient; **a ~** in the east

o'rigano sm oregano

origi'nale [oridʒi'nale] ag original; (bizzarro) eccentric ▷ sm original

origi'nario, -a [oridʒi'narjo] ag original; **essere ~ di** to be a native of; (provenire da) to originate from; to be native to

o'rigine [o'ridʒine] sf origin; **all'~** originally; **d'~ inglese** of English origin; **dare ~ a** to give rise to

origli'are [oriʎ'ʎare] vi ~ **(a)** to eavesdrop (on)

o'rina sf urine

ori'nare vi to urinate ▷ vt to pass

orizzon'tale [oriddzon'tale] ag horizontal

oriz'zonte [orid'dzonte] sm horizon

'orlo sm edge, border; (di recipiente) rim, brim; (di vestito ecc) hem

'orma sf (di persona) footprint; (di animale) track; (impronta, traccia) mark, trace

or'mai av by now, by this time; (adesso) now; (quasi) almost, nearly

ormeggi'are [ormed'dʒare] vt (Naut) to moor

or'mone sm hormone

ornamen'tale ag ornamental, decorative

or'nare vt to adorn, decorate; **ornarsi** vpr **ornarsi (di)** to deck o.s. (out) (with)

ornitolo'gia [ornitolo'dʒia] sf ornithology

'oro sm gold; **d'~, in ~** gold cpd; **d'~** (colore, occasione) golden; (persona) marvellous

oro'logio [oro'lɔdʒo] sm clock; (da tasca, da polso) watch; **orologio al quarzo** quartz watch; **orologio da polso** wristwatch

o'roscopo sm horoscope

or'rendo, -a ag (spaventoso) horrible, awful; (bruttissimo) hideous

or'ribile ag horrible

or'rore sm horror; **avere in ~ qn/qc** to loathe o detest sb/sth; **mi fanno ~** I loathe o detest them

orsacchi'otto [orsak'kjɔtto] sm teddy bear

'orso sm bear; **orso bruno/bianco** brown/polar bear

or'taggio [or'taddʒo] sm vegetable

or'tensia sf hydrangea

or'tica, -che sf (stinging) nettle

orti'caria sf nettle rash

'orto sm vegetable garden, kitchen garden; (Agr) market garden (BRIT), truck farm (US); **orto botanico** botanical garden(s) (pl)

orto'dosso, -a ag orthodox

ortogra'fia sf spelling

orto'pedico, -a, -ci, -che ag orthopaedic ▷ sm orthopaedic specialist

orzai'olo [ordza'jolo] sm (Med) stye

'orzo ['ordzo] sm barley

o'sare vt, vi to dare; **~ fare** to dare (to) do

oscenità [oʃʃeni'ta] sf inv obscenity

o'sceno, -a [oʃʃeno] ag obscene; (ripugnante) ghastly

oscil'lare [oʃʃil'lare] vi (pendolo) to swing; (dondolare: al vento ecc) to rock; (variare) to fluctuate; (Tecn) to oscillate; (fig): ~ **fra** to waver o hesitate between

oscu'rare vt to darken, obscure; (fig) to obscure; **oscurarsi** vpr (cielo) to darken, cloud over; (persona): **si oscurò in volto** his face clouded over

oscurità sf (vedi ag) darkness; obscurity

os'curo, -a ag dark; (fig) obscure; humble, lowly ▷ sm **all'~** in the dark; **tenere qn all'~ di qc** to keep sb in the dark about sth

ospe'dale sm hospital; **dov'è l'~ più vicino?** where's the nearest hospital?

ospi'tale ag hospitable

ospi'tare vt to give hospitality to; (albergo) to accommodate

'ospite sm/f (persona che ospita) host/hostess; (persona ospitata) guest

os'pizio [os'pittsjo] sm (per vecchi ecc) home

osser'vare vt to observe, watch; (esaminare) to examine; (notare, rilevare) to notice, observe; (Dir: la legge) to observe, respect; (mantenere: silenzio) to keep, observe; **far ~ qc a qn** to point sth out to sb; **osservazi'one** sf observation; (di legge ecc) observance; (considerazione critica) observation, remark; (rimprovero) reproof; **in osservazione** under observation

ossessio'nare vt to obsess, haunt; (tormentare) to torment, harass

ossessi'one sf obsession

os'sia cong that is, to be precise

'ossido sm oxide; **ossido di carbonio** carbon monoxide

ossige'nare [ossidʒe'nare] vt to oxygenate; (decolorare) to bleach; **acqua ossigenata** hydrogen peroxide

os'sigeno [os'sidʒeno] sm oxygen

'osso (pl(f) **ossa**) (nel senso Anat) sm bone; **d'~** (bottone ecc) of bone, bone cpd; **osso di seppia** cuttlebone

ostaco'lare vt to block, obstruct

os'tacolo sm obstacle; (Equitazione) hurdle, jump

os'taggio [os'taddʒo] sm hostage

os'tello sm; **ostello della gioventù** youth hostel

osten'tare vt to make a show of, flaunt

oste'ria sf inn

os'tetrico, -a, -ci, -che ag obstetric ▷ sm obstetrician

'ostia sf (Rel) host; (per medicinali) wafer

'ostico, -a, -ci, -che ag (fig) harsh; hard, difficult; unpleasant

os'tile ag hostile

osti'narsi *vpr* to insist, dig one's heels in;
~ a fare to persist (obstinately) in doing;
osti'nato, -a *ag* (*caparbio*) obstinate;
(*tenace*) persistent, determined

'ostrica, -che *sf* oyster

Attenzione! In inglese esiste la parola
ostrich, che però significa *struzzo*.

ostru'ire *vt* to obstruct, block

o'tite *sf* ear infection

ot'tanta *num* eighty

ot'tavo, -a *num* eighth

otte'nere *vt* to obtain, get; (*risultato*) to
achieve, obtain

'ottica *sf* (*scienza*) optics *sg*; (*Fot: lenti,
prismi ecc*) optics *pl*

'ottico, -a, -ci, -che *ag* (*della vista: nervo*)
optic; (*dell'ottica*) optical ▷ *sm* optician

ottima'mente *av* excellently, very well

otti'mismo *sm* optimism; **otti'mista, -i,
-e** *sm/f* optimist

'ottimo, -a *ag* excellent, very good

'otto *num* eight

ot'tobre *sm* October

otto'cento [otto'tʃɛnto] *num* eight
hundred ▷ *sm* **l'O~** the nineteenth century

ot'tone *sm* brass; **gli ottoni** (*Mus*) the
brass

ottu'rare *vt* to close (up); (*dente*) to fill; **il
lavandino è otturato** the sink is blocked;
otturarsi *vpr* to become o get blocked up;
ottura'zione *sf* closing (up); (*dentaria*)
filling

ot'tuso, -a *ag* (*Mat, fig*) obtuse; (*suono*) dull

o'vaia *sf* (*Anat*) ovary

o'vale *ag, sm* oval

o'vatta *sf* cotton wool; (*per imbottire*)
padding, wadding

'ovest *sm* west

o'vile *sm* pen, enclosure

ovulazi'one [ovulat'tsjone] *sf* ovulation

'ovulo *sm* (*Fisiol*) ovum

o'vunque *av* = **dovunque**

ovvi'are *vi* **~ a** to obviate

'ovvio, -a *ag* obvious

ozi'are [ot'tsjare] *vi* to laze, idle

'ozio ['ɔttsjo] *sm* idleness; (*tempo libero*)
leisure; **ore d'~** leisure time; **stare in ~** to
be idle

o'zono [o'dzɔno] *sm* ozone

P

P *abbr* (= *parcheggio*) P; (*Aut: = principiante*) L

p. *abbr* (= *pagina*) p.

pac'chetto [pak'ketto] *sm* packet;
pacchetto azionario (*Comm*)
shareholding

'pacco, -chi *sm* parcel; (*involto*) bundle;
pacco postale parcel

'pace ['patʃe] *sf* peace; **darsi ~** to resign
o.s.; **fare la ~ con** to make it up with

pa'cifico, -a, -ci, -che [pa'tʃi:fiko] *ag*
(*persona*) peaceable; (*vita*) peaceful; (*fig:
indiscusso*) indisputable; (: *ovvio*) obvious,
clear ▷ *sm* **il P~, l'Oceano P~** the Pacific
(Ocean)

paci'fista, -i, -e [patʃi'fista] *sm/f*
pacifist

pa'della *sf* frying pan; (*per infermi*)
bedpan

padigli'one [padiʎ'ʎone] *sm* pavilion

'Padova *sf* Padua

'padre *sm* father

pa'drino *sm* godfather

padro'nanza [padro'nantsa] *sf*
command, mastery

pa'drone, -a *sm/f* master/mistress;
(*proprietario*) owner; (*datore di lavoro*)
employer; **essere ~ di sé** to be in control
of o.s.; **padrone(a) di casa** master/
mistress of the house; (*per gli inquilini*)
landlord/lady

pae'saggio [pae'zaddʒo] sm landscape
pa'ese sm (nazione) country, nation; (terra) country, land; (villaggio) village, (small) town; **i Paesi Bassi** the Netherlands; **paese di provenienza** country of origin
'paga, -ghe sf pay, wages pl
paga'mento sm payment
pa'gare vt to pay; (acquisto, fig: colpa) to pay for; (contraccambiare) to repay, pay back ▷ vi to pay; **quanto l'hai pagato?** how much did you pay for it?; **posso ~ con la carta di credito?** can I pay by credit card?; **~ in contanti** to pay cash
pa'gella [pa'dʒella] sf (Ins) report card
pagherò [page'rɔ] sm inv acknowledgement of a debt, IOU
'pagina ['padʒina] sf page; **pagine bianche** phone book, telephone directory; **pagine gialle** Yellow Pages
'paglia ['paʎʎa] sf straw
pagli'accio [paʎ'ʎattʃo] sm clown
pagli'etta [paʎ'ʎetta] sf (cappello per uomo) (straw) boater; (per tegami ecc) steel wool
pa'gnotta [paɲ'ɲɔtta] sf round loaf
'paio (pl(f) **'paia**) sm pair; **un ~ di** (alcuni) a couple of
'Pakistan sm **il ~** Pakistan
'pala sf shovel; (di remo, ventilatore, elica) blade; (di ruota) paddle
pa'lato sm palate
pa'lazzo [pa'lattso] sm (reggia) palace; (edificio) building; **palazzo di giustizia** courthouse; **palazzo dello sport** sports stadium
'palco, -chi sm (Teatro) box; (tavolato) platform, stand; (ripiano) layer
palco'scenico, -ci [palkoʃ'ʃeniko] sm (Teatro) stage
pa'lese ag clear, evident
Pales'tina sf **la ~** Palestine
palesti'nese ag, sm/f Palestinian
pa'lestra sf gymnasium; (esercizio atletico) exercise, training; (fig) training ground, school
pa'letta sf spade; (per il focolare) shovel; (del capostazione) signalling disc
pa'letto sm stake, peg; (spranga) bolt
'palio sm (gara): **il P~** horse race run at Siena; **mettere qc in ~** to offer sth as a prize

'palla sf ball; (pallottola) bullet; **palla di neve** snowball; **palla ovale** rugby ball; **pallaca'nestro** sf basketball; **palla'mano** sf handball; **pallanu'oto** sf water polo; **palla'volo** sf volleyball
palleggi'are [palled'dʒare] vi (Calcio) to practise with the ball; (Tennis) to knock up
pallia'tivo sm palliative; (fig) stopgap measure
'pallido, -a ag pale
pal'lina sf (bilia) marble
pallon'cino [pallon'tʃino] sm balloon; (lampioncino) Chinese lantern
pal'lone sm (palla) ball; (Calcio) football; (aerostato) balloon; **gioco del ~** football
pal'lottola sf pellet; (proiettile) bullet
'palma sf (Anat) = **palmo**; (Bot, simbolo) palm; **palma da datteri** date palm
'palmo sm (Anat) palm; **restare con un ~ di naso** to be badly disappointed
'palo sm (legno appuntito) stake; (sostegno) pole; **fare da o il ~** (fig) to act as look-out
palom'baro sm diver
pal'pare vt to feel, finger
'palpebra sf eyelid
pa'lude sf marsh, swamp
pan'cetta [pan'tʃetta] sf (Cuc) bacon
pan'china [pan'kina] sf garden seat; (di giardino pubblico) (park) bench
'pancia, -ce ['pantʃa] sf belly, stomach; **mettere o fare ~** to be getting a paunch; **avere mal di ~** to have stomachache o a sore stomach
panci'otto [pan'tʃɔtto] sm waistcoat
'pancreas sm inv pancreas
'panda sm inv panda
'pane sm bread; (pagnotta) loaf (of bread); (forma): **un ~ di burro** a pat of butter; **guadagnarsi il ~** to earn one's living; **pane a cassetta** sliced bread; **pane di Spagna** sponge cake; **pane integrale** wholemeal bread; **pane tostato** toast
panette'ria sf (forno) bakery; (negozio) baker's (shop), bakery
panetti'ere, -a sm/f baker
panet'tone sm a kind of spiced brioche with sultanas, eaten at Christmas
pangrat'tato sm breadcrumbs pl
'panico, -a, -ci, -che ag, sm panic
pani'ere sm basket
pani'ficio [pani'fitʃo] sm (forno) bakery; (negozio) baker's (shop), bakery
pa'nino sm roll; **panino caldo** toasted sandwich; **panino imbottito** filled roll;

sandwich

'panna *sf* (*Cuc*) cream; (*Tecn*) = **panne**; **panna da cucina** cooking cream; **panna montata** whipped cream

'panne *sf inv* **essere in ~** (*Aut*) to have broken down

pan'nello *sm* panel; **pannello solare** solar panel

'panno *sm* cloth; **panni** *smpl* (*abiti*) clothes; **mettiti nei miei panni** (*fig*) put yourself in my shoes

pan'nocchia [pan'nɔkkja] *sf* (*di mais ecc*) ear

panno'lino *sm* (*per bambini*) nappy (BRIT), diaper (US)

pano'rama, -i *sm* panorama

panta'loni *smpl* trousers (BRIT), pants (US), pair *sg*, of trousers *o* pants

pan'tano *sm* bog

pan'tera *sf* panther

pan'tofola *sf* slipper

'Papa, -i *sm* pope

papà *sm inv* dad(dy)

pa'pavero *sm* poppy

'pappa *sf* baby cereal; **pappa reale** royal jelly

pappa'gallo *sm* parrot; (*fig: uomo*) Romeo, wolf

pa'rabola *sf* (*Mat*) parabola; (*Rel*) parable

para'bolico, -a, ci, che *ag* (*Mat*) parabolic; *vedi anche* **antenna**

para'brezza [para'breddza] *sm inv* (*Aut*) windscreen (BRIT), windshield (US)

paraca'dute *sm inv* parachute

para'diso *sm* paradise

parados'sale *ag* paradoxical

para'fulmine *sm* lightning conductor

pa'raggi [pa'raddʒi] *smpl* **nei ~** in the vicinity, in the neighbourhood

parago'nare *vt* **~ con/a** to compare with/to

para'gone *sm* comparison; (*esempio analogo*) analogy, parallel; **reggere al ~** to stand comparison

pa'ragrafo *sm* paragraph

pa'ralisi *sf* paralysis

paral'lelo, -a *ag* parallel ▷ *sm* (*Geo*) parallel; (*comparazione*): **fare un ~ tra** to draw a parallel between

para'lume *sm* lampshade

pa'rametro *sm* parameter

para'noia *sf* paranoia; **para'noico, -a, -ci, -che** *ag, sm/f* paranoid

para'occhi [para'ɔkki] *smpl* blinkers

para'petto *sm* balustrade

pa'rare *vt* (*addobbare*) to adorn, deck; (*proteggere*) to shield, protect; (*scansare: colpo*) to parry; (*Calcio*) to save ▷ *vi* **dove**

vuole andare a ~? what are you driving at?

pa'rata *sf* (*Sport*) save; (*Mil*) review, parade

para'urti *sm inv* (*Aut*) bumper

para'vento *sm* folding screen; **fare da ~ a qn** (*fig*) to shield sb

par'cella [par'tʃella] *sf* account, fee (*of lawyer etc*)

parcheggi'are [parked'dʒare] *vt* to park; **posso ~ qui?** can I park here?; **parcheggiatore, -trice** [parkeddʒa'tore] *sm/f* (*Aut*) parking attendant

par'cheggio *sm* parking *no pl*; (*luogo*) car park; (*singolo posto*) parking space

par'chimetro [par'kimetro] *sm* parking meter

'parco, -chi *sm* park; (*spazio per deposito*) depot; (*complesso di veicoli*) fleet

para'cometro *sm* (pay-and-display) ticket machine

pa'recchio, -a [pa'rekkjo] *det* quite a lot of; (*tempo*) quite a lot of, a long

pareggi'are [pared'dʒare] *vt* to make equal; (*terreno*) to level, make level; (*bilancio, conti*) to balance ▷ *vi* (*Sport*) to draw; **pa'reggio** *sm* (*Econ*) balance; (*Sport*) draw

pa'rente *sm/f* relative, relation

▍ Attenzione! In inglese esiste la parola *parent*, che però significa *genitore*.

paren'tela *sf* (*vincolo di sangue, fig*) relationship

pa'rentesi *sf* (*segno grafico*) bracket, parenthesis; (*frase incisa*) parenthesis; (*digressione*) parenthesis, digression

pa'rere *sm* (*opinione*) opinion; (*consiglio*) advice, opinion; **a mio ~** in my opinion ▷ *vi* to seem, appear ▷ *vb impers* **pare che** it seems *o* appears that, they say that; **mi pare che** it seems to me that; **mi pare di sì** I think so; **fai come ti pare** do as you like; **che ti pare del mio libro?** what do you think of my book?

pa'rete *sf* wall

'pari *ag inv* (*uguale*) equal, same; (*in giochi*) equal; drawn, tied; (*Mat*) even ▷ *sm inv* (*Pol: di Gran Bretagna*) peer ▷ *sm/f inv* peer, equal; **copiato ~ ~** copied word for word; **alla ~** on the same level; **ragazza alla ~** au pair girl; **mettersi alla ~ con** to place o.s. on the same level as; **mettersi in ~ con** to catch up with; **andare di ~ passo con qn** to keep pace with sb

Pa'rigi [pa'ridʒi] *sf* Paris

pari'gino, -a [pari'dʒino] *ag, sm/f* Parisian

parità *sf* parity, equality; (*Sport*) draw, tie

parlamen'tare *ag* parliamentary ▷ *sm/f* ≈ Member of Parliament (BRIT), ≈ Congressman/woman (US) ▷ *vi* to

negotiate, parley
parla'mento *sm* parliament

parlan'tina *(fam) sf* talkativeness; **avere ~**
to have the gift of the gab
par'lare *vi* to speak, talk; *(confidare cose
segrete)* to talk ▷ *vt* to speak; **~ (a qn) di** to
speak *o* talk (to sb) about; **posso ~ con...?**
can I speak to ...?; **parla italiano?** do you
speak Italian?; **non parlo inglese** I don't
speak English
parmigi'ano [parmi'dʒano] *sm (grana)*
Parmesan (cheese)
pa'rola *sf* word; *(facoltà)* speech; **parole**
sfpl (chiacchiere) talk *sg*; **chiedere la ~** to
ask permission to speak; **prendere la ~**
to take the floor; **parola d'onore** word of
honour; **parola d'ordine** *(Mil)* password;
parole incrociate crossword (puzzle) *sg*;
paro'laccia, -ce *sf* bad word, swearword
parrò *ecc vb vedi* **parere**
par'rocchia [par'rɔkkja] *sf* parish; parish
church
par'rucca, -che *sf* wig
parrucchi'ere, -a [parruk'kjɛre] *sm/f*
hairdresser ▷ *sm* barber
'parte *sf* part; *(lato)* side; *(quota spettante a
ciascuno)* share; *(direzione)* direction; *(Pol)*
party; faction; *(Dir)* party; **a ~** *ag* separate
▷ *av* separately; **scherzi a ~** joking aside;
a ~ ciò apart from that; **da ~** *(in disparte)*
to one side, aside; **d'altra ~** on the other
hand; **da ~ di** *(per conto di)* on behalf of; **da
~ mia** as far as I'm concerned, as for me;
da ~ a ~ right through; **da ogni ~** on all
sides, everywhere; *(moto da luogo)* from all
sides; **da nessuna ~** nowhere; **da questa
~** *(in questa direzione)* this way; **prendere
~ a qc** to take part in sth; **mettere da ~**
to put aside; **mettere qn a ~ di** to inform
sb of
parteci'pare [partetʃi'pare] *vi* **~ a** to take
part in, participate in; *(utili ecc)* to share in;
(spese ecc) to contribute to; *(dolore, successo
di qn)* to share (in)
parteggi'are [parted'dʒare] *vi* **~ per** to
side with, be on the side of
par'tenza [par'tɛntsa] *sf* departure;
(Sport) start; **essere in ~** to be about to
leave, be leaving
parti'cipio [parti'tʃipjo] *sm* participle

partico'lare *ag (specifico)* particular;
(proprio) personal, private; *(speciale)*
special, particular; *(caratteristico)*
distinctive, characteristic; *(fuori dal
comune)* peculiar ▷ *sm* detail, particular; **in
~** in particular, particularly
par'tire *vi* to go, leave; *(allontanarsi)* to go
(o drive ecc) away *o* off; *(petardo, colpo)* to
go off; *(fig: avere inizio, Sport)* to start; **sono
partita da Roma alle 7** I left Rome at 7; **a
che ora parte il treno/l'autobus?** what
time does the train/bus leave?; **il volo
parte da Ciampino** the flight leaves from
Ciampino; **a ~ da** from
par'tita *sf (Comm)* lot, consignment; *(Econ:
registrazione)* entry, item; *(Carte, Sport:
gioco)* game; *(: competizione)* match, game;
partita di caccia hunting party; **partita
IVA** VAT registration number
par'tito *sm (Pol)* party; *(decisione)* decision,
resolution; *(persona da maritare)* match
'parto *sm (Med)* delivery, (child)birth;
labour
'parvi *ecc vb vedi* **parere**
parzi'ale [par'tsjale] *ag (limitato)* partial;
(non obiettivo) biased, partial
pasco'lare *vt* to graze
'pascolo *sm* pasture
'Pasqua *sf* Easter; **Pas'quetta** *sf* Easter
Monday
pas'sabile *ag* fairly good, passable
pas'saggio [pas'saddʒo] *sm* passing *no
pl*, passage; *(traversata)* crossing *no pl*,
passage; *(luogo, prezzo della traversata,
brano di libro ecc)* passage; *(su veicolo altrui)*
lift *(BRIT)*, ride; *(Sport)* pass; **di ~** *(persona)*
passing through; **può darmi un ~ fino
alla stazione?** can you give me a lift to the
station?; **passaggio a livello** level *(BRIT) o*
grade *(US)* crossing; **passaggio pedonale**
pedestrian crossing
passamon'tagna [passamon'taɲɲa] *sm
inv* balaclava
pas'sante *sm/f* passer-by ▷ *sm* loop
passa'porto *sm* passport
pas'sare *vi (andare)* to go; *(veicolo, pedone)*
to pass (by), go by; *(fare una breve sosta:
postino ecc)* to come, call; *(: amico: per fare
una visita)* to call *o* drop in; *(sole, aria, luce)*
to get through; *(trascorrere: giorni, tempo)*
to pass, go by; *(fig: proposta di legge)* to
be passed; *(: dolore)* to pass, go away;
(Carte) to pass ▷ *vt (attraversare)* to cross;
(trasmettere: messaggio): **~ qc a qn** to pass
sth on to sb; *(dare)*: **~ qc a qn** to pass sth to
sb, give sb sth; *(trascorrere: tempo)* to spend;
(superare: esame) to pass; *(triturare: verdura)*
to strain; *(approvare)* to pass, approve;
(oltrepassare, sorpassare: anche fig) to go

beyond, pass; (fig: subire) to go through; **mi passa il sale/l'olio per favore?** could you pass the salt/oil please?; **~ da ... a** to pass from ... to; **~ di padre in figlio** to be handed down o to pass from father to son; **~ per** (anche fig) to go through; **~ per stupido/un genio** to be taken for a fool/a genius; **~ sopra** (anche fig) to pass over; **~ attraverso** (anche fig) to go through; **~ alla storia** to pass into history; **~ a un esame** to go up (to the next class) after an exam; **~ inosservato** to go unnoticed; **~ di moda** to go out of fashion; **le passo il Signor X** (al telefono) here is Mr X; I'm putting you through to Mr X; **lasciar ~ qn/qc** to let sb/sth through; **come te la passi?** how are you getting on o along?

passa'tempo sm pastime, hobby

pas'sato, -a ag past; (sfiorito) faded ▷ sm past; (Ling) past (tense); **passato prossimo/remoto** (Ling) present perfect/past historic; **passato di verdura** (Cuc) vegetable purée

passeg'gero, -a [passed'dʒɛro] ag passing ▷ sm/f passenger

passeggi'are [passed'dʒare] vi to go for a walk; (in veicolo) to go for a drive; **passeggi'ata** sf walk; drive; (luogo) promenade; **fare una passeggiata** to go for a walk (o drive); **passeg'gino** sm pushchair (BRIT), stroller (US)

passe'rella sf footbridge; (di nave, aereo) gangway; (pedana) catwalk

'passero sm sparrow

passi'one sf passion

pas'sivo, -a ag passive ▷ sm (Ling) passive; (Econ) debit; (: complesso dei debiti) liabilities pl

'passo sm step; (andatura) pace; (rumore) (foot)step; (orma) footprint; (passaggio, fig: brano) passage; (valico) pass; **a ~ d'uomo** at walking pace; **~ (a) ~** step by step; **fare due o quattro passi** to go for a walk o a stroll; **di questo ~** at this rate; **"passo carraio"** "vehicle entrance — keep clear"

'pasta sf (Cuc) dough; (: impasto per dolce) pastry; (: anche: **~ alimentare**) pasta; (massa molle di materia) paste; (fig: indole) nature; **paste** sfpl (pasticcini) pastries; **pasta in brodo** noodle soup; **pasta sfoglia** puff pastry o paste (US)

pastasci'utta [pastaʃ'ʃutta] sf pasta

pas'tella sf batter

pas'tello sm pastel

pasticce'ria [pastittʃe'ria] sf (pasticcini) pastries pl, cakes pl; (negozio) cake shop; (arte) confectionery

pasticci'ere, -a [pastit'tʃere] sm/f pastrycook; confectioner

pastic'cino [pastit'tʃino] sm petit four

pas'ticcio [pas'tittʃo] sm (Cuc) pie; (lavoro disordinato, imbroglio) mess; **trovarsi nei pasticci** to get into trouble

pas'tiglia [pas'tiʎʎa] sf pastille, lozenge

pas'tina sf small pasta shapes used in soup

'pasto sm meal

pas'tore sm shepherd; (Rel) pastor, minister; (anche: **cane ~**) sheepdog; **pastore tedesco** (Zool) Alsatian, German shepherd

pa'tata sf potato; **patate fritte** chips (BRIT), French fries (US); **pata'tine** sfpl (potato) crisps; **patatine fritte** chips

pa'tente sf licence; **patente di guida** driving licence (BRIT), driver's license (US); **patente a punti** driving licence with penalty points

> Attenzione! In inglese esiste la parola **patent**, che però significa **brevetto**.

paternità sf paternity, fatherhood

pa'tetico, -a, -ci, -che ag pathetic; (commovente) moving, touching

pa'tibolo sm gallows sg, scaffold

'patina sf (su rame ecc) patina; (sulla lingua) fur, coating

pa'tire vt, vi to suffer

pa'tito, -a sm/f enthusiast, fan, lover

patolo'gia [patolo'dʒia] sf pathology

'patria sf homeland

pa'trigno [pa'triɲɲo] sm stepfather

patri'monio sm estate, property; (fig) heritage

pa'trono sm (Rel) patron saint; (socio di patronato) patron; (Dir) counsel

patteggi'are [patted'dʒare] vt, vi to negotiate; (Dir) to plea-bargain

patti'naggio [patti'naddʒo] sm skating; **pattinaggio a rotelle/sul ghiaccio** roller-/ice-skating

patti'nare vi to skate; **~ sul ghiaccio** to ice-skate; **pattina'tore, -'trice** sm/f skater; **'pattino** sm skate; (di slitta) runner; (Aer) skid; (Tecn) sliding block; **pattini in linea** Rollerblades®; **pattini da ghiaccio/a rotelle** ice/roller skates

'patto sm (accordo) pact, agreement; (condizione) term, condition; **a ~ che** on condition that

pat'tuglia [pat'tuʎʎa] sf (Mil) patrol

pattu'ire vt to reach an agreement on

pattumi'era sf (dust)bin (BRIT), ashcan (US)

pa'ura sf fear; **aver ~ di/di fare/che** to be frightened o afraid of/of doing/that; **far ~ a** to frighten; **per ~ di/che** for fear of/that; **pau'roso, -a** ag (che fa paura) frightening; (che ha paura) fearful, timorous '**pausa** *sf* (*sosta*) break; (*nel parlare, Mus*) pause

pavi'mento *sm* floor

> Attenzione! In inglese esiste la parola *pavement*, che però significa *marciapiede*.

pa'vone *sm* peacock

pazien'tare [pattsjen'tare] *vi* to be patient

pazi'ente [pat'tsjɛnte] *ag, sm/f* patient; **pazi'enza** *sf* patience

paz'zesco, -a, -schi, -sche [pat'tsesko] *ag* mad, crazy

paz'zia [pat'tsia] *sf* (*Med*) madness, insanity; (*azione*) folly; (*di azione, decisione*) madness, folly

'**pazzo, -a** ['pattso] *ag* (*Med*) mad, insane; (*strano*) wild, mad ▷ *sm/f* madman/ woman; **~ di** (*gioia, amore ecc*) mad o crazy with; **~ per qc/qn** mad o crazy about sth/sb

PC [pit'tʃi] *sigla m inv* (= *personal computer*) PC; **PC portatile** laptop

pec'care *vi* to sin; (*fig*) to err

pec'cato *sm* sin; (*fig*) it's a pity that; **che ~!** what a shame o pity!

peccherò *ecc* [pekke'rɔ] *vb vedi* **peccare**

'**pece** ['petʃe] *sf* pitch

Pe'chino [pe'kino] *sf* Beijing

'**pecora** *sf* sheep; **peco'rino** *sm* sheep's milk cheese

pe'daggio [pe'daddʒo] *sm* toll

pedago'gia [pedago'dʒia] *sf* pedagogy, educational methods *pl*

peda'lare *vi* to pedal; (*andare in bicicletta*) to cycle

pe'dale *sm* pedal

pe'dana *sf* footboard; (*Sport: nel salto*) springboard; (*: nella scherma*) piste

pe'dante *ag* pedantic ▷ *sm/f* pedant

pe'data *sf* (*impronta*) footprint; (*colpo*) kick; **prendere a pedate qn/qc** to kick sb/sth

pedi'atra, -i, -e *sm/f* paediatrician

pedi'cure *sm/f inv* chiropodist

pe'dina *sf* (*della dama*) draughtsman (BRIT), draftsman (US); (*fig*) pawn

pedi'nare *vt* to shadow, tail

pe'dofilo, -a *ag, sm/f* paedophile

pedo'nale *ag* pedestrian

pe'done, -a *sm/f* pedestrian ▷ *sm* (*Scacchi*) pawn

'**peggio** ['pɛddʒo] *av, ag* inv worse ▷ *sm* o *f* **il** o **la ~** the worst; **alla ~** at worst, if the worst comes to the worst; **peggio'rare** *vt* to make worse, worsen ▷ *vi* to grow worse, worsen; **peggi'ore** *ag* (*comparativo*) worse; (*superlativo*) worst ▷ *sm/f* **il(la) peggiore** the worst (person)

'**pegno** ['peɲɲo] *sm* (*Dir*) security, pledge; (*nei giochi di società*) forfeit; (*fig*) pledge, token; **dare in ~ qc** to pawn sth

pe'lare *vt* (*spennare*) to pluck; (*spellare*) to skin; (*sbucciare*) to peel; (*fig*) to make pay through the nose

pe'lato, -a *ag* **pomodori pelati** tinned tomatoes

'**pelle** *sf* skin; (*di animale*) skin, hide; (*cuoio*) leather; **avere la ~ d'oca** to have goose pimples o goose flesh

pellegri'naggio [pellegri'naddʒo] *sm* pilgrimage

pelle'rossa (*pl* **pelli'rosse**) *sm/f* Red Indian

pelli'cano *sm* pelican

pel'liccia, -ce [pel'littʃa] *sf* (*mantello di animale*) coat, fur; (*indumento*) fur coat; **pelliccia ecologica** fake fur

pel'licola *sf* (*membrana sottile*) film, layer; (*Fot, Cinema*) film

'**pelo** *sm* hair; (*pelame*) coat, hair; (*pelliccia*) fur; (*di tappeto*) pile; (*di liquido*) surface; **per un ~: per un ~ non ho perduto il treno** I very nearly missed the train; **c'è mancato un ~ che affogasse** he escaped drowning by the skin of his teeth; **pe'loso, -a** *ag* hairy

'**peltro** *sm* pewter

pe'luche [pə'lyʃ] *sm* plush; **giocattoli di ~** soft toys

pe'luria *sf* down

'**pena** *sf* (*Dir*) sentence; (*punizione*) punishment; (*sofferenza*) sadness *no pl*, sorrow; (*fatica*) trouble *no pl*, effort; (*difficoltà*) difficulty; **far ~** to be pitiful; **mi fai ~** I feel sorry for you; **prendersi** o **darsi la ~ di fare** to go to the trouble of doing; **pena di morte** death sentence; **pena pecuniaria** fine; **pe'nale** *ag* penal

pen'dente *ag* hanging; leaning ▷ *sm* (*ciondolo*) pendant; (*orecchino*) drop earring

'**pendere** *vi* (*essere appeso*): **~ da** to hang from; (*essere inclinato*) to lean; (*fig: incombere*): **~ su** to hang over

pen'dio, -'dii *sm* slope, slant; (*luogo in pendenza*) slope

'**pendola** *sf* pendulum clock

pendo'lare *sm/f* commuter

pendo'lino *sm* high-speed train

pene'trante *ag* piercing, penetrating

pene'trare *vi* to come o get in ▷ *vt* to penetrate; **~ in** to enter; (*proiettile*) to penetrate; (*: acqua, aria*) to go o come into

penicil'lina [penitʃil'lina] *sf* penicillin

pe'nisola *sf* peninsula

penitenzi'ario [peniten'tsjarjo] *sm* prison

'penna sf (di uccello) feather; (per scrivere) pen; **penne** sfpl (Cuc) quills (type of pasta); **penna a sfera** ballpoint pen; **penna stilografica** fountain pen

penna'rello sm felt(-tip) pen

pen'nello sm brush; (per dipingere) (paint)brush; **a ~** (perfettamente) to perfection, perfectly; **pennello per la barba** shaving brush

pe'nombra sf half-light, dim light

pen'sare vi to think ▷ vt to think; (inventare, escogitare) to think out; **~ a** to think of; (amico, vacanze) to think of o about; (problema) to think about; **~ di fare qc** to think of doing sth; **ci penso io** I'll see to o take care of it

pensi'ero sm thought; (modo di pensare, dottrina) thinking no pl; (preoccupazione) worry, care, trouble; **stare in ~ per qn** to be worried about sb; **pensie'roso, -a** ag thoughtful

'pensile ag hanging

pensio'nato, -a sm/f pensioner

pensi'one sf (al prestatore di lavoro) pension; (vitto e alloggio) board and lodging; (albergo) boarding house; **andare in ~** to retire; **mezza ~** half board; **pensione completa** full board

pen'tirsi vpr **~ di** to repent of; (rammaricarsi) to regret, be sorry for

'pentola sf pot; **pentola a pressione** pressure cooker

pe'nultimo, -a ag last but one (BRIT), next to last, penultimate

penzo'lare [pendzo'lare] vi to dangle, hang loosely

'pepe sm pepper; **pepe in grani/macinato** whole/ground pepper

peperon'cino [peperon'tʃino] sm chilli pepper

pepe'rone sm pepper, capsicum; (piccante) chili

pe'pita sf nugget

PAROLA CHIAVE

per prep **1** (moto attraverso luogo) through; **i ladri sono passati per la finestra** the thieves got in (o out) through the window; **l'ho cercato per tutta la casa** I've searched the whole house o all over the house for it

2 (moto a luogo) for, to; **partire per la Germania/il mare** to leave for Germany/the sea; **il treno per Roma** the Rome train, the train for o to Rome

3 (stato in luogo): **seduto/sdraiato per terra** sitting/lying on the ground

4 (tempo) for; **per anni/lungo tempo** for years/a long time; **per tutta l'estate** throughout the summer, all summer long; **lo rividi per Natale** I saw him again at Christmas; **lo faccio per lunedì** I'll do it for Monday

5 (mezzo, maniera) by; **per lettera/via aerea/ferrovia** by letter/airmail/rail; **prendere qn per un braccio** to take sb by the arm

6 (causa, scopo) for; **assente per malattia** absent because of o through o owing to illness; **ottimo per il mal di gola** excellent for sore throats

7 (limitazione) for; **è troppo difficile per lui** it's too difficult for him; **per quel che mi riguarda** as far as I'm concerned; **per poco che sia** however little it may be; **per questa volta ti perdono** I'll forgive you this time

8 (prezzo, misura) for; (distributivo) a, per; **venduto per 3 milioni** sold for 3 million; **1 euro per persona** 1 euro a o per person; **uno per volta** one at a time; **uno per uno** one by one; **5 per cento** 5 per cent; **3 per 4 fa 12** 3 times 4 equals 12; **dividere/moltiplicare 12 per 4** to divide/multiply 12 by 4

9 (in qualità di) as; (al posto di) for; **avere qn per professore** to have sb as a teacher; **ti ho preso per Mario** I mistook you for Mario, I thought you were Mario; **dare per morto qn** to give sb up for dead

10 (seguito da vb: finale): **per fare qc** so as to do sth, in order to do sth; (: causale): **per aver fatto qc** for having done sth; (: consecutivo): **è abbastanza grande per andarci da solo** he's big enough to go on his own

'pera sf pear

per'bene ag inv respectable, decent ▷ av (con cura) properly, well

percentu'ale [pertʃentu'ale] sf percentage

perce'pire [pertʃe'pire] vt (sentire) to perceive; (ricevere) to receive

PAROLA CHIAVE

perché [per'ke] av why; **perché no?** why not?; **perché non vuoi andarci?** why don't you want to go?; **spiegami perché l'hai fatto** tell me why you did it

▷ cong **1** (causale) because; **non posso uscire perché ho da fare** I can't go out because o as I've a lot to do

2 (finale) in order that, so that; **te lo do perché tu lo legga** I'm giving it to you so (that) you can read it

3 (*consecutivo*): **è troppo forte perché si possa batterlo** he's too strong to be beaten
▷ *sm inv* reason; **il perché di** the reason for

perciò [per'tʃɔ] *cong* so, for this (*o* that) reason

per'correre *vt* (*luogo*) to go all over; (: *paese*) to travel up and down, go all over; (*distanza*) to cover

per'corso, -a *pp di* **percorrere** ▷ *sm* (*tragitto*) journey; (*tratto*) route

percu'otere *vt* to hit, strike

percussi'one *sf* percussion; **strumenti a ~** (*Mus*) percussion instruments

'perdere *vt* to lose; (*lasciarsi sfuggire*) to miss; (*sprecare: tempo, denaro*) to waste ▷ *vi* to lose; (*serbatoio ecc*) to leak; **perdersi** *vpr* (*smarrirsi*) to get lost; (*svanire*) to disappear, vanish; **mi sono perso** I'm lost; **ho perso il portafoglio/passaporto** I've lost my wallet/passport; **abbiamo perso il treno** we missed our train; **saper ~** to be a good loser; **lascia ~!** forget it!, never mind!

perdigi'orno [perdi'dʒorno] *sm/f inv* idler, waster

'perdita *sf* loss; (*spreco*) waste; (*fuoriuscita*) leak; **siamo in ~** (*Comm*) we are running at a loss; **a ~ d'occhio** as far as the eye can see

perdo'nare *vt* to pardon, forgive; (*scusare*) to excuse, pardon

per'dono *sm* forgiveness; (*Dir*) pardon

perduta'mente *av* desperately, passionately

pe'renne *ag* eternal, perpetual, perennial; (*Bot*) perennial

perfetta'mente *av* perfectly; **sai ~ che ...** you know perfectly well that ...

per'fetto, -a *ag* perfect ▷ *sm* (*Ling*) perfect (tense)

perfeziona'mento [perfettsjona'mento] *sm* **~ (di)** improvement (in), perfection (of); **corso di ~** proficiency course

perfezio'nare [perfettsjo'nare] *vt* to improve, perfect; **perfezionarsi** *vpr* to improve

perfezi'one [perfet'tsjone] *sf* perfection

per'fino *av* even

perfo'rare *vt* to perforate, to punch a hole (*o* holes) in; (*banda, schede*) to punch; (*trivellare*) to drill

perga'mena *sf* parchment

perico'lante *ag* precarious

pe'ricolo *sm* danger; **mettere in ~** to endanger, put in danger; **perico'loso, -a** *ag* dangerous

perife'ria *sf* (*di città*) outskirts *pl*

pe'rifrasi *sf* circumlocution

pe'rimetro *sm* perimeter

peri'odico, -a, -ci, -che *ag* periodic(al); (*Mat*) recurring ▷ *sm* periodical

pe'riodo *sm* period

peripe'zie [peripet'tsie] *sfpl* ups and downs, vicissitudes

pe'rito, -a *ag* expert, skilled ▷ *sm/f* expert; (*agronomo, navale*) surveyor; **perito chimico** qualified chemist

peri'zoma, -i [peri'dzoma] *sm* G-string

'perla *sf* pearl; **per'lina** *sf* bead

perlus'trare *vt* to patrol

perma'loso, -a *ag* touchy

perma'nente *ag* permanent ▷ *sf* permanent wave, perm; **perma'nenza** *sf* permanence; (*soggiorno*) stay

perme'are *vt* to permeate

per'messo, -a *pp di* **permettere** ▷ *sm* (*autorizzazione*) permission, leave; (*dato a militare, impiegato*) leave; (*licenza*) licence, permit; (*Mil: foglio*) pass; **~?, è ~?** (*posso entrare?*) may I come in?; (*posso passare?*) excuse me; **permesso di lavoro/pesca** work/fishing permit; **permesso di soggiorno** residence permit

per'mettere *vt* to allow, permit; **~ a qn qc/di fare qc** to allow sb sth/to do sth; **permettersi qc/di fare qc** to allow o.s. sth/to do sth; (*avere la possibilità*) to afford sth/to do sth

per'misi *ecc vb vedi* **permettere**

per'nacchia [per'nakkja] (*fam*) *sf* **fare una ~** to blow a raspberry

per'nice [per'nitʃe] *sf* partridge

'perno *sm* pivot

pernot'tare *vi* to spend the night, stay overnight

'pero *sm* pear tree

però *cong* (*ma*) but; (*tuttavia*) however, nevertheless

perpendico'lare *ag, sf* perpendicular

per'plesso, -a *ag* perplexed; uncertain, undecided

perqui'sire *vt* to search; **perquisizi'one** *sf* (*police*) search

'perse *ecc vb vedi* **perdere**

persecuzi'one [persekut'tsjone] *sf* persecution

persegui'tare *vt* to persecute

perseve'rante *ag* persevering

'persi *ecc vb vedi* **perdere**

persi'ana *sf* shutter; **persiana avvolgibile** roller shutter

per'sino *av* = **perfino**

persis'tente *ag* persistent

'perso, -a *pp di* **perdere**

per'sona *sf* person; (*qualcuno*) **una ~** someone, somebody; (*espressione interrogativa +*) anyone *o* anybody

perso'naggio [perso'naddʒo] *sm* (*persona*

ragguardevole) personality, figure; *(tipo)* character, individual; *(Letteratura)* character

perso'nale *ag* personal ▷ *sm* staff; personnel; *(figura fisica)* build

personalità *sf inv* personality

perspi'cace [perspi'katʃe] *ag* shrewd, discerning

persu'adere *vt* ~ **qn (di qc/a fare)** to persuade sb (of sth/to do)

per'tanto *cong (quindi)* so, therefore

'pertica, -che *sf* pole

perti'nente *ag* ~ **(a)** relevant (to), pertinent (to)

per'tosse *sf* whooping cough

perturbazi'one [perturbat'tsjone] *sf* disruption; perturbation; **perturbazione atmosferica** atmospheric disturbance

per'vadere *vt* to pervade

per'verso, -a *ag* depraved; perverse

perver'tito, -a *sm/f* pervert

p.es. *abbr (= per esempio)* e.g.

pe'sante *ag* heavy; **è troppo ~** it's too heavy

pe'sare *vt* to weigh ▷ *vi (avere un peso)* to weigh; *(essere pesante)* to be heavy; *(fig)* to carry weight; **~ su** *(fig)* to lie heavy on; to influence; to hang over; **pesarsi** *vpr* to weigh o.s.; **~ le parole** to weigh one's words; **~ sulla coscienza** to weigh on sb's conscience; **mi pesa ammetterlo** I don't like admitting it; **tutta la responsabilità pesa su di lui** all the responsibility rests on him; **è una situazione che mi pesa** I find the situation difficult; **il suo parere pesa molto** his opinion counts for a lot

'pesca *(pl* **pesche)** *(: frutto) sf* peach; *(il pescare)* fishing; **andare a ~** to go fishing; **~ con la lenza** angling; **pesca di beneficenza** *(lotteria)* lucky dip

pes'care *vt (pesce)* to fish for; to catch; *(qc nell'acqua)* to fish out; *(fig: trovare)* to get hold of, find; **andare a ~** to go fishing

pesca'tore *sm* fisherman; angler

'pesce ['peʃʃe] *sm* fish *gen inv;* **Pesci** *(dello zodiaco)* Pisces; **pesce d'aprile!** April Fool!; **pesce rosso** goldfish; **pesce spada** swordfish; **pesce'cane** *sm* shark

pesche'reccio [peske'rettʃo] *sm* fishing boat

pesche'ria [peske'ria] *sf* fishmonger's (shop) *(BRIT)*, fish store *(US)*

pesche'rò *ecc* [peske'rɔ] *vb vedi* **pescare**

'peso *sm* weight; *(Sport)* shot; **rubare sul ~** to give short weight; **essere di ~ a qn** *(fig)* to be a burden to sb; **peso lordo/netto** gross/net weight; **peso massimo/medio** *(Pugilato)* heavy/middleweight

pessi'mismo *sm* pessimism; **pessi'mista,**

-i, -e *ag* pessimistic ▷ *sm/f* pessimist

'pessimo, -a *ag* very bad, awful

pes'tare *vt* to tread on, trample on; *(sale, pepe)* to grind; *(uva, aglio)* to crush; *(fig: picchiare)*: **~ qn** to beat sb up

'peste *sf* plague; *(persona)* nuisance, pest

pes'tello *sm* pestle

'petalo *sm (Bot)* petal

pe'tardo *sm* firecracker, banger *(BRIT)*

petizi'one [petit'tsjone] *sf* petition

petroli'era *sf (nave)* oil tanker

pe'trolio *sm* oil, petroleum; *(per lampada, fornello)* paraffin

> Attenzione! In inglese esiste la parola *petrol* che però significa *benzina*.

pettego'lare *vi* to gossip

pettego'lezzo [pettego'leddzo] *sm* gossip *no pl;* **fare pettegolezzi** to gossip

pet'tegolo, -a *ag* gossipy ▷ *sm/f* gossip

petti'nare *vt* to comb (the hair of); **pettinarsi** *vpr* to comb one's hair; **pettina'tura** *sf (acconciatura)* hairstyle

'pettine *sm* comb; *(Zool)* scallop

petti'rosso *sm* robin

'petto *sm* chest; *(seno)* breast, bust; *(Cuc: di carne bovina)* brisket; *(: di pollo ecc)* breast; **a doppio ~** *(abito)* double-breasted

petu'lante *ag* insolent

'pezza ['pettsa] *sf* piece of cloth; *(toppa)* patch; *(cencio)* rag, cloth

pez'zente [pet'tsɛnte] *sm/f* beggar

'pezzo ['pettso] *sm (gen)* piece; *(brandello, frammento)* piece, bit; *(di macchina, arnese ecc)* part; *(Stampa)* article; *(di tempo)*: **aspettare un ~** to wait quite a while *o* some time; **in** *o* **a pezzi** in pieces; **andare in pezzi** to break into pieces; **un bel ~ d'uomo** a fine figure of a man; **abito a due pezzi** two-piece suit; **pezzo di cronaca** *(Stampa)* report; **pezzo grosso** *(fig)* bigwig; **pezzo di ricambio** spare part

pi'accio *ecc* ['pjattʃo] *vb vedi* **piacere**

pia'cente [pja'tʃɛnte] *ag* attractive

pia'cere [pja'tʃere] *vi* to please; **una ragazza che piace** a likeable girl; an attractive girl; **~ a: mi piace** I like it; **quei ragazzi non mi piacciono** I don't like those boys; **gli ~bbe andare al cinema** he would like to go to the cinema ▷ *sm* pleasure; *(favore)* favour; **"~!"** *(nelle presentazioni)* "pleased to meet you!"; **~ (di conoscerla)** nice to meet you; **con ~** certainly, with pleasure; **per ~!** please; **fare un ~ a qn** to do sb a favour; **pia'cevole** *ag* pleasant, agreeable

pi'acqui *ecc* *vb vedi* **piacere**

pi'aga, -ghe *sf (lesione)* sore; *(ferita: anche fig)* wound; *(: flagello)* scourge, curse; *(: persona)* pest, nuisance

piagnuco'lare [pjaɲɲuko'lare] *vi* to whimper

pianeggi'ante [pjaned'dʒante] *ag* flat, level

piane'rottolo *sm* landing

pia'neta *sm* (*Astr*) planet

pi'angere ['pjandʒere] *vi* to cry, weep; (*occhi*) to water ▷ *vt* to cry, weep; (*lamentare*) to bewail, lament; **~ la morte di qn** to mourn sb's death

pianifi'care *vt* to plan

pia'nista, -i, -e *sm/f* pianist

pi'ano, -a *ag* (*piatto*) flat, level; (*Mat*) plane; (*chiaro*) clear, plain ▷ *av* (*adagio*) slowly; (*a bassa voce*) softly; (*con cautela*) slowly, carefully ▷ *sm* (*Mat*) plane; (*Geo*) plain; (*livello*) level, plane; (*di edificio*) floor; (*programma*) plan; (*Mus*) piano; **a che ~ si trova?** what floor is it on?; **pian ~** very slowly; (*poco a poco*) little by little; **in primo/secondo ~** in the foreground/ background; **di primo ~** (*fig*) prominent, high-ranking

piano'forte *sm* piano, pianoforte

piano'terra *sm inv* ground floor

pi'ansi *ecc vb vedi* **piangere**

pi'anta *sf* (*Bot*) plant; (*Anat: anche:* **~ del piede**) sole (of the foot); (*grafico*) plan; (*topografica*) map; **in ~ stabile** on the permanent staff; **pian'tare** *vt* to plant; (*conficcare*) to drive *o* hammer in; (*tenda*) to put up, pitch; (*fig: lasciare*) to leave, desert; **piantarsi** *vpr* **piantarsi davanti a qn** to plant o.s. in front of sb; **piantala!** (*fam*) cut it out!

pianter'reno *sm* = **pianoterra**

pia'nura *sf* plain

pi'astra *sf* plate; (*di pietra*) slab; (*di fornello*) hotplate; **panino alla ~** ≈ toasted sandwich; **piastra di registrazione** tape deck

pias'trella *sf* tile

pias'trina *sf* (*Mil*) identity disc

piatta'forma *sf* (*anche fig*) platform

piat'tino *sm* saucer

pi'atto, -a *ag* flat; (*fig: scialbo*) dull ▷ *sm* (*recipiente, vivanda*) dish; (*portata*) course; (*parte piana*) flat (part); **piatti** *smpl* (*Mus*) cymbals; **piatto fondo** soup dish; **piatto forte** main course; **piatto del giorno** dish of the day, plat du jour; **piatto del giradischi** turntable; **piatto piano** dinner plate

pi'azza ['pjattsa] *sf* square; (*Comm*) market; **far ~ pulita** to make a clean sweep; **piazza d'armi** (*Mil*) parade ground; **piaz'zale** *sm* (large) square; **piaz'zola** [pjat'tsɔla] *sf* (*Aut*) lay-by; (*di tenda*) pitch

pic'cante *ag* hot, pungent; (*fig*) racy; biting

pic'chetto [pik'ketto] *sm* (*Mil, di scioperanti*) picket; (*di tenda*) peg

picchi'are [pik'kjare] *vt* (*persona: colpire*) to hit, strike; (*: prendere a botte*) to beat (up); (*battere*) to beat; (*sbattere*) to bang ▷ *vi* (*bussare*) to knock; (*: con forza*) to bang; (*colpire*) to hit, strike; (*sole*) to beat down; **picchi'ata** *sf* (*Aer*) dive

picchio ['pikkjo] *sm* woodpecker

pic'cino, -a [pit'tʃino] *ag* tiny, very small

picci'one [pit'tʃone] *sm* pigeon

picco, -chi *sm* peak; **a ~** vertically

piccolo, -a *ag* small; (*oggetto, mano, di età: bambino*) small, little; (*dav sostantivo: di breve durata: viaggio*) short; (*fig*) mean, petty ▷ *sm/f* child, little one

pic'cone *sm* pick(-axe)

pic'cozza [pik'kɔttsa] *sf* ice-axe

pic'nic *sm inv* picnic

pi'docchio [pi'dɔkkjo] *sm* louse

pi'ede *sm* foot; (*di mobile*) leg; **in piedi** standing; **a piedi** on foot; **a piedi nudi** barefoot; **su due piedi** (*fig*) at once; **prendere ~** (*fig*) to gain ground, catch on; **sul ~ di guerra** (*Mil*) ready for action; **piede di porco** crowbar

pi'ega, -ghe *sf* (*piegatura, Geo*) fold; (*di gonna*) pleat; (*di pantaloni*) crease; (*grinza*) wrinkle, crease; **prendere una brutta ~** (*fig*) to take a turn for the worse

pie'gare *vt* to fold; (*braccia, gambe, testa*) to bend ▷ *vi* to bend; **piegarsi** *vpr* to bend; (*fig*): **piegarsi (a)** to yield (to), submit (to)

pieghe'rò [pjege'rɔ] *vb vedi* **piegare**

pie'ghevole *ag* pliable, flexible; (*porta*) folding

Pie'monte *sm* **il ~** Piedmont

pi'ena *sf* (*di fiume*) flood, spate

pi'eno, -a *ag* full; (*muro, mattone*) solid ▷ *sm* (*colmo*) height, peak; (*carico*) full load; **~ di** full of; **in ~ giorno** in broad daylight; **il ~, per favore** (*Aut*) fill it up, please

piercing ['pirsing] *sm* piercing; **farsi il ~ all'ombelico** to have one's navel pierced

pietà *sf* pity; (*Rel*) piety; **senza ~** pitiless, merciless; **avere ~ di** (*compassione*) to pity, feel sorry for; (*misericordia*) to have pity *o* mercy on

pie'tanza [pje'tantsa] *sf* dish, course

pie'toso, -a *ag* (*compassionevole*) pitying, compassionate; (*che desta pietà*) pitiful

pi'etra *sf* stone; **pietra preziosa** precious stone, gem

piffero *sm* (*Mus*) pipe

pigi'ama, -i [pi'dʒama] *sm* pyjamas *pl*

pigli'are [piʎ'ʎare] *vt* to take, grab; (*afferrare*) to catch

'pigna ['piɲɲa] *sf* pine cone

pi'gnolo, -a [piɲ'ɔlo] *ag* pernickety

pi'grizia [pi'grittsja] *sf* laziness

'pigro, -a *ag* lazy

PIL *sigla m* (= *prodotto interno lordo*) GDP

'pila *sf* (*catasta, di ponte*) pile; (*Elettr*) battery; (*torcia*) torch (BRIT), flashlight

pi'lastro *sm* pillar

'pile ['pail] *sm inv* fleece

'pillola *sf* pill; **prendere la ~** to be on the pill

pi'lone *sm* (*di ponte*) pier; (*di linea elettrica*) pylon

pi'lota, -i, -e *sm/f* pilot; (*Aut*) driver ▷ *ag inv* pilot *cpd*; **pilota automatico** automatic pilot

pinaco'teca, -che *sf* art gallery

pi'neta *sf* pinewood

ping-'pong [piŋ'pɔŋ] *sm* table tennis

pingu'ino *sm* (*Zool*) penguin

'pinna *sf* (*di pesce*) fin; (*di cetaceo, per nuotare*) flipper

'pino *sm* pine (tree); **pi'nolo** *sm* pine kernel

'pinza ['pintsa] *sf* pliers *pl*; (*Med*) forceps *pl*; (*Zool*) pincer

pinzette [pin'tsette] *sfpl* tweezers

pi'oggia, -ge ['pjɔddʒa] *sf* rain; **pioggia acida** acid rain

pi'olo *sm* peg; (*di scala*) rung

piom'bare *vi* to fall heavily; (*gettarsi con impeto*): **~ su** to fall upon, assail ▷ *vt* (*dente*) to fill; **piomba'tura** *sf* (*di dente*) filling

piom'bino *sm* (*sigillo*) (lead) seal; (*del filo a piombo*) plummet; (*Pesca*) sinker

pi'ombo *sm* (*Chim*) lead; **a ~** (*cadere*) straight down; **senza ~** (*benzina*) unleaded

pioni'ere, -a *sm/f* pioneer

pi'oppo *sm* poplar

pi'overe *vb impers* to rain ▷ *vi* (*fig: scendere dall'alto*) to rain down; (*lettere, regali*) to pour into; **pioviggi'nare** *vb impers* to drizzle; **pio'voso, -a** *ag* rainy

pi'ovra *sf* octopus

pi'ovve *ecc vb vedi* **piovere**

'pipa *sf* pipe

pipì (*fam*) *sf* **fare ~** to have a wee (wee)

pipis'trello *sm* (*Zool*) bat

pi'ramide *sf* pyramid

pi'rata, -i *sm* pirate; **pirata della strada** hit-and-run driver; **pirata informatica** hacker

Pire'nei *smpl* **i ~** the Pyrenees

pi'romane *sm/f* pyromaniac; arsonist

pi'roscafo *sm* steamer, steamship

pisci'are [piʃʃare] (*fam!*) *vi* to piss (!), pee (!)

pi'scina [piʃʃina] *sf* (*swimming*) pool; (*stabilimento*) (swimming) baths *pl*

pi'sello *sm* pea

piso'lino *sm* nap

'pista *sf* (*traccia*) track, trail; (*di stadio*) track; (*di pattinaggio*) rink; (*da sci*) run; (*Aer*) runway; (*di circo*) ring; **pista da ballo** dance floor

pis'tacchio [pis'takkjo] *sm* pistachio (tree); pistachio (nut)

pis'tola *sf* pistol, gun

pis'tone *sm* piston

pi'tone *sm* python

pit'tore, -'trice *sm/f* painter; **pitto'resco, -a, -schi, -sche** *ag* picturesque

pit'tura *sf* painting; **pittu'rare** *vt* to paint

○ **PAROLA CHIAVE**

più *av* **1** (*in maggiore quantità*) more; **più del solito** more than usual; **in più, di più** more; **ne voglio di più** I want some more; **ci sono 3 persone in o di più** there are 3 more o extra people; **più o meno** more or less; **per di più** (*inoltre*) what's more, moreover

2 (*comparativo*) more; (*aggettivo corto +*) ...er; **più ... di/che** more ... than; **lavoro più di te/Paola** I work harder than you/ Paola; **è più intelligente che ricco** he's more intelligent than rich

3 (*superlativo*) most; (*aggettivo corto +*) ...est; **il più grande/intelligente** the biggest/most intelligent; **è quello che compro più spesso** that's the one I buy most often; **al più presto** as soon as possible; **al più tardi** at the latest

4 (*negazione*): **non ... più** no more, no longer; **non ho più soldi** I've got no more money, I don't have any more money; **non lavoro più** I'm no longer working, I don't work any more; **a più non posso** (*gridare*) at the top of one's voice; (*correre*) as fast as one can

5 (*Mat*) plus; **4 più 5 fa 9** 4 plus 5 equals 9; **più 5 gradi** 5 degrees above freezing, plus 5 ▷ *prep plus* ▷ *ag inv* **1**: **più ... (di)** more ... (than); **più denaro/tempo** more money/time; **più persone di quante ci aspettassimo** more people than we expected

2 (*numerosi, diversi*) several; **l'aspettai per più giorni** I waited for it for several days ▷ *sm* **1** (*la maggior parte*): **il più è fatto** most of it is done

2 (*Mat*) plus (sign)

3: **i più** the majority

---

pi'uma *sf* feather; **piu'mino** *sm* (eider)down; (*per letto*) eiderdown; (*: tipo* danese) duvet, continental quilt; (giacca) quilted jacket (with goose-feather padding); (per cipria) powder puff; (per spolverare) feather duster

piut'tosto av rather; ~ **che** (anziché) rather than

'**pizza** ['pittsa] sf pizza; **pizze'ria** sf place where pizzas are made, sold or eaten

pizzi'care [pittsi'kare] vt (stringere) to nip, pinch; (pungere) to sting; to bite; (Mus) to pluck ▷ vi (prudere) to itch, be itchy; (cibo) to be hot o spicy

'**pizzico, -chi** ['pittsiko] sm (pizzicotto) pinch, nip; (piccola quantità) pinch, dash; (d'insetto) sting; bite

pizzi'cotto [pittsi'kɔtto] sm pinch, nip

'**pizzo** ['pittso] sm (merletto) lace; (barbetta) goatee beard

plagi'are [pla'dʒare] vt (copiare) to plagiarize

plaid [plɛd] sm inv (travelling) rug (BRIT), lap robe (US)

pla'nare vi (Aer) to glide

'**plasma** sm plasma

plas'mare vt to mould, shape

'**plastica, -che** sf (arte) plastic arts pl; (Med) plastic surgery; (sostanza) plastic; **plastica facciale** face lift

'**platano** sm plane tree

pla'tea sf (Teatro) stalls pl

'**platino** sm platinum

plau'sibile ag plausible

pleni'lunio sm full moon

'**plettro** sm plectrum

pleu'rite sf pleurisy

'**plico, -chi** sm (pacco) parcel; **in ~ a parte** (Comm) under separate cover

plo'tone sm (Mil) platoon; **plotone d'esecuzione** firing squad

plu'rale ag, sm plural

PM abbr (Pol) = **Pubblico Ministero**; (= Polizia Militare) MP (Military Police)

pneu'matico, -a, -ci, -che ag inflatable; pneumatic ▷ sm (Aut) tyre (BRIT), tire (US)

po' av, sm vedi **poco**

○ **PAROLA CHIAVE**

'**poco, -a, -chi, -che** ag (quantità) little, not much; (numero) few, not many; **poco pane/denaro/spazio** little o not much bread/money/space; **poche persone/ idee** few o not many people/ideas; **ci vediamo tra poco** (sottinteso: tempo) see you soon

▷ av **1** (in piccola quantità) little, not much; (numero limitato) few, not many; **guadagna poco** he doesn't earn much, he earns little

2 (con ag, av) (a) little, not very; **sta poco bene** he isn't very well; **è poco più vecchia di lui** she's a little o slightly older than him

3 (tempo): **poco dopo/prima** shortly afterwards/before; **il film dura poco** the film doesn't last very long; **ci vediamo molto poco** we don't see each other very often, we hardly ever see each other

4: **un po'** a little, a bit; **è un po' corto** it's a little o a bit short; **arriverà fra un po'** he'll arrive shortly o in a little while

5: **a dir poco** to say the least; **a poco a poco** little by little; **per poco non cadevo** I nearly fell; **è una cosa da poco** it's nothing, it's of no importance; **una persona da poco** a worthless person ▷ pron (a) little

po'dere sm (Agr) farm

'**podio** sm dais, platform; (Mus) podium

po'dismo sm (Sport) track events pl

poe'sia sf (arte) poetry; (componimento) poem

po'eta, -'essa sm/f poet/poetess

poggi'are [pod'dʒare] vt to lean, rest; (posare) to lay, place; **poggia'testa** sm inv (Aut) headrest

'**poggio** ['pɔddʒo] sm hillock, knoll

'**poi** av then; (alla fine) finally, at last; **e ~** (inoltre) and besides; **questa ~ (è bella)!** (ironico) that's a good one!

poiché [poi'ke] cong since, as

'**poker** sm poker

po'lacco, -a, -chi, -che ag Polish ▷ sm/f Pole

po'lare ag polar

po'lemica, -che sf controversy

po'lemico, -a, -ci, -che ag polemic(al), controversial

po'lenta sf (Cuc) sort of thick porridge made with maize flour

'**polio(mie'lite)** sf polio(myelitis)

'**polipo** sm polyp

polisti'rolo sm polystyrene

po'litica, -che sf politics sg; (linea di condotta) policy; (anche: **politico**); **politica'mente** av politically; **politicamente corretto** politically correct

po'litico, -a, -ci, -che ag political ▷ sm/f politician

poli'zia [polit'tsia] sf police; **polizia giudiziaria** ≈ Criminal Investigation Department (BRIT), ≈ Federal Bureau of Investigation (US); **polizia stradale** traffic police; **polizi'esco, -a, -schi, -sche** ag police cpd; (film, romanzo) detective cpd; **polizi'otto** sm policeman; **cane poliziotto** police dog; **donna poliziotto**

policewoman; **poliziotto di quartiere** local police officer

polizza ['polittsa] *sf* (*Comm*) bill; **~ di assicurazione** insurance policy; **polizza di carico** bill of lading

pol'laio *sm* henhouse

pollice ['pollitʃe] *sm* thumb

polline *sm* pollen

pollo *sm* chicken

pol'mone *sm* lung; **polmone d'acciaio** (*Med*) iron lung; **polmo'nite** *sf* pneumonia; **polmonite atipica** SARS

polo *sm* (*Geo, Fisica*) pole; (*gioco*) polo; **polo nord/sud** North/South Pole

Po'lonia *sf* **la ~** Poland

polpa *sf* flesh, pulp; (*carne*) lean meat

pol'paccio [pol'pattʃo] *sm* (*Anat*) calf

polpas'trello *sm* fingertip

pol'petta *sf* (*Cuc*) meatball

polpo *sm* octopus

pol'sino *sm* cuff

polso *sm* (*Anat*) wrist; (*pulsazione*) pulse; (*fig: forza*) drive, vigour

pol'trire *vi* to laze about

pol'trona *sf* armchair; (*Teatro: posto*) seat in the front stalls (*BRIT*) o orchestra (*US*)

polvere *sf* dust; (*sostanza ridotta minutissima*) powder, dust; **latte in ~** dried o powdered milk; **caffè in ~** instant coffee; **sapone in ~** soap powder; **polvere da sparo/pirica** gunpowder

po'mata *sf* ointment, cream

po'mello *sm* knob

pome'riggio [pome'riddʒo] *sm* afternoon

pomice ['pomitʃe] *sf* pumice

pomo *sm* (*mela*) apple; (*ornamentale*) knob; (*di sella*) pommel; **pomo d'Adamo** (*Anat*) Adam's apple

pomo'doro *sm* tomato; **pomodori pelati** skinned tomatoes

pompa *sf* pump; (*sfarzo*) pomp (and ceremony); **pompe funebri** funeral parlour *sg* (*BRIT*), undertaker's *sg*; **pompa di benzina** petrol (*BRIT*) o gas (*US*) pump; (*distributore*) filling o gas (*US*) station; **pom'pare** *vt* to pump; (*trarre*) to pump out; (*gonfiare d'aria*) to pump up

pom'pelmo *sm* grapefruit

pompi'ere *sm* fireman

po'nente *sm* west

pongo, poni ecc *vb vedi* **porre**

ponte *sm* bridge; (*di nave*) deck; (: *anche:* **~ di comando**) bridge; (*impalcatura*) scaffold; **fare il ~** (*fig*) to take the extra day off (*between 2 public holidays*); **governo ~** interim government; **ponte aereo** airlift; **ponte levatoio** drawbridge; **ponte sospeso** suspension bridge

pon'tefice [pon'tɛfitʃe] *sm* (*Rel*) pontiff

popcorn ['pɔpkɔːn] *sm inv* popcorn

popo'lare *ag* popular; (*quartiere, clientela*) working-class ▷ *vt* (*rendere abitato*) to populate; **popolarsi** *vpr* to fill with people, get crowded; **popolazi'one** *sf* population

popolo *sm* people

poppa *sf* (*di nave*) stern; (*seno*) breast

porcel'lana [portʃel'lana] *sf* porcelain, china; piece of china

porcel'lino, -a [portʃel'lino] *sm/f* piglet; **porcellino d'India** guinea pig

porche'ria [porke'ria] *sf* filth, muck; (*fig: oscenità*) obscenity; (: *azione disonesta*) dirty trick; (: *cosa mal fatta*) rubbish

porcile [por'tʃile] *sm* pigsty

porcino, -a [por'tʃino] *ag* of pigs, pork *cpd* ▷ *sm* (*fungo*) type of edible mushroom

porco, -ci *sm* pig; (*carne*) pork

porcos'pino *sm* porcupine

porgere ['pɔrdʒere] *vt* to hand, give; (*tendere*) to hold out

pornogra'fia *sf* pornography; **porno'grafico, -a, -ci, -che** *ag* pornographic

poro *sm* pore

porpora *sf* purple

porre *vt* (*mettere*) to put; (*collocare*) to place; (*posare*) to lay (down), put (down); (*fig: supporre*): **poniamo (il caso) che ...** let's suppose that ...

porro *sm* (*Bot*) leek; (*Med*) wart

porsi ecc *vb vedi* **porgere**

porta *sf* door; (*Sport*) goal; **portaba'gagli** *sm inv* (*facchino*) porter; (*Aut, Ferr*) luggage rack; **porta-CD** [portatʃi'di] *sm inv* (*mobile*) CD rack; (*astuccio*) CD holder; **porta'cenere** *sm inv* ashtray; **portachi'avi** *sm inv* keyring; **porta'erei** *sf inv* (*nave*) aircraft carrier; **portafi'nestra** (*pl* **portefi'nestre**) *sf* French window; **porta'foglio** *sm* wallet; (*Pol, Borsa*) portfolio; **non trovo il portafoglio** I can't find my wallet; **portafor'tuna** *sm inv* lucky charm; mascot

por'tale *sm* (*di chiesa, Inform*) portal

porta'mento *sm* carriage, bearing

portamo'nete *sm inv* purse

por'tante *ag* (*muro ecc*) supporting, load-bearing

portan'tina *sf* sedan chair; (*per ammalati*) stretcher

portaom'brelli *sm inv* umbrella stand

porta'pacchi [porta'pakki] *sm inv* (*di moto, bicicletta*) luggage rack

por'tare *vt* (*sostenere, sorreggere: peso, bambino, pacco*) to carry; (*indossare: abito, occhiali*) to wear; (: *capelli lunghi*) to have; (*avere: nome, titolo*) to have, bear; (*recare*): ~ **qc a qn** to take (*o bring*) sth to sb; (*fig: sentimenti*) to bear

portasiga'rette *sm inv* cigarette case

por'tata *sf* (*vivanda*) course; (*Aut*) carrying (*o loading*) capacity; (*di arma*) range; (*volume d'acqua*) (rate of) flow; (*fig: limite*) scope, capability; (: *importanza*) impact, import; **alla ~ di tutti** (*conoscenza*) within everybody's capabilities; (*prezzo*) within everybody's means; **a/fuori ~ (di)** within/out of reach (of); **a ~ di mano** within (arm's) reach

por'tatile *ag* portable

por'tato, -a *ag* (*incline*): ~ **a** inclined *o* apt to

portau'ovo *sm inv* eggcup

porta'voce [porta'votʃe] *sm/f inv* spokesman/woman

por'tento *sm* wonder, marvel

porti'era *sf* (*Aut*) door

porti'ere *sm* (*portinaio*) concierge, caretaker; (*di hotel*) porter; (*nel calcio*) goalkeeper

porti'naio, -a *sm/f* concierge, caretaker

portine'ria *sf* caretaker's lodge

'porto, -a *pp di* **porgere** ⊳ *sm* (*Naut*) harbour, port ⊳ *sm inv* port (wine); **porto d'armi** (*documento*) gun licence

Porto'gallo *sm* **il** ~ Portugal; **porto'ghese** *ag, sm/f, sm* Portuguese *inv*

por'tone *sm* main entrance, main door

portu'ale *ag* harbour *cpd*, port *cpd* ⊳ *sm* dock worker

porzi'one [por'tsjone] *sf* portion, share; (*di cibo*) portion, helping

'posa *sf* (*Fot*) exposure; (*atteggiamento, di modello*) pose

po'sare *vt* to put (down), lay (down) ⊳ *vi* (*ponte, edificio, teoria*): ~ **su** to rest on; (*Fot: atteggiarsi*) to pose; **posarsi** *vpr* (*aereo*) to land; (*uccello*) to alight; (*sguardo*) to settle

po'sata *sf* piece of cutlery

pos'critto *sm* postscript

'posi *ecc vb vedi* **porre**

posi'tivo, -a *ag* positive

posizi'one [pozit'tsjone] *sf* position; **prendere ~** (*fig*) to take a stand; **luci di ~** (*Aut*) sidelights

pos'porre *vt* to place after; (*differire*) to postpone, defer

posse'dere *vt* to own, possess; (*qualità, virtù*) to have, possess

posses'sivo, -a *ag* possessive

pos'sesso *sm* ownership *no pl*; possession

posses'sore *sm* owner

pos'sibile *ag* possible ⊳ *sm* **fare tutto il** ~ to do everything possible; **nei limiti del** ~ as far as possible; **al più tardi ~** as late as possible; **possibilità** *sf inv* possibility ⊳ *sfpl* (*mezzi*) means; **aver la possibilità di fare** to be in a position to do; to have the opportunity to do

possi'dente *sm/f* landowner

possi'edo *ecc vb vedi* **possedere**

'posso *ecc vb vedi* **potere**

'posta *sf* (*servizio*) post, postal service; (*corrispondenza*) post, mail; (*ufficio postale*) post office; (*nei giochi d'azzardo*) stake; **Poste** *sfpl* (*amministrazione*) post office; **c'è ~ per me?** are there any letters for me?; **ministro delle Poste e Telecomunicazioni** Postmaster General; **posta aerea** airmail; **posta elettronica** E-mail, e-mail, electronic mail; **posta ordinaria** ≈ second-class mail; **posta prioritaria** ≈ first-class post; **pos'tale** *ag* postal, post office *cpd*

posteggi'are [posted'dʒare] *vt, vi* to park; **pos'teggio** *sm* car park (BRIT), parking lot (US); (*di taxi*) rank (BRIT), stand (US)

'poster *sm inv* poster

posteri'ore *ag* (*dietro*) back; (*dopo*) later ⊳ *sm* (*fam: sedere*) behind

postici'pare [postitʃi'pare] *vt* to defer, postpone

pos'tino *sm* postman (BRIT), mailman (US)

'posto, -a *pp di* **porre** ⊳ *sm* (*sito, posizione*) place; (*impiego*) job; (*spazio libero*) room, space; (*di parcheggio*) space; (*sedile: al teatro, in treno ecc*) seat; (*Mil*) post; **a ~** (*in ordine*) in place, tidy; (*fig*) settled; (: *persona*) reliable; **vorrei prenotare due posti** I'd like to book two seats; **al ~ di** in place of; **sul ~** on the spot; **mettere a ~** to tidy (up), put in order; (*faccende*) to straighten out; **posto di blocco** roadblock; **posto di lavoro** job; **posti in piedi** (*in teatro, in autobus*) standing room; **posto di polizia** police station

po'tabile *ag* drinkable; **acqua ~** drinking water

po'tare *vt* to prune

po'tassio *sm* potassium

po'tente *ag* (*nazione*) strong, powerful; (*veleno, farmaco*) potent, strong; **po'tenza** *sf* power; (*forza*) strength

potenzi'ale [poten'tsjale] *ag, sm* potential

 PAROLA CHIAVE

po'tere *sm* power; **al potere** (*partito ecc*) in power; **potere d'acquisto** purchasing power

▷ *vb aus* **1** (*essere in grado di*) can, be able to; **non ha potuto ripararlo** he couldn't *o* he wasn't able to repair it; **non è potuto venire** he couldn't *o* he wasn't able to come; **spiacente di non poter aiutare** sorry not to be able to help

2 (*avere il permesso*) can, may, be allowed to; **posso entrare?** can *o* may I come in?; **si può sapere dove sei stato?** where on earth have you been?

3 (*eventualità*) may, might, could; **potrebbe essere vero** it might *o* could be true; **può aver avuto un incidente** he may *o* might could have had an accident; **può darsi** perhaps; **può darsi** *o* **essere che non venga** he may *o* might not come

4 (*augurio*): **potessi almeno parlargli!** if only I could speak to him!

5 (*suggerimento*): **potresti almeno scusarti!** you could at least apologize!

▷ *vt* can, be able to; **può molto per noi** he can do a lot for us; **non ne posso più** (*per stanchezza*) I'm exhausted; (*per rabbia*) I can't take any more

potrò *ecc vb vedi* **potere**

'povero, -a *ag* poor; (*disadorno*) plain, bare ▷ *sm/f* poor man/woman; **i poveri** the poor; **~ di** lacking in, having little; **povertà** *sf* poverty

poz'zanghera [pot'tsangera] *sf* puddle

'pozzo ['pottso] *sm* well; (*cava: di carbone*) pit; (*di miniera*) shaft; **pozzo petrolifero** oil well

P.R.A. [pra] *sigla m* (= *Pubblico Registro Automobilistico*) ≈ DVLA

pran'zare [pran'dzare] *vi* to dine, have dinner; to lunch, have lunch

'pranzo ['prandzo] *sm* dinner; (*a mezzogiorno*) lunch

'prassi *sf* usual procedure

'pratica, -che *sf* practice; (*esperienza*) experience; (*conoscenza*) knowledge, familiarity; (*tirocinio*) training, practice; (*Amm: affare*) matter, case; (*: incartamento*) file, dossier; **in ~** (*praticamente*) in practice; **mettere in ~** to put into practice

prati'cabile *ag* (*progetto*) practicable, feasible; (*luogo*) passable, practicable

pratica'mente *av* (*in modo pratico*) in a practical way, practically; (*quasi*) practically, almost

prati'care *vt* to practise; (*Sport: tennis ecc*) to play; (*: nuoto, scherma ecc*) to go in for; (*eseguire: apertura, buco*) to make; **~ uno sconto** to give a discount

'pratico, -a, -ci, -che *ag* practical; **~ di** (*esperto*) experienced *o* skilled in; (*familiare*) familiar with

'prato *sm* meadow; (*di giardino*) lawn

preav'viso *sm* notice; **telefonata con ~** personal *o* person to person call

pre'cario, -a *ag* precarious; (*Ins*) temporary

precauzi'one [prekaut'tsjone] *sf* caution, care; (*misura*) precaution

prece'dente [pretʃe'dɛnte] *ag* previous ▷ *sm* precedent; **il discorso/film ~** the previous *o* preceding speech/film; **senza precedenti** unprecedented; **precedenti penali** criminal record *sg*; **prece'denza** *sf* priority, precedence; (*Aut*) right of way

pre'cedere [pre'tʃɛdere] *vt* to precede, go (*o come*) before

precipi'tare [pretʃipi'tare] *vi* (*cadere*) to fall headlong; (*fig: situazione*) to get out of control ▷ *vt* (*gettare dall'alto in basso*) to hurl, fling; (*fig: affrettare*) to rush; **precipitarsi** *vpr* (*gettarsi*) to hurl *o* fling o.s.; (*affrettarsi*) to rush; **precipi'toso, -a** *ag* (*caduta, fuga*) headlong; (*fig: avventato*) rash, reckless; (*: affrettato*) hasty, rushed

preci'pizio [pretʃi'pittsjo] *sm* precipice; **a ~** (*fig: correre*) headlong

precisa'mente [pretʃiza'mente] *av* (*gen*) precisely; (*con esattezza*) exactly

preci'sare [pretʃi'zare] *vt* to state, specify; (*spiegare*) to explain (in detail)

precisi'one [pretʃi'zjone] *sf* precision; accuracy

pre'ciso, -a [pre'tʃizo] *ag* (*esatto*) precise; (*accurato*) accurate, precise; (*deciso: idee*) precise, definite; (*uguale*): **2 vestiti precisi** 2 dresses exactly the same; **sono le 9 precise** it's exactly 9 o'clock

pre'cludere *vt* to block, obstruct

pre'coce [pre'kɔtʃe] *ag* early; (*bambino*) precocious; (*vecchiaia*) premature

precon'cetto [prekon'tʃetto] *sm* preconceived idea, prejudice

precur'sore *sm* forerunner, precursor

'preda *sf* (*bottino*) booty; (*animale, fig*) prey; **essere ~ di** to fall prey to; **essere in ~ a** to be prey to

'predica, -che *sf* sermon; (*fig*) lecture, talking-to

predi'care *vt, vi* to preach

predi'cato *sm* (*Ling*) predicate

predi'letto, -a *pp di* **prediligere** ▷ *ag, sm/f* favourite

predi'ligere [predi'lidʒere] *vt* to prefer, have a preference for

pre'dire *vt* to foretell, predict

predis'porre *vt* to get ready, prepare; **~ qn a qc** to predispose sb to sth

predizi'one [predit'tsjone] *sf* prediction

prefazi'one [prefat'tsjone] *sf* preface, foreword

prefe'renza [prefe'rɛntsa] *sf* preference

prefe'rire *vt* to prefer, like better; **~ il caffè al tè** to prefer coffee to tea, like coffee better than tea

pre'figgersi [pre'fiddʒersi] *vpr* **~ uno scopo** to set o.s. a goal

pre'fisso, -a *pp di* **prefiggere** ▷ *sm* (*Ling*) prefix; (*Tel*) dialling (BRIT) *o* dial (US) code; **qual è il ~ telefonico di Londra?** what is the dialling code for London?

pre'gare *vi* to pray ▷ *vt* (*Rel*) to pray to; (*implorare*) to beg; (*chiedere*): **~ qn di fare** to ask sb to do; **farsi ~** to need coaxing *o* persuading

pre'gevole [pre'dʒevole] *ag* valuable

pregherò *ecc* [prege'rɔ] *vb vedi* **pregare**

preghi'era [pre'gjɛra] *sf* (*Rel*) prayer; (*domanda*) request

pregi'ato, -a [pre'dʒato] *ag* (*di valore*) valuable; **vino ~** vintage wine

'pregio ['predʒo] *sm* (*stima*) esteem, regard; (*qualità*) (good) quality, merit; (*valore*) value, worth

pregiudi'care [predʒudi'kare] *vt* to prejudice, harm, be detrimental to

pregiu'dizio [predʒu'dittsjo] *sm* (*idea errata*) prejudice; (*danno*) harm *no pl*

'prego *escl* (*a chi ringrazia*) don't mention it!; (*invitando qn ad accomodarsi*) please sit down!; (*invitando qn ad andare prima*) after you!

pregus'tare *vt* to look forward to

prele'vare *vt* (*denaro*) to withdraw; (*campione*) to take; (*polizia*) to take, capture

preli'evo *sm* (*di denaro*) withdrawal; (*Med*): **fare un ~ (di)** to take a sample (of); **prelievo di sangue; fare un ~ di sangue** to take a blood sample

prelimi'nare *ag* preliminary

'premere *vt* to press ▷ *vi* **~ su** to press down on; (*fig*) to put pressure on; **~ a** (*fig: importare*) to matter to

pre'mettere *vt* to put before; (*dire prima*) to start by saying, state first

premi'are *vt* to give a prize to; (*fig: merito, onestà*) to reward

premiazi'one [premjat'tsjone] *sf* prize giving

'premio *sm* prize; (*ricompensa*) reward; (*Comm*) premium; (*Amm: indennità*) bonus

pre'misi *ecc vb vedi* **premettere**

premu'nirsi *vpr* **~ di** to provide o.s. with; **~ contro** to protect o.s. from, guard o.s. against

pre'mura *sf* (*fretta*) haste, hurry; (*riguardo*) attention, care; **premure** *sfpl* (*attenzioni, cure*) care *sg*; **aver ~** to be in a hurry; **far ~ a qn** to hurry sb; **usare ogni ~ nei riguardi di qn** to be very attentive to sb; **premu'roso, -a** *ag* thoughtful, considerate

'prendere *vt* to take; (*andare a prendere*) to get, fetch; (*ottenere*) to get; (*guadagnare*) to get, earn; (*catturare: ladro, pesce*) to catch; (*collaboratore, dipendente*) to take on; (*passeggero*) to pick up; (*chiedere: somma, prezzo*) to charge, ask; (*trattare: persona*) to handle ▷ *vi* (*colla, cemento*) to set; (*pianta*) to take; (*fuoco: nel camino*) to catch; (*voltare*): **~ a destra** to turn (to the) right; **prendersi** *vpr* (*azzuffarsi*): **prendersi a pugni** to come to blows; **dove si prende il traghetto per...** where do we get the ferry to ...; **prendi qualcosa?** (*da bere, da mangiare*) would you like something to eat (*o* drink)?; **prendo un caffè** I'll have a coffee; **~ qn/qc per** (*scambiare*) to take sb/sth for; **~ fuoco** to catch fire; **~ parte a** to take part in; **prendersi cura di qn/qc** to look after sb/sth; **prendersela** (*adirarsi*) to get annoyed; (*preoccuparsi*) to get upset, worry

preno'tare *vt* to book, reserve; **vorrei ~ una camera doppia** I'd like to book a double room; **ho prenotato un tavolo al nome di ...** I booked a table in the name of ...; **prenotazi'one** *sf* booking, reservation; **ho confermato la prenotazione per fax/e-mail** I confirmed my booking by fax/e-mail

preoccu'pare *vt* to worry; to preoccupy; **preoccuparsi** *vpr* **preoccuparsi di qn/qc** to worry about sb/sth; **preoccuparsi per qn** to be anxious for sb; **preoccupazi'one** *sf* worry, anxiety

prepa'rare *vt* to prepare; (*esame, concorso*) to prepare for; **prepararsi** *vpr* (*vestirsi*) to get ready; **prepararsi a qc/a fare** to get ready *o* prepare (o.s.) for sth/to do; **~ da mangiare** to prepare a meal; **prepara'tivi** *smpl* preparations

preposizi'one [prepozit'tsjone] *sf* (*Ling*) preposition

prepo'tente *ag* (*persona*) domineering, arrogant; (*bisogno, desiderio*) overwhelming, pressing ▷ *sm/f* bully

'presa *sf* taking *no pl*; catching *no pl*; (*di città*) capture; (*indurimento: di cemento*) setting; (*appiglio, Sport*) hold; (*di acqua, gas*) (supply) point; (*piccola quantità: di sale* ecc) pinch; (Carte) trick; **far ~** (colla) to set; **far ~ sul pubblico** to catch the public's imagination; **essere alle prese con** (fig) to be struggling with; **presa d'aria** air inlet; **presa (di corrente)** (Elettr) socket; (: al muro) point

pre'sagio [pre'zadʒo] sm omen

'presbite ag long-sighted

pres'crivere vt to prescribe

'prese ecc vb vedi **prendere**

presen'tare vt to present; (far conoscere): **~ qn (a)** to introduce sb (to); (Amm: inoltrare) to submit; **presentarsi** vpr (recarsi, farsi vedere) to present o.s., appear; (farsi conoscere) to introduce o.s.; (occasione) to arise; **presentarsi come candidato** (Pol) to stand as a candidate; **presentarsi bene/male** to have a good/poor appearance

pre'sente ag present; (questo) this ▷ sm present; **i presenti** those present; **aver ~ qc/qn** to remember sth/sb; **presenti** (persone) people present; **aver ~ qc/qn** to remember sth/sb; **tenere ~ qn/qc** to keep sth/sb in mind

presenti'mento sm premonition

pre'senza [pre'zɛntsa] sf presence; (aspetto esteriore) appearance; **presenza di spirito** presence of mind

pre'sepio, pre'sepe sm crib

preser'vare vt to protect; to save; **preserva'tivo** sm sheath, condom

'presi ecc vb vedi **prendere**

'preside sm/f (Ins) head (teacher) (BRIT), principal (US); (di facoltà universitaria) dean; **preside di facoltà** (Univ) dean of faculty

presi'dente sm (Pol) president; (di assemblea, Comm) chairman; **presidente del consiglio** prime minister

presi'edere vt to preside over ▷ vi **~ a** to direct, be in charge of

pressap'poco av about, roughly

pres'sare vt to press

pressi'one sf pressure; **far ~ su qn** to put pressure on sb; **pressione sanguigna** blood pressure; **pressione atmosferica** atmospheric pressure

'presso av (vicino) nearby, close at hand ▷ prep (vicino a) near; (accanto a) beside, next to; (in casa di): **~ qn** at sb's home; (nelle lettere) care of, c/o; (alle dipendenze di): **lavora ~ di noi** he works for o with us ▷ smpl **nei pressi di** near, in the vicinity of

pres'tante ag good-looking

pres'tare vt **~ (qc a qn)** to lend (sb sth o sth to sb); **prestarsi** vpr (offrirsi): **prestarsi a fare** to offer to do; (essere adatto): **prestarsi a** to lend itself to, be suitable for; **mi può ~ dei soldi?** can you

lend me some money?; **~ aiuto** to lend a hand; **~ attenzione** to pay attention; **~ fede a qc/qn** to give credence to sth/sb; **~ orecchio** to listen; **prestazi'one** sf (Tecn, Sport) performance

prestigia'tore, -'trice [prestidʒa'tore] sm/f conjurer

pres'tigio [pres'tidʒo] sm (fama) prestige; (illusione): **gioco di ~** conjuring trick

'prestito sm lending no pl; loan; **dar in ~** to lend; **prendere in ~** to borrow

'presto av (tra poco) soon; (in fretta) quickly; (di buon'ora) early; **a ~** see you soon; **fare ~ a fare qc** to hurry up and do sth; (non costare fatica) to have no trouble doing sth; **si fa ~ a criticare** it's easy to criticize

pre'sumere vt to presume, assume

pre'sunsi ecc vb vedi **presumere**

presuntu'oso, -a ag presumptuous

presunzi'one [prezun'tsjone] sf presumption

'prete sm priest

preten'dente sm/f pretender ▷ sm (corteggiatore) suitor

pre'tendere vt (esigere) to demand, require; (sostenere): **~ che** to claim that; **pretende di aver sempre ragione** he thinks he's always right

⚠ Attenzione! In inglese esiste il verbo to pretend, che però significa far finta.

pre'tesa sf (esigenza) claim, demand; (presunzione, sfarzo) pretentiousness; **senza pretese** unpretentious

pre'testo sm pretext, excuse

preva'lere vi to prevail

preve'dere vt (indovinare) to foresee; (presagire) to foretell; (considerare) to make provision for

preve'nire vt (anticipare) to forestall; to anticipate; (evitare) to avoid, prevent

preven'tivo, -a ag preventive ▷ sm (Comm) estimate

prevenzi'one [preven'tsjone] sf prevention; (preconcetto) prejudice

previ'dente ag showing foresight; prudent; **previ'denza** sf foresight; **istituto di previdenza** provident institution; **previdenza sociale** social security (BRIT), welfare (US)

pre'vidi ecc vb vedi **prevedere**

previsi'one sf forecast, prediction; **previsioni meteorologiche** weather forecast sg; **previsioni del tempo** weather forecast sg

pre'visto, -a pp di **prevedere** ▷ sm **più/ meno del ~** more/less than expected

prezi'oso, -a [pret'tsjoso] ag precious; invaluable ▷ sm jewel; valuable

prez'zemolo [pret'tsemolo] sm parsley

'prezzo ['prɛttso] *sm* price; **prezzo d'acquisto/di vendita** buying/selling price

prigi'one [pri'dʒone] *sf* prison; **prigioni'ero, -a** *ag* captive ▷ *sm/f* prisoner

'prima *sf* (*Teatro*) first night; (*Cinema*) première; (*Aut*) first gear; *vedi anche* **primo** ▷ *av* before; (*in anticipo*) in advance, beforehand; (*per l'addietro*) at one time, formerly; (*più presto*) sooner, earlier; (*in primo luogo*) first ▷ *cong* ~ **di fare/che parta** before doing/he leaves; ~ **di** before; ~ **o poi** sooner or later

pri'mario, -a *ag* primary; (*principale*) chief, leading, primary ▷ *sm* (*Med*) chief physician

prima'tista, -i, e *sm/f* (*Sport*) record holder

pri'mato *sm* supremacy; (*Sport*) record

prima'vera *sf* spring

primi'tivo, -a *ag* primitive; original

pri'mizie [pri'mittsje] *sfpl* early produce *sg*

'primo, -a *ag* first; (*fig*) initial; basic; prime ▷ *sm/f* first (one) ▷ *sm* (*Cuc*) first course; (*in date*): **il ~ luglio** the first of July; **le prime ore del mattino** the early hours of the morning; **ai primi di maggio** at the beginning of May; **viaggiare in prima** to travel first-class; **in ~ luogo** first of all, in the first place; **di prim'ordine** *o* **prima qualità** first-class, first-rate; **in un ~ tempo** at first; **prima donna** leading lady; (*di opera lirica*) prima donna

primordi'ale *ag* primordial

'primula *sf* primrose

princi'pale [printʃi'pale] *ag* main, principal ▷ *sm* manager, boss

principal'mente [printʃipal'mente] *av* mainly, principally

'principe ['printʃipe] *sm* prince; **principe ereditario** crown prince; **princi'pessa** *sf* princess

principi'ante [printʃi'pjante] *sm/f* beginner

prin'cipio [prin'tʃipjo] *sm* (*inizio*) beginning, start; (*origine*) origin, cause; (*concetto, norma*) principle; **al** *o* **in** ~ at first; **per** ~ on principle; **principi** *smpl* (*concetti fondamentali*) principles; **una questione di** ~ a matter of principle

priorità *sf* priority

priori'tario, -a *ag* having priority, of utmost importance

pri'vare *vt* ~ **qn di** to deprive sb of; **privarsi di** to go *o* do without

pri'vato, -a *ag* private ▷ *sm/f* private citizen; **in** ~ in private

privilegi'are [privile'dʒare] *vt* to grant a privilege to

privilegi'ato, -a [privile'dʒato] *ag* (*individuo, classe*) privileged; (*trattamento, Comm: credito*) preferential; **azioni ~e** preference shares (*BRIT*), preferred stock (*US*)

privi'legio [privi'lɛdʒo] *sm* privilege

'privo, -a *ag* ~ **di** without, lacking

pro *prep* for, on behalf of ▷ *sm inv* (*utilità*) advantage, benefit; **a che ~?** what's the use?; **il ~ e il contro** the pros and cons

pro'babile *ag* probable, likely; **probabilità** *sf inv* probability

probabil'mente *av* probably

pro'blema, -i *sm* problem

pro'boscide [pro'bɔʃʃide] *sf* (*di elefante*) trunk

pro'cedere [pro'tʃɛdere] *vi* to proceed; (*comportarsi*) to behave; (*iniziare*): ~ **a** to start; ~ **contro** (*Dir*) to start legal proceedings against; **proce'dura** *sf* (*Dir*) procedure

proces'sare [protʃes'sare] *vt* (*Dir*) to try

processi'one [protʃes'sjone] *sf* procession

pro'cesso [pro'tʃɛsso] *sm* (*Dir*) trial; proceedings *pl*; (*metodo*) process

pro'cinto [pro'tʃinto] *sm* **in ~ di fare** about to do, on the point of doing

procla'mare *vt* to proclaim

procre'are *vt* to procreate

procu'rare *vt* ~ **qc a qn** (*fornire*) to get *o* obtain sth for sb; (*causare: noie ecc*) to bring *o* give sb sth

pro'digio [pro'didʒo] *sm* marvel, wonder; (*persona*) prodigy

pro'dotto, -a *pp di* **produrre** ▷ *sm* product; **prodotti agricoli** farm produce *sg*

pro'duco *ecc vb vedi* **produrre**

pro'durre *vt* to produce

pro'dussi *ecc vb vedi* **produrre**

produzi'one *sf* production; (*rendimento*) output

Prof. *abbr* (= *professore*) Prof.

profa'nare *vt* to desecrate

profes'sare *vt* to profess; (*medicina ecc*) to practise

professio'nale *ag* professional

professi'one *sf* profession; **professio'nista, -i, -e** *sm/f* professional

profes'sore, -'essa *sm/f* (*Ins*) teacher; (: *di università*) lecturer; (: *titolare di cattedra*) professor

pro'filo *sm* profile; (*breve descrizione*) sketch, outline; **di** ~ in profile

pro'fitto *sm* advantage, profit, benefit; (*fig: progresso*) progress; (*Comm*) profit

profondità *sf inv* depth

pro'fondo, -a *ag* deep; (*rancore,*

meditazione) profound ▷ *sm* depth(s *pl*), bottom; **quanto è profonda l'acqua?** how deep is the water?; **~ 8 metri** 8 metres deep

'profugo, -a, -ghi, -ghe *sm/f* refugee

profu'mare *vt* to perfume ▷ *vi* to be fragrant; **profumarsi** *vpr* to put on perfume *o* scent

profu'mato, -a *ag (fiore, aria)* fragrant; *(fazzoletto, saponetta)* scented; *(pelle)* sweet-smelling; *(persona)* with perfume on

profume'ria *sf* perfumery; *(negozio)* perfume shop

pro'fumo *sm (prodotto)* perfume, scent; *(fragranza)* scent, fragrance

proget'tare [prodʒet'tare] *vt* to plan; *(edificio)* to plan, design; **pro'getto** *sm* plan; *(idea)* plan, project; **progetto di legge** bill

pro'gramma, -i *sm* programme; *(TV, Radio)* programmes *pl*; *(Ins)* syllabus, curriculum; *(Inform)* program; **program'mare** *vt (TV, Radio)* to put on; *(Inform)* to program; *(Econ)* to plan; **programma'tore, -'trice** *sm/f (Inform)* computer programmer

progre'dire *vi* to progress, make progress

pro'gresso *sm* progress *no pl*; **fare progressi** to make progress

proi'bire *vt* to forbid, prohibit

proiet'tare *vt (gen, Geom, Cinema)* to project; *(: presentare)* to show, screen; *(luce, ombra)* to throw, cast, project; **proi'ettile** *sm* projectile, bullet *(o shell ecc)*; **proiet'tore** *sm (Cinema)* projector; *(Aut)* headlamp; *(Mil)* searchlight; **proiezi'one** *sf (Cinema)* projection; showing

prolife'rare *vi (fig)* to proliferate

pro'lunga, -ghe *sf (di cavo ecc)* extension

prolun'gare *vt (discorso, attesa)* to prolong; *(linea, termine)* to extend

prome'moria *sm inv* memorandum

pro'messa *sf* promise

pro'mettere *vt* to promise ▷ *vi* to be *o* look promising; **~ a qn di fare** to promise sb that one will do

promi'nente *ag* prominent

pro'misi *ecc vb vedi* **promettere**

promon'torio *sm* promontory, headland

promozi'one [promot'tsjone] *sf* promotion

promu'overe *vt* to promote

proni'pote *sm/f (di nonni)* great-grandchild, great-grandson/granddaughter; *(di zii)* great-nephew/niece

pro'nome *sm (Ling)* pronoun

pron'tezza [pron'tettsa] *sf* readiness; quickness, promptness

'pronto, -a *ag* ready; *(rapido)* fast, quick, prompt; **quando saranno pronte le mie foto?** when will my photos be ready?; **~!** *(Tel)* hello!; **~ all'ira** quick-tempered; **pronto soccorso** *(cure)* first aid; *(reparto)* A&E *(BRIT)*, ER *(US)*

prontu'ario *sm* manual, handbook

pro'nuncia [pro'nuntʃa] *sf* pronunciation

pronunci'are [pronun'tʃare] *vt (parola, sentenza)* to pronounce; *(dire)* to utter; *(discorso)* to deliver; **come si pronuncia?** how do you pronounce it?

propa'ganda *sf* propaganda

pro'pendere *vi* **~ per** to favour, lean towards

propi'nare *vt* to administer

pro'porre *vt (suggerire)*: **~ qc (a qn)** to suggest sth (to sb); *(candidato)* to put forward; *(legge, brindisi)* to propose; **~ di fare** to suggest *o* propose doing; **proporsi di fare** to propose *o* intend to do; **proporsi una meta** to set o.s. a goal

proporzio'nale [proportsjo'nale] *ag* proportional

proporzi'one [propor'tsjone] *sf* proportion; **in ~ a** in proportion to; **proporzioni** *sfpl (dimensioni)* proportions; **di vaste proporzioni** huge

pro'posito *sm (intenzione)* intention, aim; *(argomento)* subject, matter; **a ~ di** regarding, with regard to; **di ~** *(apposta)* deliberately, on purpose; **a ~** by the way; **capitare a ~** *(cosa, persona)* to turn up at the right time

proposizi'one [propozit'tsjone] *sf (Ling)* clause; *(: periodo)* sentence

pro'posta *sf* proposal; *(suggerimento)* suggestion; **proposta di legge** bill

proprietà *sf inv (ciò che si possiede)* property *gen no pl*, estate; *(caratteristica)* property; *(correttezza)* correctness; **proprietà privata** private property; **proprie'tario, -a** *sm/f* owner; *(di albergo ecc)* proprietor, owner; *(per l'inquilino)* landlord/lady

'proprio, -a *ag (possessivo)* own; *(: impersonale)* one's; *(esatto)* exact, correct, proper; *(senso, significato)* literal; *(Ling: nome)* proper; *(particolare)*: **~ di** characteristic of, peculiar to ▷ *av (precisamente)* just, exactly; *(davvero)* really; *(affatto)*: **non ... ~** not ... at all; **l'ha visto con i (suoi) propri occhi** he saw it with his own eyes

proro'gare *vt* to extend; *(differire)* to postpone, defer

'prosa *sf* prose

pro'sciogliere [proʃ'ʃɔʎʎere] *vt* to release; *(Dir)* to acquit

prosciu'gare [proʃʃu'gare] *vt (terreni)* to

drain, reclaim; **prosciugarsi** vpr to dry up
prosci'utto [proʃ'ʃutto] sm ham;
prosciutto cotto/crudo cooked/cured
ham
prosegui'mento sm continuation; **buon
~!** all the best!; (a chi viaggia) enjoy the rest
of your journey!
prosegu'ire vt to carry on with, continue
▷ vi to carry on, go on
prospe'rare vi to thrive
prospet'tare vt (esporre) to point out,
show; **prospettarsi** vpr to look, appear
prospet'tiva sf (Arte) perspective; (veduta)
view; (fig: previsione, possibilità) prospect
pros'petto sm (Disegno) elevation; (veduta)
view, prospect; (facciata) façade, front;
(tabella) table; (sommario) summary;
prospetto informativo prospectus
prossimità sf nearness, proximity; **in ~ di**
near (to), close to
'prossimo, -a ag (vicino): **~ a** near (to),
close to; (che viene subito dopo) next;
(parente) close ▷ sm neighbour, fellow man
prostitu'irsi vpr to prostitute o.s.
prosti'tuta sf prostitute
protago'nista, -i, -e sm/f protagonist
pro'teggere [pro'teddʒere] vt to protect
prote'ina sf protein
pro'tendere vt to stretch out
pro'testa sf protest
protes'tante ag, sm/f Protestant
protes'tare vt, vi to protest
pro'tetto, -a pp di **proteggere**
protezi'one [protet'tsjone] sf protection;
(patrocinio) patronage
pro'totipo sm prototype
pro'trarre vt (prolungare) to prolong;
protrarsi vpr to go on, continue
protube'ranza [protube'rantsa] sf
protuberance, bulge
'prova sf (esperimento, cimento) test,
trial; (tentativo) attempt, try; (Mat,
testimonianza, documento ecc) proof; (Dir)
evidence no pl, proof; (Ins) exam, test;
(Teatro) rehearsal; (di abito) fitting; **a ~ di** (in
testimonianza a) as proof of; **a ~ di fuoco**
fireproof; **fino a ~ contraria** until it is
proved otherwise; **mettere alla ~** to put
to the test; **giro di ~** test o trial run; **prova
generale** (Teatro) dress rehearsal
pro'vare vt (sperimentare) to test; (tentare)
to try, attempt; (assaggiare) to try, taste;
(sperimentare in sé) to experience; (sentire)
to feel; (cimentare) to put to the test;
(dimostrare) to prove; (abito) to try on; **~ a
fare** to try o attempt to do
proveni'enza [prove'njɛntsa] sf origin,
source
prove'nire vi **~ da** to come from

pro'venti smpl revenue sg
pro'verbio sm proverb
pro'vetta sf test tube; **bambino in ~**
test-tube baby
pro'vider [pro'vaider] sm inv (Inform)
service provider
pro'vincia, -ce o **cie** [pro'vintʃa] sf
province
pro'vino sm (Cinema) screen test;
(campione) specimen
provo'cante ag (attraente) provocative
provo'care vt (causare) to cause, bring
about; (eccitare: riso, pietà) to arouse;
(irritare, sfidare) to provoke; **provocazi'one**
sf provocation
provve'dere vi (disporre): **~ (a)** to provide
(for); (prendere un provvedimento) to take
steps, act; **provvedi'mento** sm measure;
(di previdenza) precaution
provvi'denza [provvi'dɛntsa] sf **la ~**
providence
provvigi'one [provvi'dʒone] sf (Comm)
commission
provvi'sorio, -a ag temporary
prov'viste sfpl supplies
'prua sf (Naut) bow(s) (pl), prow
pru'dente ag cautious, prudent;
(assennato) sensible, wise; **pru'denza** sf
prudence, caution; wisdom
'prudere vi to itch, be itchy
'prugna ['pruɲɲa] sf plum; **prugna secca**
prune
pru'rito sm itchiness no pl; itch
P.S. abbr (= postscriptum) P.S.; (Polizia)
= **Pubblica Sicurezza**
pseu'donimo sm pseudonym
psica'nalisi sf psychoanalysis
psicana'lista, -i, -e sm/f psychoanalyst
'psiche ['psike] sf (Psic) psyche
psichi'atra, -i, -e [psi'kjatra] sm/f
psychiatrist; **psichi'atrico, -a, -ci, -che** ag
psychiatric
psicolo'gia [psikolo'dʒia] sf psychology;
psico'logico, -a, -ci, -che ag
psychological; **psi'cologo, -a, -gi, -ghe**
sm/f psychologist
psico'patico, -a, -ci, -che ag
psychopathic ▷ sm/f psychopath
pubbli'care vt to publish
pubblicazi'one [pubblikat'tsjone] sf
publication
pubblicità [pubblitʃi'ta] sf (diffusione)
publicity; (attività) advertising; (annunci nei
giornali) advertisements pl
'pubblico, -a, -ci, -che ag public;
(statale: scuola ecc) state cpd ▷ sm public;
(spettatori) audience; **in ~** in public; **P~
Ministero** Public Prosecutor's Office; **la
Pubblica Sicurezza** the police; **pubblico**

funzionario civil servant

'**pube** sm (Anat) pubis

pubertà sf puberty

'**pudico, -a, -ci, -che** ag modest

pu'dore sm modesty

pue'rile ag childish

pugi'lato [pudʒi'lato] sm boxing

'**pugile** ['pudʒile] sm boxer

pugna'lare [puɲɲa'lare] vt to stab

pu'gnale [puɲ'ɲale] sm dagger

'**pugno** ['puɲɲo] sm fist; (colpo) punch; (quantità) fistful

'**pulce** ['pultʃe] sf flea

pul'cino [pul'tʃino] sm chick

pu'lire vt to clean; (lucidare) to polish; **pu'lito, -a** ag (anche fig) clean; (ordinato) neat, tidy; **puli'tura** sf cleaning; **pulitura a secco** dry cleaning; **puli'zia** sf cleaning; cleanness; **fare le pulizie** to do the cleaning o the housework; **pulizia etnica** ethnic cleansing

'**pullman** sm inv coach

pul'lover sm inv pullover, jumper

pullu'lare vi to swarm, teem

pul'mino sm minibus

'**pulpito** sm pulpit

pul'sante sm (push-)button

pul'sare vi to pulsate, beat

pul'viscolo sm fine dust; **pulviscolo atmosferico** specks pl of dust

'**puma** sm inv puma

pun'gente [pun'dʒɛnte] ag prickly; stinging; (anche fig) biting

'**pungere** ['pundʒere] vt to prick; (insetto, ortica) to sting; (: freddo) to bite

pungigli'one [pundʒiʎ'ʎone] sm sting

pu'nire vt to punish; **punizi'one** sf punishment; (Sport) penalty

'**punsi** ecc vb vedi **pungere**

'**punta** sf point; (parte terminale) tip, end; (di monte) peak; (di costa) promontory; (minima parte) touch, trace; **in ~ di piedi** on tip-toe; **ore di ~** peak hours; **uomo di ~** front-rank o leading man

pun'tare vt (piedi a terra, gomiti sul tavolo) to plant; (dirigere: pistola) to point; (scommettere) to bet ▷ vi (mirare): **~ a** to aim at; **~ su** (dirigersi) to head o make for; (fig: contare) to count o rely on

pun'tata sf (gita) short trip; (scommessa) bet; (parte di opera) instalment; **romanzo a puntate** serial

punteggia'tura [punteddʒa'tura] sf (Ling) punctuation

pun'teggio [pun'teddʒo] sm score

puntel'lare vt to support

pun'tello sm prop, support

pun'tina sf; **puntina da disegno** drawing pin

pun'tino sm dot; **fare qc a ~** to do sth properly

'**punto, -a** pp di **pungere** ▷ sm (segno, macchiolina) dot; (Ling) full stop; (di indirizzo e-mail) dot; (Mat, momento, di punteggio: fig: argomento) point; (posto) spot; (a scuola) mark; (nel cucire, nella maglia, Med) stitch ▷ av **non ... ~** not at all; **punto cardinale** point of the compass, cardinal point; **punto debole** weak point; **punto esclamativo** exclamation mark; **punto interrogativo** question mark; **punto nero** (comedone) blackhead; **punto di partenza** (anche fig) starting point; **punto di riferimento** landmark; (fig) point of reference; **punto (di) vendita** retail outlet; **punto e virgola** semicolon; **punto di vista** (fig) point of view

puntu'ale ag punctual

pun'tura sf (di ago) prick; (Med) puncture; (: iniezione) injection; (dolore) sharp pain; **puntura d'insetto** sting, bite

> Attenzione! In inglese esiste la parola *puncture*, che si usa per indicare la foratura di una gomma.

punzecchi'are [puntsek'kjare] vt to prick; (fig) to tease

può ecc, **-pu'oi** vb vedi **potere**

pu'pazzo [pu'pattso] sm puppet

pu'pilla sf (Anat) pupil

purché [pur'ke] cong provided that, on condition that

'**pure** cong (tuttavia) and yet, nevertheless; (anche se) even if ▷ av (anche) too, also; **pur di** (al fine di) just to; **faccia ~!** go ahead!, please do!

purè sm (Cuc) purée; (: di patate) mashed potatoes

pu'rezza [pu'rettsa] sf purity

pur'gante sm (Med) purgative, purge

purga'torio sm purgatory

purifi'care vt to purify; (metallo) to refine

'**puro, -a** ag pure; (acqua) clear, limpid; (vino) undiluted; **puro'sangue** sm/f inv thoroughbred

pur'troppo av unfortunately

pus sm pus

'**pustola** sf pimple

puti'ferio sm rumpus, row

putre'fatto, -a pp di **putrefare**

put'tana (fam!) sf whore (!)

puz'zare [put'tsare] vi to stink

'**puzzo** ['puttso] sm stink, foul smell

'**puzzola** ['puttsola] sf polecat

puzzo'lente [puttso'lente] ag stinking

pvc [pivi'tʃi] sigla m (= polyvinyl chloride) PVC

q *abbr* (= *quintale*) q.

qua *av* here; **in ~** (*verso questa parte*) this way; **da un anno in ~** for a year now; **da ~ndo in ~?** since when?; **per di ~** (*passare*) this way; **al di ~ di** (*fiume, strada*) on this side of; **~ dentro/fuori** *ecc* in/out here *ecc*; *vedi anche* **questo**

qua'derno *sm* notebook; (*per scuola*) exercise book

qua'drante *sm* quadrant; (*di orologio*) face

qua'drare *vi* (*bilancio*) to balance, tally; (*descrizione*) to correspond ▷ *vt* (*Mat*) to square; **non mi quadra** I don't like it; **qua'drato, -a** *ag* square; (*fig: equilibrato*) level-headed, sensible; (: *peg*) square ▷ *sm* (*Mat*) square; (*Pugilato*) ring; **5 al quadrato** 5 squared

quadri'foglio [kwadri'fɔʎʎo] *sm* four-leaf clover

quadri'mestre *sm* (*periodo*) four-month period; (*Ins*) term

'quadro *sm* (*pittura*) painting, picture; (*quadrato*) square; (*tabella*) table, chart; (*Tecn*) board, panel; (*Teatro*) scene; (*fig: scena, spettacolo*) sight; (: *descrizione*) outline, description; **quadri** *smpl* (*Pol*) party organizers; (*Mil*) cadres; (*Comm*) managerial staff; (*Carte*) diamonds

'quadruplo, -a *ag, sm* quadruple

quaggiù [kwad'dʒu] *av* down here

'quaglia ['kwaʎʎa] *sf* quail

'qualche ['kwalke] *det* **1** some, a few; (*in interrogative*) any; **ho comprato qualche libro** I've bought some *o* a few books; **qualche volta** sometimes; **hai qualche sigaretta?** have you any cigarettes?
2 (*uno*): **c'è qualche medico?** is there a doctor?; **in qualche modo** somehow
3 (*un certo, parecchio*) some; **un personaggio di qualche rilievo** a figure of some importance
4: **qualche cosa = qualcosa**

qual'cosa *pron* something; (*in espressioni interrogative*) anything; **qualcos'altro** something else; anything else; **~ di nuovo** something new; anything new; **~ da mangiare** something to eat; anything to eat; **c'è ~ che non va?** is there something *o* anything wrong?

qual'cuno *pron* (*persona*) someone, somebody; (: *in espressioni interrogative*) anyone, anybody; (*alcuni*) some; **~ è favorevole a noi** some are on our side; **qualcun altro** someone *o* somebody else; anyone *o* anybody else

---

'quale (*spesso troncato in* **qual**) *det* **1** (*interrogativo*) what; (: *scegliendo tra due o più cose o persone*) which; **quale uomo/ denaro?** what man/money?, which man/ money?; **quali sono i tuoi programmi?** what are your plans?; **quale stanza preferisci?** which room do you prefer?
2 (*relativo: come*): **il risultato fu quale ci si aspettava** the result was as expected
3 (*esclamativo*) what; **quale disgrazia!** what bad luck!
▷ *pron* **1** (*interrogativo*) which; **quale dei due scegli?** which of the two do you want?
2 (*relativo*): **il (la) quale** (*persona: soggetto*) who; (: *oggetto, con preposizione*) whom; (*cosa*) which; (*possessivo*) whose; **suo padre, il quale è avvocato, ...** his father, who is a lawyer, ...; **il signore con il quale parlavo** the gentleman to whom I was speaking; **l'albergo al quale ci siamo fermati** the hotel where we stayed *o* which we stayed at; **la signora della quale ammiriamo la bellezza** the lady whose beauty we admire
3 (*relativo: in elenchi*) such as, like; **piante**

quali l'edera plants like o such as ivy; **quale sindaco di questa città** as mayor of this town

qua'lifica, -che *sf* qualification; (*titolo*) title

qualifi'cato, -a *ag* (*dotato di qualifica*) qualified; (*esperto, abile*) skilled; **non mi ritengo ~ per questo lavoro** I don't think I'm qualified for this job; **è un medico molto ~** he is a very distinguished doctor

qualificazi'one *sf* **gara di ~** (*Sport*) qualifying event

qualità *sf inv* quality; **in ~ di** in one's capacity as

qua'lora *cong* in case, if

qual'siasi *det inv* = **qualunque**

qua'lunque *det inv* any; (*quale che sia*) whatever; (*discriminativo*) whichever; (*posposto: mediocre*) poor, indifferent; ordinary; **mettiti un vestito ~** put on any old dress; **~ cosa** anything; **~ cosa accada** whatever happens; **a ~ costo** at any cost, whatever the cost; **l'uomo ~** the man in the street; **~ persona** anyone, anybody

'quando *cong, av* when; **~ sarò ricco** when I'm rich; **da ~** (*dacché*) since; (*interrogativo*): **da ~ sei qui?** how long have you been here?; **quand'anche** even if

quantità *sf inv* quantity; (*gran numero*): **una ~ di** a great deal of; a lot of; **in grande ~** in large quantities

PAROLA CHIAVE

'quanto, -a *det* **1** (*interrogativo: quantità*) how much; (*: numero*) how many; **quanto pane/denaro?** how much bread/money?; **quanti libri/ragazzi?** how many books/boys?; **quanto tempo?** how long?; **quanti anni hai?** how old are you?

2 (*esclamativo*): **quante storie!** what a lot of nonsense!; **quanto tempo sprecato!** what a waste of time!

3 (*relativo: quantità*) as much ... as; (*: numero*) as many ... as; **ho quanto denaro mi occorre** I have as much money as I need; **prendi quanti libri vuoi** take as many books as you like

▷ *pron* **1** (*interrogativo: quantità*) how much; (*: numero*) how many; (*: tempo*) how long; **quanto mi dai?** how much will you give me?; **quanti me ne hai portati?** how many did you bring me?; **da quanto sei qui?** how long have you been here?; **quanti ne abbiamo oggi?** what's the date today?

2 (*relativo: quantità*) as much as; (*: numero*) as many as; **farò quanto posso** I'll do as much as I can; **possono venire quanti**

sono stati invitati all those who have been invited can come

▷ *av* **1** (*interrogativo: con ag, av*) how; (*: con vb*) how much; **quanto stanco ti sembrava?** how tired did he seem to you?; **quanto corre la tua moto?** how fast can your motorbike go?; **quanto costa?** how much does it cost?; **quant'è?** how much is it?

2 (*esclamativo: con ag, av*) how; (*: con vb*) how much; **quanto sono felice!** how happy I am!; **sapessi quanto abbiamo camminato!** if you knew how far we've walked!; **studierò quanto posso** I'll study as much as o all I can; **quanto prima** as soon as possible

3: **in quanto** (*in qualità di*) as; (*perché, per il fatto che*) as, since; **(in) quanto a** (*per ciò che riguarda*) as for, as regards

4: **per quanto** (*nonostante, anche se*) however; **per quanto si sforzi, non ce la farà** try as he may, he won't manage it; **per quanto sia brava, fa degli errori** however good she may be, she makes mistakes; **per quanto io sappia** as far as I know

qua'ranta *num* forty

quaran'tena *sf* quarantine

quaran'tesimo, -a *num* fortieth

quaran'tina *sf* **una ~ (di)** about forty

'quarta *sf* (*Aut*) fourth (gear); *vedi anche* **quarto**

quar'tetto *sm* quartet(te)

quarti'ere *sm* district, area; (*Mil*) quarters *pl*; **quartier generale** headquarters *pl*

'quarto, -a *ag* fourth ▷ *sm* fourth; (*quarta parte*) quarter; **le 6 e un ~** a quarter past six; **quarti di finale** quarter final; **quarto d'ora** quarter of an hour

'quarzo ['kwartso] *sm* quartz

'quasi *av* almost, nearly ▷ *cong* (*anche: ~ che*) as if; **(non) ... ~ mai** hardly ever; **~ ~ me ne andrei** I've half a mind to leave

quassù *av* up here

quat'tordici [kwat'torditʃi] *num* fourteen

quat'trini *smpl* money *sg*, cash *sg*

'quattro *num* four; **in ~ e quattr'otto** in less than no time; **quattro'cento** *num* four hundred ▷ *sm* **il Quattrocento** the fifteenth century

PAROLA CHIAVE

'quello, -a (*dav sm* **quel** + C, **quell'** + V, **quello** + *s impura, gn, pn, ps, x, z; pl* **quei** + C, **quegli** + V *o s impura, gn, pn, ps, x, z; dav sf* **quella** + C, **quell'** + V; *pl* **quelle**) *det* that; those *pl*; **quella casa** that house; **quegli**

uomini those men; **voglio quella camicia (lì o là)** I want that shirt
▷ *pron* **1** (*dimostrativo*) that (one), those (ones) *pl*; (*ciò*) that; **conosci quella?** do you know that woman?; **prendo quello bianco** I'll take the white one; **chi è quello?** who's that?; **prendi quello (lì o là)** take that one (there)
2 (*relativo*): **quello(a) che** (*persona*) the one (who); (*cosa*) the one (which), the one (that); **quelli(e) che** (*persone*) those who; (*cose*) those which; **è lui quello che non voleva venire** he's the one who didn't want to come; **ho fatto quello che potevo** I did what I could

'quercia, -ce ['kwɛrtʃa] *sf* oak (tree); (*legno*) oak
que'rela *sf* (*Dir*) (legal) action
que'sito *sm* question, query; problem
questio'nario *sm* questionnaire
questi'one *sf* problem, question; (*controversia*) issue; (*litigio*) quarrel; **in ~** in question; **è ~ di tempo** it's a matter o question of time

⊙ **PAROLA CHIAVE**

'questo, -a *det* **1** (*dimostrativo*) this; these *pl*; **questo libro (qui o qua)** this book; **io prendo questo cappotto, tu quello** I'll take this coat, you take that one; **quest'oggi** today; **questa sera** this evening
2 (*enfatico*): **non fatemi più prendere di queste paure** don't frighten me like that again
▷ *pron* (*dimostrativo*) this (one); these (ones) *pl*; (*ciò*) this; **prendo questo (qui o qua)** I'll take this one; **preferisci questi o quelli?** do you prefer these (ones) or those (ones)?; **questo intendevo io** this is what I meant; **vengono Paolo e Luca: questo da Roma, quello da Palermo** Paolo and Luca are coming: the former from Palermo, the latter from Rome

ques'tura *sf* police headquarters *pl*
qui *av* here; **da o di ~** from here; **di ~ in avanti** from now on; **di ~ a poco/una settimana** in a little while/a week's time; **~ dentro/sopra/vicino** in/up/near here; *vedi anche* **questo**
quie'tanza [kwje'tantsa] *sf* receipt
qui'ete *sf* quiet, quietness; calmness; stillness; peace
qui'eto, -a *ag* quiet; (*notte*) calm, still; (*mare*) calm
'quindi *av* then ▷ *cong* therefore, so

'quindici ['kwindɪtʃi] *num* fifteen; **~ giorni** a fortnight (*BRIT*), two weeks
quindi'cina [kwindi'tʃina] *sf* (*serie*): **una ~ (di)** about fifteen; **fra una ~ di giorni** in a fortnight
quinta *sf vedi* **quinto**
quin'tale *sm* quintal (*100 kg*)
'quinto, -a *num* fifth
quiz [kwidz] *sm inv* (*domanda*) question; (*anche*): **gioco a ~** quiz game
'quota *sf* (*parte*) quota, share; (*Aer*) height, altitude; (*Ippica*) odds *pl*; **prendere/perdere ~** (*Aer*) to gain/lose height o altitude; **quota d'iscrizione** enrolment fee; (*a club*) membership fee
quotidi'ano, -a *ag* daily; (*banale*) everyday ▷ *sm* (*giornale*) daily (paper)
quozi'ente [kwot'tsjɛnte] *sm* (*Mat*) quotient; **quoziente d'intelligenza** intelligence quotient, IQ

R, r [ˈɛrre] *sf o m* (*lettera*) R, r; **R come Roma** ≈ R for Robert (BRIT), R for Roger (US)

'rabbia *sf* (*ira*) anger, rage; (*accanimento, furia*) fury; (*Med: idrofobia*) rabies *sg*

rab'bino *sm* rabbi

rabbi'oso, -a *ag* angry, furious; (*facile all'ira*) quick-tempered; (*forze, acqua ecc*) furious, raging; (*Med*) rabid, mad

rabbo'nire *vt* to calm down

rabbrivi'dire *vi* to shudder, shiver

raccapez'zarsi [rakkapet'tsarsi] *vpr* **non ~** to be at a loss

raccapricci'ante [rakkaprit'tʃante] *ag* horrifying

raccatta'palle *sm inv* (*Sport*) ballboy

raccat'tare *vt* to pick up

rac'chetta [rak'ketta] *sf* (*per tennis*) racket; (*per ping-pong*) bat; **racchetta da neve** snowshoe; **racchetta da sci** ski stick

racchi'udere [rak'kjudere] *vt* to contain

rac'cogliere [rak'kɔʎʎere] *vt* to collect; (*raccattare*) to pick up; (*frutti, fiori*) to pick, pluck; (*Agr*) to harvest; (*approvazione, voti*) to win

rac'colta *sf* collecting *no pl*; collection; (*Agr*) harvesting *no pl*, gathering *no pl*; harvest, crop; (*adunata*) gathering; **raccolta differenziata** (*dei rifiuti*) separate collection of different kinds of household waste

rac'colto, -a *pp di* **raccogliere** ▷ *ag*

(*persona: pensoso*) thoughtful; (*luogo: appartato*) secluded, quiet ▷ *sm* (*Agr*) crop, harvest

raccoman'dabile *ag* (highly) commendable; **è un tipo poco ~** he is not to be trusted

raccoman'dare *vt* to recommend; (*affidare*) to entrust; (*esortare*): **~ a qn di non fare** to tell o warn sb not to do; **raccoman'data** *sf* (*anche:* **lettera raccomandata**) recorded-delivery letter

raccon'tare *vt* **~ (a qn)** (*dire*) to tell (sb); (*narrare*) to relate (to sb), tell (sb) about; **rac'conto** *sm* telling *no pl*, relating *no pl*; (*fatto raccontato*) story, tale; **racconti per bambini** children's stories

rac'cordo *sm* (*Tecn: giunto*) connection, joint; (*Aut*): **raccordo anulare** (*Aut*) ring road (BRIT), beltway (US); **raccordo autostradale** slip road (BRIT), entrance (*o exit*) ramp (US); **raccordo ferroviario** siding; **raccordo stradale** link road

racimo'lare [ratʃimo'lare] *vt* (*fig*) to scrape together, glean

'rada *sf* (*natural*) harbour

'radar *sm* radar

raddoppi'are *vt, vi* to double

raddriz'zare [raddrit'tsare] *vt* to straighten; (*fig: correggere*) to put straight, correct

'radere *vt* (*barba*) to shave off; (*mento*) to shave; (*fig: rasentare*) to graze; to skim; **radersi** *vpr* to shave (o.s.); **~ al suolo** to raze to the ground

radi'are *vt* to strike off

radia'tore *sm* radiator

radiazi'one [radjat'tsjone] *sf* (*Fisica*) radiation; (*cancellazione*) striking off

radi'cale *ag* radical ▷ *sm* (*Ling*) root

ra'dicchio [ra'dikkjo] *sm* chicory

ra'dice [ra'ditʃe] *sf* root

'radio *sf inv* radio ▷ *sm* (*Chim*) radium; **radioat'tivo, -a** *ag* radioactive; **radio'cronaca, -che** *sf* radio commentary; **radiogra'fia** *sf* radiography; (*foto*) X-ray photograph

radi'oso, -a *ag* radiant

radios'veglia [radjoz'veʎʎa] *sf* radio alarm

'rado, -a *ag* (*capelli*) sparse, thin; (*visite*) infrequent; **di ~** rarely

radu'nare *vt* to gather, assemble; **radunarsi** *vpr* to gather, assemble

ra'dura *sf* clearing

raf'fermo, -a *ag* stale

'raffica, -che *sf* (*Meteor*) gust (of wind); (*di colpi: scarica*) burst of gunfire

raffigu'rare *vt* to represent

raffi'nato, -a *ag* refined

raffor'zare [raffor'tsare] vt to reinforce

raffredda'mento sm cooling

raffred'dare vt to cool; (fig) to dampen, have a cooling effect on; **raffreddarsi** vpr to grow cool o cold; (prendere un raffreddore) to catch a cold; (fig) to cool (off)

raffred'dato, -a ag (Med): **essere ~** to have a cold

raffred'dore sm (Med) cold

raf'fronto sm comparison

'rafia sf (fibra) raffia

rafting ['rafting] sm white-water rafting

ra'gazza [ra'gattsa] sf girl; (fam: fidanzato) girlfriend; **nome da ~** maiden name; **ragazza madre** unmarried mother

ra'gazzo [ra'gattso] sm boy; (fam: fidanzato) boyfriend; **ragazzi** smpl (figli) kids; **ciao ragazzi!** (gruppo) hi guys!

raggi'ante [rad'dʒante] ag radiant, shining

'raggio ['raddʒo] sm (di sole ecc) ray; (Mat, distanza) radius; (di ruota ecc) spoke; **raggio d'azione** range; **raggi X** X-rays

raggi'rare [raddʒi'rare] vt to take in, trick

raggi'ungere [rad'dʒundʒere] vt to reach; (persona: riprendere) to catch up (with); (bersaglio) to hit; (fig: meta) to achieve

raggomito'larsi vpr to curl up

raggranel'lare vt to scrape together

raggrup'pare vt to group (together)

ragiona'mento [radʒona'mento] sm reasoning no pl; arguing no pl; argument

ragio'nare [radʒo'nare] vi to reason; **~ di** (discorrere) to talk about

ragi'one [ra'dʒone] sf reason; (dimostrazione, prova) argument, reason; (diritto) right; **aver ~** to be right; **aver ~ di qn** to get the better of sb; **dare ~ a qn** to agree with sb; to prove sb right; **perdere la ~** to go insane; (fig) to take leave of one's senses; **in ~ di** at the rate of; to the amount of; according to; **a o con ~** rightly, justly; **a ragion veduta** after due consideration; **ragione sociale** (Comm) corporate name

ragione'ria [radʒone'ria] sf accountancy; accounts department

ragio'nevole [radʒo'nevole] ag reasonable

ragioni'ere, -a [radʒo'njere] sm/f accountant

ragli'are [raʎ'ʎare] vi to bray

ragna'tela [raɲɲa'tela] sf cobweb, spider's web

'ragno ['raɲɲo] sm spider

ragù sm inv (Cuc) meat sauce; stew

RAI-TV [raiti'vu] sigla f = **Radio televisione italiana**

ralle'grare vt to cheer up; **rallegrarsi** vpr

to cheer up; (provare allegrezza) to rejoice; **rallegrarsi con qn** to congratulate sb

rallen'tare vt to slow down; (fig) to lessen, slacken ▷ vi to slow down

rallenta'tore sm (Cinema) slow-motion camera; **al ~** (anche fig) in slow motion

raman'zina [raman'dzina] sf lecture, telling-off

'rame sm (Chim) copper

rammari'carsi vpr **~ (di)** (rincrescersi) to be sorry (about), regret; (lamentarsi) to complain (about)

rammen'dare vt to mend; (calza) to darn

'ramo sm branch

ramo'scello [ramoʃ'ʃello] sm twig

'rampa sf flight (of stairs); **rampa di lancio** launching pad

rampi'cante ag (Bot) climbing

'rana sf frog

'rancido, -a ['rantʃido] ag rancid

ran'core sm rancour, resentment

ran'dagio, -a, -gi, -gie o **ge** [ran'dadʒo] ag (gatto, cane) stray

ran'dello sm club, cudgel

'rango, -ghi sm (condizione sociale, Mil, riga) rank

rannicchi'arsi [rannik'kjarsi] vpr to crouch, huddle

rannuvo'larsi vpr to cloud over, become overcast

'rapa sf (Bot) turnip

ra'pace [ra'patʃe] ag (animale) predatory; (fig) rapacious, grasping ▷ sm bird of prey

ra'pare vt (capelli) to crop, cut very short

rapida'mente av quickly, rapidly

rapidità sf speed

'rapido, -a ag fast; (esame, occhiata) quick, rapid ▷ sm (Ferr) express (train)

rapi'mento sm kidnapping; (fig) rapture

ra'pina sf robbery; **rapina in banca** bank robbery; **rapina a mano armata** armed robbery; **rapi'nare** vt to rob; **rapina'tore, -'trice** sm/f robber

ra'pire vt (cose) to steal; (persone) to kidnap; (fig) to enrapture, delight; **rapi'tore, -'trice** sm/f kidnapper

rap'porto sm (resoconto) report; (legame) relationship; (Mat, Tecn) ratio; **rapporti sessuali** sexual intercourse sg

rappre'saglia [rappre'saʎʎa] sf reprisal, retaliation

rappresen'tante sm/f representative

rappresen'tare vt to represent; (Teatro) to perform; **rappresentazi'one** sf representation; performing no pl; (spettacolo) performance

rara'mente av seldom, rarely

rare'fatto, -a ag rarefied

'raro, -a ag rare

ra'sare vt (barba ecc) to shave off; (siepi, erba) to trim, cut; **rasarsi** vpr to shave (o.s.)

raschi'are [ras'kjare] vt to scrape; (macchia, fango) to scrape off ▷ vi to clear one's throat

ra'sente prep ~ **(a)** close to, very near

'raso, -a pp di **radere** ▷ ag (barba) shaved; (capelli) cropped; (con misure di capacità) level; (pieno: bicchiere) full to the brim ▷ sm (tessuto) satin; **un cucchiaio ~** a level spoonful; **raso terra** close to the ground

ra'soio sm razor; **rasoio elettrico** electric shaver o razor

ras'segna [ras'seɲɲa] sf (Mil) inspection, review; (esame) inspection; (resoconto) review, survey; (pubblicazione letteraria ecc) review; (mostra) exhibition, show; **passare in ~** (Mil, fig) to review

rassegnarsi vpr (accettare): **~ (a qc/a fare)** to resign o.s. (to sth/to doing)

rassicu'rare vt to reassure

rasso'dare vt to harden, stiffen; **rassodarsi** vpr to harden, to strengthen

rassomigli'anza [rassomiʎ'ʎantsa] sf resemblance

rassomigli'are [rassomiʎ'ʎare] vi **~ a** to resemble, look like ·

rastrel'lare vt to rake; (fig: perlustrare) to comb

ras'trello sm rake

'rata sf (quota) instalment; **pagare a rate** to pay by instalments o on hire purchase (BRIT)

ratifi'care vt (Dir) to ratify

'ratto sm (Dir) abduction; (Zool) rat

rattop'pare vt to patch

rattris'tare vt to sadden; **rattristarsi** vpr to become sad

'rauco, -a, -chi, -che ag hoarse

rava'nello sm radish

ravi'oli smpl ravioli sg

ravvi'vare vt to revive; (fig) to brighten up, enliven

razio'nale [rattsjo'nale] ag rational

razio'nare [rattsjo'nare] vt to ration

razi'one [rat'tsjone] sf ration; (porzione) portion, share

'razza ['rattsa] sf race; (Zool) breed; (discendenza, stirpe) stock, race; (sorta) sort, kind

razzi'ale [rat'tsjale] ag racial

raz'zismo [rat'tsizmo] sm racism, racialism

raz'zista, -i, -e [rat'tsista] ag, sm/f racist, racialist

'razzo ['raddzo] sm rocket

R.C. sigla m (= partito della Rifondazione Comunista) left-wing Italian political party

re sm inv king; (Mus) D; (: solfeggiando) re

rea'gire [rea'dʒire] vi to react

re'ale ag real; (di, da re) royal ▷ sm **il ~** reality

realiz'zare [realid'dzare] vt (progetto ecc) to realize, carry out; (sogno, desiderio) to realize, fulfil; (scopo) to achieve; (Comm: titoli ecc) to realize; (Calcio ecc) to score; **realizzarsi** vpr to be realized

real'mente av really, actually

realtà sf inv reality

re'ato sm offence

reat'tore sm (Fisica) reactor; (Aer: aereo) jet; (: motore) jet engine

reazio'nario, -a [reattsjo'narjo] ag (Pol) reactionary

reazi'one [reat'tsjone] sf reaction

'rebus sm inv rebus; (fig) puzzle; enigma

recapi'tare vt to deliver

re'capito sm (indirizzo) address; (consegna) delivery; **recapito a domicilio** home delivery (service); **recapito telefonico** phone number

re'cedere [re'tʃedere] vi to withdraw

recensi'one [retʃen'sjone] sf review

re'cente [re'tʃɛnte] ag recent; **di ~** recently; **recente'mente** av recently

re'cidere [re'tʃidere] vt to cut off, chop off

recin'tare [retʃin'tare] vt to enclose, fence off

re'cinto [re'tʃinto] sm enclosure; (ciò che recinge) fence; surrounding wall

recipi'ente [retʃi'pjɛnte] sm container

re'ciproco, -a, -ci, -che [re'tʃiproko] ag reciprocal

'recita ['rɛtʃita] sf performance

reci'tare [retʃi'tare] vt (poesia, lezione) to recite; (dramma) to perform; (ruolo) to play o act (the part of)

recla'mare vi to complain ▷ vt (richiedere) to demand

re'clamo sm complaint

recli'nabile ag (sedile) reclining

reclusi'one sf (Dir) imprisonment

'recluta sf recruit

re'condito, -a ag secluded; (fig) secret, hidden

'record ag inv record cpd ▷ sm inv record; **in tempo ~, a tempo di ~** in record time; **detenere il ~ di** to hold the record for; **record mondiale** world record

recriminazi'one [rekriminat'tsjone] sf recrimination

recupe'rare vt (rientrare in possesso di) to recover, get back; (tempo perduto) to make up for; (Naut) to salvage; (: naufraghi) to rescue; (delinquente) to rehabilitate; **~ lo svantaggio** (Sport) to close the gap

redargu'ire vt to rebuke

re'dassi ecc vb vedi **redigere**

reddi'tizio, -a [reddi'tittsjo] ag profitable

'reddito sm income; (dello Stato) revenue; (di un capitale) yield

re'digere [re'didʒere] vt to write; (contratto) to draw up

'redini sfpl reins

'reduce ['redutʃe] ag ~ da returning from, back from ▷ sm/f survivor

refe'rendum sm inv referendum

referenze [refe'rɛntse] sfpl references

re'ferto sm medical report

rega'lare vt to give (as a present), make a present of

re'galo sm gift, present

re'gata sf regatta

'reggere ['rɛddʒere] vt (tenere) to hold; (sostenere) to support, bear, hold up; (portare) to carry, bear; (resistere) to withstand; (dirigere: impresa) to manage, run; (governare) to rule, govern; (Ling) to take, be followed by ▷ vi (resistere): ~ a to stand up to, hold out against; (sopportare): ~ a to stand; (durare) to last; (fig: teoria ecc) to hold water; **reggersi** vpr (stare ritto) to stand

'reggia, -ge ['rɛddʒa] sf royal palace

reggi'calze [reddʒi'kaltse] sm inv suspender belt

reggi'mento [reddʒi'mento] sm (Mil) regiment

reggi'seno [reddʒi'seno] sm bra

re'gia, -'gie [re'dʒia] sf (TV, Cinema ecc) direction

re'gime [re'dʒime] sm (Pol) regime; (Dir: aureo, patrimoniale ecc) system; (Med) diet; (Tecn) (engine) speed

re'gina [re'dʒina] sf queen

regio'nale [redʒo'nale] ag regional ▷ sm local train (stopping frequently)

regi'one [re'dʒone] sf region; (territorio) region, district, area

re'gista, -i, -e [re'dʒista] sm/f (TV, Cinema ecc) director

regis'trare [redʒis'trare] vt (Amm) to register; (Comm) to enter; (notare) to note, take note of; (canzone, conversazione: strumento di misura) to record; (mettere a punto) to adjust, regulate; (bagagli) to check in; **registra'tore** sm (strumento) recorder, register; (magnetofono) tape recorder; **registratore di cassa** cash register; **registratore a cassette** cassette recorder

re'gistro [re'dʒistro] sm (libro, Mus, Tech) register; ledger; logbook; (Dir) registry

re'gnare [reɲ'ɲare] vi to reign, rule

'regno ['reɲɲo] sm kingdom; (periodo) reign; (fig) realm; **il R~ Unito** the United Kingdom; **regno animale/vegetale** animal/vegetable kingdom

'regola sf rule; **a ~ d'arte** duly; perfectly; **in ~** in order

rego'labile ag adjustable

regola'mento sm (complesso di norme) regulations pl; (di debito) settlement; **regolamento di conti** (fig) settling of scores

rego'lare ag regular; (in regola: domanda) in order, lawful ▷ vt to regulate, control; (apparecchio) to adjust, regulate; (questione, conto, debito) to settle; **regolarsi** vpr (moderarsi): **regolarsi nel bere/nello spendere** to control one's drinking/ spending; (comportarsi) to behave, act

rela'tivo, -a ag relative

relazi'one [relat'tsjone] sf (fra cose, persone) relation(ship); (resoconto) report, account

rele'gare vt to banish; (fig) to relegate

religi'one [reli'dʒone] sf religion

re'liquia sf relic

re'litto sm wreck; (fig) down-and-out

re'mare vi to row

remini'scenze [reminiʃ'ʃɛntse] sfpl reminiscences

remis'sivo, -a ag submissive, compliant

'remo sm oar

re'moto, -a ag remote

'rendere vt (ridare) to return, give back; (: saluto ecc) to return; (produrre) to yield, bring in; (esprimere, tradurre) to render; ~ **qc possibile** to make sth possible; **rendersi** vpr **rendersi utile** to make o.s. useful; **rendersi conto di qc** to realize sth; ~ **qc possibile** to make sth possible; ~ **grazie a qn** give thanks to sb; ~ **omaggio a qn** to pay homage to sb; ~ **un servizio a qn** to do sb a service; ~ **una testimonianza** to give evidence; **non so se rendo l'idea** I don't know if I'm making myself clear

rendi'mento sm (reddito) yield; (di manodopera, Tecn) efficiency; (capacità di produrre) output; (di studenti) performance

'rendita sf (di individuo) private o unearned income; (Comm) revenue; **rendita annua** annuity

'rene sm kidney

'renna sf reindeer inv

re'parto sm department, section; (Mil) detachment

repel'lente ag repulsive

repen'taglio [repen'taʎʎo] sm **mettere a ~** to jeopardize, risk

repen'tino, -a ag sudden, unexpected

reper'torio sm (Teatro) repertory; (elenco) index, (alphabetical) list

'replica, -che sf repetition; reply, answer;

(*obiezione*) objection; (*Teatro, Cinema*) repeat performance; (*copia*) replica

repli'care *vt* (*ripetere*) to repeat; (*rispondere*) to answer, reply

repressi'one *sf* repression

re'presso, -a *pp di* **reprimere**

re'primere *vt* to suppress, repress

re'pubblica, -che *sf* republic

reputazi'one [reputat'tsjone] *sf* reputation

requi'sire *vt* to requisition

requi'sito *sm* requirement

'resa *sf* (*l'arrendersi*) surrender; (*restituzione, rendimento*) return; **resa dei conti** rendering of accounts; (*fig*) day of reckoning

'resi *ecc vb vedi* **rendere**

resi'dente *ag* resident; **residenzi'ale** *ag* residential

re'siduo, -a *ag* residual, remaining ▷ *sm* remainder; (*Chim*) residue

'resina *sf* resin

resis'tente *ag* (*che resiste*): **~ a** resistant to; (*forte*) strong; (*duraturo*) long-lasting, durable; **~ al caldo** heat-resistant; **resis'tenza** *sf* resistance; (*di persona*: *fisica*) stamina, endurance; (: *mentale*) endurance, resistance

---

⬤ RESISTENZA
⬤
⬤ The **Resistenza** in Italy fought against
⬤ the Nazis and the Fascists during the
⬤ Second World War. Members of the
⬤ **Resistenza** spanned a wide political
⬤ spectrum and played a vital role in the
⬤ Liberation and in the formation of the
⬤ new democratic government at the end
⬤ of the war.

---

re'sistere *vi* to resist; **~ a** (*assalto, tentazioni*) to resist; (*dolore: pianta*) to withstand; (*non patir danno*) to be resistant to

reso'conto *sm* report, account

res'pingere [res'pindʒere] *vt* to drive back, repel; (*rifiutare*) to reject; (*Ins: bocciare*) to fail

respi'rare *vi* to breathe; (*fig*) to get one's breath; to breathe again ▷ *vt* to breathe (in), inhale; **respirazi'one** *sf* breathing; **respirazione artificiale** artificial respiration; **res'piro** *sm* breathing *no pl*; (*singolo atto*) breath; (*fig*) respite, rest; **mandare un respiro di sollievo** to give a sigh of relief

respon'sabile *ag* responsible ▷ *sm/f* person responsible; (*capo*) person in charge; **~ di** responsible for; (*Dir*) liable for; **responsabilità** *sf inv* responsibility; (*legale*) liability

res'ponso *sm* answer

'ressa *sf* crowd, throng

'ressi *ecc vb vedi* **reggere**

res'tare *vi* (*rimanere*) to remain, stay; (*avanzare*) to be left, remain; **~ orfano/ cieco** to become o be left an orphan/ become blind; **~ d'accordo** to agree; **non resta più niente** there's nothing left; **restano pochi giorni** there are only a few days left

restau'rare *vt* to restore

res'tio, -a, -'tii, -'tie *ag* **~ a** reluctant to

restitu'ire *vt* to return, give back; (*energie, forze*) to restore

'resto *sm* remainder, rest; (*denaro*) change; (*Mat*) remainder; **resti** *smpl* (*di cibo*) leftovers; (*di città*) remains; **del ~** moreover, besides; **tenga pure il ~** keep the change; **resti mortali** (mortal) remains

res'tringere [res'trindʒere] *vt* to reduce; (*vestito*) to take in; (*stoffa*) to shrink; (*fig*) to restrict, limit; **restringersi** *vpr* (*strada*) to narrow; (*stoffa*) to shrink

'rete *sf* net; (*fig*) trap, snare; (*di recinzione*) wire netting; (*Aut, Ferr, di spionaggio ecc*) network; **segnare una ~** (*Calcio*) to score a goal; **la R~** the Web; **rete ferroviaria** railway network; **rete del letto** (sprung) bed base; **rete stradale** road network; **rete (televisiva)** (*sistema*) network; (*canale*) channel

reti'cente [reti'tʃɛnte] *ag* reticent

retico'lato *sm* grid; (*rete*) wire netting; (*di filo spinato*) barbed wire (fence)

'retina *sf* (*Anat*) retina

re'torico, -a, -ci, -che *ag* rhetorical

retribu'ire *vt* to pay

'retro *sm inv* back ▷ *av* (*dietro*): **vedi ~** see over(leaf)

retro'cedere [retro'tʃedere] *vi* to withdraw ▷ *vt* (*Calcio*) to relegate; (*Mil*) to degrade

re'trogrado, -a *ag* (*fig*) reactionary, backward-looking

retro'marcia [retro'martʃa] *sf* (*Aut*) reverse; (: *dispositivo*) reverse gear

retro'scena [retroʃ'ʃena] *sm inv* (*Teatro*) backstage; **i ~** (*fig*) the behind-the-scenes activities

retrovi'sore *sm* (*Aut*) (rear-view) mirror

'retta *sf* (*Mat*) straight line; (*di convitto*) charge for bed and board; (*fig: ascolto*): **dar ~ a** to listen to, pay attention to

rettango'lare *ag* rectangular

ret'tangolo, -a *ag* right-angled ▷ *sm* rectangle

ret'tifica, -che sf rectification, correction

'rettile sm reptile

retti'lineo, -a ag rectilinear

'retto, -a pp di **reggere** ▷ ag straight; (Mat): **angolo ~** right angle; (onesto) honest, upright; (giusto, esatto) correct, proper, right

ret'tore sm (Rel) rector; (di università) ≈ chancellor

reuma'tismo sm rheumatism

revisi'one sf auditing no pl; audit; servicing no pl; overhaul; review; revision; **revisione di bozze** proofreading

revi'sore sm; **revisore di bozze** proofreader; **revisore di conti** auditor

revival [ri'vaivəl] sm inv revival

'revoca sf revocation

revo'care vt to revoke

re'volver sm inv revolver

ri'abbia ecc vb vedi **riavere**

riabili'tare vt to rehabilitate

rianimazi'one [rianimat'tsjone] sf (Med) resuscitation; **centro di ~** intensive care unit

ria'prire vt to reopen, open again; **riaprirsi** vpr to reopen, open again

ri'armo sm (Mil) rearmament

rias'sumere vt (riprendere) to resume; (impiegare di nuovo) to re-employ; (sintetizzare) to summarize; **rias'sunto, -a** pp di **riassumere** ▷ sm summary

riattac'care vt (attaccare di nuovo): **~ (a)** (manifesto, francobollo) to stick back (on); (bottone) to sew back (on); (quadro, chiavi) to hang back up (on); **~ (il telefono** o **il ricevitore)** to hang up (the receiver)

ria'vere vt to have again; (avere indietro) to get back; (riacquistare) to recover; **riaversi** vpr to recover

riba'dire vt (fig) to confirm

ri'balta sf flap; (Teatro: proscenio) front of the stage; (fig) limelight; **luci della ~** footlights pl

ribal'tabile ag (sedile) tip-up

ribal'tare vt, vi (anche: **ribaltarsi**) to turn over, tip over

ribas'sare vt to lower, bring down ▷ vi to come down, fall

ri'battere vt to return, hit back; (confutare) to refute; **~ che** to retort that

ribel'larsi vpr **~ (a)** to rebel (against); **ri'belle** ag (soldati) rebel; (ragazzo) rebellious ▷ sm/f rebel

'ribes sm inv currant; **ribes nero** blackcurrant; **ribes rosso** redcurrant

ri'brezzo [ri'breddzo] sm disgust, loathing; **far ~ a** to disgust

ribut'tante ag disgusting, revolting

rica'dere vi to fall again; (scendere a terra: fig: nel peccato ecc) to fall back; (vestiti, capelli ecc) to hang (down); (riversarsi: fatiche, colpe): **~ su** to fall on; **rica'duta** sf (Med) relapse

rica'mare vt to embroider

ricambi'are vt to change again; (contraccambiare) to repay, return; **ri'cambio** sm exchange, return; (Fisiol) metabolism

ri'camo sm embroidery

ricapito'lare vt to recapitulate, sum up

ricari'care vt (arma, macchina fotografica) to reload; (pipa) to refill; (orologio) to rewind; (batteria) to recharge

ricat'tare vt to blackmail; **ri'catto** sm blackmail

rica'vare vt (estrarre) to draw out, extract; (ottenere) to obtain, gain

ric'chezza [rik'kettsa] sf wealth; (fig) richness

'riccio, -a ['rittʃo] ag curly ▷ sm (Zool) hedgehog; **riccio di mare** sea urchin; **'ricciolo** sm curl

'ricco, -a, -chi, -che ag rich; (persona, paese) rich, wealthy ▷ sm/f rich man/woman; **i ricchi** the rich; **~ di** full of; rich in

ri'cerca, -che [ri'tʃerka] sf search; (indagine) investigation, inquiry; (studio): **la ~** research; **una ~** piece of research; **ricerca di mercato** market research

ricer'care [ritʃer'kare] vt (motivi, cause) to look for, try to determine; (successo, piacere) to pursue; (onore, gloria) to seek; **ricer'cato, -a** ag (apprezzato) much sought-after; (affettato) studied, affected ▷ sm/f (Polizia) wanted man/woman

ricerca'tore, -'trice [ritʃerka'tore] sm/f (Ins) researcher

ri'cetta [ri'tʃetta] sf (Med) prescription; (Cuc) recipe; **mi può fare una ~ medica?** could you write me a prescription?

ricettazi'one [ritʃettat'tsjone] sf (Dir) receiving (stolen goods)

ri'cevere [ri'tʃevere] vt to receive; (stipendio, lettera) to get, receive; (accogliere: ospite) to welcome; (vedere: cliente, rappresentante ecc) to see; **ricevi'mento** sm receiving no pl; (festa) reception; **ricevi'tore** sm (Tecn) receiver; **rice'vuta** sf receipt; **posso avere una ricevuta, per favore?** can I have a receipt, please?; **ricevuta fiscale** receipt for tax purposes; **ricevuta di ritorno** (Posta) advice of receipt

richia'mare [rikja'mare] vt (chiamare indietro, ritelefonare) to call back; (ambasciatore, truppe) to recall; (rimproverare) to reprimand; (attirare) to attract, draw; **può ~ più tardi?** can you call back later?; **richiamarsi a** (*riferirsi a*) to refer to

richi'edere [ri'kjedere] *vt* to ask again for; (*chiedere indietro*): ~ **qc** to ask for sth back; (*chiedere: per sapere*) to ask; (*: per avere*) to ask for; (*Amm: documenti*) to apply for; (*esigere*) to need, require; **richi'esta** *sf* (*domanda*) request; (*Amm*) application, request; (*esigenza*) demand, request; **a richiesta** on request

rici'clare [ritʃi'klare] *vt* to recycle

'ricino [ri'tʃino] *sm* **olio di ~** castor oil

ricognizi'one [rikoɲɲi'tsjone] *sf* (*Mil*) reconnaissance; (*Dir*) recognition, acknowledgement

ricominci'are [rikomin'tʃare] *vt, vi* to start again, begin again

ricom'pensa *sf* reward

ricompen'sare *vt* to reward

riconciliarsi *vpr* to be reconciled

ricono'scente [rikono'ʃʃente] *ag* grateful

rico'noscere [riko'noʃʃere] *vt* to recognize; (*Dir: figlio, debito*) to acknowledge; (*ammettere: errore*) to admit, acknowledge

rico'perto, -a *pp di* **ricoprire**

ricopi'are *vt* to copy

rico'prire *vt* (*coprire*) to cover; (*occupare: carica*) to hold

ricor'dare *vt* to remember, recall; (*richiamare alla memoria*): ~ **qc a qn** to remind sb of sth; **ricordarsi** *vpr* **ricordarsi (di)** to remember; **ricordarsi di qc/di aver fatto** to remember sth/having done

ri'cordo *sm* memory; (*regalo*) keepsake, souvenir; (*di viaggio*) souvenir

ricor'rente *ag* recurrent, recurring; **ricor'renza** *sf* recurrence; (*festività*) anniversary

ri'correre *vi* (*ripetersi*) to recur; ~ **a** (*rivolgersi*) to turn to; (*: Dir*) to appeal to; (*servirsi di*) to have recourse to

ricostitu'ente *ag* (*Med*): **cura ~** tonic

ricostru'ire *vt* (*casa*) to rebuild; (*fatti*) to reconstruct

ri'cotta *sf* soft white unsalted cheese made from sheep's milk

ricove'rare *vt* to give shelter to; ~ **qn in ospedale** to admit sb to hospital

ri'covero *sm* shelter, refuge; (*Mil*) shelter; (*Med*) admission (to hospital)

ricreazi'one [rikreat'tsjone] *sf* recreation, entertainment; (*Ins*) break

ri'credersi *vpr* to change one's mind

ridacchi'are [ridak'kjare] *vi* to snigger

ri'dare *vt* to return, give back

'ridere *vi* to laugh; (*deridere, beffare*): ~ **di** to laugh at, make fun of

ri'dicolo, -a *ag* ridiculous, absurd

ridimensio'nare *vt* to reorganize; (*fig*) to see in the right perspective

ri'dire *vt* to repeat; (*criticare*) to find fault with; to object to; **trova sempre qualcosa da ~** he always manages to find fault

ridon'dante *ag* redundant

ri'dotto, -a *pp di* **ridurre** ▷ *ag* (*biglietto*) reduced; (*formato*) small

ri'duco *ecc vb vedi* **ridurre**

ri'durre *vt* (*anche Chim, Mat*) to reduce; (*prezzo, spese*) to cut, reduce; (*accorciare: opera letteraria*) to abridge; (*: Radio, TV*) to adapt; **ridursi** *vpr* (*diminuirsi*) to be reduced, shrink; **ridursi a** to be reduced to; **ridursi pelle e ossa** to be reduced to skin and bone; **ri'dussi** *ecc vb vedi* **ridurre**; **ridut'tore** *sm* (*Elec*) adaptor; **riduzi'one** *sf* reduction; abridgement; adaptation; **ci sono riduzioni per i bambini/gli studenti?** is there a reduction for children/students?

ri'ebbi *ecc vb vedi* **riavere**

riem'pire *vt* to fill (up); (*modulo*) to fill in *o* out; **riempirsi** *vpr* to fill (up); ~ **qc di** to fill sth (up) with

rien'tranza [rien'trantsa] *sf* recess; indentation

rien'trare *vi* (*entrare di nuovo*) to go (*o* come) back in; (*tornare*) to return; (*fare una rientranza*) to go in, curve inwards; to be indented; (*riguardare*): ~ **in** to be included among, form part of

riepilo'gare *vt* to summarize ▷ *vi* to recapitulate

ri'esco *ecc vb vedi* **riuscire**

ri'fare *vt* to do again; (*ricostruire*) to make again; (*nodo*) to tie again, do up again; (*imitare*) to imitate, copy; **rifarsi** *vpr* (*risarcirsi*): **rifarsi di** to make up for; (*vendicarsi*): **rifarsi di qc su qn** to get one's own back on sb for sth; (*riferirsi*): **rifarsi a** to go back to; to follow; ~ **il letto** to make the bed; **rifarsi una vita** to make a new life for o.s.

riferi'mento *sm* reference; **in** *o* **con ~ a** with reference to

rife'rire *vt* (*riportare*) to report ▷ *vi* to do a report; **riferirsi** *vpr* **riferirsi a** to refer to

rifi'nire *vt* to finish off, put the finishing touches to

rifiu'tare *vt* to refuse; ~ **di fare** to refuse to do; **rifi'uto** *sm* refusal; **rifiuti** *smpl* (*spazzatura*) rubbish *sg*, refuse *sg*

riflessi'one *sf* (*Fisica, meditazione*) reflection; (*il pensare*) thought, reflection; (*osservazione*) remark

rifles'sivo, -a *ag* (*persona*) thoughtful, reflective; (*Ling*) reflexive

ri'flesso, -a pp di **riflettere** ▷ sm (di luce, allo specchio) reflection; (Fisiol) reflex; **di o per ~** indirectly

riflessologia [riflessolo'dʒia] sf reflexology

ri'flettere vt to reflect ▷ vi to think; **riflettersi** vpr to be reflected; **~ su** to think over

riflet'tore sm reflector; (proiettore) floodlight; searchlight

ri'flusso sm flowing back; (della marea) ebb; **un'epoca di ~** an era of nostalgia

ri'forma sf reform; **la R~** (Rel) the Reformation

riforma'torio sm (Dir) community home (BRIT), reformatory (US)

riforni'mento sm supplying, providing; restocking; **rifornimenti** smpl (provviste) supplies, provisions

rifor'nire vt (provvedere): **~ di** to supply o provide with; (fornire di nuovo: casa ecc) to restock; **rifornirsi** vpr **rifornirsi di qc** to stock up on sth

rifugi'arsi [rifu'dʒarsi] vpr to take refuge; **rifugi'ato, -a** sm/f refugee

ri'fugio [ri'fudʒo] sm refuge, shelter; (in montagna) shelter; **rifugio antiaereo** air-raid shelter

'riga, -ghe sf line; (striscia) stripe; (di persone, cose) line, row; (regolo) ruler; (scriminatura) parting; **mettersi in ~** to line up; **a righe** (foglio) lined; (vestito) striped

ri'gare vt (foglio) to rule ▷ vi **~ diritto** (fig) to toe the line

rigatti'ere sm junk dealer

righerò ecc [rige'rɔ] vb vedi **rigare**

'rigido, -a ['ridʒido] ag rigid, stiff; (membra ecc: indurite) stiff; (Meteor) harsh, severe; (fig) strict

rigogli'oso, -a [rigoʎ'ʎoso] ag (pianta) luxuriant; (fig: commercio, sviluppo) thriving

ri'gore sm (Meteor) harshness, rigours pl; (fig) severity, strictness; (anche: **calcio di ~**) penalty; **di ~** compulsory; **a rigor di termini** strictly speaking

riguar'dare vt to look at again; (considerare) to regard, consider; (concernere) to regard, concern; **riguardarsi** vpr (aver cura di sé) to look after o.s.

rigu'ardo sm (attenzione) care; (considerazione) regard, respect; **~ a** concerning, with regard to; **non aver riguardi nell'agire/nel parlare** to act/speak freely

rilasci'are [rilaʃ'ʃare] vt (rimettere in libertà) to release; (Amm: documenti) to issue

rilassarsi vpr to relax; (fig: disciplina) to become slack

rile'gare vt (libro) to bind

ri'leggere [ri'leddʒere] vt to reread, read again; (rivedere) to read over

ri'lento: a ~ av slowly

rile'vante ag considerable; important

rile'vare vt (ricavare) to find; (notare) to notice; (mettere in evidenza) to point out; (venire a conoscere: notizia) to learn; (raccogliere: dati) to gather, collect; (Topografia) to survey; (Mil) to relieve; (Comm) to take over

rili'evo sm (Arte, Geo) relief; (fig: rilevanza) importance; (Topografia) survey; **dar ~ a** o **mettere in ~ qc** (fig) to bring sth out, highlight sth

rilut'tante ag reluctant

'rima sf rhyme; (verso) verse

riman'dare vt to send again; (restituire, rinviare) to send back, return; (differire): **~ qc (a)** to postpone sth o put sth off (till); (fare riferimento): **~ qn a** to refer sb to; **essere rimandato** (Ins) to have to repeat one's exams

ri'mando sm (rinvio) return; (dilazione) postponement; (riferimento) cross-reference

rima'nente ag remaining ▷ sm rest, remainder; **i rimanenti** (persone) the rest of them, the others

rima'nere vi (restare) to remain, stay; (avanzare) to be left, remain; (restare stupito) to be amazed; (restare, mancare): **rimangono poche settimane a Pasqua** there are only a few weeks left till Easter; **rimane da vedere se** it remains to be seen whether; (diventare): **~ vedovo** to be left a widower; (trovarsi): **~ sorpreso** to be surprised

rimangi'are [riman'dʒare] vt to eat again; **~rsi la parola/una promessa** (fig) to go back on one's word/one's promise

ri'mango ecc vb vedi **rimanere**

rimargi'narsi vpr to heal

rimbal'zare [rimbal'tsare] vi to bounce back, rebound; (proiettile) to ricochet

rimbam'bito, -a ag senile, in one's dotage

rimboc'care vt (coperta) to tuck in; (maniche, pantaloni) to turn o roll up

rimbom'bare vi to resound

rimbor'sare vt to pay back, repay

rimedi'are vi **~ a** to remedy ▷ vt (fam: procurarsi) to get o scrape together

ri'medio sm (medicina) medicine; (cura, fig) remedy, cure

ri'mettere vt (mettere di nuovo) to put back; (indossare di nuovo): **~ qc** to put sth back on, put sth on again; (affidare) to entrust; (: decisione) to refer; (condonare) to remit; (Comm: merci) to deliver; (: denaro) to remit; (*vomitare*) to bring up; (*perdere: anche*: **rimetterci**) to lose; **rimettersi al bello** (*tempo*) to clear up; **rimettersi in salute** to get better, recover one's health

ri'misi *ecc vb vedi* **rimettere**

'rimmel® *sm inv* mascara

rimoder'nare *vt* to modernize

rimorchi'are [rimor'kjare] *vt* to tow; (*fig: ragazza*) to pick up

ri'morchio [ri'mɔrkjo] *sm* tow; (*veicolo*) trailer

ri'morso *sm* remorse

rimozi'one [rimot'tsjone] *sf* removal; (*da un impiego*) dismissal; (*Psic*) repression

rimpatri'are *vi* to return home ▷ *vt* to repatriate

rimpi'angere [rim'pjandʒere] *vt* to regret; (*persona*) to miss; **rimpi'anto, -a** *pp di* **rimpiangere** ▷ *sm* regret

rimpiaz'zare [rimpjat'tsare] *vt* to replace

rimpiccio'lire [rimpittʃo'lire] *vt* to make smaller ▷ *vi* (*anche*: **rimpicciolirsi**) to become smaller

rimpinzarsi [rimpin'tsarsi] *vpr* **~ (di qc)** to stuff o.s. (with sth)

rimprove'rare *vt* to rebuke, reprimand

rimu'overe *vt* to remove; (*destituire*) to dismiss

Rinasci'mento [rinaʃʃi'mento] *sm* **il ~** the Renaissance

ri'nascita [ri'naʃʃita] *sf* rebirth, revival

rinca'rare *vt* to increase the price of ▷ *vi* to go up, become more expensive

rinca'sare *vi* to go home

rinchi'udere [rin'kjudere] *vt* to shut (o lock) up; **rinchiudersi** *vpr* **rinchiudersi in** to shut o.s. up in; **rinchiudersi in se stesso** to withdraw into o.s.

rin'correre *vt* to chase, run after; **rin'corsa** *sf* short run

rin'crescere [rin'kreʃʃere] *vb impers* **mi rincresce che/di non poter fare** I'm sorry that/I can't do, I regret that/being unable to do

rinfacci'are [rinfat'tʃare] *vt* (*fig*): **~ qc a qn** to throw sth in sb's face

rinfor'zare [rinfor'tsare] *vt* to reinforce, strengthen ▷ *vi* (*anche*: **rinforzarsi**) to grow stronger

rinfres'care *vt* (*atmosfera, temperatura*) to cool (down); (*abito, pareti*) to freshen up ▷ *vi* (*tempo*) to grow cooler; **rinfrescarsi** *vpr* (*ristorarsi*) to refresh o.s.; (*lavarsi*) to freshen up; **rin'fresco, -schi** *sm* (*festa*) party; **rinfreschi** *smpl* refreshments

rin'fusa *sf* **alla ~** in confusion, higgledy-piggledy

ringhi'are [rin'gjare] *vi* to growl, snarl

ringhi'era [rin'gjera] *sf* railing; (*delle scale*) banister(s) (*pl*)

ringiova'nire [rindʒova'nire] *vt* (*vestito, acconciatura ecc*): **~ qn** to make sb look younger; (: *vacanze ecc*) to rejuvenate ▷ *vi* (*anche*: **ringiovanirsi**) to become (o look) younger

ringrazia'mento [ringrattsja'mento] *sm* thanks *pl*

ringrazi'are [ringrat'tsjare] *vt* to thank; **~ qn di qc** to thank sb for sth

rinne'gare *vt* (*fede*) to renounce; (*figlio*) to disown, repudiate

rinnova'mento *sm* renewal; (*economico*) revival

rinno'vare *vt* to renew; (*ripetere*) to repeat, renew

rinoce'ronte [rinotʃe'ronte] *sm* rhinoceros

rino'mato, -a *ag* renowned, celebrated

rintracci'are [rintrat'tʃare] *vt* to track down

rintro'nare *vi* to boom, roar ▷ *vt* (*assordare*) to deafen; (*stordire*) to stun

rinunci'are [rinun'tʃare] *vi* **~ a** to give up, renounce; **~ a fare qc** to give up doing sth

rinvi'are *vt* (*rimandare indietro*) to send back, return; (*differire*): **~ qc (a)** to postpone sth o put sth off (till); to adjourn sth (till); (*fare un rimando*): **~ qn a** to refer sb to

rin'vio, -'vii *sm* (*rimando*) return; (*differimento*) postponement; (: *di seduta*) adjournment; (*in un testo*) cross-reference; **rinvio a giudizio** (*Dir*) indictment

riò *ecc vb vedi* **riavere**

ri'one *sm* district, quarter

riordi'nare *vt* (*rimettere in ordine*) to tidy; (*riorganizzare*) to reorganize

riorganiz'zare [riorganid'dzare] *vt* to reorganize

ripa'gare *vt* to repay

ripa'rare *vt* (*proteggere*) to protect, defend; (*correggere: male, torto*) to make up for; (: *errore*) to put right; (*aggiustare*) to repair ▷ *vi* (*mettere rimedio*): **~ a** to make up for; **ripararsi** *vpr* (*rifugiarsi*) to take refuge o shelter; **dove lo posso far ~?** where can I get this repaired?; **riparazi'one** *sf* (*di un torto*) reparation; (*di guasto, scarpe*) repairing *no pl*; repair; (*risarcimento*) compensation

ri'paro *sm* (*protezione*) shelter, protection; (*rimedio*) remedy

ripar'tire *vt* (*dividere*) to divide up; (*distribuire*) to share out ▷ *vi* to set off again; to leave again

ripas'sare *vi* to come (o go) back ▷ *vt* (*scritto, lezione*) to go over (again)

ripen'sare *vi* to think; (*cambiare pensiero*)

to change one's mind; (*tornare col pensiero*): **~ a** to recall

ripercu'otersi *vpr* **~ su** (*fig*) to have repercussions on

ripercussi'one *sf* (*fig*): **avere una ~ o delle ripercussioni su** to have repercussions on

ripes'care *vt* (*pesce*) to catch again; (*persona, cosa*) to fish out; (*fig: ritrovare*) to dig out

ri'petere *vt* to repeat; (*ripassare*) to go over; **può ~ per favore?** can you repeat that please?; **ripetizi'one** *sf* repetition; (*di lezione*) revision; **ripetizioni** *sfpl* (*Ins*) private tutoring *o* coaching *sg*

ripi'ano *sm* (*di mobile*) shelf

ri'picca *sf* **per ~** out of spite

'ripido, -a *ag* steep

ripie'gare *vt* to refold; (*piegare più volte*) to fold (up) ▷ *vi* (*Mil*) to retreat, fall back; (*fig: accontentarsi*): **~ su** to make do with

ripi'eno, -a *ag* full; (*Cuc*) stuffed; (*: panino*) filled ▷ *sm* (*Cuc*) stuffing

ri'pone, ri'pongo *ecc vb vedi* **riporre**

ri'porre *vt* (*porre al suo posto*) to put back, replace; (*mettere via*) to put away; (*fiducia, speranza*): **~ qc in qn** to place *o* put sth in sb

ripor'tare *vt* (*portare indietro*) to bring (*o* take) back; (*riferire*) to report; (*citare*) to quote; (*vittoria*) to gain; (*successo*) to have; (*Mat*) to carry; **riportarsi a** (*anche fig*) to go back to; (*riferirsi a*) to refer to; **~ danni** to suffer damage

ripo'sare *vt, vi* to rest; **riposarsi** *vpr* to rest

ri'posi *ecc vb vedi* **riporre**

ri'poso *sm* rest; (*Mil*): **~!** at ease!; **a ~** (*in pensione*) retired; **giorno di ~** day off

ripos'tiglio [ripos'tiλλo] *sm* lumber-room

ri'prendere *vt* (*prigioniero, fortezza*) to recapture; (*prendere indietro*) to take back; (*ricominciare: lavoro*) to resume; (*andare a prendere*) to fetch, come back for; (*riassumere: impiegati*) to take on again, re-employ; (*rimproverare*) to tell off; (*restringere: abito*) to take in; (*Cinema*) to shoot; **riprendersi** *vpr* to recover; (*correggersi*) to correct o.s.; **ri'presa** *sf* recapture; resumption; (*economica, da malattia, emozione*) recovery; (*Aut*) acceleration *no pl*; (*Teatro, Cinema*) rerun; (*Cinema: presa*) shooting *no pl*; shot; (*Sport*) second half; (*: Pugilato*) round; **a più riprese** on several occasions, several times; **ripresa cinematografica** shot

ripristi'nare *vt* to restore

ripro'durre *vt* to reproduce; **riprodursi** *vpr* (*Biol*) to reproduce; (*riformarsi*) to form again

ripro'vare *vt* (*provare di nuovo: gen*) to try

again; (*vestito*) to try on again; (*: sensazione*) to experience again ▷ *vi* (*tentare*): **~ (a fare qc)** to try (to do sth) again; **riproverò più tardi** I'll try again later

ripudi'are *vt* to repudiate, disown

ripu'gnante [ripuɲ'ɲante] *ag* disgusting, repulsive

ri'quadro *sm* square; (*Archit*) panel

ri'saia *sf* paddy field

risa'lire *vi* (*ritornare in su*) to go back up; **~ a** (*ritornare con la mente*) to go back to; (*datare da*) to date back to, go back to

risal'tare *vi* (*fig: distinguersi*) to stand out; (*Archit*) to project, jut out

risa'puto, -a *ag* **è ~ che ...** everyone knows that ..., it is common knowledge that ...

risarci'mento [risartʃi'mento] *sm* **~ (di)** compensation (for); **risarcimento danni** damages

risar'cire [risar'tʃire] *vt* (*cose*) to pay compensation for; (*persona*): **~ qn di qc** to compensate sb for sth

ri'sata *sf* laugh

riscalda'mento *sm* heating; **riscaldamento centrale** central heating

riscal'dare *vt* (*scaldare*) to heat; (*: mani, persona*) to warm; (*minestra*) to reheat; **riscaldarsi** *vpr* to warm up

ris'catto *sm* ransom; redemption

rischia'rare [riskja'rare] *vt* (*illuminare*) to light up; (*colore*) to make lighter; **rischiararsi** *vpr* (*tempo*) to clear up; (*cielo*) to clear; (*fig: volto*) to brighten up; **rischiararsi la voce** to clear one's throat

rischi'are [ris'kjare] *vt* to risk ▷ *vi* **~ di fare qc** to risk *o* run the risk of doing sth

'rischio ['riskjo] *sm* risk; **rischi'oso, -a** *ag* risky, dangerous

risci'acquare [riʃʃa'kware] *vt* to rinse

riscon'trare *vt* (*rilevare*) to find

ris'cuotere *vt* (*ritirare: somma*) to collect; (*: stipendio*) to draw, collect; (*assegno*) to cash; (*fig: successo ecc*) to win, earn

'rise *ecc vb vedi* **ridere**

risenti'mento *sm* resentment

risen'tire *vt* to hear again; (*provare*) to feel ▷ *vi* **~ di** to feel (*o* show) the effects of; **risentirsi** *vpr* **risentirsi di** *o* **per** to take offence at, resent; **risen'tito, -a** *ag* resentful

ri'serbo *sm* reserve

ri'serva *sf* reserve; (*di caccia, pesca*) preserve; (*restrizione, di indigeni*) reservation; **di ~** (*provviste ecc*) in reserve

riser'vare *vt* (*tenere in serbo*) to keep, put aside; (*prenotare*) to book, reserve; **ho riservato un tavolo a nome...** I booked a table in the name of ...; **riser'vato,**

-a *ag* (*prenotato: fig: persona*) reserved; (*confidenziale*) confidential

'risi *ecc vb vedi* **ridere**

risi'edere *vi* ~ **a** *o* **in** to reside in

'risma *sf* (*di carta*) ream; (*fig*) kind, sort

'riso (*pl(f)* **risa**) (: *il ridere*) *sm* **il** ~ laughter; (*pianta*) rice ▷ *pp di* **ridere**

riso'lino *sm* snigger

ri'solsi *ecc vb vedi* **risolvere**

ri'solto, -a *pp di* **risolvere**

riso'luto, -a *ag* determined, resolute

risoluzi'one [risolut'tsjone] *sf* solving *no pl*; (*Mat*) solution; (*decisione, di schermo, immagine*) resolution

ri'solvere *vt* (*difficoltà, controversia*) to resolve; (*problema*) to solve; (*decidere*): ~ **di fare** to resolve to do; **risolversi** *vpr* (*decidersi*): **risolversi a fare** to make up one's mind to do; (*andare a finire*): **risolversi in** to end up, turn out; **risolversi in nulla** to come to nothing

riso'nanza [riso'nantsa] *sf* resonance; **aver vasta** ~ (*fig: fatto ecc*) to be known far and wide

ri'sorgere [ri'sordʒere] *vi* to rise again; **risorgi'mento** *sm* revival; **il Risorgimento** (*Storia*) the Risorgimento

● **RISORGIMENTO**
●
● The **Risorgimento** was the political
● movement which led to the
● proclamation of the Kingdom of Italy
● in 1861, and eventually to unification
● in 1871.

ri'sorsa *sf* expedient, resort; **risorse umane** human resources

ri'sorsi *ecc vb vedi* **risorgere**

ri'sotto *sm* (*Cuc*) risotto

risparmi'are *vt* to save; (*non uccidere*) to spare ▷ *vi* to save; ~ **qc a qn** to spare sb sth

ris'parmio *sm* saving *no pl*; (*denaro*) savings *pl*; **risparmi** *smpl* (*denaro*) savings

rispec'chiare [rispek'kjare] *vt* to reflect

rispet'tabile *ag* respectable

rispet'tare *vt* to respect; **farsi** ~ to command respect

rispet'tivo, -a *ag* respective

ris'petto *sm* respect; **rispetti** *smpl* (*saluti*) respects, regards; ~ **a** (*in paragone a*) compared to; (*in relazione a*) as regards, as for

ris'pondere *vi* to answer, reply; (*freni*) to respond; ~ **a** (*domanda*) to answer, reply to; (*persona*) to answer; (*invito*) to reply to; (*provocazione: veicolo, apparecchio*) to respond to; (: *corrispondere a*) to correspond to; (: *speranze, bisogno*) to answer; ~ **di** to

answer for; **ris'posta** *sf* answer, reply; **in risposta a** in reply to

'rissa *sf* brawl

ris'tampa *sf* reprinting *no pl*; reprint

risto'rante *sm* restaurant; **mi può consigliare un buon** ~? can you recommend a good restaurant?

ris'tretto, -a *pp di* **restringere** ▷ *ag* (*racchiuso*) enclosed, hemmed in; (*angusto*) narrow; (*limitato*): ~ **(a)** restricted *o* limited (to); (*Cuc: brodo*) thick; (: *caffè*) extra strong

ristruttu'rare *vt* (*azienda*) to reorganize; (*edificio*) to restore; (*appartamento*) to alter; (*crema, balsamo*) to repair

risucchi'are [risuk'kjare] *vt* to suck in

risul'tare *vi* (*dimostrarsi*) to prove (to be), turn out (to be); (*riuscire*): ~ **vincitore** to emerge as the winner; ~ **da** (*provenire*) to result from, be the result of; **mi risulta che ...** I understand that ...; **non mi risulta** not as far as I know; **risul'tato** *sm* result

risuo'nare *vi* (*rimbombare*) to resound

risurrezi'one [risurret'tsjone] *sf* (*Rel*) resurrection

risusci'tare [risuʃʃi'tare] *vt* to resuscitate, restore to life; (*fig*) to revive, bring back ▷ *vi* to rise (from the dead)

ris'veglio [riz'veʎʎo] *sm* waking up; (*fig*) revival

ris'volto *sm* (*di giacca*) lapel; (*di pantaloni*) turn-up; (*di manica*) cuff; (*di tasca*) flap; (*di libro*) inside flap; (*fig*) implication

ritagli'are [ritaʎ'ʎare] *vt* (*tagliar via*) to cut out

ritar'dare *vi* (*persona, treno*) to be late; (*orologio*) to be slow ▷ *vt* (*rallentare*) to slow down; (*impedire*) to delay, hold up; (*differire*) to postpone, delay

ri'tardo *sm* delay; (*di persona aspettata*) lateness *no pl*; (*di mentale*) backwardness; **in** ~ late; **il volo ha due ore di** ~ the flight is two hours late; **scusi il** ~ sorry I'm late

ri'tegno [ri'teɲɲo] *sm* restraint

rite'nere *vt* (*trattenere*) to hold back; (: *somma*) to deduct; (*giudicare*) to consider, believe

ri'tengo, ri'tenni *ecc vb vedi* **ritenere**

riterrò, ritiene *ecc vb vedi* **ritenere**

riti'rare *vt* to withdraw; (*Pol: richiamare*) to recall; (*andare a prendere: pacco ecc*) to collect, pick up; **ritirarsi** *vpr* to withdraw; (*da un'attività*) to retire; (*stoffa*) to shrink; (*marea*) to recede

'ritmo *sm* rhythm; (*fig*) rate; (: *della vita*) pace, tempo

'rito *sm* rite; **di** ~ usual, customary

ritoc'care *vt* (*disegno, fotografia*) to touch up; (*testo*) to alter

ritor'nare *vi* to return, go (*o come*)

back, to get back; (*ripresentarsi*) to recur; (*ridiventare*): **~ ricco** to become rich again ▷ vt (*restituire*) to return, give back; **quando ritorniamo?** when do we get back?

ritor'nello sm refrain

ri'torno sm return; **essere di ~** to be back; **avere un ~ di fiamma** (*Aut*) to backfire; (*fig: persona*) to be back in love again

ri'trarre vt (*trarre indietro, via*) to withdraw; (*distogliere: sguardo*) to turn away; (*rappresentare*) to portray, depict; (*ricavare*) to get, obtain

ritrat'tare vt (*disdire*) to retract, take back; (*trattare nuovamente*) to deal with again

ri'tratto, -a pp di **ritrarre** ▷ sm portrait

ritro'vare vt to find; (*salute*) to regain; (*persona*) to find; to meet again; **ritrovarsi** vpr (*essere, capitare*) to find o.s.; (*raccapezzarsi*) to find one's way; (*con senso reciproco*) to meet (again)

'ritto, -a ag (*in piedi*) standing, on one's feet; (*levato in alto*) erect, raised; (: *capelli*) standing on end; (*posto verticalmente*) upright

ritu'ale ag, sm ritual

riuni'one sf (*adunanza*) meeting; (*riconciliazione*) reunion

riu'nire vt (*ricongiungere*) to join (together); (*riconciliare*) to reunite, bring together (again); **riunirsi** vpr (*adunarsi*) to meet; (*tornare insieme*) to be reunited

riu'scire [riuʃʃire] vi (*uscire di nuovo*) to go out again, go back out; (*aver esito: fatti, azioni*) to go, turn out; (*aver successo*) to succeed, be successful; (*essere, apparire*) to be, prove; (*raggiungere il fine*) to manage, succeed; **~ a fare qc** to manage to do o succeed in doing o be able to do sth

'riva sf (*di fiume*) bank; (*di lago, mare*) shore

ri'vale sm/f rival; **rivalità** sf rivalry

rivalu'tare vt (*Econ*) to revalue

rive'dere vt to see again; (*ripassare*) to revise; (*verificare*) to check

rivedrò ecc vb vedi **rivedere**

rive'lare vt to reveal; (*divulgare*) to reveal, disclose; (*dare indizio*) to reveal, show; **rivelarsi** vpr (*manifestarsi*) to be revealed; **rivelarsi onesto** ecc to prove to be honest ecc; **rivelazi'one** sf revelation

rivendi'care vt to claim, demand

rivendi'tore, -'trice sm/f retailer; **rivenditore autorizzato** (*Comm*) authorized dealer

ri'verbero sm (*di luce, calore*) reflection; (*di suono*) reverberation

rivesti'mento sm covering; coating

rives'tire vt to dress again; (*ricoprire*) to cover; to coat; (*fig: carica*) to hold

ri'vidi ecc vb vedi **rivedere**

ri'vincita [ri'vintʃita] sf (*Sport*) return match; (*fig*) revenge

ri'vista sf review; (*periodico*) magazine, review; (*Teatro*) revue; variety show

ri'volgere [ri'vɔldʒere] vt (*attenzione, sguardo*) to turn, direct; (*parole*) to address; **rivolgersi** vpr to turn round; (*fig: dirigersi per informazioni*): **rivolgersi a** to go and see, go and speak to; (: *ufficio*) to enquire at

ri'volsi ecc vb vedi **rivolgere**

ri'volta sf revolt, rebellion

rivol'tella sf revolver

rivoluzio'nare [rivoluttsjo'nare] vt to revolutionize

rivoluzio'nario, -a [rivoluttsjo'narjo] ag, sm/f revolutionary

rivoluzi'one [rivolut'tsjone] sf revolution

riz'zare [rit'tsare] vt to raise, erect; **rizzarsi** vpr to stand up; (*capelli*) to stand on end

'roba sf stuff, things pl; (*possessi, beni*) belongings pl, things pl, possessions pl; **~ da mangiare** things pl to eat, food; **~ da matti** sheer madness o lunacy

'robot sm inv robot

ro'busto, -a ag robust, sturdy; (*solido: catena*) strong

roc'chetto [rok'ketto] sm reel, spool

'roccia, -ce ['rɔttʃa] sf rock; **fare ~** (*Sport*) to go rock climbing

'roco, -a, chi, che ag hoarse

ro'daggio [ro'daddʒo] sm running (BRIT) o breaking (US) in; **in ~** running (BRIT) o breaking (US)

rodi'tore sm (*Zool*) rodent

rodo'dendro sm rhododendron

ro'gnone [roɲ'ɲone] sm (*Cuc*) kidney

'rogo, -ghi sm (*per cadaveri*) (funeral) pyre; (*supplizio*): **il ~** the stake

rol'lio sm roll(ing)

'Roma sf Rome

Roma'nia sf **la ~** Romania

ro'manico, -a, -ci, -che ag Romanesque

ro'mano, -a ag, sm/f Roman

ro'mantico, -a, -ci, -che ag romantic

romanzi'ere [roman'dzjere] sm novelist

ro'manzo, -a [ro'mandzo] ag (*Ling*) romance cpd ▷ sm novel; **romanzo d'appendice** serial (story); **romanzo giallo/poliziesco** detective story; **romanzo rosa** romantic novel

'rombo sm rumble, thunder, roar; (*Mat*) rhombus; (*Zool*) turbot; brill

'rompere vt to break; (*fidanzamento*) to break off ▷ vi to break; **rompersi** vpr to break; **mi rompe le scatole** (*fam*) he (o she) is a pain in the neck; **rompersi un braccio** to break an arm; **mi si è rotta**

la macchina my car has broken down; **rompis'catole** (fam) sm/f inv pest, pain in the neck

'rondine sf (Zool) swallow

ron'zare [ron'dzare] vi to buzz, hum

ron'zio [ron'dzio] sm buzzing

'rosa sf rose ▷ ag inv, sm pink; **ro'sato, -a** ag pink, rosy ▷ sm (vino) rosé (wine)

rosicchi'are [rosik'kjare] vt to gnaw (at); (mangiucchiare) to nibble (at)

rosma'rino sm rosemary

roso'lare vt (Cuc) to brown

roso'lia sf (Med) German measles sg, rubella

ro'sone sm rosette; (vetrata) rose window

'rospo sm (Zool) toad

ros'setto sm (per labbra) lipstick

'rosso, -a ag, sm, sm/f red; **il mar R~** the Red Sea; **rosso d'uovo** egg yolk

rosticce'ria [rostitt∫e'ria] sf shop selling roast meat and other cooked food

ro'taia sf rut, track; (Ferr) rail

ro'tella sf small wheel; (di mobile) castor

roto'lare vt, vi to roll; **rotolarsi** vpr to roll (about)

'rotolo sm roll; **andare a rotoli** (fig) to go to rack and ruin

ro'tondo, -a ag round

'rotta sf (Aer, Naut) course, route; (Mil) rout; **a ~ di collo** at breakneck speed; **essere in ~ con qn** to be on bad terms with sb

rotta'mare vt to scrap

rottamazione [rottama'tsjone] sf (come incentivo) the scrapping of old vehicles in return for incentives

rot'tame sm fragment, scrap, broken bit; **rottami** smpl (di nave, aereo ecc) wreckage sg

'rotto, -a pp di **rompere** ▷ ag broken; (calzoni) torn, split; **per il ~ della cuffia** by the skin of one's teeth

rot'tura sf breaking no pl; break; breaking off; (Med) fracture, break

rou'lotte [ru'lɔt] sf caravan

ro'vente ag red-hot

'rovere sm oak

ro'vescia [ro'veʃʃa] sf **alla ~** upside-down; inside-out; **oggi mi va tutto alla ~** everything is going wrong (for me) today

rovesci'are [roveʃ'ʃare] vt (versare in giù) to pour; (: accidentalmente) to spill; (capovolgere) to turn upside down; (gettare a terra) to knock down; (: fig: governo) to overthrow; (piegare all'indietro: testa) to throw back; **rovesciarsi** vpr (sedia, macchina) to overturn; (barca) to capsize; (liquido) to spill; (fig: situazione) to be reversed

ro'vescio, -sci [ro'veʃʃo] sm other side, wrong side; (della mano) back; (di moneta) reverse; (pioggia) sudden downpour; (fig) setback; (Maglia: anche: **punto ~**) purl (stitch); (Tennis) backhand (stroke); **a ~** upside-down; inside-out; **capire qc a ~** to misunderstand sth

ro'vina sf ruin; **andare in ~** (andare a pezzi) to collapse; (fig) to go to rack and ruin; **rovine** sfpl (ruderi) ruins; **mandare in ~** to ruin

rovi'nare vi to collapse, fall down ▷ vt (danneggiare: fig) to ruin; **rovinarsi** vpr (persona) to ruin o.s.; (oggetto, vestito) to be ruined

rovis'tare vt (casa) to ransack; (tasche) to rummage in (o through)

'rovo sm (Bot) blackberry bush, bramble bush

'rozzo, -a ['roddzo] ag rough, coarse

ru'bare vt to steal; **~ qc a qn** to steal sth from sb; **mi hanno rubato il portafoglio** my wallet has been stolen

rubi'netto sm tap, faucet (US)

ru'bino sm ruby

ru'brica, -che sf (Stampa) column; (quadernetto) index book; address book; **rubrica d'indirizzi** address book; **rubrica telefonica** list of telephone numbers

'rudere sm (rovina) ruins pl

rudimen'tale ag rudimentary, basic

rudi'menti smpl rudiments; basic principles; basic knowledge sg

ruffi'ano sm pimp

'ruga, -ghe sf wrinkle

'ruggine ['ruddʒine] sf rust

rug'gire [rud'dʒire] vi to roar

rugi'ada [ru'dʒada] sf dew

ru'goso, -a ag wrinkled

rul'lino sm (Fot) spool; (: pellicola) film; **vorrei un ~ da 36 pose** I'd like a 36-exposure film

'rullo sm (di tamburi) roll; (arnese cilindrico, Tip) roller; **rullo compressore** steam roller; **rullo di pellicola** roll of film

rum sm rum

ru'meno, -a ag, sm/f, sm Romanian

rumi'nare vt (Zool) to ruminate

ru'more sm **un ~** a noise, a sound; **il ~** noise; **non riesco a dormire a causa del ~** I can't sleep for the noise; **rumo'roso, -a** ag noisy

> Attenzione! In inglese esiste la parola *rumour*, che però significa *voce* nel senso *diceria*.

ru'olo sm (Teatro: fig) role, part; (elenco) roll, register, list; **di ~** permanent, on the permanent staff

ru'ota sf wheel; **ruota anteriore/**

posteriore front/back wheel; **ruota di
scorta** spare wheel
ruo'tare vt, vi to rotate
'rupe sf cliff
'ruppi ecc vb vedi **rompere**
ru'rale ag rural, country cpd
ru'scello [ruʃʃello] sm stream
'ruspa sf excavator
rus'sare vi to snore
'Russia sf **la ~** Russia; **'russo, -a** ag, sm/f,
sm Russian
'rustico, -a, -ci, -che ag rustic; (fig) rough,
unrefined
rut'tare vi to belch; **'rutto** sm belch
'ruvido, -a ag rough, coarse

S

S. abbr (= sud) S; (= santo) St
sa vb vedi **sapere**
'sabato sm Saturday; **di** o **il ~** on Saturdays
'sabbia sf sand; **sabbie mobili**
quicksand(s); **sabbi'oso, -a** ag sandy
'sacca, -che sf bag; (bisaccia) haversack;
sacca da viaggio travelling bag
sacca'rina sf saccharin(e)
saccheggi'are [sakked'dʒare] vt to sack,
plunder
sac'chetto [sak'ketto] sm (small) bag,
(small) sack; **sacchetto di carta/di
plastica** paper/plastic bag
'sacco, -chi sm bag; (per carbone ecc) sack;
(Anat, Biol) sac; (tela) sacking; (saccheggio)
sack(ing); (fig: grande quantità): **un ~ di** lots
of, heaps of; **sacco a pelo** sleeping bag;
sacco per i rifiuti bin bag
sacer'dote [satʃer'dote] sm priest
sacrifi'care vt to sacrifice; **sacrificarsi**
vpr to sacrifice o.s.; (privarsi di qc) to make
sacrifices
sacri'ficio [sakri'fitʃo] sm sacrifice
'sacro, -a ag sacred
'sadico, -a, -ci, -che ag sadistic ▷ sm/f
sadist
sa'etta sf arrow; (fulmine) thunderbolt;
flash of lightning
sa'fari sm inv safari
sag'gezza [sad'dʒettsa] sf wisdom

'saggio, -a, -gi, -ge ['saddʒo] *ag* wise ▷ *sm* (*persona*) sage; (*esperimento*) test; (*fig: prova*) proof; (*campione*) sample; (*scritto*) essay

Sagit'tario [sadʒit'tarjo] *sm* Sagittarius

'sagoma *sf* (*profilo*) outline, profile; (*forma*) form, shape; (*Tecn*) template; (*bersaglio*) target; (*fig: persona*) character

'sagra *sf* festival

sagres'tano *sm* sacristan; sexton

sagres'tia *sf* sacristy

Sa'hara [sa'ara] *sm* **il (deserto del) ~** the Sahara (Desert)

'sai *vb vedi* **sapere**

'sala *sf* hall; (*stanza*) room; (*Cinema: Yyy: di proiezione*) cinema; **sala d'aspetto** waiting room; **sala da ballo** ballroom; **sala giochi** amusement arcade; **sala operatoria** operating theatre; **sala da pranzo** dining room; **sala per concerti** concert hall

sa'lame *sm* salami *no pl*, salami sausage

sala'moia *sf* (*Cuc*) brine

sa'lato, -a *ag* (*sapore*) salty; (*Cuc*) salted, salt *cpd*; (*fig: prezzo*) steep, stiff

sal'dare *vt* (*congiungere*) to join, bind; (*parti metalliche*) to solder; (: *con saldatura autogena*) to weld; (*conto*) to settle, pay

'saldo, -a *ag* (*resistente, forte*) strong, firm; (*fermo*) firm, steady, stable; (*fig*) firm, steadfast ▷ *sm* (*svendita*) sale; (*di conto*) settlement; (*Econ*) balance; **saldi** *smpl* (*Comm*) sales; **essere ~ nella propria fede** (*fig*) to stick to one's guns

'sale *sm* salt; (*fig*): **ha poco ~ in zucca** he doesn't have much sense; **sale fino** table salt; **sale grosso** cooking salt

'salgo *ecc vb vedi* **salire**

'salice ['salitʃe] *sm* willow; **salice piangente** weeping willow

sali'ente *ag* (*fig*) salient, main

sali'era *sf* salt cellar

sa'lire *vi* to go (*o come*) up; (*aereo ecc*) to climb, go up; (*passeggero*) to get on; (*sentiero, prezzi, livello*) to go up, rise ▷ *vt* (*scale, gradini*) to go (*o come*) up; **~ su** to climb (up); **~ sul treno/sull'autobus** to board the train/the bus; **~ in macchina** to get into the car; **sa'lita** *sf* climb, ascent; (*erta*) hill, slope; **in salita** *ag, av* uphill

sa'liva *sf* saliva

'salma *sf* corpse

'salmo *sm* psalm

sal'mone *sm* salmon

sa'lone *sm* (*stanza*) sitting room, lounge; (*in albergo*) lounge; (*su nave*) lounge, saloon; (*mostra*) show, exhibition; **salone di bellezza** beauty salon

sa'lotto *sm* lounge, sitting room; (*mobilio*) lounge suite

sal'pare *vi* (*Naut*) to set sail; (*anche: ~ l'ancora*) to weigh anchor

'salsa *sf* (*Cuc*) sauce; **salsa di pomodoro** tomato sauce

sal'siccia, -ce [sal'sittʃa] *sf* pork sausage

sal'tare *vi* to jump, leap; (*esplodere*) to blow up, explode; (: *valvola*) to blow; (*venir via*) to pop off; (*non aver luogo: corso ecc*) to be cancelled ▷ *vt* to jump (over), leap (over); (*fig: pranzo, capitolo*) to skip, miss (out); (*Cuc*) to sauté; **far ~** to blow up; to burst open; **~ fuori** (*fig: apparire all'improvviso*) to turn up

saltel'lare *vi* to skip; to hop

'salto *sm* jump; (*Sport*) jumping; **fare un ~** to jump, leap; **fare un ~ da qn** to pop over to sb's (place); **salto in alto/lungo** high/long jump; **salto con l'asta** pole vaulting; **salto mortale** somersault

saltu'ario, -a *ag* occasional, irregular

sa'lubre *ag* healthy, salubrious

salume'ria *sf* delicatessen

sa'lumi *smpl* salted pork meats

salu'tare *ag* healthy; (*fig*) salutary, beneficial ▷ *vt* (*incontrandosi*) to greet; (*congedandosi*) to say goodbye to; (*Mil*) to salute

sa'lute *sf* health; **~!** (*a chi starnutisce*) bless you!; (*nei brindisi*) cheers!; **bere alla ~ di qn** to drink (to) sb's health

sa'luto *sm* (*gesto*) wave; (*parola*) greeting; (*Mil*) salute

salvada'naio *sm* money box, piggy bank

salva'gente [salva'dʒɛnte] *sm* (*Naut*) lifebuoy; (*ciambella*) life belt; (*giubbotto*) life jacket; (*stradale*) traffic island

salvaguar'dare *vt* to safeguard

sal'vare *vt* to save; (*trarre da un pericolo*) to rescue; (*proteggere*) to protect; **salvarsi** *vpr* to save o.s.; to escape; **salvaschermo** [salvas'kermo] *sm* (*Inform*) screen saver; **salvaslip** [salva'zlip] *sm inv* panty liner; **salva'taggio** *sm* rescue

'salve (*fam*) *escl* hi!

'salvia *sf* (*Bot*) sage

salvi'etta *sf* napkin; **salvietta umidificata** baby wipe

'salvo, -a *ag* safe, unhurt, unharmed; (*fuori pericolo*) safe, out of danger ▷ *sm* **in ~ safe** ▷ *prep* (*eccetto*) except; **mettere qc in ~** to put sth in a safe place; **~ che** (*a meno che*) unless; (*eccetto che*) except (that); **~ imprevisti** barring accidents

sam'buco *sm* elder (tree)

'sandalo *sm* (*Bot*) sandalwood; (*calzatura*) sandal

'sangue *sm* blood; **farsi cattivo ~** to fret, get in a state; **sangue freddo** (*fig*) sang-froid, calm; **a ~ freddo** in cold blood;

sangui'nare vi to bleed

sanità sf health; (salubrità) healthiness; **Ministero della S~** Department of Health; **sanità mentale** sanity

sani'tario, -a ag health cpd; (condizioni) sanitary ▷ sm (Amm) doctor; **sanitari** smpl (impianti) bathroom o sanitary fittings

'sanno vb vedi **sapere**

'sano, -a ag healthy; (denti, costituzione) healthy, sound; (integro) whole, unbroken; (fig: politica, consigli) sound; **~ di mente** sane; **di sana pianta** completely, entirely; **~ e salvo** safe and sound

'santo, -a ag holy; (fig) saintly; (seguito da nome proprio) saint ▷ sm/f saint; **la Santa Sede** the Holy See

santu'ario sm sanctuary

sanzi'one [san'tsjone] sf sanction; (penale, civile) sanction, penalty

sa'pere vt to know; (essere capace di): **so nuotare** I know how to swim, I can swim ▷ vi **~ di** (aver sapore) to taste of; (aver odore) to smell of ▷ sm knowledge; **far ~ qc a qn** to inform sb about sth, let sb know sth; **mi sa che non sia vero** I don't think that's true; **non lo so** I don't know; **non so l'inglese** I don't speak English; **sa dove posso...?** do you know where I can ...?

sa'pone sm soap; **sapone da bucato** washing soap

sa'pore sm taste, flavour; **sapo'rito, -a** ag tasty

sappi'amo vb vedi **sapere**

saprò ecc vb vedi **sapere**

sarà ecc vb vedi **essere**

saraci'nesca [saratʃi'neska] sf (serranda) rolling shutter

sar'castico, -a, ci, che ag sarcastic

Sar'degna [sar'deɲɲa] sf **la ~** Sardinia

sar'dina sf sardine

sa'rei ecc vb vedi **essere**

SARS sigla f (Med: = severe acute respiratory syndrome) SARS

'sarta sf vedi **sarto**

'sarto, -a sm/f tailor/dressmaker

'sasso sm stone; (ciottolo) pebble; (masso) rock

sas'sofono sm saxophone

sas'soso, -a ag stony; pebbly

'Satana sm Satan

sa'tellite sm, ag satellite

'satira sf satire

'sauna sf sauna

sazi'are [sat'tsjare] vt to satisfy, satiate; **saziarsi** vpr **saziarsi (di)** to eat one's fill (of); (fig): **saziarsi di** to grow tired o weary of

'sazio, -a ['sattsjo] ag **~ (di)** sated (with), full (of); (fig: stufo) fed up (with), sick (of);

sono ~ I'm full (up)

sba'dato, -a ag careless, inattentive

sbadigli'are [zbadiʎ'ʎare] vi to yawn; **sba'diglio** sm yawn

sbagli'are [zbaʎ'ʎare] vt to make a mistake in, get wrong ▷ vi to make a mistake, be mistaken, be wrong; (operare in modo non giusto) to err; **sbagliarsi** vpr to make a mistake, be mistaken, be wrong; **~ strada/la mira** to take the wrong road/ miss one's aim

sbagli'ato, -a [zbaʎ'ʎato] ag (gen) wrong; (compito) full of mistakes; (conclusione) erroneous

'sbaglio sm mistake, error; (morale) error; **fare uno ~** to make a mistake

sbalor'dire vt to stun, amaze ▷ vi to be stunned, be amazed

sbal'zare [zbal'tsare] vt to throw, hurl ▷ vi (balzare) to bounce; (saltare) to leap, bound

sban'dare vi (Naut) to list; (Aer) to bank; (Aut) to skid

sba'raglio [zba'raʎʎo] sm rout; defeat; **gettarsi allo ~** to risk everything

sbaraz'zarsi [zbarat'tsarsi] vpr **~ di** to get rid of, rid o.s. of

sbar'care vt (passeggeri) to disembark; (merci) to unload ▷ vi to disembark

'sbarra sf bar; (di passaggio a livello) barrier; (Dir): **presentarsi alla ~** to appear before the court

sbar'rare vt (strada ecc) to block, bar; (assegno) to cross; **~ il passo** to bar the way; **~ gli occhi** to open one's eyes wide

'sbattere vt (porta) to slam, bang; (tappeti, ali, Cuc) to beat; (urtare) to knock, hit ▷ vi (porta, finestra) to bang; (agitarsi: ali, vele ecc) to flap; **me ne sbatto!** (fam) I don't give a damn!

sba'vare vi to dribble; (colore) to smear, smudge

'sberla sf slap

sbia'dire vi, vt to fade; **sbia'dito, -a** ag faded; (fig) colourless, dull

sbian'care vt to whiten; (tessuto) to bleach ▷ vi (impallidire) to grow pale o white

sbirci'ata [zbir'tʃata] sf **dare una ~ a qc** to glance at sth, have a look at sth

sbloc'care vt to unblock, free; (freno) to release; (prezzi, affitti) to decontrol; **sbloccarsi** vpr (gen) to become unblocked; (passaggio, strada) to clear, become unblocked

sboc'care vi **~ in** (fiume) to flow into; (strada) to lead into; (persona) to come (out) into; (fig: concludersi) to end (up) in

sboc'cato, -a ag (persona) foul-mouthed; (linguaggio) foul

sbocci'are [zbot'tʃare] vi (fiore) to bloom,

open (out)

sbol'lire vi (fig) to cool down, calm down

'sbornia (fam) sf **prendersi una ~** to get plastered

sbor'sare vt (denaro) to pay out

sbot'tare vi **~ in una risata/per la collera** to burst out laughing/explode with anger

sbotto'nare vt to unbutton, undo

sbrai'tare vi to yell, bawl

sbra'nare vt to tear to pieces

sbricio'lare [zbritʃo'lare] vt to crumble; **sbriciolarsi** vpr to crumble

sbri'gare vt to deal with; **sbrigarsi** vpr to hurry (up)

'sbronza ['zbrontsa] (fam) sf (ubriaco): **prendersi una ~** to get plastered

bron'zarsi [zbron'tsarsi] vpr (fam) to get sozzled

'sbronzo, -a ['zbrontso] (fam) ag plastered

sbruf'fone, -a sm/f boaster

sbu'care vi to come out, emerge; (improvvisamente) to pop out (o up)

sbucci'are [zbut'tʃare] vt (arancia, patata) to peel; (piselli) to shell; **sbucciarsi un ginocchio** to graze one's knee

sbucherò ecc [zbuke'rɔ] vb vedi **sbucare**

sbuf'fare vi (persona, cavallo) to snort; (ansimare) to puff, pant; (treno) to puff

sca'broso, -a ag (fig: difficile) difficult, thorny; (: imbarazzante) embarrassing; (: sconcio) indecent

scacchi smpl (gioco) chess sg; **a ~** (tessuto) check(ed)

scacchi'era [skak'kjɛra] sf chessboard

scacci'are [skat'tʃare] vt to chase away o out, drive away o out

'scaddi ecc vb vedi **scadere**

sca'dente ag shoddy, of poor quality

sca'denza [ska'dɛntsa] sf (di cambiale, contratto) maturity; (di passaporto) expiry date; **a breve/lunga ~** short-/long-term; **data di ~** expiry date

sca'dere vi (contratto ecc) to expire; (debito) to fall due; (valore, forze, peso) to decline, go down

sca'fandro sm (di palombaro) diving suit; (di astronauta) space-suit

scaf'fale sm shelf; (mobile) set of shelves

'scafo sm (Naut, Aer) hull

scagio'nare [skadʒo'nare] vt to exonerate, free from blame

'scaglia ['skaʎʎa] sf (Zool) scale; (scheggia) chip, flake

scagli'are [skaʎ'ʎare] vt (lanciare: anche fig) to hurl, fling; **scagliarsi** (anche: **vr**): **scagliarsi su** o **contro** to hurl o fling o.s. at; (fig) to rail at

'scala sf (a gradini ecc) staircase, stairs pl;

(a pioli, di corda) ladder; (Mus, Geo, di colori, valori, fig) scale; **scale** sfpl (scalinata) stairs; **su vasta ~/~ ridotta** on a large/small scale; **~ mobile (dei salari)** index-linked pay scale; **scala a libretto** stepladder; **scala mobile** escalator; (Econ) sliding scale

● **Scala**
●
● Milan's world-famous **la Scala** theatre
● first opened its doors in 1778 with a
● performance of Salieri's opera, "L'Europa
● riconosciuta". It suffered serious
● damage in the bombing of Milan in 1943
● and reopened in 1946 with a concert
● conducted by Toscanini. It also has a
● famous classical dance school.

sca'lare vt (Alpinismo, muro) to climb, scale; (debito) to scale down, reduce

scalda'bagno [skalda'baɲɲo] sm water-heater

scal'dare vt to heat; **scaldarsi** vpr to warm up, heat up; (al fuoco, al sole) to warm o.s.; (fig) to get excited

scal'fire vt to scratch

scali'nata sf staircase

sca'lino sm (anche fig) step; (di scala a pioli) rung

'scalo sm (Naut) slipway; (: porto d'approdo) port of call; (Aer) stopover; **fare ~ (a)** (Naut) to call (at), put in (at); (Aer) to land (at), make a stop (at); **scalo merci** (Ferr) goods (BRIT) o freight yard

scalop'pina sf (Cuc) escalope

scal'pello sm chisel

scal'pore sm noise, row; **far ~** (notizia) to cause a sensation o a stir

'scaltro, -a ag cunning, shrewd

'scalzo, -a ['skaltso] ag barefoot

scambi'are vt to exchange; (confondere): **~ qn/qc per** to take o mistake sb/sth for; **mi hanno scambiato il cappello** they've given me the wrong hat; **scambiarsi** vpr (auguri, confidenze, visite) to exchange; **~ qn/qc per** (confondere) to mistake sth/sb for

'scambio sm exchange; (Ferr) points pl; **fare (uno) ~** to make a swap

scampa'gnata [skampaɲ'ɲata] sf trip to the country

scam'pare vt (salvare) to rescue, save; (evitare: morte, prigione) to escape ▷ vi **~ (a qc)** to survive (sth), escape (sth); **scamparla bella** to have a narrow escape

'scampo sm (salvezza) escape; (Zool) prawn; **cercare ~ nella fuga** to seek safety in flight

'scampolo sm remnant

scanala'tura *sf (incavo)* channel, groove
scandagli'are [skanda'ʎʎare] *vt (Naut)* to
sound; *(fig)* to sound out; to probe
scandaliz'zare [skandalid'dzare] *vt* to
shock, scandalize; **scandalizzarsi** *vpr* to
be shocked
'scandalo *sm* scandal
Scandi'navia *sf* **la ~** Scandinavia;
scandi'navo, -a *ag, sm/f* Scandinavian
scanner ['skanner] *sm inv (Inform)* scanner
scansafa'tiche [skansafa'tike] *sm/f inv*
idler, loafer
scan'sare *vt (rimuovere)* to move (aside),
shift; *(schivare: schiaffo)* to dodge; *(sfuggire)*
to avoid; **scansarsi** *vpr* to move aside
scan'sia *sf* shelves *pl*; *(per libri)* bookcase
'scanso *sm* **a ~ di** in order to avoid, as a
precaution against
scanti'nato *sm* basement
scapacci'one [skapat'tʃone] *sm* clout
scapes'trato, -a *ag* dissolute
'scapola *sf* shoulder blade
'scapolo *sm* bachelor
scappa'mento *sm (Aut)* exhaust
scap'pare *vi (fuggire)* to escape; *(andare
via in fretta)* to rush off; **lasciarsi ~
un'occasione** to let an opportunity go by;
~ di prigione to escape from prison; **~ di
mano** *(oggetto)* to slip out of one's hands; **~
di mente a qn** to slip sb's mind; **mi scappò
detto** I let it slip; **scappa'toia** *sf* way out
scara'beo *sm* beetle
scarabocchi'are [skarabok'kjare] *vt*
to scribble, scrawl; **scara'bocchio** *sm*
scribble, scrawl
scara'faggio [skara'faddʒo] *sm*
cockroach
scaraman'zia [skaraman'tsia] *sf* **per ~**
for luck
scaraven'tare *vt* to fling, hurl;
scaraventarsi *vpr* to fling o.s.
scarce'rare [skartʃe'rare] *vt* to release
(from prison)
scardi'nare *vt* **~ una porta** to take a door
off its hinges
scari'care *vt (merci, camion ecc)* to unload;
(passeggeri) to set down, put off; *(arma)*
to unload; *(: sparare, Elettr)* to discharge;
(corso d'acqua) to empty, pour; *(fig: liberare
da un peso)* to unburden, relieve; *(da
Internet)* to download; **scaricarsi** *vpr
(orologio)* to run o wind down; *(batteria,
accumulatore)* to go flat o dead; *(fig:
rilassarsi)* to unwind; *(: sfogarsi)* to let off
steam
'scarico, -a, -chi, -che *ag* unloaded;
(orologio) run down; *(accumulatore)* dead,
flat ▷ *sm (di merci, materiali)* unloading; *(di
immondizie)* dumping, tipping *(BRIT)*; *(Tecn:*

deflusso) draining; *(: dispositivo)* drain; *(Aut)*
exhaust
scarlat'tina *sf* scarlet fever
scar'latto, -a *ag* scarlet
'scarpa *sf* shoe; **scarpe da ginnastica/
tennis** gym/tennis shoes
scar'pata *sf* escarpment
scarpi'era *sf* shoe rack
scar'pone *sm* boot; **scarponi da
montagna** climbing boots; **scarponi da
sci** ski-boots
scarseggi'are [skarsed'dʒare] *vi* to be
scarce; **~ di** to be short of, lack
'scarso, -a *ag (insufficiente)* insufficient,
meagre; *(povero: annata)* poor, lean; *(Ins:
voto)* poor; **~ di** lacking in; **3 chili scarsi** just
under 3 kilos, barely 3 kilos
scar'tare *vt (pacco)* to unwrap; *(idea)* to
reject; *(Mil)* to declare unfit for military
service; *(carte da gioco)* to discard; *(Calcio)*
to dodge (past) ▷ *vi* to swerve
'scarto *sm (cosa scartata: anche Comm)*
reject; *(di veicolo)* swerve; *(differenza)* gap,
difference
scassi'nare *vt* to break, force
scate'nare *vt (fig)* to incite, stir up;
scatenarsi *vpr (temporale)* to break;
(rivolta) to break out; *(persona: infuriarsi)*
to rage
'scatola *sf* box; *(di latta)* tin *(BRIT)*, can; **cibi
in ~** tinned *(BRIT)* o canned foods; **scatola
cranica** cranium; **scato'lone** *sm* (big) box
scat'tare *vt (fotografia)* to take ▷ *vi
(congegno, molla ecc)* to be released;
(balzare) to spring up; *(Sport)* to put on a
spurt; *(fig: per l'ira)* to fly into a rage; **~ in
piedi** to spring to one's feet
'scatto *sm (dispositivo)* release; *(: di arma da
fuoco)* trigger mechanism; *(rumore)* click;
(balzo) jump, start; *(Sport)* spurt; *(fig: di
ira ecc)* fit; *(: di stipendio)* increment; **di ~**
suddenly
scaval'care *vt (ostacolo)* to pass *(o* climb)
over; *(fig)* to get ahead of, overtake
sca'vare *vt (terreno)* to dig; *(legno)* to
hollow out; *(pozzo, galleria)* to bore; *(città
sepolta ecc)* to excavate
'scavo *sm* excavating *no pl*; excavation
'scegliere ['ʃeʎʎere] *vt* to choose, select
sce'icco, -chi [ʃe'ikko] *sm* sheik
'scelgo *ecc* ['ʃelgo] *vb vedi* **scegliere**
scel'lino [ʃel'lino] *sm* shilling
'scelta ['ʃelta] *sf* choice; selection; **di
prima ~** top grade o quality; **frutta o
formaggi a ~** choice of fruit or cheese
'scelto, -a ['ʃelto] *pp di* **scegliere** ▷ *ag
(gruppo)* carefully selected; *(frutta, verdura)*
choice, top quality; *(Mil: specializzato)* crack
cpd, highly skilled

'scemo, -a ['ʃemo] *ag* stupid, silly

'scena ['ʃɛna] *sf* (*gen*) scene; (*palcoscenico*) stage; **le scene** (*fig: teatro*) the stage; **fare una ~** to make a scene; **andare in ~** to be staged *o* put on *o* performed; **mettere in ~** to stage

sce'nario [ʃe'narjo] *sm* scenery; (*di film*) scenario

sce'nata [ʃe'nata] *sf* row, scene

'scendere ['ʃendere] *vi* to go (*o* come) down; (*strada, sole*) to go down; (*notte*) to fall; (*passeggero: fermarsi*) to get out, alight; (*fig: temperatura, prezzi*) to go *o* come down, fall, drop ▷ *vt* (*scale, pendio*) to go (*o* come) down; **~ dalle scale** to go (*o* come) down the stairs; **~ dal treno** to get off *o* out of the train; **dove devo ~?** where do I get off?; **~ dalla macchina** to get out of the car; **~ da cavallo** to dismount, to get off one's horse

sceneggi'ato [ʃened'dʒato] *sm* television drama

'scettico, -a, -ci, -che ['ʃettiko] *ag* sceptical

'scettro ['ʃettro] *sm* sceptre

'scheda ['skɛda] *sf* (*index*) card; **scheda elettorale** ballot paper; **scheda ricaricabile** (*Tel*) top-up card; **scheda telefonica** phone card; **sche'dario** *sm* file; (*mobile*) filing cabinet

sche'dina [ske'dina] *sf* ≈ pools coupon (BRIT)

'scheggia, -ge ['skeddʒa] *sf* splinter, sliver

'scheletro ['skɛletro] *sm* skeleton

'schema, -i ['skɛma] *sm* (*diagramma*) diagram, sketch; (*progetto, abbozzo*) outline, plan

'scherma ['skerma] *sf* fencing

scher'maglia [sker'maʎʎa] *sf* (*fig*) skirmish

'schermo ['skermo] *sm* shield, screen; (*Cinema, TV*) screen

scher'nire [sker'nire] *vt* to mock, sneer at

scher'zare [sker'tsare] *vi* to joke

'scherzo ['skertso] *sm* joke; (*tiro*) trick; (*Mus*) scherzo; **è uno ~!** (*una cosa facile*) it's child's play!, it's easy!; **per ~** in jest; for a joke *o* a laugh; **fare un brutto ~ a qn** to play a nasty trick on sb

schiaccia'noci [skjattʃa'notʃi] *sm inv* nutcracker

schiacci'are [skjat'tʃare] *vt* (*dito*) to crush; (*noci*) to crack; **~ un pisolino** to have a nap; **schiacciarsi** *vpr* (*appiattirsi*) to get squashed; (*frantumarsi*) to get crushed

schiaffeggi'are [skjaffed'dʒare] *vt* to slap

schi'affo ['skjaffo] *sm* slap

schiantarsi *vpr* to break (up), shatter

schia'rire [skja'rire] *vt* to lighten, make lighter; **schiarirsi** *vpr* to grow lighter; (*tornar sereno*) to clear, brighten up; **schiarirsi la voce** to clear one's throat

schiavitù [skjavi'tu] *sf* slavery

schi'avo, -a ['skjavo] *sm/f* slave

schi'ena ['skjɛna] *sf* (*Anat*) back; **schie'nale** *sm* (*di sedia*) back

schi'era ['skjɛra] *sf* (*Mil*) rank; (*gruppo*) group, band

schiera'mento [skjera'mento] *sm* (*Mil*, *Sport*) formation; (*fig*) alliance

schie'rare [skje'rare] *vt* (*esercito*) to line up, draw up, marshal; **schierarsi** *vpr* to line up; (*fig*): **schierarsi con** *o* **dalla parte di/contro qn** to side with/oppose sb

'schifo ['skifo] *sm* disgust; **fare ~** (*essere fatto male, dare pessimi risultati*) to be awful; **mi fa ~** it makes me sick, it's disgusting; **quel libro è uno ~** that book's rotten; **schi'foso, -a** *ag* disgusting, revolting; (*molto scadente*) rotten, lousy

schioc'care [skjok'kare] *vt* (*frusta*) to crack; (*dita*) to snap; (*lingua*) to click; **~ le labbra** to smack one's lips

schiudersi *vpr* to open

schi'uma ['skjuma] *sf* foam; (*di sapone*) lather; (*di latte*) froth; (*fig: feccia*) scum

schi'vare [ski'vare] *vt* to dodge, avoid

'schivo, -a ['skivo] *ag* (*ritroso*) stand-off-ish, reserved; (*timido*) shy

schiz'zare [skit'tsare] *vt* (*spruzzare*) to spurt, squirt; (*sporcare*) to splash, spatter; (*fig: abbozzare*) to sketch ▷ *vi* to spurt, squirt; (*saltar fuori*) to dart up (*o* off *ecc*)

schizzi'noso, -a [skittsi'noso] *ag* fussy, finicky

'schizzo ['skittso] *sm* (*di liquido*) spurt; splash, spatter; (*abbozzo*) sketch

sci [ʃi] *sm* (*attrezzo*) ski; (*attività*) skiing; **sci d'acqua** water-skiing; **sci di fondo** cross-country skiing, ski touring (US); **sci nautico** water-skiing

'scia ['ʃia] (*pl* **scie**) *sf* (*di imbarcazione*) wake; (*di profumo*) trail

scià [ʃa] *sm inv* shah

sci'abola ['ʃabola] *sf* sabre

scia'callo [ʃa'kallo] *sm* jackal

sciac'quare [ʃak'kware] *vt* to rinse

scia'gura [ʃa'gura] *sf* disaster, calamity; misfortune

scialac'quare [ʃalak'kware] *vt* to squander

sci'albo, -a ['ʃalbo] *ag* pale, dull; (*fig*) dull, colourless

sci'alle ['ʃalle] *sm* shawl

scia'luppa [ʃa'luppa] *sf*; **scialuppa di salvataggio** lifeboat

sci'ame ['ʃame] *sm* swarm

sci'are [ʃi'are] *vi* to ski

sci'arpa [ˈʃarpa] sf scarf; (fascia) sash

scia'tore, -'trice [ʃiaˈtore] sm/f skier

sci'atto, -a [ˈʃatto] ag (persona) slovenly, unkempt

scien'tifico, -a, -ci, -che [ʃenˈtifiko] ag scientific

sci'enza [ˈʃɛntsa] sf science; (sapere) knowledge; **scienze** sfpl (Ins) science sg; **scienze naturali** natural sciences; **scienzi'ato, -a** sm/f scientist

'scimmia [ˈʃimmja] sf monkey

scimpanzé [ʃimpanˈtse] sm inv chimpanzee

scin'tilla [ʃinˈtilla] sf spark; **scintil'lare** vi to spark; (acqua, occhi) to sparkle

scioc'chezza [ʃokˈkettsa] sf stupidity no pl; stupid o foolish thing; **dire sciocchezze** to talk nonsense

sci'occo, -a, -chi, -che [ˈʃokko] ag stupid, foolish

sci'ogliere [ˈʃɔʎʎere] vt (nodo) to untie; (capelli) to loosen; (persona, animale) to untie, release; (fig: persona): **~ da** to release from; (neve) to melt; (nell'acqua: zucchero ecc) to solve; (fig: mistero) to solve; (porre fine a: contratto) to cancel; (: società, matrimonio) to dissolve; (: riunione) to bring to an end; **sciogliersi** vpr to loosen, come untied; to melt; to dissolve; (assemblea ecc) to break up; **~ i muscoli** to limber up; **scioglilingua** [ʃoʎʎiˈlingwa] sm inv tongue-twister

sci'olgo ecc [ˈʃɔlgo] vb vedi **sciogliere**

sci'olto, -a [ˈʃɔlto] pp di **sciogliere** ▷ ag loose; (agile) agile, nimble; supple; (disinvolto) free and easy; **versi sciolti** (Poesia) blank verse

sciope'rare [ʃopeˈrare] vi to strike, go on strike

sci'opero [ˈʃopero] sm strike; **fare ~** to strike; **sciopero bianco** work-to-rule (BRIT), slowdown (US); **sciopero selvaggio** wildcat strike; **sciopero a singhiozzo** on-off strike

scio'via [ʃioˈvia] sf ski lift

scip'pare [ʃipˈpare] vt **~ qn** to snatch sb's bag; **mi hanno scippato** they snatched my bag

sci'rocco [ʃiˈrɔkko] sm sirocco

sci'roppo [ʃiˈrɔppo] sm syrup

'scisma, -i [ˈʃizma] sm (Rel) schism

scissi'one [ʃisˈsjone] sf (anche fig) split, division; (Fisica) fission

sciu'pare [ʃuˈpare] vt (abito, libro, appetito) to spoil, ruin; (tempo, denaro) to waste

scivo'lare [ʃivoˈlare] vi to slide o glide along; (involontariamente) to slip, slide; **'scivolo** sm slide; (Tecn) chute; **scivo'loso, -a** ag slippery

scle'rosi sf sclerosis

scoc'care vt (freccia) to shoot ▷ vi (guizzare) to shoot up; (battere: ora) to strike

scoccherò ecc [skokkeˈrɔ] vb vedi **scoccare**

scocci'are [skotˈtʃare] (fam) vt to bother, annoy; **scocciarsi** vpr to be bothered o annoyed

sco'della sf bowl

scodinzo'lare [skodintsoˈlare] vi to wag its tail

scogli'era [skoʎˈʎera] sf reef; cliff

'scoglio [ˈskɔʎʎo] sm (al mare) rock

scoi'attolo sm squirrel

scola'pasta sm inv colander

scolapi'atti sm inv drainer (for plates)

sco'lare ag **età scolare** school age ▷ vt to drain ▷ vi to drip

scola'resca sf schoolchildren pl, pupils pl

sco'laro, -a sm/f pupil, schoolboy/girl

> Attenzione! In inglese esiste la parola *scholar*, che però significa *studioso*.

sco'lastico, -a, -ci, -che ag school cpd; scholastic

scol'lato, -a ag (vestito) low-cut, low-necked; (donna) wearing a low-cut dress (o blouse ecc)

scolla'tura sf neckline

scolle'gare vt (fili, apparecchi) to disconnect

'scolo sm drainage

scolo'rire vt to fade; to discolour; **scolorirsi** vpr to fade; to become discoloured; (impallidire) to turn pale

scol'pire vt to carve, sculpt

scombusso'lare vt to upset

scom'messa sf bet, wager

scom'mettere vt, vi to bet

scomo'dare vt to trouble, bother; to disturb; **scomodarsi** vpr to put o.s. out; **scomodarsi a fare** to go to the bother o trouble of doing

'scomodo, -a ag uncomfortable; (sistemazione, posto) awkward, inconvenient

scompa'rire vi (sparire) to disappear, vanish; (fig) to be insignificant

scomparti'mento sm compartment; **uno ~ per non-fumatori** a non-smoking compartment

scompigli'are [skompiʎˈʎare] vt (cassetto, capelli) to mess up, disarrange; (fig: piani) to upset

scomuni'care vt to excommunicate

'sconcio, -a, -ci, -ce [ˈskontʃo] ag (osceno) indecent, obscene ▷ sm disgrace

scon'figgere [skonˈfiddʒere] vt to defeat, overcome

sconfi'nare vi to cross the border; (in proprietà privata) to trespass; (fig): **~ da** to

stray o digress from
scon'fitta sf defeat
scon'forto sm despondency
sconge'lare [skondʒe'lare] vt to defrost
scongiu'rare [skondʒu'rare] vt (implorare) to entreat, beseech, implore; (eludere: pericolo) to ward off, avert; **scongi'uro** sm entreaty; (esorcismo) exorcism; **fare gli scongiuri** to touch wood (BRIT), knock on wood (US)
scon'nesso, -a ag incoherent
sconosci'uto, -a [skonoʃ'ʃuto] ag unknown; new, strange ▷ sm/f stranger; unknown person
sconsigli'are [skonsiʎ'ʎare] vt **~ qc a qn** to advise sb against sth; **~ qn dal fare qc** to advise sb not to do o against doing sth
sconso'lato, -a ag inconsolable; desolate
scon'tare vt (Comm: detrarre) to deduct; (: debito) to pay off; (: cambiale) to discount; (pena) to serve; (colpa, errori) to pay for, suffer for
scon'tato, -a ag (previsto) foreseen, taken for granted; **dare per ~ che** to take it for granted that
scon'tento, -a ag **~ (di)** dissatisfied (with) ▷ sm dissatisfaction
'sconto sm discount; **fare uno ~** to give a discount; **ci sono sconti per studenti?** are there discounts for students?
scon'trarsi vpr (treni ecc) to crash, collide; (venire ad uno scontro, fig) to clash; **~ con** to crash into, collide with
scon'trino sm ticket; (di cassa) receipt; **potrei avere lo ~ per favore?** can I have a receipt, please?
'scontro sm clash, encounter; crash, collision
scon'troso, -a ag sullen, surly; (permaloso) touchy
sconveni'ente ag unseemly, improper
scon'volgere [skon'vɔldʒere] vt to throw into confusion, upset; (turbare) to shake, disturb, upset; **scon'volto, -a** pp di **sconvolgere**
scooter ['skuter] sm inv scooter
'scopa sf broom; (Carte) Italian card game; **sco'pare** vt to sweep
sco'perta sf discovery
sco'perto, -a pp di **scoprire** ▷ ag uncovered; (capo) uncovered, bare; (macchina) open; (Mil) exposed, without cover; (conto) overdrawn
'scopo sm aim, purpose; **a che ~?** what for?
scoppi'are vi (spaccarsi) to burst; (esplodere) to explode; (fig) to break out; **~ in pianto** o **a piangere** to burst out crying;

~ dalle risa o **dal ridere** to split one's sides laughing
scoppiet'tare vi to crackle
'scoppio sm explosion; (di tuono, arma ecc) crash, bang; (fig: di risa, ira) fit, outburst; (: di guerra) outbreak; **a ~ ritardato** delayed-action
sco'prire vt to discover; (liberare da ciò che copre) to uncover; (: monumento) to unveil; **scoprirsi** vpr to put on lighter clothes; (fig) to give o.s. away
scoraggi'are [skorad'dʒare] vt to discourage; **scoraggiarsi** vpr to become discouraged, lose heart
scorcia'toia [skortʃa'toja] sf short cut
'scorcio ['skortʃo] sm (Arte) foreshortening; (di secolo, periodo) end, close; **scorcio panoramico** vista
scor'dare vt to forget; **scordarsi** vpr **scordarsi di qc/di fare** to forget sth/to do
'scorgere ['skɔrdʒere] vt to make out, distinguish, see
scorpacci'ata [skorpat'tʃata] sf **fare una ~ (di)** to stuff o.s. (with), eat one's fill (of)
scorpi'one sm scorpion; (dello zodiaco): **S~** Scorpio
'scorrere vt (giornale, lettera) to run o skim through ▷ vi (liquido, fiume) to run, flow; (fune) to run; (cassetto, porta) to slide easily; (tempo) to pass (by)
scor'retto, -a ag incorrect; (sgarbato) impolite; (sconveniente) improper
scor'revole ag (porta) sliding; (fig: stile) fluent, flowing
'scorsi ecc vb vedi **scorgere**
'scorso, -a pp di **scorrere** ▷ ag last
scor'soio, -a ag **nodo ~** noose
'scorta sf (di personalità, convoglio) escort; (provvista) supply, stock
scor'tese ag discourteous, rude
'scorza ['skɔrdza] sf (di albero) bark; (di agrumi) peel, skin
sco'sceso, -a [skoʃ'ʃeso] ag steep
'scossa sf jerk, jolt, shake; (Elettr: fig) shock; **scossa di terremoto** earth tremor
'scosso, -a pp di **scuotere** ▷ ag (turbato) shaken, upset
scos'tante ag (fig) off-putting (BRIT), unpleasant
scotch [skɔtʃ] sm inv (whisky) Scotch; (nastro adesivo) Scotch tape®, Sellotape®
scot'tare vt (ustionare) to burn; (: con liquido bollente) to scald ▷ vi to burn; (caffè) to be too hot; **scottarsi** vpr to burn/scald o.s.; (fig) to have one's fingers burnt; **scotta'tura** sf burn; scald
'scotto, -a ag overcooked ▷ sm (fig):

pagare lo ~ (di) to pay the penalty (for)

sco'vare vt to drive out, flush out; (fig) to discover

'Scozia ['skɔttsia] sf **la ~** Scotland; **scoz'zese** ag Scottish ▷ sm/f Scot

scredi'tare vt to discredit

screen saver ['skriːn'sɛɪvər] sm inv (Inform) screen saver

scre'mato, -a ag skimmed; **parzialmente ~** semi-skimmed

screpo'lato, -a ag (labbra) chapped; (muro) cracked

'screzio ['skrettsjo] sm disagreement

scricchio'lare [skrikkjo'lare] vi to creak, squeak

'scrigno ['skriɲɲo] sm casket

scrimina'tura sf parting

'scrissi ecc vb vedi **scrivere**

'scritta sf inscription

'scritto, -a pp di **scrivere** ▷ ag written ▷ sm writing; (lettera) letter, note

scrit'toio sm writing desk

scrit'tore, -'trice sm/f writer

scrit'tura sf writing; (Comm) entry; (contratto) contract; (Rel): **la Sacra S~** the Scriptures pl

scrittu'rare vt (Teatro, Cinema) to sign up, engage; (Comm) to enter

scriva'nia sf desk

'scrivere vt to write; **come si scrive?** how is it spelt?, how do you write it?

scroc'cone, -a sm/f scrounger

'scrofa sf (Zool) sow

scrol'lare vt to shake; **scrollarsi** vpr (anche fig) to give o.s. a shake; (anche: **~ le spalle/il capo**) to shrug one's shoulders/shake one's head

'scrupolo sm scruple; (meticolosità) care, conscientiousness

scrupo'loso, -a ag scrupulous; conscientious

scru'tare vt to scrutinize; (intenzioni, causa) to examine, scrutinize

scu'cire [sku'tʃire] vt (orlo ecc) to unpick, undo; **scucirsi** vpr to come unstitched

scude'ria sf stable

scu'detto sm (Sport) (championship) shield; (distintivo) badge

'scudo sm shield

sculacci'are [skulat'tʃare] vt to spank

scul'tore, -'trice sm/f sculptor

scul'tura sf sculpture

scu'ola sf school; **scuola elementare/materna** primary (BRIT) o grade (US) /nursery school; **scuola guida** driving school; **scuola media** secondary (BRIT) o high (US) school; **scuola dell'obbligo** compulsory education; **scuola tecnica** technical college; **scuole serali** evening classes, night school sg

scu'otere vt to shake

'scure sf axe

'scuro, -a ag dark; (fig: espressione) grim ▷ sm darkness; dark colour; (imposta) (window) shutter; **verde/rosso** ecc **~** dark green/red ecc

'scusa sf apology; (pretesto) excuse; **chiedere ~ a qn (per)** to apologize to sb (for); **chiedo ~** I'm sorry; (disturbando ecc) excuse me

scu'sare vt to excuse; **scusarsi** vpr **scusarsi (di)** to apologize (for); **(mi) scusi** I'm sorry; (per richiamare l'attenzione) excuse me

sde'gnato, -a [zdeɲ'ɲato] ag indignant, angry

'sdegno ['zdeɲɲo] sm scorn, disdain

sdolci'nato, -a [zdoltʃi'nato] ag mawkish, oversentimental

sdrai'arsi vpr to stretch out, lie down

'sdraio sm **sedia a ~** deck chair

sdruccio'levole [zdruttʃo'levole] ag slippery

PAROLA CHIAVE

se pron vedi **si**
▷ cong 1 (condizionale, ipotetica) if; **se nevica non vengo** I won't come if it snows; **sarei rimasto se me l'avessero chiesto** I would have stayed if they'd asked me; **non puoi fare altro se non telefonare** all you can do is phone; **se mai** if, if ever; **siamo noi se mai che le siamo grati** it is we who should be grateful to you; **se no** (altrimenti) or (else), otherwise
2 (in frasi dubitative, interrogative indirette) if, whether; **non so se scrivere o telefonare** I don't know whether o if I should write or phone

sé pron (gen) oneself; (esso, essa, lui, lei, loro) itself; himself; herself; themselves; **sé stesso(a)** pron oneself; itself; himself; herself

seb'bene cong although, though

sec. abbr (= secolo) c.

'secca sf (del mare) shallows pl; vedi anche **secco**

sec'care vt to dry; (prosciugare) to dry up; (fig: importunare) to annoy, bother ▷ vi to dry; to dry up; **seccarsi** vpr to dry; to dry up; (fig) to grow annoyed

sec'cato, -a ag (fig: infastidito) bothered, annoyed; (: stufo) fed up

secca'tura sf (fig) bother no pl, trouble no pl

seccherò ecc [sekke'rɔ] vb vedi **seccare**

secchi'ello sm bucket; **secchiello del ghiaccio** ice bucket

'**secchio** ['sekkjo] sm bucket, pail

'**secco, -a, -chi, -che** ag dry; (fichi, pesce) dried; (foglie, ramo) withered; (magro: persona) thin, skinny; (fig: risposta, modo di fare) curt, abrupt; (: colpo) clean, sharp ▷ sm (siccità) drought; **restarci ~** (fig: morire sul colpo) to drop dead; **mettere in ~** (barca) to beach; **rimanere a ~** (fig) to be left in the lurch

seco'lare ag age-old, centuries-old; (laico, mondano) secular

'**secolo** sm century; (epoca) age

se'conda sf (Aut) second (gear); **viaggiare in ~** to travel second-class; vedi anche **secondo**; **seconda colazione** lunch

secon'dario, -a ag secondary

se'condo, -a ag second ▷ sm second; (di pranzo) main course ▷ prep according to; (nel modo prescritto) in accordance with; **~ me** in my opinion, to my mind; **di seconda mano** second-hand; **a seconda di** according to; in accordance with; **seconda classe** second-class

'**sedano** sm celery

seda'tivo, -a ag, sm sedative

'**sede** sf seat; (di ditta) head office; (di organizzazione) headquarters pl; **sede centrale** head office; **sede sociale** registered office

seden'tario, -a ag sedentary

se'dere vi to sit, be seated

'**sedia** sf chair; **sedia elettrica** electric chair; **sedia a rotelle** wheelchair

'**sedici** ['seditʃi] num sixteen

se'dile sm seat; (panchina) bench

sedu'cente [sedu'tʃɛnte] ag seductive; (proposta) very attractive

se'durre vt to seduce

se'duta sf session, sitting; (riunione) meeting; **seduta spiritica** séance; **seduta stante** (fig) immediately

seduzi'one [sedut'tsjone] sf seduction; (fascino) charm, appeal

SEeO abbr (= salvo errori e omissioni) E and OE

'**sega, -ghe** sf saw

'**segale** sf rye

se'gare vt to saw; (recidere) to saw off

'**seggio** ['sɛddʒo] sm seat; **seggio elettorale** polling station

'**seggiola** ['sɛddʒola] sf chair; **seggio'lone** sm (per bambini) highchair

seggio'via [sɛddʒo'via] sf chairlift

segherò ez [sege'rɔ] vb vedi **segare**

segna'lare [seɲɲa'lare] vt (manovra ecc) to signal; to indicate; (annunciare) to announce; to report; (fig: far conoscere) to point out; (: persona) to single out

se'gnale [seɲ'ɲale] sm signal; (cartello): **segnale acustico** acoustic o sound signal; **segnale d'allarme** alarm; (Ferr) communication cord; **segnale orario** (Radio) time signal; **segnale stradale** road sign

segna'libro [seɲɲa'libro] sm (anche Inform) bookmark

se'gnare [seɲ'ɲare] vt to mark; (prendere nota) to note; (indicare) to indicate, mark; (Sport: goal) to score

'**segno** ['seɲɲo] sm sign; (impronta, contrassegno) mark; (limite) limit, bounds pl; (bersaglio) target; **fare ~ di sì/no** to nod (one's head)/shake one's head; **fare ~ a qn di fermarsi** to motion (to) sb to stop; **cogliere o colpire nel ~** (fig) to hit the mark; **segno zodiacale** star sign

segre'tario, -a sm/f secretary; **segretario comunale** town clerk; **Segretario di Stato** Secretary of State

segrete'ria sf (di ditta, scuola) (secretary's) office; (d'organizzazione internazionale) secretariat; (Pol ecc: carica) office of Secretary; **segreteria telefonica** answering service

se'greto, -a ag secret ▷ sm secret; secrecy no pl; **in ~** in secret, secretly

segu'ace [se'gwatʃe] sm/f follower, disciple

segu'ente ag following, next

segu'ire vt to follow; (frequentare: corso) to attend ▷ vi to follow; (continuare: testo) to continue

segui'tare vt to continue, carry on with ▷ vi to continue, carry on

'**seguito** sm (scorta) suite, retinue; (discepoli) followers pl; (favore) following; (continuazione) continuation; (conseguenza) result; **di ~** at a stretch, on end; **in ~** later on; **in ~ a, a ~ di** following; (a causa di) as a result of, owing to

'**sei** vb vedi **essere** ▷ num six

sei'cento [sei'tʃɛnto] num six hundred ▷ sm **il S~** the seventeenth century

selci'ato [sel'tʃato] sm cobbled surface

selezio'nare [selettsjo'nare] vt to select

selezi'one [selet'tsjone] sf selection

'**sella** sf saddle

sel'lino sm saddle

selvag'gina [selvad'dʒina] sf (animali) game

sel'vaggio, -a, -gi, -ge [sel'vaddʒo] ag wild; (tribù) savage, uncivilized; (fig) savage, brutal ▷ sm/f savage

sel'vatico, -a, -ci, -che ag wild

se'maforo sm (Aut) traffic lights pl

sem'brare vi to seem ▷ vb impers **sembra che** it seems that; **mi sembra che** it seems to me that, I think (that); **~ di essere** to seem to be

'seme sm seed; (sperma) semen; (Carte) suit

se'mestre sm half-year, six-month period

semifi'nale sf semifinal

semi'freddo sm ice-cream cake

semi'nare vt to sow

semi'nario sm seminar; (Rel) seminary

seminter'rato sm basement; (appartamento) basement flat

'semola sf; **semola di grano duro** durum wheat

semo'lino sm semolina

'semplice ['semplitʃe] ag simple; (di un solo elemento) single

'sempre av always; (ancora) still; **posso ~ tentare** I can always o still try; **da ~** always; **per ~** forever; **una volta per ~** once and for all; **~ che** provided (that); **~ più** more and more; **~ meno** less and less

sempre'verde ag, sm o f (Bot) evergreen

'senape sf (Cuc) mustard

se'nato sm senate; **sena'tore, -'trice** sm/f senator

'senno sm judgment, (common) sense; **col ~ di poi** with hindsight

'seno sm (Anat: petto, mammella) breast; (: grembo, fig) womb; (: cavità) sinus

sen'sato, -a ag sensible

sensazio'nale [sensattsjo'nale] ag sensational

sensazi'one [sensat'tsjone] sf feeling, sensation; **avere la ~ che** to have a feeling that; **fare ~** to cause a sensation, create a stir

sen'sibile ag sensitive; (ai sensi) perceptible; (rilevante, notevole) appreciable, noticeable; **~ a** sensitive to

Attenzione! In inglese esiste la parola *sensible*, che però significa *ragionevole*.

'senso sm (Fisiol, istinto) sense; (impressione, sensazione) feeling, sensation; (significato) meaning, sense; (direzione) direction; **sensi** smpl (coscienza) consciousness sg; (sensualità) senses; **ciò non ha ~** that doesn't make sense; **fare ~ a** (ripugnare) to disgust, repel; **in ~ orario/antiorario** clockwise/anticlockwise; **senso di colpa** sense of guilt; **senso comune** common sense; **senso unico** (strada) one-way; **senso vietato** (Aut) no entry

sensu'ale ag sensual; sensuous

sen'tenza [sen'tentsa] sf (Dir) sentence; (massima) maxim

senti'ero sm path

sentimen'tale ag sentimental; (vita, avventura) love cpd

senti'mento sm feeling

senti'nella sf sentry

sen'tire vt (percepire al tatto, fig) to feel; (udire) to hear; (ascoltare) to listen to; (odore) to smell; (avvertire con il gusto, assaggiare) to taste ▷ vi **~ di** (avere sapore) to taste of; (avere odore) to smell of; **sentirsi** vpr (uso reciproco) to be in touch; **sentirsi bene/male** to feel well/unwell o ill; **non mi sento bene** I don't feel well; **sentirsi di fare qc** (essere disposto) to feel like doing sth

sen'tito, -a ag (sincero) sincere, warm; **per ~ dire** by hearsay

'senza ['sɛntsa] prep, cong without; **~ dir nulla** without saying a word; **fare ~ qc** to do without sth; **~ di me** without me; **~ che io lo sapessi** without my o my knowing; **senz'altro** of course, certainly; **~ dubbio** no doubt; **~ scrupoli** unscrupulous; **~ amici** friendless

sepa'rare vt to separate; (dividere) to divide; (tenere distinto) to distinguish; **separarsi** vpr (coniugi) to separate, part; (amici) to part, leave each other; **separarsi da** (coniuge) to separate o part from; (amico, socio) to part company with; (oggetto) to part with; **sepa'rato, -a** ag (letti, conto ecc) separate; (coniugi) separated

seppel'lire vt to bury

'seppi ecc vb vedi **sapere**

'seppia sf cuttlefish ▷ ag inv sepia

se'quenza [se'kwentsa] sf sequence

seques'trare vt (Dir) to impound; (rapire) to kidnap; **se'questro** sm (Dir) impoundment; **sequestro di persona** kidnapping

'sera sf evening; **di ~** in the evening; **domani ~** tomorrow evening, tomorrow night; **se'rale** ag evening cpd; **se'rata** sf evening; (ricevimento) party

ser'bare vt to keep; (mettere da parte) to put aside; **~ rancore/odio verso qn** to bear sb a grudge/hate sb

serba'toio sm tank; (cisterna) cistern

'Serbia sf la ~ Serbia

'serbo ag Serbian ▷ sm/f Serbian, Serb ▷ sm (Ling) Serbian; (il serbare): **mettere/ tenere o avere in ~ qc** to put/keep sth aside

se'reno, -a ag (tempo, cielo) clear; (fig) serene, calm

ser'gente [ser'dʒɛnte] sm (Mil) sergeant

'serie sf inv (successione) series inv; (gruppo, collezione) set; (Sport) division; league; (Comm): **modello di ~/fuori ~** standard/

custom-built model; **in ~** in quick succession; (*Comm*) mass *cpd*
serietà *sf* seriousness; reliability
'serio, -a *ag* serious; (*impiegato*) responsible, reliable; (*ditta, cliente*) reliable, dependable; **sul ~** (*davvero*) really, truly; (*seriamente*) seriously, in earnest
ser'pente *sm* snake; **serpente a sonagli** rattlesnake
'serra *sf* greenhouse; hothouse
ser'randa *sf* roller shutter
serra'tura *sf* lock
server ['sɛrver] *sm inv* (*Inform*) server
ser'vire *vt* to serve; (*clienti: al ristorante*) to wait on; (: *al negozio*) to serve, attend to; (*fig: giovare*) to aid, help; (*Carte*) to deal ▷ *vi* (*Tennis*) to serve; (*essere utile*): **~ a qn** to be of use to sb; **~ a qc/a fare** (*utensile ecc*) to be used for sth/for doing; **~ (a qn) da** to serve as (for sb); **servirsi** *vpr* (*usare*): **servirsi di** to use; (*prendere: cibo*): **servirsi (di)** to help o.s. (to); **serviti pure!** help yourself!; (*essere cliente abituale*): **servirsi da** to be a regular customer at, go to
servizi'evole [servit'tsjevole] *ag* obliging, willing to help
ser'vizio [ser'vittsjo] *sm* service; (*al ristorante: sul conto*) service (charge); (*Stampa, TV, Radio*) report; (*da tè, caffè ecc*) set, service; **servizi** *smpl* (*di casa*) kitchen and bathroom; (*Econ*) services; **essere di ~** to be on duty; **fuori ~** (*telefono ecc*) out of order; **~ compreso** service included; **servizio militare** military service; **servizio di posate** set of cutlery; **servizi segreti** secret service *sg*; **servizio da tè** tea set
ses'santa *num* sixty; **sessan'tesimo, -a** *num* sixtieth
sessi'one *sf* session
'sesso *sm* sex; **sessu'ale** *ag* sexual, sex *cpd*
ses'tante *sm* sextant
'sesto, -a *ag, sm* sixth
'seta *sf* silk
'sete *sf* thirst; **avere ~** to be thirsty
'setola *sf* bristle
'setta *sf* sect
set'tanta *num* seventy; **settan'tesimo, -a** *num* seventieth
set'tare *vt* (*Inform*) to set up
'sette *num* seven
sette'cento [sette'tʃɛnto] *num* seven hundred ▷ *sm* **il S~** the eighteenth century
set'tembre *sm* September
settentrio'nale *ag* northern
settentri'one *sm* north

setti'mana *sf* week; **settima'nale** *ag, sm* weekly

⬤ **SETTIMANA BIANCA**
⬤
⬤
⬤ **Settimana bianca** is the name given
⬤ to a week-long winter-sports holiday
⬤ taken by many Italians some time in the
⬤ skiing season.

'settimo, -a *ag, sm* seventh
set'tore *sm* sector
severità *sf* severity
se'vero, -a *ag* severe
sevizi'are [sevit'tsjare] *vt* to torture
sezio'nare [settsjo'nare] *vt* to divide into sections; (*Med*) to dissect
sezi'one [set'tsjone] *sf* section
sfacchi'nata [sfakki'nata] *sf* (*fam*) chore, drudgery *no pl*
sfacci'ato, -a [sfat'tʃato] *ag* (*maleducato*) cheeky, impudent; (*vistoso*) gaudy
sfa'mare *vt* to feed; (*cibo*) to fill; **sfamarsi** *vpr* to satisfy one's hunger, fill o.s. up
sfasci'are [sfaʃ'ʃare] *vt* (*ferita*) to unbandage; (*distruggere*) to smash, shatter; **sfasciarsi** *vpr* (*rompersi*) to smash, shatter
sfavo'revole *ag* unfavourable
'sfera *sf* sphere
sfer'rare *vt* (*fig: colpo*) to land, deal; (: *attacco*) to launch
'sfida *sf* challenge
sfi'dare *vt* to challenge; (*fig*) to defy, brave
sfi'ducia [sfi'dutʃa] *sf* distrust, mistrust
sfi'gato, -a (*fam*) *ag* (*sfortunato*) unlucky
sfigu'rare *vt* (*persona*) to disfigure; (*quadro, statua*) to deface ▷ *vi* (*far cattiva figura*) to make a bad impression
sfi'lare *vt* (*ago*) to unthread; (*abito, scarpe*) to slip off ▷ *vi* (*truppe*) to march past; (*atleti*) to parade; **sfilarsi** *vpr* (*perle ecc*) to come unstrung; (*orlo, tessuto*) to fray; (*calza*) to run, ladder; **sfi'lata** *sf* march past; parade; **sfilata di moda** fashion show
'sfinge ['sfindʒe] *sf* sphinx
sfi'nito, -a *ag* exhausted
sfio'rare *vt* to brush (against); (*argomento*) to touch upon
sfio'rire *vi* to wither, fade
sfo'cato, -a *ag* (*Fot*) out of focus
sfoci'are [sfo'tʃare] *vi* **~ in** to flow into; (*fig: malcontento*) to develop into
sfode'rato, -a *ag* (*vestito*) unlined
sfogarsi *vpr* (*sfogare la propria rabbia*) to give vent to one's anger; (*confidarsi*): **~ (con)** to pour out one's feelings (to); **non**

sfogarti su di me! don't take your bad temper out on me!

sfoggi'are [sfod'dʒare] *vt, vi* to show off

'sfoglia ['sfoʎʎa] *sf* sheet of pasta dough; **pasta ~** (*Cuc*) puff pastry

sfogli'are [sfoʎ'ʎare] *vt* (*libro*) to leaf through

'sfogo, -ghi *sm* (*eruzione cutanea*) rash; (*fig*) outburst; **dare ~ a** (*fig*) to give vent to

sfon'dare *vt* (*porta*) to break down; (*scarpe*) to wear a hole in; (*cesto, scatola*) to burst, knock the bottom out of; (*Mil*) to break through ▷ *vi* (*riuscire*) to make a name for o.s.

'sfondo *sm* background

sfor'mato *sm* (*Cuc*) type of soufflé

sfor'tuna *sf* misfortune, ill luck *no pl*; **avere ~** to be unlucky; **sfortu'nato, -a** *ag* unlucky; (*impresa, film*) unsuccessful

sforzarsi *vpr* **~ di o a o per fare** to try hard to do

'sforzo ['sfortso] *sm* effort; (*tensione eccessiva, Tecn*) strain; **fare uno ~** to make an effort

sfrat'tare *vt* to evict; **'sfratto** *sm* eviction

sfrecci'are [sfret'tʃare] *vi* to shoot o flash past

sfre'gare *vt* (*strofinare*) to rub; (*graffiare*) to scratch; **sfregarsi le mani** to rub one's hands; **~ un fiammifero** to strike a match

sfregi'are [sfre'dʒare] *vt* to slash, gash; (*persona*) to disfigure; (*quadro*) to deface

sfre'nato, -a *ag* (*fig*) unrestrained, unbridled

sfron'tato, -a *ag* shameless

sfrutta'mento *sm* exploitation

sfrut'tare *vt* (*terreno*) to overwork, exhaust; (*miniera*) to exploit, work; (*fig: operai, occasione, potere*) to exploit

sfug'gire [sfud'dʒire] *vi* to escape; **~ a** (*custode*) to escape (from); (*morte*) to escape; **~ a qn** (*dettaglio, nome*) to escape sb; **~ di mano a qn** to slip out of sb's hand (o hands)

sfu'mare *vt* (*colori, contorni*) to soften, shade off ▷ *vi* to shade (off), fade; (*fig: svanire*) to vanish, disappear; (: *speranze*) to come to nothing

sfuma'tura *sf* shading off *no pl*; (*tonalità*) shade, tone; (*fig*) touch, hint

sfuri'ata *sf* (*scatto di collera*) fit of anger; (*rimprovero*) sharp rebuke

sga'bello *sm* stool

sgabuz'zino [sgabud'dzino] *sm* lumber room

sgambet'tare *vi* to kick one's legs about

sgam'betto *sm* **far lo ~ a qn** to trip sb up; (*fig*) to oust sb

sganci'are [zgan'tʃare] *vt* to unhook; (*Ferr*) to uncouple; (*bombe: da aereo*) to release, drop; (*fig: fam: soldi*) to fork out; **sganciarsi** *vpr* (*fig*): **sganciarsi (da)** to get away (from)

sganghe'rato, -a [zgange'rato] *ag* (*porta*) off its hinges; (*auto*) ramshackle; (*risata*) wild, boisterous

sgar'bato, -a *ag* rude, impolite

'sgarbo *sm* **fare uno ~ a qn** to be rude to sb

sgargi'ante [zgar'dʒante] *ag* gaudy, showy

sgattaio'lare *vi* to sneak away o off

sge'lare [zdʒe'lare] *vi, vt* to thaw

sghignaz'zare [zgiɲɲat'tsare] *vi* to laugh scornfully

sgob'bare (*fam*) *vi* (*scolaro*) to swot; (*operaio*) to slog

sgombe'rare *vt* (*tavolo, stanza*) to clear; (*piazza, città*) to evacuate ▷ *vi* to move

'sgombro, -a *ag* **~ (di)** clear (of), free (from) ▷ *sm* (*Zool*) mackerel; (*anche:* **sgombero**) clearing; vacating; evacuation; (: *trasloco*) removal

sgonfi'are *vt* to let down, deflate; **sgonfiarsi** *vpr* to go down

'sgonfio, -a *ag* (*pneumatico, pallone*) flat

'sgorbio *sm* blot; scribble

sgra'devole *ag* unpleasant, disagreeable

sgra'dito, -a *ag* unpleasant, unwelcome

sgra'nare *vt* (*piselli*) to shell; **~ gli occhi** to open one's eyes wide

sgranchire [zgran'kire] *vt* (*anche:* **sgranchirsi**) to stretch; **~ le gambe** to stretch one's legs

sgranocchi'are [zgranok'kjare] *vt* to munch

'sgravio *sm* **~ fiscale** tax relief

sgrazi'ato, -a [zgrat'tsjato] *ag* clumsy, ungainly

sgri'dare *vt* to scold

sgual'cire [zgwal'tʃire] *vt* to crumple (up), crease

sgual'drina (*peg*) *sf* slut

sgu'ardo *sm* (*occhiata*) look, glance; (*espressione*) look (in one's eye)

sguaz'zare [zgwat'tsare] *vi* (*nell'acqua*) to splash about; (*nella melma*) to wallow; **~ nell'oro** to be rolling in money

sguinzagli'are [zgwintsaʎ'ʎare] *vt* to let off the leash; (*fig: persona*): **~ qn dietro a qn** to set sb on sb

sgusci'are [zguʃ'ʃare] *vt* to shell ▷ *vi* (*sfuggire di mano*) to slip; **~ via** to slip o slink away

'shampoo ['ʃampo] *sm inv* shampoo

shiatzu [ʃi'atstsu] *sm inv* shiatzu

shock [ʃɔk] *sm inv* shock

 PAROLA CHIAVE

si (*dav lo, la, li, le, ne diventa* **se**) *pron* **1**
(*riflessivo: maschile*) himself; (: *femminile*)
herself; (: *neutro*) itself; (: *impersonale*)
oneself; (: *pl*) themselves; **lavarsi** to wash
(oneself); **si è tagliato** he has cut himself;
si credono importanti they think a lot of
themselves
2 (*riflessivo: con complemento oggetto*):
lavarsi le mani to wash one's hands; **si
sta lavando i capelli** he (*o* she) is washing
his (*o* her) hair
3 (*reciproco*) one another, each other; **si
amano** they love one another *o* each other
4 (*passivo*): **si ripara facilmente** it is easily
repaired
5 (*impersonale*): **si dice che ...** they *o*
people say that ...; **si vede che è vecchio**
one *o* you can see that it's old
6 (*noi*) we; **tra poco si parte** we're leaving
soon

sì *av* yes; **un giorno sì e uno no** every
other day
'sia *cong* **~ ... ~** (*o ... o*): **~ che lavori, ~ che
non lavori** whether he works or not;
(*tanto ... quanto*): **verranno ~ Luigi ~ suo
fratello** both Luigi and his brother will be
coming
si'amo *vb vedi* **essere**
si'cario *sm* hired killer
sicché [sik'ke] *cong* (*perciò*) so (that),
therefore; (*e quindi*) (and) so
siccità [sittʃi'ta] *sf* drought
sic'come *cong* since, as
Si'cilia [si'tʃilja] *sf* **la ~** Sicily
si'cura *sf* safety catch; (*Aut*) safety lock
sicu'rezza [siku'rettsa] *sf* safety; security;
(*fiducia*) confidence; (*certezza*) certainty; **di
~** safety *cpd*; **la ~ stradale** road safety
si'curo, -a *ag* safe; (*ben difeso*) secure;
(*fiducioso*) confident; (*certo*) sure, certain;
(*notizia, amico*) reliable; (*esperto*) skilled
▷ *av* (*anche*: **di ~**) certainly; **essere/
mettere al ~** to be safe/put in a safe place;
~ di sé self-confident, sure of o.s.; **sentirsi
~** to feel safe *o* secure
si'edo *ecc vb vedi* **sedere**
si'epe *sf* hedge
si'ero *sm* (*Med*) serum; **sieronega'tivo,
-a** *ag* HIV-negative; **sieroposi'tivo, -a** *ag*
HIV-positive
si'ete *vb vedi* **essere**
si'filide *sf* syphilis
Sig. *abbr* (= *signore*) Mr
siga'retta *sf* cigarette

'sigaro *sm* cigar
Sigg. *abbr* (= *signori*) Messrs
sigil'lare [sidʒil'lare] *vt* to seal
si'gillo [si'dʒillo] *sm* seal
'sigla *sf* initials *pl*; acronym, abbreviation;
sigla automobilistica abbreviation of
province on vehicle number plate; **sigla
musicale** signature tune
Sig.na *abbr* (= *signorina*) Miss
signifi'care [siɲɲifi'kare] *vt* to mean;
signifi'cato *sm* meaning
si'gnora [si'ɲɲora] *sf* lady; **la ~ X** Mrs X;
buon giorno S~/Signore/Signorina
good morning; (*deferente*) good morning
Madam/Sir/Madam; (*quando si conosce
il nome*) good morning Mrs/Mr/Miss X;
Gentile S~/Signore/Signorina (*in una
lettera*) Dear Madam/Sir/Madam; **il signor
Rossi e ~** Mr Rossi and his wife; **signore e
signori** ladies and gentlemen
si'gnore [si'ɲɲore] *sm* gentleman;
(*padrone*) lord, master; (*Rel*): **il S~** the Lord;
il signor X Mr X; **i signori Bianchi** (*coniugi*)
Mr and Mrs Bianchi; *vedi anche* **signora**
signo'rile [siɲɲo'rile] *ag* refined
signo'rina [siɲɲo'rina] *sf* young lady; **la ~
X** Miss X; *vedi anche* **signora**
Sig.ra *abbr* (= *signora*) Mrs
silenzia'tore [silentsja'tore] *sm* silencer
si'lenzio [si'lɛntsjo] *sm* silence; **fare ~** to
be quiet, stop talking; **silenzi'oso, -a** *ag*
silent, quiet
si'licio [si'litʃo] *sm* silicon
sili'cone *sm* silicone
'sillaba *sf* syllable
si'luro *sm* torpedo
simboleggi'are [simboled'dʒare] *vt* to
symbolize
'simbolo *sm* symbol
'simile *sf* (*analogo*) similar; (*di questo tipo*):
un uomo ~ such a man, a man like this;
libri simili such books; **~ a** similar to; **i suoi
simili** one's fellow men; one's peers
simme'tria *sf* symmetry
simpa'tia *sf* (*qualità*) pleasantness;
(*inclinazione*) liking; **avere ~ per qn** to like
sb, have a liking for sb; **sim'patico, -a, -ci,
-che** *ag* (*persona*) nice, pleasant, likeable;
(*casa, albergo ecc*) nice, pleasant

> Attenzione! In inglese esiste la
> parola *sympathetic*, che però significa
> *comprensivo*.

simpatiz'zare [simpatid'dzare] *vi* **~ con**
to take a liking to
simu'lare *vt* to sham, simulate; (*Tecn*) to
simulate
simul'taneo, -a *ag* simultaneous
sina'goga, -ghe *sf* synagogue
sincerità [sintʃeri'ta] *sf* sincerity

sin'cero, -a [sin'tʃero] *ag* sincere; genuine; heartfelt

sinda'cale *ag* (trade-)union *cpd*

sinda'cato *sm* (*di lavoratori*) (trade) union; (*Amm, Econ, Dir*) syndicate, trust, pool

'sindaco, -ci *sm* mayor

sinfo'nia *sf* (*Mus*) symphony

singhioz'zare [singjot'tsare] *vi* to sob; to hiccup

singhi'ozzo [sin'gjottso] *sm* sob; (*Med*) hiccup; **avere il ~** to have the hiccups; **a ~** (*fig*) by fits and starts

single ['singol] *ag inv, sm/f inv* single

singo'lare *ag* (*insolito*) remarkable, singular; (*Ling*) singular ▷ *sm* (*Ling*) singular; (*Tennis*): **~ maschile/femminile** men's/women's singles

'singolo, -a *ag* single, individual ▷ *sm* (*persona*) individual; (*Tennis*) = **singolare**

si'nistra *sf* (*Pol*) left (wing); **a ~** on the left; (*direzione*) to the left

si'nistro, -a *ag* left, left-hand; (*fig*) sinister ▷ *sm* (*incidente*) accident

si'nonimo *sm* synonym; **~ di** synonymous with

sin'tassi *sf* syntax

'sintesi *sf* synthesis; (*riassunto*) summary, résumé

sin'tetico, -a, -ci, -che *ag* synthetic

sintetiz'zare [sintetid'dzare] *vt* to synthesize; (*riassumere*) to summarize

sinto'matico, -a, -ci, -che *ag* symptomatic

'sintomo *sm* symptom

sintonizzarsi *vpr* **~ su** to tune in to

si'pario *sm* (*Teatro*) curtain

si'rena *sf* (*apparecchio*) siren; (*nella mitologia, fig*) siren, mermaid

'Siria *sf* **la ~** Syria

si'ringa, -ghe *sf* syringe

'sismico, -a, -ci, -che *ag* seismic

sis'tema, -i *sm* system; method, way; **sistema nervoso** nervous system; **sistema operativo** (*Inform*) operating system; **sistema solare** solar system

siste'mare *vt* (*mettere a posto*) to tidy, put in order; (*risolvere: questione*) to sort out, settle; (*procurare un lavoro a*) to find a job for; (*dare un alloggio a*) to settle, find accommodation for; **sistemarsi** *vpr* (*problema*) to be settled; (*persona: trovare alloggio*) to find accommodation (*BRIT*) o accommodations (*US*); (*: trovarsi un lavoro*) to get fixed up with a job; **ti sistemo io!** I'll soon sort you out!

siste'matico, -a, -ci, -che *ag* systematic

sistemazi'one [sistemat'tsjone] *sf* arrangement, order; settlement; employment; accommodation (*BRIT*), accommodations (*US*)

'sito *sm* **~ Internet** website

situazi'one [situat'tsjone] *sf* situation

ski-lift ['ski:lift] *sm inv* ski tow

slacci'are [zlat'tʃare] *vt* to undo, unfasten

slanci'ato, -a [zlan'tʃato] *ag* slender

'slancio *sm* dash, leap; (*fig*) surge; **di ~** impetuously

'slavo, -a *ag* Slav(onic), Slavic

sle'ale *ag* disloyal; (*concorrenza ecc*) unfair

sle'gare *vt* to untie

slip [zlip] *sm inv* briefs *pl*

'slitta *sf* sledge; (*trainata*) sleigh

slit'tare *vi* to slip, slide; (*Aut*) to skid

s.l.m. *abbr* (= *sul livello del mare*) a.s.l.

slo'gare *vt* (*Med*) to dislocate

sloggi'are [zlod'dʒare] *vt* (*inquilino*) to turn out ▷ *vi* to move out

Slo'vacchia [zlo'vakkja] *sf* Slovakia

slo'vacco, -a, -chi, -che *ag, sm/f* Slovak

Slo'venia [zlo'venja] *sf* Slovenia

slo'veno, -a *ag, sm/f* Slovene, Slovenian ▷ *sm* (*Ling*) Slovene

smacchi'are [zmak'kjare] *vt* to remove stains from; **smacchia'tore** *sm* stain remover

'smacco, -chi *sm* humiliating defeat

smagli'ante [zmaʎ'ʎante] *ag* brilliant, dazzling

smaglia'tura [zmaʎʎa'tura] *sf* (*su maglia, calza*) ladder; (*della pelle*) stretch mark

smalizi'ato, -a [zmalit'tsjato] *ag* shrewd, cunning

smalti'mento *sm* (*di rifiuti*) disposal

smal'tire *vt* (*merce*) to sell off; (*rifiuti*) to dispose of; (*cibo*) to digest; (*peso*) to lose; (*rabbia*) to get over; **~ la sbornia** to sober up

'smalto *sm* (*anche: di denti*) enamel; (*per ceramica*) glaze; **smalto per unghie** nail varnish

smantel'lare *vt* to dismantle

smarri'mento *sm* loss; (*fig*) bewilderment; dismay

smar'rire *vt* to lose; (*non riuscire a trovare*) to mislay; **smarrirsi** *vpr* (*perdersi*) to lose one's way, get lost; (*: oggetto*) to go astray

smasche'rare [zmaske'rare] *vt* to unmask

SME *sigla m* (= *Sistema Monetario Europeo*) EMS (*European Monetary System*)

smen'tire *vt* (*negare*) to deny; (*testimonianza*) to refute; **smentirsi** *vpr* to be inconsistent

sme'raldo *sm* emerald

'smesso, -a *pp* di **smettere**

'smettere *vt* to stop; (*vestiti*) to stop wearing ▷ *vi* to stop, cease; **~ di fare** to stop doing

'smilzo, -a ['zmiltso] *ag* thin, lean

sminu'ire *vt* to diminish, lessen; (*fig*) to belittle

sminuz'zare [zminut'tsare] *vt* to break into small pieces; to crumble

'smisi *ecc vb vedi* **smettere**

smis'tare *vt* (*pacchi ecc*) to sort; (*Ferr*) to shunt

smisu'rato, -a *ag* boundless, immeasurable; (*grandissimo*) immense, enormous

smoking ['smɔukiŋ] *sm inv* dinner jacket

smon'tare *vt* (*mobile, macchina ecc*) to take to pieces, dismantle; (*fig: scoraggiare*) to dishearten ▷ *vi* (*scendere: da cavallo*) to dismount; (: *da treno*) to get off; (*terminare il lavoro*) to stop (work); **smontarsi** *vpr* to lose heart; to lose one's enthusiasm

'smorfia *sf* grimace; (*atteggiamento lezioso*) simpering; **fare smorfie** to make faces; to simper

'smorto, -a *ag* (*viso*) pale, wan; (*colore*) dull

smor'zare [zmor'tsare] *vt* (*suoni*) to deaden; (*colori*) to tone down; (*luce*) to dim; (*sete*) to quench; (*entusiasmo*) to dampen; **smorzarsi** *vpr* (*suono, luce*) to fade; (*entusiasmo*) to dampen

SMS *sigla m inv* (= *short message service*) text (message)

smu'overe *vt* to move, shift; (*fig: commuovere*) to move; (: *dall'inerzia*) to rouse, stir

snatu'rato, -a *ag* inhuman, heartless

'snello, -a *ag* (*agile*) agile; (*svelto*) slender, slim

sner'vante *ag* (*attesa, lavoro*) exasperating

snob'bare *vt* to snub

sno'dare *vt* (*rendere agile, mobile*) to loosen; **snodarsi** *vpr* to come loose; (*articolarsi*) to bend; (*strada, fiume*) to wind

sno'dato, -a *ag* (*articolazione, persona*) flexible; (*fune ecc*) undone

so *vb vedi* **sapere**

sobbar'carsi *vpr* ~ **a** to take on, undertake

'sobrio, -a *ag* sober

socchi'udere [sok'kjudere] *vt* (*porta*) to leave ajar; (*occhi*) to half-close; **socchi'uso, -a** *pp di* **socchiudere**

soc'correre *vt* to help, assist

soccorri'tore, -'trice *sm/f* rescuer

soc'corso, -a *pp di* **soccorrere** ▷ *sm* help, aid, assistance; **soccorso stradale** breakdown service

soci'ale [so'tʃale] *ag* social; (*di associazione*) club *cpd*, association *cpd*

socia'lismo [sotʃa'lizmo] *sm* socialism; **socia'lista, -i, -e** *ag, sm/f* socialist

società [sotʃe'ta] *sf inv* society; (*sportiva*) club; (*Comm*) company; ~ **a responsabilità**

limitata *type of limited liability company*; **società per azioni** limited (*BRIT*) *o* incorporated (*US*) company

soci'evole [so'tʃevole] *ag* sociable

'socio ['sɔtʃo] *sm* (*Dir, Comm*) partner; (*membro di associazione*) member

'soda *sf* (*Chim*) soda; (*bibita*) soda (water)

soddisfa'cente [soddisfa'tʃɛnte] *ag* satisfactory

soddis'fare *vt, vi* ~ **a** to satisfy; (*impegno*) to fulfil; (*debito*) to pay off; (*richiesta*) to meet, comply with; **soddis'fatto, -a** *pp di* **soddisfare** ▷ *ag* satisfied; **soddisfatto di** happy *o* satisfied with; pleased with; **soddisfazi'one** *sf* satisfaction

'sodo, -a *ag* firm, hard; (*uovo*) hard-boiled ▷ *av* (*picchiare, lavorare*) hard; (*dormire*) soundly

sofà *sm inv* sofa

soffe'renza [soffe'rɛntsa] *sf* suffering

sof'ferto, -a *pp di* **soffrire**

soffi'are *vt* to blow; (*notizia, segreto*) to whisper ▷ *vi* to blow; (*sbuffare*) to puff (and blow); **soffiarsi il naso** to blow one's nose; ~ **qc/qn a qn** (*fig*) to pinch *o* steal sth/sb from sb; ~ **via qc** to blow sth away

soffi'ata *sf* (*fam*) tip-off; **fare una ~ alla polizia** to tip off the police

'soffice ['sɔffitʃe] *ag* soft

'soffio *sm* (*di vento*) breath; **soffio al cuore** heart murmur

sof'fitta *sf* attic

sof'fitto *sm* ceiling

soffo'cante *ag* suffocating, stifling

soffo'care *vi* (*anche*: **soffocarsi**) to suffocate, choke ▷ *vt* to suffocate, choke; (*fig*) to stifle, suppress

sof'frire *vt* to suffer, endure; (*sopportare*) to bear, stand ▷ *vi* to suffer; to be in pain; ~ **(di) qc** (*Med*) to suffer from sth

sof'fritto, -a *pp di* **soffriggere** ▷ *sm* (*Cuc*) fried mixture of herbs, bacon and onions

sofisti'cato, -a *ag* sophisticated; (*vino*) adulterated

'software ['sɔftwɛə] *sm* ~ **applicativo** applications package

sogget'tivo, -a [soddʒet'tivo] *ag* subjective

sog'getto, -a [sod'dʒetto] *ag* ~ **a** (*sottomesso*) subject to; (*esposto: a variazioni, danni ecc*) subject *o* liable to ▷ *sm* subject

soggezi'one [soddʒet'tsjone] *sf* subjection; (*timidezza*) awe; **avere ~ di qn** to stand in awe of sb; to be ill at ease in sb's presence

soggi'orno *sm* (*invernale, marino*) stay; (*stanza*) living room

'soglia ['sɔʎʎa] *sf* doorstep; (*anche fig*)

threshold

'sogliola [ˈsɔʎʎola] *sf* (Zool) sole

so'gnare [soɲˈɲare] *vt, vi* to dream; **~ a occhi aperti** to daydream

'sogno [ˈsoɲɲo] *sm* dream

'soia *sf* (Bot) soya

sol *sm* (Mus) G; (: solfeggiando) so(h)

so'laio *sm* (soffitta) attic

sola'mente *av* only, just

so'lare *ag* solar, sun *cpd*

'solco, -chi *sm* (scavo, fig: ruga) furrow; (incavo) rut, track; (di disco) groove

sol'dato *sm* soldier; **soldato semplice** private

soldi *smpl* (denaro) money *sg*; **non ho ~** I haven't got any money

'sole *sm* sun; (luce) sun(light); (tempo assolato) sun(shine); **prendere il ~** to sunbathe

soleggi'ato, -a [soledˈdʒato] *ag* sunny

so'lenne *ag* solemn

soli'dale *ag* **essere ~ (con)** to be in agreement (with)

solidarietà *sf* solidarity

'solido, -a *ag* solid; (forte, robusto) sturdy, solid; (fig: ditta) sound, solid ▷ *sm* (Mat) solid

so'lista, -i, -e *ag* solo ▷ *sm/f* soloist

solita'mente *av* usually, as a rule

soli'tario, -a *ag* (senza compagnia) solitary, lonely; (solo, isolato) solitary, lone; (deserto) lonely ▷ *sm* (gioiello, gioco) solitaire

'solito, -a *ag* usual; **essere ~ fare** to be in the habit of doing; **di ~** usually; **più tardi del ~** later than usual; **come al ~** as usual

soli'tudine *sf* solitude

sol'letico *sm* tickling; **soffrire il ~** to be ticklish

solleva'mento *sm* raising; lifting; revolt; **sollevamento pesi** (Sport) weight-lifting

solle'vare *vt* to lift, raise; (fig: persona: alleggerire): **~ (da)** to relieve (of); (: dar conforto) to comfort, relieve; (: questione) to raise; (: far insorgere) to stir (to revolt); **sollevarsi** *vpr* to rise; (fig: riprendersi) to recover; (: ribellarsi) to rise up

solli'evo *sm* relief; (conforto) comfort

'solo, -a *ag* alone; (in senso spirituale: isolato) lonely; (unico): **un ~ libro** only one book, a single book; (con ag numerale): **veniamo noi tre soli** just *o* only the three of us are coming ▷ *av* (soltanto) only, just; **non ~ ... ma anche** not only ... but also; **fare qc da ~** to do sth (all) by oneself

sol'tanto *av* only

so'lubile *ag* (sostanza) soluble

soluzi'one [solutˈtsjone] *sf* solution

sol'vente *ag, sm* solvent

so'maro *sm* ass, donkey

somigli'anza [somiʎˈʎantsa] *sf* resemblance

somigli'are [somiʎˈʎare] *vi* **~ a** to be like, resemble; (nell'aspetto fisico) to look like; **somigliarsi** *vpr* to be (*o* look) alike

'somma *sf* (Mat) sum; (di denaro) sum (of money)

som'mare *vt* to add up; (aggiungere) to add; **tutto sommato** all things considered

som'mario, -a *ag* (racconto, indagine) brief; (giustizia) summary ▷ *sm* summary

sommer'gibile [sommerˈdʒibile] *sm* submarine

som'merso, -a *pp di* **sommergere**

sommità *sf inv* summit, top; (fig) height

som'mossa *sf* uprising

'sonda *sf* (Med, Meteor, Aer) probe; (Mineralogia) drill ▷ *ag inv* **pallone m ~** weather balloon

son'daggio [sonˈdaddʒo] *sm* sounding; probe; boring, drilling; (indagine) survey; **sondaggio d'opinioni** opinion poll

son'dare *vt* (Naut) to sound; (atmosfera, piaga) to probe; (Mineralogia) to bore, drill; (fig: opinione ecc) to survey, poll

so'netto *sm* sonnet

son'nambulo, -a *sm/f* sleepwalker

sonnel'lino *sm* nap

son'nifero *sm* sleeping drug (*o* pill)

'sonno *sm* sleep; **prendere ~** to fall asleep; **aver ~** to be sleepy

'sono *vb vedi* **essere**

so'noro, -a *ag* (ambiente) resonant; (voce) sonorous, ringing; (onde, film) sound *cpd*

sontu'oso, -a *ag* sumptuous; lavish

sop'palco, -chi *sm* mezzanine

soppor'tare *vt* (subire: perdita, spese) to bear, sustain; (soffrire: dolore) to bear, endure; (cosa: freddo) to withstand; (persona: freddo, vino) to take; (tollerare) to put up with, tolerate

> Attenzione! In inglese esiste il verbo *to support*, che però non significa *sopportare*.

sop'primere *vt* (carica, privilegi, testimone) to do away with; (pubblicazione) to suppress; (parola, frase) to delete

'sopra *prep* (gen) on; (al di sopra di, più in alto di) above; over; (riguardo a) about, on ▷ *av* on top; (attaccato, scritto) on it; (al di sopra) above; (al piano superiore) upstairs; **donne ~ i 30 anni** women over 30 (years of age); **abito di ~** I live upstairs; **dormirci ~** (fig) to sleep on it

so'prabito *sm* overcoat

soprac'ciglio [soprat'tʃiʎʎo] (*pl(f)* **soprac'ciglia**) *sm* eyebrow

sopraf'fare *vt* to overcome, overwhelm

sopral'luogo, -ghi *sm* (di esperti)

inspection; (*di polizia*) on-the-spot investigation

sopram'mobile *sm* ornament

soprannatu'rale *ag* supernatural

sopran'nome *sm* nickname

so'prano, -a *sm/f* (*persona*) soprano ▷ *sm* (*voce*) soprano

soprappensi'ero *av* lost in thought

sopras'salto *sm* **di ~** with a start; suddenly

soprasse'dere *vi* **~ a** to delay, put off

soprat'tutto *av* (*anzitutto*) above all; (*specialmente*) especially

sopravvalu'tare *vt* to overestimate

soprav'vento *sm* **avere/prendere il ~ su** to have/get the upper hand over

sopravvis'suto, -a *pp di* **sopravvivere**

soprav'vivere *vi* to survive; (*continuare a vivere*): **~ (in)** to live on (in); **~ a** (*incidente ecc*) to survive; (*persona*) to outlive

so'pruso *sm* abuse of power; **subire un ~** to be abused

soq'quadro *sm* **mettere a ~** to turn upside-down

sor'betto *sm* sorbet, water ice

sor'dina *sf* **in ~** softly; (*fig*) on the sly

'sordo, -a *ag* deaf; (*rumore*) muffled; (*dolore*) dull; (*odio, rancore*) veiled ▷ *sm/f* deaf person; **sordo'muto, -a** *ag* deaf-and-dumb ▷ *sm/f* deaf-mute

so'rella *sf* sister; **sorel'lastra** *sf* stepsister; (*con genitore in comune*) half-sister

sor'gente [sor'dʒɛnte] *sf* (*d'acqua*) spring; (*di fiume, Fisica, fig*) source

'sorgere ['sordʒere] *vi* to rise; (*scaturire*) to spring, rise; (*fig: difficoltà*) to arise

sorni'one, -a *ag* sly

sorpas'sare *vt* (*Aut*) to overtake; (*fig*) to surpass; (: *eccedere*) to exceed, go beyond; **~ in altezza** to be higher than; (*persona*) to be taller than

sorpren'dente *ag* surprising

sor'prendere *vt* (*cogliere: in flagrante ecc*) to catch; (*stupire*) to surprise; **sorprendersi** *vpr* **sorprendersi (di)** to be surprised (at); **sor'presa** *sf* surprise; **fare una sorpresa a qn** to give sb a surprise; **sor'preso, -a** *pp di* **sorprendere**

sor'reggere [sor'reddʒere] *vt* to support, hold up; (*fig*) to sustain; **sorreggersi** *vpr* (*tenersi ritto*) to stay upright

sor'ridere *vi* to smile; **sor'riso, -a** *pp di* **sorridere** ▷ *sm* smile

'sorsi *ecc vb vedi* **sorgere**

'sorso *sm* sip

'sorta *sf* sort, kind; **di ~** whatever, of any kind, at all

'sorte *sf* (*fato*) fate, destiny; (*evento fortuito*) chance; **tirare a ~** to draw lots

sor'teggio [sor'teddʒo] *sm* draw

sorvegli'ante [sorveʎ'ʎante] *sm/f* (*di carcere*) guard, warder (BRIT); (*di fabbrica ecc*) supervisor

sorvegli'anza [sorveʎ'ʎantsa] *sf* watch; supervision; (*Polizia, Mil*) surveillance

sorvegli'are [sorveʎ'ʎare] *vt* (*bambino, bagagli, prigioniero*) to watch, keep an eye on; (*malato*) to watch over; (*territorio, casa*) to watch o keep watch over; (*lavori*) to supervise

sorvo'lare *vt* (*territorio*) to fly over ▷ *vi* **~ su** (*fig*) to skim over

S.O.S. *sigla m* mayday, SOS

'sosia *sm inv* double

sos'pendere *vt* (*appendere*) to hang (up); (*interrompere, privare di una carica*) to suspend; (*rimandare*) to defer; (*appendere*) to hang

sospet'tare *vt* to suspect ▷ *vi* **~ di** to suspect; (*diffidare*) to be suspicious of

sos'petto, -a *ag* suspicious ▷ *sm* suspicion; **sospet'toso, -a** *ag* suspicious

sospi'rare *vi* to sigh ▷ *vt* to long for, yearn for; **sos'piro** *sm* sigh

'sosta *sf* (*fermata*) stop, halt; (*pausa*) pause, break; **senza ~** non-stop, without a break

sostan'tivo *sm* noun, substantive

sos'tanza [sos'tantsa] *sf* substance; **sostanze** *sfpl* (*ricchezze*) wealth *sg*, possessions; **in ~** in short, to sum up

sos'tare *vi* (*fermarsi*) to stop (for a while), stay; (*fare una pausa*) to take a break

sos'tegno [sos'teɲɲo] *sm* support

soste'nere *vt* to support; (*prendere su di sé*) to take on, bear; (*resistere*) to withstand, stand up to; (*affermare*): **~ che** to maintain that; **sostenersi** *vpr* to hold o.s. up, support o.s.; (*fig*) to keep up one's strength; **~ gli esami** to sit exams

sostenta'mento *sm* maintenance, support

sostitu'ire *vt* (*mettere al posto di*): **~ qn/qc a** to substitute sb/sth for; (*prendere il posto di: persona*) to substitute for; (: *cosa*) to take the place of

sosti'tuto, -a *sm/f* substitute

sostituzi'one [sostitut'tsjone] *sf* substitution; **in ~ di** as a substitute for, in place of

sotta'ceti [sotta'tʃeti] *smpl* pickles

sot'tana *sf* (*sottoveste*) underskirt; (*gonna*) skirt; (*Rel*) soutane, cassock

sotter'fugio [sotter'fudʒo] *sm* subterfuge

sotter'raneo, -a *ag* underground ▷ *sm* cellar

sotter'rare *vt* to bury

sot'tile *ag* thin; (*figura, caviglia*) thin, slim,

slender; (*fine: polvere, capelli*) fine; (*fig: leggero*) light; (: *vista*) sharp, keen; (: *olfatto*) fine, discriminating; (: *mente*) subtle; shrewd ▷ *sm* **non andare per il ~** not to mince matters

sottin'teso, -a *pp di* **sottintendere** ▷ *sm* allusion; **parlare senza sottintesi** to speak plainly

'**sotto** *prep* (*gen*) under; (*più in basso di*) below ▷ *av* underneath, beneath; below; (**al piano**) **di ~** downstairs; **~ forma di** in the form of; **~ il monte** at the foot of the mountain; **siamo ~ Natale** it's nearly Christmas; **~ la pioggia/il sole** in the rain/ sun(shine); **~ terra** underground; **chiuso ~ vuoto** vacuum-packed

sotto'fondo *sm* background; **sottofondo musicale** background music

sottoline'are *vt* to underline; (*fig*) to emphasize, stress

sottoma'rino, -a *ag* (*flora*) submarine; (*cavo, navigazione*) underwater ▷ *sm* (*Naut*) submarine

sottopas'saggio [sottopas'saddʒo] *sm* (*Aut*) underpass; (*pedonale*) subway, underpass

sotto'porre *vt* (*costringere*) to subject; (*fig: presentare*) to submit; **sottoporsi** *vpr* to submit; **sottoporsi a** (*subire*) to undergo

sottos'critto, -a *pp di* **sottoscrivere**

sotto'sopra *av* upside-down

sotto'terra *av* underground

sotto'titolo *sm* subtitle

sottovalu'tare *vt* to underestimate

sotto'veste *sf* underskirt

sotto'voce [sotto'votʃe] *av* in a low voice

sottovu'oto *av* **confezionare ~** to vacuum-pack ▷ *ag* **confezione** *f* **~** vacuum packed

sot'trarre *vt* (*Mat*) to subtract, take away; **~ qn/qc a** (*togliere*) to remove sb/sth from; (*salvare*) to save o rescue sb/sth from; **~ qc a qn** (*rubare*) to steal sth from sb; **sottrarsi** *vpr* **sottrarsi a** (*sfuggire*) to escape; (*evitare*) to avoid; **sottrazi'one** *sf* subtraction; removal

souve'nir [suv(ə)'nir] *sm inv* souvenir

sovi'etico, -a, -ci, -che *ag* Soviet ▷ *sm/f* Soviet citizen

sovrac'carico, -a, chi, che *ag* **~ (di)** overloaded (with) ▷ *sm* excess load; **~ di lavoro** extra work

sovraffol'lato, -a *ag* overcrowded

sovrannatu'rale *ag* = **soprannatu'rale**

so'vrano, -a *ag* sovereign; (*fig: sommo*) supreme ▷ *sm/f* sovereign, monarch

sovrap'porre *vt* to place on top of, put on top of

sovvenzi'one [sovven'tsjone] *sf* subsidy, grant

'**sozzo, -a** ['sottso] *ag* filthy, dirty

S.P.A. *abbr* = **società per azioni**

spac'care *vt* to split, break; (*legna*) to chop; **spaccarsi** *vpr* to split, break; **spacca'tura** *sf* split

spaccherò *ecc* [spakke'rɔ] *vb vedi* **spaccare**

spacci'are [spat'tʃare] *vt* (*vendere*) to sell (off); (*mettere in circolazione*) to circulate; (*droga*) to peddle, push; **spacciarsi** *vpr* **spacciarsi per** (*farsi credere*) to pass o.s. off as, pretend to be; **spaccia'tore, -'trice** *sm/f* (*di droga*) pusher; (*di denaro falso*) dealer; '**spaccio** *sm* (*di merce rubata, droga*): **spaccio (di)** trafficking (in); **spaccio (di)** passing (of); (*vendita*) sale; (*bottega*) shop

'**spacco, -chi** *sm* (*fenditura*) split, crack; (*strappo*) tear; (*di gonna*) slit

spac'cone *sm/f* boaster, braggart

'**spada** *sf* sword

spae'sato, -a *ag* disorientated, lost

spa'ghetti [spa'getti] *smpl* (*Cuc*) spaghetti *sg*

'**Spagna** ['spaɲɲa] *sf* **la ~** Spain; **spa'gnolo, -a** *ag* Spanish ▷ *sm/f* Spaniard ▷ *sm* (*Ling*) Spanish; **gli Spagnoli** the Spanish

'**spago, -ghi** *sm* string, twine

spai'ato, -a *ag* (*calza, guanto*) odd

spalan'care *vt* to open wide; **spalancarsi** *vpr* to open wide

spa'lare *vt* to shovel

'**spalla** *sf* shoulder; (*fig: Teatro*) stooge; **spalle** *sfpl* (*dorso*) back

spalli'era *sf* (*di sedia ecc*) back; (*di letto: da capo*) head(board); (: *da piedi*) foot(board); (*Ginnastica*) wall bars *pl*

spal'lina *sf* (*bretella*) strap; (*imbottitura*) shoulder pad

spal'mare *vt* to spread

'**spalti** *smpl* (*di stadio*) terracing

'**spandere** *vt* to spread; (*versare*) to pour (out)

spa'rare *vt* to fire ▷ *vi* (*far fuoco*) to fire; (*tirare*) to shoot; **spara'toria** *sf* exchange of shots

sparecchi'are [sparek'kjare] *vt* **~ (la tavola)** to clear the table

spa'reggio [spa'reddʒo] *sm* (*Sport*) play-off

'**spargere** ['spardʒere] *vt* (*sparpagliare*) to scatter; (*versare: vino*) to spill; (: *lacrime, sangue*) to shed; (*diffondere*) to spread; (*emanare*) to give off (*o* out); **spargersi** *vpr* to spread

spa'rire *vi* to disappear, vanish

spar'lare *vi* **~ di** to run down, speak ill of

'**sparo** *sm* shot

spar'tire vt (eredità, bottino) to share out; (avversari) to separate

spar'tito sm (Mus) score

sparti'traffico sm inv (Aut) central reservation (BRIT), median (strip) (US)

sparvi'ero sm (Zool) sparrowhawk

spasi'mante sm suitor

spassio'nato, -a ag dispassionate, impartial

'spasso sm (divertimento) amusement, enjoyment; **andare a ~** to go out for a walk; **essere a ~** (fig) to be out of work; **mandare qn a ~** (fig) to give sb the sack

'spatola sf spatula; (di muratore) trowel

spa'valdo, -a ag arrogant, bold

spaventa'passeri sm inv scarecrow

spaven'tare vt to frighten, scare; **spaventarsi** vpr to be frightened, be scared; to get a fright; **spa'vento** sm fear, fright; **far spavento a qn** to give sb a fright; **spaven'toso, -a** ag frightening, terrible; (fig: fam) tremendous, fantastic

spazientirsi [spattsjen'tirsi] vpr to lose one's patience

'spazio ['spattsjo] sm space; **spazio aereo** airspace; **spazi'oso, -a** ag spacious

spazzaca'mino [spattsaka'mino] sm chimney sweep

spazza'neve [spattsa'neve] sm inv snowplough

spaz'zare [spat'tsare] vt to sweep; (foglie ecc) to sweep up; (cacciare) to sweep away; **spazza'tura** sf sweepings pl; (immondizia) rubbish; **spaz'zino** sm street sweeper

'spazzola ['spattsola] sf brush; **spazzola da capelli** hairbrush; **spazzola per abiti** clothesbrush; **spazzo'lare** vt to brush; **spazzo'lino** sm (small) brush; **spazzolino da denti** toothbrush

specchi'arsi [spek'kjarsi] vpr to look at o.s. in a mirror; (riflettersi) to be mirrored, be reflected

specchi'etto [spek'kjetto] sm (tabella) table, chart; **specchietto da borsetta** pocket mirror; **specchietto retrovisore** (Aut) rear-view mirror

'specchio ['spɛkkjo] sm mirror

speci'ale [spe'tʃale] ag special; **specia'lista, -i, -e** sm/f specialist; **specialità** sf inv speciality; (branca di studio) special field, speciality; **vorrei assaggiare una specialità del posto** I'd like to try a local speciality; **special'mente** av especially, particularly

'specie ['spɛtʃe] sf inv (Biol, Bot, Zool) species inv; (tipo) kind, sort ▷ av especially, particularly; **una ~ di** a kind of; **fare ~ a qn** to surprise sb; **la ~ umana** mankind

specifi'care [spetʃifi'kare] vt to specify, state

spe'cifico, -a, -ci, -che [spe'tʃifiko] ag specific

specu'lare vi ~ **su** (Comm) to speculate in; (sfruttare) to exploit; (meditare) to speculate on; **speculazi'one** sf speculation

spe'dire vt to send

'spegnere ['spɛɲɲere] vt (fuoco, sigaretta) to put out, extinguish; (apparecchio elettrico) to turn o switch off; (gas) to turn off; (fig: suoni, passioni) to stifle; (debito) to extinguish; **spegnersi** vpr to go out; to go off; (morire) to pass away; **puoi ~ la luce?** could you switch off the light?; **non riesco a ~ il riscaldamento** I can't turn the heating off

spellarsi vpr to peel

'spendere vt to spend

'spengo ecc vb vedi **spegnere**

'spensi ecc vb vedi **spegnere**

spensie'rato, -a ag carefree

'spento, -a pp di **spegnere** ▷ ag (suono) muffled; (colore) dull; (sigaretta) out; (civiltà, vulcano) extinct

spe'ranza [spe'rantsa] sf hope

spe'rare vt to hope for ▷ vi ~ **in** to trust in; ~ **che/di fare** to hope that/to do; **lo spero, spero di sì** I hope so

sper'duto, -a ag (isolato) out-of-the-way; (persona: smarrita, a disagio) lost

sperimen'tale ag experimental

sperimen'tare vt to experiment with, test; (fig) to test, put to the test

'sperma, -i sm sperm

spe'rone sm spur

sperpe'rare vt to squander

'spesa sf (somma di denaro) expense; (costo) cost; (acquisto) purchase; (fam: acquisto del cibo quotidiano) shopping; **spese postali** postage sg; **spese di viaggio** travelling expenses

'spesso, -a ag (fitto) thick; (frequente) frequent ▷ av often; **spesse volte** frequently, often

spes'sore sm thickness

Spett. abbr vedi **spettabile**

spet'tabile (abbr: **Spett.**: in lettere) ag ~ **Ditta X** Messrs X and Co.

spet'tacolo sm (rappresentazione) performance, show; (vista, scena) sight; **dare ~ di sé** to make an exhibition o a spectacle of o.s.

spet'tare vi ~ **a** (decisione) to be up to; (stipendio) to be due to; **spetta a te decidere** it's up to you to decide

spetta'tore, -'trice sm/f (Cinema, Teatro) member of the audience; (di avvenimento) onlooker, witness

spettego'lare vi to gossip

spetti'nato, -a *ag* dishevelled

'spettro *sm* (*fantasma*) spectre; (*Fisica*) spectrum

'spezie ['spɛttsje] *sfpl* (*Cuc*) spices

spez'zare [spet'tsare] *vt* (*rompere*) to break; (*fig: interrompere*) to break up; **spezzarsi** *vpr* to break

spezza'tino [spettsa'tino] *sm* (*Cuc*) stew

spezzet'tare [spettset'tare] *vt* to break up (*o chop*) into small pieces

'spia *sf* spy; (*confidente della polizia*) informer; (*Elettr*) indicating light; warning light; (*fessura*) peep-hole; (*fig: sintomo*) sign, indication

spia'cente [spja'tʃɛnte] *ag* sorry; **essere ~ di qc/di fare qc** to be sorry about sth/for doing sth

spia'cevole [spja'tʃevole] *ag* unpleasant

spi'aggia, -ge ['spjaddʒa] *sf* beach; **spiaggia libera** public beach

spia'nare *vt* (*terreno*) to level, make level; (*edificio*) to raze to the ground; (*pasta*) to roll out; (*rendere liscio*) to smooth (out)

spi'are *vt* to spy on

spi'azzo ['spjattso] *sm* open space; (*radura*) clearing

'spicchio ['spikkjo] *sm* (*di agrumi*) segment; (*di aglio*) clove; (*parte*) piece, slice

spicciarsi *vpr* to hurry up

spiccioli *smpl* (small) change; **mi dispiace, non ho ~** sorry, I don't have any change

'spicco, -chi *sm* **di ~** outstanding; (*tema*) main, principal; **fare ~** to stand out

spie'dino *sm* (*utensile*) skewer; (*pietanza*) kebab

spi'edo *sm* (*Cuc*) spit

spie'gare *vt* (*far capire*) to explain; (*tovaglia*) to unfold; (*vele*) to unfurl; **spiegarsi** *vpr* to explain o.s., make o.s. clear; **~ qc a qn** to explain sth to sb; **spiegazi'one** *sf* explanation

spiegherò *ecc* [spjege'rɔ] *vb vedi* **spiegare**

spie'tato, -a *ag* ruthless, pitiless

spiffe'rare (*fam*) *vt* to blurt out, blab

'spiffero *sm* draught (*BRIT*), draft (*US*)

'spiga, -ghe *sf* (*Bot*) ear

spigli'ato, -a [spiʎ'ʎato] *ag* self-possessed, self-confident

'spigolo *sm* corner; (*Mat*) edge

'spilla *sf* brooch; (*da cravatta, cappello*) pin; **~ di sicurezza o da balia** safety pin

'spillo *sm* pin; **spillo da balia o di sicurezza** safety pin

spi'lorcio, -a, -ci, -ce [spi'lortʃo] *ag* mean, stingy

'spina *sf* (*Bot*) thorn; (*Zool*) spine, prickle; (*di pesce*) bone; (*Elettr*) plug; (*di botte*) bunghole; **birra alla ~** draught beer; **spina dorsale** (*Anat*) backbone

spinaci [spi'natʃi] *smpl* spinach *sg*

spi'nello *sm* (*Droga: gergo*) joint

'spingere ['spindʒere] *vt* to push; (*condurre: anche fig*) to drive; (*stimolare*): **~ qn a fare** to urge o press sb to do

spi'noso, -a *ag* thorny, prickly

'spinsi *ecc vb vedi* **spingere**

'spinta *sf* (*urto*) push; (*Fisica*) thrust; (*fig: stimolo*) incentive, spur; (: *appoggio*) string-pulling *no pl*; **dare una ~ a qn** (*fig*) to pull strings for sb

'spinto, -a *pp di* **spingere**

spio'naggio [spio'naddʒo] *sm* espionage, spying

spion'cino [spion'tʃino] *sm* peephole

spi'raglio [spi'raʎʎo] *sm* (*fessura*) chink, narrow opening; (*raggio di luce, fig*) glimmer, gleam

spi'rale *sf* spiral; (*contraccettivo*) coil; **a ~** spiral(-shaped)

spiri'tato, -a *ag* possessed; (*fig: persona, espressione*) wild

spiri'tismo *sm* spiritualism

'spirito *sm* (*Rel, Chim, disposizione d'animo, di legge ecc, fantasma*) spirit; (*pensieri, intelletto*) mind; (*arguzia*) wit; (*umorismo*) humour, wit; **lo S~ Santo** the Holy Spirit *o* Ghost

spirito'saggine [spirito'saddʒine] *sf* witticism; (*peg*) wisecrack

spiri'toso, -a *ag* witty

spiritu'ale *ag* spiritual

'splendere *vi* to shine

'splendido, -a *ag* splendid; (*splendente*) shining; (*sfarzoso*) magnificent, splendid

splen'dore *sm* splendour; (*luce intensa*) brilliance, brightness

spogli'are [spoʎ'ʎare] *vt* (*svestire*) to undress; (*privare, fig: depredare*): **~ qn di qc** to deprive sb of sth; (*togliere ornamenti: anche fig*): **~ qn/qc di** to strip sb/sth of; **spogliarsi** *vpr* to undress, strip; **spogliarsi di** (*ricchezze ecc*) to deprive o.s. of, give up; (*pregiudizi*) to rid o.s. of; **spoglia'rello** [spoʎʎa'rɛllo] *sm* striptease; **spoglia'toio** *sm* dressing room; (*di scuola ecc*) cloakroom; (*Sport*) changing room

'spola *sf* (*bobina di filo*) cop; **fare la ~ (fra)** to go to and fro *o* shuttle (between)

spolve'rare *vt* (*anche Cuc*) to dust; (*con spazzola*) to brush; (*con battipanni*) to beat; (*fig*) to polish off ▷ *vi* to dust

spon'taneo, -a *ag* spontaneous; (*persona*) unaffected, natural

spor'care *vt* to dirty, make dirty; (*fig*) to sully, soil; **sporcarsi** *vpr* to get dirty

spor'cizia [spor'tʃittsja] *sf* (*stato*) dirtiness; (*sudiciume*) dirt, filth; (*cosa* *sporca*) dirt *no pl*, something dirty

'sporco, -a, -chi, -che *ag* dirty, filthy

spor'genza [spor'dʒɛntsa] *sf* projection

'sporgere ['spɔrdʒere] *vt* to put out, stretch out ▷ *vi* (*venire in fuori*) to stick out; **sporgersi** *vpr* to lean out; **~ querela contro qn** (*Dir*) to take legal action against sb

'sporsi *ecc vb vedi* **sporgere**

sport *sm inv* sport

spor'tello *sm* (*di treno, auto ecc*) door; (*di banca, ufficio*) window, counter; **sportello automatico** (*Banca*) cash dispenser, automated telling machine

spor'tivo, -a *ag* (*gara, giornale, centro*) sports *cpd*; (*persona*) sporty; (*abito*) casual; (*spirito, atteggiamento*) sporting

'sposa *sf* bride; (*moglie*) wife

sposa'lizio [spoza'littsjo] *sm* wedding

spo'sare *vt* to marry; (*fig: idea, fede*) to espouse; **sposarsi** *vpr* to get married, marry; **sposarsi con qn** to marry sb, get married to sb; **spo'sato, -a** *ag* married

'sposo *sm* (bride)groom; (*marito*) husband

spos'sato, -a *ag* exhausted, weary

spos'tare *vt* to move, shift; (*cambiare: orario*) to change; **spostarsi** *vpr* to move; **può ~ la macchina, per favore?** can you move your car please?

'spranga, -ghe *sf* (*sbarra*) bar

spre'care *vt* to waste

spre'gevole [spre'dʒevole] *ag* contemptible, despicable

'spremere *vt* to squeeze

spremia'grumi *sm inv* lemon squeezer

spre'muta *sf* fresh juice; **spremuta d'arancia** fresh orange juice

sprez'zante [spret'tsante] *ag* scornful, contemptuous

sprofon'dare *vi* to sink; (*casa*) to collapse; (*suolo*) to give way, subside

spro'nare *vt* to spur (on)

sproporzio'nato, -a [sproportsjo'nato] *ag* disproportionate, out of all proportion

sproporzi'one [spropor'tsjone] *sf* disproportion

spro'posito *sm* blunder; **a ~** at the wrong time; (*rispondere, parlare*) irrelevantly

sprovve'duto, -a *ag* inexperienced, naïve

sprov'visto, -a *ag* (*mancante*): **~ di** lacking in, without; **alla sprovvista** unawares

spruz'zare [sprut'tsare] *vt* (*a nebulizzazione*) to spray; (*aspergere*) to sprinkle; (*inzaccherare*) to splash

'spugna ['spuɲɲa] *sf* (*Zool*) sponge; (*tessuto*) towelling

'spuma *sf* (*schiuma*) foam; (*bibita*) fizzy drink

spu'mante *sm* sparkling wine

spun'tare *vt* (*coltello*) to break the point of; (*capelli*) to trim ▷ *vi* (*uscire: germogli*) to sprout; (: *capelli*) to begin to grow; (: *denti*) to come through; (*apparire*) to appear (suddenly)

spun'tino *sm* snack

'spunto *sm* (*Teatro, Mus*) cue; (*fig*) starting point; **dare lo ~ a** (*fig*) to give rise to

spu'tare *vt* to spit out; (*fig*) to belch (out) ▷ *vi* to spit

'squadra *sf* (*strumento*) (set) square; (*gruppo*) team, squad; (*di operai*) gang, squad; (*Mil*) squad; (: *Aer, Naut*) squadron; (*Sport*) team; **lavoro a squadre** teamwork

squagli'arsi [skwaʎ'ʎarsi] *vpr* to melt; (*fig*) to sneak off

squa'lifica *sf* disqualification

squalifi'care *vt* to disqualify

'squallido, -a *ag* wretched, bleak

'squalo *sm* shark

'squama *sf* scale

squarcia'gola [skwartʃa'gola]: **a ~** *av* at the top of one's voice

squattri'nato, -a *ag* penniless

squili'brato, -a *ag* (*Psic*) unbalanced

squil'lante *ag* shrill, sharp

squil'lare *vi* (*campanello, telefono*) to ring (out); (*tromba*) to blare; **'squillo** *sm* ring, ringing *no pl*; blare; **ragazza f squillo** *inv* call girl

squi'sito, -a *ag* exquisite; (*cibo*) delicious; (*persona*) delightful

squit'tire *vi* (*uccello*) to squawk; (*topo*) to squeak

sradi'care *vt* to uproot; (*fig*) to eradicate

srego'lato, -a *ag* (*senza ordine: vita*) disorderly; (*smodato*) immoderate; (*dissoluto*) dissolute

S.r.l. *abbr* = **società a responsabilità limitata**

sroto'lare *vt*, **sroto'larsi** ▷ *vpr* to unroll

SS *sigla* = **strada statale**

S.S.N. *abbr* (= *Servizio Sanitario Nazionale*) ≈ NHS

sta *ecc vb vedi* **stare**

'stabile *ag* stable, steady; (*tempo: non variabile*) settled; (*Teatro: compagnia*) resident ▷ *sm* (*edificio*) building

stabili'mento *sm* (*edificio*) establishment; (*fabbrica*) plant, factory

stabi'lire *vt* to establish; (*fissare: prezzi, data*) to fix; (*decidere*) to decide; **stabilirsi** *vpr* (*prendere dimora*) to settle

stac'care *vt* (*levare*) to detach, remove; (*separare: anche fig*) to separate, divide; (*strappare*) to tear off (*o out*); (*scandire: parole*) to pronounce clearly; (*Sport*) to leave behind; **staccarsi** *vpr* (*bottone ecc*) to come off; (*scostarsi*): **staccarsi (da)**

to move away (from); (fig: separarsi): **staccarsi da** to leave; **non ~ gli occhi da qn** not to take one's eyes off sb

'**stadio** sm (Sport) stadium; (periodo, fase) phase, stage

'**staffa** sf (di sella, Tecn) stirrup; **perdere le staffe** (fig) to fly off the handle

staf'fetta sf (messo) dispatch rider; (Sport) relay race

stagio'nale [stadʒo'nale] ag seasonal

stagio'nato, -a [stadʒo'nato] ag (vedi vb) seasoned; matured; (scherzoso: attempato) getting on in years

stagi'one [sta'dʒone] sf season; **alta/ bassa ~** high/low season

stagista, -i, -e [sta'd[gh]ista] sm/f trainee, intern (US)

'**stagno, -a** ['stanno] ag watertight; (a tenuta d'aria) airtight ▷ sm (acquitrino) pond; (Chim) tin

sta'gnola [stan'nɔla] sf tinfoil

'**stalla** sf (per bovini) cowshed; (per cavalli) stable

stal'lone sm stallion

stamat'tina av this morning

stam'becco, -chi sm ibex

'**stampa** sf (Tip, Fot: tecnica) printing; (impressione, copia fotografica) print; (insieme di quotidiani, giornalisti ecc) press

stam'pante sf (Inform) printer

stam'pare vt to print; (pubblicare) to publish; (coniare) to strike, coin; (imprimere: anche fig) to impress

stampa'tello sm block letters pl

stam'pella sf crutch

'**stampo** sm mould; (fig: indole) type, kind, sort

sta'nare vt to drive out

stan'care vt to tire, make tired; (annoiare) to bore; (infastidire) to annoy; **stancarsi** vpr to get tired, tire o.s. out; **stancarsi (di)** to grow weary (of), grow tired (of)

stan'chezza [stan'kettsa] sf tiredness, fatigue

'**stanco, -a, -chi, -che** ag tired; **~ di** tired of, fed up with

stan'ghetta [stan'getta] sf (di occhiali) leg; (Mus, di scrittura) bar

'**stanno** vb vedi **stare**

sta'notte av tonight; (notte passata) last night

'**stante** prep **a sé ~** (appartamento, casa) independent, separate

stan'tio, -a, -'tii, -'tie ag stale; (burro) rancid; (fig) old

stan'tuffo sm piston

'**stanza** ['stantsa] sf room; (Poesia) stanza; **stanza da bagno** bathroom; **stanza da letto** bedroom

stap'pare vt to uncork; to uncap

'**stare** vi (restare in un luogo) to stay, remain; (abitare) to stay, live; (essere situato) to be, be situated; (anche: **~ in piedi**) to be, stand; (essere, trovarsi) to be; (dipendere): **se stesse in me** if it were up to me, if it depended on me; (seguito da gerundio): **sta studiando** he's studying; **starci** (esserci spazio): **nel baule non ci sta più niente** there's no more room in the boot; (accettare) to accept; **ci stai?** is that okay with you?; **~ a** (attenersi a) to follow, stick to; (seguito dall'infinito): **stiamo a discutere** we're talking; (toccare a): **sta a te giocare** it's your turn to play; **~ per fare qc** to be about to do sth; **come sta?** how are you?; **io sto bene/male** I'm very well/not very well; **~ a qn** (abiti ecc) to fit sb; **queste scarpe mi stanno strette** these shoes are tight for me; **il rosso ti sta bene** red suits you

starnu'tire vi to sneeze; **star'nuto** sm sneeze

sta'sera av this evening, tonight

sta'tale ag state cpd; government cpd ▷ sm/f state employee, local authority employee; (nell'amministrazione) ≈ civil servant; **strada statale** ≈ trunk (Brit) o main road

sta'tista, -i sm statesman

sta'tistica sf statistics sg

'**stato, -a** pp di **essere; stare** ▷ sm (condizione) state, condition; (Pol) state; (Dir) status; **essere in ~ d'accusa** (Dir) to be committed for trial; **~ d'assedio/ d'emergenza** state of siege/emergency; **~ civile** (Amm) marital status; **gli Stati Uniti (d'America)** the United States (of America); **stato d'animo** mood; **stato maggiore** (Mil) staff

'**statua** sf statue

statuni'tense ag United States cpd, of the United States

sta'tura sf (Anat) height, stature; (fig) stature

sta'tuto sm (Dir) statute; constitution

sta'volta av this time

stazio'nario, -a [stattsjo'narjo] ag stationary; (fig) unchanged

stazi'one [stat'tsjone] sf station; (balneare, termale) resort; **stazione degli autobus** bus station; **stazione balneare** seaside resort; **stazione ferroviaria** railway (BRIT) o railroad (US) station; **stazione invernale** winter sports resort; **stazione di polizia** police station (in small town); **stazione di servizio** service o petrol (BRIT) o filling station

'**stecca, -che** sf stick; (di ombrello) rib; (di sigarette) carton; (Med) splint; (stonatura):

fare una ~ to sing (o play) a wrong note
stec'cato *sm* fence
'stella *sf* star; **stella alpina**(*Bot*)
edelweiss; **stella cadente**shooting star;
stella di mare(*Zool*) starfish
'stelo *sm* stem; (*asta*) rod; **lampada a ~**
standard lamp
'stemma, -i *sm* coat of arms
'stemmo *vb vedi* **stare**
stempi'ato, -a *ag* with a receding hairline
'stendere *vt* (*braccia, gambe*) to stretch
(out); (*tovaglia*) to spread (out); (*bucato*)
to hang out; (*mettere a giacere*) to lay
(down); (*spalmare: colore*) to spread;
(*mettere per iscritto*) to draw up; **stendersi**
vpr (*coricarsi*) to stretch out, lie down;
(*estendersi*) to extend, stretch
stenogra'fia *sf* shorthand
sten'tare *vi* **~ a fare** to find it hard to do,
have difficulty doing
'stento *sm* (*fatica*) difficulty; **stenti** *smpl*
(*privazioni*) hardship *sg*, privation *sg*; **a ~**
with difficulty, barely
'sterco *sm* dung
stereo['stɛreo] *ag inv* stereo ▷ *sm inv*
(*impianto*) stereo
'sterile *ag* sterile; (*terra*) barren; (*fig*) futile,
fruitless
steriliz'zare [sterilid'dzare] *vt* to sterilize
ster'lina *sf* pound (sterling)
stermi'nare *vt* to exterminate, wipe out
stermi'nato, -a *ag* immense; endless
ster'minio *sm* extermination, destruction
'sterno *sm* (*Anat*) breastbone
ste'roide *sm* steroid
ster'zare[ster'tsare] *vt, vi* (*Aut*) to steer;
'sterzo *sm* steering; (*volante*) steering
wheel
'stessi *ecc vb vedi* **stare**
'stesso, -a *ag* same; (*rafforzativo: in
persona, proprio*): **il re ~** the king himself *o* in
person ▷ *pron* **lo(la) ~(a)** the same (one); **i
suoi stessi avversari lo ammirano** even
his enemies admire him; **fa lo ~** it doesn't
matter; **per me è lo ~** it's all the same to
me, it doesn't matter to me; *vedi* **io; tu** *ecc*
ste'sura *sf* drafting *no pl*, drawing up *no
pl*; draft
'stetti *ecc vb vedi* **stare**
'stia *ecc vb vedi* **stare**
sti'lare *vt* to draw up, draft
'stile *sm* style; **stile libero**freestyle;
sti'lista, -i *sm* designer
stilo'grafica, -che *sf* (*anche:* **penna ~**)
fountain pen
'stima *sf* esteem; valuation; assessment,
estimate
sti'mare *vt* (*persona*) to esteem, hold in
high regard; (*terreno, casa ecc*) to value;

(*stabilire in misura approssimativa*) to
estimate, assess; (*ritenere*): **~ che** to
consider that; **stimarsi fortunato** to
consider o.s. (to be) lucky
stimo'lare *vt* to stimulate; (*incitare*): **~ qn
(a fare)** to spur sb on (to do)
'stimolo *sm* (*anche fig*) stimulus
'stingere['stindʒere] *vt, vi* (*anche:*
stingersi) to fade; **'stinto, -a** *pp di*
stingere
sti'pare *vt* to cram, pack; **stiparsi** *vpr*
(*accalcarsi*) to crowd, throng
sti'pendio *sm* salary
'stipite *sm* (*di porta, finestra*) jamb
stipu'lare *vt* (*redigere*) to draw up
sti'rare *vt* (*abito*) to iron; (*distendere*) to
stretch; (*strappare: muscolo*) to strain;
stirarsi *vpr* to stretch (o.s.)
stiti'chezza[stiti'kettsa] *sf* constipation
'stitico, -a, -ci, -che *ag* constipated
'stiva *sf* (*di nave*) hold
sti'vale *sm* boot
'stizza['stittsa] *sf* anger, vexation
'stoffa *sf* material, fabric; (*fig*): **aver la ~ di**
to have the makings of
'stomaco, -chi *sm* stomach; **dare di ~** to
vomit, be sick
sto'nato, -a *ag* (*persona*) off-key;
(*strumento*) off-key, out of tune
stop *sm inv* (*Tel*) stop; (*Aut: cartello*) stop
sign; (*: fanalino d'arresto*) brake-light
'storcere['stɔrtʃere] *vt* to twist; **storcersi**
vpr to writhe, twist; **~ il naso** (*fig*) to turn
up one's nose; **storcersi la caviglia** to
twist one's ankle
stor'dire *vt* (*intontire*) to stun, daze;
stor'dito, -a *ag* stunned
'storia *sf* (*scienza, avvenimenti*) history;
(*racconto, bugia*) story; (*faccenda, questione*)
business *no pl*; (*pretesto*) excuse, pretext;
storie *sfpl* (*smancerie*) fuss *sg*; **'storico, -a,
-ci, -che** *ag* historic(al) ▷ *sm* historian
stori'one *sm* (*Zool*) sturgeon
'stormo *sm* (*di uccelli*) flock
'storpio, -a *ag* crippled, maimed
'storsi *ecc vb vedi* **storcere**
'storta *sf* (*distorsione*) sprain, twist
'storto, -a *pp di* **storcere** ▷ *ag* (*chiodo*)
twisted, bent; (*gamba, quadro*) crooked
sto'viglie[sto'viʎʎe] *sfpl* dishes *pl*,
crockery
'strabico, -a, -ci, -che *ag* squint-eyed;
(*occhi*) squint
strac'chino[strak'kino] *sm* type of soft
cheese
stracci'are[strat'tʃare] *vt* to tear;
stracciarsi *vpr* to tear
'straccio, -a, -ci, -ce['strattʃo] *ag* **carta
straccia** waste paper ▷ *sm* rag; (*per pulire*)

cloth, duster; **stracci** smpl (peg: indumenti) rags; **si è ridotto a uno ~** he's worn himself out; **non ha uno ~ di lavoro** he's not got a job of any sort

'**strada** sf road; (di città) street; (cammino, via, fig) way; **che ~ devo prendere per andare a …?** which road do I take for …?; **farsi ~** (fig) to do well for o.s.; **essere fuori ~** (fig) to be on the wrong track; **~ facendo** on the way; **strada senza uscita** dead end; **stra'dale** ag road cpd

strafalci'one [strafal'tʃone] sm blunder, howler

stra'fare vi to overdo it

strafot'tente ag **è ~** he doesn't give a damn, he couldn't care less

'**strage** ['stradʒe] sf massacre, slaughter

stralu'nato, -a ag (occhi) rolling; (persona) beside o.s., very upset

'**strambo, -a** ag strange, queer

strampa'lato, -a ag odd, eccentric

stra'nezza [stra'nettsa] sf strangeness

strango'lare vt to strangle

strani'ero, -a ag foreign ▷ sm/f foreigner

> Attenzione! In inglese esiste la parola stranger, che però significa sconosciuto oppure estraneo.

'**strano, -a** ag strange, odd

straordi'nario, -a ag extraordinary; (treno ecc) special ▷ sm (lavoro) overtime

strapi'ombo sm overhanging rock; **a ~** overhanging

strap'pare vt (gen) to tear, rip; (pagina ecc) to tear off, tear out; (sradicare) to pull up; (togliere): **~ qc a qn** to snatch sth from sb; (fig) to wrest sth from sb; **strapparsi** vpr (lacerarsi) to rip, tear; (rompersi) to break; **strapparsi un muscolo** to tear a muscle; '**strappo** sm pull, tug; tear, rip; **fare uno strappo alla regola** to make an exception to the rule; **strappo muscolare** torn muscle

strari'pare vi to overflow

'**strascico, -chi** ['straʃʃiko] sm (di abito) train; (conseguenza) after-effect

strata'gemma, -i [strata'dʒemma] sm stratagem

strate'gia, -'gie [strate'dʒia] sf strategy; **stra'tegico, -a, -ci, -che** ag strategic

'**strato** sm layer; (rivestimento) coat, coating; (Geo, fig) stratum; (Meteor) stratus; **strato d'ozono** ozone layer

strat'tone sm tug, jerk; **dare uno ~ a qc** to tug o jerk sth, give sth a tug o jerk

strava'gante ag odd, eccentric

stra'volto, -a pp di **stravolgere**

'**strazio** sm torture; (fig: cosa fatta male): **essere uno ~** to be appalling

'**strega, -ghe** sf witch

stre'gare vt to bewitch

stre'gone sm (mago) wizard; (di tribù) witch doctor

strepi'toso, -a ag clamorous, deafening; (fig: successo) resounding

stres'sante ag stressful

stres'sato, -a ag under stress

stretch [stretʃ] ag inv stretch

'**stretta** sf (di mano) grasp; (finanziaria) squeeze; (fig: dolore, turbamento) pang; **una ~ di mano** a handshake; **essere alle strette** to have one's back to the wall; vedi anche **stretto**

stretta'mente av tightly; (rigorosamente) strictly

'**stretto, -a** pp di **stringere** ▷ ag (corridoio, limiti) narrow; (gonna, scarpe, nodo, curva) tight; (intimo: parente, amico) close; (rigoroso: osservanza) strict; (preciso: significato) precise, exact ▷ sm (braccio di mare) strait; **a denti stretti** with clenched teeth; **lo ~ necessario** the bare minimum; **stret'toia** sf bottleneck; (fig) tricky situation

stri'ato, -a ag streaked

'**stridulo, -a** ag shrill

stril'lare vt, vi to scream, shriek; '**strillo** sm scream, shriek

strimin'zito, -a [strimin'tsito] ag (misero) shabby; (molto magro) skinny

strimpel'lare vt (Mus) to strum

'**stringa, -ghe** sf lace

strin'gato, -a ag (fig) concise

'**stringere** ['strindʒere] vt (avvicinare due cose) to press (together), squeeze (together); (tenere stretto) to hold tight, clasp, clutch; (pugno, mascella, denti) to clench; (labbra) to compress; (avvitare) to tighten; (abito) to take in; (scarpe) to pinch, be tight for; (fig: concludere: patto) to make; (: accelerare: passo, tempo) to quicken ▷ vi (essere stretto) to be tight; (tempo: incalzare) to be pressing

'**strinsi** ecc vb vedi **stringere**

'**striscia, -sce** ['striʃʃa] sf (di carta, tessuto ecc) strip; (riga) stripe; **strisce (pedonali)** zebra crossing sg

strisci'are [striʃʃare] vt (piedi) to drag; (muro, macchina) to graze ▷ vi to crawl, creep

'**striscio** ['striʃʃo] sm graze; (Med) smear; **colpire di ~** to graze

strisci'one [striʃʃone] sm banner

strito'lare vt to grind

striz'zare [strit'tsare] vt (panni) to wring (out); **~ l'occhio** to wink

'**strofa** sf strophe

strofi'naccio [strofi'nattʃo] sm duster, cloth; (per piatti) dishcloth; (per pavimenti)

floorcloth

strofi'nare vt to rub

stron'care vt to break off; (fig: ribellione) to suppress, put down; (: film, libro) to tear to pieces

'stronzo ['strontso] sm (sterco) turd; (fig fam!: persona) shit (!)

stroz'zare [strot'tsare] vt (soffocare) to choke, strangle

struccarsi vpr to remove one's make-up

strumen'tale ag (Mus) instrumental

strumentaliz'zare [strumentalid'dzare] vt to exploit, use to one's own ends

stru'mento sm (arnese, fig) instrument, tool; (Mus) instrument; ~ **a corda** o **ad arco/a fiato** stringed/wind instrument

'strutto sm lard

strut'tura sf structure

'struzzo ['struttso] sm ostrich

stuc'care vt (muro) to plaster; (vetro) to putty; (decorare con stucchi) to stucco

'stucco, -chi sm plaster; (di vetri) putty; (ornamentale) stucco; **rimanere di ~** (fig) to be dumbfounded

stu'dente, -'essa sm/f student; (scolaro) pupil, schoolboy/girl

studi'are vt to study

'studio sm studying; (ricerca, saggio, stanza) study; (di professionista) office; (di artista, Cinema, TV, Radio) studio; **studi** smpl (Ins) studies; **studio medico** doctor's surgery (BRIT) o office (US)

studi'oso, -a ag studious, hard-working ▷ sm/f scholar

'stufa sf stove; **stufa elettrica** electric fire o heater

stu'fare vt (Cuc) to stew; (fig: fam) to bore; **stufarsi** vpr (fam): **stufarsi (di)** (fig) to get fed up with (with); **'stufo, -a** (fam) ag **essere stufo di** to be fed up with, be sick and tired of

stu'oia sf mat

stupefa'cente [stupefa't∫εnte] ag stunning, astounding ▷ sm drug, narcotic

stupe'fatto, -a pp di **stupefare**

stu'pendo, -a ag marvellous, wonderful

stupi'daggine [stupi'daddʒine] sf stupid thing (to do o say)

stupidità sf stupidity

'stupido, -a ag stupid

stu'pire vt to amaze, stun ▷ vi **stupirsi**; ~ **(di)** to be amazed (at), be stunned (by)

stu'pore sm amazement, astonishment

stu'prare vt to rape

'stupro sm rape

stu'rare vt (lavandino) to clear

stuzzica'denti [stuttsika'dεnti] sm toothpick

stuzzi'care [stuttsi'kare] vt (ferita ecc)

to poke (at), prod (at); (fig) to tease; (: appetito) to whet; (: curiosità) to stimulate; ~ **i denti** to pick one's teeth

PAROLA CHIAVE

su (su +il = **sul**, su +lo = **sullo**, su +l' = **sull'**, su +la = **sulla**, su +i = **sui**, su +gli = **sugli**, su +le = **sulle**) prep **1** (gen) on; (moto) on(to); (in cima a) on (top of); **mettilo sul tavolo** put it on the table; **un paesino sul mare** a village by the sea

2 (argomento) about, on; **un libro su Cesare** a book on o about Caesar

3 (circa) about; **costerà sui 3 milioni** it will cost about 3 million; **una ragazza sui 17 anni** a girl of about 17 (years of age)

4: **su misura** made to measure; **su richiesta** on request; **3 casi su dieci** 3 cases out of 10

▷ av **1** (in alto, verso l'alto) up; **vieni su** come on up; **guarda su** look up; **su le mani!** hands up!; **in su** (verso l'alto) up(wards); (in poi) onwards; **dai 20 anni in su** from the age of 20 onwards

2 (addosso) on; **cos'hai su?** what have you got on?

▷ escl come on!; **su coraggio!** come on, cheer up!

su'bacqueo, -a ag underwater ▷ sm skin-diver

sub'buglio [sub'buʎʎo] sm confusion, turmoil

'subdolo, -a ag underhand, sneaky

suben'trare vi ~ **a qn in qc** to take over sth from sb

su'bire vt to suffer, endure

'subito av immediately, at once, straight away

subodo'rare vt (insidia ecc) to smell, suspect

subordi'nato, -a ag subordinate; (dipendente): ~ **a** dependent on, subject to

suc'cedere [sut't∫edere] vi (prendere il posto di qn): ~ **a** to succeed; (venire dopo): ~ **a** to follow; (accadere) to happen; **cos'è successo?** what happened?; **succes'sivo, -a** ag successive; **suc'cesso, -a** pp di **succedere** ▷ sm (esito) outcome; (buona riuscita) success; **di successo** (libro, personaggio) successful

succhi'are [suk'kjare] vt to suck (up); **succhi'otto** sm (per bambino) dummy

succhi'otto [suk'kjɔtto] sm dummy (BRIT), pacifier (US), comforter (US)

suc'cinto, -a [sut't∫into] ag (discorso) succinct; (abito) brief

'succo, -chi sm juice; (fig) essence, gist;

succo di frutta/pomodoro fruit/tomato juice

succur'sale *sf* branch (office)

sud *sm* south ▷ *ag inv* south; (*lato*) south, southern

Su'dafrica *sm* **il ~** South Africa; **sudafri'cano, -a** *ag, sm/f* South African

Suda'merica *sm* **il ~** South America

su'dare *vi* to perspire, sweat; **~ freddo** to come out in a cold sweat

su'dato, -a *ag* (*persona, mani*) sweaty; (*fig: denaro*) hard-earned ▷ *sf* (*anche fig*) sweat; **una vittoria sudata** a hard-won victory; **ho fatto una bella sudata per finirlo in tempo** it was a real sweat to get it finished in time

suddi'videre *vt* to subdivide

su'dest *sm* south-east

'sudicio, -a, -ci, -ce ['suditʃo] *ag* dirty, filthy

su'dore *sm* perspiration, sweat

su'dovest *sm* south-west

suffici'ente [suffi'tʃɛnte] *ag* enough, sufficient; (*borioso*) self-important; (*Ins*) satisfactory; **suffici'enza** *sf* self-importance; pass mark; **a sufficienza** enough; **ne ho avuto a sufficienza!** I've had enough of this!

suf'fisso *sm* (*Ling*) suffix

suggeri'mento [suddʒeri'mento] *sm* suggestion; (*consiglio*) piece of advice, advice *no pl*

sugge'rire [suddʒe'rire] *vt* (*risposta*) to tell; (*consigliare*) to advise; (*proporre*) to suggest; (*Teatro*) to prompt

suggestio'nare [suddʒestjo'nare] *vt* to influence

sugges'tivo, -a [suddʒes'tivo] *ag* (*paesaggio*) evocative; (*teoria*) interesting, attractive

'sughero ['sugero] *sm* cork

'sugo, -ghi *sm* (*succo*) juice; (*di carne*) gravy; (*condimento*) sauce; (*fig*) gist, essence

sui'cida, -i, -e [sui'tʃida] *ag* suicidal ▷ *sm/f* suicide

suici'darsi [suitʃi'darsi] *vpr* to commit suicide

sui'cidio [sui'tʃidjo] *sm* suicide

su'ino, -a *ag* **carne suina** pork ▷ *sm* pig

sul'tano, -a *sm/f* sultan/sultana

'suo (*f* **'sua**, *pl* **'sue, 'suoi**) *det* **il ~, la sua** *ecc* (*di lui*) his; (*di lei*) her; (*di esso*) its; (*con valore indefinito*) one's, his/her; (*anche*: **S~**: *forma di cortesia*) your ▷ *pron* **il ~, la sua** *ecc* his; hers; yours; **i ~i** his (*o* her *o* one's *o* your) family

su'ocero, -a ['swɔtʃero] *sm/f* father/mother-in-law

su'ola *sf* (*di scarpa*) sole

su'olo *sm* (*terreno*) ground; (*terra*) soil

suo'nare *vt* (*Mus*) to play; (*campana*) to ring; (*ore*) to strike; (*clacson, allarme*) to sound ▷ *vi* to play; (*telefono, campana*) to ring; (*ore*) to strike; (*clacson, fig: parole*) to sound

suone'ria *sf* alarm

su'ono *sm* sound

su'ora *sf* (*Rel*) sister

'super *sf* (*anche:* **benzina ~**) ≈ four-star (petrol) (BRIT), premium (US)

supe'rare *vt* (*oltrepassare: limite*) to exceed, surpass; (*percorrere*) to cover; (*attraversare: fiume*) to cross; (*sorpassare: veicolo*) to overtake; (*fig: essere più bravo di*) to surpass, outdo; (*: difficoltà*) to overcome; (*: esame*) to get through; **~ qn in altezza/peso** to be taller/heavier than sb; **ha superato la cinquantina** he's over fifty (years of age)

su'perbia *sf* pride; **su'perbo, -a** *ag* proud; (*fig*) magnificent, superb

superfici'ale [superfi'tʃale] *ag* superficial

super'ficie, -ci [super'fitʃe] *sf* surface

su'perfluo, -a *ag* superfluous

superi'ore *ag* (*piano, arto, classi*) upper; (*più elevato: temperatura, livello*): **~ (a)** higher (than); (*migliore*): **~ (a)** superior (to)

superla'tivo, -a *ag, sm* superlative

supermer'cato *sm* supermarket

su'perstite *ag* surviving ▷ *sm/f* survivor

superstizi'one [superstit'tsjone] *sf* superstition; **superstizi'oso, -a** *ag* superstitious

super'strada *sf* ≈ (toll-free) motorway

su'pino, -a *ag* supine

supplemen'tare *ag* extra; (*treno*) relief *cpd*; (*entrate*) additional

supple'mento *sm* supplement

sup'plente *sm/f* temporary member of staff, supply (*o* substitute) teacher

'supplica, -che *sf* (*preghiera*) plea; (*domanda scritta*) petition, request

suppli'care *vt* to implore, beseech

sup'plizio [sup'plittsjo] *sm* torture

sup'pongo, sup'poni *ecc vb vedi* **supporre**

sup'porre *vt* to suppose

sup'porto *sm* (*sostegno*) support

sup'posta *sf* (*Med*) suppository

su'premo, -a *ag* supreme

surge'lare [surdʒe'lare] *vt* to (deep-)freeze

surge'lato, -a [surdʒe'lato] *ag* (deep-)frozen ▷ *smpl* **i surgelati** frozen food *sg*

sur'plus *sm inv* (*Econ*) surplus

surriscal'dare *vt* to overheat

suscet'tibile [suʃʃet'tibile] *ag* (*sensibile*) touchy, sensitive

susci'tare [suʃʃi'tare] *vt* to provoke,

arouse

su'sina *sf* plum

susseguirsi *vpr* to follow one another

sus'sidio *sm* subsidy; **sussidi didattici** teaching aids

sussul'tare *vi* to shudder

sussur'rare *vt, vi* to whisper, murmur; **sus'surro** *sm* whisper, murmur

svagarsi *vpr* to amuse o.s.; to enjoy o.s.

'svago, -ghi *sm* (*riposo*) relaxation; (*ricreazione*) amusement; (*passatempo*) pastime

svaligi'are [zvali'dʒare] *vt* to rob, burgle (BRIT), burglarize (US)

svalu'tarsi *vpr* (*Econ*) to be devalued

svalutazi'one *sf* devaluation

sva'nire *vi* to disappear, vanish

svantaggi'ato, -a [zvantad'dʒato] *ag* at a disadvantage

svan'taggio [zvan'taddʒo] *sm* disadvantage; (*inconveniente*) drawback, disadvantage

svari'ato, -a *ag* varied; various

'svastica *sf* swastika

sve'dese *ag* Swedish ▷ *sm/f* Swede ▷ *sm* (*Ling*) Swedish

'sveglia ['zveʎʎa] *sf* waking up; (*orologio*) alarm (clock); **sveglia telefonica** alarm call

svegli'are [zveʎ'ʎare] *vt* to wake up; (*fig*) to awaken, arouse; **svegliarsi** *vpr* to wake up; (*fig*) to be revived, reawaken; **vorrei essere svegliato alle 7, per favore** could I have an alarm call at 7 am, please?

'sveglio, -a ['zveʎʎo] *ag* awake; (*fig*) quick-witted

sve'lare *vt* to reveal

'svelto, -a *ag* (*passo*) quick; (*mente*) quick, alert; **alla svelta** quickly

'svendere *vt* to sell off, clear

'svendita *sf* (*Comm*) (clearance) sale

'svengo *ecc vb vedi* **svenire**

sveni'mento *sm* fainting fit, faint

sve'nire *vi* to faint

sven'tare *vt* to foil, thwart

sven'tato, -a *ag* (*distratto*) scatterbrained; (*imprudente*) rash

svento'lare *vt, vi* to wave, flutter

sven'tura *sf* misfortune

sverrò *ecc vb vedi* **svenire**

sves'tire *vt* to undress; **svestirsi** *vpr* to get undressed

'Svezia ['zvettsja] *sf* **la ~** Sweden

svi'are *vt* to divert; (*fig*) to lead astray

svi'gnarsela [zviɲ'ɲarsela] *vpr* to slip away, sneak off

svilup'pare *vt* to develop; **svilupparsi** *vpr* to develop; **può ~ questo rullino?** can you develop this film?

svi'luppo *sm* development

'svincolo *sm* (*stradale*) motorway (BRIT) o expressway (US) intersection

'svista *sf* oversight

svi'tare *vt* to unscrew

'Svizzera ['zvittsera] *sf* **la ~** Switzerland

'svizzero, -a ['zvittsero] *ag, sm/f* Swiss

svogli'ato, -a [zvoʎ'ʎato] *ag* listless; (*pigro*) lazy

'svolgere ['zvɔldʒere] *vt* to unwind; (*srotolare*) to unroll; (*fig: argomento*) to develop; (: *piano, programma*) to carry out; **svolgersi** *vpr* to unwind; to unroll; (*fig: aver luogo*) to take place; (: *procedere*) to go on

'svolsi *ecc vb vedi* **svolgere**

'svolta *sf* (*atto*) turning *no pl*; (*curva*) turn, bend; (*fig*) turning-point

svol'tare *vi* to turn

svuo'tare *vt* to empty (out)

T, t [ti] *sf o m inv* (*lettera*) T, t; **T come Taranto** ≈ T for Tommy

t *abbr* = **tonnellata**

tabacche'ria [tabakke'ria] *sf* tobacconist's (shop)

● **TABACCHERIA**

● **Tabaccherie** sell cigarettes and tobacco
  ● and can easily be identified by their sign,
  ● a large white "T" on a black background.
  ● You can buy postage stamps and bus
  ● tickets at a **tabaccheria** and some also
  ● sell newspapers.

ta'bacco, -chi *sm* tobacco
ta'bella *sf* (*tavola*) table; (*elenco*) list
tabel'lone *sm* (*pubblicitario*) billboard; (*con orario*) timetable board
TAC *sigla f* (*Med*: = *Tomografia Assiale Computerizzata*) CAT
tac'chino [tak'kino] *sm* turkey
'tacco, -chi *sm* heel; **tacchi a spillo** stiletto heels
taccu'ino *sm* notebook
ta'cere [ta'tʃere] *vi* to be silent *o* quiet; (*smettere di parlare*) to fall silent ▷ *vt* to keep to oneself, say nothing about; **far ~ qn** to make sb be quiet; (*fig*) to silence sb
ta'chimetro [ta'kimetro] *sm* speedometer

'tacqui *ecc vb vedi* **tacere**
ta'fano *sm* horsefly
'taglia ['taʎʎa] *sf* (*statura*) height; (*misura*) size; (*riscatto*) ransom; (*ricompensa*) reward; **taglia forte** (*di abito*) large size
taglia'carte [taʎʎa'karte] *sm inv* paperknife
tagli'ando [taʎ'ʎando] *sm* coupon
tagli'are [taʎ'ʎare] *vt* to cut; (*recidere, interrompere*) to cut off; (*intersecare*) to cut across, intersect; (*carne*) to carve; (*vini*) to blend ▷ *vi* to cut; (*prendere una scorciatoia*) to take a short-cut; **tagliarsi** *vpr* to cut o.s.; **mi sono tagliato** I've cut myself; **~ corto** (*fig*) to cut short; **~ la corda** (*fig*) to sneak off; **~ i ponti (con)** (*fig*) to break off relations (with); **~ la strada a qn** to cut across sb; **mi sono tagliato** I've cut myself
taglia'telle [taʎʎa'tɛlle] *sfpl* tagliatelle *pl*
taglia'unghie [taʎʎa'ungje] *sm inv* nail clippers *pl*
tagli'ente [taʎ'ʎɛnte] *ag* sharp
'taglio ['taʎʎo] *sm* cutting *no pl*; cut; (*parte tagliente*) cutting edge; (*di abito*) cut, style; (*di stoffa: lunghezza*) length; (*di vini*) blending; **di ~** on edge, edgeways; **banconote di piccolo/grosso ~** notes of small/large denomination; **taglio cesareo** Caesarean section
tailan'dese *ag, sm/f, sm* Thai
Tai'landia *sf* **la ~** Thailand
'talco *sm* talcum powder

 PAROLA CHIAVE

'tale *det* **1** (*simile, così grande*) such; **un(a) tale ...** such (a) ...; **non accetto tali discorsi** I won't allow such talk; **è di una tale arroganza** he is so arrogant; **fa una tale confusione!** he makes such a mess!
2 (*persona o cosa indeterminata*) such-and-such; **il giorno tale all'ora tale** on such-and-such a day at such-and-such a time; **la tal persona** that person; **ha telefonato una tale Giovanna** somebody called Giovanna phoned
3 (*nelle similitudini*): **tale ... tale** like ... like; **tale padre tale figlio** like father, like son; **hai il vestito tale quale il mio** your dress is just *o* exactly like mine
▷ *pron* (*indefinito: persona*): **un(a) tale** someone; **quel (o quella) tale** that person, that man (*o* woman); **il tal dei tali** what's-his-name

tale'bano *sm* Taliban
ta'lento *sm* talent
talis'mano *sm* talisman

tallon'cino [tallon'tʃino] *sm* counterfoil
tal'lone *sm* heel
tal'mente *av* so
'talpa *sf* (Zool) mole
tal'volta *av* sometimes, at times
tambu'rello *sm* tambourine
tam'buro *sm* drum
Ta'migi [ta'midʒi] *sm* **il ~** the Thames
tampo'nare *vt* (otturare) to plug; (urtare: macchina) to crash o ram into
tam'pone *sm* (Med) wad, pad; (per timbri) ink-pad; (respingente) buffer; **tampone assorbente** tampon
'tana *sf* lair, den
'tanga *sm inv* G-string
tan'gente [tan'dʒɛnte] *ag* (Mat): **~ a** tangential to ▷ *sf* tangent; (quota) share
tangenzi'ale [tandʒen'tsjale] *sf* (Aut) bypass
'tanica *sf* (contenitore) jerry can

PAROLA CHIAVE

'tanto, -a *det* **1** (molto: quantità) a lot of, much; (: numero) a lot of, many; (così tanto: quantità) so much, such a lot of; (: numero) so many, such a lot of; **tante volte** so many times, so often; **tanti auguri!** all the best!; **tante grazie** many thanks; **tanto tempo** so long, such a long time; **ogni tanti chilometri** every so many kilometres

2: tanto ... quanto (quantità) as much ... as; (numero) as many ... as; **ho tanta pazienza quanta ne hai tu** I have as much patience as you have o as you; **ha tanti amici quanti nemici** he has as many friends as he has enemies

3 (rafforzativo) such; **ho aspettato per tanto tempo** I waited so long o for such a long time

▷ *pron* **1** (molto) much, a lot; (così tanto) so much, such a lot; **tanti, e** many, a lot; so many, such a lot; **credevo ce ne fosse tanto** I thought there was (such) a lot, I thought there was plenty

2: tanto quanto (denaro) as much as; (cioccolatini) as many as; **ne ho tanto quanto basta** I have as much as I need; **due volte tanto** twice as much

3 (indeterminato) so much; **tanto per l'affitto, tanto per il gas** so much for the rent, so much for the gas; **costa un tanto al metro** it costs so much per metre; **di tanto in tanto, ogni tanto** every so often; **tanto vale che ... I** (o we ecc) may as well ...; **tanto meglio!** so much the better!; **tanto peggio per lui!** so much the worse for him!

▷ *av* **1** (molto) very; **vengo tanto volentieri** I'd be very glad to come; **non ci vuole tanto a capirlo** it doesn't take much to understand it

2 (così tanto: con ag, av) so; (: con vb) so much, such a lot; **è tanto bella!** she's so beautiful!; **non urlare tanto** don't shout so much; **sto tanto meglio adesso** I'm so much better now; **tanto ... che** so ... (that); **tanto ... da** so ... as

3: tanto ... quanto as ... as; **conosco tanto Carlo quanto suo padre** I know both Carlo and his father; **non è poi tanto complicato quanto sembri** it's not as difficult as it seems; **tanto più insisti, tanto più non mollerà** the more you insist, the more stubborn he'll be; **quanto più ... tanto meno** the more ... the less

4 (solamente) just; **tanto per cambiare/scherzare** just for a change/a joke; **una volta tanto** for once

5 (a lungo) (for) long
▷ *cong* after all

'tappa *sf* (luogo di sosta, fermata) stop, halt; (parte di un percorso) stage, leg; (Sport) lap; **a tappe** in stages

tap'pare *vt* to plug, stop up; (bottiglia) to cork; **tapparsi** *vpr* **tapparsi in casa** to shut o.s. up at home; **tapparsi la bocca** to shut up; **tapparsi le orecchie** to turn a deaf ear

tappa'rella *sf* rolling shutter

tappe'tino *sm* (per auto) car mat; **tappetino antiscivolo** (da bagno) non-slip mat

tap'peto *sm* carpet; (anche: **tappetino**) rug; (Sport): **andare al ~** to go down for the count; **mettere sul ~** (fig) to bring up for discussion

tappez'zare [tappet'tsare] *vt* (con carta) to paper; (rivestire): **~ qc (di)** to cover sth (with); **tappezze'ria** *sf* (tessuto) tapestry; (carta da parati) wallpaper; (arte) upholstery; **far da tappezzeria** (fig) to be a wallflower

'tappo *sm* stopper; (in sughero) cork

tar'dare *vi* to be late ▷ *vt* to delay; **~ a fare** to delay doing

'tardi *av* late; **più ~** later (on); **al più ~** at the latest; **sul ~** (verso sera) late in the day; **far ~** to be late; (restare alzato) to stay up late; **è troppo ~** it's too late

'targa, -ghe *sf* plate; (Aut) number (BRIT) o license (US) plate; **tar'ghetta** *sf* (su bagaglio) name tag; (su porta) nameplate

ta'riffa *sf* (gen) rate, tariff; (di trasporti) fare; (elenco) price list; tariff

'tarlo *sm* woodworm

'**tarma** *sf* moth
tarocchi *smpl (gioco)* tarot *sg*
tarta'ruga, -ghe *sf* tortoise; *(di mare)* turtle; *(materiale)* tortoiseshell
tar'tina *sf* canapé
tar'tufo *sm (Bot)* truffle
'**tasca, -sche** *sf* pocket; **tas'cabile** *ag (libro)* pocket *cpd*
'**tassa** *sf (imposta)* tax; *(doganale)* duty; *(per iscrizione: a scuola ecc)* fee; **tassa di circolazione** road tax; **tassa di soggiorno** tourist tax
tas'sare *vt* to tax; to levy a duty on
tas'sello *sm* plug; wedge
tassì *sm inv* = **taxi**; **tas'sista, -i, -e** *sm/f* taxi driver
'**tasso** *sm (di natalità, d'interesse ecc)* rate; *(Bot)* yew; *(Zool)* badger; **tasso di cambio/d'interesse** rate of exchange/interest
tas'tare *vt* to feel; **~ il terreno** *(fig)* to see how the land lies
tasti'era *sf* keyboard
'**tasto** *sm* key; *(tatto)* touch, feel
tas'toni *av* **procedere (a) ~** to grope one's way forward
'**tatto** *sm (senso)* touch; *(fig)* tact; **duro al ~** hard to the touch; **aver ~** to be tactful, have tact
tatu'aggio [tatu'addʒo] *sm* tattooing; *(disegno)* tattoo
tatu'are *vt* to tattoo
'**tavola** *sf* table; *(asse)* plank, board; *(lastra)* tablet; *(quadro)* panel (painting); *(illustrazione)* plate; **tavola calda** snack bar; **tavola rotonda** *(fig)* round table; **tavola a vela** windsurfer
tavo'letta *sf* tablet, bar; **a ~** *(Aut)* flat out
tavo'lino *sm* small table; *(scrivania)* desk
'**tavolo** *sm* table; **un ~ per 4 per favore** a table for 4, please
'**taxi** *sm inv* taxi; **può chiamarmi un ~ per favore?** can you call me a taxi, please?
'**tazza** ['tattsa] *sf* cup; **una ~ di caffè/tè** a cup of coffee/tea; **tazza da tè/caffè** tea/coffee cup
TBC *abbr f* (= *tubercolosi*) TB
te *pron (soggetto: in forme comparative, oggetto)* you
tè *sm inv* tea; *(trattenimento)* tea party
tea'trale *ag* theatrical
te'atro *sm* theatre
techno ['tɛkno] *ag inv (musica)* techno
'**tecnica, -che** *sf* technique; *(tecnologia)* technology
'**tecnico, -a, -ci, -che** *ag* technical ▷ *sm/f* technician
tecnolo'gia [teknolo'dʒia] *sf* technology
te'desco, -a, -schi, -sche *ag, sm/f, sm* German

te'game *sm (Cuc)* pan
'**tegola** *sf* tile
tei'era *sf* teapot
tel. *abbr* (= *telefono*) tel.
'**tela** *sf (tessuto)* cloth; *(per vele, quadri)* canvas; *(dipinto)* canvas, painting; **di ~** *(calzoni)* (heavy) cotton *cpd*; *(scarpe, borsa)* canvas *cpd*; **tela cerata** oilcloth
te'laio *sm (apparecchio)* loom; *(struttura)* frame
tele'camera *sf* television camera
teleco'mando *sm* remote control
tele'cronaca *sf* television report
telefo'nare *vi* to telephone, ring; to make a phone call ▷ *vt* to telephone; **~ a** to phone up, ring up, call up
telefo'nata *sf (telephone)* call; **~ a carico del destinatario** reverse charge *(BRIT)* o collect *(US)* call
tele'fonico, -a, -ci, -che *ag* (tele)phone *cpd*
telefon'ino *sm* mobile phone
te'lefono *sm* telephone; **telefono a gettoni** ≈ pay phone
telegior'nale [teledʒor'nale] *sm* television news (programme)
tele'gramma, -i *sm* telegram
telela'voro *sm* teleworking
Tele'pass® *sm inv* automatic payment card for use on Italian motorways
telepa'tia *sf* telepathy
teles'copio *sm* telescope
teleselezi'one [teleselet'tsjone] *sf* direct dialling
telespetta'tore, -'trice *sm/f* (television) viewer
tele'vendita *sf* teleshopping
televisi'one *sf* television
televi'sore *sm* television set
'**tema, -i** *sm* theme; *(Ins)* essay, composition
te'mere *vt* to fear, be afraid of; *(essere sensibile a: freddo, calore)* to be sensitive to ▷ *vi* to be afraid; *(essere preoccupato)*: **~ per** to worry about, fear for; **~ di/che** to be afraid of/that
temperama'tite *sm inv* pencil sharpener
tempera'mento *sm* temperament
tempera'tura *sf* temperature
tempe'rino *sm* penknife
tem'pesta *sf* storm; **tempesta di sabbia/neve** sand/snowstorm
'**tempia** *sf (Anat)* temple
'**tempio** *sm (edificio)* temple
'**tempo** *sm (Meteor)* weather; *(cronologico)* time; *(epoca)* time, times *pl*; *(di film, gioco: parte)* part; *(Mus)* time; (: *battuta*) beat; *(Ling)* tense; **che ~ fa?** what's the weather like?; **un ~** once; **~ fa** some time ago; **al ~**

stesso o **a un ~** at the same time; **per ~** early; **ha fatto il suo ~** it has had its day; **primo/secondo ~** (Teatro) first/second part; (Sport) first/second half; **in ~ utile** in due time o course; **a ~ pieno** full-time; **tempo libero** free time

tempo'rale ag temporal ▷ sm (Meteor) (thunder)storm

tempo'raneo, -a ag temporary

te'nace [te'natʃe] ag strong, tough; (fig) tenacious

te'naglie [te'naʎʎe] sfpl pincers pl

'tenda sf (riparo) awning; (di finestra) curtain; (per campeggio ecc) tent

ten'denza [ten'dɛntsa] sf tendency; (orientamento) trend; **avere ~ a** o **per qc** to have a bent for sth

'tendere vt (allungare al massimo) to stretch, draw tight; (porgere: mano) to hold out; (fig: trappola) to lay, set ▷ vi **~ a qc/a fare** to tend towards sth/to do; **~ l'orecchio** to prick up one's ears; **il tempo tende al caldo** the weather is getting hot; **un blu che tende al verde** a greenish blue

'tendine sm tendon, sinew

ten'done sm (da circo) tent

'tenebre sfpl darkness sg

te'nente sm lieutenant

te'nere vt (conservare, mantenere) to keep; (ritenere, considerare) to consider; (spazio: occupare) to take up, occupy; (seguire: strada) to keep to ▷ vi to hold; (colori) to be fast; (dare importanza): **~ a** to care about; **~ a fare** to want to do, be keen to do; **tenersi** vpr (stare in una determinata posizione) to stand; (stimarsi) to consider o.s.; (aggrapparsi): **tenersi a** to hold on to; (attenersi): **tenersi a** to stick to; **~ una conferenza** to give a lecture; **~ conto di qc** to take sth into consideration; **~ presente qc** to bear sth in mind

'tenero, -a ag tender; (pietra, cera, colore) soft; (fig) tender, loving

'tengo ecc vb vedi **tenere**

'tenni ecc vb vedi **tenere**

'tennis sm tennis

ten'nista, -i, e sm/f tennis player

te'nore sm (tono) tone; (Mus) tenor; **tenore di vita** (livello) standard of living

tensi'one sf tension

ten'tare vt (indurre) to tempt; (provare): **~ qc/di fare** to attempt o try sth/to do; **tenta'tivo** sm attempt; **tentazi'one** sf temptation

tenten'nare vi to shake, be unsteady; (fig) to hesitate, waver

ten'toni av **andare a ~** (anche fig) to grope one's way

'tenue ag (sottile) fine; (colore) soft; (fig) slender, slight

te'nuta sf (capacità) capacity; (divisa) uniform; (abito) dress; (Agr) estate; **a ~ d'aria** airtight; **tenuta di strada** roadholding power

teolo'gia [teolo'dʒia] sf theology

teo'ria sf theory

te'pore sm warmth

tep'pista, -i sm hooligan

tera'pia sf therapy; **terapia intensiva** intensive care

tergicris'tallo [terdʒikris'tallo] sm windscreen (BRIT) o windshield (US) wiper

tergiver'sare [terdʒiver'sare] vi to shilly-shally

ter'male ag thermal; **stazione** sf **~** spa

'terme sfpl thermal baths

termi'nale ag, sm terminal

termi'nare vt to end; (lavoro) to finish ▷ vi to end

'termine sm term; (fine, estremità) end; (di territorio) boundary, limit; **contratto a ~** (Comm) forward contract; **a breve/lungo ~** short-/long-term; **parlare senza mezzi termini** to talk frankly, not to mince one's words

ter'mometro sm thermometer

'termos sm inv = **thermos®**

termosi'fone sm radiator

ter'mostato sm thermostat

'terra sf (gen, Elettr) earth; (sostanza) soil, earth; (opposto al mare) land no pl; (regione, paese) land; (argilla) clay; **terre** sfpl (possedimento) lands, land sg; **a** o **per ~** (stato) on the ground (o floor); (moto) to the ground, down; **mettere a ~** (Elettr) to earth

terra'cotta sf terracotta; **vasellame** sm **di ~** earthenware

terra'ferma sf dry land, terra firma; (continente) mainland

ter'razza [ter'rattsa] sf terrace

ter'razzo [ter'rattso] sm = **terrazza**

terre'moto sm earthquake

ter'reno, -a ag (vita, beni) earthly ▷ sm (suolo, fig) ground; (Comm) land no pl, plot (of land); site; (Sport, Mil) field

ter'restre ag (superficie) of the earth, earth's; (di terra: battaglia, animale) land cpd; (Rel) earthly, worldly

ter'ribile ag terrible, dreadful

terrifi'cante ag terrifying

ter'rina sf tureen

territori'ale ag territorial

terri'torio sm territory

ter'rore sm terror; **terro'rismo** sm terrorism; **terro'rista, -i, -e** sm/f terrorist

terroriz'zare [terrorid'dzare] vt to terrorize

terza ['tɛrtsa] *sf* (*Scol: elementare*) ≈ third year at primary school; (: *media*) ≈ second year at secondary school; (: *superiore*) ≈ fifth year at secondary school; (*Aut*) third gear

ter'zino [ter'tsino] *sm* (*Calcio*) fullback, back

'terzo, -a ['tɛrtso] *ag* third ▷ *sm* (*frazione*) third; (*Dir*) third party; **terza pagina** (*Stampa*) Arts page; **terzi** *smpl* (*altri*) others, other people

'teschio ['tɛskjo] *sm* skull

'tesi *sf* thesis; **tesi di laurea** degree thesis

'tesi *ecc* *vb vedi* **tendere**

'teso, -a *pp di* **tendere** ▷ *ag* (*tirato*) taut, tight; (*fig*) tense

te'soro *sm* treasure; **il Ministero del T~** the Treasury

'tessera *sf* (*documento*) card

tes'suto *sm* fabric, material; (*Biol*) tissue

test ['tɛst] *sm inv* test

'testa *sf* head; (*di cose: estremità, parte anteriore*) head, front; **di ~** (*vettura ecc*) front; **tenere ~ a qn** (*nemico ecc*) to stand up to sb; **fare di ~ propria** to go one's own way; **in ~** (*Sport*) in the lead; **~ o croce?** heads or tails?; **avere la ~ dura** to be stubborn; **testa d'aglio** bulb of garlic; **testa di serie** (*Tennis*) seed, seeded player

testa'mento *sm* (*atto*) will; **l'Antico/il Nuovo T~** (*Rel*) the Old/New Testament

tes'tardo, -a *ag* stubborn, pig-headed

tes'tata *sf* (*parte anteriore*) head; (*intestazione*) heading

tes'ticolo *sm* testicle

testi'mone *sm/f* (*Dir*) witness; **testimone oculare** eye witness

testimoni'are *vt* to testify; (*fig*) to bear witness to, testify to ▷ *vi* to give evidence, testify

'testo *sm* text; **fare ~** (*opera, autore*) to be authoritative; **questo libro non fa ~** this book is not essential reading

tes'tuggine [tes'tuddʒine] *sf* tortoise; (*di mare*) turtle

'tetano *sm* (*Med*) tetanus

'tetto *sm* roof; **tet'toia** *sf* roofing; canopy

tettuccio [tet'tuttʃo] *sm* **~ apribile** (*Aut*) sunroof

'Tevere *sm* **il ~** the Tiber

TG, Tg *abbr* = **telegiornale**

'thermos® ['tɛrmos] *sm inv* vacuum o Thermos® flask

ti *pron* (*dav lo, la, li, le, ne diventa* **te**) ▷ *pron* (*oggetto*) you; (*complemento di termine*) (to) you; (*riflessivo*) yourself

'Tibet *sm* **il ~** Tibet

'tibia *sf* tibia, shinbone

tic *sm inv* tic, (nervous) twitch; (*fig*) mannerism

ticchet'tio [tikket'tio] *sm* (*di macchina da scrivere*) clatter; (*di orologio*) ticking; (*della pioggia*) patter

'ticket *sm inv* (*su farmaci*) prescription charge

ti'ene *ecc* *vb vedi* **tenere**

ti'epido, -a *ag* lukewarm, tepid

'tifo *sm* (*Med*) typhus; (*fig*): **fare il ~ per** to be a fan of

ti'fone *sm* typhoon

ti'foso, -a *sm/f* (*Sport ecc*) fan

tigì [ti'dʒi] *sm inv* TV news

'tiglio ['tiʎʎo] *sm* lime (tree), linden (tree)

'tigre *sf* tiger

tim'brare *vt* to stamp; (*annullare: francobolli*) to postmark; **~ il cartellino** to clock in

'timbro *sm* stamp; (*Mus*) timbre, tone

'timido, -a *ag* shy; timid

'timo *sm* thyme

ti'mone *sm* (*Naut*) rudder

ti'more *sm* (*paura*) fear; (*rispetto*) awe

'timpano *sm* (*Anat*) eardrum; (*Mus*)

'tingere ['tindʒere] *vt* to dye

'tinsi *ecc* *vb vedi* **tingere**

'tinta *sf* (*materia colorante*) dye; (*colore*) colour, shade

tintin'nare *vi* to tinkle

tinto'ria *sf* (*lavasecco*) dry cleaner's (shop)

tin'tura *sf* (*operazione*) dyeing; (*colorante*) dye; **tintura di iodio** tincture of iodine

'tipico, -a, -ci, -che *ag* typical

'tipo *sm* type; (*genere*) kind, type; (*fam*) chap, fellow; **che ~ di...?** what kind of ...?

tipogra'fia *sf* typography; (*procedimento*) letterpress (printing); (*officina*) printing house

TIR *sigla m* (= *Transports Internationaux Routiers*) *International Heavy Goods Vehicle*

ti'rare *vt* (*gen*) to pull; (*estrarre*): **~ qc da** to take o pull sth out of; to get sth out of; to extract sth from; (*chiudere: tenda ecc*) to draw, pull; (*tracciare, disegnare*) to draw, trace; (*lanciare: sasso, palla*) to throw; (*stampare*) to print; (*pistola, freccia*) to fire ▷ *vi* (*pipa, camino*) to draw; (*vento*) to blow; (*abito*) to be tight; (*fare fuoco*) to fire; (*fare del tiro, Calcio*) to shoot; **~ avanti** *vi* to struggle on ▷ *vt* to keep going; **~ fuori** (*estrarre*) to take out, pull out; **~ giù** (*abbassare*) to bring down, to lower; (*da scaffale ecc.*) to take down; **~ su** to pull up; (*capelli*) to put up; (*fig: bambino*) to bring up; **tirarsi** *vpr* **tirarsi indietro** to draw back; (*fig*) to back out; **~ a indovinare** to take a guess; **~ sul prezzo** to bargain; **tirar dritto** to keep right on going; **tirati su!** (*fig*) cheer up!; **~ via** (*togliere*) to take off

tira'tura sf (azione) printing; (di libro) (print) run; (di giornale) circulation

'tirchio, -a ['tirkjo] ag mean, stingy

'tiro sm shooting no pl, firing no pl; (colpo, sparo) shot; (di palla: lancio) throwing no pl; throw; (fig) trick; **cavallo da ~** draught (BRIT) o draft (US) horse; **tiro a segno** target shooting; (luogo) shooting range; **tiro con l'arco** archery

tiro'cinio [tiro'tʃinjo] sm apprenticeship; (professionale) training

ti'roide sf thyroid (gland)

Tir'reno sm **il (mar) ~** the Tyrrhenian Sea

ti'sana sf herb tea

tito'lare sm/f incumbent; (proprietario) owner; (Calcio) regular player

'titolo sm title; (di giornale) headline; (diploma) qualification; (Comm) security; (: azione) share; **a che ~?** for what reason?; **a ~ di amicizia** out of friendship; **a ~ di premio** as a prize; **titolo di credito** share; **titoli di stato** government securities; **titoli di testa** (Cinema) credits

titu'bante ag hesitant, irresolute

toast [toust] sm inv toasted sandwich (generally with ham and cheese)

toc'cante ag touching

toc'care vt to touch; (tastare) to feel; (fig: riguardare) to concern; (: commuovere) to touch, move; (: pungere) to hurt, wound; (: far cenno a: argomento) to touch on, mention ▷ vi **~ a** (accadere) to happen to; (spettare) to be up to; **~ (il fondo)** (in acqua) to touch the bottom; **tocca a te difenderci** it's up to you to defend us; **a chi tocca?** whose turn is it?; **mi toccò pagare** I had to pay

toccherò ecc [tokke'rɔ] vb vedi **toccare**

'togliere ['tɔʎʎere] vt (rimuovere) to take away (o off), remove; (riprendere, non concedere più) to take away, remove; (Mat) to take away, subtract; **~ qc a qn** to take sth (away) from sb; **ciò non toglie che** nevertheless, be that as it may; **togliersi il cappello** to take off one's hat

toi'lette [twa'lɛt] sf inv toilet; (mobile) dressing table; **dov'è la ~?** where's the toilet?

'Tokyo sf Tokyo

'tolgo ecc vb vedi **togliere**

tolle'rare vt to tolerate

'tolsi ecc vb vedi **togliere**

'tomba sf tomb

tom'bino sm manhole cover

tom'bola sf (gioco) tombola; (ruzzolone) tumble

'tondo, -a ag round

'tonfo sm splash; (rumore sordo) thud; (caduta): **fare un ~** to take a tumble

tonifi'care vt (muscoli, pelle) to tone up; (irrobustire) to invigorate, brace

tonnel'lata sf ton

'tonno sm tuna (fish)

'tono sm (gen) tone; (Mus: di pezzo) key; (di colore) shade, tone

ton'silla sf tonsil

'tonto, -a ag dull, stupid

to'pazio [to'pattsjo] sm topaz

'topo sm mouse

'toppa sf (serratura) keyhole; (pezza) patch

to'race [to'ratʃe] sm chest

'torba sf peat

'torcere ['tɔrtʃere] vt to twist; **torcersi** vpr to twist, writhe

'torcia, -ce ['tɔrtʃa] sf torch; **torcia elettrica** torch (BRIT), flashlight (US)

torci'collo [tortʃi'kɔllo] sm stiff neck

'tordo sm thrush

To'rino sf Turin

tor'menta sf snowstorm

tormen'tare vt to torment; **tormentarsi** vpr to fret, worry o.s.

tor'nado sm tornado

tor'nante sm hairpin bend

tor'nare vi to return, go (o come) back; (ridiventare: anche fig) to become (again); (riuscire giusto, esatto: conto) to work out; (risultare) to turn out (to be), prove (to be); **~ utile** to prove o turn out (to be) useful; **~ a casa** to go (o come) home; **torno a casa martedì** I'm going home on Tuesday

tor'neo sm tournament

'tornio sm lathe

'toro sm bull; (dello zodiaco): **T~** Taurus

'torre sf tower; (Scacchi) rook, castle; **torre di controllo** (Aer) control tower

tor'rente sm torrent

torri'one sm keep

tor'rone sm nougat

'torsi ecc vb vedi **torcere**

torsi'one sf twisting; torsion

'torso sm torso, trunk; (Arte) torso

'torsolo sm (di cavolo ecc) stump; (di frutta) core

'torta sf cake

tortel'lini smpl (Cuc) tortellini

'torto, -a pp di **torcere** ▷ ag (ritorto) twisted; (storto) twisted, crooked ▷ sm (ingiustizia) wrong; (colpa) fault; **a ~** wrongly; **aver ~** to be wrong

'tortora sf turtle dove

tor'tura sf torture; **tortu'rare** vt to torture

to'sare vt (pecora) to shear; (siepe) to clip

Tos'cana sf **la ~** Tuscany

'tosse sf cough; **ho la ~** I've got a cough

'tossico, -a, -ci, -che ag toxic

tossicodipen'dente sm/f drug addict

tos'sire vi to cough

tosta'pane sm inv toaster

to'tale ag, sm total

toto'calcio [toto'kaltʃo] sm gambling pool betting on football results, ≈ (football) pools pl (BRIT)

to'vaglia [to'vaʎʎa] sf tablecloth; **tovagli'olo** sm napkin

tra prep (di due persone, cose) between; (di più persone, cose) among(st); (tempo: entro) within, in; **~ 5 giorni** in 5 days' time; **sia detto ~ noi ...** between you and me ...; **litigano ~ (di) loro** they're fighting amongst themselves; **~ breve** soon; **~ sé e sé** (parlare ecc) to oneself

traboc'care vi to overflow

traboc'chetto [trabok'ketto] sm (fig) trap

'traccia, -ce ['trattʃa] sf (segno, striscia) trail, track; (orma) tracks pl; (residuo, testimonianza) trace, sign; (abbozzo) outline

tracci'are [trat'tʃare] vt to trace, mark (out); (disegnare) to draw; (fig: abbozzare) to outline

tra'chea [tra'kɛa] sf windpipe, trachea

tra'colla sf shoulder strap; **borsa a ~** shoulder bag

tradi'mento sm betrayal; (Dir, Mil) treason

tra'dire vt to betray; (coniuge) to be unfaithful to; (doveri: mancare) to fail in; (rivelare) to give away, reveal; **tradirsi** vpr to give o.s. away

tradizio'nale [tradittsjo'nale] ag traditional

tradizi'one [tradit'tsjone] sf tradition

tra'durre vt to translate; (spiegare) to render, convey; **me lo può ~?** can you translate this for me?; **traduzi'one** sf translation

'trae vb vedi **trarre**

traffi'cante sm/f dealer; (peg) trafficker

traffi'care vi (commerciare): **~ (in)** to trade (in), deal (in); (affaccendarsi) to busy o.s. ▷ vt (peg) to traffic in

'traffico, -ci sm traffic; (commercio) trade, traffic; **traffico di armi/droga** arms/drug trafficking

tra'gedia [tra'dʒɛdja] sf tragedy

'traggo ecc vb vedi **trarre**

tra'ghetto [tra'getto] sm ferry(boat)

'tragico, -a, -ci, -che ['tradʒiko] ag tragic

tra'gitto [tra'dʒitto] sm (passaggio) crossing; (viaggio) journey

tragu'ardo sm (Sport) finishing line; (fig) goal, aim

'trai ecc vb vedi **trarre**

traiet'toria sf trajectory

trai'nare vt to drag, haul; (rimorchiare) to tow

tralasci'are [tralaʃʃare] vt (studi) to neglect; (dettagli) to leave out, omit

tra'liccio [tra'littʃo] sm (Elettr) pylon

tram sm inv tram

'trama sf (filo) weft, woof; (fig: argomento, maneggio) plot

traman'dare vt to pass on, hand down

tram'busto sm turmoil

tramez'zino [tramed'dzino] sm sandwich

'tramite prep through

tramon'tare vi to set, go down; **tra'monto** sm setting; (del sole) sunset

trampo'lino sm (per tuffi) springboard, diving board; (per lo sci) ski-jump

tra'nello sm trap

'tranne prep except (for), but (for); **~ che** unless

tranquil'lante sm (Med) tranquillizer

tranquil'lità sf calm, stillness; quietness; peace of mind

tranquilliz'zare [trankwillid'dzare] vt to reassure

> Attenzione! In inglese esiste il verbo to tranquillize, che però significa "calmare con un tranquillante".

tran'quillo, -a ag calm, quiet; (bambino, scolaro) quiet; (sereno) with one's mind at rest; **sta' ~** don't worry

transazi'one [transat'tsjone] sf compromise; (Dir) settlement; (Comm) transaction, deal

tran'senna sf barrier

transgenico, -a, -ci, -che [trans'dʒɛniko] ag genetically modified

tran'sigere [tran'sidʒere] vi (venire a patti) to compromise, come to an agreement

transi'tabile ag passable

transi'tare vi to pass

transi'tivo, -a ag transitive

'transito sm transit; **di ~** (merci) in transit; (stazione) transit cpd; **"divieto di ~"** "no entry"

'trapano sm (utensile) drill; (Med) trepan

trape'lare vi to leak, drip; (fig) to leak out

tra'pezio [tra'pɛttsjo] sm (Mat) trapezium; (attrezzo ginnico) trapeze

trapian'tare vt to transplant; **trapi'anto** sm transplanting; (Med) transplant; **trapianto cardiaco** heart transplant

'trappola sf trap

tra'punta sf quilt

'trarre vt to draw, pull; (portare) to take; (prendere, tirare fuori) to take (out), draw; (derivare) to obtain; **~ origine da qc** to have its origins o originate in sth

trasa'lire vi to start, jump

trasan'dato, -a ag shabby

trasci'nare [traʃʃi'nare] vt to drag; **trascinarsi** vpr to drag o.s. along; (fig) to drag on

tras'correre vt (tempo) to spend, pass ▷ vi to pass

tras'crivere vt to transcribe

trascu'rare vt to neglect; (non considerare) to disregard

trasferi'mento sm transfer; (trasloco) removal, move; **trasferimento di chiamata** (Tel) call forwarding

trasfe'rire vt to transfer; **trasferirsi** vpr to move; **tras'ferta** sf transfer; (indennità) travelling expenses pl; (Sport) away game

trasfor'mare vt to transform, change; **trasformarsi** vpr to be transformed; **trasformarsi in qc** to turn into sth; **trasforma'tore** sm (Elec) transformer

trasfusi'one sf (Med) transfusion

trasgre'dire vt to disobey, contravene

traslo'care vt to move, transfer; **tras'loco, -chi** sm removal

tras'mettere vt (passare): **~ qc a qn** to pass sth on to sb; (mandare) to send; (Tecn, Tel, Med) to transmit; (TV, Radio) to broadcast; **trasmissi'one** sf (gen, Fisica, Tecn) transmission; (passaggio) transmission, passing on; (TV, Radio) broadcast

traspa'rente ag transparent

traspor'tare vt to carry, move; (merce) to transport, convey; **lasciarsi ~ (da qc)** (fig) to let o.s. be carried away (by sth); **tras'porto** sm transport

'trassi ecc vb vedi **trarre**

trasver'sale ag transverse, cross(-); running at right angles

'tratta sf (Econ) draft; (di persone): **la ~ delle bianche** the white slave trade

tratta'mento sm treatment; (servizio) service

trat'tare vt (gen) to treat; (commerciare) to deal in; (svolgere: argomento) to discuss, deal with; (negoziare) to negotiate ▷ vi **~ di** to deal with; **~ con** (persona) to deal with; **si tratta di ...** it's about ...

tratte'nere vt (far rimanere: persona) to detain; (intrattenere: ospiti) to entertain; (tenere, frenare, reprimere) to hold back, keep back; (astenersi dal consegnare) to hold, keep; (detrarre: somma) to deduct; **trattenersi** vpr (astenersi) to restrain o.s., stop o.s.; (soffermarsi) to stay, remain

trat'tino sm dash; (in parole composte) hyphen

'tratto, -a pp di **trarre** ▷ sm (di penna, matita) stroke; (parte) part, piece; (di strada) stretch; (di mare, cielo) expanse; (di tempo) period (of time)

trat'tore sm tractor

tratto'ria sf restaurant

'trauma, -i sm trauma

tra'vaglio [traˈvaʎʎo] sm (angoscia) pain, suffering; (Med) pains pl

trava'sare vt to decant

tra'versa sf (trave) crosspiece; (via) side street; (Ferr) sleeper (BRIT), (railroad) tie (US); (Calcio) crossbar

traver'sata sf crossing; (Aer) flight, trip; **quanto dura la ~?** how long does the crossing take?

traver'sie sfpl mishaps, misfortunes

tra'verso, -a ag oblique; **di ~** ag askew ▷ av sideways; **andare di ~** (cibo) to go down the wrong way; **guardare di ~** to look askance at

travesti'mento sm disguise

travestirsi vpr to disguise o.s.

tra'volgere [traˈvɔldʒere] vt to sweep away, carry away; (fig) to overwhelm

tre num three

'treccia, -ce [ˈtrettʃa] sf plait, braid

tre'cento [treˈtʃento] num three hundred ▷ sm **il T~** the fourteenth century

'tredici [ˈtreditʃi] num thirteen

'tregua sf truce; (fig) respite

tre'mare vi **~ di** (freddo ecc) to shiver o tremble with; (paura, rabbia) to shake o tremble with

tre'mendo, -a ag terrible, awful

> Attenzione! In inglese esiste la parola *tremendous*, che però significa *enorme* oppure *fantastico, strepitoso*.

'tremito sm trembling no pl; shaking no pl; shivering no pl

'treno sm train; **è questo il ~ per...?** is this the train for ...?; **treno di gomme** set of tyres (BRIT) o tires (US); **treno merci** goods (BRIT) o freight train; **treno viaggiatori** passenger train

● **TRENI**
●
● There are various types of train in
● Italy. For short journeys there are
● the "Regionali" (R), which generally
● operate within a particular region,
● and the "Interregionali" (IR), which
● operate beyond regional boundaries.
● Medium- and long-distance passenger
● journeys are carried out by "Intercity" (I)
● and "Eurocity" (EC) trains. The "Eurostar"
● service (ES) offers fast connections
● between the major Italian cities. Night
● services are operated by "Intercity
● Notte" (ICN), "Euronight" (EN) and by
● "Espressi" (EXP).

'trenta num thirty; **tren'tesimo, -a** ag thirtieth; **tren'tina** sf **una trentina (di)** thirty or so, about thirty

'trepi'dante *ag* anxious

tri'angolo *sm* triangle

tribù *sf inv* tribe

tri'buna *sf* (*podio*) platform; (*in aule ecc*) gallery; (*di stadio*) stand

tribu'nale *sm* court

tri'ciclo [tri'tʃiklo] *sm* tricycle

tri'foglio [tri'fɔʎʎo] *sm* clover

'triglia ['triʎʎa] *sf* red mullet

tri'mestre *sm* period of three months; (*Ins*) term, quarter (*us*); (*Comm*) quarter

trin'cea [trin'tʃea] *sf* trench

trion'fare *vi* to triumph, win; **~ su** to triumph over, overcome; **tri'onfo** *sm* triumph

tripli'care *vt* to triple

'triplo, -a *ag* triple; treble ▷ *sm* **il ~ (di)** three times as much (as); **la spesa è tripla** it costs three times as much

'trippa *sf* (*Cuc*) tripe

'triste *ag* sad; (*luogo*) dreary, gloomy

tri'tare *vt* to mince, grind (*us*)

trivi'ale *ag* vulgar, low

tro'feo *sm* trophy

'tromba *sf* (*Mus*) trumpet; (*Aut*) horn; **tromba d'aria** whirlwind; **tromba delle scale** stairwell

trom'bone *sm* trombone

trom'bosi *sf* thrombosis

tron'care *vt* to cut off; (*spezzare*) to break off

'tronco, -a, -chi, -che *ag* cut off; broken off; (*Ling*) truncated; (*fig*) cut short ▷ *sm* (*Bot, Anat*) trunk; (*fig: tratto*) section; **licenziare qn in ~** to fire sb on the spot

'trono *sm* throne

tropi'cale *ag* tropical

◯ PAROLA CHIAVE

'troppo, -a *det* (*in eccesso: quantità*) too much; (: *numero*) too many; **c'era troppa gente** there were too many people; **fa troppo caldo** it's too hot

▷ *pron* (*in eccesso: quantità*) too much; (: *numero*) too many; **ne hai messo troppo** you've put in too much; **meglio troppi che pochi** better too many than too few

▷ *av* (*eccessivamente: con ag, av*) too; (: *con vb*) too much; too many; **troppo amaro/tardi** too bitter/late; **lavora troppo** he works too much; **costa troppo** it costs too much; **di troppo** too much; too many; **qualche tazza di troppo** a few cups too many; **2 euro di troppo** 2 euros too much; **essere di troppo** to be in the way

'trota *sf* trout

'trottola *sf* spinning top

tro'vare *vt* to find; (*giudicare*): **trovo che** I find o think that; **trovarsi** *vpr* (*reciproco: incontrarsi*) to meet; (*essere, stare*) to be; (*arrivare, capitare*) to find o.s.; **non trovo più il portafoglio** I can't find my wallet; **andare a ~ qn** to go and see sb; **~ qn colpevole** to find sb guilty; **trovarsi bene** (*in un luogo, con qn*) to get on well

truc'care *vt* (*falsare*) to fake; (*attore ecc*) to make up; (*travestire*) to disguise; (*Sport*) to fix; (*Aut*) to soup up; **truccarsi** *vpr* to make up (one's face)

'trucco, -chi *sm* trick; (*cosmesi*) make-up

'truffa *sf* fraud, swindle; **truf'fare** *vt* to swindle, cheat

truffa'tore, -'trice *sm/f* swindler, cheat

'truppa *sf* troop

tu *pron* you; **tu stesso(a)** you yourself; **dare del tu a qn** to address sb as "tu"

'tubo *sm* tube; pipe; **tubo digerente** (*Anat*) alimentary canal, digestive tract; **tubo di scappamento** (*Aut*) exhaust pipe

tuffarsi *vpr* to plunge, dive

'tuffo *sm* dive; (*breve bagno*) dip

tuli'pano *sm* tulip

tu'more *sm* (*Med*) tumour

Tuni'sia *sf* **la ~** Tunisia

'tuo (*f* 'tua, *pl* tu'oi, 'tue) *det* **il ~, la tua** *ecc* your ▷ *pron* **il ~, la tua** *ecc* yours

tuo'nare *vi* to thunder; **tuona** it is thundering, there's some thunder

tu'ono *sm* thunder

tu'orlo *sm* yolk

tur'bante *sm* turban

tur'bare *vt* to disturb, trouble

tur'bato, -a *ag* upset; (*preoccupato, ansioso*) anxious

turbo'lenza [turbo'lɛntsa] *sf* turbulence

tur'chese [tur'kese] *sf* **la** *sf* turquoise

Tur'chia [tur'kia] *sf* **la ~** Turkey

'turco, -a, -chi, -che *ag* Turkish ▷ *sm/f* Turk/Turkish woman ▷ *sm* (*Ling*) Turkish; **parlare ~** (*fig*) to talk double-dutch

tu'rismo *sm* tourism; tourist industry; **turismo sessuale** sex tourism; **tu'ristico, -a, -ci, -che** *ag* tourist *cpd*

tu'rista, -i, -e *sm/f* tourist

'turno *sm* turn; (*di lavoro*) shift; **di ~** (*soldato, medico, custode*) on duty; **a ~** (*rispondere*) in turn; (*lavorare*) in shifts; **fare a ~ a fare qc** to take turns to do sth; **è il suo ~** it's your (*o* his *ecc*) turn

'turpe *ag* filthy, vile

'tuta *sf* overalls *pl*; (*Sport*) tracksuit

tu'tela *sf* (*Dir: di minore*) guardianship; (: *protezione*) protection; (*difesa*) defence

tutta'via *cong* nevertheless, yet

○ PAROLA CHIAVE

'tutto, -a *det* **1** (*intero*) all; **tutto il latte** all the milk; **tutta la notte** all night, the whole night; **tutto il libro** the whole book; **tutta una bottiglia** a whole bottle
2 (*pl, collettivo*) all; every; **tutti i libri** all the books; **tutte le notti** every night; **tutti i venerdì** every Friday; **tutti gli uomini** all the men; (*collettivo*) all men; **tutto l'anno** all year long; **tutti e due** both *o* each of us (*o* them *o* you); **tutti e cinque** all five of us (*o* them *o* you)
3 (*completamente*): **era tutta sporca** she was all dirty; **tremava tutto** he was trembling all over; **è tutta sua madre** she's just *o* exactly like her mother
4: **a tutt'oggi** so far, up till now; **a tutta velocità** at full *o* top speed
▷ *pron* **1** (*ogni cosa*) everything, all; (*qualsiasi cosa*) anything; **ha mangiato tutto** he's eaten everything; **tutto considerato** all things considered; **in tutto: 5 euro in tutto** 5 euros in all; **in tutto eravamo 50** there were 50 of us in all
2: **tutti, e** (*ognuno*) all, everybody; **vengono tutti** they are all coming, everybody's coming; **tutti quanti** all and sundry
▷ *av* (*completamente*) entirely, quite; **è tutto il contrario** it's quite *o* exactly the opposite; **tutt'al più: saranno stati tutt'al più una cinquantina** there were about fifty of them at (the very) most; **tutt'al più possiamo prendere un treno** if the worst comes to the worst we can take a train; **tutt'altro** on the contrary; **è tutt'altro che felice** he's anything but happy; **tutt'a un tratto** suddenly ▷ *sm* **il tutto** the whole lot, all of it

tut'tora *av* still
TV [ti'vu] *sf inv* (= *televisione*) TV ▷ *sigla* = **Treviso**

ubbidi'ente *ag* obedient
ubbi'dire *vi* to obey; **~ a** to obey; (*veicolo, macchina*) to respond to
ubria'care *vt* **~ qn** to get sb drunk; (*alcool*) to make sb drunk; (*fig*) to make sb's head spin *o* reel; **ubriacarsi** *vpr* to get drunk; **ubriacarsi di** (*fig*) to become intoxicated with
ubri'aco, -a, -chi, -che *ag, sm/f* drunk
uc'cello [ut'tʃello] *sm* bird
uc'cidere [ut'tʃidere] *vt* to kill; **uccidersi** *vpr* (*suicidarsi*) to kill o.s.; (*perdere la vita*) to be killed
u'dito *sm* (sense of) hearing
UE *sigla f* (= *Unione Europea*) EU
UEM *sigla f* (= *Unione economica e monetaria*) EMU
'uffa *escl* tut!
uffici'ale [uffi'tʃale] *ag* official ▷ *sm* (*Amm*) official, officer; (*Mil*) officer; **~ di stato civile** registrar
uf'ficio [uf'fitʃo] *sm* (*gen*) office; (*dovere*) duty; (*mansione*) task, function, job; (*agenzia*) agency, bureau; (*Rel*) service; **d'~ ag** office *cpd*; official ▷ *av* officially; **ufficio di collocamento** employment office; **ufficio informazioni** information bureau; **ufficio oggetti smarriti** lost property office (*BRIT*), lost and found (*US*); **ufficio (del) personale** personnel department;

ufficio postale post office
uffici'oso, -a [uffi'tʃoso] ag unofficial
uguagli'anza [ugwaʎ'ʎantsa] sf equality
uguagli'are [ugwaʎ'ʎare] vt to make
equal; (essere uguale) to equal, be equal to;
(livellare) to level; **uguagliarsi a o con qn**
(paragonarsi) to compare o.s. to sb
ugu'ale ag equal; (identico) identical, the
same; (uniforme) level, even ▷ av **costano**
~ they cost the same; **sono bravi ~ they're**
equally good
UIL sigla f (= Unione Italiana del Lavoro) trade
union federation
'ulcera ['ultʃera] sf ulcer
U'livo sm **l'~** centre-left Italian political
grouping
u'livo = **olivo**
ulteri'ore ag further
ultima'mente av lately, of late
ulti'mare vt to finish, complete
'ultimo, -a ag (finale) last; (estremo)
farthest, utmost; (recente: notizia, moda)
latest; (fig: sommo, fondamentale) ultimate
▷ sm/f last (one); **fino all'~** to the last,
until the end; **da ~, in ~** in the end; **abitare**
all'~ piano to live on the top floor; **per ~**
(entrare, arrivare) last
ulu'lare vi to howl
umanità sf humanity
u'mano, -a ag human; (comprensivo)
humane
umidità sf dampness; humidity
'umido, -a ag damp; (mano, occhi) moist;
(clima) humid ▷ sm dampness, damp;
carne in ~ stew
'umile ag humble
umili'are vt to humiliate; **umiliarsi** vpr to
humble o.s.
u'more sm (disposizione d'animo) mood;
(carattere) temper; **di buon/cattivo ~** in a
good/bad mood
umo'rismo sm humour; **avere il senso**
dell'~ to have a sense of humour;
umo'ristico, -a, -ci, -che ag humorous,
funny
u'nanime ag unanimous
unci'netto [untʃi'netto] sm crochet hook
un'cino [un'tʃino] sm hook
undi'cenne [undi'tʃɛnne] ag, sm/f eleven-
year-old
undi'cesimo, -a [undi'tʃɛzimo] num
eleventh
'undici ['unditʃi] num eleven
'ungere ['undʒere] vt to grease, oil; (Rel) to
anoint; (fig) to flatter, butter up
unghe'rese [unge'rese] ag, sm/f, sm
Hungarian
Unghe'ria [unge'ria] sf **l'~** Hungary
'unghia ['ungja] sf (Anat) nail; (di animale)

claw; (di rapace) talon; (di cavallo) hoof
ungu'ento sm ointment
'unico, -a, -ci, -che ag (solo) only;
(ineguagliabile) unique; (singolo: binario)
single; **figlio(a) ~(a)** only son/daughter,
only child
unifi'care vt to unite, unify; (sistemi) to
standardize; **unificazi'one** sf uniting;
unification; standardization
uni'forme ag uniform; (superficie) even ▷ sf
(divisa) uniform
uni'one sf union; (fig: concordia) unity,
harmony; **Unione europea** European
Union; **ex Unione Sovietica** former
Soviet Union
u'nire vt to unite; (congiungere) to join,
connect; (: ingredienti, colori) to combine;
(in matrimonio) to unite, join together;
unirsi vpr to unite; (in matrimonio) to be
joined together; **~ qc a** to unite sth with;
to join o connect sth with; to combine sth
with; **unirsi a** (gruppo, società) to join
unità sf inv (unione, concordia) unity; (Mat,
Mil, Comm, di misura) unit; **unità di misura**
unit of measurement
u'nito, -a ag (paese) united; (amici, famiglia)
close; **in tinta unita** plain, self-coloured
univer'sale ag universal; general
università sf inv university
uni'verso sm universe

○ **PAROLA CHIAVE**

'uno, -a (dav sm **un** + C, V, **uno** + s impura, gn,
pn, ps, x, z; dav sf **un'** + V, **una** + C) art indef **1**
a; (dav vocale) an; (dav un bambino) a child; **una**
strada a street; **uno zingaro** a gypsy
2 (intensivo): **ho avuto una paura!** I got
such a fright!
▷ pron **1** one; **prendine uno** take one (of
them); **l'uno o l'altro** either (of them);
l'uno e l'altro both (of them); **aiutarsi**
l'un l'altro to help one another o each
other; **sono entrati l'uno dopo l'altro**
they came in one after the other
2 (un tale) someone, somebody
3 (con valore impersonale) one, you; **se uno**
vuole if one wants, if you want
▷ num one; **una mela e due pere** one
apple and two pears; **più uno fa due**
one plus one equals two, one and one are
two ▷ sf **è l'una** it's one (o'clock)

'unsi ecc vb vedi **ungere**
'unto, -a pp di **ungere** ▷ ag greasy, oily
▷ sm grease
u'omo (pl **u'omini**) sm man; **da ~** (abito,
scarpe) men's, for men; **uomo d'affari**
businessman; **uomo di paglia** stooge;

uomo politico politician; **uomo rana** frogman

u'ovo (pl(f) **u'ova**) sm egg; **uovo affogato/alla coque** poached/boiled egg; **uovo bazzotto/sodo** soft-/hard-boiled egg; **uovo di Pasqua** Easter egg; **uovo in camicia** poached egg; **uova strapazzate/al tegame** scrambled/fried eggs

ura'gano sm hurricane

urba'nistica sf town planning

ur'bano, -a ag urban, city cpd, town cpd; (Tel: chiamata) local; (fig) urbane

ur'gente [ur'dʒɛnte] ag urgent; **ur'genza** sf urgency; **in caso d'urgenza** in (case of) an emergency; **d'urgenza** ag emergency ▷ av urgently, as a matter of urgency

ur'lare vi (persona) to scream, yell; (animale, vento) to howl ▷ vt to scream, yell

'urlo (pl(m) **'urli**, pl(f) **'urla**) sm scream, yell; howl

urrà escl hurrah!

U.R.S.S. abbr f **l'U.R.S.S.** the USSR

ur'tare vt to bump into, knock against; (fig: irritare) to annoy ▷ vi **~ contro** o **in** to bump into, knock against, crash into; (fig: imbattersi) to come up against; **urtarsi** vpr (reciproco: scontrarsi) to collide; (: fig) to clash; (irritarsi) to get annoyed

'U.S.A. ['uza] smpl **gli U.S.A.** the USA

u'sanza [u'zantsa] sf custom; (moda) fashion

u'sare vt to use, employ ▷ vi (servirsi): **~ di** to use; (: diritto) to exercise; (essere di moda) to be fashionable; (essere solito): **~ fare** to be in the habit of doing, be accustomed to doing ▷ vb impers **qui usa così** it's the custom round here; **u'sato, -a** ag used; (consumato) worn; (di seconda mano) used, second-hand ▷ sm second-hand goods pl

u'scire [uʃ'ʃire] vi (gen) to come out; (partire, andare a passeggio, a uno spettacolo ecc) to go out; (essere sorteggiato: numero) to come up; **~ da** (gen) to leave; (posto) to go (o come) out of, leave; (solco, vasca ecc) to come out of; (muro) to stick out of; (competenza ecc) to be outside; (infanzia, adolescenza) to leave behind; (famiglia nobile ecc) to come from; **~ da** o **di casa** to go out; (fig) to leave home; **~ in automobile** to go out in the car, go for a drive; **~ di strada** (Aut) to go off o leave the road

u'scita [uʃ'ʃita] sf (passaggio, varco) exit, way out; (per divertimento) outing; (Econ: somma) expenditure; (Teatro) entrance; (fig: battuta) witty remark; **dov'è l'~?** where's the exit?; **uscita di sicurezza** emergency exit

usi'gnolo [uziɲ'ɲɔlo] sm nightingale

'uso sm (utilizzazione) use; (esercizio) practice; (abitudine) custom; **a ~ di** for (the use of); **d'~** (corrente) in use; **fuori ~** out of use; **uso esterno; per ~ esterno** for external use only

usti'one sf burn

usu'ale ag common, everyday

u'sura sf usury; (logoramento) wear (and tear)

uten'sile sm tool, implement; **utensili da cucina** kitchen utensils

u'tente sm/f user

'utero sm uterus

'utile ag useful ▷ sm (vantaggio) advantage, benefit; (Econ: profitto) profit

utiliz'zare [utilid'dzare] vt to use, make use of, utilize

'uva sf grapes pl; **uva passa** raisins pl; **uva spina** gooseberry

UVA abbr (= ultravioletto prossimo) UVA

UVB abbr (= ultravioletto remoto) UVB

V

v. *abbr* (= *vedi*) v

va, va' *vb vedi* **andare**

va'cante *ag* vacant

va'canza [va'kantsa] *sf* (*riposo, ferie*) holiday(s) *pl* (BRIT), vacation (US); (*giorno di permesso*) day off, holiday; **vacanze** *sfpl* (*periodo di ferie*) holidays (BRIT), vacation *sg* (US); **essere/andare in ~** to be/go on holiday *o* vacation; **sono qui in ~** I'm on holiday here; **vacanze estive** summer holiday(s) *o* vacation; **vacanze natalizie** Christmas holidays *o* vacation

Attenzione! In inglese esiste la parola *vacancy* che però indica un posto vacante o una camera disponibile.

'vacca, -che *sf* cow

vacci'nare [vattʃi'nare] *vt* to vaccinate

vac'cino [vat'tʃino] *sm* (*Med*) vaccine

vacil'lare [vatʃil'lare] *vi* to sway, wobble; (*luce*) to flicker; (*fig: memoria, coraggio*) to be failing, falter

'vacuo, -a *ag* (*fig*) empty, vacuous

'vado *ecc vb vedi* **andare**

vaga'bondo, -a *sm/f* tramp, vagrant

va'gare *vi* to wander

vagherò *ecc* [vage'rɔ] *vb vedi* **vagare**

va'gina [va'dʒina] *sf* vagina

'vaglia ['vaʎʎa] *sm inv* money order; **vaglia postale** postal order

vagli'are [vaʎ'ʎare] *vt* to sift; (*fig*) to weigh up

'vago, -a, -ghi, -ghe *ag* vague

va'gone *sm* (*Ferr: per passeggeri*) coach; (: *per merci*) truck, wagon; **vagone letto** sleeper, sleeping car; **vagone ristorante** dining *o* restaurant car

'vai *vb vedi* **andare**

vai'olo *sm* smallpox

va'langa, -ghe *sf* avalanche

va'lere *vi* (*avere forza, potenza*) to have influence; (*essere valido*) to be valid; (*avere vigore, autorità*) to hold, apply; (*essere capace: poeta, studente*) to be good, be able ▷ *vt* (*prezzo, sforzo*) to be worth; (*corrispondere*) to correspond to; (*procurare*): **~ qc a qn** to earn sb sth; **valersi di** to make use of, take advantage of; **far ~** (*autorità ecc*) to assert; **vale a dire** that is to say; **~ la pena** to be worth the effort *o* worth it

'valgo *ecc vb vedi* **valere**

vali'care *vt* to cross

'valico, -chi *sm* (*passo*) pass

'valido, -a *ag* valid; (*rimedio*) effective; (*aiuto*) real; (*persona*) worthwhile

vali'getta [vali'dʒetta] *sf* briefcase; **valigetta ventiquattrore** overnight bag *o* case

va'ligia, -gie *o* **-ge** [va'lidʒa] *sf* (suit)case; **fare le valigie** to pack (up)

'valle *sf* valley; **a ~** (*di fiume*) downstream; **scendere a ~** to go downhill

va'lore *sm* (*gen*) value; (*merito*) merit, worth; (*coraggio*) valour, courage; (*Comm: titolo*) security; **valori** *smpl* (*oggetti preziosi*) valuables

valoriz'zare [valorid'dzare] *vt* (*terreno*) to develop; (*fig*) to make the most of

va'luta *sf* currency, money; (*Banca*): **~ 15 gennaio** interest to run from January 15th

valu'tare *vt* (*casa, gioiello, fig*) to value; (*stabilire: peso, entrate, fig*) to estimate

'valvola *sf* (*Tecn, Anat*) valve; (*Elettr*) fuse

'valzer ['valtser] *sm inv* waltz

vam'pata *sf* (*di fiamma*) blaze; (*di calore*) blast; (: *al viso*) flush

vam'piro *sm* vampire

vanda'lismo *sm* vandalism

'vandalo *sm* vandal

vaneggi'are [vaned'dʒare] *vi* to rave

'vanga, -ghe *sf* spade

van'gelo [van'dʒɛlo] *sm* gospel

va'niglia [va'niʎʎa] *sf* vanilla

vanità *sf* vanity; (*di promessa*) emptiness; (*di sforzo*) futility; **vani'toso, -a** *ag* vain, conceited

'vanno *vb vedi* **andare**

'vano, -a *ag* vain ▷ *sm* (*spazio*) space; (*apertura*) opening; (*stanza*) room

van'taggio [van'taddʒo] *sm* advantage; **essere/portarsi in ~** (*Sport*) to be in/take the lead; **vantaggi'oso, -a** *ag* advantageous; favourable

vantarsi *vpr* **~ (di/di aver fatto)** to boast *o* brag (about/about having done)

'vanvera *sf* **a ~** haphazardly; **parlare a ~** to talk nonsense

va'pore *sm* vapour; (*anche:* **~ acqueo**) steam; (*nave*) steamer; **a ~** (*turbina ecc*) steam *cpd*; **al ~** (*Cuc*) steamed

va'rare *vt* (*Naut, fig*) to launch; (*Dir*) to pass

var'care *vt* to cross

'varco, -chi *sm* passage; **aprirsi un ~ tra la folla** to push one's way through the crowd

vare'china [vare'kina] *sf* bleach

vari'abile *ag* variable; (*tempo, umore*) changeable, variable ▷ *sf* (*Mat*) variable

vari'cella [vari'tʃɛlla] *sf* chickenpox

vari'coso, -a *ag* varicose

varietà *sf inv* variety ▷ *sm inv* variety show

'vario, -a *ag* varied; (*parecchi: col sostantivo al pl*) various; (*mutevole: umore*) changeable

'varo *sm* (*Naut: fig*) launch; (*di leggi*) passing

varrò *ecc vb vedi* **valere**

Var'savia *sf* Warsaw

va'saio *sm* potter

'vasca, -sche *sf* basin; **vasca da bagno** bathtub, bath

vas'chetta [vas'ketta] *sf* (*per gelato*) tub; (*per sviluppare fotografie*) dish

vase'lina *sf* Vaseline®

'vaso *sm* (*recipiente*) pot; (*: barattolo*) jar; (*: decorativo*) vase; (*Anat*) vessel; **vaso da fiori** vase; (*per piante*) flowerpot

vas'soio *sm* tray

'vasto, -a *ag* vast, immense

Vati'cano *sm* **il ~** the Vatican

ve *pron, av vedi* **vi**

vecchi'aia [vek'kjaja] *sf* old age

'vecchio, -a ['vɛkkjo] *ag* old ▷ *sm/f* old man/woman; **i vecchii** the old

ve'dere *vt, vi* to see; **vedersi** *vpr* to meet, see one another; **avere a che ~ con** to have something to do with; **far ~ qc a qn** to show sb sth; **farsi ~** to show o.s.; (*farsi vivo*) to show one's face; **vedi di non farlo** make sure *o* see you don't do it; **non (ci) si vede** (*è buio ecc*) you can't see a thing; **non lo posso ~** (*fig*) I can't stand him

ve'detta *sf* (*sentinella, posto*) look-out; (*Naut*) patrol boat

'vedovo, -a *sm/f* widower/widow

vedrò *ecc vb vedi* **vedere**

ve'duta *sf* view; **vedute** *sfpl* (*fig: opinioni*) views; **di larghe** *o* **ampie vedute** broad-minded; **di vedute limitate** narrow-minded

vege'tale [vedʒe'tale] *ag, sm* vegetable

vegetari'ano, -a [vedʒeta'rjano] *ag, sm/f* vegetarian; **avete piatti vegetariani?** do you have any vegetarian dishes?

vegetazi'one [vedʒetat'tsjone] *sf* vegetation

'vegeto, -a ['vɛdʒeto] *ag* (*pianta*) thriving; (*persona*) strong, vigorous

'veglia ['veʎʎa] *sf* wakefulness; (*sorveglianza*) watch; (*trattenimento*) evening gathering; **fare la ~ a un malato** to watch over a sick person

vegli'one [veʎ'ʎone] *sm* ball, dance; **veglione di Capodanno** New Year's Eve party

ve'icolo *sm* vehicle

'vela *sf* (*Naut: tela*) sail; (*Sport*) sailing

ve'leno *sm* poison; **vele'noso, -a** *ag* poisonous

veli'ero *sm* sailing ship

vel'luto *sm* velvet; **velluto a coste** cord

'velo *sm* veil; (*tessuto*) voile

ve'loce [ve'lotʃe] *ag* fast, quick ▷ *av* fast, quickly; **velocità** *sf* speed; **a forte velocità** at high speed; **velocità di crociera** cruising speed

'vena *sf* (*gen*) vein; (*filone*) vein, seam; (*fig: ispirazione*) inspiration; (*: umore*) mood; **essere in ~ di qc** to be in the mood for sth

ve'nale *ag* (*prezzo, valore*) market *cpd*; (*fig*) venal; mercenary

ven'demmia *sf* (*raccolta*) grape harvest; (*quantità d'uva*) grape crop, grapes *pl*; (*vino ottenuto*) vintage

'vendere *vt* to sell; **"vendesi"** "for sale"

ven'detta *sf* revenge

vendicarsi *vpr* **~ (di)** to avenge o.s. (for); (*per rancore*) to take one's revenge (for); **~ su qn** to revenge o.s. on sb

'vendita *sf* sale; **la ~** (*attività*) selling; (*smercio*) sales *pl*; **in ~** on sale; **vendita all'asta** sale by auction; **vendita per telefono** telesales *pl*

vene'rare *vt* to venerate

venerdì *sm inv* Friday; **di** *o* **il ~** on Fridays; **V~ Santo** Good Friday

ve'nereo, -a *ag* venereal

Ve'nezia [ve'nɛttsja] *sf* Venice

'vengo *ecc vb vedi* **venire**

veni'ale *ag* venial

ve'nire *vi* to come; (*riuscire: dolce, fotografia*) to turn out; (*come ausiliare: essere*): **viene ammirato da tutti** he is admired by everyone; **~ da** to come from; **quanto viene?** how much does it cost?; **far ~** (*mandare a chiamare*) to send for; **~ giù** to come down; **~ meno** (*svenire*) to faint; **~ meno a qc** not to fulfil sth; **~ su** to come up; **~ a trovare qn** to come and see sb; **~**

via to come away

'**venni** ecc vb vedi **venire**

ven'taglio [ven'taʎʎo] sm fan

ven'tata sf gust (of wind)

ven'tenne ag **una ragazza ~** a twenty-year-old girl, a girl of twenty

ven'tesimo, -a num twentieth

'**venti** num twenty

venti'lare vt (stanza) to air, ventilate; (fig: idea, proposta) to air; **ventila'tore** sm ventilator, fan

ven'tina sf **una ~ (di)** around twenty, twenty or so

'**vento** sm wind

'**ventola** sf (Aut, Tecn) fan

ven'tosa sf (Zool) sucker; (di gomma) suction pad

ven'toso, -a ag windy

'**ventre** sm stomach

'**vera** sf wedding ring

vera'mente av really

ve'randa sf veranda(h)

ver'bale ag verbal ▷ sm (di riunione) minutes pl

'**verbo** sm (Ling) verb; (parola) word; (Rel): **il V~** the Word

'**verde** ag, sm green; **essere al ~** to be broke; **verde bottiglia/oliva** bottle/olive green

ver'detto sm verdict

ver'dura sf vegetables pl

'**vergine** ['verdʒine] sf virgin; (dello zodiaco): **V~** Virgo ▷ ag virgin; (ragazza): **essere ~** to be a virgin

ver'gogna [ver'ɡoɲɲa] sf shame; (timidezza) shyness, embarrassment; **vergo'gnarsi** vpr **vergognarsi (di)** to o feel ashamed (of); to be shy (about), be embarrassed (about); **vergo'gnoso, -a** ag ashamed; (timido) shy, embarrassed; (causa di vergogna: azione) shameful

ve'rifica, -che sf checking no pl, check

verifi'care vt (controllare) to check; (confermare) to confirm, bear out

verità sf inv truth

'**verme** sm worm

ver'miglio [ver'miʎʎo] sm vermilion, scarlet

ver'nice [ver'nitʃe] sf (colorazione) paint; (trasparente) varnish; (pelle) patent leather; **"~ fresca"** "wet paint"; **vernici'are** vt to paint; to varnish

'**vero, -a** ag (veridico: fatti, testimonianza) true; (autentico) real ▷ sm (verità) truth; (realtà) (real) life; **un ~ e proprio delinquente** a real criminal, an out-and-out criminal

vero'simile ag likely, probable

verrò ecc vb vedi **venire**

ver'ruca, -che sf wart

versa'mento sm (pagamento) payment; (deposito di denaro) deposit

ver'sante sm slopes pl, side

ver'sare vt (fare uscire: vino, farina) to pour (out); (spargere: lacrime, sangue) to shed; (rovesciare) to spill; (Econ) to pay; (: depositare) to deposit, pay in

versa'tile ag versatile

versi'one sf version; (traduzione) translation

'**verso** sm (di poesia) verse, line; (di animale, uccello) cry; (direzione) direction; (modo) way; (di foglio di carta) verso; (di moneta) reverse; **versi** smpl (poesia) verse sg; **non c'è ~ di persuaderlo** there's no way of persuading him, he can't be persuaded prep (in direzione di) toward(s); (nei pressi di) near, around (about); (in senso temporale) about, around; (nei confronti di) for; **~ di me** towards me; **~ sera** towards evening

'**vertebra** sf vertebra

verte'brale ag vertebral; **colonna ~** spinal column, spine

verti'cale ag, sf vertical

'**vertice** ['vertitʃe] sm summit, top; (Mat) vertex; **conferenza al ~** (Pol) summit conference

ver'tigine [ver'tidʒine] sf dizziness no pl; dizzy spell; (Med) vertigo; **avere le vertigini** to feel dizzy

ve'scica, -che [veʃʃika] sf (Anat) bladder; (Med) blister

'**vescovo** sm bishop

'**vespa** sf wasp

ves'taglia [ves'taʎʎa] sf dressing gown

ves'tire vt (bambino, malato) to dress; (avere indosso) to have on, wear; **vestirsi** vpr to dress, get dressed; **ves'tito, -a** ag dressed ▷ sm garment; (da donna) dress; (da uomo) suit; **vestiti** smpl (indumenti) clothes; **vestito di bianco** dressed in white

veteri'nario, -a ag veterinary ▷ sm veterinary surgeon (BRIT), veterinarian (US), vet

'**veto** sm inv veto

ve'traio sm glassmaker; glazier

ve'trata sf glass door (o window); (di chiesa) stained glass window

ve'trato, -a ag (porta, finestra) glazed; (che contiene vetro) glass cpd ▷ sf glass door (o window); (di chiesa) stained glass window; **carta vetrata** sandpaper

ve'trina sf (di negozio) (shop) window; (armadio) display cabinet; **vetri'nista, -i, -e** sm/f window dresser

'**vetro** sm glass; (per finestra, porta) pane (of glass)

'**vetta** sf peak, summit, top

vet'tura sf (carrozza) carriage; (Ferr) carriage (BRIT), car (US); (auto) car (BRIT), automobile (US)

vezzeggia'tivo [vettseddʒa'tivo] sm (Ling) term of endearment

vi (dav lo, la, li, le, ne diventa **ve**) pron (oggetto) you; (complemento di termine) (to) you; (riflessivo) yourselves; (reciproco) each other ▷ av (lì) there; (qui) here; (per questo/quel luogo) through here/there; **vi è/sono** there is/are

'via sf (gen) way; (strada) street; (sentiero, pista) path, track; (Amm: procedimento) channels pl ▷ prep (passando per) via, by way of ▷ av away ▷ escl go away!; (suvvia) come on!; (Sport) go! ▷ sm (Sport) starting signal; **in ~ di guarigione** on the road to recovery; **per ~ di** (a causa di) because of, on account of; **in o per ~** on the way; **per ~ aerea** by air; (lettere) by airmail; **andare/essere ~** to go/be away; **~ ~ che** (a mano a mano) as; **dare il ~** (Sport) to give the starting signal; **dare il ~ a** (fig) to start; **in ~ provvisoria** provisionally; **Via lattea** (Astr) Milky Way; **via di mezzo** middle course; **via d'uscita** (fig) way out

via'dotto sm viaduct

viaggi'are [viad'dʒare] vi to travel; **viaggia'tore, -'trice** ag travelling ▷ sm traveller; (passeggero) passenger

vi'aggio ['vjaddʒo] sm travel(ling); (tragitto) journey, trip; **buon ~!** have a good trip!; **com'è andato il ~?** how was your journey?; **il ~ dura due ore** the journey takes two hours; **viaggio di nozze** honeymoon; **siamo in ~ di nozze** we're on honeymoon

vi'ale sm avenue

via'vai sm coming and going, bustle

vi'brare vi to vibrate

'vice ['vitʃe] sm/f deputy

vi'cenda [vi'tʃenda] sf event; **a ~** in turn

vice'versa [vitʃe'vɛrsa] av vice versa; **da Roma a Pisa e ~** from Rome to Pisa and back

vici'nanza [vitʃi'nantsa] sf nearness, closeness

vi'cino, -a [vi'tʃino] ag (gen) near; (nello spazio) near, nearby; (accanto) next; (nel tempo) near, close at hand ▷ sm/f neighbour ▷ av near, close; **da ~** (guardare) close up; (esaminare, seguire) closely; (conoscere) well, intimately; **~ a** near (to), close to; (accanto a) beside; **c'è una banca qui ~?** is there a bank nearby?; **~ di casa** neighbour

'vicolo sm alley; **vicolo cieco** blind alley

'video sm inv (TV: schermo) screen; **video'camera** sf camcorder;

videocas'setta sf videocassette;

videoclip [video'klip] sm inv videoclip; **videogi'oco, -chi** [video'dʒɔko] sm video game; **videoregistra'tore** sm video (recorder); **videote'lefono** sm videophone

'vidi ecc vb vedi **vedere**

vie'tare vt to forbid; (Amm) to prohibit; **~ a qn di fare** to forbid sb to do; to prohibit sb from doing; **"vietato fumare/l'ingresso"** "no smoking/admittance"

vie'tato, -a (vedi vb) forbidden; prohibited; banned; **"~ fumare/l'ingresso"** "no smoking/admittance"; **~ ai minori di 14/18 anni** prohibited to children under 14/18; **"senso ~"** (Aut) "no entry"; **"sosta vietata"** (Aut) "no parking"

Viet'nam sm il **~** Vietnam; **vietna'mita, -i, -e** ag, sm/f, sm Vietnamese inv

vi'gente [vi'dʒɛnte] ag in force

'vigile ['vidʒile] ag watchful ▷ sm (anche: **~ urbano**) policeman (in towns); **vigile del fuoco** fireman

vi'gilia [vi'dʒilja] sf (giorno antecedente) eve; **la ~ di Natale** Christmas Eve

vigli'acco, -a, -chi, -che [viʎ'ʎakko] ag cowardly ▷ sm/f coward

vi'gneto [viɲ'ɲeto] sm vineyard

vi'gnetta [viɲ'ɲetta] sf cartoon

vi'gore (Dir): **essere/entrare in ~** to be in/come into force

'vile ag (spregevole) low, mean, base; (codardo) cowardly

'villa sf villa

vil'laggio [vil'laddʒo] sm village; **villaggio turistico** holiday village

vil'lano, -a ag rude, ill-mannered

villeggia'tura [villeddʒa'tura] sf holiday(s) pl (BRIT), vacation (US)

vil'letta sf, **vil'lino** ▷ sm small house (with a garden), cottage

'vimini smpl **di ~** wicker

'vincere ['vintʃere] vt (in guerra, al gioco, a una gara) to defeat, beat; (premio, guerra, partita) to win; (fig) to overcome, conquer ▷ vi to win; **~ qn in bellezza** to be better-looking than sb; **vinci'tore** sm winner; (Mil) victor

vi'nicolo, -a ag wine cpd

'vino sm wine; **vino bianco/rosato/rosso** white/rosé/red wine; **vino da pasto** table wine

'vinsi ecc vb vedi **vincere**

vi'ola sf (Bot) violet; (Mus) viola ▷ ag, sm inv (colore) purple

vio'lare vt (chiesa) to desecrate, violate; (giuramento, legge) to violate

violen'tare vt to use violence on; (donna) to rape

vio'lento, -a ag violent; **vio'lenza** sf violence; **violenza carnale** rape

vio'letta sf (Bot) violet

vio'letto, -a ag, sm (colore) violet

violi'nista, -i, -e sm/f violinist

vio'lino sm violin

violon'cello [violon'tʃello] sm cello

vi'ottolo sm path, track

vip [vip] sigla m (= very important person) VIP

'vipera sf viper, adder

vi'rare vi (Naut, Aer) to turn; (Fot) to tone; ~ **di bordo** (Naut) to tack

'virgola sf (Ling) comma; (Mat) point; **virgo'lette** sfpl inverted commas, quotation marks

vi'rile ag (proprio dell'uomo) masculine; (non puerile, da uomo) manly, virile

virtù sf inv virtue; **in** o **per ~ di** by virtue of, by

virtu'ale ag virtual

'virus sm inv (anche Inform) virus

'viscere ['viʃʃere] sfpl (di animale) entrails pl; (fig) bowels pl

'vischio ['viskjo] sm (Bot) mistletoe; (pania) birdlime

'viscido, -a ['viʃʃido] ag slimy

vi'sibile ag visible

visibilità sf visibility

visi'era sf (di elmo) visor; (di berretto) peak

visi'one sf vision; **prendere ~ di qc** to examine sth, look sth over; **prima/seconda ~** (Cinema) first/second showing

'visita sf visit; (Med) visit, call; (: esame) examination; **visita guidata** guided tour; **a che ora comincia la ~ guidata?** what time does the guided tour start?; **visita medica** medical examination; **visi'tare** vt to visit; (Med) to visit, call on; (: esaminare) to examine; **visita'tore, -'trice** sm/f visitor

vi'sivo, -a ag visual

'viso sm face

vi'sone sm mink

'vispo, -a ag quick, lively

'vissi ecc vb vedi **vivere**

'vista sf (facoltà) (eye)sight; (fatto di vedere): **la ~ di** the sight of; (veduta) view; **sparare a ~** to shoot on sight; **in ~** in sight; **perdere qn di ~** to lose sight of sb; (fig) to lose touch with sb; **a ~ d'occhio** as far as the eye can see; (fig) before one's very eyes; **far ~ di fare** to pretend to do

'visto, -a pp di **vedere** ▷ sm visa; **~ che** seeing (that)

vis'toso, -a ag gaudy, garish; (ingente) considerable

visu'ale ag visual

'vita sf life; (Anat) waist; **a ~** for life

vi'tale ag vital

vita'mina sf vitamin

'vite sf (Bot) vine; (Tecn) screw

vi'tello sm (Zool) calf; (carne) veal; (pelle) calfskin

'vittima sf victim

'vitto sm food; (in un albergo ecc) board; **vitto e alloggio** board and lodging

vit'toria sf victory

'viva escl ~ **il re!** long live the king!

vi'vace [vi'vatʃe] ag (vivo, animato) lively; (: mente) lively, sharp; (colore) bright

vi'vaio sm (di pesci) hatchery; (Agr) nursery

vivavoce [viva'votʃe] sm inv (dispositivo) loudspeaker; **mettere il ~** to switch on the loudspeaker

vi'vente ag living, alive; **i viventi** the living

'vivere vi to live ▷ vt to live; (passare: brutto momento) to live through, go through; (sentire: gioie, pene di qn) to share ▷ sm life; (anche: **modo di ~**) way of life; **viveri** smpl (cibo) food sg, provisions; **~ di** to live on

'vivido, -a ag (colore) vivid, bright

vivisezi'one [viviset'tsjone] sf vivisection

'vivo, -a ag (vivente) alive, living; (: animale) live; (fig) lively; (: colore) bright, brilliant; **i vivi** the living; **~ e vegeto** hale and hearty; **farsi ~** to show one's face; to be heard from; **ritrarre dal ~** to paint from life; **pungere qn nel ~** (fig) to cut sb to the quick

vivrò ecc vb vedi **vivere**

vizi'are [vit'tsjare] vt (bambino) to spoil; (corrompere moralmente) to corrupt; **vizi'ato, -a** ag spoilt; (aria, acqua) polluted

'vizio ['vittsjo] sm (morale) vice; (cattiva abitudine) bad habit; (imperfezione) flaw, defect; (errore) fault, mistake

V.le abbr = **viale**

vocabo'lario sm (dizionario) dictionary; (lessico) vocabulary

vo'cabolo sm word

vo'cale ag vocal ▷ sf vowel

vocazi'one [vokat'tsjone] sf vocation; (fig) natural bent

'voce ['votʃe] sf voice; (diceria) rumour; (di un elenco, in bilancio) item; **aver ~ in capitolo** (fig) to have a say in the matter

'voga sf (Naut) rowing; (usanza): **essere in ~** to be in fashion o in vogue

vo'gare vi to row

vogherò ecc vb vedi **vogare**

'voglia ['vɔʎʎa] sf desire, wish; (macchia) birthmark; **aver ~ di qc/di fare** to feel like sth/like doing; (più forte) to want sth/to do

'voglio ecc ['vɔʎʎo] vb vedi **volere**

'voi pron you; **voi'altri** pron you

vo'lante ag flying ▷ sm (steering) wheel

volan'tino sm leaflet

vo'lare vi (uccello, aereo, fig) to fly; (cappello)

to blow away o off, fly away o off; **~ via** to fly away o off

vo'latile ag (Chim) volatile ▷ sm (Zool) bird

volente'roso, -a ag willing

volenti'eri av willingly; **"~"** "with pleasure", "I'd be glad to"

 PAROLA CHIAVE

vo'lere sm will, wish(es); **contro il volere di** against the wishes of; **per volere di qn** in obedience to sb's will o wishes
▷ vt **1** (esigere, desiderare) to want; **voler fare/che qn faccia** to want to do/sb to do; **volete del caffè?** would you like o do you want some coffee?; **vorrei questo/fare** I would o I'd like this/to do; **come vuoi** as you like; **senza volere** (inavvertitamente) without meaning to, unintentionally
2 (consentire): **vogliate attendere, per piacere** please wait; **vogliamo andare?** shall we go?; **vuole essere così gentile da ...?** would you be so kind as to ...?; **non ha voluto ricevermi** he wouldn't see me
3: **volerci** (essere necessario: materiale, attenzione) to need; (: tempo) to take; **quanta farina ci vuole per questa torta?** how much flour do you need for this cake?; **ci vuole un'ora per arrivare a Venezia** it takes an hour to get to Venice
4: **voler bene a qn** (amore) to love sb; (affetto) to be fond of sb, like sb very much; **voler male a qn** to dislike sb; **volerne a qn** to bear sb a grudge; **voler dire** to mean

vol'gare ag vulgar

voli'era sf aviary

voli'tivo, -a ag strong-willed

'volli ecc vb vedi **volere**

'volo sm flight; **al ~: colpire qc al ~** to hit sth as it flies past; **capire al ~** to understand straight away; **volo charter** charter flight; **volo di linea** scheduled flight

volontà sf will; **a ~** (mangiare, bere) as much as one likes; **buona/cattiva ~** goodwill/lack of goodwill

volon'tario, -a ag voluntary ▷ sm (Mil) volunteer

'volpe sf fox

'volta sf (momento, circostanza) time; (turno, giro) turn; (curva) turn, bend; (Archit) vault; (direzione): **partire alla ~ di** to set off for; **a mia** (o **tua** ecc) **~** in turn; **una ~** once; **una ~ sola** only once; **due volte** twice; **una cosa per ~** one thing at a time; **una ~ per tutte** once and for all; **a volte** at times, sometimes; **una ~ che** (temporale) once; (causale) since; **3 volte 4** 3 times 4

volta'faccia [volta'fattʃa] sm inv (fig) volte-face

vol'taggio [vol'taddʒo] sm (Elettr) voltage

vol'tare vt to turn; (girare: moneta) to turn over; (rigirare) to turn round ▷ vi to turn; **voltarsi** vpr to turn; to turn over; to turn round

voltas'tomaco sm nausea; (fig) disgust

'volto, -a pp di **volgere** ▷ sm face

vo'lubile ag changeable, fickle

vo'lume sm volume

vomi'tare vt, vi to vomit; **'vomito** sm vomiting no pl; vomit

'vongola sf clam

vo'race [vo'ratʃe] ag voracious, greedy

vo'ragine [vo'radʒine] sf abyss, chasm

vorrò ecc vb vedi **volere**

'vortice ['vortitʃe] sm whirlwind; whirlpool; (fig) whirl

'vostro, -a det **il(la) ~(a)** ecc your ▷ pron **il(la) ~(a)** ecc yours

vo'tante sm/f voter

vo'tare vi to vote ▷ vt (sottoporre a votazione) to take a vote on; (approvare) to vote for; (Rel): **~ qc a** to dedicate sth to

'voto sm (Pol) vote; (Ins) mark; (Rel) vow; (: offerta) votive offering; **aver voti belli/brutti** (Ins) to get good/bad marks

vs. abbr (Comm) = **vostro**

vul'cano sm volcano

vulne'rabile ag vulnerable

vu'oi, vu'ole vb vedi **volere**

vuo'tare vt to empty; **vuotarsi** vpr to empty

vu'oto, -a ag empty; (fig: privo): **~ di** (senso ecc) devoid of ▷ sm empty space, gap; (spazio in bianco) blank; (Fisica) vacuum; (fig: mancanza) gap, void; **a mani vuote** empty-handed; **vuoto d'aria** air pocket; **vuoto a rendere** returnable bottle

W X

'wafer ['vafer] *sm inv* (*Cuc, Elettr*) wafer
'water ['wɔːtəʳ] *sm inv* toilet
watt [vat] *sm inv* watt
W.C. *sm inv* WC
web [ueb] *sm* **il ~** the Web; **cercare nel ~** to search the Web ▷ *ag inv* **pagina ~** web page
'weekend ['wiːkend] *sm inv* weekend
'western ['western] *ag* (*Cinema*) cowboy *cpd* ▷ *sm inv* western, cowboy film; **western all'italiana** spaghetti western
'whisky ['wiski] *sm inv* whisky
'windsurf ['windsəːf] *sm inv* (*tavola*) windsurfer; (*sport*) windsurfing
'würstel ['vyrstəl] *sm inv* frankfurter

xe'nofobo, -a [kse'nɔfobo] *ag* xenophobic ▷ *sm/f* xenophobe
xi'lofono [ksi'lɔfono] *sm* xylophone

Y Z

yacht [jɔt] *sm inv* yacht
'yoga ['jɔga] *ag inv, sm* yoga (*cpd*)
yogurt ['jɔgurt] *sm inv* yog(h)urt

zabai'one [dzaba'jone] *sm dessert made of egg yolks, sugar and marsala*
zaf'fata [tsaf'fata] *sf (tanfo)* stench
zaffe'rano [dzaffe'rano] *sm* saffron
zaf'firo [dzaf'firo] *sm* sapphire
'zaino ['dzaino] *sm* rucksack
'zampa ['tsampa] *sf (di animale: gamba)* leg; (: *piede*) paw; **a quattro zampe** on all fours
zampil'lare [tsampil'lare] *vi* to gush, spurt
zan'zara [dzan'dzara] *sf* mosquito; **zanzari'era** *sf* mosquito net
'zappa ['tsappa] *sf* hoe
'zapping ['tsapiŋ] *sm (TV)* channel-hopping
zar, za'rina [tsar, tsa'rina] *sm/f* tsar/tsarina
'zattera ['dzattera] *sf* raft
'zebra ['dzɛbra] *sf* zebra; **zebre** *sfpl (Aut)* zebra crossing *sg (BRIT)*, crosswalk *sg (US)*
'zecca, -che ['tsekka] *sf (Zool)* tick; (*officina di monete*) mint
'zelo ['dzɛlo] *sm* zeal
'zenzero ['dzendzero] *sm* ginger
'zeppa ['tseppa] *sf* wedge
'zeppo, -a ['tseppo] *ag* **~ di** crammed *o* packed with
zer'bino [dzer'bino] *sm* doormat
'zero ['dzɛro] *sm* zero, nought; **vincere per**

tre a ~ (*Sport*) to win three-nil

'zia ['tsia] *sf* aunt

zibel'lino [dzibel'lino] *sm* sable

'zigomo ['dzigomo] *sm* cheekbone

zig'zag [dzig'dzag] *sm inv* zigzag; **andare a ~** to zigzag

Zimbabwe [tsim'babwe] *sm* **lo ~** Zimbabwe

'zinco ['dzinko] *sm* zinc

'zingaro, -a ['dzingaro] *sm/f* gipsy

'zio ['tsio] (*pl* **'zii**) *sm* uncle

zip'pare *vt* (*Inform: file*) to zip

zi'tella [dzi'tella] *sf* spinster; (*peg*) old maid

'zitto, -a ['tsitto] *ag* quiet, silent; **sta' ~!** be quiet!

'zoccolo ['tsɔkkolo] *sm* (*calzatura*) clog; (*di cavallo ecc*) hoof; (*basamento*) base; plinth

zodia'cale [dzodia'kale] *ag* zodiac *cpd*; **segno ~** sign of the zodiac

zo'diaco [dzo'diako] *sm* zodiac

'zolfo ['tsolfo] *sm* sulphur

'zolla ['dzɔlla] *sf* clod (of earth)

zol'letta [dzol'letta] *sf* sugar lump

'zona ['dzɔna] *sf* zone, area; **zona di depressione** (*Meteor*) trough of low pressure; **zona disco** (*Aut*) ≈ meter zone; **zona industriale** industrial estate; **zona pedonale** pedestrian precinct; **zona verde** (*di abitato*) green area

'zonzo ['dzondzo]: **a ~** *av*, **andare a ~** to wander about, stroll about

zoo ['dzɔo] *sm inv* zoo

zoolo'gia [dzoolo'dʒia] *sf* zoology

zoppi'care [tsoppi'kare] *vi* to limp; to be shaky, rickety

'zoppo, -a ['tsɔppo] *ag* lame; (*fig: mobile*) shaky, rickety

Z.T.L. *sigla f* (= *Zona a Traffico Limitato*) controlled traffic zone

'zucca, -che ['tsukka] *sf* (*Bot*) marrow; pumpkin

zucche'rare [tsukke'rare] *vt* to put sugar in; **zucche'rato, -a** *ag* sweet, sweetened

zuccheri'era [tsukke'rjera] *sf* sugar bowl

'zucchero ['tsukkero] *sm* sugar; **zucchero di canna** cane sugar; **zucchero filato** candy floss, cotton candy (*us*)

zuc'china [tsuk'kina] *sf* courgette (*BRIT*), zucchini (*us*)

'zuffa ['tsuffa] *sf* brawl

'zuppa ['tsuppa] *sf* soup; (*fig*) mixture, muddle; **zuppa inglese** (*Cuc*) dessert made with sponge cake, custard and chocolate, ≈ trifle (*BRIT*)

'zuppo, -a ['tsuppo] *ag* **~ (di)** drenched (with), soaked (with)

A [eɪ] *n* (*Mus*) la *m*

○ **KEYWORD**

a [ə] (*before vowel or silent h* **an**) *indef art* **1** un (uno + *s impure, gn, pn, ps, x, z*), una *f* (un' + *vowel*); **a mirror** uno specchio; **an apple** una mela; **she's a doctor** è medico
2 (*instead of the number "one"*) un(o), *f* una; **a year ago** un anno fa; **a hundred/thousand** *etc* **pounds** cento/mille *etc* sterline
3 (*in expressing ratios, prices etc*) a, per; **3 a day/week** 3 al giorno/alla settimana; **10 km an hour** 10 km all'ora; **£5 a person** 5 sterline a persona *or* per persona

A.A. *n abbr* (= *Alcoholics Anonymous*) AA; (*BRIT*: = *Automobile Association*) ≈ A.C.I. *m*
A.A.A. (*US*) *n abbr* (= *American Automobile Association*) ≈ A.C.I. *m*
aback [ə'bæk] *adv* **to be taken ~** essere sbalordito(-a)
abandon [ə'bændən] *vt* abbandonare ▷ *n* **with ~** sfrenatamente, spensieratamente
abattoir ['æbətwɑː'] (*BRIT*) *n* mattatoio
abbey ['æbɪ] *n* abbazia, badia
abbreviation [əbriːvɪ'eɪʃən] *n* abbreviazione *f*

abdomen ['æbdəmən] *n* addome *m*
abduct [æb'dʌkt] *vt* rapire
abide [ə'baɪd] *vt* **I can't ~ it/him** non lo posso soffrire *or* sopportare; **abide by** *vt fus* conformarsi a
ability [ə'bɪlɪtɪ] *n* abilità *f inv*
able ['eɪbl] *adj* capace; **to be ~ to do sth** essere capace di fare qc, poter fare qc
abnormal [æb'nɔːməl] *adj* anormale
aboard [ə'bɔːd] *adv* a bordo ▷ *prep* a bordo di
abolish [ə'bɔlɪʃ] *vt* abolire
abolition [æbəu'lɪʃən] *n* abolizione *f*
abort [ə'bɔːt] *vt* abortire; **abortion** [ə'bɔːʃən] *n* aborto; **to have an abortion** abortire

○ **KEYWORD**

about [ə'baut] *adv* **1** (*approximately*) circa, quasi; **about a hundred/thousand** *etc* un centinaio/migliaio *etc*, circa cento/mille *etc*; **it takes about 10 hours** ci vogliono circa 10 ore; **at about 2 o'clock** verso le 2; **I've just about finished** ho quasi finito
2 (*referring to place*) qua e là, in giro; **to leave things lying about** lasciare delle cose in giro; **to run about** correre qua e là; **to walk about** camminare
3: **to be about to do sth** stare per fare qc ▷ *prep* **1** (*relating to*) su, di; **a book about London** un libro su Londra; **what is it about?** di che si tratta?; (*book, film etc*) di cosa tratta?; **we talked about it** ne abbiamo parlato; **what** *or* **how about doing this?** che ne dici di fare questo?
2 (*referring to place*): **to walk about the town** camminare per la città; **her clothes were scattered about the room** i suoi vestiti erano sparsi *or* in giro per tutta la stanza

above [ə'bʌv] *adv, prep* sopra; **mentioned ~** suddetto; **~ all** soprattutto
abroad [ə'brɔːd] *adv* all'estero
abrupt [ə'brʌpt] *adj* (*sudden*) improvviso(-a); (*gruff, blunt*) brusco(-a)
abscess ['æbsɪs] *n* ascesso
absence ['æbsəns] *n* assenza
absent ['æbsənt] *adj* assente; **absent-minded** *adj* distratto(-a)
absolute ['æbsəluːt] *adj* assoluto(-a); **absolutely** [-'luːtlɪ] *adv* assolutamente
absorb [əb'zɔːb] *vt* assorbire; **to be ~ed in a book** essere immerso in un libro; **absorbent cotton** [əb'zɔːbənt-] (*US*) *n* cotone *m* idrofilo; **absorbing** *adj* avvincente, molto interessante
abstain [əb'steɪn] *vi* **to ~ (from)**

astenersi (da)
abstract ['æbstrækt] adj astratto(-a)
absurd [əb'sə:d] adj assurdo(-a)
abundance [ə'bʌndəns] n abbondanza
abundant [ə'bʌndənt] adj abbondante
abuse [n ə'bju:s, vb ə'bju:z] n abuso;
(insults) ingiurie fpl ▷ vt abusare di;
abusive adj ingiurioso(-a)
abysmal [ə'bɪzməl] adj spaventoso(-a)
academic [ækə'dɛmɪk] adj
accademico(-a); (pej: issue) puramente
formale ▷ n universitario(-a); **academic
year** n anno accademico
academy [ə'kædəmɪ] n (learned body)
accademia; (school) scuola privata;
academy of music n conservatorio
accelerate [æk'sɛləreɪt] vt, vi accelerare;
acceleration n accelerazione f;
accelerator n acceleratore m
accent ['æksɛnt] n accento
accept [ək'sɛpt] vt accettare; **acceptable**
adj accettabile; **acceptance** n
accettazione f
access ['æksɛs] n accesso; **accessible**
[æk'sɛsəbl] adj accessibile
accessory [æk'sɛsərɪ] n accessorio; (Law):
~ **to** complice m/f di
accident ['æksɪdənt] n incidente m;
(chance) caso; **I've had an ~** ho avuto
un incidente; **by ~** per caso; **accidental**
[-'dɛntl] adj accidentale; **accidentally**
[-'dɛntəlɪ] adv per caso; **Accident and
Emergency Department** n (BRIT)
pronto soccorso; **accident insurance** n
assicurazione f contro gli infortuni
acclaim [ə'kleɪm] n acclamazione f
accommodate [ə'kɔmədeɪt] vt
alloggiare; (oblige, help) favorire
accommodation [əkɔmə'deɪʃən] (US
accommodations) n alloggio
accompaniment [ə'kʌmpənɪmənt] n
accompagnamento
accompany [ə'kʌmpənɪ] vt
accompagnare
accomplice [ə'kʌmplɪs] n complice m/f
accomplish [ə'kʌmplɪʃ] vt compiere;
(goal) raggiungere; **accomplishment** n
compimento; realizzazione f
accord [ə'kɔːd] n accordo ▷ vt accordare;
of his own ~ di propria iniziativa;
accordance n **in accordance with** in
conformità con; **according: according
to** prep secondo; **accordingly** adv in
conformità
account [ə'kaunt] n (Comm) conto; (report)
descrizione f; ~**s** npl (Comm) conti mpl;
of no ~ di nessuna importanza; **on ~** in
acconto; **on no ~** per nessun motivo;
on ~ of a causa di; **to take into ~, take**

~ **of** tener conto di; **account for** vt fus
spiegare; giustificare; **accountable**
adj **accountable (to)** responsabile
(verso); **accountant** [ə'kauntənt] n
ragioniere(-a); **account number** n
numero di conto
accumulate [ə'kju:mjuleɪt] vt
accumulare ▷ vi accumularsi
accuracy ['ækjurəsɪ] n precisione f
accurate ['ækjurɪt] adj preciso(-a);
accurately adv precisamente
accusation [ækju'zeɪʃən] n accusa
accuse [ə'kju:z] vt accusare; **accused** n
accusato(-a)
accustomed [ə'kʌstəmd] adj ~ **to**
abituato(-a) a
ace [eɪs] n asso
ache [eɪk] n male m, dolore m ▷ vi (be sore)
far male, dolere; **my head ~s** mi fa male
la testa
achieve [ə'tʃi:v] vt (aim) raggiungere;
(victory, success) ottenere; **achievement** n
compimento; successo
acid ['æsɪd] adj acido(-a) ▷ n acido
acknowledge [ək'nɔlɪdʒ] vt (letter: also:
~ **receipt of**) confermare la ricevuta di;
(fact) riconoscere; **acknowledgement** n
conferma; riconoscimento
acne ['æknɪ] n acne f
acorn ['eɪkɔːn] n ghianda
acoustic [ə'ku:stɪk] adj acustico(-a)
acquaintance [ə'kweɪntəns] n
conoscenza; (person) conoscente m/f
acquire [ə'kwaɪəʳ] vt acquistare;
acquisition [ækwɪ'zɪʃən] n acquisto
acquit [ə'kwɪt] vt assolvere; **to ~ o.s. well**
comportarsi bene
acre ['eɪkəʳ] n acro, ≈ 4047 m²
acronym ['ækrənɪm] n acronimo
across [ə'krɔs] prep (on the other side)
dall'altra parte di; (crosswise) attraverso
▷ adv dall'altra parte; in larghezza; **to run/
swim ~** attraversare di corsa/a nuoto; ~
from di fronte a
acrylic [ə'krɪlɪk] adj acrilico(-a)
act [ækt] n atto; (in music-hall etc) numero;
(Law) decreto ▷ vi agire; (Theatre) recitare;
(pretend) fingere ▷ vt (part) recitare;
to ~ as agire da; **act up** (inf) vi (person)
comportarsi male; (knee, back, injury) fare
male; (machine) non funzionare; **acting**
adj che fa le funzioni di ▷ n (of actor)
recitazione f; (activity): **to do some acting**
fare del teatro (or del cinema)
action ['ækʃən] n azione f; (Mil)
combattimento; (Law) processo; **out of
~** fuori combattimento; fuori servizio; **to
take ~** agire; **action replay** n (TV) replay
m inv

activate ['æktɪveɪt] vt (mechanism) attivare

active ['æktɪv] adj attivo(-a); **actively** adv (participate) attivamente; (discourage, dislike) vivamente

activist ['æktɪvɪst] n attivista m/f

activity [æk'tɪvɪtɪ] n attività f inv; **activity holiday** n vacanza organizzata con attività ricreative per ragazzi

actor ['æktər] n attore m

actress ['æktrɪs] n attrice f

actual ['æktjʊəl] adj reale, effettivo(-a)

> Be careful not to translate **actual** by the Italian word **attuale**.

actually ['æktjʊəlɪ] adv veramente; (even) addirittura

> Be careful not to translate **actually** by the Italian word **attualmente**.

acupuncture ['ækjʊpʌŋktʃər] n agopuntura

acute [ə'kju:t] adj acuto(-a); (mind, person) perspicace

ad [æd] n abbr = **advertisement**

A.D. adv abbr (= Anno Domini) d.C.

adamant ['ædəmənt] adj irremovibile

adapt [ə'dæpt] vt adattare ▷ vi **to ~ (to)** adattarsi (a); **adapter, adaptor** n (Elec) adattatore m

add [æd] vt aggiungere ▷ vi **to ~ to** (increase) aumentare; **add up** vt (figures) addizionare ▷ vi (fig): **it doesn't ~ up** non ha senso; **add up to** vt fus (Math) ammontare a; (fig: mean) significare; **it doesn't ~ up to much** non è un granché

addict ['ædɪkt] n tossicomane m/f; (fig) fanatico(-a); **addicted** [ə'dɪktɪd] adj **to be addicted to** (drink etc) essere dedito(-a) a; (fig: football etc) essere tifoso(-a) di; **addiction** [ə'dɪkʃən] n (Med) tossicodipendenza; **addictive** [ə'dɪktɪv] adj che dà assuefazione

addition [ə'dɪʃən] n addizione f; (thing added) aggiunta; **in ~** inoltre; **in ~ to** oltre; **additional** adj supplementare

additive ['ædɪtɪv] n additivo

address [ə'drɛs] n indirizzo; (talk) discorso ▷ vt indirizzare; (speak to) fare un discorso a; (issue) affrontare; **my ~ is ...** il mio indirizzo è ...; **address book** n rubrica

adequate ['ædɪkwɪt] adj adeguato(-a), sufficiente

adhere [əd'hɪər] vi **to ~ to** aderire a; (fig: rule, decision) seguire

adhesive [əd'hi:zɪv] n adesivo; **adhesive tape** n (BRIT: for parcels etc) nastro adesivo; (US Med) cerotto adesivo

adjacent [ə'dʒeɪsənt] adj adiacente; **~ to** accanto a

adjective ['ædʒɛktɪv] n aggettivo

adjoining [ə'dʒɔɪnɪŋ] adj accanto inv, adiacente

adjourn [ə'dʒə:n] vt rimandare ▷ vi essere aggiornato(-a)

adjust [ə'dʒʌst] vt aggiustare; (change) rettificare ▷ vi **to ~ (to)** adattarsi (a); **adjustable** adj regolabile; **adjustment** n (Psych) adattamento; (of machine) regolazione f; (of prices, wages) modifica

administer [əd'mɪnɪstər] vt amministrare; (justice, drug) somministrare; **administration** [ədmɪnɪs'treɪʃən] n amministrazione f; **administrative** [əd'mɪnɪstrətɪv] adj amministrativo(-a)

administrator [əd'mɪnɪstreɪtər] n amministratore(-trice)

admiral ['ædmərəl] n ammiraglio

admiration [ædmə'reɪʃən] n ammirazione f

admire [əd'maɪər] vt ammirare; **admirer** n ammiratore(-trice)

admission [əd'mɪʃən] n ammissione f; (to exhibition, nightclub etc) ingresso; (confession) confessione f

admit [əd'mɪt] vt ammettere; far entrare; (agree) riconoscere; **admit to** vt fus riconoscere; **admittance** n ingresso; **admittedly** adv bisogna pur riconoscere (che)

adolescent [ædəu'lɛsnt] adj, n adolescente m/f

adopt [ə'dɔpt] vt adottare; **adopted** adj adottivo(-a); **adoption** [ə'dɔpʃən] n adozione f

adore [ə'dɔ:r] vt adorare

adorn [ə'dɔ:n] vt ornare

Adriatic [eɪdrɪ'ætɪk] n **the ~ (Sea)** il mare Adriatico, l'Adriatico

adrift [ə'drɪft] adv alla deriva

adult ['ædʌlt] adj adulto(-a); (work, education) per adulti ▷ n adulto(-a); **adult education** n scuola per adulti

adultery [ə'dʌltərɪ] n adulterio

advance [əd'vɑ:ns] n avanzamento; (money) anticipo ▷ adj (booking etc) in anticipo ▷ vt (money) anticipare ▷ vi avanzare; **in ~** in anticipo; **do I need to book in ~?** occorre che prenoti in anticipo?; **advanced** adj avanzato(-a); (Scol: studies) superiore

advantage [əd'vɑ:ntɪdʒ] n (also Tennis) vantaggio; **to take ~ of** approfittarsi di

advent ['ædvənt] n avvento; (Rel): **A~** Avvento

adventure [əd'vɛntʃər] n avventura; **adventurous** [əd'vɛntʃərəs] adj avventuroso(-a)

adverb ['ædvə:b] n avverbio

adversary ['ædvəsərɪ] n avversario(-a)
adverse ['ædvə:s] adj avverso(-a)
advert ['ædvə:t] (BRIT) n abbr
= **advertisement**
advertise ['ædvətaɪz] vi, vt fare pubblicità
or réclame (a); fare un'inserzione (per
vendere); **to ~ for** (staff) mettere un
annuncio sul giornale per trovare;
advertisement [əd'və:tɪsmənt] n
(Comm) réclame f inv, pubblicità f inv; (in
classified ads) inserzione f; **advertiser** n
azienda che reclamizza un prodotto; (in
newspaper) inserzionista m/f; **advertising**
['ædvətaɪzɪŋ] n pubblicità
advice [əd'vaɪs] n consiglio mpl; **piece of ~**
consiglio; **to take legal ~** consultare un
avvocato
advisable [əd'vaɪzəbl] adj consigliabile
advise [əd'vaɪz] vt consigliare; **to ~ sb of**
sth informare qn di qc; **to ~ sb against**
sth/doing sth sconsigliare qc a qn/a qn
di fare qc; **adviser** n consigliere(-a); (in
business) consulente m/f, consigliere(-a);
advisory [-ərɪ] adj consultivo(-a)
advocate [n 'ædvəkɪt, vb 'ædvəkeɪt]
n (upholder) sostenitore(-trice); (Law)
avvocato (difensore) ▷ vt propugnare
Aegean [ɪ'dʒi:ən] n **the ~ (Sea)** il mar
Egeo, l'Egeo
aerial ['eərɪəl] n antenna ▷ adj aereo(-a)
aerobics [ɛə'rəubɪks] n aerobica
aeroplane ['ɛərəpleɪn] (BRIT) n aeroplano
aerosol ['ɛərəsɔl] (BRIT) n aerosol m inv
affair [ə'fɛə²] n affare m; (also: **love ~**)
relazione f amorosa; **~s** (business) affari
affect [ə'fɛkt] vt toccare; (influence)
influire su, incidere su; (feign) fingere;
affected adj affettato(-a); **affection**
[ə'fɛkʃən] n affezione f; **affectionate** adj
affettuoso(-a)
afflict [ə'flɪkt] vt affliggere
affluent ['æfluənt] adj ricco(-a); **the ~**
society la società del benessere
afford [ə'fɔ:d] vt permettersi; (provide)
fornire; **affordable** adj (che ha un prezzo)
abbordabile
Afghanistan [æf'gænɪsta:n] n Afganistan
m
afraid [ə'freɪd] adj impaurito(-a); **to be ~**
of or **to/that** aver paura di/che; **I am ~**
so/not ho paura di sì/no
Africa ['æfrɪkə] n Africa; **African** adj, n
africano(-a); **African-American** adj, n
afroamericano(-a)
after ['ɑ:ftə²] prep, adv dopo ▷ conj dopo
che; **what/who are you ~?** che/chi
cerca?; **~ he left/having done** dopo
che se ne fu andato/dopo aver fatto; **to**
name sb ~ sb dare a qn il nome di qn; **it's**
twenty ~ eight (US) sono le otto e venti;
to ask ~ sb chiedere di qn; **~ all** dopo
tutto; **~ you!** dopo di lei!; **after-effects**
npl conseguenze fpl; (of illness) postumi
mpl; **aftermath** n conseguenze fpl; **in**
the aftermath of nel periodo dopo;
afternoon n pomeriggio; **after-shave**
(lotion) ['ɑ:ftəʃeɪv-] n dopobarba m inv;
aftersun (lotion/cream) n doposole m
inv; **afterwards** (US **afterward**) adv dopo
again [ə'gɛn] adv di nuovo; **to begin/see ~**
ricominciare/rivedere; **not ... ~** non ... più;
~ and ~ ripetutamente
against [ə'gɛnst] prep contro
age [eɪdʒ] n età f inv ▷ vt, vi invecchiare;
it's been ~s since sono secoli che; **he is**
20 years of ~ ha 20 anni; **to come of ~**
diventare maggiorenne; **~d 10** di 10 anni;
the ~d ['eɪdʒɪd] gli anziani; **age group** n
generazione f; **age limit** n limite m d'età
agency ['eɪdʒənsɪ] n agenzia
agenda [ə'dʒɛndə] n ordine m del giorno
agent ['eɪdʒənt] n agente m
aggravate ['ægrəveɪt] vt aggravare;
(person) irritare
aggression [ə'grɛʃən] n aggressione f
aggressive [ə'grɛsɪv] adj aggressivo(-a)
agile ['ædʒaɪl] adj agile
agitated ['ædʒɪteɪtɪd] adj agitato(-a),
turbato(-a)
AGM n abbr = **annual general meeting**
ago [ə'gəu] adv **2 days ~** 2 giorni fa; **not**
long ~ poco tempo fa; **how long ~?**
quanto tempo fa?
agony ['ægənɪ] n dolore m atroce; **to be in**
~ avere dolori atroci
agree [ə'gri:] vt (price) pattuire ▷ vi **to**
~ (with) essere d'accordo (con); (Ling)
concordare (con); **to ~ to sth/to do sth**
accettare qc/di fare qc; **to ~ that** (admit)
ammettere che; **to ~ on sth** accordarsi su
qc; **garlic doesn't ~ with me** l'aglio non
mi va; **agreeable** adj gradevole; (willing)
disposto(-a); **agreed** adj (time, place)
stabilito(-a); **agreement** n accordo; **in**
agreement d'accordo
agricultural [ægrɪ'kʌltʃərəl] adj
agricolo(-a)
agriculture ['ægrɪkʌltʃə²] n agricoltura
ahead [ə'hɛd] adv avanti; davanti; **~ of**
davanti a; (fig: schedule etc) in anticipo su;
~ of time in anticipo; **go right** or **straight**
~ tiri diritto
aid [eɪd] n aiuto ▷ vt aiutare; **in ~ of** a
favore di
aide [eɪd] n (person) aiutante m/f
AIDS [eɪdz] n abbr (= acquired immune
deficiency syndrome) AIDS f
ailing ['eɪlɪŋ] adj sofferente; (fig: economy,

industry etc) in difficoltà

ailment ['eɪlmənt] *n* indisposizione *f*

aim [eɪm] *vt* **to ~ sth at** (*such as gun*) mirare qc a, puntare qc a; (*camera*) rivolgere qc a; (*missile*) lanciare qc contro ▷ *vi* (*also:* **to take ~**) prendere la mira ▷ *n* mira; **to ~ at** mirare; **to ~ to do** aver l'intenzione di fare

ain't [eɪnt] (*inf*) = **am not; aren't; isn't**

air [ɛəʳ] *n* aria ▷ *vt* (*room*) arieggiare; (*clothes*) far prendere aria a; (*grievances, ideas*) esprimere pubblicamente ▷ *cpd* (*currents*) d'aria; (*attack*) aereo(-a); **to throw sth into the ~** lanciare qc in aria; **by ~** (*travel*) in aereo; **on the ~** (*Radio, TV*) in onda; **airbag** *n* airbag *m inv*; **airbed** (BRIT) *n* materassino; **airborne** ['ɛəbɔːn] *adj* (*plane*) in volo; (*troops*) aerotrasportato(-a); **as soon as the plane was airborne** appena l'aereo ebbe decollato; **air-conditioned** *adj* con or ad aria condizionata; **air conditioning** *n* condizionamento d'aria; **aircraft** *n inv* apparecchio; **airfield** *n* campo d'aviazione; **Air Force** *n* aviazione *f* militare; **air hostess** (BRIT) *n* hostess *f inv*; **airing cupboard** ['ɛərɪŋ-] *n* armadio riscaldato per asciugare panni.; **airlift** *n* ponte *m* aereo; **airline** *n* linea aerea; **airliner** *n* aereo di linea; **airmail** *n* **by airmail** per via aerea; **airplane** (US) *n* aeroplano; **airport** *n* aeroporto; **air raid** *n* incursione *f* aerea; **airsick** *adj* **to be airsick** soffrire di mal d'aria; **airspace** *n* spazio aereo; **airstrip** *n* pista d'atterraggio; **air terminal** *n* air-terminal *m inv*; **airtight** *adj* ermetico(-a); **air-traffic controller** *n* controllore *m* del traffico aereo; **airy** *adj* arioso(-a); (*manners*) noncurante

aisle [aɪl] *n* (*of church*) navata laterale; navata centrale; (*of plane*) corridoio; **aisle seat** *n* (*on plane*) posto sul corridoio

ajar [ə'dʒɑːʳ] *adj* socchiuso(-a)

à la carte [ɑːlɑː'kɑːt] *adv* alla carta

alarm [ə'lɑːm] *n* allarme *m* ▷ *vt* allarmare; **alarm call** *n* (*in hotel etc*) sveglia; **could I have an alarm call at 7 am, please?** vorrei essere svegliato alle 7, per favore; **alarm clock** *n* sveglia; **alarmed** *adj* (*person*) allarmato(-a); (*house, car etc*) dotato(-a) di allarme; **alarming** *adj* allarmante, preoccupante

Albania [æl'beɪnɪə] *n* Albania

albeit [ɔːl'biːɪt] *conj* sebbene + *sub*, benché + *sub*

album ['ælbəm] *n* album *m inv*

alcohol ['ælkəhɔl] *n* alcool *m*; **alcohol-free** *adj* analcolico(-a); **alcoholic** ['-'hɔlɪk] *adj* alcolico(-a) ▷ *n* alcolizzato(-a)

alcove ['ælkəuv] *n* alcova

ale [eɪl] *n* birra

alert [ə'ləːt] *adj* vigile ▷ *n* allarme *m* ▷ *vt* avvertire; mettere in guardia; **on the ~** all'erta

algebra ['ældʒɪbrə] *n* algebra

Algeria [æl'dʒɪərɪə] *n* Algeria

alias ['eɪlɪəs] *adv* alias ▷ *n* pseudonimo, falso nome *m*

alibi ['ælɪbaɪ] *n* alibi *m inv*

alien ['eɪlɪən] *n* straniero(-a); (*extraterrestrial*) alieno(-a) ▷ *adj* **~ (to)** estraneo(-a) (a); **alienate** *vt* alienare

alight [ə'laɪt] *adj* acceso(-a) ▷ *vi* scendere; (*bird*) posarsi

align [ə'laɪn] *vt* allineare

alike [ə'laɪk] *adj* simile ▷ *adv* sia ... sia; **to look ~** assomigliarsi

alive [ə'laɪv] *adj* vivo(-a); (*lively*) vivace

○ **KEYWORD**

all [ɔːl] *adj* tutto(-a); **all day** tutto il giorno; **all night** tutta la notte; **all men** tutti gli uomini; **all five came** sono venuti tutti e cinque; **all the books** tutti i libri; **all the food** tutto il cibo; **all the time** sempre; tutto il tempo; **all his life** tutta la vita ▷ *pron* **1** tutto(-a); **I ate it all, I ate all of it** l'ho mangiato tutto; **all of us went** tutti noi siamo andati; **all of the boys went** tutti i ragazzi sono andati

2 (*in phrases*): **above all** soprattutto; **after all** dopotutto; **at all: not at all** (*in answer to question*) niente affatto; (*in answer to thanks*) prego!, di niente!, s'immagini!; **I'm not at all tired** non sono affatto stanco(-a); **anything at all will do** andrà bene qualsiasi cosa; **all in all** tutto sommato

▷ *adv* **all alone** tutto(-a) solo(-a); **it's not as hard as all that** non è poi così difficile; **all the more/the better** tanto più/meglio; **all but** quasi; **the score is two all** il punteggio è di due a due

Allah ['ælə] *n* Allah *m*

allegation [ælɪ'geɪʃən] *n* asserzione *f*

alleged [ə'lɛdʒd] *adj* presunto(-a); **allegedly** [ə'lɛdʒɪdlɪ] *adv* secondo quanto si asserisce

allegiance [ə'liːdʒəns] *n* fedeltà

allergic [ə'ləːdʒɪk] *adj* **~ to** allergico(-a) a; **I'm ~ to penicillin** sono allergico alla penicillina

allergy ['ælədʒɪ] *n* allergia

alleviate [ə'liːvɪeɪt] *vt* sollevare

alley ['ælɪ] *n* vicolo

alliance [ə'laɪəns] *n* alleanza

allied ['ælaɪd] adj alleato(-a)

alligator ['ælɪɡeɪtə'] n alligatore m

all-in ['ɔːlɪn] adj (BRIT: also adv: charge) tutto compreso

allocate ['æləkeɪt] vt assegnare

allot [ə'lɔt] vt assegnare

all-out ['ɔːlaut] adj (effort etc) totale ▷ adv **to go all out for** mettercela tutta per

allow [ə'lau] vt (practice, behaviour) permettere; (sum to spend etc) accordare; (sum, time estimated) dare; (concede): **to ~ that** ammettere che; **to ~ sb to do** permettere a qn di fare; **he is ~ed to** lo può fare; **allow for** vt fus tener conto di; **allowance** n (money received) assegno; indennità f inv; (Tax) detrazione f di imposta; **to make allowances for** tener conto di

all right adv (feel, work) bene; (as answer) va bene

ally ['ælaɪ] n alleato

almighty [ɔːl'maɪtɪ] adj onnipotente; (row etc) colossale

almond ['ɑːmənd] n mandorla

almost ['ɔːlməust] adv quasi

alone [ə'ləun] adj, adv solo(-a); **to leave sb ~** lasciare qn in pace; **to leave sth ~** lasciare stare qc; **let ~ ...** figuriamoci poi ..., tanto meno ...

along [ə'lɔŋ] prep lungo ▷ adv **is he coming ~?** viene con noi?; **he was limping ~** veniva zoppicando; **~ with** insieme con; **all ~** (all the time) sempre, fin dall'inizio; **alongside** prep accanto a; lungo ▷ adv accanto

aloof [ə'luːf] adj distaccato(-a) ▷ adv **to stand ~** tenersi a distanza or in disparte

aloud [ə'laud] adv ad alta voce

alphabet ['ælfəbet] n alfabeto

Alps [ælps] npl **the ~** le Alpi

already [ɔːl'redɪ] adv già

alright ['ɔːl'raɪt] (BRIT) adv = **all right**

also ['ɔːlsəu] adv anche

altar ['ɔltə'] n altare m

alter ['ɔltə'] vt, vi alterare; **alteration** [ɔltə'reɪʃən] n modificazione f, alterazione f; **alterations** (Sewing, Archit) modifiche fpl; **timetable subject to alteration** orario soggetto a variazioni

alternate [adj ɔl'təːnɪt, vb 'ɔltəːneɪt] adj alterno(-a); (US: plan etc) alternativo(-a) ▷ vi **to ~ (with)** alternarsi (a); **on ~ days** ogni due giorni

alternative [ɔl'təːnətɪv] adj alternativo(-a) ▷ n (choice) alternativa; **alternatively** adv **alternatively one could ...** come alternativa si potrebbe ...

although [ɔːl'ðəu] conj benché + sub, sebbene + sub

altitude ['æltɪtjuːd] n altitudine f

altogether [ɔːltə'ɡeðə'] adv del tutto, completamente; (on the whole) tutto considerato; (in all) in tutto

aluminium [ælju'mɪnɪəm] (BRIT), **aluminum** [ə'luːmɪnəm] (US) n alluminio

always ['ɔːlweɪz] adv sempre

Alzheimer's (disease) ['æltshaɪməz-] n (malattia di) Alzheimer

am [æm] vb see **be**

amalgamate [ə'mælɡəmeɪt] vt amalgamare ▷ vi amalgamarsi

amass [ə'mæs] vt ammassare

amateur ['æmətə'] n dilettante m/f ▷ adj (Sport) dilettante

amaze [ə'meɪz] vt stupire; **amazed** adj sbalordito(-a); **to be amazed (at)** essere sbalordito (da); **amazement** n stupore m; **amazing** adj sorprendente, sbalorditivo(-a)

Amazon ['æməzən] n (Mythology) Amazzone f; (river): **the ~** il Rio delle Amazzoni ▷ cpd (basin, jungle) amazzonico(-a)

ambassador [æm'bæsədə'] n ambasciatore(-trice)

amber ['æmbə'] n ambra; **at ~** (BRIT Aut) giallo

ambiguous [æm'bɪɡjuəs] adj ambiguo(-a)

ambition [æm'bɪʃən] n ambizione f; **ambitious** [æm'bɪʃəs] adj ambizioso(-a)

ambulance ['æmbjuləns] n ambulanza; **call an ~!** chiamate un'ambulanza!

ambush ['æmbuʃ] n imboscata

amen ['ɑː'mɛn] excl così sia, amen

amend [ə'mɛnd] vt (law) emendare; (text) correggere; **to make ~s** fare ammenda; **amendment** n emendamento; correzione f

amenities [ə'miːnɪtɪz] npl attrezzature fpl ricreative e culturali

America [ə'mɛrɪkə] n America; **American** adj, n americano(-a); **American football** n (BRIT) football m americano

amicable ['æmɪkəbl] adj amichevole

amid(st) [ə'mɪd(st)] prep in mezzo a

ammunition [æmju'nɪʃən] n munizioni fpl

amnesty ['æmnɪstɪ] n amnistia; **to grant an ~ to** concedere l'amnistia a, amnistiare

among(st) [ə'mʌŋ(st)] prep fra, tra, in mezzo a

amount [ə'maunt] n somma; ammontare m; quantità f inv ▷ vi **to ~ to** (total) ammontare a; (be same as) essere come

amp(ère) ['æmp(ɛə')] n ampère m inv

ample ['æmpl] adj ampio(-a); spazioso(-a); (enough): **this is ~** questo è più che sufficiente

amplifier ['æmplɪfaɪə'] n amplificatore m
amputate ['æmpjuteɪt] vt amputare
Amtrak ['æmtræk] (us) n società ferroviaria americana
amuse [ə'mjuːz] vt divertire; **amusement** n divertimento; **amusement arcade** n sala giochi; **amusement park** n luna park m inv
amusing [ə'mjuːzɪŋ] adj divertente
an [æn] indef art see **a**
anaemia [ə'niːmɪə] (us **anemia**) n anemia
anaemic [ə'niːmɪk] (us **anemic**) adj anemico(-a)
anaesthetic [ænɪs'θetɪk] (us **anesthetic**) adj anestetico(-a) ▷ n anestetico
analog(ue) ['ænəlɔg] adj (watch, computer) analogico(-a)
analogy [ə'nælədʒɪ] n analogia; **to draw an ~ between** fare un'analogia tra
analyse ['ænəlaɪz] (us **analyze**) vt analizzare; **analysis** [ə'næləsɪs] (pl **analyses**) n analisi f inv; **analyst** ['ænəlɪst] n (Pol etc) analista m/f; (us) (psic)analista m/f
analyze ['ænəlaɪz] (us) vt = **analyse**
anarchy ['ænəkɪ] n anarchia
anatomy [ə'nætəmɪ] n anatomia
ancestor ['ænsɪstə'] n antenato(-a)
anchor ['æŋkə'] n ancora ▷ vi (also: **to drop ~**) gettare l'ancora ▷ vt ancorare; **to weigh ~** salpare or levare l'ancora
anchovy ['æntʃəvɪ] n acciuga
ancient ['eɪnʃənt] adj antico(-a); (person, car) vecchissimo(-a)
and [ænd] conj e; (often ed before vowel): **~ so on** così via; **try ~ come** cerca di venire; **he talked ~ talked** non la finiva di parlare; **better ~ better** sempre meglio
Andes ['ændiːz] npl **the ~** le Ande
anemia etc [ə'niːmɪə] (us) = **anaemia** etc
anesthetic [ænɪs'θetɪk] (us) n adj, n = **anaesthetic**
angel ['eɪndʒəl] n angelo
anger ['æŋgə'] n rabbia
angina [æn'dʒaɪnə] n angina pectoris
angle ['æŋgl] n angolo; **from their ~** dal loro punto di vista
angler ['æŋglə'] n pescatore m con la lenza
Anglican ['æŋglɪkən] adj, n anglicano(-a)
angling ['æŋglɪŋ] n pesca con la lenza
angrily ['æŋgrɪlɪ] adv con rabbia
angry ['æŋgrɪ] adj arrabbiato(-a), furioso(-a); (wound) infiammato(-a); **to be ~ with sb/at sth** essere in collera con qn/per qc; **to get ~** arrabbiarsi; **to make sb ~** fare arrabbiare qn
anguish ['æŋgwɪʃ] n angoscia
animal ['ænɪməl] adj animale ▷ n animale m

animated ['ænɪmeɪtɪd] adj animato(-a)
animation [ænɪ'meɪʃən] n animazione f
aniseed ['ænɪsiːd] n semi mpl di anice
ankle ['æŋkl] n caviglia
annex [n 'æneks, vb ə'neks] n (BRIT: also: **~e**) (edificio) annesso ▷ vt annettere
anniversary [ænɪ'vəːsərɪ] n anniversario
announce [ə'nauns] vt annunciare; **announcement** n annuncio; (letter, card) partecipazione f; **announcer** n (Radio, TV: between programmes) annunciatore(-trice); (: in a programme) presentatore(-trice)
annoy [ə'nɔɪ] vt dare fastidio a; **don't get ~ed!** non irritarti!; **annoying** adj noioso(-a)
annual ['ænjuəl] adj annuale ▷ n (Bot) pianta annua; (book) annuario; **annually** adv annualmente
annum ['ænəm] n see **per**
anonymous [ə'nɔnɪməs] adj anonimo(-a)
anorak ['ænəræk] n giacca a vento
anorexia [ænə'reksɪə] n (Med: also: **~ nervosa**) anoressia
anorexic [ænə'reksɪk] adj, n anoressico(-a)
another [ə'nʌðə'] adj **~ book** (one more) un altro libro, ancora un libro; (a different one) un altro libro ▷ pron un altro(un'altra), ancora uno(-a); see also **one**
answer ['ɑːnsə'] n risposta; soluzione f ▷ vi rispondere ▷ vt (reply to) rispondere a; (problem) risolvere; (prayer) esaudire; **in ~ to your letter** in risposta alla sua lettera; **to ~ the phone** rispondere (al telefono); **to ~ the bell** rispondere al campanello; **to ~ the door** aprire la porta; **answer back** vi ribattere; **answerphone** n (esp BRIT) segreteria telefonica
ant [ænt] n formica
Antarctic [ænt'ɑːktɪk] n **the ~** l'Antartide f
antelope ['æntɪləup] n antilope f
antenatal ['æntɪ'neɪtl] adj prenatale
antenna [æn'tenə, -niː] (pl **antennae**) n antenna
anthem ['ænθəm] n **national ~** inno nazionale
anthology [æn'θɔlədʒɪ] n antologia
anthrax ['ænθræks] n antrace m
anthropology [ænθrə'pɔlədʒɪ] n antropologia
anti [æntɪ] prefix anti; **antibiotic** ['æntɪbaɪ'ɔtɪk] n antibiotico; **antibody** ['æntɪbɔdɪ] n anticorpo
anticipate [æn'tɪsɪpeɪt] vt prevedere; pregustare; (wishes, request) prevenire; **anticipation** [æntɪsɪ'peɪʃən] n anticipazione f; (expectation) aspettative fpl
anticlimax ['æntɪ'klaɪmæks] n **it was an ~** fu una completa delusione

anticlockwise ['æntɪ'klɔkwaɪz] *adj, adv* in senso antiorario

antics ['æntɪks] *npl* buffonerie *fpl*

anti: **antidote** ['æntɪdəut] *n* antidoto; **antifreeze** ['æntɪ'friːz] *n* anticongelante *m*; **anti-globalization** [æntɪgləubəlaɪ'zeɪʃən] *n* antiglobalizzazione *f*; **antihistamine** [æntɪ'hɪstəmɪn] *n* antistaminico; **antiperspirant** ['æntɪ'pəːspərənt] *adj* antitraspirante

antique [æn'tiːk] *n* antichità *f inv* ▷ *adj* antico(-a); **antique shop** *n* negozio d'antichità

antiseptic [æntɪ'septɪk] *n* antisettico

antisocial ['æntɪ'səuʃəl] *adj* asociale

antlers ['æntləz] *npl* palchi *mpl*

anxiety [æŋ'zaɪətɪ] *n* ansia; (*keenness*): ~ **to do** smania di fare

anxious ['æŋkʃəs] *adj* ansioso(-a), inquieto(-a); (*worrying*) angosciante; (*keen*): ~ **to do/that** impaziente di fare/ che + *sub*

O **KEYWORD**

any ['enɪ] *adj* **1** (*in questions etc*): **have you any butter?** hai del burro?, hai un po' di burro?; **have you any children?** hai bambini?; **if there are any tickets left** se ci sono ancora (dei) biglietti, se c'è ancora qualche biglietto

2 (*with negative*): **I haven't any money/ books** non ho soldi/libri

3 (*no matter which*) qualsiasi, qualunque; **choose any book you like** scegli un libro qualsiasi

4 (*in phrases*): **in any case** in ogni caso; **any day now** da un giorno all'altro; **at any moment** in qualsiasi momento, da un momento all'altro; **at any rate** ad ogni modo

▷ *pron* **1** (*in questions, with negative*): **have you got any?** ne hai?; **can any of you sing?** qualcuno di voi sa cantare?; **I haven't any (of them)** non ne ho

2 (*no matter which one(s)*): **take any of those books (you like)** prendi uno qualsiasi di quei libri

▷ *adv* **1** (*in questions etc*): **do you want any more soup/sandwiches?** vuoi ancora un po' di minestra/degli altri panini?; **are you feeling any better?** ti senti meglio?

2 (*with negative*): **I can't hear him any more** non lo sento più; **don't wait any longer** non aspettare più

any: **anybody** ['enɪbɔdɪ] *pron* (*in questions etc*) qualcuno, nessuno; (*with negative*) nessuno; (*no matter who*) chiunque; **can you see anybody?** vedi qualcuno *or* nessuno?; **if anybody should phone ...** se telefona qualcuno ...; **I can't see anybody** non vedo nessuno; **anybody could do it** chiunque potrebbe farlo; **anyhow** ['enɪhau] *adv* (*at any rate*) ad ogni modo, comunque; (*haphazard*): **do it anyhow you like** fallo come ti pare; **I shall go anyhow** ci andrò lo stesso *or* comunque; **she leaves things just anyhow** lascia tutto come capita; **anyone** ['enɪwʌn] *pron* = **anybody**; **anything** ['enɪθɪŋ] *pron* (*in question etc*) qualcosa, niente; (*with negative*) niente; (*no matter what*): **you can say anything you like** puoi dire quello che ti pare; **can you see anything?** vedi niente *or* qualcosa?; **if anything happens to me ...** se mi dovesse succedere qualcosa ...; **I can't see anything** non vedo niente; **anything will do** va bene qualsiasi cosa *or* tutto; **anytime** *adv* in qualunque momento; quando vuole; **anyway** ['enɪweɪ] *adv* (*at any rate*) ad ogni modo, comunque; (*besides*) ad ogni modo; **anywhere** ['enɪwɛər] *adv* (*in questions etc*) da qualche parte; (*with negative*) da nessuna parte; (*no matter where*) da qualsiasi *or* qualunque parte, dovunque; **can you see him anywhere?** lo vedi da qualche parte?; **I can't see him anywhere** non lo vedo da nessuna parte; **anywhere in the world** dovunque nel mondo

apart [ə'pɑːt] *adv* (*to one side*) a parte; (*separately*) separatamente; **with one's legs** ~ con le gambe divaricate; **10 miles** ~ a 10 miglia di distanza (l'uno dall'altro); **to take** ~ smontare; ~ **from** a parte, eccetto

apartment [ə'pɑːtmənt] (*us*) *n* appartamento; (*room*) locale *m*; **apartment building** (*us*) *n* stabile *m*, caseggiato

apathy ['æpəθɪ] *n* apatia

ape [eɪp] *n* scimmia ▷ *vt* scimmiottare

aperitif [ə'perɪtiːf] *n* aperitivo

aperture ['æpətʃjuər] *n* apertura

APEX *n abbr* (= *advance purchase excursion*) APEX *m inv*

apologize [ə'pɔlədʒaɪz] *vi* **to** ~ **(for sth to sb)** scusarsi (di qc a qn), chiedere scusa (a qn per qc)

apology [ə'pɔlədʒɪ] *n* scuse *fpl*

apostrophe [ə'pɔstrəfɪ] *n* (*sign*) apostrofo

appal [ə'pɔːl] (*us* **appall**) *vt* scioccare; **appalling** *adj* spaventoso(-a)

apparatus [æpə'reɪtəs] *n* apparato; (*in gymnasium*) attrezzatura

apparent [ə'pærənt] *adj* evidente; **apparently** *adv* evidentemente appeal [ə'pi:l] vi (Law) appellarsi alla legge ▷ n (Law) appello; (request) richiesta; (charm) attrattiva; **to ~ for** chiedere (con insistenza); **to ~ to** (person) appellarsi a; (thing) piacere a; **it doesn't ~ to me** mi dice poco; **appealing** adj (nice) attraente

appear [ə'pɪər] vi apparire; (Law) comparire; (publication) essere pubblicato(-a); (seem) sembrare; **it would ~ that** sembra che; **appearance** n apparizione f; apparenza; (look, aspect) aspetto

appendicitis [əpɛndɪ'saɪtɪs] n appendicite f

appendix [ə'pɛndɪks] (pl appendices) n appendice f

appetite ['æpɪtaɪt] n appetito

appetizer ['æpɪtaɪzər] n stuzzichino

applaud [ə'plɔ:d] vt, vi applaudire

applause [ə'plɔ:z] n applauso

apple ['æpl] n mela; **apple pie** n torta di mele

appliance [ə'plaɪəns] n apparecchio

applicable [ə'plɪkəbl] adj applicabile; **to be ~ to** essere valido per; **the law is ~ from January** la legge entrerà in vigore in gennaio

applicant ['æplɪkənt] n candidato(-a)

application [æplɪ'keɪʃən] n applicazione f; (for a job, a grant etc) domanda; **application form** n modulo per la domanda

apply [ə'plaɪ] vt **to ~ (to)** (paint, ointment) dare (a); (theory, technique) applicare (a) ▷ vi **to ~ to** (ask) rivolgersi a; (be suitable for, relevant to) riguardare, riferirsi a; **to ~ (for)** (permit, grant, job) fare domanda (per); **to ~ o.s. to** dedicarsi a

appoint [ə'pɔɪnt] vt nominare; **appointment** n nomina; (arrangement to meet) appuntamento; **I have an appointment (with) ...** ho un appuntamento (con) ...; **I'd like to make an appointment (with)** vorrei prendere un appuntamento (con)

appraisal [ə'preɪzl] n valutazione f

appreciate [ə'pri:ʃɪeɪt] vt (like) apprezzare; (be grateful for) essere riconoscente di; (be aware of) rendersi conto di ▷ vi (Finance) aumentare; **I'd ~ your help** ti sono grato per l'aiuto; **appreciation** [əpri:ʃɪ'eɪʃən] n apprezzamento; (Finance) aumento del valore

apprehension [æprɪ'hɛnʃən] n (fear) inquietudine f

apprehensive [æprɪ'hɛnsɪv] adj apprensivo(-a)

apprentice [ə'prɛntɪs] n apprendista m/f

approach [ə'prəʊtʃ] vi avvicinarsi ▷ vt (come near) avvicinarsi a; (ask, apply to) rivolgersi a; (subject, passer-by) avvicinare ▷ n approccio; accesso; (to problem) modo di affrontare

appropriate [adj ə'prəʊprɪɪt, vb ə'prəʊprɪeɪt] adj appropriato(-a), adatto(-a) ▷ vt (take) appropriarsi

approval [ə'pru:vəl] n approvazione f; **on ~** (Comm) in prova, in esame

approve [ə'pru:v] vt, vi approvare; **approve of** vt fus approvare

approximate [ə'prɔksɪmɪt] adj approssimativo(-a); **approximately** adv circa

Apr. abbr (= April) apr.

apricot ['eɪprɪkɔt] n albicocca

April ['eɪprəl] n aprile m; **~ fool!** pesce d'aprile!; **April Fools' Day** n vedi nota nel riquadro

● **APRIL FOOLS' DAY**
●
● **April Fool's Day** è il primo aprile, il
● giorno degli scherzi e delle burle. Il nome
● deriva dal fatto che, se una persona
● cade nella trappola che gli è stata tesa,
● fa la figura del "fool", cioè dello sciocco.
● Tradizionalmente, gli scherzi vengono
● fatti entro mezzogiorno.

apron ['eɪprən] n grembiule m

apt [æpt] adj (suitable) adatto(-a); (able) capace; (likely): **to be ~ to do** avere tendenza a fare

aquarium [ə'kwɛərɪəm] n acquario

Aquarius [ə'kwɛərɪəs] n Acquario

Arab ['ærəb] adj, n arabo(-a)

Arabia [ə'reɪbɪə] n Arabia; **Arabian** [ə'reɪbɪən] adj arabo(-a); **Arabic** ['ærəbɪk] adj arabico(-a), arabo(-a) ▷ n arabo; **Arabic numerals** n numeri mpl arabi, numerazione f araba

arbitrary ['ɑ:bɪtrərɪ] adj arbitrario(-a)

arbitration [ɑ:bɪ'treɪʃən] n (Law) arbitrato; (Industry) arbitraggio

arc [ɑ:k] n arco

arcade [ɑ:'keɪd] n portico; (passage with shops) galleria

arch [ɑ:tʃ] n arco; (of foot) arco plantare ▷ vt inarcare

archaeology [ɑ:kɪ'ɔlədʒɪ] (us **archeology**) n archeologia

archbishop [ɑ:tʃ'bɪʃəp] n arcivescovo

archeology etc [ɑ:kɪ'ɔlədʒɪ] (us) = **archaeology** etc

architect ['ɑ:kɪtɛkt] n architetto; **architectural** [ɑ:kɪ'tɛktʃərəl] adj architettonico(-a); **architecture** ['ɑ:kɪtɛktʃər] n architettura

archive ['ɑːkaɪv] n (often pl: also Comput) archivio

Arctic ['ɑːktɪk] adj artico(-a) ▷ n **the ~** l'Artico

are [ɑː] vb see **be**

area ['ɛərɪə] n (Geom) area; (zone) zona; (: smaller) settore m; **area code** (US) n (Tel) prefisso

arena [ə'riːnə] n arena

aren't [ɑːnt] = **are not**

Argentina [ɑːdʒən'tiːnə] n Argentina; **Argentinian** [-'tɪnɪən] adj, n argentino(-a)

arguably ['ɑːgjuəblɪ] adv **it is ~ ...** si può sostenere che sia ...

argue ['ɑːgjuː] vi (quarrel) litigare; (reason) ragionare; **to ~ that** sostenere che

argument ['ɑːgjumənt] n (reasons) argomento; (quarrel) lite f

Aries ['ɛərɪz] n Ariete m

arise [ə'raɪz] (pt **arose**, pp **arisen**) vi (opportunity, problem) presentarsi

arithmetic [ə'rɪθmətɪk] n aritmetica

arm [ɑːm] n braccio ▷ vt armare; **~s** npl (weapons) armi fpl; **~ in ~** a braccetto; **armchair** n poltrona

armed [ɑːmd] adj armato(-a); **armed robbery** n rapina a mano armata

armour ['ɑːmə'] (US **armor**) n armatura; (Mil: tanks) mezzi mpl blindati

armpit ['ɑːmpɪt] n ascella

armrest ['ɑːmrɛst] n bracciolo

army ['ɑːmɪ] n esercito

A road n strada statale

aroma [ə'rəumə] n aroma; **aromatherapy** n aromaterapia

arose [ə'rəuz] pt of **arise**

around [ə'raund] adv attorno, intorno ▷ prep intorno a; (fig: about): **~ £5/3 o'clock** circa 5 sterline/le 3; **is he ~?** è in giro?

arouse [ə'rauz] vt (sleeper) svegliare; (curiosity, passions) suscitare

arrange [ə'reɪndʒ] vt sistemare; (programme) preparare; **to ~ to do sth** mettersi d'accordo per fare qc; **arrangement** n sistemazione f; (agreement) accordo; **arrangements** npl (plans) progetti mpl, piani mpl

array [ə'reɪ] n **~ of** fila di

arrears [ə'rɪəz] npl arretrati mpl; **to be in ~ with one's rent** essere in arretrato con l'affitto

arrest [ə'rɛst] vt arrestare; (sb's attention) attirare ▷ n arresto; **under ~** in arresto

arrival [ə'raɪvəl] n arrivo; (person) arrivato(-a); **a new ~** un nuovo venuto; (baby) un neonato

arrive [ə'raɪv] vi arrivare; **what time does the train from Rome ~?** a che ora arriva il treno da Roma?; **arrive at** vt fus arrivare a

arrogance ['ærəgəns] n arroganza

arrogant ['ærəgənt] adj arrogante

arrow ['ærəu] n freccia

arse [ɑːs] (inf!) n culo (!)

arson ['ɑːsn] n incendio doloso

art [ɑːt] n arte f; (craft) mestiere m; **art college** n scuola di belle arti

artery ['ɑːtərɪ] n arteria

art gallery n galleria d'arte

arthritis [ɑː'θraɪtɪs] n artrite f

artichoke ['ɑːtɪtʃəuk] n carciofo; **Jerusalem ~** topinambur m inv

article ['ɑːtɪkl] n articolo

articulate [adj ɑː'tɪkjulɪt, vb ɑː'tɪkjuleɪt] adj (person) che si esprime forbitamente; (speech) articolato(-a) ▷ vi articolare

artificial [ɑːtɪ'fɪʃəl] adj artificiale

artist ['ɑːtɪst] n artista m/f; **artistic** [ɑː'tɪstɪk] adj artistico(-a)

art school n scuola d'arte

 KEYWORD

as [æz] conj **1** (referring to time) mentre; **as the years went by** col passare degli anni; **he came in as I was leaving** arrivò mentre stavo uscendo; **as from tomorrow** da domani

2 (in comparisons): **as big as** grande come; **twice as big as** due volte più grande di; **as much/many as** tanto quanto/tanti quanti; **as soon as possible** prima possibile

3 (since, because) dal momento che, siccome

4 (referring to manner, way) come; **do as you wish** fa' come vuoi; **as she said** come ha detto lei

5 (concerning): **as for** or **to that** per quanto riguarda or quanto a quello

6: **as if** or **as though** come se; **he looked as if he was ill** sembrava stare male; see also **long; such; well**

▷ prep **he works as a driver** fa l'autista; **as chairman of the company he ...** come presidente della compagnia lui ...; **he gave me it as a present** me lo ha regalato

a.s.a.p. abbr = **as soon as possible**

asbestos [æz'bɛstəs] n asbesto, amianto

ascent [ə'sɛnt] n salita

ash [æʃ] n (dust) cenere f; (wood, tree) frassino

ashamed [ə'ʃeɪmd] adj vergognoso(-a); **to be ~ of** vergognarsi di

ashore [ə'ʃɔː'] adv a terra

ashtray ['æʃtreɪ] n portacenere m

Ash Wednesday n mercoledì m inv delle

Ceneri

Asia ['eɪʃə] n Asia; **Asian** adj, n asiatico(-a)

aside [ə'saɪd] adv da parte ▷ n a parte m

ask [ɑːsk] vt (question) domandare; (invite) invitare; **to ~ sb sth/sb to do sth** chiedere qc a qn/a qn di fare qc; **to ~ sb about sth** chiedere a qn di qc; **to ~ (sb) a question** fare una domanda (a qn); **to ~ sb out to dinner** invitare qn a mangiare fuori; **ask for** vt fus chiedere; (trouble etc) cercare

asleep [ə'sliːp] adj addormentato(-a); **to be ~** dormire; **to fall ~** addormentarsi

asparagus [əs'pærəgəs] n asparagi mpl

aspect ['æspɛkt] n aspetto

aspirations [æspə'reɪʃənz] npl aspirazioni fpl

aspire [əs'paɪər] vi **to ~ to** aspirare a

aspirin ['æsprɪn] n aspirina

ass [æs] n asino; (inf) scemo(-a); (US: inf!) culo(!)

assassin [ə'sæsɪn] n assassino; **assassinate** [ə'sæsɪneɪt] vt assassinare

assault [ə'sɔːlt] n (Mil) assalto; (gen: attack) aggressione f ▷ vt assaltare; aggredire; (sexually) violentare

assemble [ə'sɛmbl] vt riunire; (Tech) montare ▷ vi riunirsi

assembly [ə'sɛmblɪ] n (meeting) assemblea; (construction) montaggio

assert [ə'səːt] vt asserire; (insist on) far valere; **assertion** [ə'səːʃən] n asserzione f

assess [ə'sɛs] vt valutare; **assessment** n valutazione f

asset ['æsɛt] n vantaggio; **~s** npl (Finance: of individual) beni mpl; (: of company) attivo

assign [ə'saɪn] vt **to ~ (to)** (task) assegnare (a); (resources) riservare (a); (cause, meaning) attribuire (a); **to ~ a date to sth** fissare la data di qc; **assignment** n compito

assist [ə'sɪst] vt assistere, aiutare; **assistance** n assistenza, aiuto; **assistant** n assistente m/f; (BRIT: also: **shop assistant**) commesso(-a)

associate [adj, nə'səʊʃɪɪt, vb ə'səʊʃɪeɪt] adj associato(-a); (member) aggiunto(-a) ▷ n collega m/f ▷ vt associare ▷ vi **to ~ with sb** frequentare qn

association [əsəʊsɪ'eɪʃən] n associazione f

assorted [ə'sɔːtɪd] adj assortito(-a)

assortment [ə'sɔːtmənt] n assortimento

assume [ə'sjuːm] vt supporre; (responsibilities etc) assumere; (attitude, name) prendere

assumption [ə'sʌmpʃən] n supposizione f, ipotesi f inv; (of power) assunzione f

assurance [ə'ʃuərəns] n assicurazione f; (self-confidence) fiducia in se stesso

assure [ə'ʃuər] vt assicurare

asterisk ['æstərɪsk] n asterisco

asthma ['æsmə] n asma

astonish [ə'stɒnɪʃ] vt stupire; **astonished** adj stupito(-a), sorpreso(-a); **to be astonished (at)** essere stupito(-a) (da); **astonishing** adj sorprendente, stupefacente; **I find it astonishing that ...** mi stupisce che ...; **astonishment** n stupore m

astound [ə'staund] vt sbalordire

astray [ə'streɪ] adv **to go ~** smarrirsi; **to lead ~** portare sulla cattiva strada

astrology [əs'trɒlədʒɪ] n astrologia

astronaut ['æstrənɔːt] n astronauta m/f

astronomer [əs'trɒnəmər] n astronomo(-a)

astronomical [æstrə'nɒmɪkl] adj astronomico(-a)

astronomy [əs'trɒnəmɪ] n astronomia

astute [əs'tjuːt] adj astuto(-a)

asylum [ə'saɪləm] n (politico) asilo; (per malati) manicomio

○ **KEYWORD**

at [æt] prep **1** (referring to position, direction) a; **at the top** in cima; **at the desk** al banco, alla scrivania; **at home/school** a casa/scuola; **at the baker's** dal panettiere; **to look at sth** guardare qc; **to throw sth at sb** lanciare qc a qn

2 (referring to time) a; **at 4 o'clock** alle 4; **at night** di notte; **at Christmas** a Natale; **at times** a volte

3 (referring to rates, speed etc) a; **at £1 a kilo** a 1 sterlina al chilo; **two at a time** due alla volta, due per volta; **at 50 km/h** a 50 km/h

4 (referring to manner): **at a stroke** d'un solo colpo; **at peace** in pace

5 (referring to activity): **to be at work** essere al lavoro; **to play at cowboys** giocare ai cowboy; **to be good at sth/doing sth** essere bravo in qc/fare qc

6 (referring to cause): **shocked/surprised/ annoyed at sth** colpito da/sorpreso da/arrabbiato per qc; **I went at his suggestion** ci sono andato dietro suo consiglio

ate [eɪt] pt of **eat**

atheist ['eɪθɪɪst] n ateo(-a)

Athens ['æθɪnz] n Atene f

athlete ['æθliːt] n atleta m/f

athletic [æθ'lɛtɪk] adj atletico(-a); **athletics** n atletica

Atlantic [ət'læntɪk] adj atlantico(-a) ▷ n **the ~ (Ocean)** l'Atlantico, l'Oceano Atlantico

atlas ['ætləs] n atlante m

A.T.M. n abbr (= automated telling machine) cassa automatica prelievi, sportello automatico

atmosphere ['ætməsfɪə'] n atmosfera

atom ['ætəm] n atomo; **atomic** [ə'tɒmɪk] adj atomico(-a); **atom(ic) bomb** n bomba atomica

A to Z® n (map) stradario

atrocity [ə'trɒsɪtɪ] n atrocità f inv

attach [ə'tætʃ] vt attaccare; (document, letter) allegare; (importance etc) attribuire; **to be ~ed to sb/sth** (to like) essere affezionato(-a) a qn/qc; **attachment** [ə'tætʃmənt] n (tool) accessorio; (love): **attachment (to)** affetto (per)

attack [ə'tæk] vt attaccare; (person) aggredire; (task etc) iniziare; (problem) affrontare ▷ n attacco; **heart ~** infarto; **attacker** n aggressore m

attain [ə'teɪn] vt (also: **to ~ to**) arrivare a, raggiungere

attempt [ə'tɛmpt] n tentativo ▷ vt tentare; **to make an ~ on sb's life** attentare alla vita di qn

attend [ə'tɛnd] vt frequentare; (meeting, talk) andare a; (patient) assistere; **attend to** vt fus (needs, affairs etc) prendersi cura di; (customer) occuparsi di; **attendance** n (being present) presenza; (people present) gente f presente; **attendant** n custode m/f; persona di servizio ▷ adj concomitante

█ Be careful not to translate **attend** by the Italian word **attendere**.

attention [ə'tɛnʃən] n attenzione f ▷ excl (Mil) attenti!; **for the ~ of** (Admin) per l'attenzione di

attic ['ætɪk] n soffitta

attitude ['ætɪtjuːd] n atteggiamento; posa

attorney [ə'təːnɪ] n (lawyer) avvocato; (having proxy) mandatario; **Attorney General** n (BRIT) Procuratore m Generale; (US) Ministro della Giustizia

attract [ə'trækt] vt attirare; **attraction** [ə'trækʃən] n (gen pl: pleasant things) attrattiva; (Physics, fig: towards sth) attrazione f; **attractive** adj attraente

attribute [n 'ætrɪbjuːt, vb ə'trɪbjuːt] n attributo ▷ vt **to ~ sth to** attribuire qc a

aubergine ['əubəʒiːn] n melanzana

auburn ['ɔːbən] adj tizianesco(-a)

auction ['ɔːkʃən] n (also: **sale by ~**) asta ▷ vt (also: **to sell by ~**) vendere all'asta; (also: **to put up for ~**) mettere all'asta

audible ['ɔːdɪbl] adj udibile

audience ['ɔːdɪəns] n (people) pubblico; spettatori mpl; ascoltatori mpl; (interview) udienza

audit ['ɔːdɪt] vt rivedere, verificare

audition [ɔː'dɪʃən] n audizione f

auditor ['ɔːdɪtə'] n revisore m

auditorium [ɔːdɪ'tɔːrɪəm] n sala, auditorio

Aug. abbr (= August) ago., ag.

August ['ɔːgəst] n agosto

aunt [ɑːnt] n zia; **auntie** n zietta; **aunty** n zietta

au pair ['əu'pɛə'] n (also: **~ girl**) (ragazza f) alla pari inv

aura ['ɔːrə] n aura

austerity [ɒs'tɛrɪtɪ] n austerità f inv

Australia [ɒs'treɪlɪə] n Australia; **Australian** adj, n australiano(-a)

Austria ['ɒstrɪə] n Austria; **Austrian** adj, n austriaco(-a)

authentic [ɔː'θɛntɪk] adj autentico(-a)

author ['ɔːθə'] n autore(-trice)

authority [ɔː'θɒrɪtɪ] n autorità f inv; (permission) autorizzazione f; **the authorities** npl (government etc) le autorità

authorize ['ɔːθəraɪz] vt autorizzare

auto ['ɔːtəu] (US) n auto f inv; **autobiography** [ɔːtəbaɪ'ɒgrəfɪ] n autobiografia; **autograph** ['ɔːtəgrɑːf] n autografo ▷ vt firmare; **automatic** [ɔːtə'mætɪk] adj automatico(-a) ▷ n (gun) arma automatica; (washing machine) lavatrice f automatica; (car) automobile f con cambio automatico; **automatically** adv automaticamente; **automobile** ['ɔːtəməbiːl] (US) n automobile f; **autonomous** [ɔː'tɒnəməs] adj autonomo(-a); **autonomy** [ɔː'tɒnəmɪ] n autonomia

autumn ['ɔːtəm] n autunno

auxiliary [ɔːg'zɪlɪərɪ] adj ausiliario(-a) ▷ n ausiliare m/f

avail [ə'veɪl] vt **to ~ o.s. of** servirsi di; approfittarsi di ▷ n **to no ~** inutilmente

availability [əveɪlə'bɪlɪtɪ] n disponibilità

available [ə'veɪləbl] adj disponibile

avalanche ['ævəlɑːnʃ] n valanga

Ave. abbr = **avenue**

avenue ['ævənjuː] n viale m; (fig) strada, via

average ['ævərɪdʒ] n media ▷ adj medio(-a) ▷ vt (a certain figure) fare di or in media; **on ~** in media

avert [ə'vəːt] vt evitare, prevenire; (one's eyes) distogliere

avid ['ævɪd] adj (supporter etc) accanito(-a)

avocado [ævə'kɑːdəu] n (BRIT: also: **~ pear**) avocado m inv

avoid [ə'vɔɪd] vt evitare

await [ə'weɪt] vt aspettare

awake [ə'weɪk] (pt awoke, pp awoken, awaked) adj sveglio(-a) ▷ vt svegliare ▷ vi svegliarsi

award [ə'wɔːd] n premio; (Law) risarcimento ▷ vt assegnare; (Law: damages) accordare

aware [ə'wɛə^r] adj **~ of** (conscious) conscio(-a) di; (informed) informato(-a) di; **to become ~ of** accorgersi di; **awareness** n consapevolezza

away [ə'weɪ] adj, adv via; lontano(-a); **two kilometres ~** a due chilometri di distanza; **two hours ~ by car** a due ore di distanza in macchina; **the holiday was two weeks ~** mancavano due settimane alle vacanze; **he's ~ for a week** è andato via per una settimana; **to take ~** togliere; **he was working/pedalling** etc **~** (la particella indica la continuità e l'energia dell'azione) lavorava/pedalava etc più che poteva; **to fade/wither** etc **~** (la particella rinforza l'idea della diminuzione)

awe [ɔː] n timore m; **awesome** adj imponente

awful ['ɔːfəl] adj terribile; **an ~ lot of** un mucchio di; **awfully** adv (very) terribilmente

awkward ['ɔːkwəd] adj (clumsy) goffo(-a); (inconvenient) scomodo(-a); (embarrassing) imbarazzante

awoke [ə'wəuk] pt of **awake**

awoken [ə'wəukn] pp of **awake**

axe [æks] (US **ax**) n scure f ▷ vt (project etc) abolire; (jobs) sopprimere

axle ['æksl] n (also: **~-tree**) asse m

ay(e) [aɪ] excl (yes) sì

azalea [ə'zeɪlɪə] n azalea

B [biː] n (Mus) si m

B.A. n abbr = **Bachelor of Arts**

baby ['beɪbɪ] n bambino(-a); **baby carriage** (US) n carrozzina; **baby-sit** vi fare il (or la) baby-sitter; **baby-sitter** n baby-sitter m/f inv; **baby wipe** n salvietta umidificata

bachelor ['bætʃələ^r] n scapolo; **B~ of Arts/ Science** ≈ laureato(-a) in lettere/scienze

back [bæk] n (of person, horse) dorso, schiena; (as opposed to front) dietro; (of hand) dorso; (of train) coda; (of chair) schienale m; (of page) rovescio; (of book) retro; (Football) difensore m ▷ vt (candidate) appoggiare; (horse: at races) puntare su; (car) guidare a marcia indietro ▷ vi indietreggiare; (car etc) fare marcia indietro ▷ cpd posteriore, di dietro; (Aut: seat, wheels) posteriore ▷ adv (not forward) indietro; (returned): **he's ~** è tornato; **he ran ~** tornò indietro di corsa; (restitution): **throw the ball ~** ritira la palla; **can I have it ~?** posso riaverlo?; (again): **he called ~** ha richiamato; **back down** vi fare marcia indietro; **back out** vi (of promise) tirarsi indietro; **back up** vt (support) appoggiare, sostenere; (Comput) fare una copia di riserva di; **backache** n mal m di schiena; **backbencher** (BRIT) n membro del Parlamento senza potere amministrativo;

backbone n spina dorsale; **back door** n porta sul retro; **backfire** vi (Aut) dar ritorni di fiamma; (plans) fallire; **backgammon** n tavola reale; **background** n sfondo; (of events) background m inv; (basic knowledge) base f; (experience) esperienza; **family background** ambiente m familiare; **backing** n (fig) appoggio; **backlog** n **backlog of work** lavoro arretrato; **backpack** n zaino; **backpacker** n chi viaggia con zaino e sacco a pelo; **backslash** n backslash m inv, barra obliqua inversa; **backstage** adv nel retroscena; **backstroke** n nuoto sul dorso; **backup** adj (train, plane) supplementare; (Comput) di riserva ▷ n (support) appoggio, sostegno; (also: **backup file**) file m inv di riserva; **backward** adj (movement) indietro inv; (person) tardivo(-a); (country) arretrato(-a); **backwards** adv indietro; (fall, walk) all'indietro; **backyard** n cortile m dietro la casa

bacon ['beɪkən] n pancetta

bacteria [bæk'tɪərɪə] npl batteri mpl

bad [bæd] adj cattivo(-a); (accident, injury) brutto(-a); (meat, food) andato(-a) a male; **his ~ leg** la sua gamba malata; **to go ~** andare a male

badge [bædʒ] n insegna; (of policeman) stemma m

badger ['bædʒəʳ] n tasso

badly ['bædlɪ] adv (work, dress etc) male; **~ wounded** gravemente ferito; **he needs it ~** ne ha un gran bisogno

bad-mannered [bæd'mænəd] adj maleducato(-a), sgarbato(-a)

badminton ['bædmɪntən] n badminton m

bad-tempered ['bæd'tɛmpəd] adj irritabile; di malumore

bag [bæg] n sacco; (handbag etc) borsa; **~s of** (inf: lots of) un sacco di; **baggage** n bagagli mpl; **baggage allowance** n franchigia f bagaglio inv; **baggage reclaim** n ritiro m bagaglio inv; **baggy** adj largo(-a), sformato(-a); **bagpipes** npl cornamusa

bail [beɪl] n cauzione f ▷ vt (prisoner: also: **grant - to**) concedere la libertà provvisoria su cauzione a; (boat: also: **~ out**) aggottare; **on ~** in libertà provvisoria su cauzione

bait [beɪt] n esca ▷ vt (hook) innescare; (trap) munire di esca; (fig) tormentare

bake [beɪk] vt cuocere al forno ▷ vi cuocersi al forno; **baked beans** [-biːnz] npl fagioli mpl in salsa di pomodoro; **baked potato** n patata cotta al forno con la buccia; **baker** n fornaio(-a), panettiere(-a); **bakery** n panetteria;

baking n cottura (al forno); **baking powder** n lievito in polvere

balance ['bæləns] n equilibrio; (Comm: sum) bilancio; (remainder) resto; (scales) bilancia ▷ vt tenere in equilibrio; (budget) far quadrare; (account) pareggiare; (compensate) contrappesare; **~ of trade/ payments** bilancia commerciale/dei pagamenti; **balanced** adj (personality, diet) equilibrato(-a); **balance sheet** n bilancio

balcony ['bælkənɪ] n balcone m; (in theatre) balconata; **do you have a room with a ~?** avete una camera con balcone?

bald [bɔːld] adj calvo(-a); (tyre) liscio(-a)

Balearics [bælɪ'ærɪks] npl **the ~** le Baleari fpl

ball [bɔːl] n palla; (football) pallone m; (for golf) pallina; (of wool, string) gomitolo; (dance) ballo; **to play ~** (fig) stare al gioco

ballerina [bælə'riːnə] n ballerina

ballet ['bæleɪ] n balletto; **ballet dancer** n ballerino(-a) classico(-a)

balloon [bə'luːn] n pallone m

ballot ['bælət] n scrutinio

ballpoint (pen) ['bɔːlpɔɪnt(-)] n penna a sfera

ballroom ['bɔːlrum] n sala da ballo

Baltic ['bɔːltɪk] adj, n **the ~ Sea** il (mar) Baltico

bamboo [bæm'buː] n bambù m

ban [bæn] n interdizione f ▷ vt interdire

banana [bə'nɑːnə] n banana

band [bænd] n banda; (at a dance) orchestra; (Mil) fanfara

bandage ['bændɪdʒ] n benda, fascia

Band-Aid® ['bændeɪd] (US) n cerotto

B. & B. n abbr = **bed and breakfast**

bandit ['bændɪt] n bandito

bang [bæŋ] n (of door) lo sbattere; (of gun, blow) colpo ▷ vt battere (violentemente); (door) sbattere ▷ vi scoppiare; sbattere

Bangladesh [bɑːŋglə'dɛʃ] n Bangladesh m

bangle ['bæŋgl] n braccialetto

bangs [bæŋz] (US) npl (fringe) frangia, frangetta

banish ['bænɪʃ] vt bandire

banister(s) ['bænɪstə(z)] n(pl) ringhiera

banjo ['bændʒəu] (pl **banjoes** or **banjos**) n banjo m inv

bank [bæŋk] n banca, banco; (of river, lake) riva, sponda; (of earth) banco ▷ vi (Aviat) inclinarsi in virata; **bank on** vt fus contare su; **bank account** n conto in banca; **bank balance** n saldo; **a healthy bank balance** un solido conto in banca; **bank card** n carta f assegni inv; **bank charges** npl (BRIT) spese fpl bancarie; **banker** n banchiere m; **bank holiday** (BRIT) n giorno di festa; vedi nota nel riquadro; **banking**

n attività bancaria; professione *f* di banchiere; **bank manager** *n* direttore *m* di banca; **banknote** *n* banconota

● **BANK HOLIDAY**
●
● Una **bank holiday**, in Gran Bretagna,
● è una giornata in cui banche e molti
● negozi sono chiusi. Generalmente le
● **bank holidays** cadono di lunedì e molti
● ne approfittano per fare una breve
● vacanza fuori città.

bankrupt ['bæŋkrʌpt] *adj* fallito(-a); **to go ~** fallire; **bankruptcy** *n* fallimento
bank statement *n* estratto conto
banner ['bænəʳ] *n* striscione *m*
bannister(s) ['bænɪstə(z)] *n(pl)* see **banister(s)**
banquet ['bæŋkwɪt] *n* banchetto
baptism ['bæptɪzəm] *n* battesimo
baptize [bæp'taɪz] *vt* battezzare
bar [bɑːʳ] *n* (place) bar *m inv*; (counter) banco; (rod) barra; (of window etc) sbarra; (of chocolate) tavoletta; (fig) ostacolo; restrizione *f*; (Mus) battuta ▷ *vt* (road, window) sbarrare; (person) escludere; (activity) interdire; **~ of soap** saponetta; **the B~** (Law) l'Ordine *m* degli avvocati; **behind ~s** (prisoner) dietro le sbarre; **~ none** senza eccezione
barbaric [bɑː'bærɪk] *adj* barbarico(-a)
barbecue ['bɑːbɪkjuː] *n* barbecue *m inv*
barbed wire ['bɑːbd-] *n* filo spinato
barber ['bɑːbəʳ] *n* barbiere *m*; **barber's (shop)** (US **barber (shop)**) *n* barbiere *m*
bar code *n* (on goods) codice *m* a barre
bare [bɛəʳ] *adj* nudo(-a) ▷ *vt* scoprire, denudare; (teeth) mostrare; **the ~ necessities** lo stretto necessario; **barefoot** *adj, adv* scalzo(-a); **barely** *adv* appena
bargain ['bɑːgɪn] *n* (transaction) contratto; (good buy) affare *m* ▷ *vi* trattare; **into the ~** per giunta; **bargain for** *vt fus* **he got more than he ~ed for** gli è andata peggio di quel che si aspettasse
barge [bɑːdʒ] *n* chiatta; **barge in** *vi* (walk in) piombare dentro; (interrupt talk) intromettersi a sproposito
bark [bɑːk] *n* (of tree) corteccia; (of dog) abbaio ▷ *vi* abbaiare
barley ['bɑːlɪ] *n* orzo
barmaid ['bɑːmeɪd] *n* cameriera al banco
barman ['bɑːmən] (irreg) *n* barista *m*
barn [bɑːn] *n* granaio
barometer [bə'rɔmɪtəʳ] *n* barometro
baron ['bærən] *n* barone *m*; **baroness** *n* baronessa

barracks ['bærəks] *npl* caserma
barrage ['bærɑːʒ] *n* (Mil, dam) sbarramento; (fig) fiume *m*
barrel ['bærəl] *n* barile *m*; (of gun) canna
barren ['bærən] *adj* sterile; (soil) arido(-a)
barrette [bə'ret] (US) *n* fermaglio per capelli
barricade [bærɪ'keɪd] *n* barricata
barrier ['bærɪəʳ] *n* barriera
barring ['bɑːrɪŋ] *prep* salvo
barrister ['bærɪstəʳ] (BRIT) *n* avvocato(-essa) (con diritto di parlare davanti a tutte le corti)
barrow ['bærəu] *n* (cart) carriola
bartender ['bɑːtendəʳ] (US) *n* barista *m*
base [beɪs] *n* base *f* ▷ *vt* **to ~ sth on** basare qc su ▷ *adj* vile
baseball ['beɪsbɔːl] *n* baseball *m*; **baseball cap** *n* berretto da baseball
basement ['beɪsmənt] *n* seminterrato; (of shop) interrato
bases¹ ['beɪsiːz] *npl of* **basis**
bases² ['beɪsɪz] *npl of* **base**
bash [bæʃ] (inf) *vt* picchiare
basic ['beɪsɪk] *adj* rudimentale; essenziale; **basically** [-lɪ] *adv* fondamentalmente; sostanzialmente; **basics** *npl* **the basics** l'essenziale *m*
basil ['bæzl] *n* basilico
basin ['beɪsn] *n* (vessel: also Geo) bacino; (also: **wash~**) lavabo
basis ['beɪsɪs] (pl **bases**) *n* base *f*; **on a part-time ~** part-time; **on a trial ~** in prova
basket ['bɑːskɪt] *n* cesta; (smaller) cestino; (with handle) paniere *m*; **basketball** *n* pallacanestro *f*
bass [beɪs] *n* (Mus) basso
bastard ['bɑːstəd] *n* bastardo(-a); (inf!) stronzo (!)
bat [bæt] *n* pipistrello; (for baseball etc) mazza; (BRIT: for table tennis) racchetta ▷ *vt* **he didn't ~ an eyelid** non batté ciglio
batch [bætʃ] *n* (of bread) infornata; (of papers) cumulo
bath [bɑːθ] *n* bagno; (bathtub) vasca da bagno ▷ *vt* far fare il bagno a; **to have a ~** fare un bagno; see also **baths**
bathe [beɪð] *vi* fare il bagno ▷ *vt* (wound) lavare
bathing ['beɪðɪŋ] *n* bagni *mpl*; **bathing costume** (US **bathing suit**) *n* costume *m* da bagno
bath: bathrobe ['bɑːθrəub] *n* accappatoio; **bathroom** ['bɑːθrum] *n* stanza da bagno; **baths** [bɑːðz] *npl* bagno *mpl* pubblici; **bath towel** *n* asciugamano da bagno; **bathtub** *n* (vasca da) bagno
baton ['bætən] *n* (Mus) bacchetta;

(*Athletics*) testimone *m*; (*club*) manganello
batter ['bætə^r] *vt* battere ▷ *n* pastetta;
battered *adj* (*hat*) sformato(-a); (*pan*)
ammaccato(-a)

battery ['bætərɪ] *n* batteria; (*of torch*) pila;
battery farming *n* allevamento in batteria

battle ['bætl] *n* battaglia ▷ *vi* battagliare,
lottare; **battlefield** *n* campo di battaglia

bay [beɪ] *n* (*of sea*) baia; **to hold sb at ~**
tenere qn a bada

bazaar [bə'zɑː^r] *n* bazar *m inv*; vendita di
beneficenza

BBC *n abbr* (= *British Broadcasting
Corporation*) rete nazionale di radiotelevisione
in Gran Bretagna

● BBC
●
● La **BBC** è l'azienda statale che fornisce
● il servizio radiofonico e televisivo in
● Gran Bretagna. Ha due reti televisive
● terrestri (BBC1 e BBC2), e cinque
● stazioni radiofoniche nazionali. Oggi
● la BBC ha anche diverse stazioni
● digitali radiofoniche e televisive. Da
● molti anni fornisce inoltre un servizio
● di intrattenimento e informazione
● internazionale, il "BBC World Service",
● trasmesso in tutto il mondo.

B.C. *adv abbr* (= *before Christ*) a.C.

KEYWORD

be [biː] (*pt* **was, were**, *pp* **been**) *aux vb* **1**
(*with present participle: forming continuous
tenses*): **what are you doing?** che fa?, che
sta facendo?; **they're coming tomorrow**
vengono domani; **I've been waiting for
her for hours** sono ore che l'aspetto
2 (*with pp: forming passives*) essere; **to be
killed** essere *or* venire ucciso(-a); **the box
had been opened** la scatola era stata
aperta; **the thief was nowhere to be
seen** il ladro non si trovava da nessuna
parte
3 (*in tag questions*): **it was fun, wasn't it?** è
stato divertente, no?; **he's good-looking,
isn't he?** è un bell'uomo, vero?; **she's
back, is she?** così è tornata, eh?
4 (+ *to* + *infinitive*): **the house is
to be sold** abbiamo *or* hanno *etc*
intenzione di vendere casa; **you're to
be congratulated for all your work**
dovremo farvi i complimenti per tutto il
vostro lavoro; **he's not to open it** non
deve aprirlo
▷ *vb* + *complement* **1** (*gen*) essere; **I'm
English** sono inglese; **I'm tired** sono

stanco(-a); **I'm hot/cold** ho caldo/freddo;
he's a doctor è medico; **2 and 2 are 4** 2
più 2 fa 4; **be careful!** sta attento(-a)!; **be
good** sii buono(-a)
2 (*of health*) stare; **how are you?** come
sta?; **he's very ill** sta molto male
3 (*of age*): **how old are you?** quanti anni
hai?; **I'm sixteen (years old)** ho sedici
anni
4 (*cost*) costare; **how much was the
meal?** quant'era *or* quanto costava il
pranzo?; **that'll be £5, please** (fa) 5
sterline, per favore
▷ *vi* **1** (*exist, occur etc*) essere, esistere; **the
best singer that ever was** il migliore
cantante mai esistito *or* di tutti i tempi; **be
that as it may** comunque sia, sia come
sia; **so be it** sia pure, e sia
2 (*referring to place*) essere, trovarsi; **I won't
be here tomorrow** non ci sarò domani;
Edinburgh is in Scotland Edimburgo si
trova in Scozia
3 (*referring to movement*): **where have you
been?** dov'è stato?; **I've been to China**
sono stato in Cina
▷ *impers vb* **1** (*referring to time, distance*)
essere; **it's 5 o'clock** sono le 5; **it's the
28th of April** è il 28 aprile; **it's 10 km to
the village** di qui al paese sono 10 km
2 (*referring to the weather*) fare; **it's too
hot/cold** fa troppo caldo/freddo; **it's
windy** c'è vento
3 (*emphatic*): **it's me** sono io; **it was Maria
who paid the bill** è stata Maria che ha
pagato il conto

beach [biːtʃ] *n* spiaggia ▷ *vt* tirare in secco
beacon ['biːkən] *n* (*lighthouse*) faro;
(*marker*) segnale *m*
bead [biːd] *n* perlina; **~s** *npl* (*necklace*)
collana
beak [biːk] *n* becco
beam [biːm] *n* trave *f*; (*of light*) raggio ▷ *vi*
brillare
bean [biːn] *n* fagiolo; (*of coffee*) chicco;
runner ~ fagiolino; **beansprouts** *npl*
germogli *mpl* di soia
bear [bɛə^r] (*pt* **bore**, *pp* **borne**) *n* orso ▷ *vt*
portare; (*endure*) sopportare; (*produce*)
generare ▷ *vi* **to ~ right/left** piegare a
destra/sinistra
beard [bɪəd] *n* barba
bearer ['bɛərə^r] *n* portatore *m*
bearing ['bɛərɪŋ] *n* portamento;
(*connection*) rapporto
beast [biːst] *n* bestia
beat [biːt] (*pt* **beat**, *pp* **beaten**) *n* colpo;
(*of heart*) battito; (*Mus*) tempo; battuta;
(*of policeman*) giro ▷ *vt* battere; (*eggs,*

cream) sbattere ▷ *vi* battere; **off the ~en track** fuori mano; **~ it!** (*inf*) fila!, fuori dai piedi!; **beat up** *vt* (*person*) picchiare; (*eggs*) sbattere; **beating** *n* bastonata

beautiful ['bju:tɪful] *adj* bello(-a); **beautifully** *adv* splendidamente

beauty ['bju:tɪ] *n* bellezza; **beauty parlour** [-'pɑːlər] (*us* **beauty parlor**) *n* salone *m* di bellezza; **beauty salon** *n* istituto di bellezza; **beauty spot** (*brit*) *n* (*Tourism*) luogo pittoresco

beaver ['biːvər] *n* castoro

became [bɪ'keɪm] *pt of* **become**

because [bɪ'kɔz] *conj* perché; **~ of** a causa di

beckon ['bekən] *vt* (*also*: **~ to**) chiamare con un cenno

become [bɪ'kʌm] (*irreg: like* **come**) *vt* diventare; **to ~ fat/thin** ingrassarsi/ dimagrire

bed [bed] *n* letto; (*of flowers*) aiuola; (*of coal, clay*) strato; **single/double ~** letto a una piazza/a due piazze *or* matrimoniale; **bed and breakfast** *n* (*place*) ≈ pensione *f* familiare; (*terms*) camera con colazione; *vedi nota nel riquadro*; **bedclothes** ['bedkləʊðz] *npl* biancheria e coperte *fpl* da letto; **bedding** *n* coperte e lenzuola *fpl*; **bed linen** *n* biancheria da letto; **bedroom** *n* camera da letto; **bedside** *n* **at sb's bedside** al capezzale di qn; **bedside lamp** *n* lampada da comodino; **bedside table** *n* comodino; **bedsit(ter)** (*brit*) *n* monolocale *m*; **bedspread** *n* copriletto; **bedtime** *n* **it's bedtime** è ora di andare a letto

● **BED AND BREAKFAST**

● I **bed and breakfasts**, anche **B & Bs**, sono piccole pensioni a conduzione familiare, più economiche rispetto agli alberghi, dove al mattino viene servita la tradizionale colazione all'inglese.

bee [biː] *n* ape *f*

beech [biːtʃ] *n* faggio

beef [biːf] *n* manzo; **roast ~** arrosto di manzo; **beefburger** *n* hamburger *m inv*; **Beefeater** *n* guardia della Torre di Londra

been [biːn] *pp of* **be**

beer [bɪər] *n* birra; **beer garden** *n* (*brit*) giardino (*di pub*)

beet [biːt] (*us*) *n* (*also*: **red ~**) barbabietola rossa

beetle ['biːtl] *n* scarafaggio; coleottero

beetroot ['biːtruːt] (*brit*) *n* barbabietola

before [bɪ'fɔːr] *prep* (*in time*) prima di; (*in space*) davanti a ▷ *conj* prima che + *sub*;

prima di ▷ *adv* prima; **~ going** prima di andare; **~ she goes** prima che vada; **the week ~** la settimana prima; **I've seen it ~** l'ho già visto; **I've never seen it ~** è la prima volta che lo vedo; **beforehand** *adv* in anticipo

beg [beg] *vi* chiedere l'elemosina ▷ *vt* (*also*: **~ for**) chiedere in elemosina; (*favour*) chiedere; **to ~ sb to do** pregare qn di fare

began [bɪ'gæn] *pt of* **begin**

beggar ['begər] *n* mendicante *m/f*

begin [bɪ'gɪn] (*pt* **began**, *pp* **begun**) *vt*, *vi* cominciare; **to ~ doing** *or* **to do sth** incominciare *or* iniziare a fare qc; **beginner** *n* principiante *m/f*; **beginning** *n* inizio, principio

begun [bɪ'gʌn] *pp of* **begin**

behalf [bɪ'hɑːf] *n* **on ~ of** per conto di; a nome di

behave [bɪ'heɪv] *vi* comportarsi; (*well: also*: **~ o.s.**) comportarsi bene; **behaviour** [bɪ'heɪvjər] (*us* **behavior**) *n* comportamento, condotta

behind [bɪ'haɪnd] *prep* dietro; (*followed by pronoun*) dietro di; (*time*) in ritardo con ▷ *adv* dietro; (*leave, stay*) indietro ▷ *n* didietro; **to be ~ (schedule)** essere in ritardo rispetto al programma; **~ the scenes** (*fig*) dietro le quinte

beige [beɪʒ] *adj* beige *inv*

Beijing ['beɪ'dʒɪŋ] *n* Pechino *f*

being ['biːɪŋ] *n* essere *m*

belated [bɪ'leɪtɪd] *adj* tardo(-a)

belch [bɛltʃ] *vi* ruttare ▷ *vt* (*gen*: **belch out**: *smoke etc*) eruttare

Belgian ['bɛldʒən] *adj, n* belga *m/f*

Belgium ['bɛldʒəm] *n* Belgio

belief [bɪ'liːf] *n* (*opinion*) opinione *f*, convinzione *f*; (*trust, faith*) fede *f*

believe [bɪ'liːv] *vt, vi* credere; **to ~ in** (*God*) credere in; (*ghosts*) credere a; (*method*) avere fiducia in; **believer** *n* (*Rel*) credente *m/f*; (*in idea, activity*): **to be a believer in** credere in

bell [bel] *n* campana; (*small, on door, electric*) campanello

bellboy ['belbɔɪ] (*us* **bellhop**) ['belhɔp] *n* ragazzo d'albergo, fattorino d'albergo

bellow ['beləʊ] *vi* muggire

bell pepper (*esp us*) *n* peperone *m*

belly ['belɪ] *n* pancia; **belly button** *n* ombelico

belong [bɪ'lɔŋ] *vi* **to ~ to** appartenere a; (*club etc*) essere socio di; **this book ~s here** questo libro va qui; **belongings** *npl* cose *fpl*, roba

beloved [bɪ'lʌvɪd] *adj* adorato(-a)

below [bɪ'ləʊ] *prep* sotto, al di sotto di ▷ *adv* sotto, di sotto; giù; **see ~** vedi sotto *or* oltre

belt [bɛlt] *n* cintura; (*Tech*) cinghia ▷ *vt*
(*thrash*) picchiare ▷ *vi* (*inf*) filarsela;
beltway (*us*) *n* (*Aut: ring road*)
circonvallazione *f*; (: *motorway*) autostrada

bemused [bɪ'mju:zd] *adj* perplesso(-a),
stupito(-a)

bench [bɛntʃ] *n* panca; (*in workshop, Pol*)
banco; **the B~** (*Law*) la Corte

bend [bɛnd] (*pt, pp* **bent**) *vt* curvare; (*leg,
arm*) piegare ▷ *vi* curvarsi; piegarsi ▷ *n*
(*BRIT: in road*) curva; (*in pipe, river*) gomito;
bend down *vi* chinarsi; **bend over** *vi*
piegarsi

beneath [bɪ'ni:θ] *prep* sotto, al di sotto di;
(*unworthy of*) indegno(-a) di ▷ *adv* sotto,
di sotto

beneficial [bɛnɪ'fɪʃəl] *adj* che fa bene;
vantaggioso(-a)

benefit ['bɛnɪfɪt] *n* beneficio, vantaggio;
(*allowance of money*) indennità *f inv* ▷ *vt*
far bene a ▷ *vi* **he'll ~ from it** ne trarrà
beneficio *or* profitto

benign [bɪ'naɪn] *adj* (*person, smile*)
benevolo(-a); (*Med*) benigno(-a)

bent [bɛnt] *pt, pp of* **bend** ▷ *n* inclinazione
f ▷ *adj* (*inf: dishonest*) losco(-a); **to be ~ on**
essere deciso(-a) a

bereaved [bɪ'ri:vd] *n* **the ~** i familiari in
lutto

beret ['bɛreɪ] *n* berretto

Berlin [bə:'lɪn] *n* Berlino *f*

Bermuda [bə:'mju:də] *n* le Bermude

berry ['bɛrɪ] *n* bacca

berth [bə:θ] *n* (*bed*) cuccetta; (*for ship*)
ormeggio ▷ *vi* (*in harbour*) entrare in porto;
(*at anchor*) gettare l'ancora

beside [bɪ'saɪd] *prep* accanto a; **to be ~
o.s.** (**with anger**) essere fuori di sé (dalla
rabbia); **that's ~ the point** non c'entra;
besides [bɪ'saɪdz] *adv* inoltre, per di più
▷ *prep* oltre a; a parte

best [bɛst] *adj* migliore ▷ *adv* meglio; **the
~ part of** (*quantity*) la maggior parte di; **at
~** tutt'al più; **to make the ~ of sth** cavare
il meglio possibile da qc; **to do one's ~**
fare del proprio meglio; **to the ~ of my
knowledge** per quel che ne so; **to the ~ of
my ability** al massimo delle mie capacità;
best-before date *n* scadenza; **best
man** (*irreg*) *n* testimone *m* dello sposo;
bestseller *n* bestseller *m inv*

bet [bɛt] (*pt, pp* **bet** *or* **betted**) *n*
scommessa ▷ *vt, vi* scommettere; **to ~ sb
sth** scommettere qc con qn

betray [bɪ'treɪ] *vt* tradire

better ['bɛtər] *adj* migliore ▷ *adv* meglio
▷ *vt* migliorare ▷ *n* **to get the ~ of** avere la
meglio su; **you had ~ do it** è meglio che lo

faccia; **he thought ~ of it** cambiò idea; **to
get ~** migliorare

betting ['bɛtɪŋ] *n* scommesse *fpl*; **betting
shop** (*BRIT*) *n* ufficio dell'allibratore

between [bɪ'twi:n] *prep* tra ▷ *adv* in
mezzo, nel mezzo

beverage ['bɛvərɪdʒ] *n* bevanda

beware [bɪ'wɛər] *vt, vi* **to ~ (of)** stare
attento(-a) (a); **"~ of the dog"** "attenti
al cane"

bewildered [bɪ'wɪldəd] *adj*
sconcertato(-a), confuso(-a)

beyond [bɪ'jɔnd] *prep* (*in space*) oltre;
(*exceeding*) al di sopra di ▷ *adv* di là; **~
doubt** senza dubbio; **~ repair** irreparabile

bias ['baɪəs] *n* (*prejudice*) pregiudizio;
(*preference*) preferenza; **bias(s)ed** *adj*
parziale

bib [bɪb] *n* bavaglino

Bible ['baɪbl] *n* Bibbia

bicarbonate of soda [baɪ'kɑ:bənɪt-] *n*
bicarbonato (di sodio)

biceps ['baɪsɛps] *n* bicipite *m*

bicycle ['baɪsɪkl] *n* bicicletta; **bicycle
pump** *n* pompa della bicicletta

bid [bɪd] (*pt* **bade** *or* **bid**, *pp* **bidden** *or* **bid**)
n offerta; (*attempt*) tentativo ▷ *vi* fare
un'offerta ▷ *vt* fare un'offerta di; **to ~ sb
good day** dire buon giorno a qn; **bidder** *n*
the highest bidder il maggior offerente

bidet ['bi:deɪ] *n* bidè *m inv*

big [bɪg] *adj* grande; grosso(-a); **Big
Apple** *n* vedi nota nel riquadro; **bigheaded**
['bɪg'hɛdɪd] *adj* presuntuoso(-a); **big toe**
n alluce *m*

● **BIG APPLE**
●
●
● Tutti sanno che **The Big Apple**, la
● Grande Mela, è New York ("apple"
● in gergo significa grande città), ma
● sicuramente i soprannomi di altre città
● americane non sono così conosciuti.
● Chicago è soprannominata "the Windy
● City" perché è ventosa, New Orleans
● si chiama "the Big Easy" per il modo di
● vivere tranquillo e rilassato dei suoi
● abitanti, e l'industria automobilistica
● ha fatto sì che Detroit fosse
● soprannominata "Motown".

bike [baɪk] *n* bici *f inv*; **bike lane** *n* pista
ciclabile

bikini [bɪ'ki:nɪ] *n* bikini *m inv*

bilateral [baɪ'lætərl] *adj* bilaterale

bilingual [baɪ'lɪŋgwəl] *adj* bilingue

bill [bɪl] *n* conto; (*Pol*) atto; (*us: banknote*)
banconota; (*of bird*) becco; (*of show*)
locandina; **can I have the ~, please** il

conto, per favore; **put it on my ~** lo metta sul mio conto; **"post no ~s"** "divieto di affissione"; **to fit** or **fill the ~** (fig) fare al caso; **billboard** n tabellone m; **billfold** ['bɪlfəʊld] (US) n portafoglio

billiards ['bɪljədz] n biliardo

billion ['bɪljən] num (BRIT) bilione m; (US) miliardo

bin [bɪn] n (for coal, rubbish) bidone m; (for bread) cassetta; (dustbin) pattumiera; (litter bin) cestino

bind [baɪnd] (pt, pp **bound**) vt legare; (oblige) obbligare ▷ n (inf) scocciatura

binge [bɪndʒ] (inf) n **to go on a ~** fare baldoria

bingo ['bɪŋgəʊ] n gioco simile alla tombola

binoculars [bɪ'nɔkjuləz] npl binocolo

bio... [baɪə'...] prefix; **biochemistry** n biochimica; **biodegradable** adj biodegradabile; **biography** [baɪ'ɔgrəfɪ] n biografia; **biological** adj biologico(-a); **biology** [baɪ'ɔlədʒɪ] n biologia

birch [bə:tʃ] n betulla

bird [bə:d] n uccello; (BRIT: inf: girl) bambola; **bird of prey** n (uccello) rapace m; **birdwatching** n birdwatching m

Biro® ['baɪrəʊ] n biro f inv

birth [bə:θ] n nascita; **to give ~ to** partorire; **birth certificate** n certificato di nascita; **birth control** n controllo delle nascite; contraccezione f; **birthday** n compleanno ▷ cpd di compleanno; **birthmark** n voglia; **birthplace** n luogo di nascita

biscuit ['bɪskɪt] (BRIT) n biscotto

bishop ['bɪʃəp] n vescovo

bistro ['bi:strəʊ] n bistrò m inv

bit [bɪt] pt of **bite** ▷ n pezzo; (Comput) bit m inv; (of horse) morso; **a ~** of un po' di; **a ~ mad** un po' matto; **~ by ~** a poco a poco

bitch [bɪtʃ] n (dog) cagna; (inf!) vacca

bite [baɪt] (pt, pp **bit**, **bitten**) vt, vi mordere; (insect) pungere ▷ n morso; (insect bite) puntura; (mouthful) boccone m; **let's have a ~ to eat** mangiamo un boccone; **to ~ one's nails** mangiarsi le unghie

bitten ['bɪtn] pp of **bite**

bitter ['bɪtər] adj amaro(-a); (wind, criticism) pungente ▷ n (BRIT: beer) birra amara

bizarre [bɪ'zɑ:r] adj bizzarro(-a)

black [blæk] adj nero(-a) ▷ n nero; (person): **B~** negro(-a) ▷ vt (BRIT Industry) boicottare; **to give sb a ~ eye** fare un occhio nero a qn; **in the ~** (bank account) in attivo; **black out** vi (faint) svenire; **blackberry** n mora; **blackbird** n merlo; **blackboard** n lavagna; **black coffee** n caffè m inv nero; **blackcurrant** n ribes m inv; **black ice** n strato trasparente

di ghiaccio; **blackmail** n ricatto ▷ vt ricattare; **black market** n mercato nero; **blackout** n oscuramento; (TV, Radio) interruzione f delle trasmissioni; (fainting) svenimento; **black pepper** n pepe m nero; **black pudding** n sanguinaccio; **Black Sea** n **the Black Sea** il Mar Nero

bladder ['blædər] n vescica

blade [bleɪd] n lama; (of oar) pala; **~ of grass** filo d'erba

blame [bleɪm] n colpa ▷ vt **to ~ sb/sth for sth** dare la colpa di qc a qn/qc; **who's to ~?** chi è colpevole?

bland [blænd] adj mite; (taste) blando(-a)

blank [blæŋk] adj bianco(-a); (look) distratto(-a) ▷ n spazio vuoto; (cartridge) cartuccia a salve

blanket ['blæŋkɪt] n coperta

blast [blɑ:st] n (of wind) raffica; (of bomb etc) esplosione f ▷ vt far saltare

blatant ['bleɪtənt] adj flagrante

blaze [bleɪz] n (fire) incendio; (fig) vampata; splendore m ▷ vi (fire) ardere, fiammeggiare; (guns) sparare senza sosta; (fig: eyes) ardere ▷ vt **to ~ a trail** (fig) tracciare una via nuova; **in a ~ of publicity** circondato da grande pubblicità

blazer ['bleɪzər] n blazer m inv

bleach [bli:tʃ] n (also: **household ~**) varechina ▷ vt (material) candeggiare; **bleachers** (US) npl (Sport) posti mpl di gradinata

bleak [bli:k] adj tetro(-a)

bled [blɛd] pt, pp of **bleed**

bleed [bli:d] (pt, pp **bled**) vi sanguinare; **my nose is ~ing** mi viene fuori sangue dal naso

blemish ['blɛmɪʃ] n macchia

blend [blɛnd] n miscela ▷ vt mescolare ▷ vi (colours etc: also: **~ in**) armonizzare; **blender** n (Culin) frullatore m

bless [blɛs] (pt, pp **blessed** or **blest**) vt benedire; **~ you!** (after sneeze) salute!; **blessing** n benedizione f; fortuna

blew [blu:] pt of **blow**

blight [blaɪt] vt (hopes etc) deludere; (life) rovinare

blind [blaɪnd] adj cieco(-a) ▷ n (for window) avvolgibile m; (Venetian blind) veneziana ▷ vt accecare; **the ~** npl i ciechi; **blind alley** n vicolo cieco; **blindfold** n benda ▷ adj, adv bendato(-a) ▷ vt bendare gli occhi a

blink [blɪŋk] vi battere gli occhi; (light) lampeggiare

bliss [blɪs] n estasi f

blister ['blɪstər] n (on skin) vescica; (on paintwork) bolla ▷ vi (paint) coprirsi di bolle

blizzard ['blɪzəd] n bufera di neve

bloated ['bləʊtɪd] adj gonfio(-a)

blob [blɒb] n (drop) goccia; (stain, spot) macchia

block [blɒk] n blocco; (in pipes) ingombro; (toy) cubo; (of buildings) isolato ▷ vt bloccare; **the sink is ~ed** il lavandino è otturato; **block up** vt bloccare; (pipe) ingorgare, intasare; **blockade** [-'keɪd] n blocco; **blockage** n ostacolo; **blockbuster** n (film, book) grande successo; **block capitals** npl stampatello; **block letters** npl stampatello

bloke [bləʊk] (BRIT: inf) n tizio

blond(e) [blɒnd] adj, n biondo(-a)

blood [blʌd] n sangue m; **blood donor** n donatore(-trice) di sangue; **blood group** n gruppo sanguigno; **blood poisoning** n setticemia; **blood pressure** n pressione f sanguigna; **bloodshed** n spargimento di sangue; **bloodshot** adj **bloodshot eyes** occhi iniettati di sangue; **bloodstream** n flusso del sangue; **blood test** n analisi f inv del sangue; **blood transfusion** n trasfusione f di sangue; **blood type** n gruppo sanguigno; **blood vessel** n vaso sanguigno; **bloody** adj (fight) sanguinoso(-a); (nose) sanguinante; (BRIT: inf!): **this bloody ...** questo maledetto ...; **bloody awful/good** (inf!) veramente terribile/forte

bloom [blu:m] n fiore m ▷ vi (tree) essere in fiore; (flower) aprirsi

blossom ['blɒsəm] n fiore m; (with pl sense) fiori mpl ▷ vi essere in fiore

blot [blɒt] n macchia ▷ vt macchiare

blouse [blauz] n (feminine garment) camicetta

blow [bləʊ] (pt **blew**, pp **blown**) n colpo ▷ vi soffiare ▷ vt (fuse) far saltare; (wind) spingere; (instrument) suonare; **to ~ one's nose** soffiarsi il naso; **to ~ a whistle** fischiare; **blow away** vt portare via; **blow out** vi scoppiare; **blow up** vi saltare in aria ▷ vt far saltare in aria; (tyre) gonfiare; (Phot) ingrandire; **blow-dry** n messa in piega a föhn

blown [bləʊn] pp of **blow**

blue [blu:] adj azzurro(-a); (depressed) giù inv; **~ film/joke** film/barzelletta pornografico(-a); **out of the ~** (fig) all'improvviso; **bluebell** n giacinto dei boschi; **blueberry** n mirtillo; **blue cheese** n formaggio tipo gorgonzola; **blues** npl **the blues** (Mus) il blues; **to have the blues** (inf: feeling) essere a terra; **bluetit** n cinciarella

bluff [blʌf] vi bluffare ▷ n bluff m inv ▷ adj (person) brusco(-a); **to call sb's ~** mettere alla prova il bluff di qn

blunder ['blʌndə^r] n abbaglio ▷ vi prendere un abbaglio

blunt [blʌnt] adj smussato(-a); spuntato(-a); (person) brusco(-a)

blur [blə:^r] n forma indistinta ▷ vt offuscare; **blurred** adj (photo) mosso(-a); (TV) sfuocato(-a)

blush [blʌʃ] vi arrossire ▷ n rossore m; **blusher** n fard m inv

board [bɔ:d] n tavola; (on wall) tabellone m; (committee) consiglio, comitato; (in firm) consiglio d'amministrazione; (Naut, Aviat): **on ~** a bordo ▷ vt (ship) salire a bordo di; (train) salire su; **full ~** (BRIT) pensione completa; **half ~** (BRIT) mezza pensione; **~ and lodging** vitto e alloggio; **which goes by the ~** (fig) che viene abbandonato; **board game** n gioco da tavolo; **boarding card** n = **boarding pass**; **boarding pass** n (Aviat, Naut) carta d'imbarco; **boarding school** n collegio; **board room** n sala del consiglio

boast [bəʊst] vi **to ~ (about** or **of)** vantarsi (di)

boat [bəʊt] n nave f; (small) barca

bob [bɒb] vi (boat, cork on water: also: **~ up and down**) andare su e giù

bobby pin ['bɒbɪ-] (US) n fermaglio per capelli

body ['bɒdɪ] n corpo; (of car) carrozzeria; (of plane) fusoliera; (fig: group) gruppo; (: organization) organizzazione f; (: quantity) quantità f inv; **body-building** n culturismo; **bodyguard** n guardia del corpo; **bodywork** n carrozzeria

bog [bɒg] n palude f ▷ vt **to get ~ged down** (fig) impantanarsi

bogus ['bəʊgəs] adj falso(-a); finto(-a)

boil [bɔɪl] vt, vi bollire ▷ n foruncolo; **to come to the** (BRIT) or **a** (US) **~** raggiungere l'ebollizione; **boil over** vi traboccare (bollendo); **boiled egg** n uovo alla coque; **boiled potatoes** npl patate fpl bollite or lesse; **boiler** n caldaia; **boiling** adj bollente; **I'm boiling (hot)** (inf) sto morendo di caldo; **boiling point** n punto di ebollizione

bold [bəʊld] adj audace; (child) impudente; (colour) deciso(-a)

Bolivia [bə'lɪvɪə] n Bolivia

Bolivian [bə'lɪvɪən] adj, n boliviano(-a)

bollard ['bɒləd] (BRIT) n (Aut) colonnina luminosa

bolt [bəʊlt] n chiavistello; (with nut) bullone m ▷ adv **~ upright** diritto(-a) come un fuso ▷ vt serrare; (also: **~ together**) imbullonare; (food) mangiare in fretta ▷ vi scappare via

bomb [bɒm] n bomba ▷ vt bombardare;

bombard [bɔm'bɑ:d] vt bombardare; **bomber** n (Aviat) bombardiere m; **bomb scare** n stato di allarme (per sospetta presenza di una bomba)

bond [bɔnd] n legame m; (binding promise, Finance) obbligazione f; (Comm): **in ~** in attesa di sdoganamento

bone [bəʊn] n osso; (of fish) spina, lisca ▷ vt disossare; togliere le spine a

bonfire ['bɔnfaɪəʳ] n falò m inv

bonnet ['bɔnɪt] n cuffia; (BRIT: of car) cofano

bonus ['bəʊnəs] n premio; (fig) sovrappiù m inv

boo [bu:] excl ba! ▷ vt fischiare

book [bʊk] n libro; (of stamps etc) blocchetto ▷ vt (ticket, seat, room) prenotare; (driver) multare; (football player) ammonire; **~s** npl (Comm) conti mpl; **I'd like to ~ a double room** vorrei prenotare una camera doppia; **I ~ed a table in the name of ...** ho prenotato un tavolo al nome di...; **book in** vi (BRIT: at hotel) prendere una camera; **book up** vt riservare, prenotare; **the hotel is ~ed up** l'albergo è al completo; **all seats are ~ed up** è tutto esaurito; **bookcase** n scaffale m; **booking** n (BRIT) prenotazione f; **I confirmed my booking by fax/e-mail** ho confermato la mia prenotazione tramite fax/e-mail; **booking office** (BRIT) n (Rail) biglietteria; (Theatre) botteghino; **book-keeping** n contabilità; **booklet** n libricino; **bookmaker** n allibratore m; **bookmark** (also Comput) n segnalibro ▷ vt (Comput) mettere un segnalibro a; (Internet Explorer) aggiungere a "Preferiti"; **bookseller** n libraio; **bookshelf** n mensola (per libri); **bookshop, bookstore** n libreria

boom [bu:m] n (noise) rimbombo; (in prices etc) boom m inv ▷ vi rimbombare; andare a gonfie vele

boost [bu:st] n spinta ▷ vt spingere

boot [bu:t] n stivale m; (for hiking) scarpone m da montagna; (for football etc) scarpa; (BRIT: of car) portabagagli m inv ▷ vt (Comput) inizializzare; **to ~** (in addition) per giunta, in più

booth [bu:ð] n cabina; (at fair) baraccone m

booze [bu:z] (inf) n alcool m

border ['bɔ:dəʳ] n orlo; margine m; (of a country) frontiera; (for flowers) aiuola (laterale) ▷ vt (road) costeggiare; (another country: also: **~ on**) confinare con; **the B~s** la zona di confine tra l'Inghilterra e la Scozia; **borderline** n (fig): **on the borderline** incerto(-a)

bore [bɔ:ʳ] pt of **bear** ▷ vt (hole etc)

scavare; (person) annoiare ▷ n (person) seccatore(-trice); (of gun) calibro; **bored** adj annoiato(-a); **to be bored** annoiarsi; **he's bored to tears** or **to death** or **stiff** è annoiato a morte; **boredom** n noia

boring ['bɔ:rɪŋ] adj noioso(-a)

born [bɔ:n] adj: **to be ~** nascere; **I was ~ in 1960** sono nato nel 1960

borne [bɔ:n] pp of **bear**

borough ['bʌrə] n comune m

borrow ['bɔrəʊ] vt: **to ~ sth (from sb)** prendere in prestito qc (da qn)

Bosnia(-Herzegovina) ['bɔznɪə(hɜːzə'gəʊviːnə)] n Bosnia-Erzegovina; **Bosnian** ['bɔznɪən] n, adj bosniaco(-a) m/f

bosom ['bʊzəm] n petto; (fig) seno

boss [bɔs] n capo ▷ vt comandare; **bossy** adj prepotente

both [bəʊθ] adj entrambi(-e), tutt'e due ▷ pron: **~ of them** entrambi(-e); **~ of us went, we ~ went** ci siamo andati tutt'e due ▷ adv: **they sell ~ meat and poultry** vendono insieme la carne ed il pollame

bother ['bɔðəʳ] vt (worry) preoccupare; (annoy) infastidire ▷ vi (also: **~ o.s.**) preoccuparsi ▷ n: **it is a ~ to have to do** è una seccatura dover fare; **it was no ~** non c'era problema; **to ~ doing sth** darsi la pena di fare qc

bottle ['bɔtl] n bottiglia; (baby's) biberon m inv ▷ vt imbottigliare; **bottle bank** n contenitore m per la raccolta del vetro; **bottle-opener** n apribottiglie m inv

bottom ['bɔtəm] n fondo; (buttocks) sedere m ▷ adj più basso(-a); ultimo(-a); **at the ~ of** in fondo a

bought [bɔ:t] pt, pp of **buy**

boulder ['bəʊldəʳ] n masso (tondeggiante)

bounce [baʊns] vi (ball) rimbalzare; (cheque) essere restituito(-a) ▷ vt far rimbalzare ▷ n (rebound) rimbalzo; **bouncer** (inf) n buttafuori m inv

bound [baʊnd] pt, pp of **bind** ▷ n (gen pl) limite m; (leap) salto ▷ vi saltare ▷ vt (limit) delimitare ▷ adj: **~ by law** obbligato(-a) per legge; **to be ~ to do sth** (obliged) essere costretto(-a) a fare qc; **he's ~ to fail** (likely) fallirà di certo; **~ for** diretto(-a) a; **out of ~s** il cui accesso è vietato

boundary ['baʊndrɪ] n confine m

bouquet ['bukeɪ] n bouquet m inv

bourbon ['buəbən] (US) n (also: **~ whiskey**) bourbon m inv

bout [baʊt] n periodo; (of malaria etc) attacco; (Boxing etc) incontro

boutique [bu:'ti:k] n boutique f inv

bow¹ [bəʊ] n nodo; (weapon) arco; (Mus) archetto

bow² [baʊ] n (with body) inchino; (Naut: also: **~s**) prua ▷ vi inchinarsi; (yield): **to ~ to** or **before** sottomettersi a

bowels ['baʊəlz] npl intestini mpl; (fig) viscere fpl

bowl [baʊl] n (for eating) scodella; (for washing) bacino; (ball) boccia ▷ vi (Cricket) servire (la palla); **bowler** ['baʊlə'] n (Cricket, Baseball) lanciatore m; (BRIT: also: **bowler hat**) bombetta; **bowling** ['baʊlɪŋ] n (game) gioco delle bocce; **bowling alley** n pista da bowling; **bowling green** n campo di bocce; **bowls** [baʊlz] n gioco delle bocce

bow tie n cravatta a farfalla

box [bɔks] n scatola; (also: **cardboard ~**) cartone m; (Theatre) palco ▷ vt inscatolare ▷ vi fare del pugilato; **boxer** n (person) pugile m; **boxer shorts** ['bɔksəʃɔːts] pl n boxer; **a pair of boxer shorts** un paio di boxer; **boxing** n (Sport) pugilato; **Boxing Day** (BRIT) n ≈ Santo Stefano; vedi nota nel riquadro; **boxing gloves** npl guantoni mpl da pugile; **boxing ring** n ring m inv; **box office** n biglietteria

● **BOXING DAY**

Il **Boxing Day** è un giorno di festa e cade in genere il 26 dicembre. Prende il nome dalla tradizionale usanza di donare pacchi regalo natalizi, chiamati "Christmas boxes", a fornitori e dipendenti.

boy [bɔɪ] n ragazzo

boycott ['bɔɪkɔt] n boicottaggio ▷ vt boicottare

boyfriend ['bɔɪfrɛnd] n ragazzo

bra [brɑː] n reggipetto, reggiseno

brace [breɪs] n (on teeth) apparecchio correttore; (tool) trapano ▷ vt rinforzare, sostenere; **~s** (BRIT) npl (Dress) bretelle fpl; **to ~ o.s.** (also fig) tenersi forte

bracelet ['breɪslɪt] n braccialetto

bracket ['brækɪt] n (Tech) mensola; (group) gruppo; (Typ) parentesi f inv ▷ vt mettere fra parentesi

brag [bræg] vi vantarsi

braid [breɪd] n (trimming) passamano; (of hair) treccia

brain [breɪn] n cervello; **~s** npl (intelligence) cervella fpl; **he's got ~s** è intelligente

braise [breɪz] vt brasare

brake [breɪk] n (on vehicle) freno ▷ vi frenare; **brake light** n (fanalino dello) stop m inv

bran [bræn] n crusca

branch [brɑːntʃ] n (of tree) ramo; (Comm)

succursale f; **branch off** vi diramarsi; **branch out** vi (fig) intraprendere una nuova attività

brand [brænd] n marca; (fig) tipo ▷ vt (cattle) marcare (a ferro rovente); **brand name** n marca; **brand-new** adj nuovo(-a) di zecca

brandy ['brændɪ] n brandy m inv

brash [bræʃ] adj sfacciato(-a)

brass [brɑːs] n ottone m; **the ~** (Mus) gli ottoni; **brass band** n fanfara

brat [bræt] n (pej) marmocchio, monello(-a)

brave [breɪv] adj coraggioso(-a) ▷ vt affrontare; **bravery** n coraggio

brawl [brɔːl] n rissa

Brazil [brə'zɪl] n Brasile m; **Brazilian** adj, n brasiliano(-a)

breach [briːtʃ] vt aprire una breccia in ▷ n (gap) breccia, varco; (breaking): **~ of contract** rottura di contratto; **~ of the peace** violazione f dell'ordine pubblico

bread [brɛd] n pane m; **breadbin** n cassetta f portapane inv; **breadbox** (US) n cassetta f portapane inv; **breadcrumbs** npl briciole fpl; (Culin) pangrattato

breadth [brɛtθ] n larghezza; (fig: of knowledge etc) ampiezza

break [breɪk] (pt **broke**, pp **broken**) vt rompere; (law) violare; (record) battere ▷ vi rompersi; (storm) scoppiare; (weather) cambiare; (dawn) spuntare; (news) saltare fuori ▷ n (gap) breccia; (fracture) rottura; (rest, also Scol) intervallo; (: short) pausa; (chance) possibilità f inv; **to ~ one's leg** etc rompersi la gamba ecc; **to ~ the news to sb** comunicare per primo la notizia a qn; **to ~ even** coprire le spese; **to ~ free** or **loose** spezzare i legami; **to ~ open** (door etc) sfondare; **break down** vt (figures, data) analizzare ▷ vi (person) avere un esaurimento (nervoso); (Aut) guastarsi; **my car has broken down** mi si è rotta la macchina; **break in** vt (horse etc) domare ▷ vi (burglar) fare irruzione; (interrupt) interrompere; **break into** vt fus (house) fare irruzione in; **break off** vi (speaker) interrompersi; (branch) troncarsi; **break out** vi evadere; (war, fight) scoppiare; **to ~ out in spots** coprirsi di macchie; **break up** vi (ship) sfondarsi; (meeting) sciogliersi; (crowd) disperdersi; (marriage) andare a pezzi; (Scol) chiudere ▷ vt fare a pezzi, spaccare; (fight etc) interrompere, far cessare; **breakdown** n (Aut) guasto; (in communications) interruzione f; (of marriage) rottura; (Med: also: **nervous breakdown**) esaurimento nervoso; (of statistics) resoconto; **breakdown truck,**

breakdown van n carro m attrezzi inv
breakfast ['brɛkfəst] n colazione f; **what time is ~?** a che ora è servita la colazione?
break: break-in n irruzione f;
breakthrough n (fig) passo avanti
breast [brɛst] n (of woman) seno; (chest, Culin) petto; **breast-feed** (irreg: like **feed**) vt, vi allattare (al seno); **breast-stroke** n nuoto a rana
breath [brɛθ] n respiro; **out of ~** senza fiato
Breathalyser® ['brɛθəlaɪzər] (BRIT) n alcoltest m inv
breathe [briːð] vt, vi respirare; **breathe in** vt respirare ▷ vi inspirare; **breathe out** vt, vi espirare; **breathing** n respiro, respirazione f
breath: breathless ['brɛθlɪs] adj senza fiato; **breathtaking** ['brɛθteɪkɪŋ] adj mozzafiato inv; **breath test** n ≈ prova del palloncino
bred [brɛd] pt, pp of **breed**
breed [briːd] (pt, pp **bred**) vt allevare ▷ vi riprodursi ▷ n razza; (type, class) varietà f inv
breeze [briːz] n brezza
breezy ['briːzɪ] adj allegro(-a), ventilato(-a)
brew [bruː] vt (tea) fare un infuso di; (beer) fare ▷ vi (storm, fig: trouble etc) prepararsi; **brewery** n fabbrica di birra
bribe [braɪb] n bustarella ▷ vt comprare; **bribery** n corruzione f
bric-a-brac ['brɪkəbræk] n bric-a-brac m
brick [brɪk] n mattone m; **bricklayer** n muratore m
bride [braɪd] n sposa; **bridegroom** n sposo; **bridesmaid** n damigella d'onore
bridge [brɪdʒ] n ponte m; (Naut) ponte di comando; (of nose) dorso; (Cards) bridge m inv ▷ vt (fig: gap) colmare
bridle ['braɪdl] n briglia
brief [briːf] adj breve ▷ n (Law) comparsa; (gen) istruzioni fpl ▷ vt mettere al corrente; **~s** npl (underwear) mutande fpl; **briefcase** n cartella; **briefing** n briefing m inv; **briefly** adv (glance) di sfuggita; (explain, say) brevemente
brigadier [brɪgə'dɪər] n generale m di brigata
bright [braɪt] adj luminoso(-a); (clever) sveglio(-a); (lively) vivace
brilliant ['brɪljənt] adj brillante; (light, smile) radioso(-a); (inf) splendido(-a)
brim [brɪm] n orlo
brine [braɪn] n (Culin) salamoia
bring [brɪŋ] (pt, pp **brought**) vt portare; **bring about** vt causare; **bring back** vt riportare; **bring down** vt portare giù; abbattere; **bring in** vt (person)

fare entrare; (object) portare; (Pol: bill) presentare; (: legislation) introdurre; (Law: verdict) emettere; (produce: income) rendere; **bring on** vt (illness, attack) causare, provocare; (player, substitute) far scendere in campo; **bring out** vt tirar fuori; (meaning) mettere in evidenza; (book, album) far uscire; **bring up** vt (carry up) portare su; (child) allevare; (question) introdurre; (food: vomit) rimettere, rigurgitare
brink [brɪŋk] n orlo
brisk [brɪsk] adj (manner) spiccio(-a); (trade) vivace; (pace) svelto(-a)
bristle ['brɪsl] n setola ▷ vi rizzarsi; **bristling with** irto(-a) di
Brit [brɪt] n abbr (inf: = British person) britannico(-a)
Britain ['brɪtən] n (also: **Great ~**) Gran Bretagna
British ['brɪtɪʃ] adj britannico(-a); **British Isles** npl Isole Britanniche
Briton ['brɪtən] n britannico(-a)
brittle ['brɪtl] adj fragile
broad [brɔːd] adj largo(-a); (distinction) generale; (accent) spiccato(-a); **in ~ daylight** in pieno giorno; **broadband** adj (Comput) a banda larga ▷ n banda larga; **broad bean** n fava; **broadcast** (pt, pp **broadcast**) n trasmissione f ▷ vt trasmettere per radio (or per televisione) ▷ vi fare una trasmissione; **broaden** vt allargare ▷ vi allargarsi; **broadly** adv (fig) in generale; **broad-minded** adj di mente aperta
broccoli ['brɔkəlɪ] n broccoli mpl
brochure ['brəʊʃjuər] n dépliant m inv
broil [brɔɪl] vt cuocere a fuoco vivo
broiler ['brɔɪlər] n (US) (grill) griglia
broke [brəʊk] pt of **break** ▷ adj (inf) squattrinato(-a)
broken ['brəʊkn] pp of **break** ▷ adj rotto(-a); **a ~ leg** una gamba rotta; **in ~ English** in un inglese stentato
broker ['brəʊkər] n agente m
bronchitis [brɔŋ'kaɪtɪs] n bronchite f
bronze [brɔnz] n bronzo
brooch [brəʊtʃ] n spilla
brood [bruːd] n covata ▷ vi (person) rimuginare
broom [brum] n scopa; (Bot) ginestra
Bros. abbr (= Brothers) F.lli
broth [brɔθ] n brodo
brothel ['brɔθl] n bordello
brother ['brʌðər] n fratello; **brother-in-law** n cognato
brought [brɔːt] pt, pp of **bring**
brow [brau] n fronte f; (rare, gen: eyebrow) sopracciglio; (of hill) cima

brown [braun] *adj* bruno(-a), marrone; (*tanned*) abbronzato(-a) ▷ *n* (*colour*) color *m* bruno *or* marrone ▷ *vt* (*Culin*) rosolare; **brown bread** *n* pane *m* integrale, pane nero

Brownie ['braunɪ] *n* giovane esploratrice *f*

brown rice *n* riso greggio

brown sugar *n* zucchero greggio

browse [brauz] *vi* (*among books*) curiosare fra i libri; **to ~ through a book** sfogliare un libro; **browser** *n* (*Comput*) browser *m inv*

bruise [bru:z] *n* (*on person*) livido ▷ *vt* farsi un livido a

brunette [bru:'nɛt] *n* bruna

brush [brʌʃ] *n* spazzola; (*for painting, shaving*) pennello; (*quarrel*) schermaglia ▷ *vt* spazzolare; (*also: ~ against*) sfiorare

Brussels ['brʌslz] *n* Bruxelles *f*

Brussels sprout [spraut] *n* cavolo di Bruxelles

brutal ['bru:tl] *adj* brutale

B.Sc. *n abbr* (*Univ*) = **Bachelor of Science**

BSE *n abbr* (= *bovine spongiform encephalopathy*) encefalite *f* bovina spongiforme

bubble ['bʌbl] *n* bolla ▷ *vi* ribollire; (*sparkle: fig*) essere effervescente; **bubble bath** *n* bagnoschiuma *m inv*; **bubble gum** *n* gomma americana

buck [bʌk] *n* maschio (*di camoscio, caprone, coniglio ecc*); (*us: inf*) dollaro ▷ *vi* sgroppare; **to pass the ~ to sb** scaricare (su di qn) la propria responsabilità

bucket ['bʌkɪt] *n* secchio

buckle ['bʌkl] *n* fibbia ▷ *vt* allacciare ▷ *vi* (*wheel etc*) piegarsi

bud [bʌd] *n* gemma; (*of flower*) bocciolo ▷ *vi* germogliare; (*flower*) sbocciare

Buddhism ['budɪzəm] *n* buddismo

Buddhist ['budɪst] *adj, n* buddista (*m/f*)

buddy ['bʌdɪ] (*us*) *n* compagno

budge [bʌdʒ] *vt* scostare; (*fig*) smuovere ▷ *vi* spostarsi; smuoversi

budgerigar ['bʌdʒərɪgɑ:ʳ] *n* pappagallino

budget ['bʌdʒɪt] *n* bilancio preventivo ▷ *vi* **to ~ for sth** fare il bilancio per qc

budgie ['bʌdʒɪ] *n* = **budgerigar**

buff [bʌf] *adj* color camoscio ▷ *n* (*inf: enthusiast*) appassionato(-a)

buffalo ['bʌfələu] (*pl* **buffalo** *or* **buffaloes**) *n* bufalo; (*us*) bisonte *m*

buffer ['bʌfəʳ] *n* respingente *m*; (*Comput*) memoria tampone, buffer *m inv*

buffet[1] ['bʌfɪt] *vt* sferzare

buffet[2] ['bufeɪ] *n* (*food*, BRIT: *bar*) buffet *m inv*; **buffet car** (BRIT) *n* (*Rail*) ≈ servizio ristoro

bug [bʌg] *n* (*esp us: insect*) insetto; (*Comput, fig: germ*) virus *m inv*; (*spy device*) microfono spia ▷ *vt* mettere sotto controllo; (*inf: annoy*) scocciare

buggy ['bʌgɪ] *n* (*baby buggy*) passeggino

build [bɪld] (*pt, pp* **built**) *n* (*of person*) corporatura ▷ *vt* costruire; **build up** *vt* accumulare; aumentare; **builder** *n* costruttore *m*; **building** *n* costruzione *f*; edificio; (*industry*) edilizia; **building site** *n* cantiere *m* di costruzione; **building society** (BRIT) *n* società *f inv* immobiliare

built [bɪlt] *pt, pp of* **build**; **built-in** *adj* (*cupboard*) a muro; (*device*) incorporato(-a); **built-up** *adj* **built-up area** abitato

bulb [bʌlb] *n* (*Bot*) bulbo; (*Elec*) lampadina

Bulgaria [bʌl'gɛərɪə] *n* Bulgaria; **Bulgarian** *adj* bulgaro(-a) ▷ *n* bulgaro(-a); (*Ling*) bulgaro

bulge [bʌldʒ] *n* rigonfiamento ▷ *vi* essere protuberante *or* rigonfio(-a); **to be bulging with** essere pieno(-a) *or* zeppo(-a) di

bulimia [bə'lɪmɪə] *n* bulimia

bulimic [bju:'lɪmɪk] *adj, n* bulimico(-a)

bulk [bʌlk] *n* massa, volume *m*; **in ~** a pacchi *or* cassette *etc*; (*Comm*) all'ingrosso; **the ~ of** il grosso di; **bulky** *adj* grosso(-a), voluminoso(-a)

bull [bul] *n* toro; (*male elephant, whale*) maschio

bulldozer ['buldəuzəʳ] *n* bulldozer *m inv*

bullet ['bulɪt] *n* pallottola

bulletin ['bulɪtɪn] *n* bollettino; **bulletin board** *n* (*Comput*) bulletin board *m inv*

bullfight ['bulfaɪt] *n* corrida; **bullfighter** *n* torero; **bullfighting** *n* tauromachia

bully ['bulɪ] *n* prepotente *m* ▷ *vt* angariare; (*frighten*) intimidire

bum [bʌm] *n* (*inf*) (*backside*) culo; (*tramp*) vagabondo(-a)

bumblebee ['bʌmblbi:] *n* bombo

bump [bʌmp] *n* (*in car*) piccolo tamponamento; (*jolt*) scossa; (*on road etc*) protuberanza; (*on head*) bernoccolo ▷ *vt* battere; **bump into** *vt fus* scontrarsi con; (*person*) imbattersi in; **bumper** *n* paraurti *m inv* ▷ *adj* **bumper harvest** raccolto eccezionale; **bumpy** ['bʌmpɪ] *adj* (*road*) dissestato(-a)

bun [bʌn] *n* focaccia; (*of hair*) crocchia

bunch [bʌntʃ] *n* (*of flowers, keys*) mazzo; (*of bananas*) casco; (*of people*) gruppo; **~ of grapes** grappolo d'uva; **~es** *npl* (*in hair*) codine *fpl*

bundle ['bʌndl] *n* fascio ▷ *vt* (*also: ~ up*) legare in un fascio; (*put*): **to ~ sth/sb into** spingere qc/qn in

bungalow ['bʌŋgələu] *n* bungalow *m inv*

bungee jumping ['bʌndʒiːˈdʒʌmpɪŋ] n salto nel vuoto da ponti, grattacieli etc con un cavo fissato alla caviglia

bunion ['bʌnjən] n callo (al piede)

bunk [bʌŋk] n cuccetta; **bunk beds** npl letti mpl a castello

bunker ['bʌŋkəʳ] n (coal store) ripostiglio per il carbone; (Mil, Golf) bunker m inv

bunny ['bʌnɪ] n (also: ~ **rabbit**) coniglietto

buoy [bɔɪ] n boa; **buoyant** adj galleggiante; (fig) vivace

burden ['bəːdn] n carico, fardello ▷ vt **to ~ sb with** caricare qn di

bureau [bjuəˈrəu] (pl **bureaux**) n (BRIT: writing desk) scrivania; (US: chest of drawers) cassettone m; (office) ufficio, agenzia

bureaucracy [bjuəˈrɔkrəsɪ] n burocrazia

bureaucrat ['bjuərəkræt] n burocrate m/f

bureau de change [-dəˈʃɑːʒ] (pl **bureaux de change**) n cambiavalute m inv

bureaux [bjuəˈrəuz] npl of **bureau**

burger ['bəːgəʳ] n hamburger m inv

burglar ['bəːgləʳ] n scassinatore m; **burglar alarm** n campanello antifurto; **burglary** n furto con scasso

burial ['berɪəl] n sepoltura

burn [bəːn] (pt, pp **burned** or **burnt**) vt, vi bruciare ▷ n bruciatura, scottatura; **burn down** vt distruggere col fuoco; **burn out** vt (writer etc): **to ~ o.s. out** esaurirsi; **burning** adj in fiamme; (sand) che scotta; (ambition) bruciante

Burns Night n vedi nota nel riquadro

○ **BURNS NIGHT**
○
○ **Burns Night** è la festa celebrata il 25
○ gennaio per commemorare il poeta
○ scozzese Robert Burns (1759-1796). Gli
○ scozzesi festeggiano questa data con
○ una cena, la "Burns supper", a base di
○ "haggis", piatto tradizionale scozzese,
○ e whisky.

burnt [bəːnt] pt, pp of **burn**

burp [bəːp] (inf) n rutto ▷ vi ruttare

burrow ['bʌrəu] n tana ▷ vt scavare

burst [bəːst] (pt, pp **burst**) vt far scoppiare ▷ vi esplodere; (tyre) scoppiare ▷ n scoppio; (also: ~ **pipe**) rottura nel tubo, perdita; **a ~ of speed** uno scatto di velocità; **~ into flames/tears** scoppiare in fiamme/lacrime; **to ~ out laughing** scoppiare a ridere; **to be ~ing with** scoppiare di; **burst into** vt fus (room etc) irrompere in

bury ['berɪ] vt seppellire

bus [bʌs] (pl **buses**) n autobus m inv; bus

conductor n autista m/f (dell'autobus)

bush [buʃ] n cespuglio; (scrub land) macchia; **to beat about the ~** menare il cane per l'aia

business ['bɪznɪs] n (matter) affare m; (trading) affari mpl; (firm) azienda; (job, duty) lavoro; **to be away on ~** essere andato via per affari; **it's none of my ~** questo non mi riguarda; **he means ~** non scherza; **business class** n (Aer) business class f; **businesslike** adj serio(-a), efficiente; **businessman** (irreg) n uomo d'affari; **business trip** n viaggio d'affari; **businesswoman** (irreg) n donna d'affari

busker ['bʌskəʳ] (BRIT) n suonatore(-trice) ambulante

bus: **bus pass** n tessera dell'autobus; **bus shelter** n pensilina (alla fermata dell'autobus); **bus station** n stazione f delle corriere, autostazione f; **bus-stop** n fermata d'autobus

bust [bʌst] n busto; (Anat) seno ▷ adj (inf: broken) rotto(-a); **to go ~** fallire

bustling ['bʌslɪŋ] adj movimentato(-a)

busy ['bɪzɪ] adj occupato(-a); (shop, street) molto frequentato(-a) ▷ vt **to ~ o.s.** darsi da fare; **busy signal** (US) n (Tel) segnale m di occupato

○ **KEYWORD**

but [bʌt] conj ma; **I'd love to come, but I'm busy** vorrei tanto venire, ma ho da fare ▷ prep (apart from, except) eccetto, tranne, meno; **he was nothing but trouble** non dava altro che guai; **no-one but him can do it** nessuno può farlo tranne lui; **but for you/your help** se non fosse per te/per il tuo aiuto; **anything but that** tutto ma non questo
▷ adv (just, only) solo, soltanto; **she's but a child** è solo una bambina; **had I but known** se solo avessi saputo; **I can but try** tentar non nuoce; **all but finished** quasi finito

butcher ['butʃəʳ] n macellaio ▷ vt macellare; **butcher's (shop)** n macelleria

butler ['bʌtləʳ] n maggiordomo

butt [bʌt] n (cask) grossa botte f; (of gun) calcio; (of cigarette) mozzicone m; (BRIT: fig: target) oggetto ▷ vt cozzare

butter ['bʌtəʳ] n burro ▷ vt imburrare; **buttercup** n ranuncolo

butterfly ['bʌtəflaɪ] n farfalla; (Swimming: also: ~ **stroke**) (nuoto a) farfalla

buttocks ['bʌtəks] npl natiche fpl

button ['bʌtn] n bottone m; (US: badge)

distinctivo ▷ vt (also: **~ up**) abbottonare ▷ vi abbottonarsi

buy [baɪ] (pt, pp **bought**) vt comprare ▷ n acquisto; **where can I ~ some postcards?** dove posso comprare delle cartoline?; **to ~ sb sth/sth from sb** comprare qc per qn/qc da qn; **to ~ sb a drink** offrire da bere a qn; **buy out** vt (business) rilevare; **buy up** vt accaparrare; **buyer** n compratore(-trice)

buzz [bʌz] n ronzio; (inf: phone call) colpo di telefono ▷ vi ronzare; **buzzer** ['bʌzə^r] n cicalino

 KEYWORD

by [baɪ] prep **1** (referring to cause, agent) da; **killed by lightning** ucciso da un fulmine; **surrounded by a fence** circondato da uno steccato; **a painting by Picasso** un quadro di Picasso

2 (referring to method, manner, means): **by bus/car/train** in autobus/macchina/ treno, con l'autobus/la macchina/il treno; **to pay by cheque** pagare con (un) assegno; **by moonlight** al chiaro di luna; **by saving hard, he ...** risparmiando molto, lui ...

3 (via, through) per; **we came by Dover** siamo venuti via Dover

4 (close to, past) accanto a; **the house by the river** la casa sul fiume; **a holiday by the sea** una vacanza al mare; **she sat by his bed** si sedette accanto al suo letto; **she rushed by me** mi è passata accanto correndo; **I go by the post office every day** passo davanti all'ufficio postale ogni giorno

5 (not later than) per, entro; **by 4 o'clock** per or entro le 4; **by this time tomorrow** domani a quest'ora; **by the time I got here it was too late** quando sono arrivato era ormai troppo tardi

6 (during): **by day/night** di giorno/notte

7 (amount) a; **by the kilo/metre** a chili/ metri; **paid by the hour** pagato all'ora; **one by one** uno per uno; **little by little** poco a poco

8 (Math, measure): **to divide/multiply by 3** dividere/moltiplicare per 3; **it's broader by a metre** è un metro più largo, è più largo di un metro

9 (according to) per; **to play by the rules** attenersi alle regole; **it's all right by me** per me va bene

10: **(all) by oneself** etc (tutto(-a)) solo(-a); **he did it (all) by himself** lo ha fatto (tutto) da solo

11: **by the way** a proposito; **this wasn't**

my idea by the way tra l'altro l'idea non è stata mia

▷ adv **1** see **go**; **pass** etc

2: **by and by** (in past) poco dopo; (in future) fra breve; **by and large** nel complesso

bye(-bye) ['baɪ('baɪ)] excl ciao!, arrivederci!

by-election ['baɪɪlɛkʃən] (BRIT) n elezione f straordinaria

bypass ['baɪpɑːs] n circonvallazione f; (Med) by-pass m inv ▷ vt fare una deviazione intorno a

byte [baɪt] n (Comput) byte m inv, bicarattere m

C [si:] n (Mus) do

cab [kæb] n taxi m inv; (of train, truck) cabina

cabaret ['kæbəreɪ] n cabaret m inv

cabbage ['kæbɪdʒ] n cavolo

cabin ['kæbɪn] n capanna; (on ship) cabina; **cabin crew** n equipaggio

cabinet ['kæbɪnɪt] n (Pol) consiglio dei ministri; (furniture) armadietto; (also: **display ~**) vetrinetta; **cabinet minister** n ministro (membro del Consiglio)

cable ['keɪbl] n cavo; fune f; (Tel) cablogramma m ▷ vt telegrafare; **cable car** n funivia; **cable television** n televisione f via cavo

cactus ['kæktəs] (pl **cacti**) n cactus m inv

café ['kæfeɪ] n caffè m inv

cafeteria [kæfɪ'tɪərɪə] n self-service m inv

caffein(e) ['kæfi:n] n caffeina

cage [keɪdʒ] n gabbia

cagoule [kə'gu:l] n K-way® m inv

cake [keɪk] n (large) torta; (small) pasticcino; **cake of soap** n saponetta

calcium ['kælsɪəm] n calcio

calculate ['kælkjuleɪt] vt calcolare; **calculation** [-'leɪʃən] n calcolo; **calculator** n calcolatrice f

calendar ['kæləndə²] n calendario

calf [kɑ:f] (pl **calves**) n (of cow) vitello; (of other animals) piccolo; (also: **~skin**) (pelle f di) vitello; (Anat) polpaccio

calibre ['kælɪbə²] (us **caliber**) n calibro

call [kɔ:l] vt (gen: also Tel) chiamare; (meeting) indire ▷ vi chiamare; (visit: also: **~ in, ~ round**) passare ▷ n (shout) grido, urlo; (Tel) telefonata; **to be ~ed** (person, object) chiamarsi; **can you ~ back later?** può richiamare più tardi?; **can I make a ~ from here?** posso telefonare da qui?; **to be on ~** essere a disposizione; **call back** vi (return) ritornare; (Tel) ritelefonare, richiamare; **call for** vt fus richiedere; (fetch) passare a prendere; **call in** vt (doctor, expert, police) chiamare, far venire; **call off** vt disdire; **call on** vt fus (visit) passare da; (appeal to) chiedere a; **call out** vi (in pain) urlare; (to person) chiamare; **call up** vt (Mil) richiamare; (Tel) telefonare a; **callbox** (BRIT) n cabina telefonica; **call centre** (US **call center**) n centro informazioni telefoniche; **caller** n persona che chiama, visitatore(-trice)

callous ['kæləs] adj indurito(-a), insensibile

calm [kɑ:m] adj calmo(-a) ▷ n calma ▷ vt calmare; **calm down** vi calmarsi ▷ vt calmare; **calmly** adv con calma

Calor gas® ['kælə²-] n butano

calorie ['kælərɪ] n caloria

calves [kɑ:vz] npl of **calf**

camcorder ['kæmkɔ:də²] n camcorder f inv

came [keɪm] pt of **come**

camel ['kæməl] n cammello

camera ['kæmərə] n macchina fotografica; (Cinema, TV) cinepresa; **in ~** a porte chiuse; **cameraman** (irreg) n cameraman m inv

camouflage ['kæməflɑ:ʒ] n (Mil, Zool) mimetizzazione f ▷ vt mimetizzare

camp [kæmp] n campeggio; (Mil) campo ▷ vi accamparsi ▷ adj effeminato(-a)

campaign [kæm'peɪn] n (Mil, Pol etc) campagna ▷ vi (also fig) fare una campagna; **campaigner** n **campaigner for** fautore(-trice) di; **campaigner against** oppositore(-trice) di

camp: **campbed** n (BRIT) brandina; **camper** ['kæmpə²] n campeggiatore(-trice); (vehicle) camper m inv; **campground** (US) n campeggio; **camping** ['kæmpɪŋ] n campeggio; **to go camping** andare in campeggio; **campsite** ['kæmpsaɪt] n campeggio

campus ['kæmpəs] n campus m inv

can¹ [kæn] n (of milk) scatola; (of oil) bidone m; (of water) tanica; (tin) scatola ▷ vt

mettere in scatola

 KEYWORD

can² [kæn] (negative **cannot, can't**, conditional and pt **could**) aux vb **1** (be able to) potere; **I can't go any further** non posso andare oltre; **you can do it if you try** sei in grado di farlo — basta provarci; **I'll help you all I can** ti aiuterò come potrò; **I can't see you** non ti vedo **2** (know how to) sapere, essere capace di; **I can swim** so nuotare; **can you speak French?** parla francese? **3** (may) potere; **could I have a word with you?** posso parlarle un momento? **4** (expressing disbelief, puzzlement etc): **it can't be true!** non può essere vero!; **what can he want?** cosa può mai volere? **5** (expressing possibility, suggestion etc): **he could be in the library** può darsi che sia in biblioteca; **she could have been delayed** può aver avuto un contrattempo

Canada ['kænədə] n Canada m; **Canadian** [kə'neɪdɪən] adj, n canadese m/f

canal [kə'næl] n canale m

canary [kə'nɛərɪ] n canarino

Canary Islands, Canaries [kə'nɛərɪz] npl **the ~** le (isole) Canarie

cancel ['kænsəl] vt annullare; (train) sopprimere; (cross out) cancellare; **I want to ~ my booking** vorrei disdire la mia prenotazione; **cancellation** [-'leɪʃən] n annullamento; soppressione f; cancellazione f; (Tourism) prenotazione f annullata

cancer ['kænsə'] n cancro

Cancer ['kænsə'] n (sign) Cancro

candidate ['kændɪdeɪt] n candidato(-a)

candle ['kændl] n candela; (in church) cero; **candlestick** n bugia; (bigger, ornate) candeliere m

candy ['kændɪ] n zucchero candito; (us) caramella; caramelle fpl; **candy bar** (us) n lungo biscotto, in genere ricoperto di cioccolata; **candyfloss** ['kændɪflɒs] n (BRIT) zucchero filato

cane [keɪn] n canna; (for furniture) bambù m; (stick) verga ▷ vt (BRIT Scol) punire a colpi di verga

canister ['kænɪstə'] n scatola metallica

cannabis ['kænəbɪs] n canapa indiana

canned ['kænd] adj (food) in scatola

cannon ['kænən] (pl **cannon** or **cannons**) n (gun) cannone m

cannot ['kænɒt] = **can not**

canoe [kə'nu:] n canoa; **canoeing** n canottaggio

canon ['kænən] n (clergyman) canonico; (standard) canone m

can-opener ['kænəupnə'] n apriscatole m inv

can't [kænt] = **can not**

canteen [kæn'ti:n] n mensa; (BRIT: of cutlery) portaposate m inv

> Be careful not to translate **canteen** by the Italian word **cantina**.

canter ['kæntə'] vi andare al piccolo galoppo

canvas ['kænvəs] n tela

canvass ['kænvəs] n (Pol): **to ~ for** raccogliere voti per ▷ vt fare un sondaggio di

canyon ['kænjən] n canyon m inv

cap [kæp] n (hat) berretto; (of pen) coperchio; (of bottle, toy gun) tappo; (contraceptive) diaframma m ▷ vt (outdo) superare; (limit) fissare un tetto (a)

capability [keɪpə'bɪlɪtɪ] n capacità f inv, abilità f inv

capable ['keɪpəbl] adj capace

capacity [kə'pæsɪtɪ] n capacità f inv; (of lift etc) capienza

cape [keɪp] n (garment) cappa; (Geo) capo

caper ['keɪpə'] n (Culin) cappero; (prank) scherzetto

capital ['kæpɪtl] n (also: ~ **city**) capitale f; (money) capitale m; (also: ~ **letter**) (lettera) maiuscola; **capitalism** n capitalismo; **capitalist** adj, n capitalista m/f; **capital punishment** n pena capitale

Capitol ['kæpɪtl] n **the ~** il Campidoglio

Capricorn ['kæprɪkɔːn] n Capricorno

capsize [kæp'saɪz] vt capovolgere ▷ vi capovolgersi

capsule ['kæpsju:l] n capsula

captain ['kæptɪn] n capitano

caption ['kæpʃən] n leggenda

captivity [kæp'tɪvɪtɪ] n cattività

capture ['kæptʃə'] vt catturare; (Comput) registrare ▷ n cattura; (data) registrazione f for rilevazione f di dati

car [kɑː'] n (Aut) macchina, automobile f; (Rail) vagone m

carafe [kə'ræf] n caraffa

caramel ['kærəməl] n caramello

carat ['kærət] n carato; **18 ~ gold** oro a 18 carati

caravan ['kærəvæn] n (BRIT) roulotte f inv; (of camels) carovana; **caravan site** (BRIT) n campeggio per roulotte

carbohydrate [kɑːbəu'haɪdreɪt] n carboidrato

carbon ['kɑːbən] n carbonio; **carbon dioxide** [-daɪ'ɔksaɪd] n diossido di carbonio; **carbon monoxide** [-mɔ'nɔksaɪd] n monossido di carbonio

car boot sale n vedi nota nel riquadro

● CAR BOOT SALE
●
● Il **car boot sale** è un mercatino
● dell'usato molto popolare in Gran
● Bretagna. Normalmente ha luogo in
● un parcheggio o in un grande spiazzo,
● e la merce viene in genere esposta nei
● bagagliai, in inglese appunto "boots",
● aperti delle macchine.

carburettor [kɑ:bju'rɛtər] (US **carburetor**) n carburatore m

card [kɑ:d] n carta; (visiting card etc) biglietto; (Christmas card etc) cartolina; **cardboard** n cartone m; **card game** n gioco di carte

cardigan ['kɑ:dɪgən] n cardigan m inv

cardinal ['kɑ:dɪnl] adj cardinale ▷ n cardinale m

cardphone ['kɑ:dfəun] n telefono a scheda

care [kɛər] n cura, attenzione f; (worry) preoccupazione f ▷ vi **to ~ about** curarsi di; (thing, idea) interessarsi di; **~ of** presso; **in sb's ~** alle cure di qn; **to take ~ (to do)** fare attenzione (a fare); **to take ~ of** curarsi di; (bill, problem) occuparsi di; **I don't ~** non me ne importa; **I couldn't ~ less** non m'interessa affatto; **care for** vt fus aver cura di; (like) volere bene a

career [kə'rɪər] n carriera ▷ vi (also: **~ along**) andare di (gran) carriera

care: carefree ['kɛəfri:] adj sgombro(-a) di preoccupazioni; **careful** ['kɛəful] adj attento(-a); (cautious) cauto(-a); **(be) careful!** attenzione!; **carefully** adv con cura; cautamente; **caregiver** (US) n (professional) badante m/f; (unpaid) persona che si prende cura di un parente malato o anziano; **careless** ['kɛəlɪs] adj negligente; (heedless) spensierato(-a); **carelessness** n negligenza; mancanza di tatto; **carer** ['kɛərər] n assistente m/f (di persone malata o handicappata); **caretaker** ['kɛəteɪkə] n custode m

car-ferry ['kɑ:fɛri] n traghetto

cargo ['kɑ:gəu] (pl **cargoes**) n carico

car hire n autonoleggio

Caribbean [kærɪ'bi:ən] adj **the ~ Sea** il Mar dei Caraibi

caring ['kɛərɪŋ] adj (person) premuroso(-a); (society, organization) umanitario(-a)

carnation [kɑ:'neɪʃən] n garofano

carnival ['kɑ:nɪvəl] n (public celebration) carnevale m; (US: funfair) luna park m inv

carol ['kærəl] n **Christmas ~** canto di Natale

carousel [kærə'sɛl] (US) n giostra

car park (BRIT) n parcheggio

carpenter ['kɑ:pɪntər] n carpentiere m

carpet ['kɑ:pɪt] n tappeto ▷ vt coprire con tappeto

car rental (US) n autonoleggio

carriage ['kærɪdʒ] n vettura; (of goods) trasporto; **carriageway** (BRIT) n (part of road) carreggiata

carrier ['kærɪər] n (of disease) portatore(-trice); (Comm) impresa di trasporti; **carrier bag** (BRIT) n sacchetto

carrot ['kærət] n carota

carry ['kærɪ] vt (person) portare; (: vehicle) trasportare; (involve: responsibilities etc) comportare; (Med) essere portatore(-trice) di ▷ vi (sound) farsi sentire; **to be** or **get carried away** (fig) entusiasmarsi; **carry on** vi **to ~ on with sth/doing** continuare qc/a fare ▷ vt mandare avanti; **carry out** vt (orders) eseguire; (investigation) svolgere

cart [kɑ:t] n carro ▷ vt (inf) trascinare

carton ['kɑ:tən] n (box) scatola di cartone; (of yogurt) cartone m; (of cigarettes) stecca

cartoon [kɑ:'tu:n] n (Press) disegno umoristico; (comic strip) fumetto; (Cinema) disegno animato

cartridge ['kɑ:trɪdʒ] n (for gun, pen) cartuccia; (music tape) cassetta

carve [kɑ:v] vt (meat) trinciare; (wood, stone) intagliare; **carving** n (in wood etc) scultura

car wash n lavaggio auto

case [keɪs] n caso; (Law) causa, processo; (box) scatola; (BRIT: also: **suit~**) valigia; **in ~ of** in caso di; **in ~ he** caso mai lui; **in any ~** in ogni caso; **just in ~** in caso di bisogno

cash [kæʃ] n denaro; (coins, notes) denaro liquido ▷ vt incassare; **I haven't got any ~** non ho contanti; **to pay (in) ~** pagare in contanti; **~ on delivery** pagamento alla consegna; **cashback** n (discount) sconto; (at supermarket etc) anticipo di contanti ottenuto presso la cassa di un negozio tramite una carta di debito; **cash card** (BRIT) n tesserino di prelievo; **cash desk** (BRIT) n cassa; **cash dispenser** (BRIT) n sportello automatico

cashew [kæ'ʃu:] n (also: **~ nut**) anacardio

cashier [kæ'ʃɪər] n cassiere(-a)

cashmere ['kæʃmɪər] n cachemire m

cash point n sportello bancario automatico, Bancomat® m inv

cash register n registratore m di cassa

casino [kə'si:nəu] n casinò m inv

casket ['kɑ:skɪt] n cofanetto; (US: coffin) bara

casserole ['kæsərəul] *n* casseruola; (*food*): **chicken ~** pollo in casseruola

cassette [kæ'sɛt] *n* cassetta; **cassette player** *n* riproduttore *m* a cassette

cast [kɑːst] (*pt, pp* **cast**) *vt* (*throw*) gettare; (*metal*) gettare, fondere; (*Theatre*): **to ~ sb as Hamlet** scegliere qn per la parte di Amleto ▷ *n* (*Theatre*) cast *m inv*; (*also*: **plaster ~**) ingessatura; **to ~ one's vote** votare, dare il voto; **cast off** *vi* (*Naut*) salpare; (*Knitting*) calare

castanets [kæstə'nɛts] *npl* castagnette *fpl*

caster sugar ['kɑːstə'-] (*BRIT*) *n* zucchero semolato

cast-iron ['kɑːstaɪən] *adj* (*lit*) di ghisa; (*fig*: *case*) di ferro

castle ['kɑːsl] *n* castello

casual ['kæʒjul] *adj* (*chance*) casuale, fortuito(-a); (: *work etc*) avventizio(-a); (*unconcerned*) noncurante, indifferente; **~ wear** casual *m*

casualty ['kæʒjultɪ] *n* ferito(-a); (*dead*) morto(-a), vittima; (*Med*: *department*) pronto soccorso

cat [kæt] *n* gatto

catalogue ['kætəlɔg] (*US* **catalog**) *n* catalogo ▷ *vt* catalogare

catalytic converter [kætəlɪtɪk-] *n* marmitta catalitica, catalizzatore *m*

cataract ['kætərækt] *n* (*also Med*) cateratta

catarrh [kə'tɑː'] *n* catarro

catastrophe [kə'tæstrəfɪ] *n* catastrofe *f*

catch [kætʃ] (*pt, pp* **caught**) *vt* prendere; (*ball*) afferrare; (*surprise*: *person*) sorprendere; (*attention*) attirare; (*comment, whisper*) cogliere; (*person*) raggiungere ▷ *vi* (*fire*) prendere ▷ *n* (*fish etc caught*) retata; (*of ball*) presa; (*trick*) inganno; (*Tech*) gancio; (*game*) catch *m inv*; **to ~ fire** prendere fuoco; **to ~ sight of** scorgere; **catch up** *vi* mettersi in pari ▷ *vt* (*also*: **~ up with**) raggiungere; **catching** ['kætʃɪŋ] *adj* (*Med*) contagioso(-a)

category ['kætɪgərɪ] *n* categoria

cater ['keɪtə'] *vi* **~ for** (*BRIT*: *needs*) provvedere a; (: *readers, consumers*) incontrare i gusti di; (*Comm*: *provide food*) provvedere alla ristorazione di

caterpillar ['kætəpɪlə'] *n* bruco

cathedral [kə'θiːdrəl] *n* cattedrale *f*, duomo

Catholic ['kæθəlɪk] *adj, n* (*Rel*) cattolico(-a)

Catseye® ['kæts'aɪ] (*BRIT*) *n* (*Aut*) catarifrangente *m*

cattle ['kætl] *npl* bestiame *m*, bestie *fpl*

catwalk ['kætwɔːk] *n* passerella

caught [kɔːt] *pt, pp of* **catch**

cauliflower ['kɔlɪflauə'] *n* cavolfiore *m*

cause [kɔːz] *n* causa ▷ *vt* causare

caution ['kɔːʃən] *n* prudenza; (*warning*) avvertimento ▷ *vt* avvertire; ammonire; **cautious** ['kɔːʃəs] *adj* cauto(-a), prudente

cave [keɪv] *n* caverna, grotta; **cave in** *vi* (*roof etc*) crollare

caviar(e) ['kævɪɑː'] *n* caviale *m*

cavity ['kævɪtɪ] *n* cavità *f inv*

cc *abbr* = **cubic centimetres**; **carbon copy**

CCTV *n abbr* (= *closed-circuit television*) televisione *f* a circuito chiuso

CD *abbr* (*disc*) CD *m inv*; (*player*) lettore *m* CD *inv*; **CD player** *n* lettore *m* CD; **CD-ROM** [-rɔm] *n abbr* CD-ROM *m inv*

cease [siːs] *vt, vi* cessare; **ceasefire** *n* cessate il fuoco *m inv*

cedar ['siːdə'] *n* cedro

ceilidh ['keɪlɪ] *n* festa con musiche e danze popolari scozzesi o irlandesi

ceiling ['siːlɪŋ] *n* soffitto; (*on wages etc*) tetto

celebrate ['sɛlɪbreɪt] *vt, vi* celebrare; **celebration** [-'breɪʃən] *n* celebrazione *f*

celebrity [sɪ'lɛbrɪtɪ] *n* celebrità *f inv*

celery ['sɛlərɪ] *n* sedano

cell [sɛl] *n* cella; (*of revolutionaries, Biol*) cellula; (*Elec*) elemento (di batteria)

cellar ['sɛlə'] *n* sottosuolo; cantina

cello ['tʃɛləu] *n* violoncello

Cellophane® ['sɛləfeɪn] *n* cellophane® *m*

cellphone ['sɛləfɛn] *n* cellulare *m*

Celsius ['sɛlsɪəs] *adj* Celsius *inv*

Celtic ['kɛltɪk, 'sɛltɪk] *adj* celtico(-a)

cement [sə'mɛnt] *n* cemento

cemetery ['sɛmɪtrɪ] *n* cimitero

censor ['sɛnsə'] *n* censore *m* ▷ *vt* censurare; **censorship** *n* censura

census ['sɛnsəs] *n* censimento

cent [sɛnt] *n* (*US*: *coin*) centesimo (= 1.100 di un dollaro); (*unit of euro*) centesimo; *see also* **per**

centenary [sɛn'tiːnərɪ] *n* centenario

centennial [sɛn'tɛnɪəl] (*US*) *n* centenario

center ['sɛntə'] (*US*) *n, vt* = **centre**

centi... [sɛntɪ] *prefix*: **centigrade** ['sɛntɪgreɪd] *adj* centigrado(-a); **centimetre** ['sɛntɪmiːtə'] (*US* **centimeter**) *n* centimetro; **centipede** ['sɛntɪpiːd] *n* centopiedi *m inv*

central ['sɛntrəl] *adj* centrale; **Central America** *n* America centrale; **central heating** *n* riscaldamento centrale; **central reservation** *n* (*BRIT Aut*) banchina *f* spartitraffico *inv*

centre ['sɛntə'] (*US* **center**) *n* centro ▷ *vt* centrare; **centre-forward** *n* (*Sport*) centroavanti *m inv*; **centre-half** *n* (*Sport*) centromediano

century ['sɛntjurɪ] *n* secolo; **twentieth ~**

ventesimo secolo

CEO n abbr = **chief executive officer**

ceramic [sɪ'ræmɪk] adj ceramico(-a)

cereal ['si:rɪəl] n cereale m

ceremony ['sɛrɪmənɪ] n cerimonia; **to stand on ~** fare complimenti

certain ['sə:tən] adj certo(-a); **to make ~ of** assicurarsi di; **for ~** per certo, di sicuro; **certainly** adv certamente, certo; **certainty** n certezza

certificate [sə'tɪfɪkɪt] n certificato; diploma m

certify ['sə:tɪfaɪ] vt certificare; (award diploma to) conferire un diploma a; (declare insane) dichiarare pazzo(-a)

cf. abbr (= compare) cfr.

CFC n (= chlorofluorocarbon) CFC m inv

chain [tʃeɪn] n catena ▷ vt (also: ~ **up**) incatenare; **chain-smoke** vi fumare una sigaretta dopo l'altra

chair [tʃɛəʳ] n sedia; (armchair) poltrona; (of university) cattedra; (of meeting) presidenza ▷ vt (meeting) presiedere; **chairlift** n seggiovia; **chairman** (irreg) n presidente m; **chairperson** n presidente(-essa); **chairwoman** (irreg) n presidentessa

chalet ['ʃæleɪ] n chalet m inv

chalk [tʃɔ:k] n gesso; **chalkboard** (us) n lavagna

challenge ['tʃælɪndʒ] n sfida ▷ vt sfidare; (statement, right) mettere in dubbio; **to ~ sb to do** sfidare qn a fare; **challenging** adj (task) impegnativo(-a); (look) di sfida

chamber ['tʃeɪmbəʳ] n camera; **chambermaid** n cameriera

champagne [ʃæm'peɪn] n champagne m inv

champion ['tʃæmpɪən] n campione(-essa); **championship** n campionato

chance [tʃɑ:ns] n caso; (opportunity) occasione f; (likelihood) possibilità f inv ▷ vt **to ~ it** rischiare, provarci ▷ adj fortuito(-a); **to take a ~** rischiare; **by ~** per caso

chancellor ['tʃɑ:nsələʳ] n cancelliere m; **Chancellor of the Exchequer** [-ɪks'tʃɛkəʳ] (brit) n Cancelliere dello Scacchiere

chandelier [ʃændə'lɪəʳ] n lampadario

change [tʃeɪndʒ] vt cambiare; (transform): **to ~ sb into** trasformare qn in ▷ vi cambiare; (change one's clothes) cambiarsi; (be transformed): **to ~ into** trasformarsi in ▷ n cambiamento; (of clothes) cambio; (money returned) resto; (coins) spiccioli; **where can I ~ some money?** dove posso cambiare dei soldi?; **to ~ one's mind** cambiare idea; **keep the ~!** tenga pure il resto!; **sorry, I don't have any ~** mi dispiace, non ho spiccioli; **for a ~** tanto per

cambiare; **change over** vi (from sth to sth) passare; (players etc) scambiarsi (di posto o di campo) ▷ vt cambiare; **changeable** adj (weather) variabile; **change machine** n distributore automatico di monete; **changing room** n (brit: in shop) camerino; (: Sport) spogliatoio

channel ['tʃænl] n canale m; (of river, sea) alveo ▷ vt canalizzare; **Channel Tunnel** n **the Channel Tunnel** il tunnel sotto la Manica

chant [tʃɑ:nt] n canto; salmodia ▷ vt cantare; salmodiare

chaos ['keɪɔs] n caos m

chaotic [keɪ'ɔtɪk] adj caotico(-a)

chap [tʃæp] (brit: inf) n (man) tipo

chapel ['tʃæpəl] n cappella

chapped [tʃæpt] adj (skin, lips) screpolato(-a)

chapter ['tʃæptəʳ] n capitolo

character ['kærɪktəʳ] n carattere m; (in novel, film) personaggio; **characteristic** [-'rɪstɪk] adj caratteristico(-a) ▷ n caratteristica; **characterize** ['kærɪktəraɪz] vt caratterizzare; (describe): **to characterize (as)** descrivere (come)

charcoal ['tʃɑ:kəul] n carbone m di legna

charge [tʃɑ:dʒ] n accusa; (cost) prezzo; (responsibility) responsabilità ▷ vt (gun, battery, Mil: enemy) caricare; (customer) fare pagare a; (sum) fare pagare; (Law): **to ~ sb (with)** accusare qn (di) ▷ vi (gen with: up, along etc) lanciarsi; **charge card** n carta f clienti inv; **charger** n (also: **battery charger**) caricabatterie m inv; (old: warhorse) destriero

charismatic [kærɪz'mætɪk] adj carismatico(-a)

charity ['tʃærɪtɪ] n carità; (organization) opera pia; **charity shop** n (brit) negozi che vendono articoli di seconda mano e devolvono il ricavato in beneficenza

charm [tʃɑ:m] n fascino; (on bracelet) ciondolo ▷ vt affascinare, incantare; **charming** adj affascinante

chart [tʃɑ:t] n tabella; grafico; (map) carta nautica ▷ vt fare una carta nautica di; **~s** npl (Mus) hit parade f

charter ['tʃɑ:təʳ] vt (plane) noleggiare ▷ n (document) carta; **chartered accountant** ['tʃɑ:təd-] (brit) n ragioniere(-a) professionista; **charter flight** n volo m charter inv

chase [tʃeɪs] vt inseguire; (also: ~ **away**) cacciare ▷ n caccia

chat [tʃæt] vi (also: **have a ~**) chiacchierare ▷ n chiacchierata; **chat up** vt (brit inf: girl) abbordare; **chat room** n (Internet) chat room f inv; **chat show** (brit) n talk show *m inv*

chatter ['tʃætə'] *vi* (*person*) ciarlare; (*bird*) cinguettare; (*teeth*) battere ▷ *n* ciarle *fpl*; cinguettio

chauffeur ['ʃəufə'] *n* autista *m*

chauvinist ['ʃəuvɪnɪst] *n* (*male chauvinist*) maschilista *m*; (*nationalist*) sciovinista *m/f*

cheap [tʃi:p] *adj* economico(-a); (*joke*) grossolano(-a); (*poor quality*) di cattiva qualità ▷ *adv* a buon mercato; **can you recommend a ~ hotel/restaurant, please?** potrebbe indicarmi un albergo/ ristorante non troppo caro?; **cheap day return** *n* biglietto ridotto di andata e ritorno valido in giornata; **cheaply** *adv* a buon prezzo, a buon mercato

cheat [tʃi:t] *vi* imbrogliare; (*at school*) copiare ▷ *vt* ingannare ▷ *n* imbroglione *m*; **to ~ sb out of sth** defraudare qn di qc; **cheat on** *vt fus* (*husband, wife*) tradire

Chechnya [tʃɪtʃ'njɑ:] *n* Cecenia

check [tʃɛk] *vt* verificare; (*passport, ticket*) controllare; (*halt*) fermare; (*restrain*) contenere ▷ *n* verifica; controllo; (*curb*) freno; (*US: bill*) conto; (*pattern: gen pl*) quadretti *mpl*; (*US*) = **cheque** ▷ *adj* (*pattern, cloth*) a quadretti; **check in** *vi* (*in hotel*) registrare; (*at airport*) presentarsi all'accettazione ▷ *vt* (*luggage*) depositare; **check off** *vt* segnare; **check out** *vi* (*in hotel*) saldare il conto; **check up** *vi* **to ~ up (on sth)** investigare (qc); **to ~ up on sb** informarsi sul conto di qn; **checkbook** (*US*) *n* = **chequebook**; **checked** *adj* a quadretti; **checkers** (*US*) *n* dama; **check- in** *n* (*also:* **check-in desk**: *at airport*) check-in *m inv*, accettazione *f* (bagagli *inv*); **checking account** (*US*) *n* conto corrente; **checklist** *n* lista di controllo; **checkmate** *n* scaccomatto; **checkout** *n* (*in supermarket*) cassa; **checkpoint** *n* posto di blocco; **checkroom** (*US*) *n* deposito *m* bagagli *inv*; **checkup** *n* (*Med*) controllo medico

cheddar ['tʃɛdə'] *n* formaggio duro di latte di mucca di colore bianco o arancione

cheek [tʃi:k] *n* guancia; (*impudence*) faccia tosta; **cheekbone** *n* zigomo; **cheeky** *adj* sfacciato(-a)

cheer [tʃɪə'] *vt* applaudire; (*gladden*) rallegrare ▷ *vi* applaudire ▷ *n* grido (di incoraggiamento); **cheer up** *vi* rallegrarsi, farsi animo ▷ *vt* rallegrare; **cheerful** *adj* allegro(-a)

cheerio ['tʃɪərɪ'əu] (*BRIT*) *excl* ciao!

cheerleader ['tʃɪəli:də'] *n* cheerleader *f inv*

cheese [tʃi:z] *n* formaggio; **cheeseburger**

n cheeseburger *m inv*; **cheesecake** *n* specie di torta di ricotta, a volte con frutta

chef [ʃɛf] *n* capocuoco

chemical ['kɛmɪkəl] *adj* chimico(-a) ▷ *n* prodotto chimico

chemist ['kɛmɪst] *n* (*BRIT: pharmacist*) farmacista *m/f*; (*scientist*) chimico(-a); **chemistry** *n* chimica; **chemist's (shop)** (*BRIT*) *n* farmacia

cheque [tʃɛk] (*US* **check**) *n* assegno; **chequebook** *n* libretto degli assegni; **cheque card** *n* carta *f* assegni *inv*

cherry ['tʃɛrɪ] *n* ciliegia; (*also: ~ tree*) ciliegio

chess [tʃɛs] *n* scacchi *mpl*

chest [tʃɛst] *n* petto; (*box*) cassa

chestnut ['tʃɛsnʌt] *n* castagna; (*also: ~ tree*) castagno

chest of drawers *n* cassettone *m*

chew [tʃu:] *vt* masticare; **chewing gum** *n* chewing gum *m*

chic [ʃi:k] *adj* elegante

chick [tʃɪk] *n* pulcino; (*inf*) pollastrella

chicken ['tʃɪkɪn] *n* pollo; (*inf: coward*) coniglio; **chicken out** (*inf*) *vi* avere fifa; **chickenpox** *n* varicella

chickpea ['tʃɪkpi:] *n* cece *m*

chief [tʃi:f] *n* capo ▷ *adj* principale; **chief executive (officer)** *n* direttore *m* generale; **chiefly** *adv* per lo più, soprattutto

child [tʃaɪld] (*pl* **children**) *n* bambino(-a); **child abuse** *n* molestie *fpl* a minori; **child benefit** *n* (*BRIT*) ≈ assegni *mpl* familiari; **childbirth** *n* parto; **child-care** *n* il badare ai bambini; **childhood** *n* infanzia; **childish** *adj* puerile; **child minder** [-'maɪndə'] (*BRIT*) *n* bambinaia; **children** ['tʃɪldrən] *npl of* **child**

Chile ['tʃɪlɪ] *n* Cile *m*

Chilean ['tʃɪlɪən] *adj, n* cileno(-a)

chill [tʃɪl] *n* freddo; (*Med*) infreddatura ▷ *vt* raffreddare; **chill out** (*esp US*) *vi* (*inf*) darsi una calmata

chil(l)i ['tʃɪlɪ] *n* peperoncino

chilly ['tʃɪlɪ] *adj* freddo(-a), fresco(-a); **to feel ~** sentirsi infreddolito(-a)

chimney ['tʃɪmnɪ] *n* camino

chimpanzee [tʃɪmpæn'zi:] *n* scimpanzé *m inv*

chin [tʃɪn] *n* mento

China ['tʃaɪnə] *n* Cina

china ['tʃaɪnə] *n* porcellana

Chinese [tʃaɪ'ni:z] *adj* cinese ▷ *n inv* cinese *m/f*; (*Ling*) cinese *m*

chip [tʃɪp] *n* (*gen pl: Culin*) patatina fritta; (*: US: also:* **potato ~**) patatina; (*of wood, glass, stone*) scheggia; (*also:* **micro~**) chip *m inv* ▷ *vt* (*cup, plate*) scheggiare; **chip**

shop n (BRIT) vedi nota nel riquadro

chiropodist [kɪˈrɔpədɪst] (BRIT) n pedicure m/f inv

chisel [ˈtʃɪzl] n cesello

chives [tʃaɪvz] npl erba cipollina

chlorine [ˈklɔːriːn] n cloro

choc-ice [ˈtʃɔkaɪs] (BRIT) gelato ricoperto al cioccolato

chocolate [ˈtʃɔklɪt] ▷ n (substance) cioccolato, cioccolata; (drink) cioccolata; (a sweet) cioccolatino

choice [tʃɔɪs] n scelta ▷ adj scelto(-a)

choir [ˈkwaɪəʳ] n coro

choke [tʃəuk] vi soffocare ▷ vt soffocare; (block): **to be ~d with** essere intasato(-a) di ▷ n (Aut) valvola dell'aria

cholesterol [kəˈlɛstərɔl] n colesterolo

choose [tʃuːz] (pt **chose,**, pp **chosen**) vt scegliere; **to ~ to do** decidere di fare; preferire fare

chop [tʃɔp] vt (wood) spaccare; (Culin: also: ~ **up**) tritare ▷ n (Culin) costoletta; **chop down** vt (tree) abbattere; **chop off** vt tagliare; **chopsticks** [ˈtʃɔpstɪks] npl bastoncini mpl cinesi

chord [kɔːd] n (Mus) accordo

chore [tʃɔːʳ] n faccenda; **household ~s** faccende fpl domestiche

chorus [ˈkɔːrəs] n coro; (repeated part of song: also fig) ritornello

chose [tʃəuz] pt of **choose**

chosen [ˈtʃəuzn] pp of **choose**

Christ [kraɪst] n Cristo

christen [ˈkrɪsn] vt battezzare; **christening** n battesimo

Christian [ˈkrɪstɪən] adj, n cristiano(-a); **Christianity** [-ˈænɪtɪ] n cristianesimo; **Christian name** n nome m (di battesimo)

Christmas [ˈkrɪsməs] n Natale m; **Merry ~!** Buon Natale!; **Christmas card** n cartolina di Natale; **Christmas carol** n canto natalizio; **Christmas Day** n il giorno di Natale; **Christmas Eve** n la vigilia di Natale; **Christmas pudding** n (esp BRIT) specie di budino con frutta secca, spezie e brandy; **Christmas tree** n albero di Natale

chrome [krəum] n cromo

chronic [ˈkrɔnɪk] adj cronico(-a)

chrysanthemum [krɪˈsænθəməm] n crisantemo

chubby [ˈtʃʌbɪ] adj paffuto(-a)

chuck [tʃʌk] (inf) vt buttare, gettare; (BRIT: also: ~ **up**) piantare; **chuck out** vt buttar fuori

chuckle [ˈtʃʌkl] vi ridere sommessamente

chum [tʃʌm] n compagno(-a)

chunk [tʃʌŋk] n pezzo

church [tʃəːtʃ] n chiesa; **churchyard** n sagrato

churn [tʃəːn] n (for butter) zangola; (for milk) bidone m

chute [ʃuːt] n (also: **rubbish ~**) canale m di scarico; (BRIT: children's slide) scivolo

chutney [ˈtʃʌtnɪ] n salsa piccante (di frutta, zucchero e spezie)

CIA (US) n abbr (= Central Intelligence Agency) CIA f

CID (BRIT) n abbr (= Criminal Investigation Department) ≈ polizia giudiziaria

cider [ˈsaɪdəʳ] n sidro

cigar [sɪˈgɑːʳ] n sigaro

cigarette [sɪgəˈrɛt] n sigaretta; **cigarette lighter** n accendino

cinema [ˈsɪnəmə] n cinema m inv

cinnamon [ˈsɪnəmən] n cannella

circle [ˈsəːkl] n cerchio; (of friends etc) circolo; (in cinema) galleria ▷ vi girare in circolo ▷ vt (surround) circondare; (move round) girare intorno a

circuit [ˈsəːkɪt] n circuito

circular [ˈsəːkjuləʳ] adj circolare ▷ n circolare f

circulate [ˈsəːkjuleɪt] vi circolare ▷ vt far circolare; **circulation** [-ˈleɪʃən] n circolazione f; (of newspaper) tiratura

circumstances [ˈsəːkəmstənsɪz] npl circostanze fpl; (financial condition) condizioni fpl finanziarie

circus [ˈsəːkəs] n circo

cite [saɪt] vt citare

citizen [ˈsɪtɪzn] n (of country) cittadino(-a); (of town) abitante m/f; **citizenship** n cittadinanza

citrus fruits [ˈsɪtrəs-] npl agrumi mpl

city [ˈsɪtɪ] n città f inv; **the C~** la Città di Londra (centro commerciale); **city centre** n centro della città; **city technology college** n (BRIT) istituto tecnico superiore (finanziato dall'industria)

civic [ˈsɪvɪk] adj civico(-a)

civil [ˈsɪvl] adj civile; **civilian** [sɪˈvɪlɪən] adj, n borghese m/f

civilization [sɪvɪlaɪˈzeɪʃən] n civiltà f inv

civilized [ˈsɪvɪlaɪzd] adj civilizzato(-a); (fig) cortese

civil: **civil law** n codice m, civile; (study) diritto civile; **civil rights** npl diritti mpl civili; **civil servant** n impiegato(-a) statale; **Civil Service** n amministrazione f

statale; **civil war** n guerra civile
CJD abbr (= Creutzfeld Jacob disease) malattia di Creutzfeldt-Jacob
claim [kleɪm] vt (assert): **to ~ (that)/to be** sostenere (che)/di essere; (credit, rights etc) rivendicare; (damages) richiedere ▷ vi (for insurance) fare una domanda d'indennizzo ▷ n pretesa; rivendicazione f; richiesta; **claim form** n (gen) modulo di richiesta; (for expenses) modulo di rimborso spese
clam [klæm] n vongola
clamp [klæmp] n pinza; morsa ▷ vt stringere con una morsa; (Aut: wheel) applicare i ceppi bloccaruote a
clan [klæn] n clan m inv
clap [klæp] vi applaudire
claret ['klærət] n vino di Bordeaux
clarify ['klærɪfaɪ] vt chiarificare, chiarire
clarinet [klærɪ'nɛt] n clarinetto
clarity ['klærɪtɪ] n clarità
clash [klæʃ] n frastuono; (fig) scontro ▷ vi scontrarsi; cozzare
clasp [klɑːsp] n (hold) stretta; (of necklace, bag) fermaglio, fibbia ▷ vt stringere
class [klɑːs] n classe f ▷ vt classificare
classic ['klæsɪk] adj classico(-a) ▷ n classico; **classical** adj classico(-a)
classification [klæsɪfɪ'keɪʃən] n classificazione f
classify ['klæsɪfaɪ] vt classificare
classmate ['klɑːsmeɪt] n compagno(-a) di classe
classroom ['klɑːsrum] n aula
classy ['klɑːsɪ] adj (inf) chic inv, elegante
clatter ['klætə'] n tintinnio; scalpitio ▷ vi tintinnare; scalpitare
clause [klɔːz] n clausola; (Ling) proposizione f
claustrophobic [klɔːstrə'fəubɪk] adj claustrofobico(-a)
claw [klɔː] n (of bird of prey) artiglio; (of lobster) pinza
clay [kleɪ] n argilla
clean [kliːn] adj pulito(-a); (clear, smooth) liscio(-a) ▷ vt pulire; **clean up** vt (also fig) ripulire; **cleaner** n (person) donna delle pulizie; **cleaner's** n (also: **dry cleaner's**) tintoria; **cleaning** n pulizia
cleanser ['klɛnzə'] n detergente m
clear [klɪə'] adj chiaro(-a); (glass etc) trasparente; (road, way) libero(-a); (conscience) pulito(-a) ▷ vt sgombrare; liberare; (table) sparecchiare; (cheque) fare la compensazione di; (Law: suspect) discolpare; (obstacle) superare ▷ vi (weather) rasserenarsi; (fog) andarsene ▷ adv **~ of** distante da; **clear away** vt (things, clothes etc) mettere a posto; **to ~ away the dishes** sparecchiare la tavola;

clear up vt mettere in ordine; (mystery) risolvere; **clearance** n (removal) sgombro; (permission) autorizzazione f, permesso; **clear-cut** adj ben delineato(-a), distinto(-a); **clearing** n radura; **clearly** adv chiaramente; **clearway** (BRIT) n strada con divieto di sosta
clench [klɛntʃ] vt stringere
clergy ['klɜːdʒɪ] n clero
clerk [klɑːk, (US) klɑːrk] n (BRIT) impiegato(-a); (US) commesso(-a)
clever ['klɛvə'] adj (mentally) intelligente; (deft, skilful) abile; (device, arrangement) ingegnoso(-a)
cliché ['kliːʃeɪ] n cliché m inv
click [klɪk] vi scattare ▷ vt (heels etc) battere; (tongue) far schioccare
client ['klaɪənt] n cliente m/f
cliff [klɪf] n scogliera scoscesa, rupe f
climate ['klaɪmɪt] n clima m
climax ['klaɪmæks] n culmine m; (sexual) orgasmo
climb [klaɪm] vi salire; (clamber) arrampicarsi ▷ vt salire; (Climbing) scalare ▷ n salita; arrampicata; scalata; **climb down** vi scendere; (BRIT fig) far marcia indietro; **climber** n rocciatore(-trice); alpinista m/f; **climbing** n alpinismo
clinch [klɪntʃ] vt (deal) concludere
cling [klɪŋ] (pt, pp **clung**) vi **to ~ (to)** aggrapparsi (a); (of clothes) aderire strettamente (a)
Clingfilm® ['klɪŋfɪlm] n pellicola trasparente (per alimenti)
clinic ['klɪnɪk] n clinica
clip [klɪp] n (for hair) forcina; (also: **paper ~**) graffetta; (TV, Cinema) sequenza ▷ vt attaccare insieme; (hair, nails) tagliare; (hedge) tosare; **clipping** n (from newspaper) ritaglio
cloak [kləuk] n mantello ▷ vt avvolgere; **cloakroom** n (for coats etc) guardaroba m inv; (BRIT: W.C.) gabinetti mpl
clock [klɔk] n orologio; **clock in** or **on** vi timbrare il cartellino (all'entrata); **clock off** or **out** vi timbrare il cartellino (all'uscita); **clockwise** adv in senso orario; **clockwork** n movimento or meccanismo a orologeria ▷ adj a molla
clog [klɔg] n zoccolo ▷ vt intasare ▷ vi (also: **~ up**) intasarsi, bloccarsi
clone [kləun] n clone m
close¹ [kləus] adj **~ (to)** vicino(-a) (a); (watch, link, relative) stretto(-a); (examination) attento(-a); (contest) combattuto(-a); (weather) afoso(-a) ▷ adv vicino, dappresso; **~ to** vicino a; **~ by, ~ at hand** a portata di mano; **a ~ friend** un amico intimo; **to have a ~ shave** (fig)

scamparla bella

close² [kləʊz] vt chiudere ▷ vi (shop etc) chiudere; (lid, door etc) chiudersi; (end) finire ▷ n (end) fine f; **what time do you ~?** a che ora chiudete?; **close down** vi cessare (definitivamente); **closed** adj chiuso(-a)

closely ['kləʊslɪ] adv (examine, watch) da vicino; (related) strettamente

closet ['klɒzɪt] n (cupboard) armadio

close-up ['kləʊsʌp] n primo piano

closing time n orario di chiusura

closure ['kləʊʒəʳ] n chiusura

clot [klɒt] n (also: **blood ~**) coagulo; (inf: idiot) scemo(-a) ▷ vi coagularsi

cloth [klɒθ] n (material) tessuto, stoffa; (rag) strofinaccio

clothes [kləʊðz] npl abiti mpl, vestiti mpl; **clothes line** n corda (per stendere il bucato); **clothes peg** (us **clothes pin**) n molletta

clothing ['kləʊðɪŋ] n = **clothes**

cloud [klaʊd] n nuvola; **cloud over** vi rannuvolarsi; (fig) offuscarsi; **cloudy** adj nuvoloso(-a); (liquid) torbido(-a)

clove [kləʊv] n chiodo di garofano; **clove of garlic** n spicchio d'aglio

clown [klaʊn] n pagliaccio ▷ vi (also: ~ **about, ~ around**) fare il pagliaccio

club [klʌb] n (society) club m inv, circolo; (weapon, Golf) mazza ▷ vt bastonare ▷ vi **to ~ together** associarsi; **~s** npl (Cards) fiori mpl; **club class** n (Aviat) classe f club inv

clue [klu:] n indizio; (in crosswords) definizione f; **I haven't a ~** non ho la minima idea

clump [klʌmp] n (of flowers, trees) gruppo; (of grass) ciuffo

clumsy ['klʌmzɪ] adj goffo(-a)

clung [klʌŋ] pt, pp of **cling**

cluster ['klʌstəʳ] n gruppo ▷ vi raggrupparsi

clutch [klʌtʃ] n (grip, grasp) presa, stretta; (Aut) frizione f ▷ vt afferrare, stringere forte

cm abbr (= centimetre) cm

Co. abbr = **county**; **company**

c/o abbr (= care of) presso

coach [kəʊtʃ] n (bus) pullman m inv; (horse-drawn, of train) carrozza; (Sport) allenatore(-trice); (tutor) chi dà ripetizioni ▷ vt allenare; dare ripetizioni a; **coach station** (BRIT) n stazione f delle corriere; **coach trip** n viaggio in pullman

coal [kəʊl] n carbone m

coalition [kəʊə'lɪʃən] n coalizione f

coarse [kɔ:s] adj (salt, sand etc) grosso(-a); (cloth, person) rozzo(-a)

coast [kəʊst] n costa ▷ vi (with cycle etc) scendere a ruota libera; **coastal** adj costiero(-a); **coastguard** n guardia costiera; **coastline** n linea costiera

coat [kəʊt] n cappotto; (of animal) pelo; (of paint) mano f ▷ vt coprire; **coat hanger** n attaccapanni m inv; **coating** n rivestimento

coax [kəʊks] vt indurre (con moine)

cob [kɒb] n see **corn**

cobbled ['kɒbld] adj **~ street** strada pavimentata a ciottoli

cobweb ['kɒbwɛb] n ragnatela

cocaine [kə'keɪn] n cocaina

cock [kɒk] n (rooster) gallo; (male bird) maschio ▷ vt (gun) armare; **cockerel** n galletto

cockney ['kɒknɪ] n cockney m/f inv (abitante dei quartieri popolari dell'East End di Londra)

cockpit ['kɒkpɪt] n abitacolo

cockroach ['kɒkrəʊtʃ] n blatta

cocktail ['kɒkteɪl] n cocktail m inv

cocoa ['kəʊkəʊ] n cacao

coconut ['kəʊkənʌt] n noce f di cocco

cod [kɒd] n merluzzo

C.O.D. abbr = **cash on delivery**

code [kəʊd] n codice m

coeducational ['kəʊɛdju'keɪʃənl] adj misto(-a)

coffee ['kɒfɪ] n caffè m inv; **coffee bar** (BRIT) n caffè m inv; **coffee bean** n grano or chicco di caffè; **coffee break** n pausa per il caffè; **coffee maker** n bollitore m per il caffè; **coffeepot** n caffettiera; **coffee shop** n ≈ caffè m inv; **coffee table** n tavolino

coffin ['kɒfɪn] n bara

cog [kɒg] n dente m

cognac ['kɒnjæk] n cognac m inv

coherent [kəʊ'hɪərənt] adj coerente

coil [kɔɪl] n rotolo; (Elec) bobina; (contraceptive) spirale f ▷ vt avvolgere

coin [kɔɪn] n moneta ▷ vt (word) coniare

coincide [kəʊɪn'saɪd] vi coincidere; **coincidence** [kəʊ'ɪnsɪdəns] n combinazione f

Coke® [kəʊk] n coca

coke [kəʊk] n coke m

colander ['kɒləndəʳ] n colino

cold [kəʊld] adj freddo(-a) ▷ n freddo; (Med) raffreddore m; **it's ~** fa freddo; **to be ~** (person) aver freddo; (object) essere freddo(-a); **to catch ~** prendere freddo; **to catch a ~** prendere un raffreddore; **in ~ blood** a sangue freddo; **cold sore** n erpete m

coleslaw ['kəʊlslɔ:] n insalata di cavolo bianco

colic ['kɒlɪk] n colica

collaborate [kəˈlæbəreɪt] vi collaborare
collapse [kəˈlæps] vi crollare ▷ n crollo; (Med) collasso
collar [ˈkɔləʳ] n (of coat, shirt) colletto; (of dog, cat) collare m; **collarbone** n clavicola
colleague [ˈkɔliːg] n collega m/f
collect [kəˈlɛkt] vt (gen) raccogliere; (as a hobby) fare collezione di; (BRIT: call and pick up) prendere; (money owed, pension) riscuotere; (donations, subscriptions) fare una colletta di ▷ vi adunarsi, riunirsi; ammucchiarsi; **to call ~** (us Tel) fare una chiamata a carico del destinatario; **collection** [kəˈlɛkʃən] n raccolta; collezione f; (for money) colletta; **collective** adj collettivo(-a) ▷ n collettivo; **collector** [kəˈlɛktəʳ] n collezionista m/f
college [ˈkɔlɪdʒ] n college m inv; (of technology etc) istituto superiore
collide [kəˈlaɪd] vi **to ~ with** scontrarsi (con)
collision [kəˈlɪʒən] n collisione f, scontro
cologne [kəˈləun] n (also: **eau de ~**) acqua di colonia
Colombia [kəˈlɔmbɪə] n Colombia; **Colombian** adj, n colombiano(-a)
colon [ˈkəulən] n (sign) due punti mpl; (Med) colon m inv
colonel [ˈkəːnl] n colonnello
colonial [kəˈləunɪəl] adj coloniale
colony [ˈkɔlənɪ] n colonia
colour etc [ˈkʌləʳ] (us **color**) n colore m ▷ vt colorare; (tint, dye) tingere; (fig: affect) influenzare ▷ vi (blush) arrossire; **colour in** vt colorare; **colour-blind** adj daltonico(-a); **coloured** adj (photo) a colori; (person) di colore; **colour film** n (for camera) pellicola a colori; **colourful** adj pieno(-a) di colore, a vivaci colori; (personality) colorato(-a); **colouring** n (substance) colorante m; (complexion) colorito; **colour television** n televisione f a colori
column [ˈkɔləm] n colonna
coma [ˈkəumə] n coma m inv
comb [kəum] n pettine m ▷ vt (hair) pettinare; (area) battere a tappeto
combat [ˈkɔmbæt] n combattimento ▷ vt combattere, lottare contro
combination [kɔmbɪˈneɪʃən] n combinazione f
combine [vb kəmˈbaɪn, n ˈkɔmbaɪn] vt **to ~ (with)** combinare (con); (one quality with another) unire (a) ▷ vi unirsi; (Chem) combinarsi ▷ n (Econ) associazione f
come [kʌm] (pt **came**, pp **come**) vi venire; arrivare; **to ~ to** (decision etc) raggiungere; **I've ~ to like him** ho cominciato a piacermi; **to ~ undone** slacciarsi; **to ~**

loose allentarsi; **come across** vt fus trovare per caso; **come along** vi (pupil, work) fare progressi; **~ along!** avanti!, andiamo!, forza!; **come back** vi ritornare; **come down** vi scendere; (prices) calare; (buildings) essere demolito(-a); **come from** vt fus venire da; provenire da; **come in** vi entrare; **come off** vi (button) staccarsi; (stain) andar via; (attempt) riuscire; **come on** vi (pupil, work, project) fare progressi; (lights) accendersi; (electricity) entrare in funzione; **~ on!** avanti!, andiamo!, forza!; **come out** vi uscire; (stain) andare via; **come round** vi (after faint, operation) riprendere conoscenza, rinvenire; **come to** vi rinvenire; **come up** vi (sun) salire; (problem) sorgere; (event) essere in arrivo; (in conversation) saltar fuori; **come up with** vt fus **he came up with an idea** venne fuori con un'idea
comeback [ˈkʌmbæk] n (Theatre etc) ritorno
comedian [kəˈmiːdɪən] n comico
comedy [ˈkɔmɪdɪ] n commedia
comet [ˈkɔmɪt] n cometa
comfort [ˈkʌmfət] n comodità f inv, benessere m; (relief) consolazione f, conforto ▷ vt consolare, confortare; **comfortable** adj comodo(-a); (financially) agiato(-a); **comfort station** (us) n gabinetti mpl
comic [ˈkɔmɪk] adj (also: **~al**) comico(-a) ▷ n comico; (BRIT: magazine) giornaletto; **comic book** (us) n giornalino (a fumetti); **comic strip** n fumetto
comma [ˈkɔmə] n virgola
command [kəˈmɑːnd] n ordine m, comando; (Mil: authority) comando; (mastery) padronanza ▷ vt comandare; **to ~ sb to do** ordinare a qn di fare; **commander** n capo; (Mil) comandante m
commemorate [kəˈmɛməreɪt] vt commemorare
commence [kəˈmɛns] vt, vi cominciare; **commencement** (us) n (Univ) cerimonia di consegna dei diplomi
commend [kəˈmɛnd] vt lodare; raccomandare
comment [ˈkɔmɛnt] n commento ▷ vi **to ~ (on)** fare commenti (su); **commentary** [ˈkɔməntərɪ] n commentario; (Sport) radiocronaca; telecronaca; **commentator** [ˈkɔmənteɪtəʳ] n commentatore(-trice); radiocronista m/f; telecronista m/f
commerce [ˈkɔməːs] n commercio
commercial [kəˈməːʃəl] adj commerciale ▷ n (TV, Radio: advertisement) pubblicità f inv; **commercial break** n intervallo pubblicitario

commission [kəˈmɪʃən] n commissione
f ▷ vt (work of art) commissionare; **out
of ~** (Naut) in disarmo; **commissioner** n
(Police) questore m

commit [kəˈmɪt] vt (act) commettere;
(to sb's care) affidare; **to ~ o.s. to do**
impegnarsi (a fare); **to ~ suicide** suicidarsi;
commitment n impegno; promessa

committee [kəˈmɪtɪ] n comitato

commodity [kəˈmɔdɪtɪ] n prodotto,
articolo

common [ˈkɔmən] adj comune; (pej)
volgare; (usual) normale ▷ n terreno
comune; **the C~s** (BRIT) ▷ npl la Camera
dei Comuni; **in ~** in comune; **commonly**
adv comunemente, usualmente;
commonplace adj banale, ordinario(-a);
Commons npl (BRIT Pol): **the (House
of) Commons** la Camera dei Comuni;
common sense n buon senso;
Commonwealth n **the Commonwealth**
il Commonwealth

● **COMMONWEALTH**

● Il **Commonwealth** è un'associazione
● di stati sovrani indipendenti e di
● alcuni territori annessi che facevano
● parte dell'antico Impero Britannico.
● Nel 1931 questi assunsero il nome
● di "Commonwealth of Nations",
● denominazione successivamente
● semplificata in "Commonwealth".
● Attualmente gli stati del
● "Commonwealth" riconoscono ancora il
● proprio capo di stato.

communal [ˈkɔmjuːnl] adj (for common
use) pubblico(-a)

commune [n ˈkɔmjuːn, vb kəˈmjuːn] n
(group) comune f ▷ vi **to ~ with** mettersi in
comunione con

communicate [kəˈmjuːnɪkeɪt] vt
comunicare, trasmettere ▷ vi **to ~ with**
comunicare (con)

communication [kəmjuːnɪˈkeɪʃən] n
comunicazione f

communion [kəˈmjuːnɪən] n (also: **Holy
C~**) comunione f

communism [ˈkɔmjunɪzəm] n
comunismo; **communist** adj, n
comunista m/f

community [kəˈmjuːnɪtɪ] n comunità f
inv; **community centre** (US **community
center**) n circolo ricreativo; **community
service** n (BRIT) ≈ lavoro sostitutivo

commute [kəˈmjuːt] vi fare il pendolare
▷ vt (Law) commutare; **commuter** n
pendolare m/f

compact [adj kəmˈpækt, n ˈkɔmpækt]
adj compatto(-a) ▷ n (also: **powder
~**) portacipria m inv; **compact disc** n
compact disc m inv; **compact disc player**
n lettore m CD inv

companion [kəmˈpænɪən] n
compagno(-a)

company [ˈkʌmpənɪ] n (also Comm,
Mil, Theatre) compagnia; **to keep sb ~**
tenere compagnia a qn; **company car**
n macchina (di proprietà) della ditta;
company director n amministratore m,
consigliere m di amministrazione

comparable [ˈkɔmpərəbl] adj simile

comparative [kəmˈpærətɪv] adj
relativo(-a); (adjective etc) comparativo(-a);
comparatively adv relativamente

compare [kəmˈpɛər] vt **to ~ sth/sb
with/to** confrontare qc/qn con/a ▷ vi
to ~ (with) reggere il confronto (con);
comparison [-ˈpærɪsn] n confronto; **in
comparison (with)** in confronto (a)

compartment [kəmˈpɑːtmənt] n
compartimento; (Rail) scompartimento; **a
non-smoking ~** uno scompartimento per
non-fumatori

compass [ˈkʌmpəs] n bussola; **~es** npl
(Math) compasso

compassion [kəmˈpæʃən] n compassione
f

compatible [kəmˈpætɪbl] adj compatibile

compel [kəmˈpɛl] vt costringere,
obbligare; **compelling** adj (fig: argument)
irresistibile

compensate [ˈkɔmpənseɪt] vt risarcire
▷ vi **to ~ for** compensare; **compensation**
[-ˈseɪʃən] n compensazione f; (money)
risarcimento

compete [kəmˈpiːt] vi (take part)
concorrere; (vie): **to ~ with** fare
concorrenza (a)

competent [ˈkɔmpɪtənt] adj competente

competition [kɔmpɪˈtɪʃən] n gara;
concorso; (Econ) concorrenza

competitive [kəmˈpetɪtɪv] adj (Econ)
concorrenziale; (sport) agonistico(-a);
(person) che ha spirito di competizione; che
ha spirito agonistico

competitor [kəmˈpetɪtər] n concorrente
m/f

complacent [kəmˈpleɪsnt] adj
compiaciuto(-a) di sé

complain [kəmˈpleɪn] vi lagnarsi,
lamentarsi; **complaint** n lamento; (in
shop etc) reclamo; (Med) malattia

complement [n ˈkɔmplɪmənt, vb
ˈkɔmplɪment] n complemento; (especially
of ship's crew etc) effettivo ▷ vt (enhance)
accompagnarsi bene a; **complementary**

[kɔmplɪˈmɛntərɪ] adj complementare
complete [kəmˈpliːt] adj completo(-a)
▷ vt completare; (a form) riempire;
completely adv completamente;
completion n completamento
complex [ˈkɔmplɛks] adj complesso(-a)
▷ n (Psych, of buildings etc) complesso
complexion [kəmˈplɛkʃən] n (of face)
carnagione f
compliance [kəmˈplaɪəns] n
acquiescenza; **in ~ with** (orders, wishes etc)
in conformità con
complicate [ˈkɔmplɪkeɪt] vt complicare;
complicated adj complicato(-a);
complication [-ˈkeɪʃən] n complicazione f
compliment [n ˈkɔmplɪmənt, vb
ˈkɔmplɪmɛnt] n complimento ▷ vt fare
un complimento a; **complimentary**
[-ˈmɛntərɪ] adj complimentoso(-a),
elogiativo(-a); (free) in omaggio
comply [kəmˈplaɪ] vi **to ~ with** assentire
a; conformarsi a
component [kəmˈpəʊnənt] adj
componente ▷ n componente m
compose [kəmˈpəʊz] vt (form): **to be ~d
of** essere composto di; (music, poem etc)
comporre; **to ~ o.s.** ricomporsi; **composer**
n (Mus) compositore(-trice); **composition**
[kɔmpəˈzɪʃən] n composizione f
composure [kəmˈpəʊʒə⁰] n calma
compound [ˈkɔmpaʊnd] n (Chem, Ling)
composto; (enclosure) recinto ▷ adj
composto(-a)
comprehension [kɔmprɪˈhɛnʃən] n
comprensione f
comprehensive [kɔmprɪˈhɛnsɪv] adj
completo(-a); **comprehensive (school)**
(BRIT) n scuola secondaria aperta a tutti

> Be careful not to translate
> **comprehensive** by the Italian word
> **comprensivo**.

compress [vb kəmˈprɛs, n ˈkɔmprɛs] vt
comprimere ▷ n (Med) compressa
comprise [kəmˈpraɪz] vt (also: **be ~d**)
comprendere
compromise [ˈkɔmprəmaɪz] n
compromesso ▷ vt compromettere ▷ vi
venire a un compromesso
compulsive [kəmˈpʌlsɪv] adj (liar, gambler)
che non riesce a controllarsi; (viewing,
reading) cui non si può fare a meno
compulsory [kəmˈpʌlsərɪ] adj
obbligatorio(-a)
computer [kəmˈpjuːtə⁰] n computer
m inv, elaboratore m elettronico;
computer game n gioco per computer;
computer-generated adj realizzato(-a)
al computer; **computerize** vt
computerizzare; **computer programmer**

n programmatore(-trice); **computer
programming** n programmazione
f di computer; **computer science** n
informatica; **computer studies** npl
informatica; **computing** n informatica
con [kɔn] (inf) vt truffare ▷ n truffa
conceal [kənˈsiːl] vt nascondere
concede [kənˈsiːd] vt ammettere
conceited [kənˈsiːtɪd] adj
presuntuoso(-a), vanitoso(-a)
conceive [kənˈsiːv] vt concepire ▷ vi
concepire un bambino
concentrate [ˈkɔnsəntreɪt] vi
concentrarsi ▷ vt concentrare
concentration [kɔnsənˈtreɪʃən] n
concentrazione f
concept [ˈkɔnsɛpt] n concetto
concern [kənˈsəːn] n affare m; (Comm)
azienda, ditta; (anxiety) preoccupazione
f ▷ vt riguardare; **to be ~ed (about)**
preoccuparsi (di); **concerning** prep
riguardo a, circa
concert [ˈkɔnsət] n concerto; **concert
hall** n sala da concerti
concerto [kənˈtʃəːtəʊ] n concerto
concession [kənˈsɛʃən] n concessione f
concise [kənˈsaɪs] adj conciso(-a)
conclude [kənˈkluːd] vt concludere;
conclusion [-ˈkluːʒən] n conclusione f
concrete [ˈkɔŋkriːt] n calcestruzzo ▷ adj
concreto(-a), di calcestruzzo
concussion [kənˈkʌʃən] n commozione
f cerebrale
condemn [kənˈdɛm] vt condannare;
(building) dichiarare pericoloso(-a)
condensation [kɔndɛnˈseɪʃən] n
condensazione f
condense [kənˈdɛns] vi condensarsi ▷ vt
condensare
condition [kənˈdɪʃən] n condizione f;
(Med) malattia ▷ vt condizionare; **on ~
that** a condizione che + sub, a condizione
di; **conditional** adj condizionale; **to
be conditional upon** dipendere da;
conditioner n (for hair) balsamo; (for
fabrics) ammorbidente m
condo [ˈkɔndəʊ] (US) n abbr (inf)
= **condominium**
condom [ˈkɔndəm] n preservativo
condominium [kɔndəˈmɪnɪəm] (US) n
condominio
condone [kənˈdəʊn] vt condonare
conduct [n ˈkɔndʌkt, vb kənˈdʌkt]
n condotta ▷ vt condurre; (manage)
dirigere; amministrare; (Mus) dirigere;
to ~ o.s. comportarsi; **conducted tour**
[kənˈdʌktɪd-] n gita accompagnata;
conductor n (of orchestra) direttore m
d'orchestra; (on bus) bigliettaio; (US: on

train) controllore *m*; (*Elec*) conduttore *m*
cone [kəʊn] *n* cono; (*Bot*) pigna; (*traffic cone*) birillo
confectionery [kənˈfɛkʃənrɪ] *n* dolciumi *mpl*
confer [kənˈfəːˈ] *vt* **to ~ sth on** conferire qc a ▷ *vi* conferire
conference [ˈkɒnfərns] *n* congresso
confess [kənˈfɛs] *vt* confessare, ammettere ▷ *vi* confessare; **confession** [kənˈfɛʃən] *n* confessione *f*
confide [kənˈfaɪd] *vi* **to ~ in** confidarsi con
confidence [ˈkɒnfɪdns] *n* confidenza; (*trust*) fiducia; (*self-assurance*) sicurezza di sé; **in ~** (*speak, write*) in confidenza, confidenzialmente; **confident** *adj* sicuro(-a), sicuro(-a) di sé; **confidential** [kɒnfɪˈdɛnʃəl] *adj* riservato(-a), confidenziale
confine [kənˈfaɪn] *vt* limitare; (*shut up*) rinchiudere; **confined** *adj* (*space*) ristretto(-a)
confirm [kənˈfəːm] *vt* confermare; **confirmation** [kɒnfəˈmeɪʃən] *n* conferma; (*Rel*) cresima
confiscate [ˈkɒnfɪskeɪt] *vt* confiscare
conflict [*n* ˈkɒnflɪkt, *vb* kənˈflɪkt] *n* conflitto ▷ *vi* essere in conflitto
conform [kənˈfɔːm] *vi* **to ~ to** conformarsi (a)
confront [kənˈfrʌnt] *vt* (*enemy, danger*) affrontare; **confrontation** [kɒnfrənˈteɪʃən] *n* scontro
confuse [kənˈfjuːz] *vt* (*one thing with another*) confondere; **confused** *adj* confuso(-a); **confusing** *adj* che fa confondere; **confusion** [-ˈfjuːʒən] *n* confusione *f*
congestion [kənˈdʒɛstʃən] *n* congestione *f*
congratulate [kənˈgrætjuleɪt] *vt* **to ~ sb (on)** congratularsi con qn (per or di); **congratulations** [-ˈleɪʃənz] *npl* auguri *mpl*; (*on success*) complimenti *mpl*, congratulazioni *fpl*
congregation [kɒŋgrɪˈgeɪʃən] *n* congregazione *f*
congress [ˈkɒŋgrɛs] *n* congresso; **congressman** (*irreg*: US) *n* membro del Congresso; **congresswoman** (*irreg*: US) *n* (donna) membro del Congresso
conifer [ˈkɒnɪfəˈ] *n* conifero
conjugate [ˈkɒndʒugeɪt] *vt* coniugare
conjugation [kɒndʒəˈgeɪʃən] *n* coniugazione *f*
conjunction [kənˈdʒʌŋkʃən] *n* congiunzione *f*
conjure [ˈkʌndʒəˈ] *vi* fare giochi di prestigio

connect [kəˈnɛkt] *vt* connettere, collegare; (*Elec, Tel*) collegare; (*fig*) associare ▷ *vi* (*train*): **to ~ with** essere in coincidenza con; **to be ~ed with** (*associated*) aver rapporti con; **connecting flight** *n* volo in coincidenza; **connection** [-ʃən] ▷ *n* relazione *f*, rapporto; (*Elec*) connessione *f*; (*train, plane*) coincidenza; (*Tel*) collegamento
conquer [ˈkɒŋkəˈ] *vt* conquistare; (*feelings*) vincere
conquest [ˈkɒŋkwɛst] *n* conquista
cons [kɒnz] *npl see* **convenience**; **pro**
conscience [ˈkɒnʃəns] *n* coscienza
conscientious [kɒnʃɪˈɛnʃəs] *adj* coscienzioso(-a)
conscious [ˈkɒnʃəs] *adj* consapevole; (*Med*) cosciente; **consciousness** *n* consapevolezza; coscienza
consecutive [kənˈsɛkjutɪv] *adj* consecutivo(-a); **on 3 ~ occasions** 3 volte di fila
consensus [kənˈsɛnsəs] *n* consenso; **the ~ of opinion** l'opinione *f* unanime *or* comune
consent [kənˈsɛnt] *n* consenso ▷ *vi* **to ~ (to)** acconsentire (a)
consequence [ˈkɒnsɪkwəns] *n* conseguenza, risultato; importanza
consequently [ˈkɒnsɪkwəntlɪ] *adv* di conseguenza, dunque
conservation [kɒnsəˈveɪʃən] *n* conservazione *f*
conservative [kənˈsəːvətɪv] *adj* conservatore(-trice); (*cautious*) cauto(-a); **Conservative** (BRIT) *adj, n* (*Pol*) conservatore(-trice)
conservatory [kənˈsəːvətrɪ] *n* (*greenhouse*) serra; (*Mus*) conservatorio
consider [kənˈsɪdəˈ] *vt* considerare; (*take into account*) tener conto di; **to ~ doing sth** considerare la possibilità di fare qc; **considerable** [kənˈsɪdərəbl] *adj* considerevole, notevole; **considerably** *adv* notevolmente, decisamente; **considerate** [kənˈsɪdərɪt] *adj* premuroso(-a); **consideration** [kənsɪdəˈreɪʃən] *n* considerazione *f*; **considering** [kənˈsɪdərɪŋ] *prep* in considerazione di
consignment [kənˈsaɪnmənt] *n* (*of goods*) consegna; spedizione *f*
consist [kənˈsɪst] *vi* **to ~ of** constare di, essere composto(-a) di
consistency [kənˈsɪstənsɪ] *n* consistenza; (*fig*) coerenza
consistent [kənˈsɪstənt] *adj* coerente
consolation [kɒnsəˈleɪʃən] *n* consolazione *f*
console[1] [kənˈsəʊl] *vt* consolare

console² ['kɔnsəul] n quadro di comando
consonant ['kɔnsənənt] n consonante f
conspicuous [kən'spɪkjuəs] adj
cospicuo(-a)
conspiracy [kən'spɪrəsɪ] n congiura,
cospirazione f
constable ['kʌnstəbl] (BRIT) n ≈ poliziotto,
agente m di polizia; **chief ~** ≈ questore m
constant ['kɔnstənt] adj costante,
continuo(-a); **constantly** adv
costantemente; continuamente
constipated ['kɔnstɪpeɪtɪd] adj
stitico(-a); **constipation** [kɔnstɪ'peɪʃən]
n stitichezza
constituency [kən'stɪtjuənsɪ] n collegio
elettorale
constitute ['kɔnstɪtju:t] vt costituire
constitution [kɔnstɪ'tju:ʃən] n
costituzione f
constraint [kən'streɪnt] n costrizione f
construct [kən'strʌkt] vt costruire;
construction [-ʃən] n costruzione f;
constructive adj costruttivo(-a)
consul ['kɔnsl] n console m; **consulate**
['kɔnsjulɪt] n consolato
consult [kən'sʌlt] vt consultare;
consultant n (Med) consulente m medico;
(other specialist) consulente; **consultation**
[-'teɪʃən] n (Med) consulto; (discussion)
consultazione f; **consulting room**
[kən'sʌltɪŋ-] (BRIT) n ambulatorio
consume [kən'sju:m] vt consumare;
consumer n consumatore(-trice)
consumption [kən'sʌmpʃən] n consumo
cont. abbr = **continued**
contact ['kɔntækt] n contatto; (person)
conoscenza ▷ vt mettersi in contatto con;
contact lenses npl lenti fpl a contatto
contagious [kən'teɪdʒəs] adj (also fig)
contagioso(-a)
contain [kən'teɪn] vt contenere; **to ~ o.s.**
contenersi; **container** n recipiente m; (for
shipping etc) container m inv
contaminate [kən'tæmɪneɪt] vt
contaminare
cont'd abbr = **continued**
contemplate ['kɔntəmpleɪt] vt
contemplare; (consider) pensare a (or di)
contemporary [kən'tempərərɪ] adj, n
contemporaneo(-a)
contempt [kən'tempt] n disprezzo; **~ of
court** (Law) oltraggio alla Corte
contend [kən'tend] vt **to ~ that** sostenere
che ▷ vi **to ~ with** lottare contro
content¹ ['kɔntent] n contenuto; **~s** npl
(of box, case etc) contenuto; **(table of) ~s**
indice m
content² [kən'tent] adj contento(-a),
soddisfatto(-a) ▷ vt contentare,

soddisfare; **contented** adj contento(-a),
soddisfatto(-a)
contest [n 'kɔntest, vb kən'test] n
lotta; (competition) gara, concorso
▷ vt contestare; impugnare; (compete
for) essere in lizza per; **contestant**
[kən'testənt] n concorrente m/f; (in fight)
avversario(-a)
context ['kɔntekst] n contesto
continent ['kɔntɪnənt] n continente
m; **the C~** (BRIT) l'Europa continentale;
continental [-'nentl] adj continentale;
continental breakfast n colazione f
all'europea (senza piatti caldi); **continental
quilt** (BRIT) n piumino
continual [kən'tɪnjuəl] adj continuo(-a);
continually adv di continuo
continue [kən'tɪnju:] vi continuare ▷ vt
continuare; (start again) riprendere
continuity [kɔntɪ'nju:ɪtɪ] n continuità;
(TV, Cinema) (ordine m della) sceneggiatura
continuous [kən'tɪnjuəs] adj
continuo(-a), ininterrotto(-a); **continuous
assessment** n (BRIT) valutazione f
continua; **continuously** adv (repeatedly)
continuamente; (uninterruptedly)
ininterrottamente
contour ['kɔntuəʳ] n contorno, profilo;
(also: ~ line) curva di livello
contraception [kɔntrə'sepʃən] n
contraccezione f
contraceptive [kɔntrə'septɪv] adj
contraccettivo(-a) ▷ n contraccettivo
contract [n 'kɔntrækt, vb kən'trækt] n
contratto ▷ vi (become smaller) contrarsi;
(Comm): **to ~ to do sth** fare un contratto
per fare qc ▷ vt (illness) contrarre;
contractor n imprenditore m
contradict [kɔntrə'dɪkt] vt contraddire;
contradiction [kɔntrə'dɪkʃən] n
contraddizione f; **to be in contradiction
with** discordare con
contrary¹ ['kɔntrərɪ] adj contrario(-a);
(unfavourable) avverso(-a), contrario(-a)
▷ n contrario; **on the ~** al contrario;
unless you hear to the ~ salvo
contrordine
contrary² [kən'treərɪ] adj (perverse)
bisbetico(-a)
contrast [n 'kɔntrɑ:st, vb kən'trɑ:st] n
contrasto ▷ vt mettere in contrasto; **in ~
to** contrariamente a
contribute [kən'trɪbju:t] vi contribuire
▷ vt **to ~ £10/an article to** dare
10 sterline/un articolo a; **to ~ to**
contribuire a; (newspaper) scrivere
per; **contribution** [kɔntrɪ'bju:ʃən] n
contributo; **contributor** n (to newspaper)
collaboratore(-trice)

control [kən'trəʊl] vt controllare; (firm, operation etc) dirigere ▷ n controllo; **~s** npl (of vehicle etc) comandi mpl; (governmental) controlli mpl; **under ~** sotto controllo; **to be in ~ of** avere il controllo di; **to go out of ~** (car) non rispondere ai comandi; (situation) sfuggire di mano; **control tower** n (Aviat) torre f di controllo

controversial [kɒntrə'vəːʃl] adj controverso(-a), polemico(-a)

controversy ['kɒntrəvəːsɪ] n controversia, polemica

convenience [kən'viːnɪəns] n comodità f inv; **at your ~** a suo comodo; **all modern ~s** (BRIT), **all mod cons** tutte le comodità moderne

convenient [kən'viːnɪənt] adj comodo(-a)

> Be careful not to translate convenient by the Italian word conveniente.

convent ['kɒnvənt] n convento

convention [kən'vɛnʃən] n convenzione f; (meeting) convegno; **conventional** adj convenzionale

conversation [kɒnvə'seɪʃən] n conversazione f

conversely [kɒn'vəːslɪ] adv al contrario, per contro

conversion [kən'vəːʃən] n conversione f; (BRIT: of house) trasformazione f, rimodernamento

convert [vb kən'vəːt, n 'kɒnvəːt] vt (Comm, Rel) convertire; (alter) trasformare ▷ n convertito(-a); **convertible** n macchina decappottabile

convey [kən'veɪ] vt trasportare; (thanks) comunicare; (idea) dare; **conveyor belt** [kən'veɪə'-] n nastro trasportatore

convict [vb kən'vɪkt, n 'kɒnvɪkt] vt dichiarare colpevole ▷ n carcerato(-a); **conviction** [-ʃən] n condanna; (belief) convinzione f

convince [kən'vɪns] vt convincere, persuadere; **convinced** adj **convinced of/that** convinto(-a) di/che; **convincing** adj convincente

convoy ['kɒnvɔɪ] n convoglio

cook [kʊk] vt cucinare, cuocere ▷ vi cuocere; (person) cucinare ▷ n cuoco(-a); **cook book** n libro di cucina; **cooker** n fornello, cucina; **cookery** n cucina; **cookery book** (BRIT) n = **cook book**; **cookie** (US) n biscotto; **cooking** n cucina

cool [kuːl] adj fresco(-a); (not afraid, calm) calmo(-a); (unfriendly) freddo(-a) ▷ vt raffreddare; (room) rinfrescare ▷ vi (water) raffreddarsi; (air) rinfrescarsi; **cool down** vi raffreddarsi; (fig: person, situation) calmarsi; **cool off** vi (become

calmer) calmarsi; (lose enthusiasm) perdere interesse

cop [kɒp] (inf) n sbirro

cope [kəʊp] vi **to ~ with** (problems) far fronte a

copper ['kɒpə'] n rame m; (inf: policeman) sbirro

copy ['kɒpɪ] n copia ▷ vt copiare; **copyright** n diritto d'autore

coral ['kɒrəl] n corallo

cord [kɔːd] n corda; (Elec) filo; **~s** npl (trousers) calzoni mpl (di velluto) a coste; **cordless** adj senza cavo

corduroy ['kɔːdərɔɪ] n fustagno

core [kɔː'] n (of fruit) torsolo; (of organization etc) cuore m ▷ vt estrarre il torsolo da

coriander [kɒrɪ'ændə'] n coriandolo

cork [kɔːk] n sughero; (of bottle) tappo; **corkscrew** n cavatappi m inv

corn [kɔːn] n (BRIT: wheat) grano; (US: maize) granturco; (on foot) callo; **~ on the cob** (Culin) pannocchia cotta

corned beef ['kɔːnd-] n carne f di manzo in scatola

corner ['kɔːnə'] n angolo; (Aut) curva ▷ vt intrappolare; mettere con le spalle al muro; (Comm: market) accaparrare ▷ vi prendere una curva

corner shop (BRIT) n piccolo negozio di generi alimentari

cornflakes ['kɔːnfleɪks] npl fiocchi mpl di granturco

cornflour ['kɔːnflaʊə'] (BRIT) n farina finissima di granturco

cornstarch ['kɔːnstɑːtʃ] (US) n = **cornflour**

Cornwall ['kɔːnwəl] n Cornovaglia

coronary ['kɒrənərɪ] n **~ (thrombosis)** trombosi f coronaria

coronation [kɒrə'neɪʃən] n incoronazione f

coroner ['kɒrənə'] n magistrato incaricato di indagare la causa di morte in circostanze sospette

corporal ['kɔːpərl] n caporalmaggiore m ▷ adj **~ punishment** pena corporale

corporate ['kɔːpərɪt] adj costituito(-a) (in corporazione), comune

corporation [kɔːpə'reɪʃən] n (of town) consiglio comunale; (Comm) ente m

corps [kɔː, pl kɔːz] n inv corpo

corpse [kɔːps] n cadavere m

correct [kə'rɛkt] adj (accurate) corretto(-a), esatto(-a); (proper) corretto(-a) ▷ vt correggere; **correction** [-ʃən] n correzione f

correspond [kɒrɪs'pɒnd] vi corrispondere; **correspondence** n corrispondenza; **correspondent** n corrispondente m/f; **corresponding** adj corrispondente

corridor ['kɔrɪdɔːʳ] n corridoio

corrode [kə'rəʊd] vt corrodere ▷ vi corrodersi

corrupt [kə'rʌpt] adj corrotto(-a); (Comput) alterato(-a) ▷ vt corrompere; **corruption** n corruzione f

Corsica ['kɔːsɪkə] n Corsica

cosmetic [kɔz'metɪk] n cosmetico ▷ adj (fig: measure etc) superficiale; **cosmetic surgery** n chirurgia plastica

cosmopolitan [kɔzmə'pɔlɪtn] adj cosmopolita

cost [kɔst] (pt, pp **cost**) n costo ▷ vt costare; (find out the cost of) stabilire il prezzo di; **~s** npl (Comm, Law) spese fpl; **how much does it ~?** quanto costa?; **at all ~s** a ogni costo

co-star ['kəʊstɑːʳ] n attore/trice della stessa importanza del protagonista

Costa Rica ['kɔstə'riːkə] n Costa Rica

costly ['kɔstlɪ] adj costoso(-a), caro(-a)

cost of living adj **~ allowance** indennità f inv di contingenza

costume ['kɔstjuːm] n costume m; (lady's suit) tailleur m inv; (BRIT: also: **swimming ~**) costume m da bagno

cosy ['kəʊzɪ] (US **cozy**) adj intimo(-a); **I'm very ~ here** sto proprio bene qui

cot [kɔt] n (BRIT: child's) lettino; (US: campbed) brandina

cottage ['kɔtɪdʒ] n cottage m inv; **cottage cheese** n fiocchi mpl di latte magro

cotton ['kɔtn] n cotone m; **cotton on** vi (inf): **to ~ on (to sth)** afferrare (qc); **cotton bud** n (BRIT) cotton fioc® m inv; **cotton candy** (US) n zucchero filato; **cotton wool** (BRIT) n cotone idrofilo

couch [kautʃ] n sofà m inv

cough [kɔf] vi tossire ▷ n tosse f; **I've got a ~** ho la tosse; **cough mixture, cough syrup** n sciroppo per la tosse

could [kud] pt of **can²**

couldn't = **could not**

council ['kaunsl] n consiglio; **city or town ~** consiglio comunale; **council estate** (BRIT) n quartiere m di case popolari; **council house** (BRIT) n casa popolare; **councillor** (US **councilor**) n consigliere(-a); **council tax** n (BRIT) tassa comunale sulla proprietà

counsel ['kaunsl] n avvocato; consultazione f ▷ vt consigliare; **counselling** (US **counseling**) n (Psych) assistenza psicologica; **counsellor** (US **counselor**) n consigliere(-a); (US) avvocato

count [kaunt] vt, vi contare ▷ n (of votes etc) conteggio; (of pollen etc) livello; (nobleman) conte m; **count in** (inf) vt includere; **~ me**

in ci sto anch'io; **count on** vt fus contare su; **countdown** n conto alla rovescia

counter ['kauntəʳ] n banco ▷ vt opporsi a ▷ adv **~ to** contro; in opposizione a; **counter clockwise** [-'klɔkwaɪz] (US) adv in senso antiorario

counterfeit ['kauntəfɪt] n contraffazione f, falso ▷ vt contraffare, falsificare ▷ adj falso(-a)

counterpart ['kauntəpɑːt] n (of document etc) copia; (of person) corrispondente m/f

countess ['kauntɪs] n contessa

countless ['kauntlɪs] adj innumerevole

country ['kʌntrɪ] n paese m; (native land) patria; (as opposed to town) campagna; (region) regione f; **country and western (music)** n musica country e western, country m; **country house** n villa in campagna; **countryside** n campagna

county ['kauntɪ] n contea

coup [kuː] (pl **coups**) n colpo; (also: **~ d'état**) colpo di Stato

couple ['kʌpl] n coppia; **a ~ of** un paio di

coupon ['kuːpɔn] n buono; (detachable form) coupon m inv

courage ['kʌrɪdʒ] n coraggio; **courageous** adj coraggioso(-a)

courgette [kuə'ʒet] (BRIT) n zucchina

courier ['kurɪəʳ] n corriere m; (for tourists) guida

course [kɔːs] n corso; (of ship) rotta; (for golf) campo; (part of meal) piatto; **of ~** senz'altro, naturalmente; **~ of action** modo d'agire; **a ~ of treatment** (Med) una cura

court [kɔːt] n corte f; (Tennis) campo ▷ vt (woman) fare la corte a; **to take to ~** citare in tribunale

courtesy ['kəːtəsɪ] n cortesia; **(by) ~ of** per gentile concessione di; **courtesy bus, courtesy coach** n autobus m inv gratuito (di hotel, aeroporto)

court: **court-house** (US) n palazzo di giustizia; **courtroom** n tribunale m; **courtyard** n cortile m

cousin ['kʌzn] n cugino(-a); **first ~** cugino di primo grado

cover ['kʌvəʳ] vt coprire; (book, table) rivestire; (include) comprendere; (Press) fare un servizio su ▷ n (of pan) coperchio; (over furniture) fodera; (of bed) copriletto; (of book) copertina; (shelter) riparo; (Comm, Insurance, of spy) copertura; **~s** npl (on bed) lenzuola fpl e coperte fpl; **to take ~** (shelter) ripararsi; **under ~** al riparo; **under ~ of darkness** protetto dall'oscurità; **under separate ~** (Comm) a parte, in plico separato; **cover up** vi **to ~ up for sb** coprire qn; **coverage** n (Press, Radio,

TV): **to give full coverage to sth** fare un ampio servizio su qc; **cover charge** n coperto; **cover-up** n occultamento (di informazioni)

cow [kau] n vacca ▷ vt *(person)* intimidire

coward ['kauəd] n vigliacco(-a); **cowardly** adj vigliacco(-a)

cowboy ['kaubɔɪ] n cow-boy m inv

cozy ['kəuzɪ] *(us)* adj = **cosy**

crab [kræb] n granchio

crack [kræk] n fessura, crepa; incrinatura; *(noise)* schiocco; *(: of gun)* scoppio; *(drug)* crack m inv ▷ vt spaccare; incrinare; *(whip)* schioccare; *(nut)* schiacciare; *(problem)* risolvere; *(code)* decifrare ▷ adj *(troops)* fuori classe; **to ~ a joke** fare una battuta; **crack down on** vt fus porre freno a; **cracked** adj *(inf)* matto(-a); **cracker** n cracker m inv; petardo

crackle ['krækl] vi crepitare

cradle ['kreɪdl] n culla

craft [krɑːft] n mestiere m; *(cunning)* astuzia; *(boat)* naviglio; **craftsman** *(irreg)* n artigiano; **craftsmanship** n abilità

cram [kræm] vt *(fill)*: **to ~ sth with** riempire qc di; *(put)*: **to ~ sth into** stipare qc in ▷ vi *(for exams)* prepararsi (in gran fretta)

cramp [kræmp] n crampo; **I've got ~ in my leg** ho un crampo alla gamba; **cramped** adj ristretto(-a)

cranberry ['krænbərɪ] n mirtillo

crane [kreɪn] n gru f inv

crap [kræp] n *(inf!)* fesserie fpl; **to have a ~** cacare (!)

crash [kræʃ] n fragore m; *(of car)* incidente m; *(of plane)* caduta; *(of business etc)* crollo ▷ vt fracassare ▷ vi *(plane)* fracassarsi; *(car)* avere un incidente; *(two cars)* scontrarsi; *(business etc)* fallire, andare in rovina; **crash course** n corso intensivo; **crash helmet** n casco

crate [kreɪt] n cassa

crave [kreɪv] vt, vi **to ~ (for)** desiderare ardentemente

crawl [krɔːl] vi strisciare carponi; *(vehicle)* avanzare lentamente ▷ n *(Swimming)* crawl m

crayfish ['kreɪfɪʃ] n inv *(freshwater)* gambero (d'acqua dolce); *(saltwater)* gambero

crayon ['kreɪən] n matita colorata

craze [kreɪz] n mania

crazy ['kreɪzɪ] adj matto(-a); *(inf: keen)*: **~ about sb** pazzo(-a) di qn; **~ about sth** matto(-a) per qc

creak [kriːk] vi cigolare, scricchiolare

cream [kriːm] n crema; *(fresh)* panna ▷ adj *(colour)* color crema inv; **cream cheese** n formaggio fresco; **creamy** adj cremoso(-a)

crease [kriːs] n grinza; *(deliberate)* piega ▷ vt sgualcire ▷ vi sgualcirsi

create [kriːˈeɪt] vt creare; **creation** [-ʃən] n creazione f; **creative** adj creativo(-a); **creator** n creatore(-trice)

creature ['kriːtʃə*] n creatura

crèche [krɛʃ] n asilo infantile

credentials [krɪˈdɛnʃlz] npl credenziali fpl

credibility [krɛdɪˈbɪlɪtɪ] n credibilità

credible ['krɛdɪbl] adj credibile; *(witness, source)* attendibile

credit ['krɛdɪt] n credito; onore m ▷ vt *(Comm)* accreditare; *(believe: also: **give ~ to**)* credere, prestar fede a; **~s** *(Cinema)* titoli mpl; **to ~ sb with** *(fig)* attribuire a qn; **to be in ~** *(person)* essere creditore(-trice); *(bank account)* essere coperto(-a); **credit card** n carta di credito; **do you take credit cards?** accettate carte di credito?

creek [kriːk] n insenatura; *(us)* piccolo fiume m

creep [kriːp] *(pt, pp crept)* vi avanzare furtivamente (o pian piano)

cremate [krɪˈmeɪt] vt cremare

crematorium [krɛməˈtɔːrɪəm] *(pl **crematoria**)* n forno crematorio

crept [krɛpt] pt, pp of **creep**

crescent ['krɛsnt] n *(shape)* mezzaluna; *(street)* strada semicircolare

cress [krɛs] n crescione m

crest [krɛst] n cresta; *(of coat of arms)* cimiero

crew [kruː] n equipaggio; **crew-neck** n girocollo

crib [krɪb] n culla ▷ vt *(inf)* copiare

cricket ['krɪkɪt] n *(insect)* grillo; *(game)* cricket m; **cricketer** n giocatore m di cricket

crime [kraɪm] n crimine m; **criminal** ['krɪmɪnl] adj, n criminale m/f

crimson ['krɪmzn] adj color cremisi inv

cringe [krɪndʒ] vi acquattarsi; *(in embarrassment)* sentirsi sprofondare

cripple ['krɪpl] n zoppo(-a) ▷ vt azzoppare

crisis ['kraɪsɪs] *(pl crises)* n crisi f inv

crisp [krɪsp] adj croccante; *(fig)* frizzante; vivace; deciso(-a); **crispy** adj croccante

criterion [kraɪˈtɪərɪən] *(pl criteria)* n criterio

critic ['krɪtɪk] n critico; **critical** adj critico(-a); **criticism** ['krɪtɪsɪzm] n critica; **criticize** ['krɪtɪsaɪz] vt criticare

Croat ['krəuæt] adj, n = **Croatian**

Croatia [krəuˈeɪʃə] n Croazia; **Croatian** adj croato(-a) ▷ n croato(-a); *(Ling)* croato

crockery ['krɔkərɪ] n vasellame m

crocodile ['krɔkədaɪl] n coccodrillo

crocus ['krəʊkəs] n croco
croissant ['krwas] n brioche f inv,
croissant m inv
crook [kruk] n truffatore m; (of shepherd)
bastone m; **crooked** ['krukɪd] adj
curvo(-a), storto(-a); (action) disonesto(-a)
crop [krɔp] n (produce) coltivazione f;
(amount produced) raccolto; (riding crop)
frustino ▷ vt (hair) rapare; **crop up** vi
presentarsi
cross [krɔs] n croce f; (Biol) incrocio ▷ vt
(street etc) attraversare; (arms, legs, Biol)
incrociare; (cheque) sbarrare ▷ adj di
cattivo umore; **cross off** vt cancellare
(tirando una riga con la penna); **cross out**
vt cancellare; **cross over** vi attraversare;
cross-Channel ferry ['krɔs'tʃænl-] n
traghetto che attraversa la Manica;
crosscountry (race) n cross-country
m inv; **crossing** n incrocio; (sea passage)
traversata; (also: **pedestrian crossing**)
passaggio pedonale; **how long does the
crossing take?** quanto dura la traversata?;
crossing guard (us) n dipendente comunale
che aiuta i bambini ad attraversare la strada;
crossroads n incrocio; **crosswalk** (us) n
strisce fpl pedonali, passaggio pedonale;
crossword n cruciverba m inv
crotch [krɔtʃ] n (Anat) inforcatura; (of
garment) pattina
crouch [krautʃ] vi acquattarsi;
rannicchiarsi
crouton ['kru:tɔn] n crostino
crow [krəʊ] n (bird) cornacchia; (of cock)
canto del gallo ▷ vi (cock) cantare
crowd [kraud] n folla ▷ vt affollare, stipare
▷ vi **to ~ round/in** affollarsi intorno a/in;
crowded adj affollato(-a); **crowded with**
stipato(-a) di
crown [kraun] n corona; (of head) calotta
cranica; (of hat) cocuzzolo; (of hill) cima
▷ vt incoronare; (fig: career) coronare;
crown jewels npl gioielli mpl della Corona
crucial ['kru:ʃl] adj cruciale, decisivo(-a)
crucifix ['kru:sɪfɪks] n crocifisso
crude [kru:d] adj (materials) greggio(-a),
non raffinato(-a); (fig: basic) crudo(-a),
primitivo(-a); (: vulgar) rozzo(-a),
grossolano(-a); **crude (oil)** n (petrolio)
greggio
cruel ['kruəl] adj crudele; **cruelty** n
crudeltà f inv
cruise [kru:z] n crociera ▷ vi andare a
velocità di crociera; (taxi) circolare
crumb [krʌm] n briciola
crumble ['krʌmbl] vt sbriciolare ▷ vi
sbriciolarsi; (plaster etc) sgretolarsi; (land,
earth) franare; (building, fig) crollare
crumpet ['krʌmpɪt] n specie di frittella

crumple ['krʌmpl] vt raggrinzare,
spiegazzare
crunch [krʌntʃ] vt sgranocchiare;
(underfoot) scricchiolare ▷ n (fig) punto or
momento cruciale; **crunchy** adj croccante
crush [krʌʃ] n folla; (love): **to have a ~ on
sb** avere una cotta per qn; (drink): **lemon
~** spremuta di limone ▷ vt schiacciare;
(crumple) sgualcire
crust [krʌst] n crosta; **crusty** adj (bread)
croccante; (person) brontolone(-a);
(remark) brusco(-a)
crutch [krʌtʃ] n gruccia
cry [kraɪ] vi piangere; (shout) urlare ▷ n
urlo, grido; **cry out** vi, vt gridare
crystal ['krɪstl] n cristallo
cub [kʌb] n cucciolo; (also: **~ scout**) lupetto
Cuba ['kju:bə] n Cuba
Cuban ['kju:bən] adj, n cubano(-a)
cube [kju:b] n cubo ▷ vt (Math) elevare al
cubo; **cubic** adj cubico(-a); (metre, foot)
cubo(-a)
cubicle ['kju:bɪkl] n scompartimento
separato; cabina
cuckoo ['kuku:] n cucù m inv
cucumber ['kju:kʌmbəʳ] n cetriolo
cuddle ['kʌdl] vt abbracciare, coccolare
▷ vi abbracciarsi
cue [kju:] n (snooker cue) stecca; (Theatre
etc) segnale m
cuff [kʌf] n (BRIT: of shirt, coat etc) polsino;
(US: of trousers) risvolto; **off the ~**
improvvisando; **cufflinks** npl gemelli mpl
cuisine [kwɪ'zi:n] n cucina
cul-de-sac ['kʌldəsæk] n vicolo cieco
cull [kʌl] vt (ideas etc) scegliere ▷ n (of
animals) abbattimento selettivo
culminate ['kʌlmɪneɪt] vi **to ~ in**
culminare con
culprit ['kʌlprɪt] n colpevole m/f
cult [kʌlt] n culto
cultivate ['kʌltɪveɪt] vt (also fig) coltivare
cultural ['kʌltʃərəl] adj culturale
culture ['kʌltʃəʳ] n (also fig) cultura
cumin ['kʌmɪn] n (spice) cumino
cunning ['kʌnɪŋ] n astuzia, furberia ▷ adj
astuto(-a), furbo(-a)
cup [kʌp] n tazza; (prize, of bra) coppa
cupboard ['kʌbəd] n armadio
cup final n (BRIT Football) finale f di coppa
curator [kjuə'reɪtəʳ] n direttore m (di
museo ecc)
curb [kə:b] vt tenere a freno ▷ n freno; (US)
bordo del marciapiede
curdle ['kə:dl] vi cagliare
cure [kjuəʳ] vt guarire; (Culin) trattare;
affumicare; essiccare ▷ n rimedio
curfew ['kə:fju:] n coprifuoco
curiosity [kjuərɪ'ɔsɪtɪ] n curiosità

curious ['kjʊərɪəs] *adj* curioso(-a)

curl [kɜːl] *n* riccio ▷ *vt* ondulare; *(tightly)* arricciare ▷ *vi* arricciarsi; **curl up** *vi* rannicchiarsi; **curler** *n* bigodino; **curly** ['kɜːlɪ] *adj* ricciuto(-a)

currant ['kʌrnt] *n (dried)* sultanina; *(bush, fruit)* ribes *m inv*

currency ['kʌrnsɪ] *n* moneta; **to gain ~** *(fig)* acquistare larga diffusione

current ['kʌrnt] *adj* corrente ▷ *n* corrente *f*; **current account** (BRIT) *n* conto corrente; **current affairs** *npl* attualità *fpl*; **currently** *adv* attualmente

curriculum [kə'rɪkjʊləm] *(pl* **curriculums** *or* **curricula)** *n* curriculum *m inv*; **curriculum vitae** [-'viːtaɪ] *n* curriculum vitae *m inv*

curry ['kʌrɪ] *n* curry *m inv* ▷ *vt* **to ~ favour with** cercare di attirarsi i favori di; **curry powder** *n* curry *m*

curse [kɜːs] *vt* maledire ▷ *vi* bestemmiare ▷ *n* maledizione *f*; bestemmia

cursor ['kɜːsəʳ] *n (Comput)* cursore *m*

curt [kɜːt] *adj* secco(-a)

curtain ['kɜːtn] *n* tenda; *(Theatre)* sipario

curve [kɜːv] *n* curva ▷ *vi* curvarsi; **curved** *adj* curvo(-a)

cushion ['kʊʃən] *n* cuscino ▷ *vt (shock)* fare da cuscinetto a

custard ['kʌstəd] *n (for pouring)* crema

custody ['kʌstədɪ] *n (of child)* tutela; **to take into ~** *(suspect)* mettere in detenzione preventiva

custom ['kʌstəm] *n* costume *m*, consuetudine *f*; *(Comm)* clientela

customer ['kʌstəməʳ] *n* cliente *m/f*

customized ['kʌstəmaɪzd] *adj (car etc)* fuoriserie *inv*

customs ['kʌstəmz] *npl* dogana; **customs officer** *n* doganiere *m*

cut [kʌt] *(pt, pp* **cut)** *vt* tagliare; *(shape, make)* intagliare; *(reduce)* ridurre ▷ *vi* tagliare ▷ *n* taglio; *(in salary etc)* riduzione *f*; **I've ~ myself** mi sono tagliato; **to ~ a tooth** mettere un dente; **cut back** *vt (plants)* tagliare; *(production, expenditure)* ridurre; **cut down** *vt (tree etc)* abbattere ▷ *vt fus (also: ~ down on)* ridurre; **cut off** *vt* tagliare; *(fig)* isolare; **cut out** *vt* tagliare fuori; eliminare; ritagliare; **cut up** *vt* tagliare a pezzi; **cutback** *n* riduzione *f*

cute [kjuːt] *adj (sweet)* carino(-a)

cutlery ['kʌtlərɪ] *n* posate *fpl*

cutlet ['kʌtlɪt] *n* costoletta; *(nut etc cutlet)* cotoletta vegetariana

cut: cut-price (BRIT) *adj* a prezzo ridotto; **cut-rate** (US) *adj* = **cut-price**; **cutting** ['kʌtɪŋ] *adj* tagliente ▷ *n (from newspaper)* ritaglio *(di giornale)*; *(from plant)* talea

CV *n abbr* = **curriculum vitae**

cwt *abbr* = **hundredweight(s)**

cybercafé ['saɪbəkaefeɪ] *n* cybercaffè *m inv*

cyberspace ['saɪbəspeɪs] *n* ciberspazio

cycle ['saɪkl] *n* ciclo; *(bicycle)* bicicletta ▷ *vi* andare in bicicletta; **cycle hire** *n* noleggio *m* biciclette *inv*; **cycle lane** *n* pista ciclabile; **cycle path** *n* pista ciclabile; **cycling** ['saɪklɪŋ] *n* ciclismo; **cyclist** ['saɪklɪst] *n* ciclista *m/f*

cyclone ['saɪkləʊn] *n* ciclone *m*

cylinder ['sɪlɪndəʳ] *n* cilindro

cymbal ['sɪmbl] *n* piatto

cynical ['sɪnɪkl] *adj* cinico(-a)

Cypriot ['sɪprɪət] *adj, n* cipriota *(m/f)*

Cyprus ['saɪprəs] *n* Cipro

cyst [sɪst] *n* cisti *f inv*; **cystitis** [sɪs'taɪtɪs] *n* cistite *f*

czar [zɑːʳ] *n* zar *m inv*

Czech [tʃɛk] *adj* ceco(-a) ▷ *n* ceco(-a); *(Ling)* ceco; **Czech Republic** *n* **the Czech Republic** la Repubblica Ceca

d

D [di:] n (Mus) re m

dab [dæb] vt (eyes, wound) tamponare; (paint, cream) applicare (con leggeri colpetti)

dad, daddy [dæd, 'dædɪ] n babbo, papà m inv

daffodil ['dæfədɪl] n trombone m, giunchiglia

daft [dɑ:ft] adj sciocco(-a)

dagger ['dægəʳ] n pugnale m

daily ['deɪlɪ] adj quotidiano(-a), giornaliero(-a) ▷ n quotidiano ▷ adv tutti i giorni

dairy ['dɛərɪ] n (BRIT: shop) latteria; (on farm) caseificio ▷ adj caseario(-a); **dairy produce** npl latticini mpl

daisy ['deɪzɪ] n margherita

dam [dæm] n diga ▷ vt sbarrare; costruire dighe su

damage ['dæmɪdʒ] n danno, danni mpl; (fig) danno ▷ vt danneggiare; **~s** npl (Law) danni

damn [dæm] vt condannare; (curse) maledire ▷ n (inf): **I don't give a ~** non me ne frega niente ▷ adj (inf: also: **~ed**): **this ~ ...** questo maledetto ...; **~ it!** accidenti!

damp [dæmp] adj umido(-a) ▷ n umidità, umido ▷ vt (also: **~en**: cloth, rag) inumidire, bagnare; (: enthusiasm etc) spegnere

dance [dɑ:ns] n danza, ballo; (ball) ballo ▷ vi ballare; **dance floor** n pista da ballo; **dancer** n danzatore(-trice); (professional) ballerino(-a); **dancing** ['dɑ:nsɪŋ] n danza, ballo

dandelion ['dændɪlaɪən] n dente m di leone

dandruff ['dændrəf] n forfora

Dane [deɪn] n danese m/f

danger ['deɪndʒəʳ] n pericolo; **there is a ~ of fire** c'è pericolo di incendio; **in ~** in pericolo; **he was in ~ of falling** rischiava di cadere; **dangerous** adj pericoloso(-a)

dangle ['dæŋgl] vt dondolare; (fig) far balenare ▷ vi pendolare

Danish ['deɪnɪʃ] adj danese ▷ n (Ling) danese m

dare [dɛəʳ] vt **to ~ sb to do** sfidare qn a fare ▷ vi **to ~ to do sth** osare fare qc; **I ~ say** (I suppose) immagino (che); **daring** adj audace, ardito(-a) ▷ n audacia

dark [dɑ:k] adj (night, room) buio(-a), scuro(-a); (colour, complexion) scuro(-a); (fig) cupo(-a), tetro(-a), nero(-a) ▷ n **in the ~** al buio; **in the ~ about** (fig) all'oscuro di; **after ~** a notte fatta; **darken** vt (colour) scurire ▷ vi (sky, room) oscurarsi; **darkness** n oscurità, buio; **darkroom** n camera oscura

darling ['dɑ:lɪŋ] adj caro(-a) ▷ n tesoro

dart [dɑ:t] n freccetta; (Sewing) pince f inv ▷ vi **to ~ towards** precipitarsi verso; **to ~ away/along** sfrecciare via/lungo; **dartboard** n bersaglio (per freccette); **darts** n tiro al bersaglio (con freccette)

dash [dæʃ] n (sign) lineetta; (small quantity) punta ▷ vt (missile) gettare; (hopes) infrangere ▷ vi **to ~ towards** precipitarsi verso

dashboard ['dæʃbɔːd] n (Aut) cruscotto

data ['deɪtə] npl dati mpl; **database** n base f di dati, data base m inv; **data processing** n elaborazione f (elettronica) dei dati

date [deɪt] n data; appuntamento; (fruit) dattero ▷ vt datare; (person) uscire con; **what's the ~ today?** quanti ne abbiamo oggi?; **~ of birth** data di nascita; **to ~** (until now) fino a oggi; **dated** adj passato(-a) di moda

daughter ['dɔ:təʳ] n figlia; **daughter-in-law** n nuora

daunting ['dɔ:ntɪŋ] adj non invidiabile

dawn [dɔ:n] n alba ▷ vi (day) spuntare; (fig): **it ~ed on him that ...** gli è venuto in mente che ...

day [deɪ] n giorno; (as duration) giornata; (period of time, age) tempo, epoca; **the ~ before** il giorno avanti or prima; **the ~ after, the following ~** il giorno dopo

or seguente; **the ~ after tomorrow**
dopodomani; **the ~ before yester~**
l'altroieri; **by ~** di giorno; **day-care
centre** n scuola materna; **daydream** vi
sognare a occhi aperti; **daylight** n luce f
del giorno; **day return** (BRIT) n biglietto
giornaliero di andata e ritorno; **daytime** n
giorno; **day-to-day** adj (life, organization)
quotidiano(-a); **day trip** n gita (di un
giorno)

dazed [deɪzd] adj stordito(-a)

dazzle ['dæzl] vt abbagliare; **dazzling** adj
(light) abbagliante; (colour) violento(-a);
(smile) smagliante

DC abbr (= direct current) c.c.

dead [dɛd] adj morto(-a); (numb)
intirizzito(-a); (telephone) muto(-a);
(battery) scarico(-a) ▷ adv assolutamente,
perfettamente ▷ npl **the ~** i morti; **he
was shot ~** fu colpito a morte; **~ tired**
stanco(-a) morto(-a); **to stop ~** fermarsi di
colpo; **dead end** n vicolo cieco; **deadline**
n scadenza; **deadly** adj mortale; (weapon,
poison) micidiale; **Dead Sea** n **the Dead
Sea** il mar Morto

deaf [dɛf] adj sordo(-a); **deafen** vt
assordare; **deafening** adj fragoroso(-a),
assordante

deal [di:l] (pt, pp **dealt**) n accordo; (business
deal) affare m ▷ vt (blow, cards) dare; **a
great ~ (of)** molto(-a); **deal with** vt
fus fare affari con, trattare con;
(handle) occuparsi di; (be about: book etc)
trattare di; **dealer** n commerciante
m/f; **dealings** npl (Comm) relazioni fpl;
(relations) rapporti mpl

dealt [dɛlt] pt, pp of **deal**

dean [di:n] n (Rel) decano; (Scol) preside m
di facoltà (or di collegio)

dear [dɪə^r] adj caro(-a) ▷ n **my ~** caro mio/
cara mia ▷ excl **~ me!** Dio mio!; **D~ Sir/
Madam** (in letter) Egregio Signore/Egregia
Signora; **D~ Mr/Mrs X** Gentile Signor/
Signora X; **dearly** adv (love) moltissimo;
(pay) a caro prezzo

death [dɛθ] n morte f; (Admin) decesso;
death penalty n pena di morte; **death
sentence** n condanna a morte

debate [dɪ'beɪt] n dibattito ▷ vt dibattere;
discutere

debit ['dɛbɪt] n debito ▷ vt **to ~ a sum
to sb** or **to sb's account** addebitare una
somma a qn; **debit card** n carta di debito

debris ['dɛbri:] n detriti mpl

debt [dɛt] n debito; **to be in ~** essere
indebitato(-a)

debut ['deɪbju:] n debutto

Dec. abbr (= December) dic.

decade ['dɛkeɪd] n decennio

decaffeinated [dɪ'kæfɪneɪtɪd] adj
decaffeinato(-a)

decay [dɪ'keɪ] n decadimento; (also: **tooth
~**) carie f ▷ vi (rot) imputridire

deceased [dɪ'si:st] n defunto(-a)

deceit [dɪ'si:t] n inganno; **deceive** [dɪ'si:v]
vt ingannare

December [dɪ'sɛmbə^r] n dicembre m

decency ['di:sənsɪ] n decenza

decent ['di:sənt] adj decente; (respectable)
per bene; (kind) gentile

deception [dɪ'sɛpʃən] n inganno

deceptive [dɪ'sɛptɪv] adj ingannevole

decide [dɪ'saɪd] vt (person) far prendere una
decisione a; (question, argument) risolvere,
decidere ▷ vi decidere, decidersi; **to ~ to
do/that** decidere di fare/che; **to ~ on**
decidere per

decimal ['dɛsɪməl] adj decimale ▷ n
decimale m

decision [dɪ'sɪʒən] n decisione f

decisive [dɪ'saɪsɪv] adj decisivo(-a);
(person) deciso(-a)

deck [dɛk] n (Naut) ponte m; (of bus): **top ~**
imperiale m; (record deck) piatto; (of cards)
mazzo; **deckchair** n sedia a sdraio

declaration [dɛklə'reɪʃən] n
dichiarazione f

declare [dɪ'klɛə^r] vt dichiarare

decline [dɪ'klaɪn] n (decay) declino;
(lessening) ribasso ▷ vt declinare; rifiutare
▷ vi declinare; diminuire

decorate ['dɛkəreɪt] vt (adorn, give a medal
to) decorare; (paint and paper) tinteggiare e
tappezzare; **decoration** [-'reɪʃən] n (medal
etc, adornment) decorazione f; **decorator** n
decoratore m

decrease [n 'di:kri:s, vb di:'kri:s] n
diminuzione f ▷ vt, vi diminuire

decree [dɪ'kri:] n decreto

dedicate ['dɛdɪkeɪt] vt consacrare;
(book etc) dedicare; **dedicated**
adj coscienzioso(-a); (Comput)
specializzato(-a), dedicato(-a); **dedication**
[dɛdɪ'keɪʃən] n (devotion) dedizione f; (in
book etc) dedica

deduce [dɪ'dju:s] vt dedurre

deduct [dɪ'dʌkt] vt **to ~ sth from**
dedurre qc (da); **deduction** [dɪ'dʌkʃən] n
deduzione f

deed [di:d] n azione f, atto; (Law) atto

deem [di:m] vt (formal) giudicare,
ritenere; **to ~ it wise to do** ritenere
prudente fare

deep [di:p] adj profondo(-a); **4 metres ~**
profondo(-a) 4 metri ▷ adv **spectators
stood 20 ~** c'erano 20 file di spettatori;
how ~ is the water? quanto è profonda
l'acqua?; **deep-fry** vt friggere in olio

abbondante; **deeply** adv profondamente

deer [dɪəʳ] n inv **the ~** i cervidi; **(red) ~** cervo; **(fallow) ~** daino; **roe ~** capriolo

default [dɪˈfɔːlt] n (Comput: also: **~ value**) default m inv; **by ~** (Sport) per abbandono

defeat [dɪˈfiːt] n sconfitta ▷ vt (team, opponents) sconfiggere

defect [n ˈdiːfɛkt, vb dɪˈfɛkt] n difetto ▷ vi **to ~ to the enemy** passare al nemico; **defective** [dɪˈfɛktɪv] adj difettoso(-a)

defence [dɪˈfɛns] (us **defense**) n difesa

defend [dɪˈfɛnd] vt difendere; **defendant** n imputato(-a); **defender** n difensore(-a)

defense [dɪˈfɛns] (us) n = **defence**

defensive [dɪˈfɛnsɪv] adj difensivo(-a) ▷ n **on the ~** sulla difensiva

defer [dɪˈfəːʳ] vt (postpone) differire, rinviare

defiance [dɪˈfaɪəns] n sfida; **in ~ of** a dispetto di; **defiant** [dɪˈfaɪənt] adj (attitude) di sfida; (person) ribelle

deficiency [dɪˈfɪʃənsɪ] n deficienza; carenza; **deficient** adj deficiente; insufficiente; **to be deficient in** mancare di

deficit [ˈdɛfɪsɪt] n deficit m inv

define [dɪˈfaɪn] vt definire

definite [ˈdɛfɪnɪt] adj (fixed) definito(-a), preciso(-a); (clear, obvious) ben definito(-a), esatto(-a); (Ling) determinativo(-a); **he was ~ about it** ne era sicuro; **definitely** adv indubbiamente

definition [dɛfɪˈnɪʃən] n definizione f

deflate [diːˈfleɪt] vt sgonfiare

deflect [dɪˈflɛkt] vt deflettere, deviare

defraud [dɪˈfrɔːd] vt defraudare

defrost [diːˈfrɔst] vt (fridge) disgelare

defuse [diːˈfjuːz] vt disinnescare; (fig) distendere

defy [dɪˈfaɪ] vt sfidare; (efforts etc) resistere a; **it defies description** supera ogni descrizione

degree [dɪˈgriː] n grado; (Scol) laurea (universitaria); **a first ~ in maths** una laurea in matematica; **by ~s** (gradually) gradualmente, a poco a poco; **to some ~** fino a un certo punto, in certa misura

dehydrated [diːhaɪˈdreɪtɪd] adj disidratato(-a); (milk, eggs) in polvere

de-icer [ˈdiːaɪsəʳ] n sbrinatore m

delay [dɪˈleɪ] vt ritardare ▷ vi **to ~ (in doing sth)** ritardare (a fare qc) ▷ n ritardo; **to be ~ed** subire un ritardo; (person) essere trattenuto(-a)

delegate [n ˈdɛlɪgɪt, vb ˈdɛlɪgeɪt] n delegato(-a) ▷ vt delegare

delete [dɪˈliːt] vt cancellare

deli [ˈdɛlɪ] n = **delicatessen**

deliberate [adj dɪˈlɪbərɪt, vb dɪˈlɪbəreɪt] adj (intentional) intenzionale; (slow) misurato(-a) ▷ vi deliberare, riflettere; **deliberately** adv (on purpose) deliberatamente

delicacy [ˈdɛlɪkəsɪ] n delicatezza

delicate [ˈdɛlɪkɪt] adj delicato(-a)

delicatessen [dɛlɪkəˈtɛsn] n ≈ salumeria

delicious [dɪˈlɪʃəs] adj delizioso(-a), squisito(-a)

delight [dɪˈlaɪt] n delizia, gran piacere m ▷ vt dilettare; **to take (a) ~ in** dilettarsi in; **delighted** adj **delighted (at** or **with)** contentissimo(-a) (di), felice (di); **delighted to do** felice di fare; **delightful** adj delizioso(-a), incantevole

delinquent [dɪˈlɪŋkwənt] adj, n delinquente m/f

deliver [dɪˈlɪvəʳ] vt (mail) distribuire; (goods) consegnare; (speech) pronunciare; (Med) far partorire; **delivery** n distribuzione f; consegna; (of speaker) dizione f; (Med) parto

delusion [dɪˈluːʒən] n illusione f

de luxe [dəˈlʌks] adj di lusso

delve [dɛlv] vi **to ~ into** frugare in; (subject) far ricerche in

demand [dɪˈmɑːnd] vt richiedere; (rights) rivendicare ▷ n domanda; (claim) rivendicazione f; **in ~** ricercato(-a), richiesto(-a); **on ~** a richiesta; **demanding** adj (boss) esigente; (work) impegnativo(-a)

demise [dɪˈmaɪz] n decesso

demo [ˈdɛməʊ] (inf) n abbr (= demonstration) manifestazione f

democracy [dɪˈmɔkrəsɪ] n democrazia; **democrat** [ˈdɛməkræt] n democratico(-a); **democratic** [dɛməˈkrætɪk] adj democratico(-a)

demolish [dɪˈmɔlɪʃ] vt demolire

demolition [dɛməˈlɪʃən] n demolizione f

demon [ˈdiːmən] n (also fig) demonio ▷ cpd **a ~ squash player** un mago dello squash; **a ~ driver** un guidatore folle

demonstrate [ˈdɛmənstreɪt] vt dimostrare, provare ▷ vi dimostrare, manifestare; **demonstration** [-ˈstreɪʃən] n dimostrazione f; (Pol) dimostrazione, manifestazione f; **demonstrator** n (Pol) dimostrante m/f; (Comm) dimostratore(-trice)

demote [dɪˈməʊt] vt far retrocedere

den [dɛn] n tana, covo; (room) buco

denial [dɪˈnaɪəl] n diniego; rifiuto

denim [ˈdɛnɪm] n tessuto di cotone ritorto; **~s** npl (jeans) blue jeans mpl

Denmark [ˈdɛnmɑːk] n Danimarca

denomination [dɪnɔmɪˈneɪʃən] n (money) valore m; (Rel) confessione f

denounce [dɪ'naʊns] vt denunciare
dense [dɛns] adj fitto(-a); (smoke) denso(-a); (inf: person) ottuso(-a), duro(-a)
density ['dɛnsɪtɪ] n densità f inv
dent [dɛnt] n ammaccatura ▷ vt (also: **make a ~ in**) ammaccare
dental ['dɛntl] adj dentale; **dental floss** [-flɔs] n filo interdentale; **dental surgery** n ambulatorio del dentista
dentist ['dɛntɪst] n dentista m/f
dentures ['dɛntʃəz] npl dentiera
deny [dɪ'naɪ] vt negare; (refuse) rifiutare
deodorant [diː'əʊdərənt] n deodorante m
depart [dɪ'pɑːt] vi partire; **to ~ from** (fig) deviare da
department [dɪ'pɑːtmənt] n (Comm) reparto; (Scol) sezione f, dipartimento; (Pol) ministero; **department store** n grande magazzino
departure [dɪ'pɑːtʃər] n partenza; (fig): **~ from** deviazione f da; **a new ~** una svolta (decisiva); **departure lounge** n (at airport) sala d'attesa
depend [dɪ'pɛnd] vi **to ~ on** dipendere da; (rely on) contare su; **it ~s** dipende; **~ing on the result ...** a seconda del risultato ...; **dependant** n persona a carico; **dependent** adj **to be ~ be dependent on** dipendere da; (child, relative) essere a carico di ▷ n = **dependant**
depict [dɪ'pɪkt] vt (in picture) dipingere; (in words) descrivere
deport [dɪ'pɔːt] vt deportare; espellere
deposit [dɪ'pɔzɪt] n (Comm, Geo) deposito; (of ore, oil) giacimento; (Chem) sedimento; (part payment) acconto; (for hired goods etc) cauzione f ▷ vt depositare; dare in acconto; mettere or lasciare in deposito; **deposit account** n conto vincolato
depot ['dɛpəʊ] n deposito; (us) stazione f ferroviaria
depreciate [dɪ'priːʃɪeɪt] vi svalutarsi
depress [dɪ'prɛs] vt deprimere; (price, wages) abbassare; (press down) premere; **depressed** adj (person) depresso(-a), abbattuto(-a); (price) in ribasso; (industry) in crisi; **depressing** adj deprimente; **depression** [dɪ'prɛʃən] n depressione f
deprive [dɪ'praɪv] vt **to ~ sb of** privare qn di; **deprived** adj disgraziato(-a)
dept. abbr = **department**
depth [dɛpθ] n profondità f inv; **in the ~s of** nel profondo di; nel cuore di; **out of one's ~** (in water) dove non si tocca; (fig) a disagio
deputy ['dɛpjutɪ] adj **~ head** (BRIT Scol) vicepreside m/f ▷ n (assistant) vice m/f inv; (us: also: **~ sheriff**) vice-sceriffo
derail [dɪ'reɪl] vt **to be ~ed** deragliare
derelict ['dɛrɪlɪkt] adj abbandonato(-a)

derive [dɪ'raɪv] vt **to ~ sth from** derivare qc da; trarre qc da ▷ vi **to ~ from** derivare da
descend [dɪ'sɛnd] vt, vi discendere, scendere; **to ~ from** discendere da; **to ~ to** (lying, begging) abbassarsi a; **descendant** n discendente m/f; **descent** [dɪ'sɛnt] n discesa; (origin) discendenza, famiglia
describe [dɪs'kraɪb] vt descrivere; **description** [-'krɪpʃən] n descrizione f; (sort) genere m, specie f
desert [n 'dɛzət, vb dɪ'zɜːt] n deserto ▷ vt lasciare, abbandonare ▷ vi (Mil) disertare; **deserted** [dɪ'zɜːtɪd] adj deserto(-a)
deserve [dɪ'zɜːv] vt meritare
design [dɪ'zaɪn] n (art, sketch) disegno; (layout, shape) linea; (pattern) fantasia; (intention) intenzione f ▷ vt disegnare; progettare
designate vt [vb 'dɛzɪgneɪt, adj 'dɛzɪgnɪt] designare ▷ adj designato(-a)
designer [dɪ'zaɪnər] n (Art, Tech) disegnatore(-trice); (of fashion) modellista m/f
desirable [dɪ'zaɪərəbl] adj desiderabile; **it is ~ that** è opportuno che + sub
desire [dɪ'zaɪər] n desiderio, voglia ▷ vt desiderare, volere
desk [dɛsk] n (in office) scrivania; (for pupil) banco; (BRIT: in shop, restaurant) cassa; (in hotel) ricevimento; (at airport) accettazione f; **desk-top publishing** n desktop publishing m
despair [dɪs'pɛər] n disperazione f ▷ vi **to ~ of** disperare di
despatch [dɪs'pætʃ] n, vt = **dispatch**
desperate ['dɛspərɪt] adj disperato(-a); (fugitive) capace di tutto; **to be ~ for sth/to do** volere disperatamente qc/fare; **desperately** adv disperatamente; (very) terribilmente, estremamente; **desperation** [dɛspə'reɪʃən] n disperazione f
despise [dɪs'paɪz] vt disprezzare, sdegnare
despite [dɪs'paɪt] prep malgrado, a dispetto di, nonostante
dessert [dɪ'zɜːt] n dolce m; frutta; **dessertspoon** n cucchiaio da dolci
destination [dɛstɪ'neɪʃən] n destinazione f
destined ['dɛstɪnd] adj **to be ~ to do/for** essere destinato(-a) a fare/per
destiny ['dɛstɪnɪ] n destino
destroy [dɪs'trɔɪ] vt distruggere
destruction [dɪs'trʌkʃən] n distruzione f
destructive [dɪs'trʌktɪv] adj distruttivo(-a)
detach [dɪ'tætʃ] vt staccare, distaccare; **detached** adj (attitude) distante;

detached house n villa

detail ['di:teɪl] n particolare m, dettaglio
▷ vt dettagliare, particolareggiare;
in ~ nei particolari; **detailed** adj
particolareggiato(-a)

detain [dɪ'teɪn] vt trattenere; (in captivity)
detenere

detect [dɪ'tɛkt] vt scoprire, scorgere; (Med,
Police, Radar etc) individuare; **detection**
[dɪ'tɛkʃən] n scoperta; individuazione
f; **detective** n investigatore(-trice);
detective story n giallo

detention [dɪ'tɛnʃən] n detenzione f; (Scol)
permanenza forzata per punizione

deter [dɪ'təːʳ] vt dissuadere

detergent [dɪ'təːdʒənt] n detersivo

deteriorate [dɪ'tɪərɪəreɪt] vi deteriorarsi

determination [dɪtəːmɪ'neɪʃən] n
determinazione f

determine [dɪ'təːmɪn] vt determinare;
determined adj (person) risoluto(-a),
deciso(-a); **determined to do** deciso(-a)
a fare

deterrent [dɪ'tɛrənt] n deterrente m; **to
act as a ~** fungere da deterrente

detest [dɪ'tɛst] vt detestare

detour ['di:tuəʳ] n deviazione f

detract [dɪ'trækt] vi **to ~ from** detrarre da

detrimental [dɛtrɪ'mɛntl] adj **~ to**
dannoso(-a) a, nocivo(-a) a

devastating ['dɛvəsteɪtɪŋ] adj
devastatore(-trice), sconvolgente

develop [dɪ'vɛləp] vt sviluppare; (habit)
prendere (gradualmente) ▷ vi svilupparsi;
(facts, symptoms: appear) manifestarsi,
rivelarsi; **can you ~ this film?** può
sviluppare questo rullino?; **developing
country** n paese m in via di sviluppo;
development n sviluppo

device [dɪ'vaɪs] n (apparatus) congegno

devil ['dɛvl] n diavolo; demonio

devious ['di:vɪəs] adj (person) subdolo(-a)

devise [dɪ'vaɪz] vt escogitare, concepire

devote [dɪ'vəut] vt **~ sth to** dedicare qc
a; **devoted** adj devoto(-a); **to be devoted
to sb** essere molto affezionato(-a) a qn;
devotion [dɪ'vəuʃən] n devozione f,
attaccamento; (Rel) atto di devozione,
preghiera

devour [dɪ'vauəʳ] vt divorare

devout [dɪ'vaut] adj pio(-a), devoto(-a)

dew [dju:] n rugiada

diabetes [daɪə'bi:ti:z] n diabete m

diabetic [daɪə'bɛtɪk] adj, n diabetico(-a)

diagnose [daɪəg'nəuz] vt diagnosticare

diagnosis [daɪəg'nəusɪs] (pl **diagnoses**) n
diagnosi f inv

diagonal [daɪ'ægənl] adj diagonale ▷ n
diagonale f

diagram ['daɪəgræm] n diagramma m

dial ['daɪəl] n quadrante m; (on radio)
lancetta; (on telephone) disco combinatore
▷ vt (number) fare

dialect ['daɪəlɛkt] n dialetto

dialling code, (US **area code**) n prefisso;
what's the ~ for Paris? qual è il prefisso
telefonico di Parigi?

dialling tone ['daɪəlɪŋ-] (US **dial tone**) n
segnale m di linea libera

dialogue ['daɪəlɔg] (US **dialog**) n dialogo

diameter [daɪ'æmɪtəʳ] n diametro

diamond ['daɪəmənd] n diamante m;
(shape) rombo; **~s** npl (Cards) quadri mpl

diaper ['daɪəpəʳ] (US) n pannolino

diarrhoea [daɪə'ri:ə] (US **diarrhea**) n
diarrea

diary ['daɪərɪ] n (daily account) diario; (book)
agenda

dice [daɪs] n inv dado ▷ vt (Culin) tagliare
a dadini

dictate [dɪk'teɪt] vt dettare; **dictation**
[dɪk'teɪʃən] n dettatura; (Scol) dettato

dictator [dɪk'teɪtəʳ] n dittatore m

dictionary ['dɪkʃənrɪ] n dizionario

did [dɪd] pt of **do**

didn't [dɪdnt] = **did not**

die [daɪ] vi morire; **to be dying for sth/to
do sth** morire dalla voglia di qc/di fare
qc; **die down** vi abbassarsi; **die out** vi
estinguersi

diesel ['di:zəl] n (vehicle) diesel m inv

diet ['daɪət] n alimentazione f; (restricted
food) dieta ▷ vi (also: **be on a ~**) stare a
dieta

differ ['dɪfəʳ] vi **to ~ from sth** differire
da qc, essere diverso(-a) da qc; **to ~
from sb over sth** essere in disaccordo
con qn su qc; **difference** n differenza;
(disagreement) screzio; **different** adj
diverso(-a); **differentiate** [-'rɛnʃieɪt] vi
to differentiate between discriminare
or fare differenza fra; **differently** adv
diversamente

difficult ['dɪfɪkəlt] adj difficile; **difficulty** n
difficoltà f inv

dig [dɪg] (pt, pp **dug**) vt (hole) scavare;
(garden) vangare ▷ n (prod) gomitata;
(archaeological) scavo; (fig) frecciata; **dig
up** vt (tree etc) sradicare; (information)
scavare fuori

digest [vb daɪ'dʒɛst, n 'daɪdʒɛst] vt digerire
▷ n compendio; **digestion** [dɪ'dʒɛstʃən] n
digestione f

digit ['dɪdʒɪt] n cifra; (finger) dito; **digital**
adj digitale; **digital camera** n macchina
fotografica digitale; **digital TV** n
televisione f digitale

dignified ['dɪgnɪfaɪd] adj dignitoso(-a)

dignity ['dɪgnɪtɪ] n dignità
digs [dɪgz] (BRIT: inf) npl camera ammobiliata
dilemma [daɪ'lemə] n dilemma m
dill [dɪl] n aneto
dilute [daɪ'luːt] vt diluire; (with water) annacquare
dim [dɪm] adj (light) debole; (shape etc) vago(-a); (room) in penombra; (inf: person) tonto(-a) ▷ vt (light) abbassare
dime [daɪm] (US) n = 10 cents
dimension [daɪ'mɛnʃən] n dimensione f
diminish [dɪ'mɪnɪʃ] vt, vi diminuire
din [dɪn] n chiasso, fracasso
dine [daɪn] vi pranzare; **diner** n (person) cliente m/f; (US: place) tavola calda
dinghy ['dɪŋgɪ] n battello pneumatico; (also: **rubber ~**) gommone m
dingy ['dɪndʒɪ] adj grigio(-a)
dining car ['daɪnɪŋ-] (BRIT) n vagone m ristorante
dining room n sala da pranzo
dining table n tavolo da pranzo
dinner ['dɪnər] n (lunch) pranzo; (evening meal) cena; (public) banchetto; **dinner jacket** n smoking m inv; **dinner party** n cena; **dinner time** n ora di pranzo (or cena)
dinosaur ['daɪnəsɔːr] n dinosauro
dip [dɪp] n discesa; (in sea) bagno; (Culin) salsetta ▷ vt immergere; bagnare; (BRIT Aut: lights) abbassare ▷ vi abbassarsi
diploma [dɪ'pləumə] n diploma m
diplomacy [dɪ'pləuməsɪ] n diplomazia
diplomat ['dɪpləmæt] n diplomatico; **diplomatic** [dɪplə'mætɪk] adj diplomatico(-a)
dipstick ['dɪpstɪk] n (Aut) indicatore m di livello dell'olio
dire [daɪər] adj terribile; estremo(-a)
direct [daɪ'rɛkt] adj diretto(-a) ▷ vt dirigere; (order): **to ~ sb to do sth** dare direttive a qn di fare qc ▷ adv direttamente; **can you ~ me to ...?** mi può indicare la strada per ...?; **direct debit** n (Banking) addebito effettuato per ordine di un cliente di banca
direction [dɪ'rɛkʃən] n direzione f; **~s** npl (advice) chiarimenti mpl; **sense of ~** senso dell'orientamento; **~s for use** istruzioni fpl
directly [dɪ'rɛktlɪ] adv (in straight line) direttamente; (at once) subito
director [dɪ'rɛktər] n direttore(-trice), amministratore(-trice); (Theatre, Cinema) regista m/f
directory [dɪ'rɛktərɪ] n elenco; **directory enquiries** (US **directory assistance**) n informazioni fpl elenco abbonati inv
dirt [dəːt] n sporcizia; immondizia; (earth)

terra; **dirty** adj sporco(-a) ▷ vt sporcare
disability [dɪsə'bɪlɪtɪ] n invalidità f inv; (Law) incapacità f inv
disabled [dɪs'eɪbld] adj invalido(-a); (mentally) ritardato(-a) ▷ npl **the ~** gli invalidi
disadvantage [dɪsəd'vɑːntɪdʒ] n svantaggio
disagree [dɪsə'griː] vi (differ) discordare; (be against, think otherwise): **to ~ (with)** essere in disaccordo (con), dissentire (da); **disagreeable** adj sgradevole; (person) antipatico(-a); **disagreement** n disaccordo; (argument) dissapore m
disappear [dɪsə'pɪər] vi scomparire; **disappearance** n scomparsa
disappoint [dɪsə'pɔɪnt] vt deludere; **disappointed** adj deluso(-a); **disappointing** adj deludente; **disappointment** n delusione f
disapproval [dɪsə'pruːvəl] n disapprovazione f
disapprove [dɪsə'pruːv] vi **to ~ of** disapprovare
disarm [dɪs'ɑːm] vt disarmare; **disarmament** n disarmo
disaster [dɪ'zɑːstər] n disastro; **disastrous** [dɪ'zɑːstrəs] adj disastroso(-a)
disbelief [dɪsbə'liːf] n incredulità
disc [dɪsk] n disco; (Comput) = **disk**
discard [dɪs'kɑːd] vt (old things) scartare; (fig) abbandonare
discharge [vb dɪs'tʃɑːdʒ, n 'dɪstʃɑːdʒ] vt (duties) compiere; (Elec, waste etc) scaricare; (Med) emettere; (patient) dimettere; (employee) licenziare; (soldier) congedare; (defendant) liberare ▷ n (Elec) scarica; (Med) emissione f; (dismissal) licenziamento; congedo; liberazione f
discipline ['dɪsɪplɪn] n disciplina ▷ vt disciplinare; (punish) punire
disc jockey n disc jockey m inv
disclose [dɪs'kləuz] vt rivelare, svelare
disco ['dɪskəu] n abbr discoteca
discoloured [dɪs'kʌləd] (US **discolored**) adj scolorito(-a), ingiallito(-a)
discomfort [dɪs'kʌmfət] n disagio; (lack of comfort) scomodità f inv
disconnect [dɪskə'nɛkt] vt sconnettere, staccare; (Elec, Radio) staccare; (gas, water) chiudere
discontent [dɪskən'tɛnt] n scontentezza
discontinue [dɪskən'tɪnjuː] vt smettere, cessare; **"~d"** (Comm) "fuori produzione"
discount [n 'dɪskaunt, vb dɪs'kaunt] n sconto ▷ vt scontare; (idea) non badare a; **are there ~s for students?** ci sono sconti

per studenti?

discourage [dɪs'kʌrɪdʒ] *vt* scoraggiare

discover [dɪs'kʌvəʳ] *vt* scoprire; **discovery** *n* scoperta

discredit [dɪs'krɛdɪt] *vt* screditare; mettere in dubbio

discreet [dɪ'skriːt] *adj* discreto(-a)

discrepancy [dɪ'skrɛpənsɪ] *n* discrepanza

discretion [dɪ'skrɛʃən] *n* discrezione *f*; **use your own ~** giudichi lei

discriminate [dɪ'skrɪmɪneɪt] *vi* **to ~ between** distinguere tra; **to ~ against** discriminare contro; **discrimination** [-'neɪʃən] *n* discriminazione *f*; (*judgment*) discernimento

discuss [dɪ'skʌs] *vt* discutere; (*debate*) dibattere; **discussion** [dɪ'skʌʃən] *n* discussione *f*

disease [dɪ'ziːz] *n* malattia

disembark [dɪsɪm'baːk] *vt*, *vi* sbarcare

disgrace [dɪs'greɪs] *n* vergogna; (*disfavour*) disgrazia ▷ *vt* disonorare, far cadere in disgrazia; **disgraceful** *adj* scandaloso(-a), vergognoso(-a)

disgruntled [dɪs'grʌntld] *adj* scontento(-a), di cattivo umore

disguise [dɪs'gaɪz] *n* travestimento ▷ *vt* **to ~ (as)** travestire (da); **in ~** travestito(-a)

disgust [dɪs'gʌst] *n* disgusto, nausea ▷ *vt* disgustare, far schifo a; **disgusted** [dɪs'gʌstɪd] *adj* indignato(-a); **disgusting** [dɪs'gʌstɪŋ] *adj* disgustoso(-a), ripugnante

dish [dɪʃ] *n* piatto; **to do** *or* **wash the ~es** fare i piatti; **dishcloth** *n* strofinaccio

dishonest [dɪs'ɔnɪst] *adj* disonesto(-a)

dishtowel ['dɪʃtauəl] (*us*) *n* strofinaccio dei piatti

dishwasher ['dɪʃwɔʃəʳ] *n* lavastoviglie *f inv*

disillusion [dɪsɪ'luːʒən] *vt* disilludere, disingannare

disinfectant [dɪsɪn'fɛktənt] *n* disinfettante *m*

disintegrate [dɪs'ɪntɪgreɪt] *vi* disintegrarsi

disk [dɪsk] *n* (*Comput*) disco; **single-/ double-sided ~** disco a facciata singola/ doppia; **disk drive** *n* lettore *m*; **diskette** (*us*) *n* = **disk**

dislike [dɪs'laɪk] *n* antipatia, avversione *f*; (*gen pl*) cosa che non piace ▷ *vt* **he ~s it** non gli piace

dislocate ['dɪsləkeɪt] *vt* slogare

disloyal [dɪs'lɔɪəl] *adj* sleale

dismal ['dɪzml] *adj* triste, cupo(-a)

dismantle [dɪs'mæntl] *vt* (*machine*) smontare

dismay [dɪs'meɪ] *n* costernazione *f* ▷ *vt* sgomentare

dismiss [dɪs'mɪs] *vt* congedare; (*employee*) licenziare; (*idea*) scacciare; (*Law*) respingere; **dismissal** *n* congedo; licenziamento

disobedient [dɪsə'biːdɪənt] *adj* disubbidiente

disobey [dɪsə'beɪ] *vt* disubbidire a

disorder [dɪs'ɔːdəʳ] *n* disordine *m*; (*rioting*) tumulto; (*Med*) disturbo

disorganized [dɪs'ɔːgənaɪzd] *adj* (*person, life*) disorganizzato(-a); (*system, meeting*) male organizzato(-a)

disown [dɪs'əun] *vt* rinnegare

dispatch [dɪs'pætʃ] *vt* spedire, inviare ▷ *n* spedizione *f*, invio; (*Mil, Press*) dispaccio

dispel [dɪs'pɛl] *vt* dissipare, scacciare

dispense [dɪs'pɛns] *vt* distribuire, amministrare; **dispense with** *vt fus* fare a meno di; **dispenser** *n* (*container*) distributore *m*

disperse [dɪs'pəːs] *vt* disperdere; (*knowledge*) disseminare ▷ *vi* disperdersi

display [dɪs'pleɪ] *n* esposizione *f*; (*of feeling etc*) manifestazione *f*; (*screen*) schermo ▷ *vt* mostrare; (*goods*) esporre; (*pej*) ostentare

displease [dɪs'pliːz] *vt* dispiacere a, scontentare; **~d with** scontento di

disposable [dɪs'pəuzəbl] *adj* (*pack etc*) a perdere; (*income*) disponibile

disposal [dɪs'pəuzl] *n* eliminazione *f*; (*of property*) cessione *f*; **at one's ~** alla sua disposizione

dispose [dɪs'pəuz] *vi* **~ of** sbarazzarsi di; **disposition** [-'zɪʃən] *n* disposizione *f*; (*temperament*) carattere *m*

disproportionate [dɪsprə'pɔːʃənət] *adj* sproporzionato(-a)

dispute [dɪs'pjuːt] *n* disputa; (*also:* **industrial ~**) controversia (sindacale) ▷ *vt* contestare; (*matter*) discutere; (*victory*) disputare

disqualify [dɪs'kwɔlɪfaɪ] *vt* (*Sport*) squalificare; **to ~ sb from sth/from doing** rendere qn incapace a qc/a fare; squalificare qn da qc/da fare; **to ~ sb from driving** ritirare la patente a qn

disregard [dɪsrɪ'gaːd] *vt* non far caso a, non badare a

disrupt [dɪs'rʌpt] *vt* disturbare; creare scompiglio in; **disruption** [dɪs'rʌpʃən] *n* disordine *m*; interruzione *f*

dissatisfaction [dɪssætɪs'fækʃən] *n* scontentezza, insoddisfazione *f*

dissatisfied [dɪs'sætɪsfaɪd] *adj* **~ (with)** scontento(a) *or* insoddisfatto(-a) (di)

dissect [dɪ'sɛkt] *vt* sezionare

dissent[dɪ'sɛnt] n dissenso

dissertation[dɪsə'teɪʃən] n tesi f inv,
dissertazione f

dissolve[dɪ'zɔlv] vt dissolvere, sciogliere;
(Pol, marriage etc) sciogliere ▷ vi dissolversi,
sciogliersi

distance['dɪstns] n distanza; **in the ~** in
lontananza

distant['dɪstnt] adj lontano(-a), distante;
(manner) riservato(-a), freddo(-a)

distil[dɪs'tɪl] (US **distill**) vt distillare;
distillery n distilleria

distinct[dɪs'tɪŋkt] adj distinto(-a);
as ~ from a differenza di; **distinction**
[dɪs'tɪŋkʃən] n distinzione f; (in exam) lode
f; **distinctive** adj distintivo(-a)

distinguish[dɪs'tɪŋgwɪʃ] vt distinguere;
discernere; **distinguished** adj (eminent)
eminente

distort[dɪs'tɔ:t] vt distorcere; (Tech)
deformare

distract[dɪs'trækt] vt distrarre;
distracted adj distratto(-a); **distraction**
[dɪs'trækʃən] n distrazione f

distraught[dɪs'trɔ:t] adj stravolto(-a)

distress[dɪs'trɛs] n angoscia ▷ vt
affliggere; **distressing** adj doloroso(-a)

distribute[dɪs'trɪbju:t] vt distribuire;
distribution[-'bju:ʃən] n distribuzione f;
distributor n distributore m

district['dɪstrɪkt] n (of country) regione f;
(of town) quartiere m; (Admin) distretto;
district attorney(US) n ≈ sostituto
procuratore m della Repubblica

distrust[dɪs'trʌst] n diffidenza, sfiducia
▷ vt non aver fiducia in

disturb[dɪs'tə:b] vt disturbare;
disturbance n disturbo; (political etc)
disordini mpl; **disturbed** adj (worried,
upset) turbato(-a); **emotionally
disturbed** con turbe emotive; **disturbing**
adj sconvolgente

ditch[dɪtʃ] n fossa ▷ vt (inf) piantare in
asso

ditto['dɪtəu] adv idem

dive[daɪv] n tuffo; (of submarine)
immersione f ▷ vi tuffarsi; immergersi;
diver n tuffatore(-trice), palombaro

diverse[daɪ'və:s] adj vario(-a)

diversion[daɪ'və:ʃən] n (BRIT Aut)
deviazione f; (distraction) divertimento

diversity[daɪ'və:sɪtɪ] n diversità f inv,
varietà f inv

divert[daɪ'və:t] vt deviare

divide[dɪ'vaɪd] vt dividere; (separate)
separare ▷ vi dividersi; **divided highway**
(US) n strada a doppia carreggiata

divine[dɪ'vaɪn] adj divino(-a)

diving['daɪvɪŋ] n tuffo; **diving board** n
trampolino

division[dɪ'vɪʒən] n divisione f;
separazione f; (esp Football) serie f

divorce[dɪ'vɔ:s] n divorzio ▷ vt divorziare
da; (dissociate) separare; **divorced**
adj divorziato(-a); **divorcee**[-'si:] n
divorziato(-a)

D.I.Y.(BRIT) n abbr = **do-it-yourself**

dizzy['dɪzɪ] adj **to feel ~** avere il capogiro

DJ n abbr = **disc jockey**

DNA n abbr (= deoxyribonucleic acid) DNA m;
DNA test n test m inv del DNA

 KEYWORD

do[du:] (pt **did**, pp **done**) n (inf: party etc)
festa; **it was rather a grand do** è stato
un ricevimento piuttosto importante
▷ vb **1** (in negative constructions: non
tradotto): **I don't understand** non
capisco

2 (to form questions: non tradotto): **didn't
you know?** non lo sapevi?; **why didn't
you come?** perché non sei venuto?

3 (for emphasis, in polite expressions): **she
does seem rather late** sembra essere
piuttosto in ritardo; **do sit down** si
accomodi la prego, prego si sieda; **do
take care!** mi raccomando, sta attento!

4 (used to avoid repeating vb): **she swims
better than I do** lei nuota meglio di me;
do you agree? — yes, I do/no, I don't sei
d'accordo? — sì/no; **she lives in Glasgow
— so do I** lei vive a Glasgow — anch'io; **he
asked me to help him and I did** mi ha
chiesto di aiutarlo ed io l'ho fatto

5 (in question tags): **you like him, don't
you?** ti piace, vero?; **I don't know him,
do I?** non lo conosco, vero?

▷ vt (gen, carry out, perform etc) fare; **what
are you doing tonight?** che fa stasera?;
to do the cooking cucinare; **to do the
washing-up** fare i piatti; **to do one's
teeth** lavarsi i denti; **to do one's hair/
nails** farsi i capelli/le unghie; **the car was
doing 100** la macchina faceva i 100 all'ora

▷ vi **1** (act, behave) fare; **do as I do** faccia
come me, faccia come faccio io

2 (get on, fare) andare; **he's doing well/
badly at school** va bene/male a scuola;
how do you do? piacere!

3 (suit) andare bene; **this room will do**
questa stanza va bene

4 (be sufficient) bastare; **will £10 do?**
basteranno 10 sterline?; **that'll do** basta
così; **that'll do!** (in annoyance) ora basta!;
to make do (with) arrangiarsi (con)

do away with vt fus (kill) far fuori;
(abolish) abolire

do up vt (laces) allacciare; (dress, buttons) abbottonare; (renovate: room, house) rimettere a nuovo, rifare

do with vt fus (need) aver bisogno di; (be connected): **what has it got to do with you?** e tu che c'entri?; **I won't have anything to do with it** non voglio avere niente a che farci; **it has to do with money** si tratta di soldi

do without vi fare senza ▷ vt fus fare a meno di

dock [dɔk] n (Naut) bacino; (Law) banco degli imputati ▷ vi entrare in bacino; (Space) agganciarsi; **~s** npl (Naut) bacino m inv

doctor ['dɔktə'] n medico(-a); (Ph.D. etc) dottore(-essa) ▷ vt (drink etc) adulterare; **call a ~!** chiamate un dottore!; **Doctor of Philosophy** n dottorato di ricerca; (person) titolare m/f di un dottorato di ricerca

document ['dɔkjumənt] n documento; **documentary** [-'mɛntərɪ] adj (evidence) documentato(-a) ▷ n documentario; **documentation** [dɔkjumən'teɪʃən] n documentazione f

dodge [dɔdʒ] n trucco; schivata ▷ vt schivare, eludere

dodgy ['dɔdʒɪ] adj (inf: uncertain) rischioso(-a); (untrustworthy) sospetto(-a)

does [dʌz] vb see **do**

doesn't ['dʌznt] = **does not**

dog [dɔg] n cane m ▷ vt (follow closely) pedinare; (fig: memory etc) perseguitare; **doggy bag** n sacchetto per gli avanzi (da portare a casa)

do-it-yourself ['du:ɪtjɔː'sɛlf] n il far da sé

dole [dəul] (BRIT) n sussidio di disoccupazione; **to be on the ~** vivere del sussidio

doll [dɔl] n bambola

dollar ['dɔlə'] n dollaro

dolphin ['dɔlfɪn] n delfino

dome [dəum] n cupola

domestic [də'mɛstɪk] adj (duty, happiness, animal) domestico(-a); (policy, affairs, flights) nazionale; **domestic appliance** n elettrodomestico

dominant ['dɔmɪnənt] adj dominante

dominate ['dɔmɪneɪt] vt dominare

domino ['dɔmɪnəu] (pl **dominoes**) n domino; **dominoes** n (game) gioco del domino

donate [də'neɪt] vt donare; **donation** [də'neɪʃən] n donazione f

done [dʌn] pp of **do**

donkey ['dɔŋkɪ] n asino

donor ['dəunə'] n donatore(-trice); **donor card** n tessera di donatore di organi

don't [dəunt] = **do not**

donut ['dəunʌt] (US) n = **doughnut**

doodle ['du:dl] vi scarabocchiare

doom [du:m] n destino; rovina ▷ vt **to be ~ed (to failure)** essere predestinato(-a) (a fallire)

door [dɔː'] n porta; **doorbell** n campanello; **door handle** n maniglia; **doorknob** ['dɔːnɔb] n pomello, maniglia; **doorstep** n gradino della porta; **doorway** n porta

dope [dəup] n (inf: drugs) roba ▷ vt (horse etc) drogare

dormitory ['dɔːmɪtrɪ] n dormitorio; (US) casa dello studente

DOS [dɔs] n abbr (= disk operating system) DOS m

dosage ['dəusɪdʒ] n posologia

dose [dəus] n dose f; (bout) attacco

dot [dɔt] n punto; macchiolina ▷ vt **~ted with** punteggiato(-a) di; **on the ~** in punto; **dotted line** ['dɔtɪd-] n linea punteggiata

double ['dʌbl] adj doppio(-a) ▷ adv (twice): **to cost ~ sth** costare il doppio (di qc) ▷ n sosia m inv ▷ vt raddoppiare; (fold) piegare doppio or in due ▷ vi raddoppiarsi; **at the ~** (BRIT), **on the ~** a passo di corsa; **double back** vi (person) tornare sui propri passi; **double bass** n contrabbasso; **double bed** n letto matrimoniale; **double-check** vt, vi ricontrollare; **double-click** vi (Comput) fare doppio click; **double-cross** vt fare il doppio gioco con; **doubledecker** n autobus m inv a due piani; **double glazing** (BRIT) n doppi vetri mpl; **double room** n camera matrimoniale; **doubles** n (Tennis) doppio; **double yellow lines** npl (BRIT: Aut) linea gialla doppia continua che segnala il divieto di sosta

doubt [daut] n dubbio ▷ vt dubitare di; **to ~ that** dubitare che + sub; **doubtful** adj dubbioso(-a), incerto(-a); (person) equivoco(-a); **doubtless** adv indubbiamente

dough [dəu] n pasta, impasto; **doughnut** (US **donut**) n bombolone m

dove [dʌv] n colombo(-a)

down [daun] n piume fpl ▷ adv giù, di sotto ▷ prep giù per ▷ vt (inf: drink) scolarsi; **~ with X!** abbasso X!; **down-and-out** n barbone m; **downfall** n caduta; rovina; **downhill** adv **to go downhill** andare in discesa; (fig) lasciarsi andare; andare a rotoli

Downing Street ['daunɪŋ-] n **lo ~** residenza del primo ministro inglese

● **DOWNING STREET**
●
● Al numero 10 di **Downing Street**, nel
● quartiere di Westminster a Londra, si
● trova la residenza del primo ministro
● inglese, al numero 11 quella del
● **Chancellor of the Exchequer**.

down: **download** vt (Comput) scaricare;
downright adj franco(-a); (refusal) assoluto(-a)
Down's syndrome n sindrome f di Down
down: **downstairs** adv di sotto; al piano inferiore; **down-to-earth** adj pratico(-a); **downtown** adv in città; **down under** adv (Australia etc) agli antipodi; **downward** ['daunwəd] adj, adv in giù, in discesa; **downwards** ['daunwədz] adv = **downward**
doz. abbr = **dozen**
doze [dəuz] vi sonnecchiare
dozen ['dʌzn] n dozzina; **a ~ books** una dozzina di libri; **~s of** decine fpl di
Dr. abbr (= doctor) dott.; (in street names) = **drive**
drab [dræb] adj tetro(-a), grigio(-a)
draft [drɑːft] n abbozzo; (Pol) bozza; (Comm) tratta; (US: call-up) leva ▷ vt abbozzare; see also **draught**
drag [dræg] vt trascinare; (river) dragare ▷ vi trascinarsi ▷ n (inf) noioso(-a); noia, fatica; (women's clothing): **in ~** travestito (da donna)
dragon ['drægən] n drago
dragonfly ['drægənflaɪ] n libellula
drain [dreɪn] n (for sewage) fogna; (on resources) salasso ▷ vt (land, marshes) prosciugare; (vegetables) scolare ▷ vi (water) defluire (via); **drainage** n prosciugamento; fognatura; **drainpipe** n tubo di scarico
drama ['drɑːmə] n (art) dramma m, teatro; (play) commedia; (event) dramma; **dramatic** [drə'mætɪk] adj drammatico(-a)
drank [dræŋk] pt of **drink**
drape [dreɪp] vt drappeggiare; **~s** (US) npl (curtains) tende fpl
drastic ['dræstɪk] adj drastico(-a)
draught [drɑːft] n (US **draft**) n corrente f d'aria; (Naut) pescaggio; **on ~** (beer) alla spina; **draught beer** n birra alla spina; **draughts** (BRIT) n (gioco della) dama
draw [drɔː] (pt **drew**, pp **drawn**) vt tirare; (take out) estrarre; (attract) attirare; (picture) disegnare; (line, circle) tracciare;

(money) ritirare ▷ vi (Sport) pareggiare ▷ n pareggio; (in lottery) estrazione f; **to ~ near** avvicinarsi; **draw out** vi (lengthen) allungarsi ▷ vt (money) ritirare; **draw up** vi (stop) arrestarsi, fermarsi ▷ vt (chair) avvicinare; (document) compilare; **drawback** n svantaggio, inconveniente m
drawer [drɔːʳ] n cassetto
drawing ['drɔːɪŋ] n disegno; **drawing pin** (BRIT) n puntina da disegno; **drawing room** n salotto
drawn [drɔːn] pp of **draw**
dread [drɛd] n terrore m ▷ vt tremare all'idea di; **dreadful** adj terribile
dream [driːm] (pt, pp **dreamed** or **dreamt**) n sogno ▷ vt, vi sognare; **dreamer** n sognatore(-trice)
dreamt [drɛmt] pt, pp of **dream**
dreary ['drɪərɪ] adj tetro(-a); monotono(-a)
drench [drɛntʃ] vt inzuppare
dress [drɛs] n vestito; (no pl: clothing) abbigliamento ▷ vt vestire; (wound) fasciare ▷ vi vestirsi; **to get ~ed** vestirsi; **dress up** vi vestirsi a festa; (in fancy dress) vestirsi in costume; **dress circle** (BRIT) n prima galleria; **dresser** n (BRIT: cupboard) credenza; (US) cassettone m; **dressing** n (Med) benda; (Culin) condimento; **dressing gown** (BRIT) n vestaglia; **dressing room** n (Theatre) camerino; (Sport) spogliatoio; **dressing table** n toilette f inv; **dressmaker** n sarta
drew [druː] pt of **draw**
dribble ['drɪbl] vi (baby) sbavare ▷ vt (ball) dribblare
dried [draɪd] adj (fruit, beans) secco(-a); (eggs, milk) in polvere
drier ['draɪəʳ] n = **dryer**
drift [drɪft] n (of current etc) direzione f; forza; (of snow) cumulo; turbine m; (general meaning) senso ▷ vi (boat) essere trasportato(-a) dalla corrente; (sand, snow) ammucchiarsi
drill [drɪl] n trapano; (Mil) esercitazione f ▷ vt trapanare; (troops) addestrare ▷ vi (for oil) fare trivellazioni
drink [drɪŋk] (pt **drank**, pp **drunk**) n bevanda, bibita; (alcoholic drink) bicchierino; (sip) sorso ▷ vt, vi bere; **to have a ~** bere qualcosa; **would you like a ~?** vuoi qualcosa da bere?; **a ~ of water** un po' d'acqua; **drink-driving** n guida in stato di ebbrezza; **drinker** n bevitore(-trice); **drinking water** n acqua potabile
drip [drɪp] n goccia; gocciolamento; (Med) fleboclisi f inv ▷ vi gocciolare; (tap) sgocciolare

drive [draɪv] (*pt* **drove**, *pp* **driven**) *n* passeggiata *or* giro in macchina; (*also:* **~way**) viale *m* d'accesso; (*energy*) energia; (*campaign*) campagna; (*also:* **disk ~**) lettore *m* ▷ *vt* guidare; (*nail*) piantare; (*push*) cacciare, spingere; (*Tech: motor*) azionare; far funzionare ▷ *vi* (*Aut: at controls*) guidare; (: *travel*) andare in macchina; **left-/right-hand ~** guida a sinistra/destra; **to ~ sb mad** far impazzire qn; **drive out** *vt* (*force out*) cacciare, mandare via; **drive-in** (*esp US*) *adj*, *n* drive-in (*m inv*)
driven ['drɪvn] *pp of* **drive**
driver ['draɪvər] *n* conducente *m/f*; (*of taxi*) tassista *m*; (*chauffeur: of bus*) autista *m/f*; **driver's license** (*US*) *n* patente *f* di guida
driveway ['draɪvweɪ] *n* viale *m* d'accesso
driving ['draɪvɪŋ] *n* guida; **driving instructor** *n* istruttore(-trice) di scuola guida; **driving lesson** *n* lezione *f* di guida; **driving licence** (*BRIT*) *n* patente *f* di guida; **driving test** *n* esame *m* di guida
drizzle ['drɪzl] *n* pioggerella
droop [dru:p] *vi* (*flower*) appassire; (*head, shoulders*) chinarsi
drop [drɔp] *n* (*of water*) goccia; (*lessening*) diminuzione *f*; (*fall*) caduta ▷ *vt* lasciare cadere; (*voice, eyes, price*) abbassare; (*set down from car*) far scendere; (*name from list*) lasciare fuori ▷ *vi* cascare; (*wind*) abbassarsi; **drop in** *vi* (*inf: visit*): **to ~ in (on)** fare un salto (da), passare (da); **drop off** *vi* (*sleep*) addormentarsi ▷ *vt* (*passenger*) far scendere; **drop out** *vi* (*withdraw*) ritirarsi; (*student etc*) smettere di studiare
drought [draut] *n* siccità *f inv*
drove [drəuv] *pt of* **drive**
drown [draun] *vt* affogare; (*fig: noise*) soffocare ▷ *vi* affogare
drowsy ['drauzɪ] *adj* sonnolento(-a), assonnato(-a)
drug [drʌg] *n* farmaco; (*narcotic*) droga ▷ *vt* drogare; **to be on ~s** drogarsi; (*Med*) prendere medicinali; **hard/soft ~s** droghe pesanti/leggere; **drug addict** *n* tossicomane *m/f*; **drug dealer** *n* trafficante *m/f* di droga; **druggist** (*US*) *n* persona che gestisce un drugstore; **drugstore** (*US*) *n* drugstore *m inv*
drum [drʌm] *n* tamburo; (*for oil, petrol*) fusto ▷ *vi* tamburellare; **~s** *npl* (*set of drums*) batteria; **drummer** *n* batterista *m/f*
drunk [drʌŋk] *pp of* **drink** ▷ *adj* ubriaco(-a); ebbro(-a) ▷ *n* (*also:* **~ard**) ubriacone(-a); **drunken** *adj* ubriaco(-a); da ubriaco
dry [draɪ] *adj* secco(-a); (*day, clothes*) asciutto(-a) ▷ *vt* seccare; (*clothes, hair, hands*) asciugare ▷ *vi* asciugarsi; **dry off** *vi* asciugarsi ▷ *vt* asciugare; **dry up** *vi* seccarsi; **dry-cleaner's** *n* lavasecco *m inv*; **dry-cleaning** *n* pulitura a secco; **dryer** *n* (*for hair*) föhn *m inv*, asciugacapelli *m inv*; (*for clothes*) asciugabiancheria; (*US: spin-dryer*) centrifuga
DSS *n abbr* (= *Department of Social Security*) ministero della Previdenza sociale
DTP *n abbr* (= *desk-top publishing*) desktop publishing *m inv*
dual ['djuəl] *adj* doppio(-a); **dual carriageway** (*BRIT*) *n* strada a doppia carreggiata
dubious ['dju:bɪəs] *adj* dubbio(-a)
Dublin ['dʌblɪn] *n* Dublino *f*
duck [dʌk] *n* anatra ▷ *vi* abbassare la testa
due [dju:] *adj* dovuto(-a); (*expected*) atteso(-a); (*fitting*) giusto(-a) ▷ *n* dovuto ▷ *adv* **~ north** diritto verso nord
duel ['djuəl] *n* duello
duet [dju:'ɛt] *n* duetto
dug [dʌg] *pt*, *pp of* **dig**
duke [dju:k] *n* duca *m*
dull [dʌl] *adj* (*light*) debole; (*boring*) noioso(-a); (*slow-witted*) ottuso(-a); (*sound, pain*) sordo(-a); (*weather, day*) fosco(-a), scuro(-a) ▷ *vt* (*pain, grief*) attutire; (*mind, senses*) intorpidire
dumb [dʌm] *adj* muto(-a); (*pej*) stupido(-a)
dummy ['dʌmɪ] *n* (*tailor's model*) manichino; (*Tech, Comm*) riproduzione *f*; (*BRIT: for baby*) tettarella ▷ *adj* falso(-a), finto(-a)
dump [dʌmp] *n* (*also:* **rubbish ~**) discarica di rifiuti; (*inf: place*) buco ▷ *vt* (*put down*) scaricare; mettere giù; (*get rid of*) buttar via
dumpling ['dʌmplɪŋ] *n* specie di gnocco
dune [dju:n] *n* duna
dungarees [dʌŋgə'ri:z] *npl* tuta
dungeon ['dʌndʒən] *n* prigione *f* sotterranea
duplex ['dju:plɛks] (*US*) *n* (*house*) casa con muro divisorio in comune con un'altra; (*apartment*) appartamento su due piani
duplicate [*n* 'dju:plɪkət, *vb* 'dju:plɪkeɪt] *n* doppio ▷ *vt* duplicare; **in ~** in doppia copia
durable ['djuərəbl] *adj* durevole; (*clothes, metal*) resistente
duration [djuə'reɪʃən] *n* durata
during ['djuərɪŋ] *prep* durante, nel corso di
dusk [dʌsk] *n* crepuscolo
dust [dʌst] *n* polvere *f* ▷ *vt* (*furniture*) spolverare; (*cake etc*): **to ~ with** cospargere con; **dustbin** (*BRIT*) *n* pattumiera; **duster** *n* straccio per la polvere; **dustman** (*irreg: BRIT*) *n* netturbino; **dustpan** *n* pattumiera; **dusty** *adj* polveroso(-a)

Dutch [dʌtʃ] *adj* olandese ▷ *n* (*Ling*) olandese *m*; **the ~** *npl* gli Olandesi; **to go ~** (*inf*) fare alla romana; **Dutchman, Dutchwoman** (*irreg*) *n* olandese *m/f*

duty ['dju:tɪ] *n* dovere *m*; (*tax*) dazio, tassa; **on ~** di servizio; **off ~** libero(-a), fuori servizio; **duty-free** *adj* esente da dazio

duvet ['du:veɪ] (BRIT) *n* piumino, piumone *m*

DVD *n abbr* (= digital versatile or video disk) DVD *m inv*; **DVD player** *n* lettore *m* DVD

dwarf [dwɔːf] *n* nano(-a) ▷ *vt* far apparire piccolo

dwell [dwɛl] (*pt*, *pp* **dwelt**) *vi* dimorare; **dwell on** *vt fus* indugiare su

dwelt [dwɛlt] *pt*, *pp of* **dwell**

dwindle ['dwɪndl] *vi* diminuire

dye [daɪ] *n* tinta ▷ *vt* tingere

dying ['daɪɪŋ] *adj* morente, moribondo(-a)

dynamic [daɪ'næmɪk] *adj* dinamico(-a)

dynamite ['daɪnəmaɪt] *n* dinamite *f*

dyslexia [dɪs'lɛksɪə] *n* dislessia

dyslexic [dɪs'lɛksɪk] *adj, n* dislessico(-a)

E [iː] *n* (*Mus*) mi *m*

E111 *n abbr* (*also:* **form ~**) E111 (*modulo CEE per rimborso spese mediche*)

each [iːtʃ] *adj* ogni, ciascuno(-a) ▷ *pron* ciascuno(-a), ognuno(-a); **~ one** ognuno(-a); **~ other** si *or* ci *etc*; **they hate ~ other** si odiano (l'un l'altro); **you are jealous of ~ other** siete gelosi l'uno dell'altro; **they have 2 books ~** hanno 2 libri ciascuno

eager ['iːɡə'] *adj* impaziente, desideroso(-a); ardente; **to be ~ for** essere desideroso di, aver gran voglia di

eagle ['iːɡl] *n* aquila

ear [ɪə'] *n* orecchio; (*of corn*) pannocchia; **earache** *n* mal *m* d'orecchi; **eardrum** *n* timpano

earl [əːl] (BRIT) *n* conte *m*

earlier ['əːlɪə'] *adj* precedente ▷ *adv* prima

early ['əːlɪ] *adv* presto, di buon'ora; (*ahead of time*) in anticipo ▷ *adj* (*near the beginning*) primo(-a); (*sooner than expected*) prematuro(-a); (*quick: reply*) veloce; **at an ~ hour** di buon'ora; **to have an ~ night** andare a letto presto; **in the ~** *or* **~ in the spring/19th century** all'inizio della primavera/dell'Ottocento; **early retirement** *n* ritiro anticipato

earmark ['ɪəmɑːk] *vt* **to ~ sth for** destinare qc a

earn [əːn] vt guadagnare; (rest, reward) meritare

earnest ['əːnɪst] adj serio(-a); **in ~** sul serio

earnings ['əːnɪŋz] npl guadagni mpl; (salary) stipendio

ear: **earphones** ['ɪəfəʊnz] npl cuffia; **earplugs** npl tappi mpl per le orecchie; **earring** ['ɪərɪŋ] n orecchino

earth [əːθ] n terra ▷ vt (BRIT Elec) mettere a terra; **earthquake** n terremoto

ease [iːz] n agio, comodo ▷ vt (soothe) calmare; (loosen) allentare; **to ~ sth out/in** tirare fuori/infilare qc con delicatezza; facilitare l'uscita/l'entrata di qc; **at ~** a proprio agio; (Mil) a riposo

easily ['iːzɪlɪ] adv facilmente

east [iːst] n est m ▷ adj dell'est ▷ adv a oriente; **the E~** l'Oriente m; (Pol) l'Est; **eastbound** ['iːstbaʊnd] adj (traffic) diretto(-a) a est; (carriageway) che porta a est

Easter ['iːstər] n Pasqua; **Easter egg** n uovo di Pasqua

eastern ['iːstən] adj orientale, d'oriente; dell'est

Easter Sunday n domenica di Pasqua

easy ['iːzɪ] adj facile; (manner) disinvolto(-a) ▷ adv **to take it** or **things ~** prendersela con calma; **easy-going** adj accomodante

eat [iːt] (pt **ate**, pp **eaten**) vt, vi mangiare; **can we have something to ~?** possiamo mangiare qualcosa?; **eat out** vi mangiare fuori

eavesdrop ['iːvzdrɒp] vi **to ~ (on a conversation)** origliare (una conversazione)

e-book ['iːbuk] n libro elettronico

e-business ['iːbɪznɪs] n (company) azienda che opera in Internet; (commerce) commercio elettronico

EC n abbr (= European Community) CE f

eccentric [ɪk'sɛntrɪk] adj, n eccentrico(-a)

echo ['ɛkəʊ] (pl **echoes**) n eco m or f ▷ vt ripetere; fare eco a ▷ vi echeggiare; dare un eco

eclipse [ɪ'klɪps] n eclissi f inv

eco-friendly [iːkəʊ'frɛndlɪ] adj ecologico(-a)

ecological [iːkə'lɒdʒɪkəl] adj ecologico(-a)

ecology [ɪ'kɒlədʒɪ] n ecologia

e-commerce [iːkɒməːs] n commercio elettronico

economic [iːkə'nɒmɪk] adj economico(-a); **economical** adj economico(-a); (person) economo(-a); **economics** n economia ▷ npl lato finanziario

economist [ɪ'kɒnəmɪst] n economista m/f

economize [ɪ'kɒnəmaɪz] vi risparmiare, fare economia

economy [ɪ'kɒnəmɪ] n economia; **economy class** n (Aviat) classe f turistica; **economy class syndrome** n sindrome f della classe economica

ecstasy ['ɛkstəsɪ] n estasi f inv; **ecstatic** [ɛks'tætɪk] adj estatico(-a), in estasi

eczema ['ɛksɪmə] n eczema m

edge [ɛdʒ] n margine m; (of table, plate, cup) orlo; (of knife etc) taglio ▷ vt bordare; **on ~** (fig) = **edgy**; **to edge away from** sgattaiolare da

edgy ['ɛdʒɪ] adj nervoso(-a)

edible ['ɛdɪbl] adj commestibile; (meal) mangiabile

Edinburgh ['ɛdɪnbərə] n Edimburgo f

edit ['ɛdɪt] vt curare; **edition** [ɪ'dɪʃən] n edizione f; **editor** n (in newspaper) redattore(-trice), redattore(-trice) capo; (of sb's work) curatore(-trice); **editorial** [-'tɔːrɪəl] adj redazionale, editoriale ▷ n editoriale m

> Be careful not to translate **editor** by the Italian word **editore**.

educate ['ɛdjukeɪt] vt istruire; educare; **educated** adj istruito(-a)

education [ɛdju'keɪʃən] n educazione f; (schooling) istruzione f; **educational** adj pedagogico(-a); scolastico(-a); istruttivo(-a)

eel [iːl] n anguilla

eerie ['ɪərɪ] adj che fa accapponare la pelle

effect [ɪ'fɛkt] n effetto ▷ vt effettuare; **to take ~** (law) entrare in vigore; (drug) fare effetto; **in ~** effettivamente; **~s** npl (Theat) effetti mpl scenici; (property) effetti mpl; **effective** adj efficace; (actual) effettivo(-a); **effectively** adv efficacemente; effettivamente

efficiency [ɪ'fɪʃənsɪ] n efficienza; rendimento effettivo

efficient [ɪ'fɪʃənt] adj efficiente; **efficiently** adv efficientemente; efficacemente

effort ['ɛfət] n sforzo; **effortless** adj senza sforzo, facile

e.g. adv abbr (= exempli gratia) per esempio, p.es.

egg [ɛg] n uovo; **hard-boiled/soft-boiled ~** uovo sodo/alla coque; **eggcup** n portauovo m inv; **eggplant** (esp us) n melanzana; **eggshell** n guscio d'uovo; **egg white** n albume m, bianco d'uovo; **egg yolk** n tuorlo, rosso (d'uovo)

ego ['iːgəʊ] n ego m inv

Egypt ['iːdʒɪpt] n Egitto; **Egyptian** [ɪ'dʒɪpʃən] adj, n egiziano(-a)

eight [eɪt] num otto; **eighteen** num diciotto; **eighteenth** num diciottesimo(-a); **eighth** [eɪtθ] num

ottavo(-a); **eightieth** ['eɪtɪɪθ] *num*
ottantesimo(-a); **eighty** *num* ottanta

Eire ['ɛərə] *n* Repubblica d'Irlanda

either ['aɪðə'] *adj* l'uno(-a) o l'altro(-a);
(*both, each*) ciascuno(-a) ▷ *pron* **~ (of
them)** (o) l'uno(-a) o l'altro(-a) ▷ *adv*
neanche ▷ *conj* **~ good or bad** o buono o
cattivo; **on ~ side** su ciascun lato; **I don't
like ~** non mi piace né l'uno né l'altro; **no, I
don't ~** no, neanch'io

eject [ɪ'dʒɛkt] *vt* espellere; lanciare

elaborate [*adj* ɪ'læbərɪt, *vb* ɪ'læbəreɪt]
adj elaborato(-a), minuzioso(-a) ▷ *vt*
elaborare ▷ *vi* fornire i particolari

elastic [ɪ'læstɪk] *adj* elastico(-a) ▷ *n*
elastico; **elastic band** (BRIT) *n* elastico

elbow ['ɛlbəu] *n* gomito

elder ['ɛldə'] *adj* maggiore, più vecchio(-a)
▷ *n* (*tree*) sambuco; **one's ~s** i più anziani;
elderly *adj* anziano(-a) ▷ *npl* **the elderly**
gli anziani

eldest ['ɛldɪst] *adj*, *n* **the ~ (child)** il(la)
maggiore (dei bambini)

elect [ɪ'lɛkt] *vt* eleggere ▷ *adj* **the
president ~** il presidente designato; **to ~
to do** decidere di fare; **election** [ɪ'lɛkʃən]
n elezione *f*; **electoral** [ɪ'lɛktərəl] *adj*
elettorale; **electorate** *n* elettorato

electric [ɪ'lɛktrɪk] *adj* elettrico(-a);
electrical *adj* elettrico(-a); **electric
blanket** *n* coperta elettrica; **electric fire**
n stufa elettrica; **electrician** [ɪlɛk'trɪʃən]
n elettricista *m*; **electricity** [ɪlɛk'trɪsɪtɪ]
n elettricità; **electric shock** *n* scossa
(elettrica); **electrify** [ɪ'lɛktrɪfaɪ] *vt* (*Rail*)
elettrificare; (*audience*) elettrizzare

electronic [ɪlɛk'trɔnɪk] *adj* elettronico(-a);
electronic mail *n* posta elettronica;
electronics *n* elettronica

elegance ['ɛlɪgəns] *n* eleganza

elegant ['ɛlɪgənt] *adj* elegante

element ['ɛlɪmənt] *n* elemento; (*of heater,
kettle etc*) resistenza

elementary [ɛlɪ'mɛntərɪ] *adj* elementare;
elementary school (US) *n* scuola
elementare

elephant ['ɛlɪfənt] *n* elefante(-essa)

elevate ['ɛlɪveɪt] *vt* elevare

elevator ['ɛlɪveɪtə'] *n* elevatore *m*; (*US: lift*)
ascensore *m*

eleven [ɪ'lɛvn] *num* undici; **eleventh** *adj*
undicesimo(-a)

eligible ['ɛlɪdʒəbl] *adj* eleggibile; (*for
membership*) ▷ *n* abbraccio

eliminate [ɪ'lɪmɪneɪt] *vt* eliminare

elm [ɛlm] *n* olmo

eloquent ['ɛləkwənt] *adj* eloquente

else [ɛls] *adv* altro; **something ~**
qualcos'altro; **somewhere ~** altrove;

everywhere ~ in qualsiasi altro luogo;
nobody ~ nessun altro; **where ~?** in quale
altro luogo?; **little ~** poco altro; **elsewhere**
adv altrove

elusive [ɪ'luːsɪv] *adj* elusivo(-a)

e-mail *n abbr* (= *electronic mail*) posta
elettronica ▷ *vt* mandare un messaggio
di posta elettronica a; **e-mail address** *n*
indirizzo di posta elettronica

embankment [ɪm'bæŋkmənt] *n* (*of road,
railway*) terrapieno

embargo [ɪm'bɑːgəu] *n* (*pl* **embargoes**)
(*Comm, Naut*) embargo ▷ *vt* mettere
l'embargo su; **to put an ~ on sth** mettere
l'embargo su qc

embark [ɪm'bɑːk] *vi* **to ~ (on)** imbarcarsi
(su) ▷ *vt* imbarcare; **to ~ on** (*fig*)
imbarcarsi in

embarrass [ɪm'bærəs] *vt* imbarazzare;
embarrassed *adj* imbarazzato(-a);
embarrassing *adj* imbarazzante;
embarrassment *n* imbarazzo

embassy ['ɛmbəsɪ] *n* ambasciata

embrace [ɪm'breɪs] *vt* abbracciare ▷ *vi*
abbracciarsi ▷ *n* abbraccio

embroider [ɪm'brɔɪdə'] *vt* ricamare;
embroidery *n* ricamo

embryo ['ɛmbrɪəu] *n* embrione *m*

emerald ['ɛmərəld] *n* smeraldo

emerge [ɪ'məːdʒ] *vi* emergere

emergency [ɪ'məːdʒənsɪ] *n* emergenza;
in an ~ in caso di emergenza; **emergency
brake** (US) *n* freno a mano; **emergency
exit** *n* uscita di sicurezza; **emergency
landing** *n* atterraggio forzato;
emergency room (US: *Med*) *n* pronto
soccorso; **emergency services** *npl* (*fire,
police, ambulance*) servizi *mpl* di pronto
intervento

emigrate ['ɛmɪgreɪt] *vi* emigrare;
emigration [ɛmɪ'greɪʃən] *n* emigrazione *f*

eminent ['ɛmɪnənt] *adj* eminente

emissions [ɪ'mɪʃənz] *npl* emissioni *fpl*

emit [ɪ'mɪt] *vt* emettere

emotion [ɪ'məuʃən] *n* emozione *f*;
emotional *adj* (*person*) emotivo(-a);
(*scene*) commovente; (*tone, speech*)
carico(-a) d'emozione

emperor ['ɛmpərə'] *n* imperatore *m*

emphasis ['ɛmfəsɪs] *n* (*pl* **-ases**) enfasi *f
inv*; importanza

emphasize ['ɛmfəsaɪz] *vt* (*word, point*)
sottolineare; (*feature*) mettere in evidenza

empire ['ɛmpaɪə'] *n* impero

employ [ɪm'plɔɪ] *vt* impiegare; **employee**
[-'iː] *n* impiegato(-a); **employer** *n*
principale *m/f*, datore *m* di lavoro;
employment *n* impiego; **employment
agency** *n* agenzia di collocamento

empower [ɪm'pauəʳ] vt **to ~ sb to do** concedere autorità a qn di fare

empress ['emprɪs] n imperatrice f

emptiness ['emptɪnɪs] n vuoto

empty ['emptɪ] adj vuoto(-a); (threat, promise) vano(-a) ▷ vt vuotare ▷ vi vuotarsi; (liquid) scaricarsi; **empty-handed** adj a mani vuote

EMU n abbr (= economic and monetary union) unione f economica e monetaria

emulsion [ɪ'mʌlʃən] n emulsione f

enable [ɪ'neɪbl] vt **to ~ sb to do** permettere a qn di fare

enamel [ɪ'næməl] n smalto; (also: **~ paint**) vernice f a smalto

enchanting [ɪn'tʃɑːntɪŋ] adj incantevole, affascinante

encl. abbr (= enclosed) all.

enclose [ɪn'kləuz] vt (land) circondare, recingere; (letter etc): **to ~ (with)** allegare (con); **please find ~d** trovi qui accluso

enclosure [ɪn'kləuʒəʳ] n recinto

encore [ɔŋ'kɔːʳ] excl bis ▷ n bis m inv

encounter [ɪn'kauntəʳ] n incontro ▷ vt incontrare

encourage [ɪn'kʌrɪdʒ] vt incoraggiare; **encouragement** n incoraggiamento

encouraging [ɪn'kʌrɪdʒɪŋ] adj incoraggiante

encyclop(a)edia [ɛnsaɪkləu'piːdɪə] n enciclopedia

end [ɛnd] n fine f; (aim) fine m; (of table) bordo estremo; (of pointed object) punta ▷ vt finire; (also: **bring to an ~, put an ~ to**) mettere fine a ▷ vi finire; **in the ~** alla fine; **on ~** (object) ritto(-a); (hair) rizzarsi; **for hours on ~** per ore ed ore; **end up** vi **to ~ up in** finire in

endanger [ɪn'deɪndʒəʳ] vt mettere in pericolo

endearing [ɪn'dɪərɪŋ] adj accattivante

endeavour [ɪn'dɛvəʳ] (US **endeavor**) n sforzo, tentativo ▷ vi **to ~ to do** cercare or sforzarsi di fare

ending ['ɛndɪŋ] n fine f, conclusione f; (Ling) desinenza

endless ['ɛndlɪs] adj senza fine

endorse [ɪn'dɔːs] vt (cheque) girare; (approve) approvare, appoggiare; **endorsement** n approvazione f; (on driving licence) contravvenzione registrata sulla patente

endurance [ɪn'djuərəns] n resistenza; pazienza

endure [ɪn'djuəʳ] vt sopportare, resistere a ▷ vi durare

enemy ['ɛnəmɪ] adj, n nemico(-a)

energetic [ɛnə'dʒɛtɪk] adj energico(-a), attivo(-a)

energy ['ɛnədʒɪ] n energia

enforce [ɪn'fɔːs] vt (Law) applicare, far osservare

engaged [ɪn'geɪdʒd] adj (BRIT: busy, in use) occupato(-a); (betrothed) fidanzato(-a); **the line's ~** la linea è occupata; **to get ~** fidanzarsi; **engaged tone** (BRIT) n (Tel) segnale m di occupato

engagement [ɪn'geɪdʒmənt] n impegno, obbligo; appuntamento; (to marry) fidanzamento; **engagement ring** n anello di fidanzamento

engaging [ɪn'geɪdʒɪŋ] adj attraente

engine ['ɛndʒɪn] n (Aut) motore m; (Rail) locomotiva

engineer [ɛndʒɪ'nɪəʳ] n ingegnere m; (BRIT: for repairs) tecnico; (on ship: US: Rail) macchinista m; **engineering** n ingegneria

England ['ɪŋglənd] n Inghilterra

English ['ɪŋglɪʃ] adj inglese ▷ n (Ling) inglese m; **the ~** npl gli Inglesi; **English Channel** n **the English Channel** la Manica; **Englishman** (irreg) n inglese m; **Englishwoman** (irreg) n inglese f

engrave [ɪn'greɪv] vt incidere

engraving [ɪn'greɪvɪŋ] n incisione f

enhance [ɪn'hɑːns] vt accrescere

enjoy [ɪn'dʒɔɪ] vt godere; (have: success, fortune) avere; **to ~ o.s.** godersela, divertirsi; **enjoyable** adj piacevole; **enjoyment** n piacere m, godimento

enlarge [ɪn'lɑːdʒ] vt ingrandire ▷ vi **to ~ on** (subject) dilungarsi su; **enlargement** n (Phot) ingrandimento

enlist [ɪn'lɪst] vt arruolare; (support) procurare ▷ vi arruolarsi

enormous [ɪ'nɔːməs] adj enorme

enough [ɪ'nʌf] adj, n **~ time/books** assai tempo/libri; **have you got ~?** ne ha abbastanza or a sufficienza? ▷ adv **big ~** abbastanza grande; **he has not worked ~** non ha lavorato abbastanza; **~!** basta!; **that's ~, thanks** basta così, grazie; **I've had ~ of him** ne ho abbastanza di lui; **... which, funnily or oddly ~** ... che, strano a dirsi

enquire [ɪn'kwaɪəʳ] vt, vi (esp BRIT) = **inquire**

enquiry [ɪn'kwaɪərɪ] n (esp BRIT) = **inquiry**

enrage [ɪn'reɪdʒ] vt fare arrabbiare

enrich [ɪn'rɪtʃ] vt arricchire

enrol [ɪn'rəul] (US **enroll**) vt iscrivere ▷ vi iscriversi; **enrolment** (US **enrollment**) n iscrizione f

en route [ɔn'ruːt] adv **~ for/from/to** in viaggio per/da/a

en suite [ɔn'swiːt] adj **room with ~**

bathroom camera con bagno
ensure [ɪnˈʃuəʳ] vt assicurare; garantire
entail [ɪnˈteɪl] vt comportare
enter [ˈɛntəʳ] vt entrare in; (army)
arruolarsi in; (competition) partecipare a;
(sb for a competition) iscrivere; (write down)
registrare; (Comput) inserire ▷ vi entrare
enterprise [ˈɛntəpraɪz] n (undertaking,
company) impresa; (spirit) iniziativa;
free ~ liberalismo economico; **private
~** iniziativa privata; **enterprising**
[ˈɛntəpraɪzɪŋ] adj intraprendente
entertain [ɛntəˈteɪn] vt divertire; (invite)
ricevere; (idea, plan) nutrire; **entertainer** n
comico(-a); **entertaining** adj divertente;
entertainment n (amusement)
divertimento; (show) spettacolo
enthusiasm [ɪnˈθuːzɪæzəm] n
entusiasmo
enthusiast [ɪnˈθuːzɪæst] n entusiasta m/
f; **enthusiastic** [-ˈæstɪk] adj entusiasta,
entusiastico(-a); **to be enthusiastic
about sth/sb** essere appassionato(-a) di
qc/entusiasta di qn
entire [ɪnˈtaɪəʳ] adj intero(-a); **entirely** adv
completamente, interamente
entitle [ɪnˈtaɪtl] vt (give right): **to ~ sb to
sth/to do** dare diritto a qn a qc/a fare;
entitled adj (book) che si intitola; **to be
entitled to do** avere il diritto di fare
entrance [n ˈɛntrns, vb ɪnˈtrɑːns] n
entrata, ingresso; (of person) entrata
▷ vt incantare, rapire; **where's the ~?**
dov'è l'entrata?; **to gain ~ to** (university
etc) essere ammesso a; **entrance
examination** n esame m di ammissione;
entrance fee n tassa d'iscrizione; (to
museum etc) prezzo d'ingresso; **entrance
ramp** (us) n (Aut) rampa di accesso;
entrant [ˈɛntrnt] n partecipante m/f;
concorrente m/f
entrepreneur [ɔntrəprəˈnəːʳ] n
imprenditore m
entrust [ɪnˈtrʌst] vt **to ~ sth to** affidare
qc a
entry [ˈɛntrɪ] n entrata; (way in) entrata,
ingresso; (item: on list) iscrizione f; (in
dictionary) voce f; **no ~** vietato l'ingresso;
(Aut) divieto di accesso; **entry phone** n
citofono
envelope [ˈɛnvələup] n busta
envious [ˈɛnvɪəs] adj invidioso(-a)
environment [ɪnˈvaɪərnmənt] n
ambiente m; **environmental** [-
ˈmɛntl] adj ecologico(-a); ambientale;
environmentally [ɪnvaɪərənˈmɛntəlɪ]
adv **environmentally sound/friendly**
che rispetta l'ambiente
envisage [ɪnˈvɪzɪdʒ] vt immaginare;

prevedere
envoy [ˈɛnvɔɪ] n inviato(-a)
envy [ˈɛnvɪ] n invidia ▷ vt invidiare; **to ~ sb
sth** invidiare qn per qc
epic [ˈɛpɪk] n poema m epico ▷ adj
epico(-a)
epidemic [ɛpɪˈdɛmɪk] n epidemia
epilepsy [ˈɛpɪlɛpsɪ] n epilessia
epileptic [ɛpɪˈlɛptɪk] adj, n epilettico(-a);
epileptic fit n attacco epilettico
episode [ˈɛpɪsəud] n episodio
equal [ˈiːkwl] adj uguale ▷ n pari m/f
inv ▷ vt uguagliare; **~ to** (task) all'altezza
di; **equality** [iːˈkwɔlɪtɪ] n uguaglianza;
equalize vi pareggiare; **equally** adv
ugualmente
equation [ɪˈkweɪʃən] n (Math) equazione f
equator [ɪˈkweɪtəʳ] n equatore m
equip [ɪˈkwɪp] vt equipaggiare, attrezzare;
to ~ sb/sth with fornire qn/qc di; **to
be well ~ped** (office etc) essere ben
attrezzato(-a); **he is well ~ped for the
job** ha i requisiti necessari per quel lavoro;
equipment n attrezzatura; (electrical etc)
apparecchiatura
equivalent [ɪˈkwɪvəlnt] adj equivalente
▷ n equivalente m; **to be ~ to** equivalere a
ER abbr (BRIT) = **Elizabeth Regina** (US:
Med) = **emergency room**
era [ˈɪərə] n era, età f inv
erase [ɪˈreɪz] vt cancellare; **eraser** n
gomma
erect [ɪˈrɛkt] adj eretto(-a) ▷ vt costruire;
(assemble) montare; **erection** [ɪˈrɛkʃən]
n costruzione f; montaggio; (Physiol)
erezione f
ERM n (= Exchange Rate Mechanism) ERM m
erode [ɪˈrəud] vt erodere; (metal)
corrodere
erosion [ɪˈrəuʒən] n erosione f
erotic [ɪˈrɔtɪk] adj erotico(-a)
errand [ˈɛrnd] n commissione f
erratic [ɪˈrætɪk] adj imprevedibile; (person,
mood) incostante
error [ˈɛrəʳ] n errore m
erupt [ɪˈrʌpt] vi (volcano) mettersi (or
essere) in eruzione; (war, crisis) scoppiare;
eruption [ɪˈrʌpʃən] n eruzione f; scoppio
escalate [ˈɛskəleɪt] vi intensificarsi
escalator [ˈɛskəleɪtəʳ] n scala mobile
escape [ɪˈskeɪp] n evasione f; fuga; (of gas
etc) fuga, fuoriuscita ▷ vi fuggire; (from
jail) evadere, scappare; (leak) uscire ▷ vt
sfuggire a; **to ~ from** (place) fuggire da;
(person) sfuggire a
escort [n ˈɛskɔːt, vb ɪˈskɔːt] n scorta; (male
companion) cavaliere m ▷ vt scortare;
accompagnare
especially [ɪˈspɛʃlɪ] adv specialmente;

soprattutto; espressamente

espionage ['ɛspɪənɑːʒ] n spionaggio

essay ['ɛseɪ] n (Scol) composizione f; (Literature) saggio

essence ['ɛsns] n essenza

essential [ɪ'sɛnʃl] adj essenziale ▷ n elemento essenziale; **essentially** adv essenzialmente; **essentials** npl **the essentials** l'essenziale msg

establish [ɪ'stæblɪʃ] vt stabilire; (business) mettere su; (one's power etc) affermare; **establishment** n stabilimento; **the Establishment** la classe dirigente, l'establishment m

estate [ɪ'steɪt] n proprietà f inv; beni mpl, patrimonio; (BRIT: also: **housing ~**) complesso edilizio; **estate agent** (BRIT) n agente m immobiliare; **estate car** (BRIT) n giardiniera

estimate [n 'ɛstɪmət, vb 'ɛstɪmeɪt] n stima; (Comm) preventivo ▷ vt stimare, valutare

etc abbr (= et cetera) etc., ecc.

eternal [ɪ'təːnl] adj eterno(-a)

eternity [ɪ'təːnɪtɪ] n eternità

ethical ['ɛθɪkl] adj etico(-a), morale; **ethics** ['ɛθɪks] n etica ▷ npl morale f

Ethiopia [iːθɪ'əupɪə] n Etiopia

ethnic ['ɛθnɪk] adj etnico(-a); **ethnic minority** n minoranza etnica

etiquette ['ɛtɪkɛt] n etichetta

EU n abbr (= European Union) UE f

euro ['juərəu] n (currency) euro m inv

Europe ['juərəp] n Europa; **European** [-'piːən] adj, n europeo(-a); **European Community** n Comunità Europea; **European Union** n Unione f europea

Eurostar® ['juərəustɑː'] n Eurostar® m inv

evacuate [ɪ'vækjueɪt] vt evacuare

evade [ɪ'veɪd] vt (tax) evadere; (duties etc) sottrarsi a; (person) schivare

evaluate [ɪ'væljueɪt] vt valutare

evaporate [ɪ'væpəreɪt] vi evaporare

eve [iːv] n **on the ~ of** alla vigilia di

even ['iːvn] adj regolare; (number) pari inv ▷ adv anche, perfino; **~ if, ~ though** anche se; **~ more** ancora di più; **~ so** ciò nonostante; **not ~** nemmeno; **to get ~ with sb** dare la pari a qn

evening ['iːvnɪŋ] n sera; (as duration, event) serata; **in the ~** la sera; **evening class** n corso serale; **evening dress** n (woman's) abito da sera; **in evening dress** (man) in abito scuro; (woman) in abito lungo

event [ɪ'vɛnt] n avvenimento; (Sport) gara; **in the ~ of** in caso di; **eventful** adj denso(-a) di eventi

eventual [ɪ'vɛntʃuəl] adj finale

Be careful not to translate **eventual** by the Italian word **eventuale**.

eventually [ɪ'vɛntʃuəlɪ] adv alla fine

Be careful not to translate **eventually** by the Italian word **eventualmente**.

ever ['ɛvə'] adv mai; (at all times) sempre; **the best ~** il migliore che ci sia mai stato; **have you ~ seen it?** l'ha mai visto?; **~ since** adv da allora ▷ conj sin da quando; **~ so pretty** così bello(-a); **evergreen** n sempreverde m

every ['ɛvrɪ] adj ogni; **~ day** tutti i giorni, ogni giorno; **~ other/third day** ogni due/tre giorni; **~ other car** una macchina su due; **~ now and then** ogni tanto, di quando in quando; **everybody** pron = **everyone; everyday** adj quotidiano(-a); di ogni giorno; **everyone** pron ognuno, tutti pl; **everything** pron tutto, ogni cosa; **everywhere** adv (gen) dappertutto; (wherever) ovunque

evict [ɪ'vɪkt] vt sfrattare

evidence ['ɛvɪdns] n (proof) prova; (of witness) testimonianza; (sign): **to show ~ of** dare segni di; **to give ~** deporre

evident ['ɛvɪdnt] adj evidente; **evidently** adv evidentemente

evil ['iːvl] adj cattivo(-a), maligno(-a) ▷ n male m

evoke [ɪ'vəuk] vt evocare

evolution [iːvə'luːʃən] n evoluzione f

evolve [ɪ'vɔlv] vt elaborare ▷ vi svilupparsi, evolversi

ewe [juː] n pecora

ex- (inf) [ɛks] n **my ex** il (la) mio(-a) ex

ex- [ɛks] prefix ex

exact [ɪg'zækt] adj esatto(-a) ▷ vt **to ~ sth (from)** estorcere qc (da); esigere qc (da); **exactly** adv esattamente

exaggerate [ɪg'zædʒəreɪt] vt, vi esagerare; **exaggeration** [-'reɪʃən] n esagerazione f

exam [ɪg'zæm] n abbr (Scol) = **examination**

examination [ɪgzæmɪ'neɪʃən] n (Scol) esame m; (Med) controllo

examine [ɪg'zæmɪn] vt esaminare; **examiner** n esaminatore(-trice)

example [ɪg'zɑːmpl] n esempio; **for ~** ad or per esempio

exasperated [ɪg'zɑːspəreɪtɪd] adj esasperato(-a)

excavate ['ɛkskəveɪt] vt scavare

exceed [ɪk'siːd] vt superare; (one's powers, time limit) oltrepassare; **exceedingly** adv eccessivamente

excel [ɪk'sɛl] vi eccellere ▷ vt sorpassare; **to ~ o.s.** (BRIT) superare se stesso

excellence ['ɛksələns] n eccellenza

excellent ['ɛksələnt] *adj* eccellente
except [ɪk'sɛpt] *prep* (*also:* ~ **for, ~ing**) salvo, all'infuori di, eccetto ▷ *vt* escludere; ~ **if/when** salvo se/quando; ~ **that** salvo che; **exception** [ɪk'sɛpʃən] *n* eccezione *f*; **to take exception to** trovare a ridire su; **exceptional** [ɪk'sɛpʃənl] *adj* eccezionale; **exceptionally** [ɪk'sɛpʃənəlɪ] *adv* eccezionalmente
excerpt ['ɛksəːpt] *n* estratto
excess [ɪk'sɛs] *n* eccesso; **excess baggage** *n* bagaglio in eccedenza; **excessive** *adj* eccessivo(-a)
exchange [ɪks'tʃeɪndʒ] *n* scambio; (*also:* **telephone** ~) centralino ▷ *vt* **to** ~ **(for)** scambiare (con); **could I** ~ **this, please?** posso cambiarlo, per favore?; **exchange rate** *n* tasso di cambio
excite [ɪk'saɪt] *vt* eccitare; **to get** ~**d** eccitarsi; **excited** *adj* **to get excited** essere elettrizzato(-a); **excitement** *n* eccitazione *f*; agitazione *f*; **exciting** *adj* avventuroso(-a); (*film, book*) appassionante
exclaim [ɪk'skleɪm] *vi* esclamare; **exclamation** [ɛksklə'meɪʃən] *n* esclamazione *f*; **exclamation mark** (*US* **exclamation point**) *n* punto esclamativo
exclude [ɪk'skluːd] *vt* escludere
excluding [ɪk'skluːdɪŋ] *prep* ~ **VAT** IVA esclusa
exclusion [ɪk'skluːʒən] *n* esclusione *f*; **to the** ~ **of** escludendo
exclusive [ɪk'skluːsɪv] *adj* esclusivo(-a); ~ **of VAT** I.V.A. esclusa; **exclusively** *adv* esclusivamente
excruciating [ɪk'skruːʃɪeɪtɪŋ] *adj* straziante, atroce
excursion [ɪk'skəːʃən] *n* escursione *f*, gita
excuse [*n* ɪk'skjuːs, *vb* ɪk'skjuːz] *n* scusa ▷ *vt* scusare; **to** ~ **sb from** (*activity*) dispensare qn da; ~ **me!** mi scusi!; **now, if you will** ~ **me** ... ora, mi scusi ma ...
ex-directory ['ɛksdɪ'rɛktərɪ] (*BRIT*) *adj* (*Tel*): **to be** ~ non essere sull'elenco
execute ['ɛksɪkjuːt] *vt* (*prisoner*) giustiziare; (*plan etc*) eseguire; **execution** [ɛksɪ'kjuːʃən] *n* esecuzione *f*
executive [ɪg'zɛkjutɪv] *n* (*Comm*) dirigente *m*; (*Pol*) esecutivo ▷ *adj* esecutivo(-a)
exempt [ɪg'zɛmpt] *adj* esentato(-a) ▷ *vt* **to** ~ **sb from** esentare qn da
exercise ['ɛksəsaɪz] *n* (*keep fit*) moto; (*Scol, Mil etc*) esercizio ▷ *vt* esercitare; (*patience*) usare; (*dog*) portar fuori ▷ *vi* (*also:* **take** ~) fare del moto; **exercise book** *n* quaderno
exert [ɪg'zəːt] *vt* esercitare; **to** ~ **o.s.** sforzarsi; **exertion** [-ʃən] *n* sforzo
exhale [ɛks'heɪl] *vt, vi* espirare

exhaust [ɪg'zɔːst] *n* (*also:* ~ **fumes**) scappamento; (*also:* ~ **pipe**) tubo di scappamento ▷ *vt* esaurire; **exhausted** *adj* esaurito(-a); **exhaustion** [ɪg'zɔːstʃən] *n* esaurimento; **nervous exhaustion** sovraffaticamento mentale
exhibit [ɪg'zɪbɪt] *n* (*Art*) oggetto esposto; (*Law*) documento *or* oggetto esibito ▷ *vt* esporre; (*courage, skill*) dimostrare; **exhibition** [ɛksɪ'bɪʃən] *n* mostra, esposizione *f*
exhilarating [ɪg'zɪləreɪtɪŋ] *adj* esilarante; stimolante
exile ['ɛksaɪl] *n* esilio; (*person*) esiliato(-a) ▷ *vt* esiliare
exist [ɪg'zɪst] *vi* esistere; **existence** *n* esistenza; **existing** *adj* esistente
exit ['ɛksɪt] *n* uscita ▷ *vi* (*Theatre, Comput*) uscire; **where's the** ~? dov'è l'uscita?; **exit ramp** (*US*) *n* (*Aut*) rampa di uscita
exotic [ɪg'zɔtɪk] *adj* esotico(-a)
expand [ɪk'spænd] *vt* espandere; estendere; allargare ▷ *vi* (*business, gas*) espandersi; (*metal*) dilatarsi
expansion [ɪk'spænʃən] *n* (*gen*) espansione *f*; (*of town, economy*) sviluppo; (*of metal*) dilatazione *f*
expect [ɪk'spɛkt] *vt* (*anticipate*) prevedere, aspettarsi, prevedere *or* aspettarsi che + *sub*; (*require*) richiedere, esigere; (*suppose*) supporre; (*await, also baby*) aspettare ▷ *vi* **to be** ~**ing** essere in stato interessante; **to** ~ **sb to do** aspettarsi che qn faccia; **expectation** [ɛkspɛk'teɪʃən] *n* aspettativa; speranza
expedition [ɛkspə'dɪʃən] *n* spedizione *f*
expel [ɪk'spɛl] *vt* espellere
expenditure [ɪk'spɛndɪtʃəʳ] *n* spesa
expense [ɪk'spɛns] *n* spesa; (*high cost*) costo; ~**s** *npl* (*Comm*) spese *fpl*, indennità *fpl*; **at the** ~ **of** a spese di; **expense account** *n* conto *m* spese *inv*
expensive [ɪk'spɛnsɪv] *adj* caro(-a), costoso(-a); **it's too** ~ è troppo caro
experience [ɪk'spɪərɪəns] *n* esperienza ▷ *vt* (*pleasure*) provare; (*hardship*) soffrire; **experienced** *adj* esperto(-a)
experiment [*n* ɪk'spɛrɪmənt, *vb* ɪk'spɛrɪmɛnt] *n* esperimento, esperienza ▷ *vi* **to** ~ **(with/on)** fare esperimenti (con/su); **experimental** [ɪkspɛrɪ'mɛntl] *adj* sperimentale; **at the experimental stage** in via di sperimentazione
expert ['ɛkspəːt] *adj, n* esperto(-a); **expertise** [-'tiːz] *n* competenza
expire [ɪk'spaɪəʳ] *vi* (*period of time, licence*) scadere; **expiry** *n* scadenza; **expiry date** *n* (*of medicine, food item*) data di scadenza
explain [ɪk'spleɪn] *vt* spiegare;

explanation [ɛksplə'neɪʃən] n spiegazione f

explicit [ɪk'splɪsɪt] adj esplicito(-a)

explode [ɪk'spləud] vi esplodere

exploit [n 'ɛksplɔɪt, vb ɪk'splɔɪt] n impresa ▷ vt sfruttare; **exploitation** [-'teɪʃən] n sfruttamento

explore [ɪk'splɔːʳ] vt esplorare; (possibilities) esaminare; **explorer** n esploratore(-trice)

explosion [ɪk'spləuʒən] n esplosione f; **explosive** [ɪk'spləusɪv] adj esplosivo(-a) ▷ n esplosivo

export [vb ɛk'spɔːt, n 'ɛkspɔːt] vt esportare ▷ n esportazione f; articolo di esportazione ▷ cpd d'esportazione; **exporter** n esportatore m

expose [ɪk'spəuz] vt esporre; (unmask) smascherare; **exposed** adj (position) esposto(-a); **exposure** [ɪk'spəuʒəʳ] n esposizione f; (Phot) posa; (Med) assideramento

express [ɪk'sprɛs] adj (definite) chiaro(-a), espresso(-a); (BRIT: letter etc) espresso inv ▷ n (train) espresso ▷ vt esprimere; **expression** [ɪk'sprɛʃən] n espressione f; **expressway** (US) n (urban motorway) autostrada che attraversa la città

exquisite [ɛk'skwɪzɪt] adj squisito(-a)

extend [ɪk'stɛnd] vt (visit) protrarre; (road, deadline) prolungare; (building) ampliare; (offer) offrire, porgere ▷ vi (land, period) estendersi; **extension** [ɪk'stɛnʃən] n (of road, term) prolungamento; (of contract, deadline) proroga; (building) annesso; (to wire, table) prolunga; (telephone) interno; (: in private house) apparecchio supplementare; **extension lead** n prolunga

extensive [ɪk'stɛnsɪv] adj esteso(-a), ampio(-a); (damage) su larga scala; (coverage, discussion) esauriente; (use) grande

extent [ɪk'stɛnt] n estensione f; **to some ~** fino a un certo punto; **to such an ~ that ...** a un tal punto che ...; **to what ~?** fino a che punto?; **to the ~ of ...** fino al punto di ...

exterior [ɛk'stɪərɪəʳ] adj esteriore, esterno(-a) ▷ n esteriore m, esterno; aspetto (esteriore)

external [ɛk'stəːnl] adj esterno(-a), esteriore

extinct [ɪk'stɪŋkt] adj estinto(-a); **extinction** [ɪk'stɪŋkʃən] n estinzione f

extinguish [ɪk'stɪŋgwɪʃ] vt estinguere

extra ['ɛkstrə] adj extra inv, supplementare ▷ adv (in addition) di più ▷ n extra m inv; (surcharge) supplemento; (Cinema, Theatre) comparsa

extract [vb ɪk'strækt, n 'ɛkstrækt] vt estrarre; (money, promise) strappare ▷ n estratto; (passage) brano

extradite ['ɛkstrədaɪt] vt estradare

extraordinary [ɪk'strɔːdnrɪ] adj straordinario(-a)

extravagance [ɪk'strævəgəns] n sperpero; stravaganza

extravagant [ɪk'strævəgənt] adj (lavish) prodigo(-a); (wasteful) dispendioso(-a)

> Be careful not to translate **extravagant** by the Italian word **stravagante**.

extreme [ɪk'striːm] adj estremo(-a) ▷ n estremo; **extremely** adv estremamente

extremist [ɪk'striːmɪst] adj, n estremista (m/f)

extrovert ['ɛkstrəvəːt] n estroverso(-a)

eye [aɪ] n occhio; (of needle) cruna ▷ vt osservare; **to keep an ~ on** tenere d'occhio; **eyeball** n globo dell'occhio; **eyebrow** n sopracciglio; **eyedrops** npl gocce fpl oculari, collirio; **eyelash** n ciglio; **eyelid** n palpebra; **eyeliner** n eye-liner m inv; **eyeshadow** n ombretto; **eyesight** n vista; **eye witness** n testimone m/f oculare

F [ɛf] *n* (*Mus*) fa *m*

fabric ['fæbrɪk] *n* stoffa, tessuto

fabulous ['fæbjʊləs] *adj* favoloso(-a); (*super*) favoloso(-a), fantastico(-a)

face [feɪs] *n* faccia, viso, volto; (*expression*) faccia; (*of clock*) quadrante *m*; (*of building*) facciata ▷ *vt* essere di fronte a; (*facts, situation*) affrontare; **~ down** a faccia in giù; **to make** *or* **pull a ~** fare una smorfia; **in the ~ of** (*difficulties etc*) di fronte a; **on the ~ of it** a prima vista; **~ to ~** faccia a faccia; **face up to** *vt fus* affrontare, far fronte a; **face cloth** (*BRIT*) *n* guanto di spugna; **face pack** *n* (*BRIT*) maschera di bellezza

facial ['feɪʃəl] *adj* del viso

facilitate [fəˈsɪlɪteɪt] *vt* facilitare

facilities [fəˈsɪlɪtɪz] *npl* attrezzature *fpl*; **credit ~** facilitazioni *fpl* di credito

fact [fækt] *n* fatto; **in ~** in effetti

faction ['fækʃən] *n* fazione *f*

factor ['fæktəʳ] *n* fattore *m*; **I'd like a ~ 15 suntan lotion** vorrei una crema solare con fattore di protezione 15

factory ['fæktərɪ] *n* fabbrica, stabilimento
> Be careful not to translate **factory** by the Italian word **fattoria**.

factual ['fæktjʊəl] *adj* che si attiene ai fatti

faculty ['fækəltɪ] *n* facoltà *f inv*; (*US*) corpo insegnante

fad [fæd] *n* mania; capriccio

fade [feɪd] *vi* sbiadire, sbiadirsi; (*light, sound, hope*) attenuarsi, affievolirsi; (*flower*) appassire; **fade away** *vi* (*sound*) affievolirsi

fag [fæg] (*BRIT: inf*) *n* (*cigarette*) cicca

Fahrenheit ['fɑːrənhaɪt] *n* Fahrenheit *m inv*

fail [feɪl] *vt* (*exam*) non superare; (*candidate*) bocciare; (*courage, memory*) mancare a ▷ *vi* fallire; (*student*) essere respinto(-a); (*eyesight, health, light*) venire a mancare; **to ~ to do sth** (*neglect*) mancare di fare qc; (*be unable*) non riuscire a fare qc; **without ~** senza fallo; certamente; **failing** *n* difetto ▷ *prep* in mancanza di; **failure** ['feɪljəʳ] *n* fallimento; (*person*) fallito(-a); (*mechanical etc*) guasto

faint [feɪnt] *adj* debole; (*recollection*) vago(-a); (*mark*) indistinto(-a) ▷ *n* (*Med*) svenimento ▷ *vi* svenire; **to feel ~** sentirsi svenire; **faintest** *adj* **I haven't the faintest idea** non ho la più pallida idea; **faintly** *adv* debolmente; vagamente

fair [fɛəʳ] *adj* (*person, decision*) giusto(-a), equo(-a); (*quite large, quite good*) discreto(-a); (*hair etc*) biondo(-a); (*skin, complexion*) chiaro(-a); (*weather*) bello(-a), clemente ▷ *adv* (*play*) lealmente ▷ *n* fiera; (*BRIT: funfair*) luna park *m inv*; **fairground** *n* luna park *m inv*; **fair-haired** [fɛəˈhɛəd] *adj* (*person*) biondo(-a); **fairly** *adv* equamente; (*quite*) abbastanza; **fairway** *n* (*Golf*) fairway *m inv*

fairy ['fɛərɪ] *n* fata; **fairy tale** *n* fiaba

faith [feɪθ] *n* fede *f*; (*trust*) fiducia; (*sect*) religione *f*, fede *f*; **faithful** *adj* fedele; **faithfully** *adv* fedelmente; **yours faithfully** (*BRIT: in letters*) distinti saluti

fake [feɪk] *n* imitazione *f*; (*picture*) falso; (*person*) impostore(-a) ▷ *adj* falso(-a) ▷ *vt* (*accounts*) falsificare; (*illness*) fingere; (*painting*) contraffare

falcon ['fɔːlkən] *n* falco, falcone *m*

fall [fɔːl] (*pt* **fell**, *pp* **fallen**) *n* caduta; (*in temperature*) abbassamento; (*in price*) ribasso; (*US: autumn*) autunno ▷ *vi* cadere; (*temperature, price, night*) scendere; **~s** *npl* (*waterfall*) cascate *fpl*; **to ~ flat** (*on one's face*) cadere bocconi; (*joke*) fare cilecca; (*plan*) fallire; **fall apart** *vi* cadere a pezzi; **fall down** *vi* (*person*) cadere; (*building*) crollare; **fall for** *vt fus* (*person*) prendere una cotta per; **to ~ for a trick** (*or* **a story** *etc*) cascarci; **fall off** *vi* cadere; (*diminish*) diminuire, abbassarsi; **fall out** *vi* (*hair, teeth*) cadere; (*friends etc*) litigare; **fall over** *vi* cadere; **fall through** *vi* (*plan, project*) fallire

fallen ['fɔːlən] pp of **fall**

fallout ['fɔːlaut] n fall-out m

false [fɔːls] adj falso(-a); **under ~ pretences** con l'inganno; **false alarm** n falso allarme m; **false teeth** (BRIT) npl denti mpl finti

fame [feɪm] n fama, celebrità

familiar [fə'mɪlɪəʳ] adj familiare; (close) intimo(-a); **to be ~ with** (subject) conoscere; **familiarize** [fə'mɪlɪəraɪz] vt **to familiarize o.s. with** familiarizzare con

family ['fæmɪlɪ] n famiglia; **family doctor** n medico di famiglia; **family planning** n pianificazione f familiare

famine ['fæmɪn] n carestia

famous ['feɪməs] adj famoso(-a)

fan [fæn] n (folding) ventaglio; (Elec) ventilatore m; (person) ammiratore(-trice), tifoso(-a) ▷ vt far vento a; (fire, quarrel) alimentare

fanatic [fə'nætɪk] n fanatico(-a)

fan belt n cinghia del ventilatore

fan club n fan club m inv

fancy ['fænsɪ] n immaginazione f, fantasia; (whim) capriccio ▷ adj (hat) stravagante; (hotel, food) speciale ▷ vt (feel like, want) aver voglia di; (imagine, think) immaginare; **to take a ~ to** incapricciarsi di; **he fancies her** (inf) gli piace; **fancy dress** n costume m (per maschera)

fan heater n (BRIT) stufa ad aria calda

fantasize ['fæntəsaɪz] vi fantasticare, sognare

fantastic [fæn'tæstɪk] adj fantastico(-a)

fantasy ['fæntəsɪ] n fantasia, immaginazione f; fantasticheria; chimera

fanzine ['fænziːn] n rivista specialistica (per appassionati)

FAQs abbr (= frequently asked questions) FAQ fpl

far [fɑːʳ] adj lontano(-a) ▷ adv lontano; (much, greatly) molto; **is it ~ from here?** è molto lontano da qui?; **how ~?** quanto lontano?; (referring to activity etc) fino a dove?; **how ~ is the town centre?** quanto dista il centro da qui?; **~ away, ~ off** lontano, distante; **~ better** assai migliore; **~ from** lontano da; **by ~** di gran lunga; **go as ~ as the farm** vada fino alla fattoria; **as ~ as I know** per quel che so

farce [fɑːs] n farsa

fare [fɛəʳ] n (on trains, buses) tariffa; (in taxi) prezzo della corsa; (food) vitto, cibo; **half ~** metà tariffa; **full ~** tariffa intera

Far East n the ~ l'Estremo Oriente m

farewell [fɛə'wɛl] excl, n addio

farm [fɑːm] n fattoria, podere m ▷ vt coltivare; **farmer** n coltivatore(-trice), agricoltore(-trice); **farmhouse** n fattoria;

farming n (gen) agricoltura; (of crops) coltivazione f; (of animals) allevamento;

farmyard n aia

far-reaching [fɑː'riːtʃɪŋ] adj di vasta portata

fart [fɑːt] (inf!) vi scoreggiare (!)

farther ['fɑːðəʳ] adv più lontano ▷ adj più lontano(-a)

farthest ['fɑːðɪst] superl of **far**

fascinate ['fæsɪneɪt] vt affascinare;

fascinated adj affascinato(-a);

fascinating adj affascinante;

fascination [-'neɪʃən] n fascino

fascist ['fæʃɪst] adj, n fascista (m/f)

fashion ['fæʃən] n (manner) maniera, modo ▷ vt foggiare, formare; **in ~** alla moda; **out of ~** passato(-a) di moda;

fashionable adj alla moda, di moda;

fashion show n sfilata di moda

fast [fɑːst] adj rapido(-a), svelto(-a), veloce; (clock): **to be ~** andare avanti; (dye, colour) solido(-a) ▷ adv rapidamente; (stuck, held) saldamente ▷ n digiuno ▷ vi digiunare; **~ asleep** profondamente addormentato

fasten ['fɑːsn] vt chiudere, fissare; (coat) abbottonare, allacciare ▷ vi chiudersi, fissarsi; abbottonarsi, allacciarsi

fast food n fast food m

fat [fæt] adj grasso(-a); (book, profit etc) grosso(-a) ▷ n grasso

fatal ['feɪtl] adj fatale; mortale; disastroso(-a); **fatality** [fə'tælɪtɪ] n (road death etc) morto(-a), vittima; **fatally** adv a morte

fate [feɪt] n destino; (of person) sorte f

father ['fɑːðəʳ] n padre m; **Father Christmas** n Babbo Natale; **father-in-law** n suocero

fatigue [fə'tiːg] n stanchezza

fattening ['fætnɪŋ] adj (food) che fa ingrassare

fatty ['fætɪ] adj (food) grasso(-a) ▷ n (inf) ciccione(-a)

faucet ['fɔːsɪt] (US) n rubinetto

fault [fɔːlt] n colpa; (Tennis) fallo; (defect) difetto; (Geo) faglia ▷ vt criticare; **it's my ~** è colpa mia; **to find ~ with** trovare da ridire su; **at ~** in fallo; **faulty** adj difettoso(-a)

fauna ['fɔːnə] n fauna

favour etc ['feɪvəʳ] (US **favor**) n favore m ▷ vt (proposition) favorire, essere favorevole a; (pupil etc) favorire; (team, horse) dare per vincente; **to do sb a ~** fare un favore or una cortesia a qn; **to find ~ with** (person) entrare nelle buone grazie di; (: suggestion) avere l'approvazione di; **in ~ of** in favore di; **favourable** adj favorevole; **favourite** [-rɪt] adj, n favorito(-a)

fawn [fɔːn] *n* daino ▷ *adj* (*also:* **~-coloured**) marrone chiaro *inv* ▷ *vi* **to ~ (up)on** adulare servilmente

fax [fæks] *n* (*document*) facsimile *m inv*, telecopia; (*machine*) telecopiatrice *f* ▷ *vt* telecopiare, trasmettere in facsimile

FBI (US) *n abbr* (= *Federal Bureau of Investigation*) F.B.I. *f*

fear [fɪəʳ] *n* paura, timore *m* ▷ *vt* aver paura di, temere; **for ~ of** per paura di; **fearful** *adj* pauroso(-a); (*sight, noise*) terribile, spaventoso(-a); **fearless** *adj* intrepido(-a), senza paura

feasible ['fiːzəbl] *adj* possibile, realizzabile

feast [fiːst] *n* festa, banchetto; (*Rel: also:* **~ day**) festa ▷ *vi* banchettare

feat [fiːt] *n* impresa, fatto insigne

feather ['fɛðəʳ] *n* penna

feature ['fiːtʃəʳ] *n* caratteristica; (*Press, TV*) articolo ▷ *vt* (*film*) avere come protagonista ▷ *vi* figurare; **~s** *npl* (*of face*) fisionomia; **feature film** *n* film *m inv* principale

Feb. [fɛb] *abbr* (= *February*) feb

February ['fɛbruəri] *n* febbraio

fed [fɛd] *pt, pp of* **feed**

federal ['fɛdərəl] *adj* federale

federation [fɛdə'reɪʃən] *n* federazione *f*

fed up *adj* **to be ~** essere stufo(-a)

fee [fiː] *n* pagamento; (*of doctor, lawyer*) onorario; (*for examination*) tassa d'esame; **school ~s** tasse *fpl* scolastiche

feeble ['fiːbl] *adj* debole

feed [fiːd] (*pt, pp* **fed**) *n* (*of baby*) pappa; (*of animal*) mangime *m*; (*on printer*) meccanismo di alimentazione ▷ *vt* nutrire; (*baby*) allattare; (*horse etc*) dare da mangiare a; (*fire, machine*) alimentare; (*data, information*) **to ~ into** inserire in; **feedback** *n* feed-back *m*

feel [fiːl] (*pt, pp* **felt**) *n* consistenza; (*sense of touch*) tatto ▷ *vt* toccare; palpare; tastare; (*cold, pain, anger*) sentire; (*think, believe*): **to ~ (that)** pensare che; **to ~ hungry/cold** aver fame/freddo; **to ~ lonely/better** sentirsi solo/meglio; **I don't ~ well** non mi sento bene; **it ~s soft** è morbido al tatto; **to ~ like** (*want*) aver voglia di; **to ~ about** *or* **around for** cercare a tastoni; **feeling** *n* sensazione *f*; (*emotion*) sentimento

feet [fiːt] *npl of* **foot**

fell [fɛl] *pt of* **fall** ▷ *vt* (*tree*) abbattere

fellow ['fɛləu] *n* individuo, tipo; compagno; (*of learned society*) membro *cpd*; **fellow citizen** *n* concittadino(-a); **fellow countryman** (*irreg*) *n* compatriota *m*; **fellow men** *npl* simili *mpl*; **fellowship** *n* associazione *f*; compagnia; specie di borsa di studio universitaria

felony ['fɛlənɪ] *n* reato, crimine *m*

felt [fɛlt] *pt, pp of* **feel** ▷ *n* feltro

female ['fiːmeɪl] *n* (*Zool*) femmina; (*pej: woman*) donna, femmina ▷ *adj* (*Biol, Elec*) femmina *inv*; (*sex, character*) femminile; (*vote etc*) di donne

feminine ['fɛmɪnɪn] *adj* femminile

feminist ['fɛmɪnɪst] *n* femminista *m/f*

fence [fɛns] *n* recinto ▷ *vt* (*also:* **~ in**) recingere ▷ *vi* (*Sport*) tirare di scherma; **fencing** *n* (*Sport*) scherma

fend [fɛnd] *vi* **to ~ for o.s.** arrangiarsi; **fend off** *vt* (*attack, questions*) respingere, difendersi da

fender ['fɛndəʳ] *n* parafuoco; (*on boat*) parabordo; (*US*) parafango; paraurti *m inv*

fennel ['fɛnl] *n* finocchio

ferment [*vb* fə'mɛnt, *n* 'fəːmɛnt] *vi* fermentare ▷ *n* (*fig*) agitazione *f*, eccitazione *f*

fern [fəːn] *n* felce *f*

ferocious [fə'rəuʃəs] *adj* feroce

ferret ['fɛrɪt] *n* furetto

ferry ['fɛrɪ] *n* (*small*) traghetto; (*large: also:* **~boat**) nave *f* traghetto *inv* ▷ *vt* traghettare

fertile ['fəːtaɪl] *adj* fertile; (*Biol*) fecondo(-a); **fertilize** ['fəːtɪlaɪz] *vt* fertilizzare; fecondare; **fertilizer** ['fəːtɪlaɪzə] *n* fertilizzante *m*

festival ['fɛstɪvəl] *n* (*Rel*) festa; (*Art, Mus*) festival *m inv*

festive ['fɛstɪv] *adj* di festa; **the ~ season** (*BRIT: Christmas*) il periodo delle feste

fetch [fɛtʃ] *vt* andare a prendere; (*sell for*) essere venduto(-a) per

fête [feɪt] *n* festa

fetus ['fiːtəs] (*US*) *n* = **foetus**

feud [fjuːd] *n* contesa, lotta

fever ['fiːvəʳ] *n* febbre *f*; **feverish** *adj* febbrile

few [fjuː] *adj* pochi(-e); **a ~** *adj* qualche *inv* ▷ *pron* alcuni(-e); **fewer** *adj* meno *inv*, meno numerosi(-e); **fewest** *adj* il minor numero di

fiancé [fɪ'ɑ̃ːŋseɪ] *n* fidanzato; **fiancée** *n* fidanzata

fiasco [fɪ'æskəu] *n* fiasco

fib [fɪb] *n* piccola bugia

fibre ['faɪbəʳ] (US **fiber**) *n* fibra; **Fibreglass®** ['faɪbəglɑːs] (US **fiberglass**) *n* fibra di vetro

fickle ['fɪkl] *adj* incostante, capriccioso(-a)

fiction ['fɪkʃən] *n* narrativa, romanzi *mpl*; (*sth made up*) finzione *f*; **fictional** *adj* immaginario(-a)

fiddle ['fɪdl] *n* (*Mus*) violino; (*cheating*) imbroglio; truffa ▷ *vt* (*BRIT: accounts*) falsificare, falsare; **fiddle with** *vt fus* gingillarsi con

fidelity [fɪˈdɛlɪtɪ] n fedeltà; (accuracy) esattezza

field [fiːld] n campo; **field marshal** n feldmaresciallo

fierce [fɪəs] adj (animal, person, fighting) feroce; (loyalty) assoluto(-a); (wind) furioso(-a); (heat) intenso(-a)

fifteen [fɪfˈtiːn] num quindici; **fifteenth** num quindicesimo(-a)

fifth [fɪfθ] num quinto(-a)

fiftieth [ˈfɪftɪɪθ] num cinquantesimo(-a)

fifty [ˈfɪftɪ] num cinquanta; **fifty-fifty** adj **a fifty-fifty chance** una possibilità su due ▷ adv fifty-fifty, metà per ciascuno

fig [fɪg] n fico

fight [faɪt] (pt, pp **fought**) n zuffa, rissa; (Mil) battaglia, combattimento; (against cancer etc) lotta ▷ vt (person) azzuffarsi con; (enemy: also Mil) combattere; (cancer, alcoholism, emotion) lottare contro, combattere; (election) partecipare a ▷ vi combattere; **fight back** vi difendersi; (Sport, after illness) riprendersi ▷ vt (tears) ricacciare; **fight off** vt (attack, attacker) respingere; (disease, sleep, urge) lottare contro; **fighting** n combattimento

figure [ˈfɪgəʳ] n figura; (number, cipher) cifra ▷ vt (think: esp us) pensare ▷ vi (appear) figurare; **figure out** vt riuscire a capire; calcolare

file [faɪl] n (tool) lima; (dossier) incartamento; (folder) cartellina; (Comput) archivio; (row) fila ▷ vt (nails, wood) limare; (papers) archiviare; (Law: claim) presentare; passare agli atti; **filing cabinet** [ˈfaɪlɪŋ-] n casellario

Filipino [fɪlɪˈpiːnəu] n filippino(-a); (Ling) tagala m

fill [fɪl] vt riempire; (job) coprire ▷ n **to eat one's ~** mangiare a sazietà; **fill in** vt (hole) riempire; (form) compilare; **fill out** vt (form, receipt) riempire; **fill up** vt riempire; **~ it up, please** (Aut) il pieno, per favore

fillet [ˈfɪlɪt] n filetto; **fillet steak** n bistecca di filetto

filling [ˈfɪlɪŋ] n (Culin) impasto, ripieno; (for tooth) otturazione f; **filling station** n stazione f di rifornimento

film [fɪlm] n (Cinema) film m inv; (Phot) pellicola, rullino; (of powder, liquid) sottile strato ▷ vt, vi girare; **I'd like a 36-exposure ~** vorrei un rullino da 36 pose; **film star** n divo(-a) dello schermo

filter [ˈfɪltəʳ] n filtro ▷ vt filtrare; **filter lane** (brit) n (Aut) corsia di svincolo

filth [fɪlθ] n sporcizia; **filthy** adj lordo(-a), sozzo(-a); (language) osceno(-a)

fin [fɪn] n (of fish) pinna

final [ˈfaɪnl] adj finale, ultimo(-a); definitivo(-a) ▷ n (Sport) finale f; **~s** npl (Scol) esami mpl finali; **finale** [fɪˈnɑːlɪ] n finale m; **finalist** [ˈfaɪnəlɪst] n (Sport) finalista m/f; **finalize** [ˈfaɪnəlaɪz] vt mettere a punto; **finally** [ˈfaɪnəlɪ] adv (lastly) alla fine; (eventually) finalmente

finance [faɪˈnæns] n finanza; (capital) capitale m ▷ vt finanziare; **~s** npl (funds) finanze fpl; **financial** [faɪˈnænʃəl] adj finanziario(-a); **financial year** n anno finanziario, esercizio finanziario

find [faɪnd] (pt, pp **found**) vt trovare; (lost object) ritrovare ▷ n trovata, scoperta; **to ~ sb guilty** (Law) giudicare qn colpevole; **find out** vt (truth, secret) scoprire; (person) cogliere in fallo; **to ~ out about** informarsi su; (by chance) scoprire; **findings** npl (Law) sentenza, conclusioni fpl; (of report) conclusioni

fine [faɪn] adj bello(-a); ottimo(-a); (thin, subtle) fine ▷ adv (well) molto bene ▷ n (Law) multa ▷ vt (Law) multare; **to be ~** (person) stare bene; (weather) far bello; **fine arts** npl belle arti fpl

finger [ˈfɪŋgəʳ] n dito ▷ vt toccare, tastare; **little/index ~** mignolo/(dito) indice m; **fingernail** n unghia; **fingerprint** n impronta digitale; **fingertip** n punta del dito

finish [ˈfɪnɪʃ] n fine f; (polish etc) finitura ▷ vt, vi finire; **when does the show ~?** quando finisce lo spettacolo?; **to ~ doing sth** finire di fare qc; **to ~ third** arrivare terzo(-a); **finish off** vt compiere; (kill) uccidere; **finish up** vi, vt finire

Finland [ˈfɪnlənd] n Finlandia; **Finn** [fɪn] n finlandese m/f; **Finnish** adj finlandese ▷ n (Ling) finlandese m

fir [fəːʳ] n abete m

fire [faɪəʳ] n fuoco; (destructive) incendio; (gas fire, electric fire) stufa ▷ vt (gun) far fuoco con; (arrow) sparare; (fig) infiammare; (inf: dismiss) licenziare ▷ vi sparare, far fuoco; **~!** al fuoco!; **on ~** in fiamme; **fire alarm** n allarme m d'incendio; **firearm** n arma da fuoco; **fire brigade** [-brɪˈgeɪd] (us **fire department**) n (corpo dei) pompieri mpl; **fire engine** n autopompa; **fire escape** n scala di sicurezza; **fire exit** n uscita di sicurezza; **fire extinguisher** [-ɪkˈstɪŋgwɪʃəʳ] n estintore m; **fireman** (irreg) n pompiere m; **fireplace** n focolare m; **fire station** n caserma dei pompieri; **firetruck** (us) n = **fire engine**; **firewall** n (Internet) firewall m inv; **firewood** n legna; **fireworks** npl fuochi mpl d'artificio

firm [fəːm] adj fermo(-a) ▷ n ditta,

azienda; **firmly** adv fermamente
first [fəːst] adj primo(-a) ▷ adv (before
others) il primo, la prima; (before other
things) per primo; (when listing reasons
etc) per prima cosa ▷ n (person: in race)
primo(-a); (BRIT Scol) laurea con lode;
(Aut) prima; **at ~** dapprima, all'inizio; **~
of all** prima di tutto; **first aid** n pronto
soccorso; **first-aid kit** n cassetta pronto
soccorso; **first-class** adj di prima classe;
first-hand adj di prima mano; **first lady**
(US) n moglie f del presidente; **firstly** adv
in primo luogo; **first name** n prenome m;
first-rate adj di prima qualità, ottimo(-a)
fiscal ['fɪskəl] adj fiscale; **fiscal year** n
anno fiscale
fish [fɪʃ] n inv pesce m ▷ vt (river, area)
pescare in ▷ vi pescare; **to go ~ing** andare
a pesca; **fish and chip shop** n see **chip
shop**; **fisherman** (irreg) n pescatore m;
fish fingers (BRIT) npl bastoncini mpl
di pesce (surgelati); **fishing** n pesca;
fishing boat n barca da pesca; **fishing
line** n lenza; **fishmonger** n pescivendolo;
fishmonger's (shop) n pescheria; **fish
sticks** (US) npl = **fish fingers**; **fishy** (inf)
adj (tale, story) sospetto(-a)
fist [fɪst] n pugno
fit [fɪt] adj (Med, Sport) in forma; (proper)
adatto(-a), appropriato(-a); conveniente
▷ vt (clothes) stare bene a; (put in, attach)
mettere; installare; (equip) fornire,
equipaggiare ▷ vi (clothes) stare bene;
(parts) andare bene, adattarsi; (in space,
gap) entrare ▷ n (Med) accesso, attacco; **~
to** in grado di; **~ for** adatto(-a) a, degno(-a)
di; **a ~ of anger** un accesso d'ira; **this dress
is a good ~** questo vestito sta bene; **by ~s
and starts** a sbalzi; **fit in** vi accordarsi;
adattarsi; **fitness** n (Med) forma fisica;
fitted adj **fitted cupboards** armadi mpl
a muro; **fitted carpet** moquette f inv;
fitted kitchen (BRIT) cucina componibile;
fitting adj appropriato(-a) ▷ n (of dress)
prova; (of piece of equipment) montaggio,
aggiustaggio; **fitting room** n camerino;
fittings npl (in building) impianti mpl
five [faɪv] num cinque; **fiver** (inf) n (BRIT)
biglietto da cinque sterline; (US) biglietto
da cinque dollari
fix [fɪks] vt fissare; (mend) riparare; (meal,
drink) preparare ▷ n **to be in a ~** essere nei
guai; **fix up** vt (meeting) fissare; **to ~ sb up
with sth** procurare qc a qn; **fixed** [fɪkst]
adj (prices etc) fisso(-a); **fixture** ['fɪkstʃəʳ]
n impianto (fisso); (Sport) incontro (del
calendario sportivo)
fizzy ['fɪzɪ] adj frizzante; gassato(-a)
flag [flæg] n bandiera; (also: **~stone**) pietra

da lastricare ▷ vi stancarsi; affievolirsi;
flagpole ['flægpəʊl] n albero
flair [fleəʳ] n (for business etc) fiuto; (for
languages etc) facilità; (style) stile m
flak [flæk] n (Mil) fuoco d'artiglieria; (inf:
criticism) critiche fpl
flake [fleɪk] n (of rust, paint) scaglia; (of
snow, soap powder) fiocco ▷ vi (also: **~ off**)
sfaldarsi
flamboyant [flæm'bɔɪənt] adj sgargiante
flame [fleɪm] n fiamma
flamingo [flə'mɪŋgəʊ] n fenicottero,
fiammingo
flammable ['flæməbl] adj infiammabile
flan [flæn] (BRIT) n flan m inv
flank [flæŋk] n fianco ▷ vt fiancheggiare
flannel ['flænl] n (BRIT: also: **face ~**)
guanto di spugna; (fabric) flanella
flap [flæp] n (of pocket) patta; (of envelope)
lembo ▷ vt (wings) battere ▷ vi (sail, flag)
sbattere; (inf: also: **be in a ~**) essere in
agitazione
flare [fleəʳ] n razzo; (in skirt etc) svasatura;
~s (trousers) pantaloni mpl a zampa
d'elefante; **flare up** vi andare in fiamme;
(fig: person) infiammarsi di rabbia; (: revolt)
scoppiare
flash [flæʃ] n vampata; (also: **news ~**)
notizia f lampo inv; (Phot) flash m inv ▷ vt
accendere e spegnere; (send: message)
trasmettere; (: look, smile) lanciare ▷ vi
brillare; (light on ambulance, eyes etc)
lampeggiare; **in a ~** in un lampo; **to ~
one's headlights** lampeggiare; **he ~ed by
or past** ci passò davanti come un lampo;
flashback n flashback m inv; **flashbulb** n
cubo m flash inv; **flashlight** n lampadina
tascabile
flask [flɑːsk] n fiasco; (also: **vacuum ~**)
Thermos® m inv
flat [flæt] adj piatto(-a); (tyre) sgonfio(-a),
a terra; (battery) scarico(-a); (beer)
svampito(-a); (denial) netto(-a); (Mus)
bemolle inv; (: voice) stonato(-a); (rate, fee)
unico(-a) ▷ n (BRIT: rooms) appartamento;
(Aut) pneumatico sgonfio; (Mus) bemolle
m; **to work ~ out** lavorare a più non posso;
flatten vt (also: **flatten out**) appiattire;
(building, city) spianare
flatter ['flætəʳ] vt lusingare; **flattering** adj
lusinghiero(-a); (dress) che dona
flaunt [flɔːnt] vt fare mostra di
flavour etc ['fleɪvəʳ] (US **flavor**) n gusto
▷ vt insaporire, aggiungere sapore a;
what ~s do you have? che gusti avete?;
strawberry-~ed al gusto di fragola;
flavouring n essenza (artificiale)
flaw [flɔː] n difetto; **flawless** adj senza
difetti

flea [fliː] n pulce f; **flea market** n mercato delle pulci

flee [fliː] (pt, pp **fled**) vt fuggire da ▷ vi fuggire, scappare

fleece [fliːs] n vello ▷ vt (inf) pelare

fleet [fliːt] n flotta; (of lorries etc) convoglio; parco

fleeting [ˈfliːtɪŋ] adj fugace, fuggitivo(-a); (visit) volante

Flemish [ˈflemɪʃ] adj fiammingo(-a)

flesh [fleʃ] n carne f; (of fruit) polpa

flew [fluː] pt of **fly**

flex [fleks] n filo (flessibile) ▷ vt flettere; (muscles) contrarre; **flexibility** n flessibilità; **flexible** adj flessibile; **flexitime** [ˈfleksɪtaɪm] n orario flessibile

flick [flɪk] n colpetto; scarto ▷ vt dare un colpetto a; **flick through** vt fus sfogliare

flicker [ˈflɪkər] vi tremolare

flies [flaɪz] npl of **fly**

flight [flaɪt] n volo; (escape) fuga; (also: **~ of steps**) scalinata; **flight attendant** (US) n steward m inv, hostess f inv

flimsy [ˈflɪmzɪ] adj (shoes, clothes) leggero(-a); (building) poco solido(-a); (excuse) che non regge

flinch [flɪntʃ] vi ritirarsi; **to ~ from** tirarsi indietro di fronte a

fling [flɪŋ] (pt, pp **flung**) vt lanciare, gettare

flint [flɪnt] n selce f; (in lighter) pietrina

flip [flɪp] vt (switch) far scattare; (coin) lanciare in aria

flip-flops [ˈflɪpflɒps] npl (esp BRIT: sandals) infradito mpl

flipper [ˈflɪpər] n pinna

flirt [fləːt] vi flirtare ▷ n civetta

float [fləʊt] n galleggiante m; (in procession) carro; (money) somma ▷ vi galleggiare

flock [flɒk] n (of sheep, Rel) gregge m; (of birds) stormo ▷ vi **to ~ to** accorrere in massa a

flood [flʌd] n alluvione m; (of letters etc) marea ▷ vt allagare; (people) invadere ▷ vi (place) allagarsi; (people): **to ~ into** riversarsi in; **flooding** n inondazione f; **floodlight** n riflettore m ▷ vt illuminare a giorno

floor [flɔːr] n pavimento; (storey) piano; (of sea, valley) fondo ▷ vt (blow) atterrare; (: question) ridurre al silenzio; **which ~ is it on?** a che piano si trova?; **ground ~** (BRIT), **first ~** (US) pianterreno; **first ~** (BRIT), **second ~** (US) primo piano; **floorboard** n tavellone m di legno; **flooring** n (floor) pavimento; (material) materiale m per pavimentazioni; **floor show** n spettacolo di varietà

flop [flɒp] n fiasco ▷ vi far fiasco; (fall)

lasciarsi cadere; **floppy** [ˈflɒpɪ] adj floscio(-a), molle

floral [ˈflɔːrl] adj floreale

Florence [ˈflɒrəns] n Firenze f

Florentine [ˈflɒrəntaɪn] adj fiorentino(-a)

florist [ˈflɒrɪst] n fioraio(-a); **florist's (shop)** n fioraio(-a)

flotation [fləʊˈteɪʃən] n (Comm) lancio

flour [ˈflaʊər] n farina

flourish [ˈflʌrɪʃ] vi fiorire ▷ n (bold gesture): **with a ~** con ostentazione

flow [fləʊ] n flusso; circolazione f ▷ vi fluire; (traffic, blood in veins) circolare; (hair) scendere

flower [ˈflaʊər] n fiore m ▷ vi fiorire; **flower bed** n aiuola; **flowerpot** n vaso da fiori

flown [fləʊn] pp of **fly**

fl. oz. abbr = **fluid ounce**

flu [fluː] n influenza

fluctuate [ˈflʌktjʊeɪt] vi fluttuare, oscillare

fluent [ˈfluːənt] adj (speech) facile, sciolto(-a); corrente; **he speaks ~ Italian, he's ~ in Italian** parla l'italiano correntemente

fluff [flʌf] n lanugine f; **fluffy** adj lanuginoso(-a); (toy) di peluche

fluid [ˈfluːɪd] adj fluido(-a) ▷ n fluido; **fluid ounce** (BRIT) = 0.028 l; 0.05 pints

fluke [fluːk] (inf) n colpo di fortuna

flung [flʌŋ] pt, pp of **fling**

fluorescent [fluəˈresnt] adj fluorescente

fluoride [ˈfluəraɪd] n fluoruro

flurry [ˈflʌrɪ] n (of snow) tempesta; **a ~ of activity** uno scoppio di attività

flush [flʌʃ] n rossore m; (fig: of youth, beauty etc) rigoglio, pieno vigore ▷ vt ripulire con un getto d'acqua ▷ vi arrossire ▷ adj **~ with** a livello di, pari a; **to ~ the toilet** tirare l'acqua

flute [fluːt] n flauto

flutter [ˈflʌtər] n agitazione f; (of wings) battito ▷ vi (bird) battere le ali

fly [flaɪ] (pt **flew**, pp **flown**) n (insect) mosca; (on trousers: also: **flies**) chiusura ▷ vt pilotare; (passengers, cargo) trasportare (in aereo); (distances) percorrere ▷ vi volare; (passengers) andare in aereo; (escape) fuggire; (flag) sventolare; **fly away** vi volar via; **fly-drive** n **fly-drive holiday** fly and drive m inv; **flying** n (activity) aviazione f; (action) volo ▷ adj **flying visit** visita volante; **with flying colours** con risultati brillanti; **flying saucer** n disco volante; **flyover** (BRIT) n (bridge) cavalcavia m inv

FM abbr (= frequency modulation) FM

foal [fəʊl] n puledro

foam [fəʊm] n schiuma; (also: **~ rubber**)

gommapiuma® ▷ vi schiumare; (*soapy water*) fare la schiuma

focus ['fəukəs] (*pl* **focuses**) n fuoco; (*of interest*) centro ▷ vt (*field glasses etc*) mettere a fuoco ▷ vi **to ~ on** (*with camera*) mettere a fuoco; (*person*) fissare lo sguardo su; **in ~** a fuoco; **out of ~** sfocato(-a)

foetus ['fiːtəs] (*us* **fetus**) n feto

fog [fɔg] n nebbia; **foggy** adj **it's foggy** c'è nebbia; **fog lamp** (*us* **fog light**) n (*Aut*) faro m antinebbia inv

foil [fɔɪl] vt confondere, frustrare ▷ n lamina di metallo; (*kitchen foil*) foglio di alluminio; (*Fencing*) fioretto; **to act as a ~ to** (*fig*) far risaltare

fold [fəuld] n (*bend, crease*) piega; (*Agr*) ovile m; (*fig*) gregge m ▷ vt piegare; (*arms*) incrociare; **fold up** vi (*map, bed, table*) piegarsi; (*business*) crollare ▷ vt (*map etc*) piegare, ripiegare; **folder** n (*for papers*) cartella; cartellina; **folding** adj (*chair, bed*) pieghevole

foliage ['fəulɪdʒ] n fogliame m

folk [fəuk] npl gente f ▷ adj popolare; **~s** npl (*family*) famiglia; **folklore** ['fəuklɔːʳ] n folclore m; **folk music** n musica folk inv; **folk song** n canto popolare

follow ['fɔləu] vt seguire ▷ vi seguire; (*result*) conseguire, risultare; **to ~ suit** fare lo stesso; **follow up** vt (*letter, offer*) fare seguito a; (*case*) seguire; **follower** n seguace m/f, discepolo(-a); **following** adj seguente ▷ n seguito, discepoli mpl; **follow-up** n seguito

fond [fɔnd] adj (*memory, look*) tenero(-a), affettuoso(-a); **to be ~ of sb** volere bene a qn; **he's ~ of walking** gli piace fare camminate

food [fuːd] n cibo; **food mixer** n frullatore m; **food poisoning** n intossicazione f; **food processor** [-'prəusesə] n tritatutto m inv elettrico; **food stamp** (*us*) n buono alimentare dato agli indigenti

fool [fuːl] n sciocco(-a); (*Culin*) frullato ▷ vt ingannare ▷ vi (*gen: fool around*) fare lo sciocco; **fool about**, **fool around** vi (*waste time*) perdere tempo; **foolish** adj scemo(-a), stupido(-a); imprudente; **foolproof** adj (*plan etc*) sicurissimo(-a)

foot [fut] (*pl* **feet**) n piede m; (*measure*) piede (= 304 mm; 12 inches); (*of animal*) zampa ▷ vt (*bill*) pagare; **on ~** a piedi; **footage** n (*Cinema: length*) → metraggio; (*: material*) sequenza; **foot-and-mouth (disease)** [futənd'mauθ-] n afta epizootica; **football** n pallone m; (*sport: BRIT*) calcio; (*: US*) football m americano; **footballer** n (*BRIT*) = **football player**; **football match** n (*BRIT*) partita di calcio;

football player n (*BRIT: also:* **footballer**) calciatore m; (*US*) giocatore m di football americano; **footbridge** n passerella; **foothills** npl contrafforti fpl; **foothold** n punto d'appoggio; **footing** n (*fig*) posizione f; **to lose one's footing** mettere un piede in fallo; **footnote** n nota (a piè di pagina); **footpath** n sentiero; (*in street*) marciapiede m; **footprint** n orma, impronta; **footstep** n passo; (*footprint*) orma, impronta; **footwear** n calzatura

for [fɔːʳ] prep **1** (*indicating destination, intention, purpose*) per; **the train for London** il treno per Londra; **he went for the paper** è andato a prendere il giornale; **it's time for lunch** è ora di pranzo; **what's it for?** a che serve?; **what for?** (*why*) perché?

2 (*on behalf of, representing*) per; **to work for sb/sth** lavorare per qn/qc; **I'll ask him for you** glielo chiederò a nome tuo; **G for George** G come George

3 (*because of*) per, a causa di; **for this reason** per questo motivo

4 (*with regard to*) per; **it's cold for July** è freddo per luglio; **for everyone who voted yes, 50 voted no** per ogni voto a favore ce n'erano 50 contro

5 (*in exchange for*) per; **I sold it for £5** l'ho venduto per 5 sterline

6 (*in favour of*) per, a favore di; **are you for or against us?** è con noi o contro di noi?; **I'm all for it** sono completamente a favore

7 (*referring to distance, time*) per; **there are roadworks for 5 km** ci sono lavori in corso per 5 km; **he was away for 2 years** è stato via per 2 anni; **she will be away for a month** starà via un mese; **it hasn't rained for 3 weeks** non piove da 3 settimane; **can you do it for tomorrow?** può farlo per domani?

8 (*with infinitive clauses*): **it is not for me to decide** non sta a me decidere; **it would be best for you to leave** sarebbe meglio che lei se ne andasse; **there is still time for you to do it** ha ancora tempo per farlo; **for this to be possible ...** perché ciò sia possibile ...

9 (*in spite of*) nonostante; **for all his complaints, he's very fond of her** nonostante tutte le sue lamentele, le vuole molto bene

▷ conj (*since, as: rather formal*) dal momento che, poiché

forbid [fə'bɪd] (*pt* **forbad(e)**, *pp* **forbidden**) *vt* vietare, interdire; **to ~ sb to do sth** proibire a qn di fare qc; **forbidden** *pt of* **forbid** ▷ *adj* (*food*) proibito(-a); (*area, territory*) vietato(-a); (*word, subject*) tabù *inv*

force [fɔːs] *n* forza ▷ *vt* forzare; **forced** *adj* forzato(-a); **forceful** *adj* forte, vigoroso(-a)

ford [fɔːd] *n* guado

fore [fɔːʳ] *n* **to come to the ~** mettersi in evidenza; **forearm** ['fɔːrɑːm] *n* avambraccio; **forecast** ['fɔːkɑːst] (*irreg: like* **cast**) *n* previsione *f* ▷ *vt* prevedere; **forecourt** ['fɔːkɔːt] *n* (*of garage*) corte *f* esterna; **forefinger** ['fɔːfɪŋɡəʳ] *n* (*dito*) indice *m*; **forefront** ['fɔːfrʌnt] *n* **in the forefront of** all'avanguardia in; **foreground** ['fɔːɡraund] *n* primo piano; **forehead** ['fɔrɪd] *n* fronte *f*

foreign ['fɔrɪn] *adj* straniero(-a); (*trade*) estero(-a); (*object, matter*) estraneo(-a); **foreign currency** *n* valuta estera; **foreigner** *n* straniero(-a); **foreign exchange** *n* cambio con l'estero; (*currency*) valuta estera; **Foreign Office** (BRIT) *n* Ministero degli Esteri; **Foreign Secretary** (BRIT) *n* ministro degli Affari esteri

fore: **foreman** ['fɔːmən] (*irreg*) *n* caposquadra *m*; **foremost** ['fɔːməust] *adj* principale; più in vista ▷ *adv* **first and foremost** innanzitutto; **forename** *n* nome *m* di battesimo

forensic [fə'rɛnsɪk] *adj* **~ medicine** medicina legale

foresee [fɔː'siː] (*irreg: like* **see**) *vt* prevedere; **foreseeable** *adj* prevedibile

forest ['fɔrɪst] *n* foresta; **forestry** ['fɔrɪstrɪ] *n* silvicoltura

forever [fə'rɛvəʳ] *adv* per sempre; (*endlessly*) sempre, di continuo

foreword ['fɔːwəːd] *n* prefazione *f*

forfeit ['fɔːfɪt] *vt* perdere; (*one's happiness, health*) giocarsi

forgave [fə'ɡeɪv] *pt of* **forgive**

forge [fɔːdʒ] *n* fucina ▷ *vt* (*signature, money*) contraffare, falsificare; (*wrought iron*) fucinare, foggiare; **forger** *n* contraffattore *m*; **forgery** *n* falso; (*activity*) contraffazione *f*

forget [fə'ɡɛt] (*pt* **forgot**, *pp* **forgotten**) *vt, vi* dimenticare; **I've forgotten my key/passport** ho dimenticato la chiave/il passaporto; **forgetful** *adj* di corta memoria; **forgetful of** dimentico(-a) di

forgive [fə'ɡɪv] (*pt* **forgave**, *pp* **forgiven**) *vt* perdonare; **to ~ sb for sth** perdonare qc a qn

forgot [fə'ɡɔt] *pt of* **forget**

forgotten [fə'ɡɔtn] *pp of* **forget**

fork [fɔːk] *n* (*for eating*) forchetta; (*for gardening*) forca; (*of roads, rivers, railways*) biforcazione *f* ▷ *vi* (*road etc*) biforcarsi

forlorn [fə'lɔːn] *adj* (*person*) sconsolato(-a); (*place*) abbandonato(-a); (*attempt*) disperato(-a); (*hope*) vano(-a)

form [fɔːm] *n* forma; (*Scol*) classe *f*; (*questionnaire*) scheda ▷ *vt* formare; **in top ~** in gran forma

formal ['fɔːməl] *adj* formale; (*gardens*) simmetrico(-a), regolare; **formality** [fɔː'mælɪtɪ] *n* formalità *f inv*

format ['fɔːmæt] *n* formato ▷ *vt* (*Comput*) formattare

formation [fɔː'meɪʃən] *n* formazione *f*

former ['fɔːməʳ] *adj* vecchio(-a); (*before n*) ex *inv* (*before n*); **the ~ ... the latter** quello ... questo; **formerly** *adv* in passato

formidable ['fɔːmɪdəbl] *adj* formidabile

formula ['fɔːmjulə] *n* formula

fort [fɔːt] *n* forte *m*

forthcoming [fɔːθ'kʌmɪŋ] *adj* (*event*) prossimo(-a); (*help*) disponibile; (*character*) aperto(-a), comunicativo(-a)

fortieth ['fɔːtɪɪθ] *num* quarantesimo(-a)

fortify ['fɔːtɪfaɪ] *vt* (*city*) fortificare; (*person*) armare

fortnight ['fɔːtnaɪt] (BRIT) *n* quindici giorni *mpl*, due settimane *fpl*; **fortnightly** *adj* bimensile ▷ *adv* ogni quindici giorni

fortress ['fɔːtrɪs] *n* fortezza, rocca

fortunate ['fɔːtʃənɪt] *adj* fortunato(-a); **it is ~ that** è una fortuna che; **fortunately** *adv* fortunatamente

fortune ['fɔːtʃən] *n* fortuna; **fortune-teller** *n* indovino(-a)

forty ['fɔːtɪ] *num* quaranta

forum ['fɔːrəm] *n* foro

forward ['fɔːwəd] *adj* (*ahead of schedule*) in anticipo; (*movement, position*) in avanti; (*not shy*) aperto(-a), diretto(-a) ▷ *n* (*Sport*) avanti *m inv* ▷ *vt* (*letter*) inoltrare; (*parcel, goods*) spedire; (*career, plans*) promuovere, appoggiare; **to move ~** avanzare; **forwarding address** *n* nuovo recapito cui spedire la posta; **forward(s)** *adv* avanti; **forward slash** *n* barra obliqua

fossil ['fɔsl] *adj* fossile ▷ *n* fossile *m*

foster ['fɔstəʳ] *vt* incoraggiare, nutrire; (*child*) avere in affidamento; **foster child** *n* bambino(-a) preso(-a) in affidamento; **foster mother** *n* madre *f* affidataria

fought [fɔːt] *pt, pp of* **fight**

foul [faul] *adj* (*smell, food, temper etc*) cattivo(-a); (*weather*) brutto(-a); (*language*) osceno(-a) ▷ *n* (*Sport*) fallo ▷ *vt* sporcare; **foul play** *n* (*Law*): **the police suspect foul play** la polizia sospetta un atto

criminale
found [faund] *pt, pp of* **find** ▷ *vt (establish)*
fondare; **foundation** [-'deɪʃən] *n*
(act) fondazione *f*; *(base)* base *f*; *(also:*
foundation cream) fondo tinta;
foundations *npl (of building)* fondamenta
fpl
founder ['faundə'] *n* fondatore(-trice) ▷ *vi*
affondare
fountain ['fauntɪn] *n* fontana; **fountain
pen** *n* penna stilografica
four [fɔː'] *num* quattro; **on all ~s** a
carponi; **four-letter word** ['fɔːlɛtə-] *n*
parolaccia; **four-poster** *n (also:* **four-
poster bed**) letto a quattro colonne;
fourteen *num* quattordici; **fourteenth**
num quattordicesimo(-a); **fourth**
quarto(-a); **four-wheel drive** ['fɔːwiːl-] *n*
(Aut): **with four-wheel drive** con quattro
ruote motrici
fowl [faul] *n* pollame *m*; volatile *m*
fox [fɔks] *n* volpe *f* ▷ *vt* confondere
foyer ['fɔɪeɪ] *n* atrio; *(Theatre)* ridotto
fraction ['frækʃən] *n* frazione *f*
fracture ['fræktʃə'] *n* frattura
fragile ['frædʒaɪl] *adj* fragile
fragment ['frægmənt] *n* frammento
fragrance ['freɪɡrəns] *n* fragranza,
profumo
frail [freɪl] *adj* debole, delicato(-a)
frame [freɪm] *n (of building)* armatura,
(of human, animal) ossatura, corpo; *(of
picture)* cornice *f*; *(of door, window)* telaio;
(of spectacles: also: **~s**) montatura ▷ *vt*
(picture) incorniciare; **framework** *n*
struttura
France [frɑːns] *n* Francia
franchise ['fræntʃaɪz] *n (Pol)* diritto di
voto; *(Comm)* concessione *f*
frank [fræŋk] *adj* franco(-a), aperto(-a)
▷ *vt (letter)* affrancare; **frankly** *adv*
francamente, sinceramente
frantic ['fræntɪk] *adj* frenetico(-a)
fraud [frɔːd] *n* truffa; *(Law)* frode *f*; *(person)*
impostore(-a)
fraught [frɔːt] *adj* **~ with** pieno(-a) di,
intriso(-a) da
fray [freɪ] *vt* logorare ▷ *vi* logorarsi
freak [friːk] *n* fenomeno, mostro
freckle ['frɛkl] *n* lentiggine *f*
free [friː] *adj* libero(-a); *(gratis)* gratuito(-a)
▷ *vt (prisoner, jammed person)* liberare;
(jammed object) districare; **is this seat ~?**
è libero questo posto?; **~ of charge, for
~** gratuitamente; **freedom** ['friːdəm]
n libertà; **Freefone®** *n* numero verde;
free gift *n* regalo, omaggio; **free kick** *n*
calcio libero; **freelance** *adj* indipendente;
freely *adv* liberamente; *(liberally)*

liberamente; **Freepost®** *n* affrancatura
a carico del destinatario; **free-range** *adj*
(hen) ruspante; *(eggs)* di gallina ruspante;
freeway (US) *n* superstrada; **free will** *n*
libero arbitrio; **of one's own free will** di
spontanea volontà
freeze [friːz] (*pt* **froze**, *pp* **frozen**) *vi* gelare
▷ *vt* gelare; *(food)* congelare; *(prices,
salaries)* bloccare ▷ *n* gelo; blocco; **freezer**
n congelatore *m*; **freezing** ['friːzɪŋ] *adj*
(wind, weather) gelido(-a); **freezing point**
n punto di congelamento; **3 degrees
below freezing point** 3 gradi sotto zero
freight [freɪt] *n (goods)* merce *f*, merci
fpl; *(money charged)* spese *fpl* di trasporto;
freight train (US) *n* treno *m* merci *inv*
French [frɛntʃ] *adj* francese ▷ *n (Ling)*
francese *m*; **the ~** *npl* i Francesi; **French
bean** *n* fagiolino; **French bread** *n*
baguette *f inv*; **French dressing** *n (Culin)*
condimento per insalata; **French fried
potatoes** (US **French fries**) *npl* patate
fpl fritte; **Frenchman** *(irreg) n* francese
m; **French stick** *n* baguette *f inv*; **French
window** *n* portafinestra; **Frenchwoman**
(irreg) n francese *f*
frenzy ['frɛnzɪ] *n* frenesia
frequency ['friːkwənsɪ] *n* frequenza
frequent [*adj* 'friːkwənt, *vb* frɪ'kwɛnt] *adj*
frequente ▷ *vt* frequentare; **frequently**
adv frequentemente, spesso
fresh [frɛʃ] *adj* fresco(-a); *(new)* nuovo(-a);
(cheeky) sfacciato(-a); **freshen** *vi*
(wind, air) rinfrescare; **freshen up** *vi*
rinfrescarsi; **fresher** (BRIT: *inf*) *n (Scol)*
matricola; **freshly** *adv* di recente, di
fresco; **freshman** *(irreg:* US) *n* = **fresher**;
freshwater *adj (fish)* d'acqua dolce
fret [frɛt] *vi* agitarsi, affliggersi
Fri. *abbr* (= *Friday*) ven.
friction ['frɪkʃən] *n* frizione *f*, attrito
Friday ['fraɪdɪ] *n* venerdì *m inv*
fridge [frɪdʒ] (BRIT) *n* frigo, frigorifero
fried [fraɪd] *pt, pp of* **fry** ▷ *adj* fritto(-a)
friend [frɛnd] *n* amico(-a); **friendly** *adj*
amichevole; **friendship** *n* amicizia
fries [fraɪz] *(esp* US) *npl* patate *fpl* fritte
frigate ['frɪɡɪt] *n (Naut: modern)* fregata
fright [fraɪt] *n* paura, spavento; **to take ~**
spaventarsi; **frighten** *vt* spaventare, far
paura a; **frightened** *adj* spaventato(-a);
frightening *adj* spaventoso(-a),
pauroso(-a); **frightful** *adj* orribile
frill [frɪl] *n* balza
fringe [frɪndʒ] *n (decoration:* BRIT: *of hair)*
frangia; *(edge: of forest etc)* margine *m*
Frisbee® ['frɪzbɪ] *n* frisbee *m inv*
fritter ['frɪtə'] *n* frittella
frivolous ['frɪvələs] *adj* frivolo(-a)

fro [frəu] *see* **to**

frock [frɔk] *n* vestito

frog [frɔg] *n* rana; **frogman** (*irreg*) *n* uomo *m* rana *inv*

 KEYWORD

from [frɔm] *prep* **1** (*indicating starting place, origin etc*) da; **where do you come from?, where are you from?** da dove viene?, di dov'è?; **from London to Glasgow** da Londra a Glasgow; **a letter from my sister** una lettera da mia sorella; **tell him from me that …** gli dica da parte mia che …

2 (*indicating time*) da; **from one o'clock to** *or* **until** *or* **till two** dall'una alle due; **from January (on)** da gennaio, a partire da gennaio

3 (*indicating distance*) da; **the hotel is 1 km from the beach** l'albergo è a 1 km dalla spiaggia

4 (*indicating price, number etc*) da; **prices range from £10 to £50** i prezzi vanno dalle 10 alle 50 sterline

5 (*indicating difference*) da; **he can't tell red from green** non sa distinguere il rosso dal verde

6 (*because of, on the basis of*): **from what he says** da quanto dice lui; **weak from hunger** debole per la fame

front [frʌnt] *n* (*of house, dress*) davanti *m inv*; (*of train*) testa; (*of book*) copertina; (*promenade: also*: **sea ~**) lungomare *m*; (*Mil, Pol, Meteor*) fronte *m*; (*fig: appearances*) fronte *f* ▷ *adj* primo(-a); anteriore, davanti *inv*; **in ~ of** davanti a; **front door** *n* porta d'entrata; (*of car*) sportello anteriore; **frontier** ['frʌntɪə'] *n* frontiera; **front page** *n* prima pagina; **front-wheel drive** ['frʌntwiːl-] *n* trasmissione *f* anteriore

frost [frɔst] *n* gelo; (*also*: **hoar~**) brina; **frostbite** *n* congelamento; **frosting** (US) *n* (*on cake*) glassa; **frosty** *adj* (*weather, look*) gelido(-a)

froth ['frɔθ] *n* spuma; schiuma

frown [fraun] *vi* acciglarsi

froze [frəuz] *pt of* **freeze**

frozen ['frəuzn] *pp of* **freeze**

fruit [fruːt] *n inv* (*also fig*) frutto; (*collectively*) frutta; **fruit juice** *n* succo di frutta; **fruit machine** (BRIT) *n* macchina *f* mangiasoldi *inv*; **fruit salad** *n* macedonia

frustrate [frʌs'treɪt] *vt* frustrare; **frustrated** *adj* frustrato(-a)

fry [fraɪ] (*pt, pp* **fried**) *vt* friggere; *see also* **small**; **frying pan** *n* padella

ft. *abbr* = **foot; feet**

fudge [fʌdʒ] *n* (*Culin*) specie di caramella a base di latte, burro e zucchero

fuel [fjuəl] *n* (*for heating*) combustibile *m*; (*for propelling*) carburante *m*; **fuel tank** *n* deposito *m* nafta *inv*; (*on vehicle*) serbatoio (della benzina)

fulfil [ful'fɪl] *vt* (*function*) compiere; (*order*) eseguire; (*wish, desire*) soddisfare, appagare

full [ful] *adj* pieno(-a); (*details, skirt*) ampio(-a) ▷ *adv* **to know ~ well that** sapere benissimo che; **I'm ~ (up)** sono sazio; **a ~ two hours** due ore intere; **at ~ speed** a tutta velocità; **in ~** per intero; **full-length** *adj* (*film*) a lungometraggio; (*coat, novel*) lungo(-a); (*portrait*) in piedi; **full moon** *n* luna piena; **full-scale** *adj* (*attack, war*) su larga scala; (*model*) in grandezza naturale; **full stop** *n* punto; **full-time** *adj, adv* (*work*) a tempo pieno; **fully** *adv* interamente, pienamente, completamente; (*at least*) almeno

fumble ['fʌmbl] *vi* **to ~ with sth** armeggiare con qc

fume [fjuːm] *vi* essere furioso(-a); **fumes** *npl* esalazioni *fpl*, vapori *mpl*

fun [fʌn] *n* divertimento, spasso; **to have ~** divertirsi; **for ~** per scherzo; **to make ~ of** prendersi gioco di

function ['fʌŋkʃən] *n* funzione *f*; cerimonia, ricevimento ▷ *vi* funzionare

fund [fʌnd] *n* fondo, cassa; (*store*) riserva; **~s** *npl* (*money*) fondi *mpl*

fundamental [fʌndə'mɛntl] *adj* fondamentale

funeral ['fjuːnərəl] *n* funerale *m*; **funeral director** *n* impresario di pompe funebri; **funeral parlour** [-'pɑːlə'] *n* impresa di pompe funebri

funfair ['fʌnfɛə'] *n* luna park *m inv*

fungus ['fʌŋgəs] *n* (*pl* **fungi**) *n* fungo; (*mould*) muffa

funnel ['fʌnl] *n* imbuto; (*of ship*) ciminiera

funny ['fʌnɪ] *adj* divertente, buffo(-a); (*strange*) strano(-a), bizzarro(-a)

fur [fəː'] *n* pelo; pelliccia; (BRIT: *in kettle etc*) deposito calcare; **fur coat** *n* pelliccia

furious ['fjuərɪəs] *adj* furioso(-a); (*effort*) accanito(-a)

furnish ['fəːnɪʃ] *vt* ammobiliare; (*supply*) fornire; **furnishings** *npl* mobili *mpl*, mobilia

furniture ['fəːnɪtʃə'] *n* mobili *mpl*; **piece of ~** mobile *m*

furry ['fəːrɪ] *adj* (*animal*) peloso(-a)

further ['fəːðə'] *adj* supplementare, altro(-a); nuovo(-a); più lontano(-a) ▷ *adv* più lontano; (*more*) di più; (*moreover*) inoltre ▷ *vt* favorire, promuovere; **further**

education n ≈ corsi mpl di formazione;
college of further education istituto
statale con corsi specializzati (di formazione
professionale, aggiornamento professionale
ecc); **furthermore** [fəːðəˈmɔːʳ] adv inoltre,
per di più

furthest [ˈfəːðɪst] superl of **far**

fury [ˈfjuərɪ] n furore m

fuse [fjuːz] (US **fuze**) n fusibile m; (for bomb
etc) miccia, spoletta ▷ vt fondere ▷ vi
fondersi; **to ~ the lights** (BRIT Elec) far
saltare i fusibili; **fuse box** n cassetta dei
fusibili

fusion [ˈfjuːʒən] n fusione f

fuss [fʌs] n agitazione f; (complaining) storie
fpl; **to make a ~** fare delle storie; **fussy** adj
(person) puntiglioso(-a), esigente; che fa le
storie; (dress) carico(-a) di fronzoli; (style)
elaborato(-a)

future [ˈfjuːtʃəʳ] adj futuro(-a) ▷ n futuro,
avvenire m; (Ling) futuro; **in ~** in futuro; **~s**
npl (Comm) operazioni fpl a termine

fuze [fjuːz] (US) = **fuse**

fuzzy [ˈfʌzɪ] adj (Phot) indistinto(-a),
sfocato(-a); (hair) crespo(-a)

G [dʒiː] n (Mus) sol m

g. abbr (= gram, gravity) g.

gadget [ˈgædʒɪt] n aggeggio

Gaelic [ˈgeɪlɪk] adj gaelico(-a) ▷ n (Ling)
gaelico

gag [gæg] n bavaglio; (joke) facezia,
scherzo ▷ vt imbavagliare

gain [geɪn] n guadagno, profitto ▷ vt
guadagnare ▷ vi (clock, watch) andare
avanti; (benefit): **to ~ (from)** trarre
beneficio (da); **to ~ 3lbs (in weight)**
aumentare di 3 libbre; **to ~ on sb** (in race
etc) guadagnare su qn

gal. abbr = **gallon**

gala [ˈgɑːlə] n gala; **swimming ~**
manifestazione f di nuoto

galaxy [ˈgæləksɪ] n galassia

gale [geɪl] n vento forte; burrasca

gall bladder [ˈgɔːl-] n cistifellea

gallery [ˈgælərɪ] n galleria

gallon [ˈgælən] n gallone m (= 8 pints; BRIT
= 4.543l; US = 3.785l)

gallop [ˈgæləp] n galoppo ▷ vi galoppare

gallstone [ˈgɔːlstəun] n calcolo biliare

gamble [ˈgæmbl] n azzardo, rischio
calcolato ▷ vt, vi giocare; **to ~ on** (fig)
giocare su; **gambler** n giocatore(-trice)
d'azzardo; **gambling** n gioco d'azzardo

game [geɪm] n gioco; (event) partita;
(Tennis) game m inv; (Culin, Hunting)

selvaggina ▷ adj (ready): **to be ~ (for sth/ to do)** essere pronto(-a) (a qc/a fare); **big ~ selvaggina** grossa; **~s** npl (Scol) attività fpl sportive; **big ~** selvaggina grossa; **games console** [geimz-] n console f inv dei videogame; **game show** ['geɪmʃəu] n gioco a premi

gammon ['gæmən] n (bacon) quarto di maiale; (ham) prosciutto affumicato

gang [gæŋ] n banda, squadra ▷ vi **to ~ up on sb** far combutta contro qn

gangster ['gæŋstə'] n gangster m inv

gap [gæp] n (space) buco; (in time) intervallo; (difference): **~ (between)** divario (tra)

gape [geɪp] vi (person) restare a bocca aperta; (shirt, hole) essere spalancato(-a)

gap year n (Scol) anno di pausa durante il quale gli studenti viaggiano o lavorano

garage ['gærɑ:ʒ] n garage m inv; **garage sale** n vendita di oggetti usati nel garage di un privato

garbage ['gɑ:bɪdʒ] (US) n immondizie fpl, rifiuti mpl; (inf) sciocchezze fpl; **garbage can** (US) n bidone m della spazzatura; **garbage collector** (US) n spazzino(-a)

garden ['gɑ:dn] n giardino; **~s** npl (public park) giardini pubblici; **garden centre** n vivaio; **gardener** n giardiniere(-a); **gardening** n giardinaggio

garlic ['gɑ:lɪk] n aglio

garment ['gɑ:mənt] n indumento

garnish ['gɑ:nɪʃ] vt (food) guarnire

garrison ['gærɪsn] n guarnigione f

gas [gæs] n gas m inv; (US: gasoline) benzina ▷ vt asfissiare con il gas; **I can smell ~** sento odore di gas; **gas cooker** (BRIT) n cucina a gas; **gas cylinder** n bombola del gas; **gas fire** (BRIT) n radiatore m a gas

gasket ['gæskɪt] n (Aut) guarnizione f

gasoline ['gæsəli:n] n (US) benzina

gasp [gɑ:sp] n respiro affannoso, ansito ▷ vi ansare, ansimare; (in surprise) restare senza fiato

gas: **gas pedal** (esp US) n pedale m dell'acceleratore; **gas station** (US) n distributore m di benzina; **gas tank** (US) n (Aut) serbatoio (di benzina)

gate [geɪt] n cancello; (at airport) uscita

gateau ['gætəu, -z] (pl **gateaux**) n torta

gatecrash ['geɪtkræʃ] (BRIT) vt partecipare senza invito a

gateway ['geɪtweɪ] n porta

gather ['gæðə'] vt (flowers, fruit) cogliere; (pick up) raccogliere; (assemble) radunare; raccogliere; (understand) capire; (Sewing) increspare ▷ vi (assemble) radunarsi; **to ~ speed** acquistare velocità; **gathering** n adunanza

gauge [geɪdʒ] n (instrument) indicatore m ▷ vt misurare; (fig) valutare

gave [geɪv] pt of **give**

gay [geɪ] adj (homosexual) omosessuale; (cheerful) gaio(-a), allegro(-a); (colour) vivace, vivo(-a)

gaze [geɪz] n sguardo fisso ▷ vi **to ~ at** guardare fisso

GB abbr = **Great Britain**

GCSE (BRIT) n abbr General Certificate of Secondary Education

gear [gɪə'] n attrezzi mpl, equipaggiamento; (Tech) ingranaggio; (Aut) marcia ▷ vt (fig: adapt): **to ~ sth to** adattare qc a; **in top** or (US) **high/low ~** in quarta (or quinta)/seconda; **in ~** in marcia; **gear up** vi **to ~ up (to do)** prepararsi (a fare); **gear box** n scatola del cambio; **gear lever** n leva del cambio; **gear shift** (US), **gear stick** (BRIT) n = **gear lever**

geese [gi:s] npl of **goose**

gel [dʒɛl] n gel m inv

gem [dʒɛm] n gemma

Gemini ['dʒɛmɪnaɪ] n Gemelli mpl

gender ['dʒɛndə'] n genere m

gene [dʒi:n] n (Biol) gene m

general ['dʒɛnərl] n generale m ▷ adj generale; **in ~** in genere; **general anaesthetic** (US **general anesthetic**) n anestesia totale; **general election** n elezioni fpl generali; **generalize** vi generalizzare; **generally** adv generalmente; **general practitioner** n medico generico; **general store** n emporio

generate ['dʒɛnəreɪt] vt generare

generation [dʒɛnə'reɪʃən] n generazione f

generator ['dʒɛnəreɪtə'] n generatore m

generosity [dʒɛnə'rɔsɪtɪ] n generosità

generous ['dʒɛnərəs] adj generoso(-a); (copious) abbondante

genetic [dʒɪ'nɛtɪk] adj genetico(-a); **~ engineering** ingegneria genetica; **genetically modified** adj geneticamente modificato(-a), transgenico(-a); **genetics** n genetica

Geneva [dʒɪ'ni:və] n Ginevra

genitals ['dʒɛnɪtlz] npl genitali mpl

genius ['dʒi:nɪəs] n genio

Genoa ['dʒɛnəuə] n Genova

gent [dʒɛnt] n abbr = **gentleman**

gentle ['dʒɛntl] adj delicato(-a); (person) dolce

> Be careful not to translate **gentle** by the Italian word **gentile**.

gentleman ['dʒɛntlmən] (irreg) n signore m; (well-bred man) gentiluomo

gently ['dʒɛntlɪ] adv delicatamente

gents [dʒɛnts] n W.C. m (per signori)
genuine ['dʒɛnjuɪn] adj autentico(-a); sincero(-a); **genuinely** adv genuinamente
geographic(al) [dʒɪə'græfɪk(l)] adj geografico(-a)
geography [dʒɪ'ɔgrəfɪ] n geografia
geology [dʒɪ'ɔlədʒɪ] n geologia
geometry [dʒɪ'ɔmətrɪ] n geometria
geranium [dʒɪ'reɪnjəm] n geranio
geriatric [dʒɛrɪ'ætrɪk] adj geriatrico(-a)
germ [dʒɜːm] n (Med) microbo; (Biol, fig) germe m
German ['dʒɜːmən] adj tedesco(-a) ▷ n tedesco(-a); (Ling) tedesco; **German measles** (BRIT) n rosolia
Germany ['dʒɜːmənɪ] n Germania
gesture ['dʒɛstjər] n gesto

KEYWORD

get [gɛt] (pt, pp **got**, (US) pp **gotten**) vi **1** (become, be) diventare, farsi; **to get old** invecchiare; **to get tired** stancarsi; **to get drunk** ubriacarsi; **to get killed** venire or rimanere ucciso(-a); **when do I get paid?** quando mi pagate?; **it's getting late** si sta facendo tardi
2 (go): **to get to/from** andare a/da; **to get home** arrivare or tornare a casa; **how did you get here?** come sei venuto?
3 (begin) mettersi a, cominciare a; **to get to know sb** incominciare a conoscere qn; **let's get going** or **started** muoviamoci
4 (modal aux vb): **you've got to do it** devi farlo
▷ vt **1**: **to get sth done** (do) fare qc; (have done) far fare qc; **to get one's hair cut** farsi tagliare i capelli; **to get sb to do sth** far fare qc a qn
2 (obtain: money, permission, results) ottenere; (find: job, flat) trovare; (fetch: person, doctor) chiamare; (: object) prendere; **to get sth for sb** prendere or procurare qc a qn; **get me Mr Jones, please** (Tel) mi passi il signor Jones, per favore; **can I get you a drink?** le posso offrire da bere?
3 (receive: present, letter, prize) ricevere; (acquire: reputation) farsi; **how much did you get for the painting?** quanto le hanno dato per il quadro?
4 (catch) prendere; (hit: target etc) colpire; **to get sb by the arm/throat** afferrare qn per un braccio/alla gola; **get him!** prendetelo!
5 (take, move) portare; **to get sth to sb** far avere qc a qn; **do you think we'll get it through the door?** pensi che riusciremo a farlo passare per la porta?

6 (catch, take: plane, bus etc) prendere; **where do we get the ferry to …?** dove si prende il traghetto per …?
7 (understand) afferrare; (hear) sentire; **I've got it!** ci sono arrivato!, ci sono!; **I'm sorry, I didn't get your name** scusi, non ho capito (or sentito) il suo nome
8 (have, possess): **to have got** avere; **how many have you got?** quanti ne ha?
get along vi (agree) andare d'accordo; (depart) andarsene; (manage) = **get by**
get at vt fus (attack) prendersela con; (reach) raggiungere, arrivare a
get away vi partire, andarsene; (escape) scappare
get away with vt fus cavarsela; farla franca
get back vi (return) ritornare, tornare ▷ vt riottenere, riavere; **when do we get back?** quando ritorniamo?
get by vi (pass) passare; (manage) farcela
get down vi, vt fus scendere ▷ vt far scendere; (depress) buttare giù
get down to vt fus (work) mettersi a (fare)
get in vi entrare; (train) arrivare; (arrive home) ritornare, tornare
get into vt fus entrare in; **to get into a rage** incavolarsi
get off vi (from train etc) scendere; (depart: person, car) andare via; (escape) cavarsela ▷ vt (remove: clothes, stain) levare ▷ vt fus (train, bus) scendere da; **where do I get off?** dove devo scendere?
get on vi (at exam etc) andare; (agree): **to get on (with)** andare d'accordo (con) ▷ vt fus montare in; (horse) montare su
get out vi uscire; (of vehicle) scendere ▷ vt tirar fuori, far uscire
get out of vt fus uscire da; (duty etc) evitare
get over vt fus (illness) riaversi da
get round vt fus aggirare; (fig: person) rigirare
get through vi (Tel) avere la linea
get through to vt fus (Tel) parlare a
get together vi riunirsi ▷ vt raccogliere; (people) adunare
get up vi (rise) alzarsi ▷ vt fus salire su per
get up to vt fus (reach) raggiungere; (prank etc) fare

getaway ['gɛtəweɪ] n fuga
Ghana ['gɑːnə] n Ghana m
ghastly ['gɑːstlɪ] adj orribile, orrendo(-a); (pale) spettrale
ghetto ['gɛtəu] n ghetto
ghost [gəust] n fantasma m, spettro
giant ['dʒaɪənt] n gigante m ▷ adj gigantesco(-a), enorme

gift [gɪft] n regalo; (donation, ability) dono; **gifted** adj dotato(-a); **gift shop** (US **gift store**) n negozio di souvenir

gift token, gift voucher n buono m omaggio inv

gig [gɪg] n (inf: of musician) serata

gigabyte [giːgəbaɪt] n gigabyte m inv

gigantic [dʒaɪˈgæntɪk] adj gigantesco(-a)

giggle [ˈgɪgl] vi ridere scioccamente

gills [gɪlz] npl (of fish) branchie fpl

gilt [gɪlt] n doratura ▷ adj dorato(-a)

gimmick [ˈgɪmɪk] n trucco

gin [dʒɪn] n (liquor) gin m inv

ginger [ˈdʒɪndʒəʳ] n zenzero

gipsy [ˈdʒɪpsɪ] n zingaro(-a)

giraffe [dʒɪˈrɑːf] n giraffa

girl [gəːl] n ragazza; (young unmarried woman) signorina; (daughter) figlia, figliola; **girlfriend** n (of girl) amica; (of boy) ragazza; **Girl Scout** (US) n Giovane Esploratrice f

gist [dʒɪst] n succo

give [gɪv] (pt **gave**, pp **given**) vt dare ▷ vi cedere; **to ~ sb sth, ~ sth to sb** dare qc a qn; **I'll ~ you £5 for it** te lo pago 5 sterline; **to ~ a cry/sigh** emettere un grido/sospiro; **to ~ a speech** fare un discorso; **give away** vt dare via; (disclose) rivelare; (bride) condurre all'altare; **give back** vt rendere; **give in** vi cedere ▷ vt consegnare; **give out** vt distribuire; annunciare; **give up** vi rinunciare ▷ vt rinunciare a; **to ~ up smoking** smettere di fumare; **to ~ o.s. up** arrendersi

given [ˈgɪvn] pp of **give** ▷ adj (fixed: time, amount) dato(-a), determinato(-a) ▷ conj **~ (that) ...** dato che ...; **~ the circumstances ...** date le circostanze ...

glacier [ˈglæsɪəʳ] n ghiacciaio

glad [glæd] adj lieto(-a), contento(-a); **gladly** [ˈglædlɪ] adv volentieri

glamorous [ˈglæmərəs] adj affascinante, seducente

glamour [ˈglæməʳ] (US **glamor**) n fascino

glance [glɑːns] n occhiata, sguardo ▷ vi **to ~ at** dare un'occhiata a; **to ~ off** (bullet) rimbalzare su

gland [glænd] n ghiandola

glare [glɛəʳ] n (of anger) sguardo furioso; (of light) riverbero, luce f abbagliante; (of publicity) chiasso ▷ vi abbagliare; **to ~ at** guardare male; **glaring** adj (mistake) madornale

glass [glɑːs] n (substance) vetro; (tumbler) bicchiere m; **~es** npl (spectacles) occhiali mpl

glaze [gleɪz] vt (door) fornire di vetri; (pottery) smaltare ▷ n smalto

gleam [gliːm] vi luccicare

glen [glɛn] n valletta

glide [glaɪd] vi scivolare; (Aviat, birds) planare; **glider** n (Aviat) aliante m

glimmer [ˈglɪməʳ] n barlume m

glimpse [glɪmps] n impressione f fugace ▷ vt vedere al volo

glint [glɪnt] vi luccicare

glisten [ˈglɪsn] vi luccicare

glitter [ˈglɪtəʳ] vi scintillare

global [ˈgləubl] adj globale; **global warming** n effetto m serra inv

globe [gləub] n globo, sfera

gloom [gluːm] n oscurità, buio; (sadness) tristezza, malinconia; **gloomy** adj scuro(-a), fosco(-a), triste

glorious [ˈglɔːrɪəs] adj glorioso(-a), magnifico(-a)

glory [ˈglɔːrɪ] n gloria; splendore m

gloss [glɔs] n (shine) lucentezza; (also: **~ paint**) vernice f a olio

glossary [ˈglɔsərɪ] n glossario

glossy [ˈglɔsɪ] adj lucente

glove [glʌv] n guanto; **glove compartment** n (Aut) vano portaoggetti

glow [gləu] vi ardere; (face) essere luminoso(-a)

glucose [ˈgluːkəus] n glucosio

glue [gluː] n colla ▷ vt incollare

GM adj abbr (= genetically modified) geneticamente modificato(-a)

gm abbr = **gram**

GMO n abbr (= genetically modified organism) OGM m inv

GMT abbr (= Greenwich Mean Time) T.M.G.

gnaw [nɔː] vt rodere

go [gəu] (pt **went**, pp **gone**) (pl **goes**) vi andare; (depart) partire, andarsene; (work) funzionare; (time) passare; (break etc) rompersi; **to go for £10** essere venduto per 10 sterline; (fit, suit): **to go with** andare bene con; (become): **to go pale** diventare pallido(-a); **to go mouldy** ammuffire ▷ n **to have a go (at)** provare; **to be on the go** essere in moto; **whose go is it?** a chi tocca?; **he's going to do** sta per fare; **to go for a walk** andare a fare una passeggiata; **to go dancing/ shopping** andare a ballare/fare la spesa; **just then the bell went** proprio allora suonò il campanello; **how did it go?** com'è andato?; **to go round the back/by the shop** passare da dietro/davanti al negozio; **go ahead** vi andare avanti; **go away** vi partire, andarsene; **go back** vi tornare, ritornare; **go by** vi (years, time) scorrere ▷ vt fus attenersi a, seguire (alla lettera); prestar fede a; **go down** vi scendere; (ship) affondare; (sun) tramontare ▷ vt fus scendere; **go for** vt fus (fetch) andare a prendere; (*like*) andar matto(-a) per; (*attack*) attaccare; saltare addosso a; **go in** *vi* entrare; **go into** *vt fus* entrare in; (*investigate*) indagare, esaminare; (*embark on*) lanciarsi in; **go off** *vi* partire, andar via; (*food*) guastarsi; (*explode*) esplodere, scoppiare; (*event*) passare ▷ *vt fus* **I've ~ne off chocolate** la cioccolata non mi piace più; **the gun went off** il fucile si scaricò; **go on** *vi* continuare; (*happen*) succedere; **to ~ on doing** continuare a fare; **go out** *vi* uscire; (*couple*) **they went out for 3 years** sono stati insieme per 3 anni; (*fire, light*) spegnersi; **go over** *vi* (*ship*) ribaltarsi ▷ *vt fus* (*check*) esaminare; **go past** *vi* passare ▷ *vt fus* passare davanti a; **go round** *vi* (*circulate: news, rumour*) circolare; (*revolve*) girare; (*visit*): **to ~ round (to sb's)** passare (da qn); (*make a detour*): **to ~ round (by)** passare (per); (*suffice*) bastare (per tutti); **go through** *vt fus* (*town etc*) attraversare; (*files, papers*) passare in rassegna; (*examine: list etc*) leggere da cima a fondo; **go up** *vi* salire; **go with** *vt fus* (*accompany*) accompagnare; **go without** *vt fus* fare a meno di

go-ahead ['gəuəhɛd] *adj* intraprendente ▷ *n* via *m*

goal [gəul] *n* (*Sport*) gol *m*, rete *f*; (: *place*) porta; (*fig: aim*) fine *m*, scopo; **goalkeeper** *n* portiere *m*; **goal-post** *n* palo (della porta)

goat [gəut] *n* capra

gobble ['gɔbl] *vt* (*also:* **~ down, ~ up**) ingoiare

god [gɔd] *n* dio; **G~** Dio; **godchild** *n* figlioccio(-a); **goddaughter** *n* figlioccia; **goddess** *n* dea; **godfather** *n* padrino; **godmother** *n* madrina; **godson** *n* figlioccio

goggles ['gɔglz] *npl* occhiali *mpl* (di protezione)

going ['gəuɪŋ] *n* (*conditions*) andare *m*, stato del terreno ▷ *adj* **the ~ rate** la tariffa in vigore

gold [gəuld] *n* oro ▷ *adj* d'oro; **golden** *adj* (*made of gold*) d'oro; (*gold in colour*) dorato(-a); **goldfish** *n* pesce *m* dorato *or* rosso; **goldmine** *n* (*also fig*) miniera d'oro; **gold-plated** *adj* placcato(-a) oro *inv*

golf [gɔlf] *n* golf *m*; **golf ball** *n* (*for game*) pallina da golf; (*on typewriter*) pallina; **golf club** *n* circolo di golf; (*stick*) bastone *m or* mazza da golf; **golf course** *n* campo di golf; **golfer** *n* giocatore(-trice) di golf

gone [gɔn] *pp of* **go** ▷ *adj* partito(-a)

gong [gɔŋ] *n* gong *m inv*

good [gud] *adj* buono(-a); (*kind*) buono(-a), gentile; (*child*) bravo(-a) ▷ *n* bene *m*; **~s** *npl* (*Comm etc*) beni *mpl*; merci *fpl*; **~!** bene!, ottimo!; **to be ~ at** essere bravo(-a) in; **to be ~ for** andare bene per; **it's ~ for you** fa bene; **would you be ~ enough to ...?** avrebbe la gentilezza di ...?; **a ~ deal (of)** molto(-a), una buona quantità (di); **a ~ many** molti(-e); **to make ~** (*loss, damage*) compensare; **it's no ~ complaining** brontolare non serve a niente; **for ~** per sempre, definitivamente; **~ morning!** buon giorno!; **~ afternoon/evening!** buona sera!; **~ night!** buona notte!;

goodbye *excl* arrivederci!; **Good Friday** *n* Venerdì Santo; **good-looking** *adj* bello(-a); **good-natured** *adj* affabile; **goodness** *n* (*of person*) bontà; **for goodness sake!** per amor di Dio!; **goodness gracious!** santo cielo!, mamma mia!; **goods train** (BRIT) *n* treno *m* merci *inv*; **goodwill** *n* amicizia, benevolenza

goose [gu:s] (*pl* **geese**) *n* oca

gooseberry ['guzbərɪ] *n* uva spina; **to play ~** (BRIT) tenere la candela

goose bumps, goose pimples *npl* pelle *f* d'oca

gorge [gɔːdʒ] *n* gola ▷ *vt* **to ~ o.s. (on)** ingozzarsi (di)

gorgeous ['gɔːdʒəs] *adj* magnifico(-a)

gorilla [gə'rɪlə] *n* gorilla *m inv*

gosh (*inf*) [gɔʃ] *excl* perdinci!

gospel ['gɔspl] *n* vangelo

gossip ['gɔsɪp] *n* chiacchiere *fpl*; pettegolezzi *mpl*; (*person*) pettegolo(-a) ▷ *vi* chiacchierare; **gossip column** *n* cronaca mondana

got [gɔt] *pt, pp of* **get**

gotten ['gɔtn] (US) *pp of* **get**

gourmet ['guəmeɪ] *n* buongustaio(-a)

govern ['gʌvən] *vt* governare; **government** ['gʌvnmənt] *n* governo; **governor** ['gʌvənəʳ] *n* (*of state, bank*) governatore *m*; (*of school, hospital*) amministratore *m*; (BRIT: *of prison*) direttore(-trice)

gown [gaun] *n* vestito lungo; (*of teacher*, BRIT: *of judge*) toga

G.P. *n abbr* = **general practitioner**

grab [græb] *vt* afferrare, arraffare; (*property, power*) impadronirsi di ▷ *vi* **to ~ at** cercare di afferrare

grace [greɪs] *n* grazia ▷ *vt* onorare; **5 days' ~** dilazione di 5 giorni; **graceful** *adj* elegante, aggraziato(-a); **gracious** ['greɪʃəs] *adj* grazioso(-a), misericordioso(-a)

grade [greɪd] *n* (*Comm*) qualità *f* inv; classe *f*; categoria; (*in hierarchy*) grado; (*Scol: mark*) voto; (US: *school class*) classe ▷ *vt* classificare; ordinare; graduare; **grade**

crossing (US) n passaggio a livello; **grade school** (US) n scuola elementare

gradient ['greɪdɪənt] n pendenza, inclinazione f

gradual ['grædjuəl] adj graduale; **gradually** adv man mano, a poco a poco

graduate [n'grædjuɪt, vb'grædjueɪt] n (of university) laureato(-a); (US: of high school) diplomato(-a) ▷ vi laurearsi; diplomarsi; **graduation** [-'eɪʃən] n (ceremony) consegna delle lauree (or dei diplomi)

graffiti [grə'fiːtɪ] npl graffiti mpl

graft [grɑːft] n (Agr, Med) innesto; (bribery) corruzione f; (BRIT: hard work): **it's hard ~** è un lavoraccio ▷ vt innestare

grain [greɪn] n grano; (of sand) granello; (of wood) venatura

gram [græm] n grammo

grammar ['græmər] n grammatica; **grammar school** (BRIT) n ≈ liceo

gramme [græm] n = **gram**

gran (inf) [græn] n (BRIT) nonna

grand [grænd] adj grande, magnifico(-a); grandioso(-a); **grandad** (inf) n = **granddad**; **grandchild** (pl **-children**) n nipote m; **granddad** (inf) n nonno; **granddaughter** n nipote f; **grandfather** n nonno; **grandma** (inf) n nonna; **grandmother** n nonna; **grandpa** (inf) n = **granddad**; **grandparents** npl nonni mpl; **grand piano** n pianoforte m a coda; **Grand Prix** ['grɑ̃:'priː] n (Aut) Gran Premio, Grand Prix m inv; **grandson** n nipote m

granite ['grænɪt] n granito

granny ['grænɪ] (inf) n nonna

grant [grɑːnt] vt accordare; (a request) accogliere; (admit) ammettere, concedere ▷ n (Scol) borsa; (Admin) sussidio, sovvenzione f; **to take sth for ~ed** dare qc per scontato; **to take sb for ~ed** dare per scontata la presenza di qn

grape [greɪp] n chicco d'uva, acino

grapefruit ['greɪpfruːt] n pompelmo

graph [grɑːf] n grafico; **graphic** adj grafico(-a); (vivid) vivido(-a); **graphics** n grafica ▷ npl illustrazioni fpl

grasp [grɑːsp] vt afferrare ▷ n (grip) presa; (fig) potere m; comprensione f

grass [grɑːs] n erba; **grasshopper** n cavalletta

grate [greɪt] n graticola (del focolare) ▷ vi cigolare, stridere ▷ vt (Culin) grattugiare

grateful ['greɪtful] adj grato(-a), riconoscente

grater ['greɪtər] n grattugia

gratitude ['grætɪtjuːd] n gratitudine f

grave [greɪv] n tomba ▷ adj grave, serio(-a)

gravel ['grævl] n ghiaia

gravestone ['greɪvstəun] n pietra tombale

graveyard ['greɪvjɑːd] n cimitero

gravity ['grævɪtɪ] n (Physics) gravità; pesantezza; (seriousness) gravità, serietà

gravy ['greɪvɪ] n intingolo della carne; salsa

gray [greɪ] adj = **grey**

graze [greɪz] vi pascolare, pascere ▷ vt (touch lightly) sfiorare; (scrape) escoriare ▷ n (Med) escoriazione f

grease [griːs] n (fat) grasso; (lubricant) lubrificante m ▷ vt ingrassare; lubrificare; **greasy** adj grasso(-a), untuoso(-a)

great [greɪt] adj grande; magnifico(-a), meraviglioso(-a); **Great Britain** n Gran Bretagna; **great-grandfather** n bisnonno; **great-grandmother** n bisnonna; **greatly** adv molto

Greece [griːs] n Grecia

greed [griːd] n (also: **~iness**) avarizia; (for food) golosità, ghiottoneria; **greedy** adj avido(-a); goloso(-a), ghiotto(-a)

Greek [griːk] adj greco(-a) ▷ n greco(-a); (Ling) greco

green [griːn] adj verde; (inexperienced) inesperto(-a), ingenuo(-a) ▷ n verde m; (stretch of grass) prato; (on golf course) green m inv; **~s** npl (vegetables) verdura; **green card** n (BRIT Aut) carta verde; (US Admin) permesso di soggiorno e di lavoro; **greengage** ['griːngeɪdʒ] n susina Regina Claudia; **greengrocer** (BRIT) n fruttivendolo(-a), erbivendolo(-a); **greenhouse** n serra; **greenhouse effect** n effetto serra

Greenland ['griːnlənd] n Groenlandia

green salad n insalata verde

greet [griːt] vt salutare; **greeting** n saluto; **greeting(s) card** n cartolina d'auguri

grew [gruː] pt of **grow**

grey [greɪ] (US **gray**) adj grigio(-a); **grey-haired** adj dai capelli grigi; **greyhound** n levriere m

grid [grɪd] n grata; (Elec) rete f; **gridlock** ['grɪdlʌk] n (traffic jam) paralisi f inv del traffico; **gridlocked** adj paralizzato(-a) dal traffico; (talks etc) in fase di stallo

grief [griːf] n dolore m

grievance ['griːvəns] n lagnanza

grieve [griːv] vi addolorarsi; rattristarsi ▷ vt addolorare; **to ~ for sb** (dead person) piangere qn

grill [grɪl] n (on cooker) griglia; (also: **mixed ~**) grigliata mista ▷ vt (BRIT) cuocere ai ferri; (inf: question) interrogare senza sosta

grille [grɪl] n grata; (Aut) griglia

grim [grɪm] *adj* sinistro(-a), brutto(-a)

grime [graɪm] *n* sudiciume *m*

grin [grɪn] *n* sorriso smagliante ▷ *vi* fare un gran sorriso

grind [graɪnd] (*pt, pp* **ground**) *vt* macinare; (*make sharp*) arrotare ▷ *n* (*work*) sgobbata

grip [grɪp] *n* impugnatura; presa; (*holdall*) borsa da viaggio ▷ *vt* (*object*) afferrare; (*attention*) catturare; **to come to ~s with** affrontare; cercare di risolvere; **gripping** ['grɪpɪŋ] *adj* avvincente

grit [grɪt] *n* ghiaia; (*courage*) fegato ▷ *vt* (*road*) coprire di sabbia; **to ~ one's teeth** stringere i denti

grits [grɪts] (*US*) *npl* macinato grosso (di avena *etc*)

groan [grəʊn] *n* gemito ▷ *vi* gemere

grocer ['grəʊsə^r] *n* negoziante *m* di generi alimentari; **groceries** *npl* provviste *fpl*; **grocer's (shop)** *n* negozio di (generi) alimentari

grocery ['grəʊsərɪ] *n* (*shop*) (negozio di) alimentari

groin [grɔɪn] *n* inguine *m*

groom [gru:m] *n* palafreniere *m*; (*also*: **bride~**) sposo ▷ *vt* (*horse*) strigliare; (*fig*): **to ~ sb for** avviare qn a; **well-~ed** (*person*) curato(-a)

groove [gru:v] *n* scanalatura, solco

grope [grəʊp] *vi* **to ~ for** cercare a tastoni

gross [grəʊs] *adj* grossolano(-a); (*Comm*) lordo(-a); **grossly** *adv* (*greatly*) molto

grotesque [grəʊ'tɛsk] *adj* grottesco(-a)

ground [graʊnd] *pt, pp of* **grind** ▷ *n* suolo, terra; (*land*) terreno; (*Sport*) campo; (*reason: gen pl*) ragione *f*; (*us: also:* **~ wire**) terra ▷ *vt* (*plane*) tenere a terra; (*us Elec*) mettere la presa a terra a; **~s** *npl* (*of coffee etc*) fondi *mpl*; (*gardens etc*) terreno, giardini *mpl*; **on/to the ~** per/a terra; **to gain/lose ~** guadagnare/perdere terreno; **ground floor** *n* pianterreno; **groundsheet** (*BRIT*) *n* telone *m* impermeabile; **groundwork** *n* preparazione *f*

group [gru:p] *n* gruppo ▷ *vt* (*also:* **~ together**) raggruppare ▷ *vi* (*also:* **~ together**) raggrupparsi

grouse [graʊs] *n inv* (*bird*) tetraone *m* ▷ *vi* (*complain*) brontolare

grovel ['grɔvl] *vi* (*fig*): **to ~ (before)** strisciare (di fronte a)

grow [grəʊ] (*pt* **grew**, *pp* **grown**) *vi* crescere; (*increase*) aumentare; (*develop*) svilupparsi; (*become*): **to ~ rich/weak** arricchirsi/indebolirsi ▷ *vt* coltivare, far crescere; **grow on** *vt fus* **that painting is ~ing on me** quel quadro più lo guardo più mi piace; **grow up** *vi* farsi grande, crescere

growl [graʊl] *vi* ringhiare

grown [grəʊn] *pp of* **grow**; **grown-up** *n* adulto(-a), grande *m/f*

growth [grəʊθ] *n* crescita, sviluppo; (*what has grown*) crescita; (*Med*) escrescenza, tumore *m*

grub [grʌb] *n* larva; (*inf: food*) roba (da mangiare)

grubby ['grʌbɪ] *adj* sporco(-a)

grudge [grʌdʒ] *n* rancore *m* ▷ *vt* **to ~ sb sth** dare qc a qn di malavoglia; invidiare qc a qn; **to bear sb a ~ (for)** serbar rancore a qn (per)

gruelling ['grʊəlɪŋ] (*US* **grueling**) *adj* estenuante

gruesome ['gru:səm] *adj* orribile

grumble ['grʌmbl] *vi* brontolare, lagnarsi

grumpy ['grʌmpɪ] *adj* scorbutico(-a)

grunt [grʌnt] *vi* grugnire

guarantee [gærən'ti:] *n* garanzia ▷ *vt* garantire

guard [gɑ:d] *n* guardia; (*one man*) guardia, sentinella; (*BRIT Rail*) capotreno; (*on machine*) schermo protettivo; (*also:* **fire~**) parafuoco ▷ *vt* fare la guardia a; (*protect*): **to ~ (against)** proteggere (da); **to be on one's ~** stare in guardia; **guardian** *n* custode *m*; (*of minor*) tutore(-trice)

guerrilla [gə'rɪlə] *n* guerrigliero

guess [gɛs] *vi* indovinare ▷ *vt* indovinare; (*US*) credere, pensare ▷ *n* **to take** *or* **have a ~** provare a indovinare

guest [gɛst] *n* ospite *m/f*; (*in hotel*) cliente *m/f*; **guest house** *n* pensione *f*; **guest room** *n* camera degli ospiti

guidance ['gaɪdəns] *n* guida, direzione *f*

guide [gaɪd] *n* (*person, book etc*) guida; (*BRIT: also:* **girl ~**) giovane esploratrice *f* ▷ *vt* guidare; **is there an English-speaking ~?** c'è una guida che parla inglese?; **guidebook** *n* guida; **do you have a guidebook in English?** avete una guida in inglese?; **guide dog** *n* cane *m* guida *inv*; **guided tour** *n* visita guidata; **what time does the guided tour start?** a che ora comincia la visita guidata?; **guidelines** *npl* (*fig*) indicazioni *fpl*, linee *fpl* direttive

guild [gɪld] *n* arte *f*, corporazione *f*; associazione *f*

guilt [gɪlt] *n* colpevolezza; **guilty** *adj* colpevole

guinea pig ['gɪnɪ-] *n* cavia

guitar [gɪ'tɑ:^r] *n* chitarra; **guitarist** *n* chitarrista *m/f*

gulf [gʌlf] *n* golfo; (*abyss*) abisso

gull [gʌl] *n* gabbiano

gulp [gʌlp] *vi* deglutire; (*from emotion*) avere il nodo in gola ▷ *vt* (*also:* **~ down**) tracannare, inghiottire

gum [gʌm] n (Anat) gengiva; (glue) colla; (also: **~drop**) caramella gommosa; (also: **chewing ~**) chewing-gum m inv ▷ vt to **~ (together)** incollare

gun [gʌn] n fucile m; (small) pistola, rivoltella; (rifle) carabina; (shotgun) fucile da caccia; (cannon) cannone m; **gunfire** n spari mpl; **gunman** (irreg) n bandito armato; **gunpoint** n **at gunpoint** sotto minaccia di fucile; **gunpowder** n polvere f da sparo; **gunshot** n sparo

gush [gʌʃ] vi sgorgare; (fig) abbandonarsi ad effusioni

gust [gʌst] n (of wind) raffica; (of smoke) buffata

gut [gʌt] n intestino, budello; **~s** npl (Anat) interiora fpl; (courage) fegato

gutter ['gʌtəʳ] n (of roof) grondaia; (in street) cunetta

guy [gaɪ] n (inf: man) tipo, elemento; (also: **~rope**) cavo or corda di fissaggio; (figure) effigie di Guy Fawkes

Guy Fawkes Night [-'fɔːks-] n (BRIT) vedi nota nel riquadro

● **GUY FAWKES NIGHT**
●
● La sera del 5 novembre, in occasione
● della **Guy Fawkes Night**, altrimenti
● chiamata **Bonfire Night**, viene
● commemorato con falò e fuochi
● d'artificio il fallimento della Congiura
● delle Polveri contro Giacomo I nel 1605.
● La festa prende il nome dal principale
● congiurato della cospirazione, Guy
● Fawkes, la cui effigie viene bruciata
● durante i festeggiamenti.

gym [dʒɪm] n (also: **~nasium**) palestra; (also: **~nastics**) ginnastica; **gymnasium** [dʒɪm'neɪzɪəm] n palestra; **gymnast** ['dʒɪmnæst] n ginnasta m/f; **gymnastics** [-'næstɪks] n, npl ginnastica; **gym shoes** npl scarpe fpl da ginnastica

gynaecologist [gaɪnɪ'kɔlədʒɪst] (US **gynecologist**) n ginecologo(-a)

gypsy ['dʒɪpsɪ] n = **gipsy**

h

haberdashery ['hæbə'dæʃərɪ] (BRIT) n merceria

habit ['hæbɪt] n abitudine f; (costume) abito; (Rel) tonaca

habitat ['hæbɪtæt] n habitat m inv

hack [hæk] vt tagliare, fare a pezzi ▷ n (pej: writer) scribacchino(-a); **hacker** ['hækəʳ] n (Comput) pirata m informatico

had [hæd] pt, pp of **have**

haddock ['hædək] (pl **haddock** or **haddocks**) n eglefino

hadn't ['hædnt] = **had not**

haemorrhage ['hɛmərɪdʒ] (US **hemorrhage**) n emorragia

haemorrhoids ['hɛmərɔɪdz] (US **hemorrhoids**) npl emorroidi fpl

haggle ['hægl] vi mercanteggiare

Hague [heɪg] n **The ~** L'Aia

hail [heɪl] n grandine f; (of criticism etc) pioggia ▷ vt (call) chiamare; (flag down: taxi) fermare; (greet) salutare ▷ vi grandinare; **hailstone** n chicco di grandine

hair [hɛəʳ] n capelli mpl; (single hair: on head) capello; (: on body) pelo; **to do one's ~** pettinarsi; **hairband** ['hɛəbænd] n (elastic) fascia per i capelli; (rigid) cerchietto; **hairbrush** n spazzola per capelli; **haircut** n taglio di capelli; **hairdo** ['hɛəduː] n acconciatura, pettinatura;

hairdresser n parrucchiere(-a);
hairdresser's n parrucchiere(-a); **hair
dryer** n asciugacapelli m inv; **hair gel** n
gel m inv per capelli; **hair spray** n lacca
per capelli; **hairstyle** n pettinatura,
acconciatura; **hairy** adj irsuto(-a),
peloso(-a); (inf: frightening) spaventoso(-a)
hake [heɪk] (pl **hake** or **hakes**) n nasello
half [hɑːf] (pl **halves**) n mezzo, metà
f inv ▷ adj mezzo(-a) ▷ adv a mezzo, a
metà; **~ an hour** mezz'ora; **~ a dozen**
mezza dozzina; **~ a pound** mezza libbra;
two and a ~ due e mezzo; **a week and
a ~** una settimana e mezza; **~ (of it)** la
metà; **~ (of)** la metà di; **to cut sth in ~**
tagliare qc in due; **~ asleep** mezzo(-a)
addormentato(-a); **half board** (BRIT)
n mezza pensione; **half-brother** n
fratellastro; **half day** n mezza giornata;
half fare n tariffa a metà prezzo; **half-
hearted** adj tiepido(-a); **half-hour** n
mezz'ora; **half-price** adj, adv a metà
prezzo; **half term** (BRIT) n (Scol) vacanza
a or di metà trimestre; **half-time** n (Sport)
intervallo; **halfway** adv a metà strada
hall [hɔːl] n sala, salone m; (entrance way)
entrata
hallmark ['hɔːlmɑːk] n marchio di
garanzia; (fig) caratteristica
hallo [hə'ləʊ] excl = **hello**
hall of residence (BRIT) n casa dello
studente
Halloween [hæləʊ'iːn] n vigilia
d'Ognissanti

 ● **HALLOWEEN**
 ●
 ● Negli Stati Uniti e in Gran Bretagna il
 ● 31 ottobre si festeggia **Halloween**, la
 ● notte delle streghe e dei fantasmi. I
 ● bambini, travestiti da fantasmi, streghe
 ● o mostri, bussano alle porte e ricevono
 ● dolci e piccoli doni.

hallucination [həluːsɪ'neɪʃən] n
allucinazione f
hallway ['hɔːlweɪ] n corridoio; (entrance)
ingresso
halo ['heɪləʊ] n (of saint etc) aureola
halt [hɔːlt] n fermata ▷ vt fermare ▷ vi
fermarsi
halve [hɑːv] vt (apple etc) dividere a metà;
(expense) ridurre di metà
halves [hɑːvz] npl of **half**
ham [hæm] n prosciutto
hamburger ['hæmbəːgəʳ] n hamburger
m inv
hamlet ['hæmlɪt] n paesetto
hammer ['hæməʳ] n martello ▷ vt

martellare ▷ vi **to ~ on** or **at the door**
picchiare alla porta
hammock ['hæmək] n amaca
hamper ['hæmpəʳ] vt impedire ▷ n cesta
hamster ['hæmstəʳ] n criceto
hamstring ['hæmstrɪŋ] n (Anat) tendine
m del ginocchio
hand [hænd] n mano f; (of clock) lancetta;
(handwriting) scrittura; (at cards) mano;
(: game) partita; (worker) operaio(-a) ▷ vt
dare, passare; **to give sb a ~** dare una
mano a qn; **at ~** a portata di mano; **in
~** a disposizione; (work) in corso; **on ~**
(person) disponibile; (services) pronto(-a)
a intervenire; **to ~** (information etc) a
portata di mano; **on the one ~ ...., on
the other ~** da un lato ..., dall'altro;
hand down vt passare giù; (tradition,
heirloom) tramandare; **hand in** vt consegnare; **hand
out** vt distribuire; **hand over** vt passare;
cedere; **handbag** n borsetta; **hand
baggage** n bagaglio a mano; **handbook**
n manuale m; **handbrake** n freno a mano;
handcuffs npl manette fpl; **handful** n
manciata, pugno
handicap ['hændɪkæp] n handicap m inv
▷ vt handicappare; **to be physically ~ped**
essere handicappato(-a); **to be mentally
~ped** essere un(a) handicappato(-a)
mentale
handkerchief ['hæŋkətʃɪf] n fazzoletto
handle ['hændl] n (of door etc) maniglia; (of
cup etc) ansa; (of knife etc) impugnatura; (of
saucepan) manico; (for winding) manovella
▷ vt toccare, maneggiare; (deal with)
occuparsi di; (treat: people) trattare; **"~
with care"** "fragile"; **to fly off the ~** (fig)
perdere le staffe, uscire dai gangheri;
handlebar(s) n(pl) manubrio
hand: hand luggage n bagagli mpl a
mano; **handmade** adj fatto(-a) a mano;
handout n (money, food) elemosina;
(leaflet) volantino; (at lecture) prospetto
handsome ['hænsəm] adj bello(-a); (profit,
fortune) considerevole
handwriting ['hændraɪtɪŋ] n scrittura
handy ['hændɪ] adj (person) bravo(-a);
(close at hand) a portata di mano;
(convenient) comodo(-a)
hang [hæŋ] (pt, pp hung) vt appendere;
(criminal: pt, pp hanged) impiccare ▷ vi
(painting) essere appeso(-a); (hair)
scendere; (drapery) cadere; **to get the
~ of sth** (inf) capire come qc funziona;
hang about or **around** vi bighellonare,
ciondolare; **hang down** vi ricadere;
hang on vi (wait) aspettare; **hang out**
vt (washing) stendere (fuori); (inf: live)

stare ▷ vi penzolare, pendere; **hang round** vi = **hang around**; **hang up** vi (Tel) riattaccare ▷ vt appendere

hanger ['hæŋər] n gruccia

hang-gliding ['-glaɪdɪŋ] n volo col deltaplano

hangover ['hæŋəʊvər] n (after drinking) postumi mpl di sbornia

hankie ['hæŋkɪ] n abbr = **handkerchief**

happen ['hæpən] vi accadere, succedere; (chance): **to ~ to do sth** fare qc per caso; **what ~ed?** cos'è successo?; **as it ~s** guarda caso

happily ['hæpɪlɪ] adv felicemente; fortunatamente

happiness ['hæpɪnɪs] n felicità, contentezza

happy ['hæpɪ] adj felice, contento(-a); **~ with** (arrangements etc) soddisfatto(-a) di; **to be ~ to do** (willing) fare volentieri; **~ birthday!** buon compleanno!

harass ['hærəs] vt molestare; **harassment** n molestia

harbour ['hɑːbər] (us **harbor**) n porto ▷ vt (hope, fear) nutrire; (criminal) dare rifugio a

hard [hɑːd] adj duro(-a) ▷ adv (work) sodo; (think, try) bene; **to look ~ at** guardare fissamente; esaminare attentamente; **no ~ feelings!** senza rancore!; **to be ~ of hearing** essere duro(-a) d'orecchio; **to be ~ done by** essere trattato(-a) ingiustamente; **hardback** n libro rilegato; **hardboard** n legno precompresso; **hard disk** n (Comput) disco rigido; **harden** vt, vi indurire

hardly ['hɑːdlɪ] adv (scarcely) appena; **it's ~ the case** non è proprio il caso; **~ anyone/ anywhere** quasi nessuno/da nessuna parte; **~ ever** quasi mai

hard: hardship ['hɑːdʃɪp] n avversità f inv; privazioni fpl; **hard shoulder** (BRIT) n (Aut) corsia d'emergenza; **hard-up** (inf) adj al verde; **hardware** ['hɑːdwɛər] n ferramenta fpl; (Comput) hardware m; (Mil) armamenti mpl; **hardware shop** (us **hardware store**) n (negozio di) ferramenta fpl; **hard-working** ['-wəːkɪŋ] adj lavoratore(-trice)

hardy ['hɑːdɪ] adj robusto(-a); (plant) resistente al gelo

hare [hɛər] n lepre f

harm [hɑːm] n male m; (wrong) danno ▷ vt (person) fare male a; (thing) danneggiare; **out of ~'s way** al sicuro; **harmful** adj dannoso(-a); **harmless** adj innocuo(-a), inoffensivo(-a)

harmony ['hɑːmənɪ] n armonia

harness ['hɑːnɪs] n (for horse) bardatura, finimenti mpl; (for child) briglie fpl; (safety harness) imbracatura ▷ vt (horse) bardare; (resources) sfruttare

harp [hɑːp] n arpa ▷ vi **to ~ on about** insistere tediosamente su

harsh [hɑːʃ] adj (life, winter) duro(-a); (judge, criticism) severo(-a); (sound) rauco(-a); (light) violento(-a)

harvest ['hɑːvɪst] n raccolto; (of grapes) vendemmia ▷ vt fare il raccolto di, raccogliere; vendemmiare

has [hæz] vb see **have**

hasn't ['hæznt] = **has not**

hassle ['hæsl] (inf) n sacco di problemi

haste [heɪst] n fretta; precipitazione f; **hasten** ['heɪsn] vt affrettare ▷ vi **to hasten (to)** affrettarsi (a); **hastily** adv in fretta; precipitosamente; **hasty** adj affrettato(-a), precipitoso(-a)

hat [hæt] n cappello

hatch [hætʃ] n (Naut: also: **~way**) boccaporto; (also: **service ~**) portello di servizio ▷ vi (bird) uscire dal guscio; (egg) schiudersi

hatchback ['hætʃbæk] n (Aut) tre (or cinque) porte f inv

hate [heɪt] vt odiare, detestare ▷ n odio; **hatred** ['heɪtrɪd] n odio

haul [hɔːl] vt trascinare, tirare ▷ n (of fish) pescata; (of stolen goods etc) bottino

haunt [hɔːnt] vt (fear) pervadere; (person) frequentare ▷ n rifugio; **this house is ~ed** questa casa è abitata da un fantasma; **haunted** adj (castle etc) abitato(-a) dai fantasmi or dagli spiriti; (look) ossessionato(-a), tormentato(-a)

 KEYWORD

have [hæv] (pt, pp **had**) aux vb **1** (gen) avere; essere; **to have arrived/gone** essere arrivato(-a)/andato(-a); **to have eaten/slept** avere mangiato/dormito; **he has been kind/promoted** è stato gentile/promosso; **having finished** or **when he had finished, he left** dopo aver finito, se n'è andato

2 (in tag questions): **you've done it, haven't you?** l'hai fatto, (non è) vero?; **he hasn't done it, has he?** non l'ha fatto, vero?

3 (in short answers and questions): **you've made a mistake — no I haven't/so I have** ha fatto un errore — ma no, niente affatto/sì, è vero; **we haven't paid — yes we have!** non abbiamo pagato — ma sì che abbiamo pagato!; **I've been there before, have you?** ci sono già stato, e lei? ▷ modal aux vb (be obliged): **to have (got) to do sth** dover fare qc; **I haven't got**

or **I don't have to wear glasses** non ho bisogno di portare gli occhiali
▷ vt 1 (possess, obtain) avere; **he has (got) blue eyes/dark hair** ha gli occhi azzurri/i capelli scuri; **do you have** or **have you got a car/phone?** ha la macchina/il telefono?; **may I have your address?** potrebbe darmi il suo indirizzo?; **you can have it for £5** te lo lascio per 5 sterline
2 (+ noun: take, hold etc): **to have breakfast/a swim/a bath** fare colazione/una nuotata/un bagno; **to have lunch** pranzare; **to have dinner** cenare; **to have a drink** bere qualcosa; **to have a cigarette** fumare una sigaretta
3: **to have sth done** far fare qc; **to have one's hair cut** farsi tagliare i capelli; **to have sb do sth** far fare qc a qn
4 (experience, suffer) avere; **to have a cold/flu** avere il raffreddore/l'influenza; **she had her bag stolen** le hanno rubato la borsa
5 (inf: dupe): **you've been had!** ci sei cascato!
have out vt **to have it out with sb** (settle a problem etc) mettere le cose in chiaro con qn

haven ['heɪvn] n porto; (fig) rifugio
haven't ['hævnt] = **have not**
havoc ['hævək] n caos m
Hawaii [hə'waɪ:] n le Hawaii
hawk [hɔ:k] n falco
hawthorn ['hɔ:θɔ:n] n biancospino
hay [heɪ] n fieno; **hay fever** n febbre f da fieno; **haystack** n pagliaio
hazard ['hæzəd] n azzardo, ventura; pericolo, rischio ▷ vt (guess etc) azzardare; **hazardous** adj pericoloso(-a); **hazard warning lights** npl (Aut) luci fpl di emergenza
haze [heɪz] n foschia
hazel ['heɪzl] n (tree) nocciolo ▷ adj (eyes) (color) nocciola inv; **hazelnut** ['heɪzlnʌt] n nocciola
hazy ['heɪzɪ] adj fosco(-a); (idea) vago(-a)
he [hi:] pron lui, egli; **it is he who ...** è lui che ...
head [hɛd] n testa; (leader) capo; (of school) preside m/f ▷ vt (list) essere in testa a; (group) essere a capo di; **~s or tails** testa o croce; pari (o dispari)?; **~ first** a capofitto, di testa; **~ over heels in love** pazzamente innamorato(-a); **to ~ the ball** colpire una palla di testa; **head for** vt (threat, danger) sventare; **headache** n mal m di testa; **heading** n titolo; intestazione f; **headlamp** (BRIT) n

= **headlight**; **headlight** n fanale m; **headline** n titolo; **head office** n sede f (centrale); **headphones** npl cuffia; **headquarters** npl ufficio centrale; (Mil) quartiere m generale; **headroom** n (in car) altezza dell'abitacolo; (under bridge) altezza limite; **headscarf** n foulard m inv; **headset** n = **headphones**; **headteacher** n (of primary school) direttore(-trice); (of secondary school) preside; **head waiter** n capocameriere m
heal [hi:l] vt, vi guarire
health [hɛlθ] n salute f; **health care** n assistenza sanitaria; **health centre** (BRIT) n poliambulatorio; **health food** n cibo macrobiotico; **Health Service** (BRIT) n **the Health Service** ≈ il Servizio Sanitario Statale; **healthy** adj (person) sano(-a), in buona salute; (climate) salubre; (appetite, economy etc) sano(-a)
heap [hi:p] n mucchio ▷ vt (stones, sand): **to ~ (up)** ammucchiare; (plate, sink): **to ~ sth with** riempire qc di; **~s of** (inf) un mucchio di
hear [hɪər] (pt, pp **heard**) vt sentire; (news) ascoltare ▷ vi sentire; **to ~ about** avere notizie di; sentire parlare di; **to ~ from sb** ricevere notizie da qn
hearing ['hɪərɪŋ] n (sense) udito; (of witnesses) audizione f; (of a case) udienza; **hearing aid** n apparecchio acustico
hearse [hə:s] n carro funebre
heart [hɑ:t] n cuore m; **~s** npl (Cards) cuori mpl; **to lose ~** scoraggiarsi; **to take ~** farsi coraggio; **at ~** in fondo; **by ~** (learn, know) a memoria; **heart attack** n attacco di cuore; **heartbeat** n battito del cuore; **heartbroken** adj **to be heartbroken** avere il cuore spezzato; **heartburn** n bruciore m di stomaco; **heart disease** n malattia di cuore
hearth [hɑ:θ] n focolare m
heartless ['hɑ:tlɪs] adj senza cuore
hearty ['hɑ:tɪ] adj caloroso(-a); robusto(-a), sano(-a); vigoroso(-a)
heat [hi:t] n calore m; (fig) ardore m; fuoco; (Sport: also: **qualifying ~**) prova eliminatoria ▷ vt scaldare; **heat up** vi (liquids) scaldarsi; (room) riscaldarsi ▷ vt riscaldare; **heated** adj riscaldato(-a); (argument) acceso(-a); **heater** n radiatore m; (stove) stufa
heather ['hɛðər] n erica
heating ['hi:tɪŋ] n riscaldamento
heatwave ['hi:tweɪv] n ondata di caldo
heaven ['hɛvn] n paradiso, cielo; **heavenly** adj divino(-a), celeste
heavily ['hɛvɪlɪ] adv pesantemente; (drink, smoke) molto

heavy ['hɛvɪ] *adj* pesante; (*sea*) grosso(-a); (*rain, blow*) forte; (*weather*) afoso(-a); (*drinker, smoker*) gran (*before noun*); **it's too ~** è troppo pesante

Hebrew ['hi:bru:] *adj* ebreo(-a) ▷ *n* (*Ling*) ebraico

hectare ['hɛktɑ:ʳ] *n* (BRIT) ettaro

hectic ['hɛktɪk] *adj* movimentato(-a)

he'd [hi:d] = **he would**; **he had**

hedge [hɛdʒ] *n* siepe *f* ▷ *vi* essere elusivo(-a); **to ~ one's bets** (*fig*) coprirsi dai rischi

hedgehog ['hɛdʒhɔg] *n* riccio

heed [hi:d] *vt* (*also*: **take ~ of**) badare a, far conto di

heel [hi:l] *n* (*Anat*) calcagno; (*of shoe*) tacco ▷ *vt* (*shoe*) rifare i tacchi a

hefty ['hɛftɪ] *adj* (*person*) robusto(-a); (*parcel*) pesante; (*profit*) grosso(-a)

height [haɪt] *n* altezza; (*high ground*) altura; (*fig: of glory*) apice *m*; (: *of stupidity*) colmo; **heighten** *vt* (*fig*) accrescere

heir [ɛəʳ] *n* erede *m*; **heiress** *n* erede *f*

held [hɛld] *pt, pp of* **hold**

helicopter ['hɛlɪkɔptəʳ] *n* elicottero

hell [hɛl] *n* inferno; **~!** (*inf*) porca miseria!, accidenti!

he'll [hi:l] = **he will**; **he shall**

hello [hə'ləu] *excl* buon giorno!; ciao! (*to sb one addresses as "tu"*); (*surprise*) ma guarda!

helmet ['hɛlmɪt] *n* casco

help [hɛlp] *n* aiuto; (*charwoman*) donna di servizio ▷ *vt* aiutare; **~!** aiuto!; **can you ~ me?** può aiutarmi?; **~ yourself (to bread)** si serva (del pane); **he can't ~ it** non ci può far niente; **help out** *vi* aiutare ▷ *vt* **to ~ sb out** aiutare qn; **helper** *n* aiutante *m/f*, assistente *m/f*; **helpful** *adj* di grande aiuto; (*useful*) utile; **helping** *n* porzione *f*; **helpless** *adj* impotente; debole; **helpline** *n* ≈ telefono amico; (*Comm*) servizio *m* informazioni *inv* (*a pagamento*)

hem [hɛm] *n* orlo ▷ *vt* fare l'orlo a

hemisphere ['hɛmɪsfɪəʳ] *n* emisfero

hemorrhage ['hɛmərɪdʒ] (US) *n* = **haemorrhage**

hemorrhoids ['hɛmərɔɪdz] (US) *npl* = **haemorrhoids**

hen [hɛn] *n* gallina; (*female bird*) femmina

hence [hɛns] *adv* (*therefore*) dunque; **2 years ~** di qui a 2 anni

hen night *n* (*inf*) addio al nubilato

hepatitis [hɛpə'taɪtɪs] *n* epatite *f*

her [həːʳ] *pron* (*direct*) la, l' + *vowel*; (*indirect*) le; (*stressed, after prep*) lei ▷ *adj* il (la) suo(-a), i (le) suoi (sue); *see also* **me**; **my**

herb [həːb] *n* erba; **herbal** *adj* di erbe; **herbal tea** *n* tisana

herd [həːd] *n* mandria

here [hɪəʳ] *adv* qui, qua ▷ *excl* ehi!; **~!** (*at roll call*) presente!; **~ is/are** ecco; **~ he/she is** eccolo/eccola

hereditary [hɪ'rɛdɪtrɪ] *adj* ereditario(-a)

heritage ['hɛrɪtɪdʒ] *n* eredità; (*fig*) retaggio

hernia ['həːnɪə] *n* ernia

hero ['hɪərəu] (*pl* **heroes**) *n* eroe *m*; **heroic** [hɪ'rəuɪk] *adj* eroico(-a)

heroin ['hɛrəuɪn] *n* eroina

heroine ['hɛrəuɪn] *n* eroina

heron ['hɛrən] *n* airone *m*

herring ['hɛrɪŋ] *n* aringa

hers [həːz] *pron* il (la) suo(-a), i (le) suoi (sue); *see also* **mine¹**

herself [həː'sɛlf] *pron* (*reflexive*) si; (*emphatic*) lei stessa; (*after prep*) se stessa, sé; *see also* **oneself**

he's [hi:z] = **he is**; **he has**

hesitant ['hɛzɪtənt] *adj* esitante, indeciso(-a)

hesitate ['hɛzɪteɪt] *vi* **to ~ (about/to do)** esitare (su/a fare); **hesitation** [-'teɪʃən] *n* esitazione *f*

heterosexual ['hɛtərəu'sɛksjuəl] *adj*, *n* eterosessuale *m/f*

hexagon ['hɛksəgən] *n* esagono

hey [heɪ] *excl* ehi!

heyday ['heɪdeɪ] *n* **the ~ of** i bei giorni di, l'età d'oro di

HGV *n abbr* = **heavy goods vehicle**

hi [haɪ] *excl* ciao!

hibernate ['haɪbəneɪt] *vi* ibernare

hiccough ['hɪkʌp] *vi* singhiozzare

hiccup ['hɪkʌp] = **hiccough**

hid [hɪd] *pt of* **hide**

hidden ['hɪdn] *pp of* **hide**

hide [haɪd] (*pt* **hid**, *pp* **hidden**) *n* (*skin*) pelle *f* ▷ *vt* **to ~ sth (from sb)** nascondere qc (a qn) ▷ *vi* **to ~ (from sb)** nascondersi (da qn)

hideous ['hɪdɪəs] *adj* laido(-a); orribile

hiding ['haɪdɪŋ] *n* (*beating*) bastonata; **to be in ~** (*concealed*) tenersi nascosto(-a)

hi-fi ['haɪfaɪ] *n* stereo ▷ *adj* ad alta fedeltà, hi-fi *inv*

high [haɪ] *adj* alto(-a); (*speed, respect, number*) grande; (*wind*) forte; (*voice*) acuto(-a) ▷ *adv* alto, in alto; **20m ~** alto(-a) 20m; **highchair** *n* seggiolone *m*; **high-class** *adj* (*neighbourhood*) elegante; (*hotel*) di prim'ordine; (*person*) di gran classe; (*food*) raffinato(-a); **higher education** *n* studi *mpl* superiori; **high heels** *npl* (*heels*) tacchi *mpl* alti; (*shoes*) scarpe *fpl* con i tacchi alti; **high jump** *n* (*Sport*) salto in alto; **highlands** *npl* zona montuosa; **the Highlands** le Highlands scozzesi; **highlight** *n* (*fig: of event*) momento culminante; (*in hair*) colpo di sole ▷ *vt* mettere in evidenza; **highlights** npl (in hair) colpi mpl di sole; **highlighter** n (pen) evidenziatore m; **highly** adv molto; **to speak highly of** parlare molto bene di; **highness** n **Her Highness** Sua Altezza; **high-rise** n (also: **high-rise block, high-rise building**) palazzone m; **high school** n scuola secondaria; (US) istituto superiore d'istruzione; **high season** (BRIT) n alta stagione; **high street** (BRIT) n strada principale; **high-tech** (inf) adj high-tech inv; **highway** ['haɪweɪ] n strada maestra; **Highway Code** (BRIT) n codice m della strada

hijack ['haɪdʒæk] vt dirottare; **hijacker** n dirottatore(-trice)

hike [haɪk] vi fare un'escursione a piedi ▷ n escursione f a piedi; **hiker** n escursionista m/f; **hiking** n escursioni fpl a piedi

hilarious [hɪ'lɛərɪəs] adj (behaviour, event) spassosissimo(-a)

hill [hɪl] n collina, colle m; (fairly high) montagna; (on road) salita; **hillside** n fianco della collina; **hill walking** n escursioni fpl in collina; **hilly** adj collinoso(-a); montagnoso(-a)

him [hɪm] pron (direct) lo, l' + vowel; (indirect) gli; (stressed, after prep) lui; see also **me**; **himself** pron (reflexive) si; (emphatic) lui stesso; (after prep) se stesso, sé; see also **oneself**

hind [haɪnd] adj posteriore ▷ n cerva

hinder ['hɪndə'] vt ostacolare

hindsight ['haɪndsaɪt] n **with ~** con il senno di poi

Hindu ['hɪnduː] n indù m/f inv; **Hinduism** n (Rel) induismo

hinge [hɪndʒ] n cardine m ▷ vi (fig): **to ~ on** dipendere da

hint [hɪnt] n (suggestion) allusione f; (advice) consiglio; (sign) accenno ▷ vt **to ~ that** lasciar capire che ▷ vi **to ~ at** alludere a

hip [hɪp] n anca, fianco

hippie ['hɪpɪ] n hippy m/f inv

hippo ['hɪpəʊ] (pl **hippos**) n ippopotamo

hippopotamus [hɪpə'pɒtəməs] (pl **hippopotamuses** or **hippopotami**) n ippopotamo

hippy ['hɪpɪ] n = **hippie**

hire ['haɪə'] vt (BRIT: car, equipment) noleggiare; (worker) assumere, dare lavoro a ▷ n nolo, noleggio; **for ~** da nolo; (taxi) libero(-a); **I'd like to ~ a car** vorrei noleggiare una macchina; **hire(d) car** (BRIT) n macchina a nolo; **hire purchase** (BRIT) n acquisto (or vendita) rateale

his [hɪz] adj, pron il (la) suo (sua), i (le) suoi (sue); see also **my**; **mine**¹

Hispanic [hɪs'pænɪk] adj ispanico(-a)

hiss [hɪs] vi fischiare; (cat, snake) sibilare

historian [hɪ'stɔːrɪən] n storico(-a)

historic(al) [hɪ'stɒrɪk(l)] adj storico(-a)

history ['hɪstərɪ] n storia

hit [hɪt] (pt, pp **hit**) vt colpire, picchiare; (knock against) battere; (reach: target) raggiungere; (collide with: car) urtare contro; (fig: affect) colpire; (find: problem etc) incontrare ▷ n colpo; (success, song) successo; **to ~ it off with sb** andare molto d'accordo con qn; **hit back** vi **to ~ back at sb** restituire il colpo a qn

hitch [hɪtʃ] vt (fasten) attaccare; (also: **~ up**) tirare su ▷ n (difficulty) intoppo, difficoltà f inv; **to ~ a lift** fare l'autostop; **hitch-hike** vi fare l'autostop; **hitch-hiker** n autostoppista m/f; **hitch-hiking** n autostop m

hi-tech ['haɪ'tɛk] adj high-tech inv

hitman ['hɪtmæn] (irreg) n (inf) sicario

HIV abbr **~-negative/-positive** adj sieronegativo(-a)/sieropositivo(-a)

hive [haɪv] n alveare m

hoard [hɔːd] n (of food) provviste fpl; (of money) gruzzolo ▷ vt ammassare

hoarse [hɔːs] adj rauco(-a)

hoax [həʊks] n scherzo; falso allarme

hob [hɒb] n piastra (con fornelli)

hobble ['hɒbl] vi zoppicare

hobby ['hɒbɪ] n hobby m inv, passatempo

hobo ['həʊbəʊ] (US) n vagabondo

hockey ['hɒkɪ] n hockey m; **hockey stick** n bastone m da hockey

hog [hɒg] n maiale m ▷ vt (fig) arraffare; **to go the whole ~** farlo fino in fondo

Hogmanay [hɒgmə'neɪ] n (Scottish) ≈ San Silvestro

hoist [hɔɪst] n paranco ▷ vt issare

hold [həʊld] (pt, pp **held**) vt tenere; (contain) contenere; (keep back) trattenere; (believe) mantenere; considerare; (possess) avere, possedere; detenere ▷ vi (withstand pressure) tenere; (be valid) essere valido(-a) ▷ n presa; (control): **to have a ~ over** avere controllo su; (Naut) stiva; **~ the line!** (Tel) resti in linea!; **to ~ one's own** (fig) difendersi bene; **to catch** or **get (a) ~ of** afferrare; **hold back** vt trattenere; (secret) tenere celato(-a); **hold on** vi tener fermo; (wait) aspettare; **~ on!** (Tel) resti in linea!; **hold out** vt offrire ▷ vi (resist) resistere; **hold up** vt (raise) alzare; (support) sostenere; (delay) ritardare; (rob) assaltare; **holdall** (BRIT) n borsone m; **holder** n (container) contenitore m; (of ticket, title) possessore/posseditrice; (of office etc) incaricato(-a); (of record) detentore(-trice)

hole [həʊl] n buco, buca

holiday ['hɔlədɪ] n vacanza; (day off) giorno di vacanza; (public) giorno festivo; **on ~** in vacanza; **I'm on ~ here** sono qui in vacanza; **holiday camp** (BRIT) n (also: **holiday centre**) ≈ villaggio (di vacanze); **holiday job** n (BRIT) ≈ lavoro estivo; **holiday-maker** (BRIT) n villeggiante m/f; **holiday resort** n luogo di villeggiatura

Holland ['hɔlənd] n Olanda

hollow ['hɔləu] adj cavo(-a); (container, claim) vuoto(-a); (laugh, sound) cupo(-a) ▷ n cavità f inv; (in land) valletta, depressione f ▷ vt **to ~ out** scavare

holly ['hɔlɪ] n agrifoglio

Hollywood ['hɔlɪwud] n Hollywood f

holocaust ['hɔləkɔːst] n olocausto

holy ['həulɪ] adj santo(-a); (bread, ground) benedetto(-a), consacrato(-a)

home [həum] n casa; (country) patria; (institution) casa, ricovero ▷ cpd familiare; (cooking etc) casalingo(-a); (Econ, Pol) nazionale, interno(-a); (Sport) di casa ▷ adv a casa; in patria; (right in: nail etc) fino in fondo; **at ~** a casa; (in situation) a proprio agio; **to go** or **come ~** tornare a casa (or in patria); **make yourself at ~** si metta a suo agio; **home address** n indirizzo di casa; **homeland** n patria; **homeless** adj senza tetto; spatriato(-a); **homely** adj semplice, alla buona; accogliente; **home-made** adj casalingo(-a); **home match** n partita in casa; **Home Office** (BRIT) n ministero degli Interni; **home owner** n proprietario(-a) di casa; **home page** n (Comput) home page f inv; **Home Secretary** (BRIT) n ministro degli Interni; **homesick** adj **to be homesick** avere la nostalgia; **home town** n città f inv natale; **homework** n compiti mpl (per casa)

homicide ['hɔmɪsaɪd] (US) n omicidio

homoeopathic [həumɪə'pæθɪk] (US **homeopathic**) adj omeopatico(-a)

homoeopathy [həumɪ'ɔpəθɪ] (US **homeopathy**) n omeopatia

homosexual [hɔməu'sɛksjuəl] adj, n omosessuale m/f

honest ['ɔnɪst] adj onesto(-a); sincero(-a); **honestly** adv onestamente; sinceramente; **honesty** n onestà

honey ['hʌnɪ] n miele m; **honeymoon** n luna di miele, viaggio di nozze; **we're on honeymoon** siamo in luna di miele; **honeysuckle** n (Bot) caprifoglio

Hong Kong ['hɔŋ'kɔŋ] n Hong Kong f

honorary ['ɔnərərɪ] adj onorario(-a); (duty, title) onorifico(-a)

honour ['ɔnə⁰] (US **honor**) vt onorare ▷ n onore m; **honourable** (US **honorable**) adj onorevole; **honours degree** n (Scol) laurea specializzata

hood [hud] n cappuccio; (on cooker) cappa; (BRIT Aut) capote f; (US Aut) cofano

hoof [huːf] (pl **hooves**) n zoccolo

hook [huk] n gancio; (for fishing) amo ▷ vt uncinare; (dress) agganciare

hooligan ['huːlɪgən] n giovinastro, teppista m

hoop [huːp] n cerchio

hooray [huː'reɪ] excl = **hurray**

hoot [huːt] vi (Aut) suonare il clacson; (siren) ululare; (owl) gufare

Hoover® ['huːvə⁰] (BRIT) n aspirapolvere m inv ▷ vt **hoover** pulire con l'aspirapolvere

hooves [huːvz] npl of **hoof**

hop [hɔp] vi saltellare, saltare; (on one foot) saltare su una gamba

hope [həup] vt **to ~ that/to** do sperare che/di fare ▷ vi sperare ▷ n speranza; **I ~ so/not** spero di sì/no; **hopeful** adj (person) pieno(-a) di speranza; (situation) promettente; **hopefully** adv con speranza; **hopefully he will recover** speriamo che si riprenda; **hopeless** adj senza speranza, disperato(-a); (useless) inutile

hops [hɔps] npl luppoli mpl

horizon [hə'raɪzn] n orizzonte m; **horizontal** [hɔrɪ'zɔntl] adj orizzontale

hormone ['hɔːməun] n ormone m

horn [hɔːn] n (Zool, Mus) corno; (Aut) clacson m inv

horoscope ['hɔrəskəup] n oroscopo

horrendous [hə'rɛndəs] adj orrendo(-a)

horrible ['hɔrɪbl] adj orribile, tremendo(-a)

horrid ['hɔrɪd] adj orrido(-a); (person) odioso(-a)

horrific [hɔ'rɪfɪk] adj (accident) spaventoso(-a); (film) orripilante

horrifying ['hɔrɪfaɪɪŋ] adj terrificante

horror ['hɔrə⁰] n orrore m; **horror film** n film m inv dell'orrore

hors d'œuvre [ɔː'dəːvrə] n antipasto

horse [hɔːs] n cavallo; **horseback: on horseback** adj, adv a cavallo; **horse chestnut** n ippocastano; **horsepower** n cavallo (vapore); **horse-racing** n ippica; **horseradish** n rafano; **horse riding** n (BRIT) equitazione f

hose [həuz] n (also: **~pipe**) tubo; (also: **garden ~**) tubo per annaffiare

hospital ['hɔspɪtl] n ospedale m; **where's the nearest ~?** dov'è l'ospedale più vicino?

hospitality [hɔspɪ'tælɪtɪ] n ospitalità

host [həust] n ospite m; (Rel) ostia; (large number): **a ~ of** una schiera di

hostage ['hɔstɪdʒ] n ostaggio(-a)

hostel ['hɔstl] n ostello; (also: **youth ~**) ostello della gioventù

hostess ['həʊstɪs] n ospite f; (BRIT: air hostess) hostess f inv

hostile ['hɒstaɪl] adj ostile

hostility [hɒ'stɪlɪtɪ] n ostilità f inv

hot [hɒt] adj caldo(-a); (as opposed to only warm) molto caldo(-a); (spicy) piccante; (fig) accanito(-a); ardente; violento(-a), focoso(-a); **to be ~** (person) aver caldo; (object) essere caldo(-a); (weather) far caldo; **hot dog** n hot dog m inv

hotel [həʊ'tɛl] n albergo

hot-water bottle [hɒt'wɔːtə-] n borsa dell'acqua calda

hound [haʊnd] vt perseguitare ▷ n segugio

hour ['aʊəʳ] n ora; **hourly** adj all'ora

house [n haʊs, pl 'haʊzɪz] [vb haʊz] n (also: **firm**) casa; (Pol) camera; (Theatre) sala; pubblico; spettacolo; (dynasty) casata ▷ vt (person) ospitare, alloggiare; **on the ~** (fig) offerto(-a) dalla casa; **household** n famiglia; casa; **householder** n padrone(-a) di casa; (head of house) capofamiglia m/f; **housekeeper** n governante f; **housekeeping** n (work) governo della casa; (money) soldi mpl per le spese di casa; **housewife** (irreg) n massaia, casalinga; **house wine** n vino della casa; **housework** n faccende fpl domestiche

housing ['haʊzɪŋ] n alloggio; **housing development** (BRIT), **housing estate** n zona residenziale con case popolari e/o private

hover ['hɒvəʳ] vi (bird) librarsi; **hovercraft** n hovercraft m inv

how [haʊ] adv come; **~ are you?** come sta?; **~ do you do?** piacere!; **~ far is it to the river?** quanto è lontano il fiume?; **~ long have you been here?** da quando è qui?; **~ lovely!/awful!** che bello!/orrore!; **~ many?** quanti(-e)?; **~ much?** quanto(-a)?; **~ much milk?** quanto latte?; **~ many people?** quante persone?; **~ old are you?** quanti anni ha?

however [haʊ'ɛvəʳ] adv in qualsiasi modo or maniera che; (+ adjective) per quanto + sub; (in questions) come ▷ conj comunque, però

howl [haʊl] vi ululare; (baby, person) urlare

H.P. abbr = **hire purchase**; **horsepower**

h.p. n abbr = **H.P**

HQ n, abbr = **headquarters**

hr(s) abbr (= hour(s)) h

HTML abbr (= hypertext markup language) HTML m inv

hubcap ['hʌbkæp] n coprimozzo

huddle ['hʌdl] vi **to ~ together** rannicchiarsi l'uno contro l'altro

huff [hʌf] n **in a ~** stizzito(-a)

hug [hʌg] vt abbracciare; (shore, kerb) stringere

huge [hjuːdʒ] adj enorme, immenso(-a)

hull [hʌl] n (of ship) scafo

hum [hʌm] vt (tune) canticchiare ▷ vi canticchiare; (insect, plane, tool) ronzare

human ['hjuːmən] (irreg) adj umano(-a) ▷ n essere m umano

humane [hjuː'meɪn] adj umanitario(-a)

humanitarian [hjuːmænɪ'tɛərɪən] adj umanitario(-a)

humanity [hjuː'mænɪtɪ] n umanità

human rights npl diritti mpl dell'uomo

humble ['hʌmbl] adj umile, modesto(-a) ▷ vt umiliare

humid ['hjuːmɪd] adj umido(-a); **humidity** [hjuː'mɪdɪtɪ] n umidità

humiliate [hjuː'mɪlɪeɪt] vt umiliare; **humiliating** adj umiliante; **humiliation** [-'eɪʃən] n umiliazione f

hummus ['huməs] n purè di ceci

humorous ['hjuːmərəs] adj umoristico(-a); (person) buffo(-a)

humour ['hjuːməʳ] (US **humor**) n umore m ▷ vt accontentare

hump [hʌmp] n gobba

hunch [hʌntʃ] n (premonition) intuizione f

hundred ['hʌndrəd] num cento; **~s of** centinaia fpl di; **hundredth** [-ɪdθ] num centesimo(-a)

hung [hʌŋ] pt, pp of **hang**

Hungarian [hʌŋ'gɛərɪən] adj ungherese ▷ n ungherese m/f; (Ling) ungherese m

Hungary ['hʌŋgərɪ] n Ungheria

hunger ['hʌŋgəʳ] n fame f ▷ vi **to ~ for** desiderare ardentemente

hungry ['hʌŋgrɪ] adj affamato(-a); **to be ~** aver fame

hunt [hʌnt] vt (seek) cercare; (Sport) cacciare ▷ vi **to ~ (for)** andare a caccia (di) ▷ n caccia; **hunter** n cacciatore m; **hunting** n caccia

hurdle ['həːdl] n (Sport, fig) ostacolo

hurl [həːl] vt lanciare con violenza

hurrah [huˈrɑː] excl = **hurray**

hurray [huˈreɪ] excl urra!, evviva!

hurricane ['hʌrɪkən] n uragano

hurry ['hʌrɪ] n fretta ▷ vi (also: **~ up**) affrettarsi ▷ vt (also: **~ up**: person) affrettare; (work) far in fretta; **to be in a ~** aver fretta; **hurry up** vi sbrigarsi

hurt [həːt] (pt, pp **hurt**) vt (cause pain to) far male a; (injure, fig) ferire ▷ vi far male

husband ['hʌzbənd] n marito

hush [hʌʃ] n silenzio, calma ▷ vt zittire

husky ['hʌskɪ] adj roco(-a) ▷ n cane m eschimese

hut [hʌt] n rifugio; (shed) ripostiglio

hyacinth ['haɪəsɪnθ] n giacinto

hydrangea [haɪˈdreɪnʤə] n ortensia
hydrofoil [ˈhaɪdrəʊfɔɪl] n aliscafo
hydrogen [ˈhaɪdrədʒən] n idrogeno
hygiene [ˈhaɪʤiːn] n igiene f; **hygienic**
[haɪˈʤiːnɪk] adj igienico(-a)
hymn [hɪm] n inno; cantica
hype [haɪp] (inf) n campagna pubblicitaria
hyphen [ˈhaɪfn] n trattino
hypnotize [ˈhɪpnətaɪz] vt ipnotizzare
hypocrite [ˈhɪpəkrɪt] n ipocrita m/f
hypocritical [hɪpəˈkrɪtɪkl] adj ipocrita
hypothesis [haɪˈpɔθɪsɪs] (pl **hypotheses**)
n ipotesi f inv
hysterical [hɪˈsterɪkl] adj isterico(-a)
hysterics [hɪˈsterɪks] npl accesso di
isteria; (laughter) attacco di riso

I [aɪ] pron io
ice [aɪs] n ghiaccio; (on road) gelo; (ice
cream) gelato ▷ vt (cake) glassare ▷ vi
(also: **~ over**) ghiacciare; (also: **~ up**)
gelare; **iceberg** n iceberg m inv; **ice
cream** n gelato; **ice cube** n cubetto
di ghiaccio; **ice hockey** n hockey m su
ghiaccio
Iceland [ˈaɪslənd] n Islanda; **Icelander** n
islandese m/f; **Icelandic** [aɪsˈlændɪk] adj
islandese ▷ n (Ling) islandese m
ice: **ice lolly** (BRIT) n ghiacciolo; **ice rink**
n pista di pattinaggio; **ice skating** n
pattinaggio sul ghiaccio
icing [ˈaɪsɪŋ] n (Culin) glassa; **icing sugar**
(BRIT) n zucchero a velo
icon [ˈaɪkɔn] n icona
icy [ˈaɪsɪ] adj ghiacciato(-a); (weather,
temperature) gelido(-a)
I'd [aɪd] = I would; I had
ID card n = identity card
idea [aɪˈdɪə] n idea
ideal [aɪˈdɪəl] adj ideale ▷ n ideale m;
ideally [aɪˈdɪəlɪ] adv perfettamente,
assolutamente; **ideally the book
should have ...** l'ideale sarebbe che il
libro avesse ...
identical [aɪˈdentɪkl] adj identico(-a)
identification [aɪdentɪfɪˈkeɪʃən] n
identificazione f; **(means of) ~** carta

d'identità

identify [aɪ'dentɪfaɪ] vt identificare

identity [aɪ'dentɪtɪ] n identità finv; **identity card** n carta d'identità

ideology [aɪdɪ'ɒlədʒɪ] n ideologia

idiom ['ɪdɪəm] n idioma m; (phrase) espressione f idiomatica

idiot ['ɪdɪət] n idiota m/f

idle ['aɪdl] adj inattivo(-a); (lazy) pigro(-a), ozioso(-a); (unemployed) disoccupato(-a); (question, pleasures) ozioso(-a) ▷ vi (engine) girare al minimo

idol ['aɪdl] n idolo

idyllic [ɪ'dɪlɪk] adj idillico(-a)

i.e. adv abbr (= that is) cioè

if [ɪf] conj se; **if I were you ...** se fossi in te ..., io al tuo posto ...; **if so** se è così; **if not** se no; **if only** se solo or soltanto

ignite [ɪg'naɪt] vt accendere ▷ vi accendersi

ignition [ɪg'nɪʃən] n (Aut) accensione f; **to switch on/off the ~** accendere/spegnere il motore

ignorance ['ɪgnərəns] n ignoranza; **to keep sb in ~ of sth** tenere qn all'oscuro di qc

ignorant ['ɪgnərənt] adj ignorante; **to be ~ of** (subject) essere ignorante in; (events) essere ignaro(-a) di

ignore [ɪg'nɔːʳ] vt non tener conto di; (person, fact) ignorare

I'll [aɪl] = **I will**; **I shall**

ill [ɪl] adj (sick) malato(-a); (bad) cattivo(-a) ▷ n male m ▷ adv **to speak** etc **~ of sb** parlare etc male di qn; **to take** or **be taken ~** ammalarsi

illegal [ɪ'liːgl] adj illegale

illegible [ɪ'ledʒɪbl] adj illeggibile

illegitimate [ɪlɪ'dʒɪtɪmət] adj illegittimo(-a)

ill health n problemi mpl di salute

illiterate [ɪ'lɪtərət] adj analfabeta, illetterato(-a); (letter) scorretto(-a)

illness ['ɪlnɪs] n malattia

illuminate [ɪ'luːmɪneɪt] vt illuminare

illusion [ɪ'luːʒən] n illusione f

illustrate ['ɪləstreɪt] vt illustrare

illustration [ɪlə'streɪʃən] n illustrazione f

I'm [aɪm] = **I am**

image ['ɪmɪdʒ] n immagine f; (public face) immagine (pubblica)

imaginary [ɪ'mædʒɪnərɪ] adj immaginario(-a)

imagination [ɪmædʒɪ'neɪʃən] n immaginazione f, fantasia

imaginative [ɪ'mædʒɪnətɪv] adj immaginoso(-a)

imagine [ɪ'mædʒɪn] vt immaginare

imbalance [ɪm'bæləns] n squilibrio

imitate ['ɪmɪteɪt] vt imitare; **imitation** [-'teɪʃən] n imitazione f

immaculate [ɪ'mækjulət] adj immacolato(-a); (dress, appearance) impeccabile

immature [ɪmə'tjuəʳ] adj immaturo(-a)

immediate [ɪ'miːdɪət] adj immediato(-a); **immediately** adv (at once) subito, immediatamente; **immediately next to** proprio accanto a

immense [ɪ'mens] adj immenso(-a); enorme; **immensely** adv immensamente

immerse [ɪ'məːs] vt immergere

immigrant ['ɪmɪgrənt] n immigrante m/f; immigrato(-a); **immigration** [ɪmɪ'greɪʃən] n immigrazione f

imminent ['ɪmɪnənt] adj imminente

immoral [ɪ'mɒrl] adj immorale

immortal [ɪ'mɔːtl] adj, n immortale m/f

immune [ɪ'mjuːn] adj **~ (to)** immune (da); **immune system** n sistema m immunitario

immunize ['ɪmjunaɪz] vt immunizzare

impact ['ɪmpækt] n impatto

impair [ɪm'pεəʳ] vt danneggiare

impartial [ɪm'pɑːʃl] adj imparziale

impatience [ɪm'peɪʃəns] n impazienza

impatient [ɪm'peɪʃənt] adj impaziente; **to get** or **grow ~** perdere la pazienza

impeccable [ɪm'pɛkəbl] adj impeccabile

impending [ɪm'pɛndɪŋ] adj imminente

imperative [ɪm'pεrətɪv] adj imperativo(-a); necessario(-a), urgente; (voice) imperioso(-a)

imperfect [ɪm'pəːfɪkt] adj imperfetto(-a); (goods etc) difettoso(-a) ▷ n (Ling: also: ~ tense) imperfetto

imperial [ɪm'pɪərɪəl] adj imperiale; (measure) legale

impersonal [ɪm'pəːsənl] adj impersonale

impersonate [ɪm'pəːsəneɪt] vt impersonare; (Theatre) fare la mimica di

impetus ['ɪmpətəs] n impeto

implant [ɪm'plɑːnt] vt (Med) innestare; (fig: idea, principle) inculcare

implement [n 'ɪmplɪmənt, vb 'ɪmplɪmɛnt] n attrezzo; (for cooking) utensile m ▷ vt effettuare

implicate ['ɪmplɪkeɪt] vt implicare

implication [ɪmplɪ'keɪʃən] n implicazione f; **by ~** implicitamente

implicit [ɪm'plɪsɪt] adj implicito(-a); (complete) completo(-a)

imply [ɪm'plaɪ] vt insinuare; suggerire

impolite [ɪmpə'laɪt] adj scortese

import [vb ɪm'pɔːt, n 'ɪmpɔːt] vt importare ▷ n (Comm) importazione f

importance [ɪmˈpɔːtns] n importanza
important [ɪmˈpɔːtnt] adj importante;
it's not ~ non ha importanza
importer [ɪmˈpɔːtəʳ] n
importatore(-trice)
impose [ɪmˈpəuz] vt imporre ▷ vi **to ~
on sb** sfruttare la bontà di qn; **imposing**
[ɪmˈpəuzɪŋ] adj imponente
impossible [ɪmˈpɔsɪbl] adj impossibile
impotent [ˈɪmpətnt] adj impotente
impoverished [ɪmˈpɔvərɪʃt] adj
impoverito(-a)
impractical [ɪmˈpræktɪkl] adj non
pratico(-a)
impress [ɪmˈprɛs] vt impressionare; (mark)
imprimere, stampare; **to ~ sth on sb** far
capire qc a qn
impression [ɪmˈprɛʃən] n impressione
f; **to be under the ~ that** avere
l'impressione che
impressive [ɪmˈprɛsɪv] adj notevole
imprison [ɪmˈprɪzn] vt imprigionare;
imprisonment n imprigionamento
improbable [ɪmˈprɔbəbl] adj improbabile;
(excuse) inverosimile
improper [ɪmˈprɔpəʳ] adj scorretto(-a);
(unsuitable) inadatto(-a), improprio(-a);
sconveniente, indecente
improve [ɪmˈpruːv] vt migliorare ▷ vi
migliorare; (pupil etc) fare progressi;
improvement n miglioramento;
progresso
improvise [ˈɪmprəvaɪz] vt, vi improvvisare
impulse [ˈɪmpʌls] n impulso; **on ~**
d'impulso, impulsivamente; **impulsive**
[ɪmˈpʌlsɪv] adj impulsivo(-a)

 KEYWORD

in [ɪn] prep 1 (indicating place, position) in;
in the house/garden in casa/giardino;
in the box nella scatola; **in the fridge**
nel frigorifero; **I have it in my hand** ce
l'ho in mano; **in town/the country** in
città/campagna; **in school** a scuola; **in
here/there** qui/lì dentro
2 (with place names: of town, region,
country): **in London** a Londra; **in England**
in Inghilterra; **in the United States** negli
Stati Uniti; **in Yorkshire** nello Yorkshire
3 (indicating time: during, in the space of) in;
in spring/summer in primavera/estate;
in 1988 nel 1988; **in May** or a maggio; **I'll
see you in July** ci vediamo a luglio; **in the
afternoon** nel pomeriggio; **at 4 o'clock
in the afternoon** alle 4 del pomeriggio;
I did it in 3 hours/days l'ho fatto in 3
ore/giorni; **I'll see you in 2 weeks** or **in 2
weeks' time** ci vediamo tra 2 settimane

4 (indicating manner etc) a; **in a loud/soft
voice** a voce alta/bassa; **in pencil** a
matita; **in English/French** in inglese/
francese; **the boy in the blue shirt** il
ragazzo con la camicia blu
5 (indicating circumstances): **in the sun**
al sole; **in the shade** all'ombra; **in the
rain** sotto la pioggia; **a rise in prices** un
aumento dei prezzi
6 (indicating mood, state): **in tears** in
lacrime; **in anger** per la rabbia; **in
despair** disperato(-a); **in good condition**
in buono stato, in buone condizioni; **to
live in luxury** vivere nel lusso
7 (with ratios, numbers): **1 in 10** 1 su 10;
20 pence in the pound 20 pence per
sterlina; **they lined up in twos** si misero
in fila a due a due
8 (referring to people, works) in; **the
disease is common in children** la
malattia è comune nei bambini; **in (the
works of) Dickens** in Dickens
9 (indicating profession etc) in; **to be in
teaching** fare l'insegnante, insegnare; **to
be in publishing** essere nell'editoria
10 (after superlative) di; **the best in the
class** il migliore della classe
11 (with present participle): **in saying this**
dicendo questo, nel dire questo
▷ adv **to be in** (person: at home, work)
esserci; (train, ship, plane) essere
arrivato(-a); (in fashion) essere di moda; **to
ask sb in** invitare qn ad entrare; **to run/
limp etc in** entrare di corsa/zoppicando
etc
▷ n **the ins and outs of the problem**
tutti i particolari del problema

inability [ɪnəˈbɪlɪtɪ] n **~ (to do)** incapacità
(di fare)
inaccurate [ɪnˈækjurət] adj inesatto(-a),
impreciso(-a)
inadequate [ɪnˈædɪkwət] adj
insufficiente
inadvertently [ɪnədˈvəːtntlɪ] adv senza
volerlo
inappropriate [ɪnəˈprəuprɪət] adj
non adatto(-a); (word, expression)
improprio(-a)
inaugurate [ɪˈnɔːgjureɪt] vt inaugurare;
(president, official) insediare
Inc. (us) abbr (= incorporated) S.A.
incapable [ɪnˈkeɪpəbl] adj incapace
incense [n ˈɪnsɛns, vb ɪnˈsɛns] n incenso
▷ vt (anger) infuriare
incentive [ɪnˈsɛntɪv] n incentivo
inch [ɪntʃ] n pollice m (25 mm, 12 in a foot);
within an ~ of a un pelo da; **he didn't give
an ~** non ha ceduto di un millimetro

incidence ['ɪnsɪdns] n (of crime, disease) incidenza

incident ['ɪnsɪdnt] n incidente m; (in book) episodio

incidentally [ɪnsɪ'dɛntəlɪ] adv (by the way) a proposito

inclination [ɪnklɪ'neɪʃən] n inclinazione f

incline [n 'ɪnklaɪn, vb ɪn'klaɪn] n pendenza, pendio ▷ vt inclinare ▷ vi (surface) essere inclinato(-a); **to be ~d to do** tendere a fare; essere propenso(-a) a fare

include [ɪn'kluːd] vt includere, comprendere; **is service ~d?** il servizio è compreso?; **including** prep compreso(-a), incluso(-a); **inclusion** [ɪn'kluːʒən] n inclusione f; **inclusive** [ɪn'kluːsɪv] adj incluso(-a), compreso(-a); **inclusive of tax** etc tasse etc comprese

income ['ɪnkʌm] n reddito; **income support** n (BRIT) sussidio di indigenza or povertà; **income tax** n imposta sul reddito

incoming ['ɪnkʌmɪŋ] adj (flight, mail) in arrivo; (government) subentrante; (tide) montante

incompatible [ɪnkəm'pætɪbl] adj incompatibile

incompetence [ɪn'kɔmpɪtns] n incompetenza, incapacità

incompetent [ɪn'kɔmpɪtnt] adj incompetente, incapace

incomplete [ɪnkəm'pliːt] adj incompleto(-a)

inconsistent [ɪnkən'sɪstənt] adj incoerente; **~ with** non coerente con

inconvenience [ɪnkən'viːnjəns] n inconveniente m; (trouble) disturbo ▷ vt disturbare

inconvenient [ɪnkən'viːnjənt] adj scomodo(-a)

incorporate [ɪn'kɔːpəreɪt] vt incorporare; (contain) contenere

incorrect [ɪnkə'rɛkt] adj scorretto(-a); (statement) inesatto(-a)

increase [n 'ɪnkriːs, vb ɪn'kriːs] n aumento ▷ vi, vt aumentare; **increasingly** adv sempre più

incredible [ɪn'krɛdɪbl] adj incredibile; **incredibly** adv incredibilmente

incur [ɪn'kəː'] vt (expenses) incorrere; (anger, risk) esporsi a; (debt) contrarre; (loss) subire

indecent [ɪn'diːsnt] adj indecente

indeed [ɪn'diːd] adv infatti; veramente; **yes ~!** certamente!

indefinitely [ɪn'dɛfɪnɪtlɪ] adv (wait) indefinitamente

independence [ɪndɪ'pɛndns] n

independenza; **Independence Day** (US) n vedi nota nel riquadro

independent [ɪndɪ'pɛndnt] adj indipendente; **independent school** n (BRIT) istituto scolastico indipendente che si autofinanzia

index ['ɪndɛks] (pl **indexes**) n (in book) indice m; (: in library etc) catalogo; (pl indices: ratio, sign) indice m

India ['ɪndɪə] n India; **Indian** adj, n indiano(-a)

indicate ['ɪndɪkeɪt] vt indicare; **indication** [-'keɪʃən] n indicazione f, segno; **indicative** [ɪn'dɪkətɪv] adj **indicative of** indicativo(-a) di; **indicator** ['ɪndɪkeɪtə'] n indicatore m; (Aut) freccia

indices ['ɪndɪsiːz] npl of **index**

indict [ɪn'daɪt] vt accusare; **indictment** [ɪn'daɪtmənt] n accusa

indifference [ɪn'dɪfrəns] n indifferenza

indifferent [ɪn'dɪfrənt] adj indifferente; (poor) mediocre

indigenous [ɪn'dɪdʒɪnəs] adj indigeno(-a)

indigestion [ɪndɪ'dʒɛstʃən] n indigestione f

indignant [ɪn'dɪgnənt] adj **~ (at sth/with sb)** indignato(-a) (per qc/contro qn)

indirect [ɪndɪ'rɛkt] adj indiretto(-a)

indispensable [ɪndɪ'spɛnsəbl] adj indispensabile

individual [ɪndɪ'vɪdjuəl] n individuo ▷ adj individuale; (characteristic) particolare, originale; **individually** adv singolarmente, uno(-a) per uno(-a)

Indonesia [ɪndə'niːzɪə] n Indonesia

indoor ['ɪndɔː'] adj da interno; (plant) d'appartamento; (swimming pool) coperto(-a); (sport, games) fatto(-a) al coperto; **indoors** [ɪn'dɔːz] adv all'interno

induce [ɪn'djuːs] vt persuadere; (bring about, Med) provocare

indulge [ɪn'dʌldʒ] vt (whim) compiacere, soddisfare; (child) viziare ▷ vi **to ~ in sth** concedersi qc; abbandonarsi a qc; **indulgent** adj indulgente

industrial [ɪn'dʌstrɪəl] adj industriale; (injury) sul lavoro; **industrial estate** (BRIT) n zona industriale; **industrialist**

[ɪn'dʌstrɪəlɪst] n industriale m; **industrial park** (US) n = **industrial estate**

industry ['ɪndəstrɪ] n industria; (diligence) operosità

inefficient [ɪnɪ'fɪʃənt] adj inefficiente

inequality [ɪnɪ'kwɔlɪtɪ] n ineguaglianza

inevitable [ɪn'ɛvɪtəbl] adj inevitabile; **inevitably** adv inevitabilmente

inexpensive [ɪnɪk'spɛnsɪv] adj poco costoso(-a)

inexperienced [ɪnɪks'pɪərɪənst] adj inesperto(-a), senza esperienza

inexplicable [ɪnɪk'splɪkəbl] adj inesplicabile

infamous ['ɪnfəməs] adj infame

infant ['ɪnfənt] n bambino(-a)

infantry ['ɪnfəntrɪ] n fanteria

infant school (BRIT) scuola elementare (per bambini dall'età di 5 a 7 anni)

infect [ɪn'fɛkt] vt infettare; **infection** [ɪn'fɛkʃən] n infezione f; **infectious** [ɪn'fɛkʃəs] adj (disease) infettivo(-a), contagioso(-a); (person: fig: enthusiasm) contagioso(-a)

infer [ɪn'fəːr] vt inferire, dedurre

inferior [ɪn'fɪərɪər] adj inferiore; (goods) di qualità scadente ▷ n inferiore m/f; (in rank) subalterno(-a)

infertile [ɪn'fəːtaɪl] adj sterile

infertility [ɪnfəː'tɪlɪtɪ] n sterilità

infested [ɪn'fɛstɪd] adj ~ **(with)** infestato(-a) (di)

infinite ['ɪnfɪnɪt] adj infinito(-a); **infinitely** adv infinitamente

infirmary [ɪn'fəːmərɪ] n ospedale m; (in school, factory) infermeria

inflamed [ɪn'fleɪmd] adj infiammato(-a)

inflammation [ɪnflə'meɪʃən] n infiammazione f

inflatable [ɪn'fleɪtəbl] adj gonfiabile

inflate [ɪn'fleɪt] vt (tyre, balloon) gonfiare; (fig) esagerare; gonfiare; **inflation** [ɪn'fleɪʃən] n (Econ) inflazione f

inflexible [ɪn'flɛksɪbl] adj inflessibile, rigido(-a)

inflict [ɪn'flɪkt] vt **to ~ on** infliggere a

influence ['ɪnfluəns] n influenza ▷ vt influenzare; **under the ~ of alcohol** sotto l'effetto dell'alcool; **influential** [ɪnflu'ɛnʃl] adj influente

influx ['ɪnflʌks] n afflusso

info (inf) ['ɪnfəu] n = **information**

inform [ɪn'fɔːm] vt **to ~ sb (of)** informare qn (di) ▷ vi **to ~ on sb** denunciare qn

informal [ɪn'fɔːml] adj informale; (announcement, invitation) non ufficiale

information [ɪnfə'meɪʃən] n informazioni fpl; particolari mpl; **a piece of ~** un'informazione; **information office** n

ufficio m informazioni inv; **information technology** n informatica

informative [ɪn'fɔːmətɪv] adj istruttivo(-a)

infra-red [ɪnfrə'rɛd] adj infrarosso(-a)

infrastructure ['ɪnfrəstrʌktʃər] n infrastruttura

infrequent [ɪn'friːkwənt] adj infrequente, raro(-a)

infuriate [ɪn'fjuərɪeɪt] vt rendere furioso(-a)

infuriating [ɪn'fjuərɪeɪtɪŋ] adj molto irritante

ingenious [ɪn'dʒiːnjəs] adj ingegnoso(-a)

ingredient [ɪn'griːdɪənt] n ingrediente m; elemento

inhabit [ɪn'hæbɪt] vt abitare; **inhabitant** [ɪn'hæbɪtnt] n abitante m/f

inhale [ɪn'heɪl] vt inalare ▷ vi (in smoking) aspirare; **inhaler** n inalatore m

inherent [ɪn'hɪərənt] adj ~ **(in or to)** inerente (a)

inherit [ɪn'hɛrɪt] vt ereditare; **inheritance** n eredità

inhibit [ɪn'hɪbɪt] vt (Psych) inibire; **inhibition** [-'bɪʃən] n inibizione f

initial [ɪ'nɪʃl] adj iniziale ▷ n iniziale f ▷ vt siglare; **~s** npl (of name) iniziali fpl; (as signature) sigla; **initially** adv inizialmente, all'inizio

initiate [ɪ'nɪʃɪeɪt] vt (start) avviare; intraprendere; iniziare; (person) iniziare; **to ~ sb into a secret** mettere qn a parte di un segreto; **to ~ proceedings against sb** (Law) intentare causa contro qn

initiative [ɪ'nɪʃətɪv] n iniziativa

inject [ɪn'dʒɛkt] vt (liquid) iniettare; (patient): **to ~ sb with sth** fare a qn un'iniezione di qc; (funds) immettere; **injection** [ɪn'dʒɛkʃən] n iniezione f, puntura

injure ['ɪndʒər] vt ferire; (damage: reputation etc) nuocere a; **injured** adj ferito(-a); **injury** ['ɪndʒərɪ] n ferita

injustice [ɪn'dʒʌstɪs] n ingiustizia

ink [ɪŋk] n inchiostro; **ink-jet printer** ['ɪŋkdʒɛt-] n stampante f a getto d'inchiostro

inland [adj 'ɪnlənd, adv ɪn'lænd] adj interno(-a), dell'interno ▷ adv all'interno; **Inland Revenue** (BRIT) n Fisco

in-laws ['ɪnlɔːz] npl suoceri mpl; famiglia del marito (or della moglie)

inmate ['ɪnmeɪt] n (in prison) carcerato(-a); (in asylum) ricoverato(-a)

inn [ɪn] n locanda

inner ['ɪnər] adj interno(-a), interiore; **inner-city** n centro di una zona urbana

inning ['ɪnɪŋ] n (US: Baseball) ripresa; **~s**

(Cricket) turno di battuta

innocence ['ɪnəsns] n innocenza

innocent ['ɪnəsnt] adj innocente

innovation [ɪnəu'veɪʃən] n innovazione f

innovative ['ɪnəu'veɪtɪv] adj innovativo(-a)

in-patient ['ɪnpeɪʃənt] n ricoverato(-a)

input ['ɪnput] n input m

inquest ['ɪnkwɛst] n inchiesta

inquire [ɪn'kwaɪər] vi informarsi ▷ vt domandare, informarsi su; **inquiry** n domanda; (Law) indagine f, investigazione f; **"inquiries"** "informazioni"

ins. abbr = **inches**

insane [ɪn'seɪn] adj matto(-a), pazzo(-a); (Med) alienato(-a)

insanity [ɪn'sænɪtɪ] n follia; (Med) alienazione f mentale

insect ['ɪnsɛkt] n insetto; **insect repellent** n insettifugo

insecure [ɪnsɪ'kjuər] adj malsicuro(-a); (person) insicuro(-a)

insecurity [ɪnsɪ'kjuərɪtɪ] n mancanza di sicurezza

insensitive [ɪn'sɛnsɪtɪv] adj insensibile

insert [ɪn'sə:t] vt inserire, introdurre

inside ['ɪn'saɪd] n interno, parte f interiore ▷ adj interno(-a), interiore ▷ adv dentro, all'interno ▷ prep dentro, all'interno di; (of time): **~ 10 minutes** entro 10 minuti; **inside lane** n (Aut) corsia di marcia; **inside out** adv (turn) a rovescio; (know) a fondo

insight ['ɪnsaɪt] n acume m, perspicacia; (glimpse, idea) percezione f

insignificant [ɪnsɪg'nɪfɪknt] adj insignificante

insincere [ɪnsɪn'sɪər] adj insincero(-a)

insist [ɪn'sɪst] vi insistere; **to ~ on doing** insistere per fare; **to ~ that** insistere perché + sub; (claim) sostenere che; **insistent** adj insistente

insomnia [ɪn'sɒmnɪə] n insonnia

inspect [ɪn'spɛkt] vt ispezionare; (BRIT: ticket) controllare; **inspection** [ɪn'spɛkʃən] n ispezione f; controllo; **inspector** n ispettore(-trice); (BRIT: on buses, trains) controllore m

inspiration [ɪnspə'reɪʃən] n ispirazione f; **inspire** [ɪn'spaɪər] vt ispirare; **inspiring** adj stimolante

instability [ɪnstə'bɪlɪtɪ] n instabilità

install [ɪn'stɔ:l] (us **instal**) vt installare; **installation** [ɪnstə'leɪʃən] n installazione f

instalment [ɪn'stɔ:lmənt] (us **installment**) n rata; (of TV serial etc) puntata; **in ~s** (pay) a rate; (receive) una parte per volta; (: publication) a fascicoli

instance ['ɪnstəns] n esempio, caso; **for ~**

per or ad esempio; **in the first ~** in primo luogo

instant ['ɪnstənt] n istante m, attimo ▷ adj immediato(-a); urgente; (coffee, food) in polvere; **instantly** adv immediatamente, subito

instead [ɪn'stɛd] adv invece; **~ of** invece di

instinct ['ɪnstɪŋkt] n istinto; **instinctive** adj istintivo(-a)

institute ['ɪnstɪtju:t] n istituto ▷ vt istituire, stabilire; (inquiry) avviare; (proceedings) iniziare

institution [ɪnstɪ'tju:ʃən] n istituzione f; (educational institution, mental institution) istituto

instruct [ɪn'strʌkt] vt **to ~ sb in sth** insegnare qc a qn; **to ~ sb to do** dare ordini a qn di fare; **instruction** [ɪn'strʌkʃən] n istruzione f; **instructions (for use)** istruzioni per l'uso; **instructor** n istruttore(-trice); (for skiing) maestro(-a)

instrument ['ɪnstrəmənt] n strumento; **instrumental** [-'mɛntl] adj (Mus) strumentale; **to be instrumental in** essere d'aiuto in

insufficient [ɪnsə'fɪʃənt] adj insufficiente

insulate ['ɪnsjuleɪt] vt isolare; **insulation** [-'leɪʃən] n isolamento

insulin ['ɪnsjulɪn] n insulina

insult [n 'ɪnsʌlt, vb ɪn'sʌlt] n insulto, affronto ▷ vt insultare; **insulting** adj offensivo(-a), ingiurioso(-a)

insurance [ɪn'ʃuərəns] n assicurazione f; **fire/life ~** assicurazione contro gli incendi/sulla vita; **insurance company** n società di assicurazioni; **insurance policy** n polizza d'assicurazione

insure [ɪn'ʃuər] vt assicurare

intact [ɪn'tækt] adj intatto(-a)

intake ['ɪnteɪk] n (Tech) immissione f; (of food) consumo; (BRIT: of pupils etc) afflusso

integral ['ɪntɪgrəl] adj integrale; (part) integrante

integrate ['ɪntɪgreɪt] vt integrare ▷ vi integrarsi

integrity [ɪn'tɛgrɪtɪ] n integrità

intellect ['ɪntəlɛkt] n intelletto; **intellectual** [-'lɛktjuəl] adj, n intellettuale m/f

intelligence [ɪn'tɛlɪdʒəns] n intelligenza; (Mil etc) informazioni fpl

intelligent [ɪn'tɛlɪdʒənt] adj intelligente

intend [ɪn'tɛnd] vt (gift etc): **to ~ sth for** destinare qc a; **to ~ to do** aver l'intenzione di fare

intense [ɪn'tɛns] adj intenso(-a); (person) di forti sentimenti

intensify [ɪn'tɛnsɪfaɪ] vt intensificare

intensity [ɪn'tɛnsɪtɪ] n intensità

intensive [ɪnˈtɛnsɪv] *adj* intensivo(-a);
intensive care *n* terapia intensiva;
intensive care unit (ICU) *n* reparto
terapia intensiva

intent [ɪnˈtɛnt] *n* intenzione *f* ▷ *adj* **~ (on)**
intento(-a) (a), immerso(-a) (in); **to all ~s
and purposes** a tutti gli effetti; **to be ~ on
doing sth** essere deciso a fare qc

intention [ɪnˈtɛnʃən] *n* intenzione
f; **intentional** *adj* intenzionale,
deliberato(-a)

interact [ɪntərˈækt] *vi* interagire;
interaction [ɪntərˈækʃən] *n* azione *f*
reciproca, interazione *f*; **interactive** *adj*
(*Comput*) interattivo(-a)

intercept [ɪntəˈsɛpt] *vt* intercettare;
(*person*) fermare

interchange [ˈɪntətʃeɪndʒ] *n* (*exchange*)
scambio; (*on motorway*) incrocio
pluridirezionale

intercourse [ˈɪntəkɔːs] *n* rapporti *mpl*

interest [ˈɪntrɪst] *n* interesse *m*; (*Comm:
stake, share*) interessi *mpl* ▷ *vt* interessare;
interested *adj* interessato(-a); **to be
interested in** interessarsi di; **interesting**
adj interessante; **interest rate** *n* tasso di
interesse

interface [ˈɪntəfeɪs] *n* (*Comput*) interfaccia

interfere [ɪntəˈfɪəˈ] *vi* **to ~ in** (*quarrel, other
people's business*) immischiarsi in; **to ~ with**
(*object*) toccare; (*plans, duty*) interferire
con; **interference** [ɪntəˈfɪərəns] *n*
interferenza

interim [ˈɪntərɪm] *adj* provvisorio(-a) ▷ *n*
in the ~ nel frattempo

interior [ɪnˈtɪəriəˈ] *n* interno; (*of
country*) entroterra ▷ *adj* interno(-a);
(*minister*) degli Interni; **interior design** *n*
architettura d'interni

intermediate [ɪntəˈmiːdɪət] *adj*
intermedio(-a)

intermission [ɪntəˈmɪʃən] *n* pausa;
(*Theatre, Cinema*) intermissione *f*, intervallo

intern [*vb* ɪnˈtɜːn, *n* ˈɪntɜːn] *vt* internare
▷ *n* (*us*) medico interno

internal [ɪnˈtɜːnl] *adj* interno(-a); **Internal
Revenue Service** (*us*) *n* Fisco

international [ɪntəˈnæʃənl] *adj*
internazionale ▷ *n* (*BRIT Sport*) incontro
internazionale

Internet [ˈɪntənɛt] *n* **the ~** Internet *f*;
Internet café *n* cybercaffè *m inv*; **Internet
Service Provider** *n* Provider *m inv*;
Internet user *n* utente *m/f* Internet

interpret [ɪnˈtɜːprɪt] *vt* interpretare
▷ *vi* fare da interprete; **interpretation**
[ɪntəːprɪˈteɪʃən] *n* interpretazione *f*;
interpreter *n* interprete *m/f*; **could you
act as an interpreter for us?** ci potrebbe

fare da interprete?

interrogate [ɪnˈtɛrəʊgeɪt] *vt* interrogare;
interrogation [-ˈgeɪʃən] *n* interrogazione
f; (*of suspect etc*) interrogatorio

interrogative [ɪntəˈrɒgətɪv] *adj*
interrogativo(-a). ▷ *n* (*Ling*) interrogativo

interrupt [ɪntəˈrʌpt] *vt, vi* interrompere;
interruption [-ˈrʌpʃən] *n* interruzione *f*

intersection [ɪntəˈsɛkʃən] *n* intersezione
f; (*of roads*) incrocio

interstate [ˈɪntəsteɪt] (*us*) *n* fra stati

interval [ˈɪntəvl] *n* intervallo; **at ~s** a
intervalli

intervene [ɪntəˈviːn] *vi* (*time*) intercorrere;
(*event, person*) intervenire

interview [ˈɪntəvjuː] *n* (*Radio, TV
etc*) intervista; (*for job*) colloquio ▷ *vt*
intervistare; avere un colloquio con;
interviewer *n* intervistatore(-trice)

intimate [*adj* ˈɪntɪmət, *vb* ˈɪntɪmeɪt] *adj*
intimo(-a); (*knowledge*) profondo(-a) ▷ *vt*
lasciar capire

intimidate [ɪnˈtɪmɪdeɪt] *vt* intimidire,
intimorire

intimidating [ɪnˈtɪmɪdeɪtɪŋ] *adj* (*sight*)
spaventoso(-a); (*appearance, figure*)
minaccioso(-a)

into [ˈɪntuː] *prep* dentro, in; **come ~ the
house** entra in casa; **he worked late ~ the
night** lavorò fino a tarda notte; **~ Italian**
in italiano

intolerant [ɪnˈtɔlərnt] *adj* **~ of**
intollerante di

intranet [ˈɪntrənɛt] *n* intranet *f*

intransitive [ɪnˈtrænsɪtɪv] *adj*
intransitivo(-a)

intricate [ˈɪntrɪkət] *adj* intricato(-a),
complicato(-a)

intrigue [ɪnˈtriːg] *n* intrigo ▷ *vt*
affascinare; **intriguing** *adj* affascinante

introduce [ɪntrəˈdjuːs] *vt* introdurre;
to ~ sb (to sb) presentare qn (a qn); **to
~ sb to** (*pastime, technique*) iniziare qn a;
introduction [-ˈdʌkʃən] *n* introduzione
f; (*of person*) presentazione *f*; (*to new
experience*) iniziazione *f*; **introductory** *adj*
introduttivo(-a)

intrude [ɪnˈtruːd] *vi* (*person*): **to ~ (on)**
intromettersi (in); **intruder** *n* intruso(-a)

intuition [ɪntjuːˈɪʃən] *n* intuizione *f*

inundate [ˈɪnʌndeɪt] *vt* **to ~ with**
inondare di

invade [ɪnˈveɪd] *vt* invadere

invalid [*n* ˈɪnvəlɪd, *adj* ɪnˈvælɪd] *n*
malato(-a); (*with disability*) invalido(-a)
▷ *adj* (*not valid*) invalido(-a), non valido(-a)

invaluable [ɪnˈvæljuəbl] *adj* prezioso(-a);
inestimabile

invariably [ɪnˈvɛəriəblɪ] *adv*

invariabilmente; sempre

invasion [ɪnˈveɪʒən] n invasione f

invent [ɪnˈvɛnt] vt inventare; **invention** [ɪnˈvɛnʃən] n invenzione f; **inventor** n inventore m

inventory [ˈɪnvəntrɪ] n inventario

inverted commas [ɪnˈvə:tɪd-] (BRIT) npl virgolette fpl

invest [ɪnˈvɛst] vt investire ▷ vi **to ~ (in)** investire (in)

investigate [ɪnˈvɛstɪɡeɪt] vt investigare, indagare; (crime) fare indagini su; **investigation** [-ˈɡeɪʃən] n investigazione f; (of crime) indagine f

investigator [ɪnˈvɛstɪɡeɪtər] n investigatore(-trice); **a private ~** un investigatore privato, un detective

investment [ɪnˈvɛstmənt] n investimento

investor [ɪnˈvɛstər] n investitore(-trice); azionista m/f

invisible [ɪnˈvɪzɪbl] adj invisibile

invitation [ɪnvɪˈteɪʃən] n invito

invite [ɪnˈvaɪt] vt invitare; (opinions etc) sollecitare; **inviting** adj invitante, attraente

invoice [ˈɪnvɔɪs] n fattura ▷ vt fatturare

involve [ɪnˈvɔlv] vt (entail) richiedere, comportare; (associate): **to ~ sb (in)** implicare qn (in); coinvolgere qn (in); **involved** adj involuto(-a), complesso(-a); **to be involved in** essere coinvolto(-a) in; **involvement** n implicazione f; coinvolgimento

inward [ˈɪnwəd] adj (movement) verso l'interno; (thought, feeling) interiore, intimo(-a); **inward(s)** adv verso l'interno

IQ n abbr (= intelligence quotient) quoziente m d'intelligenza

IRA n abbr (= Irish Republican Army) IRA f

Iran [ɪˈrɑ:n] n Iran m; **Iranian** adj, n iraniano(-a)

Iraq [ɪˈrɑ:k] n Iraq m; **Iraqi** adj, n iracheno(-a)

Ireland [ˈaɪələnd] n Irlanda

iris [ˈaɪrɪs] (pl irises) n iride f; (Bot) giaggiolo, iride

Irish [ˈaɪrɪʃ] adj irlandese ▷ npl **the ~** gli Irlandesi; **Irishman** (irreg) n irlandese m; **Irish Sea** n Mar m d'Irlanda; **Irishwoman** (irreg) n irlandese f

iron [ˈaɪən] n ferro; (for clothes) ferro da stiro ▷ adj di or in ferro ▷ vt (clothes) stirare

ironic(al) [aɪˈrɔnɪk(l)] adj ironico(-a); **ironically** adv ironicamente

ironing [ˈaɪənɪŋ] n (act) stirare m; (clothes) roba da stirare; **ironing board** n asse f da stiro

irony [ˈaɪrənɪ] n ironia

irrational [ɪˈræʃənl] adj irrazionale

irregular [ɪˈrɛɡjulər] adj irregolare

irrelevant [ɪˈrɛləvənt] adj non pertinente

irresistible [ɪrɪˈzɪstɪbl] adj irresistibile

irresponsible [ɪrɪˈspɔnsɪbl] adj irresponsabile

irrigation [ɪrɪˈɡeɪʃən] n irrigazione f

irritable [ˈɪrɪtəbl] adj irritabile

irritate [ˈɪrɪteɪt] vt irritare; **irritating** adj (person, sound etc) irritante; **irritation** [-ˈteɪʃən] n irritazione f

IRS (US) n abbr = **Internal Revenue Service**

is [ɪz] vb see **be**

ISDN n abbr (= Integrated Services Digital Network) I.S.D.N. f

Islam [ˈɪzlɑ:m] n Islam m; **Islamic** [ɪzˈlæmɪk] adj islamico(-a)

island [ˈaɪlənd] n isola; **islander** n isolano(-a)

isle [aɪl] n isola

isn't [ˈɪznt] = **is not**

isolated [ˈaɪsəleɪtɪd] adj isolato(-a)

isolation [aɪsəˈleɪʃən] n isolamento

ISP n abbr (= Internet Service Provider) provider m inv

Israel [ˈɪzreɪl] n Israele m; **Israeli** [ɪzˈreɪlɪ] adj, n israeliano(-a)

issue [ˈɪʃjuː] n questione f, problema m; (of banknotes etc) emissione f; (of newspaper etc) numero ▷ vt (statement) rilasciare; (rations, equipment) distribuire; (book) pubblicare; (banknotes, cheques, stamps) emettere; **at ~** in gioco, in discussione; **to take ~ with sb (over sth)** prendere posizione contro qn (riguardo a qc); **to make an ~ of sth** fare un problema di qc

○ KEYWORD

it [ɪt] pron **1** (specific: subject) esso(-a); (: direct object) lo (la), l'; (: indirect object) gli (le); **where's my book? — it's on the table** dov'è il mio libro? — è sulla savola; **I can't find it** non lo (or la) trovo; **give it to me** dammelo (or dammela); **about/from/of it** ne; **I spoke to him about it** gliene ho parlato; **what did you learn from it?** quale insegnamento ne hai tratto?; **I'm proud of it** ne sono fiero; **did you go to it?** ci sei andato?; **put the book in it** mettici il libro

2 (impers): **it's raining** piove; **it's Friday tomorrow** domani è venerdì; **it's 6 o'clock** sono le 6; **who is it? — it's me** chi è? — sono io

IT n abbr see **information technology**

Italian [ɪˈtæljən] adj italiano(-a) ▷ n

italiano(-a); (Ling) italiano; **the ~s** gli Italiani; **what's the ~ (word) for ...?** come si dice in italiano ...?

italics [ɪˈtælɪks] npl corsivo

Italy [ˈɪtəlɪ] n Italia

itch [ɪtʃ] n prurito ▷ vi (person) avere il prurito; (part of body) prudere; **to ~ to do sth** aver una gran voglia di fare qc; **itchy** adj che prude; **to be itchy = to itch**

it'd [ɪtd] = **it would**; **it had**

item [ˈaɪtəm] n articolo; (on agenda) punto; (also: **news ~**) notizia

itinerary [aɪˈtɪnərərɪ] n itinerario

it'll [ɪtl] = **it will**; **it shall**

its [ɪts] adj il (la) suo(-a), i (le) suoi (sue)

it's [ɪts] = **it is**; **it has**

itself [ɪtˈsɛlf] pron (emphatic) esso(-a) stesso(-a); (reflexive) si

ITV (BRIT) n abbr (= Independent Television) rete televisiva in concorrenza con la BBC

I've [aɪv] = **I have**

ivory [ˈaɪvərɪ] n avorio

ivy [ˈaɪvɪ] n edera

◆

J

jab [dʒæb] vt dare colpetti a ▷ n (Med: inf) puntura; **to ~ sth into** affondare or piantare qc dentro

jack [dʒæk] n (Aut) cricco; (Cards) fante m

jacket [ˈdʒækɪt] n giacca; (of book) copertura; **jacket potato** n patata cotta al forno con la buccia

jackpot [ˈdʒækpɔt] n primo premio (in denaro)

Jacuzzi® [dʒəˈkuːzɪ] n vasca per idromassaggio Jacuzzi®

jagged [ˈdʒægɪd] adj seghettato(-a); (cliffs etc) frastagliato(-a)

jail [dʒeɪl] n prigione f ▷ vt mandare in prigione; **jail sentence** n condanna al carcere

jam [dʒæm] n marmellata; (also: **traffic ~**) ingorgo; (inf) pasticcio ▷ vt (passage etc) ingombrare, ostacolare; (mechanism, drawer etc) bloccare; (Radio) disturbare con interferenze ▷ vi incepparsi; **to ~ sth into** forzare qc dentro; infilare qc a forza dentro

Jamaica [dʒəˈmeɪkə] n Giamaica

jammed [dʒæmd] adj (door) bloccato(-a); (rifle, printer) inceppato(-a)

Jan. abbr (= January) gen., genn.

janitor [ˈdʒænɪtər] n (caretaker) portiere m; (: Scol) bidello

January [ˈdʒænjuərɪ] n gennaio

Japan [dʒəˈpæn] n Giappone m; **Japanese**

[dʒæpə'niːz] adj giapponese ▷ n inv giapponese m/f; (Ling) giapponese m

jar [dʒɑːʳ] n (glass) barattolo, vasetto ▷ vi (sound) stridere; (colours etc) stonare

jargon ['dʒɑːgən] n gergo

javelin ['dʒævlɪn] n giavellotto

jaw [dʒɔː] n mascella

jazz [dʒæz] n jazz m

jealous ['dʒɛləs] adj geloso(-a); **jealousy** n gelosia

jeans [dʒiːnz] npl (blue-)jeans mpl

Jello® ['dʒɛləu] (US) n gelatina di frutta

jelly ['dʒɛlɪ] n gelatina; **jellyfish** n medusa

jeopardize ['dʒɛpədaɪz] vt mettere in pericolo

jerk [dʒəːk] n sobbalzo, scossa; sussulto; (inf: idiot) tonto(-a) ▷ vt dare una scossa a ▷ vi (vehicles) sobbalzare

Jersey ['dʒəːzɪ] n Jersey m

jersey ['dʒəːzɪ] n maglia; (fabric) jersey m

Jesus ['dʒiːzəs] n Gesù m

jet [dʒɛt] n (of gas, liquid) getto; (Aviat) aviogetto; **jet lag** n (problemi mpl dovuti allo) sbalzo dei fusi orari; **jet-ski** vi acquascooter m inv

jetty ['dʒɛtɪ] n molo

Jew [dʒuː] n ebreo

jewel ['dʒuːəl] n gioiello; **jeweller** (US **jeweler**) n orefice m, gioielliere(-a); **jeweller's (shop)** (US **jewelry store**) n oreficeria, gioielleria; **jewellery** (US **jewelry**) n gioielli mpl

Jewish ['dʒuːɪʃ] adj ebreo(-a), ebraico(-a)

jigsaw ['dʒɪgsɔː] n (also: ~ **puzzle**) puzzle m inv

job [dʒɔb] n lavoro; (employment) impiego, posto; **it's not my ~** (duty) non è compito mio; **it's a good ~ that ...** meno male che ...; **just the ~!** proprio quello che ci vuole; **job centre** (BRIT) n ufficio di collocamento; **jobless** adj senza lavoro, disoccupato(-a)

jockey ['dʒɔkɪ] n fantino, jockey m inv ▷ vi **to ~ for position** manovrare per una posizione di vantaggio

jog [dʒɔg] vt urtare ▷ vi (Sport) fare footing, fare jogging; **to ~ sb's memory** rinfrescare la memoria a qn; **to ~ along** trottare; (fig) andare avanti piano piano; **jogging** n footing m, jogging m

join [dʒɔɪn] vt unire, congiungere; (become member of) iscriversi a; (meet) raggiungere; riunirsi a ▷ vi (roads, rivers) confluire ▷ n giuntura; **join in** vi partecipare ▷ vt fus unirsi a; **join up** vi incontrarsi; (Mil) arruolarsi

joiner ['dʒɔɪnəʳ] (BRIT) n falegname m

joint [dʒɔɪnt] n (Tech) giuntura; giunto; (Anat) articolazione f, giuntura; (BRIT Culin) arrosto; (inf: place) locale m; (: of cannabis) spinello ▷ adj comune; **joint account** n (at bank etc) conto in partecipazione, conto comune; **jointly** adv in comune, insieme

joke [dʒəuk] n scherzo; (funny story) barzelletta; (also: **practical ~**) beffa ▷ vi scherzare; **to play a ~ on sb** fare uno scherzo a qn; **joker** n (Cards) matta, jolly m inv

jolly ['dʒɔlɪ] adj allegro(-a), gioioso(-a) ▷ adv (BRIT: inf) veramente, proprio

jolt [dʒəult] n scossa, sobbalzo ▷ vt urtare

Jordan ['dʒɔːdən] n (country) Giordania; (river) Giordano

journal ['dʒəːnl] n giornale m; rivista; diario; **journalism** n giornalismo; **journalist** n giornalista m/f

journey ['dʒəːnɪ] n viaggio; (distance covered) tragitto; **how was your ~?** com'è andato il viaggio?; **the ~ takes two hours** il viaggio dura due ore

joy [dʒɔɪ] n gioia; **joyrider** n chi ruba un'auto per farvi un giro; **joy stick** n (Aviat) barra di comando; (Comput) joystick m inv

Jr abbr = **junior**

judge [dʒʌdʒ] n giudice m/f ▷ vt giudicare

judo ['dʒuːdəu] n judo

jug [dʒʌg] n brocca, bricco

juggle ['dʒʌgl] vi fare giochi di destrezza; **juggler** n giocoliere(-a)

juice [dʒuːs] n succo; **juicy** ['dʒuːsɪ] adj succoso(-a)

Jul. abbr (= July) lug., lu.

July [dʒuː'laɪ] n luglio

jumble ['dʒʌmbl] n miscuglio ▷ vt (also: ~ **up**) mischiare; **jumble sale** n (BRIT) n vendita di beneficenza

● **JUMBLE SALE**

● Una **jumble sale** è un mercatino di
● oggetti di seconda mano organizzato
● in chiese, scuole o in circoli ricreativi,
● i cui proventi vengono devoluti in
● beneficenza.

jumbo ['dʒʌmbəu] adj ~ **jet** jumbo-jet m inv; ~ **size** formato gigante

jump [dʒʌmp] vi saltare, balzare; (start) sobbalzare; (increase) rincarare ▷ vt saltare ▷ n salto, balzo; sobbalzo

jumper ['dʒʌmpəʳ] n (BRIT: pullover) maglione m, pullover m inv; (US: dress) scamiciato

jumper cables (US) npl = **jump leads**

jump leads (BRIT) npl cavi mpl per batteria

Jun. abbr = **junior**

junction ['dʒʌŋkʃən] n (BRIT: of roads) incrocio; (of rails) nodo ferroviario

June [dʒuːn] n giugno
jungle ['dʒʌŋgl] n giungla
junior ['dʒuːnɪə'] adj, n **he's ~ to me by 2 years, he's my ~ by 2 years** è più giovane di me (di 2 anni); **he's ~ to me** (seniority) è al di sotto di me, ho più anzianità di lui; **junior high school** (US) n scuola media (da 12 a 15 anni); **junior school** (BRIT) n scuola elementare (da 8 a 11 anni)
junk [dʒʌŋk] n cianfrusaglie fpl; (cheap goods) robaccia; **junk food** n porcherie fpl
junkie ['dʒʌŋkɪ] (inf) n drogato(-a)
junk mail n stampe fpl pubblicitarie
Jupiter ['dʒuːpɪtə'] n (planet) Giove m
jurisdiction [dʒuərɪs'dɪkʃən] n giurisdizione f; **it falls** or **comes within/outside our ~** è/non è di nostra competenza
jury ['dʒuərɪ] n giuria
just [dʒʌst] adj giusto(-a) ▷ adv **he's ~ done it/left** lo ha appena fatto/è appena partito; **~ right** proprio giusto; **~ 2 o'clock** le 2 precise; **she's ~ as clever as you** è in gamba proprio quanto te; **it's ~ as well that …** meno male che …; **~ as I arrived** proprio mentre arrivavo; **it was ~ before/enough/here** era poco prima/appena assai/proprio qui; **it's ~ me** sono solo io; **~ missed/caught** appena perso/preso; **~ listen to this!** senta un po' questo!
justice ['dʒʌstɪs] n giustizia
justification [dʒʌstɪfɪ'keɪʃən] n giustificazione f; (Typ) giustezza
justify ['dʒʌstɪfaɪ] vt giustificare
jut [dʒʌt] vi (also: **~ out**) sporgersi
juvenile ['dʒuːvənaɪl] adj giovane, giovanile; (court) dei minorenni; (books) per ragazzi ▷ n giovane m/f, minorenne m/f

K

K abbr (= one thousand) mille; (= kilobyte) K
kangaroo [kæŋgə'ruː] n canguro
karaoke [kɑːrə'əukɪ] n karaoke m inv
karate [kə'rɑːtɪ] n karatè m
kebab [kə'bæb] n spiedino
keel [kiːl] n chiglia; **on an even ~** (fig) in uno stato normale
keen [kiːn] adj (interest, desire) vivo(-a); (eye, intelligence) acuto(-a); (competition) serrato(-a); (edge) affilato(-a); (eager) entusiasta; **to be ~ to do** or **on doing sth** avere una gran voglia di fare qc; **to be ~ on sth** essere appassionato(-a) di qc; **to be ~ on sb** avere un debole per qn
keep [kiːp] (pt, pp kept) vt tenere; (hold back) trattenere; (feed: one's family etc) mantenere, sostenere; (a promise) mantenere; (chickens, bees, pigs etc) allevare ▷ vi (food) mantenersi; (remain: in a certain state or place) restare ▷ n (of castle) maschio; (food etc): **enough for his ~** abbastanza per vitto e alloggio; (inf): **for ~s** per sempre; **to ~ doing sth** continuare a fare qc; fare qc di continuo; **to ~ sb from doing** impedire a qn di fare; **to ~ sb busy/a place tidy** tenere qn occupato(-a)/un luogo in ordine; **to ~ sth to o.s.** tenere qc per sé; **to ~ sth (back) from sb** celare qc a qn; **to ~ time** (clock) andar bene; **keep away** vt **to ~ sth/sb away from sb**

tenere qc/qn lontano da qn ▷ *vi* **to ~ away (from)** stare lontano (da); **keep back** *vt* (*crowds, tears, money*) trattenere ▷ *vi* tenersi indietro; **keep off** *vt* (*dog, person*) tenere lontano da ▷ *vi* stare alla larga; **~ your hands off!** non toccare!, giù le mani!; **"~ off the grass"** "non calpestare l'erba"; **keep on** *vi* **to ~ on doing** continuare a fare; **to ~ on (about sth)** continuare a insistere (su qc); **keep out** *vt* tener fuori; **"~ out"** "vietato l'accesso"; **keep up** *vt* continuare, mantenere ▷ *vi* **to ~ up with** tener dietro a, andare di pari passo con; (*work etc*) farcela a seguire; **keeper** *n* custode *m/f*, guardiano(-a); **keeping** *n* (*care*) custodia; **in keeping with** in armonia con; in accordo con

kennel ['kɛnl] *n* canile *m*; **~s** *npl* canile *m*; **to put a dog in ~s** mettere un cane al canile

Kenya ['kɛnjə] *n* Kenia *m*

kept [kɛpt] *pt, pp of* **keep**

kerb [kəːb] (*BRIT*) *n* orlo del marciapiede

kerosene ['kɛrəsiːn] *n* cherosene *m*

ketchup ['kɛtʃəp] *n* ketchup *m inv*

kettle ['kɛtl] *n* bollitore *m*

key [kiː] *n* (*gen, Mus*) chiave *f*; (*of piano, typewriter*) tasto ▷ *adj* chiave *inv* ▷ *vt* (*also: ~ in*) digitare; **can I have my ~?** posso avere la mia chiave?; **keyboard** *n* tastiera; **keyhole** *n* buco della serratura; **keyring** *n* portachiavi *m inv*

kg *abbr* (= *kilogram*) Kg

khaki ['kɑːkɪ] *adj* cachi ▷ *n* cachi *m*

kick [kɪk] *vt* calciare, dare calci a; (*inf: habit etc*) liberarsi di ▷ *vi* (*horse*) tirar calci ▷ *n* calcio; (*thrill*): **he does it for ~s** lo fa giusto per il piacere di farlo; **kick off** *vi* (*Sport*) dare il primo calcio; **kick-off** *n* (*Sport*) calcio d'inizio

kid [kɪd] *n* (*inf: child*) ragazzino(-a); (*animal, leather*) capretto ▷ *vi* (*inf*) scherzare

kidnap ['kɪdnæp] *vt* rapire, sequestrare; **kidnapping** *n* sequestro (di persona)

kidney ['kɪdnɪ] *n* (*Anat*) rene *m*; (*Culin*) rognone *m*; **kidney bean** *n* fagiolo borlotto

kill [kɪl] *vt* uccidere, ammazzare ▷ *n* uccisione *f*; **killer** *n* uccisore *m*, killer *m inv*; assassino(-a); **killing** *n* assassinio; **to make a killing** (*inf*) fare un bel colpo

kiln [kɪln] *n* forno

kilo ['kiːləu] *n* chilo; **kilobyte** *n* (*Comput*) kilobyte *m inv*; **kilogram(me)** ['kɪləugræm] *n* chilogrammo; **kilometre** ['kɪləmiːtə'] (*us* **kilometer**) *n* chilometro; **kilowatt** ['kɪləuwɔt] *n* chilowatt *m inv*

kilt [kɪlt] *n* gonnellino scozzese

kin [kɪn] *n see* **next**; **kith**

kind [kaɪnd] *adj* gentile, buono(-a) ▷ *n* sorta, specie *f*; (*species*) genere *m*; **what ~ of ...?** che tipo di ...?; **to be two of a ~** essere molto simili; **in ~** (*Comm*) in natura

kindergarten ['kɪndəgɑːtn] *n* giardino d'infanzia

kindly ['kaɪndlɪ] *adj* pieno(-a) di bontà, benevolo(-a) ▷ *adv* con bontà, gentilmente; **will you ~ ...** vuole ... per favore

kindness ['kaɪndnɪs] *n* bontà, gentilezza

king [kɪŋ] *n* re *m inv*; **kingdom** *n* regno, reame *m*; **kingfisher** *n* martin *m inv* pescatore; **king-size(d) bed** *n* letto king-size

kiosk ['kiːɔsk] *n* edicola, chiosco; (*BRIT Tel*) cabina (telefonica)

kipper ['kɪpə'] *n* aringa affumicata

kiss [kɪs] *n* bacio ▷ *vt* baciare; **to ~ (each other)** baciarsi; **kiss of life** *n* respirazione *f* bocca a bocca

kit [kɪt] *n* equipaggiamento, corredo; (*set of tools etc*) attrezzi *mpl*; (*for assembly*) scatola di montaggio

kitchen ['kɪtʃɪn] *n* cucina

kite [kaɪt] *n* (*toy*) aquilone *m*

kitten ['kɪtn] *n* gattino(-a), micino(-a)

kiwi ['kiːwiː] *n* (*also: ~ fruit*) kiwi *m inv*

km *abbr* (= *kilometre*) km

km/h *abbr* (= *kilometres per hour*) km/h

knack [næk] *n* **to have the ~ of** avere l'abilità di

knee [niː] *n* ginocchio; **kneecap** *n* rotula

kneel [niːl] (*pt, pp* **knelt**) *vi* (*also: ~ down*) inginocchiarsi

knelt [nɛlt] *pt, pp of* **kneel**

knew [njuː] *pt of* **know**

knickers ['nɪkəz] (*BRIT*) *npl* mutandine *fpl*

knife [naɪf] (*pl* **knives**) *n* coltello ▷ *vt* accoltellare, dare una coltellata a

knight [naɪt] *n* cavaliere *m*; (*Chess*) cavallo

knit [nɪt] *vt* fare a maglia ▷ *vi* lavorare a maglia; (*broken bones*) saldarsi; **to ~ one's brows** aggrottare le sopracciglia; **knitting** *n* lavoro a maglia; **knitting needle** *n* ferro (da calza); **knitwear** *n* maglieria

knives [naɪvz] *npl of* **knife**

knob [nɔb] *n* bottone *m*; manopola

knock [nɔk] *vt* colpire; urtare; (*fig: inf*) criticare ▷ *vi* (*at door etc*): **to ~ at/on** bussare a ▷ *n* bussata; colpo, botta; **knock down** *vt* abbattere; **knock off** *vi* (*inf: finish*) smettere (di lavorare) ▷ *vt* (*from price*) far abbassare; (*inf: steal*) sgraffignare; **knock out** *vt* stendere; (*Boxing*) mettere K.O.; (*defeat*) battere; **knock over** *vt* (*person*) investire; (*object*) far cadere; **knockout** *n* (*Boxing*) knock out *m inv* ▷ *cpd* a eliminazione

knot [nɔt] n nodo ▷ vt annodare

know [nəu] (pt **knew**, pp **known**) vt sapere; (person, author, place) conoscere; **I don't ~** non lo so; **do you ~ where I can …?** sa dove posso …?; **to ~ how to do** sapere fare; **to ~ about** or **of sth/sb** conoscere qc/qn; **know-all** n sapientone(-a); **know-how** n tecnica; pratica; **knowing** adj (look etc) d'intesa; **knowingly** adv (purposely) consapevolmente; (smile, look) con aria d'intesa; **know-it-all** (US) n = **know-all**

knowledge ['nɔlɪdʒ] n consapevolezza; (learning) conoscenza, sapere m; **knowledgeable** adj ben informato(-a)

known [nəun] pp of **know**

knuckle ['nʌkl] n nocca

koala [kəu'ɑːlə] n (also: **~ bear**) koala m inv

Koran [kɔ'rɑːn] n Corano

Korea [kə'rɪə] n Corea; **Korean** adj, n coreano(-a)

kosher ['kəuʃər] adj kasher inv

Kosovar, Kosovan ['kɔsəvər, 'kɔsəvən] adj kosovaro(-a)

Kosovo ['kusəvəu] n Kosovo

Kremlin ['kremlɪn] n **the ~** il Cremlino

Kuwait [ku'weɪt] n Kuwait m

L (BRIT) abbr = **learner driver**

l. abbr (= litre) l

lab [læb] n abbr (= laboratory) laboratorio

label ['leɪbl] n etichetta, cartellino; (brand: of record) casa ▷ vt etichettare

labor etc ['leɪbər] (US) = **labour** etc

laboratory [lə'bɔrətərɪ] n laboratorio

Labor Day (US) n festa del lavoro

● **LABOR DAY**
●
● Negli Stati Uniti e nel Canada il **Labor**
● **Day**, la festa del lavoro, cade il primo
● lunedì di settembre, contrariamente a
● quanto accade nella maggior parte dei
● paesi europei dove tale celebrazione ha
● luogo il primo maggio.

labor union (US) n sindacato

labour ['leɪbər] (US **labor**) n (task) lavoro; (workmen) manodopera; (Med): **to be in ~** avere le doglie ▷ vi **to ~ (at)** lavorare duro (a); **L~, the L~ party** (BRIT) il partito laburista, i laburisti; **hard ~** lavori mpl forzati; **labourer** n manovale m; **farm labourer** lavoratore m agricolo

lace [leɪs] n merletto, pizzo; (of shoe etc) laccio ▷ vt (shoe: also: **~ up**) allacciare

lack [læk] n mancanza ▷ vt mancare di; **through** or **for ~ of** per mancanza di; **to be**

~ing mancare; **to be ~ing in** mancare di

lacquer ['lækə'] n lacca

lacy ['leɪsɪ] adj (like lace) che sembra un pizzo

lad [læd] n ragazzo, giovanotto

ladder ['lædə'] n scala; (BRIT: in tights) smagliatura

ladle ['leɪdl] n mestolo

lady ['leɪdɪ] n signora; dama; **L~ Smith** lady Smith; **the ladies' (room)** i gabinetti per signore; **ladybird** (US **ladybug**) n coccinella

lag [læg] n (of time) lasso, intervallo ▷ vi (also: ~ **behind**) trascinarsi ▷ vt (pipes) rivestire di materiale isolante

lager ['lɑːgə'] n lager m inv

lagoon [lə'guːn] n laguna

laid [leɪd] pt, pp of **lay**; **laid back** (inf) adj rilassato(-a), tranquillo(-a)

lain [leɪn] pp of **lie**

lake [leɪk] n lago

lamb [læm] n agnello

lame [leɪm] adj zoppo(-a); (excuse etc) zoppicante

lament [lə'mɛnt] n lamento ▷ vt lamentare, piangere

lamp [læmp] n lampada; **lamppost** ['læmppəust] (BRIT) n lampione m; **lampshade** ['læmpʃeɪd] n paralume m

land [lænd] n (as opposed to sea) terra (ferma); (country) paese m; (soil) terreno; suolo; (estate) terreni mpl, terre fpl ▷ vi (from ship) sbarcare; (Aviat) atterrare; (fig: fall) cadere ▷ vt (passengers) sbarcare; (goods) scaricare; **to ~ sb with sth** affibbiare qc a qn; **landing** n atterraggio; (of staircase) pianerottolo; **landing card** n carta di sbarco; **landlady** n padrona or proprietaria di casa; **landlord** n padrone m or proprietario di casa; (of pub etc) padrone m; **landmark** n punto di riferimento; (fig) pietra miliare; **landowner** n proprietario(-a) terriero(-a); **landscape** n paesaggio; **landslide** n (Geo) frana; (fig: Pol) valanga

lane [leɪn] n stradina; (Aut, in race) corsia; **"get in ~"** "immettersi in corsia"

language ['læŋgwɪdʒ] n lingua; (way one speaks) linguaggio; **what ~s do you speak?** che lingue parla?; **bad ~** linguaggio volgare; **language laboratory** n laboratorio linguistico

lantern ['læntən] n lanterna

lap [læp] n (of track) giro; (of body): **in** or **on one's ~** in grembo ▷ vt (also: ~ **up**) papparsi, leccare ▷ vi (waves) sciabordare

lapel [lə'pɛl] n risvolto

lapse [læps] n lapsus m inv; (longer) caduta ▷ vi (law) cadere; (membership, contract)

scadere; **to ~ into bad habits** pigliare cattive abitudini; **~ of time** spazio di tempo

laptop (computer) ['læptɔp-] n laptop m inv

lard [lɑːd] n lardo

larder ['lɑːdə'] n dispensa

large [lɑːdʒ] adj grande; (person, animal) grosso(-a); **at ~** (free) in libertà; (generally) in generale; nell'insieme; **largely** adv in gran parte; **large-scale** adj (map, drawing etc) in grande scala; (reforms, business activities) su vasta scala

lark [lɑːk] n (bird) allodola; (joke) scherzo, gioco

laryngitis [lærɪn'dʒaɪtɪs] n laringite f

lasagne [lə'zænjə] n lasagne fpl

laser ['leɪzə'] n laser m; **laser printer** n stampante f laser inv

lash [læʃ] n frustata; (also: **eye~**) ciglio ▷ vt frustare; (tie): **to ~ to/together** legare a insieme; **lash out** vi **to ~ out (at or against sb)** attaccare violentemente (qn)

lass [læs] n ragazza

last [lɑːst] adj ultimo(-a); (week, month, year) scorso(-a), passato(-a) ▷ adv per ultimo ▷ vi durare; **~ week** la settimana scorsa; **~ night** ieri sera, la notte scorsa; **at ~** finalmente, alla fine; **~ but one** penultimo(-a); **lastly** adv infine, per finire; **last-minute** adj fatto(-a) (or preso(-a) etc) all'ultimo momento

latch [lætʃ] n chiavistello; **latch onto** vt fus (cling to: person) attaccarsi a, appiccicarsi a; (: idea) afferrare, capire

late [leɪt] adj (not on time) in ritardo; (far on in day etc) tardi inv; tardo(-a); (former) ex; (dead) defunto(-a) ▷ adv tardi; (behind time, schedule) in ritardo; **sorry I'm ~** scusi il ritardo; **the flight is two hours ~** il volo ha due ore di ritardo; **it's too ~** è troppo tardi; **of ~** di recente; **in the ~ afternoon** nel tardo pomeriggio; **in ~ May** verso la fine di maggio; **latecomer** n ritardatario(-a); **lately** adv recentemente; **later** ['leɪtə'] adj (date etc) posteriore; (version etc) successivo(-a) ▷ adv più tardi; **later on** più avanti; **latest** ['leɪtɪst] adj ultimo(-a), più recente; **at the latest** al più tardi

lather ['lɑːðə'] n schiuma di sapone ▷ vt insaponare

Latin ['lætɪn] n latino ▷ adj latino(-a); **Latin America** n America Latina; **Latin American** adj sudamericano(-a)

latitude ['lætɪtjuːd] n latitudine f; (fig) libertà d'azione

latter ['lætə'] adj secondo(-a), più recente ▷ n **the ~** quest'ultimo, il secondo

laugh [lɑːf] n risata ▷ vi ridere; **laugh at**

vt fus (*misfortune etc*) ridere di; **laughter** *n* riso; risate *fpl*

launch [lɔːntʃ] *n* (*of rocket, Comm*) lancio; (*of new ship*) varo; (*also:* **motor ~**) lancia ▷ *vt* (*rocket, Comm*) lanciare; (*ship, plan*) varare; **launch into** *vt fus* lanciarsi in

launder ['lɔːndə'] *vt* lavare e stirare

Launderette® [lɔːn'drɛt] (*BRIT*) *n* lavanderia (automatica)

Laundromat® ['lɔːndrəmæt] (*US*) *n* lavanderia automatica

laundry ['lɔːndrɪ] *n* lavanderia; (*clothes*) biancheria; (: *dirty*) panni *mpl* da lavare

lava ['lɑːvə] *n* lava

lavatory ['lævətərɪ] *n* gabinetto

lavender ['lævəndə'] *n* lavanda

lavish ['lævɪʃ] *adj* copioso(-a), abbondante; (*giving freely*): **~ with** prodigo(-a) di, largo(-a) in ▷ *vt* **to ~ sth on sb** colmare qn di qc

law [lɔː] *n* legge *f*; **civil/criminal ~** diritto civile/penale; **lawful** *adj* legale, lecito(-a); **lawless** *adj* che non conosce nessuna legge

lawn [lɔːn] *n* tappeto erboso; **lawnmower** *n* tosaerba *m* or *f inv*

lawsuit ['lɔːsuːt] *n* processo, causa

lawyer ['lɔːjə'] *n* (*for sales, wills etc*) ≈ notaio; (*partner, in court*) ≈ avvocato(-essa)

lax [læks] *adj* rilassato(-a), negligente

laxative ['læksətɪv] *n* lassativo

lay [leɪ] (*pt, pp* **laid**) *pt of* **lie** ▷ *adj* laico(-a); (*not expert*) profano(-a) ▷ *vt* posare, mettere; (*eggs*) fare; (*trap*) tendere; (*plans*) fare, elaborare; **to ~ the table** apparecchiare la tavola; **lay down** *vt* mettere giù; (*rules etc*) formulare, fissare; **to ~ down the law** dettar legge; **to ~ down one's life** dare la propria vita; **lay off** *vt* (*workers*) licenziare; **lay on** *vt* (*provide*) fornire; **lay out** *vt* (*display*) presentare, disporre; **lay-by** (*BRIT*) *n* piazzola (di sosta)

layer ['leɪə'] *n* strato

layman ['leɪmən] (*irreg*) *n* laico; profano

layout ['leɪaut] *n* lay-out *m inv*, disposizione *f*; (*Press*) impaginazione *f*

lazy ['leɪzɪ] *adj* pigro(-a)

lb. *abbr* = **pound** (*weight*)

lead¹ [liːd] (*pt, pp* **led**) *n* (*front position*) posizione *f* di testa; (*distance, time ahead*) vantaggio; (*clue*) indizio; (*Elec*) filo (elettrico); (*for dog*) guinzaglio; (*Theatre*) parte *f* principale ▷ *vt* guidare, condurre; (*induce*) indurre; (*be leader of*) essere a capo di ▷ *vi* condurre; (*Sport*) essere in testa; **in the ~** in testa; **to ~ the way** fare strada; **lead up to** *vt fus* portare a

lead² [lɛd] *n* (*metal*) piombo; (*in pencil*) mina

leader ['liːdə'] *n* capo; leader *m inv*; (*in newspaper*) articolo di fondo; (*Sport*) chi è in testa; **leadership** *n* direzione *f*; capacità di comando

lead-free ['lɛdfriː] *adj* senza piombo

leading ['liːdɪŋ] *adj* primo(-a), principale

lead singer *n* cantante alla testa di un gruppo

leaf [liːf] (*pl* **leaves**) *n* foglia ▷ *vi* **to ~ through sth** sfogliare qc; **to turn over a new ~** cambiar vita

leaflet ['liːflɪt] *n* dépliant *m inv*; (*Pol, Rel*) volantino

league [liːg] *n* lega; (*Football*) campionato; **to be in ~ with** essere in lega con

leak [liːk] *n* (*out*) fuga; (*in*) infiltrazione *f*; (*security leak*) fuga d'informazioni ▷ *vi* (*roof, bucket*) perdere; (*liquid*) uscire; (*shoes*) lasciar passare l'acqua ▷ *vt* (*information*) divulgare

lean [liːn] (*pt, pp* **leaned** *or* **leant**) *adj* magro(-a) ▷ *vt* **to ~ sth on sth** appoggiare qc su qc ▷ *vi* (*slope*) pendere; (*rest*): **to ~ against** appoggiarsi contro; essere appoggiato(-a) a; **to ~ on** appoggiarsi a; **lean forward** *vi* sporgersi in avanti; **lean over** *vi* inclinarsi; **leaning** *n* **leaning (towards)** propensione *f* (per)

leant [lɛnt] *pt, pp of* **lean**

leap [liːp] (*pt, pp* **leaped** *or* **leapt**) *n* salto, balzo ▷ *vi* saltare, balzare

leapt [lɛpt] *pt, pp of* **leap**

leap year *n* anno bisestile

learn [ləːn] (*pt, pp* **learned** *or* **learnt**) *vt, vi* imparare; **to ~ about sth** (*hear, read*) apprendere qc; **to ~ to do sth** imparare a fare qc; **learner** *n* principiante *m/f*; apprendista *m/f*; (*BRIT: also:* **learner driver**) guidatore(-a) principiante; **learning** *n* erudizione *f*, sapienza

learnt [ləːnt] *pt, pp of* **learn**

lease [liːs] *n* contratto d'affitto ▷ *vt* affittare

leash [liːʃ] *n* guinzaglio

least [liːst] *adj* **the ~** (+ *noun*) il (la) più piccolo(-a), il (la) minimo(-a); (*smallest amount of*) il (la) meno ▷ *adv* (+ *verb*) meno; **the ~** (+ *adjective*): **the ~ beautiful girl** la ragazza meno bella; **the ~ possible effort** il minimo sforzo possibile; **I have the ~ money** ho meno denaro di tutti; **at ~** almeno; **not in the ~** affatto, per nulla

leather ['lɛðə'] *n* cuoio

leave [liːv] (*pt, pp* **left**) *vt* lasciare; (*go away from*) partire da ▷ *vi* partire, andarsene; (*bus, train*) partire ▷ *n* (*time off*) congedo; (*Mil, consent*) licenza; **what time does the train/bus ~?** a che ora parte il treno/

l'autobus?; **to be left** rimanere; **there's some milk left over** c'è rimasto del latte; **on ~** in congedo; **leave behind** vt (person, object) lasciare; (: forget) dimenticare; **leave out** vt omettere, tralasciare

leaves [liːvz] npl of **leaf**

Lebanon ['lɛbənən] n Libano

lecture ['lɛktʃəʳ] n conferenza; (Scol) lezione f ▷ vi fare conferenze; fare lezioni ▷ vt (scold): **to ~ sb on** or **about sth** rimproverare qn or fare una ramanzina a qn per qc; **to give a ~ on** tenere una conferenza su; **lecture hall** n aula magna; **lecturer** ['lɛktʃərəʳ] (BRIT) n (at university) professore(-essa), docente m/f; **lecture theatre** n = **lecture hall**

led [lɛd] pt, pp of **lead**

ledge [lɛdʒ] n (of window) davanzale m; (on wall etc) sporgenza; (of mountain) cornice f, cengia

leek [liːk] n porro

left [lɛft] pt, pp of **leave** ▷ adj sinistro(-a) ▷ adv a sinistra ▷ n sinistra; **on the ~, to the ~** a sinistra; **the L~** (Pol) la sinistra; **left-hand** adj **the left-hand side** il lato sinistro; **left-hand drive** adj guida a sinistra; **left-handed** adj mancino(-a); **left-luggage locker** n armadietto per deposito bagagli; **left-luggage (office)** (BRIT) n deposito m bagagli inv; **left-overs** npl avanzi mpl, resti mpl; **left-wing** adj (Pol) di sinistra

leg [lɛg] n gamba; (of animal) zampa; (of furniture) piede m; (Culin: of chicken) coscia; (of journey) tappa; **1st/2nd ~** (Sport) partita di andata/ritorno

legacy ['lɛgəsɪ] n eredità f inv

legal ['liːgl] adj legale; **legal holiday** (US) n giorno festivo, festa nazionale; **legalize** vt legalizzare; **legally** adv legalmente; **legally binding** legalmente vincolante

legend ['lɛdʒənd] n leggenda; **legendary** ['lɛdʒəndərɪ] adj leggendario(-a)

leggings ['lɛgɪŋz] npl ghette fpl

legible ['lɛdʒəbl] adj leggibile

legislation [lɛdʒɪs'leɪʃən] n legislazione f

legislative ['lɛdʒɪslətɪv] adj legislativo(-a)

legitimate [lɪ'dʒɪtɪmət] adj legittimo(-a)

leisure ['lɛʒəʳ] n agio, tempo libero; ricreazioni fpl; **at ~** con comodo; **leisure centre** n centro di ricreazione; **leisurely** adj tranquillo(-a), fatto(-a) con comodo or senza fretta

lemon ['lɛmən] n limone m; **lemonade** [-'neɪd] n limonata; **lemon tea** n tè m inv al limone

lend [lɛnd] (pt, pp **lent**) vt **to ~ sth (to sb)** prestare qc (a qn); **could you ~ me some**

money? mi può prestare dei soldi?

length [lɛŋθ] n lunghezza; (distance) distanza; (section: of road, pipe etc) pezzo, tratto; (of time) periodo; **at ~** (at last) finalmente, alla fine; (lengthily) a lungo; **lengthen** vt allungare, prolungare ▷ vi allungarsi; **lengthways** adv per il lungo; **lengthy** adj molto lungo(-a)

lens [lɛnz] n lente f; (of camera) obiettivo

Lent [lɛnt] n Quaresima

lent [lɛnt] pt, pp of **lend**

lentil ['lɛntl] n lenticchia

Leo ['liːəu] n Leone m

leopard ['lɛpəd] n leopardo

leotard ['liːətɑːd] n calzamaglia

leprosy ['lɛprəsɪ] n lebbra

lesbian ['lɛzbɪən] n lesbica

less [lɛs] adj, pron, adv meno ▷ prep **~ tax/10% discount** meno tasse/il 10% di sconto; **~ than ever** meno che mai; **~ than half** meno della metà; **~ and ~** sempre meno; **the ~ he works ...** meno lavora ...; **lessen** ['lɛsn] vi diminuire, attenuarsi ▷ vt diminuire, ridurre; **lesser** ['lɛsəʳ] adj minore, più piccolo(-a); **to a lesser extent** in grado or misura minore

lesson ['lɛsn] n lezione f; **to teach sb a ~** dare una lezione a qn

let [lɛt] (pt, pp **let**) vt lasciare; (BRIT: lease) dare in affitto; **to ~ sb do sth** lasciar fare qc a qn, lasciare che qn faccia qc; **to ~ sb know sth** far sapere qc a qn; **~'s go** andiamo; **~ him come** lo lasci venire; **"to ~"** "affittasi"; **let down** vt (lower) abbassare; (dress) allungare; (hair) sciogliere; (tyre) sgonfiare; (disappoint) deludere; **let in** vt lasciare entrare; (visitor etc) far entrare; **let off** vt (allow to go) lasciare andare; (firework etc) far partire; **let out** vt lasciare uscire; (scream) emettere

lethal ['liːθl] adj letale, mortale

letter ['lɛtəʳ] n lettera; **letterbox** (BRIT) n buca delle lettere

lettuce ['lɛtɪs] n lattuga, insalata

leukaemia [luː'kiːmɪə] (US **leukemia**) n leucemia

level ['lɛvl] adj piatto(-a), piano(-a); orizzontale ▷ adv **to draw ~ with** mettersi alla pari di ▷ n livello ▷ vt livellare, spianare; **to be ~ with** essere alla pari di; **level crossing** (BRIT) n passaggio a livello

lever ['liːvəʳ] n leva; **leverage** n **leverage (on** or **with)** forza (su); (fig) ascendente m (su)

levy ['lɛvɪ] n tassa, imposta ▷ vt imporre

liability [laɪə'bɪlətɪ] n responsabilità f inv; (handicap) peso

liable ['laɪəbl] adj (subject): **~ to**

soggetto(-a) a; passibile di; (*responsible*): **~ for** responsabile (di); (*likely*): **~ to do** propenso(-a) a fare

liaise [liː'eɪz] vt **to ~ (with)** mantenere i contatti (con)

liar ['laɪəʳ] n bugiardo(-a)

liberal ['lɪbərl] adj liberale; (*generous*): **to be ~ with** distribuire liberalmente; **Liberal Democrat** n liberaldemocratico(-a)

liberate ['lɪbəreɪt] vt liberare

liberation [lɪbə'reɪʃən] n liberazione f

liberty ['lɪbətɪ] n libertà f inv; **at ~** (*criminal*) in libertà; **at ~ to do** libero(-a) di fare

Libra ['liːbrə] n Bilancia

librarian [laɪ'brɛərɪən] n bibliotecario(-a)

library ['laɪbrərɪ] n biblioteca

Libya ['lɪbɪə] n Libia

lice [laɪs] npl of **louse**

licence ['laɪsns] (US **license**) n autorizzazione f, permesso; (*Comm*) licenza; (*Radio*, *TV*) canone m, abbonamento; (*also*: **driving ~**: US: also: **driver's license**) patente f di guida; (*excessive freedom*) licenza

license ['laɪsns] n (US) = **licence** ▷ vt dare una licenza a; **licensed** adj (*for alcohol*) che ha la licenza di vendere bibite alcoliche; **license plate** (*esp US*) n (Aut) targa (automobilistica); **licensing hours** (BRIT) npl orario d'apertura (*di un pub*)

lick [lɪk] vt leccare; (*inf: defeat*) stracciare; **to ~ one's lips** (*fig*) leccarsi i baffi

lid [lɪd] n coperchio; (*eyelid*) palpebra

lie [laɪ] (pt **lay**, pp **lain**) vi (*rest*) giacere, star disteso(-a); (*of object: be situated*) trovarsi, essere; (*tell lies*: pt, pp **lied**) mentire, dire bugie ▷ n bugia, menzogna; **to ~ low** (*fig*) latitare; **lie about** or **around** vi (*things*) essere in giro; (*person*) bighellonare; **lie down** vi stendersi, sdraiarsi

Liechtenstein ['lɪktənstaɪn] n Liechtenstein (m)

lie-in ['laɪɪn] (BRIT) n **to have a ~** rimanere a letto

lieutenant [lef'tɛnənt, (US) luː'tɛnənt] n tenente m

life [laɪf] (pl **lives**) n vita ▷ cpd di vita; della vita; a vita; **to come to ~** rianimarsi; **life assurance** (BRIT) n = **life insurance**; **lifeboat** n scialuppa di salvataggio; **lifeguard** n bagnino; **life insurance** n assicurazione f sulla vita; **life jacket** n giubbotto di salvataggio; **lifelike** adj verosimile; rassomigliante; **life preserver** [-prɪ'zəːvəʳ] (US) n salvagente m; giubbotto di salvataggio; **life sentence** n ergastolo; **lifestyle** n stile m di vita; **lifetime** n **in his lifetime** durante la sua vita; **once in a lifetime** una volta nella vita

lift [lɪft] vt sollevare; (*ban*, *rule*) levare ▷ vi (*fog*) alzarsi ▷ n (BRIT: *elevator*) ascensore m; **to give sb a ~** (BRIT) dare un passaggio a qn; **can you give me a ~ to the station?** può darmi un passaggio fino alla stazione?; **lift up** vt sollevare, alzare; **lift-off** n decollo

light [laɪt] (pt, pp **lighted** or **lit**) n luce f, lume m; (*daylight*) luce f, giorno; (*lamp*) lampada; (Aut: *rear light*) luce f di posizione; (: *headlamp*) fanale m; (*for cigarette etc*): **have you got a ~?** ha da accendere?; **~s** npl (Aut: *traffic lights*) semaforo vt (*candle*, *cigarette*, *fire*) accendere; (*room*): **to be lit by** essere illuminato(-a) da adj (*room*, *colour*) chiaro(-a); (*not heavy*, *also fig*) leggero(-a); **to come to ~** venire alla luce, emergere; **light up** vi illuminarsi ▷ vt illuminare; **light bulb** n lampadina; **lighten** vt (*make less heavy*) alleggerire; **lighter** n (*also*: **cigarette lighter**) accendino; **light-hearted** adj gioioso(-a), gaio(-a); **lighthouse** n faro; **lighting** n illuminazione f; **lightly** adv leggermente; **to get off lightly** cavarsela a buon mercato

lightning ['laɪtnɪŋ] n lampo, fulmine m

lightweight ['laɪtweɪt] adj (*suit*) leggero(-a) ▷ n (Boxing) peso leggero

like [laɪk] vt (*person*) volere bene a; (*activity*, *object*, *food*): **I ~ swimming/ that book/chocolate** mi piace nuotare/quel libro/il cioccolato ▷ prep come ▷ adj simile, uguale ▷ n **the ~** uno(-a) uguale; **his ~s and dis~s** i suoi gusti; **I would ~**, **I'd ~** mi piacerebbe, vorrei; **would you ~ a coffee?** gradirebbe un caffè?; **to be/look ~ sb/sth** somigliare a qn/qc; **what does it look/taste ~?** che aspetto/gusto ha?; **what does it sound ~?** come fa?; **that's just ~ him** è proprio da lui; **do it ~ this** fallo così; **it is nothing ~ ...** non è affatto come ...; **likeable** adj simpatico(-a)

likelihood ['laɪklɪhud] n probabilità

likely ['laɪklɪ] adj probabile; plausibile; **he's ~ to leave** probabilmente partirà, è probabile che parta; **not ~!** neanche per sogno!

likewise ['laɪkwaɪz] adv similmente, nello stesso modo

liking ['laɪkɪŋ] n **~ (for)** debole m (per); **to be to sb's ~** piacere a qn

lilac ['laɪlək] n lilla m inv

Lilo® ['laɪləu] n materassino gonfiabile

lily ['lɪlɪ] n giglio

limb [lɪm] n arto

limbo ['lɪmbəu] n **to be in ~** (fig) essere lasciato(-a) nel dimenticatoio

lime [laɪm] n (tree) tiglio; (fruit) limetta; (Geo) calce f

limelight ['laɪmlaɪt] n **in the ~** (fig) alla ribalta, in vista

limestone ['laɪmstəun] n pietra calcarea; (Geo) calcare m

limit ['lɪmɪt] n limite m ▷ vt limitare; **limited** adj limitato(-a), ristretto(-a); **to be limited to** limitarsi a

limousine ['lɪməzi:n] n limousine f inv

limp [lɪmp] n **to have a ~** zoppicare ▷ vi zoppicare ▷ adj floscio(-a), flaccido(-a)

line [laɪn] n linea; (rope) corda; (for fishing) lenza; (wire) filo; (of poem) verso; (row, series) fila, riga; coda; (on face) ruga ▷ vt (clothes): **to ~ (with)** foderare (di); (box): **to ~ (with)** rivestire or foderare (di); (trees, crowd) fiancheggiare; **~ of business** settore m or ramo d'attività; **in ~ with** in linea con; **line up** vi allinearsi, mettersi in fila ▷ vt mettere in fila; (event, celebration) preparare

linear ['lɪnɪəʳ] adj lineare

linen ['lɪnɪn] n biancheria, panni mpl; (cloth) tela di lino

liner ['laɪnəʳ] n nave f di linea; (for bin) sacchetto

line-up ['laɪnʌp] n allineamento, fila; (Sport) formazione f di gioco

linger ['lɪŋgəʳ] vi attardarsi; indugiare; (smell, tradition) persistere

lingerie ['lænʒəri:] n biancheria intima femminile

linguist ['lɪŋgwɪst] n linguista m/f; poliglotta m/f; **linguistic** adj linguistico(-a)

lining ['laɪnɪŋ] n fodera

link [lɪŋk] n (of a chain) anello; (relationship) legame m; (connection) collegamento ▷ vt collegare, unire, congiungere; (associate): **to ~ with** or **to** collegare a; **~s** npl (Golf) pista or terreno da golf; **link up** vt collegare, unire ▷ vi riunirsi; associarsi

lion ['laɪən] n leone m; **lioness** n leonessa

lip [lɪp] n labbro; (of cup etc) orlo; **lip-read** vi leggere sulle labbra; **lip salve** [-sælv] n burro di cacao; **lipstick** n rossetto

liqueur [lɪ'kjuəʳ] n liquore m

liquid ['lɪkwɪd] n liquido ▷ adj liquido(-a); **liquidizer** n frullatore m (a brocca)

liquor ['lɪkəʳ] n alcool m; **liquor store** (US) n negozio di liquori

Lisbon ['lɪzbən] n Lisbona

lisp [lɪsp] n pronuncia blesa della "s"

list [lɪst] n lista, elenco ▷ vt (write down) mettere in lista; fare una lista di; (enumerate) elencare

listen ['lɪsn] vi ascoltare; **to ~ to** ascoltare; **listener** n ascoltatore(-trice)

lit [lɪt] pt, pp of **light**

liter ['li:təʳ] (US) n = **litre**

literacy ['lɪtərəsɪ] n il sapere leggere e scrivere

literal ['lɪtərl] adj letterale; **literally** adv alla lettera, letteralmente

literary ['lɪtərərɪ] adj letterario(-a)

literate ['lɪtərət] adj che sa leggere e scrivere

literature ['lɪtərɪtʃəʳ] n letteratura; (brochures etc) materiale m

litre ['li:təʳ] (US **liter**) n litro

litter ['lɪtəʳ] n (rubbish) rifiuti mpl; (young animals) figliata; **litter bin** (BRIT) n cestino per rifiuti; **littered** adj **littered with** coperto(-a) di

little ['lɪtl] adj (small) piccolo(-a); (not much) poco(-a) ▷ adv poco; **a ~** un po' (di); **a ~ bit** un pochino; **~ by ~** a poco a poco; **little finger** n mignolo

live¹ [lɪv] vi vivere; (reside) vivere, abitare; **where do you ~?** dove abita?; **live together** vi vivere insieme, convivere; **live up to** vt fus tener fede a, non venir meno a

live² [laɪv] adj (animal) vivo(-a); (wire) sotto tensione; (bullet, missile) inesploso(-a); (broadcast) diretto(-a); (performance) dal vivo

livelihood ['laɪvlɪhud] n mezzi mpl di sostentamento

lively ['laɪvlɪ] adj vivace, vivo(-a)

liven up ['laɪvn ʌp] vt (discussion, evening) animare ▷ vi ravvivarsi

liver ['lɪvəʳ] n fegato

lives [laɪvz] npl of **life**

livestock ['laɪvstɔk] n bestiame m

living ['lɪvɪŋ] adj vivo(-a), vivente ▷ n **to earn** or **make a ~** guadagnarsi la vita; **living room** n soggiorno

lizard ['lɪzəd] n lucertola

load [ləud] n (weight) peso; (thing carried) carico ▷ vt (also: **~ up**): **to ~ (with)** (lorry, ship) caricare (di); (gun, camera, Comput) caricare (con); **a ~ of**, **~s of** (fig) un sacco di; **loaded** adj (vehicle): **loaded (with)** carico(-a) (di); (question) capzioso(-a); (inf: rich) carico(-a) di soldi

loaf [ləuf] (pl **loaves**) n pane m, pagnotta

loan [ləun] n prestito ▷ vt dare in prestito; **on ~** in prestito

loathe [ləuð] vt detestare, aborrire

loaves [ləuvz] npl of **loaf**

lobby ['lɔbɪ] n atrio, vestibolo; (Pol: pressure group) gruppo di pressione ▷ vt fare pressione su

lobster ['lɔbstə^r] n aragosta
local ['ləukl] adj locale ▷ n (BRIT: pub) ≈ bar m inv all'angolo; **the ~s** npl (local inhabitants) la gente della zona; **local anaesthetic** n anestesia locale; **local authority** n ente m locale; **local government** n amministrazione f locale; **locally** ['ləukəlɪ] adv da queste parti, nel vicinato
locate [ləu'keɪt] vt (find) trovare; (situate) collocare; situare
location [ləu'keɪʃən] n posizione f; **on ~** (Cinema) all'esterno
loch [lɔx] n lago
lock [lɔk] n (of door, box) serratura; (of canal) chiusa; (of hair) ciocca, riccio ▷ vt (with key) chiudere a chiave ▷ vi (door etc) chiudersi; (wheels) bloccarsi, incepparsi; **lock in** vt chiudere dentro (a chiave); **lock out** vt chiudere fuori; **lock up** vt (criminal, mental patient) rinchiudere; (house) chiudere a chiave) ▷ vi chiudere tutto (a chiave)
locker ['lɔkə^r] n armadietto; **locker-room** (US) n (Sport) spogliatoio
locksmith ['lɔksmɪθ] n magnano
locomotive [ləukə'məutɪv] n locomotiva
lodge [lɔdʒ] n casetta, portineria; (hunting lodge) casino di caccia ▷ vi (person): **to ~ (with)** essere a pensione (presso or da); (bullet etc) conficcarsi ▷ vt (appeal etc) presentare, fare; **to ~ a complaint** presentare un reclamo; **lodger** n affittuario(-a); (with room and meals) pensionante m/f
lodging ['lɔdʒɪŋ] n alloggio; see also **board**
loft [lɔft] n solaio, soffitta
log [lɔg] n (of wood) ceppo; (also: **~book**: Naut, Aviat) diario di bordo; (Aut) libretto di circolazione ▷ vt registrare; **log in** vi (Comput) aprire una sessione (con codice di riconoscimento); **log off** vi (Comput) terminare una sessione
logic ['lɔdʒɪk] n logica; **logical** adj logico(-a)
logo ['ləugəu] n logo m inv
lollipop ['lɔlɪpɔp] n lecca lecca m inv
lolly ['lɔlɪ] (inf) n lecca lecca m inv; (also: **ice ~**) ghiacciolo; (money) grana
London ['lʌndən] n Londra; **Londoner** n londinese m/f
lone [ləun] adj solitario(-a)
loneliness ['ləunlɪnɪs] n solitudine f, isolamento
lonely ['ləunlɪ] adj solo(-a); solitario(-a), isolato(-a)
long [lɔŋ] adj lungo(-a) ▷ adv a lungo,

per molto tempo ▷ vi **to ~ for sth/to do** desiderare qc/di fare, non veder l'ora di aver qc/di fare; **so** or **as ~ as** (while) finché; (provided that) sempre che + sub; **don't be ~!** fai presto!; **how ~ is this river/course?** quanto è lungo questo fiume/corso?; **6 metres ~** lungo 6 metri; **6 months ~** che dura 6 mesi, di 6 mesi; **all night ~** tutta la notte; **he no ~er comes** non viene più; **~ before** molto tempo prima; **before ~** (+ future) presto, fra poco; (+ past) poco tempo dopo; **at ~ last** finalmente; **long-distance** adj (race) di fondo; (call) interurbano(-a); **long-haul** ['lɔŋhɔ:l] adj (flight) a lunga percorrenza inv; **longing** n desiderio, voglia, brama
longitude ['lɔŋgɪtju:d] n longitudine f
long: long jump n salto in lungo; **long-life** adj (milk) a lunga conservazione; (batteries) di lunga durata; **long-sighted** adj presbite; **long-standing** adj di vecchia data; **long-term** adj a lungo termine
loo [lu:] (BRIT: inf) n W.C. m inv, cesso
look [luk] vi guardare; (seem) sembrare, parere; (building etc): **to ~ south/on to the sea** dare a sud/sul mare ▷ n sguardo; (appearance) aspetto, aria; **~s** npl (good looks) bellezza; **look after** vt fus occuparsi di, prendere cura di; (keep an eye on) guardare, badare a; **look around** vi guardarsi intorno; **look at** vt fus guardare; **look back** vi **to ~ back on** (event etc) ripensare a; **look down on** vt fus (fig) guardare dall'alto, disprezzare; **look for** vt fus cercare; **we're ~ing for a hotel/restaurant** stiamo cercando un albergo/ristorante; **look forward to** vt fus non veder l'ora di; (in letters): **we ~ forward to hearing from you** in attesa di una vostra gentile risposta; **look into** vt fus esaminare; **look out** vi (beware): **to ~ out (for)** stare in guardia (per); **look out for** vt fus cercare; **look round** vi (turn) girarsi, voltarsi; (in shop) dare un'occhiata; **look through** vt fus (papers, book) scorrere; (telescope) guardare attraverso; **look up** vi alzare gli occhi; (improve) migliorare ▷ vt (word) cercare; (friend) andare a trovare; **look up to** vt fus avere rispetto per; **lookout** n posto d'osservazione; guardia; **to be on the lookout (for)** stare in guardia (per)
loom [lu:m] n telaio ▷ vi (also: **~ up**) apparire minaccioso(-a); (event) essere imminente
loony ['lu:nɪ] (inf) n pazzo(-a)
loop [lu:p] n cappio ▷ vt **to ~ sth round sth** passare qc intorno a qc; **loophole** n

via d'uscita; scappatoia
loose [lu:s] *adj* (*knot*) sciolto(-a);
(*screw*) allentato(-a); (*stone*) cadente;
(*clothes*) ampio(-a), largo(-a); (*animal*)
in libertà, scappato(-a); (*life, morals*)
dissoluto(-a) ▷ *n* **to be on the ~** essere
in libertà; **loosely** *adv* senza stringere;
approssimativamente; **loosen** *vt*
sciogliere; (*belt etc*) allentare
loot [lu:t] *n* bottino ▷ *vt* saccheggiare
lop-sided ['lɔp'saɪdɪd] *adj* non
equilibrato(-a), asimmetrico(-a)
lord [lɔːd] *n* signore *m*; **L~ Smith** lord
Smith; **the L~** il Signore; **good L~!** buon
Dio!; **the (House of) L~s** (BRIT) la Camera
dei Lord
lorry ['lɔrɪ] (BRIT) *n* camion *m inv*; **lorry
driver** (BRIT) *n* camionista *m*
lose [lu:z] (*pt, pp* **lost**) *vt* perdere ▷ *vi*
perdere; **I've lost my wallet/passport**
ho perso il portafoglio/passaporto; **to
~ (time)** (*clock*) ritardare; **lose out** *vi*
rimetterci; **loser** *n* perdente *m/f*
loss [lɔs] *n* perdita; **to be at a ~** essere
perplesso(-a)
lost [lɔst] *pt, pp of* **lose** ▷ *adj* perduto(-a);
I'm ~ mi sono perso; **lost property** (US
lost and found) *n* oggetti *mpl* smarriti
lot [lɔt] *n* (*at auctions*) lotto; (*destiny*)
destino, sorte *f*; **the ~** tutto(-a) quanto(-a);
tutti(-e) quanti(-e); **a ~** molto; **a ~ of**
una gran quantità di, un sacco di; **~s of**
molto(-i); **to draw ~s (for sth)** tirare a
sorte (per qc)
lotion ['ləʊʃən] *n* lozione *f*
lottery ['lɔtərɪ] *n* lotteria
loud [laud] *adj* forte, alto(-a); (*gaudy*)
vistoso(-a), sgargiante ▷ *adv* (*speak
etc*) forte; (BRIT) ~ (*read etc*) ad alta voce;
loudly *adv* fortemente, ad alta voce;
loudspeaker *n* altoparlante *m*
lounge [laundʒ] *n* salotto, soggiorno; (*at
airport, station*) sala d'attesa; (BRIT: *also*: ~
bar) bar *m inv* con servizio a tavolino ▷ *vi*
oziare
louse [laus] (*pl* **lice**) *n* pidocchio
lousy ['lauzɪ] (*inf*) *adj* orrendo(-a),
schifoso(-a); **to feel ~** stare da cani
love [lʌv] *n* amore *m* ▷ *vt* amare;
voler bene a; **to ~ to do: I ~ to do** mi
piace fare; **to be/fall in ~ with** essere
innamorato(-a)/innamorarsi di; **to make
~** fare l'amore; **"15 ~"** (*Tennis*) "15 a zero";
love affair *n* relazione *f*; **love life** *n* vita
sentimentale
lovely ['lʌvlɪ] *adj* bello(-a); (*delicious: smell,
meal*) buono(-a)
lover ['lʌvər] *n* amante *m/f*; (*person in love*)
innamorato(-a); (*amateur*): **a ~ of** un(-un')

amante di; un(-un') appassionato(-a) di
loving ['lʌvɪŋ] *adj* affettuoso(-a)
low [ləu] *adj* basso(-a) ▷ *adv* in basso ▷ *n*
(*Meteor*) depressione *f*; **to be ~ on** (*supplies
etc*) avere scarsità di; **to feel ~** sentirsi
giù; **low-alcohol** *adj* a basso contenuto
alcolico; **low-calorie** *adj* a basso
contenuto calorico
lower ['ləuər] *adj* (*bottom: of 2 things*) più
basso; (*less important*) meno importante
▷ *vt* calare; (*prices, eyes, voice*) abbassare
low-fat ['ləu'fæt] *adj* magro(-a)
loyal ['lɔɪəl] *adj* fedele, leale; **loyalty** *n*
fedeltà, lealtà; **loyalty card** *n* carta che
offre sconti a clienti abituali
L.P. *n abbr* = **long-playing record**
L-plates ['ɛlpleɪts] (BRIT) *npl* contrassegno
P principiante
Lt *abbr* (= *lieutenant*) Ten.
Ltd *abbr* (= *limited*) ≈ S.r.l.
luck [lʌk] *n* fortuna, sorte *f*; **bad ~**
sfortuna, mala sorte; **good ~!** buona
fortuna!; **luckily** *adv* fortunatamente, per
fortuna; **lucky** *adj* fortunato(-a); (*number
etc*) che porta fortuna
lucrative ['lu:krətɪv] *adj* lucrativo(-a),
lucroso(-a), profittevole
ludicrous ['lu:dɪkrəs] *adj* ridicolo(-a)
luggage ['lʌgɪdʒ] *n* bagagli *mpl*; **our ~
hasn't arrived** i nostri bagagli non sono
arrivati; **luggage rack** *n* portabagagli
m inv
lukewarm ['lu:kwɔːm] *adj* tiepido(-a)
lull [lʌl] *n* intervallo di calma ▷ *vt* **to ~ sb to
sleep** cullare qn finché si addormenta
lullaby ['lʌləbaɪ] *n* ninnananna
lumber ['lʌmbər] *n* (*wood*) legname *m*;
(*junk*) roba vecchia
luminous ['lu:mɪnəs] *adj* luminoso(-a)
lump [lʌmp] *n* pezzo; (*in sauce*) grumo;
(*swelling*) gonfiore *m*; (*also*: **sugar ~**)
zolletta ▷ *vt* (*also*: ~ **together**) riunire,
mettere insieme; **lump sum** *n* somma
globale; **lumpy** *adj* (*sauce*) pieno(-a) di
grumi; (*bed*) bitorzoluto(-a)
lunatic ['lu:nətɪk] *adj* pazzo(-a),
matto(-a)
lunch [lʌntʃ] *n* pranzo, colazione *f*; **lunch
break** *n* intervallo del pranzo; **lunch time**
n ora di pranzo
lung [lʌŋ] *n* polmone *m*
lure [luər] *n* richiamo; lusinga ▷ *vt* attirare
(con l'inganno)
lurk [lɜːk] *vi* stare in agguato
lush [lʌʃ] *adj* lussureggiante
lust [lʌst] *n* lussuria; cupidigia; desiderio;
(*fig*): ~ **for** sete *f* di
Luxembourg ['lʌksəmbəːg] *n* (*state*)
Lussemburgo *m*; (*city*) Lussemburgo *f*

luxurious [lʌgˈzjuəriəs] *adj* sontuoso(-a), di lusso

luxury [ˈlʌkʃəri] *n* lusso ▷ *cpd* di lusso

> Be careful not to translate **luxury** by the Italian word **lussuria**.

Lycra® [ˈlaɪkrə] *n* lycra® *f inv*

lying [ˈlaɪɪŋ] *n* bugie *fpl*, menzogne *fpl* ▷ *adj* bugiardo(-a)

lyrics [ˈlɪrɪks] *npl* (*of song*) parole *fpl*

m. *abbr* = **metre**; **mile**; **million**

M.A. *abbr* = **Master of Arts**

ma (*inf*) [mɑː] *n* mamma

mac [mæk] (BRIT) *n* impermeabile *m*

macaroni [mækəˈrəuni] *n* maccheroni *mpl*

Macedonia [mæsɪˈdəuniə] *n* Macedonia; **Macedonian** [mæsɪˈdəuniən] *adj* macedone ▷ *n* macedone *m/f*; (*Ling*) macedone *m*

machine [məˈʃiːn] *n* macchina ▷ *vt* (*Tech*) lavorare a macchina; (*dress etc*) cucire a macchina; **machine gun** *n* mitragliatrice *f*; **machinery** *n* macchinario, macchine *fpl*; (*fig*) macchina; **machine washable** *adj* lavabile in lavatrice

macho [ˈmætʃəu] *adj* macho *inv*

mackerel [ˈmækrl] *n inv* sgombro

mackintosh [ˈmækɪntɔʃ] (BRIT) *n* impermeabile *m*

mad [mæd] *adj* matto(-a), pazzo(-a); (*foolish*) sciocco(-a); (*angry*) furioso(-a); **to be ~ about** (*keen*) andare pazzo(-a) per

Madagascar [mædəˈgæskəʳ] *n* Madagascar *m*

madam [ˈmædəm] *n* signora

mad cow disease *n* encefalite *f* bovina spongiforme

made [meɪd] *pt, pp of* **make**; **made-to-measure** (BRIT) *adj* fatto(-a) su misura; **made-up** ['meɪdʌp] *adj* (*story*) inventato(-a)

madly ['mædlɪ] *adv* follemente

madman ['mædmən] (*irreg*) *n* pazzo, alienato

madness ['mædnɪs] *n* pazzia

Madrid [mə'drɪd] *n* Madrid *f*

Mafia ['mæfɪə] *n* mafia *f*

mag [mæg] *n abbr* (BRIT *inf*) = **magazine** (*Press*)

magazine [mægə'zi:n] *n* (*Press*) rivista; (*Radio, TV*) rubrica

> Be careful not to translate *magazine* by the Italian word *magazzino*.

maggot ['mægət] *n* baco, verme *m*

magic ['mædʒɪk] *n* magia ▷ *adj* magico(-a); **magical** *adj* magico(-a); **magician** [mə'dʒɪʃən] *n* mago(-a)

magistrate ['mædʒɪstreɪt] *n* magistrato; giudice *m/f*

magnet ['mægnɪt] *n* magnete *m*, calamita; **magnetic** [-'nɛtɪk] *adj* magnetico(-a)

magnificent [mæg'nɪfɪsnt] *adj* magnifico(-a)

magnify ['mægnɪfaɪ] *vt* ingrandire; **magnifying glass** *n* lente *f* d'ingrandimento

magpie ['mægpaɪ] *n* gazza

mahogany [mə'hɔgənɪ] *n* mogano

maid [meɪd] *n* domestica; (*in hotel*) cameriera

maiden name ['meɪdn-] *n* nome *m* da nubile *or* da ragazza

mail [meɪl] *n* posta ▷ *vt* spedire (per posta); **mailbox** (US) *n* cassetta delle lettere; **mailing list** *n* elenco d'indirizzi; **mailman** (*irreg*: US) *n* portalettere *m inv*, postino; **mail-order** *n* vendita (*or* acquisto) per corrispondenza

main [meɪn] *adj* principale ▷ *n* (*pipe*) conduttura principale; **main course** *n* (*Culin*) piatto principale, piatto forte; **mainland** *n* continente *m*; **mainly** *adv* principalmente, soprattutto; **main road** *n* strada principale; **mainstream** *n* (*fig*) corrente *f* principale; **main street** *n* strada principale

maintain [meɪn'teɪn] *vt* mantenere; (*affirm*) sostenere; **maintenance** ['meɪntənəns] *n* manutenzione *f*; (*alimony*) alimenti *mpl*

maisonette [meɪzə'nɛt] *n* (BRIT) appartamento a due piani

maize [meɪz] *n* granturco, mais *m*

majesty ['mædʒɪstɪ] *n* maestà *f inv*

major ['meɪdʒə'] *n* (*Mil*) maggiore *m* ▷ *adj* (*greater, Mus*) maggiore; (*in importance*) principale, importante

Majorca [mə'jɔ:kə] *n* Maiorca

majority [mə'dʒɔrɪtɪ] *n* maggioranza

make [meɪk] (*pt, pp* **made**) *vt* fare; (*manufacture*) fare, fabbricare; (*cause to be*): **to ~ sb sad** *etc* rendere qn triste *etc*; (*force*): **to ~ sb do sth** costringere qn a fare qc, far fare qc a qn; (*equal*): **2 and 2 ~ 4** 2 più 2 fa 4 ▷ *n* fabbricazione *f*; (*brand*) marca; **to ~ a fool of sb** far fare a qn la figura dello scemo; **to ~ a profit** realizzare un profitto; **to ~ a loss** subire una perdita; **to ~ it** (*arrive*) arrivare; (*achieve sth*) farcela; **what time do you ~ it?** che ora fai?; **to ~ do with** arrangiarsi con; **make off** *vi* svignarsela; **make out** *vt* (*write out*) scrivere; (: *cheque*) emettere; (*understand*) capire; (*see*) distinguere; (: *numbers*) decifrare; **make up** *vt* (*constitute*) formare; (*invent*) inventare; (*parcel*) fare ▷ *vi* conciliarsi; (*with cosmetics*) truccarsi; **make up for** *vt fus* compensare; ricuperare; **makeover** ['meɪkəuvə'] *n* (*change of image*) cambiamento di immagine; (*of room, house*) trasformazione *f*; **maker** *n* (*of programme etc*) creatore(-trice); (*manufacturer*) fabbricante *m*; **makeshift** *adj* improvvisato(-a); **make-up** *n* trucco

making ['meɪkɪŋ] *n* (*fig*): **in the ~** in formazione; **to have the ~s of** (*actor, athlete etc*) avere la stoffa di

malaria [mə'lɛərɪə] *n* malaria

Malaysia [mə'leɪzɪə] *n* Malaysia

male [meɪl] *n* (*Biol*) maschio ▷ *adj* maschile; maschio(-a)

malicious [mə'lɪʃəs] *adj* malevolo(-a); (*Law*) doloso(-a)

malignant [mə'lɪgnənt] *adj* (*Med*) maligno(-a)

mall [mɔ:l] *n* (*also*: **shopping ~**) centro commerciale

mallet ['mælɪt] *n* maglio

malnutrition [mælnju:'trɪʃən] *n* denutrizione *f*

malpractice [mæl'præktɪs] *n* prevaricazione *f*; negligenza

malt [mɔ:lt] *n* malto

Malta ['mɔ:ltə] *n* Malta; **Maltese** [mɔ:l'ti:z] *adj*, *n* (*pl inv*) maltese (*m/f*); (*Ling*) maltese *m*

mammal ['mæml] *n* mammifero

mammoth ['mæməθ] *adj* enorme, gigantesco(-a)

man [mæn] (*pl* **men**) *n* uomo ▷ *vt* fornire d'uomini; stare a; **an old ~** un vecchio; **~ and wife** marito e moglie

manage ['mænɪdʒ] *vi* farcela ▷ *vt* (*be in charge of*) occuparsi di; gestire; **to ~ to do sth** riuscire a far qc; **manageable** *adj* maneggevole; fattibile; **management** *n* amministrazione f, direzione f; **manager** n direttore m; (of shop, restaurant) gerente m; (of artist, Sport) manager m inv; **manageress** [-ə'rɛs] n direttrice f; gerente f; **managerial** [-ə'dʒɪərɪəl] adj dirigenziale; **managing director** n amministratore m delegato

mandarin ['mændərɪn] n (person, fruit) mandarino

mandate ['mændeɪt] n mandato

mandatory ['mændətərɪ] adj obbligatorio(-a), ingiuntivo(-a)

mane [meɪn] n criniera

mangetout ['mɔnʒ'tu:] n pisello dolce, taccola

mango ['mæŋgəʊ] (pl **mangoes**) n mango

man: manhole ['mænhəʊl] n botola stradale; **manhood** ['mænhʊd] n età virile; virilità

mania ['meɪnɪə] n mania; **maniac** ['meɪnɪæk] n maniaco(-a)

manic ['mænɪk] adj (behaviour, activity) maniacale

manicure ['mænɪkjʊəʳ] n manicure f inv

manifest ['mænɪfɛst] vt manifestare ▷ adj manifesto(-a), palese

manifesto [mænɪ'fɛstəʊ] n manifesto

manipulate [mə'nɪpjʊleɪt] vt manipolare

man: mankind [mæn'kaɪnd] n umanità, genere m umano; **manly** ['mænlɪ] adj virile; coraggioso(-a); **man-made** adj sintetico(-a); artificiale

manner ['mænəʳ] n maniera, modo; (behaviour) modo di fare; (type, sort): **all ~ of things** ogni genere di cosa; **~s** npl (conduct) maniere fpl; **bad ~s** maleducazione f

manoeuvre [mə'nu:vəʳ] (US **maneuver**) vt manovrare ▷ vi far manovre ▷ n manovra

manpower ['mænpaʊəʳ] n manodopera

mansion ['mænʃən] n casa signorile

manslaughter ['mænslɔ:təʳ] n omicidio preterintenzionale

mantelpiece ['mæntlpi:s] n mensola del caminetto

manual ['mænjʊəl] adj manuale ▷ n manuale m

manufacture [mænjʊ'fæktʃəʳ] vt fabbricare ▷ n fabbricazione f, manifattura; **manufacturer** n fabbricante m

manure [mə'njʊəʳ] n concime m

manuscript ['mænjʊskrɪpt] n manoscritto

many ['mɛnɪ] adj molti(-e) ▷ pron molti(-e); **a great ~** moltissimi(-e), un gran numero (di); **~ a time** molte volte

map [mæp] n carta (geografica); (of city)

cartina; **can you show it to me on the ~?** può indicarmelo sulla cartina?

maple ['meɪpl] n acero

mar [mɑ:ʳ] vt sciupare

Mar. abbr (= March) mar.

marathon ['mærəθən] n maratona

marble ['mɑ:bl] n marmo; (toy) pallina, bilia

March [mɑ:tʃ] n marzo

march [mɑ:tʃ] vi marciare; sfilare ▷ n marcia

mare [mɛəʳ] n giumenta

margarine [mɑ:dʒə'ri:n] n margarina

margin ['mɑ:dʒɪn] n margine m; **marginal** adj marginale; **marginal seat** (Pol) seggio elettorale ottenuto con una stretta maggioranza; **marginally** adv (bigger, better) lievemente, di poco; (different) un po'

marigold ['mærɪgəʊld] n calendola

marijuana [mærɪ'wɑ:nə] n marijuana

marina [mə'ri:nə] n marina

marinade n [mærɪ'neɪd] marinata ▷ vt ['mærɪneɪd] = **marinate**

marinate ['mærɪneɪt] vt marinare

marine [mə'ri:n] adj (animal, plant) marino(-a); (forces, engineering) marittimo(-a) ▷ n (BRIT) fante m di marina; (US) marine m inv

marital ['mærɪtl] adj maritale, coniugale; **marital status** n stato civile

maritime ['mærɪtaɪm] adj marittimo(-a)

marjoram ['mɑ:dʒərəm] n maggiorana

mark [mɑ:k] n segno; (stain) macchia; (of skid etc) traccia; (BRIT Scol) voto; (Sport) bersaglio; (currency) marco ▷ vt segnare; (stain) macchiare; (indicate) indicare; (BRIT Scol) dare un voto a; correggere; **to ~ time** segnare il passo; **marked** adj spiccato(-a), chiaro(-a); **marker** n (sign) segno; (bookmark) segnalibro

market ['mɑ:kɪt] n mercato ▷ vt (Comm) mettere in vendita; **marketing** n marketing m; **marketplace** n (piazza del) mercato; (world of trade) piazza, mercato; **market research** n indagine f or ricerca di mercato

marmalade ['mɑ:məleɪd] n marmellata d'arance

maroon [mə'ru:n] vt (also fig): **to be ~ed (in or at)** essere abbandonato(-a) (in) ▷ adj bordeaux inv

marquee [mɑ:'ki:] n padiglione m

marriage ['mærɪdʒ] n matrimonio; **marriage certificate** n certificato di matrimonio

married ['mærɪd] adj sposato(-a); (life, love) coniugale, matrimoniale

marrow ['mærəʊ] n midollo; (vegetable) zucca

marry ['mærɪ] vt sposare, sposarsi con; (vicar, priest etc) dare in matrimonio ▷ vi (also: **get married**) sposarsi

Mars [mɑːz] n (planet) Marte m

marsh [mɑːʃ] n palude f

marshal ['mɑːʃl] n maresciallo; (us: fire) capo; (: police) capitano ▷ vt (thoughts, support) ordinare; (soldiers) adunare

martyr ['mɑːtə^r] n martire m/f

marvel ['mɑːvl] n meraviglia ▷ vi **to ~ (at)** meravigliarsi (di); **marvellous** (us **marvelous**) adj meraviglioso(-a)

Marxism ['mɑːksɪzəm] n marxismo

Marxist ['mɑːksɪst] adj, n marxista m/f

marzipan ['mɑːzɪpæn] n marzapane m

mascara [mæs'kɑːrə] n mascara m

mascot ['mæskət] n mascotte f inv

masculine ['mæskjulɪn] adj maschile; (woman) mascolino(-a)

mash [mæʃ] vt passare, schiacciare; **mashed potatoes** npl purè m di patate

mask [mɑːsk] n maschera ▷ vt mascherare

mason ['meɪsn] n (also: **stone~**) scalpellino; (also: **free~**) massone m; **masonry** n muratura

mass [mæs] n moltitudine f, massa; (Physics) massa; (Rel) messa ▷ cpd di massa ▷ vi ammassarsi; **the ~es** npl (ordinary people) le masse; **~es of** (inf) una montagna di

massacre ['mæsəkə^r] n massacro

massage ['mæsɑːʒ] n massaggio

massive ['mæsɪv] adj enorme, massiccio(-a)

mass media npl mass media mpl

mass-produce ['mæsprə'djuːs] vt produrre in serie

mast [mɑːst] n albero

master ['mɑːstə^r] n padrone m; (Art etc, teacher: in primary school) maestro; (: in secondary school) professore m; (title for boys): **M~ X** Signorino X ▷ vt domare; (learn) imparare a fondo; (understand) conoscere a fondo; **mastermind** n mente f superiore ▷ vt essere il cervello di; **Master of Arts/Science** n Master m inv in lettere/scienze; **masterpiece** n capolavoro

masturbate ['mæstəbeɪt] vi masturbare

mat [mæt] n stuoia; (also: **door~**) stoino, zerbino; (also: **table ~**) sottopiatto ▷ adj = **matt**

match [mætʃ] n fiammifero; (game) partita, incontro; (fig) uguale m/f; matrimonio; partito ▷ vt intonare; (go well with) andare benissimo con; (equal) uguagliare; (correspond to) corrispondere a; (pair: also: **~ up**) accoppiare ▷ vi

combaciare; **to be a good ~** andare bene; **matchbox** n scatola per fiammiferi; **matching** adj ben assortito(-a)

mate [meɪt] n compagno(-a) di lavoro; (inf: friend) amico(-a); (animal) compagno(-a); (in merchant navy) secondo ▷ vi accoppiarsi

material [mə'tɪərɪəl] n (substance) materiale m, materia; (cloth) stoffa ▷ adj materiale; **~s** npl (equipment) materiali mpl

materialize [mə'tɪərɪəlaɪz] vi materializzarsi, realizzarsi

maternal [mə'təːnl] adj materno(-a)

maternity [mə'təːnɪtɪ] n maternità; **maternity hospital** n ≈ clinica ostetrica; **maternity leave** n congedo di maternità

math [mæθ] (us) n = **maths**

mathematical [mæθə'mætɪkl] adj matematico(-a)

mathematician [mæθəmə'tɪʃən] n matematico(-a)

mathematics [mæθə'mætɪks] n matematica

maths [mæθs] (us **math**) n matematica

matinée ['mætɪneɪ] n matinée f inv

matron ['meɪtrən] n (in hospital) capoinfermiera; (in school) infermiera

matt [mæt] adj opaco(-a)

matter ['mætə^r] n questione f; (Physics) materia, sostanza; (content) contenuto; (Med: pus) pus m ▷ vi importare; **it doesn't ~** non importa; (I don't mind) non fa niente; **what's the ~?** che cosa c'è?; **no ~ what** qualsiasi cosa accada; **as a ~ of course** come cosa naturale; **as a ~ of fact** in verità; **~s** npl (affairs) questioni

mattress ['mætrɪs] n materasso

mature [mə'tjuə^r] adj maturo(-a); (cheese) stagionato(-a) ▷ vi maturare; stagionare; **mature student** n studente universitario che ha più di 25 anni; **maturity** n maturità

maul [mɔːl] vt lacerare

mauve [məuv] adj malva inv

max abbr = **maximum**

maximize ['mæksɪmaɪz] vt (profits etc) massimizzare; (chances) aumentare al massimo

maximum ['mæksɪməm] (pl **maxima**) adj massimo(-a) ▷ n massimo

May [meɪ] n maggio

may [meɪ] (conditional **might**) vi (indicating possibility): **he ~ come** può darsi che venga; (be allowed to): **~ I smoke?** posso fumare?; (wishes): **~ God bless you!** Dio la benedica!; **you ~ as well go** tanto vale che tu te ne vada

maybe ['meɪbiː] adv forse, può darsi; **~ he'll ...** può darsi che lui ... + sub, forse lui ...

May Day n il primo maggio

mayhem ['meɪhɛm] n cagnara

mayonnaise [meɪə'neɪz] n maionese f
mayor [mɛəʳ] n sindaco; **mayoress** n
sindaco (donna); moglie f del sindaco
maze [meɪz] n labirinto, dedalo
MD n abbr (= Doctor of Medicine) titolo di
studio; (Comm) see **managing director**
me [miː] pron mi, m' + vowel or silent "h";
(stressed, after prep) me; **he heard me** mi ha
or m'ha sentito; **give me a book** dammi (or
mi dia) un libro; **it's me** sono io; **with me**
con me; **without me** senza di me
meadow ['mɛdəu] n prato
meagre ['miːgəʳ] (us **meager**) adj
magro(-a)
meal [miːl] n pasto; (flour) farina;
mealtime n l'ora di mangiare
mean [miːn] (pt, pp **meant**) adj (with
money) avaro(-a), gretto(-a); (unkind)
meschino(-a), maligno(-a); (shabby)
misero(-a); (average) medio(-a) ▷ vt
(signify) significare, voler dire; (intend):
to ~ to do aver l'intenzione di fare ▷ n
mezzo; (Math) media; **~s** npl (way, money)
mezzi mpl; **by ~s of** per mezzo di; **by all
~s** ma certo, prego; **to be ~t for** essere
destinato(-a) a; **do you ~ it?** dice sul serio?;
what do you ~? che cosa vuol dire?
meaning ['miːnɪŋ] n significato, senso;
meaningful adj significativo(-a);
meaningless adj senza senso
meant [mɛnt] pt, pp of **mean**
meantime ['miːntaɪm] adv (also: **in the ~**)
nel frattempo
meanwhile ['miːnwaɪl] adv nel frattempo
measles ['miːzlz] n morbillo
measure ['mɛʒəʳ] vt, vi misurare ▷ n
misura; (also: **tape ~**) metro
measurement ['mɛʒəmənt] n (act)
misurazione f; (measure) misura; **chest/
hip ~** giro petto/fianchi; **to take sb's ~s**
prendere le misure di qn
meat [miːt] n carne f; **I don't eat ~** non
mangio carne; **cold ~** affettato; **meatball**
n polpetta di carne
Mecca ['mɛkə] n (also fig) la Mecca
mechanic [mɪ'kænɪk] n meccanico;
can you send a ~? può mandare
un meccanico?; **mechanical** adj
meccanico(-a)
mechanism ['mɛkənɪzəm] n meccanismo
medal ['mɛdl] n medaglia; **medallist**
(us **medalist**) n (Sport): **to be a gold
medallist** essere medaglia d'oro
meddle ['mɛdl] vi **to ~ in** immischiarsi in,
mettere le mani in; **to ~ with** toccare
media ['miːdɪə] npl media mpl
mediaeval [mɛdɪ'iːvl] adj = **medieval**
mediate ['miːdɪeɪt] vi fare da
mediatore(-trice)

medical ['mɛdɪkl] adj medico(-a) ▷ n visita
medica; **medical certificate** n certificato
medico
medicated ['mɛdɪkeɪtɪd] adj medicato(-a)
medication [mɛdɪ'keɪʃən] n medicinali
mpl, farmaci mpl
medicine ['mɛdsɪn] n medicina
medieval [mɛdɪ'iːvl] adj medievale
mediocre [miːdɪ'əukəʳ] adj mediocre
meditate ['mɛdɪteɪt] vi **to ~ (on)** meditare
(su)
meditation [mɛdɪ'teɪʃən] n meditazione f
Mediterranean [mɛdɪtə'reɪnɪən] adj
mediterraneo(-a); **the ~ (Sea)** il (mare)
Mediterraneo
medium ['miːdɪəm] (pl **media**) adj
medio(-a) ▷ n (means) mezzo; (pl **mediums**:
person) medium m inv; **medium-sized** adj
(tin etc) di grandezza media; (clothes) di
taglia media; **medium wave** n onde fpl
medie
meek [miːk] adj dolce, umile
meet [miːt] (pt, pp **met**) vt incontrare; (for
the first time) fare la conoscenza di; (go and
fetch) andare a prendere; (fig) affrontare;
soddisfare; raggiungere ▷ vi incontrarsi;
(in session) riunirsi; (join: objects) unirsi;
nice to ~ you piacere (di conoscerla);
meet up vi **to ~ up with sb** incontrare
qn; **meet with** vt fus incontrare; **meeting**
n incontro; (session: of club etc) riunione f;
(interview) intervista; **she's at a meeting**
(Comm) è in riunione; **meeting place** n
luogo d'incontro
megabyte ['mɛgəbaɪt] n (Comput)
megabyte m inv
megaphone ['mɛgəfəun] n megafono
melancholy ['mɛlənkəlɪ] n malinconia
▷ adj malinconico(-a)
melody ['mɛlədɪ] n melodia
melon ['mɛlən] n melone m
melt [mɛlt] vi (gen) sciogliersi, struggersi;
(metals) fondersi ▷ vt sciogliere, struggere;
fondere
member ['mɛmbəʳ] n membro; **Member
of Congress** (us) n membro del
Congresso; **Member of Parliament** (BRIT)
n deputato(-a); **Member of the European
Parliament** (BRIT) n eurodeputato(-a);
Member of the Scottish Parliament
(BRIT) n deputato(-a) del Parlamento
scozzese; **membership** n iscrizione
f, (numero d')iscritti mpl, membri mpl;
membership card n tessera (di iscrizione)
memento [mə'mɛntəu] n ricordo,
souvenir m inv
memo ['mɛməu] n appunto; (Comm etc)
comunicazione f di servizio
memorable ['mɛmərəbl] adj memorabile

memorandum [mɛmə'rændəm] (pl **memoranda**) n appunto; (Comm etc) comunicazione f di servizio

memorial [mɪ'mɔːrɪəl] n monumento commemorativo ▷ adj commemorativo(-a)

memorize ['mɛməraɪz] vt memorizzare

memory ['mɛmərɪ] n (also Comput) memoria; (recollection) ricordo

men [mɛn] npl of **man**

menace ['mɛnəs] n minaccia ▷ vt minacciare

mend [mɛnd] vt aggiustare, riparare; (darn) rammendare ▷ n **on the ~** in via di guarigione

meningitis [mɛnɪn'dʒaɪtɪs] n meningite f

menopause ['mɛnəupɔːz] n menopausa

men's room n **the men's room** (esp US) la toilette degli uomini

menstruation [mɛnstru'eɪʃən] n mestruazione f

menswear ['mɛnzwɛəʳ] n abbigliamento maschile

mental ['mɛntl] adj mentale; **mental hospital** n ospedale m psichiatrico; **mentality** [mɛn'tælɪtɪ] n mentalità f inv; **mentally** adv **to be mentally handicapped** essere minorato psichico

menthol ['mɛnθɒl] n mentolo

mention ['mɛnʃən] n menzione f ▷ vt menzionare, far menzione di; **don't ~ it!** non c'è di che!, prego!

menu ['mɛnjuː] n (set menu, Comput) menù m inv; (printed) carta; **could we see the ~?** ci può portare il menù?

MEP n abbr = **Member of the European Parliament**

mercenary ['məːsɪnərɪ] adj venale ▷ n mercenario

merchandise ['məːtʃəndaɪz] n merci fpl

merchant ['məːtʃənt] n mercante m, commerciante m; **merchant navy** (US **merchant marine**) n marina mercantile

merciless ['məːsɪlɪs] adj spietato(-a)

mercury ['məːkjurɪ] n mercurio

mercy ['məːsɪ] n pietà f; (Rel) misericordia; **at the ~ of** alla mercé di

mere [mɪəʳ] adj semplice; **by a ~ chance** per mero caso; **merely** adv semplicemente, non ... che

merge [məːdʒ] vt unire ▷ vi fondersi, unirsi; (Comm) fondersi; **merger** n (Comm) fusione f

meringue [mə'ræŋ] n meringa

merit ['mɛrɪt] n merito, valore m ▷ vt meritare

mermaid ['məːmeɪd] n sirena

merry ['mɛrɪ] adj gaio(-a), allegro(-a); **M~ Christmas!** Buon Natale!; **merry-go-round** n carosello

mesh [mɛʃ] n maglia; rete f

mess [mɛs] n confusione f, disordine m; (fig) pasticcio; (dirt) sporcizia; (Mil) mensa; **mess about** or **around** (inf) vi trastullarsi; **mess with** (inf) vt fus (challenge, confront) litigare con; (drugs, drinks) abusare di; **mess up** vt sporcare; fare un pasticcio di; rovinare

message ['mɛsɪdʒ] n messaggio; **can I leave a ~?** posso lasciare un messaggio?; **are there any ~s for me?** ci sono messaggi per me?

messenger ['mɛsɪndʒəʳ] n messaggero(-a)

Messrs ['mɛsəz] abbr (on letters) Spett.

messy ['mɛsɪ] adj sporco(-a), disordinato(-a)

met [mɛt] pt, pp of **meet**

metabolism [mɛ'tæbəlɪzəm] n metabolismo

metal ['mɛtl] n metallo; **metallic** [-'tælɪk] adj metallico(-a)

metaphor ['mɛtəfəʳ] n metafora

meteor ['miːtɪəʳ] n meteora; **meteorite** ['miːtɪəraɪt] n meteorite m

meteorology [miːtɪə'rɒlədʒɪ] n meteorologia

meter ['miːtəʳ] n (instrument) contatore m; (parking meter) parchimetro; (US: unit) = **metre**

method ['mɛθəd] n metodo; **methodical** [mɪ'θɒdɪkl] adj metodico(-a)

meths [mɛθs] (BRIT) n alcool m denaturato

meticulous [mɛ'tɪkjuləs] adj meticoloso(-a)

metre ['miːtəʳ] (US **meter**) n metro

metric ['mɛtrɪk] adj metrico(-a)

metro ['mɛtrəu] n metro m inv

metropolitan [mɛtrə'pɒlɪtən] adj metropolitano(-a)

Mexican ['mɛksɪkən] adj, n messicano(-a)

Mexico ['mɛksɪkəu] n Messico

mg abbr (= milligram) mg

mice [maɪs] npl of **mouse**

micro... ['maɪkrəu] prefix micro...; **microchip** n microcircuito integrato; **microphone** n microfono; **microscope** n microscopio; **microwave** n (also: **microwave oven**) forno a microonde

mid [mɪd] adj **~ May** metà maggio; **~ afternoon** metà pomeriggio; **in ~ air** a mezz'aria; **midday** n mezzogiorno

middle ['mɪdl] n mezzo; centro; (waist) vita ▷ adj di mezzo; **in the ~ of the night** nel bel mezzo della notte; **middle-aged** adj di mezza età; **Middle Ages** npl **the Middle Ages** il Medioevo; **middle-class** adj ≈ borghese; **Middle East** n Medio

Oriente *m*; **middle name** *n* secondo nome *m*; **middle school** *n* (*us*) *scuola media per ragazzi dagli 11 ai 14 anni*; (*BRIT*) *scuola media per ragazzi dagli 8 o 9 ai 12 o 13 anni*

midge [mɪdʒ] *n* moscerino

midget ['mɪdʒɪt] *n* nano(-a)

midnight ['mɪdnaɪt] *n* mezzanotte *f*

midst [mɪdst] *n* **in the ~ of** in mezzo a

midsummer [mɪd'sʌmə^r] *n* mezza *or* piena estate *f*

midway [mɪd'weɪ] *adj, adv* **~ (between)** a mezza strada (fra); **~ (through)** a metà (di)

midweek [mɪd'wiːk] *adv* a metà settimana

midwife ['mɪdwaɪf] (*pl* **midwives**) *n* levatrice *f*

midwinter [mɪd'wɪntə^r] *n* pieno inverno

might [maɪt] *vb see* **may** ▷ *n* potere *m*, forza; **mighty** *adj* forte, potente

migraine ['miːgreɪn] *n* emicrania

migrant ['maɪgrənt] *adj* (*bird*) migratore(-trice); (*worker*) emigrato(-a)

migrate [maɪ'greɪt] *vi* (*bird*) migrare; (*person*) emigrare

migration [maɪ'greɪʃən] *n* migrazione *f*

mike [maɪk] *n abbr* (= *microphone*) microfono

Milan [mɪ'læn] *n* Milano *f*

mild [maɪld] *adj* mite; (*person, voice*) dolce; (*flavour*) delicato(-a); (*illness*) leggero(-a); (*interest*) blando(-a) ▷ *n* (*beer*) birra leggera; **mildly** ['maɪldlɪ] *adv* mitemente; dolcemente; delicatamente; leggermente; blandamente; **to put it mildly** a dire poco

mile [maɪl] *n* miglio; **mileage** *n* distanza in miglia, ≈ chilometraggio; **mileometer** [maɪ'lɔmɪtə^r] *n* ≈ contachilometri *m inv*; **milestone** ['maɪlstəun] *n* pietra miliare

military ['mɪlɪtərɪ] *adj* militare

militia [mɪ'lɪʃə] *n* milizia

milk [mɪlk] *n* latte *m* ▷ *vt* (*cow*) mungere; (*fig*) sfruttare; **milk chocolate** *n* cioccolata al latte; **milkman** (*irreg*) *n* lattaio; **milky** *adj* lattiginoso(-a); (*colour*) latteo(-a)

mill [mɪl] *n* mulino; (*small: for coffee, pepper etc*) macinino; (*factory*) fabbrica; (*spinning mill*) filatura ▷ *vt* macinare ▷ *vi* (*also: ~ about*) brulicare

millennium [mɪ'lɛnɪəm] (*pl* **millenniums** *or* **millennia**) *n* millennio

milli... ['mɪlɪ] *prefix*: **milligram(me)** *n* milligrammo; **millilitre** ['mɪlɪliːtə^r] (*us* **milliliter**) *n* millilitro; **millimetre** (*us* **millimeter**) *n* millimetro

million ['mɪljən] *num* milione *m*; **millionaire** *n* milionario, ≈ miliardario; **millionth** *num* milionesimo(-a)

milometer [maɪ'lɔmɪtə^r] *n* = **mileometer**

mime [maɪm] *n* mimo ▷ *vt, vi* mimare

mimic ['mɪmɪk] *n* imitatore(-trice) ▷ *vt* fare la mimica di

min. *abbr* = **minute(s)**; **minimum**

mince [mɪns] *vt* tritare, macinare ▷ *n* (*BRIT Culin*) carne *f* tritata *or* macinata; **mincemeat** *n* frutta secca tritata per uso in pasticceria; (*us*) carne *f* tritata *or* macinata; **mince pie** *n* specie di torta con frutta secca

mind [maɪnd] *n* mente *f* ▷ *vt* (*attend to, look after*) badare a, occuparsi di; (*be careful*) fare attenzione a, stare attento(-a) a; (*object to*): **I don't ~ the noise** il rumore non mi dà alcun fastidio; **I don't ~** non m'importa; **do you ~ if ...?** le dispiace se...?; **it is on my ~** mi preoccupa; **to my ~** secondo me, a mio parere; **to be out of one's ~** essere uscito(-a) di mente; **to keep** *or* **bear sth in ~** non dimenticare qc; **to make up one's ~** decidersi; **~ you, ...** sì, però va detto che ...; **never ~** non importa, non fa niente; (*don't worry*) non preoccuparti; **"~ the step"** "attenzione allo scalino"; **mindless** *adj* idiota

mine¹ [maɪn] *pron* il (la) mio(-a); (*pl*) i (le) miei (mei); **that book is ~** quel libro è mio; **yours is red, ~ is green** il tuo è rosso, il mio è verde; **a friend of ~** un mio amico

mine² [maɪn] *n* miniera; (*explosive*) mina ▷ *vt* (*coal*) estrarre; (*ship, beach*) minare; **minefield** *n* (*also fig*) campo minato; **miner** ['maɪnə^r] *n* minatore *m*

mineral ['mɪnərəl] *adj* minerale ▷ *n* minerale *m*; **mineral water** *n* acqua minerale

mingle ['mɪŋgl] *vi* **to ~ with** mescolarsi a, mischiarsi con

miniature ['mɪnətʃə^r] *adj* in miniatura ▷ *n* miniatura

minibar ['mɪnɪbɑː^r] *n* minibar *m inv*

minibus ['mɪnɪbʌs] *n* minibus *m inv*

minicab ['mɪnɪkæb] *n* (*BRIT*) ≈ taxi *m inv*

minimal ['mɪnɪml] *adj* minimo(-a)

minimize ['mɪnɪmaɪz] *vt* minimizzare

minimum ['mɪnɪməm] (*pl* **minima**) *n* minimo ▷ *adj* minimo(-a)

mining ['maɪnɪŋ] *n* industria mineraria

miniskirt ['mɪnɪskəːt] *n* minigonna

minister ['mɪnɪstə^r] *n* (*BRIT Pol*) ministro; (*Rel*) pastore *m*

ministry ['mɪnɪstrɪ] *n* ministero

minor ['maɪnə^r] *adj* minore, di poca importanza; (*Mus*) minore ▷ *n* (*Law*) minorenne *m/f*

Minorca [mɪ'nɔːkə] *n* Minorca

minority [maɪ'nɔrɪtɪ] *n* minoranza

mint [mɪnt] *n* (*plant*) menta; (*sweet*) pasticca di menta ▷ *vt* (*coins*) battere; **the (Royal) M~** (*BRIT*), **the (US) M~** (*us*) la Zecca; **in ~ condition** come nuovo(-a) di zecca

minus ['maɪnəs] n (also: **~ sign**) segno meno ▷ prep meno

minute [adj maɪ'njuːt, n 'mɪnɪt] adj minuscolo(-a); (detail) minuzioso(-a) ▷ n minuto; **~s** npl (of meeting) verbale m

miracle ['mɪrəkl] n miracolo

miraculous [mɪ'rækjuləs] adj miracoloso(-a)

mirage ['mɪrɑːʒ] n miraggio

mirror ['mɪrə^r] n specchio; (in car) specchietto

misbehave [mɪsbɪ'heɪv] vi comportarsi male

misc. abbr = **miscellaneous**; **miscarriage** ['mɪskærɪdʒ] n (Med) aborto spontaneo; **miscarriage of justice** errore m giudiziario

miscellaneous [mɪsɪ'leɪnɪəs] adj (items) vario(-a); (selection) misto(-a)

mischief ['mɪstʃɪf] n (naughtiness) birichineria; (maliciousness) malizia; **mischievous** adj birichino(-a)

misconception ['mɪskən'sepʃən] n idea sbagliata

misconduct [mɪs'kɔndʌkt] n cattiva condotta; **professional ~** reato professionale

miser ['maɪzə^r] n avaro

miserable ['mɪzərəbl] adj infelice; (wretched) miserabile; (weather) deprimente; (offer, failure) misero(-a)

misery ['mɪzərɪ] n (unhappiness) tristezza; (wretchedness) miseria

misfortune [mɪs'fɔːtʃən] n sfortuna

misgiving [mɪs'gɪvɪŋ] n apprensione f; **to have ~s about** avere dei dubbi per quanto riguarda

misguided [mɪs'gaɪdɪd] adj sbagliato(-a), poco giudizioso(-a)

mishap ['mɪshæp] n disgrazia

misinterpret [mɪsɪn'təːprɪt] vt interpretare male

misjudge [mɪs'dʒʌdʒ] vt giudicare male

mislay [mɪs'leɪ] (irreg) vt smarrire

mislead [mɪs'liːd] (irreg) vt sviare; **misleading** adj ingannevole

misplace [mɪs'pleɪs] vt smarrire

misprint ['mɪsprɪnt] n errore m di stampa

misrepresent [mɪsreprɪ'zɛnt] vt travisare

Miss [mɪs] n Signorina

miss [mɪs] vt (fail to get) perdere; (fail to hit) mancare; (fail to see): **you can't ~ it** non puoi non vederlo; (regret the absence of): **I ~ him** sento la sua mancanza ▷ vi mancare ▷ n (shot) colpo mancato; **we ~ed our train** abbiamo perso il treno; **miss out** (BRIT) vt omettere; **miss out on**

vt fus (fun, party) perdersi; (chance, bargain) lasciarsi sfuggire

missile ['mɪsaɪl] n (Mil) missile m; (object thrown) proiettile m

missing ['mɪsɪŋ] adj perso(-a), smarrito(-a); (person) scomparso(-a); (: after disaster, Mil) disperso(-a); (removed) mancante; **to be ~** mancare

mission ['mɪʃən] n missione f; **missionary** n missionario(-a)

misspell [mɪs'spɛl] vt (irreg: like **spell**) sbagliare l'ortografia di

mist [mɪst] n nebbia, foschia ▷ vi (also: **~ over, ~ up**) annebbiarsi; (: BRIT: windows) appannarsi

mistake [mɪs'teɪk] (irreg: like **take**) n sbaglio, errore m ▷ vt sbagliarsi di; fraintendere; **to make a ~** fare uno sbaglio, sbagliare; **there must be some ~** ci dev'essere un errore; **by ~** per sbaglio; **to ~ for** prendere per; **mistaken** pp of **mistake** ▷ adj (idea etc) sbagliato(-a); **to be mistaken** sbagliarsi

mister ['mɪstə^r] (inf) n signore m; see **Mr**

mistletoe ['mɪsltəu] n vischio

mistook [mɪs'tuk] pt of **mistake**

mistress ['mɪstrɪs] n padrona; (lover) amante f; (BRIT Scol) insegnante f

mistrust [mɪs'trʌst] vt diffidare di

misty ['mɪstɪ] adj nebbioso(-a), brumoso(-a)

misunderstand [mɪsʌndə'stænd] (irreg) vt, vi capire male, fraintendere; **misunderstanding** n malinteso, equivoco; **there's been a misunderstanding** c'è stato un malinteso

misunderstood [mɪsʌndə'stud] pt, pp of **misunderstand**

misuse [n mɪs'juːs, vb mɪs'juːz] n cattivo uso; (of power) abuso ▷ vt far cattivo uso di; abusare di

mitt(en) ['mɪt(n)] n mezzo guanto; manopola

mix [mɪks] vt mescolare ▷ vi (people): **to ~ with** avere a che fare con ▷ n mescolanza; preparato; **mix up** vt mescolare; (confuse) confondere; **mixed** adj misto(-a); **mixed grill** n (BRIT) misto alla griglia; **mixed salad** n insalata mista; **mixed-up** adj (confused) confuso(-a); **mixer** n (for food: electric) frullatore m; (: hand) frullino; (person): **he is a good mixer** è molto socievole; **mixture** n mescolanza; (blend: of tobacco etc) miscela; (Med) sciroppo; **mix-up** n confusione f

ml abbr (= millilitre(s)) ml

mm abbr (= millimetre) mm

moan [məun] n gemito ▷ vi (inf: complain): **to ~ (about)** lamentarsi (di)

moat [məut] n fossato

mob [mɔb] n calca ▷ vt accalcarsi intorno a

mobile ['məubaɪl] adj mobile ▷ n (decoration) mobile m; **mobile home** n grande roulotte f inv (utilizzata come domicilio); **mobile phone** n telefono portatile, telefonino

mobility [məu'bɪlɪtɪ] n mobilità; (of applicant) disponibilità a viaggiare

mobilize ['məubɪlaɪz] vt mobilitare ▷ vi mobilitarsi

mock [mɔk] vt deridere, burlarsi di ▷ adj falso(-a); **~s** npl (BRIT: Scol: inf) simulazione f degli esami; **mockery** n derisione f; **to make a mockery of** burlarsi di; (exam) rendere una farsa

mod cons ['mɔd'kɔnz] npl abbr (BRIT) = **modern conveniences**; see **convenience**

mode [məud] n modo

model ['mɔdl] n modello; (person: for fashion) indossatore(-trice); (: for artist) modello(-a) ▷ adj (small-scale: railway etc) in miniatura; (child, factory) modello inv ▷ vt modellare ▷ vi fare l'indossatore (or l'indossatrice); **to ~ clothes** presentare degli abiti

modem ['məudɛm] n modem m inv

moderate [adj 'mɔdərət, vb 'mɔdəreɪt] adj moderato(-a) ▷ vi moderarsi, placarsi ▷ vt moderare

moderation [mɔdə'reɪʃən] n moderazione f, misura; **in ~** in quantità moderata, con moderazione

modern ['mɔdən] adj moderno(-a); **mod cons** comodità fpl moderne; **modernize** vt modernizzare; **modern languages** npl lingue fpl moderne

modest ['mɔdɪst] adj modesto(-a); **modesty** n modestia

modification [mɔdɪfɪ'keɪʃən] n modificazione f; **to make ~s** fare or apportare delle modifiche

modify ['mɔdɪfaɪ] vt modificare

module ['mɔdjuːl] n modulo

mohair ['məuhɛər] n mohair m

Mohammed [məu'hæmɪd] n Maometto

moist [mɔɪst] adj umido(-a); **moisture** ['mɔɪstʃər] n umidità; (on glass) goccioline fpl di vapore; **moisturizer** ['mɔɪstʃəraɪzər] n idratante f

mold etc [məuld] (US) n, vt = **mould**

mole [məul] n (animal, fig) talpa; (spot) neo

molecule ['mɔlɪkjuːl] n molecola

molest [məu'lɛst] vt molestare

molten ['məultən] adj fuso(-a)

mom [mɔm] (US) n = **mum**

moment ['məumənt] n momento, istante m; **at that ~** in quel momento; **at the ~** al momento, in questo momento; **momentarily** ['məumərtərɪlɪ] adv per un momento; (US: very soon) da un momento all'altro; **momentary** adj momentaneo(-a), passeggero(-a); **momentous** [-'mɛntəs] adj di grande importanza

momentum [məu'mɛntəm] n (Physics) momento; (fig) impeto; **to gather ~** aumentare di velocità

mommy ['mɔmɪ] (US) n = **mummy**

Mon. abbr (= Monday) lun.

Monaco ['mɔnəkəu] n Principato di Monaco

monarch ['mɔnək] n monarca m; **monarchy** n monarchia

monastery ['mɔnəstərɪ] n monastero

Monday ['mʌndɪ] n lunedì m inv

monetary ['mʌnɪtərɪ] adj monetario(-a)

money ['mʌnɪ] n denaro, soldi mpl; **I haven't got any ~** non ho soldi; **money belt** n marsupio (per soldi); **money order** n vaglia m inv

mongrel ['mʌŋgrəl] n (dog) cane m bastardo

monitor ['mɔnɪtər] n (TV, Comput) monitor m inv ▷ vt controllare

monk [mʌŋk] n monaco

monkey ['mʌŋkɪ] n scimmia

monologue ['mɔnəlɔg] n monologo

monopoly [mə'nɔpəlɪ] n monopolio

monosodium glutamate [mɔnə'səudɪəm'gluːtəmeɪt] n glutammato di sodio

monotonous [mə'nɔtənəs] adj monotono(-a)

monsoon [mɔn'suːn] n monsone m

monster ['mɔnstər] n mostro

month [mʌnθ] n mese m; **monthly** adj mensile ▷ adv al mese; ogni mese

monument ['mɔnjumənt] n monumento

mood [muːd] n umore m; **to be in a good/ bad ~** essere di buon/cattivo umore; **moody** adj (variable) capriccioso(-a), lunatico(-a); (sullen) imbronciato(-a)

moon [muːn] n luna; **moonlight** n chiaro di luna

moor [muər] n brughiera ▷ vt (ship) ormeggiare ▷ vi ormeggiarsi

moose [muːs] n inv alce m

mop [mɔp] n lavapavimenti m inv; (also: ~ of hair) zazzera ▷ vt lavare con lo straccio; (face) asciugare; **mop up** vt asciugare con uno straccio

mope [məup] vi fare il broncio

moped ['məupɛd] n (BRIT) ciclomotore m

moral ['mɔrl] adj morale ▷ n morale f; **~s** npl (principles) moralità

morale [mɔ'rɑːl] n morale m

morality [mə'rælɪtɪ] n moralità
morbid ['mɔːbɪd] adj morboso(-a)

 KEYWORD

more [mɔːʳ] adj 1 (greater in number etc) più; **more people/letters than we expected** più persone/lettere di quante ne aspettavamo; **I have more wine/money than you** ho più vino/soldi di te; **I have more wine than beer** ho più vino che birra

2 (additional) altro(-a), ancora; **do you want (some) more tea?** vuole dell'altro tè?, vuole ancora del tè?; **I have no** or **I don't have any more money** non ho più soldi

▷ pron 1 (greater amount) più; **more than 10** più di 10; **it cost more than we expected** ha costato più di quanto ci aspettavamo

2 (further or additional amount) ancora; **is there any more?** ce n'è ancora?; **there's no more** non ce n'è più; **a little more** ancora un po'; **many/much more** molti(-e)/molto(-a) di più

▷ adv **more dangerous/easily (than)** più pericoloso/facilmente (di); **more and more** sempre più; **more and more difficult** sempre più difficile; **more or less** più o meno; **more than ever** più che mai

moreover [mɔːˈrəuvəʳ] adv inoltre, di più
morgue [mɔːg] n obitorio
morning ['mɔːnɪŋ] n mattina, mattino; (duration) mattinata ▷ cpd del mattino; **in the ~** la mattina; **7 o'clock in the ~** le 7 di or della mattina; **morning sickness** n nausee fpl mattutine
Moroccan [mə'rɔkən] adj, n marocchino(-a)
Morocco [mə'rɔkəu] n Marocco
moron ['mɔːrɔn] (inf) n deficiente m/f
morphine ['mɔːfiːn] n morfina
morris dancing n vedi nota nel riquadro

● MORRIS DANCING
●
● Il **morris dancing** è una danza
● folcloristica inglese tradizionalmente
● riservata agli uomini. Vestiti di bianco
● e con dei campanelli attaccati alle
● caviglie, i ballerini eseguono una danza
● tenendo in mano dei fazzoletti bianchi
● e lunghi bastoni. Questa danza è molto
● popolare nelle feste paesane.

Morse [mɔːs] n (also: ~ code) alfabeto Morse
mortal ['mɔːtl] adj mortale ▷ n mortale m

mortar ['mɔːtəʳ] n (Constr) malta; (dish) mortaio
mortgage ['mɔːgɪdʒ] n ipoteca; (loan) prestito ipotecario ▷ vt ipotecare
mortician [mɔːˈtɪʃən] (US) n impresario di pompe funebri
mortified ['mɔːtɪfaɪd] adj umiliato(-a)
mortuary ['mɔːtjuərɪ] n camera mortuaria; obitorio
mosaic [məu'zeɪɪk] n mosaico
Moscow ['mɔskəu] n Mosca
Moslem ['mɔzləm] adj, n = Muslim
mosque [mɔsk] n moschea
mosquito [mɔs'kiːtəu] (pl mosquitoes) n zanzara
moss [mɔs] n muschio
most [məust] adj (almost all) la maggior parte di; (largest, greatest): **who has (the) ~ money?** chi ha più soldi di tutti? ▷ pron la maggior parte ▷ adv più; (work, sleep etc) di più; (very) estremamente; **the ~ (also: + adjective)** il(-la) più; **~ of** la maggior parte di; **~ of them** quasi tutti; **I saw (the) ~** ho visto più io; **at the (very) ~** al massimo; **to make the ~ of** trarre il massimo vantaggio da; **a ~ interesting book** un libro estremamente interessante; **mostly** adv per lo più
MOT (BRIT) n abbr = **Ministry of Transport; the ~ (test)** revisione annuale obbligatoria degli autoveicoli
motel [məu'tɛl] n motel m inv
moth [mɔθ] n farfalla notturna; tarma
mother ['mʌðəʳ] n madre f ▷ vt (care for) fare da madre a; **motherhood** n maternità; **mother-in-law** n suocera; **mother-of-pearl** [mʌðərəv'pəːl] n madreperla; **Mother's Day** n la festa della mamma; **mother-to-be** [mʌðətə'biː] n futura mamma; **mother tongue** n madrelingua
motif [məu'tiːf] n motivo
motion ['məuʃən] n movimento, moto; (gesture) gesto; (at meeting) mozione f ▷ vt, vi **to ~ (to) sb to do** fare cenno a qn di fare; **motionless** adj immobile; **motion picture** n film m inv
motivate ['məutɪveɪt] vt (act, decision) dare origine a, motivare; (person) spingere
motivation [məutɪ'veɪʃən] n motivazione f
motive ['məutɪv] n motivo
motor ['məutəʳ] n motore m; (BRIT: inf: vehicle) macchina ▷ cpd automobilistico(-a); **motorbike** n moto f inv; **motorboat** n motoscafo; **motorcar** (BRIT) n automobile f; **motorcycle** n motocicletta; **motorcyclist** n motociclista m/f; **motoring** (BRIT) n

turismo automobilistico; **motorist** n automobilista m/f; **motor racing** (BRIT) n corse fpl automobilistiche; **motorway** (BRIT) n autostrada

motto ['mɔtəu] (pl **mottoes**) n motto

mould [məuld] (US **mold**) n forma, stampo; (mildew) muffa ▷ vt formare; (fig) foggiare; **mouldy** adj ammuffito(-a); (smell) di muffa

mound [maund] n rialzo, collinetta; (heap) mucchio

mount [maunt] n (Geo) monte m ▷ vt montare; (horse) montare a ▷ vi (increase) aumentare; **mount up** vi (build up) accumularsi

mountain ['mauntɪn] n montagna ▷ cpd di montagna; **mountain bike** n mountain bike f inv; **mountaineer** [-'nɪəʳ] n alpinista m/f; **mountaineering** [-'nɪərɪŋ] n alpinismo; **mountainous** adj montagnoso(-a); **mountain range** n catena montuosa

mourn [mɔːn] vt piangere, lamentare ▷ vi **to ~ (for sb)** piangere (la morte di qn); **mourner** n parente m/f or amico(-a) del defunto; **mourning** n lutto; **in mourning** in lutto

mouse [maus] (pl **mice**) n topo; (Comput) mouse m inv; **mouse mat**, **mouse pad** n (Comput) tappetino del mouse

moussaka [mu'saːkə] n moussaka

mousse [muːs] n mousse f inv

moustache [məs'taːʃ] (US **mustache**) n baffi mpl

mouth [mauθ, pl mauðz] n bocca; (of river) foce f; (opening) orifizio; **mouthful** n boccata; **mouth organ** n armonica; **mouthpiece** n (Mus) imboccatura, bocchino; (spokesman) portavoce m/f inv; **mouthwash** n collutorio

move [muːv] n (movement) movimento; (in game) mossa; (: turn to play) turno; (change: of house) trasloco; (: of job) cambiamento ▷ vt muovere; (change position of) spostare; (emotionally) commuovere; (Pol: resolution etc) proporre ▷ vi (gen) muoversi, spostarsi; (also: **~ house**) cambiar casa, traslocare; **to get a ~ on** affrettarsi, sbrigarsi; **can you ~ your car, please?** può spostare la macchina, per favore?; **to ~ sb to do sth** indurre or spingere qn a fare qc; **to ~ towards** andare verso; **move back** vi (return) ritornare; **move in** vi (to a house) entrare (in una nuova casa); (police etc) intervenire; **move off** vi partire; **move on** vi riprendere la strada; **move out** vi (of house) sgombrare; **move over** vi spostarsi; **move up** vi avanzare; **movement** ['muːvmənt] n (gen)

movimento; (gesture) gesto; (of stars, water, physical) moto

movie ['muːvɪ] n film m inv; **the ~s** il cinema; **movie theater** (US) n cinema m inv

moving ['muːvɪŋ] adj mobile; (causing emotion) commovente

mow [məu] (pt **mowed**, pp **mowed** or **mown**) vt (grass) tagliare; (corn) mietere; **mower** n (also: **lawnmower**) tagliaerba m inv

Mozambique [məuzæm'biːk] n Mozambico

MP n abbr = **Member of Parliament**

MP3 n abbr M3; **MP3 player** n lettore m MP3

mpg n abbr = **miles per gallon** (30 mpg = 9.4 l. per 100 km)

m.p.h. n abbr = **miles per hour** (60 m.p.h = 96 km/h)

Mr ['mɪstəʳ] (US **Mr.**) n **Mr X** Signor X, Sig. X

Mrs ['mɪsɪz] (US **Mrs.**) n **Mrs X** Signora X, Sig.ra X

Ms [mɪz] (US **Ms.**) n = **Miss or Mrs**; **Ms X** ≈ Signora X, ≈ Sig.ra X

- **Ms**
-
- In inglese si usa **Ms** al posto di "Mrs"
- (Signora) o "Miss" (Signorina) per evitare
- la distinzione tradizionale tra le donne
- sposate e quelle nubili.

MSP n abbr = **Member of the Scottish Parliament**

Mt abbr (Geo: = mount) M.

◯ KEYWORD

much [mʌtʃ] adj, pron molto(-a); **he's done so much work** ha lavorato così tanto; **I have as much money as you** ho tanti soldi quanti ne hai tu; **how much is it?** quant'è?; **it costs too much** costa troppo; **as much as you want** quanto vuoi ▷ adv **1** (greatly) molto, tanto; **thank you very much** molte grazie; **he's very much the gentleman** è il vero gentiluomo; **I read as much as I can** leggo quanto posso; **as much as you** tanto quanto te **2** (by far) molto; **it's much the biggest company in Europe** è di gran lunga la più grossa società in Europa **3** (almost) grossomodo, praticamente; **they're much the same** sono praticamente uguali

muck [mʌk] n (dirt) sporcizia; **muck up** (inf) vt (ruin) rovinare; **mucky** adj (dirty) sporco(-a), lordo(-a)

mucus ['mju:kəs] n muco

mud [mʌd] n fango

muddle ['mʌdl] n confusione f, disordine m; pasticcio ▷ vt (also: ~ **up**) confondere

muddy ['mʌdɪ] adj fangoso(-a)

mudguard ['mʌdɡɑːd] n parafango

muesli ['mju:zlɪ] n muesli m

muffin ['mʌfɪn] n specie di pasticcino soffice da tè

muffled ['mʌfld] adj smorzato(-a), attutito(-a)

muffler ['mʌflər] (US) n (Aut) marmitta; (: on motorbike) silenziatore m

mug [mʌɡ] n (cup) tazzone m; (for beer) boccale m; (inf: face) muso; (: fool) scemo(-a) ▷ vt (assault) assalire; **mugger** ['mʌɡər] n aggressore m; **mugging** n assalto

muggy ['mʌɡɪ] adj afoso(-a)

mule [mju:l] n mulo

multicoloured ['mʌltɪkʌləd] (US **multicolored**) adj multicolore, variopinto(-a)

multimedia ['mʌltɪ'mi:dɪə] adj multimedia inv

multinational [mʌltɪ'næʃənl] adj, n multinazionale (f)

multiple ['mʌltɪpl] adj multiplo(-a), molteplice ▷ n multiplo; **multiple choice (test)** n esercizi mpl a scelta multipla; **multiple sclerosis** [-sklɪ'rəusɪs] n sclerosi f a placche

multiplex cinema ['mʌltɪplɛks-] n cinema m inv multisala inv

multiplication [mʌltɪplɪ'keɪʃən] n moltiplicazione f

multiply ['mʌltɪplaɪ] vt moltiplicare ▷ vi moltiplicarsi

multistorey ['mʌltɪ'stɔːrɪ] (BRIT) adj (building, car park) a più piani

mum [mʌm] (BRIT: inf) n mamma ▷ adj **to keep ~** non aprire bocca

mumble ['mʌmbl] vt, vi borbottare

mummy ['mʌmɪ] n (BRIT: mother) mamma; (embalmed) mummia

mumps [mʌmps] n orecchioni mpl

munch [mʌntʃ] vt, vi sgranocchiare

municipal [mju:'nɪsɪpl] adj municipale

mural ['mjuərl] n dipinto murale

murder ['məːdər] n assassinio, omicidio ▷ vt assassinare; **murderer** n omicida m, assassino

murky ['məːkɪ] adj tenebroso(-a)

murmur ['məːmər] n mormorio ▷ vt, vi mormorare

muscle ['mʌsl] n muscolo; (fig) forza; **muscular** ['mʌskjulər] adj muscolare; (person, arm) muscoloso(-a)

museum [mju:'zɪəm] n museo

mushroom ['mʌʃrum] n fungo ▷ vi crescere in fretta

music ['mju:zɪk] n musica; **musical** adj musicale; (person) portato(-a) per la musica ▷ n (show) commedia musicale; **musical instrument** n strumento musicale; **musician** [-'zɪʃən] n musicista m/f

Muslim ['mʌzlɪm] adj, n musulmano(-a)

muslin ['mʌzlɪn] n mussola

mussel ['mʌsl] n cozza

must [mʌst] aux vb (obligation): **I ~ do it** devo farlo; (probability): **he ~ be there by now** dovrebbe essere arrivato ormai; **I ~ have made a mistake** devo essermi sbagliato ▷ n **it's a ~** è d'obbligo

mustache ['mʌstæʃ] (US) n = **moustache**

mustard ['mʌstəd] n senape f, mostarda

mustn't ['mʌsnt] = **must not**

mute [mju:t] adj, n muto(-a)

mutilate ['mju:tɪleɪt] vt mutilare

mutiny ['mju:tɪnɪ] n ammutinamento

mutter ['mʌtər] vt, vi borbottare, brontolare

mutton ['mʌtn] n carne f di montone

mutual ['mju:tʃuəl] adj mutuo(-a), reciproco(-a)

muzzle ['mʌzl] n muso; (protective device) museruola; (of gun) bocca ▷ vt mettere la museruola a

my [maɪ] adj il (la) mio(-a); (pl) i (le) miei (mie); **my house** la mia casa; **my books** i miei libri; **my brother** mio fratello; **I've washed my hair/cut my finger** mi sono lavato i capelli/tagliato il dito

myself [maɪ'sɛlf] pron (reflexive) mi; (emphatic) io stesso(-a); (after prep) me; see also **oneself**

mysterious [mɪs'tɪərɪəs] adj misterioso(-a)

mystery ['mɪstərɪ] n mistero

mystical ['mɪstɪkəl] adj mistico(-a)

mystify ['mɪstɪfaɪ] vt mistificare; (puzzle) confondere

myth [mɪθ] n mito; **mythology** [mɪ'θɔlədʒɪ] n mitologia

n/a *abbr* = **not applicable**
nag [næg] *vt* tormentare ▷ *vi* brontolare in continuazione
nail [neɪl] *n* (*human*) unghia; (*metal*) chiodo ▷ *vt* inchiodare; **to ~ sb down to (doing) sth** costringere qn a (fare) qc; **nailbrush** *n* spazzolino da *or* per unghie; **nailfile** *n* lima da *or* per unghie; **nail polish** *n* smalto da *or* per unghie; **nail polish remover** *n* acetone *m*, solvente *m*; **nail scissors** *npl* forbici *fpl* da *or* per unghie; **nail varnish** (BRIT) *n* = **nail polish**
naïve [naɪˈiːv] *adj* ingenuo(-a)
naked [ˈneɪkɪd] *adj* nudo(-a)
name [neɪm] *n* nome *m*; (*reputation*) nome, reputazione *f* ▷ *vt* (*baby etc*) chiamare; (*plant, illness*) nominare; (*person, object*) identificare; (*price, date*) fissare; **what's your ~?** come si chiama?; **by ~** di nome; **she knows them all by ~** li conosce tutti per nome; **namely** *adv* cioè
nanny [ˈnænɪ] *n* bambinaia
nap [næp] *n* (*sleep*) pisolino; (*of cloth*) peluria; **to be caught ~ping** essere preso alla sprovvista
napkin [ˈnæpkɪn] *n* (*also*: **table ~**) tovagliolo
nappy [ˈnæpɪ] (BRIT) *n* pannolino
narcotics [nɑːˈkɔtɪkz] *npl* (*drugs*) narcotici, stupefacenti *mpl*

narrative [ˈnærətɪv] *n* narrativa
narrator [nəˈreɪtəʳ] *n* narratore(-trice)
narrow [ˈnærəu] *adj* stretto(-a); (*fig*) limitato(-a), ristretto(-a) ▷ *vi* restringersi; **to have a ~ escape** farcela per un pelo; **narrow down** *vt* (*search, investigation, possibilities*) restringere; (*list*) ridurre; **narrowly** *adv* per un pelo; (*time*) per poco; **narrow-minded** *adj* meschino(-a)
nasal [ˈneɪzl] *adj* nasale
nasty [ˈnɑːstɪ] *adj* (*person, remark: unpleasant*) cattivo(-a); (: *rude*) villano(-a); (*smell, wound, situation*) brutto(-a)
nation [ˈneɪʃən] *n* nazione *f*
national [ˈnæʃənl] *adj* nazionale ▷ *n* cittadino(-a); **national anthem** *n* inno nazionale; **national dress** *n* costume *m* nazionale; **National Health Service** (BRIT) *n* servizio nazionale di assistenza sanitaria, ≈ S.S.N. *m*; **National Insurance** (BRIT) *n* ≈ Previdenza Sociale; **Nationalist** *adj, n* nazionalista (*m/f*); **nationality** [-ˈnælɪtɪ] *n* nazionalità *f inv*; **nationalize** *vt* nazionalizzare; **national park** *n* parco nazionale; **National Trust** *n* sovrintendenza ai beni culturali e ambientali

● **NATIONAL TRUST**
●
● Fondato nel 1895, il **National Trust** è
● un'organizzazione che si occupa della
● tutela e della salvaguardia di luoghi
● di interesse storico o ambientale nel
● Regno Unito.

nationwide [ˈneɪʃənwaɪd] *adj* diffuso(-a) in tutto il paese ▷ *adv* in tutto il paese
native [ˈneɪtɪv] *n* abitante *m/f* del paese ▷ *adj* indigeno(-a); (*country*) natio(-a); (*ability*) innato(-a); **a ~ of Russia** un nativo della Russia; **a ~ speaker of French** una persona di madrelingua francese; **Native American** *n* discendente di tribù dell'America settentrionale
NATO [ˈneɪtəu] *n abbr* (= *North Atlantic Treaty Organization*) N.A.T.O. *f*
natural [ˈnætʃrəl] *adj* naturale; (*ability*) innato(-a); (*manner*) semplice; **natural gas** *n* gas *m* metano; **natural history** *n* storia naturale; **naturally** *adv* naturalmente; (*by nature: gifted*) di natura; **natural resources** *npl* risorse *fpl* naturali
nature [ˈneɪtʃəʳ] *n* natura; (*character*) natura, indole *f*; **by ~** di natura; **nature reserve** *n* (BRIT) parco naturale
naughty [ˈnɔːtɪ] *adj* (*child*) birichino(-a), cattivello(-a); (*story, film*) spinto(-a)
nausea [ˈnɔːsɪə] *n* (*Med*) nausea; (*fig: disgust*) schifo

naval ['neɪvl] *adj* navale

navel ['neɪvl] *n* ombelico

navigate ['nævɪgeɪt] *vt* percorrere navigando ▷ *vi* navigare; (*Aut*) fare da navigatore; **navigation** [-'geɪʃən] *n* navigazione *f*

navy ['neɪvɪ] *n* marina

Nazi ['nɑːtsɪ] *n* nazista *m/f*

NB *abbr* (= *nota bene*) N.B.

near [nɪəʳ] *adj* vicino(-a); (*relation*) prossimo(-a) ▷ *adv* vicino ▷ *prep* (*also:* **~ to**) vicino a, presso; (: *time*) verso ▷ *vt* avvicinarsi a; **nearby** [nɪə'baɪ] *adj* vicino(-a) ▷ *adv* vicino; **is there a bank nearby?** c'è una banca qui vicino?; **nearly** *adv* quasi; **I nearly fell** per poco non sono caduto; **near-sighted** [nɪə'saɪtɪd] *adj* miope

neat [niːt] *adj* (*person, room*) ordinato(-a); (*work*) pulito(-a); (*solution, plan*) ben indovinato(-a), azzeccato(-a); (*spirits*) liscio(-a); **neatly** *adv* con ordine; (*skilfully*) abilmente

necessarily ['nɛsɪsrɪlɪ] *adv* necessariamente

necessary ['nɛsɪsrɪ] *adj* necessario(-a)

necessity [nɪ'sɛsɪtɪ] *n* necessità *f inv*

neck [nɛk] *n* collo; (*of garment*) colletto ▷ *vi* (*inf*) pomiciare, sbaciucchiarsi; **~ and ~** testa a testa; **necklace** ['nɛklɪs] *n* collana; **necktie** ['nɛktaɪ] *n* cravatta

nectarine ['nɛktərɪn] *n* nocepesca

need [niːd] *n* bisogno ▷ *vt* aver bisogno di; **do you ~ anything?** ha bisogno di qualcosa?; **to ~ to do** dover fare; aver bisogno di fare; **you don't ~ to go** non devi andare, non c'è bisogno che tu vada

needle ['niːdl] *n* ago; (*on record player*) puntina ▷ *vt* punzecchiare

needless ['niːdlɪs] *adj* inutile

needlework ['niːdlwəːk] *n* cucito

needn't ['niːdnt] = **need not**

needy ['niːdɪ] *adj* bisognoso(-a)

negative ['nɛgətɪv] *n* (*Ling*) negazione *f*; (*Phot*) negativo ▷ *adj* negativo(-a)

neglect [nɪ'glɛkt] *vt* trascurare ▷ *n* (*of person, duty*) negligenza; (*of child, house etc*) scarsa cura; **state of ~** stato di abbandono

negotiate [nɪ'gəuʃɪeɪt] *vi* **to ~ (with)** negoziare (con) ▷ *vt* (*Comm*) negoziare; (*obstacle*) superare; **negotiations** [nɪgəuʃɪ'eɪʃənz] *pl n* trattative *fpl*, negoziati *mpl*

negotiator [nɪ'gəuʃɪeɪtəʳ] *n* negoziatore(-trice)

neighbour ['neɪbəʳ] (*us* **neighbor**) *n* vicino(-a); **neighbourhood** *n* vicinato; **neighbouring** *adj* vicino(-a)

neither ['naɪðəʳ] *adj, pron* né l'uno(-a) né l'altro(-a), nessuno(-a) dei (delle) due ▷ *conj* neanche, nemmeno, neppure ▷ *adv* **~ good nor bad** né buono né cattivo; **I didn't move and ~ did Claude** io non mi mossi e nemmeno Claude; **..., ~ did I refuse** ..., ma non ho nemmeno rifiutato

neon ['niːɔn] *n* neon *m*

Nepal [nɪ'pɔːl] *n* Nepal *m*

nephew ['nɛvjuː] *n* nipote *m*

nerve [nəːv] *n* nervo; (*fig*) coraggio; (*impudence*) faccia tosta; **~s** (*nervousness*) nervoso; **a fit of ~s** una crisi di nervi

nervous ['nəːvəs] *adj* nervoso(-a); (*anxious*) agitato(-a), in apprensione; **nervous breakdown** *n* esaurimento nervoso

nest [nɛst] *n* nido ▷ *vi* fare il nido, nidificare

net [nɛt] *n* rete *f* ▷ *adj* netto(-a) ▷ *vt* (*fish etc*) prendere con la rete; (*profit*) ricavare un utile netto di; **the N~** (*Internet*) Internet *f*; **netball** *n* specie di pallacanestro

Netherlands ['nɛðələndz] *npl* **the ~** i Paesi Bassi

nett [nɛt] *adj* = **net**

nettle ['nɛtl] *n* ortica

network ['nɛtwəːk] *n* rete *f*

neurotic [njuə'rɔtɪk] *adj, n* nevrotico(-a)

neuter ['njuːtəʳ] *adj* neutro(-a) ▷ *vt* (*cat etc*) castrare

neutral ['njuːtrəl] *adj* neutro(-a); (*person, nation*) neutrale ▷ *n* (*Aut*): **in ~** in folle

never ['nɛvəʳ] *adv* (non...) mai; **I've ~ been to Spain** non sono mai stato in Spagna; **~ again** mai più; **I'll ~ go there again** non ci vado più; **~ in my life** mai in vita mia; *see also* **mind**; **never-ending** *adj* interminabile; **nevertheless** [nɛvəðə'lɛs] *adv* tuttavia, ciò nonostante, ciò nondimeno

new [njuː] *adj* nuovo(-a); (*brand new*) nuovo(-a) di zecca; **New Age** *n* New Age *f inv*; **newborn** *adj* neonato(-a); **newcomer** ['njuːkʌməʳ] *n* nuovo(-a) venuto(-a); **newly** *adv* di recente

news [njuːz] *n* notizie *fpl*; (*Radio*) giornale *m* radio; (*TV*) telegiornale *m*; **a piece of ~** una notizia; **news agency** *n* agenzia di stampa; **newsagent** (*BRIT*) *n* giornalaio; **newscaster** *n* (*Radio, TV*) annunciatore(-trice); **news dealer** (*US*) *n* = **newsagent**; **newsletter** *n* bollettino; **newspaper** *n* giornale *m*; **newsreader** *n* = **newscaster**

newt [njuːt] *n* tritone *m*

New Year *n* Anno Nuovo; **New Year's Day** *n* il Capodanno; **New Year's Eve** *n* la vigilia di Capodanno

New York [-'jɔ:k] n New York f

New Zealand [-'zi:lənd] n Nuova Zelanda; **New Zealander** n neozelandese m/f

next [nɛkst] adj prossimo(-a) ▷ adv accanto; (in time) dopo; **the ~ day** il giorno dopo, l'indomani; **~ time** la prossima volta; **~ year** l'anno prossimo; **when do we meet ~?** quando ci rincontriamo?; **~ to** accanto a; **~ to nothing** quasi niente; **~ please!** (avanti) il prossimo!; **next door** adv, adj accanto inv; **next-of-kin** n parente m/f prossimo(-a)

NHS n abbr = **National Health Service**

nibble ['nɪbl] vt mordicchiare

nice [naɪs] adj (holiday, trip) piacevole; (flat, picture) bello(-a); (person) simpatico(-a), gentile; **nicely** adv bene

niche [ni:ʃ] n (Archit) nicchia

nick [nɪk] n taglietto; tacca ▷ vt (inf) rubare; **in the ~ of time** appena in tempo

nickel ['nɪkl] n nichel m; (us) moneta da cinque centesimi di dollaro

nickname ['nɪkneɪm] n soprannome m

nicotine ['nɪkəti:n] n nicotina

niece [ni:s] n nipote f

Nigeria [naɪ'dʒɪərɪə] n Nigeria

night [naɪt] n notte f; (evening) sera; **at ~** la sera; **by ~** di notte; **the ~ before last** l'altro ieri notte (or sera); **night club** n locale m notturno; **nightdress** n camicia da notte; **nightie** ['naɪtɪ] n = **nightdress**; **nightlife** ['naɪtlaɪf] n vita notturna; **nightly** ['naɪtlɪ] adj di ogni notte or sera; (by night) notturno(-a) ▷ adv ogni notte or sera; **nightmare** ['naɪtmɛəʳ] n incubo

night: **night school** n scuola serale; **night shift** n turno di notte; **night-time** n notte f

nil [nɪl] n nulla m; (BRIT Sport) zero

nine [naɪn] num nove; **nineteen** num diciannove; **nineteenth** [naɪn'ti:nθ] num diciannovesimo(-a); **ninetieth** ['naɪntɪɪθ] num novantesimo(-a); **ninety** num novanta; **ninth** [naɪnθ] num nono(-a)

nip [nɪp] vt pizzicare; (bite) mordere

nipple ['nɪpl] n (Anat) capezzolo

nitrogen ['naɪtrədʒən] n azoto

 KEYWORD

no [nəu] (pl **noes**) adv (opposite of "yes") no; **are you coming? — no (I'm not)** viene? — no (non vengo); **would you like some more? — no thank you** ne vuole ancora un po'? — no, grazie
▷ adj (not any) nessuno(-a); **I have no money/time/books** non ho soldi/

tempo/libri; **no student would have done it** nessuno studente lo avrebbe fatto; **"no parking"** "divieto di sosta"; **"no smoking"** "vietato fumare"
▷ n no m inv

nobility [nəu'bɪlɪtɪ] n nobiltà

noble ['nəubl] adj nobile

nobody ['nəubədɪ] pron nessuno

nod [nɔd] vi accennare col capo, fare un cenno; (in agreement) annuire con un cenno del capo; (sleep) sonnecchiare ▷ vt **to ~ one's head** fare di sì col capo ▷ n cenno; **nod off** vi assopirsi

noise [nɔɪz] n rumore m; (din, racket) chiasso; **I can't sleep for the ~** non riesco a dormire a causa del rumore; **noisy** adj (street, car) rumoroso(-a); (person) chiassoso(-a)

nominal ['nɔmɪnl] adj nominale; (rent) simbolico(-a)

nominate ['nɔmɪneɪt] vt (propose) proporre come candidato; (elect) nominare; **nomination** [nɔmɪ'neɪʃən] n nomina; candidatura; **nominee** [nɔmɪ'ni:] n persona nominata, candidato(-a)

none [nʌn] pron (not one thing) niente; (not one person) nessuno(-a); **~ of you** nessuno(-a) di voi; **I've ~ left** non ne ho più; **he's ~ the worse for it** non ne ha risentito

nonetheless [nʌnðə'lɛs] adv nondimeno

non-fiction [nɔn'fɪkʃən] n saggistica

nonsense ['nɔnsəns] n sciocchezze fpl

non: **non-smoker** n non fumatore(-trice); **non-smoking** adj (person) che non fuma; (area, section) per non fumatori; **non-stick** adj antiaderente, antiadesivo(-a)

noodles ['nu:dlz] npl taglierini mpl

noon [nu:n] n mezzogiorno

no-one ['nəuwʌn] pron = **nobody**

nor [nɔ:ʳ] conj = **neither** ▷ adv see **neither**

norm [nɔ:m] n norma

normal ['nɔ:ml] adj normale; **normally** adv normalmente

north [nɔ:θ] n nord m, settentrione m ▷ adj nord inv, del nord, settentrionale ▷ adv verso nord; **North America** n America del Nord; **North American** adj, n nordamericano(-a); **northbound** ['nɔ:θbaund] adj (traffic) diretto(-a) a nord; (carriageway) nord inv; **northeast** n nord-est m; **northeastern** adj nordorientale; **northern** ['nɔ:ðən] adj del nord, settentrionale; **Northern Ireland** n Irlanda del Nord; **North Korea** n Corea del Nord; **North Pole** n Polo Nord; **North**

Sea n Mare m del Nord; **north-west** n nord-ovest m; **northwestern** adj nordoccidentale

Norway ['nɔːweɪ] n Norvegia; **Norwegian** [nɔː'wiːdʒən] adj norvegese ▷ n norvegese m/f; (Ling) norvegese m

nose [nəʊz] n naso; (of animal) muso ▷ vi **to ~ about** aggirarsi; **nosebleed** n emorragia nasale; **nosey** (inf) adj = **nosy**

nostalgia [nɔs'tældʒɪə] n nostalgia

nostalgic [nɔs'tældʒɪk] adj nostalgico(-a)

nostril ['nɔstrɪl] n narice f; (of horse) frogia

nosy ['nəʊzɪ] (inf) adj curioso(-a)

not [nɔt] adv non; **he is ~** or **isn't here** non è qui, non c'è; **you must ~** or **you mustn't do that** non devi fare quello; **it's too late, isn't it** or **is it ~?** è troppo tardi, vero?; **~ that I don't like him** non che (lui) non mi piaccia; **~ yet/now** non ancora/ora; see also **all**; **only**

notable ['nəʊtəbl] adj notevole; **notably** ['nəʊtəblɪ] adv (markedly) notevolmente; (particularly) in particolare

notch [nɔtʃ] n tacca; (in saw) dente m

note [nəʊt] n nota; (letter, banknote) biglietto ▷ vt (also: **~ down**) prendere nota di; **to take ~s** prendere appunti; **notebook** n taccuino; **noted** ['nəʊtɪd] adj celebre; **notepad** n bloc-notes m inv; **notepaper** n carta da lettere

nothing ['nʌθɪŋ] n nulla m, niente m; (zero) zero; **he does ~** non fa niente; **~ new/much** etc niente di nuovo/speciale etc; **for ~** per niente

notice ['nəʊtɪs] n avviso; (of leaving) preavviso ▷ vt notare, accorgersi di; **to take ~ of** fare attenzione a; **to bring sth to sb's ~** far notare qc a qn; **at short ~** con un breve preavviso; **until further ~** fino a nuovo avviso; **to hand in one's ~** licenziarsi; **noticeable** adj evidente

notify ['nəʊtɪfaɪ] vt **to ~ sth to sb** far sapere qc a qn; **to ~ sb of sth** avvisare qn di qc

notion ['nəʊʃən] n idea; (concept) nozione f; **~s** npl (US: haberdashery) merceria

notorious [nəʊ'tɔːrɪəs] adj famigerato(-a)

notwithstanding [nɔtwɪθ'stændɪŋ] adv nondimeno ▷ prep nonostante, malgrado

nought [nɔːt] n zero

noun [naʊn] n nome m, sostantivo

nourish ['nʌrɪʃ] vt nutrire; **nourishment** n nutrimento

Nov. abbr (= November) nov.

novel ['nɔvl] n romanzo ▷ adj nuovo(-a); **novelist** n romanziere(-a); **novelty** n novità f inv

November [nəʊ'vɛmbə^r] n novembre m

novice ['nɔvɪs] n principiante m/f; (Rel) novizio(-a)

now [naʊ] adv ora, adesso ▷ conj **~ (that)** adesso che, ora che; **by ~** ormai; **just ~** proprio ora; **right ~** subito, immediatamente; **~ and then, ~ and again** ogni tanto; **from ~ on** da ora in poi; **nowadays** ['naʊədeɪz] adv oggidì

nowhere ['nəʊwɛə^r] adv in nessun luogo, da nessuna parte

nozzle ['nɔzl] n (of hose etc) boccaglio; (of fire extinguisher) lancia

nr abbr (BRIT) = **near**

nuclear ['njuːklɪə^r] adj nucleare

nucleus ['njuːklɪəs] (pl nuclei) n nucleo

nude [njuːd] adj nudo(-a) ▷ n (Art) nudo; **in the ~** tutto(-a) nudo(-a)

nudge [nʌdʒ] vt dare una gomitata a

nudist ['njuːdɪst] n nudista m/f

nudity ['njuːdɪtɪ] n nudità

nuisance ['njuːsns] n **it's a ~** è una seccatura; **he's a ~** è uno scocciatore

numb [nʌm] adj **~ (with)** intorpidito(-a) (da); (with fear) impietrito(-a) (da); **~ with cold** intirizzito(-a) (dal freddo)

number ['nʌmbə^r] n numero ▷ vt numerare; (include) contare; **a ~ of** un certo numero di; **to be ~ed among** venire annoverato(-a) tra; **they were 10 in ~** erano in tutto 10; **number plate** (BRIT) n (Aut) targa; **Number Ten** n (BRIT: = 10 Downing Street) residenza del Primo Ministro del Regno Unito

numerical [njuː'mɛrɪkl] adj numerico(-a)

numerous ['njuːmərəs] adj numeroso(-a)

nun [nʌn] n suora, monaca

nurse [nəːs] n infermiere(-a); (also: **~maid**) bambinaia ▷ vt (patient, cold) curare; (baby: BRIT) cullare; (: US) allattare, dare il latte a

nursery ['nəːsərɪ] n (room) camera dei bambini; (institution) asilo; (for plants) vivaio; **nursery rhyme** n filastrocca; **nursery school** n scuola materna; **nursery slope** (BRIT) n (Ski) pista per principianti

nursing ['nəːsɪŋ] n (profession) professione f di infermiere (or di infermiera); (care) cura; **nursing home** n casa di cura

nurture ['nəːtʃə^r] vt allevare; nutrire

nut [nʌt] n (of metal) dado; (fruit) noce f

nutmeg ['nʌtmɛg] n noce f moscata

nutrient ['njuːtrɪənt] adj nutriente ▷ n sostanza nutritiva

nutrition [njuːˈtrɪʃən] n nutrizione f
nutritious [njuːˈtrɪʃəs] adj nutriente
nuts [nʌts] (inf) adj matto(-a)
NVQ n abbr (BRIT) = **National Vocational Qualification**
nylon [ˈnaɪlɔn] n nailon m ▷ adj di nailon

O

oak [əuk] n quercia ▷ adj di quercia
O.A.P. (BRIT) n, abbr = **old age pensioner**
oar [ɔːʳ] n remo
oasis [əuˈeɪsɪs] (pl **oases**) n oasi f inv
oath [əuθ] n giuramento; (swear word) bestemmia
oatmeal [ˈəutmiːl] n farina d'avena
oats [əuts] npl avena
obedience [əˈbiːdɪəns] n ubbidienza
obedient [əˈbiːdɪənt] adj ubbidiente
obese [əuˈbiːs] adj obeso(-a)
obesity [əuˈbiːsɪtɪ] n obesità
obey [əˈbeɪ] vt ubbidire a; (instructions, regulations) osservare
obituary [əˈbɪtjuərɪ] n necrologia
object [n ˈɔbdʒɪkt, vb əbˈdʒɛkt] n oggetto; (purpose) scopo, intento; (Ling) complemento oggetto ▷ vi **to ~ to** (attitude) disapprovare; (proposal) protestare contro, sollevare delle obiezioni contro; **expense is no ~** non si bada a spese; **to ~ that** obiettare che; **objection** [əbˈdʒɛkʃən] n obiezione f; **objective** n obiettivo
obligation [ɔblɪˈgeɪʃən] n obbligo, dovere m; **without ~** senza impegno
obligatory [əˈblɪɡətərɪ] adj obbligatorio(-a)
oblige [əˈblaɪdʒ] vt (force): **to ~ sb to do** costringere qn a fare; (do a favour) fare una

cortesia a; **to be ~d to sb for sth** essere
grato a qn per qc
oblique [ə'bli:k] *adj* obliquo(-a); (*allusion*)
indiretto(-a)
obliterate [ə'blɪtəreɪt] *vt* cancellare
oblivious [ə'blɪvɪəs] *adj* **~ of** incurante di;
inconscio(-a) di
oblong ['ɔblɔŋ] *adj* oblungo(-a) ▷ *n*
rettangolo
obnoxious [əb'nɔkʃəs] *adj* odioso(-a);
(*smell*) disgustoso(-a), ripugnante
oboe ['əubəu] *n* oboe *m*
obscene [əb'si:n] *adj* osceno(-a)
obscure [əb'skjuər] *adj* oscuro(-a) ▷ *vt*
oscurare; (*hide: sun*) nascondere
observant [əb'zə:vnt] *adj* attento(-a)

> Be careful not to translate **observant**
> by the Italian word **osservante**.

observation [ɔbzə'veɪʃən] *n* osservazione
f; (*by police etc*) sorveglianza
observatory [əb'zə:vətrɪ] *n*
osservatorio
observe [əb'zə:v] *vt* osservare;
(*remark*) fare osservare; **observer** *n*
osservatore(-trice)
obsess [əb'sɛs] *vt* ossessionare; **obsession**
[əb'sɛʃən] *n* ossessione *f*; **obsessive** *adj*
ossessivo(-a)
obsolete ['ɔbsəli:t] *adj* obsoleto(-a)
obstacle ['ɔbstəkl] *n* ostacolo
obstinate ['ɔbstɪnɪt] *adj* ostinato(-a)
obstruct [əb'strʌkt] *vt* (*block*) ostruire,
ostacolare; (*halt*) fermare; (*hinder*)
impedire; **obstruction** [əb'strʌkʃən] *n*
ostruzione *f*; ostacolo
obtain [əb'teɪn] *vt* ottenere
obvious ['ɔbvɪəs] *adj* ovvio(-a), evidente;
obviously *adv* ovviamente; certo
occasion [ə'keɪʒən] *n* occasione *f*;
(*event*) avvenimento; **occasional** *adj*
occasionale; **occasionally** *adv* ogni
tanto
occult [ɔ'kʌlt] *adj* occulto(-a) ▷ *n* **the ~**
l'occulto
occupant ['ɔkjupənt] *n* occupante *m/f*; (*of
boat, car etc*) persona a bordo
occupation [ɔkju'peɪʃən] *n* occupazione *f*;
(*job*) mestiere *m*, professione *f*
occupy ['ɔkjupaɪ] *vt* occupare; **to ~ o.s. in
doing** occuparsi a fare
occur [ə'kə:r] *vi* succedere, capitare; **to ~
to sb** venire in mente a qn; **occurrence** *n*
caso, fatto; presenza

> Be careful not to translate **occur** by
> the Italian word **occorrere**.

ocean ['əuʃən] *n* oceano
o'clock [ə'klɔk] *adv* **it is 5 o'clock** sono le 5
Oct. *abbr* (= *October*) ott.
October [ɔk'təubər] *n* ottobre *m*

octopus ['ɔktəpəs] *n* polpo, piovra
odd [ɔd] *adj* (*strange*) strano(-a),
bizzarro(-a); (*number*) dispari *inv*; (*not of a
set*) spaiato(-a); **60-~** 60 e oltre; **at ~ times**
di tanto in tanto; **the ~ one out** l'eccezione
f; **oddly** *adv* stranamente; **odds** *npl* (*in
betting*) quota
odometer [ɔ'dɔmɪtər] *n* odometro
odour ['əudər] (*US* **odor**) *n* odore *m*;
(*unpleasant*) cattivo odore

 KEYWORD

of [ɔv, əv] *prep* **1** (*gen*) di; **a boy of 10** un
ragazzo di 10 anni; **a friend of ours** un
nostro amico; **that was kind of you** è
stato molto gentile da parte sua
2 (*expressing quantity, amount, dates etc*)
di; **a kilo of flour** un chilo di farina; **how
much of this do you need?** quanto gliene
serve?; **there were 3 of them** (*people*)
erano in 3; (*objects*) ce n'erano 3; **3 of us
went** 3 di noi sono andati; **the 5th of July**
il 5 luglio
3 (*from, out of*) di, in; **of made of wood**
(fatto) di *or* in legno

 KEYWORD

off [ɔf] *adv* **1** (*distance, time*): **it's a long way
off** è lontano; **the game is 3 days off** la
partita è tra 3 giorni
2 (*departure, removal*) via; **to go off to
Paris** andarsene a Parigi; **I must be off**
devo andare via; **to take off one's coat**
togliersi il cappotto; **the button came off**
il bottone è venuto via *or* si è staccato; **10%
off** con lo sconto del 10%
3 (*not at work*): **to have a day off** avere un
giorno libero; **to be off sick** essere assente
per malattia
▷ *adj* (*engine*) spento(-a); (*tap*) chiuso(-a);
(*cancelled*) sospeso(-a); (*BRIT: food*)
andato(-a) a male; **on the off chance**
nel caso; **to have an off day** non essere in
forma
▷ *prep* **1** (*motion, removal etc*) da; (*distant
from*) a poca distanza da; **a street off the
square** una strada che parte dalla piazza
2: **to be off meat** non mangiare più la
carne

offence [ə'fɛns] (*US* **offense**) *n* (*Law*)
contravvenzione *f*; (: *more serious*) reato; **to
take ~ at** offendersi per
offend [ə'fɛnd] *vt* (*person*) offendere;
offender *n* delinquente *m/f*; (*against
regulations*) contravventore(-trice)
offense [ə'fɛns] (*US*) *n* = **offence**

offensive [ə'fɛnsɪv] *adj* offensivo(-a); (*smell etc*) sgradevole, ripugnante ▷ *n* (*Mil*) offensiva

offer ['ɔfər] *n* offerta, proposta ▷ *vt* offrire; **"on ~"** (*Comm*) "in offerta speciale"

offhand [ɔf'hænd] *adj* disinvolto(-a), noncurante ▷ *adv* su due piedi

office ['ɔfɪs] *n* (*place*) ufficio; (*position*) carica; **doctor's ~** (*US*) studio; **to take ~** entrare in carica; **office block** (*US* **office building**) *n* complesso di uffici; **office hours** *npl* orario d'ufficio; (*US Med*) orario di visite

officer ['ɔfɪsər] *n* (*Mil etc*) ufficiale *m*; (*also*: **police ~**) agente *m* di polizia; (*of organization*) funzionario

office worker *n* impiegato(-a) d'ufficio

official [ə'fɪʃl] *adj* (*authorized*) ufficiale ▷ *n* ufficiale *m*; (*civil servant*) impiegato(-a) statale; funzionario

off: off-licence (*BRIT*) *n* (*shop*) spaccio di bevande alcoliche; **off-line** *adj, adv* (*Comput*) off-line *inv*, fuori linea; (*: switched off*) spento(-a); **off-peak** *adj* (*ticket, heating etc*) a tariffa ridotta; (*time*) non di punta; **off-putting** (*BRIT*) *adj* sgradevole, antipatico(-a); **off-season** *adj, adv* fuori stagione; **offset** ['ɔfsɛt] (*irreg*) *vt* (*counteract*) controbilanciare, compensare; **offshore** [ɔf'ʃɔːr] *adj* (*breeze*) di terra; (*island*) vicino alla costa; (*fishing*) costiero(-a); **offside** ['ɔf'saɪd] *adj* (*Sport*) fuori gioco; (*Aut: in Britain*) destro(-a); (*: in Italy etc*) sinistro(-a); **offspring** ['ɔfsprɪŋ] *n inv* prole *f*, discendenza

often ['ɔfn] *adv* spesso; **how ~ do you go?** quanto spesso ci vai?

oh [əu] *excl* oh!

oil [ɔɪl] *n* olio; (*petroleum*) petrolio; (*for central heating*) nafta ▷ *vt* (*machine*) lubrificare; **oil filter** *n* (*Aut*) filtro dell'olio; **oil painting** *n* quadro a olio; **oil refinery** *n* raffineria di petrolio; **oil rig** *n* derrick *m inv*; (*at sea*) piattaforma per trivellazioni subacquee; **oil slick** *n* chiazza d'olio; **oil tanker** *n* (*ship*) petroliera; (*truck*) autocisterna per petrolio; **oil well** *n* pozzo petrolifero; **oily** *adj* unto(-a), oleoso(-a); (*food*) grasso(-a)

ointment ['ɔɪntmənt] *n* unguento

O.K. ['əu'keɪ] *excl* d'accordo! ▷ *adj* non male *inv* ▷ *vt* approvare; **is it O.K.?, are you O.K.?** tutto bene?

old [əuld] *adj* vecchio(-a); (*ancient*) antico(-a), vecchio(-a); (*person*) vecchio(-a), anziano(-a); **how ~ are you?** quanti anni ha?; **he's 10 years ~** ha 10 anni; **~er brother** fratello maggiore; **old age** *n*

vecchiaia; **old-age pension** ['əuldeɪdʒ-] *n* (*BRIT*) pensione *f* di vecchiaia; **old-age pensioner** (*BRIT*) *n* pensionato(-a); **old-fashioned** *adj* antiquato(-a), fuori moda; (*person*) all'antica; **old people's home** *n* ricovero per anziani

olive ['ɔlɪv] *n* (*fruit*) oliva; (*tree*) olivo ▷ *adj* (*also*: **~-green**) verde oliva *inv*; **olive oil** *n* olio d'oliva

Olympic [əu'lɪmpɪk] *adj* olimpico(-a); **the ~ Games, the ~s** i giochi olimpici, le Olimpiadi

omelet(te) ['ɔmlɪt] *n* omelette *f inv*

omen ['əumən] *n* presagio, augurio

ominous ['ɔmɪnəs] *adj* minaccioso(-a); (*event*) di malaugurio

omit [əu'mɪt] *vt* omettere

 KEYWORD

on [ɔn] *prep* **1** (*indicating position*) su; **on the wall** sulla parete; **on the left** a *or* sulla sinistra

2 (*indicating means, method, condition etc*): **on foot** a piedi; **on the train/plane** in treno/aereo; **on the telephone** al telefono; **on the radio/television** alla radio/televisione; **to be on drugs** drogarsi; **on holiday** in vacanza

3 (*of time*): **on Friday** venerdì; **on Fridays** il *or* di venerdì; **on June 20th** il 20 giugno; **on Friday, June 20th** venerdì, 20 giugno; **a week on Friday** venerdì a otto; **on his arrival** al suo arrivo; **on seeing this** vedendo ciò

4 (*about, concerning*) su, di; **information on train services** informazioni sui collegamenti ferroviari; **a book on Goldoni/physics** un libro su Goldoni/di *or* sulla fisica

▷ *adv* **1** (*referring to dress, covering*): **to have one's coat on** avere indosso il cappotto; **to put one's coat on** mettersi il cappotto; **what's she got on?** cosa indossa?; **she put her boots/gloves/hat on** si mise gli stivali/i guanti/il cappello; **screw the lid on tightly** avvita bene il coperchio

2 (*further, continuously*): **to walk on, go on** *etc* continuare, proseguire *etc*; **to read on** continuare a leggere; **on and off** ogni tanto

▷ *adj* **1** (*in operation: machine, TV, light*) acceso(-a); (*: tap*) aperto(-a); (*: brake*) inserito(-a); **is the meeting still on?** (*in progress*) la riunione è ancora in corso?; (*not cancelled*) è confermato l'incontro?; **there's a good film on at the cinema** danno un buon film al cinema

z (inf): **that's not on!** (not acceptable) non si fa così!; (not possible) non se ne parla neanche!

once [wʌns] adv una volta ▷ conj non appena, quando; **~ he had left/it was done** dopo che se n'era andato/fu fatto; **at ~** subito; (simultaneously) a un tempo; **~ a week** una volta per settimana; **~ more** ancora una volta; **~ and for all** una volta per sempre; **~ upon a time** c'era una volta

oncoming ['ɔnkʌmɪŋ] adj (traffic) che viene in senso opposto

KEYWORD

one [wʌn] num uno(-a); **one hundred and fifty** centocinquanta; **one day** un giorno ▷ adj **1** (sole) unico(-a); **the one book which** l'unico libro che; **the one man who** l'unico che
2 (same) stesso(-a); **they came in the one car** sono venuti nella stessa macchina ▷ pron **1**: **this one** questo(-a); **that one** quello(-a); **I've already got one/a red one** ne ho già uno/uno rosso; **one by one** uno per uno
2: **one another** l'un l'altro; **to look at one another** guardarsi; **to help one another** aiutarsi l'un l'altro or a vicenda
3 (impersonal) si; **one never knows** non si sa mai; **to cut one's finger** tagliarsi un dito; **one needs to eat** bisogna mangiare

one: **one-off** (BRIT: inf) n fatto eccezionale
oneself [wʌn'sɛlf] pron (reflexive) si; (after prep) se stesso(-a), sé; **to do sth (by) ~** fare qc da sé; **to hurt ~** farsi male; **to keep sth for ~** tenere qc per sé; **to talk to ~** parlare da solo
one: **one-shot** [wʌn'ʃɔt] (US) n = **one-off**; **one-sided** adj (argument) unilaterale; **one-to-one** adj (relationship) univoco(-a); **one-way** adj (street, traffic) a senso unico
ongoing ['ɔngəʊɪŋ] adj in corso; in attuazione
onion ['ʌnjən] n cipolla
on-line ['ɔnlaɪn] adj, adv (Comput) on-line inv
onlooker ['ɔnlʊkər] n spettatore(-trice)
only ['əʊnlɪ] adv solo, soltanto ▷ adj solo(-a), unico(-a) ▷ conj solo che, ma; **an ~ child** un figlio unico; **not ~ ... but also** non solo ... ma anche
on-screen [ɔn'skriːn] adj sullo schermo inv
onset ['ɔnsɛt] n inizio
onto ['ɔntu] prep = **on to**
onward(s) ['ɔnwəd(z)] adv (move) in avanti; **from that time onward(s)** da quella volta in poi

oops [ups] excl ops! (esprime rincrescimento per un piccolo contrattempo); **~-a-daisy!** oplà!
ooze [uːz] vi stillare
opaque [əʊ'peɪk] adj opaco(-a)
open ['əʊpn] adj aperto(-a); (road) libero(-a); (meeting) pubblico(-a) ▷ vt aprire ▷ vi (eyes, door, debate) aprirsi; (flower) sbocciare; (shop, bank, museum) aprire; (book etc: commence) cominciare; **is it ~ to the public?** è aperto al pubblico?; **in the ~ (air)** all'aperto; **what time do you ~?** a che ora aprite?; **open up** vt aprire; (blocked road) sgombrare ▷ vi (shop, business) aprire; **open-air** adj all'aperto; **opening** adj (speech) di apertura ▷ n apertura; (opportunity) occasione f, opportunità f inv; sbocco; **opening hours** npl orario d'apertura; **open learning** n sistema educativo secondo il quale lo studente ha maggior controllo e gestione delle modalità di apprendimento; **openly** adv apertamente; **open-minded** adj che ha la mente aperta; **open-necked** adj col collo slacciato; **open-plan** adj senza pareti divisorie; **Open University** n (BRIT) vedi nota nel riquadro

OPEN UNIVERSITY

La **Open University**, fondata in Gran Bretagna nel 1969, organizza corsi di laurea per corrispondenza o via Internet. Alcune lezioni possono venir seguite per radio o alla televisione e vengono organizzati regolari corsi estivi.

opera ['ɔpərə] n opera; **opera house** n opera; **opera singer** n cantante m/f d'opera or lirico(-a)
operate ['ɔpəreɪt] vt (machine) azionare, far funzionare; (system) usare ▷ vi funzionare; (drug) essere efficace; **to ~ on sb (for)** (Med) operare qn (di)
operating room (US) n = **operating theatre**
operating theatre n (Med) sala operatoria
operation [ɔpə'reɪʃən] n operazione f; **to be in ~** (machine) essere in azione or funzionamento; (system) essere in vigore; **to have an ~** (Med) subire un'operazione; **operational** adj in funzione; d'esercizio
operative ['ɔpərətɪv] adj (measure) operativo(-a)
operator ['ɔpəreɪtər] n (of machine) operatore(-trice); (Tel) centralinista m/f

opinion [ə'pɪnɪən] n opinione f, parere m;
in my ~ secondo me, a mio avviso; **opinion
poll** n sondaggio di opinioni
opponent [ə'pəunənt] n avversario(-a)
opportunity [ɔpə'tjuːnɪtɪ] n opportunità
f inv, occasione f; **to take the ~ of doing**
cogliere l'occasione per fare
oppose [ə'pəuz] vt opporsi a; **~d to**
contrario(-a) a; **as ~d to** in contrasto con
opposite ['ɔpəzɪt] adj opposto(-a); (house
etc) di fronte ▷ adv di fronte, dirimpetto
▷ prep di fronte a ▷ n **the ~** il contrario,
l'opposto; **the ~ sex** l'altro sesso
opposition [ɔpə'zɪʃən] n opposizione f
oppress [ə'prɛs] vt opprimere
opt [ɔpt] vi **to ~ for** optare per; **to ~ to do**
scegliere di fare; **opt out** vi **to ~ out of**
ritirarsi da
optician [ɔp'tɪʃən] n ottico
optimism ['ɔptɪmɪzəm] n ottimismo
optimist ['ɔptɪmɪst] n ottimista m/f;
optimistic [-'mɪstɪk] adj ottimistico(-a)
optimum ['ɔptɪməm] adj ottimale
option ['ɔpʃən] n scelta; (Scol) materia
facoltativa; (Comm) opzione f; **optional**
adj facoltativo(-a); (Comm) a scelta
or [ɔːʳ] conj o, oppure; (with negative): **he
hasn't seen or heard anything** non
ha visto né sentito niente; **or else** se no,
altrimenti; oppure
oral ['ɔːrəl] adj orale ▷ n esame m orale
orange ['ɔrɪndʒ] n (fruit) arancia ▷ adj
arancione; **orange juice** n succo
d'arancia; **orange squash** n succo
d'arancia (da diluire con l'acqua)
orbit ['ɔːbɪt] n orbita ▷ vt orbitare intorno
a
orchard ['ɔːtʃəd] n frutteto
orchestra ['ɔːkɪstrə] n orchestra; (us:
seating) platea
orchid ['ɔːkɪd] n orchidea
ordeal [ɔː'diːl] n prova, travaglio
order ['ɔːdəʳ] n ordine m; (Comm)
ordinazione f ▷ vt ordinare; **can I ~ now,
please?** posso ordinare, per favore?; **in
~** in ordine; (of document) in regola; **in
(working) ~** funzionante; **in ~ to do** per
fare; **in ~ that** affinché + sub; **on ~** (Comm)
in ordinazione; **out of ~** non in ordine; (not
working) guasto; **to ~ sb to do** ordinare
a qn di fare; **order form** n modulo
d'ordinazione; **orderly** n (Mil) attendente
m; (Med) inserviente m ▷ adj (room) in
ordine; (mind) metodico(-a); (person)
ordinato(-a), metodico(-a)
ordinary ['ɔːdnrɪ] adj normale, comune;
(pej) mediocre; **out of the ~** diverso dal
solito, fuori dell'ordinario
ore [ɔːʳ] n minerale m grezzo

oregano [ɔrɪ'gaːnəu] n origano
organ ['ɔːgən] n organo; **organic**
[ɔː'gænɪk] adj organico(-a); (of food)
biologico(-a); **organism** n organismo
organization [ɔːgənaɪ'zeɪʃən] n
organizzazione f
organize ['ɔːgənaɪz] vt organizzare;
to get ~d organizzarsi; **organized** ['ɔː
gənaɪzd] adj organizzato(-a); **organizer**
n organizzatore(-trice)
orgasm ['ɔːgæzəm] n orgasmo
orgy ['ɔːdʒɪ] n orgia
oriental [ɔːrɪ'ɛntl] adj, n orientale m/f
orientation [ɔːrɪɛn'teɪʃən] n
orientamento
origin ['ɔrɪdʒɪn] n origine f
original [ə'rɪdʒɪnl] adj originale; (earliest)
originario(-a) ▷ n originale m; **originally**
adv (at first) all'inizio
originate [ə'rɪdʒɪneɪt] vi **to ~ from** essere
originario(-a) di; (suggestion) provenire da;
to ~ in avere origine in
Orkneys ['ɔːknɪz] npl **the ~** (also: **the
Orkney Islands**) le Orcadi
ornament ['ɔːnəmənt] n ornamento;
(trinket) ninnolo; **ornamental** [-'mɛntl]
adj ornamentale
ornate [ɔː'neɪt] adj molto ornato(-a)
orphan ['ɔːfn] n orfano(-a)
orthodox ['ɔːθədɔks] adj ortodosso(-a)
orthopaedic [ɔːθə'piːdɪk] (us **orthopedic**)
adj ortopedico(-a)
osteopath ['ɔstɪəpæθ] n specialista m/f di
osteopatia
ostrich ['ɔstrɪtʃ] n struzzo
other ['ʌðəʳ] adj altro(-a) ▷ pron **the ~
(one)** l'altro(-a); **~s** (other people) altri mpl;
~ than altro che; a parte; **otherwise** adv,
conj altrimenti
otter ['ɔtəʳ] n lontra
ouch [autʃ] excl ohi!, ahi!
ought [ɔːt] (pt **ought**) aux vb **I ~ to do
it** dovrei farlo; **this ~ to have been
corrected** questo avrebbe dovuto essere
corretto; **he ~ to win** dovrebbe vincere
ounce [auns] n oncia (= 28.35 g, 16 in a
pound)
our ['auəʳ] adj il (la) nostro(-a); (pl) i (le)
nostri(-e); see also **my**; **ours** pron il (la)
nostro(-a); (pl) i (le) nostri(-e); see also
mine; **ourselves** pron pl (reflexive) ci; (after
preposition) noi; (emphatic) noi stessi(-e);
see also **oneself**
oust [aust] vt cacciare, espellere
out [aut] adv (gen) fuori; **~ here/there**
qui/là fuori; **to speak ~ loud** parlare
forte; **to have a night ~** uscire una sera;
the boat was 10 km ~ la barca era a 10
km dalla costa; **3 days ~ from Plym~h** a 3

giorni da Plymouth; **~ of** (*outside*) fuori di; (*because of*) per; **~ of 10** su 10; **~ of petrol** senza benzina; **outback** ['autbæk] n (*in Australia*) interno, entroterra; **outbound** adj **outbound (for** or **from)** in partenza (per or da); **outbreak** ['autbreɪk] n scoppio; epidemia; **outburst** ['autbə:st] n scoppio; **outcast** ['autka:st] n esule m/f; (*socially*) paria m inv; **outcome** ['autkʌm] n esito, risultato; **outcry** ['autkraɪ] n protesta, clamore m; **outdated** [aut'deɪtɪd] adj (*custom, clothes*) fuori moda; (*idea*) sorpassato(-a); **outdoor** [aut'dɔːʳ] adj all'aperto; **outdoors** adv fuori; all'aria aperta

outer ['autəʳ] adj esteriore; **outer space** n spazio cosmico

outfit ['autfɪt] n (*clothes*) completo; (: *for sport*) tenuta

out: **outgoing** ['autgəuɪŋ] adj (*character*) socievole; **outgoings** (BRIT) npl (*expenses*) spese fpl, uscite fpl; **outhouse** ['authaus] n costruzione f annessa

outing ['autɪŋ] n gita; escursione f

out: **outlaw** ['autlɔ:] n fuorilegge m/f ▷ vt bandire; **outlay** ['autleɪ] n spese fpl; (*investment*) sborsa, spesa; **outlet** ['autlet] n (*for liquid etc*) sbocco, scarico; (US Elec) presa di corrente; (*also*: **retail outlet**) punto di vendita; **outline** ['autlaɪn] n contorno, profilo; (*summary*) abbozzo, grandi linee fpl ▷ vt (*fig*) descrivere a grandi linee; **outlook** ['autluk] n prospettiva, vista; **outnumber** [aut'nʌmbəʳ] vt superare in numero; **out-of-date** adj (*passport*) scaduto(-a); (*clothes*) fuori moda inv; **out-of-doors** [autəv'dɔ:z] adv all'aperto; **out-of-the-way** adj (*place*) fuori mano inv; **out-of-town** [autəv'taun] adj (*shopping centre etc*) fuori città; **outpatient** ['autpeɪʃənt] n paziente m/f esterno(-a); **outpost** ['autpəust] n avamposto; **output** ['autput] n produzione f; (*Comput*) output m inv

outrage ['autreɪdʒ] n oltraggio; scandalo ▷ vt oltraggiare; **outrageous** [-'reɪdʒəs] adj oltraggioso(-a), scandaloso(-a)

outright [adv aut'raɪt, adj 'autraɪt] adv completamente; schiettamente; apertamente; sul colpo ▷ adj completo(-a), schietto(-a) e netto(-a)

outset ['autset] n inizio

outside [aut'saɪd] n esterno, esteriore m ▷ adj esterno(-a), esteriore ▷ adv fuori, all'esterno ▷ prep fuori di, all'esterno di; **at the ~** (*fig*) al massimo; **outside lane** n (Aut) corsia di sorpasso; **outside line** n (Tel) linea esterna; **outsider** n (*in race etc*) outsider m inv; (*stranger*) estraneo(-a)

out: **outsize** ['autsaɪz] adj (*clothes*) per taglie forti; **outskirts** ['autskə:ts] npl sobborghi mpl; **outspoken** [aut'spəukən] adj molto franco(-a); **outstanding** [aut'stændɪŋ] adj eccezionale, di rilievo; (*unfinished*) non completo(-a); non evaso(-a); non regolato(-a)

outward ['autwəd] adj (*sign, appearances*) esteriore; (*journey*) d'andata; **outwards** ['autwədz] adv (*esp* BRIT) = **outward**

outweigh [aut'weɪ] vt avere maggior peso di

oval ['əuvl] adj ovale ▷ n ovale m

ovary ['əuvərɪ] n ovaia

oven ['ʌvn] n forno; **oven glove** n guanto da forno; **ovenproof** adj da forno; **oven-ready** adj pronto(-a) da infornare

over ['əuvəʳ] adv al di sopra ▷ adj (or adv) (*finished*) finito(-a), terminato(-a); (*too*) troppo; (*remaining*) che avanza ▷ prep su; sopra; (*above*) al di sopra di; (*on the other side of*) di là di; (*more than*) più di; (*during*) durante; **~ here** qui; **~ there** là; **all ~** (*everywhere*) dappertutto; (*finished*) tutto(-a) finito(-a); **~ and ~ (again)** più e più volte; **~ and above** oltre (a); **to ask sb ~** invitare qn (a passare)

overall [adj, n 'əuvərɔ:l, adv əuvər'ɔ:l] adj totale ▷ n (BRIT) grembiule m ▷ adv nell'insieme, complessivamente; **~s** npl (*worker's overalls*) tuta (da lavoro)

overboard ['əuvəbɔ:d] adv (Naut) fuori bordo, in mare

overcame [əuvə'keɪm] pt of **overcome**

overcast ['əuvəkɑ:st] adj (*sky*) coperto(-a)

overcharge [əuvə'tʃɑ:dʒ] vt **to ~ sb for sth** far pagare troppo caro a qn per qc

overcoat ['əuvəkəut] n soprabito, cappotto

overcome [əuvə'kʌm] (*irreg*) vt superare; sopraffare

over: **overcrowded** [əuvə'kraudɪd] adj sovraffollato(-a); **overdo** [əuvə'du:] (*irreg*) vt esagerare; (*overcook*) cuocere troppo; **overdone** [əuvə'dʌn] adj troppo cotto(-a); **overdose** ['əuvədəus] n dose f eccessiva; **overdraft** ['əuvədrɑ:ft] n scoperto (di conto); **overdrawn** [əuvə'drɔ:n] adj (*account*) scoperto(-a); **overdue** [əuvə'dju:] adj in ritardo; **overestimate** [əuvər'estɪmeɪt] vt sopravvalutare

overflow [vb əuvə'fləu, n 'əuvəfləu] vi traboccare ▷ n (*also*: **~ pipe**) troppopieno

overgrown [əuvə'grəun] adj (*garden*) ricoperto(-a) di vegetazione

overhaul [vb əuvə'hɔ:l, n 'əuvəhɔ:l] vt revisionare ▷ n revisione f

overhead [adv əuvə'hed, adj, n 'əuvəhed] adv di sopra ▷ adj aereo(-a); (*lighting*)

verticale ▷ *n* (*us*) = **overheads**;
overhead projector *n* lavagna luminosa;
overheads *npl* spese *fpl* generali
over: **overhear** [əuvəˈhɪər] (*irreg*) *vt* sentire
(per caso); **overheat** [əuvəˈhiːt] *vi* (*engine*)
surriscaldare; **overland** *adj*, *adv* per via di
terra; **overlap** [əuvəˈlæp] *vi* sovrapporsi;
overleaf [əuvəˈliːf] *adv* a tergo; **overload**
[əuvəˈləud] *vt* sovraccaricare; **overlook**
[əuvəˈluk] *vt* (*have view of*) dare su; (*miss*)
trascurare; (*forgive*) passare sopra a
overnight [əuvəˈnaɪt] *adv* (*happen*)
durante la notte; (*fig*) tutto ad un tratto
▷ *adj* di notte; **he stayed there ~** ci ha
passato la notte; **overnight bag** *n* borsa
da viaggio
overpass [ˈəuvəpɑːs] *n* cavalcavia *m inv*
overpower [əuvəˈpauər] *vt* sopraffare;
overpowering *adj* irresistibile; (*heat*,
stench) soffocante
over: **overreact** [əuvəriˈækt] *vi* reagire
in modo esagerato; **overrule** [əuvəˈruːl]
vt (*decision*) annullare; (*claim*) respingere;
overrun [əuvəˈrʌn] (*irreg*: *like* run) *vt*
(*country*) invadere; (*time limit*) superare
overseas [əuvəˈsiːz] *adv* oltremare;
(*abroad*) all'estero ▷ *adj* (*trade*) estero(-a);
(*visitor*) straniero(-a)
oversee [əuvəˈsiː] *vt irreg* sorvegliare
overshadow [əuvəˈʃædəu] *vt* far ombra
su; (*fig*) eclissare
oversight [ˈəuvəsaɪt] *n* omissione *f*, svista
oversleep [əuvəˈsliːp] (*irreg*) *vt* dormire
troppo a lungo
overspend [əuvəˈspɛnd] *vi irreg* spendere
troppo; **we have overspent by 5000
dollars** abbiamo speso 5000 dollari di
troppo
overt [əuˈvəːt] *adj* palese
overtake [əuvəˈteɪk] (*irreg*) *vt* sorpassare
over: **overthrow** [əuvəˈθrəu] (*irreg*)
vt (*government*) rovesciare; **overtime**
[ˈəuvətaɪm] *n* (*lavoro*) straordinario
overtook [əuvəˈtuk] *pt of* **overtake**
over: **overturn** [əuvəˈtəːn] *vt* rovesciare
▷ *vi* rovesciarsi; **overweight** [əuvəˈweɪt]
adj (*person*) troppo grasso(-a); **overwhelm**
[əuvəˈwɛlm] *vt* sopraffare; sommergere;
schiacciare; **overwhelming** *adj* (*victory*,
defeat) schiacciante; (*heat*, *desire*)
intenso(-a)
ow [au] *excl* ahi!
owe [əu] *vt* **to ~ sb sth, to ~ sth to sb**
dovere qc a qn; **how much do I ~ you?**
quanto le devo?; **owing to** *prep* a causa di
owl [aul] *n* gufo
own [əun] *vt* possedere ▷ *adj* proprio(-a);
a room of my ~ la mia propria camera; **to
get one's ~ back** vendicarsi; **on one's ~**
tutto(-a) solo(-a); **own up** *vi* confessare;
owner *n* proprietario(-a); **ownership** *n*
possesso
ox [ɔks] (*pl* **oxen**) *n* bue *m*
Oxbridge [ˈɔksbrɪdʒ] *n le università di
Oxford e/o Cambridge*
oxen [ˈɔksn] *npl of* **ox**
oxygen [ˈɔksɪdʒən] *n* ossigeno
oyster [ˈɔɪstər] *n* ostrica
oz. *abbr* = **ounce(s)**
ozone [ˈəuzəun] *n* ozono; **ozone friendly**
adj che non danneggia l'ozono; **ozone
layer** *n* fascia d'ozono

p [pi:] *abbr* = **penny**; **pence**
P.A. *n abbr* = **personal assistant**; **public address system**
p.a. *abbr* = **per annum**
pace [peɪs] *n* passo; (*speed*) passo; velocità ▷ *vi* **to ~ up and down** camminare su e giù; **to keep ~ with** camminare di pari passo a; (*events*) tenersi al corrente di; **pacemaker** *n* (*Med*) segnapasso; (*Sport: also*: **pace setter**) battistrada *m inv*
Pacific [pə'sɪfɪk] *n* **the ~ (Ocean)** il Pacifico, l'Oceano Pacifico
pacifier ['pæsɪfaɪəʳ] (*US*) *n* (*dummy*) succhiotto, ciuccio (*col*)
pack [pæk] *n* pacco; (*US: of cigarettes*) pacchetto; (*backpack*) zaino; (*of hounds*) muta; (*of thieves etc*) banda; (*of cards*) mazzo ▷ *vt* (*in suitcase etc*) mettere; (*box*) riempire; (*cram*) stipare, pigiare; **to ~ (one's bags)** fare la valigia; **to ~ sb off** spedire via qn; **~ it in!** (*inf*) dacci un taglio!; **pack in** (*BRIT inf*) *vi* (*watch, car*) guastarsi ▷ *vt* mollare, piantare; **~ it in!** piantala!; **pack up** *vi* (*BRIT inf: machine*) guastarsi; (: *person*) far fagotto ▷ *vt* (*belongings, clothes*) mettere in una valigia; (*goods, presents*) imballare
package ['pækɪdʒ] *n* pacco; balla; (*also*: **~ deal**) pacchetto; forfait *m inv*; **package holiday** *n* vacanza organizzata; **package tour** *n* viaggio organizzato
packaging ['pækɪdʒɪŋ] *n* confezione *f*, imballo
packed [pækt] *adj* (*crowded*) affollato(-a); **packed lunch** *n* pranzo al sacco
packet ['pækɪt] *n* pacchetto
packing ['pækɪŋ] *n* imballaggio
pact [pækt] *n* patto, accordo; trattato
pad [pæd] *n* blocco; (*to prevent friction*) cuscinetto; (*inf: flat*) appartamentino ▷ *vt* imbottire; **padded** *adj* imbottito(-a)
paddle ['pædl] *n* (*oar*) pagaia; (*US: for table tennis*) racchetta da ping-pong ▷ *vi* sguazzare ▷ *vt* **to ~ a canoe** *etc* vogare con la pagaia; **paddling pool** (*BRIT*) *n* piscina per bambini
paddock ['pædək] *n* prato recintato; (*at racecourse*) paddock *m inv*
padlock ['pædlɔk] *n* lucchetto
paedophile ['pi:dəufaɪl] (*US* **pedophile**) *adj, n* pedofilo(-a)
page [peɪdʒ] *n* pagina; (*also*: **~ boy**) paggio ▷ *vt* (*in hotel etc*) (far) chiamare
pager ['peɪdʒəʳ] *n* (*Tel*) cercapersone *m inv*
paid [peɪd] *pt, pp of* **pay** ▷ *adj* (*work, official*) rimunerato(-a); **to put ~ to** (*BRIT*) mettere fine a
pain [peɪn] *n* dolore *m*; **to be in ~** soffrire, aver male; **to take ~s to do** mettercela tutta per fare; **painful** *adj* doloroso(-a), che fa male; difficile, penoso(-a); **painkiller** *n* antalgico, antidolorifico; **painstaking** ['peɪnzteɪkɪŋ] *adj* (*person*) sollecito(-a); (*work*) accurato(-a)
paint [peɪnt] *n* vernice *f*, colore *m* ▷ *vt* dipingere; (*walls, door etc*) verniciare; **to ~ the door blue** verniciare la porta di azzurro; **paintbrush** *n* pennello; **painter** *n* (*artist*) pittore *m*; (*decorator*) imbianchino; **painting** *n* pittura; verniciatura; (*picture*) dipinto, quadro
pair [pɛəʳ] *n* (*of shoes, gloves etc*) paio; (*of people*) coppia; duo *m inv*; **a ~ of scissors/ trousers** un paio di forbici/pantaloni
pajamas [pɪ'dʒɑːməz] (*US*) *npl* pigiama *m*
Pakistan [pɑːkɪ'stɑːn] *n* Pakistan *m*; **Pakistani** *adj, n* pakistano(-a)
pal [pæl] (*inf*) *n* amico(-a), compagno(-a)
palace ['pæləs] *n* palazzo
pale [peɪl] *adj* pallido(-a) ▷ *n* **to be beyond the ~** aver oltrepassato ogni limite
Palestine ['pælɪstaɪn] *n* Palestina; **Palestinian** [-'tɪnɪən] *adj, n* palestinese *m/f*
palm [pɑːm] *n* (*Anat*) palma, palmo; (*also*: **~ tree**) palma ▷ *vt* **to ~ sth off on sb** (*inf*) rifilare qc a qn
pamper ['pæmpəʳ] *vt* viziare, coccolare
pamphlet ['pæmflət] *n* dépliant *m inv*

pan [pæn] n (also: **sauce~**) casseruola; (also: **frying ~**) padella

pancake ['pænkeɪk] n frittella

panda ['pændə] n panda m inv

pane [peɪn] n vetro

panel ['pænl] n (of wood, cloth etc) pannello; (Radio, TV) giuria

panhandler ['pænhændlər] (us) n (inf) accattone(-a)

panic ['pænɪk] n panico ▷ vi perdere il sangue freddo

panorama [pænə'rɑːmə] n panorama m

pansy ['pænzɪ] n (Bot) viola del pensiero, pensée f inv; (inf: pej) femminuccia

pant [pænt] vi ansare

panther ['pænθər] n pantera

panties ['pæntɪz] npl slip m, mutandine fpl

pantomime ['pæntəmaɪm] (BRIT) n pantomima

● **PANTOMIME**

In Gran Bretagna la **pantomime** è una sorta di libera interpretazione delle favole più conosciute, che vengono messe in scena a teatro durante il periodo natalizio. È uno spettacolo per tutta la famiglia che prevede la partecipazione del pubblico.

pants [pænts] npl mutande fpl, slip m; (us: trousers) pantaloni mpl

paper ['peɪpər] n carta; (also: **wall~**) carta da parati, tappezzeria; (also: **news~**) giornale m; (study, article) saggio; (exam) prova scritta ▷ adj di carta ▷ vt tappezzare; **~s** npl (also: **identity ~s**) carte fpl, documenti mpl; **paperback** n tascabile m; edizione f economica; **paper bag** n sacchetto di carta; **paper clip** n graffetta, clip f inv; **paper shop** n (BRIT) giornalaio (negozio); **paperwork** n lavoro amministrativo

paprika ['pæprɪkə] n paprica

par [pɑːr] n parità, pari f; (Golf) norma; **on a ~ with** alla pari con

paracetamol [pærə'siːtəmɔl] (BRIT) n paracetamolo

parachute ['pærəʃuːt] n paracadute m inv

parade [pə'reɪd] n parata ▷ vt (fig) fare sfoggio di ▷ vi sfilare in parata

paradise ['pærədaɪs] n paradiso

paradox ['pærədɔks] n paradosso

paraffin ['pærəfɪn] (BRIT) n ~ **(oil)** paraffina

paragraph ['pærəgrɑːf] n paragrafo

parallel ['pærəlel] adj parallelo(-a); (fig) analogo(-a) ▷ n (line) parallela; (fig, Geo) parallelo

paralysed ['pærəlaɪzd] adj paralizzato(-a)

paralysis [pə'rælɪsɪs] n paralisi f inv

paramedic [pærə'medɪk] n paramedico

paranoid ['pærənɔɪd] adj paranoico(-a)

parasite ['pærəsaɪt] n parassita m

parcel ['pɑːsl] n pacco, pacchetto ▷ vt (also: **~ up**) impaccare

pardon ['pɑːdn] n perdono; grazia ▷ vt perdonare; (Law) graziare; **~ me!** mi scusi!; **I beg your ~!** scusi!; **I beg your ~?** (BRIT), **~ me?** (US) prego?

parent ['pɛərənt] n genitore m; **~s** npl (mother and father) genitori mpl; **parental** [pə'rentl] adj dei genitori

▌ Be careful not to translate **parent** by the Italian word **parente**.

Paris ['pærɪs] n Parigi f

parish ['pærɪʃ] n parrocchia; (BRIT: civil) ≈ municipio

Parisian [pə'rɪzɪən] adj, n parigino(-a)

park [pɑːk] n parco ▷ vt, vi parcheggiare; **can I ~ here?** posso parcheggiare qui?

parking ['pɑːkɪŋ] n parcheggio; **"no ~"** "sosta vietata"; **parking lot** (us) n posteggio, parcheggio; **parking meter** n parchimetro; **parking ticket** n multa per sosta vietata

parkway ['pɑːkweɪ] (us) n viale m

parliament ['pɑːləmənt] n parlamento; **parliamentary** [pɑːlə'mentərɪ] adj parlamentare

Parmesan [pɑːmɪ'zæn] n (also: **~ cheese**) parmigiano

parole [pə'rəul] n **on ~** in libertà per buona condotta

parrot ['pærət] n pappagallo

parsley ['pɑːslɪ] n prezzemolo

parsnip ['pɑːsnɪp] n pastinaca

parson ['pɑːsn] n prete m; (Church of England) parroco

part [pɑːt] n parte f; (of machine) pezzo; (us: in hair) scriminatura ▷ adj in parte ▷ adv = **partly** ▷ vt separare ▷ vi (people) separarsi; **to take ~ in** prendere parte a; **for my ~** per parte mia; **to take sth in good ~** prendere bene qc; **to take sb's ~** parteggiare per o prendere le parti di qn; **for the most ~** in generale; nella maggior parte dei casi; **part with** vt fus separarsi da; rinunciare a

partial ['pɑːʃl] adj parziale; **to be ~ to** avere un debole per

participant [pɑː'tɪsɪpənt] n **~ (in)** partecipante m/f(a)

participate [pɑː'tɪsɪpeɪt] vi **to ~ (in)** prendere parte a, partecipare (a)

particle ['pɑːtɪkl] n particella

particular [pə'tɪkjulər] adj particolare;

speciale; (*fussy*) difficile; meticoloso(-a);
in ~ in particolare, particolarmente;
particularly *adv* particolarmente; in
particolare; **particulars** *npl* particolari
mpl, dettagli *mpl*; (*information*)
informazioni *fpl*

parting ['pɑ:tɪŋ] *n* separazione *f*; (*BRIT: in hair*) scriminatura ▷ *adj* d'addio

partition [pɑ:'tɪʃən] *n* (*Pol*) partizione *f*; (*wall*) tramezzo

partly ['pɑ:tlɪ] *adv* parzialmente; in parte

partner ['pɑ:tnə^r] *n* (*Comm*) socio(-a); (*wife, husband etc, Sport*) compagno(-a); (*at dance*) cavaliere/dama; **partnership** *n* associazione *f*; (*Comm*) società *f inv*

part of speech *n* parte *f* del discorso

partridge ['pɑ:trɪdʒ] *n* pernice *f*

part-time ['pɑ:t'taɪm] *adj, adv* a orario ridotto

party ['pɑ:tɪ] *n* (*Pol*) partito; (*group*) gruppo; (*Law*) parte *f*; (*celebration*) ricevimento; serata; festa ▷ *cpd* (*Pol*) del partito, di partito

pass [pɑ:s] *vt* (*gen*) passare; (*place*) passare davanti a; (*exam*) passare, superare; (*candidate*) promuovere; (*overtake, surpass*) sorpassare, superare; (*approve*) approvare ▷ *vi* passare ▷ *n* (*permit*) lasciapassare *m inv*; permesso; (*in mountains*) passo, gola; (*Sport*) passaggio; (*Scol*): **to get a ~** prendere la sufficienza; **could you ~ the salt/oil, please?** mi passa il sale/l'olio, per favore?; **to ~ sth through a hole** *etc* far passare qc attraverso un buco *etc*; **to make a ~ at sb** (*inf*) fare delle proposte *or* delle avances a qn; **pass away** *vi* morire; **pass by** *vi* passare ▷ *vt* trascurare; **pass on** *vt* passare; **pass out** *vi* svenire; **pass over** *vi* (*die*) spirare ▷ *vt* lasciare da parte; **pass up** *vt* (*opportunity*) lasciarsi sfuggire, perdere; **passable** *adj* (*road*) praticabile; (*work*) accettabile

passage ['pæsɪdʒ] *n* (*gen*) passaggio; (*also: ~way*) corridoio; (*in book*) brano, passo; (*by boat*) traversata

passenger ['pæsɪndʒə^r] *n* passeggero(-a)

passer-by [pɑ:sə'baɪ] *n* passante *m/f*

passing place *n* (*Aut*) piazzola di sosta

passion ['pæʃən] *n* passione *f*; amore *m*; **passionate** *adj* appassionato(-a); **passion fruit** *n* frutto della passione

passive ['pæsɪv] *adj* (*also Ling*) passivo(-a)

passport ['pɑ:spɔ:t] *n* passaporto; **passport control** *n* controllo *m* passaporti *inv*; **passport office** *n* ufficio *m*, passaporti *inv*

password ['pɑ:swə:d] *n* parola d'ordine

past [pɑ:st] *prep* (*further than*) oltre, di là di; dopo; (*later than*) dopo ▷ *adj* passato(-a);

(*president etc*) ex *inv* ▷ *n* passato; **he's ~ forty** ha più di quarant'anni; **ten ~ eight** le otto e dieci; **for the ~ few days** da qualche giorno; in questi ultimi giorni; **to run ~** passare di corsa

pasta ['pæstə] *n* pasta

paste [peɪst] *n* (*glue*) colla; (*Culin*) pâté *m inv*; pasta ▷ *vt* collare

pastel ['pæstl] *adj* pastello *inv*

pasteurized ['pæstəraɪzd] *adj* pastorizzato(-a)

pastime ['pɑ:staɪm] *n* passatempo

pastor ['pɑ:stə^r] *n* pastore *m*

past participle [-'pɑ:tɪsɪpl] *n* (*Ling*) participio passato

pastry ['peɪstrɪ] *n* pasta

pasture ['pɑ:stʃə^r] *n* pascolo

pasty¹ ['pæstɪ] *n* pasticcio di carne

pasty² ['peɪstɪ] *adj* (*face etc*) smorto(-a)

pat [pæt] *vt* accarezzare, dare un colpetto (affettuoso) a

patch [pætʃ] *n* (*of material, on tyre*) toppa; (*eye patch*) benda; (*spot*) macchia ▷ *vt* (*clothes*) rattoppare; **(to go through) a bad ~** (attraversare) un brutto periodo; **patchy** *adj* irregolare

pâté ['pæteɪ] *n* pâté *m inv*

patent ['peɪtnt] *n* brevetto ▷ *vt* brevettare ▷ *adj* patente, manifesto(-a)

paternal [pə'tə:nl] *adj* paterno(-a)

paternity leave [pə'tə:nɪtɪ-] *n* congedo di paternità

path [pɑ:θ] *n* sentiero, viottolo; viale *m*; (*fig*) via, strada; (*of planet, missile*) traiettoria

pathetic [pə'θetɪk] *adj* (*pitiful*) patetico(-a); (*very bad*) penoso(-a)

pathway ['pɑ:θweɪ] *n* sentiero

patience ['peɪʃns] *n* pazienza; (*BRIT Cards*) solitario

patient ['peɪʃnt] *n* paziente *m/f*, malato(-a) ▷ *adj* paziente

patio ['pætɪəu] *n* terrazza

patriotic [pætrɪ'ɔtɪk] *adj* patriottico(-a)

patrol [pə'trəul] *n* pattuglia ▷ *vt* pattugliare; **patrol car** *n* autoradio *f inv* (della polizia)

patron ['peɪtrən] *n* (*in shop*) cliente *m/f*; (*of charity*) benefattore(-trice); **~ of the arts** mecenate *m/f*

patronizing ['pætrənaɪzɪŋ] *adj* condiscendente

pattern ['pætən] *n* modello; (*design*) disegno, motivo; **patterned** *adj* a disegni, a motivi; (*material*) fantasia *inv*

pause [pɔ:z] *n* pausa ▷ *vi* fare una pausa, arrestarsi

pave [peɪv] *vt* pavimentare; **to ~ the way for** aprire la via a

pavement ['peɪvmənt] (BRIT) n
marciapiede m

> Be careful not to translate *pavement*
> by the Italian word *pavimento*.

pavilion [pə'vɪlɪən] n (Sport) edificio
annesso a campo sportivo
paving ['peɪvɪŋ] n pavimentazione f
paw [pɔː] n zampa
pawn [pɔːn] n (Chess) pedone m; (fig)
pedina ▷ vt dare in pegno; **pawn broker** n
prestatore m su pegno
pay [peɪ] (pt, pp **paid**) n stipendio; paga
▷ vt pagare ▷ vi (be profitable) rendere;
can I ~ by credit card? posso pagare
con la carta di credito?; **to ~ attention
(to)** fare attenzione (a); **to ~ sb a visit**
far visita a qn; **to ~ one's respects to sb**
porgere i propri rispetti a qn; **pay back** vt
rimborsare; **pay for** vt fus pagare; **pay
in** vt versare; **pay off** vt (debt) saldare;
(person) pagare; (employee) pagare e
licenziare ▷ vi (scheme, decision) dare
dei frutti; **pay out** vt (money) sborsare,
tirar fuori; (rope) far allentare; **pay up** vt
saldare; **payable** adj pagabile; **pay day**
n giorno di paga; **pay envelope** (US) n
= **pay packet**; **payment** n pagamento;
versamento; saldo; **payout** n pagamento;
(in competition) premio; **pay packet** (BRIT)
n busta f paga inv; **pay phone** n cabina
telefonica; **payroll** n ruolo (organico); **pay
slip** n foglio m paga inv; **pay television** n
televisione f a pagamento, pay-tv f inv
PC n abbr = **personal computer** ▷ adv abbr
= **politically correct**
p.c. abbr = **per cent**
PDA n abbr (= personal digital assistant) PDA
m inv
PE n abbr (= physical education) ed. fisica
pea [piː] n pisello
peace [piːs] n pace f; **peaceful** adj
pacifico(-a), calmo(-a)
peach [piːtʃ] n pesca
peacock ['piːkɔk] n pavone m
peak [piːk] n (of mountain) cima, vetta;
(mountain itself) picco; (of cap) visiera; (fig)
apice m, culmine m; **peak hours** npl ore
fpl di punta
peanut ['piːnʌt] n arachide f, nocciolina
americana; **peanut butter** n burro di
arachidi
pear [pɛər] n pera
pearl [pəːl] n perla
peasant ['pɛznt] n contadino(-a)
peat [piːt] n torba
pebble ['pɛbl] n ciottolo
peck [pɛk] vt (also: ~ **at**) beccare ▷ n colpo
di becco; (kiss) bacetto; **peckish** (BRIT: inf)
adj **I feel peckish** ho un languorino

peculiar [pɪ'kjuːlɪər] adj strano(-a),
bizzarro(-a); peculiare; ~ **to** peculiare di
pedal ['pɛdl] n pedale m ▷ vi pedalare
pedalo ['pɛdaləu] n pedalò m inv
pedestal ['pɛdəstl] n piedestallo
pedestrian [pɪ'dɛstrɪən] n pedone(-a)
▷ adj pedonale; (fig) prosaico(-a),
pedestre; **pedestrian crossing** (BRIT) n
passaggio pedonale; **pedestrianized**
adj **a pedestrianized street** una zona
pedonalizzata; **pedestrian precinct**
(BRIT), **pedestrian zone** (US) n zona
pedonale
pedigree ['pɛdɪɡriː] n (of animal) pedigree
m inv; (fig) background m inv ▷ cpd (animal)
di razza
pedophile ['piːdəufaɪl] (US) n
= **paedophile**
pee [piː] (inf) vi pisciare
peek [piːk] vi guardare furtivamente
peel [piːl] n buccia; (of orange, lemon) scorza
▷ vt sbucciare ▷ vi (paint etc) staccarsi
peep [piːp] n (BRIT: look) sguardo furtivo,
sbirciata; (sound) pigolio ▷ vi (BRIT)
guardare furtivamente
peer [pɪər] vi **to ~ at** scrutare ▷ n (noble)
pari m inv; (equal) pari m/f inv, uguale m/f;
(contemporary) contemporaneo(-a)
peg [pɛɡ] n caviglia; (for coat etc)
attaccapanni m inv; (BRIT: also: **clothes ~**)
molletta
pelican ['pɛlɪkən] n pellicano; **pelican
crossing** (BRIT) n (Aut) attraversamento
pedonale con semaforo a controllo manuale
pelt [pɛlt] vt **to ~ sb (with)** bombardare qn
(con) ▷ vi (rain) piovere a dirotto; (inf: run)
filare ▷ n pelle f
pelvis ['pɛlvɪs] n pelvi f inv, bacino
pen [pɛn] n penna; (for sheep) recinto
penalty ['pɛnltɪ] n penalità f inv;
sanzione f penale; (fine) ammenda; (Sport)
penalizzazione f
pence [pɛns] (BRIT) npl of **penny**
pencil ['pɛnsl] n matita; **pencil in**
vt scrivere a matita; **pencil case** n
astuccio per matite; **pencil sharpener** n
temperamatite m inv
pendant ['pɛndnt] n pendaglio
pending ['pɛndɪŋ] prep in attesa di ▷ adj
in sospeso
penetrate ['pɛnɪtreɪt] vt penetrare
penfriend ['pɛnfrɛnd] (BRIT) n
corrispondente m/f
penguin ['pɛŋɡwɪn] n pinguino
penicillin [pɛnɪ'sɪlɪn] n penicillina
peninsula [pə'nɪnsjulə] n penisola
penis ['piːnɪs] n pene m
penitentiary [pɛnɪ'tɛnʃərɪ] (US) n carcere
m

penknife ['pɛnnaɪf] n temperino
penniless ['pɛnɪlɪs] adj senza un soldo
penny ['pɛnɪ] (pl **pennies** or **pence**) (BRIT) n penny m; (US) centesimo
penpal ['pɛnpæl] n corrispondente m/f
pension ['pɛnʃən] n pensione f; **pensioner** (BRIT) n pensionato(-a)
pentagon ['pɛntəgən] n pentagono; **the P~** (US Pol) il Pentagono
penthouse ['pɛnthaus] n appartamento (di lusso) nell'attico
penultimate [pɪ'nʌltɪmət] adj penultimo(-a)
people ['pi:pl] npl gente f; persone fpl; (citizens) popolo ▷ n (nation, race) popolo; **4/several ~ came** 4/parecchie persone sono venute; **~ say that ...** si dice che ...
pepper ['pɛpəʳ] n pepe m; (vegetable) peperone m ▷ vt (fig): **to ~ with** spruzzare di; **peppermint** n (sweet) pasticca di menta
per [pəːʳ] prep per; a; **~ hour** all'ora; **~ kilo** etc il chilo etc; **~ day** al giorno
perceive [pə'siːv] vt percepire; (notice) accorgersi di
per cent adv per cento
percentage [pə'sɛntɪdʒ] n percentuale f
perception [pə'sɛpʃən] n percezione f; sensibilità; perspicacia
perch [pəːtʃ] n (fish) pesce m persico; (for bird) sostegno, ramo ▷ vi appollaiarsi
percussion [pə'kʌʃən] n percussione f; (Mus) strumenti mpl a percussione
perfect [adj, n 'pəːfɪkt, vb pə'fɛkt] adj perfetto(-a) ▷ n (also: **~ tense**) perfetto, passato prossimo ▷ vt perfezionare; mettere a punto; **perfection** [pə'fɛkʃən] n perfezione f; **perfectly** adv perfettamente, alla perfezione
perform [pə'fɔːm] vt (carry out) eseguire, fare; (symphony etc) suonare; (play, ballet) dare; (opera) fare ▷ vi suonare; recitare; **performance** n esecuzione f; (at theatre etc) rappresentazione f, spettacolo; (of an artist) interpretazione f; (of player etc) performance f; (of car, engine) prestazione f; **performer** n artista m/f
perfume ['pəːfjuːm] n profumo
perhaps [pə'hæps] adv forse
perimeter [pə'rɪmɪtəʳ] n perimetro
period ['pɪərɪəd] n periodo; (History) epoca; (Scol) lezione f; (full stop) punto; (Med) mestruazioni fpl ▷ adj (costume, furniture) d'epoca; **periodical** [-'ɔdɪkl] n periodico; **periodically** adv periodicamente
perish ['pɛrɪʃ] vi perire, morire; (decay) deteriorarsi
perjury ['pəːdʒərɪ] n spergiuro
perk [pəːk] (inf) n vantaggio

perm [pəːm] n (for hair) permanente f
permanent ['pəːmənənt] adj permanente; **permanently** adv definitivamente
permission [pə'mɪʃən] n permesso
permit [n 'pəːmɪt, vb pə'mɪt] n permesso ▷ vt permettere; **to ~ sb to do** permettere a qn di fare
perplex [pə'plɛks] vt lasciare perplesso(-a)
persecute ['pəːsɪkjuːt] vt perseguitare
persecution [pəːsɪ'kjuːʃən] n persecuzione f
persevere [pəːsɪ'vɪəʳ] vi perseverare
Persian ['pəːʃən] adj persiano(-a) ▷ n (Ling) persiano; **the (~) Gulf** n il Golfo Persico
persist [pə'sɪst] vi **to ~ (in doing)** persistere (nel fare); ostinarsi (a fare); **persistent** adj persistente; ostinato(-a)
person ['pəːsn] n persona; **in ~** di or in persona, personalmente; **personal** adj personale; individuale; **personal assistant** n segretaria personale; **personal computer** n personal computer m inv; **personality** [-'nælɪtɪ] n personalità f inv; **personally** adv personalmente; **to take sth personally** prendere qc come una critica personale; **personal organizer** n (Filofax®) Fulltime®; (electronic) agenda elettronica; **personal stereo** n Walkman® m inv
personnel [pəːsə'nɛl] n personale m
perspective [pə'spɛktɪv] n prospettiva
perspiration [pəːspɪ'reɪʃən] n traspirazione f, sudore m
persuade [pə'sweɪd] vt **to ~ sb to do sth** persuadere qn a fare qc
persuasion [pə'sweɪʒən] n persuasione f; (creed) convinzione f, credo
persuasive [pə'sweɪsɪv] adj persuasivo(-a)
perverse [pə'vəːs] adj perverso(-a)
pervert [n 'pəːvəːt, vb pə'vəːt] n pervertito(-a) ▷ vt pervertire
pessimism ['pɛsɪmɪzəm] n pessimismo
pessimist ['pɛsɪmɪst] n pessimista m/f; **pessimistic** [-'mɪstɪk] adj pessimistico(-a)
pest [pɛst] n animale m (or insetto) pestifero; (fig) peste f
pester ['pɛstəʳ] vt tormentare, molestare
pesticide ['pɛstɪsaɪd] n pesticida m
pet [pɛt] n animale m domestico ▷ cpd favorito(-a) ▷ vt accarezzare; **teacher's ~** favorito(-a) del maestro
petal ['pɛtl] n petalo
petite [pə'tiːt] adj piccolo(-a) e aggraziato(-a)
petition [pə'tɪʃən] n petizione f
petrified ['pɛtrɪfaɪd] adj (fig) morto(-a) di paura

petrol ['pɛtrəl] (BRIT) n benzina; **two/four-star ~** ≈ benzina normale/super; **I've run out of ~** sono rimasto senza benzina
⚠ Be careful not to translate **petrol** by the Italian word **petrolio**.

petroleum [pə'trəʊlɪəm] n petrolio
petrol: **petrol pump** (BRIT) n (in car, at garage) pompa di benzina; **petrol station** (BRIT) n stazione f di rifornimento; **petrol tank** (BRIT) n serbatoio della benzina
petticoat ['pɛtɪkəʊt] n sottana
petty ['pɛtɪ] adj (mean) meschino(-a); (unimportant) insignificante
pew [pju:] n panca (di chiesa)
pewter ['pju:tər] n peltro
phantom ['fæntəm] n fantasma m
pharmacist ['fɑ:məsɪst] n farmacista m/f
pharmacy ['fɑ:məsɪ] n farmacia
phase [feɪz] n fase f, periodo; **phase in** vt introdurre gradualmente; **phase out** vt (machinery) eliminare gradualmente; (product) ritirare gradualmente; (job, subsidy) abolire gradualmente
Ph.D. n abbr = **Doctor of Philosophy**
pheasant ['fɛznt] n fagiano
phenomena [fə'nɒmɪnə] npl of **phenomenon**
phenomenal [fɪ'nɒmɪnl] adj fenomenale
phenomenon [fə'nɒmɪnən] (pl **phenomena**) n fenomeno
Philippines ['fɪlɪpi:nz] npl **the ~** le Filippine
philosopher [fɪ'lɒsəfər] n filosofo(-a)
philosophical [fɪlə'sɒfɪkl] adj filosofico(-a)
philosophy [fɪ'lɒsəfɪ] n filosofia
phlegm [flɛm] n flemma
phobia ['fəʊbjə] n fobia
phone [fəʊn] n telefono ▷ vt telefonare; **to be on the ~** avere il telefono; (be calling) essere al telefono; **phone back** vt, vi richiamare; **phone up** vt telefonare a ▷ vi telefonare; **phone book** n guida del telefono, elenco telefonico; **phone booth** n = **phone box**; **phone box** n cabina telefonica; **phone call** n telefonata; **phonecard** n scheda telefonica; **phone number** n numero di telefono
phonetics [fə'nɛtɪks] n fonetica
phoney ['fəʊnɪ] adj falso(-a), fasullo(-a)
photo ['fəʊtəʊ] n foto f inv
photo... ['fəʊtəʊ] prefix: **photo album** n (new) album m inv per fotografie; (containing photos) album m inv delle fotografie; **photocopier** n fotocopiatrice f; **photocopy** n fotocopia ▷ vt fotocopiare
photograph ['fəʊtəgræf] n fotografia ▷ vt fotografare; **photographer** [fə'tɒgrəfər]

n fotografo; **photography** [fə'tɒgrəfɪ] n fotografia
phrase [freɪz] n espressione f; (Ling) locuzione f; (Mus) frase f ▷ vt esprimere; **phrase book** n vocabolarietto
physical ['fɪzɪkl] adj fisico(-a); **physical education** n educazione f fisica; **physically** adv fisicamente
physician [fɪ'zɪʃən] n medico
physicist ['fɪzɪsɪst] n fisico
physics ['fɪzɪks] n fisica
physiotherapist [fɪzɪəʊ'θɛrəpɪst] n fisioterapista m/f
physiotherapy [fɪzɪəʊ'θɛrəpɪ] n fisioterapia
physique [fɪ'zi:k] n fisico; costituzione f
pianist ['pi:ənɪst] n pianista m/f
piano [pɪ'ænəʊ] n pianoforte m
pick [pɪk] n (tool: also: **~-axe**) piccone m ▷ vt scegliere; (gather) cogliere; (remove) togliere; (lock) far scattare; **take your ~** scelga; **the ~ of** il fior fiore di; **to ~ one's nose** mettersi le dita nel naso; **to ~ one's teeth** pulirsi i denti con lo stuzzicadenti; **to ~ a quarrel** attaccar briga; **pick on** vt fus (person) avercela con; **pick out** vt scegliere; (distinguish) distinguere; **pick up** vi (improve) migliorarsi ▷ vt raccogliere; (Police, Radio) prendere; (collect) passare a prendere; (Aut: give lift to) far salire; (person: for sexual encounter) rimorchiare; (learn) imparare; **to ~ up speed** acquistare velocità; **to ~ o.s. up** rialzarsi
pickle ['pɪkl] n (also: **~s**: as condiment) sottaceti mpl; (fig: mess) pasticcio ▷ vt mettere sottaceto; mettere in salamoia
pickpocket ['pɪkpɔkɪt] n borsaiolo
pick-up ['pɪkʌp] n (BRIT: on record player) pick-up m inv; (small truck: also: **~ truck, ~ van**) camioncino
picnic ['pɪknɪk] n picnic m inv; **picnic area** n area per il picnic
picture ['pɪktʃər] n quadro; (painting) pittura; (photograph) foto(grafia); (drawing) disegno; (film) film m inv ▷ vt raffigurarsi; **~s** (BRIT) npl (cinema): **the ~s** il cinema; **would you take a ~ of us, please?** può farci una foto, per favore?; **picture frame** n cornice m inv; **picture messaging** n picture messaging m, invio di messaggini con disegni
picturesque [pɪktʃə'rɛsk] adj pittoresco(-a)
pie [paɪ] n torta; (of meat) pasticcio
piece [pi:s] n pezzo; (of land) appezzamento; (item): **a ~ of furniture/ advice** un mobile/consiglio ▷ vt **to ~ together** mettere insieme; **to take to ~s** smontare

pie chart n grafico a torta

pier [pɪəʳ] n molo; (of bridge etc) pila

pierce [pɪəs] vt forare; (with arrow etc) trafiggere; **pierced** adj **I've got pierced ears** ho i buchi per gli orecchini

pig [pɪg] n maiale m, porco

pigeon [ˈpɪdʒən] n piccione m

piggy bank [ˈpɪgɪ-] n salvadanaro

pigsty [ˈpɪgstaɪ] n porcile m

pigtail [ˈpɪgteɪl] n treccina

pike [paɪk] n (fish) luccio

pilchard [ˈpɪltʃəd] n specie di sardina

pile [paɪl] n (pillar, of books) pila; (heap) mucchio; (of carpet) pelo; **to ~ into** (car) stiparsi or ammucchiarsi in; **pile up** vt ammucchiare ▷ vi ammucchiarsi; **piles** [paɪlz] npl emorroidi fpl; **pile-up** [ˈpaɪlʌp] n (Aut) tamponamento a catena

pilgrimage [ˈpɪlgrɪmɪdʒ] n pellegrinaggio

pill [pɪl] n pillola; **the ~** la pillola

pillar [ˈpɪləʳ] n colonna

pillow [ˈpɪləu] n guanciale m; **pillowcase** n federa

pilot [ˈpaɪlət] n pilota m/f ▷ cpd (scheme etc) pilota inv ▷ vt pilotare; **pilot light** n fiamma pilota

pimple [ˈpɪmpl] n foruncolo

pin [pɪn] n spillo; (Tech) perno ▷ vt attaccare con uno spillo; **~s and needles** formicolio; **to ~ sb down** (fig) obbligare qn a pronunziarsi; **to ~ sth on sb** (fig) addossare la colpa di qc a qn

PIN n abbr (= personal identification number) codice m segreto

pinafore [ˈpɪnəfɔːʳ] n (also: **~ dress**) grembiule m (senza maniche)

pinch [pɪntʃ] n pizzicotto, pizzico ▷ vt pizzicare; (inf: steal) grattare; **at a ~** in caso di bisogno

pine [paɪn] n (also: **~ tree**) pino ▷ vi **to ~ for** struggersi dal desiderio di

pineapple [ˈpaɪnæpl] n ananas m inv

ping [pɪŋ] n (noise) tintinnio; **ping-pong**® n ping-pong® m

pink [pɪŋk] adj rosa inv ▷ n (colour) rosa m inv; (Bot) garofano

pinpoint [ˈpɪnpɔɪnt] vt indicare con precisione

pint [paɪnt] n pinta (BRIT = 0.57l; US = 0.47l); (BRIT: inf) ≈ birra da mezzo

pioneer [paɪəˈnɪəʳ] n pioniere(-a)

pious [ˈpaɪəs] adj pio(-a)

pip [pɪp] n (seed) seme m; (BRIT: time signal on radio) segnale m orario

pipe [paɪp] n tubo; (for smoking) pipa ▷ vt portare per mezzo di tubazione; **pipeline** n conduttura; (for oil) oleodotto; **piper** n piffero; suonatore(-trice) di cornamusa

pirate [ˈpaɪərət] n pirata m ▷ vt riprodurre

abusivamente

Pisces [ˈpaɪsiːz] n Pesci mpl

piss [pɪs] (inf) vi pisciare; **pissed** (inf) adj (drunk) ubriaco(-a) fradicio(-a)

pistol [ˈpɪstl] n pistola

piston [ˈpɪstən] n pistone m

pit [pɪt] n buca, fossa; (also: **coal ~**) miniera; (quarry) cava ▷ vt **to ~ sb against sb** opporre qn a qn

pitch [pɪtʃ] n (BRIT Sport) campo; (Mus) tono; (tar) pece f; (fig) grado, punto ▷ vt (throw) lanciare ▷ vi (fall) cascare; **to ~ a tent** piantare una tenda; **pitch-black** adj nero(-a) come la pece

pitfall [ˈpɪtfɔːl] n trappola

pith [pɪθ] n (of plant) midollo; (of orange) parte f interna della scorza; (fig) essenza, succo; vigore m

pitiful [ˈpɪtɪful] adj (touching) pietoso(-a)

pity [ˈpɪtɪ] n pietà ▷ vt aver pietà di; **what a ~!** che peccato!

pizza [ˈpiːtsə] n pizza

placard [ˈplækɑːd] n affisso

place [pleɪs] n posto, luogo; (proper position, rank, seat) posto; (house) casa, alloggio; (home): **at/to his ~** a casa sua ▷ vt (object) posare, mettere; (identify) riconoscere; individuare; **to take ~** aver luogo; succedere; **to change ~s with sb** scambiare il posto con qn; **out of ~** (not suitable) inopportuno(-a); **in the first ~** in primo luogo; **to ~ an order** dare un'ordinazione; **to be ~d** (in race, exam) classificarsi; **place mat** n sottopiatto; (in linen etc) tovaglietta; **placement** n collocamento; (job) lavoro

placid [ˈplæsɪd] adj placido(-a), calmo(-a)

plague [pleɪg] n peste f ▷ vt tormentare

plaice [pleɪs] n inv pianuzza

plain [pleɪn] adj (clear) chiaro(-a), palese; (simple) semplice; (frank) franco(-a), aperto(-a); (not handsome) bruttino(-a); (without seasoning etc) scondito(-a); naturale; (in one colour) tinta unita inv ▷ adv francamente, chiaramente ▷ n pianura; **plain chocolate** n cioccolato fondente; **plainly** adv chiaramente; (frankly) francamente

plaintiff [ˈpleɪntɪf] n attore(-trice)

plait [plæt] n treccia

plan [plæn] n pianta; (scheme) progetto, piano ▷ vt (think in advance) progettare; (prepare) organizzare ▷ vi far piani or progetti; **to ~ to do** progettare di fare

plane [pleɪn] n (Aviat) aereo; (tree) platano; (tool) pialla; (Art, Math etc) piano ▷ adj piano(-a), piatto(-a) ▷ vt (with tool) piallare

planet [ˈplænɪt] n pianeta m

plank [plæŋk] n tavola, asse f

planning ['plænɪŋ] n progettazione f;
family ~ pianificazione f delle nascite
plant [plɑːnt] n pianta; (machinery)
impianto; (factory) fabbrica ▷ vt piantare;
(bomb) mettere
plantation [plæn'teɪʃən] n piantagione f
plaque [plæk] n placca
plaster ['plɑːstəʳ] n intonaco; (also: **~
of Paris**) gesso; (BRIT: also: **sticking ~**)
cerotto ▷ vt intonacare; ingessare; (cover):
to ~ with coprire di; **plaster cast** n (Med)
ingessatura, gesso; (model, statue) modello
in gesso
plastic ['plæstɪk] n plastica ▷ adj (made
of plastic) di or in plastica; **plastic bag** n
sacchetto di plastica; **plastic surgery** n
chirurgia plastica
plate [pleɪt] n (dish) piatto; (in book) tavola;
(dental plate) dentiera; **gold/silver ~**
vasellame m d'oro/d'argento
plateau ['plætəʊ] n (pl **plateaus** or
plateaux) n altipiano
platform ['plætfɔːm] n (stage, at meeting)
palco; (Rail) marciapiede m; (BRIT: of bus)
piattaforma; **which ~ does the train for
Rome go from?** da che binario parte il
treno per Roma?
platinum ['plætɪnəm] n platino
platoon [plə'tuːn] n plotone m
platter ['plætəʳ] n piatto
plausible ['plɔːzɪbl] adj plausibile,
credibile; (person) convincente
play [pleɪ] n gioco; (Theatre) commedia
▷ vt (game) giocare a; (team, opponent)
giocare contro; (instrument, piece of music)
suonare; (record, tape) ascoltare; (role,
part) interpretare ▷ vi giocare; suonare;
recitare; **to ~ safe** giocare sul sicuro;
play back vt riascoltare, risentire;
play up vi (cause trouble) fare i capricci;
player n giocatore(-trice); (Theatre)
attore(-trice); (Mus) musicista m/f;
playful adj giocoso(-a); **playground** n
(in school) cortile m per la ricreazione; (in
park) parco m giochi inv; **playgroup** n
giardino d'infanzia; **playing card** n carta
da gioco; **playing field** n campo sportivo;
playschool n = **playgroup**; **playtime**
n (Scol) ricreazione f; **playwright** n
drammaturgo(-a)
plc abbr (= public limited company) società
per azioni a responsabilità limitata quotata
in borsa
plea [pliː] n (request) preghiera, domanda;
(Law) (argomento di) difesa
plead [pliːd] vt patrocinare; (give as excuse)
addurre a pretesto ▷ vi (Law) perorare la
causa; (beg): **to ~ with sb** implorare qn
pleasant ['plɛznt] adj piacevole, gradevole

please [pliːz] excl per piacere!, per favore!;
(acceptance): **yes, ~** sì, grazie ▷ vt piacere
a ▷ vi piacere; (think fit): **do as you ~**
faccia come le pare; **~ yourself!** come ti
(or le) pare!; **pleased** adj **pleased (with)**
contento(-a) (di); **pleased to meet you!**
piacere!
pleasure ['plɛʒəʳ] n piacere m; **"it's a ~"**
"prego"
pleat [pliːt] n piega
pledge [plɛdʒ] n pegno; (promise)
promessa ▷ vt impegnare; promettere
plentiful ['plɛntɪful] adj abbondante,
copioso(-a)
plenty ['plɛntɪ] n **~ of** tanto(-a), molto(-a);
un'abbondanza di
pliers ['plaɪəz] npl pinza
plight [plaɪt] n situazione f critica
plod [plɔd] vi camminare a stento; (fig)
sgobbare
plonk [plɔŋk] (inf) n (BRIT: wine) vino da
poco ▷ vt **to ~ sth down** buttare giù qc
bruscamente
plot [plɔt] n congiura, cospirazione f; (of
story, play) trama; (of land) lotto ▷ vt (mark
out) fare la pianta di; rilevare; (: diagram etc)
tracciare; (conspire) congiurare, cospirare
▷ vi congiurare
plough [plaʊ] (US **plow**) n aratro ▷ vt
(earth) arare; **to ~ money into** (company
etc) investire danaro in; **ploughman's
lunch** ['plaʊmənz-] (BRIT) n pasto a base di
pane, formaggio e birra
plow [plaʊ] (US) n = **plough**
ploy [plɔɪ] n stratagemma m
pluck [plʌk] vt (fruit) cogliere; (musical
instrument) pizzicare; (bird) spennare;
(hairs) togliere ▷ n coraggio, fegato; **to ~
up courage** farsi coraggio
plug [plʌg] n tappo; (Elec) spina; (Aut: also:
spark(ing) ~) candela ▷ vt (hole) tappare;
(inf: advertise) spingere; **plug in** vt (Elec)
attaccare a una presa; **plughole** n (BRIT)
scarico
plum [plʌm] n (fruit) susina
plumber ['plʌməʳ] n idraulico
plumbing ['plʌmɪŋ] n (trade) lavoro di
idraulico; (piping) tubature fpl
plummet ['plʌmɪt] vi **to ~ (down)** cadere
a piombo
plump [plʌmp] adj grassoccio(-a) ▷ vi **to ~
for** (inf: choose) decidersi per
plunge [plʌndʒ] n tuffo; (fig) caduta ▷ vt
immergere ▷ vi (fall) cadere, precipitare;
(dive) tuffarsi; **to take the ~** saltare il fosso
plural ['plʊərl] adj plurale ▷ n plurale m
plus [plʌs] n (also: **~ sign**) segno più ▷ prep
più; **ten/twenty ~** più di dieci/venti
ply [plaɪ] vt (a trade) esercitare ▷ vi (ship)

fare il servizio ▷ n (of wool, rope) capo; **to ~ sb with drink** dare di bere continuamente a qn; **plywood** n legno compensato

P.M. n abbr = **prime minister**

p.m. adv abbr (= post meridiem) del pomeriggio

PMS n abbr (= premenstrual syndrome) sindrome f premestruale

PMT n abbr (= premenstrual tension) sindrome f premestruale

pneumatic drill [nju:'mætik-] n martello pneumatico

pneumonia [nju:'məunɪə] n polmonite f

poach [pəutʃ] vt (cook: egg) affogare; (: fish) cuocere in bianco; (steal) cacciare (or pescare) di frodo ▷ vi fare il bracconiere; **poached** adj (egg) affogato(-a)

P.O. Box n abbr = **Post Office Box**

pocket ['pɔkɪt] n tasca ▷ vt intascare; **to be out of ~** (BRIT) rimetterci; **pocketbook** (US) n (wallet) portafoglio; **pocket money** n paghetta, settimana

pod [pɔd] n guscio

podiatrist [pɔ'di:ətrɪst] (US) n callista m/f, pedicure m/f

podium ['pəudɪəm] n podio

poem ['pəuɪm] n poesia

poet ['pəuɪt] n poeta/essa; **poetic** [-'ɛtɪk] adj poetico(-a); **poetry** n poesia

poignant ['pɔɪnjənt] adj struggente

point [pɔɪnt] n (gen) punto; (tip: of needle etc) punta; (in time) punto, momento; (Scol) voto; (main idea, important part) nocciolo; (Elec) presa (di corrente); (also: **decimal ~**): **2 ~ 3 (2.3)** 2 virgola 3 (2,3) ▷ vt (show) indicare; (gun etc): **to ~ sth at** puntare qc contro ▷ vi **to ~ at** mostrare a dito; **~s** npl (Aut) puntine fpl; (Rail) scambio; **to be on the ~ of doing sth** essere sul punto di or stare per fare qc; **to make a ~** fare un'osservazione; **to get/miss the ~** capire/non capire; **to come to the ~** venire al fatto; **there's no ~ in doing** è inutile (fare); **point out** vt far notare; **point-blank** adv (also: **at point-blank range**) a bruciapelo; (fig) categoricamente; **pointed** adj (shape) aguzzo(-a), appuntito(-a); (remark) specifico(-a); **pointer** n (needle) lancetta; (fig) indicazione f, consiglio; **pointless** adj inutile, vano(-a); **point of view** n punto di vista

poison ['pɔɪzn] n veleno ▷ vt avvelenare; **poisonous** adj velenoso(-a)

poke [pəuk] vt (fire) attizzare; (jab with finger, stick etc) punzecchiare; (put): **to ~ sth in(to)** spingere qc dentro; **poke about** or **around** vi frugare; **poke out** vi (stick out) sporger fuori

poker ['pəukər] n attizzatoio; (Cards) poker m

Poland ['pəulənd] n Polonia

polar ['pəulər] adj polare; **polar bear** n orso bianco

Pole [pəul] n polacco(-a)

pole [pəul] n (of wood) palo; (Elec, Geo) polo; **pole bean** (US) n (runner bean) fagiolino; **pole vault** n salto con l'asta

police [pə'li:s] n polizia ▷ vt mantenere l'ordine in; **police car** n macchina della polizia; **police constable** (BRIT) n agente m di polizia; **police force** n corpo di polizia, polizia; **policeman** (irreg) n poliziotto, agente m di polizia; **police officer** n = **police constable**; **police station** n posto di polizia; **policewoman** (irreg) n donna f poliziotto inv

policy ['pɔlɪsɪ] n politica; (also: **insurance ~**) polizza (d'assicurazione)

polio ['pəulɪəu] n polio f

Polish ['pəulɪʃ] adj polacco(-a) ▷ n (Ling) polacco

polish ['pɔlɪʃ] n (for shoes) lucido; (for floor) cera; (for nails) smalto; (shine) lucentezza, lustro; (fig: refinement) raffinatezza ▷ vt lucidare; (fig: improve) raffinare; **polish off** vt (food) mangiarsi; **polished** adj (fig) raffinato(-a)

polite [pə'laɪt] adj cortese; **politeness** n cortesia

political [pə'lɪtɪkl] adj politico(-a); **politically** adv politicamente; **politically correct** politicamente corretto(-a)

politician [pɔlɪ'tɪʃən] n politico

politics ['pɔlɪtɪks] n politica ▷ npl (views, policies) idee fpl politiche

poll [pəul] n scrutinio; (votes cast) voti mpl; (also: **opinion ~**) sondaggio (d'opinioni) ▷ vt ottenere

pollen ['pɔlən] n polline m

polling station ['pəulɪŋ-] (BRIT) n sezione f elettorale

pollute [pə'lu:t] vt inquinare

pollution [pə'lu:ʃən] n inquinamento

polo ['pəuləu] n polo; **polo-neck** n collo alto; (also: **polo-neck sweater**) dolcevita ▷ adj a collo alto; **polo shirt** n polo f inv

polyester [pɔlɪ'ɛstər] n poliestere m

polystyrene [pɔlɪ'staɪri:n] n polistirolo

polythene ['pɔlɪθi:n] n politene m; **polythene bag** n sacco di plastica

pomegranate ['pɔmɪgrænɪt] n melagrana

pompous ['pɔmpəs] adj pomposo(-a)

pond [pɔnd] n pozza; stagno

ponder ['pɔndər] vt ponderare, riflettere su

pony ['pəunɪ] n pony m inv; **ponytail** n coda di cavallo; **pony trekking**

[-trekɪŋ] (BRIT) n escursione f a cavallo
poodle ['puːdl] n barboncino, barbone m
pool [puːl] n (puddle) pozza; (pond) stagno; (also: **swimming ~**) piscina; (fig: of light) cerchio; (billiards) specie di biliardo a buca ▷ vt mettere in comune; **~s** npl (football pools) ≈ totocalcio; **typing ~** servizio comune di dattilografia
poor [puə^r] adj povero(-a); (mediocre) mediocre, cattivo(-a) ▷ npl **the ~** i poveri; **~ in** povero(-a) di; **poorly** adv poveramente; male ▷ adj indisposto(-a), malato(-a)
pop [pɔp] n (noise) schiocco; (Mus) musica pop; (drink) bibita gasata; (US: inf: father) babbo ▷ vt (put) mettere (in fretta) ▷ vi scoppiare; (cork) schioccare; **pop in** vi passare; **pop out** vi fare un salto fuori; **popcorn** n pop-corn m
poplar ['pɔplə^r] n pioppo
popper ['pɔpə^r] n bottone m a pressione
poppy ['pɔpɪ] n papavero
Popsicle® ['pɔpsɪkl] (US) n (ice lolly) ghiacciolo
pop star n pop star f inv
popular ['pɔpjulə^r] adj popolare; (fashionable) in voga; **popularity** [-'lærɪtɪ] n popolarità
population [pɔpju'leɪʃən] n popolazione f
porcelain ['pɔːslɪn] n porcellana
porch [pɔːtʃ] n veranda
pore [pɔː^r] n poro ▷ vi **to ~ over** essere immerso(-a) in
pork [pɔːk] n carne f di maiale; **pork chop** n braciola or costoletta di maiale; **pork pie** n (BRIT: Culin) pasticcio di maiale in crosta
porn [pɔːn] (inf) n pornografia ▷ adj porno inv; **pornographic** [pɔːnə'græfɪk] adj pornografico(-a); **pornography** [pɔː'nɔgrəfɪ] n pornografia
porridge ['pɔrɪdʒ] n porridge m
port [pɔːt] n (gen, wine) porto; (Naut: left side) babordo
portable ['pɔːtəbl] adj portatile
porter ['pɔːtə^r] n (for luggage) facchino, portabagagli m inv; (doorkeeper) portiere m, portinaio
portfolio [pɔːt'fəulɪəu] n (case) cartella; (Pol, Finance) portafoglio; (of artist) raccolta dei propri lavori
portion ['pɔːʃən] n porzione f
port of call n (porto di) scalo
portrait ['pɔːtreɪt] n ritratto
portray [pɔː'treɪ] vt fare il ritratto di; (character on stage) rappresentare; (in writing) ritrarre
Portugal ['pɔːtjugl] n Portogallo
Portuguese [pɔːtju'giːz] adj portoghese ▷ n inv portoghese m/f; (Ling) portoghese m

pose [pəuz] n posa ▷ vi posare; (pretend): **to ~ as** atteggiarsi a, posare a ▷ vt porre
posh [pɔʃ] (inf) adj elegante; (family) per bene
position [pə'zɪʃən] n posizione f; (job) posto ▷ vt sistemare
positive ['pɔzɪtɪv] adj positivo(-a); (certain) sicuro(-a), certo(-a); (definite) preciso(-a), definitivo(-a); **positively** adv (affirmatively, enthusiastically) positivamente; (decisively) decisamente; (really) assolutamente
possess [pə'zɛs] vt possedere; **possession** [pə'zɛʃən] n possesso; **possessions** npl (belongings) beni mpl; **possessive** adj possessivo(-a)
possibility [pɔsɪ'bɪlɪtɪ] n possibilità f inv
possible ['pɔsɪbl] adj possibile; **as big as ~** il più grande possibile; **possibly** ['pɔsɪblɪ] adv (perhaps) forse; **if you possibly can** se le è possibile; **I cannot possibly come** proprio non posso venire
post [pəust] n (BRIT) posta; (: collection) levata; (job, situation) posto; (Mil) postazione f; (pole) palo ▷ vt (BRIT: send by post) imbucare; (: appoint): **to ~ to** assegnare a; **where can I ~ these cards?** dove posso imbucare queste cartoline?; **postage** n affrancatura; **postal** adj postale; **postal order** n vaglia m inv postale; **postbox** (BRIT) n cassetta postale; **postcard** n cartolina; **postcode** n (BRIT) codice m (di avviamento) postale
poster ['pəustə^r] n manifesto, affisso
postgraduate ['pəust'grædjuət] n laureato/a che continua gli studi
postman ['pəustmən] (irreg) n postino
postmark ['pəustmɑːk] n bollo or timbro postale
post-mortem [-'mɔːtəm] n autopsia
post office n (building) ufficio postale; (organization): **the Post Office** ≈ le Poste e Telecomunicazioni
postpone [pəs'pəun] vt rinviare
posture ['pɔstʃə^r] n portamento; (pose) posa, atteggiamento
postwoman ['pəustwumən] (BRIT: irreg) n postina
pot [pɔt] n (for cooking) pentola; casseruola; (teapot) teiera; (coffeepot) caffettiera; (for plants, jam) vaso; (inf: marijuana) erba ▷ vt (plant) piantare in vaso; **a ~ of tea for two** tè per due; **to go to ~** (inf: work, performance) andare in malora
potato [pə'teɪtəu] (pl **potatoes**) n patata; **potato peeler** n sbucciapatate m inv
potent ['pəutnt] adj potente, forte
potential [pə'tɛnʃl] adj potenziale ▷ n possibilità fpl
pothole ['pɔthəul] n (in road) buca; (BRIT:

underground) caverna

pot plant n pianta in vaso

potter ['pɔtə'] n vasaio ▷ vi **to ~ around, ~ about** (BRIT) lavoracchiare; **pottery** n ceramiche fpl; *(factory)* fabbrica di ceramiche

potty ['pɔtɪ] adj *(inf: mad)* tocco(-a) ▷ n *(child's)* vasino

pouch [pautʃ] n borsa; *(Zool)* marsupio

poultry ['pəultrɪ] n pollame m

pounce [pauns] vi **to ~ (on)** piombare (su)

pound [paund] n *(weight)* libbra; *(money)* (lira) sterlina ▷ vt *(beat)* battere; *(crush)* pestare, polverizzare ▷ vi *(beat)* battere, martellare; **pound sterling** n sterlina (inglese)

pour [pɔː'] vt versare ▷ vi riversarsi; *(rain)* piovere a dirotto; **pour in** vi affluire in gran quantità; **pour out** vi *(people)* uscire a fiumi ▷ vt vuotare; versare; *(fig)* sfogare; **pouring** adj **pouring rain** pioggia torrenziale

pout [paut] vi sporgere le labbra; fare il broncio

poverty ['pɔvətɪ] n povertà, miseria

powder ['paudə'] n polvere f ▷ vt **to ~ one's face** incipriarsi il viso; **powdered milk** n latte m in polvere

power ['pauə'] n *(strength)* potenza, forza; *(ability, Pol: of party, leader)* potere m; *(Elec)* corrente f; **to be in ~** *(Pol etc)* essere al potere; **power cut** (BRIT) n interruzione f or mancanza di corrente; **power failure** n interruzione f della corrente elettrica; **powerful** adj potente, forte; **powerless** adj impotente; **powerless to do** impossibilitato(-a) a fare; **power point** (BRIT) n presa di corrente; **power station** n centrale f elettrica

p.p. abbr = **per procurationem; p.p. J. Smith** per J. Smith; *(= pages)* p.p.

PR abbr = **public relations**

practical ['præktɪkl] adj pratico(-a); **practical joke** n beffa; **practically** adv praticamente

practice ['præktɪs] n pratica; *(of profession)* esercizio; *(at football etc)* allenamento; *(business)* gabinetto; clientela ▷ vt, vi (US) = **practise; in ~** *(in reality)* in pratica; **out of ~** fuori esercizio

practise ['præktɪs] (US **practice**) vt *(work at: piano, one's backhand etc)* esercitarsi a; *(train for: skiing, running etc)* allenarsi a; *(a sport, religion)* praticare; *(method)* usare; *(profession)* esercitare ▷ vi esercitarsi; *(train)* allenarsi; *(lawyer, doctor)* esercitare; **practising** adj *(Christian etc)* praticante; *(lawyer)* che esercita la professione

practitioner [præk'tɪʃənə'] n professionista m/f

pragmatic [præg'mætɪk] adj pragmatico(-a)

prairie ['preərɪ] n prateria

praise [preɪz] n elogio, lode f ▷ vt elogiare, lodare

pram [præm] (BRIT) n carrozzina

prank [præŋk] n burla

prawn [prɔːn] n gamberetto; **prawn cocktail** n cocktail m inv di gamberetti

pray [preɪ] vi pregare; **prayer** [prɛə'] n preghiera

preach [priːtʃ] vt, vi predicare; **preacher** n predicatore(-trice); *(US: minister)* pastore m

precarious [prɪ'kɛərɪəs] adj precario(-a)

precaution [prɪ'kɔːʃən] n precauzione f

precede [prɪ'siːd] vt precedere; **precedent** ['presɪdənt] n precedente m; **preceding** [prɪ'siːdɪŋ] adj precedente

precinct ['priːsɪŋkt] (US) n circoscrizione f

precious ['prɛʃəs] adj prezioso(-a)

precise [prɪ'saɪs] adj preciso(-a); **precisely** adv precisamente

precision [prɪ'sɪʒən] n precisione f

predator ['predətə'] n predatore m

predecessor ['priːdɪsɛsə'] n predecessore(-a)

predicament [prɪ'dɪkəmənt] n situazione f difficile

predict [prɪ'dɪkt] vt predire; **predictable** adj prevedibile; **prediction** [prɪ'dɪkʃən] n predizione f

predominantly [prɪ'dɔmɪnəntlɪ] adv in maggior parte; soprattutto

preface ['prɛfəs] n prefazione f

prefect ['priːfɛkt] n *(BRIT: in school)* studente(-essa) con funzioni disciplinari; *(French etc, Admin)* prefetto

prefer [prɪ'fəː'] vt preferire; **to ~ doing** or **to do** preferire fare; **preferable** ['prɛfrəbl] adj preferibile; **preferably** ['prɛfrəblɪ] adv preferibilmente; **preference** ['prɛfrəns] n preferenza

prefix ['priːfɪks] n prefisso

pregnancy ['prɛgnənsɪ] n gravidanza

pregnant ['prɛgnənt] adj incinta ag

prehistoric ['priːhɪs'tɔrɪk] adj preistorico(-a)

prejudice ['prɛdʒudɪs] n pregiudizio; *(harm)* torto, danno; **prejudiced** adj **prejudiced (against)** prevenuto(-a) (contro); **prejudiced (in favour of)** ben disposto(-a) (verso)

preliminary [prɪ'lɪmɪnərɪ] adj preliminare

prelude ['prɛljuːd] n preludio

premature ['prɛmətʃuə'] adj prematuro(-a)

premier ['prɛmɪə'] adj primo(-a) ▷ n *(Pol)* primo ministro

première ['prɛmɪɛəʳ] n prima
Premier League n ≈ serie A
premises ['prɛmɪsɪz] npl locale m; **on the ~** sul posto; **business ~** locali commerciali
premium ['pri:mɪəm] n premio; **to be at a ~** essere ricercatissimo
premonition [prɛmə'nɪʃən] n premonizione f
preoccupied [pri:'ɔkjupaɪd] adj preoccupato(-a)
prepaid [pri:'peɪd] adj pagato(-a) in anticipo
preparation [prɛpə'reɪʃən] n preparazione f; **~s** npl (for trip, war) preparativi mpl
preparatory school [prɪ'pærətərɪ-] n scuola elementare privata
prepare [prɪ'pɛəʳ] vt preparare ▷ vi **to ~ for** prepararsi a; **~d to** pronto(-a) a
preposition [prɛpə'zɪʃən] n preposizione f
prep school n = **preparatory school**
prerequisite [pri:'rɛkwɪzɪt] n requisito indispensabile
preschool ['pri:'sku:l] adj (age) prescolastico(-a); (child) in età prescolastica
prescribe [prɪ'skraɪb] vt (Med) prescrivere
prescription [prɪ'skrɪpʃən] n prescrizione f; (Med) ricetta; **could you write me a ~?** mi può fare una ricetta medica?
presence ['prɛzns] n presenza; **~ of mind** presenza di spirito
present [adj, n 'prɛznt, vb prɪ'zɛnt] adj presente; (wife, residence, job) attuale ▷ n (actuality): **the ~** il presente; (gift) regalo ▷ vt presentare; (give): **to ~ sb with sth** offrire qc a qn; **to give sb a ~** fare un regalo a qn; **at ~** al momento; **presentable** [prɪ'zɛntəbl] adj presentabile;
presentation [-'teɪʃən] n presentazione f; (ceremony) consegna ufficiale; **present-day** adj attuale, d'oggigiorno; **presenter** n (Radio, TV) presentatore(-trice);
presently adv (soon) fra poco, presto; (at present) al momento; **present participle** n participio presente
preservation [prɛzə'veɪʃən] n preservazione f, conservazione f
preservative [prɪ'zə:vətɪv] n conservante m
preserve [prɪ'zə:v] vt (keep safe) preservare, proteggere; (maintain) conservare; (food) mettere in conserva ▷ n (often pl: jam) marmellata; (: fruit) frutta sciroppata
preside [prɪ'zaɪd] vi **to ~ (over)** presiedere (a)
president ['prɛzɪdənt] n presidente m; **presidential** [-'dɛnʃl] adj presidenziale

press [prɛs] n (newspapers etc): **the P~** la stampa; (tool, machine) pressa; (for wine) torchio ▷ vt (push) premere, pigiare; (squeeze) spremere; (: hand) stringere; (clothes: iron) stirare; (pursue) incalzare; (insist): **to ~ sth on sb** far accettare qc da qn ▷ vi premere; accalcare; **we are ~ed for time** ci manca il tempo; **to ~ for sth** insistere per avere qc; **press conference** n conferenza f stampa inv; **pressing** adj urgente; **press stud** (BRIT) n bottone m a pressione; **press-up** (BRIT) n flessione f sulle braccia
pressure ['prɛʃəʳ] n pressione f; **to put ~ on sb (to do)** mettere qn sotto pressione (affinché faccia); **pressure cooker** n pentola a pressione; **pressure group** n gruppo di pressione
prestige [prɛs'ti:ʒ] n prestigio
prestigious [prɛs'tɪdʒəs] adj prestigioso(-a)
presumably [prɪ'zju:məblɪ] adv presumibilmente
presume [prɪ'zju:m] vt supporre
pretence (US **pretense**) n (claim) pretesa; **to make a ~ of doing** far finta di fare; **under false ~s** con l'inganno
pretend [prɪ'tɛnd] vt (feign) fingere ▷ vi far finta; **to ~ to do** far finta di fare
pretense [prɪ'tɛns] (US) n = **pretence**
pretentious [prɪ'tɛnʃəs] adj pretenzioso(-a)
pretext ['pri:tɛkst] n pretesto
pretty ['prɪtɪ] adj grazioso(-a), carino(-a) ▷ adv abbastanza, assai
prevail [prɪ'veɪl] vi (win, be usual) prevalere; (persuade): **to ~ (up)on sb to do** persuadere qn a fare; **prevailing** adj dominante
prevalent ['prɛvələnt] adj (belief) predominante; (customs) diffuso(-a); (fashion) corrente; (disease) comune
prevent [prɪ'vɛnt] vt **to ~ sb from doing** impedire a qn di fare; **to ~ sth from happening** impedire che qc succeda; **prevention** [-'vɛnʃən] n prevenzione f; **preventive** adj preventivo(-a)
preview ['pri:vju:] n (of film) anteprima
previous ['pri:vɪəs] adj precedente; anteriore; **previously** adv prima
prey [preɪ] n preda ▷ vi **to ~ on** far preda di; **it was ~ing on his mind** lo stava ossessionando
price [praɪs] n prezzo ▷ vt (goods) fissare il prezzo di; valutare; **priceless** adj inapprezzabile; **price list** n listino (dei) prezzi
prick [prɪk] n puntura ▷ vt pungere; **to ~ up one's ears** drizzare gli orecchi

prickly ['prɪklɪ] *adj* spinoso(-a)

pride [praɪd] *n* orgoglio; superbia ▷ *vt* **to ~ o.s. on** essere orgoglioso(-a) di, vantarsi di

priest [priːst] *n* prete *m*, sacerdote *m*

primarily ['praɪmərɪlɪ] *adv* principalmente, essenzialmente

primary ['praɪmərɪ] *adj* primario(-a); (*first in importance*) primo(-a) ▷ *n* (*us: election*) primarie *fpl*; **primary school** *n* scuola elementare

prime [praɪm] *adj* primario(-a), fondamentale; (*excellent*) di prima qualità ▷ *vt* (*wood*) preparare; (*fig*) mettere al corrente ▷ *n* **in the ~ of life** nel fiore della vita; **Prime Minister** *n* primo ministro

primitive ['prɪmɪtɪv] *adj* primitivo(-a)

primrose ['prɪmrəuz] *n* primavera

prince [prɪns] *n* principe *m*

princess [prɪn'sɛs] *n* principessa

principal ['prɪnsɪpl] *adj* principale ▷ *n* (*headmaster*) preside *m*; **principally** *adv* principalmente

principle ['prɪnsɪpl] *n* principio; **in ~** in linea di principio; **on ~** per principio

print [prɪnt] *n* (*mark*) impronta; (*letters*) caratteri *mpl*; (*fabric*) tessuto stampato; (*Art, Phot*) stampa ▷ *vt* imprimere; (*publish*) stampare, pubblicare; (*write in capitals*) scrivere in stampatello; **out of ~** esaurito(-a); **print out** *vt* (*Comput*) stampare; **printer** *n* tipografo; (*machine*) stampante *f*; **printout** *n* tabulato

prior ['praɪə*r*] *adj* precedente; (*claim etc*) più importante; **~ to doing** prima di fare

priority [praɪ'ɔrɪtɪ] *n* priorità *f inv*; precedenza

prison ['prɪzn] *n* prigione *f* ▷ *cpd* (*system*) carcerario(-a); (*conditions, food*) nelle *or* delle prigioni; **prisoner** *n* prigioniero(-a); **prisoner-of-war** *n* prigioniero(-a) di guerra

pristine ['prɪstiːn] *adj* immacolato(-a)

privacy ['prɪvəsɪ] *n* solitudine *f*, intimità

private ['praɪvɪt] *adj* privato(-a); personale ▷ *n* soldato semplice; **"~"** (*on envelope*) "riservata"; (*on door*) "privato"; **in ~** in privato; **privately** *adv* in privato; (*within oneself*) dentro di sé; **private property** *n* proprietà privata; **private school** *n* scuola privata

privatize ['praɪvɪtaɪz] *vt* privatizzare

privilege ['prɪvɪlɪdʒ] *n* privilegio

prize [praɪz] *n* premio ▷ *adj* (*example, idiot*) perfetto(-a); (*bull, novel*) premiato(-a) ▷ *vt* apprezzare, pregiare; **prize-giving** *n* premiazione *f*; **prizewinner** *n* premiato(-a)

pro [prəu] *n* (*Sport*) professionista *m/f* ▷ *prep* pro; **the ~s and cons** il pro e il contro

probability [prɔbə'bɪlɪtɪ] *n* probabilità *f inv*; **in all ~** con tutta probabilità

probable ['prɔbəbl] *adj* probabile

probably ['prɔbəblɪ] *adv* probabilmente

probation [prə'beɪʃən] *n* **on ~** (*employee*) in prova; (*Law*) in libertà vigilata

probe [prəub] *n* (*Med, Space*) sonda; (*enquiry*) indagine *f*, investigazione *f* ▷ *vt* sondare, esplorare; indagare

problem ['prɔbləm] *n* problema *m*

procedure [prə'siːdʒə*r*] *n* (*Admin, Law*) procedura; (*method*) metodo, procedimento

proceed [prə'siːd] *vi* (*go forward*) avanzare, andare avanti; (*go about it*) procedere; (*continue*): **to ~ (with)** continuare; **to ~ to** andare a; passare a; **to ~ to do** mettersi a fare; **proceedings** *npl* misure *fpl*; (*Law*) procedimento; (*meeting*) riunione *f*; (*records*) rendiconti *mpl*; atti *mpl*; **proceeds** ['prəusiːdz] *npl* profitto, incasso

process ['prəusɛs] *n* processo; (*method*) metodo, sistema *m* ▷ *vt* trattare; (*information*) elaborare

procession [prə'sɛʃən] *n* processione *f*, corteo; **funeral ~** corteo funebre

proclaim [prə'kleɪm] *vt* proclamare, dichiarare

prod [prɔd] *vt* dare un colpetto a; pungolare ▷ *n* colpetto

produce [*n* 'prɔdjuːs, *vb* prə'djuːs] *n* (*Agr*) prodotto, prodotti *mpl* ▷ *vt* produrre; (*show*) esibire, mostrare; (*cause*) cagionare, causare; **producer** *n* (*Theatre*) regista *m/f*; (*Agr, Cinema*) produttore *m*

product ['prɔdʌkt] *n* prodotto; **production** [prə'dʌkʃən] *n* produzione *f*; **productive** [prə'dʌktɪv] *adj* produttivo(-a); **productivity** [prɔdʌk'tɪvɪtɪ] *n* produttività

Prof. *abbr* (= *professor*) Prof.

profession [prə'fɛʃən] *n* professione *f*; **professional** *n* professionista *m/f* ▷ *adj* professionale; (*work*) da professionista

professor [prə'fɛsə*r*] *n* professore *m* (*titolare di una cattedra*); (*us*) professore(-essa)

profile ['prəufaɪl] *n* profilo

profit ['prɔfɪt] *n* profitto; beneficio ▷ *vi* **to ~ (by** *or* **from)** approfittare (di); **profitable** *adj* redditizio(-a)

profound [prə'faund] *adj* profondo(-a)

programme ['prəugræm] (*us* **program**) *n* programma *m* ▷ *vt* programmare; **programmer** (*us* **programer**) *n* programmatore(-trice); **programming** (*us* **programing**) *n* programmazione *f*

progress [*n* 'prəugrɛs, *vb* prə'grɛs] *n*

progresso ▷ *vi* avanzare, procedere;
in ~ in corso; **to make ~** far progressi;
progressive [-'grɛsɪv] *adj* progressivo(-a);
(*person*) progressista
prohibit [prə'hɪbɪt] *vt* proibire, vietare
project [*n* 'prɒdʒɛkt, *vb* prə'dʒɛkt] *n* (*plan*)
piano; (*venture*) progetto; (*Scol*) studio
▷ *vt* proiettare ▷ *vi* (*stick out*) sporgere;
projection [prə'dʒɛkʃən] *n* proiezione
f; sporgenza; **projector** [prə'dʒɛktə[r]] *n*
proiettore *m*
prolific [prə'lɪfɪk] *adj* (*artist etc*)
fecondo(-a)
prolong [prə'lɒŋ] *vt* prolungare
prom [prɒm] *n abbr* = **promenade**; (*us:
ball*) ballo studentesco

● **PROM**

● In Gran Bretagna i **Proms**, o
● "promenade concerts", sono concerti di
● musica classica, i più noti dei quali sono
● eseguiti nella prestigiosa **Royal Albert
Hall** a Londra. Si chiamano così perché
● un tempo il pubblico seguiva i concerti
● in piedi, passeggiando (in inglese
● "promenade" voleva dire, appunto,
● passeggiata). Negli Stati Uniti, invece,
● con **prom**, si intende l'annuale ballo
● studentesco di un'università o di una
● scuola secondaria.

promenade [prɒmə'nɑːd] *n* (*by sea*)
lungomare *m*
prominent ['prɒmɪnənt] *adj*
(*standing out*) prominente; (*important*)
importante
promiscuous [prə'mɪskjuəs] *adj* (*sexually*)
di facili costumi
promise ['prɒmɪs] *n* promessa ▷ *vt*,
vi promettere; **to ~ sb sth, ~ sth to sb**
promettere qc a qn; **to ~ (sb) that/to
do sth** promettere (a qn) che/di fare qc;
promising *adj* promettente
promote [prə'məut] *vt* promuovere;
(*venture, event*) organizzare; **promotion**
[-'məuʃən] *n* promozione *f*
prompt [prɒmpt] *adj* rapido(-a),
svelto(-a); puntuale; (*reply*) sollecito(-a)
▷ *adv* (*punctually*) in punto ▷ *n* (*Comput*)
prompt *m* ▷ *vt* incitare; provocare;
(*Theatre*) suggerire a; **to ~ sb to do** incitare
qn a fare; **promptly** *adv* prontamente;
puntualmente
prone [prəun] *adj* (*lying*) prono(-a); **~ to**
propenso(-a) a, incline a
prong [prɒŋ] *n* rebbio, punta
pronoun ['prəunaun] *n* pronome *m*
pronounce [prə'nauns] *vt* pronunciare;

how do you ~ it? come si pronuncia?
pronunciation [prənʌnsɪ'eɪʃən] *n*
pronuncia
proof [pruːf] *n* prova; (*of book*) bozza; (*Phot*)
provino ▷ *adj* **~ against** a prova di
prop [prɒp] *n* sostegno, appoggio ▷ *vt*
(*also:* **~ up**) sostenere, appoggiare; (*lean*):
to ~ sth against appoggiare qc contro
ora; **~s** oggetti *m inv* di scena; **prop up** *vt*
sostenere, appoggiare
propaganda [prɒpə'gændə] *n*
propaganda
propeller [prə'pɛlə[r]] *n* elica
proper ['prɒpə[r]] *adj* (*suited, right*)
adatto(-a), appropriato(-a); (*seemly*)
decente; (*authentic*) vero(-a); (*inf: real:
noun*) + vero(-a) e proprio(-a); **properly**
['prɒpəlɪ] *adv* (*eat, study*) bene; (*behave*)
come si deve; **proper noun** *n* nome *m*
proprio
property ['prɒpətɪ] *n* (*things owned*) beni
mpl; (*land, building*) proprietà *f inv*; (*Chem
etc: quality*) proprietà
prophecy ['prɒfɪsɪ] *n* profezia
prophet ['prɒfɪt] *n* profeta *m*
proportion [prə'pɔːʃən] *n* proporzione *f*;
(*share*) parte *f*; **~s** *npl* (*size*) proporzioni *fpl*;
proportional *adj* proporzionale
proposal [prə'pəuzl] *n* proposta; (*plan*)
progetto; (*of marriage*) proposta di
matrimonio
propose [prə'pəuz] *vt* proporre, suggerire
▷ *vi* fare una proposta di matrimonio; **to
~ to do** proporsi di fare, aver l'intenzione
di fare
proposition [prɒpə'zɪʃən] *n* proposizione
f; (*offer*) proposta
proprietor [prə'praɪətə[r]] *n*
proprietario(-a)
prose [prəuz] *n* prosa
prosecute ['prɒsɪkjuːt] *vt* processare;
prosecution [-'kjuːʃən] *n* processo;
(*accusing side*) accusa; **prosecutor** *n* (*also:
public prosecutor*) ≈ procuratore *m* della
Repubblica
prospect [*n* 'prɒspɛkt, *vb* prə'spɛkt] *n*
prospettiva; (*hope*) speranza ▷ *vi* **to ~ for**
cercare; **~s** *npl* (*for work etc*) prospettive
fpl; **prospective** [-'spɛktɪv] *adj* possibile;
futuro(-a)
prospectus [prə'spɛktəs] *n* prospetto,
programma *m*
prosper ['prɒspə[r]] *vi* prosperare;
prosperity [prɒ'spɛrɪtɪ] *n* prosperità;
prosperous *adj* prospero(-a)
prostitute ['prɒstɪtjuːt] *n* prostituta;
male ~ uomo che si prostituisce
protect [prə'tɛkt] *vt* proteggere,
salvaguardare; **protection** *n* protezione *f*;

protective adj protettivo(-a)

protein ['prəuti:n] n proteina

protest [n 'prəutest, vb prə'test] n protesta ▷ vt, vi protestare

Protestant ['prɔtɪstənt] adj, n protestante m/f

protester [prə'testə^r] n dimostrante m/f

protractor [prə'træktə^r] n (Geom) goniometro

proud [praud] adj fiero(-a), orgoglioso(-a); (pej) superbo(-a)

prove [pru:v] vt provare, dimostrare ▷ vi **to ~ (to be) correct** etc risultare vero(-a) etc; **to ~ o.s.** mostrare le proprie capacità

proverb ['prɔvə:b] n proverbio

provide [prə'vaɪd] vt fornire, provvedere; **to ~ sb with sth** fornire or provvedere qn di qc; **provide for** vt fus provvedere a; (future event) prevedere; **provided** conj **provided (that)** purché + sub, a condizione che + sub; **providing** [prə'vaɪdɪŋ] conj purché +sub, a condizione che +sub

province ['prɔvɪns] n provincia; **provincial** [prə'vɪnʃəl] adj provinciale

provision [prə'vɪʒən] n (supply) riserva; (supplying) provvista; (stipulation) condizione f; **~s** npl (food) provviste fpl; **provisional** adj provvisorio(-a)

provocative [prə'vɔkətɪv] adj (aggressive) provocatorio(-a); (thought-provoking) stimolante; (seductive) provocante

provoke [prə'vəuk] vt provocare; incitare

prowl [praul] vi (also: **~ about, ~ around**) aggirarsi ▷ n **to be on the ~** aggirarsi

proximity [prɔk'sɪmɪtɪ] n prossimità

proxy ['prɔksɪ] n **by ~** per procura

prudent ['pru:dnt] adj prudente

prune [pru:n] n prugna secca ▷ vt potare

pry [praɪ] vi **to ~ into** ficcare il naso in

PS abbr (= postscript) P.S.

pseudonym ['sju:dənɪm] n pseudonimo

psychiatric [saɪkɪ'ætrɪk] adj psichiatrico(-a)

psychiatrist [saɪ'kaɪətrɪst] n psichiatra m/f

psychic ['saɪkɪk] adj (also: **~al**) psichico(-a); (person) dotato(-a) di qualità telepatiche

psychoanalysis [saɪkəuə'nælɪsɪs, -si:z] (pl **-ses**) n psicanalisi f inv

psychological [saɪkə'lɔdʒɪkl] adj psicologico(-a)

psychologist [saɪ'kɔlədʒɪst] n psicologo(-a)

psychology [saɪ'kɔlədʒɪ] n psicologia

psychotherapy [saɪkəu'θerəpɪ] n psicoterapia

pt abbr (= pint; point) pt.

PTO abbr (= please turn over) v.r.

pub [pʌb] n abbr (= public house) pub m inv

puberty ['pju:bətɪ] n pubertà

public ['pʌblɪk] adj pubblico(-a) ▷ n pubblico; **in ~** in pubblico

publication [pʌblɪ'keɪʃən] n pubblicazione f

public: **public company** n società f inv per azioni (costituita tramite pubblica sottoscrizione); **public convenience** (BRIT) n gabinetti mpl; **public holiday** n giorno festivo, festa nazionale; **public house** (BRIT) n pub m inv

publicity [pʌb'lɪsɪtɪ] n pubblicità

publicize ['pʌblɪsaɪz] vt rendere pubblico(-a)

public: **public limited company** n ≈ società per azioni a responsabilità limitata (quotata in Borsa); **publicly** ['pʌblɪklɪ] adv pubblicamente; **public opinion** n opinione f pubblica; **public relations** n pubbliche relazioni fpl; **public school** n (BRIT) scuola privata; (US) scuola statale; **public transport** n mezzi mpl pubblici

publish ['pʌblɪʃ] vt pubblicare; **publisher** n editore m; **publishing** n (industry) editoria; (of a book) pubblicazione f

pub lunch n pranzo semplice ed economico servito nei pub

pudding ['pudɪŋ] n budino; (BRIT: dessert) dolce m; **black ~**, (US) **blood ~** sanguinaccio

puddle ['pʌdl] n pozza, pozzanghera

Puerto Rico ['pwə:təu'ri:kəu] n Portorico

puff [pʌf] n sbuffo ▷ vt **to ~ one's pipe** tirare sboccate di fumo ▷ vi (pant) ansare; **puff pastry** n pasta sfoglia

pull [pul] n (tug): **to give sth a ~** tirare su qc ▷ vt tirare; (muscle) strappare; (trigger) premere ▷ vi tirare; **to ~ to pieces** fare a pezzi; **to ~ one's punches** (Boxing) risparmiare l'avversario; **to ~ one's weight** dare il proprio contributo; **to ~ o.s. together** ricomporsi, riprendersi; **to ~ sb's leg** prendere in giro qn; **pull apart** vt (break) fare a pezzi; **pull away** vi (move off: vehicle) muoversi, partire; (boat) staccarsi dal molo, salpare; (draw back: person) indietreggiare; **pull back** vt (lever etc) tirare indietro; (curtains) aprire ▷ vi (from confrontation etc) tirarsi indietro; (Mil: withdraw) ritirarsi; **pull down** vt (house) demolire; (tree) abbattere; **pull in** vi (Aut: at the kerb) accostarsi; (Rail) entrare in stazione; **pull off** vt (clothes) togliere; (deal etc) portare a compimento; **pull out** vi partire; (Aut: come out of line) spostarsi sulla mezzeria ▷ vt staccare; far uscire; (withdraw) ritirare; **pull over** vi (Aut) accostare; **pull up** vi (stop) fermarsi ⊳ vt (raise) sollevare; (uproot) sradicare

pulley ['pulɪ] n puleggia, carrucola

pullover ['puləuvər] n pullover m inv

pulp [pʌlp] n (of fruit) polpa

pulpit ['pulpɪt] n pulpito

pulse [pʌls] n polso; (Bot) legume m; **~s** npl (Culin) legumi mpl

puma ['pju:mə] n puma m inv

pump [pʌmp] n pompa; (shoe) scarpetta ⊳ vt pompare; **pump up** vt gonfiare

pumpkin ['pʌmpkɪn] n zucca

pun [pʌn] n gioco di parole

punch [pʌntʃ] n (blow) pugno; (tool) punzone m; (drink) ponce m ⊳ vt (hit): **to ~ sb/sth** dare un pugno a qn/qc; **punch-up** (BRIT: inf) n rissa

punctual ['pʌŋktjuəl] adj puntuale

punctuation [pʌŋktju'eɪʃən] n interpunzione f, punteggiatura

puncture ['pʌŋktʃər] n foratura ⊳ vt forare

⬛ Be careful not to translate *puncture* by the Italian word *puntura*.

punish ['pʌnɪʃ] vt punire; **punishment** n punizione f

punk [pʌŋk] n (also: **~ rocker**) punk m/f inv; (also: **~ rock**) musica punk, punk rock m; (US: inf: hoodlum) teppista m

pup [pʌp] n cucciolo(-a)

pupil ['pju:pl] n allievo(-a), (Anat) pupilla

puppet ['pʌpɪt] n burattino

puppy ['pʌpɪ] n cucciolo(-a), cagnolino(-a)

purchase ['pə:tʃɪs] n acquisto, compera ⊳ vt comprare

pure [pjuər] adj puro(-a); **purely** ['pjuəlɪ] adv puramente

purify ['pjuərɪfaɪ] vt purificare

purity ['pjuərɪtɪ] n purezza

purple ['pə:pl] adj di porpora; viola inv

purpose ['pə:pəs] n intenzione f, scopo; **on ~** apposta

purr [pə:r] vi fare le fusa

purse [pə:s] n (BRIT) borsellino; (US) borsetta ⊳ vt contrarre

pursue [pə'sju:] vt inseguire; (fig: activity etc) continuare con; (: aim etc) perseguire

pursuit [pə'sju:t] n inseguimento; (fig) ricerca; (pastime) passatempo

pus [pʌs] n pus m

push [puʃ] n spinta; (effort) grande sforzo; (drive) energia ⊳ vt spingere; (button) premere; (thrust): **to ~ sth (into)** ficcare qc (in); (fig) fare pubblicità a ⊳ vi spingere; premere; **to ~ for** (fig) insistere per; **push in** vi introdursi a forza; **push off** (inf) vi filare; **push on** vi (continue) continuare; **push over** vt far cadere; **push through** vi farsi largo spingendo ⊳ vt (measure) far approvare; **pushchair** (BRIT)

n passeggino; **pusher** n (drug pusher) spacciatore(-trice); **push-up** (US) n (press-up) flessione f sulle braccia

pussy(-cat) ['pusɪ(-)] (inf) n micio

put [put] (pt, pp put) vt mettere, porre; (say) dire, esprimere; (a question) fare; (estimate) stimare; **put away** vt (return) mettere a posto; **put back** vt (replace) rimettere (a posto); (postpone) rinviare; (delay) ritardare; **put by** vt (money) mettere da parte; **put down** vt (parcel etc) posare, mettere giù; (pay) versare; (in writing) mettere per iscritto; (revolt, animal) sopprimere; (attribute) attribuire; **put forward** vt (ideas) avanzare, proporre; **put in** vt (application, complaint) presentare; (time, effort) mettere; **put off** vt (postpone) rimandare, rinviare; (discourage) dissuadere; **put on** vt (clothes, lipstick etc) mettere; (light etc) accendere; (play etc) mettere in scena; (food, meal) mettere su; (brake) mettere; **to ~ on weight** ingrassare; **to ~ on airs** darsi delle arie; **put out** vt mettere fuori; (one's hand) porgere; (light etc) spegnere; (person: inconvenience) scomodare; **put through** vt (Tel: call) passare; (: person) mettere in comunicazione; (plan) far approvare; **put up** vt (raise) sollevare, alzare; (: umbrella) aprire; (tent) montare; (pin up) affiggere; (hang) appendere; (build) costruire, erigere; (increase) aumentare; (accommodate) alloggiare; **put aside** vt (lay down: book etc) mettere da una parte, posare; (save) mettere da parte; (in shop) tenere da parte; **put together** vt mettere insieme, riunire; (assemble: furniture) montare; (: meal) improvvisare; **put up with** vt fus sopportare

putt [pʌt] n colpo leggero; **putting green** n green m inv; campo da putting

puzzle ['pʌzl] n enigma m, mistero; (jigsaw) puzzle m; (also: **crossword ~**) parole fpl incrociate, cruciverba m inv ⊳ vt confondere, rendere perplesso(-a) ⊳ vi scervellarsi; **puzzled** adj perplesso(-a); **puzzling** adj (question) poco chiaro(-a); (attitude, set of instructions) incomprensibile

pyjamas [pɪ'dʒɑ:məz] (BRIT) npl pigiama m

pylon ['paɪlən] n pilone m

pyramid ['pɪrəmɪd] n piramide f

Pyrenees [pɪrɪ'ni:z] npl **the ~** i Pirenei

q

quack [kwæk] n (of duck) qua qua m inv; (pej: doctor) dottoruccio(-a)

quadruple [kwɔˈdrupl] vt quadruplicare ▷ vi quadruplicarsi

quail [kweɪl] n (Zool) quaglia ▷ vi (person): **to ~ at** or **before** perdersi d'animo davanti a

quaint [kweɪnt] adj bizzarro(-a); (old-fashioned) antiquato(-a); grazioso(-a), pittoresco(-a)

quake [kweɪk] vi tremare ▷ n abbr = **earthquake**

qualification [kwɔlɪfɪˈkeɪʃən] n (degree etc) qualifica, titolo; (ability) competenza, qualificazione f; (limitation) riserva, restrizione f

qualified [ˈkwɔlɪfaɪd] adj qualificato(-a); (able): **~ to** competente in, qualificato(-a) a; (limited) condizionato(-a)

qualify [ˈkwɔlɪfaɪ] vt abilitare; (limit: statement) modificare, precisare ▷ vi **to ~ (as)** qualificarsi (come); **to ~ (for)** acquistare i requisiti necessari (per); (Sport) qualificarsi (per or a)

quality [ˈkwɔlɪtɪ] n qualità f inv

qualm [kwɑ:m] n dubbio; scrupolo

quantify [ˈkwɔntɪfaɪ] vt quantificare

quantity [ˈkwɔntɪtɪ] n quantità f inv

quarantine [ˈkwɔrntiːn] n quarantena

quarrel [ˈkwɔrl] n lite f, disputa ▷ vi litigare

quarry [ˈkwɔrɪ] n (for stone) cava; (animal) preda

quart [kwɔ:t] n ≈ litro

quarter [ˈkwɔ:tə^r] n quarto; (us: coin) quarto di dollaro; (of year) trimestre m; (district) quartiere m ▷ vt dividere in quattro; (Mil) alloggiare; **~s** npl (living quarters) alloggio; (Mil) alloggi mpl, quadrato; **a ~ of an hour** un quarto d'ora; **quarter final** n quarto di finale; **quarterly** adj trimestrale ▷ adv trimestralmente

quartet(te) [kwɔ:ˈtɛt] n quartetto

quartz [kwɔ:ts] n quarzo

quay [ki:] n (also: **~side**) banchina

queasy [ˈkwi:zɪ] adj (stomach) delicato(-a); **to feel ~** aver la nausea

queen [kwi:n] n (gen) regina; (Cards etc) regina, donna

queer [kwɪə^r] adj strano(-a), curioso(-a) ▷ n (inf) finocchio

quench [kwɛntʃ] vt **to ~ one's thirst** dissetarsi

query [ˈkwɪərɪ] n domanda, questione f ▷ vt mettere in questione

quest [kwɛst] n cerca, ricerca

question [ˈkwɛstʃən] n domanda, questione f ▷ vt (person) interrogare; (plan, idea) mettere in questione or in dubbio; **it's a ~ of doing** si tratta di fare; **beyond ~** fuori di dubbio; **out of the ~** fuori discussione, impossibile; **questionable** adj discutibile; **question mark** n punto interrogativo; **questionnaire** [kwɛstʃəˈnɛə^r] n questionario

queue [kju:] (BRIT) n coda, fila ▷ vi fare la coda

quiche [ki:ʃ] n torta salata a base di uova, formaggio, prosciutto o altro

quick [kwɪk] adj rapido(-a), veloce; (reply) pronto(-a); (mind) pronto(-a), acuto(-a) ▷ n **cut to the ~** (fig) toccato(-a) sul vivo; **be ~!** fa presto!; **quickly** adv rapidamente, velocemente

quid [kwɪd] (BRIT: inf) n inv sterlina

quiet [ˈkwaɪət] adj tranquillo(-a), quieto(-a); (ceremony) semplice ▷ n tranquillità, calma ▷ vt, vi (US) = **quieten**; **keep ~!** sta zitto!; **quieten** (also: **quieten down**) vi calmarsi, chetarsi ▷ vt calmare, chetare; **quietly** adv tranquillamente, calmamente; sommessamente

quilt [kwɪlt] n trapunta; (continental quilt) piumino

quirky [ˈkwəːkɪ] adj stravagante

quit [kwɪt] (pt, pp **quit** or **quitted**) vt mollare; (premises) lasciare, partire da ▷ vi (give up) mollare; (resign) dimettersi

quite [kwaɪt] *adv* (*rather*) assai; (*entirely*) completamente, del tutto; **I ~ understand** capisco perfettamente; **that's not ~ big enough** non è proprio sufficiente; **~ a few of them** non pochi di loro; **~ (so)!** esatto!

quits [kwɪts] *adj* **~ (with)** pari (con); **let's call it ~** adesso siamo pari

quiver ['kwɪvə'] *vi* tremare, fremere

quiz [kwɪz] *n* (*game*) quiz *m inv*; indovinello ▷ *vt* interrogare

quota ['kwəʊtə] *n* quota

quotation [kwəʊ'teɪʃən] *n* citazione *f*; (*of shares etc*) quotazione *f*; (*estimate*) preventivo; **quotation marks** *npl* virgolette *fpl*

quote [kwəʊt] *n* citazione *f* ▷ *vt* (*sentence*) citare; (*price*) dare, fissare; (*shares*) quotare ▷ *vi* **to ~ from** citare; **~s** *npl* = **quotation marks**

rabbi ['ræbaɪ] *n* rabbino

rabbit ['ræbɪt] *n* coniglio

rabies ['reɪbiːz] *n* rabbia

RAC (*BRIT*) *n abbr* = **Royal Automobile Club**

rac(c)oon [rə'kuːn] *n* procione *m*

race [reɪs] *n* razza; (*competition, rush*) corsa ▷ *vt* (*horse*) far correre ▷ *vi* correre; (*engine*) imballarsi; **race car** (*US*) *n* = **racing car**; **racecourse** *n* campo di corse, ippodromo; **racehorse** *n* cavallo da corsa; **racetrack** *n* pista

racial ['reɪʃl] *adj* razziale

racing ['reɪsɪŋ] *n* corsa; **racing car** (*BRIT*) *n* macchina da corsa; **racing driver** (*BRIT*) *n* corridore *m* automobilista

racism ['reɪsɪzəm] *n* razzismo; **racist** *adj*, *n* razzista *m/f*

rack [ræk] *n* rastrelliera; (*also*: **luggage ~**) rete *f*, portabagagli *m inv*; (*also*: **roof ~**) portabagagli; (*dish rack*) scolapiatti *m inv* ▷ *vt* **~ed by** torturato(-a) da; **to ~ one's brains** scervellarsi

racket ['rækɪt] *n* (*for tennis*) racchetta; (*noise*) fracasso; baccano; (*swindle*) imbroglio, truffa; (*organized crime*) racket *m inv*

racquet ['rækɪt] *n* racchetta

radar ['reɪdɑː'] *n* radar *m*

radiation [reɪdɪ'eɪʃən] *n* irradiamento;

(*radioactive*) radiazione f
radiator ['reidieitə'] n radiatore m
radical ['rædikl] adj radicale
radio ['reidiəu] n radio f inv; **on the ~** alla radio; **radioactive** [reidiəu'æktiv] adj radioattivo(-a); **radio station** n stazione f radio inv
radish ['rædiʃ] n ravanello
RAF n abbr = **Royal Air Force**
raffle ['ræfl] n lotteria
raft [rɑːft] n zattera; (also: **life ~**) zattera di salvataggio
rag [ræg] n straccio, cencio; (pej: newspaper) giornalaccio, bandiera; (for charity) iniziativa studentesca a scopo benefico; **~s** npl (torn clothes) stracci mpl, brandelli mpl
rage [reidʒ] n (fury) collera, furia ▷ vi (person) andare su tutte le furie; (storm) infuriare; **it's all the ~** fa furore
ragged ['rægid] adj (edge) irregolare; (clothes) logoro(-a); (appearance) pezzente
raid [reid] n (Mil) incursione f; (criminal) rapina; (by police) irruzione f ▷ vt fare un'incursione in; rapinare; fare irruzione in
rail [reil] n (on stair) ringhiera; (on bridge, balcony) parapetto; (of ship) battagliola; **railcard** n (BRIT) tessera di riduzione ferroviaria; **railing(s)** n(pl) ringhiera f pl; **railroad** (US) n = **railway**; **railway** (BRIT: irreg) n ferrovia; **railway line** (BRIT) n linea ferroviaria; **railway station** (BRIT) n stazione f ferroviaria
rain [rein] n pioggia ▷ vi piovere; **in the ~** sotto la pioggia; **it's ~ing** piove; **rainbow** n arcobaleno; **raincoat** n impermeabile m; **raindrop** n goccia di pioggia; **rainfall** n pioggia; (measurement) piovosità; **rainforest** n foresta pluviale; **rainy** adj piovoso(-a)
raise [reiz] n aumento ▷ vt (lift) alzare; sollevare; (increase) aumentare; (a protest, doubt, question) sollevare; (cattle, family) allevare; (crop) coltivare; (army, funds) raccogliere; (loan) ottenere; **to ~ one's voice** alzare la voce
raisin ['reizn] n uva secca
rake [reik] n (tool) rastrello ▷ vt (garden) rastrellare
rally ['ræli] n (Pol etc) riunione f; (Aut) rally m inv; (Tennis) scambio ▷ vt riunire, radunare ▷ vi (sick person, Stock Exchange) riprendersi
RAM [ræm] n abbr (= random access memory) memoria ad accesso casuale
ram [ræm] n montone m, ariete m ▷ vt conficcare; (crash into) cozzare, sbattere contro; percuotere; speronare
Ramadan [ræmə'dæn] n Ramadan m inv

ramble ['ræmbl] n escursione f ▷ vi (pej: also: **~ on**) divagare; **rambler** n escursionista m/f; (Bot) rosa rampicante; **rambling** adj (speech) sconnesso(-a); (house) tutto(-a) a nicchie e corridoi; (Bot) rampicante
ramp [ræmp] n rampa; **on/off ~** (US Aut) raccordo di entrata/uscita
rampage [ræm'peidʒ] n **to go on the ~** scatenarsi in modo violento
ran [ræn] pt of **run**
ranch [rɑːntʃ] n ranch m inv
random ['rændəm] adj fatto(-a) or detto(-a) per caso; (Comput, Math) casuale ▷ n **at ~** a casaccio
rang [ræŋ] pt of **ring**
range [reindʒ] n (of mountains) catena; (of missile, voice) portata; (of proposals, products) gamma; (Mil: also: **shooting ~**) campo di tiro; (also: **kitchen ~**) fornello, cucina economica ▷ vt disporre ▷ vi **to ~ over** coprire; **to ~ from … to** andare da … a
ranger ['reindʒə'] n guardia forestale
rank [ræŋk] n fila; (status, Mil) grado; (BRIT: also: **taxi ~**) posteggio di taxi ▷ vi **to ~ among** essere tra ▷ adj puzzolente; vero(-a) e proprio(-a); **the ~ and file** (fig) la gran massa
ransom ['rænsəm] n riscatto; **to hold sb to ~** (fig) esercitare pressione su qn
rant [rænt] vi vociare
rap [ræp] vt bussare a; picchiare su ▷ n (music) rap m inv
rape [reip] n violenza carnale, stupro; (Bot) ravizzone m ▷ vt violentare
rapid ['ræpid] adj rapido(-a); **rapidly** adv rapidamente; **rapids** npl (Geo) rapida
rapist ['reipist] n violentatore m
rapport [ræ'pɔː'] n rapporto
rare [rɛə'] adj raro(-a); (Culin: steak) al sangue; **rarely** ['rɛəli] adv raramente
rash [ræʃ] adj imprudente, sconsiderato(-a) ▷ n (Med) eruzione f; (of events etc) scoppio
rasher ['ræʃə'] n fetta sottile (di lardo or prosciutto)
raspberry ['rɑːzbəri] n lampone m
rat [ræt] n ratto
rate [reit] n (proportion) tasso, percentuale f; (speed) velocità f inv; (price) tariffa ▷ vt giudicare; stimare; **~s** npl (BRIT: property tax) imposte fpl comunali; (fees) tariffe fpl; **to ~ sb/sth as** valutare qn/qc come
rather ['rɑːðə'] adv piuttosto; **it's ~ expensive** è piuttosto caro; (too) è un po' caro; **there's ~ a lot** ce n'è parecchio; **I would** or **I'd ~ go** preferirei andare
rating ['reitiŋ] n (assessment) valutazione f; (score) punteggio di merito; **~s** npl (Radio,

TV) indice *m* di ascolto

ratio ['reɪʃɪəu] *n* proporzione *f*, rapporto

ration ['ræʃən] *n* (*gen pl*) razioni *fpl* ▷ *vt* razionare; **~s** *npl* razioni *fpl*

rational ['ræʃənl] *adj* razionale, ragionevole; (*solution, reasoning*) logico(-a)

rattle ['rætl] *n* tintinnio; (*louder*) strepito; (*for baby*) sonaglino ▷ *vi* risuonare, tintinnare; fare un rumore di ferraglia ▷ *vt* scuotere (con strepito)

rave [reɪv] *vi* (*in anger*) infuriarsi; (*with enthusiasm*) andare in estasi; (*Med*) delirare ▷ *n* (BRIT: *inf: party*) rave *m inv*

raven ['reɪvən] *n* corvo

ravine [rə'viːn] *n* burrone *m*

raw [rɔː] *adj* (*uncooked*) crudo(-a); (*not processed*) greggio(-a); (*sore*) vivo(-a); (*inexperienced*) inesperto(-a); (*weather, day*) gelido(-a)

ray [reɪ] *n* raggio; **a ~ of hope** un barlume di speranza

razor ['reɪzər] *n* rasoio; **razor blade** *n* lama di rasoio

Rd *abbr* = **road**

re [riː] *prep* con riferimento a

RE *n abbr* (BRIT Mil: = Royal Engineers) ≈ G. M. (*Genio Militare*); (BRIT) = **religious education**

reach [riːtʃ] *n* portata; (*of river etc*) tratto ▷ *vt* raggiungere; arrivare a ▷ *vi* stendersi; **out of/within ~** fuori/a portata di mano; **within ~ of the shops/station** vicino ai negozi/alla stazione; **reach out** *vt* (*hand*) allungare ▷ *vi* **to ~ out for** stendere la mano per prendere

react [riː'ækt] *vi* reagire; **reaction** [-'ækʃən] *n* reazione *f*; **reactor** [riː'æktər] *n* reattore *m*

read [riːd, *pt, pp* red] (*pt, pp* **read**) *vi* leggere ▷ *vt* leggere; (*understand*) intendere, interpretare; (*study*) studiare; **read out** *vt* leggere ad alta voce; **reader** *n* lettore(-trice); (BRIT: *at university*) professore con funzioni preminenti di ricerca

readily ['redɪlɪ] *adv* volentieri; (*easily*) facilmente; (*quickly*) prontamente

reading ['riːdɪŋ] *n* lettura; (*understanding*) interpretazione *f*; (*on instrument*) indicazione *f*

ready ['redɪ] *adj* pronto(-a); (*willing*) pronto(-a), disposto(-a); (*available*) disponibile ▷ *n* **at the ~** (*Mil*) pronto a sparare; **when will my photos be ~?** quando saranno pronte le mie foto?; **to get ~** *vi* prepararsi ▷ *vt* preparare; **ready-made** *adj* prefabbricato(-a); (*clothes*) confezionato(-a)

real [rɪəl] *adj* reale; vero(-a); **in ~ terms** in realtà; **real ale** *n* birra ad effervescenza

naturale; **real estate** *n* beni *mpl* immobili; **realistic** [-'lɪstɪk] *adj* realistico(-a); **reality** [riː'ælɪtɪ] *n* realtà *f inv*

realization [rɪəlaɪ'zeɪʃən] *n* presa di coscienza; realizzazione *f*

realize ['rɪəlaɪz] *vt* (*understand*) rendersi conto di

really ['rɪəlɪ] *adv* veramente, davvero; **~!** (*indicating annoyance*) oh, insomma!

realm [rɛlm] *n* reame *m*, regno

Realtor® ['rɪəltɔː-] (US) *n* agente *m* immobiliare

reappear [riːə'pɪər] *vi* ricomparire, riapparire

rear [rɪər] *adj* di dietro; (*Aut: wheel etc*) posteriore ▷ *n* didietro, parte *f* posteriore ▷ *vt* (*cattle, family*) allevare ▷ *vi* (*also: ~ up*: *animal*) impennarsi

rear: rear-view mirror ['rɪəvju:-] *n* (*Aut*) specchio retrovisore; **rear-wheel drive** *n* trazione *fpl* posteriore

reason ['riːzn] *n* ragione *f*; (*cause, motive*) ragione, motivo ▷ *vi* **to ~ with sb** far ragionare qn; **it stands to ~ that** è ovvio che; **reasonable** *adj* ragionevole; (*not bad*) accettabile; **reasonably** *adv* ragionevolmente; **reasoning** *n* ragionamento

reassurance [riːə'ʃuərəns] *n* rassicurazione *f*

reassure [riːə'ʃuər] *vt* rassicurare; **to ~ sb of** rassicurare qn di or su

rebate ['riːbeɪt] *n* (*on tax etc*) sgravio

rebel [*n* 'rɛbl, *vb* rɪ'bɛl] *n* ribelle *m/f* ▷ *vi* ribellarsi; **rebellion** *n* ribellione *f*; **rebellious** *adj* ribelle

rebuild [riː'bɪld] *vt irreg* ricostruire

recall [rɪ'kɔːl] *vt* richiamare; (*remember*) ricordare, richiamare alla mente ▷ *n* richiamo

rec'd *abbr* = **received**

receipt [rɪ'siːt] *n* (*document*) ricevuta; (*act of receiving*) ricevimento; **~s** *npl* (*Comm*) introiti *mpl*; **can I have a ~, please?** posso avere una ricevuta, per favore?

receive [rɪ'siːv] *vt* ricevere; (*guest*) ricevere, accogliere; **receiver** [rɪ'siː-vər] *n* (*Tel*) ricevitore *m*; (*Radio, TV*) apparecchio ricevente; (*of stolen goods*) ricettatore(-trice); (*Comm*) curatore *m* fallimentare

recent ['riːsnt] *adj* recente; **recently** *adv* recentemente

reception [rɪ'sɛpʃən] *n* ricevimento; (*welcome*) accoglienza; (*TV etc*) ricezione *f*; **reception desk** *n* (*in hotel*) reception *f inv*; (*in hospital, at doctor's*) accettazione *f*; (*in offices etc*) portineria; **receptionist** *n* receptionist *m/f inv*

recession [rɪ'sɛʃən] *n* recessione *f*

recharge [riː'tʃɑːdʒ] *vt* (*battery*) ricaricare

recipe ['rɛsɪpɪ] *n* ricetta

recipient [rɪ'sɪpɪənt] *n* beneficiario(-a); (*of letter*) destinatario(-a)

recital [rɪ'saɪtl] *n* recital *m inv*

recite [rɪ'saɪt] *vt* (*poem*) recitare

reckless ['rɛkləs] *adj* (*driver etc*) spericolato(-a); (*spending*) folle

reckon ['rɛkən] *vt* (*count*) calcolare; (*think*): **I ~ that ...** penso che ...

reclaim [rɪ'kleɪm] *vt* (*demand back*) richiedere, reclamare; (*land*) bonificare; (*materials*) recuperare

recline [rɪ'klaɪn] *vi* stare sdraiato(-a)

recognition [rɛkəg'nɪʃən] *n* riconoscimento; **transformed beyond ~** irriconoscibile

recognize ['rɛkəgnaɪz] *vt* **to ~ (by/as)** riconoscere (a *or* da/come)

recollection [rɛkə'lɛkʃən] *n* ricordo

recommend [rɛkə'mɛnd] *vt* raccomandare; (*advise*) consigliare; **can you ~ a good restaurant?** mi può consigliare un buon ristorante?; **recommendation** [rɛkəmɛn'deɪʃən] *n* raccomandazione *f*; consiglio

reconcile ['rɛkənsaɪl] *vt* (*two people*) riconciliare; (*two facts*) conciliare, quadrare; **to ~ o.s. to** rassegnarsi a

reconsider [riːkən'sɪdəʳ] *vt* riconsiderare

reconstruct [riːkən'strʌkt] *vt* ricostruire

record [*n* 'rɛkɔːd, *vb* rɪ'kɔːd] *n* ricordo, documento; (*of meeting etc*) nota, verbale *m*; (*register*) registro; (*file*) pratica, dossier *m inv*; (*Comput*) record *m inv*; (*also*: **criminal ~**) fedina penale sporca; (*Mus: disc*) disco; (*Sport*) record *m inv*, primato ▷ *vt* (*set down*) prendere nota di, registrare; (*Mus: song etc*) registrare; **in ~ time** a tempo di record; **off the ~** *adj* ufficioso(-a) ▷ *adv* ufficiosamente; **recorded delivery** (BRIT) *n* (*Post*): **recorded delivery letter** *etc* lettera *etc* raccomandata; **recorder** *n* (*Mus*) flauto diritto; **recording** *n* (*Mus*) registrazione *f*; **record player** *n* giradischi *m inv*

recount [rɪ'kaʊnt] *vt* raccontare, narrare

recover [rɪ'kʌvəʳ] *vt* ricuperare ▷ *vi* **to ~ (from)** riprendersi (da); **recovery** [rɪ'kʌvərɪ] *n* ricupero; ristabilimento; ripresa

⬛ Be careful not to translate **recover** by the Italian word **ricoverare**.

recreate [riːkrɪ'eɪt] *vt* ricreare

recreation [rɛkrɪ'eɪʃən] *n* ricreazione *f*; svago; **recreational drug** [rɛkrɪ'eɪʃənl-] *n* sostanza stupefacente usata a scopo ricreativo;

recreational vehicle (US) *n* camper *m inv*

recruit [rɪ'kruːt] *n* recluta; (*in company*) nuovo(-a) assunto(-a) ▷ *vt* reclutare; **recruitment** *n* reclutamento

rectangle ['rɛktæŋgl] *n* rettangolo; **rectangular** [-'tæŋgjʊləʳ] *adj* rettangolare

rectify ['rɛktɪfaɪ] *vt* (*error*) rettificare; (*omission*) riparare

rector ['rɛktəʳ] *n* (*Rel*) parroco (*anglicano*)

recur [rɪ'kəːʳ] *vi* riaccadere; (*symptoms*) ripresentarsi; **recurring** *adj* (*Math*) periodico(-a)

recyclable [riː'saɪkləbl] *adj* riciclabile

recycle [riː'saɪkl] *vt* riciclare

recycling [riː'saɪklɪŋ] *n* riciclaggio

red [rɛd] *n* rosso; (*Pol: pej*) rosso(-a) ▷ *adj* rosso(-a); **in the ~** (*account*) scoperto; (*business*) in deficit; **Red Cross** *n* Croce *f* Rossa; **redcurrant** *n* ribes *m inv*

redeem [rɪ'diːm] *vt* (*debt*) riscattare; (*sth in pawn*) ritirare; (*fig, also Rel*) redimere

red: **red-haired** [-'hɛəd] *adj* dai capelli rossi; **redhead** ['rɛdhɛd] *n* rosso(-a); **red-hot** *adj* arroventato(-a); **red light** *n* **to go through a red light** (*Aut*) passare col rosso; **red-light district** ['rɛdlaɪt-] *n* quartiere *m* a luci rosse; **red meat** *n* carne *f* rossa

reduce [rɪ'djuːs] *vt* ridurre; (*lower*) ridurre, abbassare; **"~ speed now"** (*Aut*) "rallentare"; **at a ~d price** scontato(-a); **reduced** *adj* (*decreased*) ridotto(-a); **at a reduced price** a prezzo ribassato *or* ridotto; **"greatly reduced prices"** "grandi ribassi"; **reduction** [rɪ'dʌkʃən] *n* riduzione *f*; (*of price*) ribasso; (*discount*) sconto; **is there a reduction for children/students?** ci sono riduzioni per i bambini/gli studenti?

redundancy [rɪ'dʌndənsɪ] *n* licenziamento

redundant [rɪ'dʌndnt] *adj* (*worker*) licenziato(-a); (*detail, object*) superfluo(-a); **to be made ~** essere licenziato (per eccesso di personale)

reed [riːd] *n* (*Bot*) canna; (*Mus: of clarinet etc*) ancia

reef [riːf] *n* (*at sea*) scogliera

reel [riːl] *n* bobina, rocchetto; (*Fishing*) mulinello; (*Cinema*) rotolo; (*dance*) danza veloce scozzese ▷ *vi* (*sway*) barcollare

ref [rɛf] (*inf*) *n abbr* (= *referee*) arbitro

refectory [rɪ'fɛktərɪ] *n* refettorio

refer [rɪ'fəːʳ] *vt* **to ~ sth to** (*dispute, decision*) deferire qc a; **to ~ sb to** (*inquirer, Med: patient*) indirizzare qn a; (*reader: to text*) rimandare qn a ▷ *vi* **~ to** (*allude to*) accennare a; (*consult*) rivolgersi a

referee [rɛfə'ri:] n arbitro; (BRIT: for job application) referenza ▷ vt arbitrare

reference ['rɛfrəns] n riferimento; (mention) menzione f, allusione f; (for job application) referenza; **with ~ to** (Comm: in letter) in or con riferimento a; **reference number** n numero di riferimento

refill [vb ri:'fɪl, n 'ri:fɪl] vt riempire di nuovo; (pen, lighter etc) ricaricare ▷ n (for pen etc) ricambio

refine [rɪ'faɪn] vt raffinare; **refined** adj (person, taste) raffinato(-a); **refinery** n raffineria

reflect [rɪ'flɛkt] vt (light, image) riflettere; (fig) rispecchiare ▷ vi (think) riflettere, considerare; **it ~s badly/well on him** si ripercuote su di lui in senso negativo/positivo; **reflection** [-'flɛkʃən] n riflessione f; (image) riflesso; (criticism): **reflection on** giudizio su; attacco a; **on reflection** pensandoci sopra

reflex ['ri:flɛks] adj riflesso(-a) ▷ n riflesso

reform [rɪ'fɔ:m] n (of sinner etc) correzione f; (of law etc) riforma ▷ vt correggere; riformare

refrain [rɪ'freɪn] vi **to ~ from doing** trattenersi dal fare ▷ n ritornello

refresh [rɪ'frɛʃ] vt rinfrescare; (food, sleep) ristorare; **refreshing** adj (drink) rinfrescante; (sleep) riposante, ristoratore(-trice); **refreshments** npl rinfreschi mpl

refrigerator [rɪ'frɪdʒəreɪtər] n frigorifero

refuel [ri:'fjuəl] vi far rifornimento (di carburante)

refuge ['rɛfju:dʒ] n rifugio; **to take ~ in** rifugiarsi in; **refugee** [rɛfju'dʒi:] n rifugiato(-a), profugo(-a)

refund [n 'ri:fʌnd, vb rɪ'fʌnd] n rimborso ▷ vt rimborsare

refurbish [ri:'fə:bɪʃ] vt rimettere a nuovo

refusal [rɪ'fju:zəl] n rifiuto; **to have first ~ on** avere il diritto d'opzione su

refuse [n 'rɛfju:s, vb rɪ'fju:z] n rifiuti mpl ▷ vt, vi rifiutare; **to ~ to do** rifiutare di fare

regain [rɪ'geɪn] vt riguadagnare; riacquistare, ricuperare

regard [rɪ'gɑ:d] n riguardo, stima ▷ vt considerare, stimare; **to give one's ~s to** porgere i suoi saluti a; **"with kindest ~s"** "cordiali saluti"; **regarding** prep riguardo a, per quanto riguarda; **regardless** adv lo stesso; **regardless of** a dispetto di, nonostante

regenerate [rɪ'dʒɛnəreɪt] vt rigenerare

reggae ['rɛgeɪ] n reggae m

regiment ['rɛdʒɪmənt] n reggimento

region ['ri:dʒən] n regione f; **in the ~ of** (fig) all'incirca di; **regional** adj regionale

register ['rɛdʒɪstər] n registro; (also: **electoral ~**) lista elettorale ▷ vt registrare; (vehicle) immatricolare; (letter) assicurare; (instrument) segnare ▷ vi iscriversi; (at hotel) firmare il registro; (make impression) entrare in testa; **registered** (BRIT) adj (letter) assicurato(-a)

registrar ['rɛdʒɪstrɑ:r] n ufficiale m di stato civile; segretario

registration [rɛdʒɪs'treɪʃən] n (act) registrazione f; iscrizione f; (Aut: also: **~ number**) numero di targa

registry office (BRIT) n anagrafe f; **to get married in a ~** ≈ sposarsi in municipio

regular ['rɛgjulər] adj regolare; (usual) abituale, normale; (soldier) dell'esercito regolare ▷ n (client etc) cliente m/f abituale; **regularly** adv regolarmente

regulate ['rɛgjuleɪt] vt regolare; **regulation** [-'leɪʃən] n regolazione f; (rule) regola, regolamento

rehabilitation ['ri:həbɪlɪ'teɪʃən] n (of offender) riabilitazione f; (of disabled) riadattamento

rehearsal [rɪ'hə:səl] n prova

rehearse [rɪ'hə:s] vt provare

reign [reɪn] n regno ▷ vi regnare

reimburse [ri:ɪm'bə:s] vt rimborsare

rein [reɪn] n (for horse) briglia

reincarnation [ri:ɪnkɑ:'neɪʃən] n reincarnazione f

reindeer ['reɪndɪər] n inv renna

reinforce [ri:ɪn'fɔ:s] vt rinforzare; **reinforcements** npl (Mil) rinforzi mpl

reinstate [ri:ɪn'steɪt] vt reintegrare

reject [n 'ri:dʒɛkt, vb rɪ'dʒɛkt] n (Comm) scarto ▷ vt rifiutare, respingere; (Comm: goods) scartare; **rejection** [rɪ'dʒɛkʃən] n rifiuto

rejoice [rɪ'dʒɔɪs] vi **to ~ (at or over)** provare diletto in

relate [rɪ'leɪt] vt (tell) raccontare; (connect) collegare ▷ vi **to ~ to** (connect) riferirsi a; (get on with) stabilire un rapporto con; **relating to** che riguarda, rispetto a; **related** adj **related (to)** imparentato(-a) (con); collegato(-a) or connesso(-a) a

relation [rɪ'leɪʃən] n (person) parente m/f; (link) rapporto, relazione f; **~s** npl (relatives) parenti mpl; **relationship** n rapporto; (personal ties) rapporti mpl, relazioni fpl; (also: **family relationship**) legami mpl di parentela

relative ['rɛlətɪv] n parente m/f ▷ adj relativo(-a); (respective) rispettivo(-a); **relatively** adv relativamente; (fairly, *rather)* abbastanza

relax [rɪˈlæks] *vi* rilasciarsi; *(person: unwind)* rilassarsi ▷ *vt* rilasciare; *(mind, person)* rilassare; **relaxation** [riːlækˈseɪʃən] *n* rilasciamento; rilassamento; *(entertainment)* ricreazione *f*, svago; **relaxed** *adj* rilassato(-a); **relaxing** *adj* rilassante

relay [ˈriːleɪ] *n (Sport)* corsa a staffetta ▷ *vt (message)* trasmettere

release [rɪˈliːs] *n (from prison)* rilascio; *(from obligation)* liberazione *f*; *(of gas etc)* emissione *f*; *(of film etc)* distribuzione *f*; *(record)* disco; *(device)* disinnesto ▷ *vt (prisoner)* rilasciare; *(from obligation, wreckage etc)* liberare; *(book, film)* fare uscire; *(news)* rendere pubblico(-a); *(gas etc)* emettere; *(Tech: catch, spring etc)* disinnestare

relegate [ˈrɛləɡeɪt] *vt* relegare; *(BRIT Sport)*: **to be ~d** essere retrocesso(-a)

relent [rɪˈlɛnt] *vi* cedere; **relentless** *adj* implacabile

relevant [ˈrɛləvənt] *adj* pertinente; *(chapter)* in questione; **~ to** pertinente a

▌ Be careful not to translate *relevant* by the Italian word *rilevante*.

reliable [rɪˈlaɪəbl] *adj (person, firm)* fidato(-a), che dà affidamento; *(method)* sicuro(-a); *(machine)* affidabile

relic [ˈrɛlɪk] *n (Rel)* reliquia; *(of the past)* resto

relief [rɪˈliːf] *n (from pain, anxiety)* sollievo; *(help, supplies)* soccorsi *mpl*; *(Art, Geo)* rilievo

relieve [rɪˈliːv] *vt (pain, patient)* sollevare; *(bring help)* soccorrere; *(take over from: gen)* sostituire; *(: guard)* rilevare; **to ~ sb of sth** *(load)* alleggerire qn di qc; **to ~ o.s.** fare i propri bisogni; **relieved** *adj* sollevato(-a); **to be relieved that ...** essere sollevato(-a) (dal fatto) che ...; **I'm relieved to hear it** mi hai tolto un peso con questa notizia

religion [rɪˈlɪdʒən] *n* religione *f*

religious [rɪˈlɪdʒəs] *adj* religioso(-a); **religious education** *n* religione *f*

relish [ˈrɛlɪʃ] *n (Culin)* condimento; *(enjoyment)* gran piacere *m* ▷ *vt (food etc)* godere; **to ~ doing** adorare fare

relocate [ˈriːləʊˈkeɪt] *vt* trasferire ▷ *vi* trasferirsi

reluctance [rɪˈlʌktəns] *n* riluttanza

reluctant [rɪˈlʌktənt] *adj* riluttante, mal disposto(-a); **reluctantly** *adv* di mala voglia, a malincuore

rely [rɪˈlaɪ]: **to ~ on** *vt fus* contare su; *(be dependent)* dipendere da

remain [rɪˈmeɪn] *vi* restare, rimanere; **remainder** *n* resto; *(Comm)* rimanenza; **remaining** *adj* che rimane; **remains** *npl*

resti *mpl*

remand [rɪˈmɑːnd] *n* **on ~** in detenzione preventiva ▷ *vt* **to ~ in custody** rinviare in carcere; trattenere a disposizione della legge

remark [rɪˈmɑːk] *n* osservazione *f* ▷ *vt* osservare, dire; **remarkable** *adj* notevole; eccezionale

remarry [riːˈmærɪ] *vi* risposarsi

remedy [ˈrɛmədɪ] *n* **~ (for)** rimedio (per) ▷ *vt* rimediare a

remember [rɪˈmɛmbəʳ] *vt* ricordare, ricordarsi di; **~ me to him** salutalo da parte mia; **Remembrance Day** [rɪˈmɛmbrəns-] *n 11 novembre, giorno della commemorazione dei caduti in guerra*

● **REMEMBRANCE DAY**
●
● In Gran Bretagna, il **Remembrance**
● **Day** è un giorno di commemorazione
● dei caduti in guerra. Si celebra ogni anno
● la domenica più vicina all'11 novembre,
● anniversario della firma dell'armistizio
● con la Germania nel 1918.

remind [rɪˈmaɪnd] *vt* **to ~ sb of sth** ricordare qc a qn; **to ~ sb to do** ricordare a qn di fare; **reminder** *n* richiamo; *(note etc)* promemoria *m inv*

reminiscent [rɛmɪˈnɪsnt] *adj* **~ of** che fa pensare a, che richiama

remnant [ˈrɛmnənt] *n* resto, avanzo

remorse [rɪˈmɔːs] *n* rimorso

remote [rɪˈməʊt] *adj* remoto(-a), lontano(-a); *(person)* distaccato(-a); **remote control** *n* telecomando; **remotely** *adv* remotamente; *(slightly)* vagamente

removal [rɪˈmuːvəl] *n (taking away)* rimozione *f*; soppressione *f*; *(BRIT: from house)* trasloco; *(from office: dismissal)* destituzione *f*; *(Med)* ablazione *f*; **removal man** *(irreg) n (BRIT)* addetto ai traslochi; **removal van** *(BRIT) n* furgone *m* per traslochi

remove [rɪˈmuːv] *vt* togliere, rimuovere; *(employee)* destituire; *(stain)* far sparire; *(doubt, abuse)* sopprimere, eliminare

Renaissance [rɪˈneɪsɑ̃ːns] *n* **the ~** il Rinascimento

rename [riːˈneɪm] *vt* ribattezzare

render [ˈrɛndəʳ] *vt* rendere

rendezvous [ˈrɔndɪvuː] *n* appuntamento; *(place)* luogo d'incontro; *(meeting)* incontro

renew [rɪˈnjuː] *vt* rinnovare; *(negotiations)* riprendere

renovate [ˈrɛnəveɪt] *vt* rinnovare; *(art work)* restaurare

renowned [rɪ'naund] adj rinomato(-a)

rent [rɛnt] n affitto ▷ vt (take for rent) prendere in affitto; (also: **~ out**) dare in affitto; **rental** n (for television, car) fitto

reorganize [riːˈɔːɡənaɪz] vt riorganizzare

rep [rɛp] n abbr (Comm: = representative) rappresentante m/f; (Theatre: = repertory) teatro di repertorio

repair [rɪ'pɛəʳ] n riparazione f ▷ vt riparare; **in good/bad ~** in buone/cattive condizioni; **where can I get this ~ed?** dove lo posso far riparare?; **repair kit** n corredo per riparazioni

repay [riː'peɪ] (irreg) vt (money, creditor) rimborsare, ripagare; (sb's efforts) ricompensare; (favour) ricambiare; **repayment** n pagamento; rimborso

repeat [rɪ'piːt] n (Radio, TV) replica ▷ vt ripetere; (pattern) riprodurre; (promise, attack, also Comm: order) rinnovare ▷ vi ripetere; **can you ~ that, please?** può ripetere, per favore?; **repeatedly** adv ripetutamente, spesso; **repeat prescription** n (BRIT) ricetta ripetibile

repellent [rɪ'pɛlənt] adj repellente n ▷ n **insect ~** prodotto m anti-insetti inv

repercussions [riːpə'kʌʃənz] npl ripercussioni fpl

repetition [rɛpɪ'tɪʃən] n ripetizione f

repetitive [rɪ'pɛtɪtɪv] adj (movement) che si ripete; (work) monotono(-a); (speech) pieno(-a) di ripetizioni

replace [rɪ'pleɪs] vt (put back) rimettere a posto; (take the place of) sostituire; **replacement** n rimessa; sostituzione f; (person) sostituto(-a)

replay ['riːpleɪ] n (of match) partita ripetuta; (of tape, film) replay m inv

replica ['rɛplɪkə] n replica, copia

reply [rɪ'plaɪ] n risposta ▷ vi rispondere

report [rɪ'pɔːt] n rapporto; (Press etc) cronaca; (BRIT: also: **school ~**) pagella; (of gun) sparo ▷ vt riportare; (Press etc) fare una cronaca su; (bring to notice: occurrence) segnalare; (: person) denunciare ▷ vi (make a report) fare un rapporto (or una cronaca); (present o.s.): **to ~ (to sb)** presentarsi (a qn); **I'd like to ~ a theft** vorrei denunciare un furto; **report card** (US, Scottish) n pagella; **reportedly** adv stando a quanto si dice; **he reportedly told them to ...** avrebbe detto loro di ...; **reporter** n reporter m inv

represent [rɛprɪ'zɛnt] vt rappresentare; **representation** [-'teɪʃən] n rappresentazione f; (petition) rappresentanza; **representative** n rappresentante m/f; (US Pol) deputato(-a) ▷ adj rappresentativo(-a)

repress [rɪ'prɛs] vt reprimere; **repression** [-'prɛʃən] n repressione f

reprimand ['rɛprɪmaːnd] n rimprovero ▷ vt rimproverare

reproduce [riːprə'djuːs] vt riprodurre ▷ vi riprodursi; **reproduction** [-'dʌkʃən] n riproduzione f

reptile ['rɛptaɪl] n rettile m

republic [rɪ'pʌblɪk] n repubblica; **republican** adj, n repubblicano(-a)

reputable ['rɛpjutəbl] adj di buona reputazione; (occupation) rispettabile

reputation [rɛpju'teɪʃən] n reputazione f

request [rɪ'kwɛst] n domanda; (formal) richiesta ▷ vt **to ~ (of** or **from sb)** chiedere (a qn); **request stop** (BRIT) n (for bus) fermata facoltativa or a richiesta

require [rɪ'kwaɪəʳ] vt (need: person) aver bisogno di; (: thing, situation) richiedere; (want) volere; esigere; (order): **to ~ sb to do sth** ordinare a qn di fare qc; **requirement** n esigenza; bisogno; requisito

resat [riː'sæt] pt, pp of **resit**

rescue ['rɛskjuː] n salvataggio; (help) soccorso ▷ vt salvare

research [rɪ'səːtʃ] n ricerca, ricerche fpl ▷ vt fare ricerche su

resemblance [rɪ'zɛmbləns] n somiglianza

resemble [rɪ'zɛmbl] vt assomigliare a

resent [rɪ'zɛnt] vt risentirsi di; **resentful** adj pieno(-a) di risentimento; **resentment** n risentimento

reservation [rɛzə'veɪʃən] n (booking) prenotazione f; (doubt) dubbio; (protected area) riserva; (BRIT: on road: also: **central ~**) spartitraffico m inv; **reservation desk** (US) n (in hotel) reception f inv

reserve [rɪ'zəːv] n riserva ▷ vt (seats etc) prenotare; **reserved** adj (shy) riservato(-a)

reservoir ['rɛzəvwɑːʳ] n serbatoio

residence ['rɛzɪdəns] n residenza; **residence permit** (BRIT) n permesso di soggiorno

resident ['rɛzɪdənt] n residente m/f; (in hotel) cliente m/f fisso(-a) ▷ adj residente; (doctor) fisso(-a); (course, college) a tempo pieno con pernottamento; **residential** [-'dɛnʃəl] adj di residenza; (area) residenziale

residue ['rɛzɪdjuː] n resto; (Chem, Physics) residuo

resign [rɪ'zaɪn] vt (one's post) dimettersi da ▷ vi dimettersi; **to ~ o.s. to** rassegnarsi a; **resignation** [rɛzɪɡ'neɪʃən] n dimissioni fpl; rassegnazione f

resin ['rɛzɪn] n resina

resist [rɪ'zɪst] vt resistere a; **resistance** n resistenza

resit ['riːsɪt] (BRIT) (pt, pp **resat**) vt (exam) ripresentarsi a; (subject) ridare l'esame di

▷ *n* **he's got his French ~ on Friday** deve ridare l'esame di francese venerdì
resolution [rɛzə'luːʃən] *n* risoluzione *f*
resolve [rɪ'zɔlv] *n* risoluzione *f* ▷ *vi* (*decide*): **to ~ to do** decidere di fare ▷ *vt* (*problem*) risolvere
resort [rɪ'zɔːt] *n* (*town*) stazione *f*; (*recourse*) ricorso ▷ *vi* **to ~ to** aver ricorso a; **in the last ~** come ultima risorsa
resource [rɪ'sɔːs] *n* risorsa; **resourceful** *adj* pieno(-a) di risorse, intraprendente
respect [rɪs'pɛkt] *n* rispetto ▷ *vt* rispettare; **respectable** *adj* rispettabile; **respectful** *adj* rispettoso(-a); **respective** [rɪs'pɛktɪv] *adj* rispettivo(-a); **respectively** *adv* rispettivamente
respite ['rɛspaɪt] *n* respiro, tregua
respond [rɪs'pɔnd] *vi* rispondere; **response** [rɪs'pɔns] *n* risposta
responsibility [rɪspɔnsɪ'bɪlɪtɪ] *n* responsabilità *f inv*
responsible [rɪs'pɔnsɪbl] *adj* (*trustworthy*) fidato(-a); (*job*) di (grande) responsabilità; **~ (for)** responsabile (di); **responsibly** *adv* responsabilmente
responsive [rɪs'pɔnsɪv] *adj* che reagisce
rest [rɛst] *n* riposo; (*stop*) sosta, pausa; (*Mus*) pausa; (*object: to support sth*) appoggio, sostegno; (*remainder*) resto, avanzi *mpl* ▷ *vi* riposarsi; (*remain*) rimanere, restare; (*be supported*): **to ~ on** appoggiarsi su ▷ *vt* (*far*) riposare; (*lean*): **to ~ sth on/against** appoggiare qc su/ contro; **the ~ of them** gli altri; **it ~s with him to decide** sta a lui decidere
restaurant ['rɛstərɔŋ] *n* ristorante *m*; **restaurant car** (*BRIT*) *n* vagone *m* ristorante
restless ['rɛstlɪs] *adj* agitato(-a), irrequieto(-a)
restoration [rɛstə'reɪʃən] *n* restauro; restituzione *f*
restore [rɪ'stɔːʳ] *vt* (*building, to power*) restaurare; (*sth stolen*) restituire; (*peace, health*) ristorare
restrain [rɪs'treɪn] *vt* (*feeling, growth*) contenere, frenare; (*person*): **to ~ (from doing)** trattenere (dal fare); **restraint** *n* (*restriction*) limitazione *f*; (*moderation*) ritegno; (*of style*) contenutezza
restrict [rɪs'trɪkt] *vt* restringere, limitare; **restriction** [-kʃən] *n* **restriction (on)** restrizione *f* (di), limitazione *f*
rest room (*US*) *n* toletta
restructure [riː'strʌktʃəʳ] *vt* ristrutturare
result [rɪ'zʌlt] *n* risultato ▷ *vi* **to ~ in** avere per risultato; **as a ~ of** in or di conseguenza a, in seguito a
resume [rɪ'zjuːm] *vt, vi* (*work, journey*) riprendere

résumé ['reɪzjumeɪ] *n* riassunto; (*US*) curriculum *m inv* vitae
resuscitate [rɪ'sʌsɪteɪt] *vt* (*Med*) risuscitare
retail ['riːteɪl] *adj, adv* al minuto ▷ *vt* vendere al minuto; **retailer** *n* commerciante *m/f* al minuto, dettagliante *m/f*
retain [rɪ'teɪn] *vt* (*keep*) tenere, serbare
retaliation [rɪtælɪ'eɪʃən] *n* rappresaglie *fpl*
retarded [rɪ'tɑːdɪd] *adj* ritardato(-a)
retire [rɪ'taɪəʳ] *vi* (*give up work*) andare in pensione; (*withdraw*) ritirarsi, andarsene; (*go to bed*) andare a letto, ritirarsi; **retired** *adj* (*person*) pensionato(-a); **retirement** *n* pensione *f*; (*act*) pensionamento
retort [rɪ'tɔːt] *vi* rimbeccare
retreat [rɪ'triːt] *n* ritirata; (*place*) rifugio ▷ *vi* battere in ritirata
retrieve [rɪ'triːv] *vt* (*sth lost*) ricuperare, ritrovare; (*situation, honour*) salvare; (*error, loss*) rimediare a
retrospect ['rɛtrəspɛkt] *n* **in ~** guardando indietro; **retrospective** [-'spɛktɪv] *adj* retrospettivo(-a); (*law*) retroattivo(-a)
return [rɪ'təːn] *n* (*going or coming back*) ritorno; (*of sth stolen etc*) restituzione *f*; (*Finance: from land, shares*) profitto, reddito ▷ *cpd* (*journey, match*) di ritorno; (*BRIT: ticket*) di andata e ritorno ▷ *vi* tornare, ritornare ▷ *vt* rendere, restituire; (*bring back*) riportare; (*send back*) mandare indietro; (*put back*) rimettere; (*Pol: candidate*) eleggere; **~s** *npl* (*Comm*) incassi *mpl*; profitti *mpl*; **in ~ (for)** in cambio (di); **by ~ of post** a stretto giro di posta; **many happy ~s (of the day)!** cento di questi giorni!; **return ticket** *n* (*esp BRIT*) biglietto di andata e ritorno
reunion [riː'juːnɪən] *n* riunione *f*
reunite [riːjuː'naɪt] *vt* riunire
revamp ['riː'væmp] *vt* (*firm*) riorganizzare
reveal [rɪ'viːl] *vt* (*make known*) rivelare, svelare; (*display*) rivelare, mostrare; **revealing** *adj* rivelatore(-trice); (*dress*) scollato(-a)
revel ['rɛvl] *vi* **to ~ in sth/in doing** dilettarsi di qc/a fare
revelation [rɛvə'leɪʃən] *n* rivelazione *f*
revenge [rɪ'vɛndʒ] *n* vendetta ▷ *vt* vendicare; **to take ~ on** vendicarsi di
revenue ['rɛvənjuː] *n* reddito
Reverend ['rɛvərənd] *adj* (*in titles*) reverendo(-a)
reversal [rɪ'vəːsl] *n* capovolgimento
reverse [rɪ'vəːs] *n* contrario, opposto; (*back, defeat*) rovescio; (*Aut: also: ~ gear*) marcia indietro ▷ *adj* (*order, direction*)

contrario(-a), opposto(-a) ▷ vt (turn)
invertire, rivoltare; (change) capovolgere,
rovesciare; (Law: judgment) cassare; (car)
fare marcia indietro con ▷ vi (BRIT Aut,
person etc) fare marcia indietro; **reverse-
charge call** [rɪ'vəːstʃɑːdʒ-] (BRIT) n (Tel)
telefonata con addebito al ricevente;
reversing lights (BRIT) npl (Aut) luci fpl per
la retromarcia
revert [rɪ'vəːt] vi **to ~ to** tornare a
review [rɪ'vjuː] n rivista; (of book, film)
recensione f; (of situation) esame m ▷ vt
passare in rivista; fare la recensione di; fare
il punto di
revise [rɪ'vaɪz] vt (manuscript) rivedere,
correggere; (opinion) emendare,
modificare; (study: subject, notes) ripassare;
revision [rɪ'vɪʒən] n revisione f; ripasso
revival [rɪ'vaɪvəl] n ripresa; ristabilimento;
(of faith) risveglio
revive [rɪ'vaɪv] vt (person) rianimare;
(custom) far rivivere; (hope, courage,
economy) ravvivare; (play, fashion)
riesumare ▷ vi (person) rianimarsi; (hope)
ravvivarsi; (activity) riprendersi
revolt [rɪ'vəult] n rivolta, ribellione f ▷ vi
rivoltarsi, ribellarsi ▷ vt (far) rivoltare;
revolting adj ripugnante
revolution [rɛvə'luːʃən] n rivoluzione f; (of
wheel etc) rivoluzione, giro; **revolutionary**
adj, n rivoluzionario(-a)
revolve [rɪ'vɔlv] vi girare
revolver [rɪ'vɔlvəʳ] n rivoltella
reward [rɪ'wɔːd] n ricompensa, premio
▷ vt **to ~ (for)** ricompensare (per);
rewarding adj (fig) gratificante
rewind [riː'waɪnd] (irreg) vt (watch)
ricaricare; (ribbon etc) riavvolgere
rewrite [riː'raɪt] vt irreg riscrivere
rheumatism ['ruːmətɪzəm] n
reumatismo
rhinoceros [raɪ'nɔsərəs] n rinoceronte m
rhubarb ['ruːbɑːb] n rabarbaro
rhyme [raɪm] n rima; (verse) poesia
rhythm ['rɪðm] n ritmo
rib [rɪb] n (Anat) costola ▷ vt (tease)
punzecchiare
ribbon ['rɪbən] n nastro; **in ~s** (torn) a
brandelli
rice [raɪs] n riso; **rice pudding** n budino
di riso
rich [rɪtʃ] adj ricco(-a); (clothes)
sontuoso(-a); (abundant): **~ in** ricco(-a) di
rid [rɪd] (pt, pp **rid**) vt **to ~ sb of** sbarazzare
or liberare qn di; **to get ~ of** sbarazzarsi di
riddle ['rɪdl] n (puzzle) indovinello ▷ vt **to
be ~d with** (holes) essere crivellato(-a) di;
(doubts) essere pieno(-a) di
ride [raɪd] (pt **rode**, pp **ridden**) n (on horse)

cavalcata; (outing) passeggiata; (distance
covered) cavalcata; corsa ▷ vi (as sport)
cavalcare; (go somewhere: on horse, bicycle)
andare (a cavallo or in bicicletta etc);
(journey: on bicycle, motorcycle, bus) andare,
viaggiare ▷ vt (a horse) montare, cavalcare;
to take sb for a ~ (fig) prendere in giro qn;
fregare qn; **to ~ a horse/bicycle/camel**
montare a cavallo/in bicicletta/in groppa a
un cammello; **rider** n cavalcatore(-trice);
(in race) fantino; (on bicycle) ciclista m/f; (on
motorcycle) motociclista m/f
ridge [rɪdʒ] n (of hill) cresta; (of roof) colmo;
(of object) riga (in rilievo)
ridicule ['rɪdɪkjuːl] n ridicolo; scherno
▷ vt mettere in ridicolo; **ridiculous**
[rɪ'dɪkjuləs] adj ridicolo(-a)
riding ['raɪdɪŋ] n equitazione f; **riding
school** n scuola d'equitazione
rife [raɪf] adj diffuso(-a); **to be ~ with**
abbondare di
rifle ['raɪfl] n carabina ▷ vt vuotare
rift [rɪft] n fessura, crepatura; (fig:
disagreement) incrinatura, disaccordo
rig [rɪg] n (also: **oil ~**: on land) derrick m inv;
(: at sea) piattaforma di trivellazione ▷ vt
(election etc) truccare
right [raɪt] adj giusto(-a); (suitable)
appropriato(-a); (not left) destro(-a)
▷ n giusto; (title, claim) diritto; (not left)
destra ▷ adv (answer) correttamente;
(not on the left) a destra ▷ vt raddrizzare;
(fig) riparare ▷ excl bene!; **to be ~** (person)
aver ragione; (answer) essere giusto(-a) or
corretto(-a); **by ~s** di diritto; **on the ~** a
destra; **to be in the ~** aver ragione, essere
nel giusto; **~ now** proprio adesso; subito;
~ away subito; **right angle** n angolo
retto; **rightful** adj (heir) legittimo(-a);
right-hand adj **right-hand drive** guida
a destra; **the right-hand side** il lato
destro; **right-handed** adj (person) che
adopera la mano destra; **rightly** adv bene,
correttamente; (with reason) a ragione;
right of way n diritto di passaggio; (Aut)
precedenza; **right-wing** adj (Pol) di destra
rigid ['rɪdʒɪd] adj rigido(-a); (principle)
rigoroso(-a)
rigorous ['rɪgərəs] adj rigoroso(-a)
rim [rɪm] n orlo; (of spectacles) montatura;
(of wheel) cerchione m
rind [raɪnd] n (of bacon) cotenna; (of lemon
etc) scorza
ring [rɪŋ] (pt **rang**, pp **rung**) n anello; (of
people, objects) cerchio; (of spies) giro;
(of smoke etc) spirale m; (arena) pista,
arena; (for boxing) ring m inv; (sound of bell)
scampanio ▷ vi (person, bell, telephone)
suonare; (also: **~ out**: voice, words)

risuonare; (Tel) telefonare; (ears) fischiare
▷ vt (BRIT Tel) telefonare a; (: bell, doorbell)
suonare; **to give sb a ~** (BRIT Tel) dare un
colpo di telefono a qn; **ring back** vt, vi (Tel)
richiamare; **ring off** (BRIT) vi (Tel) mettere
giù, riattaccare; **ring up** (BRIT) vt (Tel)
telefonare a; **ringing tone** (BRIT) n (Tel)
segnale m di libero; **ringleader** n (of gang)
capobanda m; **ring road** (BRIT) n raccordo
anulare

ring tone n suoneria
rink [rɪŋk] n (also: **ice ~**) pista di
pattinaggio
rinse [rɪns] n risciacquatura; (hair tint)
cachet m inv ▷ vt sciacquare
riot ['raɪət] n sommossa, tumulto; (of
colours) orgia ▷ vi tumultuare; **to run ~**
creare disordine
rip [rɪp] n strappo ▷ vt strappare ▷ vi
strapparsi; **rip off** vt (inf: cheat) fregare;
rip up vt stracciare
ripe [raɪp] adj (fruit, grain) maturo(-a);
(cheese) stagionato(-a)
rip-off ['rɪpɔf] n (inf): **it's a ~!** è un furto!
ripple ['rɪpl] n increspamento,
ondulazione f; mormorio ▷ vi incresparsi
rise [raɪz] (pt **rose**, pp **risen**) n (slope) salita,
pendio; (hill) altura; (increase: in wages:
BRIT) aumento; (: in prices, temperature)
rialzo, aumento; (fig: to power etc) ascesa
▷ vi alzarsi, levarsi; (prices) aumentare;
(waters, river) crescere; (sun, wind, person:
from chair, bed) levarsi; (also: ~ **up**: building)
ergersi; (: rebel) insorgere; ribellarsi; (in
rank) salire; **to give ~ to** provocare, dare
origine a; **to ~ to the occasion** essere
all'altezza; **risen** ['rɪzn] pp of **rise**; **rising**
adj (increasing: number) sempre crescente;
(: prices) in aumento; (tide) montante; (sun,
moon) nascente, che sorge
risk [rɪsk] n rischio; pericolo ▷ vt rischiare;
to take or **run the ~ of doing** correre il
rischio di fare; **at ~** in pericolo; **at one's
own ~** a proprio rischio e pericolo; **risky**
adj rischioso(-a)
rite [raɪt] n rito; **last ~s** l'estrema unzione
ritual ['rɪtjuəl] adj rituale ▷ n rituale m
rival ['raɪvl] n rivale m/f; (in business)
concorrente m/f ▷ adj rivale; che fa
concorrenza ▷ vt essere in concorrenza
con; **to ~ sb/sth in** competere con qn/qc
in; **rivalry** n rivalità; concorrenza
river ['rɪvə˟] n fiume m ▷ cpd (port, traffic)
fluviale; **up/down ~** a monte/valle;
riverbank n argine m
rivet ['rɪvɪt] n ribattino, rivetto ▷ vt (fig)
concentrare, fissare
Riviera [rɪvɪˈeərə] n **the (French) ~** la
Costa Azzurra; **the Italian ~** la Riviera

road [rəud] n strada; (small) cammino;
(in town) via ▷ cpd stradale; **major/
minor ~** strada con/senza diritto di
precedenza; **which ~ do I take for ...?**
che strada devo prendere per andare
a...?; **roadblock** n blocco stradale; **road
map** n carta stradale; **road rage** n
comportamento aggressivo al volante; **road
safety** n sicurezza sulle strade; **roadside**
n margine m della strada; **roadsign** n
cartello stradale; **road tax** n (BRIT) tassa
di circolazione; **roadworks** npl lavori mpl
stradali
roam [rəum] vi errare, vagabondare
roar [rɔ:˟] n ruggito; (of crowd) tumulto;
(of thunder, storm) muggito; (of laughter)
scoppio ▷ vi ruggire; tumultuare;
muggire; **to ~ with laughter** scoppiare
dalle risa; **to do a ~ing trade** fare affari
d'oro
roast [rəust] n arrosto ▷ vt arrostire;
(coffee) tostare, torrefare; **roast beef** n
arrosto di manzo
rob [rɔb] vt (person) rubare; (bank)
svaligiare; **to ~ sb of sth** derubare qn di
qc; (fig: deprive) privare qn di qc; **robber** n
ladro; (armed) rapinatore m; **robbery** n
furto; rapina
robe [rəub] n (for ceremony etc) abito; (also:
bath ~) accappatoio; (US: also: **lap ~**)
coperta
robin ['rɔbɪn] n pettirosso
robot ['rəubɔt] n robot m inv
robust [rəuˈbʌst] adj robusto(-a);
(economy) solido(-a)
rock [rɔk] n (substance) roccia; (boulder)
masso; roccia; (in sea) scoglio; (US: pebble)
ciottolo; (BRIT: sweet) zucchero candito
▷ vt (swing gently: cradle) dondolare; (:
child) cullare; (shake) scrollare, far tremare
▷ vi dondolarsi; scrollarsi, tremare; **on
the ~s** (drink) col ghiaccio; (marriage etc) in
crisi; **rock and roll** n rock and roll m; **rock
climbing** n roccia
rocket ['rɔkɪt] n razzo
rocking chair n sedia a dondolo
rocky ['rɔkɪ] adj (hill) roccioso(-a); (path)
sassoso(-a); (marriage etc) instabile
rod [rɔd] n (metallic, Tech) asta; (wooden)
bacchetta; (also: **fishing ~**) canna da pesca
rode [rəud] pt of **ride**
rodent ['rəudnt] n roditore m
rogue [rəug] n mascalzone m
role [rəul] n ruolo; **role-model** n modello
(di comportamento)
roll [rəul] n rotolo; (of banknotes) mazzo;
(also: **bread ~**) panino; (register) lista;
(sound: of drums etc) rullo ▷ vt rotolare;
(also: ~ **up**: string) aggomitolare; (: sleeves)

rimboccare; (*cigarettes*) arrotolare; (*eyes*) roteare; (*also*: **~ out**: *pastry*) stendere; (*lawn, road etc*) spianare ▷ *vi* rotolare; (*wheel*) girare; (*drum*) rullare; (*vehicle*: *also*: **~ along**) avanzare; (*ship*) rollare; **roll over** *vi* rivoltarsi; **roll up** (*inf*) *vi* (*arrive*) arrivare ▷ *vt* (*carpet*) arrotolare; **roller** *n* rullo; (*wheel*) rotella; (*for hair*) bigodino; **Rollerblades®** *npl* pattini *mpl* in linea; **roller coaster** [-'kəustə'] *n* montagne *fpl* russe; **roller skates** *npl* pattini *mpl* a rotelle; (*for skating*) pattinaggio a rotelle; **to go roller-skating** andare a pattinare (*con i pattini a rotelle*); **rolling pin** *n* matterello

ROM [rɔm] *n abbr* (= *read only memory*) memoria di sola lettura

Roman ['rəumən] *adj*, *n* romano(-a); **Roman Catholic** *adj*, *n* cattolico(-a)

romance [rə'mæns] *n* storia (*or* avventura *or* film *m inv*) romantico(-a); (*charm*) poesia; (*love affair*) idillio

Romania [rəu'meɪnɪə] *n* Romania

Romanian [rəu'meɪnɪən] *adj* romeno(-a) ▷ *n* romeno; (*Ling*) romeno

Roman numeral *n* numero romano

romantic [rə'mæntɪk] *adj* romantico(-a); sentimentale

Rome [rəum] *n* Roma

roof [ru:f] *n* tetto; (*of tunnel, cave*) volta ▷ *vt* coprire (con un tetto); **~ of the mouth** palato; **roof rack** *n* (*Aut*) portabagagli *m inv*

rook [ruk] *n* (*bird*) corvo nero; (*Chess*) torre *f*

room [ru:m] *n* (*in house*) stanza; (*bedroom, in hotel*) camera; (*in school etc*) sala; (*space*) posto, spazio; **roommate** *n* compagno(-a) di stanza; **room service** *n* servizio da camera; **roomy** *adj* spazioso(-a); (*garment*) ampio(-a)

rooster ['ru:stə'] *n* gallo

root [ru:t] *n* radice *f* ▷ *vi* (*plant, belief*) attecchire

rope [rəup] *n* corda, fune *f*; (*Naut*) cavo ▷ *vt* (*box*) legare; (*climbers*) legare in cordata; (*area*: *also*: **~ off**) isolare cingendo con cordoni; **to know the ~s** (*fig*) conoscere i trucchi del mestiere

rose [rəuz] *pt of* **rise** ▷ *n* rosa; (*also*: **~ bush**) rosaio; (*on watering can*) rosetta

rosé ['rəuzeɪ] *n* vino rosato

rosemary ['rəuzmərɪ] *n* rosmarino

rosy ['rəuzɪ] *adj* roseo(-a)

rot [rɔt] *n* (*decay*) putrefazione *f*; (*inf*: *nonsense*) stupidaggini *fpl* ▷ *vt*, *vi* imputridire, marcire

rota ['rəutə] *n* tabella dei turni

rotate [rəu'teɪt] *vt* (*revolve*) far girare; (*change round*: *jobs*) fare a turno ▷ *vi*

(*revolve*) girare

rotten ['rɔtn] *adj* (*decayed*) putrido(-a); marcio(-a); (*dishonest*) corrotto(-a); (*inf*: *bad*) brutto(-a); (: *action*) vigliacco(-a); **to feel ~** (*ill*) sentirsi da cani

rough [rʌf] *adj* (*skin, surface*) ruvido(-a); (*terrain, road*) accidentato(-a); (*voice*) rauco(-a); (*person, manner*: *coarse*) rozzo(-a), aspro(-a); (: *violent*) brutale; (*district*) malfamato(-a); (*weather*) cattivo(-a); (*sea*) mosso(-a); (*plan*) abbozzato(-a); (*guess*) approssimativo(-a) ▷ *n* (*Golf*) macchia; **to ~ it** far vita dura; **to sleep ~** (*BRIT*) dormire all'addiaccio; **roughly** *adv* (*handle*) svegliare, brutalmente; (*make*) grossolanamente; (*speak*) bruscamente; (*approximately*) approssimativamente

roulette [ru:'let] *n* roulette *f*

round [raund] *adj* rotondo(-a); (*figures*) tondo(-a) ▷ *n* (*BRIT*: *of toast*) fetta; (*duty*: *of policeman, milkman etc*) giro; (: *of doctor*) visite *fpl*; (*game*: *of cards, golf, in competition*) partita; (*of ammunition*) cartuccia; (*Boxing*) round *m inv*; (*of talks*) serie *f inv* ▷ *vt* (*corner*) girare; (*bend*) prendere ▷ *prep* intorno a ▷ *adv* **all ~** tutt'attorno; **to go the long way ~** fare il giro più lungo; **all the year ~** tutto l'anno; **it's just ~ the corner** (*also fig*) è dietro l'angolo; **~ the clock** ininterrottamente; **to go ~ to sb's house** andare da qn; **go ~ the back** passi dietro; **enough to go ~** abbastanza per tutti; **~ of applause** applausi *mpl*; **~ of drinks** giro di bibite; **~ of sandwiches** sandwich *m inv*; **round off** *vt* (*speech etc*) finire; **round up** *vt* radunare; (*criminals*) fare una retata di; (*prices*) arrotondare; **roundabout** *n* (*BRIT Aut*) rotatoria; (: *at fair*) giostra ▷ *adj* (*route, means*) indiretto(-a); **round trip** *n* (*viaggio di*) andata e ritorno; **roundup** *n* raduno; (*of criminals*) retata

rouse [rauz] *vt* (*wake up*) svegliare; (*stir up*) destare; provocare; risvegliare

route [ru:t] *n* itinerario; (*of bus*) percorso

routine [ru:'ti:n] *adj* (*work*) corrente, abituale; (*procedure*) solito(-a) ▷ *n* (*pej*) routine *f*, tran tran *m*; (*Theatre*) numero

row¹ [rəu] *n* (*line*) riga, fila; (*Knitting*) ferro; (*behind one another*: *of cars, people*) fila; (*in boat*) remata ▷ *vi* (*in boat*) remare; (*as sport*) vogare ▷ *vt* (*boat*) manovrare a remi; **in a ~** (*fig*) di fila

row² [rau] *n* (*racket*) baccano, chiasso; (*dispute*) lite *f*; (*scolding*) sgridata ▷ *vi* (*argue*) litigare

rowboat ['rəubəut] *n* (*US*) barca a remi

rowing ['rəuɪŋ] *n* canottaggio; **rowing boat** (*BRIT*) *n* barca a remi

royal [ˈrɔɪəl] *adj* reale; **royalty** [ˈrɔɪəltɪ] *n* (*royal persons*) (membri *mpl* della) famiglia reale; (*payment: to author*) diritti *mpl* d'autore

rpm *abbr* (= *revolutions per minute*) giri/min.

R.S.V.P. *abbr* (= *répondez s'il vous plaît*) R.S.V.P.

Rt. Hon. (BRIT) *abbr* (= *Right Honourable*) ≈ Onorevole

rub [rʌb] *n* **to give sth a ~** strofinare qc; (*sore place*) massaggiare qc ▷ *vt* strofinare; massaggiare; (*hands: also:* **~ together**) sfregarsi; **to ~ sb up** (BRIT) or **~ sb the wrong way** (US) lisciare qn contro pelo; **rub in** *vt* (*ointment*) far penetrare (massaggiando or frizionando); **rub off** *vi* andare via; **rub out** *vt* cancellare

rubber [ˈrʌbəʳ] *n* gomma; **rubber band** *n* elastico; **rubber gloves** *npl* guanti *mpl* di gomma

rubbish [ˈrʌbɪʃ] *n* (*from household*) immondizie *fpl*, rifiuti *mpl*; (*fig, pej*) cose *fpl* senza valore; robaccia; sciocchezze *fpl*; **rubbish bin** (BRIT) *n* pattumiera; **rubbish dump** *n* (*in town*) immondezzaio

rubble [ˈrʌbl] *n* macerie *fpl*; (*smaller*) pietrisco

ruby [ˈruːbɪ] *n* rubino

rucksack [ˈrʌksæk] *n* zaino

rudder [ˈrʌdəʳ] *n* timone *m*

rude [ruːd] *adj* (*impolite: person*) scortese, rozzo(-a); (*: word, manners*) grossolano(-a), rozzo(-a); (*shocking*) indecente

ruffle [ˈrʌfl] *vt* (*hair*) scompigliare; (*clothes, water*) increspare; (*fig: person*) turbare

rug [rʌg] *n* tappeto; (BRIT: *for knees*) coperta

rugby [ˈrʌgbɪ] *n* (*also:* **~ football**) rugby *m*

rugged [ˈrʌgɪd] *adj* (*landscape*) aspro(-a); (*features, determination*) duro(-a); (*character*) brusco(-a)

ruin [ˈruːɪn] *n* rovina ▷ *vt* rovinare; **~s** *npl* (*of building, castle etc*) rovine *fpl*, ruderi *mpl*

rule [ruːl] *n* regola, regola; (*regulation*) regolamento, regola; (*government*) governo; (*ruler*) riga ▷ *vt* (*country*) governare; (*person*) dominare ▷ *vi* regnare; decidere; (*Law*) dichiarare; **as a ~** normalmente; **rule out** *vt* escludere; **ruler** *n* (*sovereign*) sovrano(-a); (*for measuring*) regolo, riga; **ruling** *adj* (*party*) al potere; (*class*) dirigente ▷ *n* (*Law*) decisione *f*

rum [rʌm] *n* rum *m*

Rumania *etc* [ruːˈmeɪnɪə] *n* = **Romania** *etc*

rumble [ˈrʌmbl] *n* rimbombo; brontolio ▷ *vi* rimbombare; (*stomach, pipe*) brontolare

rumour [ˈruːməʳ] *n* (US **rumor**) voce *f* ▷ *vt*

it is ~ed that corre voce che

Be careful not to translate *rumour* by the Italian word *rumore*.

rump steak [rʌmp-] *n* bistecca di girello

run [rʌn] (*pt* **ran**, *pp* **run**) *n* corsa; (*outing*) gita (in macchina); (*distance travelled*) percorso, tragitto; (*Ski*) pista; (*Cricket, Baseball*) meta; (*series*) serie *f*; (*Theatre*) periodo di rappresentazione; (*in tights, stockings*) smagliatura ▷ *vt* (*distance*) correre; (*operate: business*) gestire, dirigere; (*: competition, course*) organizzare; (*: hotel*) gestire; (*: house*) governare; (*Comput*) eseguire; (*water, bath*) far scorrere; (*force through: rope, pipe*) **to ~ sth through** far passare qc attraverso; (*pass: hand, finger*): **to ~ sth over** passare qc su; (*Press: feature*) presentare ▷ *vi* correre; (*flee*) scappare; (*pass: road etc*) passare; (*work: machine, factory*) funzionare, andare; (*bus, train: operate*) far servizio; (*: travel*) circolare; (*continue: play, contract*) durare; (*slide: drawer; flow: river, bath*) scorrere; (*colours, washing*) stemperarsi; (*in election*) presentarsi candidato; (*nose*) colare; **there was a ~ on ...** c'era una corsa a ...; **in the long ~** a lungo andare; **on the ~** in fuga; **to ~ a race** partecipare a una gara; **I'll ~ you to the station** la porto alla stazione; **to ~ a risk** correre un rischio; **run after** *vt fus* (*to catch up*) rincorrere; (*chase*) correre dietro a; **run away** *vi* fuggire; **run down** *vt* (*production*) ridurre gradualmente; (*factory*) rallentare l'attività di; (*Aut*) investire; (*criticize*) criticare; **to be ~ down** (*person: tired*) essere esausto(-a); **run into** *vt fus* (*meet: person*) incontrare per caso; (*: trouble*) incontrare, trovare; (*collide with*) andare a sbattere contro; **run off** *vi* fuggire ▷ *vt* (*water*) far scolare; (*copies*) fare; **run out** *vi* (*person*) uscire di corsa; (*liquid*) colare; (*lease*) scadere; (*money*) esaurirsi; **run out of** *vt fus* rimanere a corto di; **run over** *vt* (*Aut*) investire, mettere sotto ▷ *vt fus* (*revise*) rivedere; **run through** *vt fus* (*instructions*) dare una scorsa a; (*rehearse: play*) riprovare, ripetere; **run up** *vt* (*debt*) lasciar accumulare; **to ~ up against** (*difficulties*) incontrare; **runaway** *adj* (*person*) fuggiasco(-a); (*horse*) in libertà; (*truck*) fuori controllo

rung [rʌŋ] *pp* of **ring** ▷ *n* (*of ladder*) piolo

runner [ˈrʌnəʳ] *n* (*in race*) corridore *m*; (*: horse*) partente *m/f*; (*on sledge*) pattino; (*for drawer etc*) guida; **runner bean** (BRIT) *n* fagiolo rampicante; **runner-up** *n* secondo(-a) arrivato(-a)

running [ˈrʌnɪŋ] *n* corsa; direzione *f*; organizzazione *f*; funzionamento

▷ adj (water) corrente; (commentary) simultaneo(-a); **to be in/out of the ~ for sth** essere/non essere più in lizza per qc; **6 days ~** 6 giorni di seguito

runny ['rʌnɪ] adj che cola

run-up ['rʌnʌp] n **~ to** (election etc) periodo che precede

runway ['rʌnweɪ] n (Aviat) pista (di decollo)

rupture ['rʌptʃəʳ] n (Med) ernia

rural ['rurəl] adj rurale

rush [rʌʃ] n corsa precipitosa; (hurry) furia, fretta; (sudden demand): **~ for** corsa a; (current) flusso; (of emotion) impeto; (Bot) giunco ▷ vt mandare or spedire velocemente; (attack: town etc) prendere d'assalto ▷ vi precipitarsi; **rush hour** n ora di punta

Russia ['rʌʃə] n Russia; **Russian** adj russo(-a) ▷ n russo(-a); (Ling) russo

rust [rʌst] n ruggine f ▷ vi arrugginirsi

rusty ['rʌstɪ] adj arrugginito(-a)

ruthless ['ru:θlɪs] adj spietato(-a)

RV abbr (= revised version) versione riveduta della Bibbia ▷ n abbr (us) see **recreational vehicle**

rye [raɪ] n segale f

S

Sabbath ['sæbəθ] n (Jewish) sabato; (Christian) domenica

sabotage ['sæbətɑːʒ] n sabotaggio ▷ vt sabotare

saccharin(e) ['sækərɪn] n saccarina

sachet ['sæʃeɪ] n bustina

sack [sæk] n (bag) sacco ▷ vt (dismiss) licenziare, mandare a spasso; (plunder) saccheggiare; **to get the ~** essere mandato a spasso

sacred ['seɪkrɪd] adj sacro(-a)

sacrifice ['sækrɪfaɪs] n sacrificio ▷ vt sacrificare

sad [sæd] adj triste

saddle ['sædl] n sella ▷ vt (horse) sellare; **to be ~d with sth** (inf) avere qc sulle spalle

sadistic [sə'dɪstɪk] adj sadico(-a)

sadly ['sædlɪ] adv tristemente; (regrettably) sfortunatamente; **~ lacking in** penosamente privo di

sadness ['sædnɪs] n tristezza

s.a.e. n abbr (= stamped addressed envelope) busta affrancata e con indirizzo

safari [sə'fɑːrɪ] n safari m inv

safe [seɪf] adj sicuro(-a); (out of danger) salvo(-a), al sicuro; (cautious) prudente ▷ n cassaforte f; **~ from** al sicuro da; **~ and sound** sano(-a) e salvo(-a); **(just) to be on the ~ side** per non correre rischi; **could you put this in the ~, please?** lo potrebbe mettere nella cassaforte, per favore?; **safely** *adv* sicuramente; sano(-a) e salvo(-a); prudentemente; **safe sex** *n* sesso sicuro

safety ['seɪftɪ] *n* sicurezza; **safety belt** *n* cintura di sicurezza; **safety pin** *n* spilla di sicurezza

saffron ['sæfrən] *n* zafferano

sag [sæg] *vi* incurvarsi; afflosciarsi

sage [seɪdʒ] *n* (*herb*) salvia; (*man*) saggio

Sagittarius [sædʒɪ'tɛərɪəs] *n* Sagittario

Sahara [sə'hɑːrə] *n* **the ~ (Desert)** il (deserto del) Sahara

said [sɛd] *pt, pp of* **say**

sail [seɪl] *n* (*on boat*) vela; (*trip*): **to go for a ~** fare un giro in barca a vela ▷ *vt* (*boat*) condurre, governare ▷ *vi* (*travel: ship*) navigare; (*: passenger*) viaggiare per mare; (*set off*) salpare; (*sport*) fare della vela; **they ~ed into Genoa** entrarono nel porto di Genova; **sailboat** (*Us*) *n* barca a vela; **sailing** *n* (*sport*) vela; **to go sailing** fare della vela; **sailing boat** *n* barca a vela; **sailor** *n* marinaio

saint [seɪnt] *n* santo(-a)

sake [seɪk] *n* **for the ~ of** per, per amore di

salad ['sæləd] *n* insalata; **salad cream** (*BRIT*) *n* (tipo di) maionese *f*; **salad dressing** *n* condimento per insalata

salami [sə'lɑːmɪ] *n* salame *m*

salary ['sælərɪ] *n* stipendio

sale [seɪl] *n* vendita; (*at reduced prices*) svendita, liquidazione *f*; (*auction*) vendita all'asta; **"for ~"** "in vendita"; **on ~** in vendita; **on ~ or return** da vendere o rimandare; **~s** *npl* (*total amount sold*) vendite *fpl*; **sales assistant** (*Us* **sales clerk**) *n* commesso(-a); **salesman/woman** (*irreg*) *n* commesso(-a); (*representative*) rappresentante *m/f*; **salesperson** (*irreg*) *n* (*in shop*) commesso; (*representative*) rappresentante *m/f* di commercio; **sales rep** *n* rappresentante *m/f* di commercio

saline ['seɪlaɪn] *adj* salino(-a)

saliva [sə'laɪvə] *n* saliva

salmon ['sæmən] *n inv* salmone *m*

salon ['sælɔn] *n* (*hairdressing salon*) parrucchiere(-a); (*beauty salon*) salone *m* di bellezza

saloon [sə'luːn] *n* (*Us*) saloon *m inv*, bar *m inv*; (*BRIT*: *Aut*) berlina; (*ship's lounge*) salone *m*

salt [sɔlt] *n* sale *m* ▷ *vt* salare; **saltwater** *adj* di mare; **salty** *adj* salato(-a)

salute [sə'luːt] *n* saluto ▷ *vt* salutare

salvage ['sælvɪdʒ] *n* (*saving*) salvataggio; (*things saved*) beni *mpl* salvati *or* recuperati ▷ *vt* salvare, mettere in salvo

Salvation Army [sæl'veɪʃən-] *n* Esercito della Salvezza

same [seɪm] *adj* stesso(-a), medesimo(-a) ▷ *pron* **the ~** lo (la) stesso(-a), gli (le) stessi(-e); **the ~ book as** lo stesso libro di (*o* che); **at the ~ time** allo stesso tempo; **all** *or* **just the ~** tuttavia; **to do the ~ as sb** fare come qn; **the ~ to you!** altrettanto a te!

sample ['sɑːmpl] *n* campione *m* ▷ *vt* (*food*) assaggiare; (*wine*) degustare

sanction ['sæŋkʃən] *n* sanzione *f* ▷ *vt* sancire, sanzionare; **~s** *npl* (*Pol*) sanzioni *fpl*

sanctuary ['sæŋktjuərɪ] *n* (*holy place*) santuario; (*refuge*) rifugio; (*for wildlife*) riserva

sand [sænd] *n* sabbia ▷ *vt* (*also*: **~ down**) cartavetrare

sandal ['sændl] *n* sandalo

sand: **sandbox** ['sændbɔks] (*Us*) *n* = **sandpit**; **sandcastle** ['sændkɑːsl] *n* castello di sabbia; **sand dune** *n* duna di sabbia; **sandpaper** ['sændpeɪpə'] *n* carta vetrata; **sandpit** ['sændpɪt] *n* (*for children*) buca di sabbia; **sands** *npl* spiaggia; **sandstone** ['sændstəun] *n* arenaria

sandwich ['sændwɪtʃ] *n* tramezzino, panino, sandwich *m inv* ▷ *vt* **~ed between** incastrato(-a) fra; **cheese/ham ~** sandwich al formaggio/prosciutto

sandy ['sændɪ] *adj* sabbioso(-a); (*colour*) color sabbia *inv*, biondo(-a) rossiccio(-a)

sane [seɪn] *adj* (*person*) sano(-a) di mente; (*outlook*) sensato(-a)

sang [sæŋ] *pt of* **sing**

sanitary towel ['sænɪtərɪ-] (*Us* **sanitary napkin**) *n* assorbente *m* (igienico)

sanity ['sænɪtɪ] *n* sanità mentale; (*common sense*) buon senso

sank [sæŋk] *pt of* **sink**

Santa Claus [sæntə'klɔːz] *n* Babbo Natale

sap [sæp] *n* (*of plants*) linfa ▷ *vt* (*strength*) fiaccare

sapphire ['sæfaɪə'] *n* zaffiro

sarcasm ['sɑːkæzm] *n* sarcasmo

sarcastic [sɑː'kæstɪk] *adj* sarcastico(-a); **to be ~** fare del sarcasmo

sardine [sɑː'diːn] *n* sardina

Sardinia [sɑː'dɪnɪə] *n* Sardegna

SASE (*Us*) *n abbr* (= *self-addressed stamped envelope*) busta affrancata e con indirizzo

sat [sæt] *pt, pp of* **sit**

Sat. *abbr* (= *Saturday*) sab.

satchel ['sætʃl] *n* cartella

satellite ['sætəlaɪt] *adj* satellite ▷ *n* satellite *m*; **satellite dish** *n* antenna parabolica; **satellite television** *n* televisione *f* via satellite

satin ['sætɪn] n raso ▷ adj di raso
satire ['sætaɪə'] n satira
satisfaction [sætɪs'fækʃən] n
soddisfazione f
satisfactory [sætɪs'fæktərɪ] adj
soddisfacente
satisfied ['sætɪsfaɪd] adj (customer)
soddisfatto(-a); **to be ~ (with sth)** essere
soddisfatto(-a) (di qc)
satisfy ['sætɪsfaɪ] vt soddisfare; (convince)
convincere
Saturday ['sætədɪ] n sabato
sauce [sɔːs] n salsa; (containing meat, fish)
sugo; **saucepan** n casseruola
saucer ['sɔːsə'] n sottocoppa m, piattino
Saudi Arabia ['saʊdɪ-] n Arabia Saudita
sauna ['sɔːnə] n sauna
sausage ['sɔsɪdʒ] n salsiccia; **sausage roll**
n rotolo di pasta sfoglia ripieno di salsiccia
sautéed ['səʊteɪd] adj saltato(-a)
savage ['sævɪdʒ] adj (cruel, fierce)
selvaggio(-a), feroce; (primitive)
primitivo(-a) ▷ n selvaggio(-a) ▷ vt
attaccare selvaggiamente
save [seɪv] vt (person, belongings, Comput)
salvare; (money) risparmiare, mettere
da parte; (time) risparmiare; (food)
conservare; (avoid: trouble) evitare; (Sport)
parare ▷ vi (also: **~ up**) economizzare ▷ n
(Sport) parata ▷ prep salvo, a eccezione di
savings ['seɪvɪŋz] npl (money) risparmi mpl;
savings account n libretto di risparmio;
savings and loan association (US) n
≈ società di credito immobiliare
savoury ['seɪvərɪ] (US **savory**) adj (dish: not
sweet) salato(-a)
saw [sɔː] (pt **sawed**, pp **sawed** or **sawn**) pt
of **see** ▷ n (tool) sega ▷ vt segare; **sawdust**
n segatura
sawn [sɔːn] pp of **saw**
saxophone ['sæksəfəʊn] n sassofono
say [seɪ] (pt, pp **said**) n **to have one's ~**
fare sentire il proprio parere; **to have**
a or **some ~** avere voce in capitolo ▷ vt
dire; **could you ~ that again?** potrebbe
ripeterlo?; **that goes without ~ing** va da
sé; **saying** n proverbio, detto
scab [skæb] n crosta; (pej) crumiro(-a)
scaffolding ['skæfəldɪŋ] n impalcatura
scald [skɔːld] n scottatura ▷ vt scottare
scale [skeɪl] n scala; (of fish) squama ▷ vt
(mountain) scalare; **~s** npl (for weighing)
bilancia; **on a large ~** su vasta scala; **~ of**
charges tariffa
scallion ['skæljən] n cipolla; (US: shallot)
scalogna; (: leek) porro
scallop ['skɔləp] n (Zool) pettine m;
(Sewing) smerlo
scalp [skælp] n cuoio capelluto ▷ vt

scotennare
scalpel ['skælpl] n bisturi m inv
scam [skæm] n (inf) truffa
scampi ['skæmpɪ] npl scampi mpl
scan [skæn] vt scrutare; (glance at
quickly) scorrere, dare un'occhiata a; (TV)
analizzare; (Radar) esplorare ▷ n (Med)
ecografia
scandal ['skændl] n scandalo; (gossip)
pettegolezzi mpl
Scandinavia [skændɪ'neɪvɪə] n
Scandinavia; **Scandinavian** adj, n
scandinavo(-a)
scanner ['skænə'] n (Radar, Med) scanner
m inv
scapegoat ['skeɪpgəʊt] n capro espiatorio
scar [skɑː] n cicatrice f ▷ vt sfregiare
scarce [skɛəs] adj scarso(-a); (copy, edition)
raro(-a); **to make o.s. ~** (inf) squagliarsela;
scarcely adv appena
scare [skɛə'] n spavento; panico ▷ vt
spaventare, atterrire; **there was a bomb ~**
at the bank hanno evacuato la banca per
paura di un attentato dinamitardo; **to ~ sb**
stiff spaventare a morte qn; **scarecrow** n
spaventapasseri m inv; **scared** adj **to be**
scared aver paura
scarf [skɑːf] (pl **scarves** or **scarfs**) n (long)
sciarpa; (square) fazzoletto da testa,
foulard m inv
scarlet ['skɑːlɪt] adj scarlatto(-a)
scarves [skɑːvz] npl of **scarf**
scary ['skɛərɪ] adj che spaventa
scatter ['skætə'] vt spargere; (crowd)
disperdere ▷ vi disperdersi
scenario [sɪ'nɑːrɪəʊ] n (Theatre, Cinema)
copione m; (fig) situazione f
scene [siːn] n (Theatre, fig etc) scena;
(of crime, accident) scena, luogo; (sight,
view) vista, veduta; **scenery** n (Theatre)
scenario; (landscape) panorama m; **scenic**
adj scenico(-a); panoramico(-a)
scent [sɛnt] n profumo; (sense of smell)
olfatto, odorato; (fig: track) pista
sceptical ['skɛptɪkəl] (US **skeptical**) adj
scettico(-a)
schedule ['ʃɛdjuːl, (US) 'skɛdjuːl] n
programma m, piano; (of trains) orario; (of
prices etc) lista, tabella ▷ vt fissare; **on ~** in
orario; **to be ahead of/behind ~** essere in
anticipo/ritardo sul previsto; **scheduled**
flight n volo di linea
scheme [skiːm] n piano, progetto;
(method) sistema m; (dishonest plan, plot)
intrigo, trama; (arrangement) disposizione
f, sistemazione f; (pension scheme etc)
programma m ▷ vi fare progetti; (intrigue)
complottare
schizophrenic [skɪtsə'frɛnɪk] adj, n

schizofrenico(-a)

scholar ['skɒləʳ] n (expert) studioso(-a);
scholarship n erudizione f; (grant) borsa
di studio

school [sku:l] n (primary, secondary)
scuola; (university: us) università f
inv ⊳ cpd scolare, scolastico(-a) ⊳ vt
(animal) addestrare; **schoolbook** n libro
scolastico; **schoolboy** n scolaro; **school
children** npl scolari mpl; **schoolgirl**
n scolara; **schooling** n istruzione f;
schoolteacher n insegnante m/f,
docente m/f; (primary) maestro(-a)

science ['saɪəns] n scienza; **science
fiction** n fantascienza; **scientific**
[-'tɪfɪk] adj scientifico(-a); **scientist** n
scienziato(-a)

sci-fi ['saɪfaɪ] n abbr (inf) = **science fiction**

scissors ['sɪzəz] npl forbici fpl

scold [skəʊld] vt rimproverare

scone [skɔn] n focaccina da tè

scoop [sku:p] n mestolo; (for ice cream)
cucchiaio dosatore; (Press) colpo
giornalistico, notizia (in) esclusiva

scooter ['sku:təʳ] n (motor cycle)
motoretta, scooter m inv; (toy)
monopattino

scope [skəʊp] n (capacity: of plan,
undertaking) portata; (: of person) capacità
fpl; (opportunity) possibilità fpl

scorching ['skɔ:tʃɪŋ] adj cocente,
scottante

score [skɔːʳ] n i punti mpl, punteggio;
(Mus) partitura, spartito; (twenty) venti
⊳ vt (goal, point) segnare, fare; (success)
ottenere ⊳ vi segnare; (Football) fare un
goal; (keep score) segnare i punti; **~s of**
(very many) un sacco di; **on that ~** a questo
riguardo; **to ~ 6 out of 10** prendere 6 su
10; **score out** vt cancellare con un segno;
scoreboard n tabellone m segnapunti;
scorer n marcatore(-trice); (keeping score)
segnapunti m inv

scorn [skɔːn] n disprezzo ⊳ vt
disprezzare

Scorpio ['skɔːpɪəʊ] n Scorpione m

scorpion ['skɔːpɪən] n scorpione m

Scot [skɒt] n scozzese m/f

Scotch tape® n scotch® m

Scotland ['skɒtlənd] n Scozia

Scots [skɒts] adj scozzese; **Scotsman**
(irreg) n scozzese m; **Scotswoman** (irreg) n
scozzese f; **Scottish** ['skɒtɪʃ] adj scozzese;
Scottish Parliament n Parlamento
scozzese

scout [skaʊt] n (Mil) esploratore m; (also:
boy ~) giovane esploratore, scout m inv

scowl [skaʊl] vi accigliarsi, aggrottare le
sopracciglia; **to ~ at** guardare torvo

scramble ['skræmbl] n arrampicata ⊳ vi
inerpicarsi; **to ~ out** etc uscire etc in fretta;
to ~ for azzuffarsi per; **scrambled eggs**
npl uova fpl strapazzate

scrap [skræp] n pezzo, pezzetto; (fight)
zuffa; (also: **~ iron**) rottami mpl di ferro,
ferraglia ⊳ vt demolire; (fig) scartare ⊳ vi
to ~ (with sb) fare a botte (con qn); **~s** npl
(waste) scarti mpl; **scrapbook** n album m
inv di ritagli

scrape [skreɪp] vt, vi raschiare, grattare ⊳ n
to get into a ~ cacciarsi in un guaio

scrap paper n cartaccia

scratch [skrætʃ] n graffio ⊳ cpd **~ team**
squadra raccogliticcia ⊳ vt graffiare,
rigare ⊳ vi grattare; (paint, car) graffiare;
to start from ~ cominciare or partire
da zero; **to be up to ~** essere all'altezza;
scratch card n (BRIT) cartolina f gratta
e vinci

scream [skri:m] n grido, urlo ⊳ vi urlare,
gridare

screen [skri:n] n schermo; (fig) muro,
cortina, velo ⊳ vt schermare, fare schermo
a; (from the wind etc) riparare; (film)
proiettare; (book) adattare per lo schermo;
(candidates etc) selezionare; **screening**
n (Med) dépistage m inv; **screenplay** n
sceneggiatura; **screen saver** n (Comput)
screen saver m inv

screw [skru:] n vite f ⊳ vt avvitare; **screw
up** vt (paper etc) spiegazzare; (inf: ruin)
rovinare; **to ~ up one's eyes** strizzare gli
occhi; **screwdriver** n cacciavite m

scribble ['skrɪbl] n scarabocchio ⊳ vt
scribacchiare in fretta ⊳ vi scarabocchiare

script [skrɪpt] n (Cinema etc) copione m; (in
exam) elaborato or compito d'esame

scroll [skrəʊl] n rotolo di carta

scrub [skrʌb] n (land) boscaglia ⊳ vt pulire
strofinando; (reject) annullare

scruffy ['skrʌfɪ] adj sciatto(-a)

scrum(mage) ['skrʌm(ɪdʒ)] n mischia

scrutiny ['skru:tɪnɪ] n esame m accurato

scuba diving ['sku:bə-] n immersioni fpl
subacquee

sculptor ['skʌlptəʳ] n scultore m

sculpture ['skʌlptʃəʳ] n scultura

scum [skʌm] n schiuma; (pej: people) feccia

scurry ['skʌrɪ] vi sgambare, affrettarsi

sea [si:] n mare m ⊳ cpd marino(-a), del
mare; (bird, fish) di mare; (route, transport)
marittimo(-a); (travel) per mare; **on
the ~** (boat) in mare; (town) di mare; **to be
all at ~** (fig) non sapere che pesci pigliare;
out to ~ al largo; **(out) at ~** in mare;
seafood n frutti mpl di mare; **sea front** n
lungomare m; **seagull** n gabbiano

seal [si:l] n (animal) foca; (stamp) sigillo;

(*impression*) impronta del sigillo ▷ vt sigillare; **seal off** vt (*close*) sigillare; (*forbid entry to*) bloccare l'accesso a
sea level n livello del mare
seam [siːm] n cucitura; (*of coal*) filone m
search [səːtʃ] n ricerca; (*Law: at sb's home*) perquisizione f ▷ vt frugare ▷ vi **to ~ for** ricercare; **in ~ of** alla ricerca di; **search engine** n (*Comput*) motore m di ricerca; **search party** n squadra di soccorso
sea: **seashore** ['siːʃɔːʳ] n spiaggia; **seasick** ['siːsɪk] adj che soffre il mal di mare; **seaside** ['siːsaɪd] n spiaggia; **seaside resort** n stazione f balneare
season ['siːzn] n stagione f ▷ vt condire, insaporire; **seasonal** adj stagionale; **seasoning** n condimento; **season ticket** n abbonamento
seat [siːt] n sedile m; (*in bus, train: place*) posto; (*Parliament*) seggio; (*buttocks*) didietro; (*of trousers*) fondo ▷ vt far sedere; (*have room for*) avere or essere fornito(-a) di posti a sedere per; **I'd like to book two ~s** vorrei prenotare due posti; **to be ~ed** essere seduto(-a); **seat belt** n cintura di sicurezza; **seating** n posti mpl a sedere
sea: **sea water** n acqua di mare; **seaweed** ['siːwiːd] n alghe fpl
sec. abbr = **second(s)**
secluded [sɪˈkluːdɪd] adj isolato(-a), appartato(-a)
second ['sɛkənd] num secondo(-a) ▷ adv (*in race etc*) al secondo posto ▷ n (*unit of time*) secondo; (*Aut: also: ~ gear*) seconda; (*Comm: imperfect*) scarto; (*BRIT: Scol: degree*) laurea con punteggio discreto ▷ vt (*motion*) appoggiare; **secondary** adj secondario(-a); **secondary school** n scuola secondaria; **second-class** adj di seconda classe ▷ adv in seconda classe; **secondhand** adj di seconda mano, usato(-a); **secondly** adv in secondo luogo; **second-rate** adj scadente; **second thoughts** npl ripensamenti mpl; **on second thoughts** (BRIT) or **thought** (US) ripensandoci bene
secrecy ['siːkrəsɪ] n segretezza
secret ['siːkrɪt] adj segreto(-a) ▷ n segreto; **in ~** in segreto
secretary ['sɛkrətrɪ] n segretario(-a); **S~ of State (for)** (BRIT: Pol) ministro (di)
secretive ['siːkrətɪv] adj riservato(-a)
secret service n servizi mpl segreti
sect [sɛkt] n setta
section ['sɛkʃən] n sezione f
sector ['sɛktəʳ] n settore m
secular ['sɛkjuləʳ] adj secolare
secure [sɪˈkjuəʳ] adj sicuro(-a); (*firmly fixed*)

assicurato(-a), ben fermato(-a); (*in safe place*) al sicuro ▷ vt (*fix*) fissare, assicurare; (*get*) ottenere, assicurarsi; **securities** npl (*Stock Exchange*) titoli mpl
security [sɪˈkjuərɪtɪ] n sicurezza; (*for loan*) garanzia; **security guard** n guardia giurata
sedan [səˈdæn] (US) n (*Aut*) berlina
sedate [sɪˈdeɪt] adj posato(-a), calmo(-a) ▷ vt calmare
sedative ['sɛdɪtɪv] n sedativo, calmante m
seduce [sɪˈdjuːs] vt sedurre; **seductive** [-'dʌktɪv] adj seducente
see [siː] (pt **saw**, pp **seen**) vt vedere; (*accompany*): **to ~ sb to the door** accompagnare qn alla porta ▷ vi vedere; (*understand*) capire ▷ n sede f vescovile; **to ~ that** (*ensure*) badare che + sub, fare in modo che + sub; **~ you soon!** a presto!; **see off** vt salutare alla partenza; **see out** vt (*take to the door*) accompagnare alla porta; **see through** vt portare a termine ▷ vt fus non lasciarsi ingannare da; **see to** vt fus occuparsi di
seed [siːd] n seme m; (*fig*) germe m; (*Tennis etc*) testa di serie; **to go to ~** fare seme; (*fig*) scadere
seeing ['siːɪŋ] conj **~ (that)** visto che
seek [siːk] (pt, pp **sought**) vt cercare
seem [siːm] vi sembrare, parere; **there ~s to be ...** sembra che ci sia ...; **seemingly** adv apparentemente
seen [siːn] pp of **see**
seesaw ['siːsɔː] n altalena a bilico
segment ['sɛgmənt] n segmento
segregate ['sɛgrɪgeɪt] vt segregare, isolare
seize [siːz] vt (*grasp*) afferrare; (*take possession of*) impadronirsi di; (*Law*) sequestrare
seizure ['siːʒəʳ] n (*Med*) attacco; (*Law*) confisca, sequestro
seldom ['sɛldəm] adv raramente
select [sɪˈlɛkt] adj scelto(-a) ▷ vt scegliere, selezionare; **selection** [-'lɛkʃən] n selezione f, scelta; **selective** adj selettivo(-a)
self [sɛlf] n **the ~** l'io m ▷ prefix auto...; **self-assured** adj sicuro(-a) di sé; **self-catering** (BRIT) adj in cui ci si cucina da sé; **self-centred** (US **self-centered**) adj egocentrico(-a); **self-confidence** n sicurezza di sé; **self-confident** adj sicuro(-a) di sé; **self-conscious** adj timido(-a); **self-contained** (BRIT) adj (*flat*) indipendente; **self-control** n autocontrollo; **self-defence** (US **self-defense**) n autodifesa; (*Law*) legittima difesa; **self-drive** adj (BRIT: *rented car*)

senza autista; **self-employed** adj che
lavora in proprio; **self-esteem** n amor
proprio m; **self-indulgent** adj indulgente
verso se stesso(-a); **self-interest** n
interesse m personale; **selfish** adj egoista;
self-pity n autocommiserazione f; **self-
raising** (US **self-rising**) adj **self-raising
flour** miscela di farina e lievito; **self-
respect** n rispetto di sé, amor proprio;
self-service n autoservizio, self-service m

sell [sɛl] (pt, pp **sold**) vt vendere ▷ vi
vendersi; **to ~ at** or **for 1000 euros**
essere in vendita a 1000 euro; **sell off** vt
svendere, liquidare; **sell out** vi **to ~ out
(of sth)** esaurire (qc); **the tickets are all
sold out** i biglietti sono esauriti; **sell-by
date** ['sɛlbaɪ-] n data di scadenza; **seller** n
venditore(-trice)

Sellotape® ['sɛləuteɪp] (BRIT) n nastro
adesivo, scotch® m

selves [sɛlvz] npl of **self**

semester [sɪ'mɛstəʳ] (US) n semestre m

semi... ['sɛmɪ] prefix semi...; **semicircle**
n semicerchio; **semidetached (house)**
[sɛmɪdɪ'tætʃt-] (BRIT) n casa gemella;
semi-final n semifinale f

seminar ['sɛmɪnɑːʳ] n seminario

semi-skimmed ['sɛmɪ'skɪmd] adj (milk)
parzialmente scremato(-a)

senate ['sɛnɪt] n senato; **senator** n
senatore(-trice)

send [sɛnd] (pt, pp **sent**) vt mandare;
send back vt rimandare; **send for** vt fus
mandare a chiamare, far venire; **send in** vt
(report, application, resignation) presentare;
send off vt (goods) spedire; (BRIT: Sport:
player) espellere; **send on** vt (BRIT: letter)
inoltrare; (luggage etc: in advance) spedire
in anticipo; **send out** vt (invitation)
diramare; **send up** vt (person, price) far
salire; (BRIT: parody) mettere in ridicolo;
sender n mittente m/f; **send-off** n **to
give sb a good send-off** festeggiare la
partenza di qn

senile ['siːnaɪl] adj senile

senior ['siːnɪəʳ] adj (older) più vecchio(-a);
(of higher rank) di grado più elevato; **senior
citizen** n persona anziana; **senior high
school** (US) n ≈ liceo

sensation [sɛn'seɪʃən] n sensazione
f; **sensational** adj sensazionale;
(marvellous) eccezionale

sense [sɛns] n senso; (feeling) sensazione
f, senso; (meaning) senso, significato;
(wisdom) buonsenso ▷ vt sentire,
percepire; **it makes ~** ha senso; **senseless**
adj sciocco(-a); (unconscious) privo(-a) di
sensi; **sense of humour** (BRIT) n senso
dell'umorismo

sensible ['sɛnsɪbl] adj sensato(-a),
ragionevole

> Be careful not to translate **sensible** by
> the Italian word **sensibile**.

sensitive ['sɛnsɪtɪv] adj sensibile; (skin,
question) delicato(-a)

sensual ['sɛnsjuəl] adj sensuale

sensuous ['sɛnsjuəs] adj sensuale

sent [sɛnt] pt, pp of **send**

sentence ['sɛntns] n (Ling) frase f;
(Law: judgment) sentenza; (: punishment)
condanna ▷ vt **to ~ sb to death/to 5
years** condannare qn a morte/a 5 anni

sentiment ['sɛntɪmənt] n sentimento;
(opinion) opinione f; **sentimental** [-
'mɛntl] adj sentimentale

Sep. abbr (= September) Sett.

separate [adj 'sɛprɪt, vb 'sɛpəreɪt] adj
separato(-a) ▷ vt separare ▷ vi separarsi;
separately adv separatamente;
separates npl (clothes) coordinati mpl;
separation [-'reɪʃən] n separazione f

September [sɛp'tɛmbəʳ] n settembre m

septic ['sɛptɪk] adj settico(-a); (wound)
infettato(-a); **septic tank** n fossa settica

sequel ['siːkwl] n conseguenza; (of story)
seguito; (of film) sequenza

sequence ['siːkwəns] n (series) serie f;
(order) ordine m

sequin ['siːkwɪn] n lustrino, paillette f inv

Serb [səːb] adj, n = **Serbian**

Serbia ['səːbɪə] n Serbia

Serbian ['səːbɪən] adj serbo(-a) ▷ n
serbo(-a); (Ling) serbo

sergeant ['sɑːdʒənt] n sergente m; (Police)
brigadiere m

serial ['sɪərɪəl] n (Press) romanzo a
puntate; (Radio, TV) trasmissione f a
puntate, serial m inv; **serial killer** n serial-
killer m/f inv; **serial number** n numero
di serie

series ['sɪəriːz] n inv serie f inv; (Publishing)
collana

serious ['sɪərɪəs] adj serio(-a), grave;
seriously adv seriamente

sermon ['səːmən] n sermone m

servant ['səːvənt] n domestico(-a)

serve [səːv] vt (employer etc) servire, essere
a servizio di; (purpose) servire a; (customer,
food, meal) servire; (apprenticeship) fare;
(prison term) scontare ▷ vi (also Tennis)
servire; (be useful): **to ~ as/for/to do**
servire da/per/per fare ▷ n (Tennis)
servizio; **it ~s him right** ben gli sta, se l'è
meritata; **server** n (Comput) server m inv

service ['səːvɪs] n servizio; (Aut:
maintenance) assistenza, revisione f ▷ vt
(car, washing machine) revisionare; **to be of
~ to sb** essere d'aiuto a qn; **~ included/**

not included servizio compreso/escluso; **~s** (BRIT: on motorway) stazione f di servizio; (Mil): **the S~s** le Forze Armate; **service area** n (on motorway) area di servizio; **service charge** (BRIT) n servizio; **serviceman** (irreg) n militare m; **service station** n stazione f di servizio

serviette [sə:vɪˈɛt] (BRIT) n tovagliolo

session ['sɛʃən] n (sitting) seduta, sessione f; (Scol) anno scolastico (or accademico)

set [sɛt] (pt, pp **set**) n serie f inv; (of cutlery etc) servizio; (Radio, TV) apparecchio; (Tennis) set m inv; (group of people) mondo, ambiente m; (Cinema) scenario; (Theatre: stage) scene fpl; (: scenery) scenario; (Math) insieme m; (Hairdressing) messa in piega ▷ adj (fixed) stabilito(-a), determinato(-a); (ready) pronto(-a) ▷ vt (place) posare, mettere; (arrange) sistemare; (fix) fissare; (adjust) regolare; (decide: rules etc) stabilire, fissare ▷ vi (sun) tramontare; (jam, jelly) rapprendersi; (concrete) fare presa; **to be ~ on doing** essere deciso a fare; **to ~ to music** mettere in musica; **to ~ on fire** dare fuoco a; **to ~ free** liberare; **to ~ sth going** mettere in moto qc; **to ~ sail** prendere il mare; **set aside** vt mettere da parte; **set down** vt (bus, train) lasciare; **set in** vi (infection) svilupparsi; (complications) intervenire; **the rain has ~ in for the day** ormai pioverà tutto il giorno; **set off** vi partire ▷ vt (bomb) far scoppiare; (cause to start) mettere in moto; (show up well) dare risalto a; **set out** vi partire ▷ vt (arrange) disporre; (state) esporre, presentare; **to ~ out to do** proporsi di fare; **set up** vt (organization) fondare, costituire; **setback** n (hitch) contrattempo, inconveniente m; **set menu** n menù m inv fisso

settee [sɛˈtiː] n divano, sofà m inv

setting ['sɛtɪŋ] n (background) ambiente m; (of controls) posizione f; (of sun) tramonto; (of jewel) montatura

settle ['sɛtl] vt (argument, matter) appianare; (accounts) regolare; (Med: calm) calmare ▷ vi (bird, dust etc) posarsi; (sediment) depositarsi; **to ~ for sth** accontentarsi di qc; **to ~ on sth** decidersi per qc; **settle down** vi (get comfortable) sistemarsi; (calm down) calmarsi; (get back to normal: situation) tornare alla normalità; **settle in** vi sistemarsi; **settle up** vi **to ~ up with sb** regolare i conti con qn; **settlement** n (payment) pagamento, saldo; (agreement) accordo; (colony) colonia; (village etc) villaggio, comunità f inv

setup ['sɛtʌp] n (arrangement) sistemazione f; (situation) situazione f

seven ['sɛvn] num sette; **seventeen** num diciassette; **seventeenth** [sɛvnˈtiːnθ] num diciassettesimo(-a); **seventh** num settimo(-a); **seventieth** ['sɛvntɪɪθ] num settantesimo(-a); **seventy** num settanta

sever ['sɛvəʳ] vt recidere, tagliare; (relations) troncare

several ['sɛvərl] adj, pron alcuni(-e), diversi(-e); **~ of us** alcuni di noi

severe [sɪˈvɪəʳ] adj severo(-a); (serious) serio(-a), grave; (hard) duro(-a); (plain) semplice, sobrio(-a)

sew [səʊ] (pt sewed, pp sewn) vt, vi cucire

sewage ['suːɪdʒ] n acque fpl di scolo

sewer ['suːəʳ] n fogna

sewing ['səʊɪŋ] n cucitura; cucito; **sewing machine** n macchina da cucire

sewn [səʊn] pp of **sew**

sex [sɛks] n sesso; **to have ~ with** avere rapporti sessuali con; **sexism** ['sɛksɪzəm] n sessismo; **sexist** adj, n sessista m/f; **sexual** ['sɛksjuəl] adj sessuale; **sexual intercourse** n rapporti mpl sessuali; **sexuality** [sɛksjuˈælɪtɪ] n sessualità; **sexy** ['sɛksɪ] adj provocante, sexy inv

shabby ['ʃæbɪ] adj malandato(-a); (behaviour) vergognoso(-a)

shack [ʃæk] n baracca, capanna

shade [ʃeɪd] n ombra; (for lamp) paralume m; (of colour) tonalità f inv; (small quantity): **a ~ (more/too large)** un po' (di più/troppo grande) ▷ vt ombreggiare, fare ombra a; **in the ~** all'ombra; **~s** (US) npl (sunglasses) occhiali mpl da sole

shadow ['ʃædəʊ] n ombra ▷ vt (follow) pedinare; **shadow cabinet** (BRIT) n (Pol) governo m ombra inv

shady ['ʃeɪdɪ] adj ombroso(-a); (fig: dishonest) losco(-a), equivoco(-a)

shaft [ʃɑːft] n (of arrow, spear) asta; (Aut, Tech) albero; (of mine) pozzo; (of lift) tromba; (of light) raggio

shake [ʃeɪk] (pt shook, pp shaken) vt scuotere; (bottle, cocktail) agitare ▷ vi tremare; **to ~ one's head** (in refusal, dismay) scuotere la testa; **to ~ hands with sb** stringere or dare la mano a qn; **shake off** vt scrollare (via); (fig) sbarazzarsi di; **shake up** vt scuotere; **shaky** adj (hand, voice) tremante; (building) traballante

shall [ʃæl] aux vb **I ~ go** andrò; **~ I open the door?** apro io la porta?; **I'll get some, ~ I?** ne prendo un po', va bene?

shallow ['ʃæləʊ] adj poco profondo(-a); (fig) superficiale

sham [ʃæm] n finzione f, messinscena; (jewellery, furniture) imitazione f

shambles ['ʃæmblz] n confusione f, baraonda, scompiglio

shame [ʃeɪm] n vergogna ▷ vt far vergognare; **it is a ~ (that/to do)** è un peccato! (che + sub/fare); **what a ~!** che peccato!; **shameful** adj vergognoso(-a); **shameless** adj sfrontato(-a); (immodest) spudorato(-a)

shampoo [ʃæmˈpuː] n shampoo m inv ▷ vt fare lo shampoo a

shandy [ˈʃændɪ] n birra con gassosa

shan't [ʃɑːnt] = **shall not**

shape [ʃeɪp] n forma ▷ vt formare; (statement) formulare; (sb's ideas) condizionare; **to take ~** prendere forma

share [ʃɛəʳ] n (thing received, contribution) parte f; (Comm) azione f ▷ vt dividere; (have in common) condividere, avere in comune; **shareholder** n azionista m/f

shark [ʃɑːk] n squalo, pescecane m

sharp [ʃɑːp] adj (razor, knife) affilato(-a); (point) acuto(-a), acuminato(-a); (nose, chin) aguzzo(-a); (outline, contrast) netto(-a); (cold, pain) pungente; (voice) stridulo(-a); (person: quick-witted) sveglio(-a); (: unscrupulous) disonesto(-a); (Mus): **C ~** do diesis ▷ n (Mus) diesis m inv ▷ adv **at 2 o'clock ~** alle due in punto; **sharpen** vt affilare; (pencil) fare la punta a; (fig) acuire; **sharpener** n (also: **pencil sharpener**) temperamatite m inv; **sharply** adv (turn, stop) bruscamente; (stand out, contrast) nettamente; (criticize, retort) duramente, aspramente

shatter [ˈʃætəʳ] vt mandare in frantumi, frantumare; (fig: upset) distruggere; (: ruin) rovinare ▷ vi frantumarsi, andare in pezzi; **shattered** adj (grief-stricken) sconvolto(-a); (exhausted) a pezzi, distrutto(-a)

shave [ʃeɪv] vt radere, rasare ▷ vi radersi, farsi la barba ▷ n **to have a ~** farsi la barba; **shaver** n (also: **electric shaver**) rasoio elettrico

shaving cream n crema da barba

shaving foam n = **shaving cream**

shavings [ˈʃeɪvɪŋz] npl (of wood etc) trucioli mpl

shawl [ʃɔːl] n scialle m

she [ʃiː] pron ella, lei; **~-cat** gatta; **~-elephant** elefantessa

sheath [ʃiːθ] n fodero, guaina; (contraceptive) preservativo

shed [ʃɛd] (pt, pp **shed**) n capannone m ▷ vt (leaves, fur etc) perdere; (tears, blood) versare; (workers) liberarsi di

she'd [ʃiːd] = **she had; she would**

sheep [ʃiːp] n inv pecora; **sheepdog** n cane m da pastore; **sheepskin** n pelle f di pecora

sheer [ʃɪəʳ] adj (utter) vero(-a);

(e proprio(-a)); (steep) a picco, perpendicolare; (almost transparent) sottile ▷ adv a picco

sheet [ʃiːt] n (on bed) lenzuolo; (of paper) foglio; (of glass, ice) lastra; (of metal) foglio, lamina

sheik(h) [ʃeɪk] n sceicco

shelf [ʃɛlf] (pl **shelves**) n scaffale m, mensola

shell [ʃɛl] n (on beach) conchiglia; (of egg, nut etc) guscio; (explosive) granata; (of building) scheletro ▷ vt (peas) sgranare; (Mil) bombardare

she'll [ʃiːl] = **she will; she shall**

shellfish [ˈʃɛlfɪʃ] n inv (crab etc) crostaceo; (scallop etc) mollusco; (as food) crostacei; molluschi

shelter [ˈʃɛltəʳ] n riparo, rifugio ▷ vt riparare, proteggere; (give lodging to) dare rifugio or asilo a ▷ vi ripararsi, mettersi al riparo; **sheltered** adj riparato(-a)

shelves [ˈʃɛlvz] npl of **shelf**

shelving [ˈʃɛlvɪŋ] n scaffalature fpl

shepherd [ˈʃɛpəd] n pastore m ▷ vt (guide) guidare; **shepherd's pie** (BRIT) n timballo di carne macinata e purè di patate

sheriff [ˈʃɛrɪf] (US) n sceriffo

sherry [ˈʃɛrɪ] n sherry m inv

she's [ʃiːz] = **she is; she has**

Shetland [ˈʃɛtlənd] n (also: **the ~s, the ~ Isles**) le isole Shetland, le Shetland

shield [ʃiːld] n scudo; (trophy) scudetto; (protection) schermo ▷ vt **to ~ (from)** riparare (da), proteggere (da or contro)

shift [ʃɪft] n (change) cambiamento; (of workers) turno ▷ vt spostare, muovere; (remove) rimuovere ▷ vi spostarsi, muoversi

shin [ʃɪn] n tibia

shine [ʃaɪn] (pt, pp **shone**) n splendore m, lucentezza ▷ vi (ri)splendere, brillare ▷ vt far brillare, far risplendere; (torch): **to ~ sth on** puntare qc verso

shingles [ˈʃɪŋglz] n (Med) herpes zoster m

shiny [ˈʃaɪnɪ] adj lucente, lucido(-a)

ship [ʃɪp] n nave f ▷ vt trasportare (via mare); (send) spedire (via mare); **shipment** n carico; **shipping** n (ships) naviglio; (traffic) navigazione f; **shipwreck** n relitto; (event) naufragio ▷ vt **to be shipwrecked** naufragare, fare naufragio; **shipyard** n cantiere m navale

shirt [ʃəːt] n camicia; **in ~ sleeves** in maniche di camicia

shit [ʃɪt] (infl) excl merda (!)

shiver [ˈʃɪvəʳ] n brivido ▷ vi rabbrividire, tremare

shock [ʃɔk] n (impact) urto, colpo; (Elec) scossa; (emotional) colpo, shock m inv;

(Med) shock ▷ vt colpire, scioccare; scandalizzare; **shocking** adj scioccante, traumatizzante; scandaloso(-a)

shoe [ʃuː] (pt, pp **shod**) n scarpa; (also: **horse~**) ferro di cavallo ▷ vt (horse) ferrare; **shoelace** n stringa; **shoe polish** n lucido per scarpe; **shoeshop** n calzoleria

shone [ʃɔn] pt, pp of **shine**

shook [ʃuk] pt of **shake**

shoot [ʃuːt] (pt, pp **shot**) n (on branch, seedling) germoglio ▷ vt (game) cacciare, andare a caccia di; (person) sparare a; (execute) fucilare; (film) girare ▷ vi (with gun): **to ~ (at)** sparare (a), fare fuoco (su); (with bow): **to ~ (at)** tirare (su); (Football) sparare, tirare (forte); **shoot down** vt (plane) abbattere; **shoot up** vi (fig) salire alle stelle; **shooting** n (shots) sparatoria; (Hunting) caccia

shop [ʃɔp] n negozio; (workshop) officina ▷ vi (also: **go ~ping**) fare spese; **shop assistant** (BRIT) n commesso(-a); **shopkeeper** n negoziante m/f, bottegaio(-a); **shoplifting** n taccheggio; **shopping** n (goods) spesa, acquisti mpl; **shopping bag** n borsa per la spesa; **shopping centre** (US **shopping center**) n centro commerciale; **shopping mall** n centro commerciale; **shopping trolley** n (BRIT) carrello del supermercato; **shop window** n vetrina

shore [ʃɔːʳ] n (of sea) riva, spiaggia; (of lake) riva ▷ vt **to ~ (up)** puntellare; **on ~** a riva

short [ʃɔːt] adj (not long) corto(-a); (soon finished) breve; (person) basso(-a); (curt) brusco(-a), secco(-a); (insufficient) insufficiente ▷ n (also: **~ film**) cortometraggio; **to be ~ of sth** essere a corto di o mancare di qc; **in ~** in breve; **~ of doing** a meno che non si faccia; **everything ~ of** tutto fuorché; **it is ~ for** è l'abbreviazione or il diminutivo di; **to cut ~** (speech, visit) accorciare, abbreviare; **to fall ~ of** venir meno a; non soddisfare; **to run ~ of** rimanere senza; **to stop ~** fermarsi di colpo; **to stop ~ of** non arrivare fino a; **shortage** n scarsezza, carenza; **shortbread** n biscotto di pasta frolla; **shortcoming** n difetto; **short(crust) pastry** (BRIT) n pasta frolla; **shortcut** n scorciatoia; **shorten** vt accorciare, ridurre; **shortfall** n deficit m; **shorthand** (BRIT) n stenografia; **short-lived** adj di breve durata; **shortly** adv fra poco; **shorts** npl (also: **a pair of shorts**) i calzoncini; **short-sighted** (BRIT) adj miope; **short-sleeved** adj a maniche corte; **short story** n racconto, novella; **short-tempered** adj irascibile;

short-term adj (effect) di o a breve durata; (borrowing) a breve scadenza

shot [ʃɔt] pt, pp of **shoot** ▷ n sparo, colpo; (try) prova; (Football) tiro; (injection) iniezione f; (Phot) foto f inv; **like a ~** come un razzo; (very readily) immediatamente; **shotgun** n fucile m da caccia;

should [ʃud] aux vb **I ~ go now** dovrei andare ora; **he ~ be there now** dovrebbe essere arrivato ora; **I ~ go if I were you** se fossi in te andrei; **I ~ like to** mi piacerebbe

shoulder [ˈʃəuldəʳ] n spalla; (BRIT: of road): **hard ~** banchina ▷ vt (fig) addossarsi, prendere sulle proprie spalle; **shoulder blade** n scapola

shouldn't [ˈʃudnt] = **should not**

shout [ʃaut] n urlo, grido ▷ vt gridare ▷ vi (also: **~ out**) urlare, gridare

shove [ʃʌv] vt spingere; (inf: put): **to ~ sth in** ficcare qc in

shovel [ˈʃʌvl] n pala ▷ vt spalare

show [ʃəu] (pt **showed**, pp **shown**) n (of emotion) dimostrazione f, manifestazione f; (semblance) apparenza; (exhibition) mostra, esposizione f; (Theatre, Cinema) spettacolo ▷ vt far vedere, mostrare; (courage etc) dimostrare, dar prova di; (exhibit) esporre ▷ vi vedersi, essere visibile; **for ~** per fare scena; **on ~** (exhibits etc) esposto(-a); **can you ~ me where it is, please?** può mostrarmi dov'è, per favore?; **show in** vt (person) far entrare; **show off** vi (pej) esibirsi, mettersi in mostra ▷ vt (display) mettere in risalto; (pej) mettere in mostra; **show out** vt (person) accompagnare alla porta; **show up** vi (stand out) essere ben visibile; (inf: turn up) farsi vedere ▷ vt mettere in risalto; **show business** n industria dello spettacolo

shower [ˈʃauəʳ] n (rain) acquazzone m; (of stones etc) pioggia; (also: **~bath**) doccia ▷ vi fare la doccia ▷ vt **to ~ sb with** (gifts, abuse etc) coprire qn di; (missiles) lanciare contro qn una pioggia di; **to have a ~** fare la doccia; **shower cap** n cuffia da doccia; **shower gel** n gel m doccia inv

showing [ˈʃəuɪŋ] n (of film) proiezione f

show jumping n concorso ippico (di salto ad ostacoli)

shown [ʃəun] pp of **show**

show: **show-off** (inf) n (person) esibizionista m/f; **showroom** n sala d'esposizione

shrank [ʃræŋk] pt of **shrink**

shred [ʃred] n (gen pl) brandello ▷ vt fare a brandelli; (Culin) sminuzzare, tagliuzzare

shrewd [ʃruːd] adj astuto(-a), scaltro(-a)

shriek [ʃriːk] n strillo ▷ vi strillare

shrimp [ʃrimp] n gamberetto

shrine [ʃraɪn] n reliquario; (place) santuario

shrink [ʃrɪŋk] (pt **shrank**, pp **shrunk**) vi restringersi; (fig) ridursi; (also: **~ away**) ritrarsi ▷ vt (wool) far restringere ▷ n (inf: pej) psicanalista m/f; **to ~ from doing sth** rifuggire dal fare qc

shrivel ['ʃrɪvl] (also: **~ up**) vt raggrinzare, avvizzire ▷ vi raggrinzirsi, avvizzire

shroud [ʃraud] n lenzuolo funebre ▷ vt **~ed in mystery** avvolto(-a) nel mistero

Shrove Tuesday ['ʃrəuv-] n martedì m grasso

shrub [ʃrʌb] n arbusto

shrug [ʃrʌg] n scrollata di spalle ▷ vt, vi **to ~ (one's shoulders)** alzare le spalle, fare spallucce; **shrug off** vt passare sopra a

shrunk [ʃrʌŋk] pp of **shrink**

shudder ['ʃʌdəʳ] n brivido ▷ vi rabbrividire

shuffle ['ʃʌfl] vt (cards) mescolare; **to ~ (one's feet)** strascicare i piedi

shun [ʃʌn] vt sfuggire, evitare

shut [ʃʌt] (pt, pp **shut**) vt chiudere ▷ vi chiudersi, chiudere; **shut down** vt, vi chiudere definitivamente; **shut up** vi (inf: keep quiet) stare zitto(-a), fare silenzio ▷ vt (close) chiudere; (silence) far tacere; **shutter** n imposta; (Phot) otturatore m

shuttle ['ʃʌtl] n spola, navetta; (space shuttle) navetta (spaziale); (also: **~ service**) servizio m navetta inv; **shuttlecock** ['ʃʌtlkɔk] n volano

shy [ʃaɪ] adj timido(-a)

sibling ['sɪblɪŋ] n (formal) fratello/sorella

Sicily ['sɪsɪlɪ] n Sicilia

sick [sɪk] adj (ill) malato(-a); (vomiting): **to be ~** vomitare; (humour) macabro(-a); **to feel ~** avere la nausea; **to be ~ of** (fig) averne abbastanza di; **sickening** adj (fig) disgustoso(-a), rivoltante; **sick leave** n congedo per malattia; **sickly** adj malaticcio(-a); (causing nausea) nauseante; **sickness** n malattia; (vomiting) vomito

side [saɪd] n lato; (of lake) riva; (team) squadra ▷ cpd (door, entrance) laterale ▷ vi **to ~ with sb** parteggiare per qn, prendere le parti di qn; **by the ~ of** a fianco di; (road) sul ciglio di; **~ by ~** fianco a fianco; **from ~ to ~** da una parte all'altra; **to take ~s (with)** schierarsi (con); **sideboard** n credenza; **sideboards** (BRIT), **sideburns** ['saɪdbə:nz] npl (whiskers) basette fpl; **sidelight** n (Aut) luce f di posizione; **sideline** n (Sport) linea laterale; (fig) attività secondaria; **side order** n contorno (pietanza); **side road** n strada secondaria; **side street** n traversa; **sidetrack** vt (fig) distrarre; **sidewalk** (US) n marciapiede m; **sideways** adv (move) di lato, di fianco

siege [siːdʒ] n assedio

sieve [sɪv] n setaccio ▷ vt setacciare

sift [sɪft] vt passare al crivello; (fig) vagliare

sigh [saɪ] n sospiro ▷ vi sospirare

sight [saɪt] n (faculty) vista; (spectacle) spettacolo; (on gun) mira ▷ vt avvistare; **in ~** in vista; **on ~** a vista; **out of ~** non visibile; **sightseeing** n giro turistico; **to go sightseeing** visitare una località

sign [saɪn] n segno; (with hand etc) segno, gesto; (notice) insegna, cartello ▷ vt firmare; (player) ingaggiare; **where do I ~?** dove devo firmare?; **sign for** vt fus (item) firmare per l'accettazione di; **sign in** vi firmare il registro (all'arrivo); **sign on** vi (Mil) arruolarsi; (as unemployed) iscriversi sulla lista (dell'ufficio di collocamento) ▷ vt (Mil) arruolare; (employee) assumere; **sign up** vi (Mil) arruolarsi; (for course) iscriversi ▷ vt (player) ingaggiare; (recruits) reclutare

signal ['sɪgnl] n segnale m ▷ vi (Aut) segnalare, mettere la freccia ▷ vt (person) fare segno a; (message) comunicare per mezzo di segnali

signature ['sɪgnətʃəʳ] n firma

significance [sɪg'nɪfɪkəns] n significato; importanza

significant [sɪg'nɪfɪkənt] adj significativo(-a)

signify ['sɪgnɪfaɪ] vt significare

sign language n linguaggio dei muti

signpost ['saɪnpəust] n cartello indicatore

Sikh [siːk] adj, n sikh (m/f) inv

silence ['saɪlns] n silenzio ▷ vt far tacere, ridurre al silenzio

silent ['saɪlnt] adj silenzioso(-a); (film) muto(-a); **to remain ~** tacere, stare zitto

silhouette [sɪluː'ɛt] n silhouette f inv

silicon chip ['sɪlɪkən-] n piastrina di silicio

silk [sɪlk] n seta ▷ adj di seta

silly ['sɪlɪ] adj stupido(-a), sciocco(-a)

silver ['sɪlvəʳ] n argento; (money) monete da 5, 10, 20 or 50 pence; (also: **~ware**) argenteria ▷ adj d'argento; **silver-plated** adj argentato(-a)

similar ['sɪmɪləʳ] adj **~ (to)** simile (a); **similarity** [sɪmɪ'lærɪtɪ] n somiglianza, rassomiglianza; **similarly** adv allo stesso modo; così pure

simmer ['sɪməʳ] vi cuocere a fuoco lento

simple ['sɪmpl] adj semplice; **simplicity** [-'plɪsɪtɪ] n semplicità; **simplify** vt semplificare; **simply** adv semplicemente

simulate ['sɪmjuleɪt] vt fingere, simulare

simultaneous [sɪməl'teɪnɪəs] adj simultaneo(-a); **simultaneously** adv simultaneamente, contemporaneamente

sin [sɪn] n peccato ▷ vi peccare

since [sɪns] adv da allora ▷ prep da ▷ conj

(*time*) da quando; (*because*) poiché, dato che; **~ then, ever ~** da allora
sincere [sɪn'sɪə'] *adj* sincero(-a); **sincerely** *adv* **yours sincerely** (*in letters*) distinti saluti
sing [sɪŋ] (*pt* **sang**, *pp* **sung**) *vt*, *vi* cantare
Singapore [sɪŋgə'pɔː'] *n* Singapore *f*
singer ['sɪŋə'] *n* cantante *m/f*
singing ['sɪŋɪŋ] *n* canto
single ['sɪŋgl] *adj* solo(-a), unico(-a); (*unmarried: man*) celibe; (: *woman*) nubile; (*not double*) semplice ▷ *n* (*BRIT: also:* **~ ticket**) biglietto di (sola) andata; (*record*) 45 giri *m*; **~s** *n* (*Tennis*) singolo; **single out** *vt* scegliere; (*distinguish*) distinguere; **single bed** *n* letto singolo; **single file** *n* **in single file** in fila indiana; **single-handed** *adv* senza aiuto, da solo(-a); **single-minded** *adj* tenace, risoluto(-a); **single parent** *n* (*mother*) ragazza *f* madre *inv*; (*father*) ragazzo *m* padre *inv*; **single-parent family** famiglia monoparentale; **single room** *n* camera singola
singular ['sɪŋgjulə'] *adj* (*exceptional, Ling*) singolare ▷ *n* (*Ling*) singolare *m*
sinister ['sɪnɪstə'] *adj* sinistro(-a)
sink [sɪŋk] (*pt* **sank**, *pp* **sunk**) *n* lavandino, acquaio ▷ *vt* (*ship*) (fare) affondare, colare a picco; (*piles etc*) scavare; (*piles etc*) scavare: **to ~ sth into** conficcare qc in ▷ *vi* affondare, andare a fondo; (*ground etc*) cedere, avvallarsi; **my heart sank** mi sentii venir meno; **sink in** *vi* penetrare
sinus ['saɪnəs] *n* (*Anat*) seno
sip [sɪp] *n* sorso ▷ *vt* sorseggiare
sir [sə'] *n* signore *m*; **S~ John Smith** Sir John Smith; **yes ~** sì, signore
siren ['saɪərn] *n* sirena
sirloin ['sə:lɔɪn] *n* controfiletto
sister ['sɪstə'] *n* sorella; (*nun*) suora; (*BRIT: nurse*) infermiera *f* caposala *inv*; **sister-in-law** *n* cognata
sit [sɪt] (*pt*, *pp* **sat**) *vi* sedere, sedersi; (*assembly*) essere in seduta; (*for painter*) posare ▷ *vt* (*exam*) sostenere, dare; **sit back** *vi* (*in seat*) appoggiarsi allo schienale; **sit down** *vi* sedersi; **sit on** *vt fus* (*jury, committee*) far parte di; **sit up** *vi* tirarsi a sedere; (*not go to bed*) stare alzato(-a) fino a tardi
sitcom ['sɪtkɔm] *n abbr* (= *situation comedy*) commedia di situazione; (*TV*) telefilm *m inv* comico d'interni
site [saɪt] *n* posto; (*also:* **building ~**) cantiere *m* ▷ *vt* situare
sitting ['sɪtɪŋ] *n* (*of assembly etc*) seduta; (*in canteen*) turno; **sitting room** *n* soggiorno
situated ['sɪtjueɪtɪd] *adj* situato(-a)
situation [sɪtju'eɪʃən] *n* situazione *f*; (*job*)

lavoro; (*location*) posizione *f*; **"~s vacant"** (*BRIT*) "offerte *fpl* di impiego"
six [sɪks] *num* sei; **sixteen** *num* sedici; **sixteenth** [sɪks'tiːnθ] *num* sedicesimo(-a); **sixth** *num* sesto(-a); **sixth form** *n* (*BRIT*) ultimo biennio delle scuole superiori; **sixth-form college** *n* istituto che offre corsi di preparazione all'esame di maturità per ragazzi dai 16 ai 18 anni; **sixtieth** ['sɪkstɪθ] *num* sessantesimo(-a) ▷ *pron* (*in series*) sessantesimo(-a); (*fraction*) sessantesimo; **sixty** *num* sessanta
size [saɪz] *n* dimensioni *fpl*; (*of clothing*) taglia, misura; (*of shoes*) numero; (*glue*) colla; **sizeable** *adj* considerevole
sizzle ['sɪzl] *vi* sfrigolare
skate [skeɪt] *n* pattino; (*fish: pl inv*) razza ▷ *vi* pattinare; **skateboard** *n* skateboard *m inv*; **skateboarding** *n* skateboard *m inv*; **skater** *n* pattinatore(-trice); **skating** *n* pattinaggio; **skating rink** *n* pista di pattinaggio
skeleton ['skɛlɪtn] *n* scheletro
skeptical ['skɛptɪkl] (*US*) *adj* = **sceptical**
sketch [skɛtʃ] *n* (*drawing*) schizzo, abbozzo; (*Theatre*) scenetta comica, sketch *m inv* ▷ *vt* abbozzare, schizzare
skewer ['skjuː'] *n* spiedo
ski [skiː] *n* sci *m inv* ▷ *vi* sciare; **ski boot** *n* scarpone *m* da sci
skid [skɪd] *n* slittamento ▷ *vi* slittare
ski: skier ['skiː'] *n* sciatore(-trice); **skiing** ['skiːɪŋ] *n* sci *m*
skilful ['skɪlful] (*US* **skillful**) *adj* abile
ski lift *n* sciovia
skill [skɪl] *n* abilità *f inv*, capacità *f inv*; **skilled** *adj* esperto(-a); (*worker*) qualificato(-a), specializzato(-a)
skim [skɪm] *vt* (*milk*) scremare; (*glide over*) sfiorare ▷ *vi* **to ~ through** (*fig*) scorrere, dare una scorsa a; **skimmed milk** (*US* **skim milk**) *n* latte *m* scremato
skin [skɪn] *n* pelle *f* ▷ *vt* (*fruit etc*) sbucciare; (*animal*) scuoiare, spellare; **skinhead** *n* skinhead *m/f inv*; **skinny** *adj* molto magro(-a), pelle e ossa *inv*
skip [skɪp] *n* saltello, balzo; (*BRIT: container*) benna ▷ *vi* saltare; (*with rope*) saltare la corda ▷ *vt* saltare
ski: ski pass *n* ski pass *m*; **ski pole** *n* racchetta (da sci)
skipper ['skɪpə'] *n* (*Naut, Sport*) capitano
skipping rope ['skɪpɪŋ-] (*US* **skip rope**) *n* corda per saltare
skirt [skəːt] *n* gonna, sottana ▷ *vt* fiancheggiare, costeggiare
skirting board (*BRIT*) *n* zoccolo
ski slope *n* pista da sci
ski suit *n* tuta da sci

skull [skʌl] n cranio, teschio

skunk [skʌŋk] n moffetta

sky [skaɪ] n cielo; **skyscraper** n grattacielo

slab [slæb] n lastra; (of cake, cheese) fetta

slack [slæk] adj (loose) allentato(-a); (slow) lento(-a); (careless) negligente; **slacks** npl (trousers) pantaloni mpl

slain [sleɪn] pp of **slay**

slam [slæm] vt (door) sbattere; (throw) scaraventare; (criticize) stroncare ▷ vi sbattere

slander ['slɑːndəʳ] n calunnia; diffamazione f

slang [slæŋ] n gergo, slang m

slant [slɑːnt] n pendenza, inclinazione f; (fig) angolazione f, punto di vista

slap [slæp] n manata, pacca; (on face) schiaffo ▷ vt dare una manata a; schiaffeggiare ▷ adv (directly) in pieno; ~ **a coat of paint on it** dagli una mano di vernice

slash [slæʃ] vt tagliare; (face) sfregiare; (fig: prices) ridurre drasticamente, tagliare

slate [sleɪt] n ardesia; (piece) lastra di ardesia ▷ vt (fig: criticize) stroncare, distruggere

slaughter ['slɔːtəʳ] n strage f, massacro ▷ vt (animal) macellare; (people) trucidare, massacrare; **slaughterhouse** n macello, mattatoio

Slav [slɑːv] adj, n slavo(-a)

slave [sleɪv] n schiavo(-a) ▷ vi (also: ~ **away**) lavorare come uno schiavo; **slavery** n schiavitù f

slay [sleɪ] (pt **slew**, pp **slain**) vt (formal) uccidere

sleazy ['sliːzɪ] adj trasandato(-a)

sled [slɛd] (US) = **sledge**

sledge [slɛdʒ] n slitta

sleek [sliːk] adj (hair, fur) lucido(-a), lucente; (car, boat) slanciato(-a), affusolato(-a)

sleep [sliːp] (pt, pp **slept**) n sonno ▷ vi dormire; **to go to ~** addormentarsi; **sleep in** vi (oversleep) dormire fino a tardi; **sleep together** vi (have sex) andare a letto insieme; **sleeper** (BRIT) n (Rail: on track) traversina; (: train) treno di vagoni letto; **sleeping bag** n sacco a pelo; **sleeping car** n vagone m letto inv, carrozza f letto inv; **sleeping pill** n sonnifero; **sleepover** n notte f che un ragazzino passa dai amici; **sleepwalk** vi camminare nel sonno; (as a habit) essere sonnambulo(-a); **sleepy** adj assonnato(-a), sonnolento(-a); (fig) addormentato(-a)

sleet [sliːt] n nevischio

sleeve [sliːv] n manica; (of record) copertina; **sleeveless** adj (garment) senza maniche

sleigh [sleɪ] n slitta

slender ['slɛndəʳ] adj snello(-a), sottile; (not enough) scarso(-a), esiguo(-a)

slept [slɛpt] pt, pp of **sleep**

slew [sluː] pt of **slay** ▷ vi (BRIT) girare

slice [slaɪs] n fetta ▷ vt affettare, tagliare a fette

slick [slɪk] adj (skilful) brillante; (clever) furbo(-a) ▷ n (also: **oil ~**) chiazza di petrolio

slide [slaɪd] (pt, pp **slid**) n scivolone m; (in playground) scivolo; (Phot) diapositiva; (BRIT: also: **hair ~**) fermaglio (per capelli) ▷ vt far scivolare ▷ vi scivolare; **sliding** adj (door) scorrevole

slight [slaɪt] adj (slim) snello(-a), sottile; (frail) delicato(-a), fragile; (trivial) insignificante; (small) piccolo(-a) ▷ n offesa, affronto; **not in the ~est** affatto, neppure per sogno; **slightly** adv lievemente, un po'

slim [slɪm] adj magro(-a), snello(-a) ▷ vi dimagrire; fare (or seguire) una dieta dimagrante; **slimming** ['slɪmɪŋ] adj (diet) dimagrante; (food) ipocalorico(-a)

slimy ['slaɪmɪ] adj (also fig: person) viscido(-a); (covered with mud) melmoso(-a)

sling [slɪŋ] (pt, pp **slung**) n (Med) fascia al collo; (for baby) marsupio ▷ vt lanciare, tirare

slip [slɪp] n scivolata, scivolone m; (mistake) errore m, sbaglio; (underskirt) sottoveste f; (of paper) striscia di carta; tagliando, scontrino ▷ vt (slide) far scivolare ▷ vi (slide) scivolare; (move smoothly): **to ~ into/out of** scivolare in/fuori da; (decline) declinare; **to ~ sth on/off** infilarsi/togliersi qc; **to give sb the ~** sfuggire qn; **a ~ of the tongue** un lapsus linguae; **slip up** vi sbagliarsi

slipper ['slɪpəʳ] n pantofola

slippery ['slɪpərɪ] adj scivoloso(-a)

slip road (BRIT) n (to motorway) rampa di accesso

slit [slɪt] (pt, pp **slit**) n fessura, fenditura; (cut) taglio ▷ vt fendere; tagliare

slog [slɔg] (BRIT) n faticata ▷ vi lavorare con accanimento, sgobbare

slogan ['sləʊgən] n motto, slogan m inv

slope [sləʊp] n pendio; (side of mountain) versante m; (ski slope) pista; (of roof) pendenza; (of floor) inclinazione f ▷ vi **to ~ down** declinare; **to ~ up** essere in salita; **sloping** adj inclinato(-a)

sloppy ['slɔpɪ] adj (work) tirato(-a) via; (appearance) sciatto(-a)

slot [slɔt] n fessura ▷ vt **to ~ sth into** infilare qc in; **slot machine** n

(BRIT: *vending machine*) distributore *m* automatico; (*for gambling*) slot-machine *f inv*

Slovakia [sləu'vækɪə] *n* Slovacchia

Slovene ['sləuviːn] *adj* sloveno(-a) ▷ *n* sloveno(-a); (*Ling*) sloveno

Slovenia [sləu'viːnɪə] *n* Slovenia; **Slovenian** *adj*, *n* = **Slovene**

slow [sləu] *adj* lento(-a); (*watch*): **to be ~** essere indietro ▷ *adv* lentamente ▷ *vt, vi* (*also: ~ down, ~ up*) rallentare; "~" (*road sign*) "rallentare"; **slow down** *vi* rallentare; **slowly** *adv* lentamente; **slow motion** *n*: **in slow motion** al rallentatore

slug [slʌg] *n* lumaca; (*bullet*) pallottola; **sluggish** *adj* lento(-a); (*trading*) stagnante

slum [slʌm] *n* catapecchia

slump [slʌmp] *n* crollo, caduta; (*economic*) depressione *f*, crisi *f inv* ▷ *vi* crollare

slung [slʌŋ] *pt, pp of* **sling**

slur [sləːʳ] *n* (*fig*): **~ (on)** calunnia (su) ▷ *vt* pronunciare in modo indistinto

sly [slaɪ] *adj* (*smile, remark*) sornione(-a); (*person*) furbo(-a)

smack [smæk] *n* (*slap*) pacca; (*on face*) schiaffo ▷ *vt* schiaffeggiare; (*child*) picchiare ▷ *vi*: **to ~ of** puzzare di

small [smɔːl] *adj* piccolo(-a); **small ads** (BRIT) *npl* piccola pubblicità; **small change** *n* moneta, spiccioli *mpl*

smart [smɑːt] *adj* elegante; (*fashionable*) alla moda; (*clever*) intelligente; (*quick*) sveglio(-a); *vi* bruciare; **smartcard** ['smɑːtkɑːd] *n* smartcard *f inv*, carta intelligente

smash [smæʃ] *n* (*also*: **~-up**) scontro, collisione *f*; (*smash hit*) successone *m* ▷ *vt* frantumare, fracassare; (*Sport: record*) battere ▷ *vi* frantumarsi, andare in pezzi; **smashing** (*inf*) *adj* favoloso(-a), formidabile

smear [smɪəʳ] *n* macchia; (*Med*) striscio ▷ *vt* spalmare; (*make dirty*) sporcare; **smear test** *n* (BRIT Med) Pap-test *m inv*

smell [smɛl] (*pt* **smelt** *or* **smelled**) *n* odore *m*; (*sense*) olfatto, odorato ▷ *vt* sentire (l')odore di ▷ *vi* (*food etc*): **to ~ (of)** avere odore (di); (*pej*) puzzare, avere un cattivo odore; **smelly** *adj* puzzolente

smelt [smɛlt] *pt, pp of* **smell** ▷ *vt* (*ore*) fondere

smile [smaɪl] *n* sorriso ▷ *vi* sorridere

smirk [sməːk] *n* sorriso furbo; sorriso compiaciuto

smog [smɔg] *n* smog *m*

smoke [sməuk] *n* fumo ▷ *vt, vi* fumare; **do you mind if I ~?** le dà fastidio se fumo?; **smoke alarm** *n* rivelatore *f* di fumo; **smoked** *adj* (*bacon, glass*) affumicato(-a);

smoker *n* (*person*) fumatore(-trice); (*Rail*) carrozza per fumatori; **smoking** *n* fumo; **"no smoking"** (*sign*) "vietato fumare"; **smoky** *adj* fumoso(-a); (*taste*) affumicato(-a)

smooth [smuːð] *adj* liscio(-a); (*sauce*) omogeneo(-a); (*flavour, whisky*) amabile; (*movement*) regolare; (*person*) mellifluo(-a) ▷ *vt* (*also: ~ out*) lisciare, spianare; (: *difficulties*) appianare

smother ['smʌðəʳ] *vt* soffocare

SMS *abbr* (= *short message service*) SMS; **SMS message** *n* SMS *m inv*, messaggino

smudge [smʌdʒ] *n* macchia; sbavatura ▷ *vt* imbrattare, sporcare

smug [smʌg] *adj* soddisfatto(-a), compiaciuto(-a)

smuggle ['smʌgl] *vt* contrabbandare; **smuggling** *n* contrabbando

snack [snæk] *n* spuntino; **snack bar** *n* tavola calda, snack bar *m inv*

snag [snæg] *n* intoppo, ostacolo imprevisto

snail [sneɪl] *n* chiocciola

snake [sneɪk] *n* serpente *m*

snap [snæp] *n* (*sound*) schianto, colpo secco; (*photograph*) istantanea ▷ *adj* improvviso(-a) ▷ *vt* (*far*) schioccare; (*break*) spezzare di netto ▷ *vi* spezzarsi con un rumore secco; (*fig: person*) parlare con tono secco; **to ~ shut** chiudersi di scatto; **snap at** *vt fus* (*dog*) cercare di mordere; **snap up** *vt* afferrare; **snapshot** *n* istantanea

snarl [snɑːl] *vi* ringhiare

snatch [snætʃ] *n* (*small amount*) frammento ▷ *vt* strappare (con violenza); (*fig*) rubare

sneak [sniːk] (*pt* (US) **snuck**) *vi*: **to ~ in/out** entrare/uscire di nascosto ▷ *n* spione(-a); **to ~ up on sb** avvicinarsi quatto quatto a qn; **sneakers** *npl* scarpe *fpl* da ginnastica

sneer [snɪəʳ] *vi* sogghignare; **to ~ at** farsi beffe di

sneeze [sniːz] *n* starnuto ▷ *vi* starnutire

sniff [snɪf] *n* fiutata, annusata ▷ *vi* tirare su col naso ▷ *vt* fiutare, annusare

snigger ['snɪgəʳ] *vi* ridacchiare, ridere sotto i baffi

snip [snɪp] *n* pezzetto; (*bargain*) (buon) affare *m*, occasione *f* ▷ *vt* tagliare

sniper ['snaɪpəʳ] *n* (*marksman*) franco tiratore *m*, cecchino

snob [snɔb] *n* snob *m/f inv*

snooker ['snuːkəʳ] *n* tipo di gioco del biliardo

snoop ['snuːp] *vi*: **to ~ about** curiosare

snooze [snuːz] *n* sonnellino, pisolino ▷ *vi* fare un sonnellino

snore [snɔːʳ] *vi* russare

snorkel ['snɔːkl] *n* (*of swimmer*) respiratore

m a tubo
snort [snɔːt] *n* sbuffo ▷ *vi* sbuffare
snow [snəʊ] *n* neve *f* ▷ *vi* nevicare;
  snowball *n* palla di neve ▷ *vi* (*fig*) crescere
  a vista d'occhio; **snowstorm** *n* tormenta
snub [snʌb] *vt* snobbare ▷ *n* offesa,
  affronto
snug [snʌg] *adj* comodo(-a); (*room, house*)
  accogliente, comodo(-a)

KEYWORD

so [səʊ] *adv* 1 (*thus, likewise*) così; **if so** se è
  così, quand'è così; **I didn't do it — you did
  so!** non l'ho fatto io — sì che l'hai fatto!;
  so do I, so am I *etc* anch'io; **it's 5 o'clock
  — so it is!** sono le 5 — davvero!; **I hope
  so** lo spero; **I think so** penso di sì; **so far**
  finora, fin qui; (*in past*) fino ad allora
  2 (*in comparisons etc: to such a degree*) così;
  so big (that) così grande (che); **she's not
  so clever as her brother** lei non è (così)
  intelligente come suo fratello
  3: **so much** *adj* tanto(-a)
  ▷ *adv* tanto; **I've got so much work/
  money** ho tanto lavoro/tanti soldi; **I love
  you so much** ti amo tanto; **so many**
  tanti(-e)
  4 (*phrases*): **10 or so** circa 10; **so long!** (*inf:
  goodbye*) ciao!, ci vediamo!
  ▷ *conj* 1 (*expressing purpose*): **so as to do**
  in modo *or* così da fare; **we hurried so as
  not to be late** ci affrettammo per non fare
  tardi; **so (that)** affinché + *sub*, perché + *sub*
  2 (*expressing result*): **he didn't arrive so I
  left** non è venuto così me ne sono andata;
  so you see, I could have gone vedi, sarei
  potuto andare

soak [səʊk] *vt* inzuppare; (*clothes*) mettere
  a mollo ▷ *vi* (*clothes etc*) essere a mollo;
  soak up *vt* assorbire; **soaking** *adj* (*also:*
  soaking wet) fradicio(-a)
so-and-so [ˈsəʊənsəʊ] *n* (*somebody*) un
  tale; **Mr/Mrs ~** signor/signora tal dei tali
soap [səʊp] *n* sapone *m*; **soap opera** *n*
  soap opera *f inv*; **soap powder** *n* detersivo
soar [sɔːr] *vi* volare in alto; (*price etc*) salire
  alle stelle; (*building*) ergersi
sob [sɔb] *n* singhiozzo ▷ *vi* singhiozzare
sober [ˈsəʊbər] *adj* sobrio(-a); (*not drunk*)
  non ubriaco(-a); (*moderate*) moderato(-a);
  sober up *vt* far passare la sbornia a ▷ *vi*
  farsi passare la sbornia
so-called [ˈsəʊˈkɔːld] *adj* cosiddetto(-a)
soccer [ˈsɔkər] *n* calcio
sociable [ˈsəʊʃəbl] *adj* socievole
social [ˈsəʊʃl] *adj* sociale ▷ *n* festa, serata;
  socialism *n* socialismo; **socialist** *adj, n*

socialista *m/f*; **socialize** *vi* **to socialize
  (with)** socializzare (con); **social life** *n*
  vita sociale; **socially** *adv* socialmente,
  in società; **social security** (*BRIT*) *n*
  previdenza sociale; **social services** *npl*
  servizi *mpl* sociali; **social work** *n* servizio
  sociale; **social worker** *n* assistente *m/f*
  sociale
society [səˈsaɪətɪ] *n* società *f inv*; (*club*)
  società, associazione *f*; (*also:* **high ~**) alta
  società
sociology [səʊsɪˈɔlədʒɪ] *n* sociologia
sock [sɔk] *n* calzino
socket [ˈsɔkɪt] *n* cavità *f inv*; (*of eye*) orbita;
  (*BRIT: Elec: also:* **wall ~**) presa di corrente
soda [ˈsəʊdə] *n* (*Chem*) soda; (*also:* **~
  water**) acqua di seltz; (*US: also:* **~ pop**)
  gassosa
sodium [ˈsəʊdɪəm] *n* sodio
sofa [ˈsəʊfə] *n* sofà *m inv*; **sofa bed** *n*
  divano *m* letto *inv*
soft [sɔft] *adj* (*not rough*) morbido(-a); (*not
  hard*) soffice; (*not loud*) sommesso(-a); (*not
  bright*) tenue; (*kind*) gentile; **soft drink**
  n analcolico; **soft drugs** *npl* droghe *fpl*
  leggere; **soften** [ˈsɔfn] *vt* ammorbidire;
  addolcire; attenuare ▷ *vi* ammorbidirsi;
  addolcirsi; attenuarsi; **softly** *adv*
  dolcemente, morbidamente; **software**
  [ˈsɔftwεər] *n* (*Comput*) software *m*
soggy [ˈsɔgɪ] *adj* inzuppato(-a)
soil [sɔɪl] *n* terreno ▷ *vt* sporcare
solar [ˈsəʊlər] *adj* solare; **solar power** *n*
  energie solare; **solar system** *n* sistema
  m solare
sold [səʊld] *pt, pp of* **sell**
soldier [ˈsəʊldʒər] *n* soldato, militare *m*
sold out *adj* (*Comm*) esaurito(-a)
sole [səʊl] *n* (*of foot*) pianta (del piede);
  (*of shoe*) suola; (*fish: pl inv*) sogliola
  ▷ *adj* solo(-a), unico(-a); **solely** *adv*
  solamente, unicamente; **I will hold you
  solely responsible** la considererò il solo
  responsabile
solemn [ˈsɔləm] *adj* solenne
solicitor [səˈlɪsɪtər] (*BRIT*) *n* (*for wills etc*)
  ≈ notaio; (*in court*) ≈ avvocato
solid [ˈsɔlɪd] *adj* solido(-a); (*not hollow*)
  pieno(-a); (*meal*) sostanzioso(-a) ▷ *n*
  solido
solitary [ˈsɔlɪtərɪ] *adj* solitario(-a)
solitude [ˈsɔlɪtjuːd] *n* solitudine *f*
solo [ˈsəʊləʊ] *n* assolo; **soloist** *n* solista
  m/f
soluble [ˈsɔljubl] *adj* solubile
solution [səˈluːʃən] *n* soluzione *f*
solve [sɔlv] *vt* risolvere
solvent [ˈsɔlvənt] *adj* (*Comm*) solvibile ▷ *n*
  (*Chem*) solvente *m*

sombre ['sɔmbə^r] (US **somber**) adj
scuro(-a); (mood, person) triste

 KEYWORD

some [sʌm] adj **1** (a certain amount or number
of): **some tea/water/cream** del tè/
dell'acqua/della panna; **some children/
apples** dei bambini/delle mele
2 (certain: in contrasts) certo(-a); **some
people say that ...** alcuni dicono che ...,
certa gente dice che ...
3 (unspecified) un(a) certo(-a), qualche;
some woman was asking for you una
tale chiedeva di lei; **some day** un giorno;
some day next week un giorno della
prossima settimana
▷ pron **1** (a certain number) alcuni(-e),
certi(-e); **I've got some** (books etc) ne ho
alcuni; **some (of them) have been sold**
alcuni sono stati venduti
2 (a certain amount) un po'; **I've got some**
(money, milk) ne ho un po'; **I've read some
of the book** ho letto parte del libro
▷ adv **some 10 people** circa 10 persone

some: somebody ['sʌmbədɪ] pron
= **someone**; **somehow** ['sʌmhau] adv
in un modo o nell'altro, in qualche modo;
(for some reason) per qualche ragione;
someone ['sʌmwʌn] pron qualcuno;
someplace ['sʌmpleɪs] (US) adv
= **somewhere**; **something** ['sʌmθɪŋ]
pron qualcosa, qualche cosa; **something
nice** qualcosa di bello; **something to do**
qualcosa da fare; **sometime** ['sʌmtaɪm]
adv (in future) una volta o l'altra; (in past):
sometime last month durante il mese
scorso; **sometimes** ['sʌmtaɪmz] adv
qualche volta; **somewhat** ['sʌmwɔt] adv
piuttosto; **somewhere** ['sʌmweə^r] adv in
or da qualche parte

son [sʌn] n figlio
song [sɔŋ] n canzone f
son-in-law ['sʌnɪnlɔ:] n genero
soon [su:n] adv presto, fra poco; (early, a
short time after) presto; **~ afterwards** poco
dopo; see also **as**; **sooner** adv (time) prima;
(preference): **I would sooner do** preferirei
fare; **sooner or later** prima o poi
soothe [su:ð] vt calmare
sophisticated [sə'fɪstɪkeɪtɪd]
adj sofisticato(-a); raffinato(-a);
complesso(-a)
sophomore ['sɔfəmɔ:^r] (US) n
studente(-essa) del secondo anno
soprano [sə'prɑ:nəu] n (voice) soprano m;
(singer) soprano m/f
sorbet ['sɔ:beɪ] n sorbetto

sordid ['sɔ:dɪd] adj sordido(-a)
sore [sɔ:^r] adj (painful) dolorante ▷ n piaga
sorrow ['sɔrəu] n dolore m
sorry ['sɔrɪ] adj spiacente; (condition,
excuse) misero(-a); **~!** scusa! (or scusi! or
scusate!); **to feel ~ for sb** rincrescersi
per qn
sort [sɔ:t] n specie f, genere m; **sort out** vt
(papers) classificare; ordinare; (: letters etc)
smistare; (: problems) risolvere; (Comput)
ordinare
SOS n abbr (= save our souls) S.O.S. m inv
so-so ['səusəu] adv così così
sought [sɔ:t] pt, pp of **seek**
soul [səul] n anima
sound [saund] adj (healthy) sano(-a); (safe,
not damaged) solido(-a), in buono stato;
(reliable, not superficial) solido(-a); (sensible)
giudizioso(-a), di buon senso ▷ adv **~
asleep** profondamente addormentato
▷ n suono; (noise) rumore m; (Geo) stretto
▷ vt (alarm) suonare ▷ vi suonare; (fig:
seem) sembrare; **to ~ like** rassomigliare a;
soundtrack n (of film) colonna sonora
soup [su:p] n minestra; brodo; zuppa
sour ['sauə^r] adj aspro(-a); (fruit)
acerbo(-a); (milk) acido(-a); (fig)
arcigno(-a); acido(-a); **it's ~ grapes** è
soltanto invidia
source [sɔ:s] n fonte f, sorgente f; (fig)
fonte
south [sauθ] n sud m, meridione m,
mezzogiorno ▷ adj del sud, sud inv,
meridionale ▷ adv verso sud; **South
Africa** n Sudafrica m; **South African**
adj, n sudafricano(-a); **South America** n
Sudamerica m, America del sud; **South
American** adj, n sudamericano(-a);
southbound ['sauθbaund] adj (gen)
diretto(-a) a sud; (carriageway) sud
inv; **southeastern** [sauθ'i:stən] adj
sudorientale; **southern** ['sʌðən] adj
del sud, meridionale; esposto(-a) a sud;
South Korea n Corea f del Sud; **South
Pole** n Polo Sud; **southward(s)** adv
verso sud; **south-west** n sud-ovest
m; **southwestern** [sauθ'westən] adj
sudoccidentale
souvenir [su:və'nɪə^r] n ricordo, souvenir
m inv
sovereign ['sɔvrɪn] adj, n sovrano(-a)
sow[1] [səu] (pt **sowed**, pp **sown**) vt
seminare
sow[2] [sau] n scrofa
soya ['sɔɪə] (US **soy**) n **~ bean** n seme m di
soia; **soya sauce** n salsa di soia
spa [spɑ:] n (resort) stazione f termale; (US:
also: **health ~**) centro di cure estetiche
space [speɪs] n spazio; (room) posto;

spazio; (*length of time*) intervallo ▷ *cpd*
spaziale ▷ *vt* (*also*: **~ out**) distanziare;
spacecraft *n inv* veicolo spaziale;
spaceship *n* = **spacecraft**

spacious [ˈspeɪʃəs] *adj* spazioso(-a),
ampio(-a)

spade [speɪd] *n* (*tool*) vanga; pala; (*child's*)
paletta; **~s** *npl* (*Cards*) picche *fpl*

spaghetti [spəˈɡɛtɪ] *n* spaghetti *mpl*

Spain [speɪn] *n* Spagna

spam [spæm] (*Comput*) *n* spamming ▷ *vt*
to ~ sb inviare a qn messaggi pubblicitari
non richiesti via email

span [spæn] *n* (*of bird, plane*) apertura
alare; (*of arch*) campata; (*in time*) periodo;
durata ▷ *vt* attraversare; (*fig*) abbracciare

Spaniard [ˈspænjəd] *n* spagnolo(-a)

Spanish [ˈspænɪʃ] *adj* spagnolo(-a) ▷ *n*
(*Ling*) spagnolo; **the ~** *npl* gli Spagnoli

spank [spæŋk] *vt* sculacciare

spanner [ˈspænəʳ] (*BRIT*) *n* chiave *f* inglese

spare [spɛəʳ] *adj* di riserva, di scorta;
(*surplus*) in più, d'avanzo ▷ *n* (*part*) pezzo
di ricambio ▷ *vt* (*do without*) fare a meno
di; (*afford to give*) concedere; (*refrain from
hurting, using*) risparmiare; **to ~** (*surplus*)
d'avanzo; **spare part** *n* pezzo di ricambio;
spare room *n* stanza degli ospiti; **spare
time** *n* tempo libero; **spare tyre** (*US* **spare
tire**) *n* (*Aut*) gomma di scorta; **spare
wheel** *n* (*Aut*) ruota di scorta

spark [spɑːk] *n* scintilla; **spark(ing) plug**
n candela

sparkle [ˈspɑːkl] *n* scintillio, sfavillio ▷ *vi*
scintillare, sfavillare

sparrow [ˈspærəu] *n* passero

sparse [spɑːs] *adj* sparso(-a), rado(-a)

spasm [ˈspæzəm] *n* (*Med*) spasmo; (*fig*)
accesso, attacco

spat [spæt] *pt, pp of* **spit**

spate [speɪt] *n* (*fig*): **~ of** diluvio *or* fiume
m di

spatula [ˈspætjulə] *n* spatola

speak [spiːk] (*pt* **spoke**, *pp* **spoken**) *vt*
(*language*) parlare; (*truth*) dire ▷ *vi* parlare;
I don't ~ Italian non parlo italiano; **do you
~ English?** parla inglese?; **to ~ to sb/of** *or*
about sth parlare a qn/di qc; **can I ~ to …?**
posso parlare con…?; **~ up!** parla più forte!;
speaker *n* (*in public*) oratore(-trice);
(*also*: **loudspeaker**) altoparlante *m*; (*Pol*):
the Speaker *il presidente della Camera dei
Comuni* (*BRIT*) *or dei Rappresentanti* (*US*)

spear [spɪəʳ] *n* lancia ▷ *vt* infilzare

special [ˈspɛʃl] *adj* speciale; **special
delivery** *n* (*Post*): **by special delivery**
per espresso; **special effects** *npl*
(*Cine*) effetti *mpl* speciali; **specialist** *n*
specialista *m/f*; **speciality** [spɛʃɪˈælɪtɪ]

n specialità *f inv*; **I'd like to try a local
speciality** vorrei assaggiare una specialità
del posto; **specialize** *vi* **to specialize
(in)** specializzarsi (in); **specially** *adv*
specialmente, particolarmente;
special needs *adj* **special needs
children** bambini *mpl* con difficoltà di
apprendimento; **special offer** *n* (*Comm*)
offerta speciale; **special school** *n* (*BRIT*)
scuola speciale (*per portatori di handicap*);
specialty (*US*) *n* = **speciality**

species [ˈspiːʃiːz] *n inv* specie *f inv*

specific [spəˈsɪfɪk] *adj* specifico(-a);
preciso(-a); **specifically** *adv*
esplicitamente; (*especially*) appositamente

specify [ˈspɛsɪfaɪ] *vt* specificare, precisare;
unless otherwise specified salvo
indicazioni contrarie

specimen [ˈspɛsɪmən] *n* esemplare *m*,
modello; (*Med*) campione *m*

speck [spɛk] *n* puntino, macchiolina;
(*particle*) granello

spectacle [ˈspɛktəkl] *n* spettacolo; **~s**
npl (*glasses*) occhiali *mpl*; **spectacular**
[-ˈtækjulə] *adj* spettacolare

spectator [spɛkˈteɪtəʳ] *n* spettatore *m*

spectrum [ˈspɛktrəm] (*pl* **spectra**) *n*
spettro

speculate [ˈspɛkjuleɪt] *vi* speculare; (*try to
guess*): **to ~ about** fare ipotesi su

sped [spɛd] *pt, pp of* **speed**

speech [spiːtʃ] *n* (*faculty*) parola; (*talk,
Theatre*) discorso; (*manner of speaking*)
parlata; **speechless** *adj* ammutolito(-a),
muto(-a)

speed [spiːd] *n* velocità *f inv*; (*promptness*)
prontezza; **at full** *or* **top ~** a tutta velocità;
speed up *vi, vt* accelerare; **speedboat** *n*
motoscafo; **speeding** *n* (*Aut*) eccesso
di velocità; **speed limit** *n* limite *m* di
velocità; **speedometer** [spɪˈdɔmɪtəʳ] *n*
tachimetro; **speedy** *adj* veloce, rapido(-a);
pronto(-a)

spell [spɛl] (*pt, pp* **spelt** (*BRIT*) *or* **spelled**) *n*
(*also*: **magic ~**) incantesimo; (*period of time*)
(*breve*) periodo ▷ *vt* (*in writing*) scrivere
(lettera per lettera); (*aloud*) dire lettera per
lettera; (*fig*) significare; **to cast a ~ on sb**
fare un incantesimo a qn; **he can't ~** fa
errori di ortografia; **spell out** *vt* (*letter by
letter*) dettare lettera per lettera; (*explain*):
to ~ sth out for sb spiegare qc a qn per
filo e per segno; **spellchecker** [ˈspɛltʃɛkəʳ]
n correttore *m* ortografico; **spelling** *n*
ortografia

spelt [spɛlt] (*BRIT*) *pt, pp of* **spell**

spend [spɛnd] (*pt, pp* **spent**) *vt* (*money*)
spendere; (*time, life*) passare; **spending** *n*
government spending spesa pubblica

spent [spɛnt] *pt, pp of* **spend**

sperm [spɜːm] *n* sperma *m*

sphere [sfɪəʳ] *n* sfera

spice [spaɪs] *n* spezia ▷ *vt* aromatizzare

spicy [ˈspaɪsɪ] *adj* piccante

spider [ˈspaɪdəʳ] *n* ragno

spike [spaɪk] *n* punta

spill [spɪl] (*pt, pp* **spilt** *or* **spilled**) *vt* versare, rovesciare ▷ *vi* versarsi, rovesciarsi

spin [spɪn] (*pt, pp* **spun**) *n* (*revolution of wheel*) rotazione *f*; (*Aviat*) avvitamento; (*trip in car*) giretto ▷ *vt* (*wool etc*) filare; (*wheel*) far girare ▷ *vi* girare

spinach [ˈspɪnɪtʃ] *n* spinacio; (*as food*) spinaci *mpl*

spinal [ˈspaɪnl] *adj* spinale

spin doctor (*inf*) *n* esperto di comunicazioni responsabile dell'immagine di un partito politico

spin-dryer [spɪnˈdraɪəʳ] (*BRIT*) *n* centrifuga

spine [spaɪn] *n* spina dorsale; (*thorn*) spina

spiral [ˈspaɪərl] *n* spirale *f* ▷ *vi* (*fig*) salire a spirale

spire [ˈspaɪəʳ] *n* guglia

spirit [ˈspɪrɪt] *n* spirito; (*ghost*) spirito, fantasma *m*; (*mood*) stato d'animo, umore *m*; (*courage*) coraggio; **~s** *npl* (*drink*) alcolici *mpl*; **in good ~s** di buon umore

spiritual [ˈspɪrɪtjuəl] *adj* spirituale

spit [spɪt] (*pt, pp* **spat**) *n* (*for roasting*) spiedo; (*saliva*) sputo; saliva ▷ *vi* sputare; (*fire, fat*) scoppiettare

spite [spaɪt] *n* dispetto ▷ *vt* contrariare, far dispetto a; **in ~ of** nonostante, malgrado; **spiteful** *adj* dispettoso(-a)

splash [splæʃ] *n* spruzzo; (*sound*) splash *m inv*; (*of colour*) schizzo ▷ *vt* spruzzare ▷ *vi* (*also:* **~ about**) sguazzare; **splash out** (*inf*) *vi* (*BRIT*) far spese folli

splendid [ˈsplɛndɪd] *adj* splendido(-a), magnifico(-a)

splinter [ˈsplɪntəʳ] *n* scheggia ▷ *vi* scheggiarsi

split [splɪt] (*pt, pp* **split**) *n* spaccatura; (*fig: division, quarrel*) scissione *f* ▷ *vt* spaccare; (*party*) dividere; (*work, profits*) spartire, ripartire ▷ *vi* (*divide*) dividersi; **split up** *vi* (*couple*) separarsi, rompere; (*meeting*) sciogliersi

spoil [spɔɪl] (*pt, pp* **spoilt** *or* **spoiled**) *vt* (*damage*) rovinare, guastare; (*mar*) sciupare; (*child*) viziare

spoilt [spɔɪlt] *pt, pp of* **spoil**

spoke [spəuk] *pt of* **speak** ▷ *n* raggio

spoken [ˈspəukn] *pp of* **speak**

spokesman [ˈspəuksmən] (*irreg*) *n* portavoce *m inv*

spokesperson [ˈspəukspəːsn] *n* portavoce *m/f*

spokeswoman [ˈspəukswumən] (*irreg*) *n* portavoce *f inv*

sponge [spʌndʒ] *n* spugna; (*also:* **~ cake**) pan *m* di spagna ▷ *vt* spugnare, pulire con una spugna ▷ *vi* **to ~ off** *or* **on** scroccare a; **sponge bag** (*BRIT*) *n* nécessaire *m inv*

sponsor [ˈspɔnsəʳ] *n* (*Radio, TV, Sport etc*) sponsor *m inv*; (*Pol: of bill*) promotore(-trice) ▷ *vt* sponsorizzare; (*bill*) presentare; **sponsorship** *n* sponsorizzazione *f*

spontaneous [spɔnˈteɪnɪəs] *adj* spontaneo(-a)

spooky [ˈspuːkɪ] (*inf*) *adj* che fa accapponare la pelle

spoon [spuːn] *n* cucchiaio; **spoonful** *n* cucchiaiata

sport [spɔːt] *n* sport *m inv*; (*person*) persona di spirito ▷ *vt* sfoggiare; **sport jacket** (*US*) *n* = **sports jacket**; **sports car** *n* automobile *f* sportiva; **sports centre** (*BRIT*) *n* centro sportivo; **sports jacket** (*BRIT*) *n* giacca sportiva; **sportsman** (*irreg*) *n* sportivo; **sportswear** *n* abiti *mpl* sportivi; **sportswoman** (*irreg*) *n* sportiva; **sporty** *adj* sportivo(-a)

spot [spɔt] *n* punto; (*mark*) macchia; (*dot: on pattern*) pallino; (*pimple*) foruncolo; (*place*) posto; (*Radio, TV*) spot *m inv*; (*small amount*): **a ~ of** un po' di ▷ *vt* (*notice*) individuare, distinguere; **on the ~** sul posto; (*immediately*) su due piedi; (*in difficulty*) nei guai; **spotless** *adj* immacolato(-a), impeccabile; **spotlight** *n* proiettore *m*; (*Aut*) faro ausiliario

spouse [spauz] *n* sposo(-a)

sprain [spreɪn] *n* storta, distorsione *f* ▷ *vt* **to ~ one's ankle** storcersi una caviglia

sprang [spræŋ] *pt of* **spring**

sprawl [sprɔːl] *vi* sdraiarsi (in modo scomposto); (*place*) estendersi (disordinatamente)

spray [spreɪ] *n* spruzzo; (*container*) nebulizzatore *m*, spray *m inv*; (*of flowers*) mazzetto ▷ *vt* spruzzare; (*crops*) irrorare

spread [sprɛd] (*pt, pp* **spread**) *n* diffusione *f*; (*distribution*) distribuzione *f*; (*Culin*) pasta (da spalmare); (*inf: food*) banchetto ▷ *vt* (*cloth*) stendere, distendere; (*butter etc*) spalmare; (*disease, knowledge*) propagare, diffondere ▷ *vi* stendersi, distendersi; spalmarsi; propagarsi, diffondersi; **spread out** *vi* (*move apart*) separarsi; **spreadsheet** *n* foglio elettronico ad espansione

spree [spriː] *n* **to go on a ~** fare baldoria

spring [sprɪŋ] (*pt* **sprang**, *pp* **sprung**) *n* (*leap*) salto, balzo; (*coiled metal*) molla;

(*season*) primavera; (*of water*) sorgente
f ▷ vi saltare, balzare; **spring up** vi
(*problem*) presentarsi; **spring onion** n
(BRIT) cipollina
sprinkle ['sprɪŋkl] vt spruzzare; spargere;
to ~ water etc **on, ~ with water** etc
spruzzare dell'acqua etc su
sprint [sprɪnt] n scatto ▷ vi scattare
sprung [sprʌŋ] pp of **spring**
spun [spʌn] pt, pp of **spin**
spur [spəːʳ] n sperone m; (*fig*) sprone m,
incentivo ▷ vt (*also:* **~ on**) spronare; **on the**
~ of the moment lì per lì
spurt [spəːt] n (*of water*) getto; (*of energy*)
scatto ▷ vi sgorgare
spy [spaɪ] n spia ▷ vi **to ~ on** spiare ▷ vt
(*see*) scorgere
sq. abbr = **square**
squabble ['skwɔbl] vi bisticciarsi
squad [skwɔd] n (*Mil*) plotone m; (*Police*)
squadra
squadron ['skwɔdrn] n (*Mil*) squadrone m;
(*Aviat, Naut*) squadriglia
squander ['skwɔndəʳ] vt dissipare
square [skwɛəʳ] n quadrato; (*in town*)
piazza ▷ adj quadrato(-a); (*inf: ideas,*
person) di vecchio stampo ▷ vt (*arrange*)
regolare; (*Math*) elevare al quadrato;
(*reconcile*) conciliare; **all ~** pari; **a ~ meal** un
pasto abbondante; **2 metres ~** di 2 metri
per 2; **1 ~ metre** 1 metro quadrato; **square**
root n radice f quadrata
squash [skwɔʃ] n (*Sport*) squash m; (BRIT:
drink): **lemon/orange ~** sciroppo di
limone/arancia; (US) zucca; (*Sport*) squash
m ▷ vt schiacciare
squat [skwɔt] adj tarchiato(-a), tozzo(-a)
▷ vi (*also:* **~ down**) accovacciarsi; **squatter**
n occupante m/f abusivo(-a)
squeak [skwiːk] vi squittire
squeal [skwiːl] vi strillare
squeeze [skwiːz] n pressione f; (*also Econ*)
stretta ▷ vt premere; (*hand, arm*) stringere
squid [skwɪd] n calamaro
squint [skwɪnt] vi essere strabico(-a) ▷ n
he has a ~ è strabico
squirm [skwəːm] vi contorcersi
squirrel ['skwɪrəl] n scoiattolo
squirt [skwəːt] vi schizzare; zampillare
▷ vt spruzzare
Sr abbr = **senior**
Sri Lanka [srɪ'læŋkə] n Sri Lanka m
St abbr = **saint; street**
stab [stæb] n (*with knife etc*) pugnalata; (*of*
pain) fitta; (*inf: try*): **to have a ~ at (doing)**
sth provare (a fare) qc ▷ vt pugnalare
stability [stə'bɪlɪtɪ] n stabilità
stable ['steɪbl] n (*for horses*) scuderia; (*for*
cattle) stalla ▷ adj stabile

stack [stæk] n catasta, pila ▷ vt
accatastare, ammucchiare
stadium ['steɪdɪəm] n stadio
staff [stɑːf] n (*work force: gen*) personale
m; (: BRIT: *Scol*) personale insegnante ▷ vt
fornire di personale
stag [stæg] n cervo
stage [steɪdʒ] n palcoscenico; (*profession*):
the ~ il teatro, la scena; (*point*) punto;
(*platform*) palco ▷ vt (*play*) allestire,
mettere in scena; (*demonstration*)
organizzare; **in ~s** per gradi; a tappe
stagger ['stægəʳ] vi barcollare ▷ vt (*person*)
sbalordire; (*hours, holidays*) scaglionare;
staggering adj (*amazing*) sbalorditivo(-a)
stagnant ['stægnənt] adj stagnante
stag night, stag party n festa di addio
al celibato
stain [steɪn] n macchia; (*colouring*)
colorante m ▷ vt macchiare; (*wood*)
tingere; **stained glass** [steɪnd'glɑːs] n
vetro colorato; **stainless steel** n acciaio
inossidabile
staircase ['stɛəkeɪs] n scale fpl, scala
stairs [stɛəz] npl (*flight of stairs*) scale fpl,
scala
stairway ['stɛəweɪ] n = **staircase**
stake [steɪk] n palo, piolo; (*Comm*)
interesse m; (*Betting*) puntata, scommessa
▷ vt (*bet*) scommettere; (*risk*) rischiare; **to**
be at ~ essere in gioco
stale [steɪl] adj (*bread*) raffermo(-a);
(*food*) stantio(-a); (*air*) viziato(-a); (*beer*)
svaporato(-a); (*smell*) di chiuso
stalk [stɔːk] n gambo, stelo ▷ vt inseguire
stall [stɔːl] n bancarella; (*in stable*) box m
inv di stalla ▷ vt (*Aut*) far spegnere; (*fig*)
bloccare ▷ vi (*Aut*) spegnersi, fermarsi; (*fig*)
temporeggiare
stamina ['stæmɪnə] n vigore m, resistenza
stammer ['stæməʳ] n balbuzie f ▷ vi
balbettare
stamp [stæmp] n (*postage stamp*)
francobollo; (*implement*) timbro; (*mark,*
also fig) marchio, impronta; (*on document*)
bollo; timbro ▷ vi (*also:* **~ one's foot**)
battere il piede ▷ vt battere; (*letter*)
affrancare; (*mark with a stamp*) timbrare;
stamp out vt (*fire*) estinguere; (*crime*)
eliminare; (*opposition*) soffocare; **stamped**
addressed envelope (BRIT) busta
affrancata e indirizzata

> Be careful not to translate **stamp** the
> Italian word by *stampa*.

stampede [stæm'piːd] n fuggi fuggi m inv
stance [stæns] n posizione f
stand [stænd] (pt, pp **stood**) n (*position*)
posizione f; (*for taxis*) posteggio; (*structure*)
supporto, sostegno; (*at exhibition*)

stand m inv; (in shop) banco; (at market) bancarella; (booth) chiosco; (Sport) tribuna ▷ vi stare in piedi; (rise) alzarsi in piedi; (be placed) trovarsi ▷ vt (place) mettere, porre; (tolerate, withstand) resistere, sopportare; (treat) offrire; **to make a ~** prendere posizione; **to ~ for parliament** (BRIT) presentarsi come candidato (per il parlamento); **stand back** vi prendere le distanze; **stand by** vi (be ready) tenersi pronto(-a) ▷ vt fus (opinion) sostenere; **stand down** vi (withdraw) ritirarsi; **stand for** vt fus (signify) rappresentare, significare; (tolerate) sopportare, tollerare; **stand in for** vt fus sostituire; **stand out** vi (be prominent) spiccare; **stand up** vi (rise) alzarsi in piedi; **stand up for** vt fus difendere; **stand up to** vt fus tener testa a, resistere a

standard ['stændəd] n modello, standard m inv; (level) livello; (flag) stendardo ▷ adj (size etc) normale, standard inv; **~s** npl (morals) principi mpl, valori mpl; **standard of living** n livello di vita

stand-by ['stændbaɪ] n riserva, sostituto; **to be on ~** (gen) tenersi pronto(-a); (doctor) essere di guardia; **stand-by ticket** n (Aviat) biglietto senza garanzia

standing ['stændɪŋ] adj diritto(-a), in piedi; (permanent) permanente ▷ n rango, condizione f, posizione f; **of many years' ~** che esiste da molti anni; **standing order** (BRIT) n (at bank) ordine m di pagamento (permanente)

stand: **standpoint** ['stændpɔɪnt] n punto di vista; **standstill** ['stændstɪl] n **at a standstill** fermo(-a); (fig) a un punto morto; **to come to a standstill** fermarsi; giungere a un punto morto

stank [stæŋk] pt of **stink**

staple ['steɪpl] n (for papers) graffetta ▷ adj (food etc) di base ▷ vt cucire

star [stɑː'] n stella; (celebrity) divo(-a) ▷ vi **to ~ (in)** essere il (or la) protagonista (di) ▷ vt (Cinema) essere interpretato(-a) da; **the ~s** npl (Astrology) le stelle

starboard ['stɑːbəd] n dritta

starch [stɑːtʃ] n amido

stardom ['stɑːdəm] n celebrità

stare [steə'] n sguardo fisso ▷ vi **to ~ at** fissare

stark [stɑːk] adj (bleak) desolato(-a) ▷ adv **~ naked** completamente nudo(-a)

start [stɑːt] n inizio; (of race) partenza; (sudden movement) sobbalzo; (advantage) vantaggio ▷ vt cominciare, iniziare; (car) mettere in moto ▷ vi cominciare; (on journey) partire, mettersi in viaggio; (jump) sobbalzare; **when does the film ~?**

a che ora comincia il film?; **to ~ doing** or **to do sth** (in)cominciare a fare qc; **start off** vi cominciare; (leave) partire; **start out** vi (begin) cominciare; (set out) partire; **start up** vi cominciare; (car) avviarsi ▷ vt iniziare; (car) avviare; **starter** n (Aut) motorino d'avviamento; (Sport: official) starter m inv; (BRIT: Culin) primo piatto; **starting point** n punto di partenza

startle ['stɑːtl] vt far trasalire; **startling** adj sorprendente

starvation [stɑːˈveɪʃən] n fame f, inedia

starve [stɑːv] vi morire di fame; soffrire la fame ▷ vt far morire di fame, affamare

state [steɪt] n stato ▷ vt dichiarare, affermare; annunciare; **the S~s** (USA) gli Stati Uniti; **to be in a ~** essere agitato(-a); **statement** n dichiarazione f; **state school** n scuola statale; **statesman** (irreg) n statista m

static ['stætɪk] n (Radio) scariche fpl ▷ adj statico(-a)

station ['steɪʃən] n stazione f ▷ vt collocare, disporre

stationary ['steɪʃənərɪ] adj fermo(-a), immobile

stationer's (shop) n cartoleria

stationery ['steɪʃnərɪ] n articoli mpl di cancelleria

station wagon (US) n giardinetta

statistic [stəˈtɪstɪk] n statistica; **statistics** n (science) statistica

statue ['stætjuː] n statua

stature ['stætʃər] n statura

status ['steɪtəs] n posizione f, condizione f sociale; prestigio; stato; **status quo** [-ˈkwəʊ] n **the status quo** lo statu quo

statutory ['stætjutrɪ] adj stabilito(-a) dalla legge, statutario(-a)

staunch [stɔːntʃ] adj fidato(-a), leale

stay [steɪ] n (period of time) soggiorno, permanenza ▷ vi rimanere; (reside) alloggiare, stare; (spend some time) trattenersi, soggiornare; **to ~ put** non muoversi; **to ~ the night** fermarsi per la notte; **stay away** vi (from person, building) stare lontano (from event) non andare; **stay behind** vi restare indietro; **stay in** vi (at home) stare in casa; **stay on** vi restare, rimanere; **stay out** vi (of house) rimanere fuori (di casa); **stay up** vi (at night) rimanere alzato(-a)

steadily ['stɛdɪlɪ] adv (firmly) saldamente; (constantly) continuamente; (fixedly) fisso; (walk) con passo sicuro

steady ['stɛdɪ] adj (not wobbling) fermo(-a); (regular) costante; (person, character) serio(-a); (: calm) calmo(-a), tranquillo(-a) ▷ vt stabilizzare; calmare

steak [steɪk] n (meat) bistecca; (fish) trancia

steal [stiːl] (pt **stole**, pp **stolen**) vt rubare ▷ vi rubare; (move) muoversi furtivamente; **my wallet has been stolen** mi hanno rubato il portafoglio

steam [stiːm] n vapore m ▷ vt (Culin) cuocere a vapore ▷ vi fumare; **steam up** vi (window) appannarsi; **to get ~ed up about sth** (fig) andare in bestia per qc; **steamy** adj (room) pieno(-a) di vapore; (window) appannato(-a)

steel [stiːl] n acciaio ▷ adj di acciaio

steep [stiːp] adj ripido(-a), scosceso(-a); (price) eccessivo(-a) ▷ vt inzuppare; (washing) mettere a mollo

steeple ['stiːpl] n campanile m

steer [stɪəʳ] vt guidare ▷ vi (Naut: person) governare; (car) guidarsi; **steering** n (Aut) sterzo; **steering wheel** n volante m

stem [stɛm] n (of flower, plant) stelo; (of tree) fusto; (of glass) gambo; (of fruit, leaf) picciolo ▷ vt contenere, arginare

step [stɛp] n passo; (stair) gradino, scalino; (action) mossa, azione f ▷ vi **to ~ forward/back** fare un passo avanti/indietro; **~s** npl (BRIT) = **stepladder**; **to be in/out of ~ (with)** stare/non stare al passo (con); **step down** vi (fig) ritirarsi; **step in** vi fare il proprio ingresso; **step up** vt aumentare; intensificare; **stepbrother** n fratellastro; **stepchild** n figliastro(-a); **stepdaughter** n figliastra; **stepfather** n patrigno; **stepladder** n scala a libretto; **stepmother** n matrigna; **stepsister** n sorellastra; **stepson** n figliastro

stereo ['stɛrɪəʊ] n (system) sistema m stereofonico; (record player) stereo m inv ▷ adj (also: **~phonic**) stereofonico(-a)

stereotype ['stɪərɪətaɪp] n stereotipo

sterile ['stɛraɪl] adj sterile; **sterilize** ['stɛrɪlaɪz] vt sterilizzare

sterling ['stəːlɪŋ] adj (gold, silver) di buona lega ▷ n (Econ) (lira) sterlina; **a pound ~** una lira sterlina

stern [stəːn] adj severo(-a) ▷ n (Naut) poppa

steroid ['stɛrɔɪd] n steroide m

stew [stjuː] n stufato ▷ vt cuocere in umido

steward ['stjuːəd] n (Aviat, Naut, Rail) steward m inv; (in club etc) dispensiere m; **stewardess** n assistente f di volo, hostess f inv

stick [stɪk] (pt, pp **stuck**) n bastone m; (of rhubarb, celery) gambo; (of dynamite) candelotto ▷ vt (glue) attaccare; (thrust): **to ~ sth into** conficcare or piantare or infiggere qc in; (inf: put) ficcare; (inf:

tolerate) sopportare ▷ vi attaccarsi; (remain) restare, rimanere; **stick out** vi sporgere, spuntare; **stick up** vi sporgere, spuntare; **stick up for** vt fus difendere; **sticker** n cartellino adesivo; **sticking plaster** n cerotto adesivo; **stick shift** (US) n (Aut) cambio manuale

sticky ['stɪkɪ] adj attaccaticcio(-a), vischioso(-a); (label) adesivo(-a); (fig: situation) difficile

stiff [stɪf] adj rigido(-a), duro(-a); (muscle) legato(-a), indolenzito(-a); (difficult) difficile, arduo(-a); (cold) freddo(-a), formale; (strong) forte; (high: price) molto alto(-a) ▷ adv **bored ~** annoiato(-a) a morte

stifling ['staɪflɪŋ] adj (heat) soffocante

stigma ['stɪgmə] n (fig) stigma m

stiletto [stɪ'lɛtəʊ] n (BRIT) (also: **~ heel**) tacco a spillo

still [stɪl] adj fermo(-a); silenzioso(-a) ▷ adv (up to this time, even) ancora; (nonetheless) tuttavia, ciò nonostante

stimulate ['stɪmjʊleɪt] vt stimolare

stimulus ['stɪmjʊləs] (pl **stimuli**) n stimolo

sting [stɪŋ] (pt, pp **stung**) n puntura; (organ) pungiglione m ▷ vt pungere

stink [stɪŋk] (pt **stank**, pp **stunk**) n fetore m, puzzo ▷ vi puzzare

stir [stəːʳ] n agitazione f, clamore m ▷ vt mescolare; (fig) risvegliare ▷ vi muoversi; **stir up** vt provocare, suscitare; **stir-fry** vt saltare in padella ▷ n pietanza al salto

stitch [stɪtʃ] n (Sewing) punto; (Knitting) maglia; (Med) punto (di sutura); (pain) fitta ▷ vt cucire, attaccare; suturare

stock [stɔk] n riserva, provvista; (Comm) giacenza, stock m inv; (Agr) bestiame m; (Culin) brodo; (descent) stirpe f; (Finance) titoli mpl; azioni fpl ▷ adj (fig: reply etc) consueto(-a); classico(-a) ▷ vt (have in stock) avere, vendere; **~s and shares** valori mpl di borsa; **in ~** in magazzino; **out of ~** esaurito(-a); **stockbroker** ['stɔkbrəʊkəʳ] n agente m di cambio; **stock cube** (BRIT) n dado; **stock exchange** n Borsa (valori); **stockholder** ['stɔkhəʊldəʳ] n (Finance) azionista m/f

stocking ['stɔkɪŋ] n calza

stock market n Borsa, mercato finanziario

stole [stəʊl] pt of **steal** ▷ n stola

stolen ['stəʊln] pp of **steal**

stomach ['stʌmək] n stomaco; (belly) pancia ▷ vt sopportare, digerire; **stomachache** n mal m di stomaco

stone [stəʊn] n pietra; (pebble) sasso, ciottolo; (in fruit) nocciolo; (Med) calcolo;

(BRIT: *weight*) = 6.348 kg; 14 *libbre* ▷ *adj*
di pietra ▷ *vt* lapidare; (*fruit*) togliere il
nocciolo a
stood [stud] *pt, pp of* **stand**
stool [stu:l] *n* sgabello
stoop [stu:p] *vi* (*also:* **have a ~**) avere una
curvatura; (*also:* **~ down**) chinarsi, curvarsi
stop [stɔp] *n* arresto; (*stopping place*)
fermata; (*in punctuation*) punto
▷ *vt* arrestare, fermare; (*break off*)
interrompere; (*also:* **put a ~ to**) porre fine
a ▷ *vi* fermarsi; (*rain, noise etc*) cessare,
finire; **to ~ doing sth** cessare or finire di
fare qc; **could you ~ here/at the corner?**
può fermarsi qui/all'angolo?; **to ~ dead**
fermarsi di colpo; **stop by** *vi* passare, fare
un salto; **stop off** *vi* sostare brevemente;
stopover *n* breve sosta; (*Aviat*) scalo;
stoppage ['stɔpɪdʒ] *n* arresto, fermata;
(*of pay*) trattenuta; (*strike*) interruzione *f*
del lavoro
storage ['stɔ:rɪdʒ] *n* immagazzinamento
store [stɔ:ʳ] *n* provvista, riserva; (*depot*)
deposito; (*BRIT: department store*) grande
magazzino; (*US: shop*) negozio ▷ *vt*
immagazzinare; **~s** *npl* (*provisions*)
rifornimenti *mpl*, scorte *fpl*; **in ~** di riserva;
in serbo; **storekeeper** (*US*) *n* negoziante
m/f
storey ['stɔ:rɪ] (*US* **story**) *n* piano
storm [stɔ:m] *n* tempesta, temporale
m, burrasca; uragano ▷ *vi* (*fig*) infuriarsi
▷ *vt* prendere d'assalto; **stormy** *adj*
tempestoso(-a), burrascoso(-a)
story ['stɔ:rɪ] *n* storia; favola; racconto;
(*US*) = **storey**
stout [staut] *adj* solido(-a), robusto(-a);
(*friend, supporter*) tenace; (*fat*)
corpulento(-a), grasso(-a) ▷ *n* birra scura
stove [stəuv] *n* (*for cooking*) fornello; (:
small) fornelletto; (*for heating*) stufa
straight [streɪt] *adj* dritto(-a); (*frank*)
onesto(-a), franco(-a); (*simple*) semplice
▷ *adv* diritto; (*drink*) liscio; **to put** or **get**
~ mettere in ordine, mettere ordine in; **~**
away, ~ off (*at once*) immediatamente;
straighten *vt* (*also:* **straighten out**)
raddrizzare; **straightforward** *adj*
semplice; onesto(-a), franco(-a)
strain [streɪn] *n* (*Tech*) sollecitazione
f; (*physical*) sforzo; (*mental*) tensione *f*;
(*Med*) strappo; distorsione *f*; (*streak, trace*)
tendenza; elemento ▷ *vt* tendere; (*muscle*)
sforzare; (*ankle*) storcere; (*resources*) pesare
su; (*food*) colare; passare; **strained** *adj*
(*muscle*) stirato(-a); (*laugh etc*) forzato(-a);
(*relations*) teso(-a); **strainer** *n* passino,
colino
strait [streɪt] *n* (*Geo*) stretto; **~s** *npl* **to be**

in dire ~s (*fig*) essere nei guai
strand [strænd] *n* (*of thread*) filo; **stranded**
adj nei guai; senza mezzi di trasporto
strange [streɪndʒ] *adj* (*not known*)
sconosciuto(-a); (*odd*) strano(-a),
bizzarro(-a); **strangely** *adv* stranamente;
stranger *n* sconosciuto(-a); estraneo(-a)
strangle ['stræŋgl] *vt* strangolare
strap [stræp] *n* cinghia; (*of slip, dress*)
spallina, bretella
strategic [strə'ti:dʒɪk] *adj* strategico(-a)
strategy ['strætɪdʒɪ] *n* strategia
straw [strɔ:] *n* paglia; (*drinking straw*)
cannuccia; **that's the last ~!** è la goccia
che fa traboccare il vaso!
strawberry ['strɔ:bərɪ] *n* fragola
stray [streɪ] *adj* (*animal*) randagio(-a);
(*bullet*) vagante; (*scattered*) sparso(-a) ▷ *vi*
perdersi
streak [stri:k] *n* striscia; (*of hair*) mèche
f inv ▷ *vt* striare, screziare ▷ *vi* **to ~ past**
passare come un fulmine
stream [stri:m] *n* ruscello; corrente *f*;
(*of people, smoke etc*) fiume *m* ▷ *vt* (*Scol*)
dividere in livelli di rendimento ▷ *vi*
scorrere; **to ~ in/out** entrare/uscire a fiotti
street [stri:t] *n* strada, via; **streetcar** (*US*)
n tram *m inv*; **street light** *n* lampione *m*;
street map *n* pianta (di una città)
street plan *n* pianta (di una città)
strength [streŋθ] *n* forza; **strengthen** *vt*
rinforzare; fortificare; consolidare
strenuous ['strenjuəs] *adj* vigoroso(-a),
energico(-a); (*tiring*) duro(-a), pesante
stress [strɛs] *n* (*force, pressure*) pressione *f*;
(*mental strain*) tensione *f*; (*accent*) accento
▷ *vt* insistere su, sottolineare; accentare;
stressed *adj* (*tense: person*) stressato(-a);
(*Ling, Poetry: syllable*) accentato(-a);
stressful *adj* (*job*) difficile, stressante
stretch [strɛtʃ] *n* (*of sand etc*) distesa
▷ *vi* stirarsi; (*extend*): **to ~ to** or **as far as**
estendersi fino a ▷ *vt* tendere, allungare;
(*spread*) distendere; (*fig*) spingere (al
massimo); **stretch out** *vi* allungarsi,
estendersi ▷ *vt* (*arm etc*) allungare,
tendere; (*to spread*) distendere
stretcher ['strɛtʃəʳ] *n* barella, lettiga
strict [strɪkt] *adj* (*severe*) rigido(-a),
severo(-a); (*precise*) preciso(-a), stretto(-a);
strictly *adv* severamente; rigorosamente;
strettamente
stride [straɪd] (*pt* **strode**, *pp* **stridden**) *n*
passo lungo ▷ *vi* camminare a grandi passi
strike [straɪk] (*pt, pp* **struck**) *n* sciopero;
(*of oil etc*) scoperta; (*attack*) attacco
▷ *vt* colpire; (*oil etc*) scoprire, trovare;
(*bargain*) fare; (*fig*): **the thought** or **it**
~s me that ... mi viene in mente che ...

▷ vi scioperare; (attack) attaccare; (clock) suonare; **on ~** (workers) in sciopero; **to ~ a match** accendere un fiammifero; **striker** n scioperante m/f; (Sport) attaccante m; **striking** adj che colpisce

string [strɪŋ] (pt, pp **strung**) n spago; (row) fila; sequenza; catena; (Mus) corda ▷ vt **to ~ out** disporre di fianco; **to ~ together** (words, ideas) mettere insieme; **the ~s** npl (Mus) gli archi; **to pull ~s for sb** (fig) raccomandare qn

strip [strɪp] n striscia ▷ vt spogliare; (paint) togliere; (also: ~ **down**: machine) smontare ▷ vi spogliarsi; **strip off** vt (paint etc) staccare ▷ vi (person) spogliarsi

stripe [straɪp] n striscia, riga; (Mil, Police) gallone m; **striped** adj a strisce or righe

stripper ['strɪpər] n spogliarellista m/f

strip-search ['strɪpsəːtʃ] vt **to ~ sb** perquisire qn facendolo(-a) spogliare ▷ n perquisizione (facendo spogliare il perquisito)

strive [straɪv] (pt **strove**, pp **striven**) vi **to ~ to do** sforzarsi di fare

strode [strəud] pt of **stride**

stroke [strəuk] n colpo; (Swimming) bracciata; (: style) stile m; (Med) colpo apoplettico ▷ vt accarezzare; **at a ~** in un attimo

stroll [strəul] n giretto, passeggiatina ▷ vi andare a spasso; **stroller** (us) n passeggino

strong [strɔŋ] adj (gen) forte; (sturdy: table, fabric etc) robusto(-a); **they are 50 ~** sono in 50; **stronghold** n (also fig) roccaforte f; **strongly** adv fortemente, con forza; energicamente; vivamente

strove [strəuv] pt of **strive**

struck [strʌk] pt, pp of **strike**

structure ['strʌktʃər] n struttura; (building) costruzione f, fabbricato

struggle ['strʌgl] n lotta ▷ vi lottare

strung [strʌŋ] pt, pp of **string**

stub [stʌb] n mozzicone m; (of ticket etc) matrice f, talloncino ▷ vt **to ~ one's toe** urtare or sbattere il dito del piede; **stub out** vt schiacciare

stubble ['stʌbl] n stoppia; (on chin) barba ispida

stubborn ['stʌbən] adj testardo(-a), ostinato(-a)

stuck [stʌk] pt, pp of **stick** ▷ adj (jammed) bloccato(-a)

stud [stʌd] n bottoncino; borchia; (also: ~ **earring**) orecchino a pressione; (also: ~ **farm**) scuderia, allevamento di cavalli; (also: ~ **horse**) stallone m ▷ vt (fig): **~ded with** tempestato(-a) di

student ['stjuːdənt] n studente(-essa) ▷ cpd studentesco(-a); universitario(-a);

degli studenti; **student driver** (us) n conducente m/f principiante; **students' union** n (BRIT: association) circolo universitario; (: building) sede f del circolo universitario

studio ['stjuːdɪəu] n studio; **studio flat** (us **studio apartment**) n monolocale m

study ['stʌdɪ] n studio ▷ vt studiare; esaminare ▷ vi studiare

stuff [stʌf] n roba; (substance) sostanza, materiale m ▷ vt imbottire; (Culin) farcire; (dead animal) impagliare; (inf: push) ficcare; **stuffing** n imbottitura; (Culin) ripieno; **stuffy** adj (room) mal ventilato(-a), senz'aria; (ideas) antiquato(-a)

stumble ['stʌmbl] vi inciampare; **to ~ across** (fig) imbattersi in

stump [stʌmp] n ceppo; (of limb) moncone m ▷ vt **to be ~ed** essere sconcertato(-a)

stun [stʌn] vt stordire; (amaze) sbalordire

stung [stʌŋ] pt, pp of **sting**

stunk [stʌŋk] pp of **stink**

stunned [stʌnd] adj (from blow) stordito(-a); (amazed, shocked) sbalordito(-a)

stunning ['stʌnɪŋ] adj sbalorditivo(-a); (girl etc) fantastico(-a)

stunt [stʌnt] n bravata; trucco pubblicitario

stupid ['stjuːpɪd] adj stupido(-a); **stupidity** [-'pɪdɪtɪ] n stupidità f inv, stupidaggine f

sturdy ['stəːdɪ] adj robusto(-a), vigoroso(-a); solido(-a)

stutter ['stʌtər] n balbuzie f ▷ vi balbettare

style [staɪl] n stile m; (distinction) eleganza, classe f; **stylish** adj elegante; **stylist** n **hair stylist** parrucchiere(-a)

sub... [sʌb] prefix sub..., sotto...; **subconscious** adj subcosciente ▷ n subcosciente m

subdued [səb'djuːd] adj pacato(-a); (light) attenuato(-a)

subject [n 'sʌbdʒɪkt, vb səb'dʒɛkt] n soggetto; (citizen etc) cittadino(-a); (Scol) materia ▷ vt **to ~ to** sottomettere a; esporre a; **to be ~ to** (law) essere sottomesso(-a) a; (disease) essere soggetto(-a) a; **subjective** [-'dʒɛktɪv] adj soggettivo(-a); **subject matter** n argomento; contenuto

subjunctive [səb'dʒʌŋktɪv] adj congiuntivo(-a) ▷ n congiuntivo

submarine [sʌbməˈriːn] n sommergibile m

submission [səb'mɪʃən] n sottomissione f; (claim) richiesta

submit [səb'mɪt] vt sottomettere ▷ vi sottomettersi

subordinate [sə'bɔːdɪnət] *adj, n* subordinato(-a)

subscribe [səb'skraɪb] *vi* contribuire; **to ~ to** (*opinion*) approvare, condividere; (*fund*) sottoscrivere a; (*newspaper*) abbonarsi a; essere abbonato(-a) a

subscription [səb'skrɪpʃən] *n* sottoscrizione *f*, abbonamento

subsequent ['sʌbsɪkwənt] *adj* successivo(-a), seguente; conseguente; **subsequently** *adv* in seguito, successivamente

subside [səb'saɪd] *vi* cedere, abbassarsi; (*flood*) decrescere; (*wind*) calmarsi

subsidiary [səb'sɪdɪərɪ] *adj* sussidiario(-a); accessorio(-a) ▷ *n* filiale *f*

subsidize ['sʌbsɪdaɪz] *vt* sovvenzionare

subsidy ['sʌbsɪdɪ] *n* sovvenzione *f*

substance ['sʌbstəns] *n* sostanza

substantial [səb'stænʃl] *adj* solido(-a); (*amount, progress etc*) notevole; (*meal*) sostanzioso(-a)

substitute ['sʌbstɪtjuːt] *n* (*person*) sostituto(-a); (*thing*) succedaneo, surrogato ▷ *vt* **to ~ sth/sb for** sostituire qc/qn a; **substitution** [sʌbstɪ'tjuːʃən] *n* sostituzione *f*

subtle ['sʌtl] *adj* sottile

subtract [səb'trækt] *vt* sottrarre

suburb ['sʌbəːb] *n* sobborgo; **the ~s** la periferia; **suburban** [sə'bəːbən] *adj* suburbano(-a)

subway ['sʌbweɪ] *n* (US: *underground*) metropolitana; (BRIT: *underpass*) sottopassaggio

succeed [sək'siːd] *vi* riuscire; avere successo ▷ *vt* succedere a; **to ~ in doing** riuscire a fare

success [sək'sɛs] *n* successo; **successful** *adj* (*venture*) coronato(-a) da successo, riuscito(-a); **to be successful (in doing)** riuscire (a fare); **successfully** *adv* con successo

succession [sək'sɛʃən] *n* successione *f*

successive [sək'sɛsɪv] *adj* successivo(-a); consecutivo(-a)

successor [sək'sɛsər] *n* successore *m*

succumb [sə'kʌm] *vi* soccombere

such [sʌtʃ] *adj* tale; (*of that kind*): **~ a book** un tale libro, un libro del genere; **~ books** tali libri, libri del genere; (*so much*): **~ courage** tanto coraggio ▷ *adv* talmente, così; **~ a long trip** un viaggio così lungo; **~ a lot of** talmente or così tanto(-a); **~ as** (*like*) come; **as ~** come or in quanto tale; **such-and-such** *adj* tale (*after noun*)

suck [sʌk] *vt* succhiare; (*breast, bottle*) poppare

Sudan [suː'dɑːn] *n* Sudan *m*

sudden ['sʌdn] *adj* improvviso(-a); **all of a ~** improvvisamente, all'improvviso; **suddenly** *adv* bruscamente, improvvisamente, di colpo

sue [suː] *vt* citare in giudizio

suede [sweɪd] *n* pelle *f* scamosciata

suffer ['sʌfər] *vt* soffrire, patire; (*bear*) sopportare, tollerare ▷ *vi* soffrire; **to ~ from** soffrire di; **suffering** *n* sofferenza

suffice [sə'faɪs] *vi* essere sufficiente, bastare

sufficient [sə'fɪʃənt] *adj* sufficiente; **~ money** abbastanza soldi

suffocate ['sʌfəkeɪt] *vi* (*have difficulty breathing*) soffocare; (*die through lack of air*) asfissiare

sugar ['ʃugər] *n* zucchero ▷ *vt* zuccherare

suggest [sə'dʒɛst] *vt* proporre, suggerire; indicare; **suggestion** [-'dʒɛstʃən] *n* suggerimento, proposta; indicazione *f*

suicide ['suːɪsaɪd] *n* (*person*) suicida *m/f*; (*act*) suicidio; *see also* **commit**; **suicide bombing** *n* attentato suicida

suit [suːt] *n* (*man's*) vestito; (*woman's*) completo, tailleur *m inv*; (*Law*) causa; (*Cards*) seme *m*, colore *m* ▷ *vt* andar bene a or per; essere adatto(-a) a or per; (*adapt*): **to ~ sth to** adattare qc a; **well ~ed** ben assortito(-a); **suitable** *adj* adatto(-a); appropriato(-a); **suitcase** ['suːtkeɪs] *n* valigia

suite [swiːt] *n* (*of rooms*) appartamento; (*Mus*) suite *f inv*; (*furniture*): **bedroom/dining room ~** arredo or mobilia per la camera da letto/sala da pranzo

sulfur ['sʌlfər] (US) *n* = **sulphur**

sulk [sʌlk] *vi* fare il broncio

sulphur ['sʌlfər] (US **sulfur**) *n* zolfo

sultana [sʌl'tɑːnə] *n* (*fruit*) uva (secca) sultanina

sum [sʌm] *n* somma; (*Scol etc*) addizione *f*; **sum up** *vt, vi* riassumere

summarize ['sʌməraɪz] *vt* riassumere, riepilogare

summary ['sʌmərɪ] *n* riassunto

summer ['sʌmər] *n* estate *f* ▷ *cpd* d'estate, estivo(-a); **summer holidays** *npl* vacanze *fpl* estive; **summertime** *n* (*season*) estate *f*

summit ['sʌmɪt] *n* cima, sommità; (*Pol*) vertice *m*

summon ['sʌmən] *vt* chiamare, convocare

Sun. *abbr* (= *Sunday*) dom.

sun [sʌn] *n* sole *m*; **sunbathe** *vi* prendere un bagno di sole; **sunbed** *n* lettino solare; **sunblock** *n* protezione *f* solare totale; **sunburn** *n* (*painful*) scottatura; **sunburned, sunburnt** *adj* abbronzato(-a); (*painfully*) scottato(-a)

Sunday ['sʌndɪ] *n* domenica

Sunday paper n giornale m della domenica

sunflower ['sʌnflauəʳ] n girasole m

sung [sʌŋ] pp of **sing**

sunglasses ['sʌŋglɑːsɪz] npl occhiali mpl da sole

sunk [sʌŋk] pp of **sink**

sun: **sunlight** n (luce f del) sole m; **sun lounger** n sedia a sdraio; **sunny** adj assolato(-a), soleggiato(-a); (fig) allegro(-a), felice; **sunrise** n levata del sole, alba; **sun roof** n (Aut) tetto apribile; **sunscreen** n (cream) crema solare protettiva; **sunset** n tramonto; **sunshade** n parasole m; **sunshine** n luce f (del) sole m; **sunstroke** n insolazione f, colpo di sole; **suntan** n abbronzatura; **suntan lotion** n lozione f solare; **suntan oil** n olio solare

super ['suːpəʳ] (inf) adj fantastico(-a)

superb [suː'pəːb] adj magnifico(-a)

superficial [suːpə'fɪʃəl] adj superficiale

superintendent [suːpərɪn'tɛndənt] n direttore(-trice); (Police) ≈ commissario (capo)

superior [suː'pɪərɪəʳ] adj, n superiore m/f

superlative [suː'pəːlətɪv] adj superlativo(-a), supremo(-a) ▷ n (Ling) superlativo

supermarket ['suːpəmɑːkɪt] n supermercato

supernatural [suːpə'nætʃərəl] adj soprannaturale ▷ n soprannaturale m

superpower ['suːpəpauəʳ] n (Pol) superpotenza

superstition [suːpə'stɪʃən] n superstizione f

superstitious [suːpə'stɪʃəs] adj superstizioso(-a)

superstore ['suːpəstɔːʳ] n (BRIT) grande supermercato

supervise ['suːpəvaɪz] vt (person etc) sorvegliare; (organization) soprintendere a; **supervision** [-'vɪʒən] n sorveglianza; supervisione f; **supervisor** n sorvegliante m/f; soprintendente m/f; (in shop) capocommesso(-a)

supper ['sʌpəʳ] n cena

supple ['sʌpl] adj flessibile; agile

supplement [n 'sʌplɪmənt, vb sʌplɪ'mɛnt] n supplemento ▷ vt completare, integrare

supplier [sə'plaɪəʳ] n fornitore m

supply [sə'plaɪ] vt (provide) fornire; (equip): **to ~ (with)** approvvigionare (di), attrezzare (con) ▷ n riserva, provvista; (supplying) approvvigionamento; (Tech) alimentazione f; **supplies** npl (food) viveri mpl; (Mil) sussistenza

support [sə'pɔːt] n (moral, financial etc) sostegno, appoggio; (Tech) supporto ▷ vt sostenere; (financially) mantenere; (uphold) sostenere, difendere; **supporter** n (Pol etc) sostenitore(-trice), fautore(-trice); (Sport) tifoso(-a)

▮ Be careful not to translate **support** by the Italian word **sopportare**.

suppose [sə'pəuz] vt supporre; immaginare; **to be ~d to do** essere tenuto(-a) a fare; **supposedly** [sə'pəuzɪdlɪ] adv presumibilmente; **supposing** conj se, ammesso che + sub

suppress [sə'prɛs] vt reprimere; sopprimere; occultare

supreme [su'priːm] adj supremo(-a)

surcharge ['səːtʃɑːdʒ] n supplemento

sure [ʃuəʳ] adj sicuro(-a); (definite, convinced) sicuro(-a), certo(-a); **~!** (of course) senz'altro!, certo!; **~ enough** infatti; **to make ~ of sth/that** assicurarsi di qc/che; **surely** adv sicuramente; certamente

surf [səːf] n (waves) cavalloni mpl; (foam) spuma

surface ['səːfɪs] n superficie f ▷ vt (road) asfaltare ▷ vi risalire alla superficie; (fig: news, feeling) venire a galla

surfboard ['səːfbɔːd] n tavola per surfing

surfing ['səːfɪŋ] n surfing m

surge [səːdʒ] n (strong movement) ondata; (of feeling) impeto ▷ vi gonfiarsi; (people) riversarsi

surgeon ['səːdʒən] n chirurgo

surgery ['səːdʒərɪ] n chirurgia; (BRIT: room) studio or gabinetto medico, ambulatorio; (: also: **~ hours**) orario delle visite or di consultazione; **to undergo ~** subire un intervento chirurgico

surname ['səːneɪm] n cognome m

surpass [səː'pɑːs] vt superare

surplus ['səːpləs] n eccedenza; (Econ) surplus m inv ▷ adj eccedente, d'avanzo

surprise [sə'praɪz] n sorpresa; (astonishment) stupore m ▷ vt sorprendere; stupire; **surprised** [sə'praɪzd] adj (look, smile) sorpreso(-a); **to be surprised** essere sorpreso, sorprendersi; **surprising** adj sorprendente, stupefacente; **surprisingly** adv (easy, helpful) sorprendentemente

surrender [sə'rɛndəʳ] n resa, capitolazione f ▷ vi arrendersi

surround [sə'raund] vt circondare; (Mil etc) accerchiare; **surrounding** adj circostante; **surroundings** npl dintorni mpl; (fig) ambiente m

surveillance [sə:'veɪləns] n sorveglianza, controllo

survey [n 'sə:veɪ, vb sə:'veɪ] n quadro generale; (study) esame m; (in housebuying etc) perizia; (of land) rilevamento, rilievo topografico ▷ vt osservare; esaminare; valutare; rilevare; **surveyor** n perito; geometra m; (of land) agrimensore m

survival [sə'vaɪvl] n sopravvivenza; (relic) reliquia, vestigio

survive [sə'vaɪv] vi sopravvivere ▷ vt sopravvivere a; **survivor** n superstite m/f, sopravvissuto(-a)

suspect [adj, n 'sʌspɛkt, vb səs'pɛkt] adj sospetto(-a) ▷ n persona sospetta ▷ vt sospettare; (think likely) supporre; (doubt) dubitare

suspend [səs'pɛnd] vt sospendere; **suspended sentence** n condanna con la condizionale; **suspenders** npl (BRIT) giarrettiere fpl; (US) bretelle fpl

suspense [səs'pɛns] n apprensione f; (in film etc) suspense m; **to keep sb in ~** tenere qn in sospeso

suspension [səs'pɛnʃən] n sospensione f; (of driving licence) ritiro temporaneo; **suspension bridge** n ponte m sospeso

suspicion [səs'pɪʃən] n sospetto; **suspicious** [səs'pɪʃəs] adj (suspecting) sospettoso(-a); (causing suspicion) sospetto(-a)

sustain [səs'teɪn] vt sostenere; sopportare; (Law: charge) confermare; (suffer) subire

swallow ['swɔləu] n (bird) rondine f ▷ vt inghiottire; (fig: story) bere

swam [swæm] pt of **swim**

swamp [swɔmp] n palude f ▷ vt sommergere

swan [swɔn] n cigno

swap [swɔp] vt **to ~ (for)** scambiare (con)

swarm [swɔ:m] n sciame m ▷ vi (bees) sciamare; (people) brulicare; (place) **to be ~ing with** brulicare di

sway [sweɪ] vi (tree) ondeggiare; (person) barcollare ▷ vt (influence) influenzare, dominare

swear [swɛəʳ] (pt **swore**, pp **sworn**) vi (curse) bestemmiare, imprecare ▷ vt (promise) giurare; **swear in** vt prestare giuramento a; **swearword** n parolaccia

sweat [swɛt] n sudore m, traspirazione f ▷ vi sudare

sweater ['swɛtəʳ] n maglione m

sweatshirt ['swɛtʃə:t] n felpa

sweaty ['swɛtɪ] adj sudato(-a), bagnato(-a) di sudore

Swede [swi:d] n svedese m/f

swede [swi:d] n (BRIT) rapa svedese

Sweden ['swi:dn] n Svezia; **Swedish** ['swi:dɪʃ] adj svedese ▷ n (Ling) svedese m

sweep [swi:p] (pt, pp **swept**) n spazzata; (also: **chimney ~**) spazzacamino ▷ vt spazzare, scopare; (current) spazzare ▷ vi (hand) muoversi con gesto ampio; (wind) infuriare

sweet [swi:t] n (BRIT: pudding) dolce m; (candy) caramella ▷ adj dolce; (fresh) fresco(-a); (fig) piacevole; delicato(-a), grazioso(-a); gentile; **sweetcorn** n granturco dolce; **sweetener** ['swi:tnəʳ] n (Culin) dolcificante m; **sweetheart** n innamorato(-a); **sweetshop** n (BRIT) ≈ pasticceria

swell [swɛl] (pt **swelled**, pp **swollen**, **swelled**) n (of sea) mare m lungo ▷ adj (US: inf: excellent) favoloso(-a) ▷ vt gonfiare, ingrossare; aumentare ▷ vi gonfiarsi, ingrossarsi; (sound) crescere; (also: **~ up**) gonfiarsi; **swelling** n (Med) tumefazione f, gonfiore m

swept [swɛpt] pt, pp of **sweep**

swerve [swə:v] vi deviare; (driver) sterzare; (boxer) scartare

swift [swɪft] n (bird) rondone m ▷ adj rapido(-a), veloce

swim [swɪm] (pt **swam**, pp **swum**) n **to go for a ~** andare a fare una nuotata ▷ vi nuotare; (Sport) fare del nuoto; (head, room) girare ▷ vt (river, channel) attraversare or percorrere a nuoto; (length) nuotare; **swimmer** n nuotatore(-trice); **swimming** n nuoto; **swimming costume** (BRIT) n costume m da bagno; **swimming pool** n piscina; **swimming trunks** npl costume m da bagno (da uomo); **swimsuit** n costume m da bagno

swing [swɪŋ] (pt, pp **swung**) n altalena; (movement) oscillazione f; (Mus) ritmo; swing m ▷ vt dondolare, far oscillare; (also: **~ round**) far girare ▷ vi oscillare, dondolare; (also: **~ round**: object) roteare; (: person) girarsi, voltarsi; **to be in full ~** (activity) essere in piena attività; (party etc) essere nel pieno

swipe card n tessera magnetica

swirl [swə:l] vi turbinare, far mulinello

Swiss [swɪs] adj, n inv svizzero(-a)

switch [swɪtʃ] n (for light, radio etc) interruttore m; (change) cambiamento ▷ vt (change) cambiare; scambiare; **switch off** vt spegnere; **could you ~ off the light?** puoi spegnere la luce?; **switch on**

vt accendere; (*engine, machine*) mettere in moto, avviare; **switchboard** *n* (*Tel*) centralino

Switzerland ['swɪtsələnd] *n* Svizzera

swivel ['swɪvl] *vi* (*also:* **~ round**) girare

swollen ['swəulən] *pp of* **swell**

swoop [swu:p] *n* incursione *f* ▷ *vi* (*also:* **~ down**) scendere in picchiata, piombare

swop [swɔp] *n*, *vt* = **swap**

sword [sɔ:d] *n* spada; **swordfish** *n* pesce *m* spada *inv*

swore [swɔ:ᵣ] *pt of* **swear**

sworn [swɔ:n] *pp of* **swear** ▷ *adj* giurato(-a)

swum [swʌm] *pp of* **swim**

swung [swʌŋ] *pt*, *pp of* **swing**

syllable ['sɪləbl] *n* sillaba

syllabus ['sɪləbəs] *n* programma *m*

symbol ['sɪmbl] *n* simbolo; **symbolic(al)** [sɪm'bɔlɪk(l)] *adj* simbolico(-a); **to be symbolic(al) of sth** simboleggiare qc

symmetrical [sɪ'mɛtrɪkl] *adj* simmetrico(-a)

symmetry ['sɪmɪtrɪ] *n* simmetria

sympathetic [sɪmpə'θɛtɪk] *adj* (*showing pity*) compassionevole; (*kind*) comprensivo(-a); **~ towards** ben disposto(-a) verso

> Be careful not to translate *sympathetic* by the Italian word *simpatico*.

sympathize ['sɪmpəθaɪz] *vi* **to ~ with** (*person*) compatire; partecipare al dolore di; (*cause*) simpatizzare per

sympathy ['sɪmpəθɪ] *n* compassione *f*

symphony ['sɪmfənɪ] *n* sinfonia

symptom ['sɪmptəm] *n* sintomo; indizio

synagogue ['sɪnəgɔg] *n* sinagoga

syndicate ['sɪndɪkɪt] *n* sindacato

syndrome ['sɪndrəum] *n* sindrome *f*

synonym ['sɪnənɪm] *n* sinonimo

synthetic [sɪn'θɛtɪk] *adj* sintetico(-a)

Syria ['sɪrɪə] *n* Siria

syringe [sɪ'rɪndʒ] *n* siringa

syrup ['sɪrəp] *n* sciroppo; (*also:* **golden ~**) melassa raffinata

system ['sɪstəm] *n* sistema *m*; (*order*) metodo; (*Anat*) organismo; **systematic** [-'mætɪk] *adj* sistematico(-a); metodico(-a); **systems analyst** *n* analista *m* di sistemi

ta [tɑ:] (*BRIT: inf*) *excl* grazie!

tab [tæb] *n* (*loop on coat etc*) laccetto; (*label*) etichetta; **to keep ~s on** (*fig*) tenere d'occhio

table ['teɪbl] *n* tavolo, tavola; (*Math, Chem etc*) tavola ▷ *vt* (*BRIT: motion etc*) presentare; **a ~ for 4, please** un tavolo per 4, per favore; **to lay** *or* **set the ~** apparecchiare *or* preparare la tavola; **tablecloth** *n* tovaglia; **table d'hôte** [tɑ:bl'dəut] *adj* (*meal*) a prezzo fisso; **table lamp** *n* lampada da tavolo; **tablemat** *n* sottopiatto; **tablespoon** *n* cucchiaio da tavola; (*also:* **tablespoonful**: *as measurement*) cucchiaiata

tablet ['tæblɪt] *n* (*Med*) compressa; (*of stone*) targa

table tennis *n* tennis *m* da tavolo, ping-pong® *m*

tabloid ['tæblɔɪd] *n* (*newspaper*) tabloid *m inv* (*giornale illustrato di formato ridotto*); **the ~s, the ~ press** i giornali popolari

taboo [tə'bu:] *adj*, *n* tabù *m inv*

tack [tæk] *n* (*nail*) bulletta; (*fig*) approccio ▷ *vt* imbullettare; imbastire ▷ *vi* bordeggiare

tackle ['tækl] *n* attrezzatura, equipaggiamento; (*for lifting*) paranco; (*Football*) contrasto; (*Rugby*) placcaggio ▷ *vt* (*difficulty*) affrontare; (*Football*)

contrastare; (*Rugby*) placcare
tacky ['tækɪ] *adj* appiccicaticcio(-a); (*pej*)
scadente
tact [tækt] *n* tatto: **tactful** *adj*
delicato(-a), discreto(-a)
tactics ['tæktɪks] *n, npl* tattica
tactless ['tæktlɪs] *adj* che manca di tatto
tadpole ['tædpəʊl] *n* girino
taffy ['tæfɪ] (*us*) *n* caramella *f* mou *inv*
tag [tæg] *n* etichetta
tail [teɪl] *n* coda; (*of shirt*) falda ▷ *vt* (*follow*)
seguire, pedinare; **~s** *npl* (*formal suit*) frac
m inv
tailor ['teɪlə'] *n* sarto
Taiwan [taɪ'wɑːn] *n* Taiwan *m*; **Taiwanese**
[taɪwə'niːz] *adj, n* taiwanese
take [teɪk] (*pt* **took**, *pp* **taken**) *vt* prendere;
(*gain: prize*) ottenere, vincere; (*require:
effort, courage*) occorrere, volerci; (*tolerate*)
accettare, sopportare; (*hold: passengers etc*)
contenere; (*accompany*) accompagnare;
(*bring, carry*) portare; (*exam*) sostenere,
presentarsi a; **to ~ a photo/a shower**
fare una fotografia/una doccia; **I ~ it
that** suppongo che; **take after** *vt fus*
assomigliare a; **take apart** *vt* smontare;
take away *vt* portare via, togliere; **take
back** *vt* (*return*) restituire; riportare; (*one's
words*) ritirare; **take down** *vt* (*building*)
demolire; (*letter etc*) scrivere; **take in**
vt (*deceive*) imbrogliare, abbindolare;
(*understand*) capire; (*include*) comprendere,
includere; (*lodger*) prendere, ospitare;
take off *vi* (*Aviat*) decollare; (*go away*)
andarsene ▷ *vt* (*remove*) togliere; **take
on** *vt* (*work*) accettare, intraprendere;
(*employee*) assumere; (*opponent*) sfidare,
affrontare; **take out** *vt* portare fuori;
(*remove*) togliere; (*licence*) prendere,
ottenere; **to ~ sth out of sth** (*drawer,
pocket etc*) tirare qc fuori da qc; estrarre qc
da qc; **take over** *vt* (*business*) rilevare ▷ *vi*
to ~ over from sb prendere le consegne
or il controllo da qn; **take up** *vt* (*dress*)
accorciare; (*occupy: time, space*) occupare;
(*engage in: hobby etc*) mettersi a; **to ~ sb
up on sth** accettare qc da qn; **takeaway**
(*BRIT*) *n* (*shop etc*) ≈ rosticceria; (*food*)
pasto per asporto; **taken** *pp of* **take**;
takeoff *n* (*Aviat*) decollo; **takeout** (*us*)
n = **takeaway**; **takeover** *n* (*Comm*)
assorbimento; **takings** ['teɪkɪŋz] *npl*
(*Comm*) incasso
talc [tælk] *n* (*also*: **~um powder**) talco
tale [teɪl] *n* racconto, storia; **to tell ~s** (*fig:
to teacher, parent etc*) fare la spia
talent ['tælnt] *n* talento; **talented** *adj* di
talento
talk [tɔːk] *n* discorso; (*gossip*) chiacchiere

fpl; (*conversation*) conversazione *f*;
(*interview*) discussione *f* ▷ *vi* parlare; **~s** *npl*
(*Pol etc*) colloqui *mpl*; **to ~ about** parlare di;
to ~ sb out of/into doing dissuadere qn
da/convincere qn a fare; **to ~ shop** parlare
di lavoro *or* di affari; **talk over** *vt* discutere;
talk show *n* conversazione *f* televisiva,
talk show *m inv*
tall [tɔːl] *adj* alto(-a); **to be 6 feet ~** ≈ essere
alto 1 metro e 80
tambourine [tæmbə'riːn] *n* tamburello
tame [teɪm] *adj* addomesticato(-a); (*fig:
story, style*) insipido(-a), scialbo(-a)
tamper ['tæmpə'] *vi* **to ~ with**
manomettere
tampon ['tæmpɔn] *n* tampone *m*
tan [tæn] *n* (*also*: **sun~**) abbronzatura
▷ *vi* abbronzarsi ▷ *adj* (*colour*) marrone
rossiccio *inv*
tandem ['tændəm] *n* tandem *m inv*
tangerine [tændʒə'riːn] *n* mandarino
tangle ['tæŋgl] *n* groviglio; **to get into a ~**
aggrovigliarsi; (*fig*) combinare un pasticcio
tank [tæŋk] *n* serbatoio; (*for fish*) acquario;
(*Mil*) carro armato
tanker ['tæŋkə'] *n* (*ship*) nave *f* cisterna *inv*;
(*truck*) autobotte *f*, autocisterna
tanned [tænd] *adj* abbronzato(-a)
tantrum ['tæntrəm] *n* accesso di collera
Tanzania [tænzə'niə] *n* Tanzania
tap [tæp] *n* (*on sink etc*) rubinetto; (*gentle
blow*) colpetto ▷ *vt* dare un colpetto a;
(*resources*) sfruttare, utilizzare; (*telephone*)
mettere sotto controllo; **on ~** (*fig:
resources*) a disposizione; **tap dancing** *n*
tip tap *m*
tape [teɪp] *n* nastro; (*also*: **magnetic ~**)
nastro (magnetico); (*sticky tape*) nastro
adesivo ▷ *vt* (*record*) registrare (su nastro);
(*stick*) attaccare con nastro adesivo;
tape measure *n* metro a nastro; **tape
recorder** *n* registratore *m* (a nastro)
tapestry ['tæpɪstrɪ] *n* arazzo; tappezzeria
tar [tɑː'] *n* catrame *m*
target ['tɑːgɪt] *n* bersaglio; (*fig: objective*)
obiettivo
tariff ['tærɪf] *n* tariffa
tarmac ['tɑːmæk] *n* (*BRIT: on road*)
macadam *m* al catrame; (*Aviat*) pista di
decollo
tarpaulin [tɑː'pɔːlɪn] *n* tela incatramata
tarragon ['tærəgən] *n* dragoncello
tart [tɑːt] *n* (*Culin*) crostata; (*BRIT: inf:
pej: woman*) sgualdrina ▷ *adj* (*flavour*)
aspro(-a), agro(-a)
tartan ['tɑːtn] *n* tartan *m inv*
tartar(e) sauce *n* salsa tartara
task [tɑːsk] *n* compito; **to take to ~**
rimproverare

taste [teɪst] n gusto; (*flavour*) sapore m, gusto; (*sample*) assaggio; (*fig: glimpse, idea*) idea ▷ vt gustare; (*sample*) assaggiare ▷ vi **to ~ of** or **like** (*fish etc*) sapere or avere sapore di; **in good/bad ~** di buon/cattivo gusto; **can I have a ~?** posso assaggiarlo?; **you can ~ the garlic (in it)** (ci) si sente il sapore dell'aglio; **tasteful** adj di buon gusto; **tasteless** adj (*food*) insipido(-a); (*remark*) di cattivo gusto; **tasty** adj saporito(-a), gustoso(-a)

tatters ['tætəz] npl **in ~** a brandelli

tattoo [tə'tu:] n tatuaggio; (*spectacle*) parata militare ▷ vt tatuare

taught [tɔ:t] pt, pp of **teach**

taunt [tɔ:nt] n scherno ▷ vt schernire

Taurus ['tɔ:rəs] n Toro

taut [tɔ:t] adj teso(-a)

tax [tæks] n (*on goods*) imposta; (*on services*) tassa; (*on income*) imposte fpl, tasse fpl ▷ vt tassare; (*fig: strain: patience etc*) mettere alla prova; **tax-free** adj esente da imposte

taxi ['tæksɪ] n taxi m inv ▷ vi (*Aviat*) rullare; **can you call me a ~, please?** può chiamarmi un taxi, per favore?; **taxi driver** n tassista m/f; **taxi rank** (BRIT) n = **taxi stand**; **taxi stand** n posteggio dei taxi

tax payer n contribuente m/f

TB n abbr = **tuberculosis**

tea [ti:] n tè m inv; (BRIT: *snack: for children*) merenda; **high ~** (BRIT) cena leggera (*presa nel tardo pomeriggio*); **tea bag** n bustina di tè; **tea break** (BRIT) n intervallo per il tè

teach [ti:tʃ] (pt, pp **taught**) vt **to ~ sb sth, ~ sth to sb** insegnare qc a qn ▷ vi insegnare; **teacher** n insegnante m/f; (*in secondary school*) professore(-essa); (*in primary school*) maestro(-a); **teaching** n insegnamento

tea: **tea cloth** n (*for dishes*) strofinaccio; (BRIT: *for trolley*) tovaglietta da tè; **teacup** ['ti:kʌp] n tazza da tè

tea leaves npl foglie fpl di tè

team [ti:m] n squadra; (*of animals*) tiro; **team up** vi **to ~ up (with)** mettersi insieme (a)

teapot ['ti:pɔt] n teiera

tear¹ [tɛəʳ] (pt **tore**, pp **torn**) n strappo ▷ vt strappare ▷ vi strapparsi; **tear apart** vt (*also fig*) distruggere; **tear down** vt +adv (*building, statue*) demolire; (*poster, flag*) tirare giù; **tear off** vt (*sheet of paper etc*) strappare; (*one's clothes*) togliersi di dosso; **tear up** vt (*sheet of paper etc*) strappare

tear² [tɪəʳ] n lacrima; **in ~s** in lacrime; **tearful** ['tɪəful] adj piangente, lacrimoso(-a); **tear gas** n gas m lacrimogeno

tearoom ['ti:ru:m] n sala da tè

tease [ti:z] vt canzonare; (*unkindly*) tormentare

tea: **teaspoon** n cucchiaino da tè; (*also:* **teaspoonful**: *as measurement*) cucchiaino; **teatime** n ora del tè; **tea towel** (BRIT) n strofinaccio (per i piatti)

technical ['tɛknɪkl] adj tecnico(-a)

technician [tɛk'nɪʃən] n tecnico(-a)

technique [tɛk'ni:k] n tecnica

technology [tɛk'nɔlədʒɪ] n tecnologia

teddy (bear) ['tɛdɪ-] n orsacchiotto

tedious ['ti:dɪəs] adj noioso(-a), tedioso(-a)

tee [ti:] n (*Golf*) tee m inv

teen [ti:n] adj = **teenage** ▷ n (US) = **teenager**

teenage ['ti:neɪdʒ] adj (*fashions etc*) per giovani, per adolescenti; **teenager** n adolescente m/f

teens [ti:nz] npl **to be in one's ~** essere adolescente

teeth [ti:θ] npl of **tooth**

teetotal ['ti:'təutl] adj astemio(-a)

telecommunications ['tɛlɪkəmju:nɪ'keɪʃənz] n telecomunicazioni fpl

telegram ['tɛlɪgræm] n telegramma m

telegraph pole n palo del telegrafo

telephone ['tɛlɪfəun] n telefono ▷ vt (*person*) telefonare a; (*message*) comunicare per telefono; **telephone book** n elenco telefonico; **telephone booth** (BRIT), **telephone box** n cabina telefonica; **telephone call** n telefonata; **telephone directory** n elenco telefonico; **telephone number** n numero di telefono

telesales ['tɛlɪseɪlz] n vendita per telefono

telescope ['tɛlɪskəup] n telescopio

televise ['tɛlɪvaɪz] vt teletrasmettere

television ['tɛlɪvɪʒən] n televisione f; **on ~** alla televisione; **television programme** n programma m televisivo

tell [tɛl] (pt, pp **told**) vt dire; (*relate: story*) raccontare; (*distinguish*): **to ~ sth from** distinguere qc da ▷ vi (*talk*): **to ~ (of)** parlare (di); (*have effect*) farsi sentire, avere effetto; **to ~ sb to do** dire a qn di fare; **tell off** vt rimproverare, sgridare; **teller** n (*in bank*) cassiere(-a)

telly ['tɛlɪ] (BRIT: *inf*) n abbr (= *television*) tivù f inv

temp [tɛmp] n abbr (= *temporary*) segretaria temporanea

temper ['tɛmpəʳ] n (*nature*) carattere m; (*mood*) umore m; (*fit of anger*) collera ▷ vt (*moderate*) moderare; **to be in a ~** essere in collera; **to lose one's ~** andare in collera

temperament ['tɛmprəmənt] n (*nature*) temperamento; **temperamental** [-'mɛntl] adj capriccioso(-a)

temperature ['tɛmprətʃəʳ] n

temperatura; **to have** or **run a ~** avere la febbre

temple ['templ] n (building) tempio; (Anat) tempia

temporary ['tempərəri] adj temporaneo(-a); (job, worker) avventizio(-a), temporaneo(-a)

tempt [tempt] vt tentare; **to ~ sb into doing** indurre qn a fare; **temptation** [-'teɪʃən] n tentazione f; **tempting** adj allettante

ten [ten] num dieci

tenant ['tenənt] n inquilino(-a)

tend [tend] vt badare a, occuparsi di ▷ vi **to ~ to do** tendere a fare; **tendency** ['tendənsɪ] n tendenza

tender ['tendə'] adj tenero(-a); (sore) dolorante ▷ n (Comm: offer) offerta; (money): **legal ~** moneta in corso legale ▷ vt offrire

tendon ['tendən] n tendine m

tenner ['tenə'] n (BRIT inf) (banconota da) dieci sterline fpl

tennis ['tenɪs] n tennis m; **tennis ball** n palla da tennis; **tennis court** n campo da tennis; **tennis match** n partita di tennis; **tennis player** n tennista m/f; **tennis racket** n racchetta da tennis

tenor ['tenə'] n (Mus) tenore m

tenpin bowling ['tenpɪn-] n bowling m

tense [tens] adj teso(-a) ▷ n (Ling) tempo

tension ['tenʃən] n tensione f

tent [tent] n tenda

tentative ['tentətɪv] adj esitante, incerto(-a); (conclusion) provvisorio(-a)

tenth [tenθ] num decimo(-a)

tent: tent peg n picchetto da tenda; **tent pole** n palo da tenda, montante m

tepid ['tepɪd] adj tiepido(-a)

term [tə:m] n termine m; (Scol) trimestre m; (Law) sessione f ▷ vt chiamare, definire; **~s** npl (conditions) condizioni fpl; (Comm) prezzi mpl, tariffe fpl; **in the short/long ~** a breve/lunga scadenza; **to be on good ~s with sb** essere in buoni rapporti con qn; **to come to ~s with** (problem) affrontare

terminal ['tə:mɪnl] adj finale, terminale; (disease) terminale ▷ n (Elec) morsetto; (Comput) terminale m; (Aviat, for oil, ore etc) terminal m inv; (BRIT: also: **coach ~**) capolinea m

terminate ['tə:mɪneɪt] vt mettere fine a

termini ['tə:mɪnaɪ] npl of **terminus**

terminology [tə:mɪ'nɔlədʒɪ] n terminologia

terminus ['tə:mɪnəs] (pl **termini**) n (for buses) capolinea m; (for trains) stazione f terminale

terrace ['terəs] n terrazza; (BRIT: row of houses) fila di case a schiera; **terraced** adj (garden) a terrazze

terrain [tɛ'reɪn] n terreno

terrestrial [tɪ'restrɪəl] adj (life) terrestre; (BRIT: channel) terrestre

terrible ['terɪbl] adj terribile; **terribly** adv terribilmente; (very badly) malissimo

terrier ['terɪə'] n terrier m inv

terrific [tə'rɪfɪk] adj incredibile, fantastico(-a); (wonderful) formidabile, eccezionale

terrified ['terɪfaɪd] adj atterrito(-a)

terrify ['terɪfaɪ] vt terrorizzare; **terrifying** adj terrificante

territorial [terɪ'tɔ:rɪəl] adj territoriale

territory ['terɪtərɪ] n territorio

terror ['terə'] n terrore m; **terrorism** n terrorismo; **terrorist** n terrorista m/f

test [test] n (trial, check: of courage etc) prova; (Med) esame m; (Chem) analisi f inv; (exam: of intelligence etc) test m inv; (: in school) compito in classe; (also: **driving ~**) esame m di guida ▷ vt provare; esaminare; analizzare; sottoporre ad esame; **to ~ sb in history** esaminare qn in storia

testicle ['testɪkl] n testicolo

testify ['testɪfaɪ] vi (Law) testimoniare, deporre; **to ~ to sth** (Law) testimoniare qc; (gen) comprovare or dimostrare qc

testimony ['testɪmənɪ] n (Law) testimonianza, deposizione f

test: test match n (Cricket, Rugby) partita internazionale; **test tube** n provetta

text [tekst] n testo; (on mobile phone) SMS m inv, messaggino m ▷ vt **to ~ sb** (inf) mandare un SMS a qn; **textbook** n libro di testo

textile ['tekstaɪl] n tessile m

text message n (Tel) SMS m inv, messaggino

text messaging [-'mesɪdʒɪŋ] n il mandarsi SMS

texture ['tekstʃə'] n tessitura; (of skin, paper etc) struttura

Thai [taɪ] adj tailandese ▷ n tailandese m/f; (Ling) tailandese m

Thailand ['taɪlænd] n Tailandia

Thames [temz] n **the ~** il Tamigi

than [ðæn, ðən] conj (in comparisons) che; (with numerals, pronouns, proper names) di; **more ~ 10/once** più di 10/una volta; **I have more/less ~ you** ne ho più/meno di te; **I have more pens ~ pencils** ho più penne che matite; **she is older ~ you think** è più vecchia di quanto tu (non) pensi

thank [θæŋk] vt ringraziare; **~ you (very much)** grazie (tante); **~s** npl ringraziamenti mpl, grazie fpl excl grazie!;

~s to grazie a; **thankfully** adv con riconoscenza; con sollievo; **thankfully there were few victims** grazie al cielo ci sono state poche vittime; **Thanksgiving (Day)** n giorno del ringraziamento

● THANKSGIVING (DAY)

● Negli Stati Uniti il quarto giovedì di
● novembre ricorre il **Thanksgiving**
● **(Day)**, festa che rievoca la celebrazione
● con cui i Padri Pellegrini, fondatori della
● colonia di Plymouth in Massachusetts,
● ringraziarono Dio del buon raccolto
● del 1621.

○ KEYWORD

that [ðæt] (pl **those**) adj (demonstrative) quel (quell', quello) m; quella (quell') f; **that man/woman/book** quell'uomo/quella donna/quel libro; (not "this") quell'uomo/quella donna/quel libro là; **that one** quello(-a) là
▷ pron 1 (demonstrative) ciò; (not "this one") quello(-a); **who's that?** chi è?; **what's that?** cos'è quello?; **is that you?** sei tu?; **I prefer this to that** preferisco questo a quello; **that's what he said** questo è ciò che ha detto; **what happened after that?** che è successo dopo?; **that is (to say)** cioè
2 (relative: direct) che; (: indirect) cui; **the book (that) I read** il libro che ho letto; **the box (that) I put it in** la scatola in cui l'ho messo; **the people (that) I spoke to** le persone con cui or con le quali ho parlato
3 (relative: of time) in cui; **the day (that) he came** il giorno in cui è venuto
▷ conj che; **he thought that I was ill** pensava che io fossi malato
▷ adv (demonstrative) così; **I can't work that much** non posso lavorare (così) tanto; **that high** così alto; **the wall's about that high and that thick** il muro è alto circa così e spesso circa così

thatched [θætʃt] adj (roof) di paglia
thaw [θɔː] n disgelo ▷ vi (ice) sciogliersi; (food) scongelarsi ▷ vt (food: also: ~ **out**) (fare) scongelare

○ KEYWORD

the [ðiː, ðə] def art 1 (gen) il (lo, l') m; la (l') f; i (gli) mpl; le fpl; **the boy/girl/ink** il ragazzo/la ragazza/l'inchiostro; **the books/pencils** i libri/le matite; **the history of the world** la storia del mondo; **give it to the postman** dallo al postino;

I haven't the time/money non ho tempo/soldi; **the rich and the poor** i ricchi e i poveri
2 (in titles): **Elizabeth the First** Elisabetta prima; **Peter the Great** Pietro il grande
3 (in comparisons): **the more he works, the more he earns** più lavora più guadagna

theatre ['θɪətər] (US **theater**) n teatro; (also: **lecture ~**) aula magna; (also: **operating ~**) sala operatoria
theft [θɛft] n furto
their [ðɛər] adj il (la) loro; (pl) i (le) loro; **theirs** pron il (la) loro; (pl) i (le) loro; see also **my**; **mine**
them [ðɛm, ðəm] pron (direct) li (le); (indirect) gli (loro) (after vb)); (stressed, after prep: people) loro; (: people, things) essi(-e); see also **me**
theme [θiːm] n tema m; **theme park** n parco di divertimenti (intorno a un tema centrale)
themselves [ðəm'sɛlvz] pl pron (reflexive) si; (emphatic) loro stessi(-e); (after prep) se stessi(-e)
then [ðɛn] adv (at that time) allora; (next) poi, dopo; (and also) e poi ▷ conj (therefore) perciò, dunque, quindi ▷ adj **the ~ president** il presidente di allora; **by ~** allora; **from ~ on** da allora in poi
theology [θɪ'ɒlədʒɪ] n teologia
theory ['θɪərɪ] n teoria
therapist ['θɛrəpɪst] n terapista m/f
therapy ['θɛrəpɪ] n terapia

○ KEYWORD

there [ðɛər] adv 1: **there is, there are** c'è, ci sono; **there are 3 of them** (people) sono in 3; (things) ce ne sono 3; **there is no-one here** non c'è nessuno qui; **there has been an accident** c'è stato un incidente
2 (referring to place) là, lì; **up/in/down there** lassù/là dentro/laggiù; **he went there on Friday** ci è andato venerdì; **I want that book there** voglio quel libro là or lì; **there he is!** eccolo!
3: **there, there** (esp to child) su, su

there: thereabouts [ðɛərə'bauts] adv (place) nei pressi, da quelle parti; (amount) giù di lì, all'incirca; **thereafter** [ðɛər'ɑːftər] adv da allora in poi; **thereby** [ðɛə'baɪ] adv con ciò; **therefore** ['ðɛəfɔː'] adv perciò, quindi; **there's** [ðɛəz] = **there is**; **there has**
thermal ['θəːml] adj termico(-a)
thermometer [θə'mɒmɪtər] n

termometro
thermostat ['θə:məstæt] n termostato
these [ðiːz] pl pron, adj questi(-e)
thesis ['θiːsɪs] (pl **theses**) n tesi f inv
they [ðeɪ] pl pron essi (esse); (people only)
loro; **~ say that ...** (it is said that) si dice
che ...; **they'd = they had; they would;
they'll = they shall; they will; they're
= they are; they've = they have**
thick [θɪk] adj spesso(-a); (crowd)
compatto(-a); (stupid) ottuso(-a), lento(-a)
▷ n **in the ~ of** nel folto di; **it's 20 cm ~**
ha uno spessore di 20 cm; **thicken** vi
ispessire ▷ vt (sauce etc) ispessire, rendere
più denso(-a); **thickness** n spessore m
thief [θiːf] (pl **thieves**) n ladro(-a)
thigh [θaɪ] n coscia
thin [θɪn] adj sottile; (person) magro(-a);
(soup) poco denso(-a) ▷ vt **to ~ (down)**
(sauce, paint) diluire
thing [θɪŋ] n cosa; (object) oggetto;
(mania): **to have a ~ about** essere
fissato(-a) con; **~s** npl (belongings) cose fpl;
poor ~ poverino(-a); **the best ~ would be
to** la cosa migliore sarebbe di; **how are ~s?**
come va?
think [θɪŋk] (pt, pp **thought**) vi pensare,
riflettere ▷ vt pensare, credere; (imagine)
immaginare; **to ~** of pensare a; **what did
you ~ of them?** cosa ne ha pensato?; **to
~ about sth/sb** pensare a qc/qn; **I'll ~
about it** ci penserò; **to ~ of doing** pensare
di fare; **I ~ so/not** penso di sì/no; **to ~ well
of** avere una buona opinione di; **think
over** vt riflettere su; **think up** vt ideare
third [θəːd] num terzo(-a) ▷ n terzo(-a);
(fraction) terzo, terza parte f; (Aut) terza;
(BRIT: Scol: degree) laurea col minimo dei voti;
thirdly adv in terzo luogo; **third party
insurance** (BRIT) n assicurazione f contro
terzi; **Third World** n **the Third World** il
Terzo Mondo
thirst [θəːst] n sete f; **thirsty** adj (person)
assetato(-a), che ha sete
thirteen [θəːˈtiːn] num tredici; **thirteenth**
[-ˈtiːnθ] num tredicesimo(-a)
thirtieth ['θəːtɪɪθ] num trentesimo(-a)
thirty ['θəːtɪ] num trenta

KEYWORD

this [ðɪs] (pl **these**) adj (demonstrative)
questo(-a); **this man/woman/book**
quest'uomo/questa donna/questo libro;
(not "that") quest'uomo/questa donna/
questo libro qui; **this one** questo(-a) qui
▷ pron (demonstrative) questo(-a); (not "that
one") questo(-a) qui; **who/what is this?**
chi è/che cos'è questo?; **I prefer this to**

that preferisco questo a quello; **this is
where I live** io abito qui; **this is what he
said** questo è ciò che ha detto; **this is Mr
Brown** (in introductions, photo) questo è il
signor Brown; (on telephone) sono il signor
Brown
▷ adv (demonstrative): **this high/long** etc
alto/lungo etc così; **I didn't know things
were this bad** non sapevo andasse così
male

thistle ['θɪsl] n cardo
thorn [θɔːn] n spina
thorough ['θʌrə] adj (search)
minuzioso(-a); (knowledge, research)
approfondito(-a), profondo(-a);
(person) coscienzioso(-a); (cleaning)
a fondo; **thoroughly** adv (search)
minuziosamente; (wash, study) a fondo;
(very) assolutamente
those [ðəuz] pl pron quelli(-e) ▷ pl adj quei
(quegli) mpl; quelle fpl
though [ðəu] conj benché, sebbene ▷ adv
comunque
thought [θɔːt] pt, pp of **think** ▷ n pensiero;
(opinion) opinione f; **thoughtful** adj
pensieroso(-a), pensoso(-a); (considerate)
premuroso(-a); **thoughtless** adj
sconsiderato(-a); (behaviour) scortese
thousand ['θauzənd] num mille; **one ~**
mille; **~s of** migliaia di; **thousandth** num
millesimo(-a)
thrash [θræʃ] vt picchiare; bastonare;
(defeat) battere
thread [θrɛd] n filo; (of screw) filetto ▷ vt
(needle) infilare
threat [θrɛt] n minaccia; **threaten** vi
(storm) minacciare ▷ vt **to threaten sb
with/to do** minacciare qn con/di fare;
threatening adj minaccioso(-a)
three [θriː] num tre; **three-
dimensional** adj tridimensionale; (film)
stereoscopico(-a); **three-piece suite**
['θriːpiːs-] n salotto comprendente un
divano e due poltrone; **three-quarters**
npl tre quarti mpl; **three-quarters full**
pieno per tre quarti
threshold ['θrɛʃhəuld] n soglia
threw [θruː] pt of **throw**
thrill [θrɪl] n brivido ▷ vt (audience)
elettrizzare; **to be ~ed** (with gift etc) essere
elettrizzato(-a); **thrilled** adj **I was thrilled
to get your letter** la tua lettera mi ha
fatto veramente piacere; **thriller** n thriller
m inv; **thrilling** adj (book) pieno(-a) di
suspense; (news, discovery) elettrizzante
thriving ['θraɪvɪŋ] adj fiorente
throat [θrəut] n gola; **to have a sore ~**
avere (un or il) mal di gola

throb [θrɔb] vi palpitare; pulsare; vibrare
throne [θrəʊn] n trono
through [θruː] prep attraverso; (time) per, durante; (by means of) per mezzo di; (owing to) a causa di ▷ adj (ticket, train, passage) diretto(-a) ▷ adv attraverso; **to put sb ~ to sb** (Tel) passare qn a qn; **to be ~** (Tel) ottenere la comunicazione; (have finished) essere finito(-a); **"no ~ road"** (BRIT) "strada senza sbocco"; **throughout** prep (place) dappertutto in; (time) per or durante tutto(-a) ▷ adv dappertutto; sempre
throw [θrəʊ] (pt **threw**, pp **thrown**) n (Sport) lancio, tiro ▷ vt tirare, gettare; (Sport) lanciare, tirare; (rider) disarcionare; (fig) confondere; **to ~ a party** dare una festa; **throw away** vt gettare or buttare via; **throw in** vt (Sport: ball) rimettere in gioco; (include) aggiungere; **throw off** vt sbarazzarsi di; **throw out** vt buttare fuori; (reject) respingere; **throw up** vi vomitare
thru [θruː] (US) prep, adj, adv = **through**
thrush [θrʌʃ] n tordo
thrust [θrʌst] (pt, pp **thrust**) vt spingere con forza; (push in) conficcare
thud [θʌd] n tonfo
thug [θʌg] n delinquente m
thumb [θʌm] n (Anat) pollice m; **to ~ a lift** fare l'autostop; **thumbtack** (US) n puntina da disegno
thump [θʌmp] n colpo forte; (sound) tonfo ▷ vt (person) picchiare; (object) battere su ▷ vi picchiare; battere
thunder [ˈθʌndəʳ] n tuono ▷ vi tuonare; (train etc): **to ~ past** passare con un rombo; **thunderstorm** n temporale m
Thur(s). abbr (= Thursday) gio.
Thursday [ˈθəːzdɪ] n giovedì m inv
thus [ðʌs] adv così
thwart [θwɔːt] vt contrastare
thyme [taɪm] n timo
Tiber [ˈtaɪbəʳ] n **the ~** il Tevere
Tibet [tɪˈbɛt] n Tibet m
tick [tɪk] n (sound: of clock) tic tac m inv; (mark) segno; spunta; (Zool) zecca; (BRIT: inf): **in a ~** in un attimo ▷ vi fare tic tac ▷ vt spuntare; **tick off** vt spuntare; (person) sgridare
ticket [ˈtɪkɪt] n biglietto; (in shop: on goods) etichetta; (parking ticket) multa; (for library) scheda; **a single/return ~ to ...** un biglietto di sola andata/di andata e ritorno per...; **ticket barrier** n (BRIT: Rail) cancelletto d'ingresso; **ticket collector** n bigliettaio; **ticket inspector** n controllore m; **ticket machine** n distributore m di biglietti; **ticket office** n biglietteria
tickle [ˈtɪkl] vt fare il solletico a; (fig) solleticare ▷ vi **it ~s** mi (or gli etc) fa il

solletico; **ticklish** [-lɪʃ] adj che soffre il solletico; (problem) delicato(-a)
tide [taɪd] n marea; (fig: of events) corso; **high/low ~** alta/bassa marea
tidy [ˈtaɪdɪ] adj (room) ordinato(-a), lindo(-a); (dress, work) curato(-a), in ordine; (person) ordinato(-a) ▷ vt (also: **~ up**) riordinare, mettere in ordine
tie [taɪ] n (string etc) legaccio; (BRIT: also: **neck~**) cravatta; (fig: link) legame m; (Sport: draw) pareggio ▷ vt (parcel) legare; (ribbon) annodare ▷ vi (Sport) pareggiare; **to ~ sth in a bow** annodare qc; **to ~ a knot in sth** fare un nodo a qc; **tie down** vt legare; (to price etc) costringere ad accettare; **tie up** vt (parcel, dog) legare; (boat) ormeggiare; (arrangements) concludere; **to be ~d up** (busy) essere occupato(-a) or preso(-a)
tier [tɪəʳ] n fila; (of cake) piano, strato
tiger [ˈtaɪgəʳ] n tigre f
tight [taɪt] adj (rope) teso(-a), tirato(-a); (money) poco(-a); (clothes, budget, bend etc) stretto(-a); (control) severo(-a), fermo(-a); (inf: drunk) sbronzo(-a) ▷ adv (squeeze) fortemente; (shut) ermeticamente; **tighten** vt (rope) tendere; (screw) stringere; (control) rinforzare ▷ vi tendersi; stringersi; **tightly** adv (grasp) bene, saldamente; **tights** (BRIT) npl collant m inv
tile [taɪl] n (on roof) tegola; (on wall or floor) piastrella, mattonella
till [tɪl] n registratore m di cassa ▷ vt (land) coltivare ▷ prep, conj = **until**
tilt [tɪlt] vt inclinare, far pendere ▷ vi inclinarsi, pendere
timber [ˈtɪmbəʳ] n (material) legname m
time [taɪm] n tempo; (epoch: often pl) epoca, tempo; (by clock) ora; (moment) momento; (occasion) volta; (Mus) tempo ▷ vt (race) cronometrare; (programme) calcolare la durata di; (fix moment for) programmare; (remark etc) dire (or fare) al momento giusto; **a long ~** molto tempo; **what ~ does the museum/shop open?** a che ora apre il museo/negozio?; **for the ~ being** per il momento; **4 at a ~** 4 per or alla volta; **from ~ to ~** ogni tanto; **at ~s** a volte; **in ~** (soon enough) in tempo; (after some time) col tempo; (Mus) a tempo; **in a week's ~** fra una settimana; **in no ~** in un attimo; **any ~** in qualsiasi momento; **on ~** puntualmente; **5 ~s 5** 5 volte 5, 5 per 5; **what ~ is it?** che ora è?, che ore sono?; **to have a good ~** divertirsi; **time limit** n limite m di tempo; **timely** adj opportuno(-a); **timer** n (time switch) temporizzatore m; (in kitchen) contaminuti m inv; **time-share** adj **time-share apartment/villa** appartamento/villa in

multiproprietà; **timetable** n orario; **time zone** n fuso orario

timid ['tɪmɪd] adj timido(-a); (easily scared) pauroso(-a)

timing ['taɪmɪŋ] n (Sport) cronometraggio; (fig) scelta del momento opportuno

tin [tɪn] n stagno; (also: ~ plate) latta; (container) scatola; (BRIT: can) barattolo (di latta), lattina; **tinfoil** n stagnola

tingle ['tɪŋgl] vi pizzicare

tinker ['tɪŋkər]: ~ with vt fus armeggiare intorno a; cercare di riparare

tinned [tɪnd] (BRIT) adj (food) in scatola

tin opener ['-əupnər] (BRIT) n apriscatole m inv

tint [tɪnt] n tinta; **tinted** adj (hair) tinto(-a); (spectacles, glass) colorato(-a)

tiny ['taɪnɪ] adj minuscolo(-a)

tip [tɪp] n (end) punta; (gratuity) mancia; (BRIT: for rubbish) immondezzaio; (advice) suggerimento ▷ vt (waiter) dare la mancia a; (tilt) inclinare; (overturn: also: ~ over) capovolgere; (empty: also: ~ out) scaricare; **how much should I ~?** quanto devo lasciare di mancia?; **tip off** vt fare una soffiata a

tiptoe ['tɪptəu] n **on ~** in punta di piedi

tire ['taɪər] n (US) = **tyre** ▷ vt stancare ▷ vi stancarsi; **tired** adj stanco(-a); **to be tired of** essere stanco or stufo di; **tire pressure** (US) n = **tyre pressure**; **tiring** adj faticoso(-a)

tissue ['tɪʃuː] n tessuto; (paper handkerchief) fazzoletto di carta; **tissue paper** n carta velina

tit [tɪt] n (bird) cinciallegra; **to give ~ for tat** rendere pan per focaccia

title ['taɪtl] n titolo

T-junction ['tiː'dʒʌŋkʃən] n incrocio a T

TM abbr = **trademark**

KEYWORD

to [tuː, tə] prep 1 (direction) a; **to go to France/London/school** andare in Francia/a Londra/a scuola; **to go to Paul's/the doctor's** andare da Paul/dal dottore; **the road to Edinburgh** la strada per Edimburgo; **to the left/right** a sinistra/destra

2 (as far as) (fino) a; **from here to London** da qui a Londra; **to count to 10** contare fino a 10; **from 40 to 50 people** da 40 a 50 persone

3 (with expressions of time): **a quarter to 5** le 5 meno un quarto; **it's twenty to 3** sono le 3 meno venti

4 (for, of): **the key to the front door** la chiave della porta d'ingresso; **a letter to his wife** una lettera per la moglie

5 (expressing indirect object) a; **to give sth to sb** dare qc a qn; **to talk to sb** parlare a qn; **to be a danger to sb/sth** rappresentare un pericolo per qn/qc

6 (in relation to) a; **3 goals to 2** 3 goal a 2; **30 miles to the gallon** ≈ 11 chilometri con un litro

7 (purpose, result): **to come to sb's aid** venire in aiuto a qn; **to sentence sb to death** condannare a morte qn; **to my surprise** con mia sorpresa

▷ with vb 1 (simple infinitive): **to go/eat etc** andare/mangiare etc

2 (following another vb): **to want/try/start to do** volere/cercare di/cominciare a fare

3 (with vb omitted): **I don't want to** non voglio (farlo); **you ought to** devi (farlo)

4 (purpose, result) per; **I did it to help you** l'ho fatto per aiutarti

5 (equivalent to relative clause): **I have things to do** ho da fare; **the main thing is to try** la cosa più importante è provare

6 (after adjective etc): **ready to go** pronto a partire; **too old/young to ...** troppo vecchio/giovane per ...

▷ adv **to push the door to** accostare la porta

toad [təud] n rospo; **toadstool** n fungo (velenoso)

toast [təust] n (Culin) pane m tostato; (drink, speech) brindisi m inv ▷ vt (Culin) tostare; (drink to) brindare a; **a piece or slice of ~** una fetta di pane tostato; **toaster** n tostapane m inv

tobacco [tə'bækəu] n tabacco

toboggan [tə'bɔgən] n toboga m inv

today [tə'deɪ] adv oggi ▷ n (also fig) oggi m

toddler ['tɔdlər] n bambino(-a) che impara a camminare

toe [təu] n dito del piede; (of shoe) punta; **to ~ the line** (fig) stare in riga, conformarsi; **toenail** n unghia del piede

toffee ['tɔfɪ] n caramella

together [tə'geðər] adv insieme; (at same time) allo stesso tempo; **~ with** insieme a

toilet ['tɔɪlət] n (BRIT: lavatory) gabinetto ▷ cpd (bag, soap etc) da toletta; **where's the ~?** dov'è il bagno?; **toilet bag** n (BRIT) nécessaire m inv da toilette; **toilet paper** n carta igienica; **toiletries** npl articoli mpl da toletta; **toilet roll** n rotolo di carta igienica

token ['təukən] n (sign) segno; (substitute coin) gettone m; **book/record/gift ~** (BRIT) buono-libro/disco/regalo

Tokyo ['təukjəu] n Tokyo f

told [təuld] *pt, pp of* **tell**

tolerant ['tɔlərnt] *adj* **~ (of)** tollerante (nei confronti di)

tolerate ['tɔləreɪt] *vt* sopportare; (*Med, Tech*) tollerare

toll [təul] *n* (*tax, charge*) pedaggio ▷ *vi* (*bell*) suonare; **the accident ~ on the roads** il numero delle vittime della strada; **toll call** (*US*) *n* (*Tel*) (telefonata) interurbana; **toll-free** (*US*) *adj* senza addebito, gratuito(-a) ▷ *adv* gratuitamente; **toll-free number** ≈ numero verde

tomato [tə'mɑːtəu] (*pl* **tomatoes**) *n* pomodoro; **tomato sauce** *n* salsa di pomodoro

tomb [tuːm] *n* tomba; **tombstone** ['tuːmstəun] *n* pietra tombale

tomorrow [tə'mɔrəu] *adv* domani ▷ *n* (*also fig*) domani *m inv*; **the day after ~** dopodomani; **~ morning** domani mattina

ton [tʌn] *n* tonnellata; (*BRIT*: 1016 *kg*; *US*: 907 *kg*; *metric* 1000 *kg*): **~s of** (*inf*) un mucchio *or* sacco di

tone [təun] *n* tono ▷ *vi* (*also*: **~ in**) intonarsi; **tone down** *vt* (*colour, criticism, sound*) attenuare

tongs [tɔŋz] *npl* tenaglie *fpl*; (*for coal*) molle *fpl*; (*for hair*) arricciacapelli *m inv*

tongue [tʌŋ] *n* lingua; **~ in cheek** (*say, speak*) ironicamente

tonic ['tɔnɪk] *n* (*Med*) tonico; (*also*: **~ water**) acqua tonica

tonight [tə'naɪt] *adv* stanotte; (*this evening*) stasera ▷ *n* questa notte; questa sera

tonne [tʌn] *n* (*BRIT*: *metric ton*) tonnellata

tonsil ['tɔnsl] *n* tonsilla; **tonsillitis** [-'laɪtɪs] *n* tonsillite *f*

too [tuː] *adv* (*excessively*) troppo; (*also*) anche; (*also*: **~ much**) ▷ *adv* troppo ▷ *adj* troppo(-a); **~ many** troppi(-e)

took [tuk] *pt of* **take**

tool [tuːl] *n* utensile *m*, attrezzo; **tool box** *n* cassetta *f* portautensili; **tool kit** *n* cassetta di attrezzi

tooth [tuːθ] (*pl* **teeth**) *n* (*Anat, Tech*) dente *m*; **toothache** *n* mal *m* di denti; **toothbrush** *n* spazzolino da denti; **toothpaste** *n* dentifricio; **toothpick** *n* stuzzicadenti *m inv*

top [tɔp] *n* (*of mountain, page, ladder*) cima; (*of box, cupboard, table*) sopra *m inv*, parte *f* superiore; (*lid*: *of box, jar*) coperchio; (: *of bottle*) tappo; (*blouse etc*) sopra *m inv*; (*toy*) trottola ▷ *adj* più alto(-a); (*in rank*) primo(-a); (*best*) migliore ▷ *vt* (*exceed*) superare; (*be first in*) essere in testa a; **on ~ of** sopra, in cima a; (*in addition to*) oltre a; **from ~ to bottom** da cima a fondo;

top up (*US* **top off**) *vt* riempire; (*salary*) integrare; **top floor** *n* ultimo piano; **top hat** *n* cilindro

topic ['tɔpɪk] *n* argomento; **topical** *adj* d'attualità

topless ['tɔplɪs] *adj* (*bather etc*) col seno scoperto

topping ['tɔpɪŋ] *n* (*Culin*) guarnizione *f*

topple ['tɔpl] *vt* rovesciare, far cadere ▷ *vi* cadere; traballare

torch [tɔːtʃ] *n* torcia; (*BRIT*: *electric*) lampadina tascabile

tore [tɔːʳ] *pt of* **tear¹**

torment [*n* 'tɔːmɛnt, *vb* tɔː'mɛnt] *n* tormento ▷ *vt* tormentare

torn [tɔːn] *pp of* **tear¹**

tornado [tɔː'neɪdəu] (*pl* **tornadoes**) *n* tornado

torpedo [tɔː'piːdəu] (*pl* **torpedoes**) *n* siluro

torrent ['tɔrnt] *n* torrente *m*; **torrential** [tɔ'rɛnʃl] *adj* torrenziale

tortoise ['tɔːtəs] *n* tartaruga

torture ['tɔːtʃəʳ] *n* tortura ▷ *vt* torturare

Tory ['tɔːrɪ] (*BRIT*: *Pol*) *adj* dei tories, conservatore(-trice) ▷ *n* tory *m/f inv*, conservatore(-trice)

toss [tɔs] *vt* gettare, lanciare; (*one's head*) scuotere; **to ~ a coin** fare a testa o croce; **to ~ up for sth** fare a testa o croce per qc; **to ~ and turn** (*in bed*) girarsi e rigirarsi

total ['təutl] *adj* totale ▷ *n* totale *m* ▷ *vt* (*add up*) sommare; (*amount to*) ammontare a

totalitarian [təutælɪ'tɛərɪən] *adj* totalitario(-a)

totally ['təutəlɪ] *adv* completamente

touch [tʌtʃ] *n* tocco; (*sense*) tatto; (*contact*) contatto ▷ *vt* toccare; **a ~ of** (*fig*) un tocco di; un pizzico di; **to get in ~ with** mettersi in contatto con; **to lose ~** (*friends*) perdersi di vista; **touch down** *vi* (*on land*) atterrare; **touchdown** *n* atterraggio; (*on sea*) ammaraggio; (*US*: *Football*) meta; **touched** *adj* commosso(-a); **touching** *adj* commovente; **touchline** *n* (*Sport*) linea laterale; **touch-sensitive** *adj* sensibile al tatto

tough [tʌf] *adj* duro(-a); (*resistant*) resistente

tour ['tuəʳ] *n* viaggio; (*also*: **package ~**) viaggio organizzato *or* tutto compreso; (*of town, museum*) visita; (*by artist*) tournée *f inv* ▷ *vt* visitare; **tour guide** *n* guida turistica

tourism ['tuərɪzəm] *n* turismo

tourist ['tuərɪst] *n* turista *m/f* ▷ *adv* (*travel*) in classe turistica ▷ *cpd* turistico(-a); **tourist office** *n* pro loco *f inv*

tournament ['tuənəmənt] n torneo
tour operator n (BRIT) operatore m
turistico
tow [təu] vt rimorchiare; **"on ~"** (BRIT), **"in
~"** (US) "veicolo rimorchiato"; **tow away** vt
rimorchiare
toward(s) [tə'wɔːd(z)] prep verso; (of
attitude) nei confronti di; (of purpose) per
towel ['tauəl] n asciugamano; (also:
tea ~) strofinaccio; **towelling** n (fabric)
spugna
tower ['tauər] n torre f; **tower block** (BRIT)
n palazzone m
town [taun] n città f inv; **to go to ~** andare
in città; (fig) mettercela tutta; **town
centre** n centro (città); **town hall** n
≈ municipio
tow truck (US) n carro m, attrezzi inv
toxic ['tɔksɪk] adj tossico(-a)
toy [tɔɪ] n giocattolo; **toy with** vt
fus giocare con; (idea) accarezzare,
trastullarsi con; **toyshop** n negozio di
giocattoli
trace [treɪs] n traccia ▷ vt (draw) tracciare;
(follow) seguire; (locate) rintracciare
track [træk] n (of person, animal) traccia;
(on tape, Sport, path: gen) pista; (: of bullet
etc) traiettoria; (: of suspect, animal) pista,
tracce fpl; (Rail) binario, rotaie fpl ▷ vt
seguire le tracce di; **to keep ~ of** seguire;
track down vt (prey) scovare; snidare;
(sth lost) rintracciare; **tracksuit** n tuta
sportiva
tractor ['træktər] n trattore m
trade [treɪd] n commercio; (skill, job)
mestiere m ▷ vi commerciare ▷ vt **to ~
sth (for sth)** barattare qc (con qc); **to
~ with/in** commerciare con/in; **trade
in** vt (old car etc) dare come pagamento
parziale; **trademark** n marchio di
fabbrica; **trader** n commerciante
m/f; **tradesman** (irreg) n fornitore m;
(shopkeeper) negoziante m; **trade union**
n sindacato
trading ['treɪdɪŋ] n commercio
tradition [trə'dɪʃən] n tradizione f;
traditional adj tradizionale
traffic ['træfɪk] n traffico ▷ vi **to ~ in** (pej:
liquor, drugs) trafficare in; **traffic circle**
(US) n isola rotatoria; **traffic island** n
salvagente m, isola f, spartitraffico inv;
traffic jam n ingorgo (del traffico); **traffic
lights** npl semaforo; **traffic warden** n
addetto(-a) al controllo del traffico e del
parcheggio
tragedy ['trædʒədɪ] n tragedia
tragic ['trædʒɪk] adj tragico(-a)
trail [treɪl] n (tracks) tracce fpl, pista; (path)
sentiero; (of smoke etc) scia ▷ vt trascinare,

strascicare; (follow) seguire ▷ vi essere
al traino; (dress etc) strusciare; (plant)
arrampicarsi; strisciare; (in game) essere
in svantaggio; **trailer** n (Aut) rimorchio;
(US) roulotte f inv; (Cinema) prossimamente
m inv
train [treɪn] n treno; (of dress) coda,
strascico ▷ vt (apprentice, doctor etc)
formare; (sportsman) allenare; (dog)
addestrare; (memory) esercitare; (point:
gun etc): **to ~ sth on** puntare qc contro
▷ vi formarsi; allenarsi; **what time
does the ~ from Rome get in?** a che
ora arriva il treno da Roma?; **is this the
~ for ...?** è questo il treno per...?; **one's
~ of thought** il filo dei propri pensieri;
trainee [treɪ'niː] n (in trade) apprendista
m/f; **trainer** n (Sport) allenatore(-trice);
(: shoe) scarpa da ginnastica; (of dogs
etc) addestratore(-trice); **trainers**
npl (shoes) scarpe fpl da ginnastica;
training n formazione f; allenamento;
addestramento; **in training** (Sport) in
allenamento; **training course** n corso di
formazione professionale; **training shoes**
npl scarpe fpl da ginnastica
trait [treɪt] n tratto
traitor ['treɪtər] n traditore m
tram [træm] (BRIT) n (also: **~car**) tram
m inv
tramp [træmp] n (person) vagabondo(-a);
(inf: pej: woman) sgualdrina
trample ['træmpl] vt **to ~ (underfoot)**
calpestare
trampoline ['træmpəliːn] n trampolino
tranquil ['træŋkwɪl] adj tranquillo(-a);
tranquillizer (US **tranquilizer**) n (Med)
tranquillante m
transaction [træn'zækʃən] n
transazione f
transatlantic ['trænzət'læntɪk] adj
transatlantico(-a)
transcript ['trænskrɪpt] n trascrizione f
transfer [n 'trænsfər, vb træns'fəːr] n (gen:
also Sport) trasferimento; (Pol: of power)
passaggio; (picture, design) decalcomania;
(: stick-on) autoadesivo ▷ vt trasferire;
passare; **to ~ the charges** (BRIT: Tel) fare
una chiamata a carico del destinatario
transform [træns'fɔːm] vt trasformare;
transformation n trasformazione f
transfusion [træns'fjuːʒən] n
trasfusione f
transit ['trænzɪt] n **in ~** in transito
transition [træn'zɪʃən] n passaggio,
transizione f
transitive ['trænzɪtɪv] adj (Ling)
transitivo(-a)
translate [trænz'leɪt] vt tradurre; **can**

you ~ this for me? me lo può tradurre?;
translation [-'leɪʃən] n traduzione f;
translator n traduttore(-trice)
transmission [trænz'mɪʃən] n
trasmissione f
transmit [trænz'mɪt] vt trasmettere;
transmitter n trasmettitore m
transparent [træns'pærnt] adj
trasparente
transplant [vb træns'plɑːnt, n
'trænsplɑːnt] vt trapiantare ▷ n (Med)
trapianto
transport [n 'trænspɔːt, vb træns'pɔː:
t] n trasporto ▷ vt trasportare;
transportation [-'teɪʃən] n (mezzo di)
trasporto
transvestite [trænz'vɛstaɪt] n
travestito(-a)
trap [træp] n (snare, trick) trappola;
(carriage) calesse m ▷ vt prendere in
trappola, intrappolare
trash [træʃ] (pej) n (goods) ciarpame m;
(nonsense) sciocchezze fpl; **trash can** (US)
secchio della spazzatura
trauma ['trɔːmə] n trauma m; **traumatic**
[-'mætɪk] adj traumatico(-a)
travel ['trævl] n viaggio; viaggi mpl ▷ vi
viaggiare ▷ vt (distance) percorrere;
travel agency n agenzia (di) viaggi;
travel agent n agente m di viaggio;
travel insurance n assicurazione f
di viaggio; **traveller** (US **traveler**) n
viaggiatore(-trice); **traveller's cheque**
(US **traveler's check**) n assegno turistico;
travelling (US **traveling**) n viaggi mpl;
travel-sick adj **to get travel-sick** (in
vehicle) soffrire di mal d'auto; (in aeroplane)
soffrire di mal d'aria; (in boat) soffrire di mal
di mare; **travel sickness** n mal m d'auto
(or di mare or d'aria)
tray [treɪ] n (for carrying) vassoio; (on desk)
vaschetta
treacherous ['trɛtʃərəs] adj infido(-a)
treacle ['triːkl] n melassa
tread [trɛd] (pt **trod**, pp **trodden**) n passo;
(sound) rumore m di passi; (of stairs) pedata;
(of tyre) battistrada m inv ▷ vi camminare;
tread on vt fus calpestare
treasure ['trɛʒəʳ] n tesoro ▷ vt (value)
tenere in gran conto, apprezzare molto;
(store) custodire gelosamente; **treasurer**
['trɛʒərəʳ] n tesoriere(-a)
treasury ['trɛʒərɪ] n **the T~** (BRIT),
the T~
Department (US) il ministero del Tesoro
treat [triːt] n regalo ▷ vt trattare; (Med)
curare; **to ~ sb to sth** offrire qc a qn;
treatment ['triːtmənt] n trattamento
treaty ['triːtɪ] n patto, trattato
treble ['trɛbl] adj triplo(-a), triplice ▷ vt

triplicare ▷ vi triplicarsi
tree [triː] n albero
trek [trɛk] n escursione f a piedi;
escursione f in macchina; (tiring walk)
camminata sfiancante ▷ vi (as holiday) fare
dell'escursionismo
tremble ['trɛmbl] vi tremare
tremendous [trɪ'mɛndəs] adj (enormous)
enorme; (excellent) fantastico(-a),
strepitoso(-a)

> Be careful not to translate
> **tremendous** by the Italian word
> **tremendo**.

trench [trɛntʃ] n trincea
trend [trɛnd] n (tendency) tendenza; (of
events) corso; (fashion) moda; **trendy** adj
(idea) di moda; (clothes) all'ultima moda
trespass ['trɛspəs] vi **to ~ on** entrare
abusivamente in; **"no ~ing"** "proprietà
privata", "vietato l'accesso"
trial ['traɪəl] n (Law) processo; (test: of
machine etc) collaudo; **on ~** (Law) sotto
processo; **trial period** n periodo di prova
triangle ['traɪæŋgl] n (Math, Mus)
triangolo
triangular [traɪ'æŋgjuləʳ] adj triangolare
tribe [traɪb] n tribù f inv
tribunal [traɪ'bjuːnl] n tribunale m
tribute ['trɪbjuːt] n tributo, omaggio; **to
pay ~ to** rendere omaggio a
trick [trɪk] n trucco; (joke) tiro; (Cards) presa
▷ vt imbrogliare, ingannare; **to play a ~
on sb** giocare un tiro a qn; **that should do
the ~** vedrai che funziona
trickle ['trɪkl] n (of water etc) rivolo;
gocciolio ▷ vi gocciolare
tricky ['trɪkɪ] adj difficile, delicato(-a)
tricycle ['traɪsɪkl] n triciclo
trifle ['traɪfl] n sciocchezza; (BRIT: Culin)
≈ zuppa inglese ▷ adv **a ~ long** un po'
lungo
trigger ['trɪgəʳ] n (of gun) grilletto
trim [trɪm] adj (house, garden) ben
tenuto(-a); (figure) snello(-a) ▷ n (haircut
etc) spuntata, regolata; (embellishment)
finiture fpl; (on car) guarnizioni fpl ▷ vt
spuntare; (decorate): **to ~ (with)** decorare
(con); (Naut: a sail) orientare
trio ['triːəu] n trio
trip [trɪp] n viaggio; (excursion) gita,
escursione f; (stumble) passo falso ▷ vi
inciampare; (go lightly) camminare con
passo leggero; **on a ~** in viaggio; **trip up** vi
inciampare ▷ vt fare lo sgambetto a
triple ['trɪpl] adj triplo(-a)
triplets ['trɪplɪts] npl bambini(-e)
trigemini(-e)
tripod ['traɪpɔd] n treppiede m
triumph ['traɪʌmf] n trionfo ▷ vi **to**

~ (over) trionfare (su); **triumphant** [traɪˈʌmfənt] adj trionfante

trivial [ˈtrɪvɪəl] adj insignificante; (commonplace) banale

> Be careful not to translate **trivial** by the Italian word **triviale**.

trod [trɔd] pt of **tread**

trodden [ˈtrɔdn] pp of **tread**

trolley [ˈtrɔlɪ] n carrello

trombone [trɔmˈbəun] n trombone m

troop [truːp] n gruppo; (Mil) squadrone m; **~s** npl (Mil) truppe fpl

trophy [ˈtrəufɪ] n trofeo

tropical [ˈtrɔpɪkl] adj tropicale

trot [trɔt] n trotto ▷ vi trottare; **on the ~** (BRIT: fig) di fila, uno(-a) dopo l'altro(-a)

trouble [ˈtrʌbl] n difficoltà f inv, problema m; difficoltà fpl, problemi; (worry) preoccupazione f; (bother, effort) sforzo; (Pol) conflitti mpl, disordine m; (Med): **stomach** etc ~ disturbi mpl gastrici etc ▷ vt disturbare; (worry) preoccupare ▷ vi **to ~ to do** disturbarsi a fare; **~s** npl (Pol etc) disordini mpl; **to be in ~** avere dei problemi; **it's no ~!** di niente!; **what's the ~?** cosa c'è che non va?; **I'm sorry to ~ you** scusi il disturbo; **troubled** adj (person) preoccupato(-a), inquieto(-a); (epoch, life) agitato(-a), difficile; **troublemaker** n elemento disturbatore, agitatore(-trice); (child) disloco(-a); **troublesome** adj fastidioso(-a), seccante

trough [trɔf] n (drinking trough) abbeveratoio; (also: **feeding ~**) trogolo, mangiatoia; (channel) canale m

trousers [ˈtrauzəz] npl pantaloni mpl, calzoni mpl; **short ~** calzoncini mpl

trout [traut] n inv trota

trowel [ˈtrauəl] n cazzuola

truant [ˈtruənt] (BRIT) n **to play ~** marinare la scuola

truce [truːs] n tregua

truck [trʌk] n autocarro, camion m inv; (Rail) carro merci aperto; (for luggage) carrello m portabagagli inv; **truck driver** n camionista m/f

true [truː] adj vero(-a); (accurate) accurato(-a), esatto(-a); (genuine) reale; (faithful) fedele; **to come ~** avverarsi

truly [ˈtruːlɪ] adv veramente; (truthfully) sinceramente; (faithfully): **yours ~** (in letter) distinti saluti

trumpet [ˈtrʌmpɪt] n tromba

trunk [trʌŋk] n (of tree, person) tronco; (of elephant) proboscide f; (case) baule m; (us: Aut) bagagliaio; **~s** (also: **swimming ~s**) calzoncini mpl da bagno

trust [trʌst] n fiducia; (Law) amministrazione f fiduciaria; (Comm) trust m inv ▷ vt (rely on) contare su; (hope) sperare; (entrust): **to ~ sth to sb** affidare qc a qn; **trusted** adj fidato(-a); **trustworthy** adj fidato(-a), degno(-a) di fiducia

truth [truːθ, pl truːðz] n verità f inv; **truthful** adj (person) sincero(-a); (description) veritiero(-a), esatto(-a)

try [traɪ] n prova, tentativo; (Rugby) meta ▷ vt (Law) giudicare; (test: also: **~ out**) provare; (strain) mettere alla prova ▷ vi provare; **to have a ~** fare un tentativo; **to ~ to do** (seek) cercare di fare; **try on** vt (clothes) provare; **trying** adj (day, experience) logorante, pesante; (child) difficile, insopportabile

T-shirt [ˈtiːʃəːt] n maglietta

tub [tʌb] n tinozza; mastello; (bath) bagno

tube [tjuːb] n tubo; (BRIT: underground) metropolitana, metrò m inv; (for tyre) camera d'aria

tuberculosis [tjubəːkjuˈləusɪs] n tubercolosi f inv

tube station (BRIT) n stazione f della metropolitana

tuck [tʌk] vt (put) mettere; **tuck away** vt riporre; (building): **to be ~ed away** essere in un luogo isolato; **tuck in** vt mettere dentro; (child) rimboccare ▷ vi (eat) mangiare di buon appetito; abbuffarsi; **tuck shop** n negozio di pasticceria (in una scuola)

Tue(s). abbr (= Tuesday) mar.

Tuesday [ˈtjuːzdɪ] n martedì m inv

tug [tʌg] n (ship) rimorchiatore m ▷ vt tirare con forza

tuition [tjuːˈɪʃən] n (BRIT) lezioni fpl; (: private tuition) lezioni fpl private; (us: school fees) tasse fpl scolastiche

tulip [ˈtjuːlɪp] n tulipano

tumble [ˈtʌmbl] n (fall) capitombolo ▷ vi capitombolare, ruzzolare; **to ~ to sth** (inf) realizzare qc; **tumble dryer** (BRIT) n asciugatrice f

tumbler [ˈtʌmbləʳ] n bicchiere m (senza stelo)

tummy [ˈtʌmɪ] (inf) n pancia

tumour [ˈtjuːməʳ] (us **tumor**) n tumore m

tuna [ˈtjuːnə] n inv (also: **~ fish**) tonno

tune [tjuːn] n (melody) melodia, aria ▷ vt (Mus) accordare; (Radio, TV, Aut) regolare, mettere a punto; **to be in/out of ~** (instrument) essere accordato(-a)/ scordato(-a); (singer) essere intonato(-a)/ stonato(-a); **tune in** vi **to ~ in (to)** (Radio, TV) sintonizzarsi (su); **tune up** vi (musician) accordare lo strumento

tunic [ˈtjuːnɪk] n tunica

Tunisia [tjuːˈnɪzɪə] n Tunisia

tunnel ['tʌnl] n galleria ▷ vi scavare una galleria

turbulence ['tə:bjuləns] n (Aviat) turbolenza

turf [tə:f] n terreno erboso; (clod) zolla ▷ vt coprire di zolle erbose

Turin [tjuə'rɪn] n Torino f

Turk [tə:k] n turco(-a)

Turkey ['tə:kɪ] n Turchia

turkey ['tə:kɪ] n tacchino

Turkish ['tə:kɪʃ] adj turco(-a) ▷ n (Ling) turco

turmoil ['tə:mɔɪl] n confusione f, tumulto

turn [tə:n] n giro; (change) cambiamento; (in road) curva; (tendency: of mind, events) tendenza; (performance) numero; (chance) turno; (Med) crisi f inv, attacco ▷ vt girare, voltare; (change): **to ~ sth into** trasformare qc in ▷ vi girare; (person: look back) girarsi, voltarsi; (reverse direction) girare; (change) cambiare; (milk) andare a male; (become) diventare; **a good ~** un buon servizio; **it gave me quite a ~** mi ha fatto prendere un bello spavento; **"no left ~"** (Aut) "divieto di svolta a sinistra"; **it's your ~** tocca a lei; **in ~** a sua volta; a turno; **to take ~s (at sth)** fare (qc) a turno; **~ left/right at the next junction** al prossimo incrocio, giri a sinistra/destra; **turn around** vi (person) girarsi; (rotate) girare ▷ vt (object) girare; **turn away** vi girarsi (dall'altra parte) ▷ vt mandare via; **turn back** vi ritornare, tornare indietro ▷ vt far tornare indietro; (clock) spostare indietro; **turn down** vt (refuse) rifiutare; (reduce) abbassare; (fold) ripiegare; **turn in** vi (inf: go to bed) andare a letto ▷ vt (fold) voltare in dentro; **turn off** vi (from road) girare, voltare ▷ vt (light, radio, engine etc) spegnere; **I can't ~ the heating off** non riesco a spegnere il riscaldamento; **turn on** vt (light, radio etc) accendere; **I can't ~ the heating on** non riesco ad accendere il riscaldamento; **turn out** vt (light, gas) chiudere; spegnere ▷ vi (voters) presentarsi; **to ~ out to be ...** rivelarsi ..., risultare ...; **turn over** vi (person) girarsi ▷ vt girare; **turn round** vi girare; (person) girarsi; **turn to** vt fus **to ~ to sb** girarsi verso qn; **to ~ to sb for help** rivolgersi a qn per aiuto; **turn up** vi (person) arrivare, presentarsi; (lost object) saltar fuori ▷ vt (collar, sound) alzare; **turning** n (in road) curva; **turning point** n (fig) svolta decisiva

turnip ['tə:nɪp] n rapa

turn: **turnout** ['tə:naut] n presenza, affluenza; **turnover** ['tə:nəuvə[r]] n (Comm) turnover m inv; (Culin): **apple** etc **turnover** sfogliatella alle melle ecc; **turnstile** ['tə:nstaɪl] n tornella; **turn-up** (BRIT) n (on trousers) risvolto

turquoise ['tə:kwɔɪz] n turchese m ▷ adj turchese

turtle ['tə:tl] n testuggine f; **turtleneck (sweater)** ['tə:tlnɛk-] n maglione m con il collo alto

Tuscany ['tʌskənɪ] n Toscana

tusk [tʌsk] n zanna

tutor ['tju:tə[r]] n (in college) docente m/f (responsabile di un gruppo di studenti); (private teacher) precettore m; **tutorial** [-'tɔ:rɪəl] n (Scol) lezione f con discussione (a un gruppo limitato)

tuxedo [tʌk'si:dəu] (US) n smoking m inv

TV [ti:'vi:] n abbr (= television) tivù f inv

tweed [twi:d] n tweed m inv

tweezers ['twi:zəz] npl pinzette fpl

twelfth [twɛlfθ] num dodicesimo(-a)

twelve [twɛlv] num dodici; **at ~ o'clock** alle dodici, a mezzogiorno; (midnight) a mezzanotte

twentieth ['twɛntɪɪθ] num ventesimo(-a)

twenty ['twɛntɪ] num venti

twice [twaɪs] adv due volte; **~ as much** due volte tanto; **~ a week** due volte alla settimana

twig [twɪg] n ramoscello ▷ vt, vi (inf) capire

twilight ['twaɪlaɪt] n crepuscolo

twin [twɪn] adj, n gemello(-a) ▷ vt **to ~ one town with another** fare il gemellaggio di una città con un'altra; **twin(-bedded) room** n stanza con letti gemelli; **twin beds** npl letti mpl gemelli

twinkle ['twɪŋkl] vi scintillare; (eyes) brillare

twist [twɪst] n torsione f; (in wire, flex) piega; (in road) curva; (in story) colpo di scena ▷ vt attorcigliare; (ankle) slogare; (weave) intrecciare; (roll around) arrotolare; (fig) distorcere ▷ vi (road) serpeggiare

twit [twɪt] (inf) n cretino(-a)

twitch [twɪtʃ] n tiratina; (nervous) tic m inv ▷ vi contrarsi

two [tu:] num due; **to put ~ and ~ together** (fig) fare uno più uno

type [taɪp] n (category) genere m; (model) modello; (example) tipo; (Typ) tipo, carattere m ▷ vt (letter etc) battere (a macchina), dattilografare; **typewriter** n macchina da scrivere

typhoid ['taɪfɔɪd] n tifoidea

typhoon [taɪ'fu:n] n tifone m

typical ['tɪpɪkl] adj tipico(-a); **typically** adv tipicamente; **typically, he arrived**

late come al solito è arrivato tardi
typing ['taɪpɪŋ] *n* dattilografia
typist ['taɪpɪst] *n* dattilografo(-a)
tyre ['taɪəʳ] (*US* **tire**) *n* pneumatico, gomma; **I've got a flat ~** ho una gomma a terra; **tyre pressure** *n* pressione *f* (delle gomme)

UFO ['juːfəu] *n abbr* (= *unidentified flying object*) UFO *m inv*
Uganda [juːˈgændə] *n* Uganda
ugly ['ʌglɪ] *adj* brutto(-a)
UHT *abbr* (= *ultra heat treated*) UHT *inv*, a lunga conservazione
UK *n abbr* = **United Kingdom**
ulcer ['ʌlsəʳ] *n* ulcera; (*also:* **mouth ~**) afta
ultimate ['ʌltɪmət] *adj* ultimo(-a), finale; (*authority*) massimo(-a), supremo(-a); **ultimately** *adv* alla fine; in definitiva, in fin dei conti
ultimatum [ʌltɪˈmeɪtəm, -tə] (*pl* **ultimatums** *or* **ultimata**) *n* ultimatum *m inv*
ultrasound [ʌltrəˈsaund] *n* (*Med*) ultrasuono
ultraviolet ['ʌltrəˈvaɪəlɪt] *adj* ultravioletto(-a)
umbrella [ʌmˈbrɛlə] *n* ombrello
umpire ['ʌmpaɪəʳ] *n* arbitro
UN *n abbr* (= *United Nations*) ONU *f*
unable [ʌnˈeɪbl] *adj* **to be ~ to** non potere, essere nell'impossibilità di; essere incapace di
unacceptable [ʌnəkˈsɛptəbl] *adj* (*proposal, behaviour*) inaccettabile; (*price*) impossibile
unanimous [juːˈnænɪməs] *adj* unanime
unarmed [ʌnˈɑːmd] *adj* (*without a weapon*)

disarmato(-a); (*combat*) senz'armi
unattended [ʌnə'tɛndɪd] *adj* (*car, child, luggage*) incustodito(-a)
unattractive [ʌnə'træktɪv] *adj* poco attraente
unavailable [ʌnə'veɪləbl] *adj* (*article, room, book*) non disponibile; (*person*) impegnato(-a)
unavoidable [ʌnə'vɔɪdəbl] *adj* inevitabile
unaware [ʌnə'wɛəʳ] *adj* **to be ~ of** non sapere, ignorare; **unawares** *adv* di sorpresa, alla sprovvista
unbearable [ʌn'bɛərəbl] *adj* insopportabile
unbeatable [ʌn'biːtəbl] *adj* imbattibile
unbelievable [ʌnbɪ'liːvəbl] *adj* incredibile
unborn [ʌn'bɔːn] *adj* non ancora nato(-a)
unbutton [ʌn'bʌtn] *vt* sbottonare
uncalled-for [ʌn'kɔːldfɔːʳ] *adj* (*remark*) fuori luogo *inv*; (*action*) ingiustificato(-a)
uncanny [ʌn'kænɪ] *adj* misterioso(-a), strano(-a)
uncertain [ʌn'səːtn] *adj* incerto(-a); dubbio(-a); **uncertainty** *n* incertezza
unchanged [ʌn'tʃeɪndʒd] *adj* invariato(-a)
uncle ['ʌŋkl] *n* zio
unclear [ʌn'klɪəʳ] *adj* non chiaro(-a); **I'm still ~ about what I'm supposed to do** non ho ancora ben capito cosa dovrei fare
uncomfortable [ʌn'kʌmfətəbl] *adj* scomodo(-a); (*uneasy*) a disagio, agitato(-a); (*unpleasant*) fastidioso(-a)
uncommon [ʌn'kɔmən] *adj* raro(-a), insolito(-a), non comune
unconditional [ʌnkən'dɪʃənl] *adj* incondizionato(-a), senza condizioni
unconscious [ʌn'kɔnʃəs] *adj* privo(-a) di sensi, svenuto(-a); (*unaware*) inconsapevole, inconscio(-a) ▷ *n* **the ~** l'inconscio
uncontrollable [ʌnkən'trəuləbl] *adj* incontrollabile; indisciplinato(-a)
unconventional [ʌnkən'vɛnʃənl] *adj* poco convenzionale
uncover [ʌn'kʌvəʳ] *vt* scoprire
undecided [ʌndɪ'saɪdɪd] *adj* indeciso(-a)
undeniable [ʌndɪ'naɪəbl] *adj* innegabile, indiscutibile
under ['ʌndəʳ] *prep* sotto; (*less than*) meno di; al disotto di; (*according to*) secondo, in conformità a ▷ *adv* (al) disotto; **~ there** là sotto; **~ repair** in riparazione; **undercover** *adj* segreto(-a), clandestino(-a); **underdone** *adj* (*Culin*) al sangue; (*pej*) poco cotto(-a); **underestimate** *vt* sottovalutare; **undergo** *vt* (*irreg*) subire; (*treatment*) sottoporsi a; **undergraduate** *n* studente(-essa) universitario(-a); **underground** *n* (*BRIT:*

railway) metropolitana; (*Pol*) movimento clandestino ▷ *adj* sotterraneo(-a); (*fig*) clandestino(-a) ▷ *adv* sottoterra; **to go underground** (*fig*) darsi alla macchia; **undergrowth** *n* sottobosco; **underline** *vt* sottolineare; **undermine** *vt* minare; **underneath** [ʌndə'niːθ] *adv* sotto, disotto ▷ *prep* sotto, al di sotto di; **underpants** *npl* mutande *fpl*, slip *m inv*; **underpass** (*BRIT*) *n* sottopassaggio; **underprivileged** *adj* non abbiente; meno favorito(-a); **underscore** *vt* sottolineare; **undershirt** (*US*) *n* maglietta; **underskirt** (*BRIT*) *n* sottoveste *f*
understand [ʌndə'stænd] (*irreg: like* **stand**) *vt*, *vi* capire, comprendere; **I don't ~** non capisco; **I ~ that ...** sento che ...; credo di capire che ...; **understandable** *adj* comprensibile; **understanding** *adj* comprensivo(-a) ▷ *n* comprensione *f*; (*agreement*) accordo
understatement [ʌndə'steɪtmənt] *n* **that's an ~!** a dire poco!
understood [ʌndə'stud] *pt*, *pp of* **understand** ▷ *adj* inteso(-a); (*implied*) sottinteso(-a)
undertake [ʌndə'teɪk] (*irreg: like* **take**) *vt* intraprendere; **to ~ to do sth** impegnarsi a fare qc
undertaker ['ʌndəteɪkəʳ] *n* impresario di pompe funebri
undertaking [ʌndə'teɪkɪŋ] *n* impresa; (*promise*) promessa
under: underwater [ʌndə'wɔːtəʳ] *adv* sott'acqua ▷ *adj* subacqueo(-a); **underway** [ʌndə'weɪ] *adj* **to be underway** essere in corso; **underwear** ['ʌndəwɛəʳ] *n* biancheria (intima); **underwent** [ʌndə'wɛnt] *vb see* **undergo**; **underworld** ['ʌndəwəːld] *n* (*of crime*) malavita
undesirable [ʌndɪ'zaɪərəbl] *adj* sgradevole
undisputed [ʌndɪs'pjuːtɪd] *adj* indiscusso(-a)
undo [ʌn'duː] *vt* (*irreg*) disfare
undone [ʌn'dʌn] *pp of* **undo**; **to come ~** slacciarsi
undoubtedly [ʌn'dautɪdlɪ] *adv* senza alcun dubbio
undress [ʌn'drɛs] *vi* spogliarsi
unearth [ʌn'əːθ] *vt* dissotterrare; (*fig*) scoprire
uneasy [ʌn'iːzɪ] *adj* a disagio; (*worried*) preoccupato(-a); (*peace*) precario(-a)
unemployed [ʌnɪm'plɔɪd] *adj* disoccupato(-a) ▷ *npl* **the ~** i disoccupati
unemployment [ʌnɪm'plɔɪmənt] *n* disoccupazione *f*; **unemployment**

benefit (US **unemployment compensation**) n sussidio di disoccupazione

unequal [ʌn'i:kwəl] adj (length, objects) disuguale; (amounts) diverso(-a); (division of labour) ineguale

uneven [ʌn'i:vn] adj ineguale; irregolare

unexpected [ʌnɪk'spɛktɪd] adj inatteso(-a), imprevisto(-a);
unexpectedly adv inaspettatamente

unfair [ʌn'fɛəʳ] adj ~ (to) ingiusto(-a) (nei confronti di)

unfaithful [ʌn'feɪθful] adj infedele

unfamiliar [ʌnfə'mɪlɪəʳ] adj sconosciuto(-a), strano(-a); **to be ~ with** non avere familiarità con

unfashionable [ʌn'fæʃnəbl] adj (clothes) fuori moda; (district) non alla moda

unfasten [ʌn'fɑ:sn] vt slacciare; sciogliere

unfavourable [ʌn'feɪvərəbl] (US **unfavorable**) adj sfavorevole

unfinished [ʌn'fɪnɪʃt] adj incompleto(-a)

unfit [ʌn'fɪt] adj (ill) malato(-a), in cattiva salute; (incompetent): ~ (for) incompetente (in); (: unsuitable): ~ (for) inabile (a)

unfold [ʌn'fəuld] vt spiegare ▷ vi (story, plot) svelarsi

unforgettable [ʌnfə'gɛtəbl] adj indimenticabile

unfortunate [ʌn'fɔ:tʃnət] adj sfortunato(-a); (event, remark) infelice;
unfortunately adv sfortunatamente, purtroppo

unfriendly [ʌn'frɛndlɪ] adj poco amichevole, freddo(-a)

unfurnished [ʌn'fə:nɪʃt] adj non ammobiliato(-a)

unhappiness [ʌn'hæpɪnɪs] n infelicità

unhappy [ʌn'hæpɪ] adj infelice; ~ **about/with** (arrangements etc) insoddisfatto(-a) di

unhealthy [ʌn'hɛlθɪ] adj (gen) malsano(-a); (person) malaticcio(-a)

unheard-of [ʌn'hə:dɔv] adj inaudito(-a), senza precedenti

unhelpful [ʌn'hɛlpful] adj poco disponibile

unhurt [ʌn'hə:t] adj illeso(-a)

unidentified [ʌnaɪ'dɛntɪfaɪd] adj non identificato(-a)

uniform ['ju:nɪfɔ:m] n uniforme f, divisa ▷ adj uniforme

unify ['ju:nɪfaɪ] vt unificare

unimportant [ʌnɪm'pɔ:tənt] adj senza importanza, di scarsa importanza

uninhabited [ʌnɪn'hæbɪtɪd] adj disabitato(-a)

unintentional [ʌnɪn'tɛnʃənəl] adj involontario(-a)

union ['ju:njən] n unione f; (also: **trade ~**)

sindacato ▷ cpd sindacale, dei sindacati;
Union Jack n bandiera nazionale britannica

unique [ju:'ni:k] adj unico(-a)

unisex ['ju:nɪsɛks] adj unisex inv

unit ['ju:nɪt] n unità f inv; (section: of furniture etc) elemento; (team, squad) reparto, squadra

unite [ju:'naɪt] vt unire ▷ vi unirsi; **united** adj unito(-a); unificato(-a); (efforts) congiunto(-a); **United Kingdom** n Regno Unito; **United Nations (Organization)** n (Organizzazione f delle) Nazioni Unite; **United States (of America)** n Stati mpl Uniti (d'America)

unity ['ju:nɪtɪ] n unità

universal [ju:nɪ'və:sl] adj universale

universe ['ju:nɪvə:s] n universo

university [ju:nɪ'və:sɪtɪ] n università f inv

unjust [ʌn'dʒʌst] adj ingiusto(-a)

unkind [ʌn'kaɪnd] adj scortese; crudele

unknown [ʌn'nəun] adj sconosciuto(-a)

unlawful [ʌn'lɔ:ful] adj illecito(-a), illegale

unleaded [ʌn'lɛdɪd] adj (petrol, fuel) verde, senza piombo

unleash [ʌn'li:ʃ] vt (fig) scatenare

unless [ʌn'lɛs] conj a meno che (non) + sub

unlike [ʌn'laɪk] adj diverso(-a) ▷ prep a differenza di, contrariamente a

unlikely [ʌn'laɪklɪ] adj improbabile

unlimited [ʌn'lɪmɪtɪd] adj illimitato(-a)

unlisted [ʌn'lɪstɪd] (US) adj (Tel): **to be ~** non essere sull'elenco

unload [ʌn'ləud] vt scaricare

unlock [ʌn'lɔk] vt aprire

unlucky [ʌn'lʌkɪ] adj sfortunato(-a); (object, number) che porta sfortuna

unmarried [ʌn'mærɪd] adj non sposato(-a); (man only) scapolo, celibe; (woman only) nubile

unmistak(e)able [ʌnmɪs'teɪkəbl] adj inconfondibile

unnatural [ʌn'nætʃrəl] adj innaturale; contro natura

unnecessary [ʌn'nɛsəsərɪ] adj inutile, superfluo(-a)

UNO ['ju:nəu] n abbr (= United Nations Organization) ONU f

unofficial [ʌnə'fɪʃl] adj non ufficiale; (strike) non dichiarato(-a) dal sindacato

unpack [ʌn'pæk] vi disfare la valigia (or le valigie) ▷ vt disfare

unpaid [ʌn'peɪd] adj (holiday) non pagato(-a); (work) non retribuito(-a); (bill, debt) da pagare

unpleasant [ʌn'plɛznt] adj spiacevole

unplug [ʌn'plʌg] vt staccare

unpopular [ʌn'pɔpjuləʳ] adj impopolare

unprecedented [ʌn'prɛsɪdəntɪd] adj senza precedenti

unpredictable [ʌnprɪ'dɪktəbl] *adj* imprevedibile

unprotected ['ʌnprə'tɛktɪd] *adj* (*sex*) non protetto(-a)

unqualified [ʌn'kwɔlɪfaɪd] *adj* (*teacher*) non abilitato(-a); (*success*) assoluto(-a), senza riserve

unravel [ʌn'rævl] *vt* dipanare, districare

unreal [ʌn'rɪəl] *adj* irreale

unrealistic [ʌnrɪə'lɪstɪk] *adj* non realistico(-a)

unreasonable [ʌn'riːznəbl] *adj* irragionevole

unrelated [ʌnrɪ'leɪtɪd] *adj* ~ **(to)** senza rapporto (con); non imparentato(-a) (con)

unreliable [ʌnrɪ'laɪəbl] *adj* (*person, machine*) che non dà affidamento; (*news, source of information*) inattendibile

unrest [ʌn'rɛst] *n* agitazione *f*

unroll [ʌn'rəul] *vt* srotolare

unruly [ʌn'ruːlɪ] *adj* indisciplinato(-a)

unsafe [ʌn'seɪf] *adj* pericoloso(-a), rischioso(-a)

unsatisfactory ['ʌnsætɪs'fæktərɪ] *adj* che lascia a desiderare, insufficiente

unscrew [ʌn'skruː] *vt* svitare

unsettled [ʌn'sɛtld] *adj* (*person*) turbato(-a); indeciso(-a); (*weather*) instabile

unsettling [ʌn'sɛtlɪŋ] *adj* inquietante

unsightly [ʌn'saɪtlɪ] *adj* brutto(-a), sgradevole a vedersi

unskilled [ʌn'skɪld] *adj* non specializzato(-a)

unspoiled ['ʌn'spɔɪld], **unspoilt** ['ʌn'spɔɪlt] *adj* (*place*) non deturpato(-a)

unstable [ʌn'steɪbl] *adj* (*gen*) instabile; (*mentally*) squilibrato(-a)

unsteady [ʌn'stɛdɪ] *adj* instabile, malsicuro(-a)

unsuccessful [ʌnsək'sɛsful] *adj* (*writer, proposal*) che non ha successo; (*marriage, attempt*) mal riuscito(-a), fallito(-a); **to be** ~ (*in attempting sth*) non avere successo

unsuitable [ʌn'suːtəbl] *adj* inadatto(-a); inopportuno(-a); sconveniente

unsure [ʌn'ʃuə] *adj* incerto(-a); **to be** ~ **of o.s** essere insicuro(-a)

untidy [ʌn'taɪdɪ] *adj* (*room*) in disordine; (*appearance*) trascurato(-a); (*person*) disordinato(-a)

untie [ʌn'taɪ] *vt* (*knot, parcel*) disfare; (*prisoner, dog*) slegare

until [ʌn'tɪl] *prep* fino a; (*after negative*) prima di ▷ *conj* finché, fino a quando; (*in past, after negative*) prima che + *sub*, prima di + *infinitive*; ~ **he comes** finché o fino a quando non arriva; ~ **now** finora; ~ **then** fino ad allora

untrue [ʌn'truː] *adj* (*statement*) falso(-a), non vero(-a)

unused [ʌn'juːzd] *adj* nuovo(-a)

unusual [ʌn'juːʒuəl] *adj* insolito(-a), eccezionale, raro(-a); **unusually** *adv* insolitamente

unveil [ʌn'veɪl] *vt* scoprire; svelare

unwanted [ʌn'wɔntɪd] *adj* (*clothing*) smesso(-a); (*child*) non desiderato(-a)

unwell [ʌn'wɛl] *adj* indisposto(-a); **to feel** ~ non sentirsi bene

unwilling [ʌn'wɪlɪŋ] *adj* **to be** ~ **to do** non voler fare

unwind [ʌn'waɪnd] (*irreg: like* **wind'**) *vt* svolgere, srotolare ▷ *vi* (*relax*) rilassarsi

unwise [ʌn'waɪz] *adj* poco saggio(-a)

unwittingly [ʌn'wɪtɪŋlɪ] *adv* senza volerlo

unwrap [ʌn'ræp] *vt* disfare; aprire

unzip [ʌn'zɪp] *vt* aprire (la chiusura lampo di); (*Comput*) dezippare

○ KEYWORD

up [ʌp] *prep* **he went up the stairs/the hill** è salito su per le scale/sulla collina; **the cat was up a tree** il gatto era su un albero; **they live further up the street** vivono un po' più su nella stessa strada
▷ *adv* **1** (*upwards, higher*) su, in alto; **up in the sky/the mountains** su nel cielo/in montagna; **up there** lassù; **up above** su in alto
2: **to be up** (*out of bed*) essere alzato(-a); (*prices, level*) essere salito(-a)
3: **up to** (*as far as*) fino a; **up to now** finora
4: **to be up to** (*depending on*): **it's up to you** sta a lei, dipende da lei; (*equal to*): **he's not up to it** (*job, task etc*) non ne è all'altezza; (*inf: be doing*): **what is he up to?** cosa sta combinando?
▷ *n* **ups and downs** alti e bassi *mpl*

up-and-coming ['ʌpənd'kʌmɪŋ] *adj* pieno(-a) di promesse, promettente

upbringing ['ʌpbrɪŋɪŋ] *n* educazione *f*

update [ʌp'deɪt] *vt* aggiornare

upfront [ʌp'frʌnt] *adj* (*inf*) franco(-a), aperto(-a) ▷ *adv* (*pay*) subito

upgrade [ʌp'greɪd] *vt* (*house, job*) migliorare; (*employee*) avanzare di grado

upheaval [ʌp'hiːvl] *n* sconvolgimento; tumulto

uphill [ʌp'hɪl] *adj* in salita; (*fig: task*) difficile ▷ *adv* **to go** ~ andare in salita, salire

upholstery [ʌp'həulstərɪ] *n* tappezzeria

upmarket [ʌp'mɑːkɪt] *adj* (*product*) che si rivolge ad una fascia di mercato superiore

upon [ə'pɔn] *prep* su

upper ['ʌpə'] *adj* superiore ▷ *n* (*of shoe*)

tomaia; **upper-class** *adj* dell'alta
borghesia

upright ['Apraɪt] *adj* diritto(-a); verticale;
(*fig*) diritto(-a), onesto(-a)

uprising ['Apraɪzɪŋ] *n* insurrezione *f*,
rivolta

uproar ['Aprɔːʳ] *n* tumulto, clamore *m*

upset [*n* 'Apset, *vb, adj* Ap'set] (*irreg:
like* **set**) *n* (*to plan etc*) contrattempo;
(*stomach upset*) disturbo ▷ *vt* (*glass etc*)
rovesciare; (*plan, stomach*) scombussolare;
(*person: offend*) contrariare; (: *grieve*)
addolorare; sconvolgere ▷ *adj*
contrariato(-a), addolorato(-a); (*stomach*)
scombussolato(-a)

upside-down [Apsaɪd'daun] *adv*
sottosopra

upstairs [Ap'stɛəz] *adv, adj* di sopra, al
piano superiore ▷ *n* piano di sopra

up-to-date ['Aptə'deɪt] *adj* moderno(-a);
aggiornato(-a)

uptown ['Aptaun] (*us*) *adv* verso i quartieri
residenziali ▷ *adj* dei quartieri residenziali

upward ['Apwəd] *adj* ascendente; verso
l'alto; **upward(s)** *adv* in su, verso l'alto

uranium [juə'reɪnɪəm] *n* uranio

Uranus [juə'reɪnəs] *n* (*planet*) Urano

urban ['əːbən] *adj* urbano(-a)

urge [əːdʒ] *n* impulso; stimolo; forte
desiderio ▷ *vt* **to ~ sb to do** esortare qn a
fare, spingere qn a fare; raccomandare a
qn di fare

urgency ['əːdʒənsɪ] *n* urgenza; (*of tone*)
insistenza

urgent ['əːdʒənt] *adj* urgente; (*voice*)
insistente

urinal ['juərɪnl] *n* (*BRIT: building*)
vespasiano; (: *vessel*) orinale *m*, pappagallo

urinate ['juərɪneɪt] *vi* orinare

urine ['juərɪn] *n* orina

us [As] *pron* ci; (*stressed, after prep*) noi; *see
also* **me**

US(A) *n abbr* (= *United States (of America)*)
USA *mpl*

use [*n* juːs, *vb* juːz] *n* uso; impiego,
utilizzazione *f* ▷ *vt* usare, utilizzare,
servirsi di; **in ~** in uso; **out of ~** fuori uso; **to
be of ~** essere utile, servire; **it's no ~** non
serve, è inutile; **she ~d to do it** lo faceva
(una volta), era solita farlo; **to be ~d to**
avere l'abitudine di; **use up** *vt* consumare;
esaurire; **used** *adj* (*object, car*) usato(-a);
useful *adj* utile; **useless** *adj* inutile;
(*person*) inetto(-a); **user** *n* utente *m/f*;
user-friendly *adj* (*computer*) di facile uso

usual ['juːʒuəl] *adj* solito(-a); **as ~** come
al solito, come d'abitudine; **usually** *adv*
di solito

utensil [juː'tɛnsl] *n* utensile *m*; **kitchen ~s**

utensili da cucina

utility [juː'tɪlɪtɪ] *n* utilità; (*also:* **public ~**)
servizio pubblico

utilize ['juːtɪlaɪz] *vt* utilizzare; sfruttare

utmost ['Atməust] *adj* estremo(-a) ▷ *n* **to
do one's ~** fare il possibile *or* di tutto

utter ['Atəʳ] *adj* assoluto(-a), totale ▷ *vt*
pronunciare, proferire; emettere; **utterly**
adv completamente, del tutto

U-turn ['juː'təːn] *n* inversione *f* a U

V

v. *abbr* = **verse**; **versus**; **volt**; (= *vide*) vedi, vedere

vacancy ['veɪkənsɪ] *n* (BRIT: *job*) posto libero; (*room*) stanza libera; **"no vacancies"** "completo"

> Be careful not to translate *vacancy* by the Italian word *vacanza*.

vacant ['veɪkənt] *adj* (*job, seat etc*) libero(-a); (*expression*) assente

vacate [vəˈkeɪt] *vt* lasciare libero(-a)

vacation [vəˈkeɪʃən] (*esp* US) *n* vacanze *fpl*; **vacationer** (US **vacationist**) *n* vacanziere(-a)

vaccination [væksɪˈneɪʃən] *n* vaccinazione *f*

vaccine ['væksiːn] *n* vaccino

vacuum ['vækjuːm] *n* vuoto; **vacuum cleaner** *n* aspirapolvere *m inv*

vagina [vəˈdʒaɪnə] *n* vagina

vague [veɪg] *adj* vago(-a); (*blurred: photo, memory*) sfocato(-a)

vain [veɪn] *adj* (*useless*) inutile, vano(-a); (*conceited*) vanitoso(-a); **in ~** inutilmente, invano

Valentine's Day ['væləntaɪnzdeɪ] *n* San Valentino *m*

valid ['vælɪd] *adj* valido(-a), valevole; (*excuse*) valido(-a)

valley ['vælɪ] *n* valle *f*

valuable ['væljuəbl] *adj* (*jewel*) di (grande) valore; (*time, help*) prezioso(-a); **valuables** *npl* oggetti *mpl* di valore

value ['væljuː] *n* valore *m* ▷ *vt* (*fix price*) valutare, dare un prezzo a; (*cherish*) apprezzare, tenere a; **~s** *npl* (*principles*) valori *mpl*

valve [vælv] *n* valvola

vampire ['væmpaɪə^r] *n* vampiro

van [væn] *n* (Aut) furgone *m*; (BRIT: *Rail*) vagone *m*

vandal ['vændl] *n* vandalo(-a); **vandalism** *n* vandalismo; **vandalize** *vt* vandalizzare

vanilla [vəˈnɪlə] *n* vaniglia ▷ *cpd* (*ice cream*) alla vaniglia

vanish ['vænɪʃ] *vi* svanire, scomparire

vanity ['vænɪtɪ] *n* vanità

vapour ['veɪpə^r] (US **vapor**) *n* vapore *m*

variable ['vɛərɪəbl] *adj* variabile; (*mood*) mutevole

variant ['vɛərɪənt] *n* variante *f*

variation [vɛərɪˈeɪʃən] *n* variazione *f*; (*in opinion*) cambiamento

varied ['vɛərɪd] *adj* vario(-a), diverso(-a)

variety [vəˈraɪətɪ] *n* varietà *f inv*; (*quantity*) quantità, numero

various ['vɛərɪəs] *adj* vario(-a), diverso(-a); (*several*) parecchi(-e), molti(-e)

varnish ['vɑːnɪʃ] *n* vernice *f*; (*nail varnish*) smalto ▷ *vt* verniciare; mettere lo smalto su

vary ['vɛərɪ] *vt, vi* variare, mutare

vase [vɑːz] *n* vaso

Vaseline® ['væsɪliːn] *n* vaselina

vast [vɑːst] *adj* vasto(-a); (*amount, success*) enorme

VAT [væt] *n abbr* (= *value added tax*) I.V.A. *f*

Vatican ['vætɪkən] *n* **the ~** il Vaticano

vault [vɔːlt] *n* (*of roof*) volta; (*tomb*) tomba; (*in bank*) camera blindata ▷ *vt* (*also:* **~ over**) saltare (d'un balzo)

VCR *n abbr* = **video cassette recorder**

VDU *n abbr* = **visual display unit**

veal [viːl] *n* vitello

veer [vɪə^r] *vi* girare; virare

vegan ['viːgən] *n* vegetaliano(-a)

vegetable ['vɛdʒtəbl] *n* verdura, ortaggio ▷ *adj* vegetale

vegetarian [vɛdʒɪˈtɛərɪən] *adj, n* vegetariano(-a); **do you have any ~ dishes?** avete piatti vegetariani?

vegetation [vɛdʒɪˈteɪʃən] *n* vegetazione *f*

vehicle ['viːɪkl] *n* veicolo

veil [veɪl] *n* velo

vein [veɪn] *n* vena; (*on leaf*) nervatura

Velcro® ['vɛlkrəu] *n* velcro® *m inv*

velvet ['vɛlvɪt] *n* velluto ▷ *adj* di velluto

vending machine ['vɛndɪŋ-] *n* distributore *m* automatico

vendor ['vɛndə^r] *n* venditore(-trice)

vengeance ['vɛndʒəns] n vendetta; **with a ~** (fig) davvero; furiosamente
Venice ['vɛnɪs] n Venezia
venison ['vɛnɪsn] n carne f di cervo
venom ['vɛnəm] n veleno
vent [vɛnt] n foro, apertura; (in dress, jacket) spacco ▷ vt (fig: one's feelings) sfogare, dare sfogo a
ventilation [vɛntɪ'leɪʃən] n ventilazione f
venture ['vɛntʃə^r] n impresa (rischiosa) ▷ vt rischiare, azzardare ▷ vi avventurarsi; **business ~** iniziativa commerciale
venue ['vɛnjuː] n luogo (designato) per l'incontro
Venus ['viːnəs] n (planet) Venere m
verb [vəːb] n verbo; **verbal** adj verbale; (translation) orale
verdict ['vəːdɪkt] n verdetto
verge [vəːdʒ] n bordo, orlo; **"soft ~s"** (BRIT: Aut) banchine fpl cedevoli; **on the ~ of doing** sul punto di fare
verify ['vɛrɪfaɪ] vt verificare; (prove the truth of) confermare
versatile ['vəːsətaɪl] adj (person) versatile; (machine, tool etc) (che si presta) a molti usi
verse [vəːs] n versi mpl; (stanza) stanza, strofa; (in bible) versetto
version ['vəːʃən] n versione f
versus ['vəːsəs] prep contro
vertical ['vəːtɪkl] adj verticale ▷ n verticale m
very ['vɛrɪ] adv molto ▷ adj **the ~ book which** proprio il libro che; **the ~ last** proprio l'ultimo; **at the ~ least** almeno; **~ much** moltissimo
vessel ['vɛsl] n (Anat) vaso; (Naut) nave f; (container) recipiente m
vest [vɛst] n (BRIT) maglia; (: sleeveless) canottiera; (US: waistcoat) gilè m inv
vet [vɛt] n abbr (BRIT: = veterinary surgeon) veterinario ▷ vt esaminare minuziosamente
veteran ['vɛtərn] n (also: **war ~**) veterano
veterinary surgeon ['vɛtrɪnərɪ-] (US **veterinarian**) n veterinario
veto ['viːtəʊ] (pl **vetoes**) n veto ▷ vt opporre il veto a
via ['vaɪə] prep (by way of) via; (by means of) tramite
viable ['vaɪəbl] adj attuabile; vitale
vibrate [vaɪ'breɪt] vi **to ~ (with)** vibrare (di); (resound) risonare (di)
vibration [vaɪ'breɪʃən] n vibrazione f
vicar ['vɪkə^r] n pastore m
vice [vaɪs] n (evil) vizio; (Tech) morsa; **vice-chairman** (irreg) n vicepresidente m
vice versa ['vaɪsɪ'vəːsə] adv viceversa
vicinity [vɪ'sɪnɪtɪ] n vicinanze fpl
vicious ['vɪʃəs] adj (remark, dog) cattivo(-a);

(blow) violento(-a)
victim ['vɪktɪm] n vittima
victor ['vɪktə^r] n vincitore m
Victorian [vɪk'tɔːrɪən] adj vittoriano(-a)
victorious [vɪk'tɔːrɪəs] adj vittorioso(-a)
victory ['vɪktərɪ] n vittoria
video ['vɪdɪəʊ] cpd video... ▷ n (video film) video m inv; (also: **~ cassette**) videocassetta; (also: **~ cassette recorder**) videoregistratore m; **video camera** n videocamera; **video (cassette) recorder** n videoregistratore m; **video game** n videogioco; **video shop** n videonoleggio; **video tape** n videotape m inv; **video wall** n schermo m multivideo inv
vie [vaɪ] vi **to ~ with** competere con, rivaleggiare con
Vienna [vɪ'ɛnə] n Vienna
Vietnam [vjɛt'næm] n Vietnam m; **Vietnamese** adj, n inv vietnamita m/f
view [vjuː] n vista, veduta; (opinion) opinione f ▷ vt (look at: also fig) considerare; (house) visitare; **on ~** (in museum etc) esposto(-a); **in full ~ of** sotto gli occhi di; **in ~ of the weather/the fact that** considerato il tempo/che; **in my ~** a mio parere; **viewer** n spettatore(-trice); **viewpoint** n punto di vista; (place) posizione f
vigilant ['vɪdʒɪlənt] adj vigile
vigorous ['vɪgərəs] adj vigoroso(-a)
vile [vaɪl] adj (action) vile; (smell) disgustoso(-a), nauseante; (temper) pessimo(-a)
villa ['vɪlə] n villa
village ['vɪlɪdʒ] n villaggio; **villager** n abitante m/f di villaggio
villain ['vɪlən] n (scoundrel) canaglia; (BRIT: criminal) criminale m; (in novel etc) cattivo
vinaigrette [vɪneɪ'grɛt] n vinaigrette f inv
vine [vaɪn] n vite f; (climbing plant) rampicante m
vinegar ['vɪnɪgə^r] n aceto
vineyard ['vɪnjɑːd] n vigna, vigneto
vintage ['vɪntɪdʒ] n (year) annata, produzione f ▷ cpd d'annata
vinyl ['vaɪnl] n vinile m
viola [vɪ'əʊlə] n viola
violate ['vaɪəleɪt] vt violare
violation [vaɪə'leɪʃən] n violazione f; **in ~ of sth** violando qc
violence ['vaɪələns] n violenza
violent ['vaɪələnt] adj violento(-a)
violet ['vaɪələt] adj (colour) viola inv, violetto(-a) ▷ n (plant) violetta; (colour) violetto
violin [vaɪə'lɪn] n violino
VIP n abbr (= very important person) V.I.P. m/f inv

virgin ['vɜːdʒɪn] n vergine f ▷ adj vergine inv

Virgo ['vɜːgəʊ] n (sign) Vergine f

virtual ['vɜːtjʊəl] adj effettivo(-a), vero(-a); (Comput, Physics) virtuale; (in effect): **it's a ~ impossibility** è praticamente impossibile; **the ~ leader** il capo all'atto pratico; **virtually** ['vɜːtjʊəlɪ] adv (almost) praticamente; **virtual reality** n (Comput) realtà virtuale

virtue ['vɜːtjuː] n virtù f inv; (advantage) pregio, vantaggio; **by ~ of** grazie a

virus ['vaɪərəs] n (also Comput) virus m inv

visa ['viːzə] n visto

vise [vaɪs] (US) n (Tech) = **vice**

visibility [vɪzɪ'bɪlɪtɪ] n visibilità

visible ['vɪzəbl] adj visibile

vision ['vɪʒən] n (sight) vista; (foresight, in dream) visione f

visit ['vɪzɪt] n visita; (stay) soggiorno ▷ vt (person: US: also: **~ with**) andare a trovare; (place) visitare; **visiting hours** npl (in hospital etc) orario delle visite; **visitor** n visitatore(-trice); (guest) ospite m/f; **visitor centre** (US **visitor center**) n centro informazioni per visitatori di museo, zoo, parco ecc

visual ['vɪzjʊəl] adj visivo(-a); visuale; ottico(-a); **visualize** ['vɪzjʊəlaɪz] vt immaginare, figurarsi; (foresee) prevedere

vital ['vaɪtl] adj vitale

vitality [vaɪ'tælɪtɪ] n vitalità

vitamin ['vɪtəmɪn] n vitamina

vivid ['vɪvɪd] adj vivido(-a)

V-neck ['viːnɛk] n maglione m con lo scollo a V

vocabulary [vəʊ'kæbjʊlərɪ] n vocabolario

vocal ['vəʊkl] adj (Mus) vocale; (communication) verbale

vocational [vəʊ'keɪʃənl] adj professionale

vodka ['vɔdkə] n vodka f inv

vogue [vəʊg] n moda; (popularity) popolarità, voga

voice [vɔɪs] n voce f ▷ vt (opinion) esprimere; **voice mail** n servizio di segretaria telefonica

void [vɔɪd] n vuoto ▷ adj (invalid) nullo(-a); (empty): **~ of** privo(-a) di

volatile ['vɔlətaɪl] adj volatile; (fig) volubile

volcano [vɔl'keɪnəʊ] (pl **volcanoes**) n vulcano

volleyball ['vɔlɪbɔːl] n pallavolo f

volt [vəʊlt] n volt m inv; **voltage** n tensione f, voltaggio

volume ['vɔljuːm] n volume m

voluntarily ['vɔləntrɪlɪ] adv volontariamente; gratuitamente

voluntary ['vɔləntərɪ] adj volontario(-a); (unpaid) gratuito(-a), non retribuito(-a)

volunteer [vɔlən'tɪəʳ] n volontario(-a) ▷ vt offrire volontariamente ▷ vi (Mil) arruolarsi volontario; **to ~ to do** offrire (volontariamente) di fare

vomit ['vɔmɪt] n vomito ▷ vt, vi vomitare

vote [vəʊt] n voto, suffragio; (cast) voto; (franchise) diritto di voto ▷ vt **to be ~d chairman** etc venir eletto presidente etc; (propose): **to ~ that** approvare la proposta che ▷ vi votare; **~ of thanks** discorso di ringraziamento; **voter** n elettore(-trice); **voting** n scrutinio

voucher ['vaʊtʃəʳ] n (for meal, petrol etc) buono

vow [vaʊ] n voto, promessa solenne ▷ vt **to ~ to do/that** giurare di fare/che

vowel ['vaʊəl] n vocale f

voyage ['vɔɪɪdʒ] n viaggio per mare, traversata

vulgar ['vʌlgəʳ] adj volgare

vulnerable ['vʌlnərəbl] adj vulnerabile

vulture ['vʌltʃəʳ] n avvoltoio

Wales [weɪlz] n Galles m
walk [wɔːk] n passeggiata; (short) giretto; (gait) passo, andatura; (path) sentiero; (in park etc) sentiero, vialetto ▷ vi camminare; (for pleasure, exercise) passeggiare ▷ vt (distance) fare or percorrere a piedi; (dog) accompagnare, portare a passeggiare; **10 minutes' ~ from** 10 minuti di cammino or a piedi da; **from all ~s of life** di tutte le condizioni sociali; **walk out** vi (audience) andarsene; (workers) scendere in sciopero; **walker** n (person) camminatore(-trice); **walkie-talkie** ['wɔːkɪ'tɔːkɪ] n walkie-talkie m inv; **walking** n camminare m; **walking shoes** npl pedule fpl; **walking stick** n bastone m da passeggio; **Walkman®** ['wɔːkmən] n Walkman® m inv; **walkway** n passaggio pedonale
wall [wɔːl] n muro; (internal, of tunnel, cave) parete f
wallet ['wɔlɪt] n portafoglio; **I can't find my ~** non trovo il portafoglio
wallpaper ['wɔːlpeɪpəʳ] n carta da parati ▷ vt (room) mettere la carta da parati in
walnut ['wɔːlnʌt] n noce f; (tree, wood) noce m
walrus ['wɔːlrəs] (pl **walrus** or **walruses**) n tricheco
waltz [wɔːlts] n valzer m inv ▷ vi ballare il valzer
wand [wɔnd] n (also: **magic ~**) bacchetta (magica)
wander ['wɔndəʳ] vi (person) girare senza meta, girovagare; (thoughts) vagare ▷ vt girovagare per
want [wɔnt] vt volere; (need) aver bisogno di ▷ n **for ~ of** per mancanza di; **wanted** adj (criminal) ricercato(-a); **"wanted"** (in adverts) "cercasi"
war [wɔːʳ] n guerra; **to make ~ (on)** far guerra (a)
ward [wɔːd] n (in hospital: room) corsia; (: section) reparto; (Pol) circoscrizione f; (Law: child: also: **~ of court**) pupillo(-a)
warden ['wɔːdn] n (of park, game reserve, youth hostel) guardiano(-a); (BRIT: of institution) direttore(-trice); (BRIT: also: **traffic ~**) addetto(-a) al controllo del traffico e del parcheggio
wardrobe ['wɔːdrəub] n (cupboard) guardaroba m inv, armadio; (clothes) guardaroba; (Cinema, Theatre) costumi mpl
warehouse ['wɛəhaus] n magazzino
warfare ['wɔːfɛəʳ] n guerra
warhead ['wɔːhɛd] n (Mil) testata
warm [wɔːm] adj caldo(-a); (thanks, welcome, applause) caloroso(-a); (person) cordiale; **it's ~** fa caldo; **I'm ~** ho caldo; **warm up** vi scaldarsi, riscaldarsi

waddle ['wɔdl] vi camminare come una papera
wade [weɪd] vi **to ~ through** camminare a stento in; (fig: book) leggere con fatica
wafer ['weɪfəʳ] n (Culin) cialda
waffle ['wɔfl] n (Culin) cialda; (inf) ciance fpl ▷ vi cianciare
wag [wæg] vt agitare, muovere ▷ vi agitarsi
wage [weɪdʒ] n (also: **~s**) salario, paga ▷ vt **to ~ war** fare la guerra
wag(g)on ['wægən] n (horse-drawn) carro; (BRIT: Rail) vagone m (merci)
wail [weɪl] n gemito; (of siren) urlo ▷ vi gemere; urlare
waist [weɪst] n vita, cintola; **waistcoat** (BRIT) n panciotto, gilè m inv
wait [weɪt] n attesa ▷ vi aspettare, attendere; **to lie in ~ for** stare in agguato a; **to ~ for** aspettare; **~ for me, please** aspettami, per favore; **I can't ~ to** (fig) non vedo l'ora di; **wait on** vt fus servire; **waiter** n cameriere m; **waiting list** n lista di attesa; **waiting room** n sala d'aspetto or d'attesa; **waitress** n cameriera
waive [weɪv] vt rinunciare a, abbandonare
wake [weɪk] (pt **woke, waked**, pp **woken, waked**) vt (also: **~ up**) svegliare ▷ vi (also: **~ up**) svegliarsi ▷ n (for dead person) veglia funebre; (Naut) scia

▷ vt scaldare, riscaldare; (*engine*) far scaldare; **warmly** adv (*applaud, welcome*) calorosamente; (*dress*) con abiti pesanti; **warmth** n calore m

warn [wɔːn] vt **to ~ sb that/(not) to do/of** avvertire or avvisare qn che/di (non) fare/di; **warning** n avvertimento; (*notice*) avviso; (*signal*) segnalazione f; **warning light** n spia luminosa

warrant ['wɔrnt] n (*voucher*) buono; (*Law: to arrest*) mandato di cattura; (: *to search*) mandato di perquisizione

warranty ['wɔrənti] n garanzia

warrior ['wɔrɪəʳ] n guerriero(-a)

Warsaw ['wɔːsɔː] n Varsavia

warship ['wɔːʃɪp] n nave f da guerra

wart [wɔːt] n verruca

wartime ['wɔːtaɪm] n **in ~** in tempo di guerra

wary ['wɛərɪ] adj prudente

was [wɔz] pt of **be**

wash [wɔʃ] vt lavare ▷ vi lavarsi; (*sea*): **to ~ over/against sth** infrangersi su/contro qc ▷ n lavaggio; (*of ship*) scia; **to give sth a ~** lavare qc, dare una lavata a qc; **to have a ~** lavarsi; **wash up** vi (BRIT) lavare i piatti; (US) darsi una lavata; **washbasin** (US **washbowl**) n lavabo; **wash cloth** (US) n pezzuola (per lavarsi); **washer** n (Tech) rondella; **washing** n (*linen etc*) bucato; **washing line** n (BRIT) corda del bucato; **washing machine** n lavatrice f; **washing powder** (BRIT) n detersivo (in polvere)

Washington ['wɔʃɪŋtən] n Washington f

wash: **washing-up** n rigovernatura, lavatura dei piatti; **washing-up liquid** n detersivo liquido (per stoviglie); **washroom** n gabinetto

wasn't ['wɔznt] = **was not**

wasp [wɔsp] n vespa

waste [weɪst] n spreco; (*of time*) perdita; (*rubbish*) rifiuti mpl; (*also*: **household ~**) immondizie fpl ▷ adj (*material*) di scarto; (*food*) avanzato(-a); (*land*) incolto(-a) ▷ vt sprecare; **waste ground** (BRIT) n terreno incolto or abbandonato; **wastepaper basket** ['weɪstpeɪpə-] n cestino per la carta straccia

watch [wɔtʃ] n (*also*: **wrist ~**) orologio (da polso); (*act of watching, vigilance*) sorveglianza; (*guard: Mil, Naut*) guardia; (*Naut: spell of duty*) quarto ▷ vt (*look at*) osservare; (: *match, programme*) guardare; (*spy on, guard*) sorvegliare, tenere d'occhio; (*be careful of*) fare attenzione a ▷ vi osservare, guardare; (*keep guard*) fare or montare la guardia; **watch out** vi fare attenzione; **watchdog** n (*also fig*) cane m da guardia; **watch strap** n cinturino da orologio

water ['wɔːtəʳ] n acqua ▷ vt (*plant*) annaffiare ▷ vi (*eyes*) lacrimare; (*mouth*): **to make sb's mouth ~** far venire l'acquolina in bocca a qn; **in British ~s** nelle acque territoriali britanniche; **water down** vt (*milk*) diluire; (*fig: story*) edulcorare; **watercolour** (US **watercolor**) n acquerello; **watercress** n crescione m; **waterfall** n cascata; **watering can** n annaffiatoio; **watermelon** n anguria, cocomero; **waterproof** adj impermeabile; **water-skiing** n sci m acquatico

watt [wɔt] n watt m inv

wave [weɪv] n onda; (*of hand*) gesto, segno; (*in hair*) ondulazione f; (*fig: surge*) ondata ▷ vi fare un cenno con la mano; (*branches, grass*) ondeggiare; (*flag*) sventolare ▷ vt (*hand*) fare un gesto con; (*handkerchief*) sventolare; (*stick*) brandire; **wavelength** n lunghezza d'onda

waver ['weɪvəʳ] vi esitare; (*voice*) tremolare

wavy ['weɪvɪ] adj ondulato(-a); ondeggiante

wax [wæks] n cera ▷ vt dare la cera a; (*car*) lucidare ▷ vi (*moon*) crescere

way [weɪ] n via, strada; (*path, access*) passaggio; (*distance*) distanza; (*direction*) parte f, direzione f; (*manner*) modo, stile m; (*habit*) abitudine f; **which ~? — this ~** da che parte or in quale direzione? — da questa parte or per di qua; **on the ~** (*en route*) per strada; **to be on one's ~** essere in cammino or sulla strada; **to be in the ~** bloccare il passaggio; (*fig*) essere tra i piedi or d'impiccio; **to go out of one's ~ to do** (*fig*) mettercela tutta or fare di tutto per fare; **under ~** (*project*) in corso; **to lose one's ~** perdere la strada; **in a ~** in un certo senso; **in some ~s** sotto certi aspetti; **no ~!** (*inf*) neanche per idea!; **by the ~ ...** a proposito ...; **"~ in"** (BRIT) "entrata", "ingresso"; **"~ out"** (BRIT) "uscita"; **the ~ back** la strada del ritorno; **"give ~"** (BRIT: Aut) "dare la precedenza"

W.C. ['dʌblju:si:] (BRIT) n W.C. m inv, gabinetto

we [wiː] pl pron noi

weak [wiːk] adj debole; (*health*) precario(-a); (*beam etc*) fragile; (*tea*) leggero(-a); **weaken** vi indebolirsi ▷ vt indebolire; **weakness** n debolezza; (*fault*) punto debole, difetto; **to have a weakness for** avere un debole per

wealth [wɛlθ] n (*money, resources*) ricchezza, ricchezze fpl; (*of details*) abbondanza, profusione f; **wealthy** adj ricco(-a)

weapon ['wɛpən] n arma; **~s of mass**

destruction armi *mpl* di distruzione di massa

wear [wɛəʳ] (*pt* **wore**, *pp* **worn**) *n* (*use*) uso; (*damage through use*) logorìo, usura; (*clothing*): **sports/baby ~** abbigliamento sportivo/per neonati ▷ *vt* (*clothes*) portare; (*put on*) mettersi; (*damage: through use*) consumare ▷ *vi* (*last*) durare; (*rub etc through*) consumarsi; **evening ~** abiti *mpl or* tenuta da sera; **wear off** *vi* sparire lentamente; **wear out** *vt* consumare; (*person, strength*) esaurire

weary ['wɪərɪ] *adj* stanco(-a) ▷ *vi* **to ~ of** stancarsi di

weasel ['wi:zl] *n* (*Zool*) donnola

weather ['wɛðəʳ] *n* tempo ▷ *vt* (*storm, crisis*) superare; **What's the ~ like?** che tempo fa?; **under the ~** (*fig: ill*) poco bene; **weather forecast** *n* previsioni *fpl* del tempo, bollettino meteorologico

weave [wi:v] (*pt* **wove**, *pp* **woven**) *vt* (*cloth*) tessere; (*basket*) intrecciare

web [wɛb] *n* (*of spider*) ragnatela; (*on foot*) palma; (*fabric, also fig*) tessuto; **the (World Wide) W~** la Rete; **web page** *n* (*Comput*) pagina *f* web *inv*; **website** *n* (*Comput*) sito (Internet)

wed [wɛd] (*pt, pp* **wedded**) *vt* sposare ▷ *vi* sposarsi

we'd [wi:d] = **we had**; **we would**

Wed. *abbr* (= *Wednesday*) mer.

wedding ['wɛdɪŋ] *n* matrimonio; **wedding anniversary** *n* anniversario di matrimonio; **wedding day** *n* giorno delle nozze *or* del matrimonio; **wedding dress** *n* abito nuziale; **wedding ring** *n* fede *f*

wedge [wɛdʒ] *n* (*of wood etc*) zeppa; (*of cake*) fetta ▷ *vt* (*fix*) fissare con zeppe; (*pack tightly*) incastrare

Wednesday ['wɛdnzdɪ] *n* mercoledì *m inv*

wee [wi:] (*Scottish*) *adj* piccolo(-a)

weed [wi:d] *n* erbaccia ▷ *vt* diserbare; **weedkiller** *n* diserbante *m*

week [wi:k] *n* settimana; **a ~ today/on Friday** oggi/venerdì a otto; **weekday** *n* giorno feriale; (*Comm*) giornata lavorativa; **weekend** *n* fine settimana *m or f inv*, weekend *m inv*; **weekly** *adv* ogni settimana, settimanalmente ▷ *adj* settimanale ▷ *n* settimanale *m*

weep [wi:p] (*pt, pp* **wept**) *vi* (*person*) piangere

weigh [weɪ] *vt, vi* pesare; **to ~ anchor** salpare l'ancora; **weigh up** *vt* valutare

weight [weɪt] *n* peso; **to lose/put on ~** dimagrire/ingrassare; **weightlifting** *n* sollevamento pesi

weir [wɪəʳ] *n* diga

weird [wɪəd] *adj* strano(-a), bizzarro(-a);

(*eerie*) soprannaturale

welcome ['wɛlkəm] *adj* benvenuto(-a) ▷ *n* accoglienza, benvenuto ▷ *vt* dare il benvenuto a; (*be glad of*) rallegrarsi di; **thank you — you're ~!** grazie — prego!

weld [wɛld] *n* saldatura ▷ *vt* saldare

welfare ['wɛlfɛəʳ] *n* benessere *m*; **welfare state** *n* stato assistenziale

well [wɛl] *n* pozzo ▷ *adv* bene ▷ *adj* **to be ~** (*person*) stare bene ▷ *excl* allora!; ma!; ebbene!; **as ~** anche; **as ~ as** così come; oltre a; **~ done!** bravo(-a)!; **get ~ soon!** guarisci presto!; **to do ~** andare bene

we'll [wi:l] = **we will**; **we shall**

well: **well-behaved** *adj* ubbidiente; **well-built** *adj* (*person*) ben fatto(-a); **well-dressed** *adj* ben vestito(-a), vestito(-a) bene

wellies (*inf*) ['wɛlɪz] *npl* (*BRIT*) stivali *mpl* di gomma

well: **well-known** *adj* noto(-a), famoso(-a); **well-off** *adj* benestante, danaroso(-a); **well-paid** [wɛl'peɪd] *adj* ben pagato(-a)

Welsh [wɛlʃ] *adj* gallese ▷ *n* (*Ling*) gallese *m*; **Welshman** (*irreg*) *n* gallese *m*; **Welshwoman** (*irreg*) *n* gallese *f*

went [wɛnt] *pt of* **go**

wept [wɛpt] *pt, pp of* **weep**

were [wəːʳ] *pt of* **be**

we're [wɪəʳ] = **we are**

weren't [wəːnt] = **were not**

west [wɛst] *n* ovest *m*, occidente *m*, ponente *m* ▷ *adj* (a) ovest *inv*, occidentale ▷ *adv* verso ovest; **the W~** l'Occidente *m*; **westbound** ['wɛstbaund] *adj* (*traffic*) diretto(-a) a ovest; (*carriageway*) ovest *inv*; **western** *adj* occidentale, dell'ovest ▷ *n* (*Cinema*) western *m inv*; **West Indian** *adj* delle Indie Occidentali ▷ *n* abitante *m/f* delle Indie Occidentali; **West Indies** [-'ɪndɪz] *npl* Indie *fpl* Occidentali

wet [wɛt] *adj* umido(-a), bagnato(-a); (*soaked*) fradicio(-a); (*rainy*) piovoso(-a) ▷ *n* (*BRIT: Pol*) politico moderato; **to get ~** bagnarsi; **"~ paint"** "vernice fresca"; **wetsuit** *n* tuta da sub

we've [wi:v] = **we have**

whack [wæk] *vt* picchiare, battere

whale [weɪl] *n* (*Zool*) balena

wharf [wɔːf] *n* (*pl* **wharves**) *n* banchina

 KEYWORD

what [wɔt] *adj* **1** (*in direct/indirect questions*) che; quale; **what size is it?** che taglia è?; **what colour is it?** di che colore è?; **what books do you want?** quali *or* che libri vuole?

2 (*in exclamations*) che; **what a mess!** che

disordine!
▷ *pron* **1** (*interrogative*) che cosa, cosa, che; **what are you doing?** che *or* (che) cosa fai?; **what are you talking about?** di che cosa parli?; **what is it called?** come si chiama?; **what about me?** e io?; **what about doing …?** e se facessimo …?
2 (*relative*) ciò che, quello che; **I saw what you did/was on the table** ho visto quello che hai fatto/quello che era sul tavolo
3 (*indirect use*) (che) cosa; **he asked me what she had said** mi ha chiesto che cosa avesse detto; **tell me what you're thinking about** dimmi a cosa stai pensando
▷ *excl* (*disbelieving*) cosa!, come!

whatever [wɔt'ɛvə] *adj* **~ book** qualunque *or* qualsiasi libro + *sub* ▷ *pron* **do ~ is necessary/you want** faccia qualunque *or* qualsiasi cosa sia necessaria/lei voglia; **~ happens** qualunque cosa accada; **no reason ~** *or* **whatsoever** nessuna ragione affatto *or* al mondo; **nothing ~** proprio niente

whatsoever [wɔtsəu'ɛvə] *adj* = **whatever**

wheat [wi:t] *n* grano, frumento

wheel [wi:l] *n* ruota; (*Aut: also:* **steering ~**) volante *m*; (*Naut*) (ruota del) timone *m* ▷ *vt* spingere ▷ *vi* (*birds*) roteare; (*also:* **~ round**) girare; **wheelbarrow** *n* carriola; **wheelchair** *n* sedia a rotelle; **wheel clamp** *n* (*Aut*) morsa che blocca la ruota di una vettura in sosta vietata

wheeze [wi:z] *vi* ansimare

 KEYWORD

when [wɛn] *adv* quando; **when did it happen?** quando è successo?
▷ *conj* **1** (*at, during, after the time that*) quando; **she was reading when I came in** quando sono entrato lei leggeva; **that was when I needed you** era allora che avevo bisogno di te
2 (*on, at which*): **on the day when I met him** il giorno in cui l'ho incontrato; **one day when it was raining** un giorno che pioveva
3 (*whereas*) quando, mentre; **you said I was wrong when in fact I was right** mi hai detto che avevo torto, quando in realtà avevo ragione

whenever [wɛn'ɛvə] *adv* quando mai ▷ *conj* quando; (*every time that*) ogni volta che

where [wɛə^r] *adv, conj* dove; **this is ~** è qui che; **whereabouts** *adv* dove ▷ *n* **sb's**

whereabouts luogo dove qn si trova; **whereas** *conj* mentre; **whereby** *pron* per cui; **wherever** [-'ɛvə^r] *conj* dovunque + *sub*; (*interrogative*) dove mai

whether ['wɛðə^r] *conj* se; **I don't know ~ to accept or not** non so se accettare o no; **it's doubtful ~** è poco probabile che; **~ you go or not** che lei vada o no

O KEYWORD

which [wɪtʃ] *adj* **1** (*interrogative: direct, indirect*) quale; **which picture do you want?** quale quadro vuole?; **which one?** quale?; **which one of you did it?** chi di voi lo ha fatto?
2: **in which case** nel qual caso
▷ *pron* **1** (*interrogative*) quale; **which (of these) are yours?** quali di questi sono suoi?; **which of you are coming?** chi di voi viene?
2 (*relative*) che; (: *indirect*) cui, il (la) quale; **the apple which you ate/which is on the table** la mela che hai mangiato/che è sul tavolo; **the chair on which you are sitting** la sedia sulla quale *or* su cui sei seduto; **he said he knew, which is true** ha detto che lo sapeva, il che è vero; **after which** dopo di che

whichever [wɪtʃ'ɛvə] *adj* **take ~ book you prefer** prenda qualsiasi libro che preferisce; **~ book you take** qualsiasi libro prenda

while [waɪl] *n* momento ▷ *conj* mentre; (*as long as*) finché; (*although*) sebbene + *sub*; per quanto + *sub*; **for a ~** per un po'

whilst [waɪlst] *conj* = **while**

whim [wɪm] *n* capriccio

whine [waɪn] *n* gemito ▷ *vi* gemere; uggiolare; piagnucolare

whip [wɪp] *n* frusta; (*for riding*) frustino; (*Pol: person*) capogruppo (*che sovrintende alla disciplina dei colleghi di partito*) ▷ *vt* frustare; (*cream, eggs*) sbattere; **whipped cream** *n* panna montata

whirl [wə:l] *vt* (far) girare rapidamente, (far) turbinare ▷ *vi* (*dancers*) volteggiare; (*leaves, water*) sollevarsi in vortice

whisk [wɪsk] *n* (*Culin*) frusta; frullino ▷ *vt* sbattere, frullare; **to ~ sb away** *or* **off** portar via qn a tutta velocità

whiskers ['wɪskəz] *npl* (*of animal*) baffi *mpl*; (*of man*) favoriti *mpl*

whisky ['wɪskɪ] (*us, Ireland* **whiskey**) *n* whisky *m inv*

whisper ['wɪspə^r] *n* sussurro ▷ *vt, vi* sussurrare

whistle ['wɪsl] *n* (*sound*) fischio; (*object*)

fischietto ▷ *vi* fischiare
white [waɪt] *adj* bianco(-a); (*with fear*)
pallido(-a) ▷ *n* bianco; (*person*) bianco(-a);
White House *n* Casa Bianca; **whitewash**
n (*paint*) bianco di calce ▷ *vt* imbiancare;
(*fig*) coprire
whiting ['waɪtɪŋ] *n inv* (*fish*) merlango
Whitsun ['wɪtsn] *n* Pentecoste *f*
whittle ['wɪtl] *vt* **to ~ away, ~ down**
ridurre, tagliare
whizz [wɪz] *vi* **to ~ past** *or* **by** passare
sfrecciando

O **KEYWORD**

who [huː] *pron* **1** (*interrogative*) chi; **who is
it?, who's there?** chi è?
2 (*relative*) che; **the man who spoke to
me** l'uomo che ha parlato con me; **those
who can swim** quelli che sanno nuotare

whoever [huːˈɛvə] *pron* **~ finds it**
chiunque lo trovi; **ask ~ you like** lo chieda
a chiunque vuole; **~ she marries** chiunque
sposerà, non importa chi sposerà; **~ told
you that?** chi mai gliel'ha detto?
whole [həʊl] *adj* (*complete*) tutto(-a),
completo(-a); (*not broken*) intero(-a),
intatto(-a) ▷ *n* (*all*) **the ~ of** tutto(-a) il
(la); (*entire unit*) tutto; (*not broken*) tutto;
the ~ of the town tutta la città, la città
intera; **on the ~, as a ~** nel complesso,
nell'insieme; **wholefood(s)** *n(pl)* cibo
integrale; **wholeheartedly** [həʊlˈhɑː
tɪdlɪ] *adv* sentitamente, di tutto cuore;
wholemeal *adj* (*bread, flour*) integrale;
wholesale *n* commercio *or* vendita
all'ingrosso ▷ *adj* all'ingrosso; (*destruction*)
totale; **wholewheat** *adj* = **wholemeal**;
wholly *adv* completamente, del tutto

O **KEYWORD**

whom [huːm] *pron* **1** (*interrogative*) chi;
whom did you see? chi hai visto?; **to
whom did you give it?** a chi lo hai dato?
2 (*relative*) che, prep + il (la) quale (*check
syntax of Italian verb used*): **the man whom
I saw/to whom I spoke** l'uomo che ho
visto/al quale ho parlato

whore [hɔː] (*inf: pej*) *n* puttana

O **KEYWORD**

whose [huːz] *adj* **1** (*possessive: interrogative*)
di chi; **whose book is this?, whose is
this book?** di chi è questo libro?; **whose
daughter are you?** di chi sei figlia?

2 (*possessive: relative*): **the man whose
son you rescued** l'uomo il cui figlio hai
salvato; **the girl whose sister you were
speaking to** la ragazza alla cui sorella
stavi parlando
▷ *pron* di chi; **whose is this?** di chi è
questo?; **I know whose it is** so di chi è

O **KEYWORD**

why [waɪ] *adv* perché; **why not?** perché
no?; **why not do it now?** perché non farlo
adesso?
▷ *conj* **I wonder why he said that** mi
chiedo perché l'abbia detto; **that's not
why I'm here** non è questo il motivo per
cui sono qui; **the reason why** il motivo
per cui
▷ *excl* (*surprise*) ma guarda un po'!;
(*remonstrating*) ma (via)!; (*explaining*)
ebbene!

---

wicked ['wɪkɪd] *adj* cattivo(-a),
malvagio(-a); maligno(-a); perfido(-a)
wicket ['wɪkɪt] *n* (*Cricket*) porta; area tra
le due porte
wide [waɪd] *adj* largo(-a); (*area, knowledge*)
vasto(-a); (*choice*) ampio(-a) ▷ *adv* **to open
~** spalancare; **to shoot ~** tirare a vuoto
or fuori bersaglio; **widely** *adv* (*differing*)
molto, completamente; (*travelled, spaced*)
molto; (*believed*) generalmente; **widen**
vt allargare, ampliare; **wide open** *adj*
spalancato(-a); **widespread** *adj* (*belief etc*)
molto *or* assai diffuso(-a)
widow ['wɪdəʊ] *n* vedova; **widower** *n*
vedovo
width [wɪdθ] *n* larghezza
wield [wiːld] *vt* (*sword*) maneggiare;
(*power*) esercitare
wife [waɪf] (*pl* **wives**) *n* moglie *f*
wig [wɪg] *n* parrucca
wild [waɪld] *adj* selvatico(-a);
selvaggio(-a); (*sea, weather*)
tempestoso(-a); (*idea, life*) folle;
stravagante; (*applause*) frenetico(-a);
wilderness ['wɪldənɪs] *n* deserto;
wildlife *n* natura; **wildly** *adv*
selvaggiamente; (*applaud*)
freneticamente; (*hit, guess*) a casaccio;
(*happy*) follemente

O **KEYWORD**

will [wɪl] (*pt, pp* **willed**) *aux vb* **1** (*forming
future tense*): **I will finish it tomorrow** lo
finirò domani; **I will have finished it by
tomorrow** lo finirò entro domani; **will you
do it? — yes I will/no I won't** lo farai? — sì

(lo farò)/no (non lo farò)
2 (*in conjectures, predictions*): **he will** or **he'll be there by now** dovrebbe essere arrivato ora; **that will be the postman** sarà il postino
3 (*in commands, requests, offers*): **will you be quiet!** vuoi stare zitto?; **will you come?** vieni anche tu?; **will you help me?** mi aiuti?, mi puoi aiutare?; **will you have a cup of tea?** vorrebbe una tazza di tè?; **I won't put up with it!** non lo accetterò!
▷ *vt* **to will sb to do** volere che qn faccia; **he willed himself to go on** continuò grazie a un grande sforzo di volontà
▷ *n* volontà; testamento

willing ['wɪlɪŋ] *adj* volonteroso(-a); **~ to do** disposto(-a) a fare; **willingly** *adv* volentieri
willow ['wɪləʊ] *n* salice *m*
willpower ['wɪlpaʊə'] *n* forza di volontà
wilt [wɪlt] *vi* appassire
win [wɪn] (*pt*, *pp* **won**) *n* (*in sports etc*) vittoria ▷ *vt* (*battle*, *prize*, *money*) vincere; (*popularity*) conquistare ▷ *vi* vincere; **win over** *vt* convincere
wince [wɪns] *vi* trasalire
wind¹ [waɪnd] (*pt*, *pp* **wound**) *vt* attorcigliare; (*wrap*) avvolgere; (*clock*, *toy*) caricare ▷ *vi* (*road*, *river*) serpeggiare; **wind down** *vt* (*car window*) abbassare; (*fig: production*, *business*) diminuire; **wind up** *vt* (*clock*) caricare; (*debate*) concludere
wind² [wɪnd] *n* vento; (*Med*) flatulenza; (*breath*) respiro, fiato ▷ *vt* (*take breath away*) far restare senza fiato; **~ power** energia eolica
windfall ['wɪndfɔ:l] *n* (*money*) guadagno insperato
winding ['waɪndɪŋ] *adj* (*road*) serpeggiante; (*staircase*) a chiocciola
windmill ['wɪndmɪl] *n* mulino a vento
window ['wɪndəʊ] *n* finestra; (*in car*, *train*, *plane*) finestrino; (*in shop etc*) vetrina; (*also:* **~ pane**) vetro; **I'd like a ~ seat** vorrei un posto vicino al finestrino; **window box** *n* cassetta da fiori; **window cleaner** (*person*) pulitore *m* di finestre; **window pane** *n* vetro; **window seat** *n* posto finestrino; **windowsill** *n* davanzale *m*
windscreen ['wɪndskri:n] (*us* **windshield**) *n* parabrezza *m inv*; **windscreen wiper** (*us* **windshield wiper**) *n* tergicristallo
windsurfing ['wɪndsə:fɪŋ] *n* windsurf *m inv*
windy ['wɪndɪ] *adj* ventoso(-a); **it's ~** c'è vento
wine [waɪn] *n* vino; **wine bar** *n* enoteca

(*per degustazione*); **wine glass** *n* bicchiere *m* da vino; **wine list** *n* lista dei vini; **wine tasting** *n* degustazione *f* dei vini
wing [wɪŋ] *n* ala; (*Aut*) fiancata; **wing mirror** *n* (BRIT) specchietto retrovisore esterno
wink [wɪŋk] *n* ammiccamento ▷ *vi* ammiccare, fare l'occhiolino; (*light*) baluginare
winner ['wɪnə'] *n* vincitore(-trice)
winning ['wɪnɪŋ] *adj* (*team*, *goal*) vincente; (*smile*) affascinante
winter ['wɪntə'] *n* inverno; **winter sports** *npl* sport *mpl* invernali; **wintertime** *n* inverno, stagione *f* invernale
wipe [waɪp] *n* pulita, passata ▷ *vt* pulire (strofinando); (*erase: tape*) cancellare; **wipe out** *vt* (*debt*) pagare, liquidare; (*memory*) cancellare; (*destroy*) annientare; **wipe up** *vt* asciugare
wire ['waɪə'] *n* filo; (*Elec*) filo elettrico; (*Tel*) telegramma *m* ▷ *vt* (*house*) fare l'impianto elettrico di; (*also:* **~ up**) collegare, allacciare; (*person*) telegrafare a
wiring ['waɪərɪŋ] *n* impianto elettrico
wisdom ['wɪzdəm] *n* saggezza; (*of action*) prudenza; **wisdom tooth** *n* dente *m* del giudizio
wise [waɪz] *adj* saggio(-a); prudente; giudizioso(-a)
wish [wɪʃ] *n* (*desire*) desiderio; (*specific desire*) richiesta ▷ *vt* desiderare, volere; **best ~es** (*on birthday etc*) i migliori auguri; **with best ~es** (*in letter*) cordiali saluti, con i migliori saluti; **to ~ sb goodbye** dire arrivederci a qn; **he ~ed me well** mi augurò di riuscire; **to ~ to do/sb to do** desiderare or volere fare/che qn faccia; **to ~ for** desiderare
wistful ['wɪstful] *adj* malinconico(-a)
wit [wɪt] *n* (*also:* **~s**) intelligenza; presenza di spirito; (*wittiness*) spirito, arguzia; (*person*) bello spirito
witch [wɪtʃ] *n* strega

 KEYWORD

with [wɪð, wɪθ] *prep* **1** (*in the company of*) con; **I was with him** ero con lui; **we stayed with friends** siamo stati da amici; **I'll be with you in a minute** vengo subito
2 (*descriptive*) con; **a room with a view** una stanza con vista sul mare (*or* sulle montagne *etc*); **the man with the grey hat/blue eyes** l'uomo con il cappello grigio/gli occhi blu
3 (*indicating manner, means, cause*): **with tears in her eyes** con le lacrime agli occhi; **red with anger** rosso dalla rabbia; **to**

shake with fear tremare di paura
4: **I'm with you** (*I understand*) la seguo;
to be with it (*inf: up-to-date*) essere alla
moda; (: *alert*) essere sveglio(-a)

withdraw [wɪθˈdrɔː] (*irreg: like* draw) *vt*
ritirare; (*money from bank*) ritirare; prelevare
▷ *vi* ritirarsi; **withdrawal** *n* ritiro; prelievo;
(*of army*) ritirata; **withdrawal symptoms**
n (*Med*) crisi *f* di astinenza; **withdrawn** *adj*
(*person*) distaccato(-a)
withdrew [wɪθˈdruː] *pt of* **withdraw**
wither [ˈwɪðəʳ] *vi* appassire
withhold [wɪθˈhəuld] (*irreg: like* hold)
vt (*money*) trattenere; (*permission*): **to ~
(from)** rifiutare (a); (*information*): **to ~
(from)** nascondere (a)
within [wɪðˈɪn] *prep* all'interno; (*in time,
distances*) entro ▷ *adv* all'interno, dentro; **~
reach (of)** alla portata (di); **~ sight (of)** in
vista (di); **~ a mile of** entro un miglio da; **~
the week** prima della fine della settimana
without [wɪðˈaut] *prep* senza; **to go ~ sth**
fare a meno di qc
withstand [wɪθˈstænd] (*irreg: like* stand)
vt resistere a
witness [ˈwɪtnɪs] *n* (*person, also Law*)
testimone *m/f* ▷ *vt* (*event*) essere
testimone di; (*document*) attestare
l'autenticità di
witty [ˈwɪtɪ] *adj* spiritoso(-a)
wives [waɪvz] *npl of* **wife**
wizard [ˈwɪzəd] *n* mago
wk *abbr* = **week**
wobble [ˈwɔbl] *vi* tremare; (*chair*)
traballare
woe [wəu] *n* dolore *m*; disgrazia
woke [wəuk] *pt of* **wake**
woken [ˈwəukn] *pp of* **wake**
wolf [wulf] (*pl* **wolves**) *n* lupo
woman [ˈwumən] (*pl* **women**) *n* donna
womb [wuːm] *n* (*Anat*) utero
women [ˈwɪmɪn] *npl of* **woman**
won [wʌn] *pt, pp of* **win**
wonder [ˈwʌndəʳ] *n* meraviglia ▷ *vi* **to ~
whether/why** domandarsi se/perché; **to
~ at** essere sorpreso(-a) di; meravigliarsi
di; **to ~ about** domandarsi di; pensare
a; **it's no ~ that** c'è poco *or* non c'è da
meravigliarsi che + *sub*; **wonderful** *adj*
meraviglioso(-a)
won't [wəunt] = **will not**
wood [wud] *n* legno; (*timber*) legname *m*;
(*forest*) bosco; **wooden** *adj* di legno; (*fig*)
rigido(-a); inespressivo(-a); **woodwind** *npl*
(*Mus*): **the woodwind** i legni; **woodwork**
n (*craft, subject*) falegnameria
wool [wul] *n* lana; **to pull the ~ over sb's
eyes** (*fig*) imbrogliare qn; **woollen** (*us*

woolen) *adj* di lana; (*industry*) laniero(-a);
woolly (*us* **wooly**) *adj* di lana; (*fig: ideas*)
confuso(-a)
word [wəːd] *n* parola; (*news*) notizie *fpl*
▷ *vt* esprimere, formulare; **in other ~s** in
altre parole; **to break/keep one's ~** non
mantenere/mantenere la propria parola;
to have ~s with sb avere un diverbio con
qn; **wording** *n* formulazione *f*; **word
processing** *n* elaborazione *f* di testi, word
processing *m*; **word processor** *n* word
processor *m inv*
wore [wɔːʳ] *pt of* **wear**
work [wəːk] *n* lavoro; (*Art, Literature*)
opera ▷ *vi* lavorare; (*mechanism, plan etc*)
funzionare; (*medicine*) essere efficace
▷ *vt* (*clay, wood etc*) lavorare; (*mine etc*)
sfruttare; (*machine*) far funzionare;
(*cause: effect, miracle*) fare; **to be out of
~** essere disoccupato(-a); **~s** *n* (*BRIT:
factory*) fabbrica *npl* (*of clock, machine*)
meccanismo; **how does this ~?** come
funziona?; **the TV isn't ~ing** la TV non
funziona; **to ~ loose** allentarsi; **work
out** *vi* (*plans etc*) riuscire, andare bene
▷ *vt* (*problem*) risolvere; (*plan*) elaborare;
it ~s out at £100 fa 100 sterline; **worker**
n lavoratore(-trice), operaio(-a); **work
experience** *n* (*previous jobs*) esperienze
fpl lavorative; (*student training placement*)
tirocinio; **workforce** *n* forza lavoro;
working class *n* classe *f* operaia;
working week *n* settimana lavorativa;
workman (*irreg*) *n* operaio; **work of
art** *n* opera d'arte; **workout** *n* (*Sport*)
allenamento; **work permit** *n* permesso
di lavoro; **workplace** *n* posto di lavoro;
workshop *n* officina; (*practical session*)
gruppo di lavoro; **work station** *n* stazione
f di lavoro; **work surface** *n* piano di
lavoro; **worktop** *n* piano di lavoro
world [wəːld] *n* mondo ▷ *cpd* (*champion*)
del mondo; (*power, war*) mondiale; **to
think the ~ of sb** (*fig*) pensare un gran
bene di qn; **World Cup** *n* (*Football*) Coppa
del Mondo; **world-wide** *adj* universale;
World-Wide Web *n* World Wide Web *m*
worm [wəːm] *n* (*also:* **earth~**) verme *m*
worn [wɔːn] *pp of* **wear** ▷ *adj* usato(-a);
worn-out *adj* (*object*) consumato(-a),
logoro(-a); (*person*) sfinito(-a)
worried [ˈwʌrɪd] *adj* preoccupato(-a)
worry [ˈwʌrɪ] *n* preoccupazione *f* ▷ *vt*
preoccupare ▷ *vi* preoccuparsi; **worrying**
adj preoccupante
worse [wəːs] *adj* peggiore ▷ *adv, n* peggio;
a change for the ~ un peggioramento;
worsen *vt, vi* peggiorare; **worse off** *adj* in
condizioni (economiche) peggiori

worship ['wəːʃɪp] n culto ▷ vt (God) adorare, venerare; (person) adorare; **Your W~** (BRIT: to mayor) signor sindaco; (: to judge) signor giudice

worst [wəːst] adj il (la) peggiore ▷ adv, n peggio; **at ~** al peggio, per male che vada

worth [wəːθ] n valore m ▷ adj **to be ~ valere; it's ~ it** ne vale la pena; **it is ~ one's while (to do)** vale la pena (fare); **worthless** adj di nessun valore; **worthwhile** adj (activity) utile; (cause) lodevole

worthy ['wəːðɪ] adj (person) degno(-a); (motive) lodevole; **~ of** degno di

 KEYWORD

would [wud] aux vb **1** (conditional tense): **if you asked him he would do it** se glielo chiedesse lo farebbe; **if you had asked him he would have done it** se glielo avesse chiesto lo avrebbe fatto
2 (in offers, invitations, requests): **would you like a biscuit?** vorrebbe or vuole un biscotto?; **would you ask him to come in?** lo faccia entrare, per cortesia; **would you open the window please?** apra la finestra, per favore
3 (in indirect speech): **I said I would do it** ho detto che l'avrei fatto
4 (emphatic): **it would have to snow today!** doveva proprio nevicare oggi!
5 (insistence): **she wouldn't do it** non ha voluto farlo
6 (conjecture): **it would have been midnight** sarà stato mezzanotte; **it would seem so** sembrerebbe proprio di sì
7 (indicating habit): **he would go there on Mondays** andava lì ogni lunedì

wouldn't ['wudnt] = **would not**
wound¹ [waund] pt, pp of **wind¹**
wound² [wuːnd] n ferita ▷ vt ferire
wove [wəuv] pt of **weave**
woven ['wəuvn] pp of **weave**
wrap [ræp] vt avvolgere; (pack: also: **~ up**) incartare; **wrapper** n (on chocolate) carta; (BRIT: of book) copertina; **wrapping** ['ræpɪŋ] n carta; **wrapping paper** n carta da pacchi; (for gift) carta da regali
wreath [riːθ, pl riːðz] n corona
wreck [rɛk] n (sea disaster) naufragio; (ship) relitto; (pej: person) rottame m ▷ vt demolire; (ship) far naufragare; (fig) rovinare; **wreckage** n rottami mpl; (of building) macerie fpl; (of ship) relitti mpl
wren [rɛn] n (Zool) scricciolo
wrench [rɛntʃ] n (Tech) chiave f; (tug) torsione f brusca; (fig) strazio ▷ vt strappare; storcere; **to ~ sth from** strappare qc a or da
wrestle ['rɛsl] vi **to ~ (with sb)** lottare (con qn); **wrestler** n lottatore(-trice); **wrestling** n lotta
wretched ['rɛtʃɪd] adj disgraziato(-a); (inf: weather, holiday) orrendo(-a), orribile; (: child, dog) pestifero(-a)
wriggle ['rɪgl] vi (also: **~ about**) dimenarsi; (: snake, worm) serpeggiare, muoversi serpeggiando
wring [rɪŋ] (pt, pp **wrung**) vt torcere; (wet clothes) strizzare; (fig): **to ~ sth out of** strappare qc a
wrinkle ['rɪŋkl] n (on skin) ruga; (on paper etc) grinza ▷ vt (nose) torcere; (forehead) corrugare ▷ vi (skin, paint) raggrinzirsi
wrist [rɪst] n polso
write [raɪt] (pt **wrote**, pp **written**) vt, vi scrivere; **write down** vt annotare; (put in writing) mettere per iscritto; **write off** vt (debt, plan) cancellare; **write out** vt mettere per iscritto; (cheque, receipt) scrivere; **write-off** n perdita completa; **writer** n autore(-trice), scrittore(-trice)
writing ['raɪtɪŋ] n scrittura; (of author) scritto, opera; **in ~** per iscritto; **writing paper** n carta da lettere
written ['rɪtn] pp of **write**
wrong [rɒŋ] adj sbagliato(-a); (not suitable) inadatto(-a); (wicked) cattivo(-a); (unfair) ingiusto(-a) ▷ adv in modo sbagliato, erroneamente ▷ n (injustice) torto ▷ vt fare torto a; **I took a ~ turning** ho sbagliato strada; **you are ~ to do it** ha torto a farlo; **you are ~ about that, you've got it ~** si sbaglia; **to be in the ~** avere torto; **what's ~?** cosa c'è che non va?; **to go ~** (person) sbagliarsi; (plan) fallire, non riuscire; (machine) guastarsi; **wrongly** adv (incorrectly, by mistake) in modo sbagliato; **wrong number** n (Tel): **you've got the wrong number** ha sbagliato numero
wrote [rəut] pt of **write**
wrung [rʌŋ] pt, pp of **wring**
WWW n abbr = **World Wide Web**; **the ~** la Rete

XL *abbr* = **extra large**
Xmas [ˈɛksməs] *n abbr* = **Christmas**
X-ray [ˈɛksreɪ] *n* raggio X; (*photograph*)
radiografia ▷ *vt* radiografare
xylophone [ˈzaɪləfəun] *n* xilofono

yacht [jɔt] *n* panfilo, yacht *m inv*;
yachting *n* yachting *m*, sport *m* della
vela
yard [jɑːd] *n* (*of house etc*) cortile *m*;
(*measure*) iarda (= 914 mm; 3 feet); **yard sale**
(*US*) *n* vendita di oggetti usati nel cortile di
una casa privata
yarn [jɑːn] *n* filato; (*tale*) lunga storia
yawn [jɔːn] *n* sbadiglio ▷ *vi* sbadigliare
yd. *abbr* = **yard(s)**
yeah [jɛə] (*inf*) *adv* sì
year [jɪəʳ] *n* anno; (*referring to harvest,
wine etc*) annata; **he is 8 ~s old** ha 8 anni;
an eight-~-old child un(a) bambino(-a)
di otto anni; **yearly** *adj* annuale ▷ *adv*
annualmente
yearn [jəːn] *vi* **to ~ for sth/to do**
desiderare ardentemente qc/di fare
yeast [jiːst] *n* lievito
yell [jɛl] *n* urlo ▷ *vi* urlare
yellow [ˈjɛləu] *adj* giallo(-a); **Yellow
Pages**® *npl* pagine *fpl* gialle
yes [jɛs] *adv* sì ▷ *n* sì *m inv*; **to say/answer
~** dire/rispondere di sì
yesterday [ˈjɛstədɪ] *adv* ieri ▷ *n* ieri *m inv*;
~ morning/evening ieri mattina/sera; **all
day ~** ieri per tutta la giornata
yet [jɛt] *adv* ancora; già ▷ *conj* ma,
tuttavia; **it is not finished ~** non
è ancora finito; **the best ~** finora il

migliore; **as ~** finora
yew [juː] n tasso *(albero)*
Yiddish ['jɪdɪʃ] n yiddish m
yield [jiːld] n produzione f, resa; reddito
▷ vt produrre, rendere; *(surrender)*
cedere ▷ vi cedere; *(US: Aut)* dare la
precedenza
yob(bo) ['jɔb(əu)] n *(BRIT inf)* bullo
yoga ['jəugə] n yoga m
yog(h)urt ['jəugət] n iogurt m inv
yolk [jəuk] n tuorlo, rosso d'uovo

 KEYWORD

you [juː] pron **1** *(subject)* tu; (: *polite form)* lei;
(: *pl)* voi; (: *very formal)* loro; **you Italians
enjoy your food** a voi Italiani piace
mangiare bene; **you and I will go** tu ed io
or lei ed io andiamo
2 *(object: direct)* ti; la; vi; loro *(after vb)*; (:
indirect) ti; le; vi; loro *(after vb)*; **I know you**
ti *or* la *or* vi conosco; **I gave it to you** te
l'ho dato; gliel'ho dato; ve l'ho dato; l'ho
dato loro
3 *(stressed, after prep, in comparisons)* te; lei;
voi; loro; **I told you to do it** ho detto a TE
(*or* a LEI *etc)* di farlo; **she's younger than
you** è più giovane di te (*or* lei *etc)*
4 *(impers: one)* si; **fresh air does you good**
l'aria fresca fa bene; **you never know** non
si sa mai

you'd [juːd] **= you had; you would**
you'll [juːl] **= you will; you shall**
young [jʌŋ] adj giovane ▷ npl *(of animal)*
piccoli mpl; *(people)*: **the ~** i giovani, la
gioventù; **youngster** n giovanotto,
ragazzo; *(child)* bambino(-a)
your [jɔːʳ] adj il (la) tuo(-a) pl, i (le) tuoi
(tue); il (la) suo(-a); *(pl)* i (le) suoi (sue); il
(la) vostro(-a); *(pl)* i (le) vostri(-e); il (la)
loro; *(pl)* i (le) loro; *see also* **my**
you're [juəʳ] **= you are**
yours [jɔːz] pron il (la) tuo(-a); *(pl)* i (le)
tuoi (tue); *(polite form)* il (la) suo(-a); *(pl)*
i (le) suoi (sue); *(pl)* il (la) vostro(-a); *(pl)*
i (le) vostri(-e); (: *very formal)* il (la) loro;
(pl) i (le) loro; *see also* **mine; faithfully;
sincerely**
yourself [jɔːˈsɛlf] pron *(reflexive)* ti;
si; *(after prep)* te; sé; *(emphatic)* tu
stesso(-a); lei stesso(-a); **yourselves** pl
pron *(reflexive)* vi; si; *(after prep)* voi; loro;
(emphatic) voi stessi(-e); loro stessi(-e); *see
also* **oneself**
youth [juːθ, pl juːðz] n gioventù f; *(young
man)* giovane m, ragazzo; **youth club** n
centro giovanile; **youthful** adj giovane;
da giovane; giovanile; **youth hostel** n

ostello della gioventù
you've [juːv] **= you have**
Yugoslavia ['juːgəu'slaːvɪə] n *(Hist)*
Jugoslavia

Z

zeal [ziːl] *n* zelo; entusiasmo
zebra ['ziːbrə] *n* zebra; **zebra crossing**
(BRIT) *n* (passaggio pedonale a) strisce *fpl*,
zebre *fpl*
zero ['zɪərəʊ] *n* zero
zest [zɛst] *n* gusto; (*Culin*) buccia
zigzag ['zɪgzæg] *n* zigzag *m inv* ▷ *vi*
zigzagare
Zimbabwe [zɪmˈbɑːbwɪ] *n* Zimbabwe *m*
zinc [zɪŋk] *n* zinco
zip [zɪp] *n* (*also*: **~ fastener**, (US) **zipper**)
chiusura *f* or cerniera *f* lampo *inv* ▷ *vt* (*also*:
~ up) chiudere con una cerniera lampo;
zip code (US) *n* codice *m* di avviamento
postale; **zipper** (US) *n* cerniera *f* lampo *inv*
zit [zɪt] *n* brufolo
zodiac ['zəʊdɪæk] *n* zodiaco
zone [zəʊn] *n* (*also Mil*) zona
zoo [zuː] *n* zoo *m inv*
zoology [zuːˈɔlədʒɪ] *n* zoologia
zoom [zuːm] *vi* **to ~ past** sfrecciare; **zoom**
lens *n* zoom *m inv*, obiettivo a focale
variabile
zucchini [zuːˈkiːnɪ] (US) *npl* (*courgettes*)
zucchine *fpl*